Indiana:
A New Historical Guide

Robert M. Taylor, Jr.
Errol Wayne Stevens
Mary Ann Ponder
Paul Brockman

Indiana Historical Society
Indianapolis
1989

Library of Congress Cataloging-in-Publication Data

Indiana: a new historical guide / by Robert M. Taylor, Jr. . . . [et al.].
  p. cm.
  ISBN 0-87195-049-9 : $45.00. — ISBN 0-87195-048-0 (pbk.) : $19.95
  1. Historic sites—Indiana—Guide-books. 2. Indiana—Description and travel—1981-
—Guide-books. 3. Indiana—History, Local. I. Taylor, Robert M., 1941-   . II. Indiana
Historical Society.
F527.I54 1989
917.7204′43—dc20   89-19807
                                                               CIP

Cover identifications are found on the last page of the book.

Table of Contents

Introduction

In 1921 the *American Magazine* ran an article by Hoosier journalist George Ade entitled "Do You Run a Motor-Car or a Moveable Madhouse?" The next year Ade, in *Single Blessedness and Other Observations*, a selection of his writings, republished the piece with a new title: "The Tortures of Touring." He contended that the automobile of his day went too fast and its passengers were too intent on reaching a destination to relax and behold the countryside. "All of our motorists are rushing past the things worth seeing, instead of stopping to enjoy them. There is no township, however remote, but has within its boundaries some exhibit which will instruct or entertain the caller." Ade goes on to give his remedy for the traveler's indifference to roadside settings. "In order to insure more leisurely habits of travel and arouse a proper interest in the varied charms of all outlying regions, we need in this country an entirely new sort of guide book for motorists. The kind of book now in use devotes too much attention to the roadway, instead of giving spicy information about what may be seen from the roadway. It is a mere chart, whereas it might be made a document bubbling with human interest." Ade then presses his argument with a humorous example.

Route 23A, mile 0.0, Hicksville. Started by Truman Hicks about 1800. The town is famous on account of the Liberty Hotel (large faded structure on Main Street), it being claimed that more traveling men have committed suicide within its walls than in any two other hotels in the state. The elderly persons seen along the business thoroughfares are retired farmers. They are talking about the taxes. The small vacant room next to the post office was used as a manicure parlor for three weeks in 1917, but the public sentiment prevailed. In order to get out of town as soon as possible proceed east on Main Street. Note on the left the drug store owned by Henry F. Pilsbry. After local option went into effect, and before the Eighteenth Amendment was passed, Mr. Pilsbry bought two large farms. Look out for stretch of bad pavement. The contractor who did the work was related to the mayor. Cross R.R.

Through this artifice, Ade accentuates his message, as clear in our era of speedy cars and superhighways as in his day: let us have road guides, he advises, "which will keep the tourists sitting up and interested."

Writers came close to Ade's ideal with the splendid series of state guides produced by the Federal Writers' Project of the Work Projects Administration in the late 1930s and early 1940s. Enthusiasm for these WPA Guides has not abated as witnessed by the recent nationwide reprinting, updating, and abstracting of the books. The Indiana volume went on sale in September 1941 and was an immediate success. New York City papers judged it to be among the finest of the state guides. It has been reprinted several times, and people still refer to it, though its primary value today is that of a document chronicling the face of Indiana around 1940. Still, it is a highly readable work, filled with entertaining anecdotal, folkloric accounts, and peppered with maps, illustrations, and competent, though dated, thematic essays on Indiana history and its principal cities.

In 1978 the Indiana Historical Society took a fresh look at the *Guide* in response to the widening interest in local history and preservation, and to that era's rising fuel costs which initiated a decline in long-distance excursions. With a surge in state travel and tourism imminent, the Society weighed the options of revising the old standby or creating a new book. The reviewers did not have to read far into the old *Guide* to see that it was so obsolete in many parts, so deficient in its coverage, that only an entirely new guide made sense. Less than fifty percent of the described sites in the major cities section, for example, existed forty years later. This lack of carryover was most acute in highly industrialized areas, such as Lake County, where businesses, so vulnerable to economic change, were the focus of portrayals. The book's sites most likely to survive through the 1940-80 period were located in old historic cities like New Harmony, Vincennes, and Corydon. Even in these venerable places, and generally throughout the state, the sheer multiplication of worthy candidates for inclusion in a guidebook rendered a new publication inevitable. (For additional information about the

Writers' Project and conceptualization of the new guide see the two articles in the June 1980 *Indiana Magazine of History*: Robert K. O'Neill, "The Federal Writers' Project Files for Indiana," and Errol Wayne Stevens, "The Federal Writers' Project Revisited: The Indiana Historical Society's New Guide to the State of Indiana.")

The Indiana Historical Society's Guide Project was launched therefore in August 1978. Over the following decade staff members, no more than four at any one time, drove and redrove the entire state and researched hundreds of sites and pieces of information to compile the present work. A preliminary survey of the state in 1978-79 alerted the staff to the enormous changes that had occurred in towns, cities, and countrysides in the previous forty years. Many old buildings had been demolished, replaced, or restored. Significant structures had been erected. Books and articles on local history had multiplied. Numerous historical markers had been installed; new roads, built; museums, pioneer villages, and historical societies, established or revived. What seemed an overwhelming task in 1978, to write a new guidebook, became more problematic in the 1980s, a decade which saw the Hoosier landscape virtually revamped. The *Guide* staff was hard pressed to keep up with the ever-changing material and natural environment, not to mention the institutions, organizations, and personalities. Updating the text became a prime consideration in the project's last years, a process that, finally, had to be drawn to a close.

The format of the *Guide* differs decisively from the old one. The authors decided not to incorporate a listing of restaurants, motels, hospitals, public conveyances, and other amenities. To have done so would have considerably expanded the size of the book. But more important, this kind of data becomes quickly extinct, and there are any number of available resources for such specifics. The popular travel guides on the newsstands have to make thousands of changes to their annual publications along these lines, and we intentionally avoided printing information of any sort that would shorten the usefulness of the text.

The second major decision was to abandon the old *Guide*'s plan of touring the state in a north-south, east-west pattern, and rather lay out a series of large circular tours, nineteen in all. Each of the nineteen tours, the outlines of which are mapped on the insides of the front and back covers of the book, were designed to pass through or touch upon a series of counties so that all of the state's counties, with the exception of Marion County and most of Lake County, would be represented. The traveler is guided by maps and by geographical and directional descriptors from county to county, town to town, attraction to attraction. When the narrative crosses a county line there follows a brief overview of that county's history. The circuits provide a means of guiding readers conveniently to sites and attractions; they are not intended to be traveled in one day. One can pick up a tour at any point and continue on with the help of that tour's text.

The nineteen large circular tours begin and end at one of fourteen "lead" cities, so called. For our purposes, the Calumet Region is considered a lead city, rather than counted among the large circular tours. Indianapolis is a lead city that encompasses Marion County. Sometimes one city, in this case Fort Wayne, Evansville, Terre Haute, Lafayette, and South Bend, introduces two circular tours. The lead cities, including the Calumet Region, are treated to a brief narrative of their historical and contemporary development. The essay is followed by descriptions of the chief attractions, each site numbered to correspond to its location on the accompanying city map.

A thorough search and investigation of sites all over the state helped determine the route of each tour. The criteria for inclusion took into account the site's historical or architectural significance, its commercial, industrial, social, or political importance to the community generally, its link to a personality, group, or event, its uniqueness, its capacity to add variety to the tour narrative, and its accessibility for viewing. Finally, we had to know there existed enough information about the site to warrant its consideration.

In casting the tours in the above fashion it is evident that a considerable portion of the state is not covered. A number of communities and roadsides are not explored. Even in the designated locales, we did not include all the properties listed in the National Register of Historic Places, or all the historic markers, or all designated historic districts, or all the local officially or unofficially recognized mansions, farms, churches, downtown commercial buildings, covered or iron bridges, railroads, fossil beds, mineral waters, or natural phenomena. Nevertheless, we think our sizable sample of more than 2,000 sites and 425 cities and towns affords the armchair traveler and the eyewitness a familiarity with most of Indiana's major features. However, just as we offer the *Guide* as a means to exit the interstates and explore the state's byways, so too we encourage the curious to break away from the *Guide*'s maps and search and research the remainder of Indiana's inexhaustible riches. For further information we suggest the visitor's centers (named usually at the start of a city tour), which will have available tourist literature.

Initially the staff intended to write and incorporate a section surveying the state's history similar to the one provided in the old *Guide*. As time passed and the stack of tour texts grew, we realized that an addition of a lengthy narrative history would necessitate limiting tour sites, the number of which was already being circumscribed by time and space constraints. We opted to insert as many sites as possible. In coming to this decision we kept in mind that much of the history of the state can be discovered through the reading of the *Guide*'s city essays and tour sketches. We also were aware of the recent appearance of several excellent histories of Indiana: James H. Madison's *The Indiana Way* (1986); Patrick J. Furlong's *Indiana: An Illustrated History* (1985), Justin E. Walsh's *The Centennial History of the Indiana General Assembly, 1816-1978* (1987), and Peter T. Harstad's essay "Indiana and the Art of Adjustment," in James H. Madison, ed., *Heartland* (1988). The *Indiana Magazine of History* and the Indiana Historical Society's new popular history magazine *Traces of Indiana and Midwestern History* present quarterly glimpses into aspects of Hoosier history. The Indiana Historical Society has available a catalog, free for the asking, of not only IHS publications, but those Indiana-related books offered by Indiana University Press, along with selections from other presses.

Though the *Guide* is largely self-explanatory, there are a few final explanations and counsels required for its full and effective use. The Contents page at the front lists the order of appearance of the lead cities and the larger tours emanating from them. The population figures for counties, cities, and towns are taken from the 1980 federal census. The mileage figures between sites in the circular tours are

reasonably accurate though reference points for determining the exact mileage interval could not always be fixed. Abbreviations have been held to a minimum and are usually placed at the end of a site's description. The ones employed indicate a special recognition of a structure: *NRHP* stands for the National Register of Historic Places; *HABS* refers to the Historic American Buildings Survey; *HABSI* denotes the Historic American Buildings Survey Inventory; and *HAER* designates the Historic American Engineering Record. The reader may learn more about the latter three programs by consulting Thomas M. Slade, ed., *Historic American Buildings Survey in Indiana* (Bloomington: Indiana University Press, 1983). The tourist should also be alerted that the city maps do not indicate all the one-way streets, which are ever-changing components of urban life. In addition we want to underscore the need to be sensitive to the property of others. The appearance of a house or building in this book does not grant license to enter its premises. Indeed, probably the majority of listings are private and do not permit visitors. Please check on the accessibility to a site before approaching it.

Finally, we anticipate disagreement on some facts presented in this book. We have tried to subject each item to meticulous scrutiny, but we are also aware of the many instances where we have made choices among equally reputable secondary sources. We want to be informed of possible errors and sources to correct them. Although the components selected for this book, we think, are of significance, we are painfully aware that many other items could have been included. The features listed will undergo change. We have a continuing concern for the state's heritage and we implore readers to communicate to us changes occurring with the sites mentioned in the book, and report any attraction they deem worthy of bringing to our attention.

Acknowledgments

Hoosiers take great interest in the vanished past as well as in the extant relics of bygone days. We were reminded of this again and again as we crisscrossed the state in search of material for this new guide. In putting together a book of this size with so many bits and pieces of information, the authors have incurred a debt to scores of people who have taken time to answer our questions in person, by phone, or by letter, and we want to acknowledge them.

First and foremost we want to recognize the board of trustees of the Indiana Historical Society and its then executive secretary, Gayle Thornbrough, who brought the Guide Project into existence in 1978 and supervised its early years. In 1984, upon her retirement, Peter T. Harstad became executive director and he and the trustees have continued to give the project unwavering support. Two of the project's initial staff, MaryJo Wagner and Deirdre Spencer, deserve our thanks for helping launch the guide. In particular the *Guide* staff is obliged to Richard S. Simons, of Marion, Indiana, a member of the board of trustees, a former newspaper editor and a longtime feature writer for the *Indianapolis Star*. In 1987-88, he read the *Guide* manuscript and redrove the tours noting corrections or additions. His knowledge of Indiana, especially its railroads and, as author of *The Rivers of Indiana* (1985), its waterways, saved us from many mistakes in fact and emphasis, while reinforcing and augmenting the accounts.

Certainly we want to thank the dedicated staffs of Indiana's 238 central public libraries, who so competently and graciously researched our inquiries. We would be remiss if we did not single out the Indiana Division of the Indiana State Library and the William Henry Smith Memorial Library of the Indiana Historical Society. The *Guide* staff spent the bulk of its research time in these two fine repositories, and the courtesies extended deserve our acknowledgment and sincere appreciation. Newspapers are a major source of historical data, and the *Guide* project would have faltered without this record of events and personages. We thank the many reporters, feature writers, and columnists for their historical contributions, and especially to John Selch and his staff in the Newspaper Division of the Indiana State Library for their assistance these many years. The specialized collections of the Genealogy Division of the State Library and the Commission on Public Records also proved to be indispensable research tools. We esteem also the relationship we have had with the Indiana Historical Bureau and its director Pamela J. Bennett. The Bureau's book publications, along with the *Indiana History Bulletin*, and its files on local historical societies and state historical markers, added considerable detail to the book's contents. Shirley S. McCord, the Bureau's editor, read the text and contributed valuable comments. The architectural studies of Hoosier settlements compiled by the Indiana Junior Historical Society from 1968 through 1976 furnished a handy visual reference to houses and buildings.

An untold number of individuals throughout the state, along with town and city officials, staffs of Chambers of Commerce and municipal development offices, supervisors in factories and stores, and owners of historical homes and buildings have been vital to this project. The historical community—the ninety-two county historians, leaders of local historical societies, caretakers of historical sites and memorials, museum personnel, history professors in our colleges and universities, and history enthusiasts in all walks of life—has made a major contribution. In particular we are grateful to the work of the Indiana Department of Natural Resources and the State Division of Historic Preservation and Archaeology, whose ongoing published reports on Indiana's historic sites and structures have been requisite reading, not to mention the DNR's fine magazine, *Outdoor Indiana*. The same can be said for the Historic Landmarks Foundation of Indiana's *The Indiana Preservationist*, which along with its news on preservation efforts kept us abreast of the National Register of Historic Places listings. We thank J. Reid Williamson, Jr., and his fine staff at the Historic Landmarks Foundation for their investment in Indiana's legacy. Mention should also be made of the Indiana Humanities Council (formerly Indiana Committee for the Humanities) which under the direction of Kenneth Gladish has funded such history projects as Freetown Village and cooperated with the Indiana Historical Society in supporting Indiana Heritage Research Grants, thereby generating valuable studies. Our knowledge of recent Hoosier history and progress would have been considerably less had it not been for the finance, business, and economics experts who contributed information on cities and regions through the *Indianapolis Business Journal* and the *Indiana Business Review*, the latter a publication of the Indiana Business Research Center, Indiana University School of Business. Our appreciation also goes to the Indiana Department of Commerce and its Tourism Development office. We drew upon its resources many times in the course of writing the *Guide*.

The following listing gives credit to those persons who at points in the last decade have given us particular help in research, or read and commented on the manuscript, and are not mentioned elsewhere in this introduction:

Nancy A. Adams, Tom Adams, Frank P. Albertson, Jane Alexis, C. D. Alig, Jr., Leona Alig, Harold W. Allison, Louis Alyea, O. K. Anderson, Ruth Ascherman, Carolyn Autry, Mrs. Birney G. Bailey, Diane Bainbridge, Donald E. Baker, Kenneth L. Baker, Dorothy Ballantyne, Robert G. Barrows, Betty Jo Bartley, Van P. Batterton, Kitsey Beck, Cecil Beeson, James Bellis, Wayne Bessinger, Darrel E. Bigham, Thelma Bingham, Julia Binkley, Keith Bishop, Josephus C. Blachly, Betty Black, Mildred B. Blake, Edwin J. Boley, Marian E. Bollinger, Shirley Boltz, Edward E. Breen, Velma Bright, Don Bucove, Edna E. Burns, Virgil V. Burns, Eugene H. Burrell, Ned A. Bush, Sr., Eleanore Cammack, Ron Campbell, Vickey Campbell, Rosemary Canright, Donald F. Carmony, Jared Carter, Bernice Carver, A. W. Cavins, William L. Casteel, Florence A. Chitwood, Leslie Choitz, Ellen Christianson, Dorothy Clark, Pauline Clark, Pat Clements, Linda Cochran,

Jean Cohoon, Christine M. Connor, Gayle Cook, Vesper Cook, Mary C. Crandall, Beth A. Crawford, Owen L. Crecelius, Donna Creek, Michael F. Crowe, Mimi Crump, Leigh Darbee, Lulie Davis, Richard Day, the Rev. Merris M. Dice, Franklin Dillman, Esther Dittlinger, James J. Divita, Richard R. Dodd, R. J. Doherty, Nora L. Donovan, Wilma Dulin, Douglas A. Dunn, the Rev. Joseph J. Dunne, Brian L. Dunnigan, Mary Durnan, Howard Eldon, Josephine M. Elliott, Thomas S. Emison, Kenneth Englund, M. Enneking, Mary A. Falls, Bert Fenn, Dave Ferrebee, Camille B. Fife, Norma Fink, Jerry Finley, Carol Fisher, Dale L. Flesher, Josephine Ford, Florence Fosler, Alan H. Fox, Paul Fox, John R. Frank, Jeanne Frederick, Russell F. Frehse, Arville L. Funk, Patrick J. Furlong, Betty Gehrke, George W. Geib, Albert Gengnagel, David W. Girton, Gene Gladson, James A. Glass, David Graham, Shaun Granum, Margaret Greenamyer, Wanda Griess, Robert G. Gunderson, Lois Hagedorn, Hester Anne Hale, Judy Hamilton, Ruth Hammond, F. Gerald Handfield, Jr., Pat Hanson, Don Hardin, Walter H. Harmon, John M. Harris, Mrs. William H. Harris, William O. Harris, Michael Hawfield, Paulette Haynes, Don Heady, J. Michael Heagy, Wilbur Heidbreder, Walter H. Harmen, Sylvia Hendricks, Rachel Henry, Marjory Hershberger, Kay Hinds, Bert Hindmarsh, E. G. Hoffman, Robert J. Holden, Robert A. Holt, Floyd Hopper, David E. Horn, Beatrice Horner, Helen Horstman, Joan Hostetler, Andrew K. Houk, Sr., Mrs. F. V. Howell, Lea Hudson, Hank Huffman, Jennie Huntzinger, Frank Hurdis, Gail Hursey, Paul A. Hutton, Vernon Iliff, Dorothy Jerse, Susanna Jones, James H. Kellar, Maria Thiesan Kelsay, Elizabeth Kelso, Karen Kiemnec, Robert Kirby, Randy Kirkendall, Herbert Korra, Thomas K. Krasean, Bob Kreibel, Robert Lagemann, Carol Lamar, Frederick D. Lane, Mrs. Howard Lane, James B. Lane, Mrs. George C. Langdon, Gernice Lanman, Jim Lawton, Robert B. Leggat, Mrs. John G. Lemmon, Joseph Levine, Larry Lidster, R. Kent Liffick, Carol Lindauer, Lydia Lowrey, Mrs. Ray Lumpkin, Mrs. Jesse W. McAtee, Constance McBirney, Gladys McCommon, Kenneth P. McCutchan, Jim McDonald, Katherine M. McDonell, James A. McFeul, Ray McIntire, Simon McTighe, James H. Madison, Phyllis Manago, Martin D. Marciniak, Frank R. "Skip" Marketti, Robert C. Martin, Jeanette M. Matthew, Florence Maxwell, Dharathula Millender, Isabel J. Miller, John W. Miller, Ralph Wayne Miller, Howard Mitchener, Pauline Montgomery, Freeman E. Morgan, Jr., Thomas Moriarity, Mary P. Mountz, Eric Mundell, Mrs. Robert C. Munger, Cheryl Ann Munson, L. Rex Myers, Vivian Myers, Charles R. Niehaus, Raymond J. Neiner, Glenda Nobles, Alan T. Nolan, Harriet A. O'Connor, Robert K. O'Neill, John Oxian, Marsha L. Patterson, Robert Peirce, Michael D. Peyton, William B. Pickett, Robert Peirce, Joe Pike, Rebecca E. Pitts, Clara Plum, Barbara Poore, Mabel Potter, Eric Pumroy, Gladys Ratke, Anne Raymer, Clifford Richards, Linda Robertson, Ernestine Bradford Rose, Dorothy Rowley, Margorie Runyan, Mary M. Rust, Martha Samuels, Jane Sandburg, James Sandrick, Wayne Sanford, Charles M. Sappenfield, Garry Schalliol, Thomas J. Schlereth, August Schultheis, Charles Schreiber, Charles J. Schuttrow, Ralph Grayson Schwarz, Barbara Schweitzer, Brig. Gen. Eugene D. Scott, Lucinda Scotton, Virgil Scowden, William L. Selm, Jane Sheller, Jerry Showalter, Linda J. Shultz, Sue Ellen Small, Harry M. Smith, Jewell Smith, Martina Smith, Mary Lou Smith, Mrs. Noble Smith, Mark Souder, W. J. Spangler, Paul Sprague, Wiley W. Spurgeon, Jr., Pat Spurlock, Paul F. Stabile, Bertha Stalbaum, John Stamper, Ralph W. Stark, Patrick H. Steele, Jack R. Stephenson, Robert R. Stevens, Rita Stewart, Jesse Stiles, Georgianne Strange, Ervin Stuntz, Susan S. Sutton, June Swango, Lucian A. Szlizewski, Lois H. Thompson, Lloyd Thoren, Emma Lou Thornbrough, Bernice Tolchinsky, Don Tolliver, Robert W. Topping, Patty Sue Trotman, Lance Trusty, Howard M. Utter, M. W. Vahlsing, Carole Vance, David G. Vanderstel, Viola A. Van Loo, Lawrence R. Walsh, Mrs. Harold Walters, John A. Ward, Ann and Harry Warr, Paul Warrick, Bill Weathers, William R. Wepler, T. Perry Wesley, Donald West, Mig Wilkhack, Margarie Wilkinson, Shirley Willard, Stephen R. Williams, Wanda Lou Willis, Jay Wilson, Jr., John T. Windle, Ann Windle, Eleanor Wittenberg, Al Wright, Don Yehle, Paul S. Zahara, Darrell Zink, Geneva Zink.

A very special thank you goes to Joan C. Marchand, who is Historic Preservation Officer for the city of Evansville. Over the course of this project, she not only undertook an enormous amount of original research into Evansville's past on our behalf but also took time to keep us informed of current developments in the city and read many drafts of the Evansville text. Her constancy of interest in the guide has been an inspiration to us all.

A critical component in the utility of travel books is the maps. John M. Hollingsworth, Professor of Geography at Indiana University, Bloomington, prepared the large circular tour maps and several of the city maps. Terry J.

Christie of the Geography Department at Indiana University, Indianapolis, executed the bulk of the city maps. We are grateful to both of these individuals for the evident skill they brought to their work.

To bring about a book of this scope requires massive editorial input, and we were fortunate to have a group of editors at the Society equal to fulfilling the task. Their expertise shaped many coarse and disparate pages delivered to them over the last decade into an orderly and readable text. Editors Gayle Thornbrough, Lana Ruegamer, Amy Schutt, J. Kent Calder, Douglas E. Clanin, Kathleen M. Breen, Ruth Dorrel, and Megan McKee have contributed to the final product. Thomas A. Mason, the Society's director of publications, read the manuscript and suggested many improvements. Paula Corpuz, the Society's senior editor, had the major editorial responsibility. She worked with the guide staff for the greater portion of the project. Besides the usual duties of copyediting, arranging, indexing, preparing the text for type, working on design and illustrations, and seeing the manuscript through production, she also grappled with many substantive research questions. We owe much to her and the entire editorial staff for the quality of the guide.

With this, a combination guidebook and history in hand, we urge you onto the road, confident that you will find, perhaps to your amazement, that Indiana has its fair share of attractions and distractions, enough at least to keep you "sitting up and interested." A final piece of advice from George Ade: "Every incorporated town has some hold upon fame. Travel slowly. Stop often. Get under the cover of every neighborhood."

Robert M. Taylor, Jr.

About the Authors

Dr. Robert M. Taylor, Jr., is a staff member of the Indiana Historical Society. With the project since 1979, he directed it after mid-1984. He has degrees from Franklin College, Andover Newton Theological School, the University of Iowa, and Kent State University. His articles have appeared in such journals as the *Indiana Magazine of History*, *Journal of Social History*, and *Traces of Indiana and Midwestern History*, for which he is contributing editor. He edited (with Ralph Crandall) *Generations and Change: Genealogical Perspectives in Social History* (1986), coauthored (with John T. Windle) *The Early Architecture of Madison, Indiana* (1986), and edited *The Northwest Ordinance: A Bicentennial Handbook* (1987). He is secretary of the Indiana Association of Historians.

Dr. Errol Wayne Stevens is Head, Seaver Center for Western History Research at the Natural History Museum Los Angeles County, California. Stevens directed the project from its beginning until mid-1984. Stevens received his undergraduate and graduate degrees from Indiana University. He has had articles published in the *Indiana Magazine of History*, *Journal of* the *Illinois State Historical Society*, *Labor History*, and *Terrae Incognitae*. His essay on socialism in Marion, Indiana, appeared in *Socialism in the Heartland*, ed. by Donald T. Critchlow (1987), and he has edited a diary on an 1849 voyage to California during the gold rush.

Mary Ann Ponder is Literacy Program Coordinator at the Colton Public Library, Colton, California. An experienced editor and writer, Ponder served on the project staff from 1980 to 1985. She received her master's degree in English from Iowa State University and took postgraduate work at the University of Arizona.

Paul Brockman is Archivist of the William Henry Smith Library of the Indiana Historical Society. Brockman received his master's degree in history from Purdue University. He researched and wrote for the project from 1982 to 1984. He assisted in the writing of the *Indiana Newspaper Bibliography* (1982) and wrote (with Eric Pumroy) *A Guide to Manuscript Collections of the Indiana Historical Society and Indiana State Library* (1986). He presently edits *The Indiana German Heritage Society Newsletter*.

Preface to the 1992 Printing

When a second printing of this book became necessary, the Indiana Historical Society solicited information from the county historians concerning possible additions or corrections. The Society could not make changes in the text, but the editors wanted to provide updated information in the preface to the new printing. The editors are deeply grateful to the county historians for their most helpful efforts and the useful information that they provided. The Society's president, Richard S. Simons, made available his wide knowledge and provided a wealth of information on Indiana's history and geography in making the information in this preface as complete and up-to-date as possible. The editors thankfully acknowledge his contribution. Not all information received on recent developments could be included, and the editors focused on providing information that would affect how a visitor would reach a site. For example, if a building has been demolished, or its name has changed, or its occupant has moved, those facts are included below. The Indiana Historical Society plans to publish a comprehensive revision of the *Guide* in the future, so more wide-ranging suggestions will be kept on file and incorporated then. The updated information below is keyed to the pages on which the subject appears.

17 **Poinsette Motors** no longer occupies the site at 200 S. Clinton St. A furniture outlet currently operates on the site, where the **bronze plaque** can still be found.

25 The **Hillsdale County Railroad** is operating a steam train from Pleasant Lake north to Angola.

33 The **Garrett Railroad Museum** has moved, around the corner, to a new location on Randolph St. The **Gengnagel Lumber Company** is no longer in business. The four old railroad cars that were on the site have been sold.

35 Adjacent to the **Auburn-Cord-Duesenberg Museum** is the **National Automotive and Truck Museum of the United States** (NATMUS). Housed in the former Service Building and L-29 Cord/Experimental Building, the facility contains 112,000 feet of floor space for display of postwar cars and trucks of all eras. A museum within a museum, the **National Automotive and Truck Model and Toy Museum of the United States** (NATMATMUS) uses toys and models to illustrate the history of the automobile. The **Midwestern United Life Insurance Company** no longer occupies the site on W. Jefferson Blvd.

43 A **state historical marker** was erected on Fourth St., two blocks east of the courthouse, marking an **early narrow gauge railroad** and describing the national significance of this type of road. The **Octogenarian Museum** was demolished in 1991. Its collection is not available.

46 The **circus winter headquarters** are the property of the **International Circus Hall of Fame,** and a restoration is planned. The **Miami County Historical Society Museum** has moved to the former Senger Dry Goods Company building at 51 N. Broadway.

50 **Chief Richardville's house** is located on US 24 at IND 9 on the right.

59 The **Muncie Visitors Bureau** is still located at 425 N. High St. The **National Headquarters of the Academy for Model Aviation** has moved to Muncie from Washington, D.C. It is located 1 m. east of the city limits on Memorial Dr., which is 1 m. south of IND 32. The facility covers more than 100 acres, with large flying fields, a paved runway for model craft, and parking areas. The Academy's museum is scheduled to be located on the site. For information contact the Muncie Visitors Bureau.

60 The **Radisson Hotel** has gone through reorganization and again is the **Roberts Hotel** (NRHP).

78 The **Ex-Cell-O Corporation** is closed. The **Wendell L. Willkie High School** has been razed and only the front entrance stands.

79 The **St. Clair Glass Works, Inc.,** is now the **House of Glass.**

80 The **Indiana Rockwool Division of the Susquehanna Corporation** is no longer in business in Alexandria.

88 The **Radisson Hotel** is closed and for sale.

92 There is no longer a **zoo** in the **Glen Miller Park.**

104 The **Fayette County Courthouse** was demolished in May 1992. The **new courthouse** is located at 401 Central Ave.

105 The **Whitewater Valley Railroad** is currently using a diesel engine.

114 The **Union County Historical Society Museum** is in the renovated **Liberty Depot** on Union St. The artifacts were formerly in the courthouse basement.

150 The **Dumont house** was demolished by the county.

167 The **Old Goshen Church** has been reconstructed on the same site as the old church. Work was completed in 1991 from funds left by the Ray Boone Estate.

171 The **Louisville, New Albany and Corydon Railroad** is running passenger excursions.

184 The old **United States Quartermaster Depot** is now called the **Quadrangle**.

186 The **Falls of the Ohio State Park** is located on the banks of the Ohio River in Clarksville. The park's 350-million-year-old fossil beds are the largest exposed Devonian fossil beds in the world. A 16,000-sq.-ft. interpretive center overlooking the fossil beds is scheduled to open in 1993. For information, tours, and directions, contact the park office at 914 E. Main St., New Albany.

197 The **Evansville Convention and Visitors Bureau** is now located at 601 Walnut St., on the first floor of the Executive Inn Parking Garage.

224 The structure that housed the **Tell City Pretzel Company** was razed in February 1992, and the company moved to 532 Main St. The former **Schreiber's Drugstore** burned in late October 1989. The **depot of the old Southern Railway** burned in early November 1989.

231 As a result of a June 1990 flood, plans are under way to move the town of **ENGLISH** to higher ground 1 m. northeast of its present location. The old town will be leveled.

236 The **Ferdinand and Huntingburg Railroad** is no longer operating.

306 The **Army Ammunition Plant** is operated by Mason & Hanger-Silas Mason Co., Inc.

332 The **stone inscribed Red Cross Farm** is now at the Red Cross office located at 2119 29th St., Bedford, Indiana. The **Hindostan Whetstone Company** is now doing business as **Hindostone Products, Inc.,** located at 6355 Morenci Trail, Indianapolis.

333 The Bedford **Chamber of Commerce** office has moved to 116 16th St.

335 The **Carpenter Body Works** is now **Carpenter Manufacturing, Inc.**

341 The **West Baden Springs Hotel** is closed and for sale.

344 The **Larkin Brothers Department Store** in Loogootee is out of business.

370 The Nashville **Chamber of Commerce** has moved to Main St., one-half block west of Van Buren. It is next to the First America Bank. Park where possible and proceed on foot. Thus the **John Dillinger Historical Museum** can no longer be cited as "approximately one-half block north of the Chamber of Commerce."

374 The **Homelawn Sanitarium** has burned; only a few of the outbuildings remain. The official name of **Drake's Phonograph Museum** is the **Midwest Phonograph Museum.** It is open by appointment through the Martinsville Chamber of Commerce, and groups are welcome.

376 The **Morgan County Historical Society** in Mooresville is no longer active.

377 The **Johnson County Historical Museum** has moved to the **Masonic Temple** at 135 N. Main St. The **Lewis Hendricks Pioneer Log Cabin** has been moved and is currently in storage. The **Suckow house** has been returned to the family.

421 **Fort Benjamin Harrison** is scheduled to be closed.

434 **The Coca-Cola plant** in Crawfordsville is scheduled for demolition in 1992.

437 The **old Normal School** building in Ladoga is scheduled for demolition.

459 The **railroad museum,** in the **Big Four Railroad Station,** has been closed.

469 The **Knightstown Spring Rest Park** has been closed by the Department of Natural Resources and the State Highway Department. Nothing remains at the site.

477 The **Winchester Methodist Episcopal Church** was demolished in 1991.

478 The **Cedar Ford Covered Bridge** has been removed.

480 **Riley Elementary School** has burned, and all that remains are the arches. A local doctor has built his offices around the arches.

489 The **Greater Lafayette Convention and Visitors Bureau, Inc.,** has moved to 301 Frontage Rd. (I-65 and IND 26).

492 The **Scott St. Pavilion** is now the **Rush Pavilion.**

503 **Grissom Air Force Base** is scheduled to be closed.

508 The **Indiana Transportation Museum** is running steam excursions and is purchasing the former Norfolk Southern line between Indianapolis and Tipton.

509 A new **Hamilton County Courthouse** is being completed in Noblesville.

529 **Discovery Hall Museum** moved out of the Century Center in June 1991 and is no longer in existence. The *Violin Woman* sculpture, across the street from the Morris Civic Auditorium, is no longer mounted on a fountain. It is now located north of the fountain.

531 The segment of a blazed tree from the 1679 La Salle landing is no longer displayed at the **Northern Indiana Historical Society Museum.**

532 The address of **St. Paul's Memorial United Methodist Church** is 1001 W. Colfax Ave. The address of the **Studebaker National Museum** is 525 S. Main St.

533 The **Council Oak** blew down in August 1991.

544 **Papakeechie Rd.** has been renamed **East Wawasee Dr.**

546 The **International Palace of Sports** is no longer operating.

548 The **Billy Sunday Tabernacle** at Winona Lake has been razed.

550 The **Roann Covered Bridge** was burned and has been reconstructed.

566 After being damaged by a tornado in 1989, the **Larry Paxton Round Barn** was donated to the Fulton County Historical Society. It was moved to the FCHS grounds on New US 31 and reconstructed with the help of a $40,000 loan from Historic Landmarks Foundation of Indiana. Total cost of the reconstruction was $65,000. It is now the **Fulton County Round Barn Museum** with horse-drawn farm implements and old-time tools. It is located beside the Fulton County Museum.

568 The **Rochester Depot Museum** is scheduled to move in October 1992 to US 31 by the Fulton County Museum.

583 **Calumet College of St. Joseph** is now **Calumet College.**

593 Commuter trains no longer operate through the **Pennsylvania Railroad Station** at Hobart.

598 The **Perfection Musical String Company** is no longer operating.

604 The building in Pinhook referred to as a "**grocery store,** recently closed" no longer exists.

607 The **Allis-Chalmers Corporation factory** on Pine Lake Ave. has been demolished and replaced with the Pine Lake Community Shopping Center. The **Sage Ice Cream Company** is no longer in business.

619 **Valparaiso Technical Institute** is closed. The **Wilbur H. Cummings Museum of Electronics** is located at 1 Center St. **I G Technologies** is now **UGIMAG, Inc.**

Fort Wayne

Fort Wayne, Indiana's second largest city (p. 172,196) and Allen County's seat of government, was platted in 1824. For more than a century prior to its founding, the site served as a trading and military post to a succession of nations—Miamis, Iroquois, France, England, and United States. To these rivals for control of the Old Northwest the area possessed exceptional geographical value. Here the St. Joseph and St. Marys rivers came together to form the Maumee River. The conjunction of three rivers invested the locale with transportation and communication significance. The Indians called it the "Glorious Gate." Moreover, the Maumee-Wabash portage, a small patch of land lying southwest of the present city, connected the great water networks of the Great Lakes and the Mississippi Valley. The seven-mile pathway linked Lake Erie, via the Maumee River, to a tributary of the Wabash River. Once afloat on the Wabash, a craft could reach the Gulf of Mexico without leaving the water.

The French were the first Europeans to occupy the magnificent forests at the three-rivers junction. To gain its objective, France negotiated a tentative truce with the ruling Iroquois and persuaded the pro-French Miamis, who had relinquished the area to the Iroquois in the 1600s, to remigrate to the Maumee headwaters. By the early 1700s the Miamis had repossessed much of the Wabash valley. They located their principal village, Kiskakon, or Kekionga, in the lakeside section of present Fort Wayne. Fort Miami, the first French fort, went up in 1722 about a half-mile west of Kiskakon. A new Fort Miami was completed in 1750 on the St. Joseph River's east bank above Kiskakon. The minimally staffed forts served primarily as trade centers and as meeting places for French-Indian diplomacy.

The smoldering contest between France and England for sovereignty in North America erupted in the 1750s into a full-fledged conflict historically known as the French and Indian War. The English decisively won the war and thereby gained nominal authority over half a continent. England took command of Fort Miami in 1760. In 1763 the local Miamis captured the stockade on behalf of Pontiac, an Ottawa chief, whose pan-Indian movement sought to halt further white advance. Upon the failure of Pontiac's mission, the English returned, soothed the Miamis, and restored business with cooperative French traders. However, they did not reoccupy the fort, which harbored French families. Around the fort clustered traders, outlaws, officials, Miamis, Shawnees, and Delawares in seven distinct villages collectively called Miamitown. Among the inhabitants were the infamous renegade Simon Girty and the powerful Miami chief Little Turtle. Miamitown became a headquarters for Indian raiding parties.

A series of military thrusts by Americans during the Revolutionary War and up through 1791 failed to dislodge the Miami Confederacy from the Northwest. Anthony Wayne finally routed the Indian league in 1794 at Fallen Timbers in present northwest Ohio. Wayne proceeded west to Miamitown, torching fields and villages in his path. On arrival, he selected the high ground south of the river junction as the site of the first United States fort. Lt. Col. John Hamtramck, who supervised construction, dedicated the garrison on October 22, 1794, and named it Fort Wayne in his commander's honor. The next year the United States acquired from the Miamis through the Treaty of Greenville six square miles encircling Fort Wayne. Congress soon established an Indian agency at the fort and in 1800 approved the building of a new fort nearby. In the vicinity homes and business houses of government representatives, French and American traders, Indians, and sutlers (post provisioners) arose.

The area's last serious threat from Indians occurred in 1812 when Tecumseh, the Shawnee chief, laid siege to Fort Wayne. William Henry

Harrison, the territorial governor, rescued the fort, but the ravaged countryside and fleeing inhabitants delayed the planting of a viable community. In 1815 Maj. John Whistler, the grandfather of artist James Abbott McNeill Whistler, replaced the fort with one better built and more compact. The presence of Whistler's fort and the ending of the War of 1812 drew squatters back to the government property. As the only settlement between Fort Dearborn (Chicago) and St. Marys, Ohio, Fort Wayne commanded the regional trade; however, before it could tap the burgeoning population in central and southern Indiana, the peripheral Indian lands had to be taken over. This was accomplished by the St. Marys Treaty of 1818, which shifted to the United States ownership of most of the land south of Fort Wayne. By virtue of the treaty, the Fort Wayne countryside was accessible to the land- and job-hungry throng pushing northward from the Ohio River.

The provisions of the St. Marys Treaty did not immediately transform Fort Wayne into a flourishing town. The sale of government lands was five years away. Meanwhile, the largely French-Canadian tenants of the crude log cabins around the fort lived not for city-building but for fur trade profits, illicitly gained at times. The fort's termination as a military garrison in 1819 increased the precariousness of existence in this rough-and-tumble frontier hamlet. Still, the government's influence persisted, for good or ill, in the person of the Indian agent. Moreover, residents could choose to set up housekeeping in the abandoned barracks. Isaac McCoy, a Baptist missionary, organized a school in the fort in 1820, the same year the backwoods settlement acquired a post office.

An indication that Fort Wayne was about to enter a new phase of its history came with the establishment of a federal land office at the fort in 1822. All public lands south of Fort Wayne went on sale October 22, 1823, excluding the fort, thirty acres reserved for Indian encampments, and specified grants. The original plat of Fort Wayne city was purchased by John T. Barr of Baltimore, Maryland, and John McCorkle of Piqua, Ohio. The two speculators promptly had their property surveyed and laid out into lots.

ALLEN COUNTY (p. 294,335; 659 sq. m.), comprising most of northeastern Indiana, was created by the state legislature in 1823.

The county's name memorialized John Allen, a liberator of Fort Wayne in 1812. In the spring of 1824 the county commissioners accepted Barr and McCorkle's offer of several public lots from their tract. In return the officials awarded the two businessmen the exclusive right to develop their tract as the county seat. The exchange led to the establishment of the town of Fort Wayne.

The county seat placement and the sale of town lots, beginning in September 1824, drew new settlers from Kentucky, Ohio, and Virginia primarily. By 1825 the fledgling village had about 150 inhabitants. An 1826 treaty gave the United States the land above Fort Wayne, and in 1828 the Indian agency transferred to Logansport. Both actions irritated local traders who risked losing their major means of support. The decreasing dependence on the Indian trade, however, prompted other types of business ventures critical to the town's survival. Moreover, new lands encouraged residential and commerical expansion, much needed agricultural development, and construction of a canal that could link the settlement more closely with the rest of the nation.

The town's incorporation in 1829 served notice to the state legislature that the now organized community expected action on the Wabash and Erie Canal. The route through Fort Wayne had been traced in 1828, but opposition from railroad proponents and insufficient sales of canal lands for construction funds held up digging the channel. In 1832 the lawmakers finally authorized the canal commissioners to borrow funds to launch the project.

Fort Wayne hosted the official canal ground breaking in 1832 as well as its grand dedication in 1843. The artificial waterway hastened the transition of Fort Wayne from an isolated frontier hamlet, subsisting on fur processing, to a prosperous cosmopolitan and industrial city tied to agriculture. This conversion began in the 1830s with feverish land sales, the influx of farmers and skilled artisans from Germany and canal workers from Ireland, plus the emergence of sawmills, breweries, cabinet shops, slaughterhouses, and marble works. By decade's end the original town plat had expanded by four additions, and the population had increased fivefold. In 1840 the Indiana General Assembly approved a city charter.

The fervor of church plantings, courthouse construction, farm development, and the general enterprise of city-building undermined the fur and Indian trades, though both activities pulled the community through the lean years following the financial panic of 1837. Inevitably, though, the fur business moved westward, and the Indians were persuaded to cede their last reserve in 1840. In late 1846 the local Miamis boarded canalboats for their long and sorrowful journey to Kansas.

During the heyday of the canal era, from 1842 to 1854, Fort Wayne rapidly evolved into the state's fifth largest city and a leader in manufacturing. A key to the progress was the interrelationship between the canal and agriculture. The canalboats, crafted with lumber from farmers' cleared fields, facilitated the movement east and west of goods and people. The ripening and specialization of agriculture meant raw materials for saw, flour, and woolen mills, tanneries, and textile factories, while stimulating the erection of foundries and tile manufacturers, for example, to meet the farmers' needs.

The core of the city, encompassing warehouses, docks, boatyards, stores, and offices, developed along the south side of the canal. Around the public square, which sported a new courthouse in 1847, churches and schools went up with increasing regularity in the 1840s. The first Catholic school, the first public schools, and the first colleges were established between 1845 and 1853. The Fort Wayne Female College (1846) and the Fort Wayne Collegiate Institute (1852) merged into the Fort Wayne College, which in time became Taylor University at Upland, Indiana. The state's first Jewish congregation began in 1848 as the Society for Visiting the Sick and Burying the Dead. Allen Hamilton, a land office employee in 1823, founded a bank in 1853. Edith Hamilton (1867–1963), the banker's granddaughter, grew up in Fort Wayne and went on to become an acclaimed classical scholar, author of the popular *The Greek Way* (1930). Her sister, Alice Hamilton (1869–1970), reformer and pacifist, associated with Jane Addams at Hull House and pioneered in industrial diseases. In 1845 John Chapman, better known as Johnny Appleseed, died and was buried in Fort Wayne. In 1846 Samuel Bigger, the state's seventh governor, was buried in the City Cemetery.

In the 1850s the railroad came to Fort Wayne, and canal use rapidly declined. The Ohio and Indiana (1850) and the Fort Wayne and Chicago (1852) railroads merged in 1856 to form the Pittsburgh, Fort Wayne and Chicago Railroad. The "Pennsy"shops, manufacturing engines and cars, evolved from the Jones, Bass and Company foundry established in 1853 and was sold to the railroad in 1857. Located at the site of the present main post office on Clinton Street, the Pennsy shops was a major employer for 70 years. In 1858 John H. Bass (1835–1922) founded the Bass Foundry and Machine Works, which became the nation's primary producer of railroad wheels and axles.

By 1860 Fort Wayne ranked second in Indiana in manufacturing establishments. The city's population topped 9,000, and Allen County had the state's second highest number of foreign born. A new courthouse went up during the Civil War. The Summit City Club, Fort Wayne's first baseball team, organized in 1862. The Summit City sobriquet came about because Fort Wayne proved to be the highest point, or the summit level, on the Wabash and Erie Canal route, which, in addition, is on the continental divide between the Great Lakes and the Mississippi Valley. The major new industry begun in the war years was Charles Lewis Centlivre's French Brewery in 1862, subsequently Centlivre Brewery. The company, later named Crown Brewery, ceased operations in 1973. Fort Wayne's first telegraph dispatch occurred in 1848. In 1864 Thomas Edison, a young telegrapher and soon-to-be inventor, stayed about six months in the city working for the railroad. Around the same time the Hoagland brothers and Thomas Biddle, druggists, formulated what soon became Royal Baking Powder. John Paul Dreiser, the father of Theodore Dreiser, the author, and Paul Dresser, the songwriter, worked in the giant woolen mill of French, Hanna and Company. George Westinghouse came to Fort Wayne in 1869 to test his first air brake.

By 1870 only Evansville and Indianapolis surpassed Fort Wayne in population, a ranking the Summit City would hold for the next 50 years. The railroad, textile, beer, brick, and tile products of the 1860s were supplemented before the end of the century by pianos and organs, valves and pumps, washing machines and hosiery, electrical items, and more beer. Horton Manufacturing Company, founded in 1871, pioneered in the development of the self-contained washing machine. General Electric, the city's largest employer by the mid-20th century, began in 1881 as the Fort Wayne Jenney Electric Light Company. Centlivre Brewery had to compete with Berghoff Brewery. Wayne Knitting Mills, formed in 1891, received widespread recognition for its hosiery. A revolution in the handling and measuring of gas and oil got under way with the pump inventions of Sylvanus F. Bowser, who organized his factory in 1885, and the appearance of the Wayne Oil Tank Company (Wayne Pump) in 1891. Today's computing gasoline pump was created at the Wayne Pump facility. Scottish-born James Bain White (1835–1897) parlayed his cloth printing and tailoring skills into the fashioning of a leading department store. He also owned a wheel-making factory and a bank and served as a congressman, 1887–89. His great-grandson, astronaut Ed White, made America's first space walk.

The city's borders widened in 1894 with the annexation of the South Wayne community. The wetlands southwest of town, known as the Portage Marsh, attained agricultural and business value when the miles of swamp were dredged in the late 1880s. More railroads, including the Nickel Plate, the construction of bridges, and the introduction of streetcars, free mail delivery, and the telephone helped tie together the enlarged metropolis while furthering its connections to the outside world. In 1901 the interurbans began regular service.

By 1915 Fort Wayne had become the state's second largest city, eclipsing Evansville. Turn-of-the-century reform mayors, particularly William J. Hosey, guided the unprecedented growth. Their regard for public morals, city-owned utilities, park development, pure water and food, railroad overpasses, paved streets, clean alleys, and flood control attracted to the city increasing numbers of residents, including Italian and East European immigrants. Only the occasional labor-management dispute, a police chief's indictment, or a devastating flood or fire could shake the community's sense of well-being.

The prosperous prewar years gave way to the super-patriotism and xenophobia of the European conflict. Ninety-four men and women from Fort Wayne died in the First World War. Fort Wayne native Paul Frank Baer was an ace combat pilot and the first aviator to receive the Distinguished Service Cross. In 1925 the city's first municipal airport carried Baer's name. On the home front, official and unauthorized actions forced German citizens to refrain from using their native language in churches, schools, and on the streets. The German-American National Bank changed its name to Lincoln National Bank.

Between the war and the onset of the Great Depression of the 1930s, Fort Wayne rose to the fore among America's affluent communities. By 1929 the city had acquired within its 17 square miles some 300 factories, 26,760 dwellings, 1,500 wholesale and retail firms, 140 churches and schools, 29 parks, 21 hotels, 18 theaters, and 8 hospitals. Air passenger service was established in 1928. Major new plants, the fruit of efforts by the Greater Fort Wayne Development Corporation, included International Harvester, Zollner Machine Works, and several wire manufacturers. Fort Wayne claimed to be the nation's leading producer of oil tanks and pumps, rail car wheels, lisle hosiery, auto trucks, and copper wire. Besides stimulating an increase in population, which surpassed the 100,000 mark in the mid-1920s, the vigorous business activity spelled new jobs and housing. Few American cities could match Fort Wayne's low tax rate, the wage standard, the average $688 family bank deposit, the 66 percent home ownership, the 122 cars per 100 families, or the sums spent on education.

For entertainment and recreation residents could choose from 18 theaters, 2 country clubs and golf courses, 150 restaurants, 29 parks, and unknown numbers of speakeasies. A big public entertainer was the phonograph, perhaps one made by the firm of the future United States senator Homer E. Capehart, who located his company in Fort Wayne in 1929. People tuned in WOWO radio, which call letters evoked the slogan Wayne Offers Wonderful Opportunity. Founded in 1925 WOWO soon became one of the 15 most powerful stations in the country. Sports fans cheered for the Fort Wayne Hoosiers of the American Professional Basketball League. Six libraries catered to the reading public. Devotees of the performing arts here and elsewhere caught Fort Wayne native George Jean Nathan's witty and biting drama columns in the *Smart Set* or the *American Mercury*, magazines Nathan edited with H. L. Mencken.

To a city as financially strong as Fort Wayne in the 1920s, the economic debacle of the subsequent decade seemed that much more severe. Prominent buildings went up between

1929 and 1933: the 22-story Lincoln National Bank, which was Indiana's tallest, a Federal Building, and a huge water filtration plant. These structures, normal undertakings for a thriving community, seemed out of place in a city that could muster only 34 new home starts from 1932 through 1934. Meanwhile 10 of Fort Wayne's 12 banks failed. Unemployment soared, particularly in the metal trades. International Harvester provided 66 acres of plowed land for its furloughed employees to garden. Local relief efforts, briefly successful, experienced added strains from hobos, always attracted to larger railroad towns. The rusty sheet metal and packing box hovels of impoverished families composed a large shantytown on the St. Marys River flats. These conditions, along with the deepening of the depression and the continuation of liquor prohibition, bred crime. Police and special agents raided speakeasies and roadhouses, ran down tips on arsons and bombings, arrested increasing numbers of loiterers, and kept sharp eyes for John Dillinger and his gang of mostly Fort Wayne hoodlums. The period's most sensational crime was the Broadway Bank holdup by the Kelly Gang in 1930. George "Machine Gun" Kelly, captured later, stood trial in Fort Wayne and served a sentence at the Michigan City prison.

Show business flourished as persons paused from depression realities. The Community Concert Association, the Civic Symphony, the Civic Youththeatre, and the Old Fort Players were organized in the 1930s. Moviegoers viewed with special interest the meteoric career of Fort Wayne's Carole Lombard. Across the country listeners enjoyed the high jinks on the Hoosier Hop, a WOWO production. Vanguard technical developments in the entertainment world occurred in Fort Wayne. In 1929 Magnavox moved its speaker and phonograph firm from California to Fort Wayne, and Homer E. Capehart brought in his radio and phonograph company from nearby Huntington. Capehart lost his company in the early years of the Great Depression and took a position with the Rudolph Wurlitzer Manufacturing Company in North Tonawanda, New York. His patented record changing device, fashioned in Fort Wayne, enabled Wurlitzer to introduce the jukebox in 1934.

An economic upturn in Fort Wayne originated with the end of national prohibition in 1933 and the reopening of the Centlivre and Berghoff breweries. Relief programs emanating from all government levels put people back to work. Pro-labor legislation breathed new life into that long-dormant movement. The United Electrical Workers was formed in Fort Wayne in 1936. Also established was Local 57 of the United Auto Workers, eventually the city's largest union. New attempts to economize in municipal government, in a city well-known for its low bonded indebtedness and tax rates, received nationwide exposure in 1940. The National Consumers Tax Commission produced a pamphlet detailing Fort Wayne's efficiency measures and its schooling of citizens to the exact costs of service. By 1940 Fort Wayne stood second highest in its population class in per family income, and fourth highest in per capita income.

America's entry into World War II contributed to Fort Wayne's recovery process. Virtually every type of war-related equipment was produced in the city. Older plants expanded facilities. New factories were constructed. The Studebaker Corporation built a huge installation to manufacture airplane engine gear. South of the city the army constructed an air base that took the name Baer Field, which happened to be the name of the municipal airport. The latter redesignated its field to honor another local aviator, Art Smith. A jump in employment and, despite the restrictions, consumer spending rippled through the local economy, thus terminating a decade of stagnation.

On balance, Fort Wayne demonstrated resilience to the typical urban trauma of postwar reconversion. As expected, employment opportunities initially fell as several large businesses, including Studebaker, shut down, and as major industries reduced work forces. Much of the surplus labor returned to neighboring farms and towns. The job market was affected also by labor-management disputes, work stoppages, and shortages in industrial tools and equipment. New jobs emerged, nevertheless, because of a steadily increasing population, up 12.8 percent in the 1940s as compared to 3 percent in the depressed 1930s. The job vacuum after 1945 was filled partially by the needs of new factories, such as United States Rubber, non-defense-related plants, and new government contracts. Considerable aid in revitalizing postwar industry derived from the flow of swollen wartime savings into the marketplace to purchase previously scarce houses, cars, and appliances.

Look magazine in 1949 featured Fort Wayne in an article entitled "America's Happiest Town." The writer portrayed the community as relaxed and pleasant, void of socioeconomic extremes, progressive but colorless, a center of the precision tool industry, a population of skilled labor and well-adjusted youth, and beneficiaries of a relatively prosperous environment. A more discerning observer would have offered a less flattering image. Fort Wayne was due for a major physical overhaul, and, after 1950, a renewal of confidence in city government, following the indictment of the mayor, police chief, and others on conspiracy to commit grand larceny in regard to the city's coal purchases.

Fort Wayne's business district in the early 1950s was characterized by chronic traffic congestion, deteriorating buildings, and nearby pockets of blight. A few stores, most notably Sears, had relocated outside the core area. The population began spilling outside the city line, thus calling forth an aggressive annexation policy that by 1983 would add 39 square miles to the city. Measures taken to relieve the traffic situation included increasing parking areas, repairing roads, instituting one-way street patterns, constructing the Circumurban (US 30 Bypass), and elevating the Nickel Plate tracks. The two-mile-long rail elevation, dedicated in 1955, opened north Fort Wayne for residential and commercial development. Interstate 69, skirting the city to the west and the north, was built in the 1960s. The Circumurban, I-69, and the push of population northward attracted business to the city's northern rim. Eventually the bypass would become as traffic-choked as the downtown bottleneck it was supposed to remedy and necessitated new bypass construction, which began in 1987.

Fort Wayne took up urban renewal belatedly due to the gradual exit of retailers, the reluctance of shopkeepers to upgrade their stores, the unconcern of absentee landowners, the lack of heavy private investment, and the too-rapid changeover of city administrations. Federal moneys were earmarked for water, sewer, and street mending rather than more visible sprucing-up. But in the late 1960s urban renewal began in earnest. Over 140 acres were leveled at this time. About 150 aging buildings were torn down between 1967 and 1983. In the same period almost $200 million went into over 30 new buildings and the expansion or renovation of 60 businesses and institutions. Fort Wayne's skyline was dramatically changed. Altered, too, was the nature of activity in the central city as office buildings, hotels, banks, government buildings, and cultural institutions replaced the once dominant retail firms. By the early 1980s only 4 percent of the core land area was designated as retail oriented.

In the wake of the wrecking ball, aroused citizens sought to salvage what remained of bygone days. Initial steps were taken in the 1960s to restore a block of structures along Columbia Street at the old canal landing. Historic Fort Wayne, a likeness of one of the early forts, opened to the public in 1976. ARCH, a special committee of the Fort Wayne Bicentennial Commission, began a fruitful period of surveying, rescuing, restoring, and legally protecting representative historic buildings.

The upheaval of urban renewal was accompanied by similar convulsions in the social arena. In the 1970s Fort Wayne, for the first time in its history, recorded a loss in population. Many persons who left the city kept their jobs in Fort Wayne and took up residence in nearby communities. Apparently newly installed sewage systems had as much to do with the appeal of the small towns as their proximity or overall quality of life. Despite an ambitious annexation program and, not surprisingly, massive sewer and water projects, the slippage could not be halted. Fort Wayne ended the decade with a net loss of 6,073 residents, whereas the county's count increased by almost 14,000.

Throughout the 1970s persons experiencing or perceiving serious deprivation of one kind or another let their voices be heard. Labor-management agitations punctuated the decade. Police and firemen conducted work slowdowns. City employees and schoolteachers held walkouts. Youth battled police on several occasions. Fort Wayne blacks, comprising 10 percent of the population, protested urban renewal practices, the closing of neighborhood schools, and one-way busing for school integration. The courts adjudicated increasing numbers of civil rights cases. A Ku Klux Klan march in 1979 and the sniper wounding of Vernon Jordan, National Urban League President, in 1980 kept racial issues at the forefront of local concerns. A jump in crime, largely tied to drugs and arson, brought public attention to a major group of victims, the elderly. To assist the aged, a number of federal, state, and local programs, from meal delivery to legal services, were implemented. A new Senior Citizens Center, low cost housing, and a dozen new nursing homes helped fulfill a variety of needs.

Major economic adjustments underlay much of the unsettling dynamics of modern Fort Wayne. All sectors proved vulnerable to the decade's energy crunch and inflation. Prices on homes and consumer goods shot upwards as the era of cheap fuels ended. Some businesses retrenched in the face of spiraling utility rates, government mandated environmental standards, and labor demands for wage adjustments. During the recession of 1973–75 unemployment peaked at 12.6 percent. Small retailers felt the pinch of higher costs of living and the pressures from large-volume department stores. On the other side of the ledger, builders of apartments, condominiums, hotels and motels, along with big discount houses, leisure and recreation dealers, and pump companies were among the profit-taking enterprises. The pump companies flourished as gas stations added equipment and converted to self-service islands.

Events surrounding the recession of the early 1980s speeded up and clearly revealed the shifting nature of the city's economy. The downturn in housing construction and vehicle purchases directly affected such giants as General Electric and International Harvester. Double-digit inflation checked the consumer's appetite for GE's heavy-duty appliances and for Harvester's trucks. Both manufacturers and their suppliers began laying off workers in 1979. The city's unemployment rate, determined largely within the durable goods sector, climbed past 13 percent by mid-1982. The financially strapped International Harvester closed the doors of its truck facility in 1983, and with it went 8,000 jobs, a loss of such magnitude to the community that the full effects are still unknown. What is recognized is that the recession-vulnerable smokestack industries on which Fort Wayne grew to depend after World War II can no longer form the leading edge of the local economy. In the place of heavy manufacturing the emerging economic framework rests in high tech industry, the wholesale and retail trades, financial services, insurance, and government.

While Fort Wayne grappled with inflation and increasing joblessness a literal sea of troubles brought added burdens. For one week in March 1982 melting snow and rain caused the three rivers to inundate the city with its worst flood since 1913. The waters crested at 25.93 ft., just shy of the 1913 record of 26.1 ft. The battle to stem the overflow captured the country's admiration. Some 50,000 volunteers, mostly of school age, filled and stacked an estimated one million sandbags along eight miles of dikes. Termed the "children's crusade," the youthful effort to reinforce floodwalls drew to the site the national television networks and President Ronald Reagan to witness and report the community's heroic endeavor. Still, the damage totaled about $21.8 million. Approximately 3,000 homes and businesses were affected by the deluge, and 9,000 individuals were put up in shelters. Although the flood could not have come at a worse time, in some respects the wide attention given the disaster and the banding together of residents raised morale. Subsequent projects to strengthen the dikes, install early warning systems, and improve the channels and backwater gates, make it less likely that the 1982 catastrophe will be repeated.

By the mid to late 1980s, Fort Wayne, helped considerably by the national economic recovery, verged on gaining the upper hand in reestablishing economic stability. In fact, in 1987 the city showed a five-year growth in employment that exceeded that of the Great Lakes region. Apparently the pullout of International Harvester had not, as predicted, wrecked the local economy. Harvester's former property filled with new tenants, and because of the company's high wage scale its going lowered the community's pay structure, an appealing aspect to potential new employers. A multimillion dollar job promotion plan, a national advertising campaign, and tax incentives offered to businesses locating in a demarcated Enterprise Zone, contributed to Fort Wayne's attractiveness as a location for new firms. A major boost to the economy came in 1985 with the building just south of the city of a 2.1 million-sq.-ft. General Motors light-duty, truck-assembly plant with the potential for 3,000 employees. In the meantime Fort Wayne received selection as an All American City, and the United States Council of Mayors voted it the Most Livable City, the only municipality to garner both honors in the same year. A transformed downtown boasted a new civic center and hotel, a unusual Botanical Conservatory, a Performing Arts Center, a Museum of Art, a Historical Museum, a midtown fountained plaza, and a variety of other historical and cultural attractions. The Rivergreenway Project, begun in 1975, is reviving waterfront usage by creating parks, boardwalks, trails, bikeways, and landscapes along the three rivers. Fort Wayne continues to be one of the least expensive places to live of any city its size, and by many accounts one of the most pleasurable.

Fort Wayne Attractions

The **Fort Wayne Convention & Visitors Bureau** is located in the Chamber of Commerce Building, 826 Ewing St., Fort Wayne. It is open weekdays, but not weekends.

1. The **Allen County-Fort Wayne Historical Society Museum**, 302 E. Berry St., exhibits an extensive body of local and regional historical objects in attractive chronological or thematic settings. The museum is located in the Old City Hall, a sandstone fortress completed in 1893 at a cost of almost $70,000. In time community growth forced officials to seek added space in scattered locales and finally in 1971 to consolidate services in the new City-County Building. Meanwhile, the Historical Society's museum was outgrowing its quarters in the Swinney house. The Society, formed in 1921, had removed a collection of miscellaneous artifacts from the courthouse to the historic Swinney residence in 1926. By the 1970s only a portion of the organization's holdings could be displayed in the old home. The Society's desire for a new location met the needs of the city, which was looking for a tenant for the Old City Hall, and which had funds for the Hall's renovation. The remodeling was finished in 1979, and the Society's museum was transferred in 1980. (*NRHP*)

2. The **Performing Arts Center**, 303 E. Main St., opened in 1973 as the community's initial effort to centralize and clothe in modern wrap its long and distinguished cultural tradition. Plans surfaced in 1961 to house the city's various artistic pursuits in a complex of buildings to be constructed in the downtown urban renewal area. The Fine Arts Foundation's ambitious venture had to be scaled down to the one building as years passed and costs accelerated. From the beginning the architect was the noted Philadelphian Louis I. Kahn. The creator of the Yale Art Center, among other eminent designs, Kahn employed ungarnished brick and con-

crete throughout his first and only theater project. The exterior forms a shell concealing a 682-seat detached auditorium. The building-in-a-building motif utilizes the double walls to maximize soundproofing. A large movable lift can increase the seating capacity, extend the stage, or make room for an orchestra pit. The Civic Theatre, housed at the Center, is the principal user along with the Youththeatre, which celebrated its 50th birthday in 1984. Other groups availing themselves of the facility include the Fort Wayne Ballet and the Fort Wayne Philharmonic. A small gallery on the second floor occasionally holds exhibits, and community organizations can lease space for special events. In front of the building is a helitec, or sundial, carved from limestone by Timothy Doyle. A copy of the helitec is in Takaoka, Japan, Fort Wayne's sister city. This relationship blossomed during the mid-1970s and resulted in the Japanese city presenting Fort Wayne a gift of an authentic Japanese garden in 1979. The garden can be viewed at the side of the Performing Arts Center. In return, Fort Wayne sent to Takaoka one of the two sundials.

3. The **Fort Wayne Museum of Art**, 311 E. Main St., is situated directly east of the Performing Arts Center. The $3.5 million museum, opened in 1984, traces its beginnings to 1888 when local patrons launched an art school taught by J. Ottis Adams. A more formal organization, the Fort Wayne Art School, was established in 1897. In 1922 Theodore F. Thieme, founder of Wayne Knitting Mills, underwrote the incorporation and housing of the Fort Wayne Art School and Museum. From 1949 to 1984 the museum was quartered in the B. Paul Mossman stone mansion at 1202 Wayne St. The Wayne St. gallery's increasing space problem, physical deterioration, and its relative remoteness appeared solved with the Arts Foundation's announcement in the early 1960s to build a downtown complex. The failure of the

Fort Wayne Attractions

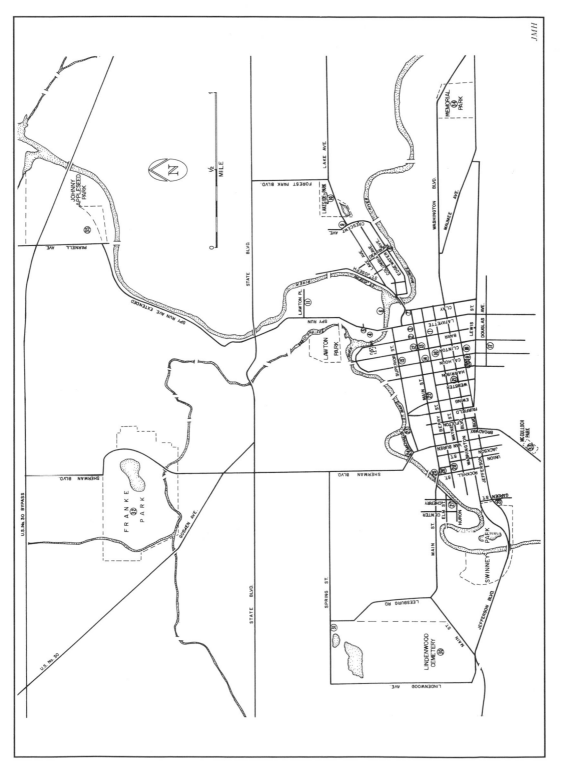

plan to materialize demoralized the arts community. Alarmed at the critical status of the museum, civic leaders amassed enough corporate funds, matching grants, and small contributions to break ground for a new building in 1982. Walter A. Netsch of Chicago designed the red brick structure. Its floor plan divides into exhibition, education, and community service areas, each entered from a central two-story sculpture court. Skylights give an airy and spacious feel to the 39,000-sq.-ft. interior, painted in the colors of watermelon and Spanish raisin. The museum includes a 108-seat auditorium, museum shop, and sales and rental gallery. Fronting the building is an 18 x 40-ft. aluminum sculpture entitled Crossings, executed by David Black, a retired Ohio State University professor of art who holds a MFA degree from Indiana University.

4. **Historic Fort Wayne**, 107 S. Clinton St., is a faithful copy of Maj. John Whistler's post constructed in 1815–16. Reputedly one of the finest military fort re-creations in the Midwest, it features a well-rehearsed staff of authentically clothed historical interpreters who portray life at the fort in 1816. The 10 wood-hewn buildings, including a museum, are situated on four and one-half acres about three blocks north of the original site of the fort. When plans were formulated in the mid-1960s to reconstruct the facility, its former location at E. Main and Clay sts. was unavailable, and the developers opted for the nearest sizable downtown place. For guidance in reproducing the fort, the last remnants of which vanished in the 1850s, historians and architects turned to the records housed in the National Archives including Major Whistler's diagram of the installation. Ground breaking took place in November 1974. The fort opened to the public in 1976. In front of the fort's entrance is a relic of the Battle of Lake Erie in 1813. The six-pound naval gun was used in the dedication of the Wabash and Erie Canal in 1843. Its present carriage is a reproduction made from old canal timbers. The Old Fort Visitors Center is at 211 S. Baar St.

5. The **William Wells Marker**, Spy Run Ave. and Baltes St., indicates the site of the home of a major figure in Indian-white relations in the Old Northwest. Captured by the Miamis in 1784, the 14-year-old Wells was adopted by a Wea chief, Gaviahatte (the Porcupine), and quickly conformed to tribal customs. Wells went on Indian raids of white settlements, became friends with Little Turtle, who died at Wells's home in 1812, and married his daughter Sweet Breeze. Wells gave up his Indian life for the security of white civilization in the late 1790s. He became a scout, government interpreter, and Indian agent. His unique position as a "white Indian" made him invaluable as a go-between in negotiations, but it also rendered him marginally acceptable by either side. Involved in some way with most of the treaty dealings and military conflicts up to the War of 1812, Wells presents a tragic figure trying to forge an honorable and just relation between two incompatible cultures. He was killed by Potawatomi Indians in 1812 while leading some Miamis and soldiers from the besieged Fort Dearborn (Chicago). He was beheaded, and his heart was devoured by his attackers, who hoped to ingest their victim's courage. His descendants acquired much land in the Fort Wayne area by dint of Federal grants and treaty reservations. One section, called "Wells preemption," took up a square mile between the Maumee and St. Joseph rivers.

6. The **Jesuit Statue**, representing the priests-explorers who arrived at the three-rivers junction in the 1600s, stands at riverside in front of the filtration plant at the end of Baltes St. east off Spy Run Ave. Commissioned by the Joseph W. Parrot family, the 7-ft., 9-in.-tall bronze figure points to the spot where the St. Marys and St. Joseph rivers form the Maumee River. Dedicated in 1976, the sculpture is the work of Hector Garcia of Indiana University-Purdue University at Fort Wayne. The stone Gothic filtration plant was constructed in the early 1930s as an answer to the city's chronic water needs. Dependent on drying and polluted wells the city turned to the St. Joseph River for water. The new plant, costing $2.5 million, met the water deficiency by purifying 20 million gallons of the precious liquid daily.

7. The **Old Fort Well**, Main and Clay sts., is a replica of the one constructed sometime around 1800 for use in the second, and newly completed, Fort Wayne. The reconstructed well rests on the site of Col. Thomas Hunt's fort, but some 20 ft. south of the location of the original well. In 1863 the grounds of the post became the city's first park. Old Fort Park, as it was

called, had its historical and natural character spoiled by the erection of the railroad elevation in the 1950s. At the edge of the railroad embankment, about 6 ft. underground, traces of the old well were uncovered in 1959 by a team of county historical society members. Using some of the stones from the initial well, a copy was built as a gift from the local chapter of the Daughters of the American Revolution (DAR). The well along with an identifying plaque was dedicated in 1960.

8. The **Harmar Crossing Marker**, Dearborn St. and Edgewater Ave., designates the area where Miami warriors turned back a United States force in 1790. Indians north of the Ohio River had continued to war against white settlers even after the American defeat of the British in the Revolutionary War appeared to settle the issue of who won the choice land. President George Washington instructed Brig. Gen. Josiah Harmar to lead United States troops and Kentucky militiamen against the Indians of Kekionga (Fort Wayne). Harmar with almost 1,500 soldiers met only frustration in the campaign. Forewarned, the Miamis under Little Turtle bested the Americans on two occasions, the first being the rout of Col. John Hardin's mounted force, and the second being the defeat and death of Maj. John Wyllys and almost all of his 60 infantrymen. The Harmar marker, to the memory of John Wyllys and his company, was dedicated in 1916.

9. The **Gen. Henry W. Lawton Monument**, Lake and Crescent aves., honors a Fort Wayne military hero. Born in Ohio in 1843, Lawton moved to Fort Wayne with his family in 1848. He was educated at the Fort Wayne Methodist Episcopal College, the site of which is marked at Thieme Dr. and Wayne St. Lawton was the first city man to be awarded the Congressional Medal of Honor, having earned the decoration at Atlanta in the Civil War. After the war he served as an officer in a black regiment. He pursued Geronimo in 1886 and arranged the warrior's surrender. Likewise, Lawton was one of the commissioners who accepted the surrender of Spain in Cuba in 1898. While Lawton fought the rebels in the Philippines in 1899, he was shot and killed. He was buried in Arlington National Cemetery. Old Northside Park, Clinton and 4th sts., acquired by the city in 1864, was renamed Lawton Park. The bronze statue of the general was executed by noted Chicago artist Frederick C. Hibbard and dedicated in 1921.

10. **Lakeside Park**, Lake Ave. and Forest Park Blvd., was acquired by the city in 1908 largely through donations of land from realty companies. The park was enlarged in 1912, and lakes were created. The dirt from the carved-out lakes went toward bolstering river levees. In the mid-1920s the park board created a rose garden complete with a trellis of wood latticework supported by stone columns. The garden area also received a landscape of walks and fencing and elaborate sunken gardens with foliage neatly clipped and patterned. For a few years in the early 1930s the lakes became municipal fish hatcheries, the first in the United States. Today the **Lakeside Rose Garden** is a major attraction. It is considered the largest municipal rose garden in Indiana, displaying several hundred varieties. The best time to see the display is in mid-June during the annual Rose Walk.

11. **Little Turtle's Grave**, 634 Lawton Pl., was discovered in 1912, a century after the great Miami chief's death. While digging a cellar for Dr. George Gillie's new home, workmen uncovered an Indian burial ground, including a grave containing an exceptional amount of decorative metalwork, a sign of an important figure. Jacob M. Stouder, a local historian, claimed the relics to be associated with Little Turtle. His prime evidence was a ceremonial sword thought to be the one presented to Little Turtle by George Washington. Little Turtle's skull, avidly sought by the Smithsonian Institution, was inadvertently given away and never recovered. A small stone slab marked the grave until 1959 when Mary Catherine Smeltzly, a former high school history teacher in Fort Wayne, bought the lot and presented it to the city for a small memorial park, on behalf of herself and her sister, Eleanor, also a history teacher. The house on the site was razed, and a bronze plaque attached to a granite boulder was erected and dedicated in 1960. Little Turtle's sword is among the Indian artifacts on display in the museum of the Old Fort.

12. **Freimann Square**, located between the City-County Building and the Performing Arts Center, is a landscaped urban park, a delight to the lunchtime crowd, weary shoppers, and tourists.

The $750,000, six-acre plaza was dedicated in 1973. The funds came from the Frank Freimann Charitable Trust. Freimann was president and chief executive of Magnavox Corporation from 1950 until his death in 1968. The trust's timely decision to underwrite the development of a downtown park set aside prior considerations to use the site for a new county jail. Fort Wayne's Strauss Associates, Inc., supervised the project, designed by Indianapolis landscape architects James E. Browning and Alan Day. The park's centerpieces are a large square fountain and the Maj. Gen. Anthony Wayne Equestrian Monument. The 19-ton bronze statue of Wayne astride his horse was executed by Chicago artist George E. Ganiere and was dedicated July 4, 1918, in Hayden Park. The monument, minus its large base, was relocated to Freimann Square in 1973. The park with its fountains, benches, trees, shrubbery, flowers, and brick and concrete walkways has become an integral part of the arts and civic theme of midtown Fort Wayne.

13. The **Journal-Gazette Building**, 701 S. Clinton St., is one of the few remaining examples of early 20th-century commercial architecture in the city. Constructed in 1928, the four-story brick office building was designed by local architect Charles R. Weatherhogg. In 1982 the structure was renovated and restored under the direction of Archonics of Fort Wayne. The reddish metallic color of the exterior copper panels, exhumed from layers of paint, extends to the interior mirrors, handrails, and elevators. The corporate offices of the newspaper are housed in the building. The remaining space has been converted to offices. (*NRHP*)

14. The **Allen County Courthouse**, 715 S. Calhoun St., is an example of a Beaux Arts Classicism style of architecture. The grandiose composition, copious detail, projecting pavilions, colossal columns, and free standing and relief statuary reflect the synthesis of classical design imported from Paris and popularized in the buildings at the 1893 Chicago World's Fair. The Fort Wayne structure built in 1897–1902 represents the fourth courthouse erected on the public square. The architect, Fort Wayne's Brentwood S. Tolan, was as well known as his father, Thomas J. Tolan, for courthouse and jail creations. The three-story, fireproof, blue limestone edifice cost $817,553.59. The resplendent interior features tiled floors, Italian marble walls and stairways, imitation marble columns, and an open rotunda that extends upwards to a stained-glass dome encircled with murals by Charles Holloway of Clinton, Iowa. The courtrooms' decor is carried out in rich woods, murals, and bas-relief panels. Most of the offices were removed in 1971 to the new City-County Building. The old courthouse was remodeled in 1972 to serve as a government annex. (*NRHP*)

15. The **Canal House**, 114 E. Superior St., is considered a significant structure because of its age and its connections with the Wabash and Erie Canal. John Brown, a Scottish stonemason, built the two-story business and residence on the north bank of the canal in 1852, the year before the canal was completed to Evansville. Brown no doubt used the canal commercially; however, several later tenants of the house piloted canal craft, and it is these boatmen who best establish the house's relation to the canal. In 1885 the railroad bought the house to serve primarily as storage space. The Norfolk and Western Railway deeded the old stone building to Fort Wayne in 1970. Restoration of the Canal House took place in 1975–76 under the auspices of the Fort Wayne Bicentennial Com-

Indiana Historical Society (C4213)
Allen County Courthouse, photographed by Edward J. Vadas in 1977

mittee. Navy Seabees performed the actual reconstruction as a civic project. In 1976 the Fort Wayne Fine Arts Foundation occupied the building.

16. The **Lincoln National Bank and Trust Building**, 116 E. Berry St., was the tallest building in Indiana when constructed in 1929-30. The 22-story steel, limestone, and marble skyscraper, patterned after the Chicago Tribune Building, outstripped Indianapolis's Merchants Bank by 5 stories. The Lincoln Tower, as the structure was designated, is now overshadowed in its own backyard by the Fort Wayne National Bank and One Summit Square buildings of 26 levels each. The $1.3 million Lincoln Tower opened in 1930 on the silver anniversary of the bank's founding. In 1905 the bank organized as the German-American National Bank. The bank's stockholders in 1914 formed a sister institution, the German-American Trust Company. In the anti-German atmosphere of World War I both organizations substituted the name Lincoln for German-American. The bank merged with the trust company in 1928 and adopted its present title. J. M. Strauss, Fort Wayne, collaborating with the Cleveland firm of Walker and Weeks, designed the Lincoln Tower. On top was placed a powerful beacon,

Lincoln National Bank and Trust Building, ca. 1930

which was in service until 1971. The outer entrance is faced with a series of copper panels depicting events in the life of Abraham Lincoln. The golden terra-cotta bands near the building's summit are striking details. The rays of the sun decorating the ceiling of the bank's main lobby and the murals on the end walls were the work of Cleveland artist Glenn M. Shaw.

17. The **Louis A. Warren Lincoln Library and Museum**, 1300 S. Clinton St., is a corporately established and endowed institution dedicated to the collection and dissemination of materials connected with Abraham Lincoln. The museum houses the nation's largest body of Lincolniana. The Great Emancipator set foot in Fort Wayne only once, to change trains, and he failed to capture the local vote in the 1860 and 1864 presidential elections. Hugh McCulloch, a Fort Wayne banker and Lincoln's secretary of the treasury, was probably the president's closest link with the Summit City. In 1905 when a newly reorganized insurance company wanted to promote an image of honesty, it received permission from Robert Todd Lincoln to use his father's name and portrait. Grateful for the consent, the Lincoln National Life Insurance Company determined to take an active role in perpetuating Lincoln's memory. One of the company's first contributions was to place a replica of Lincoln's birthplace in Foster Park in 1916. The log cabin still sits in the park. In 1923 the firm moved into its new headquarters in the 1300 block of Harrison St., two blocks west of Clinton St. For the front plaza, the company in 1928 commissioned New York artist Paul Manship to sculpt an heroic-scale bronze of a 21-year-old Lincoln. The statue, over 12 ft. high, depicting the young Lincoln reclining against an oak stump, was dedicated in September 1932. The artwork is entitled Abraham Lincoln, the Hoosier Youth. Also in 1928, Lincoln National set up the Lincoln Historical Research Foundation. In 1931 the foundation dedicated its museum, which occupied the fourth floor of the headquarters building. In 1978 the museum moved to its present location in a two-story section of the new glass and steel company offices on Clinton St. At the same time the museum was renamed for its first director, Louis A. Warren. The library, studded with Lincoln busts, is situated on the ground level and consists of thousands

of books, manuscripts, clippings, microfilms, and graphics. On the lower level is an interpretive museum, a winding corridor lined with 60 display cases, and three reconstructed period rooms.

18. The **Cathedral of the Immaculate Conception**, situated on Cathedral Square, bounded by Calhoun, Lewis, Clinton, and Jefferson sts., was dedicated in 1860, three years after the founding of the diocese of Fort Wayne. Local Catholics began organizing in the 1830s under the direction of Father Stephen Badin. Two small chapels preceded the cathedral on the land that formerly had been an Indian burial site. Jean Baptiste Richardville, a Miami chieftain of French and Indian heritage, is buried on the square, as a marker on the front lawn indicates. Richardville's well-respected diplomatic and business skills earned him such wealth that at the time of his death in 1841 he was considered the nation's richest Indian. The $54,000 cathedral was designed by the then pastor Father Julian Benoit. The twin-spired French Gothic church has since undergone change, the most extensive occurring in the early 1950s when the exterior of brick and sandstone was faced with Indiana and Wisconsin stone. The 14 beautiful stained-glass windows created in Munich, Germany, were installed in the late 1890s. Much of the wood furnishings and carvings were put in during the 1920s and the 1930s. (*NRHP*) A Cathedral Museum was established in 1980 in the Cathedral Center at the corner of Clinton and Jefferson sts. The one-room repository holds a variety of articles associated with the cathedral's long history.

19. The **Foellinger-Freimann Botanical Conservatory**, 1100 S. Calhoun St., is one of the few Midwest urban exhibition halls of horticultural varieties. Almost an acre of seasonal flowers, rare and exotic plants, and desert cacti is under glass. The trio of connected roof-shaped display modules, partially solar heated, was designed by Archonics of Fort Wayne. Dedicated in 1983, the botanical gardens, lavishly laid out in authentic settings, are intended for scholarly research, for conserving threatened plants, for practical demonstrations of floral cultivation, and for the public's simple pleasure of observing the natural processes. Funding for the $4.5 million greenhouse came from the Foellinger Foundation and the Freimann Charitable

Trust. The Foellinger family, publishers of the *Fort Wayne News Sentinel* from 1920 to 1981, incorporated its foundation in 1958. Helene Foellinger, who first conceived of the conservatory, was named to the Indiana Journalism Hall of Fame in 1974, the first woman to be so honored. The botanical attraction is owned and operated by the Fort Wayne Parks and Recreation Department.

20. The **Embassy Theatre**, 121 W. Jefferson Blvd., is a classic 1920s grand theater and movie palace. Completed in 1928 at a cost exceeding $1.5 million and financed by the Fox Realty Company, the theater was considered one of the nation's most luxurious. The facility opened as the Emboyd Theatre, a name given it by manager W. C. Quimby, to honor his mother Emily Boyd. Built at the time and under the same roof was the Indiana Hotel, which stayed in business until the 1960s. A. M. Strauss, the architect, employed brick and terra-cotta trim on the exterior. The richly decorated interior of Italian and Spanish design featured 20-ft. mirrors, a grand staircase, and towering columns. An 80-ft.-high ceiling rose above the 3,100-seat auditorium. A huge Page Theatre Organ, one of only four made, graced the orchestra pit. The organ and much of the original grandeur remains. The Alliance Amusement Company bought the theater in 1952, sold it to Cinecom Corporation in 1970, and Cinecom filed for bankruptcy in 1972. At this point the Embassy Theatre Foundation was formed to try and save the building. From 1972 to 1975 a volunteer group simply maintained the now closed theater. The foundation raised $250,000 in 1975 to buy the structure from Sports-Services, Inc., of Buffalo, New York. Restoration of the auditorium was completed in 1980. Presently the theater hosts the Fort Wayne Philharmonic Orchestra, a classic film series, organ recitals, special entertainment bookings, meetings, and receptions. (*NRHP*)

21. The **Fort Wayne Fire Fighters Museum**, 226 W. Washington Blvd., is located in Old Engine House No. 3, a registered landmark. Constructed of brick with cut-stone trim, the two-story Richardsonian Romanesque firehouse, designed by Wing and Mahurin, cost $5,300 when completed in 1893. Expanded in 1907 and 1909, the station remained the city's largest until Firehouse No. 1 went up in 1971 just east of the more recently built Museum of Art.

Old No. 3 closed in 1973. In 1975 the Fort Wayne Fire Fighters Museum, Inc., leased the building, commenced showing its holdings on special occasions in 1981, and began opening once a week in 1983. The museum exhibits a variety of fire vehicles and paraphernalia of historic and contemporary interest. Perhaps its greatest attraction is the Fire Safety Maze, a realistic adventure for children in learning how to detect, escape, and report fires. (*NRHP*)

22. The **Edsall house**, 305 W. Main St., is the oldest building in downtown Fort Wayne. William S. Edsall, a merchant and civic leader well known among his contemporaries for making and losing money, built the two-story rectangular brick home in 1839. The transitional style of architecture encompasses elements of Greek Revival and Italianate. The Italianate roof brackets were probably added in the 1870s. Edsall died impoverished in 1876. The house changed numerous hands, even serving two weeks as the city's first hospital. ARCH, the local preservation group, found the house in sad condition in 1975. It also learned that the Redevelopment Commission, having bought the property, planned to raze the whole block and have a private developer put up senior citizens housing. Negotiations over the fate of the house resulted in the commission selling the land to developer Gene B. Glick Company of Indianapolis, but stipulating that Glick had to save the Edsall house and restore the exterior. This the company did, spending some $80,000 to sandblast the old brick, remove rear additions, solidify and reshingle the sagging roof, rebuild the south wall, replace windowsills and several brackets, replaster the foundation, and build new chimneys. (*NRHP*)

23. The **Hugh McCulloch house**, 616 W. Superior St., is another older Fort Wayne home, though extensively remodeled since its erection in 1839-43. Hugh McCulloch (1808-1895) was a lawyer and banker who presided over the State Bank of Indiana. In the 1860s he achieved wide prominence by becoming in 1863 the nation's first comptroller of the currency, putting in operation the new national banking system. From fathering this important innovation in America's banking structure, McCulloch went on to serve as secretary of the treasury in the cabinets of presidents Abraham Lincoln, Andrew Johnson, and Chester Arthur.

McCulloch's image appears on the $20 bill, 1902 series. McCulloch situated his Greek Revival-style home on the highest point of his 100-acre tract lying between the St. Marys River and the Wabash and Erie Canal. The original house, designed by local architect Henry Williams, was a brick story-and-a-half rectangular block flanked by one-story wings. The front portico featured four tall square columns. The low-pitched roof supported an observation tower. The tower is gone now, and other alterations, beginning with an Italianate rear addition in 1862, have reshaped the structure. The family sold the home in 1887 and converted the expansive grounds to housing tracts. The Fort Wayne College of Medicine founded in 1879 purchased the house in 1892. The medical college, eventually absorbed into the Indiana University School of Medicine, changed the roof lines, replaced the portico and substituted round columns, and attached new two-story side porches. The Turnverein Vorwaerts Hall Association used the house as a German athletic and cultural center from 1906 to 1966. The Turners created an interior gymnasium in addition to a two-story north wing. The Fort Wayne Poster Company held the property for a few years before it was bought in 1968 by the International Brotherhood of Electrical Workers Local 723. The union filed for bankruptcy in 1976, and Anthony Wayne Bank repossessed and turned over the McCulloch homestead to ARCH, the local preservation organization. Sold to a private party in 1983, it now houses several shops. (*NRHP*)

24. The **site of the first French fort** is marked at Van Buren and Michaels sts., just north of W. Superior St. Known as Fort St. Philippe, and later as Fort Miamis, the fortification was completed in 1722 by Capt. Charles Regnault Dubuisson, a former commander of the French fort at Detroit. The log outpost reigned as the hub of French military and commercial influence in the Miami country for 25 years. In 1747 it was partially destroyed by Indians, and a new fort was constructed to the east on the left bank of the St. Joseph River (the site is designated by a bronze plaque by the Van Buren St. bridge at Guldlin Park). The first French fort was then occupied by Chief Cold Foot, and an Indian settlement known as Cold Foot Village grew up around the old garrison.

25. The **Old Aqueduct** Club-More Swimmers Monument, Orff Park, commemorates a group of westside youngsters who frolicked in the structure that spanned St. Marys River near the memorial site. The oak-timbered aqueduct, 204 ft. long and 17.5 ft. wide, was constructed in 1834 to carry the Wabash and Erie Canal over the St. Marys. The canal waters flowed through the aqueduct at a depth of 4.5 ft. The covered-bridge structure was dismantled by the railroad in 1883. To remember the halcyon days in the aqueduct, the former participants organized the Old Aqueduct Club and held a yearly dinner. Members were limited to those born before 1867, who swam in the aqueduct, and lived west of Calhoun St. prior to 1872. The monument to the club was erected in Orff Park in 1927. Orff Park was much larger than at present when purchased by the city from John Orff in 1892.

26. The brick home at the corner of Main and Union sts. is the **birthplace of actress Carole Lombard**. Born Jane Alice Peters on October 6, 1908, the future screen star left her hometown for California at the age of six. In 1921 she debuted in her first feature length film with 56 more to follow before her tragic death in 1942. The tall, blonde actress perfected what has been described as the screwball comedy, a farcical story about mismatched couples. In 1939 she married Clark Gable in what is still regarded as one of Hollywood's greatest love stories. Returning to the West Coast from Indianapolis where she helped raise $2 million from bond sales for the war effort, her plane crashed on January 16, 1942, near Las Vegas, killing Carole, her mother, press agent, and 19 servicemen and crew. She was buried in Hollywood. Other prominent personalities from Fort Wayne include the humorist Herb Shriner, actress Shelly Long, and fashion designer Bill Blass.

27. Fort Wayne has had interesting ties to the world of sports. **Camp Allen Park**, Camp Allen Dr., a recruiting station during the Civil War, was the site of America's first professional league baseball game. The Fort Wayne Kekiongas, organized in 1869, became a charter member in 1871 of the first professional baseball league, the National Association of Professional Baseball Players. The league's opening game, won by the Kekiongas over the Cleveland Forest Citys, took place on the Camp Allen diamond May 4, 1871. Although disputed, Fort Wayne also claims the first night baseball game. The Jenny Electric Light Company illuminated a contest held June 2, 1883, between an Illinois pro team and players from the Fort Wayne Methodist College. A bronze plaque on the north side of Poinsette Motors, 200 S. Clinton St., marks the location of the game. Prior to penning his many tales of the wild west, Zane Grey played outfield in 1896 for Fort Wayne's entry in the Interstate Pro League. Around 1909 Louis Heilbroner established here the Heilbroner Baseball Service and began publishing his Blue Book of baseball statistics. Fort Wayne's Zollner Corporation, maker of aluminum alloy pistons, fielded a national champion softball team in the 1940s and 1950s. The Zollner Pistons basketball team played professional basketball from 1948 to 1957. The franchise became the Detroit Pistons after its move to Michigan in 1957.

28. The **Sponhauer house**, 1017 W. Berry St., was the city's first major preservation project. The attention the house received, from the initial fear of its razing through its dramatic relocation 12 blocks west, educated the community to the process of saving old buildings. The Neoclassical-style home was built for the German immigrant grocer Christian G. Strunz in 1886. It is noted for the plaster mermaid under the front eaves that appears to be holding up or clinging to the large elaborate Flemish gable. Strunz's granddaughter, Helen Sponhauer, lived in the house all her life. Upon her death in 1976 the property was auctioned to the General Telephone Company of Indiana. An energetic preservation alliance of ARCH and the Junior League began negotiations to rescue the house. In 1977 GenTel offered the preservationists the house if it could be moved. A determined effort to amass federal, state, and local moneys, plus the purchase of the present site, formerly a parking lot, prepared the way for the house-move in July 1980. Transporting the 204-ton house was facilitated by alert utility crews lowering electricity lines, trimming trees, and dismantling traffic lights along the route. A private party bought the house in 1981. (*NRHP*)

29. The **Swinney home**, 1424 W. Jefferson Blvd., is distinguished as a longtime family residence and, more recently, as a center for historical preservation and education. Thomas W.

Swinney (1803–1875), Indian trader, Whig politician, businessman, and agriculturalist constructed the first section of his home, one-and-a-half stories, in 1844. A second level and servants' wing were added in 1885. In 1922 after the death of the last Swinney daughter the property went to the city park board in accordance with Thomas Swinney's will of 1875. The present house and environs including the 94.5 acres of East and West Swinney parks make up the family's legacy to Fort Wayne. From 1926 to 1980 the home housed the Allen County-Fort Wayne Historical Society Museum. After the museum moved to the Old City Hall, the Old Fort Settlers, an offshoot of the historical society dedicated to the perpetuation of bygone domestic skills, leased the house for its headquarters. Besides actively refurbishing the homestead, the organization has reconstructed an 1849 log cabin found in Huntington County as a focus for its classes and demonstrations in pioneer crafts. The cabin on the northwest lawn stands near a well-maintained herb garden. Among the various items scattered about the front yard of the Swinney home is a Spanish-American War cannon dedicated in 1900 at Old Fort Park and removed to its present site in 1956. (*NRHP/HABS*)

30. **Lindenwood Cemetery**, 2324 W. Main St., was privately established in 1860 as the city's first large landscaped graveyard. A dozen public-spirited citizens purchased the original 152 acres of timber and marshland. The cemetery's name derived from the abundance of linden (basswood) trees on the property. John Chislett, Sr., a landscape architect, selected the Lindenwood site and designed the ornamental layout of the garden-like burial grounds. Chislett later platted Crown Hill Cemetery in Indianapolis. Among the noteworthy buildings in Lindenwood is the Chapel of the Woods, erected in 1895 and restored in 1973, and the office constructed in 1884. Both structures were designed by the Fort Wayne firm of Wing and Mahurin. The present 175-acre cemetery contains the graves of practically all the prominent figures and families of Fort Wayne's past, along with some other memorable persons: Sammy Morris, from western Liberia, who attended Fort Wayne College before his premature death at the school in 1893, and who became well known upon the publication of an inspirational biography by Thaddeus Reade in

1896; "Mother George," a renowned Civil War nurse who died of typhoid fever in 1865 and was buried with full military honors (a marker to Mother George is in the 300 block of E. Berry St.); and Adolph "Germany" Schulz, center for the University of Michigan football team, 1904–8, and often touted as the greatest ever to play the game at that position. (*NRHP*) In 1974 the cemetery corporation leased 110 acres to the city's Park Board for development as a city park. The Lindenwood Park Environmental Study Area offers hiking trails for fair weather enjoyment of the flora and fauna and for cross-country skiing in the winter.

31. The **Bass Mansion**, 2701 Spring St., serves as the library for St. Francis College, but in the first third of the 20th century it reigned as Fort Wayne's most sumptuous residence. John H. Bass (1835–1922), foundry owner, streetcar line officer, bank president, piano company founder, and philanthropist, built his first home on his large estate in 1887–91. Brookside, the name given the house, was designed by local architects John Wing and Marshall Mahurin. It burned in 1902. The second Brookside, the present imposing sandstone Romanesque Revival castle, towered up from the old foundation in 1902–6. The 33-roomed, tall-ceilinged mansion still grandly displays its curved main entrance door, textile wall coverings, murals, fireplaces, exquisite woodwork, stained-glass, and magnificent staircase. The original room furnishings are now gone, but displayed photographs recall the posh settings —each room outfitted in a particular European period style. The well-maintained grounds exhibited a variety of trees, plants, and wildlife. In 1944 Mrs. Grace Bass Leslie, a daughter of John Bass, sold the house and lot to the Sisters of Saint Francis of the Perpetual Adoration, who operated a college in Lafayette, Indiana. St. Francis College, chartered in 1940, had functioned as a normal or junior college from 1923 to 1937, after which time it evolved into a four-year women's college. The institution moved from Lafayette to its 70-acre campus in Fort Wayne in 1944. By the 1960s men were being admitted, and a graduate degree program had been established. The Bass mansion, the school library since 1947, has recently undergone an extensive renovation and restoration program, largely the work of faculty and students. (*NRHP*)

32. **Franke Park**, Sherman Blvd., is a veritable storehouse of things to do and see. John B. Franke, president of the Perfection Biscuit Company which he founded in 1901, presented the city in 1921 an 80-acre tract for a park. Since 1921 the park's area has expanded to 280 acres. A 13-acre lake was created in 1939. Major attractions include the Children's Zoo opened in 1965. The zoo features a miniature train ride, horse rides, and a contact area. The African Veldt, established in 1975, is a part of the 33-acre zoo complex. The Veldt re-creates the landscape and animal world of East Africa. The visitor can go on safari, take in the Probstville African Village, or survey the grounds from the elevated boardwalk. Also in Franke Park is the Jack D. Diehm Museum of Natural History. The museum was formed by Mr. and Mrs. Berlen Diehm and named for their son who died in a car accident in 1959. The museum was dedicated in 1965, but subsequently burned and was replaced by the present museum, dedicated in 1981. The popularity of the Diehm taxidermy studio among schoolchildren led to the building of the museum. The large display area includes over 60 exhibits of mounted animals, birds, and fish. The Foellinger Theatre, constructed in 1948–49, is a 3,000-seat, covered open air facility that draws a variety of live entertainment by name performers and local talent. Funds for the theater were given in memory of Oscar Foellinger, publisher of the *News-Sentinel*. Also of popular interest in the park is the soap box derby track that in the winter is employed as a toboggan slide.

33. The **Samuel Bigger Grave Marker**, McCulloch Park on Broadway, denotes the burial plot of Indiana's seventh governor. Bigger (1802–1846) was born and educated in Ohio. He moved to Indiana in 1829 and after a time settled in Rushville. He served in the state's lower house in 1833–35 before capturing the governorship on the Whig ticket in 1840. Defeated for a second term, Bigger moved to Fort Wayne to practice law. At his death in 1846 he was interred in Broadway Cemetery, the city's first burial ground. Hugh McCulloch had purchased the four acres in 1837 and had it fenced and laid off as a cemetery. In 1860 bodies were transferred to the newly founded Lindenwood Cemetery. Bigger's remains were not removed because no next of kin existed to sanction the reburial. In 1886 McCulloch deeded the prop-erty to the city, stipulating that it be made into a park. On September 30, 1923, a bronze plaque donated by General Electric was placed on a concrete slab over the grave.

34. The **Art Smith Memorial**, Memorial Park between Washington Blvd. and Maumee Ave., pays tribute to Fort Wayne's pioneer aviator. Arthur Roy Smith (1890–1926) built his first plane in 1910. His parents mortgaged their home in order to buy a $350 engine to power his frail contraption of wood, cloth, and wire. Although he did not participate, Smith no doubt was present when in the autumn of 1910 Fort Wayne held its first aviation meet. In this early competition Blanche Stuart Scott, a student of the famed Glenn H. Curtiss, soloed across the field and became, as the papers reported, the first woman to make a public flight in an airplane. Art Smith went on to star on the daredevil circuit. It is said that the barnstormer initiated skywriting and airborne fireworks displays. He tested planes and during World War I served as an aviation instructor in Japan and in the United States. After 1923 he flew the night routes for the postal department. Smith was flying the Cleveland-Chicago route in February 1926 when he crashed and died near Montpelier, Ohio. Smith's memorial, designed by New York artist James Novelli, was dedicated in 1928. The 8-ft.-high bronze figure crowning the tall granite shaft depicts a youth flying skyward, his feet barely touching the globe, representing the earth.

35. The **Johnny Appleseed Grave Site**, off Parnell Ave., is located at the approximate burial spot of John Chapman, an almost mythical figure in middle America lore. Chapman was born in Massachusetts in 1774. He came to the Ohio country around 1800 and began his life's work of planting fruit trees and spreading the religious beliefs of Emanuel Swedenborg. The ascetic orchardist, proverbially attired in a tin-pan hat and flour sack, disposed of apple, plum, and cherry seeds on purchased land fractions, or on others' property, gratuitously. A vegetarian and respecter of all living things, Chapman gained the affection of Indians and whites and many old, lame, or cruelly treated animals that he rescued and cared for. Between 1838 and 1845 he worked his way around northern Indiana. He died near Fort Wayne in 1845 and was buried in the Archer family plot,

the exact place of interment long since lost to view. The grave site is situated within the Johnny Appleseed Memorial Park. (*NRHP*) The feeder canal to the Wabash and Erie Canal, dug in the 1830s, ran along the east base of the grave site mound. The Appleseed grave overlooks to the northwest the Allen County War Memorial Coliseum dedicated in 1952.

Tour 1

Tour 1 begins at the Allen County Courthouse, on the square bounded by Main, Berry, Calhoun, and Clinton sts. in downtown Fort Wayne. Go east two blocks on Main St. to Lafayette St. and turn left, crossing the St. Marys River, where the street name changes to Spy Run Ave. Continue *1.4 m.* where the street merges into N. Clinton. Continue north *1.6 m.* past Coliseum Blvd. (US 33/24/30), to the **Concordia Theological Seminary** on the right. The seminary is a private institution operated by the Lutheran Church, Missouri Synod, to prepare students for professional church and church-related careers. Founded by Lutherans in Fort Wayne in 1846, the seminary subsequently relocated in Missouri and, later, in Springfield, Illinois. In 1977 the school returned to Fort Wayne and to its present quarters on the site of Concordia Senior College, established as a junior college in the early 1950s, which closed in 1977.

In the 1950s the Lutheran Church, Missouri Synod, commissioned Finnish architect Eero Saarinen, who designed the St. Louis Arch and the Air Force Academy Chapel at Colorado Springs, to design the campus of the future Concordia Senior College. The integration of art and utilitarianism is readily apparent throughout the 191-acre campus, from the Martin Luther statue at the entrance drive to the dorms and classrooms bordering the shore of a man-made lake. Saarinen designed the campus to resemble a North European village, and the college chapel best exemplifies his work. Situated in the center of the campus, the A-frame structure stands above a central plaza and surrounding buildings as in the village tradition. Inside the chapel natural light, filtering through the skylight in the peak of the roof and through the side-aisle baffles below, creates a dramatic lighting effect, emphasizing the altar and cross at the east end. A specially designed 2,900-pipe organ occupies the west end. All campus buildings feature pitched roofs with clay tiles, light airy rooms, and functional furnishings. American and European craftsmen produced the art works which decorate the interior walls of the college facilities. Outstanding are the massive Te Deum mosaic at the library entrance and a fascinating incised brick bas-relief carving on a dining hall wall.

From the seminary, proceed north on Clinton St. (Leo Rd.) for *3.7 m.* to IND 1. Turn right and continue northeast for *3.2 m.* to Clay St. in **CEDARVILLE**. This unincorporated bedroom community of Fort Wayne was once the site of a Potawatomi Indian village. Chief Metea, reputedly a great orator and Indian spokesman, lived here and in the vicinity of Fort Wayne until he died of poisoning in 1827. Disgruntled by Metea's adherence to the Treaty of 1826, his followers allegedly administered the poison.

Continue north on IND 1 (Leo Rd.) for *1.7 m.*, following the contours of the Cedarville Reservoir and the St. Joseph River, to Grabill Rd. in **LEO**. Platted in 1849, this unincorporated village was first called Hamilton then renamed Leo in honor of Pope Leo XII. Turn right and proceed east *2.4 m.* on Grabill Rd., crossing the bridge over the St. Joseph River. The river begins in Hillsdale County, Michigan, and flows to Fort Wayne where it joins the St. Marys River to form the Maumee, which flows into Lake Erie. Navigating the river in flatboats, settlers arrived in Leo and Cedarville during the 1830s.

On the southwest corner of Grabill Rd. (State St.) and Main St. in **GRABILL** (p. 658), an old windmill stands on the site of the Joseph Grabill homestead. Grabill is a resort town located in the center of an Old Order Amish farm community. Joseph Grabill laid out the town in 1901 and organized the first bank. Grabill developed as a railroad town situated on the Wabash (now Norfolk and Western) Railroad between Detroit and St. Louis. Many original "old town" structures have been converted into shops and businesses selling Amish goods. In 1907 the Souders established a store at the southwest corner of Grabill Rd. and Main St. comprised of parts from several buildings including a bank, firehouse, school, jail, two post offices, a saloon, and a hotel.

Return to Leo. Proceed north on Leo Rd. (IND 1) for *5 m.* to the **DE KALB COUNTY** (p. 33,606; 364 sq. m.) line. Previously a part of Lagrange County, De Kalb County was laid out in 1835, organized in 1837, and named for Bavarian baron Johann De Kalb who served as a general during the American Revolutionary War and died at Camden, South Carolina, in 1780. The main business of the county is agriculture. Though farmland still covers more than 80 percent of the county's acreage, De Kalb has become increasingly industrialized. The county's manufactured products include plastics, iron castings, rubber products, closures, gears, auto jacks, automotive parts, and wiring harnesses. The county is noted for its former auto industry headquartered at Auburn.

Continue north on IND 1 for *1.1 m.* to the unincorporated village of **SPENCERVILLE**. According to a bronze tablet at the front of St. Peter's Lutheran Church, the first white settlement in De Kalb County took place in 1828 at the Spencerville site. This statement is difficult to substantiate. What is known, through land entries, is that a number of the first settlers arrived in the county in the mid-1830s, among whom was Thomas L. Yates. Yates came up the river from Fort Wayne in 1833 and recorded the first piece of land on the future site of Spencerville. Reuben J. Dawson bought the Yates farm in 1836 and erected a dam, sawmill, and gristmill. Dawson then platted the town in 1842 and named it Spencerville in honor of his brother-in-law, Col. John Spencer, a clerk at the United States land office in Fort Wayne.

Turn right at the principal intersection at *.3 m.* and continue *.4 m.* east to the **Spencerville Bridge**, the only survivor of five covered bridges built in De Kalb County during the 19th century. Contractors John A. McKay and Alpheus Wheelock erected the 168-ft.-long bridge in 1873. It is made of Michigan white pine which was precut and shipped to the site for assembly by the Smith Bridge Company of Toledo, Ohio. Spanning the St. Joseph River, the bridge has withstood many high waters including the destructive flood of 1898. The installation of new concrete piers in 1983

increased the load capacity from 4 to 12 tons. (*NRHP*)

From Spencerville, follow IND 1 northeast for *11.6 m.* to **BUTLER** (p. 2,509), passing through St. Joe. Originally called Norristown after pioneer Charles Norris who arrived here in 1840 and built his cabin on the north bank of Big Run, the town name was subsequently changed to Jarvis and finally Butler. It developed as a distribution center for agricultural products following arrival of the Lake Shore and Michigan Southern Railroad in 1856. Butler became the junction of two major trunk lines when the Detroit, Eel River and Illinois Railroad opened its freight operations here in 1873. Products manufactured in the Butler area today include car jacks, aluminum castings, paper containers, and wiring harnesses.

From Butler, proceed north on IND 1 for *7.8 m.* to the **STEUBEN COUNTY** (p. 24,694; 308 sq. m.) line. When white settlers arrived at this northeast corner of the state in the early 1830s, Indians still occupied the rolling glaciated terrain and fished from the sparkling rivers and spring-fed lakes which number more than 100. Prehistoric relics indicate the presence of mound builders and record the passage of Iroquois warriors through the region. Almost all of the Indians in this area were herded together and marched west, under government orders, in 1838. In the early days fur traders conducted a lucrative business in this part of the state, exchanging elk, moose, beaver, and buffalo skins for imported goods.

Until 1835 Lagrange County encompassed the entire northeast section of the state. Steuben County was separated from Lagrange in 1835 and officially organized in 1837. The county is named in honor of Baron Friedrich von Steuben, a Prussian-born general who served in the American Revolutionary War.

Continue north on IND 1 for *.7 m.* to IND 427 in **HAMILTON** (p. 587), crossing the railroad which divides the north and south sides of town. A Dr. Tuttle platted the village as Enterprise in 1836. About two years later the name changed to Hamilton, after Alexander Hamilton. The town, which was incorporated in 1914, straddles the line between De Kalb and Steuben counties with a population of 121 residents in the former and 466 in the latter. A mural immediately south of the main intersection portrays Hamilton's history.

Tour I

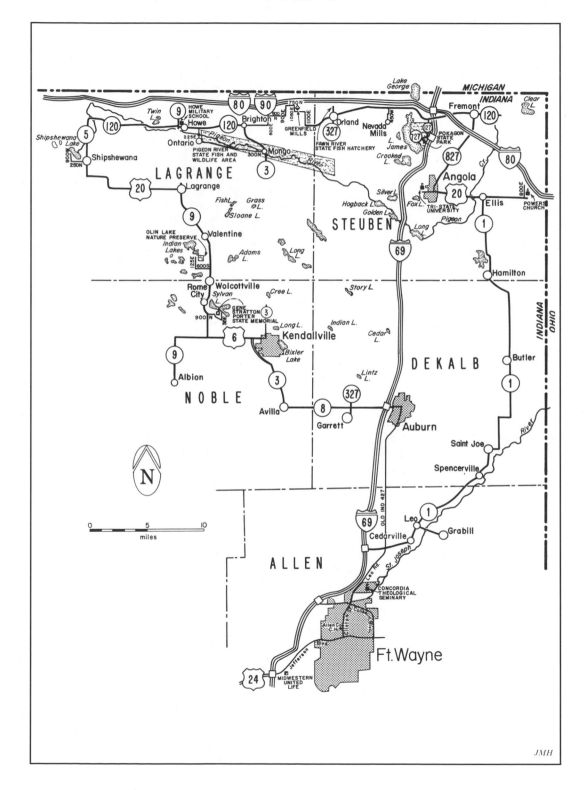

JMH

Continue on IND 1 past the southern tip of Hamilton Lake, the fifth largest in the state. Located on the beachfront *1.8 m.* north of town and *.5 m.* west of IND 1 is one of the county's oldest resorts, the **Cold Springs Hotel**, which occasionally features the sounds of the big name bands of the late 1930s. Homer Watkins started the resort in the 1880s on the site of the family farm. The first dance hall was built just after the turn of the century, and the dance craze reached its peak in the 1920s. During the 1940s disc jockeys from Fort Wayne's radio station WOWO spun records for young people at weekly "hops." Following a period of playing contemporary rock music, the management returned to engaging the big bands.

Continue north on IND 1 for *5.7 m.* to US 20 at Ellis. Turn right and go east *4 m.* to Old Rd 1 (CR 800E). **Powers Church** is situated *.4 m.* north. The picturesque New England-style frame chapel dates to 1876. Clark Powers donated the land for a nondenominational church in 1839. The local historic landmark, restored in 1976, contains two pump organs and original furnishings. The last regular services were held in the 1920s.

Return to US 20 and continue west for *8.5 m.* to IND 127 in downtown **ANGOLA** (p. 5,486). Most early settlers came from New York, Pennsylvania, and the New England states. Thomas Gale and Cornelius Gilmore of Ohio platted the town in 1838 and named it for Angola, New York. The old Fort Wayne to Coldwater, Michigan, road (later US 27) and the Maumee Trail (US 20) to Toledo, Ohio, intersected in Angola. Indians traded at the local stores, and farmers tethered their horses and ox teams at the public square when they came to town. Gale selected his name for the first street south of the crossroads and his wife's name, Martha, for the first street to the east. Gilmore gave his name to the first street to the north of the crossroads and his wife's name, Elizabeth, to the first street west. Gale and Gilmore donated the courthouse lots and county buildings in order to obtain the location of the county seat at Angola.

The Fort Wayne, Jackson and Saginaw Railroad, now the Hillsdale County Railroad, reached Angola in 1871. The town was incorporated as a city in 1906. Angola today has a diversified industrial base producing automobile parts, business forms, wiring, security equipment, and castings. Seasonal residents and tourists swell the population during the summer months.

Dedicated in 1917, the **Soldiers and Sailors Monument** at the center of Angola commemorates the 1,278 county soldiers who served in the Civil War. Topped by a figure of Columbia and flanked by four bronze statues —representing infantry, artillery, cavalry, and navy—the 300,000-lb. monument with a granite shaft stands 85 ft. high.

Thomas Gale built the first **Steuben County Courthouse**, a frame structure which stood on the southeast quadrant of the public square. Architect Freeborn Patterson designed the present two-story brick courthouse with decorative wood brackets, arched windows, and an ornate belfry and weathervane. Constructed in 1867-68 of native materials, the New England-style courthouse occupies the site of the original 1841 structure. (*NRHP*)

Behind the courthouse, at the corner of Wayne and Gale sts., is the **Steuben County Jail**, completed in 1877. Architects Biggs and Moser designed the brick and concrete building to house the jail and the sheriff's office and residence. Now mellowed with age, the bricks for both the jail and the courthouse were made with blue clay and marl from Lake James, north of Angola. The present jail replaced an 1839 frame structure built around an earlier log cell. (*NRHP*)

East of the public square, at 313 E. Maumee St., is the **Cline Memorial Home**, a house museum operated by the Steuben County Historical Society. Built by Cyrus and Jennie Cline about 1891, the two-story Queen Anne-style house with gingerbread trim across the eaves contains original wood flooring and decorative fireplaces. Among the exhibits is a restored hand loom dating back to the 1840s. Cyrus Cline (1856–1923) was a prominent citizen who practiced law in Angola for many years. He also served for a time as the county superintendent of schools, president of the First National Bank, and four-term congressman.

Return to the public square and proceed west on Maumee St. for four blocks then left two blocks on Darling St. to the **Tri-State University** campus. Visitor parking is available in the northwest corner of Darling and South sts. Founded in 1884, Tri-State University is a four-year, private, coeducational institution granting the B.S. and B.A. degrees in business, arts and sciences, and engineering. Associate degree programs are also available in accounting, computer technology, drafting and design, criminal justice, and secretarial science.

Tri-State began as a normal college concerned almost exclusively with training teachers for the public schools. The school reorganized as Tri-State College in 1946 and Tri-State University in 1975. The School of Engineering, which today enrolls about 65 percent of the university's students, was established in 1902. For the most part constructed of brick, more than 25 major buildings occupy the 400-acre campus.

On the west edge of the campus, just south of Park St., the Hershey Hall Physical Education Building houses the **Gen. Lewis B. Hershey Museum**. A graduate of Tri-State, Hershey served on its board of trustees from 1950 until his death in 1977. He was a four-star general and director of the Selective Service System, 1941–70. The museum contains personal letters, furniture, papers, and military memorabilia.

On the north end of the campus, off W. Gale St., an old wood freight station along the **Hillsdale County Railroad** recently served a steam train running between Angola and Pleasant Lake. Pleasant Lake became a resort in the 1870s, and excursion trains from Fort Wayne ran four times a day each way. A restored 1911 steam engine, believed to be the smallest standard gauge Pacific type ever built, began making the nine-mile trip in 1976. Pacific locomotives were favorites in passenger service. The railroad, a nonprofit organization manned by volunteers, now operates south from Pleasant Lake to Steubenville.

Return to Darling and Maumee sts. and proceed west four blocks to Woodard St. The Steuben County Historical Society maintains the **Hartman house**, on the southwest corner at 901 W. Maumee St., as its headquarters and as a museum. The society has furnished the house with many historical items, including a woven tapestry which hung in the first territorial capitol at Vincennes. The large, gray house was built around the 1890s by Dr. W. F. Waller. It was later owned by the Brokaw family, managers of the local theater, and subsequently owned by Dr. John J. Hartman.

Fox Lake, just southwest of Angola, has been a resort, tourist, and residential spot for Hoosier and midwest blacks since the late 1920s. Fostered by white investors, the lake

front became a haven for blacks desiring summer entertainment and recreation, especially during the years from 1930 into the 1960s. Today, blacks still own much of the property around the lake.

Return to IND 127 at the public square. Proceed north for *.6 m.* to Mechanic St. Turn right and follow IND 827 east *.2 m.* then north *6.9 m.* to IND 120 (Toledo St.) at **FREMONT** (p. 1,180). A historical marker posted on the northwest corner notes the history of the town. What is now IND 120 follows the old Vistula Rd. which originally ran between Fort Dearborn (now Chicago) and Vistula (now Toledo, Ohio). More than 250 years ago, French Jesuit missionaries used the trail to bring Christianity to the Indians. The Mormons followed Brigham Young along the trail on their way west. Originally called Willow Prairie but platted as Brockville in 1837, Frémont was an early settlement on the Vistula Trail. To avoid confusion with another Brockville, Indiana, the name was changed to Frémont in honor of John C. Frémont, the famous explorer.

The Fort Wayne, Jackson and Saginaw Railroad, which later became the New York Central, arrived at Fremont in 1870, running north into Michigan. For several years Fremont was an active shipping center for horses being sent to market in Buffalo, New York. The large grain elevators located at the railroad on the south side of town still operate, but passenger service on the railroad was discontinued in 1943. Other industries in the area manufacture automobile parts, plastic products, baked goods, castings, and wiring.

Proceed left on IND 120 (Toledo St.) for *3.5 m.* to IND 127 and turn left *1.8 m.* to IND 727, the entrance to **Pokagon State Park**. Located on the east shore of Lake James, the fourth largest lake in Indiana, the park encompasses 1,195 acres, including another small lake and a nature preserve. Established in 1925, the park offers swimming, boating, fishing, sailing, horseback riding, water skiing, and bicycling in the summer plus sledding, cross-country skiing, and ice skating in the winter. Park facilities include a public bathing beach, boat rentals, five campgrounds, picnic areas, hiking trails, a 1,780-ft.-long refrigerated toboggan slide, a nature center, and a wildlife exhibit of elk, deer, and buffalo.

The state-owned Potawatomi Inn, built in 1927, provides 81 guest rooms, conference

Potawatomi Inn, Pokagon State Park

rooms, tennis courts, and a swimming pool in a lakeside setting. The Civilian Conservation Corps (CCC) did much of the actual construction in the park between 1934 and 1942. The 208-acre Potawatomi Nature Preserve in the southeastern portion of the park was dedicated in 1973. Hiking trails from the inn pass a small lake, cattail and sedge marshes, and tamarack and yellow birch stands.

The inn takes its name from the Potawatomi Indians who once lived in the area surrounding Lake James. The park is named after a famous Potawatomi Indian chief, Simon Pokagon, youngest son of Leopold Pokagon. Leopold Pokagon transferred to the government approximately a million acres of land by treaty, at a price of three cents per acre. This included the present site of Chicago. He then retired to 700 acres on Long Lake, Michigan, not included in the ceded areas, where he died in 1841. At age 14, Simon Pokagon went to Notre Dame preparatory school in South Bend and later attended Oberlin College in Ohio. He made numerous public addresses and wrote articles on Indian subjects which were published in national magazines. He also made two visits to Washington and pleaded the Indian cause with Lincoln at the White House.

Return north to IND 120 and go west for *4 m.*, past the newly developed housing at the north end of Snow Lake, to the old **Collins School** on the south side of the road. Surrounded by oak trees, the rural one-room schoolhouse served the area from 1877 to 1943. Restored in 1967, the building has arched windows, a wood belfry, and 19th-century furnishings.

Continue to the next crossroad, turn left, and proceed *1.8 m.* to the village of **NEVADA MILLS**. Although the mill on Crooked Creek is gone, the dam remains and controls the levels of Snow Lake, Lake James, and Jimerson Lake.

Return to IND 120, turn left, and continue *2.7 m.* to CR 750W. Turn right and continue *.1 m.* to the parking lot of the **Ropchan Memorial Nature Preserve**. Acres, Inc., a nonprofit organization, owns this 77-acre preserve, featuring a small glacial lake surrounded by morainal ridges, woodlands, swamps, and bogs. A nature trail is available to the public.

Return to IND 120 and proceed west *2 m.* to IND 327 at **ORLAND** (p. 424), passing large gladioli fields in season on the left at *1.4 m.* Located on the old Vistula Rd., Orland is believed to be the oldest town in Steuben County. Many early residents followed John Stocker here from Vermont in 1834–35. Though first settled about 1835, the town was not incorporated until 1915. The church fathers opened a hymn book at random to select the name for the settlement.

Proceed north on Wayne Rd. (IND 327), passing a round barn, for *.6 m.* to the fieldstone gateway on the right for the **Fawn River State Fish Hatchery**. Located on Crooked Creek, the hatchery, which covers 23 acres, is the second largest facility in the state. Works Progress Administration (WPA) labor and money developed the hatchery, beginning with nine ponds in 1935. The state later purchased land on the west side of the highway to build a caretaker's house and additional ponds. A water quality and fish disease laboratory was established in 1978. The hatchery produces bluegill, bass, catfish, pike, and trout. It is the state's only hatchery with multi-temperature controls adaptable for both warm-water and cold-water fish.

Return to Orland and continue west on IND 120 for *1.5 m.* to the **LAGRANGE COUNTY** (p. 25,550; 380 sq. m.) line. All of Lagrange and Steuben and three-fourths of De Kalb and Noble counties were originally part of Elkhart County, then called the township of Mongoquinong. In 1832 this land was separated and organized into a county named Lagrange after the country residence, near Paris, France, of the Marquis de Lafayette. Further separations followed before the county reached its present size.

A glacial deposit called the Knobs forms the county's highest elevation. Farmland dotted with lakes and forests characterizes more than 85 percent of the county's terrain. The Indiana Toll Road crosses the length of the county's northern border. Industrial development began in the early 1900s, and today the county manufactures pleasure boats, mobile homes, upholstery padding, electric wiring, and equipment related to the recreational vehicle industry.

Nearly 40 percent of the county's church adherents are Old Order Amish, whose ancestors were German-speaking farmers from Lancaster County, Pennsylvania. Many Amish adhere to traditional farming and social and religious practices. (See description of Amish lifestyles in Tour 17.)

Continue west for *1 m.* on IND 120. Turn right on CR 1100E, proceed *1.4 m.*, and angle left through a beautiful archway of trees *.4 m.* to CR 1050E. Turn right and continue *.5 m.* to **Greenfield Mills**. In 1834 Samuel Burnside erected a sawmill on this site along the Fawn River. About 1846 Peter Bisel added a gristmill using the same water power, and a village grew

up around the mill. Four generations of the Rinkel family have operated the two mills housed in a large frame structure constructed with 50-ft.-long, hand-hewn beams in the upper floor. In the 1920s the Rinkels added self-generated hydroelectricity to supplement the water power.

Proceed west on CR 750N for *1.4 m.* to CR 900E, turn left, and continue *1.5 m.* to CR 600N. Turn right and go west *1 m.*, passing the Camsco Products plant on the right, where ingredients are processed for Campbell soups. Continue west, turn left at the first road, and after *.5 m.* turn right on IND 120. Two miles west is **BRIGHTON**, once known as Lexington, where a commune which called itself the Congregation of Saints sprang up in 1843. Its constitution, which decried the evils of a "social and political system at variance with the principles of Christianity and rendered contemporary society little more than a pandemonium," embraced the Golden Rule and agreed to "secure the rights and extend the privileges of women." Despite its generous promises, the commune was short-lived.

At Brighton turn left on IND 3 and proceed *3.3 m.* to **MONGO**. Originally called Mongoquinong, an Indian name meaning Big Squaw Prairie or White Squaw, Mongo straddles the Pigeon River at the site of a former Indian encampment. The picturesque Mongo mill pond is the river's origin. In the early 1830s French fur traders from Fort Wayne established a post here to barter with the Potawatomi Indians. The town was platted in 1840, and the Indian name was later shortened to Mongo. A dam was constructed across the Pigeon River, and a distillery and gristmill operated for several years. A fish and wildlife preserve now surrounds the unincorporated village of about 300 persons. The outlying area is noted for its muskmelon and gladioli farms.

On the northeast corner of West and 2nd sts. stands a two-story wood frame and clapboard structure of Greek Revival design built in 1832 by John O'Ferrell. It became Mongo's first general store and post office. (*NRHP/HABS*) Continue east on CR 300N, passing the former **Mongo Hotel**, a large two-story Victorian frame house which now contains small shops.

The Lagrange Phalanx, located near Mongo, was a Fourierist commune established in 1844. It attracted about 40 families who lived in a 200-ft.-long building, which also housed a common dining hall. They were governed by a legislative charter and a 30-article constitution and owned 1,500 acres of choice farmland on which they raised crops and livestock. Although completely socialistic, the group issued stock and paid dividends. Dissension caused the experiment to fail in about two years.

Just east of Mongo on CR 300N is the **Pigeon River State Fish and Wildlife Area** headquarters. Created in the 1950s, the 11,500-acre state facility contains former farmland, marshes, and three hydroelectric dams with adjacent mill ponds at Mongo, Nasby, and Ontario. Also within its borders is a 100-acre nature preserve featuring the largest tamarack bog forest in Indiana. In 1965 the state developed the 694-acre Shallow Lake Marsh for use as a waterfowl production area to reintroduce free-flying giant Canada geese in Indiana after several years of near extinction. Fields, lakes, and streams are stocked to supply ample game for state-regulated hunting and fishing. The facility also offers camping, canoeing, picnicking, bird-watching, and mushroom and berry picking. Continue west from Mongo on CR 300N, immediately crossing Pigeon River and paralleling it *3.8 m.* past numerous wildlife areas and the Nasby Dam area. Turn right and travel *.7 m.* to the **Curtis Creek State Trout Rearing Station**. The cold-water hatchery annually raises about 67,000 rainbow and brown trout to stock inland lakes and streams.

Return to the end of the road, turn right, and travel *2.2 m.* to **ONTARIO**, an early industrial community whose mills and factories produced flour, wool, tanned leathers, shoes, gloves, potash, and wood products. Unsuccessful efforts also were made to produce silk from local sources. Ontario fought with nearby Howe over location of the county seat but lost, although it did find solace in snaring the Lagrange Collegiate Institute, which operated until it encountered financial difficulties in 1881. It earned more lasting fame, however, as the birthplace of two internationally-known astronomers, Dr. Charles L. Doolittle and his son, Eric. Ontario today consists of an open square bordered by an 1885 schoolhouse and a church which reflects the New England background of its first settlers.

After turning right to pass through Ontario, continue north *1.6 m.* on CR 225E and turn left at IND 120. Proceed *1.6 m.* to **HOWE**. The village originally was called by the Indian name Mongoquinong, which was changed to Lima about 1833 and finally Howe in 1909. John Badlam Howe, a frontier lawyer for whom the town and the local military academy are named, taught school in the county as early as 1833. He organized the Lagrange Bank of Lima with Samuel P. Williams in 1854. He was a lifelong benefactor of the community. Still unincorporated, Howe maintains a small-town character with spacious wooded yards and well-preserved old houses.

Built as a restaurant and hotel, the **Kingsbury house**, 409 3rd St., a handsome two-story structure with arched windows and a wrought-iron balcony, stands on the east side of the town square. Norman Merriman opened a hotel on this site in 1835 which burned in 1859. N. R. Kingsbury began operating the present building as a hotel in 1863. The renovated Italianate-style building now serves as commercial office space.

From the Kingsbury house, proceed north on 3rd St. for three blocks to Union St. and turn west to 6th St., entering the 150-acre campus of the **Howe Military School**. Now the chaplain's residence, the small frame structure of Greek Revival design on the southeast corner is the house John B. Howe built in 1840. The house became the first classroom building for the grammar school founded through a bequest by Howe in 1884. Affiliated with the Episcopal church (Diocese of Northern Indiana), the school became a military academy in 1895. Cadets still wear uniforms, but the school, grades 5-12, is now coed.

Howe's second home is a Second Empire-style house built in 1875 and located on Union St. between 6th St. and IND 9. This building served as the school rectory until 1958 when it was converted into the administration building. Administrative offices were housed here until August 1985. Now known as the Howe mansion, this building is primarily used for special functions and receptions.

Just west of this building, facing IND 9, **St. James Chapel** was built in three stages between 1902 and 1914. Modeled after the Magdalen College chapel in Oxford, England, the chapel features a Norman-style exterior and an interior with stone floors, hand-carved walnut pews, a triptych by an Italian painter named Ducci, and a hammer-beamed arched ceiling.

In 1955 the sacristy and chaplain's office were added, and the brick exterior was refaced with limestone. A crypt chapel in the basement contains the graves of several Episcopal bishops.

Most buildings on campus were part of a major construction project in the 1950s. A military review and parade, held Sunday afternoons at noon during the spring and fall, is a traditional event.

From the school entrance at Union St., go south three blocks on IND 9. Turn right on IND 120 and proceed west *8.3 m.* to IND 5. Turn left for *3.2 m.* to Main St. in **SHIPSHEWANA** (p. 466). Founded in 1889, the town and the nearby lake were named after Chief Shipshewana, leader of Potawatomi Indians who lived on the east shore. A large Amish population now inhabits Lagrange County, and Shipshewana has become the bustling center for buying and selling Amish goods. Visitors, antique buyers, and bargain hunters gather here on Tuesdays and Wednesdays from early spring to late fall to visit the flea market, auctions, and local stores. Amish farmers mingle with the crowds, and their distinctive horse and buggy rigs share the streets and parking lots with motor vehicles. Restaurants, boutiques, and gift shops occupy the old business district situated two blocks east of IND 5.

A **Railroad Depot**, at Morton and Main sts., was the first building erected in the town proper. The Lake Shore and Michigan Southern Railroad constructed the station in 1888 along its line between Goshen and Sturgis, Michigan. A store now occupies the depot that has been partially refaced with stone.

In 1891 pioneer Hezekiah Davis built the **Davis Hotel** on Main St., west of Morton. It later housed a feed store and now contains several specialty shops. Davis also owned a planing mill and lumberyard on property east of IND 5 which was known as Davistown in the early 1900s. The town of Shipshewana was incorporated in 1916.

Return to Main St. and IND 5. Proceed south two blocks to Middlebury St. (CR 250N), turn right, and go west for *1 m.*, passing an unusual cement round barn. Turn right and follow CR 900W north for *.2 m.* to the marker on the left dedicated to **Chief Shipshewana**, located at the entrance of the Brethren Retreat Center. A public access site to Lake Shipshewana begins *.2 m.* to the left. In 1838 the federal government moved Chief Shipshewana, whose name

means "vision of a lion," from his ancestral grounds on the east shore of Lake Shipshewana to a Kansas reservation. He was allowed to return to Lagrange County, however, where he died in 1841.

Return to IND 5 at Shipshewana and proceed south for *.2 m.* to the 30-acre site of the **Shipshewana Auction and Flea Market**. Begun in the 1920s as an ordinary country auction, the horse and livestock auctions and flea market now draw thousands of people every summer and is one of the largest in the Middle West. Facilities include a livestock sales barn, an antique auction building, three restaurants, and hundreds of outdoor booths.

Continue south on IND 5 for *1.2 m.* to US 20 and turn left for *9.5 m.* to IND 9 at **LAGRANGE** (p. 2,164). Turn north and proceed *.2 m.* to the courthouse square bounded by Detroit, Michigan, Spring, and High sts. Platted in 1836, Lagrange became the county seat in 1844 and was incorporated in 1855. Lagrange is a small town in a largely rural area settled by Amish who migrated from Lancaster County, Pennsylvania. The town's largest manufacturer, Duo-Therm, specializes in heating/air conditioning units for mobile homes.

The county's first courthouse was located at Howe. Architects T. J. Tolan and Son designed the present **Lagrange County Courthouse**, an attractive Renaissance Revival-style structure of brick with sandstone trim and a 125-ft.-high clock tower, built in 1879. It replaced the courthouse built in 1843. A hitching rail along the west side of the courthouse square provides a place for Amish people to tie their horses and buggies when they come to town. A wrought-iron fence surrounding the courthouse is gone, but brick-paved streets still border the square. (*NRHP/HABSI*)

Return to US 20 and continue south on IND 9 for *6.9 m.* to CR 600S. Turn right and proceed *1.8 m.* to CR 125E. Turn right and continue *.5 m.* to the parking lot of the **Olin Lake Nature Preserve**. A hiking trail leads to the 269-acre, public- and privately-owned preserve, which includes the 103-acre Olin Lake. Olin Lake, the largest lake in the state with an undeveloped shoreline, is 82 ft. deep and is connected to the 371-acre Oliver Lake. The lake bottom is covered with marl, and most of the shoreline is marshy. Skunk cabbage and tamaracks grow in profusion. A part of the present preserve was acquired by the state for dedication in 1975.

Return to IND 9. Turn right for *1.7 m.* to a picturesque park on the left along the upper Elkhart River on the north side of **WOLCOTT-VILLE** (p. 890). W. H. Crone donated the property for Wolcott Park in honor of George Wolcott—a town founder and owner of a gristmill, sawmill, carding mill, and a distillery—who settled here in 1837. First called Wolcott's Mills, the town was surveyed in 1849 and recorded in 1853. Wolcottville doubled in population following the arrival of the Grand Rapids and Indiana Railroad in 1870. The present population is divided between Lagrange and Noble counties.

Continue south on IND 9 for *.2 m.* to the Lagrange/Noble county line. Formed by statute in 1835, **NOBLE COUNTY** (p. 35,443; 413 sq. m.) was officially organized by an act of the legislature in 1836 and was formed from Elkhart, Lagrange, and Allen counties. The county is named for James Noble, who was the first United States senator of Indiana, elected in 1816, and reelected in 1821 and 1827.

The centrally located town of Albion became the county seat in 1847. The seat of Noble County resided at three other sites before moving to Albion. In the 1830s and 1840s, a strip mine operated near the early county seats. Bog iron ore was hauled to a nearby forge until the mines were abandoned in 1854. Traditionally, Noble County is agricultural in nature though some of the county's larger towns now support a diversified industrial base. The county ranks number one in sheep production for the state.

York Township in central Noble County is the birthplace of Dr. Earl L. Butz, the former dean of agriculture at Purdue University, 1957-67, who became the United States secretary of agriculture in 1971.

From the county line at Wolcottville, proceed south on IND 9 for *1.4 m.* to Northport Rd. On the hillside just west of the highway are several old brick buildings surrounding a central courtyard on the grounds of the **Kneipp Sanatorium**, occupied since 1976 by The Way College of Biblical Research. Msgr. Sebastian Kneipp, of Bavaria, popularized the principles of his "water cure" which the Catholic Sisters of the Most Precious Blood administered at this hospital, established in 1895 by Dr. G. W. Giermann on the site of an old mineral springs spa. The sisters purchased the site in 1902. Until the late 1960s, patients suffering from a variety of ailments and diseases found a haven of "rest, recuperation, and restoration." Treatments entailed the use and application of water in the form of packs, wading, douches, ablutions, and baths. The sanatorium provided accommodations for more than 200 guests at one time. Many herbs, medicinal plants, vegetables, and dairy products used for the special Kneipp diet were raised on the sanatorium property. Promotional materials extolled the virtues of nearby Sylvan Lake and the temperate climate.

At the **Old Northport Cemetery**, just east of IND 9 and *.2 m.* north of Northport Rd. on CR 300E, is the grave of McGregor McDougle, variously spelled Gregory McDougall and McDougal, who died in 1858 at the age of 27. Since his death, McDougle's exploits have achieved legendary proportions. McDougle was a member of a band of outlaws known as "blacklegs," involved in robbing, horse stealing, counterfeiting, murdering, and jail breaking over a five-state area and Canada. In 1852 the state passed an act authorizing the formation of companies for the detection and apprehension of horse thieves and other felons. A group of these "regulators," called the Noble County Invincibles, arrested McDougle at Rome City. He was brought to trial at Ligonier (some accounts hold he never was tried), hanged from a tree near Diamond Lake, then buried at Northport.

The old cemetery marks the site of what once was the village of Northport, laid out by Francis Comparct, a Frenchman, in 1838. A tavern, two stores, and a tannery operated here for a short time before the village was overshadowed by nearby Rome City.

From Northport Rd., follow IND 9 south for *.8 m.* to Front St. at **ROME CITY** (p. 1,319). Turn right and proceed west one block to North St. and turn right again to the dam on the north branch of the Elkhart River which forms **Sylvan Lake**. The 630-acre lake was created in the 1830s as a reservoir for a canal to connect Lake Michigan with the Wabash and Erie Canal at Fort Wayne. The state abandoned the program before the canal project was well under way. The original Northport Feeder Dam was constructed in 1840, and the waterpower rights subsequently were leased to various mills which operated for a time.

While working on the feeder canal, workers divided into two camps on the north and south sides representing the French and Irish population of the work camp, respectively. The men on the north side received the best living quarters. When the Irish complained about their working conditions, the project foreman ordered that all workers on the south side, who incidentally were Roman Catholic, or Romans, must "do as the Romans do." The south side soon became known as Rome, the name officially adopted in 1839 when the town was laid out and platted. To avoid confusion with another town named Rome in Perry County, the post office changed the name to Rome City in 1868.

Sylvan Lake developed as a resort beginning with the construction of a dance hall which stood from 1876 to 1927 on the island connected by a bridge to the railroad station grounds. During the summer months, excursion trains from Fort Wayne brought thousands of visitors to the lake. Several steamers operated as passenger ferries between the island and the mainland. A number of hotels around the lake flourished at the turn of the century as did a skating rink, ice cream parlor, and an art gallery.

Return to IND 9 and proceed south through town for *1 m.* Turn left on CR 900N and follow signs *1.4 m.* to the entrance of the **Gene Stratton Porter State Historic Site** on the left. In 1913 Mrs. Porter came to the south shore of Sylvan Lake where she built her beloved "Cabin in Wildflower Woods," a two-story house of Wisconsin white cedar logs and native stone. Here, from 1914 to 1919, Mrs. Porter lived and worked in the natural setting that provided the background for much of her writing. She wandered around the lake region collecting specimens for what she called her "bog garden" and frequently visited the Atwood farm where she wrote *Michael O'Halloran.* Born in Wabash County in 1863, Mrs. Porter was already the author of several popular books before she left "Limberlost," her cabin at Geneva (see Tour 2), to relocate at Rome City. Among her best-known works are *Freckles, A Girl of the Limberlost, The Song of the Cardinal, Laddie, The Harvester,* and *Morning Face.* In 1919 Mrs. Porter established her permanent residence in California where she wrote and supervised the filming of her stories, although she continued to make regular visits

to Wildflower Woods. She erected a home on Catalina Island before 1924 when, at the age of 61, she was killed in an automobile accident in Los Angeles. Mrs. Porter's cabin in Wildflower Woods became the property of the state and opened as a memorial park in 1938.

Return to IND 9 and proceed south *8.8 m.* to Main St. in **ALBION** (p. 1,637). Called simply "the center" in its early days, the town takes its name from Albion, New York, the home of a county commissioner. Albion became the seat of Noble County in 1846. The first courthouse was completed in 1847, but it was destroyed by fire in 1859. Two years later the next courthouse was constructed of brick and designed to be fireproof but proved too small for Noble County's growing administrative system. In 1888-89 the Malone Brothers of Toledo, Ohio, built the present **Noble County Courthouse** on the square bounded by Main, Jefferson, York, and Orange sts. The brick and limestone structure with a central clock tower is of a Richardsonian Romanesque design. (*NRHP*)

The **Noble County Old Jail Museum** at 217 W. Main St. is maintained by the Noble County Historical Society. Built in 1875, the two-story brick structure with an elaborate roofline trim,

Gene Stratton Porter

Indiana State Library

constructed by George Harvey, served as a jail until 1968. Only one jailbreak, in 1907, has been recorded in its history. (*NRHP*)

From Albion, return north on IND 9 to US 6. Follow US 6 east for *7.5 m.* to IND 3 at **KENDALLVILLE** (p. 7,299). William Mitchell of New York settled here in 1836 and platted the town in 1849. It was named after Amos Kendall, the postmaster general of the United States under President Andrew Jackson. Kendallville was incorporated as a town in 1863 and as a city three years later. It is the county's largest city and also is an industrial center which proudly claims, "the world takes what Kendallville makes."

The **Kraft Foods Company**, confectionary plant, is Kendallville's largest employer. Located on the south side of town, the company occupies the site of the former Breyer Ice Cream Company started in 1927. Kraft bought the plant in 1934 and turned it into a cheddar cheese manufacturing plant, but a year later began the production of its famous vanilla and chocolate carmels and phased out the cheese-making operation.

Other products manufactured in the Kendallville area include water pumps, grey iron castings, plastics, machine tools, appliance controls, furniture and bed springs, machine parts, and electrical magnet wire.

Proceed *.6 m.* on US 6 to IND 3 North. Turn north and proceed approximately *1.5 m.* to the **Stutley Whitford mansion** on the left. Whitford returned from a trip west with a bag of gold and built this southern-style mansion for his bride in 1844. The two-story brick structure with a wrought-iron balcony and tall central tower originally featured five porches with 24-ft.-high pillars. Four original pillars still grace the front of the house. The north wing was added in 1855 after Whitford returned from a second trip to California. Whitford supposedly used the house as an "underground railroad" station until he sold the farm in 1860. The mansion changed hands many times before the present owner began its restoration.

Return to US 6 (North St.) and go east two blocks to BUS IND 3 (Main St.). Turn right and continue south *.6 m.* to Mitchell St. in the business district. The block to the north of the intersection contains some fine examples of 19th-century commercial architecture. The storefront at 217 S. Main St., for instance, features an elaborate pressed-tin facade. Further

south, at Lisle St., Hoosier poet Arthur Franklin Mapes (1913–1986) was born. Mapes wrote "Indiana," the official state poem adopted by the General Assembly in 1963.

> God crowned her hills with beauty,
>   Gave her lakes and winding streams,
> Then He edged them all with woodlands
>   As the settings for our dreams.
> Lovely are her moonlit rivers,
>   Shadowed by the sycamores,
> Where the fragrant winds of Summer
>   Play along the willowed shores.
> I must roam those wooded hillsides,
>   I must heed the native call,
> For a Pagan voice within me
>   Seems to answer to it all.
> I must walk where squirrels scamper
>   Down a rustic old rail fence,
> Where a choir of birds is singing
>   In the woodland . . . green and dense.
> I must learn more of my homeland
>   For it's paradise to me,
> There's no haven quite as peaceful,
>   There's no place I'd rather be.
> Indiana . . . is a garden
>   Where the seeds of peace have grown,
> Where each tree, and vine, and flower
>   Has a beauty . . . all its own.
> Lovely are the fields and meadows,
>   That reach out to hills that rise
> Where the dreamy Wabash River
>   Wanders on . . . through paradise.

From Mitchell and Main sts., proceed east for eight blocks to Park. Turn south and go one block to Lake Park Dr., then east and south to **Bixler Lake**. The 117-acre lake is named for Daniel Bixler, who once owned much of the land around it. In the past there has been a steamboat on the lake and a brewery, an icehouse, a restaurant, and a dance hall on its shores. Since 1917 the city has slowly acquired land for a park along the lake on the east edge of town. The 170-acre city park contains campgrounds, lakeshore pavilions, and picnic areas. There is a swimming beach on each side of the lake, which the state has stocked with bluegill and perch for fishing.

Return to Main St. Proceed south for *5.5 m.* to IND 8 at Avilla and turn left for *5.3 m.* to IND 327, reentering De Kalb County. Turn right on IND 327 (Randolph St.) and continue south *1 m.* to Quincy St. in downtown **GAR-**

RETT (p. 4,874). Garrett began as a railroad town. The area was first surveyed in 1853 but abandoned because of the swampy conditions. In 1871 the Baltimore and Ohio Railroad conducted another survey and filled in the roadbed for railroad tracks over a three-year period. Fifty acres selected for the site of a division point between Akron and Chicago became the town of Garrett, named for the president of the B and O, John W. Garrett. Platted in 1875, Garrett was populated quickly and incorporated in the same year. It became a city in 1893.

The first passenger train passed through Garrett in 1874. Between 1875 and the 1910s the town experienced a boom. The B and O erected a roundhouse with a turntable and 32 stalls for engines just west of Randolph St. Car shops for repairing steam locomotives and numerous other facilities used to service the trains employed hundreds of workers in Garrett. In 1929 the car shops moved to Willard, Ohio, and the town's railroad-related services declined. In 1958 diesel-electric locomotives replaced the last steam engines, and the Garrett facilities became outdated. The brick roundhouse was demolished in 1968, and the last passenger train stopped in Garrett in 1971.

The B and O, now a part of the CSX System, still uses a brick passenger depot and an oil house which stand along the railroad at Randolph St. The Italianate-style depot was built in 1876, and the second floor office was added in 1910.

Just east of IND 327 is the **Garrett Railroad Museum**, 210 E. Quincy St. At the northeast corner of Randolph and Quincy sts., on the south side of the B and O tracks, stands a Gothic-style freighthouse, built in 1875, of board and batten siding. The Garrett Historical Society owns the freighthouse and houses a museum in the former agent's office. The exterior has been restored to its original colors. The historical society also owns a switching shanty, a parlor car, mail car, crew car, several carts, and a collection of railroad artifacts.

In 1983, 46 historical homes and buildings, of which 26 are located in central Garrett, were designated as the **Keyser Township Multiple Resource Area**. Most of the properties are homes and farmhouses dating from Garrett's boom period which have been occupied by descendants of the town's early railroad workers. (*NRHP*)

Proceed south on Randolph St. for three blocks through the business district to Houston St. The **Garrett Public Library**, 107 W. Houston St., a Carnegie-funded facility which opened in 1914, stands on the southwest corner. It houses the Indian artifact collection of Cameron Park, a local high school teacher and authority on Indiana's prehistory.

Turn east on Houston St. and go four blocks to the **Peter Mountz house** at 507 E. Houston St. Between 1893 and 1896 Herman M. Coffinberry, the president of the Garrett Banking Company, erected this large frame house featuring elaborate wood carving at the peak of the roof with money embezzled from the bank. When the police came to the door, Coffinberry fatally shot himself. Howard Wesley Mountz, an attorney, purchased the property, including a carriage house to the rear of the main house, in 1906. Four generations of the Mountz family have lived in the house. (*NRHP*)

Return to IND 327 and IND 8, north of Garrett. Proceed east on IND 8 for *3.7 m.*, past the I-69 interchange, to the railroad on the west side of Auburn. In the yard of the **Gengnagel Lumber Company**, on the south side of the road, are four old railroad cars. A renovated 1933 Pullman passenger car now serves as company offices, and the boxcars provide storage space. The lumber store occupies the former New York Central freight station, built at the turn of the century.

The brick factory building across the street is the home of **Rieke Corporation**, producer and distributor of closures for drums and pails. In the 1910s the W. H. McIntyre Company, one of several early automotive companies in Auburn, housed its administrative headquarters in this facility, known as Plant No. 5. The McIntyre Company manufactured automobiles from 1908 to 1915. The early McIntyres are classified as "highwheelers," a buggy type vehicle with a tiller or simple wheel steering mechanism, a one or two cylinder engine, and solid tires. By 1911 the company carried pneumatic-tired models with two and four cylinder motors. The company introduced a six-cylinder model with a touring body in 1913, but achieved its fame for the short-lived Imp Cycle Car, a tandem-seated compact economy car with belt drive, produced in 1914, which sold for $375. The Imp was assembled at Plant No.

5 until 1915 when the company ceased operations. Very few lightweight Imps have survived.

Continue east on IND 8 (7th St.) for *.4 m.* to Main St. in downtown **AUBURN** (p. 8,122). Wesley Park and John Badlam Howe platted the village of Auburn in 1835. It was selected for the county seat shortly after De Kalb County was organized in 1837. Park's cabin served as the county courthouse and jail until 1843 when a schoolhouse replaced it. The first courthouse on the public square, a 30 x 40-ft. frame structure, was completed in the fall of 1843. Construction of a new courthouse began in 1863. In the fall of 1864 the townspeople made a bonfire of the former courthouse to celebrate the siege of Richmond by federal troops. Architects Mahurin and Mahurin of Fort Wayne designed the present **De Kalb County Courthouse**, a three-story Bedford limestone building, erected in 1911. A jail was built in 1918.

From one block west of 7th and Main sts., go south on Jackson St. for six blocks to the **Eckhart Public Library**, located between 12th and 13th sts. Charles Eckhart (1841–1915), founder of the Eckhart Buggy Works, which was a forerunner of the Auburn Automobile Company, donated the funds to build this magnificent library of Chicago Prairie School design, completed in 1911. Architects Patton and Miller of Chicago modeled it after the library at Clinton, Indiana. The Bedford limestone and salt-glazed brick building features a green barrel-tile roof with wide heavy overhangs, an oversized fireplace and chimneys, and stained-glass windows. Eckhart also donated the property for a park behind the library and commissioned the W. L. Mott Iron Works of New York to cast the fountain, topped with figures of two boys struggling with a goose, erected about 1916. (*NRHP*)

Continue south on Jackson St. for two blocks to 15th St. Three blocks east on the northwest corner of 15th and Union sts. and across from the county fairgrounds is the former **Union Depot**. Around 1875 the B and O Railroad built the rectangular board and batten station which originally stood at Auburn Junction. Since then, the station has been moved twice, made into a restaurant, converted into a four-unit apartment building, and condemned by the Health Department following a fire. In the 1980s the present owner restored the depot to its original appearance and colors on the exterior and adapted the interior for commercial space.

Return two blocks west of 15th and Union sts., turn south, and proceed five and one-half blocks to the foot of Main St. Continue southwest on Ensley St. then Wayne St. for two blocks to the **Auburn-Cord-Duesenberg Museum**, 1600 S. Wayne St. There is parking across the street. The museum occupies the Auburn Automobile Company administrative building and factory showroom, erected in 1930. A grand staircase, ornate chandeliers, and terrazzo floors grace the main floor of the 80,000-sq.-ft. building of art deco design and provide the setting for more than 120 classic and antique cars on display. Auburn-built cars such as the McIntyre, Kiblinger, Imp, and Zimmerman share floor space with roadsters, touring cars, phaetons, speedsters, convertibles, and sedans of all makes. The museum, which opened in 1974, also houses a collection of antiquarian clothing, historical radios, televisions, phonographs, automotive literature, photographs, and memorabilia from the 1933 Chicago World's Fair. Restored offices on the second floor re-create the company's advertising, engineering, and accounting departments of the 1930s. A reproduction of the Art Smith Aeroplane of Fort Wayne, flown in 1911, hangs from the showroom ceiling.

Charles Eckhart established Auburn as an early auto manufacturing center when, in 1900, he built his first experimental automobile and converted his buggy works to an automotive operation. Three local buggy companies and early auto manufacturers—Eckhart, Kiblinger, and Zimmerman—formed the Auburn Automobile Company. A group of Chicago financiers, which included William Wrigley, Jr., bought the firm in 1919. Errett Lobban Cord (1894–1974) of Chicago became the vice-president and general sales manager in 1924. Sales doubled within a year, and Cord became president of the company. Under Cord's guidance, Auburn became a pioneer in advancing the fields of automotive engineering, design, and production. He promoted the mass production of front-wheel drive cars, straight eight-cylinder engines, and two-tone color schemes—innovations followed by the rest of the auto industry. Duesenberg Motors, founded at Indianapolis in 1920, joined the Cord Corporation in 1926. The Auburns, Cords, and Duesenbergs produced in the 1920s and 1930s achieved worldwide acclaim for their avant-garde styling and engineering and reached a sales peak of 28,103 vehicles sold in 1931. Between 1928 and 1932 the Auburn Automobile Company introduced the Auburn Boatail Speedster, the revolutionary front-wheel drive Cord, the Duesenberg Model J, and the 12-cylinder models. However, even production of the memorable Auburn 851 Speedster in 1935 and 1936 could not combat the overall slump in sales and depressed economy of the 1930s. In 1937 Cord sold his interests in the business and the company folded in 1938. (*NRHP*)

Proceed south on old IND 427 for *5.5 m.* to CR 68. Turn right and follow Cedar Chapel Rd. west for *.7 m.* to the **Cornell homestead** on the south side. William and Mary Cornell came to Butler Township from Maryland in 1850 and cleared 80 acres for a farm. About 1863 they erected a two-story brick mansion of Italianate design on a knoll overlooking a sweeping expanse of lawn. The beautifully restored exterior features ornamental brackets under the eaves and an octagonal tower. A log cabin stands west of the main house. (*NRHP*)

Return to old IND 427 (Tonkel Rd.) and proceed south, crossing the county line, for *7 m.* to IND 1. Turn right for *1.4 m.* to the I-69 interchange. Take I-69 south to Exit 102 on the west side of Fort Wayne. Follow US 24 (W. Jefferson Blvd.) *.8 m.* east to the **Midwestern United Life Insurance Company**. Construction began on its headquarters in 1961. Architect Leo Daly of Omaha, Nebraska, designed the facility constructed of glass, steel, aluminum, and stone. The directors' meeting room features a modern stained-glass window created by French artist Jean Barillet. Bill J. Hammon of Islamorada, Florida, executed the frieze on the exterior of the south building. The bas-relief in stone aggregate depicts the history of Allen County from the glacier age to the present.

At the entrance road to Midwestern United's home office, a historical marker indicates the "**Glorious Gate**." This stretch of valley floor was the only land barrier separating a water trade route between Quebec and New Orleans in the 18th century. First the Indians, then the French, British, and American fur traders portaged the eight miles from the St. Marys River in Fort Wayne to a tiny stream called Little River, leading to the Wabash and eventually to the Ohio and Mississippi rivers. The travel route was used for well over a century before canals, railroads, and highways pushing through the valley supplanted it.

From the roadside marker, follow Jefferson Blvd. east for *6.1 m.* to Harrison St. in Fort Wayne. Turn north and go four blocks to W. Main. Turn right and proceed one block to the Allen County Courthouse and the conclusion of Tour 1.

Tour 2

Tour 2 begins at Clinton and Main Sts. in downtown Fort Wayne, one block east of the Allen County Courthouse. Drive south on Clinton St. (US 27/33) *14 m.* to the **ADAMS COUNTY** (p. 29,619; 340 sq. m.) line. Formed from Allen County in 1835 and organized under a legislative act in 1836, it was named for John Quincy Adams, sixth president of the United States. In 1980 Adams County ranked 48th of Indiana's 92 counties in population and 72nd in area. Overwhelmingly agricultural in its economy, ranking first in the state in the percentage of farm population (36.85 percent), Adams County is a leading producer of oats, winter wheat, and livestock, particularly horses.

Continue south on US 27/33 for *6.7 m.* The massive complex of grain elevators on the left is the Decatur plant of **Central Soya Company, Inc.**, 1200 N. 2nd St. Dale W. McMillen, a pioneer in soybean cultivation in the United States, founded the corporation in Decatur in October 1934. From its modest beginnings in a former sugar-beet processing plant, Central Soya has grown into a multinational corporation with 75 plants in the United States, Europe, the Caribbean, and South and Central America. Headquartered in Fort Wayne, it is one of Indiana's largest industries. The Decatur plant can process 70,000 bushels of soybeans a day—equivalent to the output of a 2,000-acre farm. In 1970 Central Soya opened its first edible vegetable oil refinery at the Decatur plant, which also serves as a grain merchandising center. The plant can store 12 million bushels of grain in silos, which stand up to 120 ft. high and 80 ft. in diameter. Each has a 400,000-bushel capacity.

Continue south on 13th St. (US 27/33) into **DECATUR** (p. 8,649), the seat of Adams County. At *1.1 m.* beyond the Central Soya plant, turn left on Monroe St. where US 33 branches from US 27. Founded in 1836 by Thomas Johnson and Samuel L. Rugg, the city is named for Stephen Decatur, naval hero of the Tripolitan War.

Go east on Monroe St. (US 224) to 5th St. On the left is the **Dugan mansion**, 420 W. Monroe St., home of the Adams County Historical Society Museum. Charles A. Dugan, then cashier and later president of Decatur's First National Bank, had the home built in 1902. Collections relate to the history of Adams County and vicinity.

Continue east on Monroe St. to 2nd St., turn right, and go one block to the **Adams County Courthouse** at Madison St. Constructed in 1872, this brick structure is the third building to serve as the Adams County courthouse. The Second Empire-style tower at the front was added in 1900 when the original tower, located at the center of the building, proved unstable and had to be razed. In front of the courthouse is a memorial to Gene Stratton Porter attached to a 50-ton boulder known as the Elephant Rock, which was taken from the St. Marys River bed. At the rear of the building is a limestone monument to Adams County's war dead. Dedicated in 1913, the monument was touted as the first "peace" monument in the country. Instead of the usual display of servicemen and armaments, it exhibits an heroic-sized "female figure of the nation" posed by Margaret McMaster Van Slyke, "Chicago's most perfectly formed woman." Chicago sculptor Charles J. Mulligan created the design, which was executed in Bedford limestone by Charles M. Dodd. The idea was to symbolize the peace that results from war rather than represent the means of the conflict.

An annual event in Decatur is the **Callithumpian parade**, held near Halloween night. Callithumpian, which means a noisy boisterous parade, began in 1926 as an activity to keep schoolchildren out of mischief. It features costumed marchers, floats, marching bands, antique autos, drill teams, and other attractions.

Tour 2

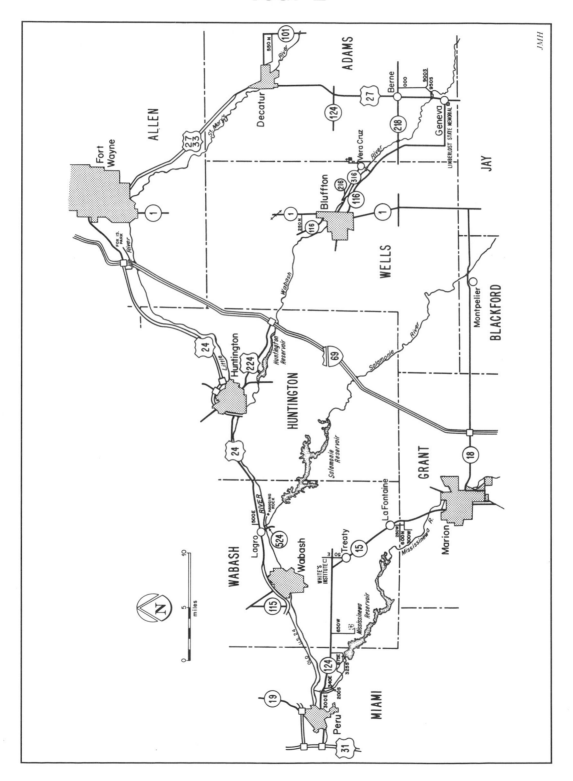

In 1979 the event was expanded into Callithumpian week.

An interesting local institution is **Reppert's School of Auctioneering**, 141 Madison St. Col. Fred Reppert, Jr.—the "Boy Auctioneer of Indiana"—founded the school in 1921. To reach the auction barn where classes are held, drive east from 2nd and Monroe sts. *4.5 m.* to IND 101 south. Turn right and drive *1 m.* to CR 550N. Turn right again and go *.8 m.* to the auction barn, a low white building on the right. Continue west *1.7 m.* to Piqua Rd., angle right, and return to Decatur.

Return to Monroe and 13th sts. Drive south *12.2 m.* on US 27 to **BERNE** (p. 3,300), which Swiss Mennonites from the Jura region of canton Berne settled in 1852. The town was not platted until 1871 when the Grand Rapids and Indiana Railroad built through the area. Berne serves as a marketing center for the many Amish families that live in the neighborhood, and many interesting shops which cater to their needs may be found. Originally surrounded by a great hardwood forest, Berne developed a small furniture industry. Three factories still operate. The Berne Furniture Company, Behring and Berne sts., offers tours. The Berne Public Library, 116 Springer St., maintains a small tourist information center.

Turn left on Main St. (IND 218) at the traffic light and go one block. On the right is the **First Mennonite Church**, a Gothic-style structure dedicated on April 7, 1912, and nicknamed the "Big M" because it had the world's largest Mennonite congregation until the mid-1970s. The Mennonites, who take their name from Menno Simons, a Dutch Anabaptist reformer, trace their origins to the 16th-century Protestant Reformation. They rejected infant baptism and believed in voluntary church membership and completely separate church and state. They also were pacifists and refused to serve in the military. Rulers of church and state regarded the Mennonites as heretical and subversive, and to escape persecution many migrated to America in the 18th and 19th centuries. Today there are more than 200,000 Mennonites in the United States divided into many groups. The Berne church is affiliated with the General Conference Mennonites. The church's Moeller organ with 2,281 pipes was installed in 1914.

Drive east on Main St. *1 m.* past US 27 and turn right on CR 000 (a marker just south of Berne on US 27 designates the continental divide between the Atlantic Ocean and Gulf of Mexico watersheds). This is the so-called **Amish Turnpike**, where numerous Amish farms may be seen and are conspicuous by their windmills, the absence of power lines, the many horses, and Amish working in the fields. Be alert for horse-drawn traffic.

In the late 17th century, a group led by Jacob Ammann split from the Mennonites, who they claimed had grown lax in following the teachings of the New Testament. The Amish, as Ammann's followers came to be called, emphasized plain dress, the simple life, and strictly observed the *Meidung*, or the banning of all social intercourse with excommunicated members. Like the Mennonites, the Amish were persecuted in Europe, and many migrated to America. The first to settle in Indiana came in 1841.

Unlike the Mennonites, the Amish have rigidly adhered to their traditional way of life, which has changed little since the 18th century. Following the admonition of Paul—"And be not conformed to this world"—the Amish have resisted use of modern conveniences such as automobiles or electricity. Their dress-black, wide-brimmed hats and broadfall trousers for men and long dresses and black bonnets for women emphasize Amish separation from the world. Indiana ranks only behind Ohio and Pennsylvania in the number of its Amish.

Continue south *2.8 m.* to CR 900S. Bear left. Drive east *.9 m.* to **Amishville, U.S.A.**, a commercially-operated campground, gift shop, and restaurant complex on a 120-acre former Amish farm. Guided tours of an authentic Amish home are available. There are also buggy rides and a barnyard with farm animals.

Return to the intersection of CR 900S and CR 000. Proceed west on CR 900S and CR 950S to the **Ceylon Covered Bridge**. (*HABS*) This Howe-truss structure, built in 1860, was the last covered bridge to span the Wabash River, although it no longer stands over the channel. Closed to traffic since 1948, it has been preserved as part of Limberlost Park.

Continue southwest *.9 m.* to US 27. Turn left and drive south on US 27 *1 m.* to Line St. (blinker light) in **GENEVA** (p. 1,430). Founded in 1871 from the consolidation of the villages of Alexander and Buffalo, Geneva took its name from a station on the Grand Rapids and Indiana Railroad.

Amishville, late 1960s

Continue south two blocks to **Limberlost State Historic Site**, 200 E. 6th St. From 1895 to 1913 this was the home of writer and naturalist Gene Stratton Porter (1863–1924). Porter selected this location because it was near the center of a vast forest and swamp wilderness known as the Limberlost. The region supposedly took its name from "Limber Jim" Corbus, a pioneer who was lost here for several days. The forest and swamps have since been cleared, drained, and replaced with fertile farmlands. During the 18 years that she lived at Limberlost, Porter achieved fame as a novelist who used the wilderness as a background for her stories, a naturalist, and an illustrator and photographer. While living at her home in Geneva, Porter produced six novels: *The Song of the Cardinal* (1903); *Freckles* (1904); *At the Foot of the Rainbow* (1907); *A Girl of the Limberlost* (1909); *The Harvester* (1911); and *Laddie* (1913); and five nature studies: *What I Have Done with Birds* (1907); *Birds of the Bible* (1909); *Music of the Wild* (1910); *Moths of the Limberlost* (1912); and *Wings* (1923). In 1913, after the Limberlost swamp was drained, Porter

and her family moved to Rome City. (See Tour 1.)

Porter designed the 14-room home constructed of white cedar logs. Redwood shingles cover the upper story and roof. Many furnishings were used by Porter and her family when she lived here. An interesting display is the moths she collected in 1912 as part of her research for *Moths of the Limberlost*. (*NRHP*)

Return to US 27 and Line St. Turn left and drive west and north *10.8 m.* on IND 116 to the **WELLS COUNTY** (p. 25,401; 370 sq. m.) line. Much of this route parallels at trackside the Bluffton, Geneva and Celina Traction Company's former right-of-way. Part of Indiana's vast interurban system and its shortest-lived line, it was opened in 1910 and conceived as a connection with the sprawling Ohio traction network at Celina. However, it never was extended beyond Geneva and was abandoned in 1917. It typifies the interurban craze that swept Indiana early in the century when many economically unjustified lines were built.

Wells County is named for William Wells, the legendary "white Indian." Captured by the

Miamis when he was 14, Wells became a fierce warrior and son-in-law of the Miami chief Little Turtle. He participated in the bloody defeat of Maj. Gen. Arthur St. Clair's army in 1791, but later switched sides and served as a scout for Maj. Gen. Anthony Wayne. Wells died in the Fort Dearborn massacre in 1812. Created by the state legislature from Allen, Delaware, and Randolph counties in 1835 and organized by an 1837 act, Wells County is one of the state's leading producers of soybeans, oats, and winter wheat.

Continue northwest on IND 116 for *1.4 m.* to IND 316. Turn right, drive *.2 m.*, and cross the Wabash River. Parallel to the new steel and concrete span is an **iron bridge**, built in 1887 by the Indiana Bridge Builders of Muncie. Examples, such as this, of a double-intersection Pratt through-truss are disappearing quickly. (*HAER*) From Vera Cruz, at the north end of the bridge, continue north *1.1 m.* to one of Indiana's most imposing rural churches. Apostolic Christians, a small denomination, built it in 1951, spending $530,000 and paying for it in 18 months. The contemporary brick building is 170 ft. long, has a 76-ft. bell tower, and seats 1,400 worshipers in a breathtaking, fully-carpeted sanctuary. The congregation is largely of Swiss descent, and the soft sounds of Schwyzer Dutsch may still be heard in everyday conversation.

Return to Vera Cruz and continue *3.2 m.* northwest on IND 316 to IND 216, the entrance to **Ouabache State Park.** This 1,089-acre tract contains a small lake, live animal exhibits, and recreational facilities. Continue northwest on IND 316 for *2.9 m.* to the courthouse at S. Main and W. Market sts. in downtown **BLUFFTON** (p. 8,705). It was selected the Wells County seat in March 1838 and platted soon thereafter. Local industries produce electric motors, grey iron castings, rubber products, and foods.

The Romanesque-style **Courthouse**, 100 W. Market St., is unusual in that it is located on a busy corner rather than on a public square. Designed by the Indianapolis architectural firm of G. W. Bunting and Son, the building was dedicated on August 29, 1889, and is the third structure to have served as Wells County's seat of government. (*NRHP/HABSI*)

Three blocks west, the **Wells County Historical Society Museum**, 420 W. Market St., occupies the former Stewart-Studebaker house. John Studebaker of Ohio came to the area in the 1840s, purchased land here, and established a trading post. He sold a lot to Alvin Stewart, a railroad engineer, who erected this well-preserved three-story brick Victorian house in 1882. Ten years later Studebaker re-bought the lot and resided in the house until his death in 1912, at age 95. The house remained in the family for many years, then served as a funeral home before the Wells County Historical Society purchased it in 1974. It now exhibits displays depicting the history of Wells County in such fields as early transportation, industry, agriculture, education, prominent residents, and war memorabilia. In the basement is the vault and teller's cage from a turn-of-the-century bank at Uniondale. The work of local artist Harry Lindstrand enhances many exhibits. (*NRHP*)

From the courthouse drive north on Main St. (IND 116/IND 1) for *1.2 m.*, then follow IND 116 northwest *2.3 m.* to the **Deam Oak** on the right. This rare hybrid, a cross between the white and chinquapin oaks, was discovered by L. A. Williamson and his son E. Bruce Williamson in 1904 and named for Charles C. Deam, Indiana's first state forester and Wells County native, who saved it from destruction by purchasing in 1915 the land on which it grew and deeding it to the state.

Continue east on CR 250N *2.3 m.* to IND 1. Two and one-half miles north, the worst interurban disaster in the nation's history claimed 41 lives on September 21, 1910. A car returning empty from Fort Wayne crashed into a car loaded with passengers headed for a fair in Fort Wayne. The collision was instrumental in causing the legislature to require block signals on heavily traveled lines.

Turn south on IND 1 and continue *16 m.* to IND 18, passing the Wells County courthouse and crossing the **JAY COUNTY** (p. 23,239; 384 sq. m.) line. The state legislature in 1835 passed an omnibus bill creating Jay and 14 other counties. In 1836 the county was organized by a legislative act. The name given the new county honored John Jay, first chief justice of the Supreme Court, minister to England, and governor of New York. The coming of the railroads in 1867, 1871, and 1879 and the subsequent boom in natural gas brought some prosperity to the largely rural county. Since the turn of the century, Jay's population has actually dropped about 10 percent. In the last several decades, the economic base has been shifting from agriculture to manufacturing and service, following the trends in many other parts of the state and nation. Continue south *1.3 m.* on IND 1 to a stone monument on the left which marks the purported location of an "underground railroad" station. Tradition has it that the real Eliza Harris, whom Harriet Beecher Stowe portrayed in her novel *Uncle Tom's Cabin*, rested here during her freedom flight to Canada.

Return to the junction of IND 1 and IND 18. Turn west, immediately crossing the abandoned right-of-way of the Cincinnati, Bluffton and Chicago Railroad, known from its initials as the "Corned Beef and Cabbage." Opened in successive segments from 1903 to 1908, it extended 50 miles between Portland and Huntington and was Indiana's original hard luck railroad, as well as one of its shortest lived. Before it was abandoned in 1917, it had undergone two receiverships, lost proceeds of a $300,000 bond issue to an unscrupulous broker, been forced to reimburse the bond holders and to issue a second group of bonds to replace the first, and lost its tracks in three locations when a trunk line railroad charged breach of contract in a joint operation and took them out. In addition, the 1913 flood washed out its Wabash River bridge north of Bluffton, and two months later the new bridge collapsed beneath a train with fatal results. Also, a runaway locomotive in Huntington demolished a confectionery.

Drive *2.7 m.* to the **BLACKFORD COUNTY** (p. 15,570; 166 sq. m.) line. In 1838 state lawmakers detached a slice of Jay County to form Blackford, Indiana's third smallest county, and in 1839 Blackford County was organized by a legislative act. The name honors Isaac Blackford (1786-1859), speaker of the first state legislature, state supreme court member for 35 years, and an unsuccessful candidate for governor and for United States senator. Today, the majority of Blackford's residents live in the two major cities of Montpelier and Hartford City, the county seat. Continue *3.7 m.* on IND 18 to **MONTPELIER** (p. 1,995). Sometimes called the "zinnia city" for the flowers in its unusual downtown parks, located at the four corners of its principal intersections, the city dates from 1837 when Abel Baldwin platted it and named it for his Vermont home. Like many cities in this region, Montpelier expanded rapidly with the oil and gas boom, and for many years it was known as the "Oil City." The city also was known as a harness racing center;

some of the country's best trotters and pacers raced here from 1923 to 1976.

Continue west on IND 18 for *8.7 m.* to the **GRANT COUNTY** (p. 80,934; 415 sq. m.) line. Organized in 1831 and named for Kentuckians Samuel and Moses Grant who were killed by Indians near present-day Switzerland County in 1789, Grant County is a state leader in both agriculture and industry. Because of its location within the Trenton natural gas field, the county played a major role in the gas boom of the late 19th century.

Drive west *10.5 m.* from the county line past the World Gospel Mission headquarters (at *8.2 m.*) to the traffic light at Pennsylvania St. in **MARION** (p. 35,874). On the right is the multimillion dollar **Tucker Career Center**, a vocational building operated by Marion community schools. In 1831 the county commissioners selected the rude settlement that had grown up near the mouth of Boots Creek as the seat of newly formed Grant County. A town was platted and named for Revolutionary War hero Francis Marion. It remained a quiet county seat until 1887, when discovery of natural gas propelled it into an industrial boom town nearly overnight. The population increased from 3,182 in 1880 to 17,337 in 1900. Marion became known for its iron foundries, paper and glass factories, and, more recently, auto parts, plastics, and cable plants. From 1945 to 1952 the Crosley, America's first compact car, was made here. The community still has many industries, including the Foster-Forbes Glass Company, General Motors's Chevrolet-Pontiac-Canada division, Thomson (formerly RCA), which produces TV picture tubes, DiversiTech General, and Dana Corporation.

Turn left *2.5 m.* to 38th St. and left again *.2 m.* to the entrance to the **Veterans Administration Medical Center** on the right. Opened in 1890, it now is a self-sustaining 99-building city spread over 189 acres. Return to 38th St. and continue west *1.5 m.* to Washington St., passing on the right the former **Superior Paperware plant**, last of Marion's paper plate manufacturers. In the industry's early days, when only nine factories in the United States produced paper plates, five were located in Marion. Superior's predecessor, St. Regis, could produce 17,500,000 plates daily. Peerless Machine and Tool Corporation of Marion is one of two paper plate-making machinery manufacturers in the world. Beyond Superior *.5 m.*

to the right is the Thomson television picture tube plant.

Turn left at Washington St. .2 m. to **Indiana Wesleyan University** (formerly Marion College), a private institution operated by the Wesleyan Church. Most of the campus lies to the east and south. The Wesleyan Methodist Church chartered the university in 1920, having the previous year purchased the property of Marion Normal Institute, a successor to Marion Normal College, established in 1887 on the site. Upon its founding in 1920 Indiana Wesleyan absorbed the denomination's bible school at Fairmount, which became the new institution's religion department. Most students are enrolled in courses leading to degrees in teaching, nursing, or ministerial fields. The university also offers masters' programs in Christian ministries and nursing education. A small museum is located on the third floor of the administration building in the "Old Triangle" section of campus. The name change occurred in 1988.

Continue south *1.3 m.* to the **Shugart house**, 4689 Strawtown Pike, which is IND 37 and an extension of Washington St. Constructed by Quaker leader George Shugart in 1847, the outside walls are four bricks thick and the inside walls are three bricks thick. Over 8,500 bricks were used for the rear fireplace and chimney. Shugart used the space between the walls to hide runaway slaves during the "underground railroad" era. The house has been restored to fit this period, and a log cabin has been added to commemorate Shugart's first home on this site, which was erected in 1846.

Return *.6 m.* to IND 9, angle left *2.4 m.*, and turn right on IND 18 (4th St.). On the right at Garfield St. is the **Hostess house**, a mansion built by banker J. Wood Wilson and now used for community events. Continue east on 4th St. past the **Grant County Courthouse**, which is the third building to house the county offices. Constructed in 1880, this Classical Revival-style building was once topped by a dome which rose 40 ft. above the roof. The dome was removed in 1943 following a fire.

Continue east *.2 m.* to the Sheraton-Marion Hotel, passing the Grant County Office and Security Complex on the right (formerly the Spencer Hotel) and the City Building on the left. An unusual Celebrity Audio Walking tour which leads to homes and work places of actor James Dean, baseball commissioner Kenesaw Mountain Landis, United States Supreme Court Justice Willis Vandevanter, composer Cole Porter, cartoonist Jim Davis, and other nationally known persons begins at the Sheraton. A combination of on-location markers, audio presentations, and visual descriptions on TV makes it unique in Indiana. The Indiana Historical Society provided major funding for the tour development.

From the Sheraton, return west on 3rd St. three blocks to Adams St., passing the former Grant County jail. Turn right, left at the end of the street, and right after one block. Cross the Mississinewa River. Each spring since 1937, except during World War II, nearly 4,000 local volunteers present an Easter Pageant in the **Marion Coliseum**, right one block, which portrays the last week of Christ's life in pantomime and music.

Drive two blocks to the **Swayzee-Love home**, 224 N. Washington St., an impressive Greek Revival-style mansion once owned by Henry Erlewine, a Marion manufacturer. It also was the residence of George W. Steele, Sr., and his son, George, Jr. The elder Steele was instrumental in having the Soldiers' Home (now the Veterans' Administration Medical Center) located in Marion. He later became the first governor of the Oklahoma Territory. His son flew across the Atlantic in a dirigible four years before Lindbergh's celebrated flight. (*NRHP*) A celebrity walking tour station is located here.

Return on Washington St., turn right at the end of the river bridge, and right at the first street to River Rd. At *1.8 m.* the **Charles Mill**, built in 1856, stands across the river. Since its active milling days, it has been converted into shops and apartments. Continue on River Rd. to Matter Park, where the **Octogenarian Museum** is located. Its collections consist mostly of local pioneer and Indian artifacts. Continue through the park, turn right on River Rd. at the far end of the park, then immediately turn left into Shady Hills, a residential area which contains a **Frank Lloyd Wright-designed home**, the front resembling a tepee, at *.5 m.* on the left. Continue on Overlook Dr. to IND 15, turn right, and continue *3.9 m.*, turning left on CR 600N. Go *1.1 m.* to the **Miami Indian Cemetery**, on the right. Now a one-acre plot, the hilltop cemetery was once part of a 6,400-acre Indian reservation. Most of those buried here are descended from Chief Metocinyah. The cemetery and church ground were set up near the home of Metocinyah's son, Chief Mesh-ingomesia (1782–1879), when the reservation was formed in 1840. The earliest grave stone dates from 1873. Since burial was not part of Indian tradition, these markers indicate that those interred here were converts to Christianity. The Union Baptist Church that once stood here is gone and the Indian school has been moved to a farm a short distance east of the cemetery and south on the first road, where it serves as a storage shed. The large brick house opposite was built by Nelson Tawataw, son of Chief Meshingomesia, after the reservation was divided.

Continue west on CR 600N, turning south at *.2 m.* onto CR 300W. Drive *.7 m.* to the probable site of the **Mississinewa Battlefield**. (The exact location of the battle is still debated.) In December 1812 Gen. William Henry Harrison sent Lt. Col. John B. Campbell and nearly 600 men north from Greenville, Ohio, to destroy Miami villages along the Mississinewa River. On the morning of December 18 the Miamis attacked Campbell's position. After a furious battle the attackers were repulsed; but 12 Americans were killed, as were about 48 Miami and Delaware Indians. Fearing another attack, Campbell withdrew toward Greenville the same day, the bitter winter cold taking a toll on his men. The United States claimed a victory, but heavy American casualties and Campbell's withdrawal suggest that the Miamis had an equal right to such a claim. A historical marker indicates the probable battle site, and monuments to the fallen combatants in the battle were dedicated in 1988.

Return to the Indian Cemetery, continue east *.2 m.*, and turn left. Cross the Grant-Wabash county line at *1 m.* **WABASH COUNTY** (p. 36,640; 398 sq. m.) was formed by statute in 1832, organized in 1835, and named for the Wabash River, which flows across the area. Most of the county is farmland with some industry in the Wabash and North Manchester areas. In addition to the Wabash, the county also is drained by the Salamonie, Mississinewa, and Eel rivers, which create a gently rolling terrain. The first settlements in the county were made in the vicinity of what is now the city of Wabash, following treaty negotiations with the Miami and Potawatomi Indians. The site of the **Treaty at Paradise Spring** (Kincomaong), signed October 16 and 23, 1826, is at the east

end of Market St. near the northwest bank of the Wabash River.

Continue *1.3 m.* to IND 15 at Lafontaine. Turn left. Continue *4.8 m.* to Treaty, turn north, and continue *1.6 m.* to **White's Institute**, which was incorporated in 1852 on land bequeathed by Josiah White, a Pennsylvania Quaker. The first enrollees at this Society of Friends school, which was designed to teach farming to boys and housework to girls, arrived in 1861. The school served children of all races and creeds from grades 1-8. Many up to the mid-1890s were Indians, and for several years the institute received government aid for their training. The school later served children from various Indiana counties, most of whom were there by court order. White's Institute (also known as White's Indiana Manual Labor Institute) later expanded to include a high school designed for technical training. The Society of Friends continues to maintain this training school for needy school-age children. The brick Romanesque-style administration/school building dates from 1904. It replaced the original building, erected in 1860 and destroyed by fire in 1903.

Return *.6 m.* to IND 124, turn right, and continue *6.8 m.* to CR 650W. Turn left and

Indiana State Library
Frances Slocum (reproduction from a 1916 painting by J. M. Wilmore, Montpelier, Indiana)

drive *2.8 m.* to the **Frances Slocum Cemetery**. Frances Slocum was born in Rhode Island in 1773 and moved with her family to the Susquehanna Valley in Pennsylvania a short time later. Three Delaware braves attacked the family cabin and stole Frances when she was five. She was assimilated into the Delaware nation and adopted by a childless couple who gave her the name Weletawash. The family and the tribe traveled throughout the middle Atlantic states, Canada, and parts of the Old Northwest before settling in the Miami village of Kekionga, near present-day Fort Wayne. In the early 1790s she married the Miami war chief Shepoconah and adopted the Miami name, Maconaqua, which means "Little Bear Woman." (Slocum had previously been married to a Delaware brave, but the union was short-lived because he mistreated her.) In 1817 the couple moved to Miami lands just east of Peru and built a log cabin, where a small settlement of Indians soon sprang up. Since Shepoconah had become deaf as a result of a battle injury, the area was known as Deaf Man's Village. Shepoconah died in 1833, but Maconaqua remained in the village along with her two daughters and their families. Slocum's family members never stopped their quest to find Frances, and in 1837 they were notified of her location and went to her. Frances, however, remained with her adopted race until her death in 1847 and was buried next to Shepoconah just outside the village. The cemetery where Slocum and her family were buried was originally named Bundy Cemetery, but the name was changed to Slocum Cemetery in 1900 when Frances's descendants erected a monument. Potential flooding caused by creation of Mississinewa Lake in the late 1960s forced the cemetery to be relocated.

Return to IND 124 and turn left. Continue *1 m.* to **Asherwood** on the right, a nature study laboratory owned by Marion Community Schools and made possible in part by a contribution by William and Daniel Resneck, Marion merchants. Continue *1.4 m.* to the **MIAMI COUNTY** (p. 39,820; 369 sq. m.) line. Named for the Miami Indian nation, the county was formed in 1832 and organized by law in 1834, but original boundaries have been changed. A northern section became part of Fulton County upon its creation. A section south of the Wabash River remained unattached to the county until the last of a series of treaties with the Mi-

ami tribe was concluded in 1840. Gently rolling hills and picturesque valleys, created by the county's three main waterways, the Wabash, Eel, and Mississinewa rivers, characterize the countryside. Economically, Miami County is one of the state's leaders in livestock and crop production, with some light industry.

Continue west *.4 m.* to CR 675E. Turn left at the sign marked **Mississinewa Reservoir**. Drive *1.1 m.* to CR 325S, turn right, and drive *.2 m.* to the **Mississinewa Dam**. Located on the Mississinewa River, the 140-ft.-high, 8,000-ft.-long earth-filled dam also helps prevent damage along the Wabash and Ohio rivers downstream. The lake/reservoir, which is noted for boating and fishing, has a capacity of 12,830 acres for expansion during flood season. The dam's observation pavilion offers a panoramic view. The area generally serves 550,000 visitors a year.

Continue across the dam, turn right at the end of the road, and continue *2 m.* to the Seven Pillars of the Mississinewa, which are beneath the road and not easily accessible for viewing (see below). Continue *.9 m.* to a small brick house and a garden which is said to have inspired Cole Porter to write the song "The Old Fashioned Garden." The house was constructed between 1910 and 1913 and used by Porter and his mother to entertain friends.

Continue *1.1 m.* to IND 124, turn right, and go *1 m.* to the **Godfroy Cemetery** on the right, a Miami burial ground formerly called Massasinaway. Only Indians and their white spouses were allowed burial in this now overcrowded cemetery. Among those interred here are the last Miami war chief Francis Godfroy and his descendants. (*NRHP*)

Godfroy, the son of a French trader and a Miami mother, became his nation's chief when Shepoconah became deaf. He later became one of the largest landowners in the area as a result of various treaties with the United States government. In addition, Godfroy was the second wealthiest Indian merchant behind Chief Richardville and maintained two highly successful trading posts. Godfroy's major source of wealth came from the sale of furs to large eastern companies, and at the time of his death in 1840, New York City merchants owed him $15,000. Although he claimed to be a member of the Catholic Church, Godfroy had two wives, Sacachequah and Saccaquatah, one residing at each of his trading posts. Across the highway from the cemetery is the site of one of Godfroy's trading posts, known as Mount Pleasant. The wood house was built by Godfroy's son Gabriel in 1893.

Return on IND 124. About *.9 m.* ahead on the right is Valley Farms, Inc., the former site of the **Great Wallace Show and Expedition's (later Hagenbeck-Wallace Circus) winter headquarters.** (*NRHP*) After the circuses left, Emil Schramm, retired president of the New York Stock Exchange, bought the farms. In 1884 Col. Benjamin Wallace acquired a number of small circuses and formed a traveling road show. Wallace wintered his circus in Peru where he resided and formerly owned a livery stable. The showman acquired this 500-acre site from Gabriel Godfroy in 1891 and constructed his headquarters. Other great circuses such as Cole Brothers-Clyde Beatty Shows, Sells-Floto, and Buffalo Bill's Wild West Show also moved their winter quarters to this region. At the industry's peak, seven circuses called Peru home, and many famous stars such as Emmett Kelly, Sr., Clyde Beatty, Terrell Jacobs, and the Great Wilno ("The Human Cannonball") resided here. Wallace sold his interests to a corporation in 1913, and in 1921 it sold to the American Circus Corporation, a conglomerate that owned five other local circuses. From 1921 to 1929 the Hagenbeck-Wallace site boasted the world's largest menagerie. Ringling Brothers-Barnum and Bailey acquired the headquarters and the American Circus Corporation in 1929, and they moved the operation to their main headquarters in Sarasota, Florida, a short time later. Some remodeled houses and a barn are the only reminders from the Hegenbeck-Wallace days. The Great Depression took its toll on the remaining circuses, and the last show, the Terrell Jacobs Circus, moved out in 1944.

Continue on IND 124, cross the Mississinewa River, and drive west *.6 m.* to CR 300E. Turn left and drive south *1.2 m.* to CR 200S. Turn left again. Drive another *1.3 m.* to the **Seven Pillars of the Mississinewa** on the opposite bank of the river. These 60-ft. cliffs of Liston Creek limestone were cut over the centuries by the Mississinewa River. To the Miamis, the pillars symbolized "the Great Father," and the area was the site of tribal rituals, meetings, and celebrations. Young braves were educated and enemies were tortured at the foot of the formation. An Indian legend is related of the "Little Indians," fairy-like creatures who

guided lost Indian boys home. The Little Indians lived in the stream below the pillars and played in the caves, and they could only be seen by old women. The first white (French) trading post in the region supposedly was located in one of the caves.

Return to IND 124, which becomes Riverside Dr., and continue west *2.4 m.* to IND 19 (Broadway). Turn right, cross the Wabash River, and drive north *.3 m.* to the courthouse square in **PERU** (p. 13,764). The city was platted as the county seat by William H. Hood in 1834 and named for the South American country. The land previously had been the site of Miamisport, which Joseph Holman had laid out in 1829. The town developed into an important trade center on the Wabash and Erie Canal in the 1830s and 1840s until the train replaced the canalboat in the 1850s. The 1913 flood caused 11 deaths in the city and an estimated $2 million in property loss. Peru continues to serve as a transportation center for agricultural products into the 1980s. The city also relies on local manufacturing.

The first **Miami County Courthouse** was built on the square bounded by Broadway, Main, 5th, and Court sts. in 1843. It burned the same year. This ill-fated building was not replaced until 1858 when a new courthouse, in the "Norman castle" style, was completed. The present courthouse was dedicated on April 6, 1911. The architectural firm of Lehman and Schmitt of Cleveland, Ohio, designed the Neoclassical-style structure.

Located on the fourth floor of the courthouse is the **Miami County Historical Society Museum.** The museum's collections, which are rich in circus and Indian artifacts, are largely the product of years of work by Judge Hal C. Phelps who searched the county for items of historical interest. Phelps was one of the incorporators of the society which was organized on April 22, 1916. It also maintains the **Puterbaugh Museum,** 11 N. Huntington St., which is located two blocks east in the public library annex. The collections of both museums eventually will be transferred to the Senger Dry Goods Building located on the northeast corner of Broadway and 5th sts. immediately north of the courthouse square. The Senger Building, a gift of Richard Riebel of Grand Rapids, Michigan, is being restored to its 1910 appearance.

From Broadway, drive west on Bus US 24 (W. Main St.) for *1.6 m.*, continuing *.5 m.* past the junction with US 31. Turn left on an unmarked road just before the Northern Indiana Public Service Building. Follow this road south *.1 m.*, turn sharply west, and drive another *1 m.* to the **Old Stone House**. Now covered with blue stucco, this building, the only two-story house between Fort Wayne and Logansport, was constructed around 1838 for use of the Wabash and Erie Canal lockmaster.

Return to Broadway and Main sts. Turn left and drive three blocks to the **Circus City Center and Museum**, 154 N. Broadway St. Since 1960 the community has revived its circus tradition in the annual Circus City Festival. For one week, which begins the third Wednesday in July, the people of Peru put on an amateur circus. Most performers are children, some descended from local circus stars, who must be enrolled in a Miami County school to be eligible. All participants are volunteers. Before the present Circus Center building was purchased in 1967, performances were conducted in a tent. The museum's collections include memorabilia from circuses that made Peru their home, including posters, costumes, a wild animal cage, and furniture from the Wallace Circus Train.

Continue north on Broadway for five blocks. On the right is the **Peru High School**, which houses an exceptional art collection. Most of the collection (70 of 91 pieces, not including ceramics) was donated by steel magnate G. David Thompson, a 1913 graduate. Thompson started donating pieces in 1938 in memory of his former junior high principal, to whom he credited his success in life. The collection contains a wide sampling of works from different styles and time periods. Several are on loan to the Indianapolis Museum of Art. The high school stands on the site of the Wabash Railroad Employees Hospital, which indicates Peru's one-time importance as a rail center.

Return to Main St. Turn left and continue east two blocks to Huntington St. Turn right. Drive one block to **Cole Porter's birthplace**, 102 E. 3rd St. Porter (1891–1964), the composer of more than 30 musical comedies including *Kiss Me Kate* (1948) and *Can Can* (1953), was the son of a Peru druggist and the grandson of one of the richest men in the nation. Porter's grandfather, James Omar Cole, who made millions by prospecting for gold in California and speculating in West Virginia timber and coal, built the house at 27 E. 3rd St., in 1883, one block

west of the Porter home. Porter received his undergraduate degree from Yale in 1913, attended Harvard Music School in 1915–16, went to North Africa to entertain the French Foreign Legion, and served in the French army during World War I. His first successful Broadway musical was *Paris* (1928). Among Porter's more popular songs were *Begin the Beguine*, *Anything Goes*, and *In the Still of the Night*. A 1937 horseback riding accident left him severely crippled, but he continued to compose until 1958, when failing health and the amputation of his right leg forced his retirement. Porter then went into a life of seclusion at his Santa Monica, California, home where he remained until his death in 1964.

Many other notables called Peru home. Among them were comedian John (Ole) Olsen of the Olsen and Johnson shows; Gens. William E. Kepner, George E. Stratemeyer, and William R. Arnold of World War II fame; Admiral Sidney Kraus, who flew the Atlantic before Lindbergh; Frank Whiting, president of the Chicago Merchandise Mart Corporation; and Emil Schramm, president of the New York Stock Exchange.

Return to Main St. and continue east *7 m.* on Business US 24 to the **Omar Cole Public Access Site**, formerly Transportation Park. The entire tapestry of inland transportation unrolled at this location along the Wabash River. First were the Indian foot paths along the river bank, followed by Indian canoes upon the river. Next came the Wabash and Erie Canal, used until it was put out of business by the paralleling railroad. After these came the electric interurban which was driven to extinction by modern highways.

Continue east, crossing into Wabash County, *5 m.* to US 24. Turn right and at *.3 m.* right again to rejoin Business US 24. At *.8 m.* on the right is **GenCorp Automotive** (formerly DiversiTech), which manufactures rubber automotive equipment. The plant originally housed the Service Motor Truck Company, the developer after World War I of the most popular gasoline-powered railroad car in the United States. The model was so successful that J. G. Brill, probably the leading manufacturer in its field, bought out Service Motor's rail car business and provided many cars for such rail giants as the Pennsylvania, Reading, and Seaboard lines.

From GenCorp Automotive, continue *.4 m.* to Vermont St. in downtown **WABASH** (p.

12,985), the county seat. Named for the river on which it is located, Wabash (from the Indian Ouabache meaning "water over white stones") was laid out in 1834, seven years after the first white settlers arrived. The town developed into a trade center with the Wabash and Erie Canal opening in 1837, and its progress continued with the arrival of the railroad in 1856. The name "Wabash Cannon Ball" refers to a train of the Wabash Railroad (later the Norfolk and Western Railway) that ran between Detroit and St. Louis. The name was attached to the train in 1950 after a ballad published in 1943 had made it famous. Prior to 1950 the train had been designated the Detroit and St. Louis Special and still earlier was nationally known as the Continental Limited. Special excursions along the route of the old "Cannon Ball" are occasionally conducted by the Fort Wayne Railroad Historical Society using a restored Nickel Plate Road locomotive, not the original "Cannon Ball." Wabash became famous in 1880 as the purported first municipally electrically lighted city in the world. On March 31 of that year, four Brush electric arc lights were installed on the courthouse tower and tested at twilight. The city's economy depends on agriculture and manufacturing.

At Vermont St., turn right and immediately pass on the left a small park overlooking a waterfall in Charley Creek. Continue along the winding drive through Charley Park, named for an early Indian. Turn left on Hill St. and at .4 m. turn right on Carroll St. At the bottom of the hill, on the left, is the **Honeywell Memorial Community Center**, 275 W. Market St. Wabash industrialist and philanthropist Mark C. Honeywell developed the center in the 1940s as a memorial to his first wife, Olive Lutz Honeywell. The lavishly structured and furnished building was designed to host conferences, meetings, cultural events, and recreational activities. In addition to a large auditorium, the center contains meeting rooms and lounges, dining rooms, galleries, and a combination roller-skating rink and banquet hall. A sauna was among the later additions. Paintings by such famous artists as T. C. Steele, Marie Goth, and C. Curry Bohm hang in the building. (*NRHP*)

Turn left on Canal St. and left on Wabash St. to the **Wabash County Courthouse** bounded by Hill, Wabash, Main, and Miami sts. From its location at the top of a hill, the courthouse stands majestically over the city. Constructed by L. and P. Gable of Eaton, Ohio, 1878–79, and remodeled, 1958–60, the building is a combination of Greek Revival, Romanesque, and Italianate architectural styles. The structure, which has a height of 178 ft., is the third building to house the county government.

In the courthouse foyer is one of the four 3,000 candle-power **Brush electric arc lamps** installed atop the courthouse tower for the 1880 demonstration. The town fathers, who had been criticized for Wabash's dark streets, contacted the Brush Electric Light Company of Cleveland, Ohio, that had been searching for a city in which to demonstrate its product. The publicity resulted in a crowd of about 10,000 from Illinois, Ohio, and Indiana cities. The demonstration began at 8:00 P.M., and the light could be seen on farms up to five miles away. After a two-week trial, Brush sold the lighting to the city. The lamps cost $60 each. A $1,800 dynamo in the basement and a $600 steam engine in the courtyard provided the energy. Brush guaranteed the lights to burn for 10 hours at a cost of $2.50 a night, which was considerably less than the existing gas lights. The discarded arc lamp was found in the basement of the Northern Indiana Power Company in 1935.

The bronze **statue of Abraham Lincoln** on the courthouse lawn was erected in 1932. Alexander New, a Wabash native who pursued a lucrative legal career in Kansas City and New York City, commissioned Charles Keck to construct the 8-ft.-high statue of a seated Lincoln atop a 54 x 72-in. marble base at a cost of around $35,000. New, who admired Lincoln, donated the statue in memory of his parents.

Immediately west of the courthouse is the **Wabash Historical Museum**, 89 W. Hill St. This Romanesque-style building was constructed by the Grand Army of the Republic (GAR) in 1899 as a memorial to Union soldiers of the Civil War and was designed for patriotic meetings, memorial services, and as a place where all ex-service people could meet. J. C. Gault served as the architect. The Wabash Historical Museum moved into the building in 1938. Previously, the museum had been located in the courthouse basement after its establishment in 1924. The museum contains a wide variety of historical artifacts with local relevance. Included are Indian artifacts, war mementos, and articles related to canal construction.

Return to Wabash St. Drive north to the **Honeywell house**, 720 N. Wabash St. The mansion was built for Mark C. Honeywell from 1959 to 1964. Honeywell (1874–1964) was born in Wabash and started a heating contracting business there in 1900. He specialized in developing automatically controlled heating, and in 1902 he founded Honeywell Heating Specialties Company, merging his business with his chief competitor in 1927 to form Minneapolis-Honeywell Regulator Company. It became Honeywell, Inc., in 1964 and is now one of the 100 largest United States businesses with 47 heat control/thermostat plants worldwide. In addition to business interests that included banking, philanthropy, and finance, Honeywell enjoyed many leisure-time activities that included music, gardening, photography, and many civic organizations. In 1942 Honeywell married Eugenia Hubbard Nixon, a former concert pianist with the Cleveland Symphony Orchestra, who controlled the Nixon newspaper chain. Both were widowed at the time. Mrs. Honeywell (1896–1974) furnished the mansion with many Louis XIV and XV pieces, and it often is referred to as the French House. A fire which devastated the mansion in 1974 resulted in Mrs. Honeywell's death by suffocation. The house was bequeathed to the Indiana University Foundation for use by the people of Wabash and is used for special events.

Continue north on Wabash St. Turn right at Harrison Ave. and left at Manchester Ave. Continue north to US 24 and turn right. Turn right again at **LAGRO** (p. 549), *3.7 m.* onto IND 524. The town was founded in 1829 and named for the Miami chief Le Gros or Les Gros who lived in the area. Lagro became one of the main towns along the Wabash and Erie Canal, but its importance declined with that of the canal.

Cross the railroad tracks and turn right on Main St. At the end of the block on the left is **St. Patrick's Catholic Church**, Main and Harrison sts., which was started when the first Irish canal workers arrived in 1834. Many remained in Lagro when the work was completed, and the first frame church was erected in 1838. The cornerstone for the present brick church was laid in 1870, and the structure was completed three years later. Only minor modifications have been made. The bell, which was hauled by wagon from Buffalo, New York, in the 1840s, hangs in the tall tower. The hand-carved religious statuary inside was imported from Europe. A large stained-glass window with the figure of St. Patrick overlooks the main altar.

Return to IND 524. Turn right. Go to the bottom of the hill and turn left on Washington St. to the end of the third block. On the right, in a small park, are the **Kerr Locks**, a reminder of Lagro's prominent role in the Wabash and Erie Canal days. The locks date from 1834 to 1838, the years the canal was constructed through Lagro. During the building of the canal, Irish laborers engaged in a protracted internal conflict that culminated in 1835 in a pitched battle near Lagro. State troops quelled the disturbance and jailed 200 participants. Most were freed as the canal work had to go on. The ringleaders were tried in Indianapolis, with some serving short jail terms. This encounter has come down in history as the Irish War.

Return to IND 524. Turn south, cross the Wabash River, and drive *1.7 m.* to Division Rd., which continues east from IND 524. Follow Division Rd. across the Salamonie River just above its mouth *.8 m.* east to **Hanging Rock**, a natural formation which juts over the Wabash River. The top is reached by a steep and narrow path. The turnoff by the rock is marked by a sign reading Hanging Rock. The site is leased by Acres, Inc., a nature preservation group. Once part of a Silurian coral reef covered by prehistoric oceans, the rock has a flat top 84 ft. high, which provides an ideal observation point from which to see the Wabash and Salamonie rivers and surrounding countryside. Near the Hanging Rock are the **Salamonie River State Forest** and the **Salamonie Reservoir**. The small forest of 619 acres, designated a state possession in 1939, contains campsites, picnic facilities, an 11-acre lake for fishing, boat ramps, and trails for hikers, horses, and skiers. Hunting is permitted. Next door to the forest, the Salamonie Reservoir, completed in 1966 for the purpose of flood control, sits behind a 6,100-ft. dam which is 133 ft. high. The reservoir's pool covers 2,855 acres and stretches for 17 miles. The total area of the reservoir property is 11,506 acres and includes, besides the lake, a variety of camping, swimming, boating, fishing, hiking, and hunting opportunities.

Return to IND 524 and US 24. Turn east on US 24 and drive *1.5 m.* to CR 500E. Turn left and drive *1.9 m.* to CR 300N. Here is **Hopewell Church**—Gene Stratton Porter's girlhood church. Buried in the cemetery is Porter's brother Leander Elliott Stratton who drowned in the Wabash River in 1872. Leander served as the model for Laddie who appeared in Porter's 1913 novel, *Laddie*. Now used as a museum and community center (open occasionally) to perpetuate the memory of Mrs. Porter, the church was built in 1872 on land donated by the Rev. Mark Stratton. The youngest of 12 children, Mrs. Porter was born on a 240-acre farm, one-half mile north. Besides Leander, nine members of the Stratton family are buried in the church cemetery.

Return to CR 500E and US 24. Turn east and drive *3.2 m.* to the **HUNTINGTON COUNTY** (p. 35,596; 366 sq. m.) line. Formed in 1832 and organized by a legislative act in 1834, the county was named for Samuel Huntington, a Connecticut delegate to the Continental Congress and a signer of the Declaration of Independence. Most of the county's fertile land yields corn, soybeans, fruit, livestock, and grains, but there also is a good deal of manufacturing.

Continue east *.8 m.* on US 24 to a marker indicating the site of the **first Indian agricultural school in the West**. Chief Little Turtle had made several trips to Washington, D.C., to obtain help from Presidents George Washington, John Adams, and Thomas Jefferson for the construction of a school to teach young Indian men to farm and young women to maintain a home. In 1804 the Baltimore Meeting of the Society of Friends sent Philip Dennis and some assistants to establish such a school in the Old Northwest. Meeting with only limited success, it was destroyed during the War of 1812 and was never rebuilt.

Continue east on US 24 for *5.7 m.* to IND 9. On the left is **Chief Richardville's house**. Jean Baptiste Richardville, or Pe-she-wah (1761-1841), was born to the French fur trader Joseph Drouet de Richardville and the Miami princess, Tau-cum-wah, the sister of Little Turtle. Richardville succeeded his uncle as chief of the Miamis and is generally regarded as the tribe's last great leader. As part of the terms of the Treaty of St. Marys (1818), Richardville received a large sum of money and vast tracts of land in north central Indiana. In addition, he operated a highly profitable trading post in Fort Wayne and was regarded by many as the wealthiest Indian in the country. In 1831 Richardville moved the Miami capital from Kekionga near Fort Wayne to this site at the forks of the Wabash. Two years later he had this

Greek Revival-style house constructed. It is said to have been the first frame house in the area. Construction money came from the United States government according to treaty. Richardville's descendants continued to occupy the house until 1943. It was rented for several years, then unoccupied for 20 years before the Huntington County Junior Historical Society restored it in 1977. In recent years a two-story log cabin has been moved to the area from another location, and a round-domed teepee was constructed. (*NRHP/HABS*)

Continue straight into **HUNTINGTON** (p. 16,202) on Park Dr. (US 24) (not US 24 Bypass). The city was once the site of the Miami village of Wepecheange, meaning "place of flints." The first white settlers arrived on the site of the future city in 1831. That same year, Gen. John Tipton purchased the land, had the town laid out in 1833, and offered some of its lots to the county as a county seat, an offer accepted in 1834. The town was named for Samuel Huntington (1731-1796), a signer of the Declaration of Independence, a delegate from Connecticut to the Continental Congress, and its president from 1779 to 1781. The construction of the Wabash and Erie Canal brought prosperity to the settlement and hastened its development. Huntington was once nicknamed the "Lime City" for the numerous limestone quarries and kilns in and around the town. Michael Houseman constructed the area's first kiln around 1843, and by 1875 there were 31 kilns in the city. The product was of high quality and was both exported and used locally. The limestone supply was exhausted by the early 1900s, and since that time the city's economy has relied on manufacturing and agriculture. The city's most famous industry is *Our Sunday Visitor*, which publishes a nationally circulated weekly Catholic church newspaper and other Catholic publications.

Huntington's most famous personality is J. Danforth (Dan) Quayle, vice-president of the United States, elected with George Bush in November 1988. Born in Indianapolis in 1947, he grew up in Huntington, eventually receiving his college degree from DePauw University (1969) and his law degree from Indiana University School of Law, Indianapolis (1974). He and his wife, Marilyn, also an attorney, opened a law office in Huntington, where he also helped publish his father's newspaper, the *Huntington Herald*. Quayle was elected to Congress in 1976 and to the United States Senate in 1980 and reelected in 1986. He is the grandson of the late Eugene Pulliam, a newspaper baron, publisher of the *Indianapolis Star* and the *Indianapolis News*. Quayle makes the ninth Hoosier nominated for the vice-presidency and the fifth to be elected from a state called "The Mother of Vice-Presidents."

On the left, *.7 m.* past Chief Richardville's house, is the entrance to **Victory Noll Convent**, 1900 W. Park Dr. The Spanish mission-style building was erected in 1924 with additions being made in 1936. The facility serves as the headquarters of the congregation, Our Lady of Victory Missionary Sisters. Retired and semi-retired sisters are also housed in the convent. The name is a combination of Our Lady of Victory and former Fort Wayne Bishop John F. Noll. Further towards town left off Park Dr. on Hitzfield St. is the former **St. Felix Friary**, built for the Capuchin order in 1928 and used until recently when it was acquired by the Church of the United Brethren for use as a parish. Its tan brick walls, sprawling mass, and tile roof reflect medieval Europe.

Return to Park Dr. and continue *.7 m.* to the **sunken gardens** located in **Memorial Park**. This area was an abandoned limestone quarry until E. M. Wasmuth saw the sunken gardens in San Antonio, Texas, and decided to duplicate the attraction in Huntington. The land was cleared, landscaped, and given to the city in 1924. Flowers and trees were planted and a lake constructed. In addition, two arched stone footbridges were built that lent a Japanese motif, and a fountain was installed. The gardens were completed and dedicated in 1929.

Continue *.5 m.* to Cherry St. Turn right. Drive three blocks to W. State St. Turn left. Go 1/4 block to Franklin St. Turn left and arrive at the **Huntington County Courthouse**, Jefferson and Court sts. This Neoclassical-style structure was designed by J. W. Gaddis of Vincennes and constructed from 1904 to 1906. The interior features hand-painted murals depicting the county's early history. The large eagle design mosaic in the center of the lobby floor is made of Italian tile and was the work of a Sicilian artist. The Huntington County Historical Society operates a museum on the fourth floor that features pioneer, farm, and Indian items.

A marker on the courthouse lawn commemorates the legal decision involving Huntington lawyer **Lambdin P. Milligan** (1812-1899). Milligan was a states' rights advocate, and in the 1850s he constructed a windowless stone building on Frederick St. where he held captured runaway slaves awaiting return to the South by bounty hunters. In 1864 he was arrested, charged with treason, and taken to Indianapolis to be tried by a military tribunal. Milligan was convicted and sentenced to hang; however, he was pardoned by Secretary of War Edwin Stanton at the last minute. Milligan then took his case to the United States Supreme Court, which ruled in the landmark *Ex parte Milligan* (1866) that a civilian could not be tried by a military court as long as civil courts were in operation.

Two blocks north of the courthouse, on the northwest corner of Jefferson and Market sts., is the Federal-style **Moore Building**, constructed by John Kenower, Sr., for pioneer Samuel Moore in 1844-45. It was the first brick structure erected in Huntington. For many years this architectural gem was hidden inside an aluminum shell, but it has been restored to its original appearance and is a relic of Huntington's canal era. It is now used for offices. (*NRHP*)

From the east side of the courthouse, drive north on Warren St., turn right on Park Dr., left on Byron St. for one block, right on Tipton St. for one block, and left on College Ave. to **Huntington College**, a coeducational, liberal arts college operated by the Church of the United Brethren in Christ. Chartered in 1897 as Central College, it is the direct successor of Hartsville College in Bartholomew County (see Tour 14). In 1917 the name was changed to Huntington College. The school offers undergraduate degrees in various majors plus a master's program in Christian Education. Highlighting the 99-acre campus are the **Administration and Classroom Building**, a Romanesque-style structure that dates from the school's founding, the **Loew Botanical Garden and Arboretum**, and **Snow Tip Lake**.

At the end of College Ave., turn right on Gragg Rd., then left at the end on Stults Rd. to US 24. Turn right and go *1.1 m.* to a marker on the right side of the road commemorating Huntington as the "Lime City."

The broad valley to the right was gouged by a mighty glacial stream that drained the Great Lakes when ice blocked the St. Lawrence River outlet. After the ice sheet retreated, more than 10,000 years ago, the St. Lawrence outlet reopened, and only the tiny Little River of to-day was left to occupy the valley.

Beyond Roanoke *1.7 m.* a white barn on the left stands at the end of an earthen trough which is one of the last remnants of the Wabash and Erie Canal, once the longest artificial waterway in North America. It extended 464 miles between Toledo, Ohio, and Evansville, Indiana.

Cross the Allen County line *2.5 m.* beyond the canal channel and *.7 m.* beyond, cross Aboite Creek. On the right, historians recently found remains of the canal aqueduct that crossed the creek.

Continue *3.8 m.* to the **Fox Island County Park** turn-off to the right, a short distance before reaching I-69. Drive south and east *2.1 m.* on Ellison and Yohne rds. to the park entrance. Established in 1974, the county park encom-passes 595 acres, including a 220-acre nature preserve and a 6.5-acre lake. The park provides nature and education centers in addition to facilities for fishing, swimming, picnicking, primitive camping, and cross-country skiing in season. Nature trails run through Fox Island Nature Preserve. The preserve features a sand dune bordered by swamps and marshes which support a wide variety of plant and animal communities. More than 190 species of birds have been found. A short distance east, the May stone quarry sits on the continental divide between the Great Lakes and Mississippi Valley drainage systems. Near the nature center, a "geogarden" displays a collection of prehistoric rocks excavated in Fort Wayne.

Return to US 24. Turn right and continue east *7.4 m.* to Clinton St. in downtown Fort Wayne.

Muncie

Muncie (p. 77,216) straddles the White River some 50 miles northeast of Indianapolis. Indiana's seventh most populous city is the manufacturing hub of the state's east central region. It is the seat of government of **DELAWARE COUNTY**. The state legislature established Delaware County on January 26, 1827, with an organization date of April 1, 1827. The county comprises 392 square miles of generally level ground drained by the Mississinewa River and the west fork of the White River and their tributaries. In 1980 it was the state's eighth most populous county with 128,587 residents. Almost three-fourths of that population live in urban areas, primarily in Muncie. Muncie is widely known for its role as Middletown, USA, an object of recurring research and media attention. So many people, in this regard, have come to know Muncie as an exceptional city precisely because it is viewed as so unexceptional.

Muncie's heritage is directly connected to the Delaware Indians, specifically with the group of Delaware referred to as the Munsee clan. Around 1800 about one dozen Delaware villages were strung out along the White River from present-day Muncie to north of Indianapolis. Where Muncie now stands there existed a settlement known as Munsee Town. Some called it Tetepachsit's Town after a Munsee leader and Moravian convert. Tetepachsit, accused of witchcraft by the anti-Christian Shawnee shaman, the Prophet, was tomahawked by his son and burned alive in 1806.

The Delaware Indians relinquished their lands to the United States by the Treaty of St. Marys, Ohio, in 1818. A provision of the treaty granted 672 acres of Munsee Town to Rebecca Hackley, granddaughter of the Miami chief Little Turtle, and daughter of William Wells, the prominent Indian agent in the Fort Wayne area. The Hackley Reserve was purchased in 1825 by Goldsmith Coffeen Gilbert, frontier Muncie's most prominent proprietor. In 1827

Muncie was platted and Delaware County was organized. Gilbert, along with Lemuel Jackson and William Brown, brought the seat of justice to Muncie by donating to the county land on which to locate the government buildings.

Muncietown, so designated until the state legislature shortened the name in 1845, grew slowly at first. In 1837, 10 years after its founding, the village comprised 320 residents and the usual array of frontier businesses: groceries, taverns, tanneries, blacksmith shops, and so forth. The townsfolk foresaw a spurt of roaring trade after 1837 if, as anticipated, the Whitewater Canal terminated at Muncietown. To the villagers' dismay the canal was completed only to Hagerstown, southeast of Muncie. The long-awaited expansion of the town followed the arrival in 1852 of the Indianapolis and Bellefontaine Railroad. The population nearly tripled between 1850 and 1860. As a result of this good fortune the citizens voted in favor of incorporation as a town in 1854 and as a city in 1865. Several more railways elected to lay track through Muncie after the Civil War, thereby helping boost the population to around 6,000 by 1885 and enhancing the city's reputation as a regional trade center.

Drillers, exploring for coal in 1876 near Eaton, 10 miles north of Muncie, struck natural gas. No effort was made to capitalize on the find because natural gas had little economic worth at the time. The subsequent revelation of the energy potential of natural gas led to the reopening of the Eaton well in 1886, marking the beginning of the state's gas industry. By 1888 Delaware County had 35 producing wells. The gas boom brought overnight prosperity to east central Indiana. Companies requiring high levels of heat in manufacturing, such as glass, iron, and steel, flocked into the area. Delaware County reported 226 industrial firms in 1890; by 1900 the number had soared to 481 with almost three-fourths of these in Muncie. Among the industries attracted by the fuel deluge were the Indiana Bridge Company (1886), the Hemingray Glass Company (1890), and the Indiana Steel and Wire Company (1900). Between 1880 and 1900 Muncie's population quadrupled to almost 21,000. Promoters christened Muncie the Natural Gas City of the West, the Magic City, and the Home of the Industrial Genii.

The cheap and plentiful fuel supply drew Frank C. Ball to Muncie in 1886 after fire destroyed the family's glass canning jar factory in Buffalo, New York. Admitting he found Muncie physically unpleasant, the courteous and professional manner of the local businessmen persuaded him to settle. The inducement of a free seven-acre plant site and $5,000 to defray relocation expenses probably influenced Ball's decision. The factory opened in Muncie in 1888, and the Ball brothers—Edmund Burke, William C., Lucius, George, and Frank—set in motion what today is the oldest continuously operating home canning jar manufacturer in the world.

Muncie flourished to the roar of natural gas into the first years of the 20th century. Thereafter, the supposedly inexhaustible supply of gas rapidly decreased. As a contemporary publication expressed it, "the needles of the pressure gauges quivered the warning." With a critical letup in gas production after 1902, population growth slowed considerably.

Luckily, Muncie's economic welfare did not rest solely on the availability of natural gas. Oil had been discovered along with gas in the region, and it continued to be pumped for several years as gas resources dwindled. More important, Muncie's status as a railway and agricultural trading center helped to retain the majority of industries. Furthering the regional transportation development was the arrival in 1901 of the Union Traction Company's interurban railway. In 1910 the *Indianapolis Star* reported that Muncie was the first city in Indiana and the second in the nation, after Los Angeles, to have a depot (built in 1905) devoted exclusively to the accommodation of interurban passenger traffic.

The Union Traction Company faced a company-wide strike of its street and electric railway employees in 1908. Muncie, a strong union town, became the focus of the controversy when successive days of violence prompted Gov. James Frank Hanly to declare martial law and to send in 591 officers and men. Martial law ended after two weeks, but the walkout continued another six weeks before the workers capitulated. Hanly's action was the first such act by the state government since the Civil War. According to the Indiana Labor Commission, the strike was the state's most costly up to that time. The episode toppled Muncie's unions. The open shop became the norm until the Congress of Industrial Organizations (CIO) gained power in the city after 1937.

Muncie's adjustment to a post-gas boom economy was paralleled by boosters' efforts to install a college to add a cultural dimension to the industrialized community and, no doubt, to increase real estate values. The backers of the proposed institution, including the Ball brothers, formed an association in 1896 to implement the project. They acquired an option on 300 lots and contracted to sell them within two years with proceeds earmarked for the college. One of the many incentives offered to prospective buyers was a two-term scholarship to the prospective school. Only a last-minute purchase of 20 lots by George McCulloch, president of the Union Traction Company, salvaged the enterprise. In the meantime the association had filed incorporation papers with the secretary of state to create "a Normal University for the education of males and females."

With the completion of the University Building, now the Administration Building, in 1899, the doors of the Eastern Indiana Normal University opened to an initial class of 232. Plagued by administrative problems, the school lasted only two years. Afterwards several schools located on the site: Palmer University, 1902-3, Indiana Normal School and College of Applied Science, 1905-7, and Muncie Normal Institute (renamed Muncie National Institute), 1912-18. In 1918 the Ball brothers bought the 64 acres and two buildings and presented them to the state. The Eastern Division of the Indiana State Normal School at Muncie, a branch of the state normal school at Terre Haute, commenced operation in June 1918. Four years later the state legislature honored the Ball family's generosity by changing the school's name to Ball Teachers College, Eastern Division, Indiana State Normal School. The school separated from the Terre Haute institution in 1929 and became Ball State Teachers College. The state lawmakers awarded university status to the school in 1965.

In the early years of the 20th century automobile makers helped diversify Muncie's economy. At least seven makes of cars were produced in the city between 1908 and 1928. The earliest models included the Interstate, the Rider-Lewis, and the Sheridan. The developers of the Muncie, actually a light-service truck, ceased production after their one completed vehicle on its initial run in 1910 was involved in an accident. William C. Durant, who organized General Motors in 1908 and lost control of it in 1920, founded the Durant Motors Company in 1921. He located his Indiana plant in Muncie and manufactured the Princeton, the Star, and the Durant.

More important to Muncie in the long run was the auto parts industry. Henry Warner, designer of the ill-fated Muncie truck, created a differential gear and established his shop in 1904. Immediately successful in the transmission business, the Warner Gear Company merged in 1928 with other auto parts firms to create the Borg-Warner Corporation. Other auto parts suppliers came to Muncie following World War I. General Motors built its Muncie Products Division in 1919 to manufacture speedometers, steering gears, and transmissions. In 1928 General Motors's Delco-Remy plant in Anderson located the Delco Battery factory in Muncie, taking over the Durant car facility. By 1935 an estimated 50 percent of the city's manufacturers produced automotive components.

Muncie captured a national audience on several occasions in the interval between the world wars. In 1925 New York's Institute of Social and Religious Research sponsored a pioneering study of Muncie by Robert and Helen Lynd. The Lynds selected Muncie because it was a midwestern, medium-sized, relatively homogeneous community experiencing rapid industrialization. The sociologists clinically dissected the town's everyday life to discover the effects of modernization on American values. *Middletown: A Study in American Culture*, published in 1929, contained their findings. The conclusions confirmed their presuppositions that industrialization and commercialization wreak havoc on the quality of people's lives, particularly the lives of blue-collar workers. The authors blamed the business class, especially the "X Family" (obviously the Ball family) for the adverse circumstances. A follow-up report, *Middletown in Transition* (1937),

held few new observations. The Middletown books became standard fare for university students, and they are now considered classics. Muncie has become one of the most frequently analyzed cities in the nation. A succession of scholars, journalists, media reporters, moviemakers, and product testers, among others, have besieged the city to tap the mood of America's "typical" community.

The doubling of population between 1910 and 1930 along with a similar rate of business expansion at times outdistanced law enforcement efforts to control the strong undercurrent of lawlessness. Illicit get-rich-quick schemes, petty crime, vice, and graft found fertile ground in Muncie during and after the natural gas bonanza. Local liquor option laws and state prohibition after 1918 effectively closed Muncie's 97 taverns, but the clandestine operations of "blind tiger" establishments kept the whiskey flowing. For example, 43 percent of the 1,217 arrests in 1914 were for public intoxication in a supposedly saloonless city. The frequency of arrests often depended on the fervor of public officials, a passion occasionally tempered by their own involvement in crime. Changes in city administrations usually meant a renewal of graft charges by the losing candidates. A judge in 1920 boldly branded Muncie a lawless town, a gambler's paradise.

Within this volatile environment, a reborn Ku Klux Klan organization recruited eager rank and file. The Klan's racist ideology and its ostensible campaign to rid Indiana cities of all traces of immorality spread throughout east central Indiana and Muncie in the 1920s. These were tension-filled days for the city's black population, a group virtually ignored in the Middletown studies. The segregated black community of approximately 2,500 persons faced intense verbal and physical harassment, unfair judicial practices, and occupational and social isolation.

The menacing atmosphere also bred heroes like George R. Dale, crusading editor of Muncie's *Post-Democrat*. Dale exposed Klan activities and members during the 1920s and received national acclaim for his struggle. In the process he was spit upon, beaten, almost shot, and charged with contempt (subsequently pardoned by the governor) by a Klan-connected judge. At one point Dale lost advertising support, almost lost the paper, and his family tottered on the edge of destitution. The tide of public opinion gradually turned against the Klan. Dale's reformist editorials gained wider acceptance. A record vote in 1929 put the newspaperman in the mayor's chair. Subsequently convicted of liquor trafficking, Dale obtained another pardon, this one from President Franklin D. Roosevelt. Dale was not reelected, the members of his own party and other citizens choosing instead a former mayor, one previously indicted for political corruption.

The durable goods market undergirded the vigorous economy of the roaring twenties and proved to be the most vulnerable market during the Great Depression. Muncie particularly suffered due to its industrial concentration on automotive and machine parts, foundry products, and wire. Between 1929 and 1933, 25 percent of Muncie's workers lost jobs, an equal percentage of families ended up on relief rolls, and the dollar volume of retail sales almost halved. Even the usually upbeat Chamber of Commerce cancelled its annual dinners in the early 1930s. A bright spot in the economy was the solvency of the Ball Corporation on account of the great demand by homemakers for canning jars. To provide family assistance, so-called Muncie Plans urged the planting of home gardens and the initiating of home improvement tasks that could utilize unemployed skilled craftsmen. Various New Deal projects created jobs and led to community improvements including flood control measures, removal of unused trolley tracks, street repair, and a new city swimming pool. The reopening of General Motors's Chevrolet transmission plant in 1935 signaled the start of Muncie's climb out of the depression.

The city's economy rebounded swiftly with the onset of World War II as factories shifted to wartime production. After the war Muncie lived through its share of strikes and shortages, but it did not experience debilitating reconversion headaches common to the boom-and-bust cycle in many communities. Muncie escaped the usual plant shutdowns, massive unemployment, and financial burdens of temporary expansion because its factories made similar types of materials in peace and war. By 1950 the major concerns in the city of 58,479 persons revolved around bus fare increases, a ministerial drive against prostitution and slot machines, and inadequate garbage disposal and

sewer facilities. Issues of a more serious nature would arise in the years to come.

Over the next three decades Muncie had to contend with the effects of high unemployment, population redistribution, and urban decay. The city's periodic economic woes began after the Korean War with a slump in sales of Studebaker and American Motors cars. At the time Muncie was a major supplier of parts to these auto makers. In addition, Ball Corporation, the historical linchpin of the local economy, stepped up its process of decentralization, thereby closing the door to job-producing factory growth in the city. Other firms elected not to develop locally but to spread into southern states where operations cost less. During the energy-related recession of the early 1970s, Muncie's depressed transportation equipment sector contributed to raising unemployment figures. Manufacturing employment declined 21 percent between 1968 and 1976. The national recession of the early 1980s pushed Muncie's jobless rate to almost 17 percent, and the United States Labor Department ranked the city fifth in the nation in joblessness. To make matters worse census figures for 1980-83 showed Muncie losing 3.3 percent of its population, one among 25 cities leading the nation in population loss over this brief time span.

Notwithstanding the signs and measures of economic corrosion, the level of impairment was exaggerated. As manufacturing employment declined, jobs in government service, retailing, and wholesaling increased, indicative of an emerging trend. Ball State University, which quadrupled its student body size between 1950 and 1970, accounted in large measure for what economic health Muncie exhibited prior to the 1980s. The school's expanding physical plant meant jobs in construction, as well as in trade, service, and government.

The common pattern of decline in the central city occurred in the 1950s as schools, stores, industries, and people began to spill over Muncie's city limits. Two-thirds of Delaware County residents lived in Muncie in 1950. By 1970 the number had decreased to slightly more than half. For many years Muncie lacked a comprehensive urban strategy to combat inner city decay. Officials responded with federal urban renewal programs, suggested privately funded downtown development, experimented with redevelopment plans, removed parking meters, outfitted new parking areas, and installed a walking plaza. The completion of a plaza, bank and office buildings, a county government center, and the Ball Corporation's headquarters altered the downtown silhouette. The change from a manufacturing to a non-manufacturing base and the redistribution of population and commerce underlie the shift in the makeup of the core city from retailing to providing work space for salaried employees of government, financial institutions, private utilities, and corporations.

Despite the new physical look of Muncie brought about by adjustments in business interests and residential preferences, there were many signs in the late 1970s and early 1980s that in other ways little had changed in 50 years. City officials faced corruption proceedings. Racial tensions mounted as the Ku Klux Klan marched through the downtown. Muncie Central high school won a seventh state basketball championship in 1979 (an eighth in 1988) and holds the record for the most state crowns. A fresh cadre of sociologists, calling their project Middletown III, found slight change since the 1920s and 1930s in community structures or values—a "persistence of identity" they called it. The initial volume of findings, *Middletown Families*, came out in 1982. Another scholar, an Australian, studied Ball State as a typical American university. Incidentally, the presence and influence of Ball State, the city's largest employer, brings into question the concept of Muncie as the characteristic American community. Regardless, the Public Broadcasting System aired its Middletown series in 1982. The five non-fiction dramas, produced by the Emmy and Oscar Award-winning Peter Davis, documented slices of everyday Muncie life. In addition, the city was the backdrop for the highly successful science fiction movie *Close Encounters of the Third Kind*, though no scenes were shot in the city. The movie's director is quoted as saying he selected Muncie because "it was neither too far east nor too west. It was just right. It was Middletown, America—a symbol of a broad section of this country."

Despite contrary evidence, the native's consciousness of being *the* representative American city is ever reinforced, as for example, the selection by the Muncie Pride Task Force, in 1987, of the slogan "Muncie: America's Hometown." The Task Force is one of several organizations, made up of business, civic, university, and government leaders, ad-

dressing the themes of economic and job development, historic preservation, or tourism. A seven-year economic development program, named Horizon '91, was kicked off by the Chamber of Commerce in the fall of 1984. The plan, supported by all sectors of local government and business, anticipated creating several thousand new jobs in Muncie and Delaware County by 1991. The renovation of Muncie Mall and its expansion by some 200,000 sq. ft., announced in 1987 by Melvin Simon and Associates, Inc., was expected to boost employment. Meanwhile, the Delaware County Convention and Tourist Commission and the Muncie Visitors Bureau, established in 1983 and 1984, respectively, publicized the county and city and generated millions in tourist dollars. Their job was made somewhat easier with the renovation of the Roberts Hotel into a modern Radisson hotel in 1986 and the updating of its cross-street neighbor the former federal building and post office into the Horizon Center, a convention headquarters, opened in 1988. Together, the two structures are referred to as the "hospitality center of Muncie." The proposing of new historic districts, the care given to preserving the city's historic buildings, and the inclusion on the National Register of Historic Places of such buildings as the Boyce Block, the Rose Building, and the former Roberts Hotel, enhanced the city's quality of life and its pride. Taking charge of raising Muncie's historical consciousness is the Delaware County Historical Alliance, formed in 1987 as a merger of the Delaware County Historical Society, Historic Muncie, Inc., and the Delaware County Genealogical Society. Of central importance to the cultural life of Muncie is the Minnetrista Cultural Center, a focus for history, arts, and industry in Muncie, erected by the Ball Brothers' Foundation. Other additions to the Muncie skyline in the late 1980s included a downtown bus stop and transfer station, called T. J. Ault III MITS (Muncie Indiana Transit System) after the transit board's first chairman, and a Minnetrista Corporation building that will house several foundations and other firms.

An apparent downside to Muncie's progress in the 1980s—loss of population, relative excessive unemployment, continued decline in manufacturing employment—should be seen as part of the community's long-term transition to a different form of economy, one of diversity, as evidenced in the increase in service, construction, and transportation jobs. Its many small businesses are part of a mix of educational, medical, retail, and manufacturing components that service a wide area in east-central Indiana.

Muncie Attractions

1. The **Muncie Visitors Bureau** opened in April 1984 at 425 N. High St., as indicated on the map. In 1988 the Visitors Bureau was moved to the Horizon Convention Center, 401 S. High St. (See No. 10 below.)

2. The two-story **Moore-Youse Home Museum**, 122 E. Washington, is located in one of the oldest structures in Muncie. It was under construction in 1848. Mary Youse Maxon, who lived in the house from her birth in 1896 to her death in 1982, willed the house and its furnishings to the Delaware County Historical Society, along with money for the home's restoration. Possibly the family of Mary Maxon's mother, who was a Moore, built the house. The museum is now operated by the Delaware County Historical Alliance. It is furnished with period items. (*NRHP*)

3. Next door to the museum, at 120 E. Washington, is the **Delaware County Historical Resource Center**, housed in a renovated office building. The center, which opened in 1988, serves as a repository for local genealogical and historical records and is open to researchers. It also contains the offices of the Delaware County Historical Alliance and its director.

4. Muncie's **Civic Theatre**, 216 E. Main St., is housed in the old Star Theatre, a turn-of-the-century vaudevillian palace. The Star Theatre, hollowed out of the west section of a commercial block around 1904, was converted in the 1920s for the showing of moving pictures and was renamed the Hoosier Theatre in 1936. The local thespians purchased the playhouse in 1964 and, thereby, became one of the state's few acting troupes to own its own hall. In 1985-87 renovation and restoration of the building took in the interior and the theater's facade, including the brick sidewalk and old electric lights. The intimate 460-seat auditorium has a semicircular balcony and the original asbestos stage curtain. (*NRHP*) The Civic Theatre is located in the **Boyce Block**, which along with the theater has undergone major renewal. Constructed in 1880 by James Boyce, a textile manufacturer and a leading Muncie businessman, the two-story brick and iron Renaissance Revival-style structure first accommodated small retail stores, offices, and sleeping rooms. It was one of the first, if not the first, buildings in Muncie to have electric lights, hot and cold running water, gas, and steam heating. (*NRHP*)

5. The **Delaware County Building**, Main and Walnut sts., is the county's fourth courthouse, completed in 1969 for $2.5 million. The L-shaped structure replaced a massive 80-year-old building, the tearing down of which did not go unchallenged by local preservationists. The new three-story glass and granite courthouse has the appearance and all the comforts of a modern office building: acoustical tile ceilings, fluorescent lights, air conditioning, and carpeting. A covered promenade borders a wide concrete and landscaped plaza and entryway.

6. The **Ball Corporation Museum** is located in the Ball Corporation Headquarters, 345 S. High St. The corporation's four-story precast concrete main office building opened in 1976. Scattered throughout the interior are photo murals depicting the company's history. The museum, adjacent to the main lobby, contains company artifacts and is the nation's only museum dedicated to the history of glass food containers. Sunlight radiates through plate glass walls and glass display cases to illuminate the shades of amber, green, and blue of hundreds of rare and collectible Ball jars. Tin-jacketed kerosene cans, Frank C. Ball's rolltop desk, the company's first steam engine, and its oldest glass blowing machine are among the memorabilia on exhibit. In the **Ball Associates building**, 222 S. Mulberry St., is a bronze sculpture of the five Ball brothers executed by Anderson Uni-

versity artist Kenneth G. Ryden and placed on exhibit in the summer of 1988.

7. The **Passing of the Buffalo**, a bronze statue by Cyrus Dallin, stands at Walnut and Charles sts. in the Walnut Plaza. Portrayed is a standing Indian holding an arrowless bow and with one foot resting on a buffalo skull. The pose symbolizes the tragic end of the Indian way of life resulting from the depletion of the great buffalo herds. Muncie's treasure is Dallin's last major work, and the only one cast from the mold. Between 1931 and 1975 the statue remained hidden from public view on the Madison, New Jersey, estate of Mrs. Geraldine Rockefeller Dodge, aunt of former vice-president Nelson Rockefeller. In 1975 Muncie's Margaret Ball Petty Foundation purchased the 9-ft. statue along with its 45-ton boulder base. The Petty Foundation presented it to the city as a memorial to Fred J. Petty, a Muncie industrialist. The artwork was dedicated in April 1976.

8. The **Muncie Children's Museum**, 306 S. Walnut, is in its second home since it began in 1977. First housed at 519 S. Walnut St., the museum moved in 1982 to its present downstairs room of what originally was the Columbia Theatre, which opened in 1913. An impressive array of educational and entertaining displays await the young of age or of heart who can take full advantage of the museum's hands-on approach. The attractions include a nationally acclaimed fire safety exhibit, "Learn Not to Burn," one on how the eye perceives movement, another which explains the properties and use of water, a film on dinosaurs, a 22-ft. replica of a clipper ship, an exhibit on magnets, a farm area replete with loft, a 1948 Farmall tractor and 1915 Interstate automobile, and occasionally some live animals.

9. The **Radisson Hotel**, 420 S. High St., formerly the landmark Roberts Hotel, is directly across from the Horizon Convention Center. The hotel, which opened for business on January 17, 1921, was built by the Muncie Hotel Corporation, George D. Roberts, president. Nicol, Scholer, and Hoffman of Lafayette designed and supervised its construction. The seven-story, 200-plus rooms, brick and oolitic limestone structure went through several owners before closing in 1983. In 1986 Robert Gabbard of Danville, Kentucky, and Richard Freeman of Richmond, Indiana, initiated the hotel's renovation with the understanding that a convention center would be created. Gabbard purchased the building and financed its overhaul through the sale of limited partnerships. The $10 million renovated hotel opened April 25, 1987. A newly constructed adjoining tower has added 150 rooms.

10. The **Horizon Convention Center**, 401 S. High St., held its grand opening on April 16, 1988. The center is located in the refurbished and expanded Federal Building, which housed the local post office when it opened in 1906. An addition in the 1930s doubled its size. The building closed in 1979. In 1983 an Alaskan couple bought it as an investment and sold it in 1986 to the Delaware Advancement Corporation (DAC), the fund-raising arm of Horizon '91. The DAC operates the center, remodeled for $3.8 million, financed with bonds paid for by a tax on food and beverages. Local architect Jim Gooden, of Gooden Associates, supervised the overhaul, maintaining the integrity of the interior's ornamental detail, marble wainscoting, terrazzo floors, and oak woodwork, while furnishing modern accommodations. The center occupies 34,200 sq. ft. and has three levels affording meeting space for more than 1,400 persons.

11. The **Muncie Public Library**, 301 E. Jackson St., is considered an outstanding example of Neoclassical architecture, an expert blend of a Greek Doric facade and a Roman Classical dome. The firm of Wing and Mahurin of Fort Wayne designed the Andrew Carnegie-funded structure, completed in 1904 at a cost of $55,900. Exceptional cut stone panels of muses front the limestone building. Inside, green marbleized columns with gold colored Ionic capitals support the art glass dome, which was covered in 1951 to halt leakage. Note also the ornate ceilings of the east and west reading rooms. The interior has been altered periodically to permit greater storage space and to modernize facilities. (*NRHP*)

12. The **Charles Maberry Kimbrough house**, 615 E. Washington St., was the home of Emily Kimbrough's grandfather. The house, now missing its red roof tiles and several front dormers and drastically altered in other ways, was designed by the British-born architect Alfred

Muncie Attractions

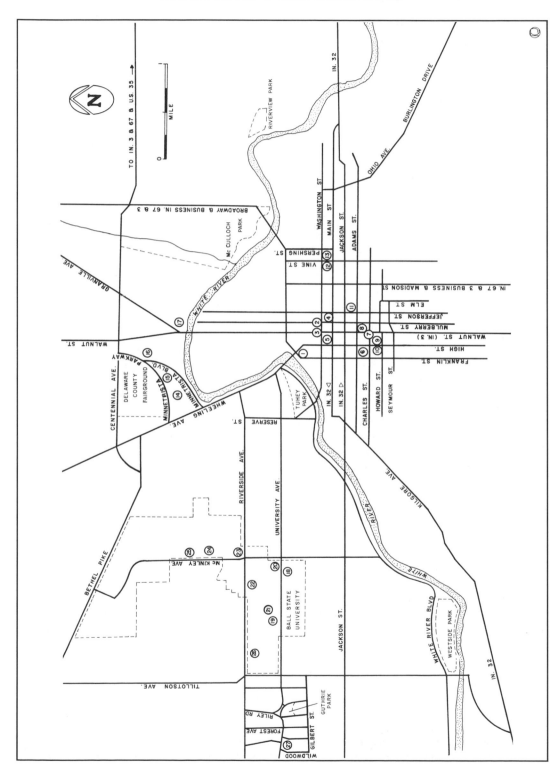

Grindle. Charles Kimbrough arrived in Muncie in 1876 and established the city's first book and stationery store. He later was president of the Indiana Bridge Company, a banker, and a state senator. Early in this century Teddy Roosevelt campaigned from the front steps of the house. In 1934 a wedding reception was held in the house, then owned by Ray and Ann Johnson, for their daughter, Margaret, and future presidential candidate Barry Goldwater. A number of community agencies have offices in the Kimbrough home.

13. The girlhood home of humorist-author **Emily Kimbrough**, 715 E. Washington St., is the centerpiece of a 12-block area of 127 Victorian-era homes designated in 1978 as the Emily Kimbrough Historic District. Born in Muncie in 1898, the future editor of the *Ladies Home Journal* and the author of 17 books spent her first 11 years in the little two-story pale green frame house on Washington St. Perhaps her most familiar works are *Our Hearts Were Young and Gay* (1942), a classic of American humor coauthored with Cornelia Otis Skinner, and *How Dear to My Heart* (1944), the story of growing up in Muncie in the early years of the century. Restoration of the home began in 1982. (*NRHP*)

14. The **E. B. and Bertha C. Ball Center for University and Community Programs** is housed in the Tudor mansion of Edmund Burke Ball, 400 Minnetrista Blvd., the boulevard of the Ball brothers' homes. The center, operated by Ball State University's School of Continuing Education, offers a variety of programs geared to the educational needs of adults not enrolled for the regular university curriculum. In 1894 the Ball brothers purchased the land along the bank of the White River for the family homes and their private drive. Edmund and Bertha Crosley Ball had Marshall Mahurin of Fort Wayne draw the plans for their dream home in 1905. Built of iron and steel, concrete, and buff limestone, with an interior of red oak, stained glass, and parquetry floors, the house was whispered to have cost around $100,000. After Bertha Ball's death in 1957 the house served as a community art center from 1963 to 1971. In 1975 Ball State was given the home. The Ball Brothers Foundation funded the renovation project, which received in 1977 the Modernization Showcase Award of Excellence from the

American Institute of Architects. The original splendor of the spacious home remains substantially unaffected by the introduction of elevators, a new stairwell, stainless steel kitchen, and other modern guest accommodations.

15. The **Ball Corporation Guesthouse**, 500 Minnestrista Blvd., is a corporate hostelry used principally to entertain and lodge company customers. The brick Georgian-style mansion was built in 1898 for William C. Ball. In 1949 the family turned the property over to the Ball Brothers Foundation. The house was used for offices in the 1950s and for apartments between 1960 and 1981. In the latter year the Ball Corporation leased the house from the Ball Foundation for the purpose of converting it into a guesthouse. Renovation began in early 1982 and was completed before the year's end. The mansion now contains a formal dining room, living room, lounge, nine guest rooms, kitchen, breakfast room, and indoor and outdoor porches.

16. The **Minnetrista Cultural Center**, Minnetrista Parkway, for preserving the heritage of East Central Indiana, opened in December 1988 on 35 acres along White River. The Minnetrista Cultural Foundation, Inc., is the $8.7 million project's financial arm largely made up of contributions from the Ball Brothers and the George and Frances Ball foundations. The center is fronted by a circle of columns that originally graced the portico of the Frank C. Ball mansion, torn down after a fire in 1967. The lower level contains storage and work areas, while the upper two levels provide public meeting rooms, a learning center, and historical and art exhibitions. Plans for an orchard shop, nature center, pioneer education center, and a Victorian education center on the grounds have been implemented or will be in the near future. A new road, Minnetrista Parkway, between Wheeling and Centennial aves., was built specifically to provide easy access to the center.

17. The **Appeal to the Great Spirit**, at the intersection of Walnut St. and Granville Ave., is a towering bronze that is a copy of Cyrus Dallin's sculpture fronting the Boston Museum of Fine Arts. The familiar piece, depicting a mounted Indian with outstretched arms, was presented to the city by Bertha Ball and family in 1929 in memory of Edmund B. Ball. The figure has be-

Minnetrista Cultural Center, photographed by Clay Calder in 1989

come an official emblem of Muncie after its adornment on the city's first flag in 1974.

Visitors to **Ball State University** wanting information about the campus can check with the Campus Information Center in the **L. A. Pittenger Student Center**, 2000 W. University Ave. (18) or the **Campus Visit Center**, Lucina Hall (19).

20. The **Administration Building**, directly across University Ave. from the Student Center, was completed in 1899, and it was the first structure erected on the campus of the newly established Eastern Indiana Normal University. The building was divided into classrooms, a chapel, a library, an auditorium, and an apartment for F. A. Z. Kumler, the first president. Today the quarters house the school's main administrative offices.

21. Just west of the Administration Building is a campus landmark, the bronze statue **Beneficence**, known adoringly as "Benny" to the university community. The sculpture, unveiled in 1937, shows a robed and winged woman dispensing jewels from a hand-held box. She stands high on a pedestal in a circular pool. A semicircle of five 20-ft.-tall columns, each with Corinthian capitals capped with bronze tripods, forms a classical setting for the heroic figure. The name, number of columns, and the posture of the statue represent, as inscribed on the base, "a civic testimonial to the beneficence of the five Ball brothers and their families." Daniel Chester French, the designer, completed the work shortly before his death in 1931 at age 81. Among French's many artistic accomplishments are the Minute Man at Concord Bridge in Massachusetts and Abraham Lincoln in the Lincoln Memorial at the nation's capital. Richard Henry Dana (1879-1933) of New York City planned the architectural features surrounding the statue. Though completed in 1930, French's creation remained in storage until enough money could be raised during the depression years for its placement in 1937. More than 11,000 Muncie citizens contributed around $65,000 for this tribute to the Ball families.

22. The **Arts Building and Art Gallery**, directly north of the Beneficence statue, is a three-story, Tudor-Gothic classroom building and art exhibition hall. It was constructed in 1934-35 and jointly funded by the state, the Federal Public Works Administration, and the Ball families. The project provided needed jobs for Muncie's unemployed during the depression. George F. Schreiber (1875-1950), the German-born architect, also designed the Scottish Rite Cathedral in Indianapolis. The gallery features collections of Roman and Syrian glass, Italian Renaissance paintings and furniture, decorative arts, and ethnographic artifacts.

Beneficence, photographed by J. Kent Calder in 1989

23. The **John R. Emens College-Community Auditorium**, Riverside and McKinley aves., is named for the sixth president of Ball State and is used for professional, university, and community dramatic and musical productions and special lecture series. When constructed in 1963-64, 17 years after the project's drawing first appeared, the red brick and stone auditorium was dovetailed into an existing complex comprising the English and Music buildings and the Ball State Theatre. This maneuver reportedly saved several millions of dollars in construction costs. The final price tag of $2,975,000 was paid for by public subscription and a bond issue. Planned by architects Walter Scholer and Associates of Lafayette, Indiana, the large balconied, 3,605-seat hall is known for its excellent acoustics. The internationally recognized acoustical engineer Heinrich Keilholz of West Germany, along with John W. Ditamore of Purdue University, a sound and stage expert, designed the system. Under a scalloped ceiling Keilholz placed mammoth vertical acoustical panels on each side of the auditorium to be opened and closed like venetian blinds to produce variable sound effects. Blues and greens predominate in the coloring scheme of seats, carpets, walls, and curtain. The Aline Brainerd Lounge, named for Emens's wife, contains paintings and sculpture on permanent loan from the Ball Brothers Foundation.

24. The **Alexander M. Bracken Library**, just north of Emens Auditorium on McKinley Ave., opened in September 1975. Named for the Muncie industrialist, attorney, and university trustee, the massive brick building contains about 230,000 sq. ft. of space and cost almost $15 million. Its one-millionth volume was cataloged in November 1979. The library's special collections include materials pertaining to John Steinbeck, Sir Norman Angell, Emily Kimbrough, and many other prominent figures, along with the files of the Center for Middletown Studies, also located in the library.

25. The **College of Architecture and Planning Building**, southeast corner of McKinley Ave. and Petty Rd., houses Indiana's first and only public school of architecture, established by the General Assembly in 1965. Ball State surmounted intense competition from other state schools to gain the college. The six-story, $2.2 million brick building designed by Melvin D. Birkey, South Bend, was completed in 1972. Visitors will want to view the exhibition of architectural compositions on the main floor. The rapid expansion of programs in the college necessitated constructing a five-story, $7.7 million addition. Crumlish/Sporleder of South Bend drew up the plans for the energy-conscious structure, dedicated in 1983. The addition features a five-story atrium space under a continuous sloping glass roof, which accommodates a solar chimney. At the east end is the newly formed Center for Energy Research, Education, and Service (CERES). The center works to keep the public abreast of developments in the energy area through literature distribution, research publication, lectures, and on-site workshops. Along with an exhibition gallery on the ground floor, the addition includes the Historic Preservation/Archives on the first floor. The archives contain thousands of plans and drawings, photographs, and documents recording historic sites and structures in Indiana.

26. **Christy Woods** is the oldest developed nature preserve among the several operated by Ball State. The 17-acre tract is situated west of the Cooper Science Building on Riverside Ave. The nature laboratory is named for Dr. Otto B. Christy, a member of the science faculty from 1918 to 1950, who was largely responsible for furbishing the arboretum in the 1930s. Used for student recreation, biology field studies, and open to the public, the woods encompasses walking paths, greenhouses, encased displays, and gardens.

27. The **Kitselman Conference Center**, 3401 W. University Ave., provides meeting and lodging space for individuals and groups from the university and community. The English manor estate was built in 1927 for Muncie industrialist E. Faye Kitselman. In 1956 the three Kitselman children donated the home and 2.65 acres to the Ball State Foundation. The beautiful oak-paneled house apparently sheltered a security-conscious owner as the glass is heavily leaded in windows and doors which bolt into concrete.

Tour 3

Leave Muncie east via Jackson St. (IND 32). Drive past the Indiana Steel and Wire complex and continue for *7.8 m.* to the Delaware-Randolph county line. **RANDOLPH COUNTY** (p. 29,997; 454 sq. m.) adjoins the state's east boundary. Though generally flat, it has the highest average elevation of Indiana's counties. This height accounts for Randolph being the headwater region for several major rivers including the Mississinewa, the West Fork of Whitewater, and the West Fork of White rivers. A journalist once referred to the county as the "mother of rivers." The county is largely rural with only two of its cities exceeding 1,500 in population. The first settlers for the most part migrated from North Carolina. When organized in 1818, Randolph was the northernmost Indiana county, containing sections obtained from the Treaty of Greenville (1795), the Twelve Mile Purchase (1809), and the Treaty of St. Marys (1818). The vast territory north of the county, stretching to the Michigan border, known as Wayne Township, came under its legal jurisdiction. The derivation of the county's name remains a mystery. The consensus is that it refers to Randolph County in North Carolina, the home area of several pioneers, or to Thomas Randolph (1771-1811), an attorney general of the Indiana Territory, and a casualty of the Battle of Tippecanoe. The county's early growth rested largely on its role as a major farming region and as an important railway crossroads. The decline in agricultural employment, improvement in roads, and growth of nearby urban centers, such as Muncie and Richmond, have reduced the importance of the county's location.

Traveling east to Winchester, the county seat, follow IND 32 through **PARKER CITY** (p. 1,414) and **FARMLAND** (p. 1,560), the county's third and fourth most populous towns. Located north of White River, both Parker City, just past the county line, originally named Morristown, and Farmland, *4.3 m.* farther, owe

their existence to the arrival of the Indianapolis and Bellefontaine Railroad in 1852. Before this time, westbound traffic followed a course south of the river from Winchester through Maxville and Windsor. The **Winchester Speedway** is *5.5 m.* east of Farmland on IND 32. Established in 1914 by Frank Funk, it is the state's second oldest racetrack. It is described as the world's fastest half-mile track, that is, it has the fastest qualifying time of any half-mile track.

In 1818 the citizens of **WINCHESTER** (p. 5,659), *1.9 m.* east of the speedway, donated 158 acres for county use and thereby captured the coveted designation as county seat. Sampletown, the county's first platted town, lost its bid by offering less land. Judge Sample, the founder of the tiny hamlet just west of Winchester, subsequently removed to Winchester where he built the town's first frame house. His namesake village faded into history. It is believed that Winchester was named for Brig. Gen. James Winchester, a leader of the War of 1812. Regardless of its status as county seat and judicial center for a large portion of northern Indiana, Winchester grew very slowly. Not more than a dozen families had located there by 1830. Winchester was incorporated as a town in 1838, but the civil administration was not firmly established until the 1850s with construction of the Indianapolis and Bellefontaine Railroad. Incorporation as a city took place in 1893 during the heyday of the natural gas boom.

The population count nudged just over the 3,500 mark by 1900, a 22 percent increase in the previous decade. In 1904 the Woodbury Glass Corporation resettled in Winchester after 11 years in Parker City, subsequently becoming part of Anchor Hocking Corporation, presently Winchester's largest employer. Another important industry is the Overmyer Corporation. Founded in 1920 by C. P. Overmyer and J. H. B. White, the company is considered the largest commercial mold producer for the glass industry in the United States. The company's production of gas mask molds for the Finnish government in 1937 represented one of the state's earliest war efforts. Today, Winchester is principally an industrial community where about half of the workers are employed in the manufacture of primary metals and glass products.

The third **Randolph County Courthouse**, on the public square in Winchester, was built in 1875-77 for about $78,000. J. C. Johnson of Fremont, Ohio, designed the stone and brick edifice. For years after its completion, citizens openly displayed their anger toward county officials for failing to have the structure fireproofed. In 1954 a flat rooftop replaced the sloping mansard roof and central spire. The interior received a thorough redecorating in 1978 by Henry Husmann of Portland, Indiana. The courthouse is .7 m. east of the city limits.

The **Winchester Historical Mural**, along the north side of the first floor corridor, depicts important places and personalities in the county's history. The 11 x 24-ft. mural was painted by local artist Roy Barnes who completed the enormous canvas in 1978. Among the 26 faces incorporated in the artwork are four Civil War soldiers including Col. Isaac Gray, from Union City, who served as governor of Indiana, 1880-81 and 1885-89. Also represented are James Eli Watson, who served as United States senator, 1916-33, and James P. Goodrich, governor of Indiana, 1917-21. Numbered among the portraits are film director Robert Wise and Nobel Prize winner in chemistry, Wendell M. Stanley.

On the northeast corner of the courthouse lawn stands the 67-ft.-high **Civil War Monument**. The familiar landmark, completed in 1892, was second in size only to the Soldiers and Sailors Monument at Indianapolis. The initial monies for the $25,659 memorial oddly enough came from the estate of a pacifist Quaker, James Moorman (1795-1888). Citizens tried with moderate success to increase the funds, even holding a lottery with a farm as a prize. The breakthrough came with the passing of a state law permitting counties to appropriate money for such memorials. A. A. McKain of Indianapolis designed the oolitic limestone and Vermont granite monument. The local committee did ask him, however, to replace the crowning figure of the war god Mars with a more suitable figure of an American soldier.

The lower section depicts a fort with 16 cannon. Above the fort, four figures, each 6 1/2 ft. high, represent the four branches of military service—infantry, artillery, cavalry, and navy. These figures were sculpted by the famed artist, Lorado Taft.

Turn right onto S. Meridian St., on the west side of the courthouse. On the right, at 416 S. Meridian, is the **Cary Goodrich home**, a two-story brick Federal-style dwelling constructed in 1839. In 1968 the Randolph County Historical Society purchased the house, which now houses the **Randolph County Museum**.

At the south end of Meridian St. is the well-preserved **Stone mansion**. The palatial three-story brick Franco-American-style home was constructed shortly after the Civil War by Brig. Gen. Asahel Stone (1817-1891). Stone led a distinguished career as a state legislator, a state quartermaster general during the Civil War, a bank president, and a manager of the Winchester Wagon Works. (*NRHP*)

On Stone St., east of the mansion, is a series of identically shaped houses known for many years as **Stone's Row**. General Stone built these low-rent, two-story frame cottages around 1880 for his tenants.

At the end of Stone St. turn left, then right on S. Main to the **Fountain Park Cemetery** located on the right on 40 acres given to the city by General Stone in 1880. The Stone family's circular plot sits in the middle of the grounds. The name Fountain Park alludes to Stone's unfulfilled dream of enclosing a landscaped rest and recreational area within the burial place.

The **James E. Watson home** is situated at 415 S. Main St. north of the cemetery on the right. The colorful "Sunny Jim" Watson, the United States representative and senator from Indiana for 28 years between 1895 and 1933, lived in Winchester until age 29 when he moved to Rushville. The humble single-level, frame bungalow with its tin roof was built in 1850.

East of the courthouse at 208 E. Washington St. is the **Hirsch-Study-Borror home**, built in 1877 by Adam Hirsch as a wedding gift to his daughter. Architectural features are its corner dormers and central chimney.

A block north of E. Washington at 133 E. North St. (the northwest corner of N. East and E. North sts.) is the brick Federal-style **James Moorman home**. Moorman not only initiated the construction of the Civil War Monument

Tour 3

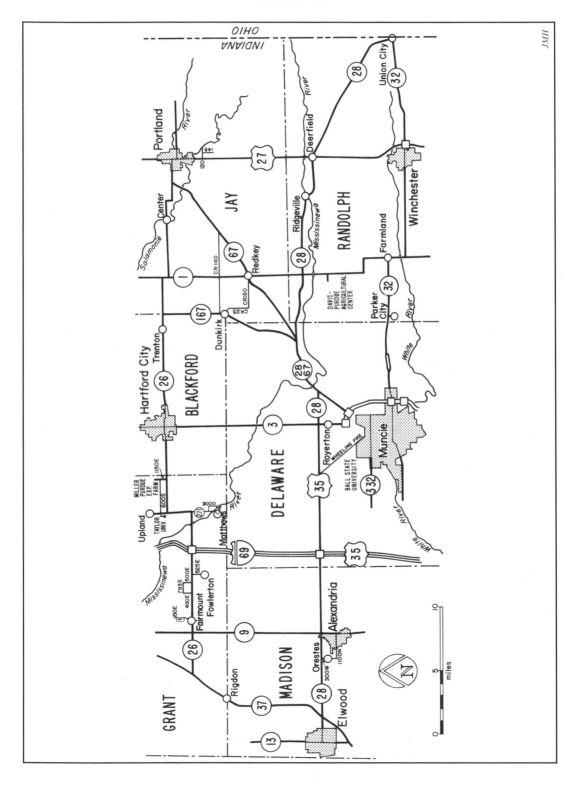

Randolph County Orphans Home, near Winchester

but also built and endowed the Randolph County Orphans Home.

Drive east on North St. to Union St. and turn left, continuing to **Silver Towne**, near the city limits. It displays gold and silver coin collections and is known nationally among numismatists. Return to Washington St. (IND 32), turn left, and continue *9 m.* to **UNION CITY**. Union City straddles the Indiana-Ohio state line, with 3,908 of its roughly 5,000 residents situated on the Indiana side. In appearance and in common municipal boundaries it is one town. The federal government recognized a unified city by establishing a single post office. Each side of town, nevertheless, functions as a separate corporation with its respective governments, tax rates, police, schools, firehouses, water systems, and even two time zones during part of the year. Rivalries between the two sections have been intense at times. A local quip goes that Union City, "the hub of two states," is sometimes "the stub of two hates." Union

City, Ohio, was first platted in 1838 and again in 1853. On the Indiana side, the town is the creation of the Smith brothers, Jeremiah and Oliver, who recognized in the late 1840s the probability of railroads intersecting at the Union City site. Hence, they purchased 160 acres in 1849 and platted Union City, Indiana. By buying a stretch of land in 1852 on the Ohio side between the two settlements and refusing to permit habitation for several decades, the Smiths subtly encouraged the building up of the Indiana side. In the early 1870s the interspace was laid out and the merging of businesses and residences into one physical entity proceeded rapidly. A major misfortune took place in 1893 when a quarter-million-dollar fire nearly destroyed the downtown section, taking with it many buildings and landmarks.

Follow IND 32 (Chestnut St.) into Union City and turn left onto Howard St. About one block on the left is the 1913-built **Union City Passenger Depot**. The Art Association of Randolph County acquired the decaying structure in 1981. The art collection includes works by Frederick Polley (1875-1957), a noted Indiana printmaker and Union City native. (*NRHP*)

Proceed north on Howard St. one block and turn left onto W. Pearl St. The **Fraze, Brooks and Davis Funeral Home**, 432 W. Pearl St. on the right, is housed in the only known Indiana work of Philadelphia architect Isaac H. Hobbs. Hobbs apparently did not personally supervise the construction, but, like many architects at the time, operated a kind of mail-order service. William P. Debolt, a Union City contractor, obtained the plans from Hobbs, modified them, and built the house for the Converse family in 1874. The Second Empire-style structure passed through a series of hands from 1880 until 1927 when S. E. Fraze bought it and converted it into a funeral home.

West .4 m. at 1015 Pearl St. is the **Union City Body Company**, founded in 1898, which provided coachwork for such early automobiles as Haynes, Apperson, Essex, Pierce-Arrow, Cord, and Duesenberg. Today it is the world's largest producer of forward control and utility truck bodies, making Step Vans, Value Vans, and High Cube Vans for General Motors.

Turn right onto Mulberry St. across from the Union City Body Company and travel north one block to Oak St. Turn right and proceed seven blocks to the City Savings Bank on the left at 200 W. Oak. This is the site of the **Isaac Gray home**. Gray (1828-1895) established the Citizens State Bank in Union City after the Civil War, and subsequently served as a state senator, 1869-71, lieutenant governor, 1877-80, acting governor, 1880-81, governor, 1885-89, and minister to Mexico, 1893-95.

Drive south on Union St. one block to Pearl St., which becomes Elm St. on the Ohio side. Turn left. The **Lambert-Parent house**, 631 E. Elm St., is a two-story Italianate-style brick structure completed in 1881 by George A. Lambert, a local businessman and a trustee of Otterbein College in Ohio for 27 years. His brother, John W. Lambert, was among the earliest automobile manufacturing pioneers. His Buckeye Works in Anderson was instrumental in producing the Union auto in Union City from 1902 to 1905.

Return to Columbia St. and turn right. Located on a corner at 413 N. Columbia, opposite the public library, is a three-story white brick painted home owned by a granddaughter of Je-

remiah Smith, a founder of Union City. The house has a transitional style, including elements of Franco-American and Neo-Jacobean, evident in its slate-gray mansard roof and side turret.

Take IND 28 (N. Columbia St.) northwest from Union City 12.4 m., through Deerfield (platted in 1833) to **RIDGEVILLE** (p. 933). Laid out twice, in 1837 and 1853, Ridgeville was named for its location on a slight elevation. A plaque on a stone next to the bank explains that between 1809 and 1818 the site of Ridgeville lay on the eastern line of the Indian frontier, known as the Twelve Mile Boundary. In its early days it was a major manufacturing center and a launching point for flatboats going down the Mississinewa River. For a brief period after replatting in 1853, the village became known as Newtown. The subsequent junction of two major railways at Ridgeville spurred the town's growth. Ridgeville College, one of Indiana's pioneer educational institutions, commenced classes in 1867 under the auspices of the Free-Will Baptists. The Congregationalists operated it between 1893 and 1900. In 1902 the three-story brick structure was sold to a manufacturing firm, and it housed factories until razed in 1932 to make way for a state highway district garage. Ridgeville was the birthplace of Wendell M. Stanley who won a 1946 Nobel Prize in chemistry for work on viruses.

From Ridgeville head west on IND 28 6 m. to IND 1. Drive south 2.8 m. to the **Davis-Purdue Agricultural Center** on the right, a 623-acre agricultural and woodlands research facility. The initial 385 acres were deeded to Purdue University in 1917 by Martha F. Davis, widow of Dr. Lewis Nelson Davis, physician and president of the Farmland State Bank. In compliance with Mrs. Davis's wishes, the farm originally was called the Herbert Davis Forestry Farm in memory of her only son who died in 1895 at the age of 19. Purdue assumed the management of the farm in 1921. The center is listed on the National Registry of Natural Landmarks. North of the Davis-Purdue farm 1.6 m., a marker on the east side of the road designates the McVey wildlife area.

Return on IND 1 and continue north to Jay County (for a description of the county see Tour 2). North of the county line 2.5 m. is **REDKEY** (p. 1,537), Jay County's third largest town. Platted in 1854 as Mount Vernon (informally called Half Way after a nearby creek), the town was renamed Redkey in 1867 for the Rev. James Redkey. The pioneer Methodist minister laid out an addition to the town in 1867 concurrent with the coming of the railroad. The town had other names given it: Skillet, Grab All, and Buzzard's Roost—designations allegedly derived from the meager meals served in a local boardinghouse. Redkey's reputation for skimpy fare was overcome by the cuisine of **Shambarger's Restaurant**. Begun in 1895, and under the Shambarger family ownership after 1928, the nationally famed gourmet establishment, situated next to the downtown railroad tracks, was the community's chief drawing card until it closed in the mid-1980s following the owner's death.

Continue north to Main St. Turn left and continue *1.9 m.* beyond the town limits. Turn right on CR 25 to **DUNKIRK** (p. 3,180). Initially called Quincy, it was platted in 1853 on a proposed railroad. The railroad project did not materialize for another 14 years, at which time the railroad officials named their new station Dunkirk. Quincy citizens were told their new post office would be named Dunkirk because another Indiana town had preempted the Quincy name. Dunkirk may derive from towns of that name in France and New York.

Dunkirk generally is considered to be the glass capital of Indiana, and there are several attractions that emphasize this industry. Its two glass companies—**Kerr Glass Manufacturing Corporation** and **Indiana Glass**—carry on a tradition harking back to the boisterous days of the natural gas boom in the 1890s when Indiana ranked second only to Pennsylvania in glass production. Today, Kerr makes food, beverage, and drug containers, while Indiana Glass continues to create tableware and other decorative glassware. Kerr is located at the approach to Dunkirk, and, like Indiana Glass, holds an open house the last weekend in July during Dunkirk's annual Glass Days Festival.

Continue northwest, paralleling the Conrail tracks, to Main St. and turn left. Turn right at Washington St. and left on Franklin to the modernistic building that houses the **Glass Museum**, which was dedicated in 1981 and contains artifacts and historical aspects of the north central Indiana glass industry. Included are numerous glass items as well as tools used in the glass manufacturing industry.

Indiana Glass can be reached by driving west to Angle St. and turning right to E St. From the glass factory, continue north under the Conrail tracks and turn right at Blackford St. At Main St. (IND 167) across from West Jay School is the **Benjamin E. Rubrecht Memorial**. Situated on a grassy triangle dividing three roads, the 6-ft. stone monument honors a pioneer of the American Flint Glass Workers Union of North America. Rubrecht (1850-1922) was the union's first secretary and an active member from 1878 to 1922.

Continue east on Blackford St., which becomes CR 140, *6 m.* to IND 67. Turn left and continue past the hamlets of Como and Blaine across the Salamonie River to **PORTLAND** (p. 7,074), the county's seat of justice. Daniel Reid of Richmond, Indiana, donated the major portion of land for the county seat in 1836, and he almost had the town named Reidville in his honor. Instead, officials named it after Portland, Maine, the hometown of Daniel W. McNeal, who surveyed the Jay County village. In the 1870s the population count jumped from approximately 500 to 3,000 persons largely because of the arrival of the railroad. Portland received its city charter in 1883 and led Indiana into the gas boom era when in 1886 the state's first commercial natural gas well was successfully sunk there. By 1900 close to 5,000 residents had made Portland their home. The pace of growth slowed once the natural gas phenomenon ended in the early years of the 20th century. Today the largest employers in Portland are Teledyne-Portland Forge and Jay Garment; the latter specializes in denim outfits.

Portland has the distinction of being the birthplace of the last soldier to die in the Civil War. Pvt. John J. Williams of Indiana's 34th Infantry Regiment was fatally wounded in a battle at Palmito Ranch, Texas, on May 13, 1865, two weeks before the last Confederate troops surrendered in Louisiana.

Travel east on Votaw St. (IND 26/67) to Meridian St. and turn right. One block on the left behind a painted block building at the northeast corner of Depot and North sts. is the unmarked **site of the state's first gas well** (1886). Continue three blocks south on Meridian and turn right onto High St. One block west at the southwest corner of High and Commerce sts. on the grounds of the Williamson Spencer Funeral Home is the site of the **birthplace of Elwood Haynes**, the designer of one of

America's first successful automobiles (see Tour 15). Haynes was born in 1857 to attorney, judge, and banker Jacob Haynes and his wife Hilinda Sophia. Elwood Haynes became superintendent of the Portland Natural Gas and Oil Company shortly after the discovery of the fuel in the area. He maintained his connection with this company for some years after he moved to Kokomo in 1892 and launched his automotive career.

Return to Meridian and continue south approximately one and one-half blocks to the **People's Bank** on the right, just north of Main St. People's was the first Indiana bank to incorporate under the 1873 state law permitting the establishment of banks under state supervision. Jacob Haynes was the first president of People's Bank. The original vaults are still in use although the exterior of the building has been refurbished and modernized.

The **Jay County Courthouse**, designed by architects from Lima, Ohio, dates from 1916 and is located one block west on Main St. The $400,000 limestone structure was dedicated in 1919. The stained-glass dome is a striking feature as is the marble-floored center court with two marble stairways leading to the second floor. (*NRHP*)

The **site of Liber College** is just south of Portland. Take US 27 (Meridian St.) south *1.6 m.* from Main St. to the turnoff to College Corner (CR 120) and travel east *.4 m.* before turning south onto CR 145 for *.1 m.* A bronze marker on a boulder in the yard of a house on the right commemorates the 25-year history of Liber College. Opened in 1853 on a six-acre lot, the school faced immediate problems when its acceptance of a black student split the organizing body and led to establishment of a rival institution, the Farmers' Academy, nearby. Liber College continued in operation until its mortgage was foreclosed in 1878. The college building was towed to the opposite side of the road and sectioned into a residence (later destroyed by fire) and a combination outhouse and stable (subsequently torn down).

Backtrack to Portland and take IND 67/26 west about *2 m.* to where IND 26 divides from IND 67. Continue west on IND 26 for *11.5 m.* past the church and cemetery at the town of Center and across IND 1 to the junction of IND 26 with IND 167. Continue into Blackford County (for a description of the county see Tour 2). To reach **HARTFORD CITY** (p.

7,622), the county seat, proceed west on IND 26 *7 m.* Hartford City originally was called "Hartford," possibly after a fordable part of Lick Creek on Jacob Hart's farm, thus Hart's Ford or Hartford. The "City" appendage was tacked on later to distinguish the Blackford County town from the Hartford in southeast Indiana. Platted in 1839 and incorporated in 1857, Hartford City remained a small agricultural trading center until the discovery of natural gas in the county in 1887. A number of paper and glass companies, taking advantage of the cheap and plentiful fuel, located there. The Hartford City Window Glass Company, established in 1891, was considered a leader. Skilled Belgian glassworkers flocked to the city and formed a community around the glass factories in the southeast section named Belgium Town. The Hartford City Paper Company, founded in 1892, introduced semitransparent and greaseproof glassine paper to the nation in 1907. Olaf Hedstrom, a native of Sweden, brought the German-perfected paper treatment to Hartford City and supervised production. In 1955 the Minnesota Mining and Manufacturing Company (3-M) bought the floundering paper company, reformed its operation, and built another plant to process its stock. Thirty years later the company divested itself of the paper processing division. Today, 3-M's audiovisual division in Hartford City produces copying supplies, paper products, encapsulated fragrances and ink, coated copy paper, and film, among other things. Though its work force was reduced with the closing of the paper division, the company remains the largest employer in the city. Another pioneering industry in Hartford City is the Overhead Door Corporation. C. G. Johnson, a Scandinavian, invented the upward swinging door in Detroit in 1921. He moved the operation to Hartford City in 1924 where it continues in the production of door sections. The corporate headquarters moved from Hartford City to Dallas, Texas, in 1965, and the name changed to Dallas Corporation in 1984.

Continue on IND 26 and turn right onto High St. at the Richardsonian/Romanesque-style **Blackford County Courthouse**. The three-story limestone structure with its 165-ft.-high clock tower and copper roof was completed in 1894 at a cost exceeding $129,000 and was modeled after Henry H. Richardson's Albany, New York, city hall, and the Allegany (New York) County courthouse. It was designed by

LaBelle and French of Marion, Indiana, who used Amherst Blue stone from Lorain, Ohio, for the outside walls. The semicircular turrets are common features on Indiana courthouses. The interior has been remodeled in recent years. (*NRHP)*

Continue north on High St. to the **Blackford Historical Museum and Cecil Beeson Library** on the southwest corner of High and Kickapoo sts. Located in an 11-room, turn-of-the-century brick home, the museum and library result largely from efforts of local historian Cecil Beeson whose lifelong collections of artifacts and documents make up the bulk of the contents. In 1976 the Blackford County Historical Society purchased the home, and the museum and library were dedicated the following year. Among its seven display rooms is a tool room containing interesting 19th-century carpenter and farm tools.

Return to Washington St. (IND 26) and turn right to the **Sinclair Glass Company**, located *.5 m.* west. The company originated in West Virginia in 1919 and moved to Hartford City in 1964 where it later linked up with the Canton Glass Company, formerly of Canton, Ohio, and Marion, Indiana. Housed in an old factory building on the grounds are the **Sinclair Shops**, operated by a group of eight artists and craftspersons who explain and demonstrate their specialties. The products of their work with wood, glass, clay, and printing press can be purchased.

After leaving the Sinclair Glass Company continue west on IND 26 *3.7 m.* to the Grant County line (for a description of the county see Tour 2). Continue an additional *.5 m.* to CR 1150E, turn right, and drive *1.4 m.* to the former **Miller-Purdue Experimental Farm**. Purdue University acquired this farm in 1938 from Isaiah M. Miller (1851-1941) in memory of his parents, Grant County pioneers. A self-educated man, Miller almost single-handedly maintained the old homestead farm, called Millerton, and wrote prodigiously. He wrote several small books of verse, largely of local historical content, including *Hoosier Halos in Hocus Pocus on Genus Homo's of Facts and Follies* in 1928. A lifelong atheist, Miller was one of six founders of the Indiana Rationalist Association in the early 1900s. Purdue sold the farm to a private party in 1988.

Return *.4 m.* to CR 600S, turn right, proceed *2.1 m.* to IND 22 in Upland, and turn left.

UPLAND (p. 3,335) is another north central Indiana town that owes its existence to the coming of the railroad and has experienced the exhilarating expansion and subsequent decline characterizing the boom and bust era of natural gas. Platted in 1867, Upland blossomed as a railway station. Railroad officials gave the town its name because they thought, mistakenly, it rested on the rail line's highest point between Union City and Logansport (between Columbus, Ohio, and Chicago, Illinois, some said). During the golden days of the natural gas marvel, Upland's population count topped 1,300 residents.

At *.6 m.* south on IND 22 is **Taylor University**. In 1893, at the height of the gas boom, the Upland Land Company offered $10,000 and 10 acres of land to this struggling Fort Wayne institution. The school, founded by Methodists in 1846 as the Fort Wayne Female College, became Fort Wayne College (coeducational) in 1855 and finally Taylor University in 1890 in honor of famed Methodist-Episcopal missionary and bishop, William Taylor. The university, faced with economic woes, accepted the Upland offer. The 240-acre campus contains 21 facilities, most dating from after 1965, and has a 10-acre lake. The modernistic building opposite the Taylor University entrance is the **Avis Industrial Corporation's national headquarters**. Avis is the parent of numerous manufacturing companies located nationwide.

Continue due south, past the two IND 26 junctions, *4.7 m.* to **MATTHEWS** (p. 745). Today it is difficult to imagine that around the turn of the century Matthews possessed at least 10 glass factories and other plants producing steel castings, foundry products, glass industry and railroad equipment, and bricks. It had 5 hotels, numerous saloons, a newspaper, 2 banks, and in 1902, during its peak, more than 100 business and professional offices. The town also had several thousand residents. Promoted as the "Wonder City," Matthews originated during the gas boom when the enterprising Matthews Land Company purchased over 2,000 acres and proceeded to promote its creation by offering a 20 percent discount on lot prices for anyone who would build immediately. The new town's name honored Claude Matthews, Indiana governor, 1893-97, and a major stockholder of the land company. So attractive was the burgeoning metropolis that the Indianapolis professional baseball team of the

Western Association was induced to relocate there in 1901. From 1905 through 1908 the gas supply dwindled rapidly, forcing the removal of most factories and businesses, and Matthews's prosperity and growth ended.

The major attraction now is the **Cumberland Covered Bridge**. Marion's William Parks built the first bridge on the site in 1867. The present Howe-truss structure was erected 10 years later by the Smith Bridge Company of Toledo, Ohio, with Peter Millspaugh and his 15-year-old son adding the exterior cover. The 1913 flood carried the 183-ft.-bridge about one-quarter mile down the Mississinewa. It was towed back, shortened by 6 ft., and replaced on higher abutments. There is a small park and picnic area near the bridge. To reach the bridge, turn left onto 6th St., which becomes Midway Ave. before becoming 4th St. Next, turn right onto High St., then left onto 3rd St. The bridge is straight ahead on 3rd St (CR 1000E). (*NRHP/HAER*)

Continue through the bridge about *.5 m.*, turn left on CR 1061S, travel about *.5 m.*, and turn right on CR 950E. At about *1.6 m.* turn left on IND 26. Beyond I-69 *1.3 m.* turn left on CR 525E to **FOWLERTON** (p. 300). A post office was placed in the vicinity in 1895, and the town named Leach after a prominent family in the township. Another family, the Fowlers, began the first industry, a mill, in 1895. Apparently the names Leach, Leachburg, and Fowlerton were used interchangeably until 1902 when the United States Post Office Department settled the question by designating the name of Fowlerton. The next year, 1903, Fowlerton was incorporated.

Benjamin F. Leach arrived in Fowlerton from neighboring Fairmount in 1896 and established a glass factory, one of several founded during the heyday of natural gas. Among Leach's products were paperweights, made from broken glass purchased from other glass factories at a penny a pound. The weights, said to have been designed and made by Leo J. Ernst and Jean Annamaugh, wholesaled for $2.50 a dozen. It has been estimated that about 25,000 weights were produced by the **Leach Glass Company**. It is this quality of mass production that at times has led paperweight connoisseurs to dismiss the Fowlerton articles as crude and unattractive. Yet the paperweights are highly sought by collectors, and some, discovered at Fowlerton in 1929, have found a permanent home at the Art Institute of Chicago.

Continue on Leach St. (CR 525E), take 2nd St. (flashing light) right to the street just before the railroad tracks, and turn right. To the left is a well-preserved tiny red-brick barn-like structure. This small **glass factory building** survives from the days when glassmaking was king in the gas-belt towns.

Continue to the end of the street, turn right, and proceed *.6 m.* to a farmhouse, white barn, and mobile home on the left. Bishop Milton Wright, father of the airplane inventors, moved to this spot in 1860. Here, Reuchlin Wright, the oldest of the five Wright children, was born in a two-story log cabin.

Return to CR 525E, turn right, proceed to IND 26, turn left, and at *.2 m.* turn right on CR 500. Take the county road for a mile to **Lake Galatia** crossing Barren Creek at approximately *.6 m.* In the valley to the left, approximately *.3 m.*, a nearly complete mammoth skeleton was unearthed in 1904 and subsequently sold to the American Museum of Natural History in New York City, where it remains on display. The discovery precipitated a suit in which the jury ruled that the skeleton was real estate belonging to the farm owner rather than personal property belonging to the tenant. The 17-acre lake and boggy shoreline, a remnant of a much larger glacial lake, has confounded observers for years by its capacity to swallow up unpredictably roads, cornfields, and utility lines. The lake has been both a haven for fishermen and a commercial success for the peat moss business. After the turn of the century, however, the Chesapeake and Ohio Railroad fought the waters for years as the wet, spongy ground persistently yielded to the pressure of the roadbed. The railroad even hired a watchman to signal approaching trains of the embankment's condition. In the 1930s a section of IND 26 disappeared in one night. CR 500E periodically sank from sight, and today the weight of a vehicle driven over the road after a rain can cause ripples of water to emanate from the marshy roadsides. The old lake bed has relinquished several prehistoric skeletons, including a giant beaver now displayed by the Field Museum of Natural History in Chicago. The lake area once was the site of two towns. A group of spiritualists platted Galatia in 1854 and established a few businesses and a newspaper, *The Galatia Messenger*. The community died out in the early 1860s because a projected rail line failed to materialize and because orthodox Protestantism made persuasive inroads into the nonconformist faith. On the opposite side of the lake, Prospertown was created for the explicit purpose of opposing its spiritualistic neighbor. The project was soon abandoned.

Leave Lake Galatia by taking the road just north of the lake (CR 793S) west .5 m. to CR 450E. Turn left, drive to IND 26, and turn right 3.1 m. to **FAIRMOUNT** (p. 3,286). Settled by Quakers for the most part, the community was platted in 1850. Residents called the place Pucker until Fairmount was officially adopted after a local visitor to Philadelphia returned with glowing reports of the magnificence of Fairmount Park in that city. The town was incorporated in 1870, and 17 years later the Fairmount Mining Company struck natural gas. Mills and glass industries proliferated, and the town's population in the decade of the 1890s jumped from 1,462 to 3,205. The citizens successfully fought against the establishment of saloons in their town from 1874 well into the 20th century. If threats of bodily harm to tavern owners did not accomplish the goals of the vigilantes, the dynamiting of saloons usually settled the question.

Fairmount boosters have made some unsubstantiated claims of greatness for their community. Not only has it been said that the Eskimo Pie ice cream treat began there, but also that the first auto was built in Fairmount by Orlie Scott, wrecked here, and subsequently sold to Elwood Haynes who simply restored it and added a brake. Whatever truth there is to these stories there is no doubt that, for its size, Fairmount has produced an extraordinary number of achievers. Nationally recognized college presidents and deans, corporate executives, authors, artists, cartoonists, reporters, actors, and professors have called Fairmount their home. During its 1950 centennial three former residents were college presidents, and listed in *Who's Who* was the equivalent of 1 of every 230 residents, which was 14 times the national average. Among them were Mary Jane Ward, author of *The Snake Pit*; Garfield V. Cox, University of Chicago dean; Marvin Coyle, General Motors vice-president; and Alvin Seale, a noted marine scientist. Among the more colorful post-Civil War heroes is Capt. David L. Payne (1836-1884), a local boy who went West to serve as a soldier and later a guide

and hunter. Payne then became doorkeeper in the United States House of Representatives, postmaster, and Kansas legislator. He is best known for his unsuccessful and illegal attempts to bring white settlements into the Unassigned Lands of the Indian Territory, now a portion of Oklahoma. Payne and others led the Boomers (those who sought to enter the territory) and intensified agitation for congressional action that ultimately led to the opening of Oklahoma lands in 1889.

James Dean, the actor, grew up near Fairmount at the home of an uncle and aunt. He attended the local high school where, in 1949, he was judged the best actor in Indiana in a state drama contest. From Fairmount he went to Hollywood and made three important pictures before he died, tragically, in a car accident in 1955 at the age of 24. The movies *East of Eden*, *Rebel Without a Cause*, and *Giant* established his stardom and gave rise to legions of fans and to cult-like followings after his death. Souvenir hunters have chipped away at Dean's gravestone and at a monument to him in Park Cemetery, located on CR 150E (N. Main St.), .7 m. north of IND 26.

Among the town's more recent famous citizens are Emmy Award-winning television news commentator Phil Jones and cartoonist Jim Davis, the creator of the comic strip *Garfield*. Davis, the only author to have five books appear simultaneously on the *New York Times* bestseller list, grew up on a Fairmount farm and learned to draw as a result of asthma attacks which kept him confined indoors.

Materials pertaining to Dean, Davis, and Fairmount history are located in the **Fairmount Historical Museum**, which was opened in 1975 and was moved into the J. W. Patterson house, 203 E. Washington St., in 1983. The home was built in 1888 by Nixon Winslow, James Dean's great-grandfather, and later occupied by Patterson, a well-known physician and town leader. To view the museum, take Main St. south from the Park Cemetery to Washington St. and turn left. The museum is on the northeast corner of Washington and Walnut sts. (*NRHP*) The **James Dean Gallery**, 425 N. Main St., opened in 1988 and displays the collection of longtime Dean researcher and memorabilia collector David Loehr. Among the items exhibited are hundreds of novelty and paper items related to Dean's career.

Return to IND 26 (8th St.), turn left, and proceed *4.6 m.* to IND 37, passing the Wesleyan Church Campground at the edge of Fairmount. Head south on IND 37 *11.4 m.*, passing through Rigdon and entering **MADISON COUNTY** (p. 139,336; 453 sq. m.) to IND 28. The county was chartered in 1823, two years after the last of the Delaware Indians, who had populated the vicinity for about three quarters of a century, left, treaty-bound, for new homes in Kansas. A series of shifts in its borders brought the county to its present rectangular shape by 1838. Favored with timber, numerous mill streams, and relatively flat land, the county's economy rested on agriculture, and largely on farm-related industries, until the late 1880s. The discovery of natural gas in 1887 radically altered the local economy, stimulating manufacturing, particularly glass. New jobs attracted workers, and the population nearly doubled during the 1890s. Afterwards, even as the gas supply diminished creating some economic dislocations, the advent of the automotive age promised to reinvigorate trade. Automobile makers and auto parts factories proliferated prior to World War I. The auto parts industry is today the largest employer, especially General Motors, and Madison County consistently ranks in the state's top 10 counties in manufacturing categories. Yet the county maintains a prosperous and important agricultural sector, which year after year stands among the top five counties in the value of all crops.

Turn west onto IND 28 and drive *.7 m.* into **ELWOOD** (p. 10,867). Elwood, the second largest city in Madison County, is located on Duck Creek about 20 miles northwest of Anderson. The town was called Quincy when platted in 1853. Two years later Duck Creek post office was established. Confusion over the names of Quincy and Duck Creek led to the adoption in 1869 of a new designation, Elwood, after Homer Elwood Frazier, seven-year-old son of one of the town founders. The first railroad came to Elwood in 1856. Fourteen years later the small agricultural center incorporated. The discovery of natural gas in 1887 transformed the community, and the population reached 2,284 in 1890. A year later Elwood became a city with the state's youngest mayor, 21-year-old William DeHority. The newly industrialized city counted almost 13,000 residents by the turn of the century. Lo-

cal boosters advertised Elwood as the Buckle of the Gas Belt.

The foundation of Elwood's new-found prosperity in the 1890s was the American Sheet and Tin Plate Company, the nation's first fully equipped mill exclusively devoted to tinplate production (putting a tin veneer onto sheet iron or steel). The doubling of duties on English and Welsh tinplate by the McKinley tariff of 1890 enabled the infant American industry to get on its feet. Daniel G. Reid and William Leeds of Richmond, Indiana, attracted by Elwood's cheap fuel, launched the company in 1892. William McKinley, sponsor of the tariff that had benefited the industry and at the time governor of Ohio, spoke at the formal opening. The company trademark was an American eagle in flight with the British lion in its talons, a logo most conspicuously displayed on the big bass drum of the popular company band. The skilled and experienced English and Welsh tin mill laborers proved indispensable in the success of the nation's and Elwood's tinplate business. The Elwood company subsequently became one of the largest tinplate producing plants in the world.

In 1898 the Elwood operation merged with 35 competitors to form the American Tin Plate Company with Daniel Reid as president. Shortly after the turn of the century this conglomerate joined with several others to form the United States Steel Corporation. Labor problems pervaded the steel industry in these early days. Management's aversion to unionization induced a number of strikes in Elwood and elsewhere and precipitated the appearance of an active Socialist party in Elwood. The party reached its zenith in 1917 when voters elected a socialist city administration including mayor John G. Lewis. One of Elwood's tinplate employees was James J. Davis (1873-1947), a Welsh immigrant who came from Louisiana to Elwood in a railroad boxcar. In 1898 he rose to the city clerk's office and subsequently to the position of secretary of labor during the Harding, Coolidge, and Hoover administrations, 1921-30. Davis later served as a United States senator from Pennsylvania, 1930-45. His name appears on the Elwood City Hall cornerstone.

Elwood's fortunes in the gas boom days were buoyed also by five glass companies. The George A. McBeth Glass Company of Pittsburgh opened plants in Elwood and neighboring Marion, merging with the Thomas Evans

Company in 1898. For a time, the McBeth-Evans complex manufactured the nation's only oil-tempered lamp chimneys, and in 1890 the Elwood plant produced the country's first successful optical glass. The process proved invaluable when European imports were cut off during World Wars I and II. Another major glassworks in Elwood was the Diamond Plate Glass Company founded in 1891 and later purchased by the Pittsburgh Plate Glass Company as their Works No. 7. These two glass concerns along with the tinplate mill survived the economic downswing in the early 1900s when the natural gas supply dwindled. In 1936-38 all three companies permanently shut down, idling about 2,000 workers. An aggressive Chamber of Commerce, the expansion of nearby industries, and the rejuvenation of agriculture supported the city through the slump. The short-lived Tomato Festival, inaugurated in 1937, the four canneries, and the building of the Continental Can Company plant in 1935 testify to the significance of this seasonal crop at that time. The major industry is the Ex-Cell-O Corporation, makers of jet airplane compressor blades. To see the Ex-Cell-O facility turn left off IND 28 (Main St.) onto 28th St. Drive .7 m.south and turn right onto J St. The plant is .2 m. west. The two large concrete gate posts at the visitors' parking lot entrance remain from the tinplate factory that once covered 33 acres.

Wendell Willkie (1892-1944) is Elwood's favorite son. The unsuccessful Republican party candidate for the presidency in 1940 was born in Elwood. His father operated a law practice while superintending the local high school. His mother joined the family law firm after her admittance to the bar in 1897, one of the first women in the state to have achieved this distinction. The young Willkie took a law degree from Indiana University in 1916, joined the army in 1918, and one year later married Edith Wilk of Rushville (see Tour 14). Afterwards, Willkie was company lawyer for Firestone Tire and Rubber Company of Akron, Ohio, and president of the Commonwealth and Southern Corporation, a giant utility holding company. Protecting his interests, Willkie fought against Franklin Roosevelt's efforts to control utilities and to establish the Tennessee Valley Authority. In the process Willkie gained a following that snowballed into a nomination for the presidency. During the 1940 campaign, Elwood citizens had to bear the ridicule of their community being portrayed in the press as a hick town, an old ghost town, a two-event town—the Tomato Festival and Willkie's nomination—and a place where teenagers spiked their cokes on Saturday night and attended Sunday school the next morning. The Republican candidate won only nine states in the electoral college. However, he won 45 percent of the popular vote, more than his two predecessors who had opposed Roosevelt. Ironically, Willkie went on to become a firm advocate of Roosevelt's policy of foreign intervention for the purpose, Willkie thought, of promoting international reconciliation. Willkie's book, *One World* (1943), called for a unified world order. Willkie died unexpectedly in 1944 and was buried at Rushville.

Three attractions pertain to Wendell Willkie in Elwood. The **Willkie boyhood home**, with its leaded windows and stone porch, sits on the northwest corner of North A and 19th sts., a block north of Main St. Farther west .2 m. on Main St. stands Willkie's old high school on the right. Built in the mid-1890s, the red-brick structure was officially renamed the **Wen-**

Indiana State Library
Wendell Willkie, campaigning in August 1940

dell L. Willkie High School in 1945. From the steps of this school on August 17, 1940, Willkie spoke briefly to an enormous crowd before moving on to a nearby park to accept officially the nomination for president. (*NRHP*) A third memento is the 1.83-acre **Wendell L. Willkie Memorial Park**, on N. Anderson St. (IND 13) *.3 m.* north of Main St. The park's centerpiece is a 2,000-lb. granite monument, crowned with a bust of Willkie, which was dedicated in 1966. The inscription includes a popular Willkie quotation: "To have peace this world must be free."

Return to Main St., turn right, and right at 5th St. to the **St. Clair Glass Works, Inc.**, *.2 m.* on the left. It represents three generations of Elwood glass workers. The St. Clairs, natives of France, moved from St. Louis to Elwood in 1890 to work at the McBeth Glass Company. Here the father, son, and grandsons perfected their skills in glass production. After the McBeth plant closed in 1938, Joe St. Clair started his own glass shop. Joined by the rest of the family, the glass business expanded after the war to include a display room, office, and gift shop. By 1949 at least 20 different handmade items were being offered. The St. Clairs began pressing glass in the 1960s using molds reproduced from glassware of the old Indiana Tumbler and Goblet Company of Greentown, Indiana (see Tour 15). In 1971 the St. Clairs sold the factory to an Elkhart, Indiana, firm, but Joe St. Clair repurchased it in 1974 and resumed operation. Joe St. Clair continued to handcraft most of the items available in the gift shop until his death in October 1987. Occasionally new molds are designed for pressed ware.

In the vicinity of the St. Clair shops is a remnant of the old **McBeth-Evans Glass Company**. Take the first right north of St. Clair (D St.) to the next stop sign (9th St.) and turn left. The smoke stack and gabled roof of the deteriorating McBeth-Evans plant are to the left at 9th and N. K sts.

Return to IND 28 (Main St.), turn left, and *4.4 m.* after crossing IND 37 turn right on CR 300W and proceed *.5 m.* to Superior (CR 300W) and S. 1st sts. in **ORESTES** (p. 539). The area was developed by Nathan Lowry as a railroad station around 1876 and was called Lowry's Station. The name was changed to Orestes after local farmer Orestes McMahan in the 1890s, when the town blossomed with industry and a business district as a result of the gas boom. The major attraction is the **Orestes**

Oak on S. 1st St., just east of the intersection on the right. Nearly 7 ft. in diameter, the roughly 300-year-old white oak tree received a memorial plaque in 1972 from the Madison County Historical Society, Inc. The arrow-shaped bronze medallion, situated on a boulder, has a fanciful inscription: "Since about 1670 this oak has been a landmark for a Delaware Indian Trail, the Fort Wayne Trace, for the Village of Orestes, and for God."

One of Indiana's last surviving electric traction lines extended from a railroad connection about *1 m.* west of Orestes southward *2.5 m.* to the Western Indiana Gravel Company pit. After the Tipton-Alexandria interurban line was abandoned in 1931, the gravel company bought the spur from Indiana Railroad and continued to operate it for many years.

Continue south on CR 300W for *.4 m.* and turn left on CR 1100N *2 m.* to **ALEXANDRIA** (p. 6,028). The third largest city in Madison County was laid out in 1836 by John D. Stephenson and William Conner, the noted frontiersmen who purchased the site in anticipation of riches to be gained when the proposed Central Canal flowed through their property. The derivation of the town's name remains a mystery—possibilities include Alexander the Great, the ancient city of Alexandria, and the wife of one of the founders. Canal fever stimulated a rapid development, but the canal never made it to Alexandria, and the village languished until 1875 when the arrival of two rail lines revitalized the community. Drillers discovered Madison County's first natural gas well in Alexandria in 1887, and the prospect of prosperity attracted venturesome businessmen and workers. The population count of 715 in 1890 multiplied tenfold to 7,221 by 1900. The abundance of fuel attracted glass factories, a huge steel mill, brickworks, and the Kelly Ax Company (makers of the Perfect Ax). Alexandria was incorporated as a city in 1893.

Meanwhile, Charles Corydon Hall, a chemist and Elwood Haynes's former classmate at Worcester Polytechnic Institute in Massachusetts, used the family kitchen in Alexandria to experiment with converting limestone into rock wool, an insulation fiber. His success in the late 1890s helped launch the nation's rock wool industry and subsequently bolstered the city's economy after the close of the natural gas era. Hall and two partners organized the **Banner Rock Products Company** in 1906, the first of a number of Indiana firms that by the 1930s made the state the nation's leader in mineral, or rock wool, production. In 1928 Hall sold the company to the Johns-Manville Products Corporation. The Indiana Rockwool Division of the Susquehanna Corporation continues to be the economic mainstay. A portion of the old Banner Rock factory can still be seen southeast of the Johns-Manville complex near the west city limits. At CR 100W, cross the railroad tracks and look to the left. The Banner Rock name stretches across the top of a red brick, stone-trimmed building in the foreground.

The Mantle Lamp Company of Chicago acquired property in Alexandria in 1926. Here the company produced its famous glass kerosene lamps, electric lamps, and other glass articles under its trademark **Aladdin**. In 1929 the company incorporated its land on the west side of Alexandria into the town of Aladdin for tax-saving purposes. Aladdin "Alacite" glass, an ivory-toned substance and a favorite among glass collectors, was manufactured between 1938 and 1953. Aladdin's 17 residents in 1940 earned it the title of "flyweight" champion in the census of that year. During World War II Aladdin produced vacuum bottles and a light-weight, gas-efficient cookstove for the allied forces. The plant moved to Nashville, Tennessee, in 1953, and a few years afterwards Alexandria annexed the town of Aladdin.

Gimco City, founded on Alexandria's southwest side in 1929 for similar tax reasons, long held the distinction of being the state's smallest incorporated municipality. When annexed in 1973, it had a population of nine.

American overseas propaganda during World War II heralded Alexandria as *Small Town, U.S.A.* in a publication of the Office of War Information. The booklet, not distributed stateside or to the armed forces, depicted Alexandria in word and picture as exemplifying democracy in action. The exposure abroad led to a succession of articles on the town appearing in nationwide media. The pamphlet was reissued by the local Chamber of Commerce during America's bicentennial celebration in 1976.

One of the first interurban lines in the state ran between Anderson and Alexandria beginning in January 1898. The terminal for the Union Traction Company cars sat at the corner of Harrison and Monroe sts. and housed the Wells-Fargo Express office, a lunch room, and a confectionery specializing in Christmas candies. Along the route of the interurban, hexagonal, steel-reinforced concrete **waiting stations** protected passengers from the elements. In 1979 a surviving, 12,000-lb. waiting station was removed from a local farm to Beulah Park, where a marker extolling the city's role in inaugurating interurbans was erected. Beulah Park is right on Clinton St. at the east end of Washington St., left at Berry St., and right on IND 9 for .2 m.

About 100 yds. north of the park on IND 9 is a marker to the right commemorating the first settler in the township and other important township dates.

Continue north on IND 9 to IND 28. Proceed east *12.5 m.* to the flashing light and angle right on Wheeling Pike. Continue *2.5 m.* to the Muncie limits.

Richmond

Richmond (p. 41,349), the Queen City of the Whitewater Valley, lies 65 miles east of Indianapolis. The **WAYNE COUNTY** (p. 76,058; 404 sq. m.) seat of justice borders on the state line and sits astride two historical thoroughfares, the Old National Rd. (US 40) and the East Fork of the Whitewater River. The lush valley, created centuries ago by meltwater from a succession of retreating ice sheets, begins at the headwaters of the Whitewater River in northern Wayne County and southern Randolph County. From near the state's highest elevation, the river falls nearly 800 ft., 5.6 ft. per mile, and drains 1,355 square miles in 10 Indiana counties before reaching the Miami River. It is the steepest and swiftest major waterway in Indiana. Whitewater River was probably named for the foaming rapids along the often narrow and shallow channel. An observer in 1817, however, claimed that the designation reflected the water's unusual transparency: "A fish or a pebble can be seen at a depth of 20 feet."

The main attraction of the Richmond area topography is the Whitewater Gorge, a large natural cleft in the valley's bedrock caused by receding meltwaters around 20,000 years ago. The gorge is at least three and one-half miles long, 800 ft. wide, and 80 ft. deep in places. The natural assets of the gorge and surrounding lands and river forks—excellent timber, plentiful game, good soil, clay for bricks, potable spring water, extractable stone, dam sites to provide water power—were prime considerations in founding Richmond.

Permanent settlement at the site began in 1806 when the first wave of southern Quakers, led by the Cox, Smith, and Hoover families, inhabited land on the gorge's east side, the former fishing and hunting domain of the Miamis, Delawares, and Shawnees. While the Indians had been pushed west by the 1795 Greenville Treaty, their eastern border lay just two and one-half miles west in 1806. In 1809 the Twelve Mile Purchase agreement relocated the Indian boundary a dozen miles farther west, and a year later the territorial legislature carved Wayne County from northern Dearborn County, designating a county seat to be named Salisbury on the old Greenville Treaty line. During the War of 1812 Wayne County's white settlers feared attack by Indians, who were futilely resisting encroachments throughout the Indiana Territory. Some 20 fortified cabins, blockhouses, and forts were built for protection in Wayne County alone. With the war's end in 1815, the signing of treaties, and statehood for Indiana in 1816, the Whitewater region increased rapidly in population.

The first recorded plat at Richmond was entered in 1816 by John Smith, who called his small collection of lots Smithville. Smith had failed earlier to interest his neighbor and fellow Quaker Jeremiah Cox into linking his lands, called Coxborough or Jericho, with Smith's lands in a single plat. Cox reportedly said, "I would rather see a Buck's tail than a tavern sign." In 1818 Cox relented. The town was laid out, incorporated, and named Richmond, suggested by surveyor David Hoover, instead of Waterford or Plainfield, which the naming committee also proposed. The village's population at incorporation stood at around 200. Also in 1818, following a four-year heated contest, the county seat was transferred from Salisbury to Centerville. Today no trace remains of the once flourishing town of Salisbury.

Richmond's Quakers dominated the town's early social and religious life. Methodist circuit riders had difficulty finding a home in which to preach. The Quakers attracted a continuous stream of coreligionists from North Carolina and Virginia seeking economic gain and freedom to speak and practice their antislavery convictions. One path across Ohio was sometimes called the Quaker Trace. By 1821 the Whitewater Friends Meeting, established in 1807, had grown to become the Indiana Yearly

Meeting with jurisdiction over the states of Indiana and Illinois and points west. Members from this vast area in the Yearly Meeting numbered almost 14,000 by 1827. The division of the Society of Friends at Philadelphia in 1827-29 into Orthodox and Hicksite factions also split the Richmond group. Elias Hicks's movement to revert to the original Quaker doctrine of the Inner Light as sole spiritual authority and his opposition to all external authorities, whether scriptures, elders, or the historical Christ, prompted the division, which lasted more than a century. Most communities, including Richmond, contained representatives of both groups and separate meetinghouses. The orthodox Friends founded the Friends' Boarding School in 1847, a high-school level institution that later became Earlham College.

Richmond was a regional farm and industrial center in the 1830s with its variety of mills, blacksmith shops, tanneries, cabinet and wagon works, and textile and carriage factories. The *Richmond Palladium*, founded in 1831 by Nelson Boon, grandnephew of Daniel Boone, is one of the three oldest Indiana newspapers and Richmond's oldest surviving business. The *Palladium*'s fourth editor and Richmond's mayor from 1852 to 1866, John Finley is credited with popularizing the term "Hoosier" through his poem *The Hoosier's Nest* that first appeared in the January 1, 1833, *Indianapolis Journal*. Between 1828 and 1836 the National Rd. was finished through Richmond with a wooden span, the National Bridge, that prompted growth on the river's west side. During this era of feverish canal construction, a local group tried to fund a canal from Richmond to Brookville. Like many other Hoosier canal projects this one failed because of lack of funds, flood destruction, and railroad competition. By 1840 Richmond's 2,070 residents elected to incorporate as a city. John Sailor, a Philadelphia-born cabinetmaker, was the first mayor.

The 1850 census discloses a 30 percent decline in Richmond's population in the decade of the 1840s. The westward movement of settlers, the slowdown of Quaker migration, the lingering effects of the late 1830s national depression discouraging new business ventures, the enrollment of volunteers in the Mexican War, and the lure of the California goldfields may have contributed to the population decrease. On the other hand, census takers may have seriously undercounted. A cholera outbreak that took 70 lives in 1849 may have caused census officials to rush the enumeration. A one-third loss of population seemed preposterous to contemporaries who claimed that the population had increased by as much as 50 percent. The census results are challenged by its own figures that credit 25,320 residents to Wayne County, making it the state's most populous county, and by signs of growth and expansion in Richmond. In 1841 members of the Gaar family, along with William Scott, all laborers in a stove foundry, fashioned one of Indiana's earliest threshers. In 1849 they bought the business and launched a successful farm implement manufactory, A. Gaar and Company, later Gaar, Scott and Company. Another firm, Robinson and Company began making agricultural machinery in 1842. Today Swayne, Robinson and Company is Richmond's oldest manufacturer and the nation's oldest continually operated family owned foundry. During the 1840s at least five religious congregations organized or built churches. Railroad fever seized Richmond in the mid-1840s. Three county turnpikes were completed late in the decade. A telegraph line connected the city with Dayton, Ohio, in 1848.

The building of factories, churches, and roads required workers, and Richmond received a considerable influx of emigrants, particularly from Germany. The Germans, escaping economic destitution and a hated five-year military conscription, came to interior towns such as Richmond to work in the mills, on railroads or turnpikes, or to set up farms or businesses. Richmond's Quakers and Germans lived together amicably due to a mutual dislike of litigation, lawyers, ostentatious display, and compulsory military service. The Irish, too, fleeing the horrid effects of their homeland's potato famine in the late 1840s, arrived in the city to labor for road or railway contractors. Progress on a variety of fronts, along with the foreign inflow, would make it appear doubtful that Richmond experienced a major loss in population.

Rail service reached the city in 1853 about the time foreign migration to the city peaked. A gasworks was inaugurated in 1854. A wholesale district spread north of Main St. in response to the needs of a rapidly developing region. Wayne County, at this juncture, held the state's highest ratio of cabinetmakers to population, about 1 to every 350 residents. A vigorous economy was taking root, but with it came charged social issues: temperance, slavery, and women's rights. The Indiana Women's Rights Association, formed in 1852 at Dublin, Wayne County, chose Richmond's Jane Morrow as its first vice-president. In 1859 Dr. Mary F. Thomas, a Richmond physician, joined two other persons in appearing before the state legislature to petition for a women's voting rights amendment to the constitution. Dr. Thomas was the first woman member of the state medical society and the second woman admitted to the American Medical Association. She served many years as president of the Indiana Woman's Suffrage Association, organized in 1860.

Two landmark institutions, still in existence, were established during the Civil War years. Indiana's oldest national bank, the First National Bank of Richmond, opened in 1863. The following year Robert Morrisson, the city's first postmaster, donated grounds and funds for outfitting a new library, known today as the Morrisson-Reeves Library.

Richmond's development took a relatively orderly course during the last half of the 19th century. The population increased at a rate of three or four thousand persons each decade. Another series of bitter courthouse wars ended in 1873 with the county seat's removal from Centerville to Richmond. The contention for the coveted courthouse and the foregone conclusion as to its outcome sparked a minor business boom in Richmond. In 1868 J. M. Hutton founded what today is the nation's oldest casket manufacturer operating under the original name. The Starr Piano Company, perhaps the first trans-Appalachian piano factory, located in Richmond in 1872. The Dille and McGuire Manufacturing Company began making lawn mowers in 1874. Soon Richmond claimed to be the lawn mower capital of the world. Wayne Corporation, currently one of America's largest producers of school buses, had been in business 38 years when it moved from Dublin to Richmond in 1875. The inception of the Adam H. Bartel Company, dry goods jobber, and Knollenberg's construction of a building on Main St. in 1877 enhanced the retail and wholesale sectors. Haynes, Spencer and Company, incorporated in 1878 but associated with desk making in Richmond since the 1860s, produced Wooton secretaries and rotary desks. William S. Wooton, the designer of the famed Patent

Cabinet Office Secretary, manufactured school desks out of the George Grant factory from 1867 until his departure for Indianapolis in 1870. His Wooton Desk Manufacturing Company relocated to Richmond in 1884 as a subsidiary of Wayne, Spencer and Company. In 1879 Micajah C. Henley built a roller skate factory destined to be a major influence in the new recreational and sports craze. Two years later Joseph Hill and his son E. Gurney Hill established what evolved into the largest wholesale rose-growing and shipping operation in the country. Richmond's industrial base of agricultural items, pianos, lawn mowers, vehicles, roller skates, office furniture, and roses was formed by the early 1880s and would remain for many years essentially the same.

Because Richmond did not possess the deep pockets of natural gas that fueled the fortunes of neighboring towns in the 1880s and the 1890s, it did not undergo the boom-and-bust economy that accompanied the wasteful use of gas. Richmond escaped the hectic and haphazard growth common in the gas belt towns but still made good use of the gas by having it pumped in from Chesterfield, 40 miles away. In return, however, the greater opportunities in the gas-rich communities deprived Richmond of new residents. The city's population increase in the 1890s was the smallest since the 1840s.

Growth and achievement in areas other than industry characterized Richmond in the century's final two decades. Utility services improved with the construction of an electric plant and a waterworks system. Two new bridges spanned the gorge. Richmond's success in skate manufacturing most likely accounted for two new roller rinks in the 1890s. The county's fifth courthouse was erected between 1890 and 1893. The Bethel African Methodist Episcopal congregation built a new sanctuary. James M. Townsend, Bethel's former pastor and a state legislator, received a presidential appointment in 1889 to the land commissioner's office in Washington, D.C. Thomas A. Mott, Richmond's superintendent of schools, restructured American education when he devised a junior high school in the mid-1890s. The inauguration of the Richmond Art Association in 1898 proved a springboard to the city's enduring involvement in artist training and fine arts appreciation.

In the early decades of the 20th century, while nearby towns stagnated due to subsiding flows of natural gas, Richmond made substantial gains. The city registered a 22.5 percent jump in population between 1900 and 1910. By 1903 the city had reaped an interurban route to Dublin, the Richmond Baking Company, and the state's largest municipal electric utility plant. Richmond earned a reputation of being panic-proof when it successfully weathered the national crisis of 1907, an accomplishment credited to Richmond's businesses being largely locally owned.

One major local industry, however, ran into serious problems and folded, creating a brief panic of sorts. Gaar, Scott and Company, longtime makers of steam-powered farm machinery and related products, failed to keep pace with the emerging technologies in the automotive field. The company overproduced steam threshers at a time when the internal combustion engine was being applied to agricultural equipment. Left holding too great an inventory of outmoded apparatus, the company sold out in 1911 and closed permanently in 1915. The shutdown idled 900 workers, and Richmond lost the benefits from an annual $500,000 payroll.

In due time automobile makers and related firms took up the slack. Eight makes of cars originated in Richmond. One, the Davis, was produced from 1909 to 1928 and pioneered in the use of a one-piece windshield and a central gearshift. Automobiles spawned dealerships, service stations, and parts industries. The National Automatic Tool Company, for example, came to Richmond in 1910 and sold to Ford Motor Company the first multiple drilling machine for cylinder blocks. In 1914 Wayne Corporation built its first motor-powered school bus frame. Ironically, Richmond held its first automobile show in 1916 in a portion of the old Garr, Scott plant. The loss of Gaar, Scott and the switch by Swayne-Robinson from farm machinery to making iron castings for lawn mowers did not diminish Richmond's prominence in the state's agricultural picture. One reason for this was the 1921 arrival of an International Harvester shop to produce farm items. The *Palladium* aided farmers by broadcasting farm reports on its own radio station, WOZ, the second newspaper radio station in the nation and the first in Indiana to transmit farm news.

A Richmond native and a Chicago restaurateur, Charles Weeghman, earned a footnote in baseball's history when in 1915 he headed a syndicate that bought the Chicago Cubs. Weeghman, the club's president, installed the team in his own field, soon to be known as Wrigley Field after the chewing gum magnate, who took control of the Cubs in the early 1920s. In 1916 the Starr Piano Company branched into the recording business. The Gennett studio, housed in the Starr plant, made classical jazz history as it recorded a succession of famous musicians, including King Oliver, Bix Beiderbecke, Hoagy Carmichael, Duke Ellington, Jelly Roll Morton, and Louis Armstrong. The Gennett label went out of existence during the depression years of the 1930s, but the studio continued to press records for major recording companies.

Richmond moved into the 1920s as the state's 12th largest city. City administrations grappled with inadequate utilities, careless drivers, illegal merchandizing of alcoholic beverages, and gambling dens. The downtown congestion of factories, stores, residences, and schools prompted the city council in 1922 to adopt a pioneering comprehensive zoning ordinance. The measure, though, did not fully alleviate a situation that plagued Richmond for years. On the eve of the depression, in 1928-29, the city welcomed the Belden Company, manufacturers of electrical wire. The local historical society's museum opened in an old Quaker meetinghouse. Not so fortunate was W. C. Davis (of Davis car fame), whose Davis Aircraft Corporation burned in 1930, thus ending his and Richmond's brief excursion into aviation history.

By January of 1931 Richmond was feeling the full effects of the depression. Building permits had dropped 86 percent from 1929 levels. New car sales lagged. Unemployment reached 18 percent in October. Farmers paid only the interest on their mortgages. All but 3 of Richmond's 35 major manufacturers were on part-time schedules by April 1932. By June unemployment stood at 26 percent. Only 1 plant operated a normal schedule, and 3 factories closed in early 1933.

By the fall of 1933 some 900 families had been removed from the relief rolls, and the government's aid programs began to put people back to work. The Works Progress Administration (WPA), for instance, helped fund such construction projects as a sewage treatment plant, a ball park, and a police station. Improvements were made on schools, streets, and parks. Johns-Manville established its insulation plant, and Crosley, makers of radios, refrigerators, and subcompact cars, relocated from Cincinnati in 1938. The same year city bus lines replaced the old streetcars.

Mobilization for war in 1941 increased employment, payrolls, and consumer spending, thus practically eliminating relief rolls and federal make-work projects. Factories converted to war materials production. Richmond Baking Company, for example, made K-rations instead of cakes. The war effort stimulated Richmond business, but the reconversion process and the variable economic conditions of the 1950s posed problems for maintaining the momentum. Industrial strikes, supply shortages, and decreased product demand immediately after the war was followed by the seesaw commercial affairs of the Eisenhower years. Industries generally were listless or folding in the 1950s. Major employers such as Starr Piano, F and N and Davis lawn mowers, Bucyrus-Erie, International Harvester, and Crosley shut down at a loss of thousands of jobs and retail dollars.

Richmond's black population, exceptionally vulnerable to economic drought and a discouraging community spirit, took steps to alter its traditional marginal station. A local branch of the National Association for the Advancement of Colored People (NAACP) was established in 1959 by Bobby Smith and Marion Williams. A year later the organization claimed to be the second largest in the state. The black leadership pressed for civil rights, decent housing, and jobs.

The downward economic trend was reversed in the 1960s due to a combination of a national business recovery and a public relations blitz by Richmond's Committee of 100, founded in 1954, and its successor, the Chamber of Commerce, established in 1966. Existing factories expanded into abandoned plants or built new ones. The huge Divco-Wayne busbody company, after announcing intentions in 1964 to move south, was persuaded to remain. The laying of the Interstate 70 Bypass drew motel, service station, and restaurant construction at the exits. Shopping centers opened east and west of the city.

Downtown merchants looked on these developments as a mixed blessing. The interstate

relieved the choking traffic on Main St. (US 40), but the shopping malls siphoned major department stores from the core district and hastened its deterioration. Twelve stores stood empty along Main St. in January 1963. Authorities tried to head off the problem by implementing plans ranging from federally funded urban renewal to free parking. By the spring of 1968 a new city hall was under construction just west of downtown, and discussions were under way for a mall-type shopping center for the central area. On April 6, 1968, an explosion leveled two downtown blocks, spread destruction over a 14-block area, killed 41 persons, and injured more than 100. The multimillion dollar blast, allegedly set off by gas leaks and gunpowder stored in a sporting goods store, hastened urban revitalization. In the tragedy's aftermath, amidst investigations and the filing of some 370 damage suits, the city administration launched a $2.8 million development program.

Between 1968 and 1983 a 10-block area east of the river was reshaped by some 10 new constructions and by a number of additions and remodelings into a dynamic retail, government, and learning center. In the shadow of the old courthouse rose the Richmond Municipal Building, the Wayne County Administration Building, housing for the Richmond Waterworks Corporation, a post office, and a modern library. The centerpiece of downtown's fresh look was the Richmond Promenade, a four-block-long pedestrian mall, later extended to five blocks. Highway 40 was rerouted, and its former path became an award-winning bricked corridor of greenery, fountains, and benches. After the Promenade's completion in 1972, business activity immediately picked up, signifying the end of shoppers' fears of entering the onetime disaster scene.

Elsewhere, the protection and restoration of old buildings got under way in 1973 with the formation of Old Richmond, Inc., now Historic Richmond, Inc., to encourage and administer historical preservation. In 1974 two historic districts, Old Richmond and Starr, together containing more than 300 structures of historical importance, were added to the National Register of Historic Places, thus safeguarding significant architecture from wanton destruction. From 1974 to the present Old Richmond, Inc., through its attractive quarterly and in cooperation with the local organizations Heritage

Restorations and Neighborhood Preservation Services has alerted homeowners and officials of the urgent need to retain the community's rich historical texture.

The downtown business resurgence was not the only bright spot in Richmond's economy in the 1970s. More than a dozen small firms began operations, and other companies expanded facilities. The community also welcomed a branch campus of Indiana University and the building projects on the campuses of Earlham College and Ivy Tech. Running counter to these advances was the lackluster performance of heavy industry. Two large plants, Avco and Huffman, closed at the height of the mid-1970s national recession. Unemployment ballooned to over 12 percent. The start-up of an American Motors engine line in 1975 softened the blow, but it phased out production by decade's end. Chrysler Corporation began factory construction in 1978 only to abandon its plans in 1980. Over the 1970s the number of county manufacturing jobs declined, and Richmond's population dropped by 6 percent.

The city's economic difficulties intensified in the early 1980s as the country's economy foundered. Richmond's major products—school bus bodies, fiberglass insulation, kitchen cabinets, wire, cable, camshafts, piston rings, machine tools, farm implements, gears—were closely linked to the faltering automobile, steel, and housing markets. The shrinking manufacture of durable goods, coupled with tight fiscal policies and consumer caution, depressed local industry. In 1982, as unemployment neared the 15 percent mark, Mayor Clifford Dickman declared the city "as poor as a fence mouse" and curtailed city services and capital improvements.

By mid-decade, however, circumstances had improved somewhat in the wake of the national recovery. All sectors of the city's economy reported better conditions. The awarding of an "enterprise zone" to the city in 1984 enlisted federal and state funds to encourage new jobs and businesses and the rehabilitation of existing structures in the north Richmond vicinity. City leaders could once again look to improving the quality of life by repairing streets and sidewalks, building new schools, easing thruway traffic, and erecting a civic center. The city's enrichment took three giant steps forward with the opening of the Whitewater Gorge Park in 1983, the establishment of an annual Jazz Festival in 1985, and the renovation of the old Leland Hotel (now the Radisson), the only downtown hotel, which promised to return some nightlife to the city's core.

Still, Richmond had to live with or near double digit unemployment. More than 1,200 jobs vanished between 1985 and 1987. Yet there continued to be bright spots. Tourism, particularly generated by the giant midsummer Richmond area Rose Festival, brought $3 million annually. The success of the Richmond Red Devils high school team on the basketball court helped galvanize community spirit. And, perhaps, the highlight of the 1980s for Richmond was its receiving an All-American City Award in 1987. Richmond was 1 of 8 chosen from 16 finalists out of 76 entrants (Seymour, Indiana, received honorable mention). Its efforts to reclaim the Whitewater River Gorge, to give incentives to increase attendance in schools, and to help laid-off workers get new jobs through Project COPE, convinced the judges that despite the city's difficulties over the last decade, it was a premier example of cooperative problem solving among citizens, business, and government.

Richmond Attractions

The **Wayne County Convention and Tourism Bureau**, 600 Main St., has available to visitors a packet of information on what to see and do in the Richmond area.

1. The **Wayne County Courthouse**, S. 4th and Main sts., is a Romanesque-style structure erected between 1890 and 1893 at a cost of nearly $300,000. James W. McLauglin, a Cincinnati architect, designed the government building, the second county courthouse to be located in Richmond. The first Richmond-based courthouse, a two-story brick structure, had been completed in 1873 for $22,700. Its replacement covered a city block and required 600 carloads of Bedford limestone, 3 million bricks, and 125 stonecutters. The massive castle-like building, scorned by critics as a white elephant to be underutilized, served Wayne County for 85 years. Beginning in 1978 the old courthouse transferred much of its business to the new center next door and received a thorough refurbishing. (*NRHP/HABS*)

2. The modern **Wayne County Courthouse and Administration Building**, just east of the old courthouse, contains the bulk of county departments. Ground breaking took place in 1976 for the two-story, L-shaped facility with its exterior of sloping glass walls. Moving into the new offices in 1978, county employees welcomed the colorful, well-lit, air-conditioned atmosphere of the spacious interior. The new government headquarters along with the adjacent Emergency Operations Center cost around $3.3 million.

3. The **Richmond Municipal Building**, across Main St. from the courthouse complex, houses the police department and city administrative offices. Begun just prior to the downtown explosion in 1968, the new $2 million city hall replaced quarters erected in 1886. One thousand roses were planted around the building in 1977.

4. The **Morrisson-Reeves Library**, 80 N. 6th St., is a new home for a very old city institution. Robert Morrisson, merchant and banker, established the library in 1864. In 1892 a memorial gift from Caroline Middleton Reeves allowed for expansion of the facility and specified its renaming. The present building, erected in 1974-75, is situated just south of the former library's location, now a parking lot. The $2.6 million brick structure includes a roomy, two-level interior with a capacity for 300,000 volumes. The Cincinnati architect Jack E. Hodell incorporated as much of the old library as possible into the new. Among the salvaged furnishings made use of are lights, clocks, tables, and paintings. Prominently displayed in a setting of four stained-glass windows from the old library is a large Tiffany-executed masterpiece entitled *Gutenburg and the Early Printers*, crafted in 1894 and dedicated to members of the Morrisson family. Architectural ornaments from the preceding building decorate the exterior walls and the courtyard at the lower level entranceway.

5. A few steps east of the government buildings and the library is the start of the **Richmond Promenade**, the five-block pedestrian mall that rose phoenix-like from the ashes of the 1968 disaster. A bird's-eye view of the 70 ft.-wide strip of the old National Rd. reveals a collage of white spherical shapes randomly plotted on a well-proportioned grid. At ground level the spheres become globes of street lights, mushroom-like canopies, masonry and fiberglass containers for plants, and rims encircling trees and fountains. Sidewalks divide expanses of brick and greenery dotted with benches, a small amphitheater, and a children's play area. A variety of business establishments border the mall. In the mid-1970s the American Associa-

tion of Nurserymen singled out the Promenade for an award for landscaping excellence.

6. Among the several points of interest along the Promenade is the **First National Bank**, a landmark at the corner of 7th and Main sts. since its founding in 1863 as the state's first chartered national bank. It is now the country's sixth oldest national bank. A million dollar building and remodeling project, launched in 1972, resulted in a new exterior of bronze-hued panels and floor-to-ceiling glass, along with a two-story addition of glass framed by quartz-white columns.

7. On the north side of the Promenade at 726 Main St. is a small wall plaque just west of the People's Federal Savings Association building. The marker commemorates the life of **Charles Francis Jenkins**. The plaque reads: "To the memory of C. Francis Jenkins, inventor of the original motion picture machine, who projected the first moving picture ever shown in Richmond in this building." Jenkins, a resident of Wayne County from 1870 to 1886, brought his invention to Richmond in 1894 and reproduced on a wall of the Jenkins Jewelry Store a moving image of a dancer. Somewhat later he sold his creation because it had attracted little interest. He went on to establish Jenkins Laboratories in Washington, D.C., where he invented a number of products including the conical paper cup. He pioneered in television through his developments in transmitting weather maps to ships at sea in the 1920s. Jenkins received an honorary Doctor of Science degree from Earlham College in 1929 and several medals from the Franklin Institute of Philadelphia.

8. **Knollenberg's** department store, between 8th and 9th sts. on the Promenade, began operation in 1866 when 18-year-old George H. Knollenberg (1848-1918) set up shop on the site of the present store. In 1877 he built the first of three buildings comprising Knollenberg's today. The three-story, mid-Victorian structure cost $13,000 and featured wrought- and cast-iron balconies. The east building was constructed in 1888 and an annex on 8th St. in 1898. Many Knollenberg employees established their own stores in Richmond and elsewhere.

9. The **Radisson Hotel** (formerly the Leland), 900 S. A St., officially opened in 1928 on the site of the Richmond Casket Factory. The Detroit-based Continental-Leland Corporation built and operated the hotel, one of a chain. Room rates in 1928 began at two dollars, more for an apartment on the top floor of the seven-story building. On its roof was painted a huge yellow arrow directing airplanes to the airport two miles away. The hotel was sold to the Miller Brothers of Dayton, Ohio, in 1963, who remodeled it into the Leland Motor Inn. Falling on hard times in recent years, the hotel seemed primed for the wrecker's ball until a group of Kentucky investors purchased the property. Richmond's only downtown hotel received a $5.5 million face-lift in 1985 and opened as a Radisson in 1986. (*NRHP*)

10. Just beyond the end of the Promenade is the **Murray Theatre**, 1003 E. Main St. The present home of the Richmond Civic Theatre was constructed in 1909 by O. G. Murray, a theater entrepreneur who earlier built the Phillips Opera House. Later the Murray Theatre became the Indiana Theatre and in 1968 the Norbert Silbiger Theatre. Silbiger came to Richmond in 1940 as an Austrian refugee. He organized the Richmond Civic Theatre in 1941 and served many years as its director. In 1952 the local troupe moved into the theater building. The three-story buff brick structure seats more than 600 persons. The 1909 fire curtain with its pastoral scene is still used occasionally, and the original seats have been restored. In 1984 the building was renamed for Murray while the theater's auditorium retained the Silbiger designation. (*NRHP*)

11. The **Indiana Football Hall of Fame**, N. A and 9th sts., was established in 1973 through the efforts of a group of local sports enthusiasts. Housed in a former post office building, the Hall of Fame's inductees number about 175. Mementos, enshrined in the gold and blue exhibit area, honor such Hoosier gridiron greats as Knute Rockne, Pete Pihos, and Weeb Eubank.

12. The **Mendenhall-Clay Marker**, N. A and 7th sts., chronicles an important incident in the life of Henry Clay. Clay spoke at a political rally held near this spot on October 1, 1842. Hiram Mendenhall, a Randolph County

Richmond Attractions

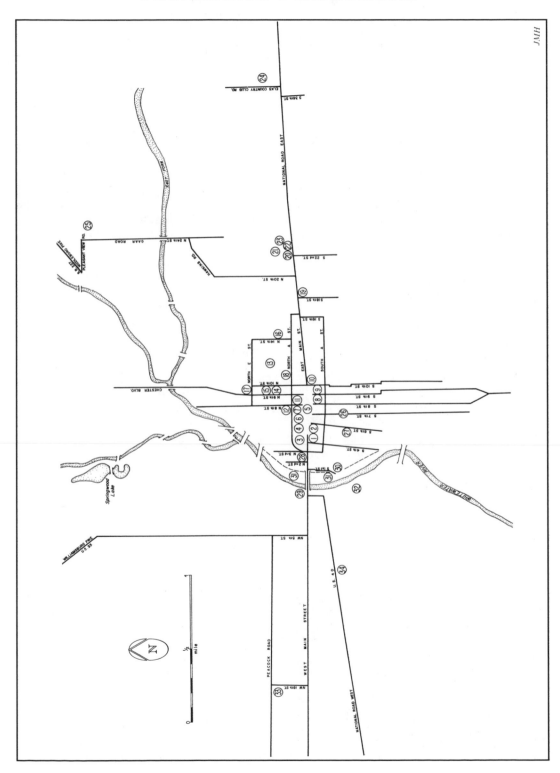

Quaker, presented Clay a petition requesting him to free his 50 slaves. Clay rejected the petition diplomatically but blundered when he, in effect, told Mendenhall to go home and mind his own business. Over time there arose a popular, but erroneous, belief that Clay's antislavery stance and his retort to Mendenhall cost him the 1844 presidential election.

13. The **Starr Historic District** (*NRHP/HABS*) stretches from the alley between N. 9th and N. 10th sts. to N. 16th St. with N. A and N. E sts. being the southern and northern boundaries, respectively. The area covers 25 blocks and contains 120 structures of historical importance. The locale always encompassed the residences of the local elite. The centerpiece of the Starr District is the **Andrew F. Scott Mansion** at 126 N. 10th St. Built in 1858, members of the Scott family resided in the Italianate structure for 119 years. The Virginia-born Andrew F. Scott, a prominent farmer and industrialist, organized the Second National Bank in 1872 and presided over the institution for 20 years. His brick house, now painted a tan with light beige trim, features an ornate cupola. In 1977 Martha Scott, a descendant, bequeathed the home to the Wayne County Historical Museum. The museum restored the home and furnished it with the museum's fine collection of Victorian furniture. (*NRHP/HABS*)

Indiana Historical Society (C1242)

Leland Hotel

14. The **Miller home**, 222 N. 10th St., is an Italianate town villa constructed in 1870 and lived in for about 40 years by John F. Miller, a Pennsylvania Railroad executive. Miller owned the property bought by the city in 1885 and developed into the Glen Miller Park. Since 1927 the house has been a funeral home.

15. The house known as **High Tower**, 326 N. 10th St., was built around 1870 by Elizabeth Starr. Her husband, Charles West Starr, a distant cousin of the noted Philadelphia painter Benjamin West, purchased 240 acres from Jeremiah Cox in 1826 and proved instrumental in the development of north Richmond. James M. Starr, a son, helped in the organization of the Starr Piano Company and lived in the eclectic-style Victorian home into the 1890s.

16. The house at 201 N. 14th, though not architecturally noteworthy, is worth mentioning because it was the residence of **Micajah C. Henley**, the "roller skate king." The roller skate was not invented in Richmond, but Henley's development of the ball-bearing skate wheel and a toe clamp fastened with a key rather than a screwdriver are milestones in the history of the skate. Henley patented his Chicago Skate in 1884, three years after he opened his factory. The large Turkish boxwood wheels became a Henley trademark. The Henley skates continued to be made until World War II. The old factory is on N. E St. one block north of N. 16th St.

17. The magnificent **Pennsylvania Railroad Depot**, between 9th and 10th sts. on N. E St., was built in 1902. The $200,000 station, the third on the site, followed the design drawn up by the renowned architect Daniel H. Burnham, whose portfolio included the plans for the Union Station in Washington, D.C. The terminal is constructed of red brick with white terra-cotta trim. The entranceway features a portico having four two-story brick columns. The architectural style of the building has been called Roman-Renaissance. The Norfolk and Western Railway purchased the station from Conrail in 1981 and planned to tear it down. The outcry from preservationists and city officials has thus far prevented its destruction. Projecting the station as the keystone of Richmond's new Enterprise Zone and the proposed Fort Wayne Ave. Historic District, the city pur-

chased the property from Norfolk and Western in 1985 and is holding it for future sale and development.

18. The **Hicksite Friends Meetinghouse/Julia Meek Gaar Wayne County Historical Museum**, 1150 N. A St., is one of Indiana's most highly regarded museums. The establishment of the museum in 1929 came about through the donation of the 1865 Hicksite Meetinghouse to the Wayne County Historical Society and through the efforts of Julia Gaar (1859-1944). She gave generously of her time, money, and worldwide acquisitions, including the 13th-century bust of Buddha on the east lawn. Additional lots were added to the grounds in 1930 and 1954. Among the collections of special interest in the brick meetinghouse is the exhibit pertaining to Gaar Williams, a Richmond native who gained fame as a cartoonist for the *Indianapolis News* and the *Chicago Tribune*. A showcase of items connected with Julia Gaar stands under her portrait by Indiana artist Wayman Adams. A pair of Henley silver skates and an unusual Henley bicycle with two movable handlebars attest to

the originality of the roller skate magnate, Micajah C. Henley. On the lower floor is a reconstructed street of well-stocked 19th-century shops, a display of locally made automobiles, and the inventions of movie and television pioneer Charles Francis Jenkins. An Egyptian room contains a mummy obtained by Mrs. Gaar in 1929 and brought out of Egypt only after personal intervention by President Herbert Hoover. The museum grounds include buildings housing farm equipment and machinery, antique hand tools, and looms. A village square features functioning reproductions of the 1890-style Palladium Printing Office and the Richmond Baking Company. Nearby is the two-story Dickinson log house along with Richmond's first schoolhouse, erected in 1812. (*NRHP/HABS*)

19. The **Gennett home,** 1829 E. Main St., is an imposing pillared, three-story Colonial Revival-style house built in 1900 by Henry Gennett (1852-1922), a founder and president of the Starr Piano Company. In 1916 Gennett launched the recording division of his piano

Indiana Historical Society (C4186)

Wayne County Historical Museum

firm and made music history with his Gennett label's parade of pioneering jazz musicians. The Gennett home was turned into apartments in 1940. The World Life and Accident Association purchased the property in 1982 for use as its home offices. While converting the interior for business purposes the insurance company has succeeded in remaining faithful to much of the original design, even to restoring the third floor T-shaped ballroom. Artworks, owned by the company or on loan, are scattered throughout the home. (*NRHP*)

20. The **Madonna of the Trail Statue** stands at the entrance to Glen Miller Park, 22nd and E. Main sts. Unveiled in 1928, the 18-ft.-high monument honors the hardy pioneer woman and was the 9th of 12 such sculptures placed along the National Old Trails Rd. (US 40), from Maryland to California, by the Daughters of the American Revolution (DAR). Utah-born artist Mahroni Young (1877-1957) executed the sculpture designed by August Leimbach of St. Louis. Among the four inscriptions on the base of the Madonna statue is one indicating the nearby site of Indiana's first tollgate on the National Rd., a fact also recorded on a marker just east of the park entrance.

21. **Glen Miller Park** comprises 194 acres of picnic grounds, golf links, tennis courts, playgrounds, a zoo, a lake, winding timber-lined roads, and the All-America City rose garden. Col. John F. Miller purchased 135 acres of the future park site in 1880. He partially developed the land as a recreational area prior to 1885 when he sold it to the city for $35,000. The old Maple Grove Cemetery, covering several acres near present E. Main and 22nd sts., was one of several plots the city added to the park. The graves were moved to Earlham College in 1887. A city park commission was formed in 1891 with E. Gurney Hill, a founder of Hill's rose companies, as an official. The park board adopted a $20,000 improvement program and imported experts, such as John Thorpe, chief of floriculture at the 1893 Columbian Exposition, to help plan and implement the Miller project. The term "glen" in the park's name is not a person's name, but rather refers to the beauty of the landscape.

22. The **E. G. Hill Memorial Rose Garden**, just east of Miller Park's entrance, is a tribute to E.

Gurney Hill, park commissioner, whose rose business bordered the park between 1887 and 1907. The memorial was dedicated in 1937 by the Richmond Garden Club. The Hill Memorial Fountain, sculpted by Jon Johnson of Frankfort, Indiana, is situated amidst dozens of varieties of roses, some 70 kinds at last count. The fountain bowl was damaged by lightning and was replaced in 1948. The gazing globe on the figural pedestal was placed there in 1957 at the time of Hill's death. The sundial at the rear of the garden is dedicated to E. G. Hill's son, Joseph H. Hill.

23. The **Samuel Charles home**, directly behind the Hill Memorial Garden, is said to have been built in 1813 by Charles (1759-1849), a native of North Carolina. The colonial house, constructed of grey stone and stucco, often hosted weary travelers of the National Rd. and fugitive slaves. Reportedly the parlor's fireplace embodied a removable flagstone revealing steps to a large cellar equipped to hide Canada-bound slaves. The home, minus its west wing, subsequently became the clubhouse of the Richmond Garden Club. It retains the garden club affiliation though the first floor is now shared with other groups renting its space and the second floor is the caretaker's apartment.

24. The **Hayes Regional Arboretum**, 801 Elks Rd., is a 355-acre botanical garden cultivated for scientific and educational aims. Ohio-born Stanley W. Hayes (1865-1963) moved his Hayes Track Appliance Company from Geneva, New York, to Richmond in 1911. The founder patented the Hayes Derail, a device to prevent fouling a main line with unauthorized side track rolling stock, and over 60 products related to railway track safety appliances. In the meantime he assembled an estate of almost 300 acres, the bulk of the arboretum. It is a "regional" garden because species of trees, shrubs, and vines, mostly planted by the Hayes family, are limited to those native to the Whitewater River Basin. Among the many features of the nature complex are a nature center in a 180-year-old barn, children's garden, wilderness-era forest of maple and beech trees, and the Native Woody Plant Preserve, containing representatives of the arboretum's 181 native plants. In addition there is a three-and-one-half-mile auto tour route, walking trails, and Indiana's first solar-heated greenhouse. The preserve provides

an outdoor classroom for scientists, home land-scapers, and children. Summer courses are held for all grades through college sophomore. Plantings from the arboretum beautify highways and public buildings. In 1983 the prestigious All-America Rose Selection, Inc. (AARS), which tests and recommends new varieties of roses, picked the Hayes facility to operate a demonstration rose garden.

25. The **Gaar mansion**, 2411 Pleasant View Rd., is one of the area's finest historical and architectural structures. Designed by Richmond native John Hasecoster, the $20,000 Franco-American brick structure went up in 1876. Abram Gaar founded Gaar, Scott and Company, manufacturers of steam threshers, and he could well afford the luxury of an opulent home with a mansard roof incorporating the name A. Gaar in its tile covering. The house is now owned by a great-granddaughter of A. Gaar. Many of the furnishings are original. (*NRHP*)

26. The **Old Richmond Historic District** (*NRHP/HABS*) covers 250 acres between S. 11th St. and the Chesapeake and Ohio Railroad and between S. A and S. E sts. Historically the district is a mixed commercial, industrial, and residential neighborhood. In 1975 restoration of some of the 213 structures of historical importance began when Old Richmond, Inc., purchased Cutter's Corner, S. 4th and D sts. Cutter's Corner consists of an 1825 two-story brick, Federal town house and an 1893 building that served the community as a grocery until 1973. Old Richmond, Inc., sold the buildings in 1978.

27. The **Bethel African Methodist Episcopal Church**, 200 S. 6th St., was organized in 1836 by Bishop William Paul Quinn, who founded more than 50 churches in the Midwest. The Bethel parishioners first worshiped in a frame warehouse. In 1869 church officials bought the German Methodist Church on the present site. In 1892 the Rev. James M. Townsend (1841-1913) remodeled the old church, adding a Romanesque-style nave. (*NRHP/HABS*) Townsend, the first black to serve in the Indiana legislature, 1885, and the recorder of deeds under President Benjamin Harrison, is credited with instigating the desegregation process in the Richmond educational system by enrolling his daughter in an all-white school. In 1921 a community center was named in honor of Townsend. A new Townsend Community Center, located in the 800 block of N. 12th St., was dedicated in 1966.

28. The **Swayne, Robinson and Company foundry**, between N. 2nd and 3rd sts. on E. Main St., dates from 1842 when Francis W. Robinson established a small machine shop. Robinson's business expanded into manufacturing steam engines, boilers, and threshing machines. The present red brick factory buildings were put up in 1854. Robinson and Company, incorporated in 1889, became Swayne, Robinson and Company in 1915. Samuel Swayne, Robinson's son-in-law, was hired as a salesman. He quickly climbed the ladder of success to the president's chair. The Robinson family eventually bought out the Swayne interests but retained the name. Between 1914 and 1920 the business discontinued its agricultural machinery line and responded to the needs of the lawn mower industry. A fifth generation Robinson today heads the company, which makes castings for a variety of regional businesses.

29. The **Richmond Gas Company Building**, north of the E. Main St. bridge, was built by the utility in 1854. The L-shaped brick structure with its copper-colored roof housed equipment to produce artificial gas for lighting streets and homes. After gas manufacturing ended in 1941 the building was used as a service center until 1977 when a new complex of buildings, along US 27 north of I-70, was completed. In the late 1970s the city purchased the vacated building, and it is presently being used by the Park Department for storage. (*NRHP/HAER*)

30. A fragment of the **Starr Piano Company** building and its subsidiary, Gennett Records, can be seen by going south on S. 1st St. at the east end of the E. Main St. bridge. Established in 1872, the Starr Piano Company complex, which numbered as many as 31 buildings, dominated the industrial makeup of the Whitewater River gorge until the factory closed in 1952. In its heyday Starr annually produced millions of records in addition to thousands of pianos and phonographs. At one time the company alternated music publishing with refrigerator manufacturing. (*NRHP/HAER*)

31. The **Whitewater Gorge Park** covers around 159 acres along three and one-half miles of the East Fork of the Whitewater River. Left barren of mills and factories as waterpower and stone gave way to other sources of energy and building materials, the slice of river bottom was neglected—but not forgotten. Transforming the gorge for public recreation got under way in 1966 with the formation of the Society for the Preservation and Use of Resources (SPUR). A series of organizations, studies, and reports led to the acquisition of land using federal, state, city, and private funds. The process of obtaining land was completed in early 1983, and the park was dedicated in April of that year. The marked trail along the west bank of the river through the gorge passes by waterfalls, steep valley walls, quarry, mill, factory sites, bridges, abundant foliage, and wildlife. There are four main entrances to the gorge trail: Test Rd. at the south end, Thistlethwaite Falls at the north end with parking in Springwood Park, at G St. and Whitewater Blvd., and on the Sim Hodgin Parkway below the N. D St. or Richmond Ave. bridge.

32. **McGuire Memorial Hall** on the campus of Richmond High School, 350 Whitewater Blvd., is the home of the Richmond Art Association, organized in 1898. In 1910 the Oliver P. Morton High School was erected at N. 9th and B sts. Art enthusiasts gained a portion of the new building for a gallery. An interesting tile facade graces the upper exterior east wall of the Morton school, now insurance company offices. Henry Mercer of Doylestown, Pennsylvania, at the time of the school's construction, inlaid tiles in the forms of figures representing industries such as glass blowing, stonecutting, blacksmithing, carpentry, and others. As an educational facility, Morton High School was inadequate from the start, but nearly three decades passed before the erection of the present school. In 1939 the academic building, named Morton Hall, was dedicated along with the gymnasium-civic auditorium. Two years later officials held dedication ceremonies for McGuire Memorial Hall. Charles McGuire, of Dille and McGuire Manufacturing Company, contributed $50,000 for the building of an art museum as a memorial to his mother. McGuire also furnished four large ceramic vases, two of which are set in exterior wall niches near the entrance. The museum contains four galleries, an auditorium, library, and workrooms. Among its most prized possessions is the self-portrait of famed Hoosier artist William Merritt Chase, painted expressly for the art association between 1911 and 1916. The valuable painting left Richmond for the first time in 1983 to be the centerpiece for a show of Chase artworks in Seattle and New York City.

33. **Hill Floral Products, Inc.**, .6 mile north of US 40 at 2117 Peacock Rd., is the administrative and sales headquarters for the **Joseph H. Hill** and the **E. G. Hill** companies, located on NW 18th St. between Peacock Rd. and the Richmond State Hospital. Hills' Roses, as the companies are known collectively, celebrated in 1981 a century of existence. With 42 acres under glass, Hills' Roses turns out 30 million flowers annually, making it a world leader in the production of cut flowers. When Joseph H. Hill died in 1958, it was estimated that he and his father, E. Gurney Hill, were responsible for developing 75 to 80 percent of all indoor roses grown in the United States. The names of Hills' rose varieties have often reflected prominent personalities or events of the day: Better Times (1932), Snow White (1939), Edith Willkie (1942), Coral Sea (1943), President Eisenhower (1953), Independence '76, and Lady Diana.

34. **Earlham College**, 1000 block of W. National Rd., since its founding has gained worldwide recognition and respect for its high academic standards (the majority of graduates work toward advanced degrees). The Quaker values of tolerance and social responsibility infuse its innovative liberal arts curriculum. The Earlham School of Religion, a college division, is the only degree-granting Quaker seminary in the world. In 1832 the Indiana Yearly Meeting of Friends authorized the purchase of 320 acres west of the Whitewater River as the site for a boarding school to supply education beyond the elementary level. A scarcity of operational funds prevented the opening of the Friends Boarding School until 1847. The school became Earlham College in 1859 when it added a collegiate department and began granting degrees. Earlham takes its name from Earlham Hall, the ancestral home of the Gurney family, well-known Quakers of Norwich, England. Joseph John Gurney visited his fellow Quakers in Richmond in 1837 and encouraged them on their educational plans. Gurney's sister, Eliza-

beth Gurney Fry, helped lead a prison reform movement in England. Between 1847 and 1887 Earlham's campus was made up of two buildings, old Earlham Hall and the observatory, and around 250 students. Today there are some 25 academic, residence, and service buildings, not counting athletic and off-campus housing facilities, and a student body of about 1,000. Attractions on the campus include the **Stout Memorial Meetinghouse**, located west of Earlham Hall. Opened in 1952, the all-purpose structure was largely paid for by descendants of an early southern Indiana family. Some of the beams, bricks, balustrade, and facing benches came from a 200-year-old meetinghouse at Wymondham, England, a few miles from the Gurney home. The **Joseph Moore Museum** is part of the Dennis Hall science complex. Joseph Moore, a student at the early boarding school, and subsequently professor of natural sciences and geology, museum curator, and president of the college, 1868-83, collected much of the museum's holdings. The displays of the cabinet, as museums were then called,

initially were mounted and exhibited in old Earlham Hall. In 1888 the specimens were moved to the newly completed Lindley Hall. When Lindley Hall burned in 1924, taking with it a quarter of the 45,000 items, the remainder was distributed around the campus until transferred to the new wing of Dennis Hall after 1952. Among the attractions in the museum are the skeleton of a mastodon over 11 ft. tall, a mummy, and the most complete fossil of a giant beaver in the country. The **Observatory**, the oldest building on the campus, cost $400 to build in 1861. It was the first observatory in Indiana and the centerpiece of possibly the sixth oldest astronomy department in the nation. The dome is mounted so precisely on its 15 x 40-ft. base that it can be turned by hand. The smaller telescope includes a transit used at Fort Sumter during the firing of the Civil War's first volley. During an epidemic in the college's early years, the last five healthy students sought refuge in the observatory until the danger passed. (*NRHP/HABS*)

Tour 4

From Earlham College travel west on US 40 *3.9 m.* to **CENTERVILLE** (p. 2,284). Four years after being platted by Henry Bryan in 1814, Centerville took possession of the seat of justice from Salisbury and subsequently became a major city on the National Rd. As business boomed and as space along the National Rd. became unavailable, structures went up in front of existing buildings thus reducing the width of the main thoroughfare from 100 to 65 ft. Row houses, with shared or "party" sidewalls, became another adjustment to the economy of space. Arched passageways or alleys, of which seven survive, led from the street to the original dwellings at the rear. Often, rooms were built above the archways to provide additional street-side accessibility. Centerville's decline paralleled Richmond's rise as a railway center after 1853. Travelers shifted from the National Rd. to trains.

In 1873 Richmond, then the acknowledged population center of the county, divested Centerville of its county seat status. Between 1870 and 1900, Centerville's population decreased by one quarter, reaching an all-time low of 785 in 1900. The city slumbered for the next 60 years. Meanwhile, its architecture remained practically untouched. Today, Centerville is essentially a tourist mecca with an outstanding ensemble of historically and architecturally significant buildings and more than a dozen antique shops. The original platted portion of the city bounded by North, 3rd, and South sts. and Willow Grove Rd. is a registered historic district. (*NRHP/HABS*)

A small stone marker erected in 1834 by the surveyors of the National Rd. rests on the front lawn of a private residence *.4 m.* east of the Centerville city limits on the north side of US 40. Its inscription, almost obliterated, tells travelers they are nine miles from the state line, four and one-half miles from Richmond, and one mile east of Centerville.

Centerville was the first town along the National Rd. to have its section paved with stone. This paving took place in 1836, about the same time that a covered bridge was being erected across the Whitewater River at Richmond and a famous hostelry was under construction in Centerville. The **Mansion House**, now the headquarters of Historic Centerville, Inc., stands on the north side of US 40 at 214 E. Main St. (*.4 m.* from the town limits sign). The three-story brick Greek Revival-style building was built by Henry Rowan and functioned for many years as a tavern, inn, and stopover for mail coaches. A plaque on the front of the Mansion House memorializes pioneer journalist John Scott, editor of Centerville's *Western Emporium* and publisher of the *Indiana Gazetteer*—the earliest scholarly description of the state (1826). Scott committed suicide in Logansport in 1838.

In the next block west, at the northwest corner of E. Main and 1st sts., stands the old **Sheriff's house**, now occupied by a Masonic lodge. It centered largely in the "courthouse wars" of the early 1870s. Built in 1868, along with a jail, at a cost of $80,000, the Italianate-style structure briefly housed county records prior to their removal to the new courthouse at Richmond. Unwilling to give up the records without a fight, Alfred Lashley and James Dearth of Centerville fired a cannon load of iron scraps at the sheriff's house from an archway across the street at 139 E. Main St. The discharge from old Black Betsy scared off the jail guard from Richmond but forced the calling in of state militiamen to restore order and help convey the ledgers to Richmond. The jail was torn down eventually. However, the sheriff's house remains along with the scars of the cannon blast evident on the wall at the upper left of the front door.

One block north of the Masonic building, on the northwest corner of N. 1st and E. Plum sts., is the former residence of **Jacob B. Julian**

(1815-1898). Julian, Centerville attorney, bank president, and two-term state legislator, 1846-49, built the L-shaped, two-story brick home, with its open porch, around 1856. His brother George served in Congress and won the candidacy for vice-president on the Free Soil party ticket in 1852. As a young Centerville lawyer, George launched the Dark Lyceum—an unusual society in which members debated in the dark to help overcome timidity. Julian's other brother, Isaac, was a writer, journalist, and Centerville's postmaster during the Civil War. In the early 1870s Jacob, fearing economic loss with the removal of the courthouse to Richmond, moved to the Indianapolis area and co-founded Irvington. He was judge of the Marion County circuit court from 1876 through 1878.

The two-story Federal-style house at 214 W. Main St. was built by **Israel Abram**, a Jewish pioneer and merchant. It contained a wagon shop on the first floor and a meeting room above it. Between 1823 and 1827 Webb Lodge No. 24 of the Masons met in the second floor room. The Masons controlled access through a specially built one-man stairway in the arch. The Lantz family, proprietors of the wagon shop, lived in the adjoining brick home.

The **Morton home**, one-time residence of Indiana governor Oliver P. Morton, sits back from the road one block west on the southeast corner of W. Main St. and Willow Grove Rd. Presently owned by Historic Centerville, Inc., the brick Greek Revival-style structure, atop a terraced knoll, was built in 1848 by Jacob Julian. Morton, born in the old county seat town of Salisbury in 1823 to a boot maker, rose from an apothecary clerk to become governor, 1861-67, and United States senator, 1867-77. Morton purchased the home from Julian in 1857 for $5,000 and sold it in 1863, living in it no more than three years. (*NRHP/HABS*)

Turn left onto Willow Grove Rd. and proceed south two blocks. Turn east onto W. School St. One block on the right, at the southeast corner of W. School and S. Ash sts. in a fenced-in area in front of the old high school building, is a memorial on the site of the **Whitewater Seminary and College**. Begun in 1827 as a county seminary, the school provided the rudiments of education for such notables as Oliver P. Morton; George Julian; Lew Wallace, author of *Ben Hur*; Maj. Gen. Ambrose E. Burnside, famed Union Civil War officer; and John Burbank, governor of the Dakota Territory in the Grant administration. The main structure and two wings of the seminary were constructed between 1827 and 1844. The seminary evolved into a college under the supervision of the Methodists by the late 1840s, becoming the Whitewater Female College and Whitewater Academy, successively. In 1853 a branch of the school was established in Richmond. During the late 1850s A. B. Shortridge taught at the college. He subsequently moved to Indianapolis to become superintendent of schools and received the honor of having a high school named after him. The Methodists withdrew their support in 1865, and the school struggled in private hands until sold to Centerville and converted to a public school in 1870. The seminary and college buildings burned in 1891.

From Centerville, return to downtown Richmond by way of US 40 and follow US 27 (off S. 8th St.) north *8.9 m.* to **FOUNTAIN CITY** (p. 839). Called New Garden when laid out in 1818, the town's name changed to Newport in 1834, and, again, to Fountain City in 1878 to end confusion with a Newport in Vermillion County. The name Fountain City supposedly was derived from the sulphur fountains located in the town.

Fountain City gained fame as the so-called Grand Central Station of the "underground railroad" in the pre-Civil War era. Several thousand slaves made their way to Fountain City along the major escape routes leading from Jeffersonville, Madison, and Cincinnati. Levi and Katherine Coffin's home was an important shelter for the fleeing slaves before they continued north. The restored **Levi Coffin house** is a Fountain City landmark, located one block north of the intersection with Fountain City Rd. on the southeast corner of US 27 and Mill St. (*HABS*) It was the first structure in the state to be listed on the National Register of Historic Places (1966). Levi Coffin (1798-1877), a North Carolina Quaker, moved with his family to Fountain City in 1826 and became a leading merchant and miller. He built the present home, his second, in 1839. Five years later Coffin began selling only free labor-produced articles in his store (goods produced in the South but not by slave labor). In 1847 Coffin moved to Cincinnati to open a wholesale free labor store to supply retail outlets. He subsequently ran a commission business in farm produce and a boardinghouse. In the midst of the Civil War, he became the general agent for the Western Freedmen's Aid Commission, raising funds for aiding the liberated Afro-Americans. The Coffin house was purchased by the state in 1967 and leased to the Wayne County Historical Society for renovation and maintenance as a museum. The building changed owners a dozen times and served as an apartment building after 1911, requiring extensive work for restoration. Once the original structure was uncovered though, it showed few signs of mistreatment. The house is now furnished with period accoutrements and some objects connected with the Coffin family. The marker on the grave of William Bush in the adjacent cemetery was placed there in 1983 by the great-granddaughter of the former slave who found shelter at the Coffin house. His wooden shoes, pictured on the marker, are on display in the house.

Return to the caution light in Fountain City and turn left onto Fountain City Rd. Proceed east *2.5 m.* to the road's end at Arba Pike. Go north on Arba Pike *2.3 m.* and turn right onto Bethel Rd., continuing *1.7 m.* into the town of **BETHEL**. The unincorporated town was settled in 1817 by the Harlan family of Kentucky. In 1844 it took the name of Bethel after the Christian Church in the locality. The **Bethel Christian Church** was organized in 1821 and is considered the first church of that denomination north of US 40. The present church building, located south of the main intersection in town on the left side of IND 227, was constructed in 1893. A plaque on the church's north lawn gives its history.

From Bethel return to Arba Pike, which follows the Quaker Trace, blazed in 1817 by pioneer Quaker settlers of the Richmond area to establish a trade route to the Miami Indians at Kekionga (Fort Wayne). Head north on Arba Pike through fairly level farmlands. The flatness of the topography is deceiving for this is actually the vicinity of the **state's highest elevation**. From the Bethel Rd. turnoff onto Arba Pike *1.3 m.* is the Wayne-Randolph county line (for a description of Randolph County see Tour 3). About a mile east along the county line road is an unmarked spot *.4 m.* south, in Wayne County, which geologists say is the highest point in the state at 1,257 ft. In this general area are the headwaters of eight major rivers including the Whitewater, the Wabash, the Big Miami, and the White rivers. Farmers in the locale note that their lands drain water in all directions.

The unincorporated town of **ARBA** lies *.2 m.* north of the county line. Although the origin of the town's name is a mystery, the town itself began with the establishment of a Friends' meetinghouse in 1815. A year earlier the Thomas Parker family had settled in the vicinity. They were probably the first residents of Randolph County. In the early years, Arba was the largest settlement in the county; the Friends' meeting reported 276 members in 1823. However, the village was not officially platted until 1855. The newer brick and frame **Friends' meetinghouse** can be seen on the left near the south edge of town.

Through Arba on Arba Pike bear slightly to the right *.6 m.* past the meetinghouse. North *3.5 m.* is the small town of **SPARTANBURG**, laid out in 1832 and called Newburg until 1842 when the new post office took the name Spartanburg. Past the town limits sign *1.2 m.*, turn right on CR 600S. At *1.9 m.*, visible from the road but on private farmland, southeast of the intersection with CR 850E, stands a two-story brick schoolhouse, the **Union Literary Institute**. Established by Friends in 1845 and chartered by the state in 1848, the school provided elementary and secondary-level education for north central Indiana students, especially blacks. Four members of the original board were blacks. In 1849 the school enrolled 230 students, over 70 percent of whom were black. Resident students lived in an L-shaped, two-story frame structure and initially attended classes in a log building. The present brick schoolhouse replaced the log building in 1860. The guiding hand of the institute was Ebenezer Tucker, principal from 1846 to 1856, who subsequently headed Liber College in Jay County from 1859 to 1868. The school's enrollment declined after the Civil War as public schools extended educational rights to black students. Most of the school property was sold in 1869, and the township leased the schoolhouse for a public school. After 1908 pupils went to the newly constructed Spartanburg High School. Finally, in 1914 officials shut down the school, and five years later the state General Assembly disposed of the property. The school left a legacy in the form of scholarship money for minority students that is given out by a committee and was raised from the sale of the school's lands in 1869.

Tour 4

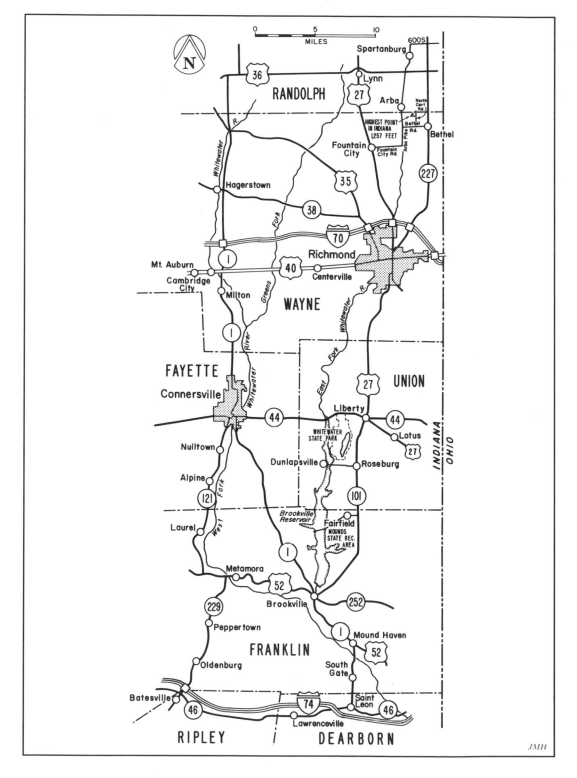

JMH

From the Union Literary Institute return west .5 m. to a stop sign and turn left onto CR 800E (IND 227). Proceed south 2 m. to US 36. Go west on US 36 6 m. to **LYNN** (p. 1,250), which was devastated by tornadoes in March 1986. The two twisters damaged 284 buildings, including the destruction of 24 homes. Amazingly there were no deaths or injuries in the $4 million catastrophe. Continue west on US 36 to Modoc and follow IND 1 west and south 9.5 m., reentering Wayne County, to IND 38. Follow IND 38 west into **HAGERSTOWN** (p. 1,950). Originally called Elizabethtown when settled by New Jersey migrants around 1815, the village became Hagerstown in 1836, so designated presumably by former residents of Hagerstown, Maryland. The town's expansion was delayed until workmen completed the section of the Whitewater Canal from Cambridge City to Hagerstown in 1847. For the next six years Hagerstown experienced a boom. Its population exceeded 600 by 1850. Financial and climatic misfortunes forced closing of the canal in 1853, and the town resumed its former pattern of snail-like growth. Hagerstown had a net gain of 32 people in the decade of the 1850s.

Today, many Hagerstown residents work for the **Perfect Circle Division of Dana Corporation**. This well-known maker of piston rings, and other machine and engine parts, had its start in Hagerstown. The Teetor brothers, bicycle repairmen of Muncie, Indiana, organized the Railway Cycle Manufacturing Company in Hagerstown in 1895 to produce a lightweight railway inspection pedal car. The product was essentially a bicycle with a pair of flanged wheels extending on either side and was pedaled like a bicycle. After 1902 the business became the Light Inspection Car Company and made automobile engines and piston rings along with the railway car. These new items soon became the company's primary products, and the firm changed names again to the Teetor-Hartley Motor Company in 1914. Four years later the engine division was sold to the Ansted Engineering Company of Connersville, Indiana. The Hagerstown plant continued making piston rings under the name of Indiana Piston Ring Company. The trade name Perfect Circle was adopted for advertising purposes and later became the company name. The firm became a subsidiary of Dana Corporation of Toledo, Ohio, in 1963. Turn right to Perfect Circle's packaging plant on the left side of IND 38, .3 m. west of IND 1. The manufacturing is done at the older complex at 552 S. Washington St. Proceed .3 m. west and turn left. The factory is .2 m. on the right.

Return to IND 38, turn right, and pass the Independent Order of Odd Fellows (IOOF) building erected in 1880 at Main and Perry sts. In 1974 Historic Hagerstown, Inc., purchased the three-story, iron front structure, renting the first floor to retailers and creating a **museum** on the second floor. Originally it was an auditorium for opera, dramas, skating, dancing, and basketball. The walls of the museum are decorated with murals painted in 1913 by local artist Charles Lucien Newcomb. In addition to the murals, the museum features a collection of historical artifacts related to the Perfect Circle Company, including a railway pedal car. Old dental tools of a local practitioner and items pertaining to the Whitewater Canal are noteworthy holdings. Beyond the museum, at the far side of the first bridge, on the right, a marker designates the Whitewater Canal's northern terminus, reached in 1847. (*NRHP*)

From Hagerstown return to IND 1 and drive south 6.8 m. to US 40 and west into **CAMBRIDGE CITY** (p. 2,407). The center of population in the area originally was at Vandalia, a village laid out by the Hawkins family in 1824. When the National Rd. was extended to the south of Vandalia in 1827, the movement to the throughway ended Vandalia's brief life and gave rise to a new settlement. In 1835 the Cambridge post office was established, and the following year a town was platted that straddled the Whitewater River and bordered the National Rd. Some citizens wanted to name the town Bridgeport, but the name Cambridge won. Named probably for the English county or town, the town was incorporated in 1841 and grew rapidly with completion of the Whitewater Canal to it in 1846. The town counted 1,217 residents by 1850. The ethnic and religious makeup of Cambridge City set it apart from other towns in the county in that it had a heavy concentration of Catholic and Protestant Germans and very few Friends. Although periodic floods between 1847 and 1853 practically eliminated the commercial importance of the northern branch of the canal from Cambridge City to Hagerstown, the arrival of the railroad in the early 1850s prevented a collapse of the town. The major industries produce milking machines, store displays, metal-bending machinery, and caskets.

A marker at the eastern edge of town at the corner of US 40 and S. Gay St. (*.5 m.* from IND 1 and US 40 on the left) memorializes the life of **Maj. Gen. Solomon A. Meredith** (1810-1875). North Carolina born, Meredith migrated in 1829 to Wayne County and in 1840 to Cambridge City, where he became a railroad promoter and breeder of prize shorthorn cattle. He served as sheriff and clerk of the county, a United States marshal, a state representative, and commander of the famed Iron Brigade in the Civil War. His daughter-in-law, **Virginia Claypool Meredith** (1848-1936), continued in the livestock business after the deaths of her husband and father-in-law. She was one of the first women to lecture on agricultural subjects and organized the University of Minnesota's department of home economics, wrote a column for the *Breeder's Gazette*, founded the Indiana Federation of Clubs, and received appointment in 1921 as the first woman trustee at Purdue University. Solomon Meredith's grave site, with its tall shaft crowned by a likeness of the general, can be seen in **Riverside Cemetery**. Continue west *.1 m.* farther and turn right onto N. Lincoln St. The cemetery is north *.6 m.* on the left (bear right around a curve).

To get to the **Meredith-Rice home**, or Oakland Farm as it was called, return to S. Gay St. and go right one block to E. Church St. Go left one block to Meredith St. Follow Meredith St. south to the farm's entrance on the right. The lovely brick mansion was built in 1836 by Ira Lackey, a town founder, and sold to Meredith in 1851. On the grounds of the 22-room palatial residence is a two-story spring house, a brick smokehouse, and a carriage barn. Converted to apartments years ago, in 1975 the home came into the hands of the Rice family, who renovated the property.

To the left of the entrance to the Meredith-Rice home is a lane leading to a circular drive fronting the old **Kimmel home**, called Rose Hill. The two-story brick Victorian house was built by Joseph Kimmel, a farmer, brewer, and grain and malt dealer. The Kimmel property once consisted of about 300 acres in the area of Cambridge City known as Walnut Levels.

At 520 E. Church St., on the southeast corner of Meredith and E. Church sts., stands the **Lackey-Overbeck home**. The two-story frame Federal-style structure, possibly the oldest house in Cambridge City, was probably built in the early 1830s by Ira Lackey. From 1911 to 1955 the Overbeck sisters, six in all, produced a style of art pottery that has achieved worldwide recognition. The Overbecks' kiln is just west of the house. (*NRHP*)

Return to Main St. and continue west. The **Conklin-Montgomery home** at 302 E. Main St. and S. Lincoln Dr. was built by Benjamin Conklin, a merchant, in 1840. The west side of the first floor was given over to his mercantile business. When the business district shifted from East to West Cambridge (names still used in the community), Conklin was the last to move. The two-story, Greek Revival-style brick building has an unusual roof treatment with a steep gable at the east end and a hipped area at the west. The recessed front door is repeated on the second story and serves as a small balcony. Pauline and Robert Montgomery carefully restored the home after its purchase in 1944. Pauline Montgomery wrote *Indiana Coverlet Weavers and Their Coverlets* (1974). (*NRHP/HABS*)

The old **Vinton house** is at 22 W. Main St. Elbridge Vinton launched his inn business in the late 1840s after apprenticing in Solomon Meredith's White Hall Tavern. The Vinton Hotel functioned as a stagecoach and canalboat stop and earned a widespread reputation for warm hospitality.

Directly northwest from the hotel at 33 W. Main St. is the **Cambridge City Public Library**. A collection of the Overbeck sisters' pottery and paintings can be seen by request in the library's Overbeck Room. Also in the library is the History Room featuring artifacts of western Wayne County. The brass bell on display was used aboard a boat that plied the canal between Cambridge City and Cincinnati from 1842 to 1855. Gen. Solomon Meredith's Civil War effects also are on exhibit.

Beginning in the 1880s to about World War I, Cambridge City was noted for its **Lackey Horse Sales**. John S. Lackey stabled horses on his farm at the south edge of the city. He annually printed over 5,000 catalogs, and on an average sale day drew around 1,500 potential buyers from America and Europe. Lackey's death in 1914 and the arrival of the automobile ended this colorful phase of the city's history.

At a Lackey sale in 1912 a Cambridge City-bred, two-year-old pacer named **Single G** was purchased for $275. Between 1913 and retirement in 1927 the stallion ran in 434 heats, set innumerable harness-racing records, and earned over $120,000 for his owners. In a 1950 vote among horsemen, Single G outpolled the famed Dan Patch as "the greatest pacer in the first half of the twentieth century." The unusually hardy horse died in 1940 at the ripe age of 30 and was buried near Tipton, Indiana. In 1951 the remains were transferred to Cambridge City and reburied. A stone monument to Single G's accomplishments is located at the corner of N. Green St. and W. Parkway Dr. Proceed *.1 m.* farther westward and take Green St. north off US 40 about two blocks (*.3 m.*) to the memorial on the right just past the firehouse.

Return to US 40 and travel west to the **Huddleston Farmhouse Inn Museum** *.8 m.* west of Cambridge City on US 40 in Mount Auburn. In 1840 John and Susannah Huddleston, having just extended their 74-acre farm to the National Rd., built the 14-room farmhouse for their 14-member household. Huddleston subsequently converted the first floor to an inn to take advantage of the heavily traveled National Rd. Unlike other inns, this one did not offer bed or board, nor did the Quaker Huddleston sell liquor. Rather, the inn rented kitchen space to migrants for preparation of their own food while resting their teams or repairing their wagons. The inn operated in this fashion from roughly 1850 to 1875. The next generation of Huddlestons to occupy the three-story Federal-style brick home changed some of the trappings to reflect the Victorian fashions of the day. The Italianate louvered cupolas on the barn and spring house are obvious additions. The house was sold out of the family in the late 1930s. In 1966 the Historic Landmarks Foundation of Indiana bought it and began restoration. The large two-story barn has been turned into a multipurpose structure for museum and community functions. The third floor of the farmhouse contains administrative offices. The living quarters of the Huddlestons on the second floor have been refurbished. A public kitchen on the first floor can be seen in its original state. Displays on the National Rd. and the Huddleston house are in other ground floor rooms. (*NRHP/HABS*)

Return to IND 1, east of Cambridge City, and drive south *7.1 m.* through **MILTON**, founded in 1824, to the **FAYETTE COUNTY** (p. 28,272; 215 sq. m.) line. This agriculturally

reliant county was formed in 1818 from parts of Wayne and Franklin counties and was named for the Marquis de Lafayette.

The city of **CONNERSVILLE** (p. 17,023) lies *.9 m.* south of the county line on IND 1. Connersville became the seat of Fayette County in 1819, six years after its founding by the pioneer tradesman, John Conner, for whom the town was named. The village grew up on the west side of the Whitewater River around John Conner's trading post and mills. The town of about 600 residents incorporated in 1840. Five years later, with the completion of the Whitewater Canal to Connersville, the city emerged as a major center of pork-packing, flour-milling, and barrel-making companies. In the 1870s furniture became an important industry. In the late decades of the century, buggies, wagons, wheelworks, and body shops became the backbone of the community's economy. With this solid base of expertise in vehicle production, the subsequent transition to automobile manufacturing was made with relative ease. Between 1905 and 1937, 10 makes of cars rolled off Connersville's production lines, including the well-known McFarlan, Lexington, Auburn, and Cord. Other plants supplied auto parts to many state carmakers. During this time, annexations, especially that of East Connersville (platted in 1857), greatly expanded the city limits. Important small industries were the Krell Auto Grand Piano Company, which made player pianos, 1908-15, and the Dan Patch Company, which delighted youngsters with hobby horses, coaster wagons, playground autos, and related items mostly of wood. After the decline of Indiana's prolific auto business in the 1920s and 1930s, delivery trucks and Jeep bodies were produced in Connersville into the 1940s. Today, the nation's car manufacturers still rely on automobile hardware, precision parts, and air-conditioning components produced here. Other major companies in the city assemble dishwashers, blowers, vacuum pumps, and casket wares.

Entering the city from the north, follow IND 1, which becomes Park Rd., *2.5 m.* to **Roberts Park**. Established in 1902, it is the scene of the annual Fayette County Free Fair, which began in 1903. Approximately 100 acres contain the usual assortment of picnic, swimming, and sports facilities. The grinding wheels that border the children's playground once helped shape springs for buggies and automobiles. James E. Roberts, a Brookville native and the park's benefactor, sold furniture in Connersville until he moved to Indianapolis in 1893. His first wife was Mary Claypool, daughter of the founder of the Claypool Hotel in the capital. In 1984 the Longwood (Fayette County) covered bridge was moved to the park and restored by vocational school students.

Proceed south on Park Rd. (which becomes Central Ave.) to where it jogs east at 9th St. (*2 m.*). Go one block on 9th St. and turn south onto Eastern Ave. To the left, in front of the Moose Lodge, is a marker noting the site of **John Conner's first trading post**, which operated from 1808 to 1815.

Continue south on Eastern Ave. to its intersection with 5th St. (IND 44). Head east *.5 m.* to Vine St. (IND 1), just past the Whitewater River bridge. Go two blocks (*.2 m.*) south on Vine St. to Howard St. On the right is the **Reynolds Museum of Science and History**. Housed in the old Vine St. Baptist Church, which was deeded to the schools in 1953, the museum exhibits Indian artifacts, pioneer and Civil War relics, and mementos from canal days. Allen Jesse Reynolds assembled most of the collection in the 1920s and displayed it in local schools before its move to the present location in 1954. Reynolds was born in Wabash, Indiana, but lived most of his life in Connersville, where he wrote a column on local history for the *Connersville News-Examiner*.

Return to Eastern Ave. and 5th St. On the southwest corner in 1815 John Conner erected a store and trading post. After 1818 the structure was used as an inn, post office, and Masonic hall until in 1854 the Heinemann family established a grocery, which remained in operation for 90 years. After 175 years of existence the building is still in use. The oldest business building in the city now contains the **Glass House**, a gift shop owned and operated by members of the Heinemann family.

Continue west one block and turn left onto Central Ave. One block south on the northwest corner of 4th and Central is the **Fayette County Courthouse**. Built in 1849 as the county's second courthouse, the structure underwent a major face-lift in 1890 that totally changed its style of architecture. As originally constructed the brick building resembled the fashionable Classic Revival architecture, with a high base of arches supporting six columns on a second-floor portico. A tall clock tower was centered

on the winged edifice. When overhauled in 1890 the appearance became Romanesque, featuring a new stone exterior and the addition of the common cone-crowned towers. The columns and clock tower were dismantled. In time the cones were removed. Today's courthouse, deficient of any well-defined architectural expressions, nevertheless contains in its framework one of the oldest extant courthouses in the state.

One of Connersville's most famous landmarks stands one-half block east of the courthouse at 111 E. 4th St. The Doric-style structure is known as the **Canal House**. Built between 1839 and 1842 and located about 200 yds. from the canal, the columned two-story brick house became the headquarters of the Whitewater Canal Company in 1843. Samuel Parker, president of the company, bought the property in 1848. In 1854 the deed was turned over to the Savings Bank of Indiana. The bank held it for three years at which time the Vance family bought it and retained ownership for 79 years. Alice G. Gray, wife of Connersville mayor and congressman Finly H. Gray, obtained the house in 1936 and restored it. The Grays bequeathed the house to the Indiana Audubon Society in 1947, and the society in turn sold the house to the local chapter of the Veterans of Foreign Wars in 1950. Historic Connersville, Inc., acquired the house in 1971 and began the process of refurbishing. The second floor is leased by the Whitewater Valley Arts Association. Its Patriot Gallery, named for the first canalboat in Connersville, is on this level. The first floor is outfitted with period furnishings. (*NRHP/HABS*)

From the Canal House take Central Ave. two blocks north to 6th St. Go west one block to Grand Ave. On the northwest corner is a marker indicating the site of the **Roots Woolen Mill** and the birthplace of the **Roots blower**. The mill, started in 1846, produced a wide variety of clothing. Two Roots brothers, Philander and Francis, ran the Connersville mill. In 1854 while experimenting with a new waterwheel to replace their overshot wheel powered by the Whitewater Canal, they discovered the principle of the rotary air blower. They found that two wooden lobes shaped like figure-eight paddles, revolving in opposite directions, did not make a good waterwheel but did discharge a force of air. The brothers parlayed their discovery into what now is the world's largest producer of rotary lobe and centrifugal blowers. The blowers were first used in foundry furnaces and in mines for ventilation, such as in the famed Comstock lode in Nevada. In 1867 a huge Roots blower, called the "Western Tornado," installed in a New York City subway literally blew a 22-seat passenger car to one end of the track and drew it back again with suction force. Fire destroyed the original building in 1875.

In the middle of 7th St., one-half block west of Grand Ave. and a block north of the Roots marker, is the **1870 First Ward Hose House**. At one time the small brick building housed the firehouse and man-drawn hose cart for Connersville's first division fire fighters. Historic Connersville, Inc., restored the building in 1966, replacing decaying timbers, a roof, and a door. The lumber for the door came from a razed structure at Laurel in Franklin County. It is presently the home of the Big Brothers and Big Sisters organizations.

Continue west on 7th St. about one and one-half blocks and turn right onto Western Ave. Travel .5 m. north (Western Ave. becomes Mount St.). On the northwest corner of Mount and Columbia sts. is the present-day **Roots Blower plant**. The first building was constructed on this site in 1893 as the Connersville Blower Company, a local rival to the P. H. and F. B. Roots Company. In 1929 both companies were purchased by a conglomerate and merged. The factories were combined on the present site two years later. Since 1944 the company has been a division of Dresser Industries, Inc., and it is now referred to as the Roots Blower Operation. Roots engines are used in a variety of worldwide industries requiring the movement of gas or air at moderate pressures. (*HAER*)

Turn right onto Columbia St. and proceed north, bearing right onto 16th St. for a short distance, then left back onto Columbia until the road ends at 18th St. On the immediate left across the street is the **H. H. Robertson Company**, which occupies the old Lexington automobile factory building. The two-story brick structure was constructed in 1900, a year after the auto firm's organization at Lexington, Kentucky, and was purchased by the Robertson Company in 1960. The building, which is now painted white with green shutters, once bustled with orders for the Lexington, the Auburn, and the Cord.

Turn right from Columbia onto 18th St. Travel east, cross the railroad to Western Ave., and turn right. From Western turn left onto 8th St., then right onto Grand Ave. (IND 121). South on Grand .6 m. on the left at Spring Hill Rd. is the dry bed of the **old Whitewater Canal**, now hardly more than a ditch. A marker at the small bridge across the canal provides a brief history of the waterway.

South on IND 121 .3 m. from the canal marker and on the left is the home of the **Whitewater Valley Railroad** that provides on the weekends nostalgic 32-mile round trips between Connersville and Metamora. The railroad began operations in 1974 along a route dating from the 1860s. Volunteer railroad buffs tenderly handle the old steam locomotive and passenger cars along the towpath of the canal. In the presence of living history and the lush scenery of the Whitewater Valley, few of the thousands of annual excursionists mind the infrequent delays caused by breakdowns or grass fires ignited by engine sparks or heed the stifling afternoon summer heat in the coaches.

Opposite the railroad station is a stately mansion sometimes referred to as the White House of Indiana. The history of the **Elmhurst mansion** dates back to 1831 when Indiana congressman Oliver Hampton Smith, author in 1858 of *Early Indiana Trials and Sketches*, selected the hillside for his new home. Smith bought 160 acres for $1,440 and constructed a four-room, two-story brick dwelling, the nucleus of the present structure. Other well-known owners have included Caleb B. Smith, congressman and Lincoln's secretary of the interior; Samuel Parker, congressman, railroad promoter, and president of the Whitewater Canal Company; and James N. Huston, state senator, Benjamin Harrison's campaign manager, and United States treasurer under Harrison, 1889-91. Huston added the north and south wings and the six huge porch columns, and he remodeled the interior. After the turn of the century the Old Elm Farm became a sanitarium under several owners with the addition of a 26-room north annex. The Elmhurst School for Girls, modeled on the exclusive boarding schools of the Northeast, used the home from 1909 to 1929. In the following two years both a military institute and a private school failed to become established. After 1931 the house stood idle until 1940 when the Connersville Masons purchased it and restored it to its present grandeur. (*NRHP/HABSI*)

From Elmhurst mansion proceed south on IND 121 *3.1 m.* Go right onto CR 350S for another *3.1 m.* to CR 425W. Where the county roads meet lies the 650-acre **Mary Gray Bird Sanctuary**. When Finly H. and Alice G. Gray bequeathed the Canal House in Connersville to the Indiana Audubon Society, they also gave the society the land for the bird haven. Although litigation over the contents of the will after 1948 deprived the society of full ownership until 1955, work continued on the sanctuary. Some funds for maintenance were received from the sale of the Canal House furnishings in 1948. The sanctuary was established as a memorial to Mary, only child of the Grays, who died in her youth. Today, the land shelters some 60 bird species and a mixture of animals and reptiles. Marked foot trails lead through many varieties of wild flowers, shrubs, and trees.

Return to IND 121 from the bird sanctuary and proceed south along the twisting road *5.2 m.* through the Fayette County villages of Nulltown and Alpine into **FRANKLIN COUNTY** (p. 19,612; 385 sq. m.). Organized in 1811 and named for Benjamin Franklin, it was the seventh county established in the Indiana Territory. It was formed from a portion of Dearborn County and included parts of the present Fayette and Union counties until 1826. The Whitewater River cuts through the heart of the county and in the early years conveyed people and produce to and from the area. **LAUREL** (p. 819), located *1.5 m.* south of the county line, began profiting from the construction of the Whitewater Canal just three years after the town was platted in 1836 by James Conwell and named for his hometown in Delaware. The Whetzel Trace, an important east-west pioneer trail across southern Indiana (completed in 1819) began at Laurel and ended at the White River Bluffs, *1.5 m.* northeast of Waverly in Morgan County. The trace first drew settlers' attention to the little hamlet in the valley. Between 1839 and 1852, during the time of major activity on the canal, Laurel prospered, particularly after 1843 when the canal reached the town from Brookville. Laurel became a major shipping point and a center of limestone quarrying. After the canal era and devastating fires in 1872 and 1886, the town languished. Just to the right when entering Laurel on IND 121 is the old **Laurel Cemetery** upon a hillside off High St. The cemetery affords a panoramic view of the town and the hills and valleys of the surrounding countryside.

On the north slope of the cemetery are the headstones of **Elizabeth Conwell Smith and Byron Forceythe Willson**, Hoosier poets. B. F. Willson (1837-1867) lived in New Albany and wrote editorials for the *Louisville Journal* when he met Elizabeth Conwell Smith (1842-1864), granddaughter of Laurel's founder and student at the city's De Pauw College for Women. After their marriage in 1863 the couple moved to Willson's home state of New York briefly and then to Cambridge, Massachusetts. Here in 1864 Elizabeth died as did the couple's infant child. In 1866 Willson published a slim volume of his wife's poetry, simply entitled *Poems*. The same year Willson printed his collection of verse, *The Old Sergeant and Other Poems*. The title poem was his most famous. Written during the Civil War, the poem is said to have attracted Lincoln's attention and that of Oliver Wendell Holmes. Holmes and Willson became friends, and through Holmes Willson hobnobbed with Boston's literati Ralph Waldo Emerson, James Russell Lowell, and Henry Wadsworth Longfellow. After his premature death in 1867 Willson's body was returned to Laurel to rest beside his wife and son.

East of the cemetery follow the main road left to a lofty bluff, an **Indian mound**, which is crowned by an **old wooden bandstand**. Reportedly, James Conwell, the town's founder, gave the knoll to the citizens for a park. From the bandstand take Washington St. south two blocks to Conwell St. Near the west end of Conwell St. on the right is the whitewashed brick with faded red trim, Federal-style home of **Elizabeth Conwell Smith Willson**, built around 1840. A block south and two blocks east (*.2 m.*) on the northwest corner of Baltimore and Washington sts. is another Federal-style home of the 1840s, the birthplace of famed vaudeville and motion picture comedian **Charles Murray** (1872-1941). He and Oliver Trumbull toured the vaudeville circuit for 20 years as the team of Murray and Mack. Murray achieved silent and talkie film stardom as the lanky Irishman in the Jewish-Irish comedy series the Cohens and the Kellys, 1926-33.

Situated on a hill at the northeast corner of Baltimore and Franklin sts., a block east of the Murray home, stands the abandoned **White**

Hall Tavern, another Federal-style structure with a stone retaining wall and an added wrap-around porch. Located near the boat landing in the canal basin, the tavern was an important hostelry in the canal and early railroad days. South of the tavern *.1 m.* at Franklin and Pearl sts. is the **Laurel Hotel**, formerly known as Hunsinger's Tavern. Built around 1850, the Italianate-style structure is the only building in Laurel facing directly east. Take Pearl St. *.3 m.* east of town, crossing the bridge, to the first road on the right. Proceed on the rough and narrow road *1.2 m.* to a small, well-groomed clearing on the right. A sign identifies the place as the **Laurel Feeder Dam**, built in 1843 and restored in 1960. Near the dam is the starting point for the Whitewater Canal Trail. Return to Pearl St., a major thoroughfare in Laurel's past that led directly to the canal basin. Some old Laurel limestone foundations of buildings on Pearl St., the main business street, are still visible.

West *.2 m.* from the Laurel Hotel on Pearl St. just to the left after crossing Lafayette St. stands the three-story brick **Laurel Collegiate High School** building erected in 1852. Local

Masons have been meeting in the building almost without interruption since its construction after they helped finance its completion in 1852 in return for use of the third floor. The public schools used the structure until 1915. Take Lafayette St. south one block to Commerce St., then a block and one-half east on Commerce to a small limestone building on a nice fenced and landscaped plot on the left. This is one of Indiana's oldest jails, estimated to have been constructed around 1850. It contains a guardroom and a cell. From the jail return one-half block. Turn left onto IND 121 and proceed south. At a bend in the road *.2 m.* on the right is a marker indicating the site of **Toner's Tavern**, the point from which Laurel's Jacob Whetzel launched his road. Edward Toner established his tavern in 1815, the same year that he platted the hamlet of Somerset, which was soon swallowed up by its neighbor Laurel.

Follow IND 121 south from Laurel about *4 m.* to US 52. Go east on US 52 *2 m.* to the turnoff sign for **OLD METAMORA** on the right. The main street and canal section of the old town is *.5 m.* farther. The Metamora area

Laurel Feeder Dam

was settled in 1811. David Mount, a resident in 1812, member of the Territorial House of Representatives and subsequently of the House and Senate of the General Assembly, platted Metamora in 1838. Mrs. John A. Matson named the town Metamora after an Indian princess character in a popular contemporary play in New York City. The Whitewater River town's prosperity rose and fell with the canal's fortunes. The canal bisected the town by the early 1840s and, as a main stop on the line, growth was rapid on both sides of the waterway. Although the canal continued as a source of water power after the railroad had taken over the towpath, Metamora's glory days were over, at least for a century. The population, probably never over 1,000, dropped to 588 by 1910. A further blow came in the 1930s when passenger trains were discontinued, and US 52, a main thoroughfare between Cincinnati and Indianapolis, was relocated outside the town. In the 1940s the town's rejuvenation began with local and state efforts to restore and preserve the canal and surviving buildings. The **Whitewater Canal State Historic Site**, 14 miles of canal from the Laurel Feeder Dam to Brookville, was established by the General Assembly in 1946. From the middle of the 1960s to the present, craftsmen, artists, antique dealers, restaurateurs, and boutique proprietors of all descriptions have descended into Metamora transforming the once somnolent village into a tourist and shopkeeper cornucopia. Over one hundred businesses are in operation, on weekends for the most part. (*NRHP/HABS*)

A popular attraction is the **Metamora Grist and Roller Mill** located at the west end of town by canal lock No. 25. It is a functioning gristmill and museum. Originally built in 1845 and rebuilt in 1900, the present structure largely dates from the 1930s. A horse-drawn canalboat, the 14-ton, 44-ft.-long **Ben Franklin**, named for one of the original packet boats on the canal, provides half-hour rides.

Across from the mill on Main St. are a number of recently constructed log and wood buildings designed to attract the tourist dollar. Some of the original buildings along the south side of the canal include the **Banes house** about one block east of the mill on the right. This Federal-style structure was built in the 1840s by Jonathan Banes, a carpenter superintendent for the canal company. In 1845 Banes built a cotton mill on the site of the present Metamora Mill. Directly east across the street is the **Odd Fellows Hall**, a three-story brick commercial structure erected in 1853. In addition to housing two lodges, the building has served as a town hall, a post office, and a general store on the first floor. Just east before the next block is the **Mill Street Gallery** or the "Leaning Gallery," so called because it was built slightly crooked in 1890 (note the bricks on the upper left wall to see the defect). Two buildings east is the **Masonic Lodge**, an 1870s Italianate-style structure noted for the cobalt-blue, second-floor windows. This is believed to be the only lodge in the state with most of its cobalt-blue windowpanes intact. Directly east is the former **Van Camp Drug Store**, built in 1853 by the Van Camp family. An 1870 gasoline explosion destroyed much of the building and killed four members of the family, including Mrs. Van Camp and one of her sons. Another son, Gilbert, later went to Indianapolis and founded the Van Camp canning industry. Two buildings east is the former **Martindale Hotel**, built in 1838 by Ezekiel Tyner, a shipping agent for the canalboats. Originally used to house Tyner's business, the building became a tavern in 1856 and was expanded into a hotel when acquired by Amos Martindale in 1870. While walking through Metamora, watch for the historical markers on several storefronts.

At the east end of town is the **Duck Creek Aqueduct**, which was constructed in 1846 to allow canalboats to pass above the stream 16 ft. below. This 60-ft.-long, water-filled bridge covered by a wooden shed is believed to be the only "covered bridge" aqueduct in existence and once was featured in Ripley's "Believe It or Not." The Whitewater Valley Railroad travels from Connersville to Metamora on weekends, May through October, on the track just south of the canal. The railroad also offers a four-mile trip which begins and ends in Metamora.

Take US 52 west from Metamora to IND 229. South *4.4 m.* on IND 229 is **PEPPERTOWN**. Platted in 1859 and named for August Pepper, a German immigrant and shopkeeper, the hamlet retains much of its primitive character with several limestone structures as excellent examples of local limestone masonry.

OLDENBURG (p. 770), another German community, lies *5 m.* south of Peppertown on IND 229. The town proudly preserves its religious, cultural, and architectural heritage. The old stone and brick structures, clapboard houses, tin facades and cornices, bilingual street signs, and the combination of shops and residences attest to the Old World influence. Settled by Irish in 1817, the town was officially platted in 1837 by German speculators who named it for the province of Oldenburg in northern Germany. The settlement rapidly took on a German flavor with the in-migration of German Catholics from Cincinnati. Incorporated in 1869, Oldenburg is called the "Village of Spires" because of its churches and religious educational institutions. The huge barn, seen on the left when entering the outskirts of the town, is called the **Sisters' Cow Barn**, referring to its former function when operated by members of the Convent of the Immaculate Conception in Oldenburg. The barn is reported to be the largest in the county.

IND 229 becomes Indiana Ave. (Indiana Allee) and soon turns into Main St. (Haupt Strasse), which leads to the **Immaculate Conception Convent** on the right, the motherhouse of the Sisters of the Third Order of St. Francis, founded by Austrian-born Mother Theresa Hackelmeier in 1851. The present convent building dates from 1901, and the next door Chapel of the Immaculate Conception dates from 1891. The Franciscan Sisters serve schools, hospitals, parishes, and missions. Their academy for girls in Oldenburg was founded in 1885. The **Holy Family Church**, across the street from the convent, at the southeast corner of Main and Pearl sts. (Perlen Strasse), was the third church built by the Alsatian-born Rev. Franz Josef Rudolph (1813-1866), pastor of Oldenburg beginning in 1844. The present church with a steeple rising 187 ft. was constructed in 1861. Father Rudolph, who is buried beneath the Holy Family sanctuary, also built a stone church in 1846 that later became part of the former **Franciscan Monastery** complex adjoining Holy Family Church to the south around the corner of Main and Pearl sts. The three-story brick monastery building, which was constructed in 1894, was closed in 1981 and demolished in 1986. At the north end of Pearl St. is the **Holy Family Parish Cemetery** and the **Immaculate Conception Convent Cemetery and shrine**. The convent cemetery is easily distinguished by its rows of simple white stone crosses and a fieldstone chapel. The parish cemetery is noted for its unusual iron grave markers. Return south on Pearl St., noting part of the convent complex on the left. At the northwest corner of Main and Pearl sts. stands **Hackman's General Store**, erected in 1861-62. It features the town's most ornate tin work, fashioned by the Prussian-born master tinsmith Casper Gaupel. Directly south on Pearl St., on the right, is **King's Tavern**. The tavern's door lintel of tin, of which the word "Saloon" is an integral part, is a Gaupel creation. The **Town Hall**, between King's Tavern and Pigtail Alley (Schweineschwanz Gasse), was built in 1878 by the Eagle Fire Company, which later turned the building over to the town. A marker in front records the history of Oldenburg. Next to the

Oldenburg in the 1910s

Town Hall is the stone **Huegal Tavern** (c. 1845), which bears an eye-catching door lintel with a moon and sun. South one block to the left on Water St. (Wasser Strasse) stands the **Waechter house** embellished with an elaborately carved unsupported balcony. The **Cradle Shop**, across the street, erected in 1845, is where Eberhard Waechter handcrafted grain cradles and spinning wheels. West on Water St. at its junction with IND 229 is **Clem Fisher's blacksmith shop**, which has been in his family for a century or more, remaining unchanged over the course of time.

From Oldenburg continue south on IND 229 *2.6 m.* to the **RIPLEY COUNTY** (p. 24,398; 447 sq. m.) line. The state General Assembly passed an act in 1816 creating Ripley County from Dearborn and Jefferson counties, and the official organization took place two years later. Its slanted and northwestern boundaries resulted from the Indian treaty lines of 1795 and 1805, and its name honors Maj. Gen. Eleazer Wheelock Ripley (1782-1839), an officer in the War of 1812. Ripley's economy is divided between agriculture and manufacturing.

Continue on IND 229 *2.2 m.* to **BATES-VILLE** (p. 4,152). The routing of a Lawrenceburg to Indianapolis railroad through the northern part of Ripley County in 1852 is the primary reason for Batesville's existence. The town was laid out in 1852 by Joshua Bates, a railroad engineer and surveyor who also worked for the land company that owned the town site. Tradition credits the town's name to Joshua Bates. The enormous stock of timber in the area attracted buyers and craftsmen, mostly Germans from Cincinnati, and they began Batesville's primary industry of woodworking. Around 1900, when Batesville's population stood at about 1,300 residents, there existed six furniture factories, two coffin and casket plants, two sawmills, a door and sash factory, and a novelty works. Three retail stores sold the wares of these woodworking businesses exclusively.

The **Hillenbrand families**, leaders in the community then and now, were among the pioneers in furniture making. The family began with a general store in the 1870s and subsequently created the American Furniture Company in the 1880s, the Batesville Casket Company in 1906, and the Batesville Cabinet Company in 1913. The Hill-Rom Company was incorporated in 1928 to make hospital furniture. In 1929 John A. Hillenbrand disposed of his interest in the household furniture line to A. W. Romweber, a brother-in-law. Today the Romweber Industries include the American Furniture Company, the Batesville Cabinet Company, Romweber Company, and Universal Equipment Company. Hillenbrand Industries, Inc., includes the Batesville Casket Company, Hill-Rom, and the Forethought Group, an insurance firm. These three are based in Batesville. Hillenbrand also is the holding company for American Tourister luggage, Medico locks, and SSI Medical Services, all out-of-state companies. The Hillenbrands have added immeasurably to the growth and stability of Batesville through four generations of active involvement in the economic and civic welfare of the community. In 1980 the town was honored in having John A. Hillenbrand II as the state's Democratic gubernatorial candidate.

IND 229 becomes Walnut St. in Batesville. Follow Walnut in a southwesterly direction to Boehinger St. and turn left. Go one block farther and turn right onto Main St. At the northwest corner of Main and George sts. (two blocks on the right) is the **Sherman House**, a historic hostelry dating from 1852. Its popularity has long been known among salesmen and travelers because of its excellent cuisine and its convenient location between Cincinnati and Indianapolis. Sometime in the late 1860s one of the several owners of the hotel named it for Gen. William T. Sherman of Civil War fame. Subsequent owners have collected valuable prints from the Sherman era to hang in the lobby. In 1922 Hillenbrand Industries purchased the building and expanded and renovated the hotel. The modernized inn now displays a decor reminiscent of an old-world Vienna cafe. It is said that during one of the fires in 1874 that destroyed the furniture factories, the Sherman House was saved by piling bags of salt on the roof.

Turn left onto George St. Travel southeast one block and turn left onto Park Ave. Located on the southwest corner of E. Pearl St. and Park Ave. is the **Romweber-American Furniture Company**. The original company, founded by John and William Hillenbrand in 1881, manufactured bedroom furniture exclusively until dining room furniture was introduced in 1913. In 1934 a subsidiary firm, the Romweber Company, was incorporated to merchandise the company's most famous product—Scandinavian oak furniture with the trade name Viking Oak. The company at present employs about 250 persons and maintains showrooms in major cities from coast to coast.

Take Park Ave. *.3 m.* south to Western Ave. and turn left. At 510 Western Ave. is the home of one of Indiana's most prolific creators of juvenile literature, **Miriam E. Mason** (1900-1973). Born in Goshen, Indiana, the author attended Indiana University and the University of Missouri. She taught school in Indiana for several years and served as an editor for *Farm Life* magazine in Spencer, Indiana, until it folded in 1935. Like other writers during the depression years of the 1930s, she earned a partial living by composing anonymous "true confession" stories. She continued free-lancing in Chicago after 1935 and moved to Batesville in 1946. Miriam Mason wrote over 400 short stories, articles, and plays, and over 50 children's books, many of them historical biographies. Her sisters, Rachel Peden and Nina Pulliam, were also writers. Her brick and frame two-story house of 1930s vintage is presently occupied by her only daughter, Kitsey Beck, who continues the family tradition as a columnist for the weekly Batesville paper, a radio talk-show host, and an active participant in the community theater.

The **Union Furniture Company**, at the northwest corner of George and Elm sts., is two blocks west of the Sherman House. Called Batesville Union Company when established in 1867, the manufacturer has grown from a four-story barn to brick buildings covering more than two acres. Production is limited to bedroom or dining room items of French Provincial styling often with elaborate carving. The company usually employs 100 to 150 persons. It has showrooms in New York City, Chicago, Los Angeles, and San Francisco. Oddly, there is no showroom in Batesville.

Back at the Sherman House, go one block north to Pearl St. and turn right. Follow Pearl St. east *.5 m.* past the Romweber-American Furniture Company. After crossing John St. note the **Batesville Casket Company** on the left and the **Hill-Rom factory** *.3 m.* farther on the right, two of the three Batesville-based units of Hillenbrand Industries, the largest employer within a 40-mile radius. The casket works produces one-fifth of the world's caskets, and it

is the world's largest single manufacturer. Batesville pioneered in the design and production of metal caskets. Its products are made of steel, copper, and bronze and are transported to 52 distribution points around the country in Hillenbrand's fleet of specially equipped trucks.

Hill-Rom is the largest maker of hospital furniture in the country, filling more than 50 percent of hospital needs in the United States and Canada. The Batesville plant invented such hospital room fixtures as the electric bed and the bed table. Pearl St. connects with IND 46 near the Hill-Rom factory. Take a sharp left onto IND 46 opposite the Weberding carving shop, and look immediately to the left for the corporate headquarters of **Hillenbrand Industries, Inc.** Hillenbrand employs around 2,500 persons in its Batesville plants and is Indiana's ninth largest firm. A new corporate headquarters office opened in 1981 *.4 m.* west of the old office complex.

In contrast to the huge furniture operations of the Union or Romweber companies is the custom wood carving found in the **Weberding Carving Shop, Inc.**, *.5 m.* east of the older Hillenbrand Industries complex on the north side of IND 46. William J. Weberding, a veteran of the Batesville furniture factories, began his shop in 1937. Over the years the master craftsman, along with his sons and father and a dozen skilled workmen, has turned out custom-made wood products for individuals, firms, and churches. William Weberding is especially known for his massive carved religious figures and scenes.

Drive east on IND 46 *8 m.* to the **DEARBORN COUNTY** (p. 34,291; 307 sq. m.) line. The state's third oldest county was formed in 1803 and named in honor of Maj. Gen. Henry Dearborn, at the time secretary of war under President Thomas Jefferson. Originally, the county encompassed an area referred to as "the Gore." The county's boundaries stretched from the Ohio River in present southwest Switzerland County to Fort Recovery on the territorial boundary line, now in Ohio just east of Portland in Jay County, straight south to the mouth of the Great Miami River near Lawrenceburg. Small farms dot the steeply sloping inland part of the county while industry dominates along the Ohio River. During the 1970s, the county's population increased 16.5 percent.

The village of **LAWRENCEVILLE**, founded in 1835 by John Lawrence, is *1.4 m.* farther. Follow IND 46 *4.6 m.* and turn left onto IND 1 *.3 m.* to **SAINT LEON**. In front of St. Joseph church and school *.3 m.* on the right is a marker noting the site of the **Saint Leon Pole Raising**. The marker refers to an event held in the town each presidential election year at which time a tall hickory pole is raised, a custom begun in the United States in 1844 when Democrats erected a hickory pole in memory of their hero, Andrew Jackson. Saint Leon commenced performing this memorial in 1892 and celebrated its 25th quadrennial pole raising in 1988, reportedly the only community in the country still observing the tradition.

Continue on IND 1 north *1 m.* and enter a scenic portion of southeast Franklin County. Travel *4.4 m.* to US 52, passing through the hamlet of South Gate. Travel through Mound Haven and turn left on US 52. On the right *2.2 m.* stands the historic **Little Cedar Grove Baptist Church**. Built in 1812, the two-story brick church is the state's oldest church on its original foundation. Membership numbered more than 150 in the 1830s but dwindled thereafter. The structure was used as a residence for a brief time before the Brookville Historical Society acquired it in 1912. Restoration was completed in 1955. Of interest are the rows of slots in the second floor exterior used as rifle ports in the early days. Inside, the hand-hewn timbers, the ash balcony, and several original pews are reminders of the woodworking skills of the pioneer craftsmen. The building is now operated by the Franklin County Historical Society.

Northwest of the Cedar Grove church *2.4 m.* on US 52 is the well-preserved city of **BROOKVILLE** (p. 2,874). Situated on a bluff and in a valley plain at the junction of the east and west forks of the Whitewater River, Brookville has long been the heart of a rich agricultural district. Founded in 1808 by Amos Butler and Jesse Thomas, Brookville became the seat of Franklin County in 1811. Thomas named it after his mother's maiden name of Brooks. Subsequently, Thomas became a United States senator from Illinois and wrote a portion of the famous Missouri Compromise of 1820. The location of a federal land office in Brookville in 1820 accelerated the community's growth as speculators and immigrants flocked into and through this gateway to the state's interior. Between 1817 and 1822 Brookville hosted the

second branch of Indiana's first chartered state bank at Vincennes. The town suffered a major setback in 1825 when the land office was removed to Indianapolis. Large numbers of people, including several future governors of Indiana, migrated to the capital or rival cities or to new lands in recently formed neighboring counties. Construction of the Whitewater Canal, beginning at Brookville in 1836, and the great German migration into the Whitewater Valley in the 1830s initiated another period of expansion. Incorporated in 1839, Brookville by 1850 counted a population of 1,200. This figure doubled in the next decade. The railroad sustained the town's economy after the collapse of canal traffic in the 1850s. Brookville then settled into quiet repose, aroused only on occasion by natural calamities such as the destructive flood of 1913. Perhaps because it avoided extreme booms and busts, Brookville has managed to retain its 19th-century architectural heritage.

Driving into Brookville from the south on Main St. (US 52), turn right at 3rd St. and go two blocks to High St. Two markers indicate the site of the home of **David Wallace** (1799-1859), governor of Indiana from 1837 to 1840, and the birthplace of his son Lew Wallace in 1827. Lew Wallace went from Brookville to fame as a Civil War general and as an author whose works included *Ben Hur*.

Just south of the Wallace homesite, on the grounds of the present St. Michael's rectory, lived the **Noble family**. Of the four Noble brothers, Ben (1809-1869) was a physician and state representative, 1837-38, Lazarus (1795-1825) directed the Federal Land Office, James (1785-1831) served in the General Assembly and the United States Senate, 1816-31, and Noah (1794-1844) governed the state of Indiana, 1831-37. Historical markers commemorate both the Nobles and St. Michael's, which was built on the site in 1845. The present building dates from 1862 with an addition being constructed in 1902.

Returning to Main St., turn right to another marker on the right side of the street and south of the courthouse which records that **Abram Hammond**, Indiana governor, 1860-61, lived in Brookville as a boy in the old Yellow Tavern, now the site of the county jail. The **Franklin County Courthouse** was essentially a new building when completed in 1912, although it incorporated a portion of the third courthouse built in the 1850s. The older building formed the center of the new, with the construction of wings on the north and south, along with a new front.

Around the corner from the courthouse at 412 5th St. is a marker recalling the history of the **Franklin County Seminary**, which underwent restoration in 1980. Built in 1829, the school opened in 1831 and functioned for two decades. The town purchased the building in 1862 for use as a public school, but eventually it went into private hands. Booth Tarkington's father, John, attended school here. (*NRHP*)

Between 6th and 7th sts. on the west side of Main St. is a wall plaque by the Fayette Federal Savings and Loan building marking the **site of an old Indian trading post**. In the next block near 766 Main St. is another wall plaque indicating the site of the **Brookville Federal Land Office, 1820-25**.

At 813 Main St. is the most palatial Brookville home. The **Howland-Goodwin-Strohmier home** was built in the 1850s by John Howland and was owned subsequently by the Goodwin family of Brookville bankers. The two-story, paired-chimney, Federal-style structure features a semicircular portico of Ionic columns, added to the house at a later date.

On the northeast corner of 9th and Main sts. is the large white frame house built by Richard Tyner, an early Brookville merchant. It is the **birthplace of James Noble Tyner**, who served as postmaster general under President Ulysses S. Grant.

Turn right onto 9th St. Go to the end of 9th St., turn right onto Market St., and follow it one block to 8th St. Turn left onto 8th St. and go about one-half block to **The Hermitage**, one of Brookville's most outstanding structures. The rambling 17-room house with a 100-ft.-long porch and skylights once hosted several of the state's most celebrated artists. The nucleus of the home was built by James Speer, who erected a paper mill nearby in 1835. Amos Butler, a grandson of the founder of Brookville, bought the Speer home in the 1880s. The old mill and woods attracted the attention of artists J. Ottis Adams and T. C. Steele who bought the old home in 1898, and Steele's wife, Libbie, named it The Hermitage. A number of painters, including William Forsyth and Otto Stark, visited with fellow artists at The Hermitage. Steele sold out to Adams around 1907 and moved to Brown County. The house remained in Adams's hands until 1929. It stayed vacant until 1945 when it was reoccupied by one family for the next 33 years. The house at one time had 27 rooms before the 1913 flood washed away 10 of them.

Return to Main St. One block east of Main St. at the northeast corner of 10th and Franklin sts., a marker on the left in front of the Brookville School denotes the site of **Brookville College**, established in 1852 and operated under Methodist auspices until its closing in 1872. The college, first named Brookville Female College, admitted women only until 1860. The town purchased the structure in 1872 for public school use, and in 1912 the old structure was demolished to make room for the present building. Brookville College graduated many who went on to establish themselves in various fields of scientific endeavor. The Julia Dumont Society, which is claimed to be the second women's club formed in the state, began at Brookville College in 1853 and included among its literary lights such notables as the poetess Elizabeth Willson. Julia Dumont (1794-1857) was a teacher at Vevay and is considered by some to be Indiana's first short-story writer.

Across the street from the college site sits the **house of James B. Ray** (1794-1848), governor of Indiana, 1825-31. The home was built in 1821. Indianapolis papers published comments about the ornamentation over the south side arched window and the fanlight over the front door, suggesting that Ray was too aristocratic to lead the Hoosier state. It has been said that such attacks almost cost Ray his political career.

Just east of the Ray home across Franklin St. is the former **First Methodist Church and Cemetery**. The church, the oldest in Brookville, was built by the Methodists in 1821-22. The building later became a Presbyterian and then a Lutheran church. Since 1923 it has been used by the Baptists as a house of worship. Many of the area's first settlers are buried in the surrounding cemetery.

North from 10th and Main sts. on IND 101 *2.1 m.* is the south entrance to **Brookville Lake**. Brookville and the surrounding countryside, situated at the juncture of the Whitewater River forks, experienced periodic devastating floods. A year after the 1937 flood, Congress authorized the Army Corps of Engineers to construct a dam and reservoir on the East Fork north of Brookville. Appropriation delays postponed ground breaking for 27 years, until 1965. Additional budget problems delayed completion of the $40 million lake another nine years. Brookville Lake is the third largest in the state, 15 miles long and covering 5,260 acres. It also is Indiana's deepest man-made lake, being 125 ft. deep in places. The reservoir property comprises 16,445 acres. The dam is over 3,000 ft. long and 182 ft. high. The recreation opportunities include fishing, boating, camping, and swimming. The lake has added immeasurably to the tourist market of southeastern Indiana while providing flood protection and an abundant water supply.

North .4 m. farther on IND 101 is a turnoff on the left for a **scenic drive** that runs *5.4 m.* along the eastern edge of the lake. North on IND 101 *4.8 m.* (*2.2 m.* upon returning to IND 101 if the scenic route is taken) is the turnoff on the left for **Mounds State Recreation Area**. Opened in 1975, the area offers camping, swimming, boating, and fishing. Continue north *.5 m.* to the turnoff for **NEW FAIRFIELD** and the Fairfield Causeway on the left. New Fairfield is a collection of modern homes erected after and named for **FAIRFIELD**. Platted in 1815 and at one time a major challenger to Brookville for county-seat status, Fairfield was razed to allow creation of the Brookville Reservoir. North on IND 101 *.9 m.* is the **UNION COUNTY** (p. 6,860; 163 sq. m.) line. Union County was organized as the state's 34th county in 1821 from parts of Wayne, Franklin, and Fayette counties. It is Indiana's second smallest county in population and third smallest in land area. The first county seat was in Brownsville in the west-central section.

Continuing north *4.3 m.* turn left at Roseburg to the Dunlapsville Causeway. Proceed *1.8 m.* west to a turnoff for **Hanna House** on the right. The building was begun in 1842 by John Hanna, Jr., and completed by Washington Hanna, his son, several years later. At one time the two-story brick house supposedly was haunted by John Hanna and a girl named Jenny. Continue west *1.2 m.*, crossing the causeway, and turn right on a road leading to the **Treaty Line Museum**. The museum is a pioneer village grouping of restored log cabins and other structures salvaged from the flooded environs.

Returning to IND 101, proceed north *1.6 m.* to **Whitewater Memorial State Park**. The park, the 16th in the state chain, was dedicated in 1949 as a living memorial to the men and women who served in World War II. Four counties joined in raising the $135,000 necessary to purchase 1,710 acres for the park. A main attraction is the 200-acre man-made lake impounded from the waters of Silver Creek. As with other state parks, Whitewater offers campsites, boating, fishing, hiking, picnicking, horseback riding, and swimming. There is no inn in the park nor are motorboats allowed.

North of Whitewater State Park *1.4 m.* on IND 101 is the town of **LIBERTY** (p. 1,844), seat of Union County. Liberty was platted in 1822, and its central location won for it the seat of justice in 1823. The present **courthouse** is the county's third and the second on this site. It was constructed in 1890 in the modified French and Spanish Romanesque style of Henry H. Richardson by George W. Bunting and Son of Indianapolis. A prolific designer of public buildings, Bunting produced a massive limestone building whose 100-ft. tower collapsed a year later. The new tower, completed in 1892, boasts a four-faced clock. A small one-room museum of Union County artifacts is located in the basement of the courthouse. (*NRHP*)

Standing on the southeast side of the courthouse lawn is the **Templeton Cabin**, the oldest surviving log structure in the county. Built a few miles south of Dunlapsville in 1804, the cabin was enlarged in 1807 and removed to Liberty in 1938 as a memorial to Union County pioneers. John Templeton (1766-1837), the cabin's builder, served in the territorial General Assembly in 1810 and 1811. The Union County Historical Society restored the cabin and maintains it.

On the northwest corner of the courthouse lawn is a marker recalling the life of **Maj. Gen. Ambrose E. Burnside** (1824-1881), a Liberty native. Burnside's father, a state senator, obtained a West Point appointment for his son in 1843. While serving in the army in the southwest, Burnside invented a breech-loading rifle, and he resigned his army commission to manufacture the weapon in Bristol, Rhode Island. Eventual bankruptcy because of a lack of government support led to reenlistment in the army. During the Civil War Burnside briefly commanded the Army of the Potomac, a promising tenure marred by his humiliating retreat at Fredericksburg, Virginia. Subsequently, Burnside became governor of Rhode Island

and a United States senator. Burnside sported magnificent side whiskers, ever after referred to as "sideburns." The two-story brick home at 102 E. Seminary St., *.2 m.* southeast of the courthouse, was built around 1876 and is said to include construction material from a former home of Burnside.

The large brick Greek Revival-style house at 106 E. Seminary St. originally housed the **Union County Seminary** when constructed in 1841. Continue east on E. Seminary St. or US 27. From the courthouse, *1.6 m.* on the left side of the road, partially obscured by overgrowth and a guardrail, is a rock-embedded plaque placed in 1936 to indicate **General Burnside's birthplace site**. Farther southeast *1.2 m.* on US 27 turn right at Lotus and proceed *.5 m.* to the **Salem Friends Church**, founded in 1818. Bear right at the church and travel nearly *.3 m.* On the right is a two-story brick home, painted white, which operated as a major "underground railroad" station. The house is said to have been built between 1816 and 1822 by John Beard, a Quaker. The two small windows at the peak of each side served as lookouts for fugitive slaves or slave hunters. An escape hatch was built into the roof.

Return to Liberty at Main and Seminary sts. and take US 27 north for *2.7 m.* On the left fronting a fenced farm field is a boulder and bronze plate denoting the birthplace of **Joaquin Miller** (1839-1913), often referred to as the "Poet of the Sierras" or the "American Byron." Miller, whose given name was Cincinnatus Hiner Miller, lived most of his life on the West Coast. At various times the writer-adventurer dressed as a frontiersman and wore his hair and beard long, fought Indians, practiced law, taught school, panned for gold, married three times, lectured, and received critical acclaim from admirers in Europe, South America, and the United States. His most famous volumes of poetry were *Songs of the Sierras* and *Pacific Poems*. North on US 27 *3.6 m.* is the Wayne County line and *5.3 m.* farther is Richmond.

Madison

Madison (p. 12,472), one of Indiana's oldest settlements, lies in **JEFFERSON COUNTY** (p. 30,419; 363 sq. m.). The county was organized in 1811 and named for president Thomas Jefferson. The county is situated near the southeastern corner of the state and features a terrain that ranges from flat and gently rolling to deep river valleys. Although traditionally an agricultural region, the county is not blessed with fertile soil, abundant minerals, surface water, or lakes. What it offers is a picturesque landscape and historical communities, characteristics that increasingly attract sightseers. Madison, laid out in 1810, is located at the uppermost part of a horseshoe bend in the river, which positioned the townsite nearer the interior of the state than any Ohio River settlement. This natural feature and Madison's location as the terminus of the Michigan Rd. and the headquarters of Indiana's first commercial railroad help explain why the town assumed a major role in the economic welfare of antebellum Indiana. Madison had few peers when it came to processing agricultural products. Its port was an important breakpoint for shippers and a prominent gateway for immigrants. In the 1850s competition from rival cities and transportation routes curtailed river traffic and diminished Madison's preeminence. Not until the 1960s did Madison recover the level of population enjoyed a century earlier. In the interval, however, the city continued to service farmers and shippers, and it found new sources of revenue in starch, syrup, and saddletree manufacturing and in the peach, poultry, coal, and tobacco trade. Today, manufacturing is concentrated in automotive equipment, electric motors, plastics, heating equipment, and shoes. Nonresidents probably best know Madison for its annual powerboat regatta, Clifty Falls State Park, and historical architecture.

Built on the river bottomlands, Madison is ringed by hills rising to heights of up to 400 ft. A boatman in 1814 observed that "the stupen-dous rocky cliffs on the opposite side just above the town of Madison, together with the singular slope of the hills altogether form a scene highly pleasant to the imagination, and one that is mixed with something of the romantic." To songstress Jenny Lind, who honored Madison in 1851 with her only Indiana appearance, the Ohio River village was "a lovely place, calm and quiet as one of the ancient towns that nestle in the arms of the old Father Rhine. It lay lapped among the green and grassy hills that circled it."

The earliest permanent settlers arrived in the Madison vicinity in 1805-6 and took up residence in the highlands. Families began inhabiting the lands near and on the site of the future city in 1808. In the same year, sensing the economic potential of a riverfront community, John Paul, Jonathan Lyons, and Lewis Davis purchased the 691.54-acre site at the Jeffersonville land office. In early 1811 Madison became the county seat of the newly organized Jefferson County. In February of that year the first sale of lots took place. Madison, it is said, was first called Wakefield before being designated the namesake of the then president, James Madison. An intriguing but unverified statement by an early settler in an 1873 newspaper suggests a different name origin: "The first man that ever lived in Madison was a negro named Madison, from whom the town got its name."

Madison contained only a dozen families in 1811, yet it held county seat status, and its future prospects brightened considerably when the General Assembly voted to move the territorial capital to Madison temporarily. Gov. William Henry Harrison vetoed the measure. Later, Madison competed against a number of towns as the permanent location for the capital. Corydon gained the prize but Madison received valuable exposure. The fledgling riverfront village quickly obtained the rudimentary institutions of a county seat. A log courthouse and jail went up in 1811. The first issue of the *Western Eagle* appeared in 1813 under the auspices of Seth Leavenworth and William Hendricks, the latter becoming the state's third governor in 1822. John Paul erected the first mill by 1814, the year that the Farmers and Mechanics Bank of Indiana incorporated. This institution was one of the first two banks legally established in the Indiana Territory. Only Main St., where the bank stood, was partially cleared of trees at this time. Improvements were in the offing though as the end of the War of 1812 ushered in a few years of prosperity. At the time Indiana became a state in 1816, Madison was its largest town. By 1818 the population had grown to more than 800 persons and a second jail had been erected. The state's second Masonic lodge and its Grand Lodge had been instituted, as well as the Methodist and Presbyterian congregations and one of the state's earliest subscription libraries.

The national depression of 1818-20 slowed the community's progress somewhat, but it finished the decade of the 1820s in fine fashion. An international demand for American farm products stimulated Madison's expansion in the mid-1820s. With a population of around 1,000 persons by May 26, 1824, the town voted for a corporation ordinance. The citizens were justly proud of their new two-story brick octagonal county courthouse. Hanover Academy, founded in 1827 in the nearby village of Hanover, provided a semblance of higher education for the Presbyterian youth of Madison. Some 30 buildings were constructed in 1829. The next year, 1830, the federal census gave Madison a population of 1,752, second only to the downriver city of New Albany.

During the next 25 years, 1830-55, Madison experienced its golden era as influence and affluence came its way. By 1855 the city had added five times more people to its rolls than it had in 1830, doubling its population each decade. Its boundary lines stretched to the full length and width of the river bottoms as land promoters platted 25 separate areas of Madison between 1835 and 1854. A major key to Madison's success lay in the completion of transportation projects that effectively tied the city to the interior. The weaving of river, road, and railroad into a comprehensive carrier system placed Madison at the funnel end of a continuous flow of raw materials for processing and for distribution.

The Michigan Rd., extending from Madison to Michigan City, was built between 1831 and 1834. It was the first significant land artery contributing to Madison's economic well-being. State assemblymen chose Madison as the road's southern terminus in 1830 after two years of wrangling among representatives from Madison, Jeffersonville, Lawrenceburg, Mauckport, and New Albany, to name a few of the contenders for the highway. Historians have played down the importance of the Michigan Rd. to Madison's economy. Certainly its quality of construction did not match that of the National Rd., and more goods tended to move north rather than south once the road was finished. Still, the road tapped the rich farming country of central Indiana for Madison, opening up new sources of supplies for its industrialists and new markets for its merchants.

Madison benefited far more from the Madison and Indianapolis Railroad. State chartered in 1832, the project lay dormant until 1836 when the legislature earmarked funds for its construction as part of the massive internal improvements program. The route ascended the high north ridge behind Madison. Irish laborers cut deeply into the limestone hills to produce an incline over 1.3 miles in length. Rising 311 ft. per mile, this railroad was one of the steepest standard gauge railroads ever built in the United States. While the upgrade was prepared work proceeded northward from the summit. The collapse of state support in 1841 shifted the burden of completion to a local group which formed the Madison and Indianapolis Railroad Company in 1843. Within four years the track reached Indianapolis. At first horses or oxen pulled cars one by one to the top of the incline where the train was reassembled, but from 1848 to 1868 locomotives were used with a rack-and-pinion system. In 1868 Reuben Wells, the Jeffersonville, Madison and Indianapolis Railroad master mechanic (the M and I had merged), built a 55-ton engine that until 1905 towed cars up the grade without the use of cogwheels. A century after it began operation, the big engine, called the Reuben Wells, was placed on exhibit in the Indianapolis Children's Museum.

Despite its status as a leading shipping center, Madison did not develop a major shipbuilding industry. It never rivaled Pittsburgh, Cincinnati, or even Louisville, Jeffersonville, and New Albany in this regard. James Howard started a boatyard in Madison in 1836 but left in 1846 for Louisville prior to establishing his famed steamboat facility at Jeffersonville. Though short-lived, Howard's tenure at Madison did result in the partial clearing of trees along the waterfront, allowing passersby, for the first time, a glimpse of one of the state's premier cities. The building and repairing of other types of rivercraft probably went on unchecked, but not until the founding of the Madison Marine Railway Shipyard in 1851 was there again a shipyard set up on a more permanent basis. The Madison Marine Railway continued in operation, with more or less success, through World War II. Railroad and steamship construction encouraged the development of feeder industries, including iron foundries, some of which designed and crafted architectural metalwork, decorative fencing, and railing found in such abundance in the city.

The work of city building paralleled the evolution of the transportation network. In the 1830s, for example, seasons of deathly cholera prompted expenditures of money to eradicate stagnant ponds and careless waste disposal. A primitive water system of iron pipes and hydrants was devised but only partially completed. The threat and actuality of fires led in 1832 to the purchase of a small hand pumper for the Volunteer Fire Fighters Club. The erratic business climate was made more secure when Madison was awarded 1 of 13 branches of the Second State Bank of Indiana, created in 1834. The citizens elected to incorporate as a city in 1838, two years after the *Madison Courier* was founded. The *Courier* is presently one of the state's oldest newspapers.

Between 1838 and 1844 a sluggish economy somewhat slowed the pace of growth, yet efforts to better fire protection went on unabated as shown by the formation of the Fair Play Fire Company in 1841, one of three fire companies organized in the 1840s. The Fair Play company is still active and is the senior fire department in all of Indiana. In other developments in this decade, new castor oil and linseed oil mills enhanced Madison's processing reputation. North Madison was platted in 1846 as a direct result of the expected completion of the Madison and Indianapolis Railroad. The railroad helped bring about an enormous expansion in pork packing, Madison's largest and most profitable industry. In

turn, the pork business drew into town German settlers who not only worked in the packinghouses but initiated a variety of other enterprises including distilleries. Madison's architectural attractiveness was magnified with the addition of the Lanier mansion, the Shrewsbury house, the Costigan house, and the Madison Presbyterian Church. In 1849 Madison's black Baptists organized St. Paul's Second Baptist Church. The first African Methodist Episcopal Church was founded in 1850 or 1851. All of this growth and much more, including a jump in population from 3,798 to 8,012, took place in the context of devastating fires, a Crooked Creek flood in 1846 that killed 11 persons, and outbreaks of cholera and smallpox.

In 1850 Jefferson County led the state in manufacturing capital and in the total of products produced. It ranked second in the number of employees. In Madison workers found construction jobs on downtown buildings, which by the mid-1850s occupied almost all available space. Laborers could find work on one of the six permanent wharfs, or at the new shipyard. Pork processors, who collectively handled 124,000 hogs in 1852 alone, employed hundreds of men. Some of these perhaps toiled in that cleaning corps that removed accumulated grease from a pork house floor, whitewashed and wallpapered its walls, draped flags, devised a lighting system, and borrowed chairs in order to provide a suitable setting for Jenny Lind's performance in 1851. If work was unavailable in pork houses, mills, or the three new saddletree factories, jobs could be had putting up street signs, preparing a west-end grove for the third Indiana State Fair in 1854, planking roads, or building the state's first city water system.

Public or free-graded schools were instituted in 1852 over the loud cries of opponents who called them "degraded" schools. Madison acquired a new courthouse after an arsonist ignited the old eight-sided structure in 1853. Six years later the interior of the new courthouse was gutted by fire and required extensive renovation. Antislavery forces were active in the 1850s. An antislavery society had been formed in 1839, and there grew up a strong tradition of underground railroading. Substantial southern sentiment prevailed also. It is said that discussions to place a bridge over the Ohio River to Kentucky fell through for fear it would further encourage northern abolitionists to entice slaves from their southern owners.

Customarily the early 1850s are regarded as the peak years for 19th-century Madison. The 1860 federal census disclosed that Madison's population had not doubled as in previous decades. The city gained less than 2 percent between 1850 and 1860. Indianapolis, with only 79 more people than Madison in 1850, increased its margin to 10,481 by 1860. Plainly Indianapolis had become the primary city of Indiana. By 1860 several major railroads crisscrossed Madison's market area, but none entered the city. River trade declined as railroads assumed a greater portion of the state's shipping requirements. Many of Madison's pork processors either failed or moved away. The effects of this key industry's troubles rippled through the local economy.

Madison's fortunes changed gradually, not cataclysmically. Jefferson County in 1860 still ranked among the state's top three counties in capital investments, employee numbers, and product value. During the Civil War supply orders inundated Madison's manufacturers, including shipbuilders. A huge military hospital on about 30 acres and containing 65 wards with bed space for about 2,000 patients opened in Madison in 1863. More than 8,000 patients received treatment at the hospital before the close of the war. Although between 1860 and 1870 the county slipped to 11th place in the crucial manufacturing categories noted above, a writer in the *Lafayette Courier* in 1871, after noting that it "had been accustomed of late years to hear Madison spoken of as one of the dead cities of the northwest," found abundant evidence of the city's good health. The correspondent mentioned that Madison had the largest coal trade south of Cincinnati and a rush of business in syrup, starch, and saddletrees (five manufacturers made 37,500 saddletrees in 1870). To buttress his argument the reporter might have pointed to Madison's 32 percent jump in population in the 1860s, to 10,709 residents by 1870. Or he might have revealed the county's step-up in the 1860s from sixth to fifth place in the state in the number of manufacturing concerns.

Madison, in effect, by 1870 probably had returned to a more normal growth pattern after some four decades of exceptional expansion. A few large plants moved away, but many smaller firms moved in. Other cities experienced rapid progress partly at Madison's expense, yet families and businesses did not frantically desert the city. A *Courier* editorial in 1871 put the matter rather well despite the usual puff: "The Madison of today is very much in advance of the Madison twenty years ago in population, manufactures and trade generally; though to a superficial observer it may not appear so. The large jobbing trade and the rush of the strangers of twenty years ago we have not now. Instead we have increased manufactures in all departments. The progress of Madison has been slow compared with that of Indianapolis, but evidently there has been progress."

Unfortunately Madison's rate of progress could not be sustained. A 50-year descent in population commenced in the 1870s, from a peak of 10,709 to a low of 6,530 in 1930. Persistent statewide shifts in population, business, and transport routes checked the city's growth. Madison's problems began to multiply when the stock market panic of 1873 triggered widespread commercial ills. The economic slowdown partially caused the closing of Madison's shipyard in 1876. It reopened in 1878 and launched 26 steamboats and barges and repaired 80 craft, but its new well-being was unenduring. In like manner, long-held dreams of additional railroads reaching the city faded when the much-discussed Ohio River railroad from Cincinnati to St. Louis, through Madison, and the narrow gauge Bedford, Brownstown, and Madison Railroad failed to materialize. In 1883 Madison experienced its worst flood up to that date. Damages ran in excess of $200,000. Several hundred persons lost their jobs, while between 125 and 150 families lost their homes. Relief committees fed 700 flood victims.

Civic leaders tried to circumvent the misfortune accompanying Wall Street panics and unprecedented floods. A Merchants and Manufacturers Club, formed in 1883 to promote business interests, attracted textile, stove, canning, tobacco, and silver plating firms. The enormous Eagle Cotton Mill Company relocated to Madison from Pittsburgh in 1884. The shipyards, along with peach, coal, lumber, flour, saddletrees, tacks, starch, furniture, and beer companies comprised Madison's economic base in the latter 19th century.

As the city struggled to uphold financial solvency, efforts continued to safeguard property and improve the quality of community life.

Upgraded fire equipment and a new water reservoir provided better fire protection. Three of the four fire companies had steam-powered fire engines by the 1890s. Electric lighting, introduced in 1886, increased in range after 1896 when the Madison Light and Railway Company contracted to illuminate streets and alleys for 10 years. The same company installed the city's first electric railway in 1898. The local Odd Fellows Lodge presented the city, in 1886, with a large fountain that had graced the Philadelphia Centennial Exposition a decade earlier. The Centennial, or Broadway, fountain, recently recast and reset, turned out to be a favorite meeting place. A new post office, completed in 1897, resulted from the Merchants and Manufacturers Club's direct appeals to Washington. As regards education, Madison in the 1890s had six public schools and two parochial schools. Its two high schools were segregated, with blacks going to the Broadway St. building. Of eight black high schools in the state around the turn of the century only Madison's Broadway School was commissioned. That is, the state universities accepted its graduates without requiring entrance examinations.

Entering the 20th century, local leaders, seeking ways to overcome the persistent population decline and to offer a commercially viable community, welcomed encouraging reports in state newspapers. For example, the *Indianapolis News* in 1903 diagnosed the city as economically sound as evidenced by its agricultural market and 75 businesses and industries. The paper drew attention to the horse and mule sale stables, claimed as the state's largest, and to the heavy river haulage chiefly in coal, lumber, poultry, peaches, and tobacco. Madison received more free publicity when the press discovered that Louis Sulzer, dealer in so-called crude drugs, or medicinal roots and herbs, was one of the nation's biggest purchasers of ginseng, yellow root, wahoo (burning bush), sarsaparilla, and other roots. Madison's cultural star ascended in this period as the renowned Hoosier author and historian Edward Eggleston took up residence and participated actively in library affairs. Construction of the Southeastern Hospital for the Insane, now the Madison State Hospital, between 1905 and 1910, again thrust Madison into the public eye.

Madison did not engage in, nor profit from, the upstate rage for establishing interurbans or producing automobiles. Consequently, it escaped the management-labor strife endemic to the transportation industry in northern cities. Still, Madison remained the center of local river trade. The freight tonnage hauled from Madison's docks actually increased by 26 percent between 1910 and 1916. Boat owners expected even better days once the deepening of the Ohio River, authorized by Congress in 1910, provided sufficient depth for large craft and stimulated yearlong shipping.

Despite signs to the contrary, the 1920 census figure continued its downward trend. Madison's population fell another 3.2 percent. While noting the absence of empty residences, the census discovered relatively fewer persons living in large houses, a fact the *Courier* interpreted as indicating that an exodus of young people lay behind the loss of population. The newspaper failed to report that population gains in contiguous settlements such as West Madison, North Madison, and Hanover easily offset Madison's losses.

Madison achieved several milestones in the 1920s, notwithstanding the ominous census revelations at the first of the decade. The work of deepening the river channel reached Jeffersonville with the result that Madison's shipyards and shippers increased business; however, the lucrative trade in mussel gathering and pearl button manufacturing ceased. In 1922 Indiana recorded its archaeological and historical heritage. Jefferson County, thanks to the efforts of the Jefferson County Historical Society organized in 1917, filed its natural and historical sites ahead of every other county. The local history group had its headquarters and museum in the James F. D. Lanier mansion. It deeded the house to Indiana in 1925 with the proviso that $12,000 be expended on its refurbishing. The Lanier home, the state's first historical memorial, opened to the public in 1926. The following year Charles Lindbergh flew nonstop to Paris in the *Spirit of St. Louis*, a plane powered by a motor designed by Charles Lanier Laurence, a great-grandson of James F. D. Lanier.

Residents of Madison and Jefferson County subscribed enough money in 1920 to purchase and present lovely Clifty Falls and surrounding land to Indiana for the establishment of a state park. On the same day, November 27, 1920, that the state received the parklands, Gov. James P. Goodrich announced the inclusion in the new state highway system of three roads leading from Madison. In 1929 came the completion of the first bridge to link Madison with Kentucky. The dedication of the toll bridge was a memorable event. Besides the parade and speeches, 10 planes led by World War I ace H. Weir Cook dropped thousands of congratulatory leaflets on the town and skillfully deposited floral arrangements onto the span. Madison's mayor and herb dealer, Marcus Sulzer, confidently predicted the end of North Vernon and Columbus, Indiana, and Campbellsburg and New Castle, Kentucky: "They will be just one big Madison." The purchase of Clifty Falls, the developments in historical preservation, and the highways and bridge gave Madison a new industry, the tourist trade, estimated at the time to equal the value of a large manufacturing plant.

Madison had very little time to capitalize on the tourist bonanza for it soon joined the nation in battling the ill effects of the 1930s economic depression. Just when it seemed things were improving, thanks in part to federal relief programs, the 1937 Ohio River flood shattered all expectations for recovery. Madison's historically worst deluge destroyed buildings slated for renovation. It forced the Marine Shipyard to end operations. Together the depression and the flood contributed to the closing or change of owners of 15 stores and severely reduced the importance of the city's mills.

The picture brightened in 1939 and during the ensuing war years. Madison's tobacco market by 1939 could claim to be the largest north of the river, and America's defense needs reversed six decades of population decline. Laborers at the site of the new smokeless powder plant in nearby Charlestown disposed of a large portion of their ample paychecks in Madison's shops. A number of new homes were built, and older homes were converted to apartments. The 1940 census gave Madison almost 400 new residents. In December 1940 government planners announced the building of a huge weapons proving ground north of the city. Completed in 1941, the Jefferson Proving Grounds took in 56,000 acres and parts of three counties. Land acquisitions uprooted about 500 families and caused the reburial of bodies from 21 cemeteries, a boon to the local morticians. The grounds swallowed up five towns, four schools, and two churches. It took only 45 days to depopulate the area. Persons reacted with mixed emotions.

Little could be done to moderate the wrenching experience of leaving a lifetime home or community. County officials worried over the loss of revenue from one-twentieth of county taxables. The good news was the prospect of increased employment, housing construction, and retail spending. About one million dollars of federal money flowed to Madison each month during the building of the military facility. At the peak of World War II, educated guesses placed Madison's population at around 10,000.

In the 1950s Madison awakened from a commonly shared postwar slump and realized its most active decade in a century. The city expanded its boundaries, revitalized the riverfront, and greeted a score of industries. In 1952 Madison annexed four near neighbors including the fast-growing North Madison. Along the river in 1952, city employees, as part of a levee improvement program, created a picnic area from a rubbish-ridden and overgrown section. In the same year, a 300-ft.-long curved concrete ramp was built to the water's edge to accommodate the increasing numbers of boaters and weekend vacationers. The annual Madison Regatta, begun on a small scale in 1949, achieved national status in 1952 when the American Power Boat Association sanctioned it. Also in 1952, a rather extraordinary year, residents heard the news that the world's largest steam-powered generating plant would be put up just west of Madison at the mouth of Clifty Creek. Built between 1953 and 1955 for more than $200 million, the facility boosted the local economy while it supplied 1,290,000 kilowatts of power for an atomic energy plant at Portsmouth, Ohio. Madison anticipated acquiring a Westinghouse plant on the hill in 1953, but the project fell through, as did the attempt to land the proposed Air Force Academy in the vicinity of Hanover. Nevertheless, industry continued to move to Madison, and established firms expanded. In 1958-59, six businesses located in the city. So, too, did Hollywood, briefly. Madison became the setting for the 1959 release *Some Came Running* starring Frank Sinatra, Dean Martin, Shirley MacLaine, Arthur Kennedy, and Martha Hyer. MacLaine, Hyer, and Kennedy received Academy Award nominations for their performances.

During this time Madison literally was becoming a city of two communities, one on the hilltop and one on the riverfront. Upper Madison grew rapidly in the 1950s and 1960s. Old Madison grew also, and the larger population, more tourists, and traffic created a demand for more businesses, better roads, and parking space. Hemmed in by the river and surrounding hills, Old Madison's development most likely had to occur through the destruction of existing structures, possibly of historical or architectural value. Given this prospect and the demolition of noteworthy landmarks, including the Second State Bank of Indiana branch building, Historic Madison, Inc. (HMI), formed in 1960 to take the lead in saving significant buildings and encouraging citywide preservation. If one theme dominates Madison's recent past it is that of historical preservation guided by HMI.

The groundwork for Madison's historical renaissance had been laid in the 1920s with the establishment of the Lanier Memorial. In the late 1940s Mr. and Mrs. John T. Windle purchased the Shrewsbury house and opened it in 1949 as a house museum. Also in 1950 Tri Kappa Sorority conducted its first home tour. With the founding of HMI in 1960 preservation activities accelerated. John Windle, president of HMI from its inception until 1981 and a 1984 recipient of a National Trust Honor Award, recruited a membership of local and state notables and launched a series of eight property purchases that, along with advising private restorations and directing educational programs, gained national recognition. In 1970 a Joint Committee for the Restoration of Downtown Madison began deliberating the reviving of the business district. More than 130 city blocks were put on the National Register of Historic Places in 1973. Four years later the National Trust for Historic Preservation selected Madison as one of three cities to demonstrate how the restoration of old retail structures could revitalize a humdrum downtown. Soon afterwards more than half of the 100 stores had undergone face-lifts. The diligence of HMI, the Jefferson County Historical Society, and a score of other organizations has netted the city a number of grants and awards, in addition to newspaper and magazine coverage and special television and film promotions.

Madison's warranted reputation as one of Indiana's most beautiful and most cared for cities seems secure. Even the trees in the historic district are inventoried. Notwithstanding economic setbacks including the stopping of construction at the nearby Marble Hill Nuclear Power Plant in January 1984 and the closing of the Jefferson Proving Grounds in 1989, the city has exerted itself to provide a balanced program of historical preservation and business incentives. The effort has been rewarded. A good example of this blend of conservation and commerce is the 1984 inauguration of the Mulberry St. Project, a feasibility study funded by the National Trust and local organizations and businesses for rehabilitating 10 commercial structures on the old commercial street. New businesses, such as Arvin Sango, Inc., which manufactures automobile exhaust systems, the W. S. Products plant built by Rotary Lift, and the construction of River Pointe Shopping Center, have bolstered the local economy. Plans have gone ahead to turn the old cotton mill, or Meese Building, into a hotel. The hotel, when complete, will overlook a new scenic riverside two-block brick walkway complete with benches, Phase I of a long-term project spearheaded by the Riverfront Development Committee. The river improvement should enhance chances for increased tourism, often viewed as the key to Madison's future. Even now, the city's seasoned menu of attractions including the annual Chautauqua of the Arts, the Madison Regatta, the Tour of Homes, and the Christmas Candlelight Tour draw huge crowds to the "Williamsburg of the West."

Madison Attractions

Information on the sites and attractions in Madison and environs can be acquired at the **Visitor Information Center** in the Community Development Complex, corner of E. Main and Jefferson sts. (301 E. Main).

1. The **Jefferson County Courthouse**, Jefferson and Main sts., is a Greek Revival-style public building designed by David Dubach and constructed in 1854-55. It features the classic high porch supporting four narrow Ionic columns. The interior was remodeled after a fire in 1859. In 1869 the building received a new slate roof which necessitated giving the roof a greater pitch and raising the dome.

2. The **Jefferson County Jail**, Courthouse Square, was completed in 1849, and it is the third jail on the same site. A new section was added in 1973. The old jail is one large room with cells in the middle covered with a vaulted roof reinforced by iron contained in the masonry. A heavy iron door leads into the cellblock. Some stones in the walls measure 3 ft. wide and 6ft. long. The belief that a secret tunnel connected the courthouse and the jail has not been substantiated. (*NRHP/HABS*)

3. The **Middleton Monument**, Courthouse Square, is a memorial to Civil War servicemen from Jefferson County. George Middleton, a Madison native and Civil War veteran who made a fortune in a chain of theaters, financed the erection of the monument, dedicated in 1908. The faces of the four figures crowning the cenotaph supposedly resemble Middleton's face. In 1863 Union troops at Vicksburg, Mississippi, fired the cannon ball now resting in front of the monument. The widow of Dr. W. A. Collins, assistant surgeon with Indiana's Sixth Regiment, presented the relic to the city. The memorial is situated where the Walnut St. Market House stood from 1846 to 1907.

4. The **Fair Play Fire Company No. 1**, 403 E. Main St., is the state's oldest volunteer fire fighters' headquarters. The company dates from 1841. In 1888 it moved to its present location, a building erected around 1875 as a trolley barn for the Madison St. Railway Company. A 52-ft.-tall canopied bell tower was added in 1888, along with Jimmy the weathervane, fashioned at John Adams's metal shop. Jimmy, with arm extended and bugle poised, stands over 5 ft. tall. The tin weathervane came down in 1945 because of the fragile condition of its standard. Ten years afterwards Clarence Hoffman, the son of Jimmy's creator, repaired the bullet holes and broken finger, repainted the figure, and supervised its replacement on the tower. In the firehouse the old horse stalls have been converted to a meeting room and kitchen. The Neptune hose reel, purchased in 1851, is displayed along with antique fire fighting mementos.

5. **St. Michael's Roman Catholic Church**, 519 E. 3rd St., is Madison's second oldest public building. St. Michael's was founded in 1837, some 20 years after the first recorded visit to Madison by a Catholic missionary. Father Michael Edgar Gordon Shawe, who later became Notre Dame University's first professor of English, guided the construction of St. Michael's in 1838-39. Francis Costigan, the architect, belonged to this parish, and it is assumed he had a hand in the design of the structure. Costigan's first assignment in Madison may have been to roof the church with a low-pitched Classic style rather than with a Gothic style. Tradition has it that the brownish sandstone of the building's exterior came from the second cut of the Madison and Indianapolis Railroad then being built. Interesting features of the church are its bell tower and its unusual placement at the rear, and the "open-book" ceiling.

Madison Attractions

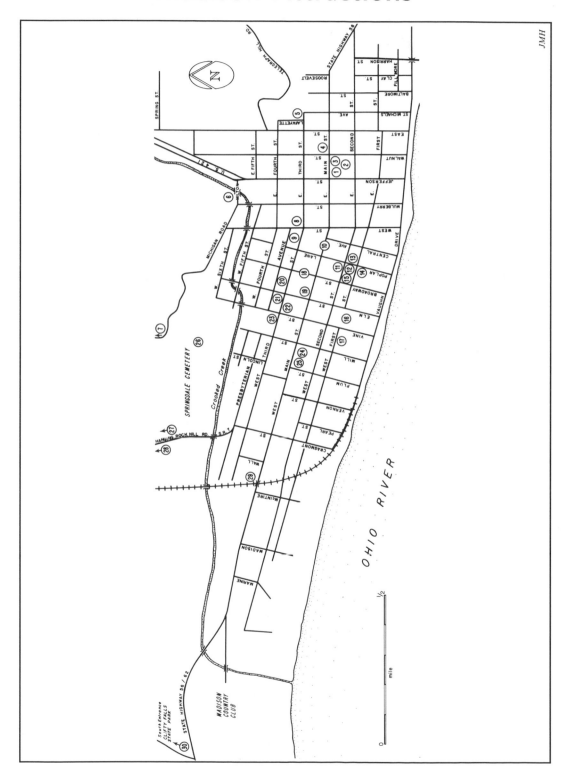

6. The **Ben Schroeder Saddletree Factory**, 106 Milton St., immediately to the right after crossing the Crooked Creek bridge, is an old Madison industry that operated for 94 years. Begun in 1878, the factory functioned until 1972. In that year Joseph Schroeder, the last of three brothers who carried on the company after their father's death in 1908, died. Without heirs to continue the business, it became in 1974 a property of Historic Madison, Inc. During its lengthy existence, the Schroeder firm supplied saddletrees of all shapes and descriptions to customers throughout the United States and South America. It outfitted cavalry and mules in five wars. Some reports have the Schroeders selling saddletrees to Kaiser Wilhelm of Germany in World War I until indignant townspeople negotiated a halt to the practice. In the 1930s the company also produced wooden clothespins. In 1972 an inspection team from the Historic American Engineering Record declared the Schroeder plant to be one of the most complete preservations of a 19th-century industry discovered in the United States. (*HAER*)

7. The **William Hendricks Grave** is located in Fairmount Cemetery north of the water tower at the top of the Michigan Rd. hill. Hendricks (1782-1850) came to Madison in 1812, set up Indiana Territory's second printing press and, with Seth Leavenworth, put out the territory's second newspaper, the *Western Eagle*. Hendricks began his notable political career in 1816 as Indiana's first elected representative to Congress. He served as Indiana's third governor, 1822-25, running unopposed, the only gubernatorial candidate in the state's history to do so. Before his tenure in the governor's chair ended, Hendricks became a United States senator. He resigned as governor and did duty two consecutive terms in the United States Senate.

8. The **John T. Windle Memorial Auditorium**, West and 3rd sts., is in Madison's oldest public building, constructed in 1833-35 as the Second Presbyterian Church. The simple and continuous lines, the low-gabled roof, and the Doric columns imitate the most ancient and least ornamented of Greek order architecture. It is one of the most important Doric Greek buildings yet standing within the boundaries of the old Northwest Territory. The barrel-vaulted ceiling with recessed panels is unique to the area. Edwin J. Peck (1806-1876), the designer, also supervised masonry work on Indiana's first statehouse, and he erected several of the State Bank's branch buildings. Dr. Lyman Beecher, a famed New England divine and father of more famous children including Harriet Beecher Stowe and Henry Ward Beecher, delivered the dedication sermon in 1835. The Presbyterians vacated the facility in the early 1920s. Since then a mortuary and several religious bodies have used the building. HMI bought it in 1961, established its offices in the basement, and called it Historic Madison, Inc., Auditorium. In 1984 the auditorium's rare 1867 Johnson tracker organ, its casing and facade pipes, underwent a complete restoration and was re-dedicated in 1985. Upon the death in 1987 of John T. Windle, the auditorium was renamed to honor the founder and longtime president of HMI.

9. The **Dr. William Hutchings's Office and Hospital**, 120 W. 3rd St., is considered one of the purest Classic Revival structures in Madison. Designed by Francis Suire and built in the 1840s, the two-story red brick office building housed an attorney and a judge prior to 1882 when Dr. Hutchings moved into the facility. He remained there until his death in 1903. His granddaughter, Elisabeth Zulauf Kelemen, chronicled his life in *A Horse-and-Buggy Doctor in Southern Indiana*, published in 1973. She presented the building to HMI in 1969. On display are many pieces of furniture and equipment Hutchings used in his daily practice.

10. The **Main St. Buildings** reflect through their refurbished appearance Madison's participation in the Main St. Project, 1978-80, and the merchants' continued interest in historical preservation. Note the exceptional lyre-patterned ironwork on the balcony of the Lotz-Greves building at 306 W. Main St. and the excellent examples of the Italianate business structure at 323-327 W. Main St. The massive moldings and heavy cornices resemble carved stone but actually they are cast metal, mostly zinc. Much of the metal ornamentation dates from the 1870s.

11. The **Jeremiah Sullivan house**, 304 W. 2nd St., is one of Madison's oldest extant buildings. Sullivan (1794-1870), a Virginia native, built the brick Federal-style home in 1818. A promi-

nent attorney, Sullivan held city and county offices and served on Indiana's Supreme Court and in the legislature, 1819-20. The naming of Indianapolis is attributed to Sullivan. His grandson and great-grandson occupied the mayoral chair of the capital city. Jeremiah Sullivan contributed to the founding of Hanover College and the Indiana Historical Society. In 1961 Historic Madison, Inc., purchased the endangered home and conducted an initial restoration largely funded by Eli Lilly. The exterior of the house features paired chimneys on one side, rear porches and side galleries, an exquisite fanlight over the front door, and bricks contoured with a lower lip to shield the mortar from weather damage. The interior whitewashed walls adjoin poplar woodwork, pit-sawed oak flooring, and variously designed mantels and doors. The full six-room basement is unusual for this time and place. Many of Judge Sullivan's effects are on display. In 1985-86 HMI reconstructed a smokehouse-bake oven on the grounds. The two-room structure and projecting usable oven helps to round out one of the most complete house museums of pioneer life in the region. (*NRHP*)

12. The **Talbott-Hyatt house and pioneer garden**, 301 W. 2nd St., is another of Madison's old Federal-style homes. Richard C. Talbott, like his neighbor Jeremiah Sullivan, acquired land in the "suburbs" of Madison on which to locate his home and garden. Talbott probably built his brick house in 1818 and planted a patch of flowers, foods, and garnishes. One of six public wells stood on his property. The fresh water pit, when discovered in 1964, yielded bushels of artifacts providing clues to the life-style of Madison's early elite. In 1962 Mr. and Mrs. Pierre McBride of Louisville, Kentucky, deeded the lot to HMI. Restoration of the house and grounds began almost immediately, and by 1965 a portion of the original garden had been opened to the public. Professionals relaid the garden in period design and helped identify and plant scores of early cuttings, roots, seeds, and seedlings contributed by friends of the project. A Victorian house built on the garden site in 1895 was removed in 1969. HMI erected in 1971 a carriage house and stable on their original foundations and added a potting shed.

13. The **Schofield house**, 217 W. 2nd St., is the birthplace of Indiana's Grand Masonic Lodge. Built around 1817, the two-story, Federal-style brick house is one of only three Grand Lodge birthplaces extant in the country. Fourteen representatives of the state's nine Masonic lodges gathered upstairs in the home on January 13, 1818, and organized a Grand Lodge. At the time the building functioned as a private residence, a tavern, a grocery store, and a post office. From 1908 to 1972 the Schofield family owned the house. The Ancient and Accepted Scottish Rite in the Valley of Indianapolis purchased the property in 1972 and turned it over to the Masonic Heritage Foundation, Inc., for restoration and visitation. It opened to the public in 1975.

14. The **Shrewsbury house**, 301 W. 1st St., is an important Francis Costigan-designed Classic Revival-style structure constructed between 1846 and 1849. Reportedly, Capt. Charles Shrewsbury, commission merchant, pork packing magnate, and flour manufacturer, wanted a residence as splendid as the Lanier mansion, completed a few years earlier. Shrewsbury hired the same architect. The result, although not as pretentious as the Lanier home, contains features, such as the twin pairs of Corinthian columns in the drawing room and the famous free standing spiral staircase, that are considered Costigan masterpieces. The 12-room dwelling has walls that reach 12 to 16 ft. high, floors of ash, poplar, and pine, 13 fireplaces, French chandeliers illuminating Shrewsbury family portraits, and appropriate pieces of European and American furniture, glass, and china. The drawing room retains its original painted walls that required 16 applications of paint by imported French artisans. The exterior brick, once painted red with mortar penciled in white, has paled to a soft pink. The foundation stone came from Maysville, Kentucky. Madison foundries forged the ornamental iron gates and the balcony grillwork. A public outcry prevented the school board from razing the house in 1927 for a new high school. Again, in 1948, interested parties wanted the old place for a boardinghouse or restaurant. Fortunately, John T. and Ann Windle, who would soon spearhead Madison's historic preservation through the founding of Historic Madison, Inc., bought Shrewsbury house and restored it.

Schofield house

15. The **Madison Presbyterian Church**, 202 Broadway, since 1921 has been the home of the reunited congregations of the First and Second Presbyterian churches. Madison's Presbyterians organized in 1815 and erected their first sanctuary in 1818. The church divided in 1833, principally over the slavery issue, and the newly formed Second Presbyterian Church built what is now HMI's Auditorium on E. 3rd St. The other body remained in the original church building until 1840 when a new meetinghouse was constructed on Main St. This church building burned in 1845. In 1848 the congregation built the present structure with its interesting octagonal bell tower in the style of Christopher Wren.

16. The **James F. D. Lanier State Historic Site**, 500 block of W. 1st St., is judged by authorities to be a premier example of the Classic Revival mode of architecture and Indiana's finest antebellum residence. The palatial house of Costigan design was built during the period 1840-44. James Franklin Doughty Lanier (1800-1881) moved to Madison in 1817 from North Carolina. An attorney and businessman, he clerked for the territorial and state legislatures, promoted the Madison and Indianapolis Railroad,

Indiana Historical Society (C2689)
Portico, Lanier State Historic Site

and presided over the Madison branch of the State Bank. Less than five years after moving into his new home, Lanier left for New York City and a partnership with his son-in-law, Richard Winslow, in a new financial firm. Lanier is fondly remembered in Indiana for having rescued the state from money difficulties during the Civil War. His unsecured loans for outfitting regiments and paying the interest on the state debt totaled more than one million dollars, an amount eventually repaid. Four generations of the Lanier family lived in the Madison home. In 1925 the state acquired the residence and opened it in 1926 as the state's first historical memorial. The mansion's dominant external features include its classical shape and its 50-ft.-wide columned portico framed by a distinctive shell-patterned iron railing. The porch's columns rise 30 ft. Highlights of the 3-floor, 18-room interior, stocked with period furnishings, include the spiral staircase with Costigan's name engraved on a small silver plaque attached to the newel post. Gold leaf wallpaper richly decorates Lanier's upstairs bedroom. The bell on the front lawn dates from 1849 and originally hung in the riverfront terminal of the Madison and Indianapolis Railroad.

17. The **Madison Railroad Station**, 615 W. 1st St., is an octagon-shaped building that was built in 1895 for the Pittsburgh, Cincinnati, Chicago, and St. Louis Railroad Company. The sandstone and buff brick station topped by a cupola was owned by the Pennsylvania Railroad until the 1960s. The Jefferson County Historical Society purchased the terminal in the late 1980s and is in the process of restoring the interior and plans to build a new structure to the southwest of the station to house the society's artifact collection. The society's museum had been in the former carriage house behind the public library. Presently the railroad station offers exhibits on the history of southeast Indiana from May through Thanksgiving. The caboose displayed west of the station dates from the time of the station's construction.

18. The **Broadway Fountain**, Broadway St., originally graced the entranceway of the agricultural building at the centennial celebration in Philadelphia in 1876. The 20-ft.-high ornate fountain, embellished with mythical figures and birds and crowned with a 5-ft.-high Greek goddess, came to Madison in 1886. The local Odd Fellows lodge purchased the fountain for around $1,000 and presented it to the city. George Middleton, immortalized in the Middleton Monument on Courthouse Square, gave much of the money for the fountain's reassembly in Madison. Designed for inside display, the fountain slowly deteriorated in the outdoors. Discovered in the 1960s to be severely corroded, the fountain's survival rested on a total bronze recasting. The city contracted in 1976 with Eleftherios Karkadoulias, a Cincinnati-based sculptor, to do the work. In August 1980, after citizens raised almost $120,000 and after innumerable delays, the replica fountain successfully went into operation. The **Trinity Methodist Church**, constructed in 1873, forms a backdrop to the fountain. To the north of the church on the southwest corner of 3rd and Broadway is the **Mrs. John Paul home** built in 1837 by the wife of Madison's founder. The large two-story brick house, enclosed by a masterfully designed iron fence, once was home to author Edward Eggleston.

19. The **Madison-Jefferson County Public Library**, 420 W. Main St., traces its beginnings to the establishment in 1818 of a subscription library, one of the first in Indiana. The library became a public institution in 1888. Its reorganization as a city-county library with township substations came about in 1921. The library had its first permanent home in 1930 when it moved into the old Powell residence at the site of the present building. In 1966 officials broke ground for the addition of wings and a new front to the Powell home. A new building, in essence, went up around the old house. Behind the library is located the former carriage house of the Powell mansion, which until 1988 housed the Jefferson County Historical Museum. The historical society obtained the services of Lee Burns, a noted Indianapolis architect and author, to convert the carriage house into a meeting place and museum, dedicated June 22, 1934. The society previously headquartered in the Lanier house.

20. The **Jesse D. Bright house**, 312 W. 3rd St., was erected sometime between 1837 and 1843. Bright, lieutenant governor, 1843-45, and United States senator, 1845-62, lived in the house from 1837 to 1853. It is not known that he built the two-story brick building. The Senate expelled Bright in 1862 for writing a letter of introduction to his old friend and president of the Confederacy Jefferson Davis. The letter provided an introduction to Davis for another longtime friend, formerly of Madison, who wished to dispose of an improved firearm. The George Wood family occupied the home from 1895 to 1934 and called it Brightwood.

21. The **Francis Costigan house**, 408 W. 3rd St., was built between 1846 and 1849 after the noted architect had achieved fame and fortune from designing the Lanier and Shrewsbury houses, among others. At a time when land was scarce and expensive, Costigan, familiar with the constricted housing in his native Baltimore, designed a narrow structure for a 22-ft.-wide lot. The architect skillfully planned the interior of the home to counter its circumscribed exterior appearance. The drawing room, for example, is 30 ft. long, with two fireplaces and a double stairs leading to an unusual push gate. Magnificent woodwork and ceiling moldings furnish a sense of grandeur in the diminutive residence. A rare sliding front door highlights the small columned portico of the Classic Revival gem. Historic Madison, Inc., acquired the property in 1988.

22. The **First Baptist Church**, 416 Vine St., is the state's oldest Baptist church in continuous existence. The earliest settlers in the vicinity of Madison professed the Baptist creed, and in 1807 they established the Crooked Creek Baptist congregation under the leadership of Elder Jesse Vawter. After worshiping four years in a log cabin, the members built a church in the hamlet of Mount Pleasant. In 1831 the Baptists bought a lot on Vine St. in Madison and constructed a new sanctuary. This building gave way in 1850 for the present church, completed in 1860. The ceiling moldings and door frames in the church suggest a Costigan influence, though no direct link has been established. Costigan lived near the church on 3rd St. The original hand-planed pews are still in use. The church built an addition in 1964. The exterior underwent restoration in 1982.

23. The **John Paul Park**, Vine and 3rd sts., began as a city cemetery donated by John and Sarah Paul early in the 19th century. Many pioneers originally buried here were eventually reburied in Fairmount or Springdale cemeteries. Some undisturbed graves remain to this day in the park and also possibly under 3rd St. In 1874, after a body was dug up from the center of 3rd St., the newspaper report observed that years ago the graveyard extended to the south side of the street, and when the street went through, the remains of 20 or 30 persons were not removed. The park grounds at one time displayed flower beds, broad pathways, and trees, some of which came from the state governors of the original 13 colonies. King Edward VII of England supposedly gave the park an English red oak. It was rumored that a weeping willow tree originated at Napoleon's tomb on St. Helena. A large coral rock fountain was the park's centerpiece. The local chapter of the Daughters of the American Revolution (DAR) acquired control of the premises in 1902. In 1984 the city took over management of the park.

24. The **Trolley Barn**, 717-719 W. Main St., is so named because it once functioned as a storage shed for Madison's trolleys. The brick building served as a city market when built in

1875 and subsequently as a substation for the local electric utility. Purchased in 1971 and renovated in 1972, the Trolley Barn houses a collection of small shops. The businesses spill over into an old brick carriage house moved to the site and reconstructed in 1976.

25. The **Cisco Meat Market Building**, 721 W. Main St., is a late Italianate-style iron-front store built in 1850. Public Service Indiana deeded the building to HMI in 1964. HMI sold the structure in 1970 to a private party but included in the transaction a clause binding the owners to leave unaltered the exterior. This strategy, used in other cities, enabled HMI to ensure the continued protection of the architecture, yet sell the property and earmark the proceeds for other preservation activities. Margie's Country Store presently occupies the building.

26. **Springdale Cemetery**, Vine and W. 5th sts., established in 1839, exhibits a tall very conspicuous granite figure of a woman with her arms upraised in a prayerful attitude. Called *Let There Be Light*, the sculpture, on the north side of the cemetery, marks the graves of the Rev. Joseph H. Barnard (d. 1926) and Martha Grey Grubb Barnard (d. 1919). Joseph Barnard pastored the Second Presbyterian Church for 25 years and subsequently held the chaplaincy at the Madison State Hospital. The statue is a replica of a bronze that sits in Bernheim Forest near Shepherdsville, Kentucky. George Grey Barnard (1863-1938), the son of Joseph and Martha Barnard and a world-renowned sculptor and art collector, designed the memorial. George Barnard did not live in Madison but visited occasionally. Through the patronage and friendship of Miss Drusilla Cravens, of Madison, a collection of plaster casts of his many works graced Lanier mansion before it became state owned. Later the Grace Methodist Church, transformed into the Barnard Museum, displayed the plaster collection. Lack of support for the museum forced the removal of the pieces from Madison in the 1930s. Most of George Barnard's original works of art and his fine assembly of medieval art is on exhibit in the Cloisters, a division of the New York Metropolitan Museum of Art.

27. The **Hanging Rock**, a stone cliff landmark projecting over a natural amphitheater, is located alongside IND 7 on its winding uphill course north from Madison. The phenomenon is the consequence of an aeon of weather erosion. The roadway at one time ran under the shelf of rock. The shade of the stone awning and the issue of spring water revived many fatigued wagoners and teams.

28. The **Waterworks Marker** is on the road leading to the Madison State Hospital. From the entrance to the hospital off IND 7 near the top of the hill, a narrow bridge crosses the old Madison and Indianapolis Railroad incline approaching the end of its precipitous climb. At .3 mile is a curved stone wall above a deep ravine. The marker on the wall gives 1868 as the year of its construction as part of the city's new waterworks system. The wall, part of a dam, permitted the stored spring water to flow down the railroad cuts through troughs to several reservoirs. The plan worked well until the apparently uncontrollable use of the reservoirs as swimming pools by Madison's youth forced authorities to experiment with alternate forms of water supply.

29. The **Madison and Indianapolis Railroad Incline** can be viewed from the bridge at the 1000 block on W. Main St. The grade, one of the nation's steepest standard gauge lines, cost more than $275,000 to complete by 1841. It gave Madison until the mid-1850s the state's sole rail outlet to the Ohio River, and it guaranteed the city several decades of prosperity. (*HAER*)

30. **Clifty Falls State Park** became the state's third park when established in 1920. Previously a succession of families owned the land including the Todd family, said to be kin to President James Buchanan and to Mary Todd Lincoln. The general course of the 1,336-acre park follows deep limestone gorges formed by Clifty Creek and Little Clifty Creek. A handful of waterfalls and moderate to rugged hiking trails are among the park's attractions. Also available are camping facilities, picnic areas, tennis courts, and an olympic size swimming pool. Clifty Falls Inn and the Riverview Annex provide modern lodging and an exceptional view of the Ohio River valley and Madison. A historical feature is the remainder of the old railroad tunnel known as "Brough's Folly," an abortive attempt to build another railroad route from Madison to the hilltop. John

Brough (1811-1865), the tunnel's designer and president of the Madison and Indianapolis Railroad, abandoned the project because of financial difficulties. Brough went on to become Ohio's Civil War governor. The park, despite the distracting towering smoke stacks of the Clifty Creek power plant, and historical Madison treat the visitor to a rare combination of natural beauty and noteworthy architecture.

Tour 5

Leave Clifty Falls by the north entrance at IND 62, go left *3 m.* to IND 56, and proceed west *1.1 m.* to the east entrance of **Hanover College**. Turn left. The twisting tree-lined Lucinda Ball Dr. leads to the 600-acre college campus overlooking the Ohio River. The town of **HANOVER** (p. 4,054) had its beginnings in 1809 when Williamson Dunn and family moved from Danville, Kentucky, onto land purchased the previous year. The site was first called Dunn's Settlement, then South Hanover, and finally, Hanover, after the former New Hampshire home of Mrs. Thomas Searle, wife of the first pastor of the local Presbyterian Church. The college's roots go back to 1827 when John Finley Crowe, the second pastor of the same church, desired an establishment to train youth for the ministry. Under Presbyterian auspices, Crowe founded an academy on land donated by Williamson Dunn. The Indiana General Assembly incorporated the academy in 1829 and in 1833 approved a change of name to Hanover College. In the same year the first substantive building was erected, called the **College Edifice**. A Presbyterian seminary instituted in 1829 as the Department of Theology of the academy moved to New Albany in 1840 and to Chicago in 1859, becoming the McCormick Theological Seminary in 1886. In 1837 a tornado severely damaged the College Edifice. The Hanover Presbyterian Church donated money earmarked for a new sanctuary to the reconstruction of the main building. After the college moved to its present location in 1857, the building was deeded to the congregation and remains the home of Hanover's Presbyterians, located at the corner of Presbyterian and Main sts.

For a brief period between 1843 and 1844, the college lost its charter to the newly formed Madison University in the nearby city. The new university, however, failed to hold the loyalties of former Hanover students or faculty, and the state rechartered the college at Hano-

ver. It became officially coeducational in 1880, but it was not until the late 1940s that the college began admitting blacks, one of the last Indiana colleges to do so. Distinguished alumni include politicians Thomas A. Hendricks and William Hayden English, journalist John H. Holliday, and historian Walter LaFeber. Most buildings date since 1940, when large private donations and successful fund drives afforded the construction of practically a complete new physical plant. On April 3, 1974, a tornado damaged most of the college's 30 buildings, 60 faculty homes, and a large number of beautiful old trees. Two years and $3 million later, the campus had recovered, although the return of the foliage would take many years. Today, Hanover is the state's oldest private four-year liberal arts school.

While on the campus, besides taking advantage of the several spectacular vistas of the Ohio River Valley, note the old frame **YMCA building** located behind several fraternity houses to the right just after entering the campus from the north on Ball Dr. Hanover's Young Men's Christian Association dates from 1870, the world's first college campus YMCA. Its hall, completed in 1883, is the oldest YMCA building in the world erected solely for that purpose. It is also the oldest building on Hanover's campus. The **observatory** north of the YMCA was constructed in 1889. Both structures were moved to their present location from other parts of the campus to make room for new buildings. **Hendricks Hall**, named for Thomas A. Hendricks, was built in 1903 and served as the first college library until 1952. Located east of the administration building, it now houses the foreign language lab and art studios. (*NRHP*)

From the YMCA building and observatory, continue to the administration building. Turn right and follow the road from the campus through downtown Hanover to Presbyterian St. Go right one block to Crowe St. The old two-

Tour 5

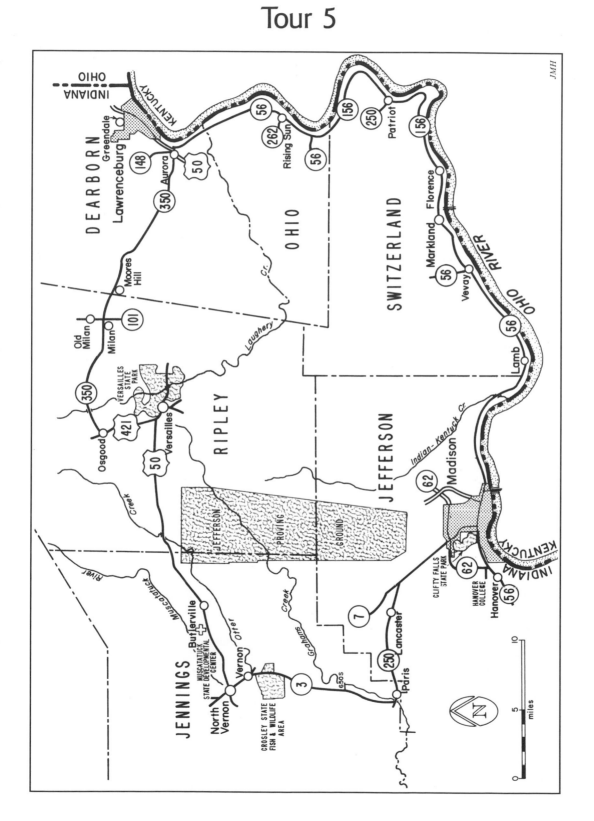

story, 12-room frame house with full-length porches on both levels is the **John Finley Crowe house**, built in 1824 by the college's founder. Owned by the college since 1960 and used for storage, the house in obvious disrepair was saved from possible demolition in 1981 by local persons who formed a nonprofit organization called Friends of the John Finley Crowe House and sold shares towards its eventual purchase. With the help of a loan from Historic Landmarks Foundation of Indiana the group completed rehabilitation in 1984, the same year the Keach family purchased it. A small plaque in the left front yard gives some particulars about the house. (*NRHP/HABSI*)

Leave Hanover and return east on IND 56 to IND 62. Turn north and continue about *4.1 m.* past the entrance to Clifty Falls State Park to IND 7. Head north on IND 7 *4.7 m.* to IND 250 and turn west *2.5 m.* to **LANCASTER**. Set back from the road to the left on the approach into Lancaster is a large three-story stone building, once the **Eleutherian College**, the second school west of the Allegheny Mountains to provide interracial education (Oberlin was first). Founded in 1848 by Thomas Craven and supported by Lancaster's Neal Creek Abolition Baptist Church and the local antislavery society, Eleutherian College (Eleutherian=freedom, liberty) opened its doors to freed and fugitive slaves. In the decade prior to the Civil War between one-fourth and one-third of the students were blacks. The college building, one of several on the campus, was completed in 1856. The school closed in 1874 but reopened in 1878 as a private high school and normal school until 1888 when Lancaster Township purchased the building for a public school. Upon consolidation of township schools in 1938, the school was closed permanently. Private owners failed in the attempt to have the State Department of Conservation take it over and convert the area into a state park. In 1973 Historic Madison, Inc., received the building as a gift. Eleutherian's most prominent black alumnus was the Rev. Moses Broyles (d. 1882), an ex-slave who attended the school between 1854 and 1857. Broyles went on to become pastor of the Second Baptist Church in Indianapolis and a prime mover in the organization of the Indiana Association of Black Baptist Churches in 1858.

From the college continue west on IND 250 *7 m.* to IND 3, entering **JENNINGS COUNTY** (p. 22,854; 378 sq. m.) and the town of **PARIS**. Jennings County was formed from Jackson and Jefferson counties in 1816. The state's 17th county took its name from **Jonathan Jennings**, Indiana's first state governor, 1816-22. Almost one-half of the county's land is used for farming. The small cluster of houses that identifies Paris today is but a remnant of what once was a thriving community boasting several dozen stores and factories. Its prosperity was due partially to its location between Madison and Brownstown, two major centers of early Indiana. Paris had a widespread reputation for its well-dressed men, catered to by the town's excellent tailoring shops. The town declined when several railroads, including the Madison and Indianapolis, bypassed it. Some early families were of French Huguenot descent, which probably accounts for the town's name.

Head north on IND 3 *5 m.* Turn right on CR 650S, at the sign for Graham Church (the first Presbyterian church in Jennings County, established in 1817). About *.5 m.* east stands the **James Covered Bridge** of Howe truss design with steel abutments, built in 1887 by Daniel Baron and still in use.

Return to IND 3 and continue north *4.5 m.* to the **Crosley State Fish and Wildlife Area**, a public hunting and fishing ground supervised by the Indiana Department of Natural Resources. In 1958 the state purchased the 4,084-acre grounds from Powell Crosley, Jr., a Cincinnati industrialist and sportsman. Crosley at one time owned the Cincinnati Reds baseball team, WLW radio station, and the Crosley Manufacturing Company, which produced a range of articles from radios to cars. The care of his Jennings County property, which included a large lodge, since destroyed, required a staff of 14. About seven miles of the Muscatatuck River meanders through the heavily timbered area. The river, along with 10 well-stocked ponds, is a popular fishing place. Outdoor archery ranges provide a variety of distances to test a person's bow and arrow skills. Hunting requires permits and prior permission and is subject to other regulations. A shooting range and a camping and picnic area are also provided.

From Crosley State Fish and Wildlife Area continue north on IND 3 about *1.8 m.* to IND 7 and **VERNON** (p. 329), a historically rich and well-preserved community. Founded in

1815 by **John Vawter** (1782-1862), a Baptist minister and pioneer in the Madison, Indiana, vicinity, Vernon became the seat of Jennings County in 1817. The town was named for Mount Vernon, George Washington's home. Its location on a plateau almost surrounded by a loop of the Muscatatuck River essentially barred outward growth. Incorporated as a town in 1851, Vernon eventually yielded economic dominance, but not the courthouse, to North Vernon, its near neighbor. Vernon elects its officials every two years in March rather than following the statewide practice of November elections every four years. Vernon's 1851 act of incorporation granted the town jurisdiction over its election laws. (*NRHP/HABSI/HAER*)

Vernon claims Indiana's first women's club, the **Clionian Society**, based on the discovery in 1922 of the club's constitution dated July 17, 1855, four years before the institution of New Harmony's Minerva group, traditionally considered the state's first women's organization.

Most Vernon attractions are within walking distance. A detailed listing of historical sites and present businesses is available at shops located around the courthouse. Construction on the Italianate-style **Jennings County Courthouse** began in 1857. Isaac Hodgson (1826-1909), the architect, designed other Indiana courthouses and public buildings, including the Rose Polytechnic Institute at Terre Haute in the 1870s. The white limestone trim on the Vernon courthouse came from a local quarry. The structure was remodeled in 1953. A display of Indian relics from the vicinity is on the first floor. In the first half of the 20th century, Vernon waged a lengthy battle to retain its status as the county seat. In 1913 the state legislature authorized a special election to relocate the courthouse at North Vernon. The election of 1916 failed to win approval, but the voters, three years later, gave their consent. Vernon, however, fought the decision until 1948 when the special election of 1919 was set aside by the courts and the courthouse was allowed to remain in Vernon.

A historical marker on the courthouse lawn describes **Morgan's Raid** into Indiana. On July 11, 1863, a small force of around 1,000 Jennings County volunteers and Union troops at Vernon prepared to battle Brig. Gen. John Hunt Morgan and several thousand Confederate raiders who sought to destroy two large bridges on the Madison and Indianapolis Railroad. The clash did not take place. In one of the few mistakes Morgan made in his military blitz through Kentucky and southern Indiana, he overestimated the defense of the town and withdrew after several fruitless demands that the defenders surrender. The next day Maj. Gen. Lew Wallace arrived from Indianapolis with a contingent of about 1,000 raw recruits. Wallace received orders not to pursue the fleeing Morgan. A house, a former school building on the northeast corner of Perry St. and IND 3/7, served as **Lew Wallace's Headquarters** during his brief stay in Vernon. On the east side of Perry St., between High and South sts., south of the courthouse, is the area where the soldiers and townspeople gathered to await the battle.

The **North American House**, on the northeast corner of Pike and Brown sts. north of the courthouse, is probably the oldest building in Vernon. Erected around 1820 as an inn and stagecoach stop, the structure now is home for Our Heritage, Inc. (Jennings County Historical Society), and contains a free museum, art gallery, and antique and gift shop.

The **Old Mill Inn**, on the east side of Pike St., two buildings north of the North American House, was built before 1840 and served through the years as a depot, tavern, and mill. Immediately north of the Old Mill Inn is the famous **Madison and Indianapolis Railroad overpass**, built between 1837 and 1841. In order to reduce the risk of flood damage and avoid a precipitous grade, the railroad built a 50-ft.-high, one-mile-long curved fill which included this masonry arch. (*HAER*)

Backtrack from the underpass to Brown St. West on Brown St. at the northwest corner of Brown and Montgomery sts. is the **Hickman New home**. The two-story brick house, painted white with blue shutters, was built in the early 1830s. The New family, with 12 children, including Hickman, came to Vernon in 1822. A lifelong cabinetmaker, Hickman New was instrumental in starting the Christian church in Vernon. New's attorney son, Jeptha, was a mayor of Vernon and a congressman.

Next to the New home, west, is the boyhood **home of Albert Edward Wiggam** (1871-1957). Wiggam, a popular lecturer and author in the early 20th century, grew up in the one-story frame house. He was graduated from Vernon High School and Hanover College. His particular interest was heredity, and he wrote several best-selling books on the subject, including *The New Decalogue of Science* (1923), *The Fruit of the Family Tree* (1924), and *Marks of the Educated Man* (1930). He belonged to a variety of heredity and eugenics organizations and served as president of the Association for the Study of Human Heredity. For many years he wrote a well-known syndicated newspaper column, "Let's Explore Your Mind." Wiggam is buried in Santa Monica, California, where he spent much of his adult life.

South on Montgomery St., between Brown St. and IND 3/7, is the old **Christian Church** building, built in 1838, in which Hickman New preached and worshiped. Successive businesses have used the brick structure since its discontinuance as a church sanctuary in 1878, the year the membership elected to join what is now North Vernon's First Christian Church. The bell in the tower once pealed from atop the courthouse. Inside, a preserved strip of wall is inscribed, "Sam Smith—Oct. 7, 1861—Going to the Army Tomorrow. Goodby, Vernon."

Return to Perry St., east of the courthouse, turn right, and drive south to the **Vernon Cemetery**. Many of Vernon's pioneers and several famous race-car drivers are buried here. Among the drivers are **Wilbur Shaw**, three-time winner of the Indianapolis 500 (1937, 1939, 1940), who died in a plane crash in 1954 at the age of 52, and **Pat O'Connor**, another Indianapolis 500 driver, who was killed in a 14-car pileup on the first lap of the 1958 race.

From the cemetery, return to Washington St., turn left, cross the Muscatatuck River, and proceed left on the first gravel road *.4 m.* to its termination at the Baldwin family cemetery. A path through the woods of several hundred yards leads to the remains of **Tunnel Mill**. An engineering feat, Tunnel Mill was built in 1824 by Ebenezer Baldwin and remained in operation until around 1900. He employed, so it is said, John Vawter, the founder of Vernon, to dig a 300-ft. tunnel through limestone to obtain water power.

Returning to Poplar St. via Washington St., rejoin IND 3/7 and head north from Vernon. To the right, beyond Vernon and behind CEW Enterprises, Inc., stands the **Smith Vawter house**. The two-story brick home was built in the 1830s by the son of John Vawter. North on IND 3/7 *.2 m.* is the entrance to the **Muscatatuck-Jennings County Park** on the left. Established in 1921 as a state park, the wooded

261 acres were turned over to the county in June 1968.

North of the park *.2 m.* is the city limits of **NORTH VERNON** (p. 5,768). In the early 1850s the prospect of the Ohio and Mississippi Railroad crossing the Madison and Indianapolis Railroad in the vicinity of the sparse settlement of Lick Skillet led directly to the founding of North Vernon. The young and alert Hagerman Tripp platted a town at the railway junction and changed the name from Lick Skillet to Tripton, in his own honor. Subsequent additions to the original plat after 1854 generally employed the name North Vernon, and this designation won out by 1867 when North Vernon was incorporated as a town. By 1876 North Vernon had grown to more than 2,000 residents, and the agricultural and industrial center of the county officially assumed city status. Although the Baltimore and Ohio Railroad was once the largest employer, the present economy is characterized by small industries and retail stores, with automotive accessories and parts and rug and plastic manufacturers clearly dominating its manufacturing.

Six blocks (*.8 m.*) beyond the city limits, turn right on Oak St. and drive to the end, which faces the **Tripp home**, at 318 Jennings St., built in 1853. The columned, two-story white brick house with green shutters is set back from the street on the left and is fronted by a circular drive.

Turn left to US 50 (first Walnut, then Buckeye sts.) then right for *5 m.* to the **Muscatatuck State Developmental Center** entrance on the left. Established in 1919 by the state legislature as the Indiana Farm Colony for Feeble Minded Youth, the center serves mentally retarded and developmentally disabled persons. Often a political football, occasionally riddled with scandal, and ever involved in public relations efforts with nearby communities, the institution houses residents from 35 southern Indiana counties. The majority of the buildings were constructed in 1938-39. Twenty-five new structures were dedicated in 1940. The original 2,071-acre farm has been trimmed to less than 100 acres of actual farmland as the school's agricultural operations have been phased out in recent years. Around 900 acres of the site became the Southeastern Indiana Purdue Agricultural Center (SEPAC) in 1977, an area the visitor will pass on the mile-long entryway to the hospital.

BUTLERVILLE, *1 m.* east of the hospital on US 50, like North Vernon, owed its existence to the railroads. Platted in 1853, Butlerville straddled the Ohio and Mississippi Railroad. It derived its name from its first postmaster's hometown of Butlerville, Ohio. Two notable personalities have close ties with the Butlerville vicinity. **Jessamyn West** (1902-1984), author of *The Friendly Persuasion* (1945) and more than a dozen other novels, was born near Butlerville. The West family moved to California when Jessamyn was six years old. She was a cousin to former president **Richard Milhous Nixon**, whose roots lie deep in Jennings County. Elizabeth Price Griffith Milhous and her nurseryman husband Joshua Milhous, the great-grandparents of Jessamyn West and Richard Nixon, moved to Jennings County from Ohio in 1854. The devout Quakers (Elizabeth was a Quaker minister) established a farm south of Butlerville on Rush Branch Creek. On an adjoining farm, Nixon's mother Hannah was born in 1885 to Franklin and Almira Burdg Milhous in a big square frame farmhouse that unfortunately burned in December 1968. Richard Nixon is one of two American presidents, Benjamin Harrison being the other, to have had a Hoosier-born parent. When Hannah was 12 years old in 1897 the family removed to the new Quaker colony of Whittier, California, where Richard was born in 1913. In June 1971 President Nixon came to the courthouse at Vernon to dedicate a plaque to his mother, Hannah. The historical marker is permanently located on the east side of Butlerville on the south side of US 50.

While driving through Butlerville take note of the **Baptist Church** at the west edge of town on the right with its interesting "wedding cake" three-tiered bell tower erected in 1881-82, 20 years after the church was built.

Hopewell Cemetery contains a number of the Milhous clan, including great-grandfather Joshua and Sarah Emily Milhous, the first wife of Franklin Milhous. To get to the quaint fenced cemetery turn right at the church, follow the road past a right turn, followed by a left turn for *1 m.* to a crossroad. The cemetery is in the northeast corner of the intersection. Turn left and at *.5 m.* turn left again. Turn right at US 50. At *.1 m.* on the right is the Milhous marker.

Continue *4.2 m.* to the Ripley County line (for a description of the county see Tour 4).

Travel *9.4 m.* east to **VERSAILLES** (pronounced Versales, p. 1,560), the seat of Ripley County. John Paul, owner of much of southeastern Indiana and founder of Madison and New Albany, donated 100 acres for the county seat in January 1818. **John Ritchie** (Ritchey or Richie), county agent, laid out the town in September 1818. The town's name obviously refers to the French city or royal palace near Paris, but the precise manner of its being named is confused. The choices include it being so designated by John Paul to honor his native French city, or to memorialize his French parents. Another possibility is that the city was named by John DePauw of Washington County, whose French father fought with Lafayette in the American Revolutionary War. It could also have been named by transplanted natives of Versailles, Kentucky, or by John Ritchie whose surname is of French derivation. Versailles became a vital link in the populating of Indiana and points beyond because it lay on the north-south Michigan Rd. (US 421) and the east-west Cincinnati-St. Louis highway (US 50). The railroads subsequently bypassed Versailles and severely curtailed its expansion.

Continue east on US 50 *1.3 m.* past the stoplight at Versailles (US 50 and Adams St.) to the **Versailles State Park** entrance on the left. The park's 5,903 acres make it the second largest in the state. The grounds were acquired by the National Park Service in 1935. Civilian Conservation Corps (CCC) workers, who lived on the site, began the park's development. Indiana received the land from the National Park Service in 1943. The first priority called for the damming of Laughery Creek to create a 230-acre lake. Legal snarls over land purchases delayed the effort until 1954. The park also offers a field-trial course (testing hunting dogs) and facilities for boat launching, fishing, camping, picnicking, hiking, and horse riding.

Between the entrance to the park and the gatehouse stands the **Busching Covered Bridge**, to the left, straddling Laughery Creek. The contract for the bridge was let to Thomas A. Hardman of Brookville in 1885. The Howe truss bridge, the only one remaining of nine covered bridges Hardman built in Indiana between 1870 and 1885, is 184 ft. long, including overhangs. The road through the bridge is part of the original Cincinnati-to-St. Louis Pike. (*HAER*)

Bat Cave, northeast of the campground in the park, is over 400 ft. long with ceilings ranging 1 to 8 ft. The legend of Silas Schimmerhorn and Bat Cave is intriguing local lore. Schimmerhorn, a fugitive from Morgan's Raiders, took refuge in the cave, surrounded himself with obliging timber wolves, and lived off the land and neighboring farmers' grain and stock. Few persons ever caught sight of him, and attempts to capture him proved futile. No one knows when or where he died, but, so the story goes, Schimmerhorn and the wolves still roam the countryside on starless nights.

From the park return west on US 50 and proceed into Versailles via Main St., one block east of the stoplight. The **Ripley County Historical Society Building and Museum** is located at 201 S. Main St. The museum is housed in the old brick Grand Army of the Republic (GAR) headquarters, a property deeded to the historical society in 1931 as a county shrine to soldiers of all wars. Initially, it was called the War Memorial Museum. War relics and Ripley County memorabilia are on display, including a mid-19th-century piano that originally belonged to Stephen Harding, a Ripley County resident who briefly served as governor of the Territory of Utah during the Civil War.

A block north of the museum is the **Ripley County Courthouse**. Constructed during the Civil War, it received additions and remodeling in 1912 and 1972. The clock tower was erected in 1932 to fulfill the bequest of Florence S. Grether for a memorial to her husband, Charles. Several markers on the courthouse lawn note the occupation of Versailles by Morgan's Raiders on July 12, 1863. Morgan and his men seized the county's available cash and the citizens' weapons, supposedly smashing the armaments on the cornerstone of the new courthouse then under construction. From the Masonic Lodge, then housed on the top floor of the nearby old courthouse, Morgan's troops stole a collection of jewels. Morgan, a Mason, returned the treasure. The gems can be seen in the Masonic Temple a block west of the courthouse on the northeast corner of Tyson and Adams sts.

Across from the Masonic Lodge on the northwest corner of Tyson and Adams sts. is the **Tyson United Methodist Church**. James H. Tyson (1856-1941), born in Versailles, cofounded the Walgreen drugstore chain in the late 19th century. Having acquired considerable wealth by the 1930s, "Uncle Jim" Tyson endowed the town with a church, a library, a waterworks, a school, and a trustee-administered block of Walgreen stock, the dividends of which continue to provide means for civic improvements as voted upon annually by the residents. Tyson had the church built as a memorial to his mother, Elizabeth Adams Tyson. The unique architectural style is a composite image of the world's great palaces and cathedrals glimpsed by Tyson during his extensive travels. The exterior is glazed ivory brick, now heavily crazed, and glass brick. The aluminum cross crowns a 65-ft.-tall aluminum spire. The roof is lead-coated copper. The vaulted interior ceiling features painted stars, placed in astronomically correct positions, on a blue background. A half-block west of the church is the library, of similar architecture, and at the end of the block is the school.

Versailles is home to the **Historic Hoosier Hills**, a resource, conservation, and development project assisted by federal, state, and local agencies and organizations, covering eight counties in southeastern Indiana. The project office is located at 207 N. Main St. in the USDA Agricultural Center.

Return to the courthouse, turn left on Main St., and right at 2nd North St. to the **Cliff Hill Cemetery**. The Tyson headstone sits in front of a tall obelisk topped by a carved flame dedicated in Tyson's memory by the citizens of Versailles and Johnson Township. Two famous incidents are connected with the cliffside area of the cemetery. One night in the 1840s Jonathan W. Gordon, a young doctor, along with John B. Glass and Bernard Mullen, medical students, crept into the cemetery to disinter a body in order to perform an autopsy. Surprised, however, by guards posted by relatives of the deceased to prevent just such an occurrence, Gordon and Mullen escaped by horse but Glass avoided capture by leaping over the 100-ft.-high cliff, surviving only by landing in tree branches. Gordon skipped the state but returned later to lead a distinguished career as an attorney. Glass and Mullen were caught and indicted but apparently the trial never commenced. For years the spot of the famed jump was called Gordon's Leap because it was mistakenly thought the doctor had taken the remarkable dive.

Clifford Gordon, reportedly Jonathan Gordon's nephew, figured in another extraordinary escapade in the cemetery 50 years later. In 1897 the citizens of Ripley County, frustrated and fearful after several months of robberies and thefts, practiced their own brand of justice. In the early morning hours of September 15, between 200 and 400 hooded vigilantes occupied Versailles and seized control of the jail. They shot or beat to death five prisoners, including Clifford Gordon, and hanged the corpses in a slippery elm tree at the cliff in the cemetery. The bold lynching created a sensation. Souvenir hunters stole or bought every piece of the hanging tree. One scavenger cut a bullet out of the body of Lyle Levi. (Interestingly, Levi, years earlier, had ridden with the famed Reno Gang of the Seymour vicinity.) A record in the state attorney general's office covered up the townsfolk's actions by ruling that the victims actually selected ropes and hung themselves, a verdict few believed.

All five victims in the Versailles lynching resided in **OSGOOD** (p. 1,554), *4.5 m.* north of Versailles on US 421. Laid out in 1856, Osgood was named for A. L. Osgood, the chief engineer of that section of the Ohio and Mississippi Railroad that ran just north of the plat. The town, incorporated in 1878, became a commercial and agricultural center. Osgood was the county's second largest town behind Batesville until the 1980 census moved Versailles into the second spot by a plurality of six persons. The **Damm Theatre** on the left side of Buckeye St. (US 421) and the **Louis Damm Building** across the street are local landmarks. The Damm family ran a bakery whose goods often were transported by wheelbarrow from the business to the depot for shipment to nearby towns. In 1914 Louis Damm, a German immigrant, built the Damm Building wherein he opened Osgood's first movie theater. Admission in the early days cost a nickel or 20 wrappers from Damm's baked bread. The family relocated the movie house to its present location in 1921. The 400-seat Damm Theatre is believed to be Indiana's oldest family-owned and operated motion picture house.

Proceed east from Osgood on IND 350, passing through the hamlets of Delaware and Pierceville, *9.5 m.* to the turnoff (IND 101) on the right to **MILAN** (p. 1,566). Just past Pierceville, Seagram's Distillery operates a warehouse complex. What is called Old Milan today, situated a mile north on IND 101, was the initial settlement. When the railroad came

through a mile south in 1854 the population gradually shifted to the new Milan. The high point in Milan's history took place in 1954. Not only did the town celebrate its centennial, but its high school won the state basketball crown by beating Muncie Central 32 to 30. With only 161 students, Milan was the smallest school to win the title since Thorntown in 1915. **Bobby Plump**, the 5'10" hero of the game, received the coveted **Arthur L. Trester** Award for Mental Attitude and was named Indiana's "Mr. Basketball." Milan was the inspiration for the 1986 movie "Hoosiers," shot in Indiana and starring Gene Hackman, Barbara Hershey, and Dennis Hopper. Hopper was nominated for an Oscar for his performance. David Anspaugh, a Decatur, Indiana, native, directed the picture, and Angelo Pizzo, Anspaugh's former roommate at Indiana University, wrote and co-produced it. The movie told the story of a small-town ("Hickory, Indiana") team that made it to the basketball finals in 1951.

From Milan travel east on IND 350 *1.8 m.* to the Ripley-Dearborn county line (for a description of Dearborn County see Tour 4). Continue east *.7 m.* and turn right at Manchester St. for the town of **MOORES HILL** (p. 566), platted in 1838 and named for Adam Moore, an early settler, miller, and Methodist preacher. Fifteen years prior to surveying the site, residents petitioned for a post office to be designated Moores Mill, after Adam Moore's gristmill business. Tradition has it that an official in Washington, D.C., misread the name and substituted "Hill" for "Mill," and thus it has remained. Adam Moore's son, John, spearheaded a drive for a college in 1853. Through his efforts the **Moores Hill Male and Female Collegiate Institute** was chartered in 1854, the second Indiana college to adopt coeducation. Moores Hill College, as it is more commonly known, existed until 1917, when, unable to meet minimum endowment requirements for accreditation, it relocated in Evansville, becoming Evansville College, more recently the University of Evansville.

Carnegie Hall is the only surviving building of the college at Moores Hill. It was built in 1907-8 on the strength of an initial gift of $18,500 from the philanthropist Andrew Carnegie. The building is located on the left (south) side of Main St. *.3 m.* west (right) of Manchester St. Three markers, including an old mill stone from Adam Moore's mill, highlight the history of Moores Hill College. A museum and library were installed in the building in 1988, the first efforts to make Carnegie Hall a cultural center for the area.

AURORA (p. 3,816), *11 m.* east of Moores Hill on IND 350, overlooks the picturesque hilly terrain that borders a prominent bend of the Ohio River. Marinas dot the banks of Hogan Creek's two branches that connect in the city before emptying into the Ohio River. The lovely tract of forested hills and waterways was purchased in 1804 by Charles Vattier of Cincinnati. In 1818 a post office was established and given the name Decatur. The following year Vattier sold 35,616 acres for $19,000 to the Aurora Association for Internal Improvements composed of about 20 men from Indiana, Ohio, and Kentucky. The land was vested in the group's presiding officer, the multitalented **Jesse Lynch Holman** (1784-1842), legislator, state and federal judge, Dearborn County school superintendent, Franklin College trustee, prominent writer of fiction and poetry, Baptist minister and organizer, and one of the first officers of the Indiana Historical Society. The Aurora Association laid out the town in 1819. Holman influenced the post office to change its name from Decatur to Aurora. Supposedly, envy of the nearby prospering town of Rising Sun led to the use of the Aurora designation. Holman reportedly wrote, "the Aurora [the Roman goddess of dawn] comes before the Rising Sun." Industry and river traffic historically have been the pillars of Aurora's economy. For years steamboats daily lined the wharves to receive and deliver passengers and goods. The importance of river commerce in Aurora's past is expressed in two unusual downtown street names, Importing and Exporting. Foundries and furniture and casket makers have existed in the area since the 19th century. Recently, the city's population dipped below 4,000, the lowest level since 1900, but the population shrinkage has not diminished the significance of this early Indiana river town or its many attractions.

IND 350 ends at its junction with US 50 and IND 56. IND 56 continues east into the downtown area as Importing St. Proceed east on IND 56 into Aurora, past the old 1887 George St. iron bridge on the left (nontraversable; *NRHP*) across Hogan Creek and around the corner onto Judiciary St. (IND 56). At the foot of 2nd St. near the river bank on the left is a marker commemorating the launching of the **Clinton**, July 4, 1824, the first steamboat built at Aurora.

From the marker, follow 3rd St. to Main St. and turn left to the **Hillforest Mansion**. Although of an Italian Renaissance style of architecture, this extraordinary edifice is sometimes referred to as Steamboat Gothic because of its circular porches, coupled columns, and round cupola, reminiscent of a pilot house. Thomas Gaff (b. 1808), a prominent industrialist and civic leader, built the home between 1852 and 1856 on a 10-acre tract. Gaff, singly or with his brother James W., is said to have launched 33 businesses in and out of state, including breweries, steamboat lines, mills, general stores, freight houses, a cotton plantation, a compressed-yeast factory, a silver mine, and a gas and coke company. He also started the First National Bank of Aurora and served on school boards, agricultural societies, the board of directors of the Ohio and Mississippi Railroad, and two terms in the Indiana Senate.

The materials used in building the spacious three-level home were the finest money could buy at the time, from the Circassian walnut used in the parquet flooring to the porcelain keyhole covers. The interior is highlighted by the elaborate 18-in.-wide plaster borders formed from molds imported from Italy. The twin drawing rooms feature bay windows, Belter-type Victorian furniture, a melodeon, a Fisher piano, Smilie engravings, and iron fireplace mantels. The upstairs bedrooms and the ladies' sitting or "morning" room are nicely furnished with period pieces. The belvedere or cupola was designed to provide a sweeping view of the river and surrounding territory and still houses Gaff's large brass telescope. To the east of the house is an unusual melon cellar made of glacial rock and built into a rise behind the mansion. Hillforest is owned and operated by Hillforest Historical Foundation, Inc. (*NRHP/HABSI*)

Hillforest affords a spectacular visual range that takes in parts of Indiana, Ohio, and Kentucky. From the porch of the mansion can be seen below, on 4th St., the construction date "1864" incorporated in the roof of St. Mary of the Immaculate Conception Catholic Church. The top of Langley Heights St., about two blocks west of Hillforest on 5th St., provides another panoramic view. Just east of the man-

Hillforest Mansion, 1966

sion on 5th St. is the small **Mary Stratton Park**, a memorial plot to the daughter of Jesse L. Holman. Stratton began the Aurora Women's Research Club in the 19th century. Continue east to the bottom of 5th St. Just after turning south onto Water St. look right at the hillside. Note the arched masonry openings that years ago were used to store locally made beer. To the left is **Riverfront Park**, developed during the 1976 bicentennial. The historical marker at the park, dedicated the same year, commemorates the lives of Jesse L. Holman and his son, William. William Steele Holman (1822-1897), elected 16 times to Congress between 1859 and 1897, earned the title "Watchdog of the Treasury" for his hostility to government appropriation bills. Return to the junction of highways 50, 350, and 56 via downtown Aurora, noting the many old business structures. At the highway intersection, on the west shoulder of US 50, stands a historical plaque denoting the birthplace of **Samuel Morrison**, the first white child born in Indiana Territory east of Vincennes (a similar

claim is made for John Henry Kluge at Hope, see Tour 14).

Proceed north on US 50 a short distance to IND 148 or Sunnyside Ave. and turn left. The homes at 340, 343, and 344 Sunnyside belonged in the **Squibb family**, early distillery magnates. The **Davis home** at 422 Sunnyside dates from 1859. In 1874 Elam and Louisa Davis purchased the large white frame house. Here **Elmer H. Davis** was born in 1890. He was a nationally recognized radio news commentator for three decades and a four-time winner of the Peabody Award for outstanding broadcasting. He also headed the Office of War Information from 1942 to 1945. The family lived in Aurora until 1913. Aurora also was the birthplace, in 1894, of nationally known commentator Edwin C. Hill, best known for his broadcasts "The Human Side of the News."

Return to US 50, turn left, and continue *1.1 m.* to **LAWRENCEBURG** (p. 4,403), Indiana's fourth oldest city and Dearborn County's largest community. Capt. Samuel C. Vance, a Revolutionary War veteran, founded the town in 1802. He named it after his wife, Mary Morris Lawrence, the granddaughter of Maj. Gen. Arthur St. Clair, governor of the Northwest Territory. Lawrenceburg became the seat of justice for Dearborn County in 1803. By 1808 a ferry-house, jail, tavern, general store, and chairmaker shop were among the 20 or so cabins that lined the bank of the Ohio River. The cabins were often constructed of buckeye logs, and when just built the new shoots growing from each length of timber gave the dwellings the appearance of a mass of green bushes. (In 1988 the Dearborn County Historical Society erected at West High and Ash sts. the first log cabin of a new Pioneer Village.) In 1809 Pinckney Jones, a shipbuilder from Rising Sun, laid out the town of Edenborough due west of Lawrenceburg. Edenborough, now **Newtown**, changed hands several times before being annexed to Lawrenceburg in 1819. By the Civil War, Lawrenceburg's population exceeded 3,500. The devastating flood of 1832 and the removal of the courthouse to nearby Wilmington between 1836 and 1844 had not seriously impeded growth. City incorporation took place in 1846. Lawrenceburg's favorable location for river trade and agricultural processing helped create a viable local economy. The area's abundance of grain stimulated whiskey distilling as early as 1809, an industry that continues today in the form of the giant Seagram plant. Both Lawrenceburg and Aurora have experienced periodic major flooding, the most destructive deluge taking place in 1937 with the inundation of both cities. The present earth and concrete levee at Lawrenceburg was constructed in the early 1940s at a height equal to the 1937 flood stage, 76.1 ft. Aurora does not have the same degree of protection. In the last 20 years, Lawrenceburg has lost population, the bulk of movement going next door to **GREENDALE** (p. 3,795), which has steadily grown since its plat was recorded in 1883. Lawrenceburg's major industries besides distilleries produce glass and veneer. In 1984 the city's downtown historic district, bounded by the Conrail tracks and Charlotte, Tate, William, and Elm sts., was listed on the National Register of Historic Places.

Proceed northeast into Lawrenceburg on US 50. That portion of US 50 connecting Lawrenceburg's Newtown with its old section is called **Eads Parkway**. The name, selected in 1972, honors **James Buchanan Eads** (1820-

1887), an engineer and inventor, who lived the first three years of his life in Lawrenceburg. Eads gained a fortune in the river salvage business, for which he devised and patented the first diving bell in 1842. During the Civil War he constructed 14 armored boats and other rivercraft on commission from Abraham Lincoln. He is best known for Eads Bridge, with its 520-ft. central span, built between 1867 and 1874 across the Mississippi River at St. Louis. **Eads Park**, *2.1 m.* past the city limits sign to the right of the parkway between Park and Main (IND 1) sts. in Newtown, exhibits a millstone monument to Eads. The small park originally was laid out as a public square in 1819 by **Isaac Dunn** (1785-1870), a Lawrenceburg merchant and banker, county judge, and territorial and state legislator. A wood fence surrounded the grounds until 1890. The old bandstand in the center gave way in 1924 to the present fountain. Picnic tables and benches, the manicured lawn, and greenery provide a tranquil setting amidst this heavily traveled section of the city. Two other memorials facing Eads Parkway at the park include a bell in memory of Lawrenceburg firemen and a marker noting the city's two governors, **Albert Gallatin Porter** (1824-1897) and **Winfield Taylor Durbin** (1847-1928), 18th and 24th governors of Indiana, respectively. Turn right on Main St. and left at the end for one block. Then turn right on Front St. Durbin Plaza Shopping Center on the left at Tate St. marks the **birthplace of Gov. Durbin**. The family moved to New Philadelphia, Indiana, when Winfield was three years old. A Civil War veteran, Durbin taught school, worked for a dry goods firm in Indianapolis, helped establish the Citizens Bank of Anderson, and served in the Spanish-American War. Durbin died in 1928 at Anderson and is buried in Crown Hill Cemetery in Indianapolis.

Continue on Front St. through the underpass and left at the Y to High St. To the right is the **Vance-Tousey house** at 508 W. High. Samuel C. Vance, founder of Lawrenceburg, began construction on the two-story, Federal-style mansion in 1818 on his plat's highest ground. Highly acclaimed in its day for its visibility along the river, its spacious lawn that reached to the river edge, and its three-floor spiral staircase, the home at present is a mere shadow of its former grandeur. The house faced the river—the rear is to the street—and the original front has been preserved. After Vance's death in 1830, the heirs established a short-lived Washington Agricultural College here. Omer Tousey next possessed the property. Albert Gallatin Porter, the future governor and Tousey's nephew by marriage, is said to have spent his youth in the home. After 1908 the house was converted to business offices, and since 1966 it has been owned by Seagram Distillery and used as the Lotus Warehouse offices.

Turning back on W. High St. past Charlotte St. on the left is the **Dearborn County Courthouse**. The first courthouse, built on this site in 1810, burned in 1826. A second building was completed in 1828, and, except for the period from 1836 to 1844, when the county seat was located in Wilmington, it served as the courthouse until 1870. The present courthouse was completed in 1873. The huge limestone building, faced with four large Corinthian columns, boasts an exceptional interior affording a view from the first floor to the dome through circular and banistered openings at each level. (*NRHP/HABSI*)

Continue northeast on W. High St. to Walnut St. The **Jesse Hunt house** (formerly the **King Hotel**), on the southeast corner, was built for tavern owner Jesse Hunt in 1817-20 and is claimed to be the first three-story structure in Dearborn County and the tallest structure in the state at the time. The "skyscraper" has always functioned as a hotel under various names. Wings have been added to the original brick corner building and most recently it was faced with stone. Andrew Jackson was apparently one of the guests in this former showplace hotel.

Turn right onto Walnut St. and proceed one block to the levee, where a marker on the crest commemorates **Abraham Lincoln's** brief stop in Lawrenceburg in February 1861 on his way to Washington to assume the duties of president. The top of the levee affords a panoramic view of the Ohio River.

The section of the **Whitewater Canal** from Lawrenceburg to West Harrison in the northeast corner of the county was completed in 1839. The canal's turning basin extended from the foot of Elm St., two blocks northeast of Walnut St., to the foot of St. Clair St. at what is now the river side of the levee. The building of the canal brought increased business and settlement to Lawrenceburg. Manufacturing establishments sprang up along the canal, and Omer and George Tousey along with Isaac Dunn laid

out an addition subsequently called Germantown after the native land of many of its inhabitants. Return to High St. and go right. There is a marker on the Elm St. levee (south of High St.) commemorating the Whitewater Canal and the subsequent use of the towpath by the Indianapolis and Cincinnati Railroad.

Return on Elm St. to William St. Go left one block and right on Short St. one-half block to the **Beecher Presbyterian Church**. Twenty-three-year-old Henry Ward Beecher, one of America's most celebrated clergymen of the 19th century, began his ministry at this site in 1837. Fresh from Lane Theological Seminary in Cincinnati and the tutelage of his father, Lyman Beecher, the young Henry accepted the position from the eight-year-old First Presbyterian body for a $450 annual salary. His congregation at first numbered 19 women and 1 man. For two years Beecher preached and acted as sexton. Here he first spoke on the slavery question and attracted the attention of the Second Presbyterian Church of Indianapolis, to which Beecher was called in 1839. The present brick Lawrenceburg church was built in 1882, partially from funds raised by Beecher from his pulpit in Plymouth Church, New York City. In 1922 the church adopted its present name of Beecher Presbyterian Church.

From Short St. turn left onto Tate St., then right onto Walnut St., and proceed northwest to US 50. Turn left a short distance to Main St. (IND 1) in Lawrenceburg's Newtown area and turn right. In the second block of Main St. is an interesting row of older homes including, at 534 Main St., what could be the oldest extant home in Newtown, the old **Ludlow family farmhouse** (ca. 1811-20), modernized with porch and stucco.

Just past Main and 6th sts. are the Lawrenceburg city limits and the start of Greendale. Main St. changes to Ridge Ave. Immediately to the left after entering Greendale are the offices of the **Joseph E. Seagram and Sons, Inc.**, distillery, the American operating company for the Canadian-based Seagram Company, Ltd. Founded at Waterloo, Ontario, Canada, in 1857, Seagram's has distilleries and wineries in 15 countries. Its Indiana plant was established in 1933 on the site of the Rossville Distillery, which began operation in 1847 but was destroyed by fire in 1932. The Greendale-Lawrenceburg complex is Seagram's largest producer and is regarded as the world's largest distillery. The facility is capable of producing 85,000 gallons of alcohol a day.

Proceed north on Ridge Ave. to Broadway St. On the southwest corner is the painted-gray brick **Bannister-Cook house**. Built in the 1860s and subsequently enlarged, the home was owned from 1891 to 1981 by the Cook family, whose fortune came from deep-well strainer and pump inventions.

One block farther north on the northwest corner of Ridge Ave. and Probasco St. stands the **William H. Probasco home**. Probasco, president of the People's National Bank, constructed the house in 1868. One of the most imposing structures in Greendale, the house features porches on two levels that run the width of the front side and an elaborate lookout on the roof.

Turn left to a marker on the southwest corner of Probasco and Nowlin sts., four blocks west of Ridge Ave., which notes the route of the **Lawrenceburg and Indianapolis Railroad**, completed in 1853 through the efforts of George H. Dunn (1796-1854), state legislator and congressman. Later the same year the name was changed to the Indianapolis and Cincinnati Railroad, with Dunn as president.

George H. Dunn was buried in **Greendale Cemetery**, .5 m. north on Nowlin St. On his stone, located in the western part of the cemetery, is carved a railroad train. Greendale Cemetery, dedicated in 1867, is situated on land given to Col. Zebulon Pike in 1803 in payment for his Revolutionary War service. His son, Brig. Gen. Zebulon Montgomery Pike (1779-1813), explored the West and discovered Pikes Peak. A marker at the entrance to this beautiful cemetery commemorates the father and son.

Return to Aurora via US 50 west and resume the tour south on IND 56 west. South of Aurora 2 m. on the right is **Riverview Cemetery**, established in 1869. The cemetery at its southern end borders the famed Laughery Creek, near the mouth of which on August 24, 1781, about 100 Indians under the command of Mohawk Joseph Brant surprised and roundly defeated Col. Archibald Lochry and 107 Pennsylvania volunteers who were en route to join George Rogers Clark in a campaign against Fort Detroit. Lochry's troops were low on food and ammunition when attacked. Lochry and about one-half of his men were killed; the remainder were taken prisoner. A **memorial to Lochry** and his comrades is in Riverview Cem-

etery near the cannon-crowned war monument. Old IND 56 fronts the cemetery and crosses Laughery Creek just above the Lochry memorial. The creek was named in honor of the colonel; however, the name was mispelled when recorded and was never changed. The **Laughery Creek Bridge** (now closed), constructed in 1878, is an extremely rare triple-intersection Pratt through-truss span. It is the oldest known metal-truss bridge in Indiana. (*NRHP/HAER*)

From the Riverview Cemetery exit, continue south on new IND 56. Another **marker to the Lochry defeat** is at the south end of the new bridge across Laughery Creek.

Laughery Creek is the boundary between Dearborn and Ohio counties. **OHIO COUNTY** (p. 5,114; 87 sq. m.) was carved from Dearborn County in 1844 by the same legislative act that returned Dearborn County's courthouse to Lawrenceburg from Wilmington. Ohio County is Indiana's smallest in size and population. It boasts an impressive archaeological history and superb scenery of steep ridges, deeply cut valleys, and the broad Ohio River, which forms the county's eastern border. With no manufacturing firms, the county's economy relies on tobacco growing, dairy farming, and tourism. The county was named for the Ohio River.

To the right, immediately after crossing Laughery Creek, is the **Tomary farm** with its grand homestead. The brick paired-chimney Federal-type structure, displaying a two-story portico and a balustraded lookout, was constructed in 1846 for Stephen Speakman.

South of the Laughery Creek bridge *3.5 m.* on the right side of IND 56 is the **Fulton Burying Ground** and marker. Seven small headstones mark the graves of John Fulton, Jane Dills Fulton, his wife, and Samuel and Thomas, their sons, in addition to some members of the sons' families. John Fulton and family made the first permanent settlement in 1798 at the site of Rising Sun, one mile south. John and Samuel Fulton served in the American Revolutionary War. In 1811 Samuel moved to the farm where the graveyard is located. The Fultons were cousins of Robert Fulton, civil engineer and steamboat inventor.

Continue *1.1 m.* to **RISING SUN** (p. 2,478), the seat of justice for Ohio County. John James, a Maryland planter, founded the river town in 1814 and, by one account, named it Rising Sun because of the beauty of an Ohio River sunrise or because a ferryboat by that name was at the site when James arrived. Other histories have John Fulton naming the place in 1798 after he viewed the sun peek over the Kentucky hills across the Ohio River. During World War II some persons sought to change the name because of its identification with Japan, the land of the rising sun, and its flag. The citizens, however, refused to switch. Rising Sun was incorporated in 1817 and became the county seat in 1844 at the same time as the formation of the county.

Enter Rising Sun on IND 56, which becomes High St., and observe the grand Victorian homes. Turn right on Main St. (IND 262) to the **Ohio County Courthouse**. Constructed in 1845, it is the oldest Greek Revival-style courthouse in Indiana to be used continuously. It sits on the highest ground in the city. The 60 by 40-ft. structure has no central hall; all offices, including the second-story courtroom, are reached from the outside.

From the courthouse, turn right at Mulberry St. and go one block. Proceed east on 4th St., crossing High St. In the middle of the next block on the right is the white-painted brick with black trim building that once housed the **Rising Sun Seminary**. Established in 1827, the school became the Indiana Teachers Seminary in 1836, which is claimed to be the first normal school in Indiana. The Rising Sun Female Seminary took over one room of the building in 1839. The Presbyterian Church acquired the property in 1854 for its Southeastern Indiana Female Seminary, which operated for many years.

At the east end of 4th St. turn right onto Front St. Floods have obliterated the many business houses that once stood on the riverside. On the west side of Front St. is a line of two-story brick **row houses** constructed in the late 1820s. In the next block of Front St. south, the large structure with columns on the first floor and a bannister around the second-floor portico was built in 1817 as **Rising Sun's first Masonic Temple**, one of the nine Indiana lodges organized under the Grand Lodge of Kentucky. In 1818 Rising Sun Masons joined with the other Hoosier lodges in establishing an Indiana Grand Lodge at Madison in the Schofield house.

Continue south on Front St. to 1st St. Head west for two blocks to Walnut St. Turn right. In the next block at 218 S. Walnut St. on the left (north) is the **Ohio County Historical Museum**. Located in a former plow factory complex, the museum features the famed Hoosier Boy racing boat of the 1920s and fascinating coin-operated musical inventions, many predating the jukebox. The museum also has a nice quilt display along with a sampling of farm implements and Ohio County artifacts and memorabilia.

Reverse direction and follow IND 56 south from Rising Sun. At 2 m., follow IND 156. Leave Ohio County at 3.4 m. and enter **SWITZERLAND COUNTY** (p. 7,153; 224 sq. m.). Separated from Jefferson and Dearborn counties in 1814, Switzerland County is the state's 11th county established and the 7th smallest. Bordered on both the east and south by the Ohio River and featuring a topography of rolling and steep hills, Switzerland County, named by its French-Swiss settlers, is one of the most picturesque sections of Indiana. Its rural charm has remained unspoiled because no railroads or giant industries have penetrated its boundaries. By 1900 the county's population reached 11,840 persons. The county's agricultural economy, however, could not sustain growth, and residents gradually migrated to more promising environs. The county's present population level represents the first decennial increase in 80 years.

On the right side of IND 156, 5.4 m. south of the county line, stands the **Merit-Tandy-Tillotson home**. James H. Merit, or Meritt, built the one-story, Federal-style brick house in the mid-1840s. He deeded it to attorney Carl S. Tandy in the 1890s to fulfill a legal debt. The hip roof, crowned with an ornamental balustraded walk, is rarely seen on single-floor cottages of Federal design. (*NRHP*) The Tandy house, as it is commonly known, is situated on a stretch of river bottomland historically referred to as the **Mexico Bottoms**, so named during the Mexican War when rough frontiersmen battled the great forests and each other to clear the area for agriculture.

PATRIOT (p. 265) lies 2.6 m. south of the Tandy home. First called Troy when laid out in 1820, the name had to be changed upon discovery of another Troy in the state. Patriot was then chosen, probably to honor Revolutionary War soldiers or George Washington. It was incorporated as a town in 1848. Its position on a wide and deep channel of the Ohio River encouraged early steamship traffic and the establishment of mills and distilleries. Several old homes along Patriot's riverfront are all that remain of those halcyon years. Entering Patriot, take the first road to the right and drive one block to a small old whitewashed **stone jail** on the north side of the street. Little is known of the history of the jail except that it probably was built in the 1820s. At the junction of IND 156 and IND 250 is a **marker to Dr. Elwood Mead** (1858-1936), a Patriot native, who headed the Interior Department's Bureau of Reclamation from 1924 until his death. Mead served as chief engineer in the construction of the Hoover Dam, and the huge lake formed by the dam was named Lake Mead in his honor.

From Patriot proceed on IND 156 south along the river which borders another section of lowland called the **Egypt Bottoms** for its fertile soil that produced bumper corn crops during lean farming seasons. Such productivity reminded settlers of Biblical Egypt, which supplied grain to a famine-plagued countryside.

Southwest of Patriot *8.9 m.* on IND 156 is the hamlet of **FLORENCE**. Benjamin Drake laid out the town in 1817 and called it New York, which designation held for three decades before the change to Florence. New York (Florence) was incorporated in 1836. At one time Florence possessed an Anti-Swearing Society with 75 members and a branch society in nearby Bethel. The organization imposed on its members a fine for uttering a profanity. Just west of Florence on IND 156 is the two-story brick **Armstrong house**, with a columned portico and green shutters, built in the 1880s by Thomas Armstrong, farmer and state legislator in 1850-51.

Continue *2 m.* to the **Markland Locks and Dam** and the **Markland Generating Station**. The locks and dam were constructed between 1956 and 1963 near the town of Markland, founded in 1874 by Charles Markland, a produce dealer and shipper. The dam is 1,416 ft. long with twelve 42-ft. high gates. The two parallel locks, on the Kentucky side of the river, are 110 ft. wide and 1,200 and 600 ft. long, respectively. The dam created a pool 95 miles long and eliminated five outmoded locks and dams. The hydroelectric station, the largest in Indiana, began operation in 1967.

VEVAY (pronounced Ve-Ve; p. 1,343), the seat of Switzerland County, lies *7 m.* west of Florence on IND 156. Swiss immigrants from the district of Vevey, Canton de Vaud, settled the area in 1802 and called it New Switzerland.

Following their vocations as winemakers, the pioneers successfully transformed the hilly countryside into terraced vineyards, producing as much as 12,000 gallons of wine annually. Jean François Dufour and his brother Jean Daniel Dufour laid out the town of Vevay in 1813, naming it for their homeland, though inexplicably spelling it differently. Besides wine, the settlers made various brandies, whiskies, and beers. The dispatching of these products, along with tobacco and hay, from Vevay docks promoted the town as a principal shipping point on the Ohio River. In time, interest in grape harvesting declined, replaced by other forms of agriculture and small retail businesses. After the Civil War furniture manufacturing in particular blossomed, but the lack of a railroad and the decrease of river trade limited industrial expansion. Vevay's population has never exceeded 2,000 persons. The town's economy at present rests on the county's cattle and sheep raising, dairy products, tobacco, hay and soybean crops, and several factories. Vevay's cultural prosperity is reflected in its exceptional collection of old homes. A recent attempt to have most of the town placed on the National Register has revealed that of 492 structures in the historical district 86 percent are over 50 years old and 63 percent were built before 1883. This concentration of Hoosier heritage drew Hollywood to Vevay in 1974 to film the television movie, *A Girl Named Sooner*. Vevay also draws hundreds of visitors who want to recapture the flavor of an old river town and to sample the fruit of the vine at the wine festivals. Only a fraction of the noteworthy structures of Vevay can be described, and most of these, in any case, are private residences. On special occasions, tours of selected Vevay homes are given.

Driving into Vevay on E. Main St. (IND 156) note the **Grisard-Sieglitz home** at 306 E. Main St. Built in 1848 by Frederick L. Grisard, a Swiss-born pioneer blacksmith, hardware dealer, and banker, the light tan-painted brick home with black shutters features a front porch of Ionic pillars and a cap of decorative iron grillwork. The timbered portions of the home were connected with wood pegs. The Sieglitz family has lived in the house for several generations.

The **Switzerland County Historical Museum** is housed in a century-old Presbyterian church that stands near the Grisard home on a grassy point dividing E. Main and Market sts. The first Presbyterian church on the site was erected in 1828. The present building, which the county historical society acquired in the late 1960s, dates from 1860. Besides Indian artifacts and other local memorabilia, the museum features the Muzio Clementi piano, claimed to be the first piano brought into the state. An upper-crust but indigent English family by the name of Wright brought the piano to Vevay in 1817. A story goes that Mary, the daughter, spurned by her English fiancé and grief-stricken, nonetheless gave weekly concerts for neighbors until her death in 1874, though never exchanging a word with her appreciative audience.

From the museum continue west toward downtown Vevay on Main St. (IND 156 ends in Vevay and Main St. becomes IND 56) to the **Switzerland County Courthouse**. The first courthouse, constructed in 1815, was also the first brick building in the town. The present courthouse was designed by David Dubach and erected in 1862-64 for about $30,000. The architecture is an adaptation of several Greek Classical forms and is similar to the courthouse in Madison, Indiana. The portico with four slim columns rests on a high base of pierced arches. The cupola's dome contains four clock faces in hooded dormers. Beneath the courthouse is a dungeon that served as a station on the "underground railroad" during the Civil War.

South of the courthouse, at 302 W. Main St., stands the **Knox house**. George G. Knox, cabinetmaker and miller, built the two-story frame house in 1830. Its architecture is referred to in old guidebooks as New Orleans French in design, probably in relation to its narrow open front porch girded by iron grilling. The Knox family entertained many distinguished personalities including Ole Bull, the famed Norwegian violinist, who was stranded in Vevay after the nearby collision of the steamboats the *United States* and the *America* in 1868. The boats, two of the most luxurious afloat, burned and sank with a loss of as many as 70 lives.

Next to the Knox home, at 306 W. Main St., is the **birthplace of Edward and George Eggleston**, major Hoosier literary figures. They were born in 1837 and 1839, respectively. Their father, Joseph Eggleston (1812-1846), a Virginia native, served in the Indiana House and Senate from Switzerland County. Their mother, Mary Jane Craig, was the daughter of George Craig (1776-1833), who settled Craig Township in the county and sat in the state Senate. The precocious Eggleston boys attended a country school west of Vevay near the Craig farm. Edward, whose cradle is in the county museum, led a varied career as Bible salesman, minister of Methodist and Congregational churches, editor, novelist, and historian. *The Hoosier Schoolmaster*, published in 1871, is his most famous novel. His *Roxy* (1878), however, is most closely associated with the Vevay locale. Eggleston also wrote several popular histories of the United States. He considered his election as president of the American Historical Association in 1900 the highlight of his career. He died in 1902 at Lake George, New York. His brother George attended Indiana Asbury College (DePauw), fought in the Confederate Army, and practiced law in Illinois before moving to New York City. He worked as an editor on the *New York Evening Post* and on Joseph Pulitzer's *New York World*, among others. Before his death in 1911 George had written more than 40 novels, generally of the romantic escapist genre. Next to the front door at the two-story brick house is a plaque that calls attention to the significance of the residence. (*NRHP*)

Continue on W. Main St. to Vineyard St. Turn right and go about three blocks to the two-story, gray-painted brick building on the left that houses the County Extension Service and Welfare offices. Known as the **Dumont house**, it was constructed by John Dumont (1787-1871), a lawyer, state legislator, and defeated gubernatorial candidate in 1837. His wife was Julia Louisa Cory Dumont (1794-1857), a schoolteacher for 35 years, and an author whom Meredith Nicholson once memorialized as the "first Hoosier to become known beyond the state through imaginative writing." At one time she taught school in an upper room of her home. Both Edward and George Eggleston studied with her. The Dumonts' son, Aurelius, was Mark Bonaby in Edward Eggleston's novel *Roxy*. It was to the Dumont home, or the House of Lombardy Pillars in *Roxy*, that Bonaby took his bride. This storybook house is now owned by the county.

Return south on Vineyard St. one block to Seminary St. and turn left to Main Cross St. Proceed north past Turnpike St. and bear left around the trailer court. Look up the hill to the right for a view of the magnificent **Benjamin**

Indiana State Library

Eggleston birthplace, 1928

Schenck home. This brick Victorian mansion, constructed in the 1870s for $67,000, features 4 porches, 7 balconies, 35 rooms, 5 copper or tin-lined walnut bathtubs, high ceilings, bay windows, and other significant architectural trappings. Benjamin Schenck (1834-1877) died before his home was finished. His father, Swiss-born Ulysses P. Schenck (1811-1884) was perhaps the wealthiest man of his day in the county. Known as the "Hay King," U. P. Schenck made his fortune largely by transporting hay on his fleet of Ohio River boats. His son Benjamin attended Franklin (Indiana) College and studied to become an attorney but instead joined his father's business. After his death in 1877 the home was completed and through the next century housed a variety of occupants including orphans, retired Baptist ministers, tearoom aficionados, and apartment dwellers.

East of the Schenck mansion is a small **Dufour cottage**, one of several homes built by Jean François Dufour (1783-1850), who along with his brother Jean Daniel Dufour (1765-1855) laid out the town of Vevay in 1813. Among his many civic contributions, Dufour served as president of the Vevay branch of the State Bank of Indiana from 1817 to 1820 and established the *Indiana Register*, Vevay's first newspaper. Jean François Dufour died in this house in 1850.

Backtrack to Main Cross St. and proceed south past the courthouse and across Main St. to Market St. To the left at 209 W. Market St. is the palatial **Ulysses P. Schenck** house, a Greek Revival-style structure built by the "Hay King" in 1844. On the far river side of the house is a broad veranda with massive pillars several stories high. Its prominence as a landmark for boat pilots can still be seen by viewing the home from Ferry St. near the river. The design of the house is attributed to George Kyle, an uncle by marriage of the Eggleston brothers and a student of famed architect Francis Costigan. The spiral staircase in the Schenck home is a Costigan trademark, fashioned by the master builder for $1,500. Mementos of the Schenck family are on display in the county museum.

At 201 W. Market St., just east of the Schenck house, is the **Armstrong Tavern**, constructed by Thomas Armstrong in 1816. The proprietor until 1838 was John M. King, a one-legged veteran and husband of Eugenie, daughter of Jean Daniel Dufour. King's portrait hangs in the county museum. A later owner was Edward Patton, an uncle by marriage of the Eggleston boys. Built with a large upper room for meetings, the place has been designated as the oldest-known building used as a Masonic meeting hall in Indiana. Masonic Lodge No. 7 assembled here beginning in 1817. Workers in the tavern in its early days were Kentucky slaves who were shuttled back and forth daily across the river. After many years as an apartment house or a private residence, the Armstrong Tavern was reopened in 1981 as a restaurant.

Another "storybook" house is located west of the Armstrong Tavern at 405 W. Market St. The two-story frame building built in 1814 is referred to as the **Roxy house** or the **Aunt Lucy Detraz home**. Aunt Lucy, Lucille Marguerite Dufour Morerod (1806-1903), married Benjamin Detraz in 1828 and moved to this home in 1853. In Eggleston's *Roxy*, she and her husband are portrayed as Monsieur and Madame Le Feur, and her daughter Twonnette is the original of the character of the same name. Julia Louisa Cory Dumont taught classes in an upper room at one time.

From the Roxy house, continue west to the end of Market St. and turn right on Arch St. On the left is the **Morerod homestead**, built in 1817 by Jean Daniel Morerod and Antoinette Dufour Morerod, the parents of Lucy Detraz. The back of the house faces Main St. The Morerod home was noted for its hospitality with dances

given in a large ballroom wing, long ago torn down. Morerod had extensive vineyards, and a 500-gallon cask still resides in the basement of the home. An oil painting of Antoinette Dufour Morerod is exhibited in the county museum.

From the Morerod residence proceed west on Main St. (IND 56) *3.3 m.* from the Vevay courthouse to the **Thiebaud house**, upon a hill to the right and framed by a fieldstone fence. Built in 1840, the two-story frame house with small rectangular windows under the front eave is the second home on the site of the French-Swiss Thiebauds, who settled here in 1817.

The town of **LAMB** lies on IND 56, *6.3 m.* southwest of the junction of IND 56 and IND 129 near Vevay. The **George Ash house** in Lamb is thought to be the state's oldest extant brick house, having been built between 1798 and 1803. George Ash, the builder, grew up among Indians and, so it is said, pirated settlers' possessions on the Ohio River. Later, he and his descendants operated a ferry on the river for over a century, and the lineage lived in the house until 1973. To get to the two-story house veer left immediately at the town's sign and go *.2 m.* to a dead end. Turn left and proceed *.3 m.*, bearing to the right along the river, to the house on the north side of the road. James and Vanna O'Banion now own the house.

Conclude the tour by continuing west on IND 56 about *9 m.* to Madison.

New Albany

The historic port city of New Albany (p. 37,103) lies across the Ohio River from Louisville, Kentucky, and 112 miles south of Indianapolis. Founded in 1813, New Albany ranked as Indiana's most populous city from the 1830s into the 1850s, thus figuring prominently in the state's cultural, industrial, and transportation development. Though eventually eclipsed in size and status by Indianapolis and Louisville, New Albany has managed to maintain its industrial diversity. In recent years New Albany citizens have taken important measures to preserve their community's heritage and surrounding natural beauty.

New Albany is positioned in a lowland east of a steep slope called the Knobstone Escarpment. Between the city and the steepest part of the escarpment is a group of hills known as the Knobs, which form a scenic backdrop and city overlook. New Albany, Jeffersonville, Clarksville, and Louisville comprise the Falls Cities, so designated because they are located at the falls of the Ohio River. The term "the falls" refers to a swift current racing over an irregular dam-like limestone shelf several miles long. Though navigable today, the stretch of rough water earlier virtually was impassable except through natural "chutes" during high water periods. Between Pittsburgh, Pennsylvania, and Cairo, Illinois, the falls was the only place on the river route that usually required shippers and travelers to portage. Consequently, the need for docks, shipyards, transshipments of goods and people, and lodging facilities accounts largely for the settlement of the locale.

Besides its historical significance, the falls vicinity is a unique geological attraction. A large exposed section of the river contains a fossil coral bank about 300 million years old. The profusion of well-preserved imprints of ancient animals and plants has been studied for more than 160 years. Over 600 species have been recorded, many for the first time. The New Albany portion of this Devonian Age deposit features a black to grey shale indicating a deoxidation of rapidly buried organisms.

The falls drew the attention of brothers Joel, Nathaniel, and Abner Scribner in the winter of 1812-13. Joel Scribner's Cincinnati shoe and leather shop, opened in 1811, had folded due to the loss of his partner, William Waring, to military service. Therefore, the brothers prospected for a townsite west along the Ohio River. They liked what they saw at the falls. To Abner Scribner, a millwright, the topography was ideal for mill operations. Even in 1812 the extent of development signified future prosperity. The territory near the falls, embracing Clark's Grant, a 150,000-acre block awarded to George Rogers Clark and his soldiers in 1784, already was occupied. John Paul, a store proprietor in Madison, Indiana, held the 322.5 acres below the falls between Clark's Grant and the Knobs. The Scribners purchased this property, which turned out to be 826 1/2 acres, from Paul for $8,000 in 1813.

The thickly forested tract was uninhabited by and large in 1813 when John Graham surveyed and platted New Albany, named by the Scribners for the capital of New York State. Within five years leaders of the flourishing village were eliciting state support for the formation of a new county with New Albany as its seat of government. Accordingly, the state legislature partitioned **FLOYD COUNTY** (p. 61,169; 150 sq. m.) from Clark and Harrison counties in 1819, and New Albany secured the county seat after overcoming a serious bid by Greenville. The county is named, it is thought, for Davis Floyd (1772-1834), a familiar figure in southern Indiana public affairs at the time. Floyd's association with Aaron Burr's conspiracy to embroil America in a war with Spain in 1807 earned him time in jail, a small fine, and the distinction of being the only Burr coconspirator tried and convicted. Just days after his sentencing, Indiana's territorial legislature elected him clerk of the lower house. In 1818

Floyd helped New Albany campaign for a new county, and subsequently he served as the county's first circuit court judge.

New Albany's pre-Civil War economy rested largely on boat construction and repair along with produce shipping. The steamboat revolutionized inland waterway commerce by allowing travel in two directions. The builders of the large passenger and freight packets set up shop near streams and within reach of light and durable timber. New Albany possessed the forests, attracting skilled workers who began boat production in 1817. Between 1817 and 1867 New Albany yards turned out more than 350 steamboats, including some of America's most famous floating palaces. New Albany-built boats held many racing records on the treacherous New Orleans to Louisville run, and such craft as the *Eclipse* and the *Robert E. Lee* were immortalized in word and song.

New Albany's waterfront always lacked sufficient accommodations for its huge volume of business, thus giving it a chaotic appearance. Steamboats, yawls, barges, towboats, snagboats, and ferries, in various stages of construction or repair, vied for space in the limited expanse with boats engaged in passenger and produce traffic. All the while, the boat business lived with disaster—wrecks, explosions, ice, debris, floods, droughts, economic panics, and competition. However, New Albany possessed some advantages. First, its boats had acquired a reputation for speed and durability. Second, the river below the falls rarely froze due to its deep channel. Third, although Kentucky had won the battle to build a canal around the falls, the locks of the Louisville and Portland Canal, completed in 1831, could not handle boats longer than 182 ft. Thus, New Albany, for all practical purposes, had a monopoly on the building of large craft below the falls.

As greater amounts of farm produce and larger numbers of immigrants, migrants, and vacationers converged in the city, hard-pressed officials worked to advance transportation links between the river and the interior. They built plank roads from New Albany to Corydon and Jeffersonville. The Paoli Pike, part of the New Albany-Vincennes Turnpike authorized by the state in 1836, became the first macadamized road in Indiana. Its covering of broken limestone gave it the appearance of "a white thread winding among the green hills." The state collected tolls on the pike between 1840

and 1851. After 1851 a private corporation continued the operation for the remainder of the century. Subsequently, the road became a section in the great Dixie Highway that reached from Miami, Florida, to Sault Sainte Marie, Michigan. After the establishment of the Indiana Highway Commission in 1919, the old pike came to be State Road 42, and, in 1926, today's federal highway 150.

Indiana's internal improvements legislation of 1836 commissioned the construction of the Jeffersonville, New Albany, and Crawfordsville Railroad. The railroad remained on paper until private enterprise took over in 1847. Now, the target was not Crawfordsville, but the fertile farmlands of Washington County and Salem, its county seat. Work started on the New Albany and Salem Railroad in 1848, and it reached Salem in 1851. Because the stockholders wished the road pushed northward, by 1854 crews had laid tracks to Michigan City, creating a 287-mile line, the longest in Indiana. At Michigan City it linked with the Michigan Central Railroad to Chicago, thus giving New Albany access to this increasingly important metropolis. Other railroad schemes of the 1850s involving New Albany failed to materialize. In 1859 the New Albany and Salem Railroad became the Louisville, New Albany, and Chicago Railroad, popularly known as the Monon in deference to the major railroad crossing in the White County town. The Monon reorganized in 1897, and its new title, the Chicago, Indianapolis and Louisville Railway, minus New Albany, clearly reflected the latter city's secondary position to its more populous northern and southern neighbors. In 1956 the C. I. and L. officially became the Monon Railroad, which merged with the Louisville and Nashville Railroad in 1971.

During the golden age of river traffic, New Albany garnered the cultural trappings befitting Indiana's largest metropolitan and commercial center. The village of taverns, general stores, and log homes in 1819 had been transformed by mid-century to a city of churches, schools, and stately homes. A heterogeneous population of 8,181 Yankees, Southerners, blacks, Germans, and Irish lived in respective ethnic neighborhoods. Nine churches had been established by 1848 with Methodists and Presbyterians having the largest congregations. School construction kept pace with the city's growth. The New Albany High School, instituted in

1853, was the state's second public high school. The Indiana Asbury Female College, one of several women's schools founded in New Albany, was established in 1852. Subsequently, it took the name DePauw College for Young Women. In 1905 its resources were transferred to DePauw University at Greencastle.

The New Albany Theological Seminary, begun in 1840, originated as the theological department of a Presbyterian academy in Hanover, Indiana. In 1847 the seminary left New Albany for Chicago, where it was renamed the Presbyterian Theological Seminary of the Northwest. In 1886 it became McCormick Theological Seminary in recognition of its principal benefactor Cyrus McCormick, the inventor of the McCormick Reaper. Such an honored lineage did not accrue to all New Albany schools. One example is the Christian College of New Albany, chartered by the state in 1833. Dr. John Cook Bennett and associates set up this short-lived paper institution to confer degrees of all types, for a fee. Bennett's Medical College, as it was popularly called, was considered for a time Indiana's first medical school. Historians divested New Albany of this laurel when evidence surfaced of a degree given but 40 days after the school's charter, thus substantiating the fraudulent nature of Bennett's scheme.

The zenith of New Albany's early history occurred in the 1850s coinciding with the peak in local boatbuilding. The city by then was linked by river, road, and rail to the principal ports and producing areas. Its boundaries had nearly doubled in size through annexations. A new wave of German immigrants helped maintain respectable increases in population though New Albany was rapidly losing its status as the state's most populous city. Officials could boast of 22 miles of macadamized streets, most illuminated with gaslight after 1852. The building of a combination city hall and firehouse, also a new jail, symbolized the city's progress. New Albany could boast also of a native in the state's top political position when Ashbel P. Willard, a local attorney and former lieutenant governor, won the governor's chair in 1856. He died three months before his term ended, the first Indiana governor to die in office.

New Albany, a cosmopolitan city, was not immune to group violence. Daylong battles marred elections in 1854 when anti-foreign groups called Know Nothings tried to keep Irish Catholics from voting. Blacks, almost 8 percent of New Albany's population, then the highest concentration in Indiana, fell victim to verbal and physical assault. During the Civil War the city's strong ties with southern commerce and fears of job competition from fugitive and freed slaves spelled trouble for black citizens. Indiana's major wartime riot broke out in New Albany in 1862 after two whites were shot by blacks. The accused had to be saved from a lynch mob, and fighting raged in the black neighborhood for 30 hours. The city's most famous lynching occurred in 1868 when a band of vigilantes from the Seymour area forced their way into the jail and hanged four members of the Reno gang, who in 1866 had committed the nation's first recorded train robbery near Seymour in Jackson County.

A decline in New Albany's fortunes set in during the Civil War. Having largely concentrated on building boats for service in the deep South, the New Albany yards experienced severe cuts in orders from that region. Moreover, payments on boats delivered before the war now went uncollected. In addition, the war drastically reduced river commerce and the need for freighters. Railroads assumed more and more of the nation's transportation needs. New Albany's Monon did not connect with Indianapolis, which had three times as many residents as New Albany in 1870.

Even as the steamboat industry diminished, the loss was partially offset by the emergence of other forms of manufacturing. Of greatest importance was the establishment of glass production. John Baptiste Ford (1811-1903) came to Floyd County in 1824 and earned a small fortune through several enterprises, including the marketing of riding gear to the United States Cavalry during the Mexican War. After 1854 he made everything from nails to steamboats in New Albany. Following the Civil War, Ford began making glass bottles and fruit jars. His New Albany Glass Works, launched in 1867, developed America's first plate glass, revolutionizing the glass industry and severing the nation's dependence on European glass. However, financial problems plagued Ford's operation. Washington C. De-Pauw (1822-1887), a native of Salem, Indiana, and Ford's wealthy cousin, came to New Albany after the Civil War and built his Star Glass Company next to Ford's. In 1872 De-Pauw bought Ford's plant and built up his business into one of the largest window, plate, and bottle glass companies in the United States. By 1881 DePauw employed 2,000 workers, and his buildings covered 25 acres of riverfront property. Two-thirds of the plate glass produced in America came from New Albany plants in 1890. Meantime, John B. Ford, after further failures in Louisville and Jeffersonville, made a successful resumption of business in Creighton, Pennsylvania. During the 1930s depression, Ford's descendants merged the company with Libbey-Owens Glass to form the Libbey-Owens-Ford Glass Company.

DePauw's great wealth filtered throughout New Albany and the state. He had interests in plank roads, banks, city utilities, insurance companies, woolen mills, and iron-working plants. His philanthropy underwrote the DePauw College for Young Women, and, subsequently, DePauw University at Greencastle.

The industrial expansion after the Civil War necessitated renewed efforts to improve transportation. The Jeffersonville, Madison, and Indianapolis Railroad laid a connecting link to New Albany in the late 1860s. A seven-mile section of track from Watson in Clark County to New Albany in 1870 tied the latter to the Ohio and Mississippi Railroad (Baltimore and Ohio) and gave New Albany an east-west route. The Louisville, New Albany, and St. Louis Air Line began construction at New Albany in 1871. The Air Line company dug a 4,311-ft.-long tunnel through the Knobs. The construction of the Edwardsville Tunnel, the longest in the state, initiated large-scale tunneling in Indiana. Sidelined temporarily by the financial panic of the early 1870s, the railroad opened in 1881 under a new name, the Louisville, Evansville, and St. Louis Air Line. The line was purchased by the Southern Railway Company in 1901.

After 1870 New Albany manufacturers had rail service to Louisville via the Jeffersonville, Madison and Indianapolis Railroad. The first direct link between the two cities came in 1886 with the completion of the Kentucky and Indiana Bridge. In 1887 the Kentucky and Indiana Bridge Company bought New Albany's street railway system, established in 1867, in order to consolidate rail connections between Louisville, New Albany, and its western suburbs. The electric trolleys of the New Albany Highland Railway Company, organized in 1890, conveyed passengers to the new residences in the Silver Hills, as the Knobs were often called.

Washington C. DePauw's industrial empire that underpinned New Albany's economy after the Civil War crumbled in the 1890s, forcing a transformation in the city's business and labor makeup. The discovery of natural gas in north-central Indiana, permitting a cheaper source of fuel for glassmaking, the slump in the iron and textile market, and the depression of the 1890s combined to overturn New Albany's previous economic structure. DePauw's glass companies moved to Alexandria in Madison County in the early 1890s, and around 4,000 of New Albany's residents left. The century ended with a net loss of population in the decade, from 21,059 to 20,628.

In 1903 the New Albany Commercial Club offered cash prizes for the essays judged best on New Albany. The essays, though tinged with boosterism, contain what amounts to an index of concerns about the city as it entered the 20th century. The writers took pride in New Albany's extensive rail connections, its huge Ohio Falls Iron Works, the new St. Edwards Hospital, Carnegie Library, the almost completed high school, the opening of an interurban line to Jeffersonville, and the establishment of Silver Creek Park (Glenwood Park) on the interurban route. The essayists, however, were cognizant that they lived in the shadow of Louisville. Many New Albany residents worked in Louisville and spent their dollars there despite the presence of over 100 retail stores in New Albany. How could New Albany compete when it had no comparable hotel, its streets were ridden with uncollected trash and litter, and its sewage system was totally inadequate? Some felt New Albany's high taxes, excessive debts, privately owned utilities, and an unimaginative city hall contributed to the city's malaise.

The writers pinned their hope for New Albany's economic recovery on the development of brick and glass factories and the proposed deepening of the Ohio River to permit year-round shipping. They could not have foreseen the city's infant wood-processing industry becoming the wellspring of economic rejuvenation. New Albany's heritage of carpentry, furniture making, and boatbuilding revived in the form of veneer and plywood production. The need for these wood articles arose because of the increasing costs of solid wood furniture and the demand for inexpensive piano and phonograph cabinets and floor coverings. Between 1898 and 1915 five plywood and veneer plants appeared in New Albany, including the New Albany Veneering Company (1907). By the 1920s New Albany was being touted as a center for this type of woodworking.

In the meantime, Samuel Insull, the utilities financier who ultimately controlled one-eighth of the nation's electric power, bought heavily into New Albany's utilities and rail lines and turned a profit. A mayor was impeached in 1906. The electorate voted to retain rather than prohibit liquor sales in order to stay competitive with Louisville's attractions. This decision, to some, demonstrated New Albany's wide-open reputation. The chautauqua meetings drew hundreds to the 24-acre Glenwood Park to hear such celebrities as William Jennings Bryan, James Whitcomb Riley, and Eugene V. Debs. New Albany joined the state's interurban network in 1908. The automobile began its revolutionary journey, and five car manufacturers between 1909 and 1916 turned out the American, the Crown, the Jonz, the Ohio Falls, the Hercules, and the Pilgrim. The old 1865 courthouse received a coat of stucco in 1913, just in time for the observance of the city's centennial. In 1917 a tornado killed more than 50 persons and left around 3,000 homeless. One-third of the homeless left the city. Devastation was witnessed again, a few months later, by New Albany's young men on the battlefields of Europe. Indiana's prohibition law went into effect in April 1918, and the city's breweries converted to soft drinks or went out of business. New Albany won the state football title in 1919. The same year New Albany learned that America's 30th Division, led by the city's own Maj. Gen. Edward M. Lewis, received credit for breaching the famous Hindenburg Line.

The prosperity of the postwar years was not limited to veneer and plywood factories, which numbered seven in 1923. The advent of truck transportation brought a thriving business to the tomato and fruit growers north of the city. The sight of trucks carrying burley tobacco through New Albany to Louisville inspired local tobacco enthusiasts to open a tobacco warehouse in 1924 in an abandoned cotton mill. Today, New Albany's tobacco market sells several million pounds of the leaves each season.

In 1920 New Albany, with 22,992 residents, ranked as the 2nd largest city in southern Indiana and the 15th largest in the state. Despite the loss of population after the 1917 tornado, the 1920 figure represented an 11.5 percent increase in the decade. The spurt in population, along with a jump in business and the loss of about 300 dwellings following the tornado, placed severe strains on housing. Real estate financing and construction boomed as a result, but shortages in housing would plague the city for years.

The Great Depression interrupted New Albany's progress. Other than the excitement of following New Albany native Billy Herman's extraordinary career with the Chicago Cubs or the satisfaction of reading New Albany-born Robert Staughton Lynd's sociological study of *Middletown* (Muncie), the 1930s afforded little cause for elation. Labor troubles, a flood, and an extremely low level of building activity impeded recovery. A strike at M. Fine and Sons work shirt factory in the fall of 1935 evolved into a riot which required state troops to restore order. Business seemed to be normalizing in 1937, just before the giant flooding of the Ohio River caused around $8 million in damages in the community. The 1940 census showed a decade loss of 405 persons, a reduction blamed on the relocation of families after the flood to higher ground in the county.

The effects of the flood alerted residents to New Albany's housing needs. One result was the Valley View Housing Project, claimed as the nation's first such project to offer prefabricated homes. Twenty prefab structures called Gunnison Homes were the brainchild of Foster Gunnison who began mass-producing houses in New Albany in 1935. Gunnison Homes subsequently merged with United States Steel Homes, a division of United States Steel Corporation. Intended to provide inexpensive housing for low-income flood victims, Valley View homes proved too costly for the poor; therefore, more affluent families occupied the dwellings. Broadview Gardens, a housing project completed in 1941, replaced what was viewed as inferior homes with new structures for workers in the defense-related facilities at Charlestown and at Jeffersonville. Its construction, federally-funded, was opposed by citizen groups bothered by its no property tax provision and by black families facing loss of homes to the bulldozer.

As happened with other cities, the supply demands of the war bolstered the local economy. Afterwards, manufacturers hurdled the problems of peacetime reconversion. By 1948 New Albany's sales were fourfold those of 1939, and by 1950 factory employment reached its highest postwar level, with wood products leading the resurgence. Cheered by the favorable turn in the business picture, New Albany citizens also could point proudly to the accomplishments of Sherman Minton (1890-1965), who was born in neighboring Georgetown, educated in New Albany schools, and appointed to the United States Supreme Court by President Harry S Truman in 1949. In 1951 Georgetown was again highlighted when its native son R. Carlyle Buley (1893-1968) was awarded the Pulitzer Prize in history for his two-volume *Old Northwest.*

Floyd County's population count in 1950 showed a decade increase of more than twice that of New Albany, a clear indication of suburban expansion. The movement to the suburbs troubled city officials, who supplied some services to fringe areas but received no tax moneys in return. The solution lay in annexation. New Albany, ranking lowest in its class size in terms of taxables per capita, jumped at the chance to possess the suburbs after the passage of a state law in 1955 simplifying annexation procedures. An annexation ordinance, adopted in 1956, more than doubled the city's area, from 4.5 to 10.9 square miles. The population gain of more than 8,000 raised New Albany from a third- to a second-class city, and the assessed valuation of property almost doubled. New Albany's venture brought it national attention, including a long article in the April 20, 1957, *Saturday Evening Post.*

The windfall expansion came at a time when New Albany had already made significant strides in improving its health and safety features. The Floyd County Memorial Hospital was completed in 1953, and a 3.5-mile-long floodwall and six pumping stations became fully operative by 1954. These achievements, however, paled in comparison to the torrent of construction in the decade between 1953 and the city's sesquicentennial in 1963. By 1963 New Albany's altered skyline included Indiana's first city-county building, a Federal Building, a double-deck bridge to Louisville, a power plant, several schools, a hospital wing, and a sewage and garbage disposal plant. The

Pillsbury Company built in the city's north section in 1959, and a civic group acquired 70 acres north of the Pillsbury plant for future industrial expansion. Recreational improvements included an 18-hole golf course and the 92-acre Jaycee Waterfront Park.

The advances made in New Albany in the remaining years of the 1960s touched on improving the quality of life for all citizens. Historic New Albany, Inc., led a drive to renovate historical structures. Hundreds of gaslights decorated residential lawns and downtown streets. The erection of a dividing plaza on Market St. further beautified the business district. A public fund campaign resulted in the purchase of land for the establishment in 1967 of Indiana University's southeastern campus. Other important activities involved finding jobs for youth, creating a human rights commission, and initiating civil rights ordinances. Plans were laid for a new vocational center. Officials inaugurated a civil defense program and built an animal shelter and a municipal swimming pool. An art gallery and an orchestra enriched New Albany's cultural life.

The agenda for the 1970s focused on three objectives: downtown revitalization, historic preservation, and industrial expansion. Competition from suburban shopping centers hurt businesses in the core city. The closing of major department stores uptown, traffic congestion, inadequate parking facilities, lack of standardized store hours, a lackluster merchants association, and a series of scandals in the police department raised serious questions about the central city's chances for survival. Yet in other areas the city continued to progress. The hospital and high school received major additions. New Albany's high school basketball team won the state championship in 1973. Indiana University's southeast campus relocated onto 180 acres in the northern section of the city. Highrise housing projects were either dismantled or rehabilitated. The New Albany/Floyd County Industrial Park gained 28 new businesses on its 183-acre tract between 1969 and 1981, thereby markedly contributing to the community's tax base, land value, employment rate, and manufacturing diversity. The location of the university and the industrial park in the Grant Rd. area rapidly changed the character of that once rural setting into a high-growth residential, commercial, and manufacturing district.

New Albany residents shared in the revived historical consciousness that accompanied the nation's bicentennial celebration. The old Carnegie Library became the site in 1971 of the Floyd County Museum. The Main St. Association, founded in 1975, pushed for restoration of historical homes on the city's so-called Mansion Row. The Culbertson Mansion, the cornerstone of Main St.'s historic architecture, was put on the National Register of Historic Places in 1974. It was deeded to the state in 1976 and reopened as a state memorial. Preservationists opposed the razing of downtown buildings for parking lots or new structures. Several interested persons purchased and improved old buildings for full or partial leasing, thus contributing to the recovery of the city's core. In 1983 a multi-block portion of the central city residential section, designated the Mansion Row Historic District, was given a place on the National Register. In a related development, the falls of the Ohio was declared a National Wildlife Conservation Area in 1981. The river also is the backdrop for New Albany's most ambitious venture of recent years, a development of its riverfront. The first step was the construction in the early 1980s of an overlook atop the city's levee. The latest addition is the New Albany River Heritage Cultural Center, a 1,500-seat amphitheater built on the floodwall and connected with auto and pedestrian access routes plus biking trails and parking lots. This $510,000 cultural center was funded principally by the Clark-Floyd Counties Convention and Tourism Bureau.

New Albany shared with its borderers, Jeffersonville, Clarksville, and Louisville, the hardships associated with the national economic debacle of the early 1980s. Because some 30 percent of New Albany's workers worked in Louisville factories, the Indiana town's fortunes became entangled with those of its Kentucky neighbor. The adjusted seasonal unemployment rate slid to 15.2 percent in December 1982. The New Albany SMSA (Standard Metropolitan Statistical Area) possessed a higher average jobless rate than both the state or nation. On the other hand, New Albany's nonmanufacturing sector increased substantially during these years, which bodes well for a more balanced local economy able to withstand severe business declines. By the mid-1980s the economic outlook in New Albany was particularly bright. City leadership projected a new role for the community in the social and economic affairs of the Falls Cities. Accessible by a network of state, federal, and interstate highways, New Albany expects by the end of the century to capture its share of the tourist traffic. Other goals include the continued upgrading of the urban core, gaining total occupancy in the industrial park, and adding concretely to the already impressive efforts to conserve the city's remarkably rich historical inheritance.

New Albany Attractions

For additional tourist information contact the **Clark-Floyd Counties Convention and Tourism Bureau**, 540 Marriott Dr., Jeffersonville.

Before touring New Albany drive the outskirts of the city to gain a perspective of its topographical setting. Take State St. (old US 150), which divides the east and west streets of New Albany, north to the village of **Floyd Knobs**, from where the populous valley and the broad Ohio River can be clearly seen. At Floyd Knobs a skyline drive winds northeast around New Albany and terminates at IND 111, or Grant Line Rd. From here IND 111 south returns to New Albany. A drive along the Ohio River presents New Albany from a different angle. Take W. 10th St. south, through the levee, to Water St. Just east on Water St. is the **Jaycee Riverfront Park**, dedicated in 1960. Continue east along the riverbank and pass under the **Sherman Minton Bridge**, the $14 million steel and aluminum structure, which opened by stages during 1961 and 1962. A short distance beyond the bridge, to the left and crowning the levee, is the riverfront overlook. Also in sight, near the Sherman Minton Bridge, is the **clock tower** of the Second Baptist Church in downtown New Albany, a landmark for river pilots. The concrete abutments to the left once supported railroad track. Visible in the distance is the Kentucky and Indiana bridge. Continue east on Water St. to the turnaround and backtrack to W. 10th St.

1. The **Robert E. Lee Steamboat Marker** on Corydon Pike (IND 62) commemorates the famed craft built in the vicinity near the mouth of Falling Run Creek. In 1870 the *Lee* "took the horns," a mounted set of stag horns, by beating the *Natchez* in a historic New Orleans to St. Louis race. In beating the *Natchez*, the *Lee* set a speed record of slightly over three and three-fourth days, a record that still stands.

2. The **Edwardsville Tunnel**, 4.4 miles on Corydon Pike (old IND 62) from the intersection of W. Main and W. 10th sts., is Indiana's longest tunnel. The 4,311-ft.-long railroad passageway cost around $1 million before its completion in 1881. The tunnel entrance is in a ravine to the south of the roadway. Keep an eye out for the railroad tracks that border Corydon Pike.

3. The **Stoy-Moody-Shader house**, 141 W. Main, was briefly the home of poet and playwright William Vaughn Moody (1869-1910). This house was built in the late 1820s by Peter Stoy, one of the city's leading citizens. The Moody family came to New Albany in 1870, 15 months after the birth of William Vaughn Moody at Spencer, Indiana. The family removed shortly afterwards to a house at 411 W. Market St., torn down in 1976. Moody attended the local schools, graduating as valedictorian from the high school in 1885, and left for New York at the age of 18. A giant in the literary world around the turn of the 20th century, Moody wrote volumes of prose and poetry, but is best known for his play *The Great Divide*.

4. The **Scribner house**, 106 E. Main St., is New Albany's oldest standing residence. Built in 1814 by one of the city's founders, Joel Scribner, and his wife Mary, the two-and-one-half-story frame house has a two-level rear porch overlooking the Ohio River. The house was purchased from Harriett Scribner in 1917 by the Piankeshaw Chapter of the Daughters of the American Revolution (DAR), which restored it in 1932 for use as a meeting place. It is furnished with 19th-century pieces collected over the years. The most recent addition to the site is the Scribner Square, a small chained courtyard in the front west yard, put up in 1980 under the auspices of the Floyd County Bicentennial Committee. (*NRHP*)

Scribner house, as it was in 1850

5. The **Clapp house**, 110 E. Main St., which abuts the Scribner property, was built in 1822. Dr. Asahel Clapp (1792-1862), one of pioneer Indiana's foremost physicians, had his home and office in the building. The New England native settled in New Albany in 1817 as the village's first permanent doctor. He married into the Scribner family. Clapp found time to help organize the Medical Society of the State of Indiana in 1849, serving as its second president. In recent years a succession of retailers has used the structure.

6. The **State Bank of Indiana Building**, 203 E. Main St., housed New Albany's first banking institution. Designed by Hugh Pugh, this branch of the state bank was built in 1837. When constructed, at a cost of around $40,000, it was the largest structure in the city, and one of the first Greek Revival-style buildings in the Falls area. The two-story interior was capped with a skylight. A first floor ceiling was added later. The building remained a state bank through several charters until 1865 when it converted to a national bank. After the First National Bank closed, as a result of the 1893 depression, the building stood empty for years. The Christian Scientists and the Knights of Pythias eventually made use of the space. Since 1941 it has been the home of a Red Cross chapter. The old bank vault is still intact. On the walls hang several World War I Red Cross posters. A large tablet to the right of the front door gives the building's history.

7. The **Town Clock Church**, 300 E. Main St., was constructed between 1849 and 1852 by members of the Second Presbyterian Church. In 1889 the Greek Revival-style structure was sold to the black congregation of the Second Baptist Church, organized in 1867. The church building, acclaimed for its conspicuous timepiece that long signaled New Albany's location to boatmen on the river, contains an early 19th-century organ and basement rooms thought to have sheltered fugitive slaves in the 1850s. The present clock tower is a much-shortened version of the original 160-ft. tower.

8. The residential area bounded by Main St. between State and 15th sts. and Market St. between 7th and 11th sts. is the **Mansion Row Historic District** (*NRHP*). Only a sampling of the stately homes are mentioned here. The **Sloan-Bicknell house**, 600 E. Main St., was built in 1852 by Dr. John Sloan. Rear Admiral George A. Bicknell (1846-1925) was a later tenant of the home. The Italianate-style house is noted for its concave window panes, the octagonal tower, and the hoods over the upper windows. Glass sheets were used between the stone and brick as insulation against moisture. The

Town Clock Church, 1931

New Albany Attractions

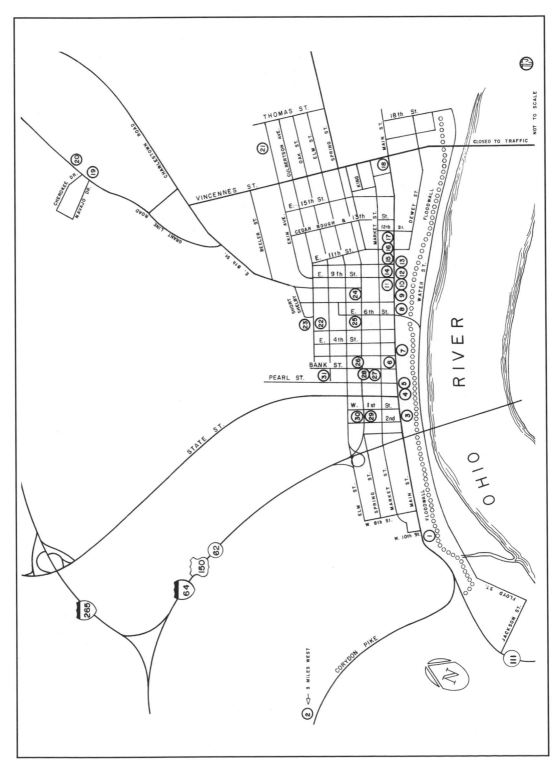

tin roof reportedly came from Edinburgh, Scotland.

9. William S. Culbertson (1814-1892), a native of Pennsylvania, came to New Albany in 1835 and proceeded to make a fortune in the dry goods business and as a result of numerous investments. The **Widow's Home**, 704 E. Main St., is an example of Culbertson's goodwill. He built the $25,000 brick home in 1873 for destitute widows, provided for its maintenance, and supervised, among other things, the purchase of food for the occupants. Architect James T. Banes designed the 20-room, three-story Italianate-style home, which, at one time, sheltered 30 widows.

10. **Washington C. DePauw's summer home,** 714 E. Main St., was constructed in the 1870s. Like Culbertson, DePauw was a leading entrepreneur and philanthropist in 19th-century New Albany. The large green-shingled house has Italianate features but is more an informal composite type of structure with the wood framing treated as masonry. Its principal attraction is its lavish display of ironwork porches and fencing.

11. The **George Rogers Clark Marker**, 809 E. Main St., denotes the western boundary of Clark's Grant. The state of Virginia awarded Clark and his men 150,000 acres of land for their service in the Illinois campaign during the Revolutionary War.

12. The **Order of Red Men Clubhouse**, 904 E. Main St., is another home built by William S. Culbertson. Culbertson built this Italianate dwelling in 1886 for his son Samuel. The house features cast-iron porches, a classical entry, and a multiple-hipped roof.

13. Next door to the Samuel Culbertson house is the **Culbertson Mansion**, 914 E. Main St. Maintained by the state as a memorial, it is considered one of the finest houses in the vicinity of the Falls of the Ohio. James T. Banes, a local architect and builder, constructed the three-story brick house between 1867 and 1869 at a cost of around $120,000. Its numerous bay windows, verandas, and French mansard roof provide the stylistic keys to the French Second Empire design. The tin roof, imported from Scotland, is edged by a 3-ft.-high iron fence.

The off-center door is almost 15 ft. high. The three levels of the interior have graduated ceiling heights from 18.5 ft. on the first floor to 11 ft. on the third floor. Its 16,000 ft. of living space is divided into 20 rooms. Culbertson drew on the skills and products of the city's boat and glassmakers. As in other Culbertson homes, glass panels served as moisture barriers between the foundation and the soil. The woodwork was created by boatbuilders. The newel post and rails of the three-story staircase are carved mohogany and rosewood. Hand-painted ceilings, marble fireplaces, and medallion-centered chandeliers reflect the opulence of the Victorian era. The home is outfitted with period furnishings, but nothing remains of Culbertson's household goods, which were auctioned after his death. The house was sold in 1899 and again in 1946 to the American Legion which headquartered there until 1964. In that year, Historic New Albany, Inc., was formed to head off the construction of a service station on the mansion site. Historic New Albany purchased the house and maintained it until the state acquired it in 1976. In 1980-81 and again in early 1989 the structure received major renovations. (*NRHP*) A marker on the mansion's front lawn documents New Albany's premier role in the manufacture of plate glass.

14. The **James Collins house**, 917 E. Main St., is a two-story, Tuscan Italianate brick house built in 1852. Collins (1802-1869) was a councilman, mayor, state legislator, and founder and editor of the *New Albany Gazette*. Angelina Maria Lorraine Collins (1820-1885), his wife, wrote *Mrs. Collins' Table Receipts; Adapted to Western Housewifery.* This was the first cookbook published in Indiana, and probably the first book to be published in Indiana by a woman resident of the state. It was printed in 1851 by John R. Nunemacher of New Albany.

15. The **Victor A. Pepin house**, 1003 E. Main St., is in the Italian Villa style, with prominent Tuscan towers. It was built between 1851 and 1866.

16. Also in the Italian Villa style is the neighboring **Phineas Kent house**, 1015 E. Main St., constructed in 1857 by Kent, a New Albany printer and lawyer. It is presently the parish house of St. Paul's Episcopal Church.

17. The **Michael Crawford Kerr home**, 1109 E. Main St., the Italianate-style brick house with the center gable, was built in 1864. Michael Kerr (1827-1876) lived in New Albany after 1852. He held positions as a city and county attorney and as a state legislator. Kerr was a five-term congressman, 1865-73, 1875-76, and speaker of the House of Representatives in 1875-76.

18. **Vincennes Street** (US 31W), off E. Main St., is a monument to the vision of Epaphras Jones. Around 1820 Jones platted a town called Providence at the foot of present Vincennes St. He hoped his creation would challenge New Albany for dominance on the Hoosier side of the falls. Jones failed as a town builder, but the road he cut northward, that would have connected Providence to major east-west routes, became the line of Vincennes St.

19. **Chester B. Stem, Inc.**, 2710 Grant Line Rd., supplies domestic and foreign veneers to the building trades. The Stem common and exotic wood coverings can be seen throughout the United States in such buildings as the John Hancock Building in Chicago, the Chase Manhattan Bank in New York City, the Smithsonian Institution, and the library at the University of Notre Dame in South Bend, Indiana. Note the four-century-old fir log on display just past the entrance to the company's grounds and observe to the right the enchanting teakwood house, an attractive facade for a lumber warehouse. To the left are the firm's offices.

20. North of the Stem plant is the **Lucas Tobacco Warehouse**, 3020 Grant Line Rd. Claimed as the leading cash crop for this part of southern Indiana, burley tobacco was sold in vacated mills a few blocks east of the present New Albany High School on Vincennes St. beginning in the 1920s. The business was called the New Albany Tobacco Warehouse. The Lucas family became associated with the enterprise in 1949. In 1961 the Lucas partners built the storage and sales barn on Grant Line Rd., and the New Albany Tobacco Warehouse became the Lucas Tobacco Warehouse. Millions of dollars in sales occur here each season from November to mid-February. Persons who have not experienced the pungent smell of tobacco leaf in thousands of stacks or hogsheads over-

laying a huge floor or heard the cry of the auctioneer should visit the Lucas warehouse.

21. The **New Albany National Cemetery**, 1900 block of Ekin Ave., was established by a congressional act in 1862 for the reinterment of servicemen buried in city and soldiers' graveyards in the vicinity and in Kentucky, Virginia, and West Virginia. The land was purchased from Dr. and Mrs. Charles Bowman for $955.50. Some 5,000 interments from the Civil War through Vietnam have taken place on the grounds. It is one of seven cemeteries established by Congress for burial of both Union and Confederate soldiers. Except for some reserved plots the cemetery is now closed.

22. The **Byron Forceythe Willson house**, 520 E. Culbertson Ave., was the home of an Indiana poet who became famous for his *The Old Sergeant*, written during the Civil War. Willson lived in New Albany from 1852 to 1864. He died in 1867 and is buried at Laurel in Franklin County. His small frame carpenter-builder-style cottage was built probably in the 1850s.

23. The **Fairview Cemetery**, across from the Willson home, opened in 1841 and was called the Northern Burial Ground until 1896. Buried in the large 61-acre cemetery are most of the local celebrities, including Michael Crawford Kerr, Ashbel P. Willard, and the Scribners.

24. **St. Mary's Roman Catholic Church**, 8th and Spring sts., was erected in 1858. The interesting feature of the Romanesque Revival architecture is the spire, a bulbous affair, called the Zwiebelturm, literally, onion tower. The 135-ft.-high onion tower is rare in this country, but it can be found in southern Germany, with variations seen in Russia.

25. The **Willard Marker** on a flag pole at the entrance to Frisch's restaurant, E. 6th and Spring sts., indicates that this is the site of Gov. Ashbel P. Willard's residence. Willard won the governor's chair in 1856, defeating Oliver P. Morton, but died in office. His large brick home, built around 1850, was sold to the New Albany School City in 1902, torn down, and replaced by the People's College Building. The latter structure subsequently housed the New Albany High School until 1926, and a junior

high school until the present restaurant went up in the early 1960s.

26. The **Floyd County Museum**, 201 E. Spring St., is located in the old Carnegie Library building. The library, built in 1904 on the original site of the New Albany High School, continued there until 1969 when it moved to its new home on E. Spring St. The Floyd County Parks and Recreation Board then leased the building from the library board for a museum, which opened in 1971. The museum, largely contained on the first floor of the structure, features a variety of local artifacts and theme exhibits along with an art gallery. The Collector's Gallery and Museum Shop sells arts and crafts, souvenirs, and gifts.

27. The **Heib Building**, 318 Pearl St., is a three-story Italianate business house with close ties to New Albany's historic glass industry. In October of 1870, the Heib Building, in which John Heib had a tailoring shop, received from John B. Ford's glassworks the first sheet of American-made plate glass. The building has been restored as part of Mutual Trust Bank's renewal of its complex on Pearl St. The historic panes of glass were removed years ago, mirrored, and installed in the homes of J. B. Ford's two granddaughters.

28. The **Kaiser Building**, 326 Pearl St., houses the Kaiser Retail Tobacco Store, which holds the record as the oldest business in New Albany, dating from 1832. The Kaiser Store, known by this name since 1866, was founded by David Gorlitz, a stepfather of the Kaiser lineage. The tobacco shop is one of eight city businesses more than a century old.

29. **Hauss Square**, Spring and 1st sts., is the governmental center of New Albany. The old city hall, jail, courthouse, and Scribner High School once were located where the City-County Building and the Federal Building now stand. In 1953 the state legislature passed a bill permitting local governments to establish a body empowered to issue revenue bonds for needed public buildings. Dr. A. P. Hauss presided over New Albany's first building authority. Between 1959 and 1961 the $2.4 million City-County Building was constructed. This structure was Indiana's first new building under the 1953 act. Four columns from the 1867 courthouse, torn down in 1961, stand on the north side of the building.

30. The **New Albany-Floyd County Public Library**, 180 W. Spring St., has on display in the lower gallery, adjacent to the Indiana History Room, two exceptional bird's-eye paintings of the city by local artist George M. Morrison (1820-1893). One entitled *New Albany from Silver Hills* was executed in 1851. The second, *View from Spickert Knobs*, is dated 1856.

31. The **New Albany and Salem Railroad Station**, Pearl and Oak sts., dedicated in 1854, was the city's first depot. The railroad was organized in 1847 and eventually reached to Michigan City on Lake Michigan and became part of the Monon system. After many years of service the depot was converted to industrial uses, including a boiler works and a grain and feed operation. The tracks may still be seen in the rear of the terminal. (*NRHP*)

Tour 6

At State and W. Market sts. is a roadside marker which tells the history of **New Albany's market houses.** Narrow street dividers have replaced the two long buildings referred to as Upper and Lower Markets. The shed-type structures had broad overhangs which allowed vendors and buyers to conduct business in any weather. The **Upper Market**, between Pearl and State sts., was torn down around 1900. The last remnants of the **Lower Market**, also called Hoosier Market, were swept away in the 1937 flood.

From New Albany, take Main St. and Corydon Pike (former IND 62) westward, leaving IND 111 at its south turn. Continue into the Knobs and cross the east portal of Edwardsville Tunnel, a 4,311-ft. bore built about 1880 by a predecessor of the Southern Railway. It is Indiana's longest tunnel. Continue to IND 62, turn left, and proceed southwest *3 m.* to IND 11. Take IND 11 *6 m.* to the **HARRISON COUNTY** (p. 27,276; 486 sq. m.) line. Harrison is the middle county of the 13 Indiana counties which border the Ohio River. It is popularly referred to as the Cradle of Indiana because the state's first capital was located at Corydon, the county seat, and the first state constitutional convention was held there. Harrison County, organized in 1808, was the fourth county established in the Indiana Territory and included present Washington and Floyd counties, and parts of Orange, Perry, and Crawford. Its present boundaries were established in 1852. The county was named for William Henry Harrison (1773-1841). Harrison County is predominantly rural and agricultural. Its topography has the rugged character typical of southern Indiana: broken, hilly, and cavernous, but with fertile valleys and a 40-mile stretch of bottomlands along its southern border adjacent to the Ohio River.

Travel *15.3 m.* on scenic IND 11 to the **site of the Old Goshen Church** and burial grounds. Until 1963, when it was razed for safety rea-sons, Harrison County's oldest church stood near the graveyard. Moses Boone and George Bartley built the log church around 1813 under the leadership of Squire Boone, brother of the famous Daniel Boone. The old church became a state memorial in 1944, but the state failed to provide funds for its upkeep. In 1956 the deed reverted to the Baptist Church, which subsequently turned it over to a local foundation maintaining the cemetery. A large memorial slab, erected in 1968, gives a history of the church and grounds and a genealogy of the Boone family.

From the Goshen monument continue on IND 11 south through the small village of **LACONIA** (p. 58), platted by John Boone in 1816 and named for a New Hampshire town. Past Laconia on IND 11 the traveler, in autumn, frequently sees barns laden with drying tobacco leaves. The broad Ohio River breaks into view as IND 11 descends from a promontory to the water's edge about *5 m.* west of Laconia. Here the **Matthew Welsh Toll Bridge**, named for the former Indiana governor, crosses the Ohio River. It opened in 1966.

IND 11 runs under the Welsh bridge and *.6 m.* farther dead-ends at the town of **MAUCKPORT** (p. 109). Called New Market when laid out in 1827, the town eventually took the name Mauckport for Frederick Mauck, an early settler and ferryman who made the original plat. In 1829 Mauckport had achieved enough status as a bustling river port to compete, unsuccessfully, with much larger cities to become the southern terminus of the Michigan Rd. Just east of Mauckport at Morvan Landing, now vanished, Brig. Gen. John Hunt Morgan and his raiders invaded Indiana in the summer of 1863. The 1937 flood devastated Mauckport and contributed to its gradual decline.

By the Welsh bridge take IND 135 north *1.1* steep miles. At the top of the grade and to the right a parallel road leads *.4 m.* back south

Tour 6

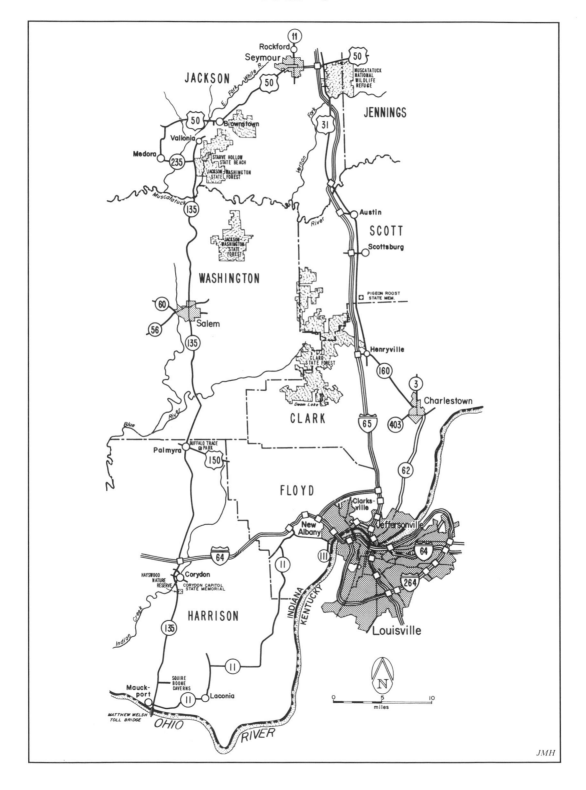

JMH

to the **Mauckport Overlook** which affords an inviting panorama of the Ohio River valley.

North *2.7 m.* past the turnoff to the overlook is the entrance road to **Squire Boone Caverns and Village**. In 1804 Boone settled near the caves, which he had discovered 14 years earlier, and built the county's first gristmill. At his death in 1815 the family fulfilled his request to be buried in a small cave near the larger one. Long known as Boone's Mill Cave, the 110-acre tract was purchased privately in 1972, developed, and opened to the public in 1973. The one-hour tour of the large cave covers one-third mile. Rare cave pearls, onyx curtains, a large rimstone formation, and an aged 48-ft.-tall column, the product of the meeting of stalactite and stalagmite, are among the cave's features. Waterfalls and two rivers fill the cavern with the sounds of constantly running water. A walnut casket on exhibit contains bones uncovered in 1974 thought to be those of Squire Boone. The cavern complex includes campgrounds, picnic areas, nature trails, a frontier village with a gristmill replica, arts and crafts shop, Indian Relic Museum, rock shop, and snack bar.

Continuing north on IND 135, the **Hayswood Nature Reserve** is *9.7 m.* from the Squire Boone Caverns. The reserve is a 160-acre park that includes a 40-acre timber stand of mixed hardwoods, Pilot Knob (a prominent local landmark overlooking Indian Creek), an 8-acre lake, shelter houses, playground, hiking trails, a blacktop trail for the handicapped, and boat and canoe rental for use on Indian Creek.

Past the entrance to the reserve *1 m.* is IND 62 which heads east into **CORYDON** (p. 2,724), the seat of government for Harrison County. Nestled in a picturesque valley at the junction of Big Indian and Little Indian creeks, Corydon rests on a tract of land originally purchased in 1804 by William Henry Harrison, then governor of the Indiana Territory. Harrison sold his property in 1807 to Harvey Heth, who laid out Corydon in 1808. The name for the town was suggested to Harrison by the words of his favorite dirge, "The Pastoral Elegy," which laments the death of the shepherd Corydon. In 1813 the village became the seat of government for the Indiana Territory. The convention called to draft a constitution for the state of Indiana convened in Corydon in 1816, and from 1816 to 1825 Corydon held the distinction of being Indiana's first capital. An-

other distinction came in the Civil War when Morgan's Raiders fought a battle with Harrison County Home Guards near Corydon: the only official pitched battle waged on Hoosier soil in the Civil War. (*NRHP*)

The place to begin a tour of Corydon is at the public square and the two convenient tourist headquarters on Walnut St. The **Corydon Capitol State Historic Site Visitor's Center** is next to the **Governor Hendricks house** on the north side of Walnut St. The center is located in a refurbished 19th-century woodshed. The Hendricks house and the Old Capitol on the public square are state historic sites, and the center supplies information and tours for both places.

Across Walnut St. at the southeast corner of Elm and Walnut sts. is Corydon's **Information Center and Chamber of Commerce building**, which opened in 1981. Details on Corydon and nearby attractions can be obtained here.

Indiana's first State Capitol, on the commons in Corydon, was begun in 1814 and completed in 1816. Dennis Pennington, a farmer, teacher, and speaker of the lower house of the territorial legislature, supervised the construction, which was nearly concluded by the time the first session of the state legislature convened in 1816. The $3,000 structure was actu-

Indiana Historical Society (Bass Photo Collection 209004)
Old State Capitol, 1915

ally built as the Harrison County Courthouse, but state offices were housed in it from 1816 to 1825. The design of the building had been approved by the Harrison County Court in 1811. The plain cube-shaped two-story gray limestone structure has walls 2 1/2 ft. thick. Two chimneys accommodate the four fireplaces. The hip roof supports an eight-sided cupola. In 1917 Indiana bought the Old Capitol, restored it, and opened it to the public as a state memorial in 1929. Restoration efforts uncovered the original flagstone floor, unsealed fireplaces, reset the original front door transom, resized the windows, and removed a deep dirt fill around the exterior walls. Doors, hardware, glass, railings, furniture, and other accoutrements were garnered from old buildings throughout the state. The reproduced cupola borrowed details from one on an Ohio courthouse. Among the furnishings are benches out of the Old Goshen Baptist Church in Boone Township.

To the north of the Old Capitol on the corner of Capitol and Walnut sts. is the present **Harrison County Courthouse**. When the state bought the Old Capitol in 1917, it allowed Harrison County its free use until the new courthouse was completed in 1929. The three-story stone structure cost about $150,000.

Across from the Harrison County Courthouse on Walnut St. at Elm St. stands the **Presbyterian Church**. The church is the oldest continuous religious organization in Corydon, which the Rev. John Finley Crowe, founder of Hanover College, helped form in 1819. The first church building was erected in 1826 on S. Capitol Ave., near Poplar St. During Morgan's raid in 1863 the little one-room brick church functioned as a Confederate hospital. The Presbyterians sold the building to the United Brethren in 1906, when they constructed their present sanctuary. In 1912 the original structure was razed.

Immediately east of the church on E. Walnut St. is the **Gov. William Hendricks residence**, opened in 1979 as a state historic site. Built by Davis Floyd in 1817, it served as William Hendricks's home when the General Assembly was in session during his term as governor, 1822-25. In 1841 the L-shaped Federal-style house was acquired by William Anderson Porter, lawyer, judge, state legislator, and speaker of the Indiana House of Representatives, 1847-48, and it remained in his family until bought by the state in 1975. Among the

furnishings is Hendricks's writing desk. A restored washhouse is at the rear of the building.

On Elm St., north of the Old Capitol, is the **Masonic Lodge**, organized in August 1817 under the Grand Lodge of Kentucky. On December 3, 1817, local Masons met at the home of Reuben Nelson, at the southwest corner of Maple and Walnut sts., to take steps to establish a Grand Lodge for the new state of Indiana. The planning meeting in Corydon resulted in the organization of the Grand Lodge of Indiana in Madison in 1818. The Pisgah Lodge of Corydon met in various buildings, including the Old Capitol, until 1926 when the present Temple was erected.

The **Old Treasury Building** or the first **State Office Building**, a one-story brick structure at Walnut and Mulberry sts., immediately northeast of the Gov. William Hendricks house, was built by Davis Floyd in 1817. Its two rooms, divided by a hall, served as the offices for the state auditor and treasurer until the capital was moved to Indianapolis in 1825. A cellar held the state's treasury vault. In 1829 it became the home of the Harrison County Seminary, then in 1851 a private residence. Over the years the house was enlarged. In 1988 Mary Sample Conrad, whose family had lived in the house since 1871, sold the structure to the state for $150,000. With this acquisition, all the extant properties associated with the government of the state prior to 1825 are owned and administered by the Indiana State Museum and Historic Sites and together form what is referred to as the Corydon Capitol State Historic Site.

In 1981 a new **bandstand** was built on the Corydon public square dedicated to Hurley B. Conrad, who died in 1979. Known as "Mr. Music Man of Harrison County," Conrad composed, conducted, sold musical instruments, and wrote "Down in Old Corydon" for Indiana's sesquicentennial celebration.

Proceed north on Mulberry St. one block, turn left on High St., and travel west to the **Constitutional Elm Memorial**. It is generally held that this once magnificent tree shaded delegates to Indiana's first constitutional convention during the sultry June days of 1816 as they composed the historic document. The elm, then, stood about 50 ft. high with a spread of approximately 132 ft. An elm disease killed the mammoth tree in the early 1920s. In 1925 its limbs were sawed off, and the 34 wagonloads of wood were stored, to be cut up eventually and fashioned into souvenirs. The surviving tree trunk, 5 ft. in diameter, first received a protective canopy. Then in 1937 a covering, constructed of 100 tons of sandstone, was erected over the trunk. The job of building the stone casing fell to the local Civilian Conservation Corps (CCC) and Works Progress Administration (WPA) laborers.

Directly west of the Constitutional Elm is the **Westfall house**, Corydon's oldest extant home. The Westfall family established a tanyard and built its log home in 1807. The property eventually came into the hands of Col. Lewis Jordan, who commanded Corydon's Home Guard during the Battle of Corydon in 1863.

Turn left for the tracks and depot of the **Louisville, New Albany and Corydon Railroad**, whose yards in front of the station include a rare stub switch in which the main track, rather than the switch points, is movable. This type generally disappeared in the Civil War era. The railroad's initial run took place in 1883, an eight-mile trip to Corydon Junction to connect with the Louisville, Evansville, and St. Louis Railroad (Southern Railway). Known locally as The Dinky, the train continues to haul freight for local manufacturers.

From the depot, go east one block and turn right on Oak St., location of the **Posey house**. Built in 1817 by Thomas L. Posey and Allen D. Thom, the house then had a south wing, and the U-shaped structure faced the commons and State Capitol. Posey (1792-1863) was the son of Thomas Posey (1750-1818), the last governor of the Indiana Territory. Thomas L. Posey was adjutant general of Indiana in 1823 and a state representative for two sessions, 1825 and 1825-26. Though a bachelor, he raised 14 orphans in his spacious house. In 1925 the Hoosier Elm Chapter of the Daughters of the American Revolution (DAR) bought the house (the south section had been torn down) and established a museum featuring local artifacts, including cannonballs from the Battle of Corydon. The museum has been partially financed by selling souvenirs made from wood of the Constitutional Elm.

Continue south, turn left at the end of the street to Chestnut St., and in three blocks turn right on Mulberry St. Cross Indian Creek and bear east about *.2 m.* to the **Zimmerman Art Glass Company**. Just west of the Indian Creek

bridge, the Louisville, New Albany and Corydon Railroad, now out of service at this point, fords the creek, a singular, if not unique, circumstance. A third generation glassmaker, Joe Zimmerman launched his Corydon glass company in 1961. Aficionados of paperweights quickly recognize the Zimmerman specialty. Executed in different sizes, the clear glass balls enclose a variety of unfolding glass flowers.

Return to Capitol Ave. (old IND 135) and head south past the Harrison County Fairgrounds and the Heidelberg Rd., bearing right. To the left is the entrance to the **Battle of Corydon Memorial Park**. The five-acre area was opened in 1975. On July 9, 1863, Confederate Brig. Gen. John Hunt Morgan's cavalry, more than 2,000 strong, met and overwhelmed roughly 450 local militia and citizens. A monument, erected in 1977, lists on its north face the Union men who died in the encounter and on the south face the Confederates. A marker beside the monument details the clash. A log cabin on the site has been refurbished, and a trail encircles the park. (*NRHP*)

Return on Capitol Ave. to High St., one block north of the Capitol, and turn right. Go two blocks to Mulberry St. and turn left to Summit St., one block away. Looking east up the Summit St. hill one can see the walls of the **Cedar Hill Cemetery**. A marker at the entrance to the cemetery provides the history of this burial ground, in existence since 1808. It contains graves of Confederate soldiers who died at the Battle of Corydon, as well as veterans from all of America's wars beginning with the Revolution. The cemetery, situated on a hill, provides a splendid view of the surrounding countryside.

Continue north one block, turn left on Elliot Ave., and right in two blocks on Capitol Ave. To the right, near the Indian Creek bridge, is **Cedar Glade**, or the **Kintner-McGrain home**. Jacob Kintner, a wealthy Virginian, purchased hundreds of acres in and around Corydon, and in 1808 he built this brick Greek Revival-style house. In 1849 Kintner heirs traded the property to Thomas McGrain, Sr., whose descendants have lived in the house since. The story is told that at the time of Morgan's raid the besieged citizens of Corydon retreated to the McGrain land because it was then some distance from the town. Morgan's gunners on their first volley into Corydon misjudged the distance and overshot the target, and some shells reached the McGrain sanctuary, putting the frightened populace to flight again. (*NRHP*)

Opposite Cedar Glade, a street leads west, then south to the **Keller Manufacturing Company**, the largest employer in Corydon. Established by William Keller, son of a German immigrant who came to Harrison County in 1847, the company first produced the Keller and Corydon wooden wagons, turning out over 250,000 between 1901 and 1935. Wagon making was phased out in 1942, being replaced by the manufacture of solid wood furniture. The three Keller plants now employ around 600 persons, of which one-half are in the Corydon facility.

Proceed north on IND 135 *12.7 m.* to **PALMYRA** (p. 692). Hays McCallen leased land on the Palmyra site in 1810. His parcel of ground became known as McCallen's Cross Roads. The story goes that McCallen got hold of the property because the owner felt crowded by two new towns emerging four and six miles from him. McCallen's Cross Roads gained a post office in 1823. In 1836 the town of Carthage was laid out on the spot, but another Indiana town claimed the name, thus leading to the adoption of Palmyra in 1839. Those who designated the town Palmyra probably had in mind King Solomon's fortified city in the Syrian desert. It became a wealthy center of caravan trade in Hellenistic and Roman times.

Hays McCallen's crossroads, originally the north-south Mauckport Rd., intersecting with the east-west New Albany-Vincennes Turnpike, eventually became IND 135 and US 150. The Buffalo Trace, "Indiana's first highway," ran in a northwesterly direction across Harrison County and through the present hamlet of Central Barren. The **Buffalo Trace Park**, *.7 m.* east of Palmyra on US 150, was opened in 1974 to commemorate the famous trail. Attractions on the 146-acre grounds include a 29-acre lake, a swimming beach, and facilities for tennis, shuffleboard, basketball, baseball, volleyball, and horseshoes. Three shelter houses are provided, along with picnic and playground equipment. A primitive camping area is available.

From Palmyra go north on IND 135 *.7 m.* to the Harrison-Washington County line. **WASHINGTON COUNTY** (p. 21,932; 516 sq. m.) was formed from Harrison and Clark counties in 1813, and by 1873 the present county boundaries were fixed. The terrain ranges from the arid barrens in the west to

steep hills and forests in the north and east. Numerous caves exist. The majority of the county's approximately 300,000 acres is given over to agriculture.

Continue north *13.7 m.* on IND 135 to **SALEM** (p. 5,290), the Washington County seat. County agent John DePauw, father of Washington C. DePauw, laid out the town in 1814 at the forks of Blue River and Brock Creek. The 174-acre site was purchased from William Lindley and Benjamin Brewer for $1,350. Mrs. William Lindley supplied the name, to honor her Salem, North Carolina, hometown. Overcoming squirrel invasions, cholera epidemics, Morgan's raiders, floods, and tornadoes, Salem throughout its history has served the region as a small agricultural and manufacturing center. Smith Cabinet Manufacturing Company, making radio and television cabinets and Child-Craft furniture, Imperial Clevite, creating powdered metal products, and O. P. Link Handle Company, manufacturing wood tools, handles, and mallets, are the city's major employers.

The present **Washington County Courthouse** on the Courthouse Square in Salem is the third such building on the site. It was completed in 1888 at a cost of $73,000. The clock tower was destroyed by fire in 1934 but was rebuilt to include the original clock and bell. On the first floor some old office furniture and other memorabilia are displayed. (*NRHP*)

A marker on the south courthouse lawn tells of Confederate Brig. Gen. John Hunt Morgan's stop in Salem on his raid into Indiana. Morgan took possession of the town on July 10, 1863, burned the depot, cut telegraph wires, and demanded ransom from the merchants for sparing their stores. The raiders moved on eastward the same day.

The stone **lion in front of the State Bank of Salem** on the square and east of the courthouse was carved at the request of Lee Sinclair (1836-1916), operator of a woolen mill and a dry goods business and after 1879 president of the State Bank. He also constructed the magnificent West Baden Springs Hotel (see Tour 11). The present State Bank occupies the site of the old bank building, Sinclair's residence, and the Sinclair Building.

A marker on the bank building identifies this location, before the erection of the Sinclair buildings, as the **homesite of Christopher Harrison** (1775-1863), Indiana's first lieutenant governor. The Maryland native and lawyer is first discovered in Indiana in 1808 living a reclusive existence on or near the present campus of Hanover College in Jefferson County. Accounts, perhaps apocryphal, of his self-imposed exile tell of his broken love affair with Elizabeth Patterson. Who came between the young lovers is unclear. Was it Elizabeth's father, Harrison's wealthy employer, who disliked the match? Or was the intruder Jerome Bonaparte, Napoleon's brother, whose social position diverted Elizabeth's attentions from Christopher? In any case, Elizabeth wed Jerome Bonaparte, but Napoleon annulled the marriage. The couple, however, had a child, Jerome Napoleon Bonaparte, whose son Charles Joseph Bonaparte served as secretary of the navy and attorney general in President Theodore Roosevelt's cabinet.

Christopher Harrison abandoned the hermit life-style in 1815. With Jonathan Lyons, John Paul's partner in the founding of Madison, Harrison moved to Salem and opened a dry goods store and built Salem's first brick house on the future bank corner. His election as the state's first lieutenant governor took place in 1816, but he resigned in 1818 over a dispute involving Gov. Jonathan Jennings, who had accepted a federal appointment as an Indian treaty negotiator. Harrison thought this violated the state constitutional provision prohibiting a sitting governor from holding a federal office. In accepting the commission, Harrison reasoned, Jennings had vacated the governor's chair and the lieutenant governor rightfully should be named governor. Neither Jennings nor the legislature sided with Harrison; thus he resigned. Among his subsequent public activities, Harrison supervised the survey of the new capital of Indianapolis, and he helped draw up a feasibility study on a canal around the Ohio River falls at Jeffersonville. In 1834 Harrison moved to one of his farms in the county and eventually returned to Maryland.

East of the courthouse, at 307 E. Market St. (IND 160) is the **John Hay Center**, comprising the **Stevens Memorial Museum**, the **John Hay house**, and a **pioneer village**. John Milton Hay (1838-1905), author and diplomat, was born in Salem, but the family moved to Warsaw, Illinois, when John Hay was three years old. After graduating from Brown University, where he was chosen class poet, he studied law and entered his uncle's law office, next to that

of Abraham Lincoln. Subsequently, Hay served as Lincoln's private secretary during his presidency. A diplomatic career followed with Hay holding posts in Paris, Vienna, Madrid, and England. He was secretary of state under Presidents William McKinley and Theodore Roosevelt. Hay's poetry is represented in his *Pike County Ballads and Other Pieces* (1871). He co-authored with John G. Nicolay the 10-volume *Abraham Lincoln, a History* (1890). *Century* magazine paid the authors the then unheard-of sum of $50,000 to serialize the Lincoln material.

The small two-room brick birthplace of John Hay was built in 1824 to house the Salem Grammar School. John Irwin Morrison (1806-1882), the school's first and only teacher, demonstrated considerable influence in Indiana's educational development. He launched Salem's Seminary and Female Collegiate Institute and subsequently taught languages and mathematics at Indiana University and chaired the school's board of trustees. While a state legislator in the 1840s, he pushed for tax-supported higher education. As a member of the state constitutional convention of 1850-51, he wrote the provision for election of a state superintendent of public instruction. A newspaperman and surveyor, Morrison also served as state treasurer in the mid-1860s. Sarah Morrison, his daughter, was the first woman to enroll (1867) in Indiana University and to graduate (1869).

In 1833 Charles Hay, John's father and a pioneer physician, moved his family into the schoolhouse. After their move to Illinois, George Teller bought the house, which remained in the Teller family possession until 1966. In conjunction with Indiana's sesquicentennial observance that year, Washington County won $1,000 for submitting to the state the most historical materials for copying. The prize money was earmarked for acquiring a facility to display the county's historical collection. The Hay house, by coincidence, came up for sale. The prize money, innumerable fund-raising projects, and the generosity of Mrs. Warda Stevens Stout, who desired a memorial to her parents, led to the procurement of the Hay home and the construction of the Stevens Museum. The John Hay Center was dedicated in 1971. The Hay house is refurbished to approximate the living conditions of the 1840s. The Stevens Museum is built of brick from old structures in Salem. It contains the genealogical library of the Washington County Historical Society and a variety of exhibits on its three floors. Mementos of John Hay are encased in the lobby. Between the museum and the Hay home a pioneer village has been laid out. (*NRHP/HABS*)

The unmarked site of the **home of Beebe and Hannah Booth** is at 311 E. Market St., two doors east of the museum. The Booths migrated to Indiana from New England after 1812. Beebe Booth was part owner of a general store, and he co-founded the *Tocsin*, Salem's first newspaper and one of the first papers in Indiana. In 1818 Booth also presided over the Salem Peace Society, an organization devoted to peace among nations. From the newspaper office above the store he and Ebenezer Patrick in 1818 published *The Life of Bonaparte*, the first literary work printed in Indiana. Beebe and Hannah's son, Newton, born in 1825 and educated under John Irwin Morrison, subsequently became California's 11th governor and a United States senator. Elizabeth, their daughter, married John Stevenson Tarkington. Newton Booth Tarkington, their offspring, became one of America's foremost authors. Beebe and Hannah Booth left Salem for Terre Haute in 1841.

Return to the courthouse, take Market St. *.3 m.* west to Shelby St., and go left about three blocks to an entrance to **Crown Hill Cemetery**, established in 1824. A marker near the Shelby St. entrance commemorates the life of **John Hay Farnham** (1791-1833), brother-in-law of Charles Hay. Born in Massachusetts, Farnham took up law after his Harvard graduation, and he is found practicing in Jeffersonville, Indiana, in 1819. He made a specialty of writing speeches and bills for the legislators at Corydon and Indianapolis. In Salem, to which he moved in 1824, he began speaking out for free public education. Farnham might have outperformed his neighbor John I. Morrison on this cause if he had lived longer. Farnham was one of the founders of the Indiana Historical Society in 1830 and was its first corresponding secretary. In 1833 a cholera epidemic wiped out about 10 percent of Salem's population, including Farnham, his wife, and child. Two children survived and lived briefly with Charles Hay.

In the vicinity of the Farnham headstone are clusters of small, weathered grave markers of others who perished in the cholera epidemic of 1833. Nearby is the iron-fenced **plot of the**

DePauw family. The only mausoleum-type structure in the cemetery is that of Lee Sinclair, located in the southwest section.

Returning to the courthouse from the cemetery, W. Market St. passes **DePauw Park** on the right. John DePauw, who sold Salem's lots in 1814, built his home on this site. His son, Washington C. DePauw, inherited the property and at his death willed that it remain in the DePauw family. Realizing that the day might come when no DePauw descendants would be living in Salem, the heirs deeded the square to the town in 1912. Upon the death in 1921 of John F. Keyes, a grandson of John DePauw and the last occupant of the homestead, the house was torn down. In 1927 Salem officials established a public park on the grounds to honor the DePauws.

Return to the courthouse and go north on Main St. (IND 135) three blocks to IND 56. Turn right and proceed east *1.4 m.* to the first paved road going north, just past the radio station. Go north *.5 m.* On the left, a small headstone-shaped monument marks the site of an **African Methodist Episcopal Church**, erected in the early 1850s, and the burial plot of **John Williams**, an ex-slave. Williams came to Salem as a slave with a family of Quakers named Lindley from North Carolina. Granted his freedom, Williams worked his own farm until 1863, when he was murdered at his home by, presumably, white racists. Williams was a victim, one of many, of Washington County's crusade of hate that reduced its black resident count from 252 in 1850 to 3 in 1880. In his will, Williams bequeathed his property to William Lindley to be held in trust and used for the education of black Americans. Proceeds from the sale of the farm, about $5,500, first were administered through the Colored Orphans Home in Indianapolis. The fund has grown considerably over the years and is still being used according to Williams's request.

Return to IND 56 and again head east. At *.5 m.* turn north *.2 m.* to the old **Blue River Friends Meetinghouse**, the site in 1815 of the beginnings of organized Friends worship in the county. The Friends Meeting ceased here in 1880, but each October a memorial service is held at the old meetinghouse. The present Blue River Friends Church, dedicated in 1902, is about two miles north and east of its former site. On the lawn stands a marker indicating the site of the **Blue River Academy**, a Friends school.

Return to Salem and proceed north on IND 135 *11.7 m.* to the Jackson County line at the Muscatatuck River. **JACKSON COUNTY** (p. 36,523; 514 sq. m.) became the 14th territorial county when established in 1815. Its name honored "Old Hickory" Andrew Jackson, who had earlier in the year repulsed the British in the Battle of New Orleans. The county's boundaries became fixed in 1859, after 11 readjustments to allow for neighboring county development. It is the state's eighth largest county. Its heavily forested landscape is bisected by the East Fork of the White River and dominated by the great Knobs in the south-central area. A leading melon producer, the county is agriculturally oriented, with some manufacturing concentrated in the Seymour vicinity.

Continue north *1.8 m.* past a round barn, 68 ft. in diameter, built in 1909. Nearby is the **Driftwood Christian Church**, the site in 1816 of the building of Jackson County's first church. North of the church *.1 m.* is the right-hand turnoff to **Starve Hollow Lake**. The 149-acre lake includes a 1,100-ft. beach. Fishing, boat and canoe rental, picnic grounds, nature trails, primitive campsites, and sports facilities are among the offerings at the 395-acre complex.

North of the entrance to Starve Hollow Lake *3.1 m.*, take the left fork to Main St. in **VALLONIA**, Jackson County's oldest community, dating from 1810 or 1812, though not recorded until 1856. Its name is open to several interpretations, but more than likely it is derived from the French "un vallon," meaning a vale or small valley or the adjective form "vallonne," which describes a small hilly landscape. The name recalls both the village's geographical setting and the tradition of the presence of a French settlement in the vicinity in the late 1700s. A version of **Fort Vallonia**, the principal stockade in the county during the War of 1812, has been built in the heart of the town, and a stone memorial to the fort stands in front of it. Near the fort's entrance on Main St. is a small museum. The proceeds from the Old Fort Vallonia Days festival held each October go to maintain the fort.

From Vallonia return *1.7 m.* on IND 135 to IND 235. Turn right, and at *1.3 m.* note the **round barn** in the left distance, built around 1910. The **Medora Covered Bridge** is along the right side of IND 235 *2.5 m.* west of IND 135.

Joseph J. Daniels built the three-span structure in 1875. Its length, 458 ft. including a 24-ft. overhang, makes it the longest of Jackson County's three covered bridges and the state's longest extant covered bridge, though no longer in use. It was saved from demolition in 1972, when preservationists won the battle to have the new bridge over the East Fork of White River constructed just south of the old one.

The town of **MEDORA** (p. 853), *1.3 m.* west of the bridge on IND 235, was laid out in 1853. West Lee Wright, the town's founder, applied his love of music to the naming of the community by juxtaposing the first three notes of the musical scale—do, re, mi. Others have suggested that the name comes from Lord Byron's poem "The Corsair," in which Medora is the loving companion of the hero Conrad. The passage of the Ohio and Mississippi Railroad through Medora in the mid-1850s benefited the town's selection as a prominent area trading center. In 1933, when US 50 was shifted from downtown Medora to several miles north, the community was deprived of a major trade artery. Nevertheless, Medora has not lost population over the last half century but has gradually grown.

Take Main St. west from downtown Medora up into the Knobs. Travel *2.7 m.* from the center of town to a block church building on the left a short distance before the road bends sharply to the right at a T-intersection. A modern ranch house rests on the southeast corner. The church sits on the foundation of a house once thought to be haunted by ghosts. On this spot around 1850 Dr. Creed Wilson constructed a fine two-story home. The physician's son, Aesop C. Wilson, died in the Civil War. The son's body was shipped home where it lay in a casket in an upstairs hallway for 12 years while his heartbroken mother refused a burial. Only after a fake seance, arranged by Dr. Wilson in 1874, in which the mother received verbal consent from her deceased son to be interred, was the burial performed. The old home, scene of this eerie story, was soon vacated and left to deteriorate, a haven for phantoms, until the present building was erected in 1958.

Bear right at the ranch house and take the next road left (Old US 50). Less than *.5 m.* on the right is **Weddleville Evangelical Lutheran Church**. The frame structure is on the site of an early log Methodist church at Weddleville, a village no longer in existence. John A. Weddle, a miller, laid out the town in 1855. The town gradually disappeared as the route of the Ohio and Mississippi Railroad drew the residents into Medora.

West of the Lutheran Church *.2 m.* on the left is the old **Weddleville High School**. Established in 1857, the school was built on land donated by George Whitfield Carr, legislator and president of the state constitutional convention, 1850-51, and his wife, Fanny Carr. The building served as a high school until 1897 and as a grade school until 1934. Long empty, it is cared for by the local Old Settlers Association.

Backtrack about *.7 m.* and turn left. Follow the main traveled road northward about *1.4 m.* and turn right on Byarlayknob Rd. Following this winding, scenic highway down through the Knobs to IND 235, turn left, and at US 50 turn right. Go east *5.7 m.* to **BROWNSTOWN** (p. 2,704), the seat of Jackson County. On the right, just beyond the CSX railroad bridge west of Brownstown, stands the **Marion-Kay Company**, an unusual factory that produces vanilla extract and other flavorings made of imports from distant lands. The town sits on a rise between the East Fork of White River and the high knobs to the southeast. In the late 1880s or early 1890s Brownstown and the community of Ewing, which grew up on the railroad about a mile to its west, merged into a civil unit. Prior to 1972 when Ewing's post office was closed, Brownstown had the rare, if not unique, distinction of having two separate post offices within its corporate boundaries. Also the horse and mule-drawn streetcar, which ran between Ewing and Brownstown starting in 1892, lasted until 1916—the last such streetcar in the state. Brownstown is also known for its annual Watermelon Fair, reflecting the flourishing crops of melons—watermelons, cantaloupes, etc.—that grow in the sandy White River Valley soil.

The present **Jackson County Courthouse**, on US 50 (Main St.) in Brownstown, actually dates from the early 1870s, though what is visible on both the outside and inside is a consequence of a 20th-century face-lifting. The 1873 courthouse, the fourth on the site, was a large brick structure with arched windows, quoined walls, and a tall wooden cupola. A massive reconstruction project in 1910-11 drastically changed the courthouse's appearance, most noticeably by the addition of wings, a columned

portico, and a brick clock tower. In 1959 lightning struck the building, causing a fire in the tower resulting in extensive damage to the glass dome and clock and also to the courtrooms and records. The old 2,500-lb. bell was damaged beyond repair; it now rests in the southwest corner of the courtyard. Fortunately, the fire did not harm the murals on either side of the second floor mezzanine. Painted in the mid-1930s by Carl Reinbold of Seymour, the murals depict scenes of important events in Jackson County's pioneer days.

Near the bell on the courthouse lawn is a marker honoring **John Ketcham** (1782-1865). A native of Maryland, Ketcham settled in the vicinity of the present Brownstown in 1811 and established a trading post. He served in the War of 1812. In 1816 the Jackson County commissioners, appointed to locate a county seat, purchased 150 acres for $1,200 from Ketcham for their purpose. The Ketcham family moved to Monroe County in 1818 where the father served as a trustee of Indiana University and several terms as a state legislator.

On the east, or backside, of the courthouse square and one-half block north, at 115 N. Sugar St., is the **Ball Memorial Museum**. Opened in 1970, the museum features local artifacts in addition to clothing, guns, telephones, tools, and old Brownstown newspaper files. The museum is under the auspices of the Jackson County Historical Society, organized in 1916.

From the museum return west to US 50 and S. Poplar St., which is one block before the highway curves north *1 m.* on the left into the business district. Poplar St. south leads directly to the **Skyline Drive** (watch for signs). Part of the Jackson State Forest project, initiated in 1931, it is a narrow gravel road that runs for nearly six miles over the ridges of the knobs outside Brownstown. At its peak 929-ft. elevation is a clearing with picnic facilities and a panoramic view into a four-county area. The drive exits onto IND 250. Take IND 250 left and return to Brownstown.

Exit from Brownstown on US 50 east and drive *3.1 m.* from the town limits, then go left onto Shields Rd. (unmarked), opposite the tall white Jackson County (water) Tank 4. The **Shieldstown Covered Bridge** is *.8 m.* from US 50 on the right. No longer in use, the bridge, 355 ft. including overhang and built by Joseph J. Daniels in 1876, once conveyed farmers and their goods from the north side of White River to the hamlet of **SHIELDS**. Shields, founded in 1866 by L. L. and William H. Shields, was a station on the railroad and a milling center.

Back on US 50 and *3.8 m.* east, on the left-hand shoulder, is a **Ten O'Clock Treaty Line marker**, erected in 1966 to commemorate the Fort Wayne Treaty of 1809 that opened up a large portion of southern Indiana for white settlement. Some 800 ft. northwest of this marker, the treaty line, which began about 90 miles northwest near Montezuma in Parke County, terminated at its juncture with the Grouseland Treaty line of 1805. Resting next to the modern marker is the treaty line's first memorial, an inscribed stone erected by the Jackson County Historical Society in 1916.

East *.4 m.* an unmarked street to the left intersects with US 50. The street (W. 2nd St.) almost immediately crosses the railroad tracks and bends eastward to run parallel with the highway. On two separate occasions in 1868, three Reno gang members were forcibly taken from their captors by local hooded vigilantes and hanged on a beech tree at a spot near the junction of W. 2nd St. and the Baltimore and Ohio railroad tracks. The spot has since been known as **Hangman's Crossing**. The hanging tree no longer exists.

Farther east on US 50 *.7 m.* are the city limits of **SEYMOUR** (p. 15,050), Jackson County's largest community. Meedy Shields (1805-1866) laid out the town on his property in 1852. At the time, the Jeffersonville and Indianapolis Railroad ran through his land. Through enticements, Shields persuaded the Ohio and Mississippi Railroad to cross the J and I tracks on his grounds. A part of the deal involved naming the town after the railroad's chief engineer, Henry C. Seymour. The O and M Railroad completed laying rails through Seymour in 1854. The next step for Shields was to get the trains to stop in his town. To achieve this, Shields, a state senator, pushed through a law requiring all trains to stop wherever tracks intersected, as they did in Seymour. With the cars now forced to halt at Seymour, the town grew rapidly, and on June 24, 1865, it incorporated as a city.

Seymour also played a role in the oft-voiced American dream of operating a true transcontinental railroad, one extending from coast to coast. For approximately 20 years, beginning in 1961, the Chicago, Milwaukee, St. Paul and Pacific Railroad, which had reached Seattle, Washington, on the west, terminated on the east at Seymour. This road had penetrated further east than any Pacific Coast road when it had reached Westport, Indiana, before the line was cut back to Seymour. It has since been abandoned from Seymour to Bedford.

On October 6, 1866, Seymour made its way into annals of crime when John and Simeon Reno and Franklin Sparks perpetrated the nation's first train robbery at the city's eastern outskirts. Later, in the 1880s, the Pinkerton Detective Agency reportedly thought Seymour was a hideaway for scores of the nation's most-wanted criminals. In the 1950s another infamous Hoosier, D. C. Stephenson, former Indiana Ku Klux Klan leader and one of the most powerful men in the state in the 1920s, lived in Seymour after his release from prison in 1956, where he served a 30-year sentence on a murder conviction. He left Seymour in 1962 and died in Tennessee four years later.

As a major railroad junction, Seymour attracted the desperado and the notorious, but it also lured business. Besides the mills and various woodworking firms, Seymour welcomed the Asa M. Fitch Company, chewing gum manufacturer. Asa Fitch launched his gum enterprise in Lexington, Indiana, in 1876. He moved it to Seymour in 1882, and to Indianapolis in 1893. By promoting the medicinal benefits of his tulip and blackstrap lines, Fitch introduced gum to an adult public. From mills and gum to the present commercial emphasis on plastics, diesel engine components, auto headlamps, and wood and metal products, Seymour historically has blended light manufacturing with agricultural services. It is also the hometown of rock musician John Cougar Mellencamp. A new museum and cultural center is being planned that will feature an extensive collection of antique telephones.

Past the city boundary *.4 m.* and at the first stoplight is the entrance to the **Freeman Field Airport and Industrial Park** on the right, which includes a municipal airport. The 2,550-acre facility was built in 1942 as a military flight-training base. The city received the grounds in 1947 from the War Assets Administration. The 309-acre industrial park includes 43 manufacturers, distributors, warehouses, and aircraft-related businesses. The airfield, one of the largest in the state, has three 5,500-

ft. runways, which are used primarily by chartered craft.

Continue on US 50 (Tipton St.) into downtown Seymour and turn left onto Chestnut to the old **Farmers' Club Building** on the right at 105 S. Chestnut St. When erected in 1914, the Farmers' Club was heralded as the first institution in America to provide farmers and their families at no charge the sorts of comforts found in big city department stores. The club building offered reading and meeting rooms, lounges, and nurseries. Families could bring dinner baskets to town, refrigerate them at the club, and, after shopping, have lunch or supper in the dining room. The benefactors were the brothers Meedy Shields Blish and Tipton S. Blish, operators of the huge Blish Milling Company in Seymour, and grandsons of the town's founder. They donated $35,000 for the construction of the building and its maintenance as a memorial to their grandfather. Tipton Blish's wife, Agnes A. Blish, founded in 1917 the county Red Cross Chapter that occupied the front room of the club until 1985. The one-story, classical-style Bedford stone building was restored to its original appearance by the Seymour Heritage Foundation, Inc., in the mid-1980s. The Seymour Chamber of Commerce moved its offices to the building in 1986. (*NRHP*)

From the Farmers' Club take Chestnut St. north three blocks to 4th St., one block west to Walnut St., and two blocks south on Walnut St. to 2nd St. The **Seymour Public Library** and the **H. Vance Swope Memorial Art Gallery** are located on the southwest corner of Walnut and 2nd sts. The library, built with a $10,000 gift from Andrew Carnegie, opened to the public in 1905. It doubled its floor space in 1928 after the library board became the first in Indiana to borrow money for such improvements under a new state law. H. Vance Swope (1879-1926), a Jefferson County native who lived his formative years in Seymour, became a prominent landscape and marine painter in New York City. Between 1916 and his death he sent to Seymour art exhibits, which were displayed under the watchful care of the Seymour Art League, founded in 1913. Through Swope's donations and the league's purchases, a respectable group of works by Indiana artists, including T. C. Steele, found a permanent home in Seymour. Swope bequeathed $3,000 and 10 more paintings to the Art League, which

erected the Swope memorial room, dedicated in 1928.

From the library take 2nd St. west four blocks to Elm St., turn right for four blocks to W. 6th St., and turn right for one block to 503 W. 6th. The large two-story frame house, called **Shadelawn**, was built in 1875 by William T. Branaman, an attorney for the Reno family.

Across the street east is the James M. Shields Memorial Gymnasium (former Shields High School gymnasium), which occupies ground that belonged to **Frank Brown Shields** (1884-1946), a Seymour native who invented brushless shaving cream in 1918. Shields established the Barbasol Company, headquartered in Indianapolis, in 1921. The famed concern was sold to Charles Pfizer and Company in 1962. Shields, known as "the Barbasol King," purchased one-half block of residences on W. 6th St. between Poplar and Pine in Seymour as a site for a gymnasium to honor his father, Dr. James M. Shields, a prominent town physician and former mayor. The gymnasium was completed in 1941, but the Army Corps of Engineers took it over the first year as a workshop for engineers drafting plans for Freeman Field.

From the gymnasium head west on W. 6th St. (IND 258) *2 m.* to the **Bell's Ford Covered Bridge** on the right, which opened to traffic in 1869. G. E. Shields and Robert Patterson, of Seymour, constructed the 325-ft.-long bridge that spans the East Fork of the White River. Rather than the usual Howe or Burr truss design, this bridge used a post truss, the only one ever built in Indiana. The Bell's Ford bridge was bypassed by the new IND 258 span in 1970.

Return to Seymour on W. 6th St. to Poplar (a side street one block east of Pine St.) and turn left for one block. On the southeast corner of Poplar and 7th is the **Edgar Whitcomb home**. The brick-and-stucco mansion was built for Thomas Groub in 1917 by Indianapolis architect Frank B. Hunter. Groub was the grandson of John C. Groub, whose grocery business, begun in 1863, developed into the present chain of Jay-C Food Stores in operation across southern Indiana. Since 1957 the mansion has been the home of the Edgar Whitcomb family. A lawyer, Whitcomb (b. 1917) was an assistant United States attorney for southern Indiana, Indiana secretary of state, 1966-68, and governor, 1969-73. Features of the 15-room residence include an underground tunnel, wine cellar, three porches, two staircases, and a 6-ft. fountain on the terraced front lawn.

Turn right and proceed two blocks to N. Chestnut St. Go two blocks south to 5th St. The **Burkholder Funeral Home** on the southwest corner occupies a Colonial-style mansion built by Meedy Shields Blish between 1898 and 1900 for his bride. The Burkholder family purchased the residence from the Blish heirs in 1961 and moved its funeral business into the remodeled home in 1963.

From the Burkholder Funeral Home return to W. 6th St. and drive east one block to N. Indianapolis Ave., which parallels the railroad. Proceed south to 410 N. Indianapolis. The two-story frame house on the east side of the tracks, painted white, with the long-columned front porch, is considered Seymour's first residence. It was built by **Travis Carter** in the early 1850s. Carter (1819-1901) came to Seymour in 1852 and established a planing mill in 1855. The Travis Carter Company, Inc., closed in 1957 after more than 100 years of supplying lumber and building supplies to the area.

From the Carter home go north to W. 6th St. and proceed two blocks east to IND 11. Follow IND 11 (Ewing St.) north to 9th St. The grounds to the left between 9th and 11th sts. comprise two cemeteries. The old **Seymour City Cemetery** is the nearest to the corner of 9th and Ewing sts. Buried here are three of the Reno brothers (Frank, William, and Simeon). The Renos and one of their gang members (Charlie Anderson) were being held in the New Albany jail when vigilantes overtook the facility and hanged the criminals from the second level of cells on December 12, 1868. The three brothers were placed in one large pine box and interred in the cemetery three days later. To view the graves turn left on 9th St. and go one-half block to a new marker atop a stone pillar on the right. The graves are located up the incline and are distinguished by a rectangular wrought iron fence. The graves were unmarked for many years until veterans' headstones were added in the early 1980s. **St. Ambrose Cemetery**, north of the city cemetery, off Ewing St., is situated on ground where, in 1812, James Shields, father of Meedy Shields, Seymour's founder, had charge of a crude blockhouse.

Proceed north on IND 11 to 15th St. Turn left, go one block west to Shields Ave., which cuts north and south through the Seymour Country Club, and turn left again. The stone wall, bordering the road and in front of the clubhouse, has incorporated into it a marker which denotes the surrounding land as **Woodstock Gardens**, the original farm of James Shields, who settled it in 1808. Meedy Shields spent his boyhood here, often visited by his cousin John Tipton, who subsequently served in the United States Senate from Indiana.

Turn around and proceed one block north on Shields Ave. to the **Riverview Cemetery** entrance at 16th St. Sarah V. Reno, wife of both John Reno, from whom she was divorced, and Frank Reno, is buried here. Laura Amanda Reno Goudy, the Reno brothers' only sister, is also buried here. To see the stones, get directions from personnel in the cemetery office at Shields Ave. and 16th St.

From Riverview Cemetery go north on IND 11 *.8 m.* to **ROCKFORD**. At Seymour's founding in 1852, Rockford was the county's commercial center. Founded in 1830, Rockford's river location drew mills and flatboat activity. This early riverfront community died out due to floodings and business relocations, but a new village emerged at a safer distance from the water. A series of fires in the 1850s leveled the new Rockford. How the fires originated remains a mystery, but the leading suspects traditionally have been the Reno family. In any case, the Reno kin quietly bought up the vacated and burned out properties at greatly reduced prices until they owned five-sixths of the lots. The overall consequences were the making of Rockford into a criminals' lair, the physical destruction of the town, and the shift of people and trade to Seymour.

From Rockford return through Seymour to US 50 via IND 11 and proceed east *.9 m.* to Burkart Blvd. Go north on Burkart Blvd. about *.3 m.* to the top of the railroad overpass. Approximately 100 ft. east on the tracks is the unmarked spot where the Reno gang committed the **nation's first train robbery**, which occurred on October 6, 1866.

Return to US 50 and proceed east. Before reaching the intersection with I-65 and with US 31, you pass on the left the headquarters of the **Kocolene Oil Corporation**. Launched in Seymour in 1938 by Carrie Myers, the company first sold gas under the name "Hoosier Pete" through its contract with the Hoosier Petroleum Company. The new firm created in 1943 its Kocolene trademark, a combination of letters from *Ke*iser *O*il *Co*mpany (an early business relation) and "lene," a rendering of the last letters of the word gasoline. Today, the Kocolene Oil Corporation is among the fifty largest privately held companies in Indiana and operates stations in four states.

Proceed east on US 50 *2.2 m.* beyond US 31 to the **Muscatatuck National Wildlife Refuge** entrance on the right just across the Jennings County line (for a description of the county see Tour 5). Established in 1966 under the supervision of the United States Fish and Wildlife Service to provide habitat for waterfowl that use the area in spring and fall migrations, it is Indiana's only national wildlife refuge. Half of its 7,702 acres is forest, the rest water, marshlands, and croplands. Fishing and hunting are allowed. The visitor information center, near the entrance, exhibits interpretive displays. Well-marked nature trails afford an education in wildlife identification and management.

Return to US 31 and turn left. **SCOTT COUNTY** (p. 20,422; 192 sq. m.), Indiana's fifth smallest county, is *14.3 m.* south. It was created from parts of five existing counties in 1820 and named after the Revolutionary War veteran and Kentucky governor Maj. Gen. Charles Scott. The land is rolling to level except for the knobs in the southwestern corner. The Muscatatuck River forms the north boundary, and the arteries of I-65 and US 31 cut through it from north to south.

Continue south on US 31 *1.1 m.* to **AUSTIN** (p. 4,857), platted in 1853. Continue *.7 m.* farther to Morgan St., location of the **Morgan Packing Company** and **American National Can Company**. Until the 1890s the town's livelihood came from timber processing for shipbuilders and barrel makers. As the timber gave out, a canning industry grew. The Austin Canning Company was organized in 1899 by Joseph F. Morgan and others who jointly put up $4,000 to build the first canning plant. In 1907 Joseph and his son Ivan formed a partnership and bought out the other stockholders, and in 1917 they changed the company's name to Morgan Packing Company. Now a major food packer, it has 50 items on its price list, covers 45 acres with 30 acres under roof, and has a regular work force of some 450, which increases considerably during peak harvesting and canning months. The American National Can Company came to Austin in 1933 to produce containers primarily for the Morgan cannery.

On May 22, 1868, the Reno gang pulled off one of the most lucrative train robberies in American history. The scene was the Marshfield station of the Jeffersonville, Madison, and Indianapolis Railroad about *1.5 m.* south of Austin. The **Marshfield caper** netted the notorious Renos and their henchmen over $96,000 and instant nationwide fame.

South of Austin *2.7 m.* on US 31 is **SCOTTSBURG** (p. 5,068), the county's seat of justice. Between 1820 and 1874 the government offices were located in Lexington. The progressive settlement of the county, and particularly the completion of rail lines some distance from Lexington, provoked sporadic calls for a centrally placed county seat. Not until 1870 did the county commissioners approve a transfer from Lexington to Centreville, a railside hamlet subsequently absorbed by Scottsburg. Scottsburg's plat was recorded in March 1871. The new town's name paid tribute to Col. Horace Scott, the general superintendent of the Jeffersonville, Madison, and Indianapolis Railroad.

Turn left on IND 56 (McClain St.) and proceed *.3 m.* to the **Scott County Courthouse** on the public square, which was built and furnished in 1873-74 by Travis Carter of Seymour for $15,995. In the front courtyard is an 18-ft.-tall monument to **William Hayden English** (1822-1896). Born in Lexington, Scott County, English's achievements included a four-term stint in Congress, 1853-61, the Democratic party nomination for vice-president in 1880, the building of the English Opera House and Hotel in Indianapolis, the presidency of the Indiana Historical Society, 1886-96, and the writing of a history of George Rogers Clark's Revolutionary War campaigns in the Northwest Territory. The bronze statue of English was sculpted by John H. Mahoney, of Indianapolis, whose many works include the figures of William Henry Harrison, George Rogers Clark, and James Whitcomb on Monument Circle in the state capital. Dedication ceremonies took place September 28, 1907, keynoted by Vice-President Charles W. Fairbanks.

From the courthouse, return to US 31 and drive *4.7 m.* south. Watch for the marker indicating the location of the **Pigeon Roost State Historic Site**, *.3 m.* east of US 31. William E. Collings founded the settlement of Pigeon Roost in 1809, naming it for the passenger pigeon, an important and plentiful food and feed item in pioneer Indiana. Collings's Kentucky relatives and neighbors occupied the village's cluster of cabins. On September 3, 1812, an Indian war party of Shawnees with some Miamis and Delawares attacked the residents, leaving 24 men, women, and children dead. Several assailants were killed, but the bulk avoided capture. The victims were buried in one or more mass graves. The cause of the horrid episode is not known fully, but it has been linked to the emotions triggered by the War of 1812 and to thievery and fraud perpetrated by the whites against the Indians. The 44-ft.-high square stone shaft, commemorating the Pigeon Roost tragedy, was dedicated in 1904. It became a state memorial in 1929.

Continue south on US 31 *.6 m.* and cross into **CLARK COUNTY** (p. 88,838; 376 sq. m.). William Henry Harrison, governor of the Indiana Territory, established Clark County by proclamation in 1801. The county was carved from Knox County, which then covered almost the whole of present Indiana and well beyond. Named for George Rogers Clark, the Revolutionary War hero, the county originally comprised almost one-fifth of the future state's land area. Fifteen alterations of Clark's boundaries, principally for creating new counties, had by 1873 reshaped the county. Fronting the Ohio River and possessing heavily timbered hinterlands, the county's early economy concentrated on agriculture, cooperage, milling, shipping, and boat building. Today, about one-third of the county's residents are rural-based. The urban dwellers are largely concentrated at the three largest cities: Charlestown, Clarksville, and Jeffersonville. Manufacturing is well balanced, with soaps, detergents, and ammunition leading the way. The recent opening of a county airport near Clarksville, construction of a key shipping port near Jeffersonville called the Clark Maritime Centre, and discussions on riverfront development and a state park near Charlestown have refocused attention on the area's tourist and transport potential.

South of the county line *3.8 m.* on US 31 is the main entrance to the **Clark State Forest** on the right. Containing 22,979 acres, Clark State Forest is the third largest state forest. Established in 1903, with an initial purchase of 2,028 acres for $16,000, the forest is the state's oldest. All of the state's experimental and forestry work was done here until 1929. Indiana's first forest nursery began here in 1925. The for-

est lies chiefly in Clark, but it extends into Scott and Washington counties. Recreational facilities in the forest include five lakes, picnic and camping areas, a 2,000-acre backpack area, and shelter houses. Fishing and turkey hunting are permitted. A rugged 32-mile-long hiking trail, known as the Knobstone Trail, was completed in 1980.

HENRYVILLE (p. 1,132) is *.3 m.* south of the Clark forest entrance on US 31. Henry Ferguson laid out the town in 1850 but named it Morristown. Three years later the county commissioners, having discovered another Hoosier town by the same name, changed the name to Henryville to honor its founder. The running of the Jeffersonville Railroad through the site provided the incentive for Ferguson, a local landowner, not only actively to support the laying of the track but also to found the town. In the late 1940s Henryville made news as the driest town in the state. The water supply had to be trucked in daily to most of the 368 residents. More recently, Henryville has gained repute as the birthplace of **Col. Harlan Sanders**, the Kentucky Fried Chicken king. He was born just east of Henryville and lived his youth in the county.

At Henryville turn left on IND 160 and go *8.5 m.* to **CHARLESTOWN** (p. 5,596). IND 160 terminates at IND 403. Turn left on IND 403 and go right on IND 3 (Market St.). Charlestown is Indiana's fifth oldest city. It was laid out in 1808 and named for one of its surveyors, Charles Beggs, who subsequently served in the territorial and state legislatures. In 1811 Charlestown wrested the county seat from Jeffersonville and held it until the larger city reclaimed it in 1878. (Clark County's first government headquarters was in Springville, no longer in existence but once situated about a mile southwest of Charlestown.) After losing the county seat, Charlestown settled into the humdrum of a small country town until World War II. Then, practically overnight, Charlestown found itself in the shadow of the world's largest smokeless powder plant and discovered the burden of caring for several thousand additional residents. Traffic jams, trailer courts, and real estate offices transformed the once pastoral landscape. From a village of 939 people in 1940, Charlestown's population count fluctuated between 15,000 and 40,000 residents during the war years. At war's end, the city experienced another massive adjustment as workers and their families packed up and left. When the dust finally settled, Powder Town had gained a fivefold increase in population, some utility improvements, government housing, and an explosives plant.

Most of Charlestown's attractions, historical or modern, pertain to **Jonathan Jennings** (1784-1834), Indiana's first governor. The New Jersey-born, Pennsylvania-raised lawyer practiced his profession in Vincennes before moving to Charlestown in 1809. Jennings presided over the constitutional convention at Corydon in 1816 and won the governor's chair the same year. Reelected in 1819, he resigned in 1822 to run for Congress. He captured the congressional seat and held it until defeated in 1830. At this time Jennings retired to his Charlestown farm, where he died in 1834.

Turn left at the second traffic light two blocks to the **Charlestown City Cemetery**, the resting place of Jennings and his two wives. Jennings was interred originally in an unmarked grave in an earlier town burial ground. In 1893 the state legislature appropriated $500 to purchase a gravestone. Jennings's body was reburied in the present city cemetery, and his headstone was erected. Fears that something could happen to the stone at its location near the entrance prompted its removal in 1981 to a spot further inside the cemetery. His grave site received a less vulnerable marker. To the left of Jennings's monument, at its new location, is a headstone marking the burial sites of Ann Hay and Clarissa Barbee, Jennings's wives.

In 1982 Indiana Masons put up a marker next to Jennings's monument in recognition of the first governor's service as an Indiana Grand Master. Charlestown figures prominently in the state's Masonic history. The Grand Lodge, in its first year of existence in 1818, headquartered in Charlestown and held its first annual meeting there. Alexander Buckner, the first Grand Master, lived in Charlestown. The Charlestown lodge was established in 1816 and was known as the Blazing Star Lodge. Local Masons built a two-story brick hall in 1827, the first floor of which for many years was the home of the Charlestown Seminary. A marker to Charlestown's historic Freemasonry is located just east of Jennings Plaza at the site of the **Blazing Star Lodge** between Main Cross and Harrison sts.

Two blocks south of the cemetery, at the northeast corner of Harrison and Water sts., is a plaque indicating the site of the **Green Tree Tavern**, built in 1812, and the location of Jennings's inaugural ball and his marriage reception in 1826. The Queen Anne-style house was built for Judge Ward Watson around 1900 after the tavern was torn down. (*NRHP*)

Continue south one block on Harrison St. and turn right on Market St. to the **Jennings Plaza**, located on the site of Clark County's first courthouse. The plaza was constructed in the late 1960s as a result of urban renewal. The Jennings Plaza marker on the site was installed by the Green Thumb Garden Club in 1977. The gazebo was constructed in 1986.

Besides Buckner and Jennings, **Dr. Andrew Jennings Hay** (1822-1897), of Charlestown, also was an Indiana Grand Master of the Masons. The Charlestown-born physician was the nephew of Ann Hay, the first wife of Jonathan Jennings. **Mary Garrett Hay**, the daughter of Dr. Hay and Rebecca Garrett, and grandniece of Jonathan Jennings, became one of America's leading suffragists, temperance reformers, and Republican party leaders. Born in Charlestown in 1857, Mary Hay left her hometown to attend college in Ohio and eventually made her career in New York. She was a confidante and companion of the noted suffragist Carrie Chapman Catt. Hay held the presidency in many New York organizations, including its Federation of Women's Clubs, the Equal Suffrage League, the Women's Suffrage party, and the League of Women Voters. She was one of the original appointees to the Republican Women's National Executive Committee in 1918, and she helped organize the first conference on the Cause and Cure of War in 1926. She died in New York in 1928 and is buried there. Her Charlestown home is now the **Grayson Funeral Home**, located at 893 High St., a block south of the Plaza and to the left.

A right turn leads to 673 High St., the two-story, Federal-style **Benjamin Ferguson house**, constructed in 1816 for Ferguson, a prominent local citizen and a member of the first Indiana House of Representatives in 1816. Ferguson owned the home only briefly, and it changed hands several times until a family of German immigrants named Spreisterbach acquired it in 1860. The house remained in the hands of this family for 100 years. (*NRHP*)

Leave Charlestown via Market St. (IND 3) and turn right on IND 62. The **Indiana Army Ammunition Plant** is a short distance on the left. The highway borders the huge 10,600-acre complex for *5.5 m.* The powder plant, put on standby after World War II, was reactivated during the Korean and Vietnam wars. In 1980 a multimillion dollar expansion and modernizing project for the continued production of ammunition for large artillery weapons helped to maintain peacetime employment levels at around 1,800 workers. Some 900 surplus acres in the facility have been discussed as a possible state park site.

JEFFERSONVILLE (p. 21,220) is *7.8 m.* south on IND 62 from the intersection with IND 3 at Charlestown. Jeffersonville is located in one of the state's most populous townships. Among Indiana's oldest cities, Jeffersonville was laid out in 1802 in a unique grid pattern suggested by then President Thomas Jefferson. He believed the sun's heat, intensified by the congestion of urban buildings, contributed to yellow fever epidemics. Jeffersonville's checkerboard plat, therefore, designated alternate squares to be unsold and be retained as open-air buffers against the spread of settlement and diseases. If the scheme for the 150-acre tract had succeeded, Jeffersonville today would exhibit a one-of-a-kind cityscape, or many other communities would have followed its lead. Instead, the press of land seekers and speculators by 1817 caused the original plan to be abandoned and the vacant lots to be sold.

Jeffersonville attracted the potential resident because the townsite bordered the Ohio River at the Falls, possessed Indiana's second land office, and, until 1811, was the county seat. The county seat was returned permanently to Jeffersonville from Charlestown in 1878. Jeffersonville's river orientation and its proximity to Louisville have meant heavy investments in transportation products and facilities. Early attempts to provide ways for boats to circumvent the Falls obstruction, either by canals or piggyback on railroad cars, were expensive failures. Of greater consequence was Jeffersonville's boat building and railroad activity. Vessels of the Howard Shipyards, established in 1848, dominated the Ohio-Mississippi river traffic into the 20th century. Railroads, beginning in the 1840s with the Jeffersonville Railroad, subsequently the Jeffersonville, Madison, and Indianapolis Railroad, gave the Falls Cities commercial preeminence in the region. The Ohio Falls Car and Locomotive Company, founded in 1864, was a leader in its day in the

manufacture of rail cars. Other institutions, such as the Indiana State Prison and the huge United States Quartermaster Depot, brought nationwide prestige to the river town. The river often tore down what it helped to build up, and Jeffersonville suffered extensively from periodic flooding. The 1937 flood destroyed or damaged up to 400 homes and businesses, while an estimated 80 percent of the 11,000 residents were evacuated. A flood wall was constructed shortly thereafter. The river continues to figure prominently in Jeffersonville's future as witness the ground breaking in the spring of 1982 for the Clark Maritime Centre, off IND 62 above the city, which has opened Jeffersonville to commercial traffic on the Ohio River.

Continue south on IND 62 *.3 m.* to the intersection with Holman Ln. and turn right (the first light past the city limits sign). Proceed northwest *1 m.* to an intersection where Holman Ln. merges into Charlestown-New Albany Pike. Located *1.6 m.* on the right is the 56-acre **Slugger Park**, the producer of Hillerich and Bradsby's **Louisville Slugger** bats and **Power-Bilt** golf clubs. The firm moved its Louisville factory to the modern Jeffersonville facility in 1974, although the corporate headquarters remains in Louisville. The Louisville Slugger had its beginning in 1884 when Louis R. (Pete) Browning of the old American Association's **Louisville Eclipse** broke his bat beyond repair or, it is also said, he was in a terrible slump. Fourteen-year-old John Andrew "Bud" Hillerich then constructed a new bat for Browning at his father's wood turning shop. At its peak, the company produced over six million wooden bats a year from white ash wood that comes from the company's private forests in Pennsylvania and New York. Jeffersonville-made Louisville Sluggers are used by more than 75 percent of all major league baseball players and comprise more than 50 percent of the world's total. While most bats are produced by semiautomatic machines, the professionals' bats are still hand turned to the individual's rigid specifications. Hillerich and Bradsby started production of Power-Bilt golf clubs in 1916, making it the oldest such producer in existence. Many of the PGA's top stars use clubs produced in the Jeffersonville plant.

Return to IND 62 and continue south into downtown Jeffersonville (IND 62 becomes E. 10th St.). At E. 10th and Meigs Ave. *3.2 m.* from the Holman Ln. intersection is the former

United States Quartermaster Depot on the right, now a series of shops called the Warehouse Barn. From the Civil War through the Korean War, the depot, one of the nation's largest, supplied the armed forces with everything from saddles to shirts. During the Civil War the storerooms and offices were spread throughout the city and beyond. Ulysses S. Grant, in his first term as president, authorized Maj. Gen. M. C. Meigs, quartermaster general of the army, to consolidate the scattered storehouses. Meigs constructed a quadrangle-shaped structure, which was completed in 1874. In World War I the depot turned out, along with other equipment, almost all the regulation shirts for enlistees. From bundles of cut cloth distributed at the depot, up to 14,000 women sewed the garments, often in their own homes. At times, new buildings went up, and in World War II Uncle Sam's Department Store covered 244 acres, handled 71,000 individual items, and dispersed a million dollars worth of equipment monthly. Officials figured that in 1944 alone the depot provided enough canvas duck to build a block-wide tent that could stretch from California eastward to Paris, France. The depot closed in 1957, and buildings not reserved for government use were auctioned off for retail and industrial conversions. Beginning in 1958, the government moved its major census processing onto the depot grounds. The main building is located at 1201 E. 10th St. The **Census Bureau** is southern Indiana's largest federal employer. Almost 2,000 persons were employed at Jeffersonville during the 1980 enumeration when the center processed around 80 million questionnaires, encoding the information on tape for telephone transmission to Washington, D.C.

Continue southwest on 10th St. about one-third mile to Spring St. and turn left, driving southeast four blocks to Court Ave. and **Warder Park**, which was established in 1881 and named for Luther Fairfax Warder, the city's mayor at the time. Elected in 1875, Warder led the successful fight to have the county seat returned to Jeffersonville in 1878. A stone marker in the park also honors the popular mayor. The old courthouse, completed in 1878, was torn down in 1970 to make way for a wing of the new City-County Building, located in the 500 block of E. Court Ave., just north of Warder Park.

Stay on Spring St., go two blocks to Chestnut St., and turn right to the **Grisamore house** at 111-113 W. Chestnut St. The unusual brick double house was built in 1837 on land that was jointly owned by local businessmen and brothers, Wilson and David Grisamore, each of whom occupied half the building. Although there is no evidence as to who designed the structure, it is thought by some that Jacob Glossbrenner, a local cabinetmaker and carpenter, might have been responsible. The Federal-style structure, fronted by three, two-story high Doric columns, combines an eclectic mixing of architecture not usually found in Indiana. In its early days, the home was the dwelling of many local notables. In 1840 presidential candidate William Henry Harrison delivered a speech from the building's front porch. A 1981 electrical fire destroyed the eastern third of the building. Local citizens led by Mrs. Rosemary Prentice and Harvey Russ were responsible for rebuilding and renovating the historic structure. It now houses several businesses, including Historic Landmarks Foundation of Indiana's Southern Regional Office. (*NRHP*)

Continue around the block, left, to Market St. and proceed .9 m. east to 1101 E. Market St. and the **Howard Steamboat Museum**. James Howard launched his shipyards at Port Fulton (now a part of Jeffersonville) in 1834 at the age of 19. From 1836 to 1843 he built his boats upriver at Madison. He returned to Jeffersonville in 1848 to stay. Between 1834 and 1940, successive generations of the Howard family directed the construction of more than 1,000 vessels. The output from the Howard yards in some years exceeded 10 percent of the total number of boats introduced on western rivers. The $103,500 *J. M. White* (1878), the most luxurious steamboat ever built, came from the Howard works, as did the *City of Louisville* (1894), history's fastest steamboat. In 1941 the United States Navy bought the yards for the production of landing ships. After the war the establishment was sold at auction. In the early 1890s E. J. Howard, son of the founder, erected the 22-room Victorian mansion which now houses the museum. Its opulence is discernible in the diversity of woods so skillfully applied by steamboat craftsmen to the interior. In 1958 the Clark County Historical Society purchased the house, and the following year the society's board of directors incorporated as the Howard

National Steamboat Museum and officially opened the house to the public. A tragic fire in 1971 extensively damaged practically every room in the mansion. However, its collection of ship wheels, woodworking tools, lanterns, bells, photographs, and steamboat models, among many other interesting artifacts of the area's old riverboat days, was not permanently harmed. (*NRHP*)

Across from the Howard Museum are the **Jeffboat** shipyards, once the largest inland shipyards in the country. Jeffboat property encompasses the old Howard shipyards, purchased at auction following World War II. The Jeffersonville Boat and Machine Company, or Jeffboat, was launched in 1938 as a subsidiary of the American Commercial Barge Lines Company. In 1969 Jeffboat became a part of the Inland Waterways Division of the Texas Gas Transmission Corporation. Besides its usual barges and towboats, Jeffboat occasionally did custom work, as when in 1979 it launched the *Mississippi Queen*, a $20 million luxury steam-pow-

ered stern paddlewheeler, the first to be built in this century.

Return to Spring St. via E. Market St., go one block south to Riverside Dr., and turn right. Docked across the street is the sternwheel excursion boat, **Bonnie Belle**. Constructed in 1969, this diesel-powered vessel is Indiana's only riverboat on the Ohio. It has a seating capacity of 160 and combines modern conveniences such as air conditioning with traditional interior design.

Proceed *.7 m.* west on Riverside Dr. passing under the John F. Kennedy and the George Rogers Clark bridges, and enter **CLARKS-VILLE** (p. 15,164), just west of the latter span. Chartered in 1783, the city is recognized as the first American settlement in the Old Northwest Territory and Indiana's oldest municipality. When Virginia ceded the 150,000-acre Clark's Grant in 1781, it authorized 1,000 acres for the establishment of Clarksville to honor George Rogers Clark, hero of Kaskaskia and Vincennes. Lacking a suitable boat landing, reportedly unhealthy, and quickly overshadowed by

City of Louisville *trial trip, April 2, 1894*

neighboring communities, Clarksville grew little until the boom years of World War II. Largely on the strength of the expansion throughout the Falls Cities region, Clarksville is about six and one-half times its size of 40 years ago.

A major threat to Clarksville's existence occurred in the mid-1850s when a group of promoters revealed well-prepared plans for a new town, **Falls City**, to be situated next to Jeffersonville and encompass most of Clarksville. The uncertain boundaries of Clarksville's original plat allowed such a scheme to be proposed. The proprietors of the projected Falls City sold lots and consummated deals with railroads and manufacturers. Before the matter went too far, however, the state Supreme Court intervened and ruled that Falls City encroached on Clarksville city limits. As a result, the elaborate Falls City project quickly disintegrated.

Immediately west of the Clark bridge and Missouri Ave., north of Riverside Dr., lies the former complex of the **Ohio Falls Car and Locomotive Company**. Established in 1864 to manufacture freight and passenger cars, it was the largest firm in its specialty in the country at one time. The concern reorganized in 1876 as the Ohio Falls Car Company, and it merged in 1898 with 12 other such railroad rolling stock producers to form the American Car and Foundry Company. The car works ceased business in 1932 and closed permanently in 1939. The factory at its height comprised 50 buildings of the one-story brick shed variety. The plant is used primarily as a private industrial park.

Take Woerner Ave., on the west side of the car works, north to its termination at S. Clark Blvd. Directly across the boulevard is the main building and huge clock of the **Colgate-Palmolive Company**. The Romanesque central structure, erected in the late 19th century, conjures up an image of a fortress, replete with battlements. In fact, the buildings once housed a state prison. Indiana's first state prison was established at Jeffersonville in 1821. In 1845 the prison was relocated to Clarksville. It became the Indiana Reformatory for Men in 1891. Thirty-two years later the reformatory was moved to Pendleton, Indiana, and the Clarksville site was purchased by the Colgate Company for the odd amount of $301,101.01. The

Colgate firm, then famous the world over for its Octagon brand cleaning products and perfumes, such as Cashmere Bouquet, converted the old penitentiary to a soap factory, which opened in 1924. The clock, the world's second largest and larger than London's Big Ben, was taken from Colgate's New Jersey plant. The timepiece is 40 ft. in diameter, and its hands measure 16 and 20 1/2 ft., respectively. The giant clock has been a major landmark for area residents for more than 60 years. The Colgate-Palmolive Company today makes between 300 and 400 items, ranging from dishwashing liquid to toothpaste. Its nearly 1,100 employees make the firm one of the largest employers in southern Indiana.

At Clark Blvd. go left *.2 m.* to State St. Turn right immediately beyond the railroad underpass and travel two blocks to the Clarksville Town Hall at 230 E. Montgomery St. In Room 203 of the Town Hall is the **Clarksville Museum**, a one-room display of local memorabilia and materials pertaining to George Rogers Clark. A key must be obtained to enter.

From the Town Hall take E. Montgomery St. west two blocks to Virginia Ave., head south two blocks to Win Bourne St., and turn right. Follow Win Bourne *.4 m.* southwest to the **Clarksville Optimist Park**. From the park, looking west, can be glimpsed the Devonian Fossil Beds, the Falls of the Ohio coral reef believed to be 300 million years old.

From the park, return to S. Clark Blvd., which intersects E. Montgomery Ave. halfway between Virginia and State sts. Turn left and proceed on S. Clark to its deadend at Harrison Ave. In a center island at this intersection is a marker that briefly tells of the founding of Clarksville. Head left on Harrison Ave. *.6 m.* On the left is a large marker which discloses the location to be near the **site of George Rogers Clark's home**. Local historians boast that Clark's younger brother William and Meriwether Lewis started their expedition west to explore the Louisiana Purchase from this vicinity on October 23, 1803.

Return on Harrison Ave. east to the intersection with Randolph Ave. and turn left. Drive *.2 m.* northwest on Randolph to IND 62 and turn left. The New Albany city limits are *1.8 m.* farther on IND 62 west.

Evansville

EVANSVILLE (p. 130,496) is Indiana's fourth largest city and the center of government for **VANDERBURGH COUNTY** (p. 167,515; 236 sq. m.). One of Indiana's smallest counties in area, Vanderburgh County ranks near the top in population, population density, and percent of its residents in urban areas. A major tourist area, the county features a sloping topography that reaches highest elevations in the northern and western sections. Evansville borders a horseshoe bend of the Ohio River. The crescent-shaped metropolis dominates the economic and cultural life of southwest Indiana, western Kentucky, and southeast Illinois. It is the most southerly of the North's larger cities, lying farther south than Louisville, Kentucky, or St. Louis, Missouri. Beginning in the mid-1800s, businessmen parlayed the area's rich natural and human resources into a succession of nationally acclaimed industries: lumber, furniture, stoves, coal, textiles, oil, cars, trucks, pharmaceuticals, refrigerators, and plastics. The unexpected loss of a dozen large and small employers in the 1950s paralyzed the city. Pessimism, deep political divisions, and management and labor strife eroded community spirit. Evansville's recovery through the 1960s, 1970s, and into the 1980s was due to a realistic assessment of the problem and an effective implementation of a plan that called for industrial diversification, center city revitalization, riverfront development, and a host of other improvements. The multitude of historical preservations undertaken over the last 25 years is a measure, partly, of the community's evolving sense of esteem. The work toward reestablishing Evansville as the tri-state hub has proved successful, and, in the process, the city has become the second largest, and fastest growing, tourist market in the state.

Hugh McGary purchased the Evansville site in 1812. He probably anticipated a great river port materializing on the forested 441 acres. If so, he received some initial encouragement when in 1814 he and Robert M. Evans, a territorial legislator and family friend, persuaded the commissioners of the newly created Warrick County to designate McGary's clearing as the county seat. The county agents named the new settlement Evansville in honor of Robert M. Evans. In all likelihood buoyed by this development, McGary, who also piloted ferries across Pigeon Creek and the Ohio River, plunged into marketing the lots, only to have his situation quickly reversed. The state legislature carved Perry and Posey counties from Warrick County, which dislodged Evansville from its central location and assured its loss of county seat status. McGary, as he had promised, compensated disgruntled lot owners, many of whom may have moved to Darlington, a thriving village east of Evansville and Warrick County's new seat of government. Evansville languished.

By 1817 McGary could show for his efforts only a dozen cabins, several uninhabited. He continued to ply his ferry across Pigeon Creek, but he gave up his Ohio River run. He, too, bought a lot at Darlington, but he stayed in Evansville and opened a store. In considerable debt, he sold 130 acres of his best property to Robert M. Evans and James W. Jones. Evans, Jones, and McGary replatted the town and explored means of regaining the county seat. The course decided upon and accomplished entailed an appeal to the political ambitions of Ratliff Boon, an influential Warrick County landowner. Boon consented to a redrawing of county lines that would enlarge his political base and give Evansville a county seat if he should win the next state senate race. Following his election Boon carried through his pledge. Two counties were formed in 1818—Spencer with Rockport as the county seat and Vanderburgh with Evansville, again, awarded county seat honors. The modified Warrick County acquired a new government center, Boonville, named for Ratliff Boon's eldest son. Darlington rapidly faded into history. Vanderburgh County memorialized Henry Vanderburgh (1760-1812), a New York native who presided over the Northwest Territory Legislative Council in 1799, became a territorial judge, and served on the first board of trustees of Vincennes University.

Soon after Evansville recaptured the county seat, Elisha Harrison, cousin to William Henry Harrison and the county's first state assemblyman, obtained a town charter. By 1819 the resourceful Hugh McGary had become the leading citizen among the village's 100 residents, and much of the political and social activity centered in his home and trading post. McGary held positions of postmaster, circuit court clerk, county recorder, associate judge, and president of the town trustees. He built the first jail and hosted the first church service. He also managed to free himself from an assortment of criminal charges, including horse stealing. Although he had some success in building a town and promoting his image as a civic leader, he seldom profited in the business world. Ill, practically destitute, and alone, in 1826 he left Evansville to spend his declining years with a daughter in the South. It is said he died in Arkansas.

McGary's money difficulties were symptomatic of the community's economy in general. Prior to the mid-1830s Evansville lacked economic inducements for attracting settlers. Evansville could not lure and hold the businessman, despite the town's reputation as an embarkation point for emigrants bound for the Wabash River, its new county buildings, its taverns, and its stage line. A cholera epidemic in 1832 wiped out 11 percent of the population. In 1833 property valuations stood lower than they had in 1819.

The tonic for the sagging community came by way of the announcement in 1834 that Evansville probably would be the southern terminus of the great Central Canal, which would run from the Wabash River between Fort Wayne and Logansport, via Muncietown and Indianapolis, then down White River to Evansville. No other event of that year—founding of the *Evansville Journal*, obtaining a State Bank branch, or christening of the first locally built steamboat—measured up to the enthusiasm incited by the canal tidings. The state approved the project in its massive internal improvements legislation of 1836. That summer work began on the basin and pushed northward some

18 miles in the first year. A flurry of land and housing business accompanied the canal's progress. A visitor in 1837 observed that townsfolk were "mad on lot speculation." The building of canal boats and the opening of the Polk Brothers cabinetmaking establishment gave Evansville its first industries. A steam sawmill went up in 1837, but the financial panic of that year and the collapse of state support for internal improvements halted canal construction and business expansion. The failure of the canal plus the deaths of 50 citizens by pneumonia in the harsh winter of 1837-38 were major setbacks. Still the 2,121 residents in 1840 represented a sevenfold gain in just 8 years. Within 30 years Evansville would be Indiana's second largest city.

A new era of prosperity for the nation and for Indiana was inaugurated in 1843. The small stretch of the Central Canal completed at Evansville had continued in use during the six years of economic doldrums. The canal section thereafter became part of the Wabash and Erie Canal project. Resumption of work on the canal helped spark economic recovery. Evansville received its city charter in 1847. Officials improved and expanded the city wharf and acquired a wharf boat. By 1853 a telegraph line from Louisville had been put into service, and the Evansville and Crawfordsville Railroad had reached Terre Haute. The Wabash and Erie Canal reached Evansville in 1853, but only a handful of boats would ever make the full 464-mile journey. The day of the canal was over, and Evansville had little to show for its many years of patient waiting. The railroad, however, did for Evansville what the completed canal was intended to do; it kindled new business aspirations. In its wake came wholesale houses, jobbers, retailers, breweries, mills, tobacco houses, and furniture factories. August and Louis Uhl, recent immigrants from Germany, laid the foundation in 1849 for the Uhl Pottery Company. The Germans concentrated in Lamasco, northwest and adjacent to Evansville. John and William Law, James McCall, and Lucius Scott platted Lamasco in 1837. They scrambled their surnames to concoct the town's name. The merger of Evansville and Lamasco in 1857 sparked an aggressive, but abortive, effort to name the composite Lamasco. In other matters, the county erected its second courthouse in 1857. The passage of free school legislation in 1853 prompted citizens to vote for a tax-supported education system. The city's first public school buildings were put up in 1854, the same year the city formed one of the state's first high schools.

The 1860 federal elections aroused considerable interest in Evansville because of the candidacies of Joseph Lane, the vice-presidential choice of the Southern Democrats, and Abraham Lincoln, the Republican party's presidential hopeful. Lane, a senator from Oregon, had been a prominent Vanderburgh County farmer, trader, and state representative. Lincoln had spent his youth in nearby Spencer County. At the polls, the electorate voted overwhelmingly for Lincoln.

The Civil War touched Evansville in many ways, though the city was spared direct military combat. The disruption of southern trade stalled the city's economy momentarily until northern supply demands re-oiled the business machine. The city's size and port facilities made it a major contributor and conduit of troops and provisions. From Vanderburgh County came over 3,600 Union army enlistees, including nine-year-old drummer boy John W. Messick, reportedly the service's youngest recruit. The Confederacy's brief capture of Newburgh, Indiana, at the time about eight miles east of Evansville, provoked as much excitement as rumors of John Hunt Morgan's imminent invasion of Indiana soil. Alvin P. Hovey of neighboring Mount Vernon, a future Indiana governor, and John Watson Foster of Evansville, Benjamin Harrison's secretary of state in the 1890s, led forays into and around Henderson, Kentucky, opposite Evansville. Kentucky annals occasionally refer to these exploits as "Hovey's Raid" and "Foster's Raid." The recorded improprieties imposed on Henderson's citizens by Indiana soldiers were no less terrifying than Morgan's oppression of Hoosiers. Incidently, Brig. Gen. James M. Shackelford, whom President Lincoln commissioned to pursue Morgan, and who helped capture the famed Confederate, settled in Evansville in 1864 to practice law.

After the war the black population of Evansville increased substantially. The number, less than 150 in 1869, soared to 7,405 by 1900, giving Evansville the largest proportion of blacks, 13 percent, among Indiana cities. These residents lived principally at the city's eastern edge near the filled-in canal area called Baptisttown, a reference to the blacks' Liberty Baptist Church, founded in 1865. The influx of blacks, along with another crest in German immigration and the annexation of Independence, west of Pigeon Creek, helped push up the city's population count to 21,830 by 1870, making it the state's second largest city.

Evansville began advertising itself as the Crescent City as it grew in population and as homes and factories crowded into the horseshoe-shaped contour. To one Evansville booster in the 1870s, "the smoke stacks of industry at countless points form a forest of progress." Perhaps to many, but few blacks could penetrate the forest of iron and brick. For the rest, jobs were plentiful. Coal, in a narrow seam stretching through the county, began to be extracted in the mid-1850s with the opening of the Bodiam Mine, owned by an English consortium. Soon 50 mines operated within a 30-mile radius. A large portion of downtown Evansville today rests on abandoned coal shafts, now water-filled. Work could also be had in the stove works, metal foundries, flour and cotton mills, breweries, brick yards, tobacco warehouses, or wood-related industries.

Evansville strengthened its hold on the commercial and cultural affairs of southwest Indiana in the 1880s and 1890s. The city professed to be the nation's leading hardwood market and to possess the biggest cotton mills outside New England, declarations meant to be attractive to potential residents and developers. Its relatively high elevation prevented serious damage by the historic floods of 1882 through 1884. Evansville, though surrounded by inundated lowlands, was scarcely touched. From this island, Clara Barton initiated in 1884 the Red Cross's first flood relief program. Once the waters receded, Evansville's port again hummed with the daily coming and going of dozens of craft. Railroad improvements enhanced the city's enviable combination of river and rail transport. In 1885 the Louisville and Nashville Railroad built a bridge across the Ohio River, thus linking Evansville and Henderson, Kentucky. At the time only this railroad bridge spanned the Ohio River west of Louisville. Trunk lines of the Louisville and Nashville, the Illinois Central, and the Southern Railroad also entered the city by 1900. On a smaller scale, the Evansville, Suburban, and Newburgh Railroad, which operated a light steam train dubbed the "Dummy Line," began its daily trips in 1889. Electricity, which illuminated some streets and fewer homes in 1884, powered the cars of the Evansville Street Railway Company by 1892. Some headway was made in bricking, curbing, and graveling the 125 miles of city streets, thus facilitating pedestrian and vehicular movement.

A new city hall, courthouse, and jail, plus new hotels, hospitals, theaters, and schools gave Evansville an ever-changing cityscape in the latter years of the century. Additional schools, as well as a high school curriculum for blacks, appeared as definite social progress to the white citizens of the segregated city. For the sports-minded, Evansville High School's death-defying football, baseball, and basketball squads, formed in the late 1890s, drew enthusiasm and concern. A primitive nine-hole course tested the skills of the few golf aficionados.

The rapid headway in civic improvements, from public buildings to waterworks, strained the city's finances. Successive administrations grappled with severe debts, not to mention bitter factional politics, police scandals, crime, and rumors of widespread vice. The seamier side of urban life could be momentarily forgotten when 50,000 people turned out to welcome President William McKinley in 1899 or when a competition with Indianapolis dominated the news. The latter occurred during the Spanish-American War when a federal decision to have Evansville as the rendezvous for all of Indiana's volunteer troops was overturned in favor of Indianapolis. The Evansville press, referring to Indianapolis as "Hogsville" for its apparent hegemony on federal favors, accused officials of purposely giving inadequate food and shelter to Evansville soldiers bivouacked at the capital.

Evansville was not behind the times in taking quick advantage of new technologies. The city's first look at a "horseless buggy" may have been in 1897 with the completion by Willis M. Copeland of such a vehicle to cost less than $1,000. Though not a center of car manufacturing, Evansville offered the more prosperous or adventurous a range of locally designed and built motorcars with such names as Zentmobile, Windsor, Worth, Single-Center, Evansville, Simplicity, and Traveler. Gasoline motors soon powered Evansville's beer wagons, mail trucks, street sprinklers, and a flying contraption that thrilled spectators at the fairgrounds in 1911. The electric interurban, first operated in 1903, linked Evansville to Newburgh, Boonville, Princeton, Rockport, and Mount Vernon. Streetcar lines expanded despite periodic management-labor problems that led to strikes in 1893, 1907, and 1909.

Evansville weathered the financial panic of 1907. Throughout, employers kept up cash payments to their workers, a rare happening and one shared by only six other cities of Evansville's size in the nation. The economic slump did not retard the city's population growth. The count in 1910 stood at 69,647, an 18 percent rise in 10 years. Among Evansville's 300 factories in 1910, the furniture manufacturers had no peers in quantity of production, which amounted to over 1.3 million items per year. The Globe-Bosse-World Furniture Company, a merger of three firms in 1910, became, it is said, the largest furniture business in the world. Benjamin Bosse, a Globe employee and organizer of the Bosse and World companies, was Evansville's mayor from 1914 to 1922. He spearheaded the drive for an "amusement field"—a stadium—to house the city's multiplying athletic and recreational activities. Bosse Field was dedicated June 17, 1915.

The tally of population in 1910 masks the fact that since 1900 Evansville had been losing its black residents. The limited opportunities in Evansville and the opening of job opportunities in other cities contributed to the gradual exodus. A race riot in the summer of 1903, which killed 11 persons and injured 50 others, is symbolic of the racial problems that also influenced blacks to move out. In 1910 Evansville had 1,252 fewer blacks than in 1900.

In times of less civic stress, citizens took to the half dozen parks, the open-air theaters, chautauqua programs, and summer gardens. The newly organized Boy Scouts, along with the YMCA and YWCA, scheduled a varied lot of activities for the city's youth. Nickelodeons appeared in 1907, and 20 of the small movie houses entertained patrons by 1917. One of two interurban ferries in the United States was operated across the Ohio River by the Evansville and Ohio Valley Railway and its predecessors from 1912 to 1928. Named the Henderson, the ferry measured 130 ft. and could carry a two-car train. It connected two segments of the Evansville-Henderson, Kentucky, line and offered hourly service most of the day.

If, after 1905, townspeople came across the lyrics of "My Gal Sal," written by Paul Dresser, or heard it sung by Louise Dresser, they might have recalled these two artists' Evansville roots. Paul Dresser (1859-1906), who penned, among other things, "On the Banks of the Wabash Far Away" (1897), Indiana's state song, lived in Evansville in the 1880s at the St. George Hotel and spent much time at Sallie Walker's well-appointed brothel. Dresser head-lined at the Apollo Theater and contributed to the *Evansville Argus* a daily column captioned "Plummy's Pointers." Living with him for a short while were his mother and several sib-lings, including Theodore Dreiser (Paul Ameri-canized the surname), who became one of the most celebrated Indiana-born authors. The Dressers were acquaintances of the Kerlin fam-ily of Evansville. Years later in Chicago, Dresser recalled his neighbors when the young Lulie Josephine Kerlin (1882-1965) sought his help in obtaining work. He obtained her em-ployment as a roof-garden singer, presenting her as his sister Louise Dresser. She introduced her benefactor's "My Gal Sal" to the music world in 1905, supposedly written with Sallie Walker in mind. For the next three decades Louise Dresser starred on stage and screen.

The record-breaking flood of 1913, which overswept Evansville's southeast side, did not deter new businesses from locating in the city. Graham Glass Works and Faultless Castor Company came to town. Three bank buildings went up on Main St., including the 10-story Citizens National Bank, Evansville's first sky-scraper. Edward Mead Johnson, baby food pro-ducer in New Jersey, wanted to be closer to the corn belt because corn starch was a basic ingre-dient in the dextri-maltose (malt sugar) used in the food. He removed to Evansville, into the old Evansville Cotton Mill building, while his brother Robert W. established Johnson and Johnson, the surgical dressing company. E. Mead guided his firm to the forefront in the nutritional and pharmaceutical field with such famous products as Pablum, Vi-Sol vitamins, Metrecal, Nutrament, and Oracon.

For a city of its size, Evansville lacked an institution of higher education. This shortcom-ing was remedied in 1917 when Evansville ac-quired Moores Hill College, a Methodist school founded in 1854 at Moores Hill, Dearborn County, Indiana. The war interrupted the pro-cess of reestablishing the college, renamed Ev-ansville College, but its doors finally opened in 1919 in temporary quarters in the building of the Young Men's Hebrew Association. The col-lege had a permanent home by 1922 with the completion of the Administration Building on Lincoln Ave. In 1934 Zerah Priestly enrolled at the college, the first black to be admitted. An-other educational achievement was the 1918 completion of the Francis Joseph Reitz High School situated west of Evansville on top of Coal Mine Hill. The facility relieved the over-crowded Evansville High School, which now became Central High School.

The very month, April 1917, when Presi-dent Woodrow Wilson proclaimed a state of war to exist, Evansville dedicated its Soldiers and Sailors Memorial Coliseum, providing the area a capacious structure for meetings and en-tertainment. Evansville's James Bethel Gresham was one of the first Americans to die in combat in this war to end all wars. At home, in the heat of anti-German attitudes, pressures mounted to take the German language out of schools and churches, even to rename German Township. The *Taglicher Demokrat*, a German-language daily, was suspended. The contin-gencies of war also severely restricted plans for Evansville's centennial celebration scheduled in the autumn of 1917.

The anti-German sentiment aided in the passage of state, then national, liquor prohibi-tion laws. Organized bootlegging operations capitalized on the convenience of the Ohio River to shuttle the illegal item between Ken-tucky and Evansville. An Evansville whiskey ring, which included the chief of police and al-most 70 other persons, was broken up in 1920. From the south through Kentucky to Evansville also came the Ku Klux Klan in 1920, founding Indiana's first klavern. D. C. Stephenson began his meteoric rise in the klan in Evansville where he had been working as a coal salesman. Soon he became Indiana's Grand Dragon and a power in state politics until 1926.

Prohibition spelled doom for Evansville's breweries and bottle makers. Joseph, Robert C., and Ray Graham relinquished their four bottle factories in 1918 and took to making all types of trucks fitted with Dodge engines and chassis. Dodge bought the Graham Brothers Truck Company in 1925, and the former own-ers took executive positions with Dodge in De-troit. In 1927 the Graham brothers purchased the old Paige Detroit Motor Car Company. They built a new factory in Evansville on East Columbia St. and began producing in early 1929 the critically acclaimed Graham-Paige automobile.

Experience in vehicle workmanship contributed to the emergence in Evansville of refrigerator production. William McCurdy, who owned, among his many enterprises, the Hercules Buggy Company and the Hercules Gas Engine Company, found his knowledge of engines served him well when in 1922 the idea of pumping refrigerants through coils was given him by a man named James Howard Dennedy. McCurdy began manufacturing home refrigerators which were first marketed through the Seaber-Johnson Company of Detroit. Hercules, then producing truck bodies (and four, only, McCurdy cars), was also in the business of designing wood refrigerator cabinets. It reorganized in 1924 as the Serv-el Corporation—the hyphen was removed in 1926—a name created from Serve Electrically, the original motto of the Detroit concern which oversaw the company affairs. Servel obtained the Swedish patents on gas refrigeration, "the miracle of ice from heat," and by 1927 it assembled both gas and electric refrigerators, most in steel cabinets. Another Evansville company, Sunbeam Electric, successor to the Schroeder Headlight Company, founded in 1883, began crafting Coldspot refrigerators for Sears, Roebuck and Company in 1929.

The extent of car and truck manufacturing in addition to the expansion into refrigerators represents a displacement of hardwood items as the city's leading commodities. Furthermore, the Detroit connection with Evansville's vehicle and refrigerator industries signals a general shift from the south to the north for financial and management direction, a change facilitated by improved roads and cheaper freight rates.

Residential development, especially in east Evansville, paralleled the reshaping of industrial interests. Two new high schools, Bosse and Reitz Memorial Catholic built in the mid-1920s, Evansville College's Administration Building, and St. Benedict Catholic Church transformed eastside farmlands into eagerly sought and highly valuable real estate.

The 1930s economic depression hit Evansville as hard as other cities. Eight banks suspended operations in the winter of 1931-32. Unemployment rose as furniture, stove, refrigerator, and car industries shut down or curtailed production. The only major building activity occurred on the Mead Johnson rail-river terminal, a $500,000 facility dedicated in early 1931, and on the Evansville-Henderson toll bridge, completed in 1932. Many families, living in temporary shanty towns, accepted doles from strained and near-empty county and state coffers. President Franklin D. Roosevelt's New Deal relief programs helped ease the city's unemployment burden. Hundreds of citizens found work, ranging from raking leaves to construction projects, such as Dress Plaza and Lincoln Gardens, both launched in 1936. Dress Plaza, named for mayor William H. Dress, was a half-million-dollar riverfront improvement plan. Lincoln Gardens was a low-rent public housing project in Baptisttown. Another promising sign of the period was the opening of a Chrysler Plymouth assembly plant in 1935.

The trend toward economic recovery in the mid-1930s suffered a setback in the winter of 1937 when the Ohio Valley's worst-ever flood took place. At Evansville, normally immune from inundation, flood waters penetrated 40 percent of the city proper, causing about $9 million damage. Some 30,000 persons vacated their homes. Refugee centers cared for about 6,000 homeless. Except for riverside businesses whose water-battered structures had to be torn down, the city's commercial flow was not seriously interrupted. Less than two weeks after the flood crested, city payrolls were back to normal.

The complete recovery from the depression is generally associated with the coming of World War II and the boom in military expenditures. Such is true for Evansville, and yet the city made great headway prior to the war as a result of the discovery of oil in the region in 1938. Within a year millions of acres in a score of southwestern Indiana counties had been leased. Vanderburgh was among the dozen most important oil-producing counties. In Evansville oilmen, lawyers, salesmen, and workers tied up every available living space, which led to a shortage of housing. Employment in the oil industry, income from land leases, and retail sales to the city's new inhabitants markedly improved Evansville's financial picture. In 1940 Evansville became one of the first 15 American cities, and the first in Indiana, to be granted a commercial FM radio license.

Evansville eventually profited from wartime product requirements, but initially it seemed as though the lucrative government work might bypass the city. The large refrigerator and car plants, adversely affected by war material priorities, were about to lay off employees. Skilled workers began transferring to more active labor fields. Evansville officials appealed to Paul V. McNutt, former Indiana governor, who in 1941 was the Federal Security Administrator. McNutt saw that Evansville was surveyed for defense plants. Soon, contracts poured in. A new shipyard made Landing Ship Tanks (LSTs) and Landing Craft Tanks (LCTs). In 1942 Republic Aviation built a factory to make P-47 Thunderbolts. Resident industries converted to making battle articles. For instance, Plymouth rebuilt army trucks, overhauled Sherman tanks, and made ammunition. Servel assembled wings for the Thunderbolt. Employment in Evansville soared from 21,000 to a peak of 64,000 workers. The consequent housing deficiency was met by special housing projects. Many of the larger older homes were converted to multi-unit dwellings. The population influx also contributed to a rise in the crime rate, which jumped 60 percent between 1943 and 1946, the largest increase of any Indiana city with over 50,000 residents.

Postwar Evansville quickly adjusted to the shutdown of defense work. Evansville College expanded its physical plant and course list to accommodate the GI Bill-funded education of returning servicemen. Jobs were plentiful in construction and in car and refrigerator companies. Wage earners demanded consumer goods, and retailers gladly obliged them. In 1946 the destruction by fire of the Globe-Bosse-World furniture factory and the closing of the county's last coal mine represented the end of a two-decade shift in the area's economic makeup. Now, refrigerators held the spotlight. Sunbeam merged with Seeger, a Minneapolis cabinet firm, in 1946, and took the name Seeger Refrigerator Company. International Harvester bought the Republic Aviation Corporation and made milk coolers and freezer chests before venturing into a refrigerator line. Servel, Seeger, and International Harvester manufactured, by 1950, one-fourth of the nation's refrigerators. Evansville earned the titles Refrigerator Capital or Ice-Box City. For many years the Chamber of Commerce sponsored the Refrigerator Bowl, a football extravaganza reigned over by Miss Refrigeradorable.

Roaring trade, full employment, and rising standards of living defined the state of affairs in Evansville through the early 1950s and the Korean War. The rosy era, however, soon ended. Evansville's economy rested on refriger-

ators and cars, two durable-goods products with sales susceptible to public taste and technological change. The arrival of the all-electric kitchen with color-matched appliances and the fully automated car-assembly plant caught Evansville with obsolete merchandise and factories. Between 1953 and 1960, 10 companies —including Servel, International Harvester, and Chrysler—closed their doors, with devastating consequences. Besides the loss of thousands of jobs, pay checks, and tax revenue, city property began to deteriorate. Local morale collapsed and management-labor problems proliferated, resulting in 29 work stoppages between 1954 and 1956. Ineffective local officials bickered and grumbled. In 1956 the government designated Evansville a "surplus labor" area, meaning it had high unemployment. In 1957 the city was officially classified as a depressed area.

Evansville Future, Inc., a quickly formed civic organization, hired an outside consultant to identify and evaluate the city's problems. The unsparing report concluded that "the city as a whole is unable to accomplish anything." Stung by the criticism, local leaders set in motion a recovery plan that attracted widespread support. The plan called for and secured new industrial parks, slum clearance, labor-management dialogues, industrial expansion, new schools, shopping centers, swimming pools, sewer and water lines, airport improvements, flood walls, a museum, and a start on downtown revitalization. By 1963 Evansville had been dropped from the labor surplus and depressed area lists. Unemployment fell below 4 percent, sparked by the establishment and expansion of the Whirlpool Corporation which, in 1956 and 1958, either merged with or purchased Servel, International Harvester, and Seeger operations. Whirlpool's combined assets made it the city's largest employer and helped perpetuate the Pocket City as a refrigeration capital. Besides Whirlpool, the Aluminum Company of America (ALCOA) constructed a huge smelting plant in neighboring Warrick County. By the early 1960s ALCOA was the second largest employer of Evansville's residents. These manufacturers, along with Mead Johnson and several hundred other companies, paced Evansville's comeback.

Other developments in the 1960s included the establishment of a branch campus of Indiana State University. Begun in a condemned grade-school building in 1965, ISUE, by 1969, was constructing a $5 million campus. In 1967 Evansville College became the University of Evansville. Almost 5,500 students attended the university in 1969, the school's 50th year in the community. Nine high schools and 61 elementary schools serviced the city's younger students. As the city expanded in population and in businesses, good roads became a paramount consideration. Efforts intensified to have US 41 dual-laned between Evansville and Terre Haute. Interstate 64's location, just north of the city, was approved in 1963, thanks to the work of local officials who persuaded planners to give it a more southerly position than originally intended. The super highway was completed in 1976, giving Evansville a direct route upriver to Louisville and downriver to St. Louis.

A highlight of Evansville's remarkable turnaround in the 1960s was the building of the Civic Center Complex, a $25 million grouping of federal and county offices and a convention center. The complex, built between 1966 and 1969, was constructed where there existed a railway switching yard, an old icehouse, the empty F. W. Cook brewery, two churches, and a mass of substandard housing. More than 200 land parcels were purchased with few hitches other than the complicated negotiations with the Vatican in Rome for the purchase of the Assumption Cathedral.

Amidst racial strife over school desegregation, crippling strikes at Whirlpool, and a vacillating national economy, Evansville plunged ahead to solidify the gains made in the 1960s. The Civic Center represented the inauguration of massive urban renewal programs. Main St., between the Civic Center and the river, became the Downtown Walkway, a tree-lined, winding, pedestrian pathway. The mall's centerpiece was the 18-story Old National Bank Building, completed in 1969. Landeco, Inc., of Indianapolis purchased 9.5 blocks of riverside property for a $50 million multipurpose development called Riverside Commons. The land transaction was the largest in Evansville history up to that time. Evansville also was picked in 1971 to be one of the first American cities to test the Revenue Sharing idea. The city qualified for more than $12 million to undertake a diversity of housing and community projects.

Interest also began to be directed toward historic preservation. Beginning in the late 1960s a number of private and semipublic groups started up to oversee preservation of specific areas or buildings; however, the city of Evansville came to be the major sponsor of preservation. Through a Historic Preservation Officer, seed money for projects, nomination of structures for inclusion on the National Register of Historic Places, and aid to individuals and corporations needing documentation on properties and also tax assistance, the local government has assumed major responsibility for the safekeeping of the community's rich historical and architectural heritage.

Tragedy engulfed Evansville in December 1977 when 29 persons, including 14 members of the University of Evansville basketball team, died aboard a chartered DC-3, which crashed on takeoff from Dress Airport. In March 1980 residents grieved again when a disgruntled citizen murdered the popular former mayor Russell G. Lloyd. Such events momentarily prostrate a community. Other incidents lift spirits. In 1978 the undefeated Reitz Memorial High School Tiger baseball team won the state championship. Don Mattingly, now a major league super star, played on that team. In the spring of 1980 the world's largest American flag was unfurled at Evansville's airport. Produced at the city's Anchor Industries, the seven-ton polyester flag is as large as one and one-half football fields. Each star measures 13 ft. from tip to tip, and each stripe is 16 ft. wide. In June 1983 the flag was donated to the federal government, which will display it in Washington, D.C., on special occasions. In 1980 an Evansville native returned to a hometown tribute. Ron Glass of television fame, well known as Detective Harris of the Barney Miller Show, received an award of excellence from his college alma mater, the University of Evansville. Two years later he was given a similar honor in Evansville by the National Association for the Advancement of Colored People. River enthusiasts welcomed to their shore the *Spirit of Evansville*, the city's new excursion boat, christened on July 5, 1981. Built by the La Crosse (Wisconsin) Riverboat Company, the 150-passenger, diesel-powered stern-wheeler offers afternoon trips and dinner cruises. Evansville also hosts the Thunder on the Ohio Regatta, held since 1981 as part of the annual Freedom Festival. The hydroplanes ran in the coveted Gold Cup race at Evansville in 1983.

The new recreational and entertainment uses of the river, coupled with the waterway's traditional commercial and industrial roles, keep the plight and promise of the downtown business district in the center of public attention. Competition from suburban malls, such as the sprawling Eastland Mall that opened in 1981, slowed efforts to revitalize the downtown fully. Setbacks in the manufacturing base, for example the closing in 1983 of one of the two Whirlpool plants, brought added pressures to improve job prospects and to plan for a more inviting city.

To accomplish these ends, officials are banking on the continued development of the riverfront, the new fascination with living at the urban core, 10 major road projects, including the completion of the Russell Lloyd Expressway, the east-west highway through the city, and Interstate 164, which will encircle the city's east and south sides. These improvements in the transportation network, along with the anticipated completion of a $20 million airport terminal, spurred growth in the construction sector, which in turn spearheaded an economic surge in the late 1980s. The housing industry also expanded, and this boom in real estate with its strong demand for refrigerators breathed life into Whirlpool. Expansions at the Warrick operation of ALCOA, and at Sunbeam Plastic Corporation, and the establishment of a huge T. J. Maxx Company, contributed to a substantial increase in industrial production and an improvement in the local employment situation.

Of central importance to the city's future is the ongoing effort to identify and safeguard historical buildings. Of particular note in this regard is the Downtown Evansville Multiple Resources Area, a designated historical district roughly bounded by the river, Division, Walnut, and Pennsylvania sts. Almost 50 of the more than 100 buildings thus far nominated for inclusion on the National Register of Historic Places have been accepted. This means that this many structures qualify for tax credits for building improvements. It is believed this incentive can have a marked impact on downtown growth.

Evansville, in fact, is rapidly becoming a city of historic districts, a significant sign that it has turned a corner in economic and cultural rehabilitation. Eleven historic districts have been locally identified and five have been placed on the Register. In addition, almost 100 landmarks lying outside these central districts have been recognized. Through the initiatives of public and private sources, Evansville is affirming in very concrete ways its desire to preserve the collective memory of the community in all its varied and colorful facets.

Evansville Attractions

For additional tour information see the first entry below.

1. The **Vanderburgh Auditorium and Convention Center**, 715 Locust St., should be the visitor's first stop in Evansville. Off its lobby is the **Evansville Convention and Visitors Bureau**. The bureau's personnel can answer questions and provide informational and tour materials. The huge round building enclosing the Visitors Bureau also contains a 2,000-seat auditorium along with floor space and meeting rooms for conventions. The $2.6 million structure opened in 1967 and was the first completed component of the Civic Center Complex.

2. The **Civic Center Complex** is composed of six buildings, including the auditorium, and is arranged in campus style on a 40-acre tract. The $25 million facility was dedicated in 1969. The largest single unit is the City-County Safety and Administrative Building that fronts on 7th St. between Locust and Sycamore sts. The three-story structure, made of Indiana limestone, concentrates city and county offices and services that formerly were spread throughout the metropolitan area. Other buildings in this ensemble include the Federal Court and Office Building, the Courts and Security Building, the Federal Post Office, and the Evansville-Vanderburgh School Corporation Building. The third-floor south windows of the City-County Building afford an excellent full-length view of the seven-block-long winding **Downtown Walkway**, which was under construction from 1971 to 1974, and which underwent major renovation in the mid-1980s.

3. The **two-story brick double building** at 611-613 Main St. was built in 1865 and is believed to be one of Evansville's oldest downtown commercial structures. Long associated with a drug store and a tobacco shop, the main level is still used for commercial space.

4. The **site of Robert M. Evans's homestead** is commemorated with a bronze marker mounted on stone in a small plaza on the north side of the Union Federal Savings and Loan Association, 501 Main St. A one-story frame cottage was built in 1828 on a rise within a grove of shade trees for Evans, for whom the city is named. Bank officials unveiled the Evans plaque in 1966 on the occasion of the opening of their new building.

5. The **Ridgway Building**, 313-315 Main St., was constructed during the Civil War. The side-by-side buildings, with a common front, originally housed a foundry and stove works. An 1895 modernization gave the building its present three-and-one-half-story round arched facade of buff brick and pale orange terra-cotta. This excellent example of 19th-century commercial architecture is named for the Ridgway Optical Company, a resident of the building since 1922. Ridgway Optical and a co-occupant, a law firm, have renovated the interior of the lower floors. (*NRHP*) In the 1870s the Evansville Foundry Association, which displayed the finished products of its membership in a Ridgway Building showroom, advertised its location as opposite the courthouse. From the beginnings of Evansville to the late 19th century the area of 3rd and Main sts. was the public square. The first and second courthouses, plus jail and sheriff facilities, were situated on the square.

6. The **Old and New Bitterman Buildings**, 200 and 202 Main St., were built between 1885 and 1906. The corner structure, possibly designed by local architect Frank J. Schlotter, was put up in 1885 and housed the jewelry firm of Isaac and Adolph Bitterman. The Bittermans, natives of Germany, brought their shop from Vincennes, Indiana, to Evansville in 1874. They occupied several Main St. stores before moving into the three-story brick building at 200 Main

Evansville

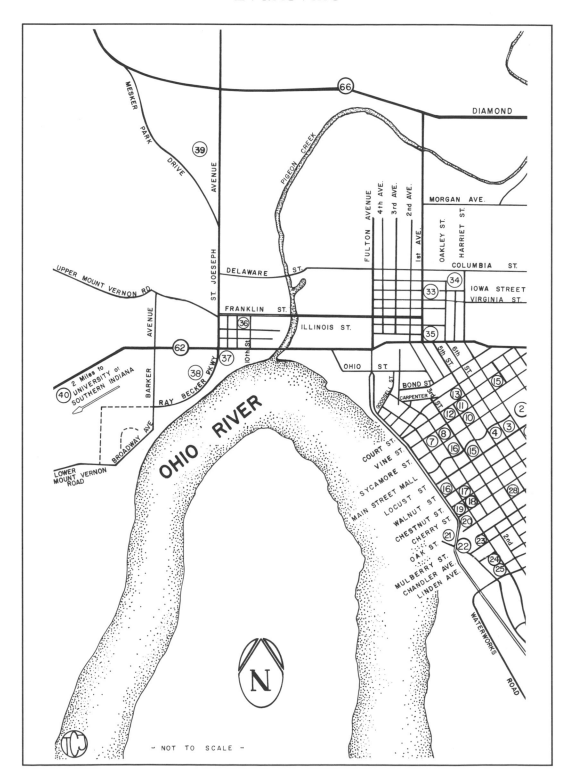

- NOT TO SCALE -

Attractions

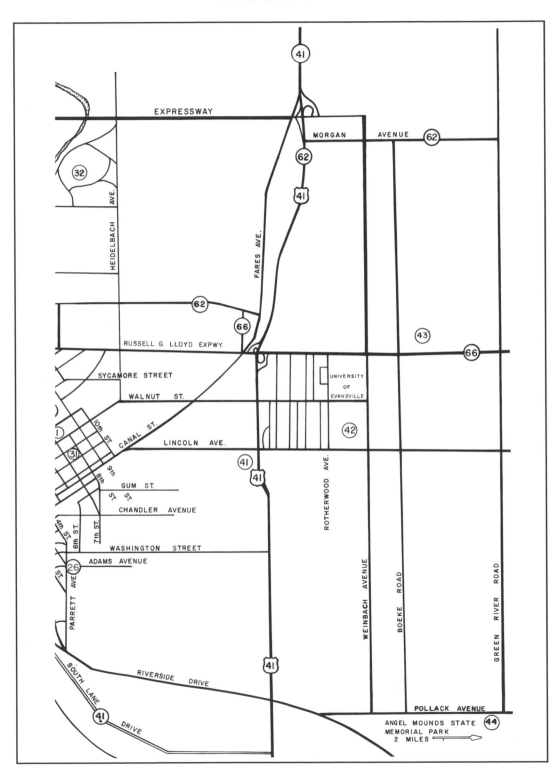

St. In 1897 the brothers relocated a block north on Main St. They again moved, in 1906, to their new building at 202 Main St., where the business remained until it closed in 1967. Clifford Shopbell and William J. Harris, of Evansville, followed the Chicago Commercial style of architecture when designing the Bittermans' building in 1906. The use of the "Chicago window," a large central glass flanked by narrower sidelights, best links the Bitterman building with the Chicago school. The total area of glass on such buildings usually exceeds the total space covered by brick or stone. The Bitterman buildings have had few alterations over the years, and they are among the few downtown structures that escaped the wrecking ball of urban renewal in the early 1960s. (*NRHP*)

7. The **Old United States Post Office, Courthouse, and Custom House**, 100 N. W. 2nd St., is a linchpin in plans for regenerating the riverfront district. The middle section of the present structure was erected between 1875 and 1879 from the designs of William A. Potter, supervising architect of the United States Treasury. The wings were added in 1918. Indicative of the period's Victorian Gothic style in government buildings, the Post Office features contrasting surface colors in stone, heavy ornamentation, a multicolored slate roof, and pointed arches at entrances and windows. In 1977 the city gained title to the century-old facility, which was deteriorating rapidly from being unoccupied for eight years. A $1.25 million rehabilitation program, funded by nine different sources, halted the dilapidation and made essential improvements. In the mid-1980s a $6 million renovation of the building became the focal point of a complex called Old Post Office Place, which included a newly constructed Retail and Office Village and a planned-for residential development featuring townhouses and condominiums. (*NRHP*)

8. The **Greyhound Bus Terminal**, 102 N. W. 3rd St., is one of Evansville's prime examples of Art Deco architecture of the 1930s. The smooth blue and white porcelainized panels, which cover the two-story brick structure, along with the arrangement of horizontal parallel lines, large sweeping curves, and the use of Broadway-style neon signage, denote trademarks of its designer, William S. Arrasmith of Louisville, Kentucky, a major architect of

Greyhound terminals. It is said that the "running greyhound" neon sign is the only one left in the country. Construction took place in 1939 on the foundation of the Cadick Theatre, an uncompleted project begun in the early 1920s. Greyhound Bus Lines continues to operate out of the old terminal, which in recent years has had extensive interior and exterior renovation. (*NRHP*)

9. The **Hulman Building**, 20 N. W. 4th St., was Evansville's first tall structure featuring the sleek modern detailing of Art Deco. The 10-story, 165-ft.-tall building was constructed in 1929-30. The McGuire and Shook firm of Indianapolis designed the skyscraper for the new Central Union Bank, which represented a merger of the Morris Plan Company and the Mercantile-Commercial Bank. Morris Plan opened in Evansville in 1916 with William H. McCurdy as its president. The following year the Mercantile-Commercial Bank commenced business. Evansville's M. J. Hoffman Construction Company, the general contractors, faced the first two stories of the bank building with Indiana limestone and used buff brick to finish it off. The luster-finished aluminum panels between the window sills and floor levels of the upper eight stories were novel architectural fine points. The entranceways featured ornamental grillwork with an arabesque motif. The interior, by Ohner, Inc., of Dayton, Ohio, emphasized Belgian walnut woodwork, marble wainscoting and counters, bronze cashier cages, elegant lighting fixtures, frescoes, and murals. The bank leased 130 suites on the upper eight floors for offices. The Central Union Bank folded during the depression. Anton "Tony" Hulman, Jr., of Terre Haute, Indiana, purchased the bank building at auction in 1935. Hulman, who married into the Fendrich family of Evansville, owned Hulman and Company of Terre Haute, manufacturer of Clabber Girl Baking Powder, and the Indianapolis Speedway. In Evansville he owned a wholesale grocery warehouse and, in the 1950s, he bought the F. W. Cook "Goldblume" Brewery, which stood on the site of the present Civic Center Complex. Renovation of the Hulman Building began in the early 1980s, including the reinstallation of amber lights atop the building to highlight the ornate stonework. Offices of the Southern Indiana Gas and Electric Company have been housed here since 1939. (*NRHP*)

10. The **McCurdy-Sears Building**, 101 N. W. 4th St., was one of the first Sears, Roebuck and Company retail stores in the nation. The McCurdy-Sears Building, a four-story reinforced concrete structure, was erected in 1920 on a design prepared by W. E. Russ of Indianapolis and Gilbert Karges of Evansville. William H. McCurdy, the wealthy head of Hercules Buggy Company, put up the building to lodge the Van Pickerill Hardware Company, of which McCurdy was one of five incorporators in 1919. The arrest of Van Pickerill on bootlegging charges, just prior to the beginning of construction, and his turning state's evidence in the sensational whiskey ring trials of 1920 apparently did not halt the building or opening of the hardware store. Shortly thereafter the business became the Mumford Hardware Company. Sears leased the building in 1925 and opened in October of that year, following remodeling directed by Gilbert Karges. Sears began opening retail outlets in 1925 in places where it had previously established catalog service. The Evansville store was the first opened by Sears in a city that had not contained a mail-order plant. Sears remained downtown for 50 years, closing in December 1975. The old Sears building has had numerous tenants since then. (*NRHP*)

11. The **Old Vanderburgh County Courthouse**, 201 N. W. 4th St., is Evansville's architectural gem. The Neo-Baroque edifice, with its profusely ornamented exterior and richly marbled interior, became a focus for preservation with the transfer of county government headquarters to the new Civic Center Complex in the late 1960s. Redesignated a multi-use facility, the massive limestone structure now houses cultural activities, meeting rooms, and a few shops. The history of the courthouse building begins in 1873. County officials then paid $52,000 for eight lots, known as the Union Block, bounded by 4th, 5th, Vine, and Division (Court) sts., on which to build a new courthouse. Opponents of the project delayed ground breaking for 15 years. Some persons contested the ownership of the old filled canal bed underlying a portion of the courthouse plot. Finally, in 1888 construction began after the last of the so-called "canal bed suits" was decided by the courts in favor of the county commissioners. German-born Henry Wolters (1845-1921), of Louisville, Kentucky, designed the courthouse, while Charles Pearce and Company of Indianapolis submitted the low bid of $379,450 to build it. Wolters unsparingly encrusted his cruciform-shaped composition with relief carvings, including 14 statues sculpted by Franz Engelsmann, a pupil of Augustus Saint-Gaudens. Materials pertaining to Engelsmann's work are on display in the courthouse. The building was completed in 1890 and occupied in January 1891. Since 1967 the Conrad Baker Foundation, awarded an unusual 99-year lease by the county, has directed the ongoing and expensive preservation efforts. Major room renovations thus far include the Wedgwood Hall, the Superior Court Room, the Governor's Parlor, the Canal Room, and the Old Courthouse Theatre. The 9-ft.-tall metal sculpture of a blacksmith, in the rotunda area, at one time rested on the site of Evansville's Vulcan Plow Works. (*NRHP*).

12. The **Vanderburgh County Jail and Sheriff's Residence**, 208 N. W. 4th St., and the courthouse went up concurrently. The contract for the jail complex was let in November 1889, and the county commissioners accepted the building in December 1890. Charles Pearce

Indiana Historical Society (C4211)
Old Vanderburgh County Courthouse, 1977, photographed by Edward J. Vadas

and Company, the courthouse contractor, also directed the construction of the jail, its boiler room, smokestack, and tunnel to the courthouse. The Pauly Jail Building and Manufacturing Company of St. Louis was responsible for the steel and iron jail cells. Henry Wolters, who designed the courthouse, drew up the blueprints for the jailhouse, the county's fourth. The lot and the building cost $67,440. The jail's architectural style is Gothic Revival, or what a reporter of the day referred to as the "old castellated [castle-like] kind with a central tower and turreted walls." The upright citizens of that era seemed to prefer in their penal institutions the security represented in the rough-hewn stone exterior and fortress-like features. The sheriff and his family lived in the front part of the building facing 4th St. The jail was leased to the Conrad Baker Foundation in 1968 but awaits creative adaptive use. (*NRHP*)

13. The **Soldiers and Sailors Memorial Coliseum**, Court and 4th sts., was erected in 1916-17, culminating years of public discussion on the need for a war memorial and a large auditorium. In 1913 a new state law and a city referendum permitted a semiprivate scheme of financing the $250,000 structure. The site selected for the coliseum received general approval because of its close proximity to the courthouse and jail, in an area considered the city's prospective civic center, although it meant putting the building partially over the old canal bed. In order to find a safe foundation, the contractor, W. H. Klaussman of Indianapolis, had to go down 30 ft. or more in places. The cornerstone laying in May 1916 occurred in conjunction with the spectacular pageantry accorded Indiana's centennial celebration, and with the sizable encampments of Civil War and Spanish-American War veterans' groups. The festivities imposed on Evansville, according to one account, an atmosphere of "a military concentration camp." Clifford Shopbell, the Evansville architect, gave the building a classic and ceremonial look by creating a broad Greek Revival entranceway featuring six, two-story Doric columns. Flanking the center section are statuary groups symbolizing the "Spirit of 1861" and the "Spirit of 1916" sculpted by Indiana native George H. Honig, then a resident of Evansville. In 1919 citizens raised $30,000 to purchase and install a Moeller organ, which had been used during the

Methodist centenary in Columbus, Ohio. The interior of the coliseum was extensively remodeled in 1932. On May 13, 1934, murals by Nelson Wilson were hung on either side of the stage. Wilson, a well-known local painter and at the time employed in the Works Progress Administration (WPA) artists program, depicted pioneer and modern scenes. Since 1971 the building has been leased from the county by the Council of Veterans' Organizations of Vanderburgh County. The huge auditorium, which once headlined such personalities as evangelist Billy Sunday, President William Howard Taft, and comedian Jack Benny, now attracts crowds to wrestling matches or an occasional stage show. Several military-related organizations maintain offices in the building. (*NRHP*)

14. The **Willard Carpenter house**, 405 Carpenter St., dates from 1848-49, and it is one of Evansville's oldest buildings. Willard Carpenter (1805-1883), a Vermont native, came to Evansville from New York State in 1837. Here he made his fortune, wholesaling dry goods and notions and speculating in land, canals, and railroads. He served in the state legislature in 1851-52. Carpenter channeled his business acumen and profits into philanthropy, providing a residence for homeless girls and endowing the Willard Library. His home sheltered escaped slaves in the pre-Civil War years, as noted on a marker at the site. The Carpenter house is a three-story, block-type brick structure of Greek Revival style, reminiscent of other Ohio River mansions of the era. Carpenter's daughter married Dr. William G. Winfrey, and during this couple's lengthy stay in the family home it was called the Winfrey-Carpenter house. Georgia Carpenter sold the house to the Funkhouser Post of the American Legion in the early 1930s. The Legion added an auditorium-gymnasium to its headquarters in 1948. The subsequent outlawing of slot machines in private clubs severely reduced the Legion's means for maintaining its center, and in 1956 it sold the complex to the television station WTVW. When the station relocated in 1974, MEDCO, an operator of nursing homes, bought the house for its headquarters. MEDCO officials had the house renovated in 1975 to accommodate offices, which included tearing down the Legion's gym, relandscaping, refurbishing the interior, and painting the outside a light gray. MEDCO moved out of the house in 1985, and it became

the home of Southwest Indiana Public Broadcasting and its WNIN television and FM radio station. (*NRHP/HABS*)

15. The **Rose Terrace, Albion, and Van Cleave apartments**, N. W. 7th and Court sts., are examples of an early 20th-century solution to slum housing. The brick buildings, designed by Evansville's Clifford Shopbell, were constructed around 1909-1910. Albert C. Rosencranz (1842-1920), owner of the Vulcan Plow Company, financed the project and named the one flat to honor Albion Fellows Bacon (1865-1933), a pioneer in housing reform. Bacon was the daughter of the Rev. Albion Fellows, pastor of Trinity Methodist Episcopal Church in Evansville. She married Hilary Edwin Bacon, who became president of the H. E. Bacon Company department store in downtown Evansville and a director of the Citizens National and Morris Plan banks. Mrs. Bacon's excursions into the city's impoverished neighborhoods around 1900 sensitized her to the needs of the poor and led to local campaigns for health and sanitation improvements. For years she fought for a statewide tenement reform law which finally was enacted in 1913. In 1917 she was instrumental in the passage of a statewide housing law. She launched the Evansville Anti-Tuberculosis League and the Working Girls' Association (which evolved into the city's YWCA). Among her other organizational credits are the National Housing Association, its Indiana branch, and the Indiana Child Welfare Association. Mrs. Bacon wrote the act that set up Indiana's Probation Department. She served on numerous local, state, and national boards and commissions. She wrote up her early struggles for fair housing in *Beauty for Ashes* (1914). The flat, having two or more units, was just beginning to take hold in the Midwest when Rosencranz, following Mrs. Bacon's lead, helped introduce apartments to Evansville. Meant to replace the existing dilapidated and overcrowded tenements, the apartments featured solid construction, spacious rooms, accessibility to fresh air, and sanitary plumbing. The Albion, for example, contained eight, two-bedroom units, each with a front veranda and rear porch, the latter opening onto a well-groomed backyard. An apartment ordinarily rented for $20 or $25 per month. (*NRHP*)

16. The **McCurdy Hotel**, 101-111 S. E. 1st St., was Evansville's largest hotel and a focal point of the city's social life from 1917 to 1970. The first hotel on the site was the elegant St. George, which opened in 1874. Fred Van Orman, a pioneer in the chain hotel business, took over the St. George in 1900. As early as 1903 the newly incorporated Van Orman Hotel Company planned to raze the St. George and build the McCurdy, named for William H. McCurdy, who had arrived in Evansville with his Hercules Buggy Company just the year before and promoted the construction of the new hotel. It was not until 1915, however, that erection of the new hotel, designed by H. Ziegler Dietz, a well-known St. Louis hotel architect, got under way. The construction specifications called for using the old brick of the St. George as rubble in the new walls. The hotel's formal opening with the Midwest's major hotelmen in attendance occurred June 25, 1917. The palatial lodging cost around $500,000 to complete. It contained 300 rooms, 2 dining rooms, and the large eighth-floor Rose Room, recently restored. Carpeted marble floors, walnut woodwork, and decorative moldings and ceilings complemented the rich furnishings. Prominent Evansville families had permanent residences in the hotel. F. Harold Van Orman, son of Fred Van Orman, managed the McCurdy during its heyday in the 1920s and the 1930s. A colorful figure, Harold Van Orman exhibited a special fondness for circuses, in which he met two of his three wives. He served as state senator and as lieutenant governor in the mid-1920s. The popular Republican politician reportedly coined the phrase: "Indiana has the best legislature money can buy." After Van Orman's death in 1959 the hotel declined due to internal management changes and competition from motels. Several private efforts failed to resuscitate the business. In 1970 MEDCO occupied the building, converting the old hotel to its present use as a retirement home, the McCurdy Residential Center. (*NRHP*)

17. The **John Augustus Reitz home**, 224 S. E. 1st St., is the cornerstone of the Riverside Historic District. Built by Reitz (1815-1891), a lumber magnate, in 1870-71, the French Second Empire structure is open to the public as Evansville's only house museum. Henry Mursinna, a noted Evansville architect, planned the 3-story, 17-room brick dwelling, which re-

ceived several "modernizations" around the turn of the century. In 1934 the Reitz descendants gave the house to the Daughters of Isabella, a Catholic women's beneficent society. When, in 1944, Evansville became a diocese of the Catholic Church, the home was purchased as a residence for the first bishop, Henry J. Grimmelson. Upon the bishop's death in 1972, the diocesan council voted to donate the house as a memorial to the prelate and to the Reitz family. The Reitz House Preservation Society was organized in 1973. Three years later the home was opened for public viewing. Highlights of the interior include the parlor's onyx mantel, which was bought at the 1893 Columbian Exhibition in Chicago, the canvas-covered and painted ceilings, the parquet floors, the huge clothes drying rack in the basement, and the restored kitchen. Through the efforts of Mary Hulman, granddaughter of Mary Reitz, the Preservation Society has placed two Victorian urns in their original places in the home's yard. (*NRHP*)

18. The **Watkins F. Nisbet house**, 310 S. E. 1st St., is considered Evansville's finest example of French Second Empire architecture. Robert Boyd and Henry Brickley, Evansville-based architects, and the local firm of French and Company, interior decorators, spared no expense in erecting and ornamenting the $60,000 brick home in 1878-80. Nisbet (1825-1886) was a leading merchant and partner in the wholesale dry goods firm of Mackey, Nisbet, and Company, and an avid investor in railroads. At the time of construction, the Nisbet home was one of the city's largest mansions, containing 28 rooms. Between 1938 and 1961 the dwelling functioned as a nursing home, and subsequently an apartment house. On the eve of the home's threatened destruction in 1961 the vacant structure was purchased and has undergone a long and expensive process of restoration.

19. The **Stockwell-Wheeler double house**, 313-315 S. E. 1st St., is believed to be the oldest extant structure in the downtown area. It was

Indiana Historical Society (Peat Collection)

John Augustus Reitz home

built in the late 1830s and is associated with Thomas Stockwell, an early town and county official and builder of a courthouse annex in 1837, and the Rev. Joseph Wheeler, an Englishman, who came to Evansville in 1819 and preached in the Methodist and Presbyterian churches intermittently until his death in 1864. The house is a simplified version of Federal architecture, similar to townhouses on the eastern seaboard. The modest brick dwelling abuts the sidewalk. Its only ostentatious feature is the arched entrances with fanlight transoms and a wooden keystone.

20. The **Charles Viele house**, 400 S. E. Riverside Dr., had only two stories and a cross-gabled roof when constructed in 1855-56. Charles Viele, a prominent wholesale grocer, returned from a European trip in the early 1870s and called for a remodeling of his home along French Second Empire lines. Evansville designers Jesse Vrydagh and Levi Clark added a third level enclosed by a steep mansard roof, a bracketed cornice, and metal corner quoins. The upper story had a fancy ballroom with gold leaf worked into the wallpaper motif. The Vieles imported statuary and other furnishings for the interior. In 1946 the last Viele descendant sold the home which was then made into apartments. In 1965 the house was purchased by a local preservation-minded couple who restored some of its original details. In 1984 a new owner took up the restoration effort. (*HABSI*)

21. The **Evansville Museum of Arts and Science**, 411 S. E. Riverside Dr., opened October 18, 1959, the third structure to house the city's aggregate of curios and artwork. The first museum, founded in 1904, occupied a mansion at the present museum's site in Sunset Park, a wedge of riverbank developed as a park after 1879. The Sunset Park Museum's home had been practically rebuilt in the 1850s and resided in by the Robert Barnes and U. W. Armstrong families prior to its conversion to a boardinghouse and subsequently to a museum. In 1910 over intense opposition, the park commissioners ordered the removal of the museum's holdings to various public buildings and the razing of the Barnes-Armstrong house for safety reasons. The Society of Fine Arts and History, formed in 1926, assembled the scattered objects and established its Temple of Fine Arts and Museum in June 1928 in the former

YWCA on N. W. 2nd St. In 1953 the City Park Board voted to return to Sunset Park and erect a new museum facility. Construction commenced in 1957. The architect was Victor Gruen Associates of California, the noted designer of malls and shopping centers. The $618,000 split-level brick and marble structure was financed mainly by local subscriptions supplemented with grants from the Lilly and the Kresge foundations. The exterior's walnut travertine marble is seldom seen in this region. The museum's wide-ranging art collection comprises 16th-century Gothic to modern European and American paintings and sculpture. The Anthropology Gallery focuses on worldwide primitive cultures and civilizations. Rivertown, USA, re-creates the trappings of frontier living and also life on Main St. around 1900. The third floor Koch Planetarium features sophisticated programs in astronomy. The Science Center Gallery offers changing exhibits on science and technology. Artifacts relating to the founding of Evansville are displayed in the main lobby. After 1976 the museum underwent interior renovation. In the mid-1980s the museum received a major 13,000-sq.-ft. addition, designed by Indianapolis architect Evans Woollen III. The new wing includes an auditorium, gift shop, and classrooms.

Alongside the walkway leading from the museum to the railroad station stands the **Dexter Cannon**. The small Civil War-era, four-pound cannon was affixed to the forecastle of Capt. Henry T. Dexter's mail boat, the *Charley Bowen*. Dexter managed to operate his craft during the war, skillfully eluding capture by Confederates. After the war the cannon was used as a hitching post in Dexter's front yard until rescued in 1910 and placed on a stone standard at the foot of Main St. as a memorial to Dexter's heroism. With the modernization of the riverfront as Dress Plaza in 1937 the cannon was assigned to storage. In 1940 it was set up in Sunset Park, and in 1969 it was installed at its present location on the museum's riverside terrace. On the base of the cannon are high water marks from the 1883-84, 1913, and 1937 floods.

On the lawn in front of the railroad station is a marker calling attention to the **Home Guard** that camped in Sunset Park during the Civil War to protect the city against rebel raids and hostile gunboats.

The **Sprinklesburg, Goosetown, and Independence Railroad** exhibit in the old Sunset Park pavilion includes a 1908 steam-powered switch engine, an equipped lounge car from the 1920s, and an early 1900s red caboose. The lounge car was used by Dwight Eisenhower in his 1952 presidential campaign and by Lady Bird Johnson in her husband's 1964 presidential campaign. The pavilion has been converted to a passenger station replete with authentic furnishings inside and outside. The railroad's name comprises the names of three of Vanderburgh County's pioneer communities. The park's shelter house, now the train station, was built in 1912 for $15,000. Its construction was held up temporarily by the litigation of Riverside Dr. residents who objected to its location which, they felt, blocked their view of the river. When completed, the shelter contained a refreshment stand, segregated rest rooms in the basement, and a roof garden surmounted by a band stand.

The **Four Freedoms Monument**, crowning the levee just east of the railroad exhibit, was Evansville's contribution to the nation's bicentennial celebration in 1976. Rupert Condict, the architect, positioned four, 26-ft.-tall Ionic columns, representing the freedoms of speech and religion and the freedoms from fear and from oppression, on a circular base, symbolizing unity. Around the edge of the base are 50 stone slabs standing for the 50 states. The 13 steps leading to the base denote the 13 original colonies. The columns came from the entrance of a railroad station built in 1905 and which had been used as a community center for some years prior to its being razed in 1966 for the Civic Center. The columns had been stored behind the waterworks garage. Plans for the bicentennial project were announced in 1975. The monument was ceremoniously illuminated on July 4, 1976. In Evansville's version of the four freedoms that of freedom from oppression is substituted for freedom from want, which President Franklin D. Roosevelt included in his famed rendering of the four freedoms in 1941.

22. **Morgan Manor**, 605 S. E. Riverside Dr., is one of the few remaining structures of mid-19th-century Greek Revival design in Evansville. It was built in 1850-51 for John M. Stockwell, a dry goods merchant and real estate speculator. In 1864 Mrs. John Henry Morgan, whose husband also dealt in dry goods, bought the house for $30,000. The three-story house, with its stucco-over-brick exterior, was a center for social life in the post-Civil War years. The grounds, stretching to the riverfront, supported servant quarters, stables, and a carriage house, besides the manor itself. The Italianate gable and brackets were later additions to the house. Amy Morgan, one of the Morgans' three daughters, and the one who married into the Viele family on Riverside Dr., lived in the Morgan home until her death in 1942. Afterwards, Morgan Manor became an apartment house. In the years after its purchase in 1975 the building received a sensitive renovation.

23. The **Samuel Orr house**, 603 S. E. 1st St., was the boyhood home of Indiana governor Robert D. Orr (b. 1917). Kirtland K. Cutter, an architect from Spokane, Washington, interpreted the English Tudor manor house for the 1904 Orr residence. Various building materials—brick, slate, stucco, stone—are embodied in the structure, which underwent expansion in 1917. Since the mid-1800s the Orr family has been closely associated with the industrial, banking, political, and educational interests of Evansville. The Orr Iron Company, the family business, had its roots in 1835 when Irish-born Samuel Orr came to Evansville and established a pork packing, wholesale grocery, and iron dealership on behalf of the Loughlin brothers of Pittsburgh. Orr became a partner in the Pittsburgh firm in 1836. Subsequently three generations of descendants from Samuel Orr took part in the business, which was sold to Shelby Steel Company in the mid-1970s. Robert D. Orr was born in Michigan because his mother wished to be under the care of her former Evansville physician who had moved to Ann Arbor. The future governor entered the Orr Iron Company after service in World War II, but eventually left to concentrate on a number of other businesses, and political and civic ventures. Orr climbed the political ladder from Republican precinct committeeman to state senator and lieutenant governor before capturing the governor's chair in 1980 by the largest vote plurality in the history of Indiana gubernatorial elections. He was reelected in 1984.

24. The **Benjamin Bosse house**, 813 S. E. 1st St., was constructed in 1916-17 for Benjamin Bosse (1872-1922), the mayor of Evansville.

The popular and progressive three-term Democratic mayor (1914-22; died in office) wielded considerable authority in business as in politics. He rose from grocery boy to the head of, or investor in, at least 28 businesses and industries. He was identified particularly with the gigantic Globe-Bosse-World Furniture Company, which he assembled in 1910. In January 1916 Bosse bought the August Bretano property for his new home. The architect, Clifford Shopbell, borrowed elements of Frank Lloyd Wright's Prairie School Architecture. He designed a low-slung, decidedly horizontal structure with characteristic wide overhanging eaves, an expanse of glass, and an open floor plan for the interior. The warm earth tones inside and outside the $10,000 home emphasize the effort to blend nature and architecture, the result standing in sharp contrast to the surrounding eclectic and ornate Victorian styles.

25. The **John H. Fendrich house**, 827 S. E. 1st St., was built in 1916-17 for the head of the Fendrich Cigar Company. During its heyday in the early decades of the 20th century, the Fendrich firm was America's largest independent cigar producer. Five Fendrich brothers began a tobacco company in Baltimore, Maryland, in 1850. They opened a buying station at Evansville in the mid-1850s. The business was known as the Fendrich Brothers until renamed the H. Fendrich Company in 1878 when Herrmann Fendrich took charge. Herrmann Fendrich married Mary Reitz, daughter of John Augustus Reitz, remembered today by the preservation of the Reitz home. Their son, John H. (1867-1952), headed the company after 1888. When a fire destroyed the Main St. factory and warehouse, the company relocated to Oakley St. and, in 1913, began manufacturing its most famous cigar, the La Fendrich. The company closed its doors in March 1969. The 15-room Fendrich house was designed by Chicago architect W. L. Klewer. The steel beamed framework is covered in Rugby brick, with a green tile roof. Italian stone carvers were employed to execute the exterior decoration, including the interesting limestone entryway arch with its three lion heads. Inside floors are of quarter-sawed oak or Carrara marble. Imported black and Circassian walnut and South American mahogany are used for moldings and stair rails. In the pantry is a sink made of nickel silver. The house reportedly cost about $100,000 to build.

In 1988 Mary Fendrich Hulman, widow of Anton Hulman, donated for resale her childhood home to Historic Landmarks Foundation of Indiana, which sold the house to Mr. and Mrs. Byron Warren. A portion of the proceeds established the Mary Fendrich Hulman Preservation Fund to assist statewide preservation efforts.

26. The **Alhambra Theatre**, 50 Adams Ave., was built in 1913 with the exotic architecture of the Near East in mind. Frank J. Schlotter, the designer, adapted to the movie house what at the time was called the Arabian motif, now referred to as Moorish Revival. The theater cost about $12,000 to construct, and it could accommodate 400 to 450 patrons, who were treated to silent and talkie films on the French-made "mirror" screen. The two-story front (one-story rear) included rented offices on the second floor and confectioner's and cigar stores, now concealed by stone facing, at the street level. The Alhambra is claimed as the first community theater in Evansville to have sound and to be "the princess among the second-run movie houses." The theater closed in 1958, reopened briefly in the late 1960s, and again in the early 1980s. At present it is not in regular use. (*NRHP*)

27. The **Matthew Watson Foster house**, 709 S. E. 2nd St., was constructed in 1860 for a leading citizen and the progenitor of several notable public figures. Matthew Foster (1800-1863) was born in England and emigrated to New York in 1815. Between 1819 and 1846 he and his family lived in and around Petersburg, Indiana, in Pike County. Foster engaged in farming, flatboating, and running a general store. In 1846 he moved to Evansville and over the course of the years became a prominent figure as a bank director, city councilman, president of the Board of Trade, and supporter of libraries, free schools, and the Presbyterian church. His son John Watson Foster became a career diplomat. He served as minister to Mexico, Russia, and Spain between 1873 and 1885 and as secretary of state under Benjamin Harrison. John W. Foster's son-in-law, Robert Lansing, was secretary of state under Woodrow Wilson. John Foster Dulles, a great-grandson, served as secretary of state, 1953-59, in the Eisenhower administration, while Allen Dulles, another great-grandson, directed the Central Intelligence Agency, 1953-61. Just before World War

I the Foster home came into the hands of Otto Hartmetz, who substituted a classical entryway and removed the cupola, shutters, and rear wing. From 1948 to the late 1960s the house was owned by the First Presbyterian Church, which used it as a parish house. It is now a single-family dwelling.

28. The **Joe Cook plaque**, behind the fence at the 4th and Oak sts. entrance to Welborn Hospital, memorializes another celebrated entertainer reared in Evansville. Cook (1890-1959) made his mark as a stage, screen, and radio comic. He was born Joseph Lopez, the son of an artist and circus performer. Orphaned at age 14, the future vaudevillian's surname changed when he was adopted by the Joseph Cook family of Evansville. The young Cook mastered practically all the tools of entertaining, from sharpshooting to magic. In 1923 he broke into big-time show business with the Carroll Vanities. A leading role in the 1930 musical comedy *Rain or Shine* vaulted him to stardom. Cook was famous for his four (actually three and a threat to do one more) mythical Hawaiian routines. The marker to Cook was dedicated in March 1931.

29. The **Wabash and Erie Canal Marker**, in Welborn Hospital's visitor's parking lot No. 2, just north of the Cook plaque, denotes the course of the canal. **Welborn Baptist Hospital** had its beginnings in 1894 when Drs. Edwin Walker and A. M. Owen built the Evansville Sanitarium. In 1914 it became the Walker Hospital. Dr. James York Welborn (1873-1948) purchased the institution from the Walker estate in 1922 and converted its name to the Welborn-Walker Hospital. Dr. Welborn, a charter member of the American College of Surgeons founded in 1917, was the third generation of his family to practice medicine locally. Prior to his becoming chief of staff at the Walker Hospital in 1916, Welborn served as Evansville's health officer from 1905 to 1913. He was a city councilman in the early 1920s, a leader in local Democratic party affairs, an owner of several farms in Posey County, and an avid genealogist. Welborn sold the hospital to the First Baptist Church of Evansville, March 1, 1944, for $175,000. The new owners changed the name to the Welborn Memorial Baptist Hospital.

30. The **Liberty Baptist Church**, 701 Oak St., houses the city's oldest continuous black congregation. The church was organized in 1865, and a frame sanctuary was completed in 1866. Brick replaced wood when a new structure, costing around $7,000, went up between 1879 and 1882. A "cyclone" in May 1886 destroyed the four-year-old meetinghouse, but the members rebuilt within the year. Over time the church has acquired additions, including an education annex. The Gothic-style building recently underwent a remodeling which involved the restoration of the original stained-glass windows. (*NRHP*)

31. The **Buckner Tower Apartments**, 717 Cherry St., though of recent vintage, honors by its name a former city physician and an American diplomat. The $1.8 million, seven-story apartment building for the elderly was constructed in 1967-68. It was named for Dr. George Washington Buckner, Sr. (1855-1943). Born into slavery at Greensburg, Kentucky, Buckner attended public school in Indianapolis and the Indiana State Normal School at Terre Haute. He taught school for 17 years in Kentucky and Indiana. After graduation in 1890 from the Eclectic Medical College in Indianapolis, he began practice in Evansville. In 1913 President Woodrow Wilson appointed him minister to Liberia, a post Buckner filled with distinction until illness forced his resignation in 1915. Afterwards, Dr. Buckner returned to his medical work in Evansville.

32. **Garvin Park**, at the end of N. Main St., was founded in 1915 when the city purchased 90 acres of woodland from the estate of Thomas E. Garvin (1826-1912), attorney, banker, and Willard Library trustee. For years Garvin had permitted community use of his "Grove." He had offered to sell it to the city, but no administration could meet his asking price. Mayor Benjamin Bosse and the Garvin heirs, however, agreed upon a $50,000 figure. The city appropriated another $30,000 for the park's beautification, directed by the American Park Builders of Chicago, which included the creation of Evansmere Lake, driveways, playgrounds, and a greenhouse. (*NRHP*) The city school took over 10 southeast acres and built **Bosse Field** for school activities, large civic affairs, and professional baseball. The 6,500-seat brick and concrete stadium was designed by Evansville

architect Harry E. Boyle. At its dedication on June 17, 1915, Evansville's Central League baseball team, behind its ace spitball hurler Jake Fromholtz, appropriately beat its Erie, Pennsylvania, rivals 4-0. Bosse Field underwent an extensive face-lift in 1930. **James Bethel Gresham** probably missed the festive inauguration of the stadium in 1915. He had joined the army in 1914 and in 1916 accompanied "Black Jack" Pershing into Mexico to fight Pancho Villa. Reenlisting in 1917, he left for France with Pershing's American Expeditionary Forces. On November 3, 1917, a German raiding party killed Corporal Gresham and two others, the first American soldiers killed in combat in World War I. The three soldiers were buried in France. In Evansville, Mrs. Alice Dodd, Gresham's twice-widowed mother, became the first of this war's dependents to receive a government pension. She also was named honorary president of the first chapter of the Service Star Legion, an organization of war mothers that began at Evansville and attracted two million members nationwide by 1918. To honor Gresham and provide needed lodging for his mother, the community raised funds to build her a Prairie School-style house, the design attributed to Clifford Shopbell, at the northeast edge of Garvin Park on a lot donated by the Evansville Real Estate Board. In 1921 Gresham's body was shipped to Indiana, where, after lying in state at Indianapolis, it was reinterred in Evansville's Locust Hill Cemetery. Mrs. Dodd lived in her stucco cottage at 2 Wedeking Ave. until about 1928, the year when the home was officially dedicated as the **Gresham Memorial Home**. Attempts failed in 1931 to have Gresham's body placed in the War Memorial Building at Indianapolis. For several decades the Service Star Legion occupied the Gresham house. In 1977 it became the Garvin Park site office of the Evansville Department of Parks and Recreation.

33. The **Heilman house**, 611 1st Ave., was built for William Heilman (1824-1890), a leading manufacturer of farm machinery. Heilman emigrated from Germany to a Posey County, Indiana, farm in 1843. By 1847 he had launched a machine shop in Evansville in partnership with his brother-in-law Christian Kratz. Heilman bought out Kratz's interest in 1864. The company's name, City Foundry and Machine Works, was changed to Heilman Machine

Works in 1884. In time the firm passed to his half-brother's sons, the Wientz brothers. The Heilman-Urie Plow Company was established in the 1870s and managed by W. Heilman's son-in-law Albert C. Rosencranz after 1877. This business became the Heilman Plow Company in 1890 and the Vulcan Plow Company in 1898. Besides his many business interests, including bank and railroad directorships, Heilman served terms as city councilman, state representative, and congressman, 1879-83. Heilman had his Italianate home built in 1869 in order to use his former residence, near the factory, as a site for a new salesroom. Henry Mursinna designed the 2-story, 24-room mansion to have brick construction and be faced with stone on the front. The $50,000 structure rested on a three-acre plot accented with fountains, gardens, and graveled walks. Yellow pine floors were edged with cedar strips to keep moths from the carpets. John Alt's elegant fresco work decorated the walls and ceilings. A shuttered plate glass window opened into a glass conservatory of exotic flowers. The finished basement reportedly included a kitchen and a billiard room. The attic led to a rooftop observatory. A reporter described the hot and cold water facilities in the kitchen and in three bathrooms as unequaled in southern Indiana. In 1930 John H. Fendrich, the cigar manufacturer, and Laura Fendrich McCarthy donated funds for the purchase and renovation of the house, which they presented that year to the St. Vincent Day Nursery, the present occupants.

34. The **Clara Barton plaque**, Mary and Iowa sts., commemorates the site of the Red Cross founder's administrative center when she initiated her new organization's first disaster relief program during the 1884 Ohio Valley floods. The plaque, designed by George H. Honig and dedicated on National Hospital Day, May 13, 1934, notes that the house used as Barton's headquarters later became the nucleus of Deaconess Hospital. The frame facility, believed built for Mayor William Baker in 1867, was bought in 1893 for $8,000 from its subsequent owner Maj. Bryan Parsons by the Protestant Deaconess Association, a charity nursing guild formed in 1892 by pastors in the German community. The deaconess order, rooted in the disposition of women's services in the New Testament, had recently been revived among main line Protestant denominations after cen-

turies of disuse. The 19-bed Protestant Deaconess Home and Hospital was dedicated June 11, 1893. Sisters from the Deaconess Motherhouse in Dayton, Ohio, began serving the hospital in 1894. Two years later the Deaconess Hospital Training School for Nurses and Deaconesses was established. A three-story brick hospital, costing $50,000, was built at the location of the Parsons home in 1897-99. Deaconess training was dropped in 1915, but nursing education continued. In 1944 Barton Hall was constructed as the School of Nursing's main facility. Subsequent additions, particularly from the 1960s to the present, to the hospital and the School of Nursing have enlarged the institution to the point where it is now one of the county's largest employers.

35. **Willard Library**, 21 1st Ave., is a century-old privately chartered free public library. In 1876 Willard and Lucinda Carpenter deeded to six trustees some $400,000 worth of land as a site and an endowment for a library available to all regardless of race. The Evansville firm of Boyd and Brickley drew up the original plans. The foundation and basement were completed in 1877 before the project was halted because of a poor realty market during the late 1870s depression. In 1882 construction resumed in conformance with extensive design alterations executed by James M. and Merritt J. Reid of Evansville, who established a well-known architectural business in California after 1888. (While in Evansville the Reid brothers designed the famed Hotel del Coronado for San Diego.) The red brick, two-story Victorian Gothic library was completed in 1884 and dedicated on March 28, 1885. Its initial book stock came from the city's school board which had inherited in 1874 the property of the Evansville Library Association, founded in 1855. Willard Library remained Evansville's only library until the opening of two Carnegie-funded buildings in 1913. Among Willard Library's popular attractions is its regional and family history center initiated in 1976 and its children's room. On permanent display is a collection of published works by Annie Fellows Johnston (1863-1931), including her Little Colonel series. Annie Johnston was a Vanderburgh County native and sister to Albion Fellows Bacon, the housing reformer. (*NRHP/HABSI*)

36. The **Rosenberger Building**, 2100 W. Franklin Ave., now the Heldt and Voelker hardware store, is generally considered the centerpiece of the West Franklin/Wabash Ave. Historic District. August Rosenberger (b. 1848) emigrated to the United States from Germany in 1860. He entered the retail grocery trade in Evansville in 1875, and in 1887 he joined with Andrew J. Klein, his brother-in-law, in establishing a broom factory. Rosenberger paid $4,000 in 1890 for four lots at the present site and constructed on two lots the extant brick building as a grocery and all-purpose farm store called Rosenberger, Klein and Company. In 1894 he placed on the remaining two lots a similarly massive warehouse, which is no longer standing. Besides his store Rosenberger held directorships in several banks and savings and loan companies. He stood high in Catholic circles, having been one of five influential westside churchmen who launched St. Boniface's parish in 1878. Rosenberger sold his store and property in 1915. Rosenberger's home, built in 1894, still stands at 409 N. Wabash Ave. Both structures are in the Independence Historic District that covers W. Franklin St. between Wabash and St. Joseph aves. (*NRHP*)

37. **Mead Johnson and Company**, 2404 Pennsylvania St., an international nutritional and pharmaceutical firm, had its headquarters in Evansville from 1915 to 1986. In 1893 Edward Mead Johnson with his brothers James W. and Robert W. launched the Johnson and Johnson Company, producers of surgical supplies and dressings. E. Mead Johnson left the family business in 1900 to start Mead Johnson and Company, incorporated in 1905 at Jersey City, New Jersey. From the beginning Johnson specialized in infant diet food. He developed Dextri-Maltose (malt sugar), the first infant formula carbohydrate modifier. When World War I cut the supply of potato starch used in Dextri-Maltose, Johnson found a substitute in corn, and in order to be closer to the grain market he relocated into a 40-year-old cotton mill in Evansville in 1915. From here Mead Johnson has introduced a number of products, including such formerly well-known household staples as Pablum, Metrecal, Enfamil, and Oracon. Over the years the Johnson family has aided needy individuals, underdeveloped countries, war victims, the city of Evansville, and even ailing zoo inhabitants. Mead Johnson, Sr., put up $500,000 for the

construction of the **Mead Johnson River-Rail-Truck Terminal**, 1830 W. Ohio St., dedicated in 1931. The terminal greatly improved dockage and shipping facilities and helped revitalize interest in inland waterway trade. The terminal was sold to the Valley Line Company of St. Louis in 1969. (*NRHP*) D. Mead Johnson, the grandson of the founder, organized Evansville Future, Inc., the major citizens' arm in the redevelopment of the city in the 1950s and 1960s. Evansville College, Vanderburgh County Society for Crippled Children and Adults, and the Museum of Arts and Science, have received grants from the company. In 1967 Mead Johnson became a subsidiary of Bristol-Myers and in 1986 changed its name to Bristol-Myers U.S. Pharmaceutical and Nutritional Group.

38. The **Francis Joseph Reitz High School** in Forest Hills is situated on a high bluff which affords an unobstructed view of the city, river, and countryside. When in 1917 a poor investment market discouraged financiers from purchasing bonds to underwrite construction of the new West Side High School, Francis Joseph Reitz (1841-1930), a banker, bought the entire issue. The school board renamed the school in tribute to Reitz's generosity. His philanthropy, especially in Catholic endeavors, gained him in 1925 the title of Commander of the Order of Pius IX. Reitz was the first Hoosier, and the third American, bestowed with the Roman Catholic Church's supreme honor to its laity. The new school's nine-acre site was originally called Coal Mine Hill to denote the whereabouts of John Ingle's Ingleside Mines, organized in 1866. Clifford Shopbell and Company designed the school in a classical style with two-story stone pillars adorning the front entrance. Reitz High School opened in September 1918.

39. **Mesker Park Zoo** with its main entrance on Bement Ave. covers 64 acres and cares for 500 furry and feathery inhabitants. Around 1900 several persons, including George L. Mesker, donated 120 acres of land to the city for a park. Mesker, a manufacturer of metal architectural articles, stipulated that any sort of development would carry his name. A key figure in the establishment of the park and zoo was Gilmore Haynie, a park board member from 1915 to 1935. Haynie's desire for a first-rate zoo meshed with the *Courier*'s cartoonist Karl Kae

Knecht's enthusiasm for the circus, and as a result Mesker Zoo was launched in 1928. The zoo's nucleus included small animals previously housed at Garvin Park, a gift of two lions from the American Circus Corporation of Peru, Indiana, and Kay, the elephant, purchased in 1929 with funds raised in a city-wide campaign. During the 1930s WPA laborers constructed many of the innovative "open" display structures, such as the "monkey ship" which received wide publicity. The Mesker Amphitheatre (Mesker Music Theatre) opened in 1952 and received a major face-lift in 1983. The George L. Kley Memorial Building, a bird sanctuary, was dedicated in 1956. More recently a shelter was built to house the zoo's two giraffes. The zoo's resources largely come from admissions, along with memberships in, and activities of, the Evansville Zoological Society.

40. The **University of Southern Indiana (USI)**, west of town on IND 62, 8600 University Blvd., began in September 1965 as a branch campus of Indiana State University. Classes were first held in the 89-year-old Centennial School building owned by Mead Johnson and Company. Southern Indiana Higher Education, Inc. (SIHE), formed in 1966 by a group of community leaders, raised nearly $1 million to buy 1,400 acres for a Mid-America University Center planned to encompass a variety of educational institutions. In the course of years SIHE purchased and donated around 300 acres to Indiana State University for its Evansville campus. Construction began in June 1968 on a two-building complex to house classrooms, faculty and administrative offices, labs, and a library. The $3.2 million concrete, brick, and steel building was almost complete in September 1969 when ISUE moved to its new location from Centennial School. Only massive traffic tie-ups on IND 62, due partially to an uncompleted parking lot, marred the opening of school. Since that time a number of new buildings have gone up, including some student housing. In July 1985 Indiana State University-Evansville became the University of Southern Indiana, the seventh independent, state-supported school, and the fifth independent liberal arts college in the state. Of special interest is the Bent Twig Outdoor Education Center, a complex of relocated and refurbished structures, several of which are of pre-Civil War vintage. The buildings are open to, and used for,

classes, school and public meetings, and a multitude of social and recreational activities. On the other side of the campus from the Center is a nature preserve and learning area nestled alongside man-made Reflection Lake, which includes the Bent Twig hiking trail and numerous types of flora and wildlife.

41. The **John W. Boehne house**, 1119 Lincoln Ave., was built in 1912-13 on three acres of a former fruit tree nursery that fronted on an improved avenue. Clifford Shopbell and Company planned the $15,000 Colonial Revival-style home to feature tall fluted columns and an intricately designed pediment. Boehne (1856-1946) helped to found the Schroeder, Fisher and Boehne Stove Company in 1881. The firm reorganized in 1887 as the Indiana Stove Works with Boehne as president. He cofounded the Globe-Bosse-World Furniture Company. Boehne contributed substantially to the new hospital facilities in 1915 at the Boehne Anti-Tuberculosis Camp, which he had nurtured since 1909. An avid officeholder, Boehne served as city councilman, 1897-1905, mayor, 1905-9, and congressman, 1909-13. After his death in 1946 the American Legion bought the property and sold it to Walter Moll, Sr., in the early 1950s. Tau Kappa Epsilon fraternity purchased the house in 1965. In the mid-1980s the house became lawyers' offices. (*NRHP*)

42. **Olmstead Administration Hall**, 1800 Lincoln Ave., is the oldest building on the campus of the University of Evansville. The school dates from 1917 when the Indiana Conference of the Methodist Church chose Evansville over Seymour for relocation of its financially strapped college at Moore's Hill, Indiana. Moore's Hill College was established in 1854. The energetic leadership of Evansville businessman George S. Clifford and the raising of $500,000 in a whirlwind, nine-day campaign tipped the scales in favor of the Crescent City. Evansville College opened in 1919 with 104 students. Until the completion of Administration Hall in 1922, the school rented space in downtown buildings. In 1919 the school's trustees had purchased 70 acres on Lincoln Ave. for a campus. The Chicago firm of Miller, Fullenwider and Dowling designed a $350,000, four-story Collegiate Gothic structure for the school's centerpiece. Its limestone surface of random-sized stones, their ends broken instead of sawed, represented a departure in American architecture. The college transferred to its new home in June 1922. The Administration Hall was the only major building besides the president's house in the college's first 25 years. Both of these buildings plus the front oval are listed on the National Register of Historic Places. The college took on university status in 1967. The school and community honored Ralph Olmstead, longtime administrator and archivist, by renaming the administration building in 1981. Today, the University of Evansville, a private, Methodist-affiliated school, can boast of 20 major structures, along with Harlaxton College, the British campus of the university, established in 1971 in a 19th-century manor house situated on 675 acres. Also worth viewing on the Evansville campus is the memorial dedicated to the university's basketball team and others who perished in an airline crash December 13, 1977. (*NRHP*)

43. **Wesselman Park**, 551 N. Boeke Rd., encompasses a recreation area and a Registered National Landmark forest, each section covering about 200 acres. For its size, the forest is unique among American cities of 100,000 or more residents. Tall oaks, sweet gum, tulip trees, and two dozen other species compactly inhabit the ancient woodland. Its density, 125 trees per acre, was without peer in Indiana until the uprooting caused by a 1982 summer storm. The park's tranquility belies the fact that in earlier days a canal, several railroads, and interurbans crisscrossed its terrain. The state acquired the farm in 1919 from the Stockwell family, who first purchased it in 1847 for use by patients of the nearby Evansville State Hospital. The city later bought 56 acres of the state's land on which to build Roberts Memorial Stadium (1956) and Hartke Pool (1959), the latter honoring Mayor Rupert Vance Hartke, subsequently United States senator, 1959-77. An abortive attempt to establish Shawnee State Park on the Evansville tract in 1959 led the same year to the state granting land to the city for park development. Albert Wesselman (1896-1962), an Evansville grocer and state senator, and his East Enders civic group coaxed the state to relinquish its property. Shortly afterwards Evansville annexed the parkland, and on October 30, 1960, Wesselman Park was dedicated. With the efforts of the Ju-

nior League, Stockwell Woods became an educative Nature Center in the 1960s. A Nature Center Building was built through a community fund drive and dedicated in January 1973. The building includes a one-way viewing area, conference rooms, and a lobby with displays. Additional features of the woods are its small amphitheater and eight miles of trails. The recreation section of the park has facilities for golf, tennis, basketball, softball, handball, and picnics.

44. **Angel Mounds State Historic Site**, 8215 Pollack Ave., is the 103-acre site of a significant Middle Mississippian Indian town of the 14th and 15th centuries. About 1,000 people lived in thatched-roofed houses in the stockaded trade center. The inhabitants placed 11 important communal buildings on earthen mounds, the grandest mound rising 44 ft. and covering four acres. In the 1930s the threat of the ground's continued erosion by cultivation and relic hunters and its piecemeal subdivision alerted the state's budding archaeology interests. Accordingly, Eli Lilly purchased the site from the Angel family and others for the Indiana Historical Society in 1938. From April 1939 to May 1942 an archaeology team, directed by Glenn A. Black and including 277 inexperienced WPA employees, conducted a systematic excavation. Some 2.3 million items turned up during the three years of research and reconstruction. In 1945 the Indiana Historical Society turned Angel Mounds over to the Indiana Conservation Department, but retained excavation rights. An Indiana University summer field school continued the work from 1945 to 1962. The registered National Historic Landmark came under joint control by the state and Indiana University when the latter received full investigatory powers from the Indiana Historical Society in 1965. In 1969 a Lilly Endowment gift underwrote construction of the Interpretive Center, which opened October 19, 1972. The center features a simulated excavation, an introductory slide show, and exhibits on Indian material culture. A self-guided tour takes in exact replicas of family dwellings, ceremonial structures, and a stockade section. (*NRHP*)

Tour 7

Take Pollack Ave. from Evansville to the Vanderburgh-Warrick county line at the east edge of Angel Mounds. **WARRICK COUNTY** (p. 41,474; 391 sq. m.), named for Capt. Jacob Warrick, a hero of the Battle of Tippecanoe, was organized in 1813. Initially the county included all or part of six present counties. The need for new counties to accommodate a rapidly expanding population reduced Warrick County by 1818 almost to its present dimensions, finally defined in 1852. The county's topography ranges from crop-rich bottomlands and gently rolling pastures to hilly uplands. Coal is the major natural resource. The population jumped 48 percent in the 1970s, the second largest increase in the state. Observers attributed the growth to developments at ALCOA (Aluminum Company of America), to a labor-hungry coal industry responding to energy concerns, and to the spillover of former Evansville inhabitants attracted to charming old Newburgh and its vicinity.

Follow Pollack Ave. to IND 662 and turn right. **NEWBURGH** (p. 2,906), *1.8 m.* east of Angel Mounds, is practically a suburb of Evansville. It dates from 1803 when the Sprinkle family flatboated from Henderson, Kentucky, and "squatted" on a high forested Ohio River bank at the present site. Sprinkle took out land grants in 1812, and in 1818 he founded Sprinklesburg, or Mount Pleasant, as it was called for several years. In 1829 Abner Luce platted Newburgh, which bordered Sprinklesburg. The state legislature merged the two towns along with a median strip of land owned by Samuel Short in 1837 under the name Newburgh. The town initially prospered as a milling, coal, and shipping center. Soon, however, railroads bypassed it. Evansville overshadowed it, and the town's protracted decline was underway. Brief economic revivals took place with an upturn in the coal industry around 1900, with the construction of Lock and Dam 47 in the mid-1920s, and with the building of the huge ALCOA rolling mills in the 1950s. The worst, however, was yet to come. In the 1970s Newburgh's retail core dried up as a result of an exodus of businessmen, disastrous fires, and the presence of unsavory motorcycle gangs. Meanwhile in and around Newburgh, old and new residents were rediscovering the river town and organizing to prevent the forfeiture of its material inheritance. As a consequence of the combined efforts of Historic Newburgh, Inc., city officials, clubs, and concerned individuals, the visitor to the town sees lovely restored homes and functional, rehabilitated, and occupied buildings. Dozens of large eye-catching green historical markers convey the new pride in Newburgh's heritage. In 1983 a four-square-block area of downtown Newburgh was included in the National Register of Historic Places. Visitors to Newburgh should stop first at the headquarters of **Historic Newburgh, Inc.**, 100 State St. (the northwest corner of State [IND 261] and Jennings [IND 662] sts.), where walking tour maps and brochures are available.

Historic Newburgh, Inc., is located in the old **Phelps-Sargeant Block**. Abraham M. Phelps (b. 1798), a successful merchant, sometime before 1837 built the upper frame level on top of a hill. In 1837 the lower brick portion was erected following the removal of the hillside to make way for street construction. The property remained in the family until 1976, during which time it housed a variety of businesses including the coal company of Eugene Sargeant, a great-nephew of A. M. Phelps.

Opposite the Phelps Block is the **Exchange Hotel** at 1 W. Jennings. Built in 1841 by Joseph Spitz, the popular hostelry received a third floor and a west wing in 1853. On July 18, 1862, Adam R. Johnson and his Confederate raiders, supported by fake cannon positioned on the Kentucky side, occupied Newburgh. The incident was the first encroachment of Indiana soil by southern troops. The Exchange Hotel housed about 85 ill and wounded Union

Tour 7

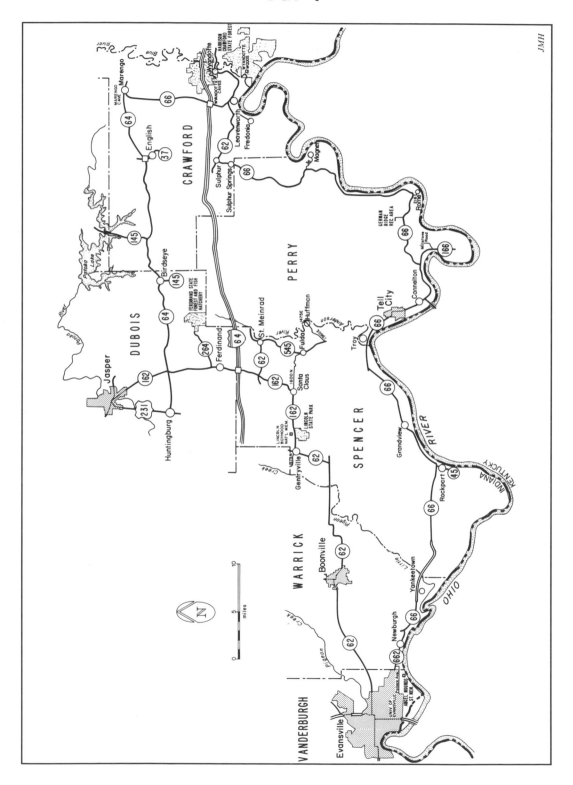

soldiers, plus commissary and hospital items and ammunition. Sabres and pistols were stored in a nearby warehouse. Johnson and his men confiscated these materials, plundered a few homes and businesses, and made good their escape. The outraged citizens fell upon and killed two suspected Southern sympathizers and informers. Johnson acquired the nickname of "Stovepipe Johnson" for the tubes he used to imitate barrels on his ominous-looking, but phony, cannon. In subsequent years the hotel became the J. W. Fuquay Dry Goods Store, which in 1902 underwent extensive remodeling including the addition of the sheet-metal clad corner tower. The Chivian Department Store took over the property in 1927 and stayed until 1973. The building is still used for retail businesses.

On State St., one block north of Phelps Block and between Main and Gray sts., is a collection of six interesting historical structures. On the northwest corner of State and Main sts. is the **Newburgh Town Hall**, a former sanctuary of the Cumberland Presbyterians, a splinter denomination formed in Tennessee in 1810. The Cumberland Presbyterian Church of Newburgh was organized in 1839. A. M. Phelps financed the construction of the church's sanctuary in 1841. A decade later, on another plot of land donated by Phelps, the building of a new church commenced. This edifice, the present Town Hall, was dedicated on June 19, 1853. Newburgh's first town hall was erected around 1900 near the corner of State and Jennings sts. Cramped for space by the 1960s, the town board approved the purchase of the Presbyterian Church for $14,000 in September 1965. The Presbyterians, at the time, had begun building a new church east of town. In May 1966 the town accepted the keys to the historical property. The yellow stucco was removed from the brick, and the interior was fitted for offices. The old bell tower received badly needed repairs in 1980, and in the same year the main meeting room acquired a mural of Newburgh's historical sites painted by four local artists. (*NRHP*)

The **Phelps-Hopkins house**, 208 State St., next to the Town Hall, is one of Newburgh's most magnificent private residences. A. M. Phelps built the home in 1850 for about $15,000. The two-story brick structure initially rested on a full block of grounds, which included a carriage house and servants' quarters.

The 90-ft.-long twin rear porches can be viewed best from behind the Town Hall. It is said that Phelps purchased the decorative iron balcony railing in New Orleans. The north wing and the cupola were later additions. The house has 22 floor-to-ceiling windows with original interior shutters. Phelps's daughter Frances married Charles Hopkins, and five generations of the Hopkins family lived in the house. During the 1930s the north wing was converted to apartments. The Edgar A. Iglehearts bought the house in 1952 and sold it in 1977 to the Gerald Bienvenus, who have restored it.

The other historically designated Civil War-era structures in the 200 block of State St. perhaps are more fascinating for episodes involving former tenants than for their architecture. In the **Corneal McCormick house**, 224 State St., built in 1869 by a local grocer and violin maker, a despondent elderly occupant hanged herself in the stairwell. Although no tragic deaths occurred in the **Pepmiller house**, 211 State St., it is said that Louis Pepmiller, a partner in the local Eagle Brewery, was sued for breach of promise and that today a tiny spirit haunts the place. **Samuel R. Weed**, who purchased the house at 217 State St. shortly after its construction in 1856, is chiefly remembered as the fifth husband of Mary Ann Castle, known as "Marrying Polly." Polly is known to have wed at least 8 times, with some unverified accounts putting the number of marriages at 17. Her fourth and sixth husband was George Boyden, a traveling salesman, who committed suicide December 28, 1900, by jumping into the kitchen cistern and drowning. Newspapers of the day attributed his suicide to Polly's refusal to marry him a third time. Another tragedy occurred at the **Garwood house** at 221 State St. The marker indicates that the house was built in the 1840s, but subsequent research puts the construction in the late 1850s or early 1860s. William Stokes Garwood, a blacksmith, accidently shot himself, according to Masonic lodge records, and died March 1, 1881. Unconfirmed stories tell of his suicide by hanging. By whatever means he died, tales still circulate of his subsequent haunting of the lovely Greek Revival-style brick home. The stone wall fronting the house is the work of **William Butterworth**, an early stonecutter, whose shop was located across Gray St. on the east side of State St. Butterworth's small frame cottage, built in the mid-1850s, is located at 8 Gray St.

Return to State and Jennings sts. and proceed west three blocks to the **Weis house** situated on the southeast corner of W. Jennings and Market sts. Newburgh's oldest extant brick house was built in 1839 by Joseph Weis, who made saddles and harnesses in a rear shop. The framework of the house consists mainly of unshaped timbers cut to the desired length and fastened with wood pegs. Branches and twigs remain on some of the small trees used as roof supports. Bricks brought by flatboat were used to wall in the dirt-floored cottage.

Newburgh's German Catholics first met in 1862 in the Weis house. The following year the members purchased a lot across the road from the Weis property at the northeast corner of Jennings and Market. Supplying labor and materials, the group erected **St. John the Baptist Church** in 1865. Its spire, bell tower, and bell were installed in the fall of 1872. Eventually a section was added to the church's north side, and a rectory and a school were built nearby. In the 1950s the body relocated to its new complex on Frame Rd. In 1964 Kurt Kluger and Marilyn Kluger, a soon-to-be author (*The Joy of Spinning* 1971, *The Wild Flavor* 1973), bought the vacant century-old church building. They rearranged the interior, put up old barn beams, and attached a side porch, entrance, and front display window in order to convert the structure to commercial use as the **Country Store**. With some imagination the architectural features of the original church can be detected.

From the Country Store go one block west and then north to 612 Jefferson St., the home of **Delaney Academy** from 1857 to 1867. The popular southern Indiana school was founded in 1842 by the Indiana Presbytery, which named it the Newburgh Cumberland Presbyterian Academy. The school, which at the outset trained ministerial students, was incorporated in February 1843 as the Delaney Academy, to honor the Rev. Henry Delaney, a revered area minister. The school initially occupied a frame building, which stood about mid-block on the north side of Jennings St. between State and Monroe sts. (site marked). It moved to the basement of the newly erected Cumberland Presbyterian Church (now Town Hall) in September 1853. Four years later, in October 1857, the academy opened its new quarters on Jefferson St. A. M. Phelps, who financed the building and supplying of the first school, liberally underwrote the construction and equipping of the

two-story brick institution on his Jefferson St. land. The academy remained in operation until 1867 when the Presbyterian Synod voted to transfer the school to Lincoln, Illinois.

Immediately north of Delaney Academy, at 700 Jefferson St., is the former home of the John M. Kuebler family. Between the Civil War and World War I the house was the centerpiece of a popular playground known as **Kuebler's Garden**. Kuebler (1835-1918), a tanner from Alsace, France, acquired the Jefferson St. property around 1860, and in 1872 he relocated his leather store to his new house north of town. Kuebler built a large tannery, which later burned, north of the house, and he maintained an office and salesroom in Evansville. On the remainder of the grounds he cultivated vineyards, established a winery, and built a greenhouse. His manicured gardens lay near a lake, and small summer cottages were scattered about. For the crowds that came to the garden for the excellent lunches and chicken dinners, Kuebler also could provide lodging, a concert by the Kuebler Band, plus facilities for baseball, horse racing, and stage shows. The house at present is an apartment, the Maples, owned by Francis Fauvres, who purchased it from Kuebler heirs in 1947.

From Kuebler's Garden follow Jefferson St. south to Water St., which borders the river, and turn left. Continue past the **Colonial Manor** (110 Water St.), a prominent business establishment when the riverfront artery was the hub of Newburgh's commerce (marked), to the south end of State St. Here, a tablet designates the landing site of **John Sprinkle** in 1803. Another marker, close by, commemorates **Johnson's raid** on Newburgh in 1862. Directly across from the Civil War marker, at 12 E. Water St., is the former station of the **Evansville, Suburban, and Newburgh Railway Company** (E. S. and N. R. R.). This steam line was organized in 1888 and in partial operation by the time of its formal opening May 31, 1889. The Suburban Motor Railroad, as it was often called, eventually traveled the 10.3 miles between the depots at Newburgh and Evansville at hourly intervals. The railway's Newburgh station was first located near the corner of W. Water and Jefferson sts. and was known as Kuebler's Station because the destination of many passengers was Kuebler's Garden. In 1905 the railroad switched from steam to electricity, thereby decreasing the travel time between the two cities. In the fall of 1911 Clifford Shopbell of Evansville designed a new station of glazed brown brick and green stained shingled roof, which probably was completed in 1912. On December 15, 1930, the traction line ended its Newburgh passenger service, replacing it with buses that would arrive and depart from Munn's garage on Jennings St., west of State St. The abandoned depot on Water St. was sold in 1937 and again in 1952 when the Crenshaws, the present occupants, converted it into a residence.

Proceed east on Water St. to IND 662 and continue past the **old Dam and Lock No. 47**, built between 1923 and 1928 at a cost of $4,412,400. One-half mile farther is the **Newburgh Presbyterian Church** at which site in 1850, it is claimed, John Hutchinson sank the state's first coal shaft mine. On the north side of IND 662, *.7 m.* east of the church, is a driveway leading up to the **Old Stone House**, an area landmark. Gaines H. Roberts (1793-1863), a timber dealer, land speculator, county official, and state senator, imported German artisans to build the Federal-style house in 1833-34. The house sits on a bluff called Indian Hill, the location of a frontier stockade, and overlooks a vast portion of the Ohio River valley. The imposing two-story, sandstone structure features paired chimneys, a substantial arched center entrance, a front of symmetrically laid stone, and sides of randomly laid stone. The twin front porticoes were later additions. Following a succession of owners after Roberts's death, Isaac and Cora Hollander in 1919 turned the house into a drug rehabilitation center. The Thomas Morton, Jrs., bought the place in 1931 and restored its former grandeur. The Old Stone House was one of 28 Indiana structures selected for review in connection with the Historic American Buildings Survey of 1934. In December 1969 the Mortons saw to it that at a future date, when they no longer required the house, it would become the property of the University of Evansville. (*NRHP/HABS*)

Continue east on IND 662 *.3 m.* and follow the indicated route to the **Newburgh Lock and Dam Overlook**. In 1953 a federal program was instituted to modernize the Ohio River's locks and dams erected in the 1920s. The newest Newburgh facility was completed in 1975, although the first towboat and barges had gone through on July 2, 1974. Old Lock and Dam No. 47, *1.5 m.* west, was removed with dyna-

mite. The new navigation system, built by the Corps of Engineers for $104.4 million, has a 1,200-ft.-long main lock, which is twice as long as its downstream predecessor. Also, the old hand-operated wickets of Dam No. 47 gave way to push-button controls on the new dam. Over the last 60 years the string of dams has raised the water level and created a succession of "moving lakes" of great recreational value. Less accepting of the advantages of river controls are bankside property owners who have watched their land slip gradually into the spreading waters. Their anger has led, on occasion, to filing remedial class-action suits. The overlook is furnished with a parking area, picnic tables, and an encased map and dam data.

Leaving the overlook proceed east on IND 66 (merges with IND 662) past the huge **ALCOA rolling mill**, a major mainstay of Warrick County's economy from its completion in the late 1950s, to the turnoff south to **YANKEETOWN** (*4.3 m.* east of the overlook). Yankeetown was laid out by Thomas Day in 1858. It is said that New England relatives of Ralph Waldo Emerson gave the village its name. Yankeetown, today, is totally residential.

East of the Yankeetown turnoff *1.5 m.* is Little Pigeon Creek, which forms the natural boundary between Warrick and Spencer counties. **SPENCER COUNTY** (p. 19,361; 400 sq. m.), Abraham Lincoln's home from 1816 to 1830 and the locale of the unique village of Santa Claus, was organized in 1818. Its name honored Capt. Spier Spencer, a Corydon sheriff and tavern keeper, who led his famous company of "Yellow Jackets" into the Battle of Tippecanoe in 1811, and who died a hero of that battle. The broad valleys and rolling hills over much of the county have contributed to the largely agricultural economy, centering on livestock products. From 1900 to 1960 the population of the county declined, but the trend has been reversed in the last two decades.

East of Pigeon Creek nearly *12 m.* on IND 45, and just south of IND 66, is **ROCKPORT** (p. 2,590), Spencer County's largest town and commercial center and the county seat. The early settlers congregated at the base of a huge bluff bordering the Ohio River. They called their tiny collection of cabins Hanging Rock, inspired by the two columnar appendages, respectively called George Washington and Lady Washington, that tilted outward from the cliff's face. One of the stone pillars, it is claimed, tumbled in the earthquake of 1811, and the other column was eventually dynamited for safety's sake. Daniel Grass, who in 1807 first entered land at the location, subsequently changed the name from Hanging Rock to Mount Duvall, in honor of a Kentucky friend. When Spencer County was formed in 1818, Mount Duvall was declared the county seat but under the new name of Rockport. Afterwards, the settlement shifted from the foot of the bluff to its present location on the crest. Rockport has had its share of notables born or raised within its bounds, including Kate Milner Rabb, author and a columnist for the *Indianapolis News*; James Clifford Veatch, Civil War general and friend of Lincoln; and Florence Henderson, star of stage, screen, and television.

Drive into Rockport on IND 45 south (5th St.). Turn east onto Main St. and proceed down the incline, bordering the towering bluff, to the river's edge. At its highest point, the nearly one-half-mile-long bluff exceeds 100 ft. Note on the cliff wall the high water marks indicating levels of past floods. A cave-like gouge in the stone face is where, according to tradition, James Lankford and family, the first permanent white settlers at the Rockport site, lived in 1808. The **Abraham Lincoln marker** at the lower end of the bluff road commemorates Abe's first New Orleans flatboat trip, which embarked from this spot in 1828. Before the new river dams raised the water and contributed to the erosion and inundation of unprotected banks, the environs of the Lincoln marker took in a greater area than observed at present. Many festivals, pageants, and social gatherings took place by the river in what was then the much larger Rocky Side Park, dedicated in 1923.

Return to the hilltop via 2nd St. just north of the Lincoln marker. Before bending left near the top of the bluff, catch sight of the large white frame house with the red tin roof, on the right. This is the **Brown-Kercheval house**, 315 S. 2nd St. Built in 1854 by Rockport banker Samuel Gibson Brown, the house passed on to his daughter, Cornelia, who married Samuel Edward Kercheval. Kercheval, who came to Spencer County from Campbell County, Kentucky, in 1853 at the age of six, manufactured farm equipment, published the *Rockport Journal*, and served as a United States marshal, county official, state legislator, and mayor of Rockport. The Kerchevals hosted such famous persons as Benjamin Harrison, Frederick Douglass, and Meredith Nicholson. Nicholson, a Hoosier author, parodied a title of one of his books when he referred to it, supposedly, as the "House of a Thousand Biscuits," in praise of the Kerchevals' generous hospitality. (*NRHP*)

The **Spencer County Courthouse** occupies the block bounded by Walnut, Main, 2nd, and 3rd sts. The courthouse, the county's fifth since 1818, was completed in 1921 at a cost of $275,926.23. The Elmer E. Dunlap Company of Indianapolis designed the building. Dunlap, a Bartholomew County native, organized his architectural firm in 1912. He chose to construct the walls with reinforced concrete and brick faced with Bedford limestone. The inside he trimmed in Italian marble and decorated the walls and ceilings. Its most attractive feature is the large stained glass dome. In October 1844 Abraham Lincoln delivered a speech in the county's third courthouse on behalf of Henry Clay, the Whig presidential candidate. On the northeast corner of Main and 2nd sts., across from the present courthouse, is a small rock marker dedicated October 28, 1926, denoting the site of the **Rockport Tavern** where Lincoln stayed while on his visit in 1844. The tavern was torn down in 1953. Another Lincoln tribute is in the **Rockport Public Library**, located just south of the courthouse at 3rd and Walnut sts. An oil painting of Lincoln surrounded by scenes of his life was presented to the library in March 1956 by local artist Myrtle Posey in memory of her father Frank B. Posey.

From the library return to Main St. and go west to 6th St. and south one block to Walnut St. and the **Rockport-Ohio Elementary School**. Just inside the school's main entrance on 6th St. is a large bronze mural, executed by George H. Honig, entitled **Abraham Lincoln and James Grigsby's "Forest College" in Spencer County, Indiana, 1816-1830**. The story behind the depiction, as related years later, is that James Grigsby and his friend Abe Lincoln took to the woods occasionally to study the textbooks brought to Grigsby by a relative who attended college in Kentucky. Eli Grigsby, a descendant of James Grigsby, unveiled Honig's bas-relief mural in the old Rockport High School on October 31, 1934, the 90th anniversary of Lincoln's return visit in 1844 to the scenes of his youth.

Head east on Walnut St. past the unusual 1859 octagonal house on the right, known as the **Crooks-Anderson home**, at 410 Walnut St. At 4th and Walnut sts. return north one block to Main St. and proceed west to 9th St. and south .2 m. to the **Lincoln Pioneer Village**, reached through the city park, on the right. The group of vintage and replica log homes, along with contents, was assembled in 1934-35 through donations of time, money, and materials, and with labor provided by the Federal Emergency Relief Administration. To Rockport native George H. Honig, the village capped his career as an artist and local historian. He voluntarily designed the memorial, laid out the four-acre tract, and mapped the building placements. Honig and other leaders of the project, in particular Bess V. Ehrmann, visualized their creation as featuring structures and furnishings familiar to young Lincoln. As a result of painstaking research the village contained accurate representations of the inn, church, school, law office, store, and homes of friends and neighbors, a total of 11 buildings, deemed significant to Lincoln during his 14-year stay in the county. Additions to the village after its dedication on July 4, 1935, expanded to about 20 the number of cabins on the grounds. For several decades the village proved to be a major attraction in southern Indiana, receiving nationwide media coverage. A museum was constructed in the complex in 1950. In 1954 the village served as a backdrop for part of the movie "The Kentuckian," starring Burt Lancaster.

From the Lincoln Pioneer Village return to Main and 5th sts. and head north out of Rockport via IND 45 to IND 66 east. Observe in the distance the twin 1,040-ft. smokestacks of the new **Indiana Michigan Power Company's plant**. Construction began at the 3,820-acre site in 1979.

Continue east of Rockport 3.6 m. on IND 66 to **GRANDVIEW** (p. 670), platted in 1851 and incorporated as a town in 1872. Settlement in the vicinity began as early as 1807 when the Ezekiel Ray family, generally regarded as the first permanent settlers of the future Spencer County, came by raft from Kentucky. The Lincoln and Ray families became acquainted after 1816. When Elizabeth Ray, Ezekiel's daughter, married Reuben Grigsby in a large double wedding, the Lincolns were not invited to the following infare. Perhaps ruffled by the snub, the 20-year-old Abe Lincoln satirized the event in a composition, "The Chronicles of Reuben," written in Biblical style, in which the two

grooms mistook their respective rooms in the Grigsby house and nearly spent the wedding night with the wrong wife. In downtown Grandview, along IND 66, in front of the local library, is a **Lincoln marker**, noting that Lincoln traveled along this route while hauling hoop poles (wood stock for barrel hoops) with an oxteam to the river for shipment.

Continue east on IND 66 11 m. to **Ferry Park** just west of the Anderson River. As settlers migrated into Troy and its environs in the early 1800s, the Anderson River, which empties into the Ohio here, became an important storage and shipping point. Here, in 1816, the Lincoln family made its first stop before moving inland, and, in subsequent years, the Lincolns often disposed of their surplus produce at the river junction. In 1825-26 Abe Lincoln worked as a ferryman on the Anderson River near the present grounds of the small roadside memorial park.

Cross the Anderson River into **PERRY COUNTY** (p. 19,346; 381 sq. m.). On Lake Erie, September 10, 1813, Oliver Hazard Perry forced the British navy, for the first time in its history, to surrender a squadron of ships. Perry related to William Henry Harrison the now famous dispatch, "We have met the enemy and they are ours." One year later, September 7, 1814, the Indiana territorial legislature carved from Gibson and Warrick counties a new county and named it Perry in honor of the naval hero of the War of 1812. Perry, one of Indiana's southernmost counties, lies about equidistant between Louisville and Evansville. More than half of its acreage is in timber, and most of the remainder is devoted to agriculture. More than 56,000 acres of county land is in the Hoosier National Forest.

TROY (p. 550), platted in 1815 and once Perry County's seat of justice, is situated .2 m. east of the Anderson River, the county's western border. For many years it was thought that the county seat probably derived its name from the ancient Homeric stronghold of Troy, the site of which today is in northwest Turkey. In 1948, however, Albert Kleber published evidence to show that the town was named for Judge Alexander Troy of Salisbury, North Carolina, by two clients and Troy settlers who, in this manner, wished to show appreciation to the judge for services rendered. When the state legislature formed Spencer County in 1818, Perry County's boundary shifted eastward from

Pigeon Creek to the Anderson River. No longer centrally located as a result of the realignment of county lines, Troy lost its advantageous county seat status and its prospects of becoming a great river city.

Approaching Troy from the west, the most visible landmark is the 142-ft.-high steeple of **St. Pius V Roman Catholic Church**. This building, erected between 1881 and 1884, replaced one constructed in 1847, the year of beginning corporate activity for Catholics in Troy.

On entering Troy a roadside marker supplies information pertaining to **Abraham Smythe Fulton**, brother of steamboat inventor Robert Fulton. Abraham Fulton arrived in Troy around 1814 to establish a woodyard and manage his brother's nearby coal mine operations. A few years later Abraham was killed in an accident while building his home, which was never completed. He is buried in **Troy Cemetery**, which is located at the end of Washington St. directly north of the Fulton marker. Fulton's gravestone, reached by going through the cemetery's middle gate and walking to the right, is a horizontal modern marble tablet.

From the cemetery return to IND 66 and proceed to the river via the street just east of the Fulton marker. Turn upstream on the riverside road and note the stone buildings, which date from the Civil War era. In the old days Troy's commerce largely centered along this brief stretch of waterfront property. Take Harrison St. to IND 66 and head eastward to Spring St. Take Spring St. to Market St. and follow the signs to **Camp Koch** on the left, which provides summer recreation and camping for handicapped children and young adults. The camp was built for $125,000 in 1948 on three acres purchased by Henry F. Koch, an Evansville businessman, from Riley Mosby. Further acquisitions of land expanded the camp to its present size of more than 35 acres. Camp Koch opened in the spring of 1949 with 150 persons attending. Since the camp's beginning and until his death in 1986, Roy Fenn, of Tell City, had been the guiding hand in its growth. The veranda of the camp's main building, situated on a high bluff, affords a magnificent view, taking in a 30-mile radius of the river and surrounding landscape. The bluff is known as Fulton Hill, because Abraham Fulton, before his tragic mishap, had started building his house near the crest.

Positioned on the side of Fulton Hill some 75 ft. above the highway, and visible from the hillside edge of Camp Koch, is the **Christ of the Ohio statue**. The 18-ft.-high representation of Christ, arms outspread, was the gift of Dr. and Mrs. John M. James, who also deeded to Camp Koch three acres on which the statue rests. Herbert Jogerst, a German sculptor and an American prisoner in World War II, came to the Catholic seminary at St. Meinrad, Indiana, after the war to work at his trade. He subsequently received the commission to execute the artwork. Jogerst cast the figure in a durable synthetic material composed of Terrazzatine dust and white cement. The Christ of the Ohio was dedicated May 1, 1957, to the community and Camp Koch and to travelers on the highway and river below. The statue is illuminated at night.

Upon returning to IND 66, by way of the steep road from the camp, head east again. When passing below the Christ of the Ohio statue, glance toward the river, beside which a number of successive potteries existed, adjacent to Troy, throughout much of the 19th century. On hindsight, the most interesting, but probably the most short-lived, was the **Indiana Pottery Company** established around 1837 by James Clews. Clews, a well-known figure among Staffordshire potters in England (J and R Clews, ca. 1818-ca. 1834), received intelligence from America that the clays at Troy were suitable for manufacturing white ware. Backed by American capital, Clews came to Troy and set up his pottery, only then to discover he had been misled as to the quality of the clay. In 1838 he left the area. The pottery produced at Troy was utilitarian ware of Rockingham or Bennington color and style.

Travel *2.3 m.* southeast of Troy on IND 66 to **TELL CITY** (p. 8,704). Perry County's largest community dates from 1857 when representatives of the Swiss Colonization Society of Cincinnati (organized 1856) chose the Indiana river site for a new industrial city. The society, composed of German and German-Swiss shareholders, purchased 4,154 acres for $85,314. The holdings of Judge Elisha Mills Huntington constituted the largest acquisition of land, upon which the bulk of Tell City would rest eventually. Huntington had obtained his property from the heirs of Robert Fulton, who in turn had bought it from Nicholas J. Roosevelt, the great uncle of President Theodore

Roosevelt and an associate of Fulton's. Nicholas Roosevelt introduced steamboats on the western waters when he built and piloted the *New Orleans* from Pittsburgh to the city of the same name in 1811. The society designated its possession Tell City in honor of William Tell, the legendary Swiss hero. It laid out 7,594 residential and garden lots, crisscrossing the plot with exceptionally wide streets named for American and European leaders in government, literature, art, and science. In 1866, nine years after its founding, Tell City had a population of 2,600 and apparently little crime, since not until the 1870s did local officials even discuss building a jail. Tell City became, as planned, a manufacturing town with mills, breweries, furniture factories, and river-related industries. It was incorporated as a city in 1886, and the following year the railroad inaugurated a new era of prosperity. Always susceptible to damaging floods, Tell City was the first Indiana community to complete a floodwall after the great inundation of 1937. In the 1970s Tell City increased its population by almost 10 percent on the strength of an economic upturn between 1976 and 1978, the opening of I-64 across Perry County in 1976, and the reconstruction of IND 37 into the city in 1980.

Continue on IND 66 to Rubens St. (two blocks beyond the second traffic light), turn left, and after one block turn right on 13th St. At 1239 13th St. is the **Old Stone House**. When the Swiss Colonization Society bought the land tract in 1857, this sandstone house was already on the property as indicated by its diagonal position in relation to the neighboring houses, which conform to the squared streets of the initial plat. The house remains on its elevated ground, while subsequent street improvements lowered the surrounding land. In the early days of Tell City the house was used as a meeting place and a school.

Continue south on 13th St., turn right at the first corner, and left at the next corner. Proceed two blocks to 12th and Tell sts., turn right, and after four blocks turn left on Main St. Continue to the **City Hall**, on the left between Jefferson and Mozart sts. The Swiss Colonization Society set aside five areas as city property, including the present City Hall block, which early on gained prominence as the hub of the city. In the early years the plank road from Cannelton to Troy cut through the grounds, and various establishments sprang up beside the road. The

businesses, subsequently, were forced off the city property and replaced by a market house, which eventually included an annex housing city offices and fire apparatus. In 1896 Tell City's education board requested a new schoolhouse be built on the square, but the board was apparently overruled in favor of a new city hall. Existing structures were dismantled. The city council offered the fence encircling the square to some needy family willing to carry it away. When no family stepped forward the fence was auctioned off for $8.70. The Rock Island stone foundation of the city hall was completed by the spring of 1896, and the brick superstructure, contracted to Fred U. Hugger of Tell City, was in place by fall. The estimated $50,000 spent for the large, three-story building represented a tidy sum for the community, though officials anticipated their headquarters to be a future county courthouse, an expectation that never materialized.

Located in front of City Hall is a **statue of William Tell and his son Walther**. It is a copy of the Tell statue near Lake Lucerne in Switzerland. The Swiss hero, Tell, was an expert archer, friend of liberty, and foe to Austrian oppressors. According to legend he was forced to shoot an apple off his young son's head when he refused to obey Herman Gessler, the Austrian bailiff. The legend is a distortion of actual events that took place in the 13th century. Tell City attorney Austin B. Corbin commissioned the statue. Donald B. Ingle, an Evansville artist, re-created the sculpture, which now rests on a foundation built for the Tell City National Bank to celebrate its 100th birthday. The long-awaited dedication of the Tell monument on August 9, 1974, almost did not take place. Less than two weeks before the ceremony the bronze casting had been completed at a Long Island, New York, foundry. Ingle, the sculptor, while driving the 500-lb., $25,000 artwork from New York to Tell City experienced mechanical problems with his rented van. He stayed overnight in Strongville, Ohio, where thieves made off with the van and its prized contents. Luckily, however, the statue was found a week later, safe in the van, in Cleveland. Ingle flew to Cleveland and drove the statue to its destination, entering Tell City behind a police car and fire truck escort. The dedication went off as scheduled.

On the east side of City Hall sit two **stone lions** sculpted by John C. Meyenberg, a Tell

City artist. Meyenberg, who lived in a chalet in southeast Tell City, was instrumental in the design or implementation of several city parks. He carved the lions for Depot Park, which he planned in 1907 for the riverfront at the south side of town. The lions guarded each end of the park for years before being moved to the front of the Tell City Municipal Swimming Pool, which opened in 1939. Next, the lions sat on the west side of City Hall prior to being transferred to their present place to make way for the Tell statue.

Continue two blocks south on Main St. to the **Tell City Pretzel Company**, bakers of a tradition in southern Indiana. Tell City has been known for its fine pretzels from the time Casper Gloor, a Swiss master baker, brought his skill to Tell City as a member of the Swiss Colonization Society. After his death in 1912, Alex Kessler, Gloor's assistant, ran the business. Jim Elder purchased the company in 1972. The hard, hand-twisted pretzels are still made from Gloor's secret formula, then glazed, salted, baked, and packaged for distribution around the country.

Near the pretzel bakery, on the northwest corner of Main and Humboldt sts., is the former home of **Schreiber's Drugstore**, Tell City's oldest retail establishment, now located in the Tell City Professional Building on IND 66, south of town. A drugstore, begun in Market Square in 1861, was bought by August Schreiber in 1866 and moved to its recently vacated location in 1876. Schreiber became the first mayor of Tell City after its incorporation in 1886. The city's first library was housed at Schreiber's from 1893 to 1905.

Take Humboldt St. west one block to 7th St. In the first block south at 417 7th St. is the main office of the **Tell City Chair Company**, established in 1865 as the Chair Makers Union of Tell City. The present name of the firm was adopted in 1924. Initially, the principal product was the common and sturdy split-bottom chair. In 1900 the management came into the hands of the partners and brothers-in-law Albert P. Fenn and Jacob Zoercher, whose descendants continue to direct the company. After 1906 three factories were in operation, and the line was expanded to include rockers and a variety of chair styles. It became known as one of the largest chair manufacturers in the world. Having purchased in 1953 the Tell City Desk Company (est. 1890), the firm began producing pieces of furniture besides chairs, and since then it has added decorative accessories. It remains one of the largest employers in the community.

On the northwest corner of the **William Tell Woodcrafters, Inc.**, building in the next block south of the Tell City Chair Company, note the marks indicating the levels reached by the 1883, 1884, 1907, 1913, and 1937 floods.

Return to Main St. and continue south. At Main and Blum sts. on the right is the **old depot of the Southern Railway**. The first depot, a frame building, was erected in 1899. J. C. Meyenberg developed Depot Park around this station after 1907. The park, largely situated along the riverbank, included Meyenberg's two stone lions, now resting on the City Hall lawn. The depot was destroyed by fire January 7, 1914, but the city council soon approved plans for the present brick structure, which was completed by the following winter. The tracks, originally west of the terminal, were moved to the east side when the flood wall went up in 1940. The Southern Railway vacated the depot in the early 1970s, and in 1978 the railroad company donated the building to the city. The city in turn signed a 20-year lease with Schweizer Fest, Inc. (Schweizer Fest is the name of Tell City's annual festival), to oversee the depot. A $23,500 federal grant, plus city and Schweizer Fest funds, paid for remodeling. The city's Chamber of Commerce utilizes the former general waiting room as its headquarters, and the other six rooms are designated for offices or meetings. Items pertaining to the history of Tell City and Perry County are displayed around the walls and in cases in the main lobby.

Beyond the depot *1.6 m.* is an unmarked outcropping of coal considered to be the **earliest site of coal extraction** west of the Appalachian Mountains. Just south of the depot go east on Guttenberg St. one block to 9th St. Follow 9th St. along the flood wall and, at the first opportunity, exit to the far side of the wall onto the old Cannelton-Tell City plank road. Continue south past the Maxon Marine yards. The road surface eventually changes to gravel. Bear left at the fork and observe to the east, on the far side of the railroad tracks, the ridge or small bluff from which the coal was taken in 1809. In that year, and two years before the history-making run of the *New Orleans*, Nicholas J. Roosevelt, in a crude flatboat, conducted a navigation survey of the Ohio and the lower

Mississippi rivers. On the voyage he spotted the coal outcropping and, understanding the potential for coal as a replacement for wood in the incipient steam engine, had bankside residents dig out a quantity and place it on the riverbank. Roosevelt picked up the coal two years later while steering the *New Orleans* on its initial trip down the Ohio River. At this time Roosevelt also purchased the 1,000 acres, including the coalfield, a portion of which subsequently would become the heart of Tell City. Soon after 1811 Roosevelt transferred the deed to Robert Fulton, but the inventor and his descendants failed to develop the mine.

From the Fulton Mine site continue *.2 m.*, turn right on IND 66, and proceed south *.1 m.* into **CANNELTON** (p. 2,373), or, from Tell City take IND 66 south to Cannelton, which is *.7 m.* from Tell City's southern limits. The county seat of Cannelton had its pre-corporate beginnings in the 1820s when several families drifted into the vicinity to farm and to mine coal. Not until 1837, however, when eastern capitalists led by James T. Hobart purchased a large tract at the site for mining purposes, did the settlement known as Coal Haven develop. In December 1837 Hobart and his associates formed the American Cannel Coal Company, Indiana's first coal company chartered by the state legislature. The firm purchased 6,456 mostly coal-bearing acres from its shareholders and others, and it commenced to build homes, factories, mills, and mines and to market its products to steamboats and river ports. The initial burst of activity was short-lived. A fire in 1839 practically wiped out the small community. The fire, coupled with some unsuccessful business ventures, drained the company of funds, and the village of inhabitants. When in 1840 only five families remained in Coal Haven, Francis Carlisle arrived, leased a mine, and gave the town a fresh start. Coal Haven was replatted in February 1841 and renamed Cannelsburg. The more popular name Cannelton was officially adopted in 1844. The brightly burning cannel coal, which gave the company and town their names, was rarely found. But enough other kinds of bituminous coal were found to attract to the locality new investors, including in 1847 the Cannelton Cotton Mill Company. More than 1,600 persons resided in Cannelton by 1851, and the following year the town incorporated. Emerging as the county's major metropolis, Cannelton

wrested the county seat from Rome in 1859. Through the ensuing years Cannelton's fortunes were tied largely to its big cotton mill. Cannelton has yet to fully recover from the mill's closing in 1954, along with the highway adjustments that detoured traffic from the business district. Today the town is optimistic once again because of the buildup of perimeter residences, the new job opportunities on the Kentucky side, the citizen enthusiasm to rehabilitate the old business section, and the potential for reuse of the giant empty mill that dominates the city's skyline.

Note the **sandstone houses** alongside IND 66 (7th St.) in north Cannelton. In the distance on the left the 156-ft.-high spire of **St. Michael's Roman Catholic Church** is clearly visible. Located one block east of IND 66 at Washington and 8th sts., St. Michael's is one of the most photographed local buildings. The church was constructed in 1858-59 for Cannelton's German Catholics. Situated on Cannelton Heights, the Gothic structure overlooks the city and surrounding areas, and its three-clock tower is a dependable timepiece once again after recent restoration.

Providing a more majestic vista is the road, variously called Cannelton Heights Rd., St. Michaels Rd., or just Hill Rd., which climbs from St. Michael's Church to the crest of the ridge east of the city. (Proceed *.2 m.* up this road and pull off to the right for the best view.) **Cliff cemetery**, established in 1854, is the first cemetery on the west side of the road at the top of the hill. About halfway down the northern side of the cemetery is the stone vault of **Hamilton Smith**, a leading industrialist in Cannelton from 1851 to 1873. Smith (1804-1875), an enlightened promoter of manufacturing in the new west, held the presidencies of the American Cannel Coal Company and the Indiana Cotton Mill.

Return to the intersection, cross IND 66, and proceed *.2 m.* to the **Cannelton Cotton Mill** on the right, at the southwest corner of 4th and Washington sts. (unmarked). Few structures of such size, age, condition, and historical influence still stand in Indiana. Built in 1849-50 for $80,000, the mill's backers, mostly New Englanders persuaded by Hamilton Smith's arguments, thought the venture would provide a healthy profit, pioneer in steam manufacturing, develop western industry, and create work for job-hungry Yankees. On land donated by the

American Cannel Coal Company, noted mill-builder Charles T. James of Rhode Island, along with engineer Alexander McGregor, supervised construction of the building, designed by Thomas A. Tefft. The four-story, sandstone structure contained 70,000 sq. ft. It required a soaring 200-ft.-tall smokestack (now gone) to catch the draft, which at lower elevations was cut off by the hills east of town. Two 100-ft.-tall towers flanked the entrance. The northern tower held the bell to summon the operatives, mostly young New England women serving two-year contracts. The building never experienced a fire thanks to built-in safety devices, such as wide staircases, lint removers, and water hoses in each room.

Success did not come overnight. Difficulties in attracting new investors and laborers, underestimates of coal supplies, work stoppages due to mechanical breakdowns, the cleaning of lime-encrusted boilers, and a strike, along with negative reports in New England and the South, a drought, and depressed markets, nearly wrecked the project. By 1853 the company had changed hands. Not until after the Civil War, when regional trade had stabilized, did the factory begin to show major earnings by selling cheap cotton sheeting. In 1899 a newspaper account noted that the "famous Hoosier Jeans" came from the Cannelton looms. Bemis Brothers Bag Company bought the property in 1946 and began making cotton feed bags. When cotton items lagged, the mills converted to producing rayon cloth, feed bags, towel, and beach set novelties. In 1954 the mill closed. The long-empty building was donated in 1982 by its owners, Hubert and Louise Bruce, to Historic Cannelton, Inc. (*NRHP/HAER*)

Across from the mill on the southeast corner of Washington and 3rd sts. (unmarked) is **St. Luke's Episcopal Church**, erected in 1845, the first house of worship in Cannelton. The Cannelton Coal Company provided the land for the building, and a group of easterners financed its construction and dedicated its use as a "union" church open to all congregations. For three years the Unitarians occupied the building. Other Christian groups had their initial services in the "Mother Church," including the Episcopalian body established in 1857. In 1897 the Episcopal congregation acquired full title to the property. The New England frame-style meetinghouse, with its square belfry, recently underwent extensive restoration through moneys furnished by a Lilly Endowment grant. (*NRHP*)

Next to St. Luke's on the east is the **Newcomb Place**, once the home of the owner of the Cannelton Cotton Mill. The Newcomb broth-

1955 view of Cannelton with the Cotton Mill in the background

Indiana State Library

ers, Dwight and Horatio, prominently served the cotton mill from its earliest days. Dwight, in his steamer, *California*, delivered the mill's first supplies of cotton. Horatio was company treasurer. The brothers acquired a lease to the firm in 1851, and they bought it outright in 1853 by assuming its $200,000 debt. Eventually the marketing of the mill's inexpensive sheeting and of the coal from leased mines to passing steamers brought the Newcombs great wealth. The Newcomb Place was Dwight Newcomb's home from 1882 to his death in 1893. Charles Mason, lawyer and newspaper owner, had built the house in 1868. It was purchased by the Cannelton schools in 1935. The home's old wraparound porch was removed in 1938. The house was remodeled in the early 1970s.

Return to 7th St. and turn south onto IND 66. The **Perry County Courthouse** stands east of IND 66, between Washington and Taylor sts. Since 1859, when Cannelton acquired the county seat from Rome and set up offices in a remodeled but too small schoolhouse, agitation for a new building or the transfer of the county seat to another town had not ceased. When in 1896 Tell City built its stately city hall, perhaps to influence the county commissioners to relocate the courthouse, Cannelton decided to build a new courthouse. Cannelton residents raised nearly $30,000, and they hired the Louisville firm of Curtin and Hutchings to design the structure. The Italian Renaissance courthouse, made of buff brick with Bedford limestone trimmings, was deeded to the county for one dollar on June 11, 1897. County officials accepted the offer, and Cannelton retained its county seat status.

On the southeastern outskirts of Cannelton, and off IND 66, is the **Bob Cummings Lincoln Trail Bridge** leading to Hawesville, Kentucky. The toll bridge, begun in 1964 and completed in 1966, was first named the Lincoln Trail Ohio River Bridge. Bob Cummings (1913-1971), editor of the *Cannelton News*, was the moving spirit behind the bridge's construction. A leader in Indiana newspaper circles, Cummings worked untiringly to inform the media and the public of the recreational and industrial potential of the Ohio River region. After his death, friends and associates successfully pushed to have the bridge renamed in Cummings's honor. At the November 17, 1974, rededication ceremony, a bronze likeness of the Cannelton newspaperman on its limestone standard was unveiled at the Indiana entrance to the bridge.

East of Cannelton *2 m.* is the **Overlook for the Cannelton Locks and Dam**. Built between 1963 and 1974 for $99.6 million, the new facility replaced three locks between Cannelton and Louisville. Continue east. The smoke stacks on the Kentucky side of the river belong to a huge paper mill, which grinds into pulp the wood residue from Tell City's furniture factories.

East *1 m.* from the overlook is **Lafayette Spring**, a small rest stop on the north side of IND 66. Here, it is believed, the Marquis de Lafayette, the famous French general and American ally in the Revolutionary War, went ashore May 9, 1825, after the steamboat *Mechanic*, plying upstream at night, struck a submerged ledge of an island and sank quickly. Rescuing few possessions, the passengers and crew safely reached the Indiana bank where they built campfires under the overhanging shelf at the spring. The stranded party was picked up the following morning by a passing craft. The property encompassing the small cliff and trickling spring originally belonged to the American Cannel Coal Company. The Lafayette Spring chapter of the Daughters of the American Revolution (DAR) paid a reported $100 to the Keating family for the four-acre site in 1934. Thinking the state highway department could better maintain the area, the DAR gave it to the state, which turned it into Roadside Rest Park No. 41. In 1957 the state complied with the local DAR chapter's request to return the historical landmark.

From Lafayette Spring drive *1.2 m.* east on IND 66 to IND 166. Follow the rough surfaced IND 166 southeast *1.6 m.* to Millstone Rd. on the left. Proceed on Millstone Rd. *.9 m.* to the **Air Crash Memorial** on the left. Here, on St. Patrick's Day, March 17, 1960, a Northwest Airlines Lockheed Electra turbojet plane, flying from Minneapolis to Miami, broke apart at 18,000 ft. and plummeted to earth killing all 63 persons aboard. Authorities eventually blamed the crash on engine structural faults, which created wing flutter that caused the wings to snap off. The plane literally buried itself on impact in George McIntire's soybean field. A blackened, smoking crater, 30 ft. wide and 20 ft. deep, lodged the remains of Flight 710. Victims' clothing hung from nearby tree limbs. It took two weeks to complete the recovery operation of Indiana's worst aerial tragedy up to that time. At Greenwood Cemetery in Tell City, a 1,800-sq.-ft. plot was set aside for 55 of the 63 victims, only 17 of whom could be positively identified. Northwest Airlines installed at the cemetery a tall obelisk, inscribed with the names of the dead, in August 1960. The Cannelton Kiwanis Club launched a fund campaign to erect a monument at the crash site. The Air Crash Memorial Monument, dedicated May 28, 1961, is 12 ft. wide and 9 ft. tall. The center granite shaft is topped by a "torch of life." Inscriptions include the victims' names, along with bas-relief religious symbols and an airliner, in addition to an engraved hope "that such tragedies will be eliminated."

Return to IND 66 and head east. The hilly blacktop road winds through *3.2 m.* of exceptional scenery before entering the Hoosier National Forest. Proceed into the forest *3.5 m.* to the north turnoff to the 250-acre **German Ridge Recreation Area**, which the Civilian Conservation Corps (CCC) constructed in 1939-40. On May 17, 1942, it was dedicated as the first Hoosier National Forest recreational facility. Ten such areas are in operation at present. Accommodations include a four-acre lake with swimming beach, campground and picnic units, and two trails.

From German Ridge proceed on IND 66 east *3.2 m.* to CR 216 and turn south *.8 m.* to the hamlet of **ROME**, the county seat from 1819 to 1859. Changes in county boundaries in 1818 brought the county seat to Rome from Troy. Rome was called Washington when laid out in 1818, designated Franklin the same year, and officially named Rome in 1819. Rome may have been named for the classical city, but others contend it took the name from Rome, New York, where, in 1817, construction began on the Erie Canal. The excitement engendered by canal building captured the imagination of inhabitants in potentially thriving waterway towns, including perhaps the citizens of the newly designated Perry County capital. The **Rome Courthouse**, still standing, was built between 1818 and 1822 and repaired several times. The square, two-story brick structure, crowned with a center cupola on a hip roof, rests on a high stone foundation. It could have been modeled after the state's capitol at Corydon or the old courthouse at Owensboro, Kentucky. Rome prospered as a river landing during the 40 years it functioned as the seat of government. Its decline, commencing with the

transfer of the county seat to Cannelton in 1859, was accelerated by its isolation from railroads and by dwindling river traffic. The old courthouse became the Rome Academy from 1860 to 1867, after which a series of private, denominational, and public schools occupied the building. The structure was remodeled in 1917 and again in the early 1930s. Since 1966, it has been used as a town hall and community center. (*NRHP*)

Back on IND 66, proceed north *3.7 m.* to the **Hines Raid Marker** on the left of the highway. On June 17, 1863, Capt. Thomas Henry Hines (1838-1898) took his company of 62 Confederate troops from Kentucky into Indiana. They disembarked at Robert's Landing near the present marker. Hines, who was heavily involved in subversive activities in the North before and after the raid, came into Indiana to contact Southern sympathizers and their Copperhead organizations. Hoosiers were not fooled by Hines's attempt to pass off his troops as a Union Army detachment looking for deserters. Home Guards maneuvered the perpetrators onto an Ohio River island above Leavenworth in Crawford County. Only Hines and a few others escaped capture or death. Hines subsequently accompanied John H. Morgan on his escapade through Indiana in July 1863. Both men were captured in Ohio and sent to the Columbus penitentiary, from which they escaped. In 1875 Hines began serving two terms as Chief Justice of the Kentucky Court of Appeals. On June 16, 1963, Perry County citizens gathered at the Rome Courthouse to relive the Hines Raid and dedicate the Hines marker.

From the Hines marker drive north *10.2 m.* to CR 36. Turn right and immediately right again to **MAGNET**. In the early 19th century a small settlement grew up around Dodson's Landing, Magnet's first name. In 1857 the community appears as the post office station Rono, supposedly the name of an aged dog in the locale. Magnet became the hamlet's third name in 1899, a change made by the post office. Though never platted, the town did considerable business in woodyards, meat packing, and general river trade. On August 21, 1865, the steamboat *Argosy III*, on its way to Cincinnati with a group of mustered-out Civil War veterans, ran into a storm near Rono. The storm hurled the boat against some rocks and caused its boiler to explode, scalding some of the passengers while others jumped into the river. Ten soldiers, on their way home after surviving years of savage warfare, drowned. Local farmers and survivors pulled the dead from the waters and buried them in a mass grave. Nine of the deceased were in the 70th Ohio Infantry Regiment; the 10th was in the 39th Indiana Infantry. The history of the accident and mass burial came to light in 1962. A row of **10 white stone markers**, supplied by the federal government, was placed near the grave site and dedicated August 22, 1965. Interestingly, the steamboat *Argosy III* was repaired and became a durable shipping vessel. To see the markers go *1.8 m.* from the IND 66 turnoff to Magnet and continue *.5 m.* to the markers, located on the right.

Return to IND 66 and continue north *10 m.* to the Perry-Crawford county line. **CRAWFORD COUNTY** (p. 9,820; 307 sq. m.), organized in 1818, was carved out of Harrison, Orange, and Perry counties. The county may have been named for Col. William Crawford (1732-1782), George Washington's land agent, Revolutionary War leader, and Indian fighter. In 1782 Crawford had led an expedition against Indians in Ohio. Coming on the heels of several foolish attacks by whites on peaceful Moravian Indian villages, Crawford faced a unified and outraged Indian front, which routed the white invaders. Crawford was captured by the Delawares, who burned him at the stake. Another possible county name source is the southerner William H. Crawford (1772-1834), a well-known public figure of that day. At the time of the county's establishment, Crawford was secretary of the treasury in the cabinet of President James Monroe. Having been named, the county encountered problems hewing out a viable economy on a heavily forested, hilly, cavernous, and thinly populated land. Forms of river commerce proved most expedient for success. When river traffic declined and railroads bypassed the river towns, employment became scarce. Crawford County has been described as the poorest real estate in Indiana. Industries are few in number, and the inevitable small farms often force owners to take second jobs. Prospects have improved, however. The 1970s witnessed a healthy 22 percent increase in population, and officials and organizations are aggressively seeking the tourist dollar. The county is rich in breathtaking scenery and recreational opportunities. Over half its total area is in timber, with almost 30,000 acres within state and national forests.

The terrain covers numerous caves, while the hills, some of which crest at 905 ft., offer frequent eye-opening vistas.

SULPHUR SPRINGS, *.1 m.* north of the county line, was one of several spas in Crawford County around the turn of the century that offered vacationers and clients the bitter-tasting but supposedly soothing and medicinal properties of its artesian well. During the Civil War, oil drillers had struck mineral water instead. Developers established the White Sulphur resort, which included a three-story hotel and annex. The water was bottled and shipped throughout the Midwest along with a boiled down, concentrated form called 16 to 1 White Sulphur Water.

Continue *1.5 m.* to IND 62 at **SULPHUR**. Head east *6.3 m.* to a south turnoff, indicated by a **FREDONIA** directional sign. Go south *.1 m.* to the first crossroad and turn right onto a blacktop road that runs *1.5 m.* to Fredonia. In the 19th century Crawford County had four successive county seats beginning in 1818 with Mount Sterling. Nothing remains today of this town, which was located about four miles southeast of the present town of English. Mount Sterling did not prosper because it lacked a water supply. A few buildings, but no courthouse, were erected. Allan D. Thom platted Fredonia on June 22, 1818. Situated at Oxbow Bend, the name given to the large horseshoe loop of the Ohio River, Fredonia had plentiful water, a potential docking area for river craft, and a marvelous view of the valley lands. Consequently, the county seat was moved to Fredonia in 1822. A two-story brick courthouse had already been built. Fredonia, meaning place of freedom, blossomed as a shipping center until it lost the county seat in 1843. Thereafter the Methodists used the courthouse as a church into the 1960s. A portion of the old building still can be seen right of the main street in Fredonia. Near the **remains of the old courthouse** is a cemetery which contains the grave of Allan D. Thom, who, it is said, never drank water and year-round wore an overcoat. A new marble headstone lists Thom's achievements. The **Fredonia Community Center** building, located just east of the main road as it enters the town, is a replica of the old courthouse.

Return to IND 62/66 and proceed east *1.5 m.* through new Leavenworth (p. 356), which sprang up in 1938, to its east limits, *1 m.* beyond which is a southerly turnoff to the old town below. The first Leavenworth, which snared the county seat from Fredonia, was founded by cousins Seth and Zebulon Leavenworth, who arrived in the vicinity in 1818. Their plat, filed July 14, 1819, located the town on a stretch of river bottomland below a 400-ft.-high bluff. Leavenworth blossomed as a busy river port, and the Leavenworth cousins, both of whom served in the state legislature, carried on much of the business activity and town promotion. They succeeded after repeated attempts to wrest the county seat from Fredonia in 1843, and it remained until 1894. Situated at the water's edge, Leavenworth was vulnerable to floods. Time after time, beginning in 1832, floodwaters inundated the site. The 1937 deluge, the worst flood in Leavenworth's water-soaked history, destroyed or damaged 111 homes and 21 businesses, leaving only 8 structures fit to live in. Faced with this degree of ruin, the townspeople voted to move to the crown of the bluff and to build a **new Leavenworth**. With the aid of the Red Cross and state and federal agencies, 78 of 113 families relocated to a town designed by Lawrence Sheridan and Merritt Harrison of the State Planning Board. IND 62, then called Wonderland Trail, was rerouted to run through the new Leavenworth. The model town, the first instance after the flood of a comprehensive community transfer, was dedicated December 15, 1938. Some resentments were created when families refused to leave their venerable but water-logged homes for the sterile, look-alike, and box-like modern cottages topside. But the future lay with the new Leavenworth. One of the attractions built into the transplanted town was an overlook on IND 62 *.6 m.* past the turnoff on the right. The Overlook Park offers a magnificent view of the river valley and the elongated horseshoe of the Ohio River.

From new Leavenworth proceed east on IND 62 *4.2 m.* to the **Wyandotte Caves** entrance road on the left. According to carbon-dated artifacts retrieved from Big Wyandotte cave, it sheltered human life almost 3,000 years ago. More recent tribes of Indians used the cave for shelter, food storage, calcite mining, flint or chert quarrying, and ceremonies. The Wyandottes may have roamed the area, but they neither lived here nor, as far as is known, used the cave. Reportedly, the first white man to enter the cave was F. I. Bentley, a fur trap-per, who in 1798 was guided by an Indian befriended by the frontiersman. William Henry Harrison, the future president, visited the cave in 1806, presumably to survey its mineral makeup. Potassium nitrate, or saltpeter, an ingredient in black gunpowder, was extracted from the cavern throughout the War of 1812 and up to 1817. In 1819 Henry P. Rothrock acquired 4,000 acres, which included the caves, and established a sawmill on the banks of the Blue River. Rothrock gave little thought to the caves until 1850 when the discovery of new passages in the cave, and the subsequent increase in curious visitors, alerted the owner to his property's commercial value. Rothrock put up a lodge in 1856, the same year that the Little Wyandotte, about 700 ft. south of Big Wyandotte, was discovered and explored. The 1941 disclosure of the Garden of Helictites is the latest find in the larger cave. The Little Wyandotte, closed for years because of wranglings over an estate settlement, reopened in 1947. The Rothrock family owned the caves until 1966 when the state bought the property and 1,174 acres of forest for $350,000. The purchase was added to the Harrison-Crawford State Forest, established in 1932. Indiana developed the Wyandotte Woods Recreation Area just south of the caves. In 1980 the Department of Natural Resources consolidated the caves, the Recreation Area, and the forest into the Harrison-Crawford Wyandotte Complex. Wyandotte caves feature some of America's largest subterranean rooms and mountains.

From the Wyandotte caves return through new Leavenworth to IND 66. Travel north for *11.4 m.* to **MARENGO** (p. 892), the site of another major Indiana cave. Located at the confluence of Whiskey Run and Brandywine Fork creeks, Marengo is the county's largest town. During the War of 1812, a blockhouse was erected on the site. A postal station named Tuckersville was established in 1824. Its name changed to Proctorsville in 1835, and it was platted in 1839. In 1852 the hamlet received the designation Marengo, honoring, probably, Napoleon's conquest of the Austrians in 1800 at Marengo, Italy. The Hoosier community grew slowly until the discovery of **Marengo Cave** generated a tourist trade. Schoolboys from the Marengo Academy found an opening September 9, 1883, and planned to explore it. A 15-year-old cook at the school, Blanche Hiestand, overheard the plans, and she and her younger brother reached the sinkhole first and discovered the cave. Farmer Samuel Stewart, who owned the property, opened the cave for tourists almost immediately. The Crystal Palace Room became the most popular attraction.

The Stewart family sold the property in 1955 to the Marengo Cave Company, and the Southern Indiana Recreation Company purchased it in 1973. A 200-ft. tunnel, blasted out in 1979, has been developed into the Dripstone Trail, a new tour that is different from the Crystal Palace Tour. Another cave section was uncovered in 1982. The 112-acre **Marengo Cave Park** above the cave offers horseback trail rides, picnic and camping areas, a swimming pool, nature trail, restaurants, and gift shops. To get to the cave, which celebrated its centennial in 1983, go through Marengo to IND 64 and turn right. The caves are *.3 m.* farther on the left.

Bordering the Marengo Cave parking lot is the **Old White Oak Tree**, one of Indiana's oldest and largest trees, standing 100 ft. tall with a circumference of 16 ft. The old **Springtown Cemetery** is situated near the white oak. Across from the cave's entrance is **Big Springs Old Town Church**, established in 1828. The present building was erected in 1858. Big Springs and Springtown were early unofficial names for Marengo.

Return west on IND 64 and proceed *7.6 m.* to IND 37. Take IND 37 south *.4 m.* to **ENGLISH** (p. 633), the Crawford County seat of justice. Platted in 1839 as Hartford, the name changed to English in 1856 in recognition of Congressman William H. English's efforts in obtaining a post office for the town. The town began to grow after the Air Line (Southern) Railroad came through in 1883. Incorporation came in 1884, and 10 years later English gained county seat status, fulfilling the public's desire to have its courthouse nearer the railroad. English's first courthouse, and the first ever to have been built with county funds, went up in 1895. The present modern brick and stone courthouse, designed by Lester Rauth of Vincennes, was erected in 1958-59 at a cost of $105,851. English's courthouses are unique in Indiana's history due to their location at the edge rather than in the center of the town. To reach the courthouse, drive through the business district, turn right on Church St. and left on Court Ave. to the southwest section of town. English made headlines in July 1979

when floodwaters nearly buried the town. Public attention focused on the local library, which lost almost all its contents. Through volunteer help and donations the county's only library was refurbished. The thrifty library board refused federal moneys to construct a new building for fear taxes would be increased eventually for library maintenance, a luxury unaffordable in the poor county. The library is situated on the northwest corner of 5th and Main sts.

After returning to the business district, go left on 5th St. three blocks to Spears St. and left *.2 m.* to the **statue of William H. English** on the right. The bronze artwork was designed by John H. Mahoney of Indianapolis and cast by the American Bronze Company of Chicago. Heirs of English paid the $3,000 for the sculpture, which was dedicated in 1900 on ground granted by the town for this purpose. The figure is supposed to represent the congressman at age 60.

Back on IND 64, drive west *9.6 m.* to IND 145, which connects with the principal entrances and through roads of **Patoka Lake**, a 25,583-acre multipurpose attraction that extends into three counties. Dedicated in 1980, the $65 million federal and state installation, built by the Army Corps of Engineers, is the largest public works project in Indiana's history. It provides a supply of water, a means of flood control, and facilities for recreation. The Army Corps, beginning in 1971, purchased 455 parcels of land including some 50 pieces taken from resisting property owners. A 1,550-ft.-long dam, which created Patoka Lake, is near Ellsworth in Dubois County. The lake itself, Indiana's second largest, takes up 8,880 acres. Four designated state recreation areas cover 8,769 acres, and 7,934 acres are devoted to wildlife lands. The Interpretive Center in the Newton Stewart Recreation Area is a large passive solar-heated building, designed to demonstrate the utility of the sun's energy.

From IND 64 and IND 145 north, proceed west *3.4 m.* to the **DUBOIS COUNTY** (p. 34,238; 429 sq. m.) line. Indiana organized its 21st county in 1817 by detaching a portion of Pike County, but between 1818 and 1820 Dubois County gave up land to Perry and Martin counties. The county was named for Toussaint Dubois, a wealthy merchant and trader of Vincennes, who, in 1807, recorded the first land in the area of the future county. Dubois, subsequently, served as captain of the Company of

Spies and Guides in the Tippecanoe campaign of 1811. He drowned in 1816. Fred T. Dubois, one of Toussaint's grandchildren, served as a delegate to Congress from the Territory of Idaho, 1887-90, and as a United States senator from Idaho, 1891-97 and 1901-7. The west half of the county is relatively flat in contrast to the hills and woods in the east. The Patoka and White rivers are the county's two major waterways. The economic backbone of the area is the lumber industry and the processing of wood products, notably furniture.

West of the county line *.5 m.*, on IND 64, is the community of **BIRDSEYE** (p. 533). One of the county's postmasters was the Rev. Benjamin Talbott Goodman, a well-known southern Indiana clergyman and state legislator, whose nickname was Bird. In 1856 when the residents of the nameless crossroads hamlet here desired a post office they sought his support. After looking over the location, Goodman is supposed to have said, "It suits Bird's eye to a T-y-tee." In gratitude for the preacher's aid, the new postal station was called Birdseye. The town incorporated in 1883, shortly after the Southern Railway cut through. With transport facilities, the local lumber business boomed, and Birdseye sorghum reached a wider market. In 1902-3 oil was discovered in the vicinity. Dozens of companies rushed in to lease land and put down wells. Headlines in the *Evansville Courier* proclaimed that "Birdseye May Become Oil Center of the U.S." Some opposed the drilling, because "Gawd had put that ile there to burn up the world," and they were not going "agin Providence." The oil supply soon dried up. The roaring trade subsided. The old brick stores that line IND 145 south from downtown Birdseye recall the atmosphere of those prosperous days. Just past the railroad tracks on IND 145 turn west and see the antique one-room **stone jail** on the left.

Continue on IND 64 west *10.4 m.* to IND 162. Head north *5.2 m.* to **JASPER** (p. 9,097), the county seat. The path of settlement in Dubois County followed the Buffalo Trace along the county's northern border. Portersville, in the northwest corner, was designated in 1818 as the first county seat. In the county's midsection, on the north side of the Patoka River and across from Benjamin Enlow's mill, a small village arose in the 1820s. Called Jasper, a Biblical reference to a highly valued quartz-like mineral, the community was laid out in 1830

and obtained the county seat the same year. Jasper's proximity to a mill, to a good water route, and to the only fordable spot on the river, naturally attracted homeseekers. A post town of 60 persons in 1833, Jasper greatly expanded when more than 100 German families moved to the vicinity between 1836 and 1841. The surrounding large oak timber stands supplied the raw materials for the German farmer, skilled worker, and tradesman to launch furniture-making operations. Jasper's manufacturers eventually specialized in wood office equipment, and the city prides itself on being recognized as the nation's wood office furniture capital. The majority of Jasper's manufacturers, most locally owned, produce wood products. In 1949 Jasper became the first city in the nation to eliminate garbage collection by requiring that a sink disposer be installed in every home. Today's downtown beautification projects and recently enacted ordinances against noise pollution reflect officials' intentions to maintain a clean and comfortable community. Jasper's self-esteem, moreover, is rooted in its European heritage. The German contribution is becoming more widely known and appreciated through its study by professionals and in the schools, and because of the organization, lately, of the Jasper Deutscherverein (German Club), becoming a Sister City to Pfaffenweiler, Germany, in 1984, and the establishment of an annual Strassenfest (street festival).

The **Dubois County Courthouse**, on the public square, was built in 1909-10. The four-story, tan brick structure, with identical porches on all sides, was the third courthouse erected on the square. Fire destroyed the first log courthouse, along with county records, in 1839. The second courthouse, built of brick, was completed in 1845. The present headquarters was designed by Milburn, Heister and Company of Washington, D.C.

On the east side of the courthouse stands the **Dubois County Soldiers' and Sailors' Monument**, dedicated in 1894 by Indiana's "farmer" governor Claude Matthews. A Monument Association composed of Civil War veterans spearheaded the drive for the memorial. Michael F. Durlauf, a prominent Jasper musician, band organizer, and architect, designed the 32-ft.-high bronze and stone memento, crowned by a 6-ft.-tall soldier at parade rest. For many years Durlauf operated the Jasper Monumental

Works. Within the iron fence encircling the monument are artillery pieces, the 1976 Jasper Bicentennial Time Capsule, and a plaque denoting the first courthouse site.

Northeast of the square, on the Gambles Store's rear wall, near 7th and Jackson sts., is a **new mural** depicting aspects of Jasper's history. Financing was by the Indiana Arts Commission and the National Endowment for the Arts, which granted funds to the Jasper Chamber of Commerce and its Strassenfest Committee. Artists David Blodgett and Linda Crimson, a South Bend husband-wife team, rendered scenes of St. Joseph Catholic Church and its early pastors, the area's agricultural and industrial past, and the Labor Day parade of boxes. The origin of the latter activity, perhaps unique, is unknown, but it could have commenced anytime after 1894, the year Labor Day was officially recognized. In the evening on this annual holiday, young children march about pulling or pushing boxes of all descriptions, some shaped like boats, some illuminated with candles. Trophies and ribbons are awarded to entries in various categories.

Two blocks north of the square on the north side of E. 8th St. between Newton and Main sts. is the **Dubois County Jail and Sheriff's Residence**. The stone-veneered-front sheriff's house was built in 1954 to replace a residence erected in 1890. The sandstone jail, at the rear of the sheriff's home, went up in 1893. John Gramelspacher, the county auditor at the time, designed and supervised the construction of the fortress-like jailhouse.

Drive north on Newton St. and turn east onto 11th St. The **Gramelspacher-Gutzweiler house**, located on the north side of 11th St., between Newton and Main sts., is Jasper's oldest extant building. When built in 1849 for Joseph and Sophia Gramelspacher, the city's first two-story brick structure stood at the corner of 7th and Main sts. Over the years it housed a variety of businesses including a general store, post office, hotel, toy shop, saloon, liquor store, nursing home, shoe repair shop, barbershop, real estate office, and apartments. Michael F. Durlauf, Jasper's musician-architect, added the stone-arched front window in the late 19th century. Historic Jasper, Inc., became the building's overseer in 1977. In 1980 its new owner, the German American Bank, wanting space for expansion, offered the Gramelspacher house to Historic Jasper, Inc., with

the stipulation that it be removed. Arnold F. Habig, a local industrialist, donated a lot on 11th St., and the local historical society raised thousands of dollars for the expensive transfer. In November 1980 the 500-ton building was moved, without incident, the four blocks north to its new foundation. (*NRHP*)

Directly east of the Gramelspacher house is the **Jasper Public Library** at 1116 Main St. The library was completed in 1952 according to plans drawn up by Warweg and Hagel of Evansville. Memorial Park, dedicated on Armistice Day, 1929, was the setting for the new library. On the front lawn of the library stands the **Freedom Lamp** erected in 1952 by the Jasper Jaycees. During the Korean War Jaycee chapters throughout the nation put up these perpetually lighted reminders of America's fundamental ideal. It is said that the notion of the Freedom Lamp originated in Winchester, Indiana. Jasper's monument was particularly meaningful because one of its own, Father Robert Greene, a Maryknoll missionary, only three months before had been released from a Communist Chinese prison after 18 months of confinement and torture. Father Greene had finally been given a mock trial and sentenced to a beheading, a fate subsequently reduced to expulsion. He was on hand, August 10, 1952, to dedicate the Freedom Lamp, a 5 1/2-ft.-high Bedford limestone shaft which was fashioned in the Schum Monument Company of Dale, Indiana. The metal lamp, made in Winchester, held a flame procured from a similar monument in Evansville, flown to Huntingburg, and carried to Jasper by runners.

On Newton St., between 11th and 13th sts., is **St. Joseph's Church**, one of the oldest and largest Catholic churches in the state. The first Mass in Jasper was offered in 1834, and a log church was constructed in 1836. Led by the Rev. Joseph Kundek, who arrived in 1838, Jasper's Catholics purchased 22 acres north of the settlement and erected a brick church in 1840-41. The present building, minus the bell and clock tower, was put up between 1867 and 1880 at a cost of $80,000. The brown sandstone Romanesque structure has walls 4 ft. to 6 ft. thick, and a 10-ft. deep foundation. The church is 193 ft. long and 82 ft. wide. The landmark tower, which Michael Durlauf helped design and build in 1904, ascends 235 ft., and it supports four bells with a combined weight of 12,650 lbs. The 1,200-seat sanctuary features carved oak pews, Italian marble altars, Swiss stained glass, and Austrian mosaics. The main altar, made of red oak, was donated by Kimball International in 1980. The 14 columns, trunks of poplar trees sheathed in stone, support a series of green arches that make up the 92-ft.-high ceiling. (*NRHP*)

On the southeast grounds is the **Plaza of the Pastors**, a semicircular landscaped walkway bordering the statues of three early leaders of the parish: Father Joseph Kundek, Father Basil Heusler, and Father Fidelis Maute. Each figure, created in Georgia marble by Elmer H. Daniels, is 14 ft. high. The plaza was dedicated July 19, 1944.

At the south entrance to the church grounds stands the **Deliverance Cross**, erected in 1848 by a grateful George Bauman, who, along with other German immigrants, was delivered from a raging ocean storm during his voyage to the United States. Lightning destroyed the cross in 1928, but it was replaced in 1932.

From St. Joseph's Church continue north on Newton St. to 15th St. and drive east eight blocks to Royal St. Follow Royal St. north one block on the right to the headquarters of **Kimball International, Inc.**, Jasper's largest employer, and a leader in the manufacture of pianos, organs, and office and home furniture. In 1950 Arnold F. Habig, along with representatives of the Sermersheim, Thyen, and Schneider families of Jasper, purchased a small furniture factory and established the Jasper Corporation. The firm initially made television cabinets, and it profited from the rapid growth of this medium. A major expansion of the corporation occurred in 1959 when it acquired the century-old W. W. Kimball Company of Melrose Park, Illinois. The moribund piano firm was revitalized by its new owners, who, in 1966, also purchased the acclaimed Bosendorfer Piano Company of Vienna, Austria. A few years later the company began manufacturing Victorian period reproduction furniture, which, added to its office furniture specialty, greatly enlarged its product line. Recognizing its worldwide market, Jasper Corporation changed its name to Kimball International, Inc., in 1974. In 1984 Kimball supplied 100 grand pianos, made at its French Lick, Indiana, plant, to accompany a choir during the torchlighting ceremony in the Los Angeles Summer Olympics. Today, the family-owned company has factories in eight states and in Mexico, Austria, and England. The Gen-

eral Office complex on Royal St. was constructed in 1975. All of the furnishings in the offices were drawn from various company divisions. In the spacious lobby note particularly the huge wall murals and the simulated wood carvings in the polyurethane ceiling tiles.

Return to the courthouse square and drive east on 6th St. five blocks to the **Jasper Desk Company**, the oldest continuously operating office furniture manufacturer in the United States. The company's forerunner dates from the mid-1860s when Jacob, John, and Joseph Alles, German cabinetmakers, began manufacturing furniture in a frame building located at the northwest corner of the public square (a marker attached to a wall on the north side of W. 6th St., just off the square, denotes the site of the Alles factory). In 1876 the Alleses sold their building to Sabastian Kuebler, John Gramelspacher, and Frank Joseph, who formed the Jasper Furniture Company, although the Alleses retained stock in the new firm. The demand became so great for the rolltop desks and other types of office furniture that the company discontinued making household furniture and concentrated on office items. Shortly after its founding, the business relocated to its present site and in 1921 took the name Jasper Desk Company.

From the Jasper Desk Company, return to Jackson St. (one block east of the courthouse) and drive south, bearing left onto 3rd St. (IND 164). After crossing the Patoka River turn west immediately onto Cemetery Rd. Just off Cemetery Rd., beside the river, is a small park in which a marker denotes the **site of Enlow Mill**, which Benjamin Enlow built around 1820. The property was sold in 1847 to J. A. Graham and William C. Graham, who turned it over to Francis X. Eckert a few years later. Known as the City Mill of Jasper, or Eckert's Mill, the facility operated until the 1930s. It served as a furniture company's warehouse until it was deeded to the Dubois County Historical Society in 1963. The society, in turn, gave the building and land to the city for park and recreational purposes. Floodwaters in 1964 so weakened the historical mill that it had to be razed.

From the mill go west on 3rd St. to Clay St. and one block south to 2nd St. West of the intersection of Clay and 2nd sts., one block (400 W. 2nd St.), stands the **Gateway to the Heart sculpture** in memory of Jasper's William

Schroeder, the world's second recipient of an artificial heart. At age 52, the retired army civilian employee received the Jarvik-7 pump on November 25, 1984, at Humana Hospital-Audubon in Louisville. Schroeder survived 620 days, providing inspiration to other heart patients and much needed information for artificial heart research before his death on August 6, 1986. The 13-ft.-tall memorial, sculpted by local artist Bernard Hagedorn, is located at the Bill Schroeder Sports Complex behind Alumni Stadium. The memorial was dedicated November 13, 1988.

Return to the courthouse square and head west on 6th St. (US 231 and IND 45/56). South of Jasper on US 231 *1.3 m.* is the **Indiana Baseball Hall of Fame** exhibited in a wing of the Holiday Inn on the left. In the summer of 1977 the Indiana High School Baseball Coaches Association selected Jasper as the Hall of Fame's permanent home. Coach Don Noblitt of Jasper High School offered to locate it in his city, and the Holiday Inn provided space in its lobby and entrance hall. The memorial to illustrious Hoosier professional and amateur ball players officially opened July 20, 1979, with 16 inductees and a visit by Mickey Mantle, the former great of the New York Yankees. The display includes plaques of the inductees, pictures of state high school championship teams, and collections of baseball memorabilia.

Continue south on US 231 *3.2 m.* to **HUNTINGBURG** (p. 5,376), which, like its neighbor Jasper, is a furniture manufacturing center. Jacob Geiger, of Jefferson County, Kentucky, purchased 1,920 acres of government land at the Huntingburg site in 1837. He had grown fond of the area as a result of successful hunting expeditions, and from favorable remarks made by his father, Capt. Frederick Geiger, who fought with the Kentucky Mountain Riflemen at the Battle of Tippecanoe. Geiger platted the town in 1837. Because of his enjoyment in stalking bears and pigeons in the vicinity, he called the townsite Huntingburgh (the post office officially dropped the final "h" in 1893). A major inducement for community growth was Geiger's construction of the county's first year-round steam gristmill in 1841. The large number of brick structures in Huntingburg recall the days when brickyards vied with tobacco as the city's economic backbone. The fine quality clay in the surrounding hills was used by Evansville's Uhl Pottery be-

ginning in the mid-19th century. In 1908 the plant moved to Huntingburg. The main office followed in 1932, while Evansville retained a retail store and a warehouse. In 1937 Uhl Pottery was producing 900 different articles of utilitarian ware and novelties. The plant closed in 1944 after a long strike. Among the interesting firms in Huntingburg today is Ahrens Strawberry Farm and Plant Nursery, IND 64 west, which ships nursery stock throughout the United States. Ahrens specializes in strawberries but sells other fruit and vegetable stock as well.

Jacob and Elizabeth Geiger's brick home, built in 1854-55, is located at 511 Geiger St., on the southeast corner of IND 64 (6th St.) and Geiger St., one block west of US 231 (Main St.). Two blocks south of the Geiger house is the former **Huntingburg Town Hall and Fire Engine House**, 311 Geiger St. When built in 1885-86, the Italianate-style building cost $13,600. Henry Mursinna, the noted Evansville architect, designed it. The rectangular structure has 14-in.-thick brick walls, and it features unusually elongated second-floor windows. The brackets under the eaves are made of tin. Huntingburg's first fire company, organized in 1887, shared space with city government offices and a variety of retail stores. Community events and entertainments took place on the upper level, and for 30 years the hall functioned as a youth center. The city discontinued its occupancy in 1971. Restoration began in 1976 with federal funds earmarked to transform the hall into a senior citizens center. The original cupola, removed around 1953, has been reproduced and stationed. The old bell, hung in 1891, was retrieved from a Catholic church in Dale, Indiana, and installed in the tower, which also boasts a new clock. (*NRHP*)

Return to Main St. (US 231) by taking Geiger St. to 3rd St. and proceed *1.2 m.* to the south edge of Huntingburg, where, on the right side of the highway, is located **Fairmount Cemetery**. The Geiger family members are buried here as is Jesse K. Stork, an Evansville native who grew up in the Dubois County town of Holland and was the first American soldier killed in the Spanish-American War. Stork's Troop "A" of the First United States Cavalry, attached to Teddy Roosevelt's Rough Riders, was marching toward Santiago, Cuba, when attacked, June 28, 1898. The 23-year-old Stork was the only American soldier killed in the first engagement of the war. The yard-long limestone marker, resting in the middle section of the cemetery, was placed on Stork's grave in 1909.

Near the flagpole at the east entrance to Southridge High School, just below the cemetery and right on Sunset Dr., is the **Eli Thomas marker**. In 1818 the Thomas family, friends of the Lincolns, made the first land entry in the township and built one of the first brick homes in Dubois County. According to tradition, Thomas built a gristmill near Duff, Indiana, with the help of Abe Lincoln and his father. The Thomas house, in unrestorable condition, was torn down in the early 1970s to make way for the new high school. The 5-ft.-high granite stone was dedicated by the Dubois County Historical Society on September 19, 1976.

Return to IND 64, turn right, and proceed east *4.7 m.* to IND 162. Turn right and proceed south *4.7 m.* to **FERDINAND** (p. 2,192), founded in 1840. The German Catholic community was established by the Rev. Joseph Kundek, who initiated church affairs over a wide area of southwest Indiana. After seeing to the formation of St. Joseph's Church in Jasper in 1838, Father Kundek set about planting and nurturing Catholicism by colonizing his forested territory. In 1839 he purchased 1,360 acres in the region of present Ferdinand Township. He laid out the town in 1840 to be one of several way stations for Catholics traversing the rugged Troy-Jasper road. Ferdinand was named for the Austrian Emperor, a patron of the Leopoldine Society, which supported missionary work in North America. As a result of Father Kundek's far-flung publicizing, Ferdinand gradually filled with Catholic families who prospered on the land, in woodworking industries, and in kindred trades. In 1905 Ferdinand incorporated as a town, and by 1909 it had rail linkage to Huntingburg. The shortline "Ferdy Flyer" traveled the 7.4 miles to Huntingburg carrying F. Kitten foundry steam engines, wheat, wood, mail, students, and commuters. Now operating as a freight train, it hauls wood, wood products, and furniture, which remain the area's dominant manufacturing interests. Occasionally, the Ferdinand train was called the "Wooden Shoe Local" in reference to the footwear, made of birch and poplar, often donned by Ferdinand's citizens. The wooden shoe carver maintained an essential position in the town well into this century. On the side

of progress, Albert F. Sondermann, a local businessman, developed and patented a self-computing gasoline dispensing unit in 1917, a gas-pump feature taken for granted today. In the course of Ferdinand's growth persons took up dwellings outside the original town boundaries. In the 1970s these adjacent properties were annexed, and Ferdinand's population ballooned more than 50 percent overnight.

Just before entering Ferdinand is the east turnoff onto IND 264 (23rd St.), which leads *5 m.* to the **Ferdinand State Forest**. The Ferdinand Fish and Game Club, desiring to preserve wildlife and timber near its usual hunting grounds, persuaded the Indiana Department of Conservation to make a survey of the forest in 1933. By early 1934 some 1,000 acres had been donated by owners or purchased to form the initial area. Workers from a CCC camp planted trees, scooped out a lake, and constructed hatchery ponds, roadways, and various buildings. A lakeside beach was dedicated on Memorial Day, 1961. The state forest now comprises 7,650 acres. It has facilities for hiking, picnicking, fishing, camping, boating, and swimming.

Overlooking Ferdinand is the massive domed church of the **Convent of the Immaculate Conception**, home of the Benedictine Sisters. To reach the convent, turn left on 10th St., then left again on Alabama to the visitors parking area. Four nuns of the ancient Benedictine Order arrived in Ferdinand on August 20, 1867, to take over a three-room cottage relinquished by the Sisters of Providence. A two-story brick convent and chapel were completed in 1870. A new quadrangular convent was constructed in 1883-87 on Mount Thabor, a hill east of town. The expanding community soon required larger facilities, and in 1915 ground was broken for the present church. St. Louis architect Victor Klutho designed the Romanesque-style structure, which embodies a side dome similar to that of the new St. Louis Cathedral. The brick-faced building has Bedford limestone and Italian terra-cotta trim. Encircling the church are promenades set off by ornamented Italian pagodas. The interior dome is 87 ft. above the floor. The numerous stained-glass windows, installed in the 1930s, were designed by Father Bede Maler of St. Meinrad and crafted by the Frei Art Glass Studios of Munich-St. Louis.

Another landmark in Ferdinand is the tall spire of **St. Ferdinand's Church**, situated below the convent, on the southeast corner of Maryland and Kundek sts. one block east of IND 162 (Main St.). The church, built in 1845-48, is Ferdinand's oldest extant structure. The church is particularly known for its having a set of paintings by the Swiss-born artist Melchior Paul von Deschwanden (1811-1881). The three paintings, all of religious themes, came from Germany in 1858.

Back on Main St., head south on IND 162 for *3.3 m.* to IND 62 in Spencer County; then go *3.3 m.* east to **ST. MEINRAD**. In shaping an environment conducive to Catholic settlement, Father Kundek recognized the need for a stable supply of priests. This meant having a seminary nearby. He turned to the Benedictines at Our Lady of Einsiedeln monastery in Switzerland. Accepting the mission, the Benedictines arrived in Indiana in 1853. Others followed, and for a year the pioneer clergy worked throughout the diocese. In 1853 the band purchased a 160-acre farm alongside the Anderson River, six miles south of Ferdinand. The new owners crowned an old two-room cabin with a cross, and they called the crude lodging **St. Meinrad**, after a Swiss Benedictine hermit murdered in 861. Einsiedeln monastery arose at the martyr's hermitage in 934. Black ravens that, by pursuit and noise, abetted the capture of their benefactor's killers, became the identifying logo of Einsiedeln and St. Meinrad monasteries. After 1854 the Indiana priests put up frame buildings to house the monks and to use for school and worship. The town of St. Meinrad was established in 1861 as a source of income from the selling of lots and as a new home for Catholic emigrants. The monastery became an independent abbey in 1870. The stone monastery, erected in 1872-74, burned in 1887. Its stone walls survived, however, and soon enclosed a new interior. The abbey church, a local landmark with its two 168-ft.-high spires, went up in 1899-1907. St. Meinrad was rewarded for its excellence by being designated an archabbey in 1953, one of two Benedictine archabbeys in America, and one of nine on the globe. The most recent major change occurred in 1982 with the completion of a new monastery and library. St. Meinrad monks' primary vocation is the operation of the seminary, which comprises a college and theological school. Its nearly 250 enrollees make it one of the largest Catholic seminaries in the western hemisphere. Many interesting buildings and artworks grace the 2,500-acre grounds, in addition to a popular gift and sausage shop. Helping to support the monastery and its schools is the Abbey Press, a multimillion dollar mail-order gift company operated by the monks. Go through town on IND 62 and turn south at the archabbey sign on the right. The Visitors' Information Center is in the Guest House Office.

Continue east on IND 62 *.4 m.* past IND 545 to the left turnoff for the **Shrine of Our Lady of Monte Cassino**. The hill, on top of which the shrine is located, was named in 1855 for Monte Cassino, a Benedictine monastery in Italy. In May 1866 a frame chapel was constructed at the spot. A formal pilgrimage to the shrine ensued, and contributions followed for the purpose of erecting a more worthy shrine. The foundation stone for the present building was laid in 1868. Nearby sandstone quarries supplied the materials, and the monks mostly completed their work by 1870, two years before the first stone monastery went up at St. Meinrad. The stone pulpit, on the front lawn, was installed in 1952.

Return to St. Meinrad and go *4.4 m.* south on IND 545 to **FULDA**, laid out in 1845 on behalf of Milton Jackson, who, along with family and kin, had settled in the vicinity in 1829. When Jackson requested suggestions for a town name, the German surveyors proposed their old world hometown of Fulda, which was accepted for the new plat. Jackson advertised his town and thus attracted an influx of German families. Father Kundek of Jasper began visiting Fulda in 1847. He built a log church, and Fulda, like Ferdinand, became a stopping place for the migrant. The construction of **St. Bonifacius Kirche** (St. Boniface Church on the left by CR 1550N) began in 1860 on land donated by Jackson. The Civil War halted construction, however, and the building was not completed or dedicated until 1866. The church sits on 7-ft.-thick sandstone slabs. Its steeple is 150 ft. above the ground. The Romanesque-style interior features 16 stained-glass windows, walnut and poplar altars, and a 535-pipe organ built in 1895. (*NRHP*)

Continue south on IND 545 *3.1 m.* and turn left for *3 m.* to the **Huffman Mill Covered Bridge** (the road becomes CR 1360E and later CR 1475E). The site of Huffman Mill was settled by George Huffman shortly after the War of 1812. At an early date Huffman erected his brick home, which stands today on the right near the bridge entrance. The Huffmans built a succession of grist and sawmills. It is said the Lincoln family did business at the mills—Abe having logs cut for his flatboats, and Thomas bartering a jug of whiskey for a day's millwork. W. T. Washer erected the covered bridge in 1864. The one-span, burr truss bridge is 15 1/2 ft. wide, 11 1/2 ft. high, and 156 ft. long, including the overhangs. Spencer and Perry counties share responsibility for the bridge because it crosses the Anderson River, the county line. The co-ownership, at times, has made for disagreements on its upkeep. In one instance, years ago, the traveler could have witnessed the strange sight of exactly half the bridge freshly painted, with the remaining half left unpainted.

Return to Fulda and at the north edge take CR 1175E left *.2 m.* before heading west on CR 1600N (unmarked on the left) for *4.2 m.* This hilly, rough, but scenic gravel country road goes directly to the intersection of IND 162 and 245 at **SANTA CLAUS** (p. 514). Travel west (straight) on IND 162 at the intersection.

The magical name of Santa Claus is identified not only with the red-suited patron saint of children, but also with a small village in Indiana of the same name. Here in the late 1920s the postmaster began replying to children's Christmas letters and to answer requests for the town's unusual postmark. The courtesy evolved into a massive postal undertaking involving the annual transit of millions of pieces of mail. The publicity on America's only town named Santa Claus led eventually to the development of a large amusement park. Santa Claus received its town incorporation papers in 1967, 115 years after a tiny group of settlers met Christmas Eve and designated Santa Claus as a fitting name for their hamlet. The Santa Claus post office was officially established in 1856. Despite its enchanting name, Santa Claus lured few permanent dwellers. When incorporated in 1967, it had only 31 residents, making it the county's smallest town. On the other hand, it covered 2,358 acres, making it the largest town in land area. This measure of land reflected previous efforts to transform Santa Claus and vicinity into a tourist mecca. A theme park, claimed as the nation's first, came in the mid-1930s when Milton Harris built medieval-looking buildings to house his "toy town." Others followed, including Curtis Candy Company, which used a castle design for its outlet. Next established was a roadside park overlooked by a giant stone Santa. The major thrust came when Evansville industrialist Louis J. Koch along with son William opened in 1946 **Santa Claus Land** nearby (renamed **Holiday World** in 1980), replete with toy land, restaurants, gift shop, dollhouse, and toy museum. The additions of rides, musicals, live shows, displays, and other improvements have helped make the 45-acre Santa Claus Land a major southern Indiana attraction. On the strength of this progress, along with the creation of several residential-recreational parcels, plus an industrial park, Santa Claus's population soared in the 1970s. The famous post office is located in its stone castle-like headquarters, built in 1957, on IND 162 just outside the park's entrance.

Continue west *5 m.* on IND 162 (the Lincoln Heritage Trail) to the entrances of the **Lincoln Boyhood National Memorial** (north) (*NRHP*) and of the **Lincoln State Park** (south). The 196-acre Lincoln memorial complex encompasses the U-shaped Memorial Building that houses the visitor's center, auditoriums, and a museum, plus the grave site of Nancy Hanks Lincoln, Abe's mother, and the Lincoln Cabin Site and Living Historical Farm. America's 16th president lived here a fourth of his life, from age 7 to age 21 (1816-30). His mother died of milk sickness in 1818, and she was buried on a wooded knoll south of the Lincoln cabin. Following the family's removal to Illinois in 1830, the 100-acre farm passed through five owners before 1871, when James Gentry sold it to four Cincinnati men, who laid out Kercheval, renamed Lincoln City. Public attention first focused on preserving and marking Nancy Lincoln's grave. The failure to maintain the grave site influenced the legislature in 1907 to create a board of commissioners of the Nancy Hanks Lincoln Burial Grounds. The organization fenced in 16 acres encircling the grave, built a new driveway, and secured the property with an iron gate flanked by sandstone lions. The area took on more the character of a memorial park with these improvements and the subsequent increase in visitors. The work on Nancy Lincoln's grave stimulated interest in designating the site of the Lincoln cabin, removed in the late 19th century. Its hearthstones were found on the playground of the Lincoln City school, and a marker was put up in 1917. The development of a large-scale memorial to Lincoln got under way in 1926 when Gov. Edward Jackson formed a group of 125 civic leaders into the Indiana Lincoln Union. The union invited Frederick Law Olmsted, the eminent landscape architect, and

Thomas Hibben, a former Hoosier architect, to submit plans for a Lincoln memorial. From this point to the opening of the Memorial Building in 1943 the area was virtually transformed. The state purchased hundreds of acres and set out thousands of trees and shrubs. Lincoln City was practically dismantled to make way for renovations around the Lincoln cabin site. The separation of the Lincoln State Memorial and Lincoln State Park took place in 1932. In 1935 the site of the Lincoln cabin was marked with an outline of bronze logs and hearth and surrounded with a stone wall. The Lincoln Boyhood National Memorial became the new name for the complex in 1962 at the time the state relinquished control of the memorial to the National Park Service. IND 162, which ran in front of the Memorial Building, was relocated. A Visitor's Center was added to the main building. In 1967 the memorial was selected as one of two Living Historical Farms operated by the National Park Service. The Lincoln cabin and outbuildings were reproduced on three acres north of the original cabin site.

Across IND 162 from the Lincoln Memorial is the **Lincoln State Park**. The park's 1,747 acres encompass 200 campsites, buildings for group camps, an 85-acre lake for swimming, fishing, and boating, shelter houses, playground areas, a tennis court, around 500 picnic spots, and hiking trails. Within the park is the **Little Pigeon Primitive Baptist Church**, erected near the site of an earlier sanctuary that Thomas Lincoln helped construct and in which he and his family worshiped. In the churchyard is the gravestone of **Sarah Lincoln Grigsby**, Abe's only sister, who died in 1828. Also in the park is the 1,514-seat **Lincoln Amphitheatre**, completed in early 1987, in which the Lincoln Boyhood Drama Association presents Tuesday through Sunday, from June to September, a drama, "The Young Lincoln."

The Gentrys were friends and neighbors of the Lincolns. James Gentry came to Spencer County in 1818. He bought a land tract on which, in 1854, Gentryville was platted and named for the pioneer family. The **James Gentry homestead site** is indicated by a sign on the north side of IND 162, *1.4 m.* west of the Lincoln memorial entrance.

GENTRYVILLE (p. 299) is located at IND 162 and US 231/IND 62, *.1 m.* west of the Gentry homesite. After turning left at the junction, take the next road west (CR 1575N) *.7 m.* to the **Col. William Jones house** on the right. A tiny settlement, Jonesboro, grew up around the trading post and cabin of William Jones, a contemporary of the Lincolns. In 1835 Jones constructed his Federal-style brick home. While campaigning for Henry Clay in 1844, Lincoln lodged at the Jones house. The Jones family sold its home in the 1850s and moved into Gentryville. In 1976 Bill and Gayle Cook, who live in Bloomington, Indiana, purchased the Jones property and restored it during the following three years. (*NRHP*)

South of Gentryville *3.8 m.* IND 62 and US 231 separate. Take IND 62 west *13 m.* to **BOONVILLE** (p. 6,300), the seat of government for Warrick County. Selected in 1818 as the new county seat of a modified Warrick County, Boonville and Boon Township were named for a member of the Boon family, of which the most prominent was Ratliff Boon (1781-1844). Boon, a cousin to Daniel Boone, came to Warrick County in 1809. While serving as the county's first treasurer, Boon participated in the territorial legislature. He served as a member of the state General Assembly and of Congress. He was Indiana's lieutenant governor, 1819-24, and the acting governor in the fall of 1822. Boonville stagnated until 1873 when the arrival of the Lake Erie, Evansville and Southwestern Railway stimulated building and production in the coal and tobacco trades particularly. Soon Boonville eclipsed Newburgh as the county's most populous community. A century later, Boonville remains Warrick County's largest city. Coal mining and related industries continue to employ the bulk of the city's working residents.

In 1904, the same year that the Evansville Suburban and Newburgh Railway traction line planned its extension to Boonville, county officials laid the cornerstone for a **new courthouse**. The public square was readied for the new $75,000 structure by the removing of many tall trees along with the 1851 red-brick courthouse. A feature of the present courthouse, designed by Evansville's William J. Harris and Clifford Shopbell, is its lofty town-clock tower. The clock, installed some years after the courthouse was completed, was the gift of Herbert Hoggatt, whose brother Wilford Bacon Hoggatt grew up in Boonville and served as governor of Alaska, 1906-9. At the entrance of the courthouse are two memorials. The one to **James A. Hemenway** (1860-1923) honors a Warrick County congressman, 1895-1905, and United States

LABOR IS THE GREAT SOURCE FROM WHICH NEARLY ALL IF NOT ALL HUMAN COMFORTS AND NECESSITIES ARE DRAWN

INDIANA 1816 1830

Indiana State Library

Lincoln's "Indiana Years" as depicted at the Lincoln Boyhood National Memorial

senator, 1905-9. The other marker pays tribute to **William Fortune** (1863-1942), a Boonville native, who gained recognition for his many civic works. While living in Indianapolis, Fortune was the moving force behind the Red Cross, the Chamber of Commerce, and the state's Board of Commerce. At his death he was credited with having raised more money for public causes than any other citizen in Indiana history. Next to the courthouse entrance, near the exterior wall, is a ground-level plaque noting the burial site of the **"Centennial Satellite,"** a time capsule filled with local memorabilia deposited in 1958 at the city's centennial and scheduled for opening in 2058. Other courthouse memorials are to Lincoln, at the northeast corner, and Boon at the southwest corner.

Ratliff Boon's home, built in 1831, still stands at 116 N. 1st St., one block west of the courthouse on the north side of the street. Presently a gray siding structure, its appearance suggests extensive alterations from the time of its construction.

One block east of the courthouse on the northwest corner of Main and 4th sts. is the **Old Warrick County Jail and Sheriff's Residence** at 124 E. Main St. Constructed in 1876-77 from a design by Boonville architect J. F. Frick, the two-story brick front part housed the sheriff and his family, and the story-and-a-half rear portion served as the jail. It has 22-in.-thick walls, a stone floor, and a ceiling of Gothic arches. The lockup comprised 12 cells. When erected, the building cost $39,250. The well-preserved structure is presently being used as a senior citizens' center and as offices for the Junior Chamber of Commerce. (*NRHP*)

The **Warrick County Museum** is located on the northwest corner of S. 1st and W. Walnut sts., a block south and west of the courthouse. The museum, opened December 4, 1977, is housed on the second floor of the former Ella Williams Elementary School, which was built in 1901 to replace the 1849 county seminary. The first floor of the school is used as a courthouse annex. Attractions in the six-room museum include a reconstructed turn-of-the-century schoolroom, a Victorian living room, an early 20th-century kitchen, a doctor's office, and a variety of local memorabilia.

From Boonville's courthouse proceed west on IND 62 *15.9 m.* to Evansville and the end of Tour 7.

Tour 8

Tour 8 of the southwest corner of Indiana, known as "the pocket," begins at the Civic Center in downtown Evansville. From the east-side parking area on 9th St., proceed west on Locust St. for two blocks then north on 7th St. for .7 m. to Division St. which becomes Pennsylvania Ave. Turn left. Follow IND 62 past the University of Southern Indiana campus, west of town, and continue another 2 m. to the Posey County line.

Named in honor of Maj. Gen. Thomas Posey (1750-1818), who was appointed governor of the Indiana Territory in 1813, **POSEY COUNTY** (p. 26,414; 410 sq. m.) was formed from parts of Gibson and Warrick counties in 1814. It previously was part of Knox County and acquired its present boundaries when Vanderburgh was formed from parts of Gibson, Warrick, and Posey counties in 1818. The first county circuit court was held at Blackford, about five miles north of what is now Mount Vernon, in 1815. Isaac Blackford, later a Supreme Court judge of Indiana, was the presiding district judge. In 1817 the county seat was moved to the site that would be called Springfield, a more central location, and a brick courthouse was erected on land granted by its owner, the Harmony Society, to the county. In 1825 the board of commissioners decided to make Mount Vernon the county seat because of its commercially advantageous position on the Ohio River. The first county buildings on the site of the present courthouse square were erected in the 1830s.

Farms interspersed with manifestations of recent industrial growth occupy much of the land between Evansville and Mount Vernon. The rich bottomland along IND 62 provides ideal soil for farming while the nearby Ohio River is a natural distribution network for commerce. Situated south of the highway, 7.6 m. within Posey County, **Mead Johnson Park** covers 600 acres. Mead Johnson and Company moved to Evansville in 1915. (See Evansville

Attractions.) The plant near Mount Vernon is a major nutritional-pharmaceutical manufacturing and warehousing facility. The first phase of the research and production complex opened in 1970, followed by major expansion projects. Dedicated in 1981, the new Drug Safety Evaluation facilities consolidate most of the company's toxicology activities under one roof.

Continue west on IND 62 for 2.1 m. to the turnoff, left, for the **Southwind Maritime Centre.** Dedicated in the summer of 1979, the river port east of Mount Vernon is linked to major highways, rail lines, and the Evansville airport and is fully equipped to handle tons of cargo going between any point on the inland waterways system—from the Great Lakes region to the Gulf of Mexico. Each year since its opening in 1979 the amount of tonnage going through has increased. In 1986 the figure was 4,053,243 tons, almost eight times the amount handled by the more recently built port at Clarksville. Clarksville, however, is a larger port, having 838 acres compared to the 745 acres at Southwind. Facilities on the Southwind site include cargo storage, cranes which lift goods directly from barge to truck, and a mile of sheltered riverfront for fleeting, mooring, drydocking, and other services. The industrial park leases space to a grain terminal, coal transfer company, fertilizer and grain companies, timber exporter, and shippers of bulk commodities.

During construction of the Southwind Maritime Centre evidence of a **prehistoric Indian village** was discovered. Archaeologists found remains of a village comprised of at least 96 structures surrounding a central plaza and bounded by a 430 by 465-ft. rectangular stockade. On the basis of excavations of the six-acre site during the summers of 1981 and 1982, staff from the Glenn A. Black Laboratory of Archaeology at Indiana University surmised that about 300 Indians of the Mississippian culture occupied the site for less than 50 years

Tour 8

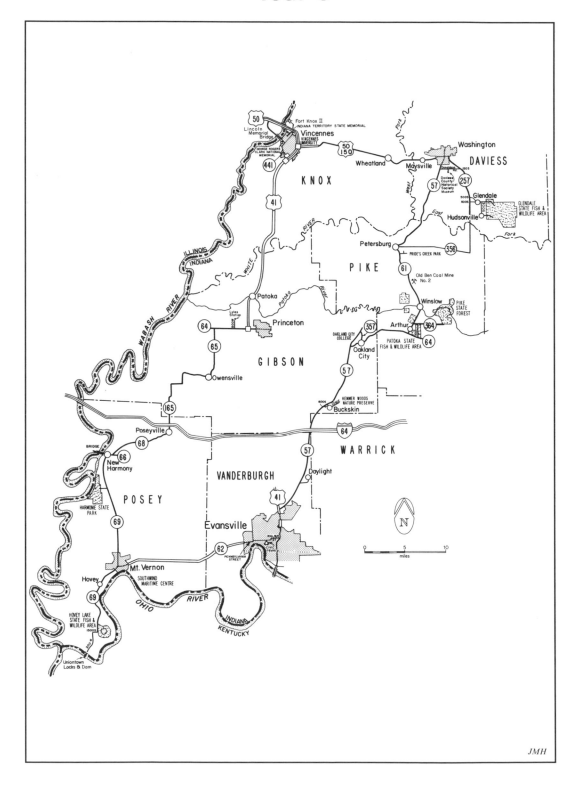

around 1200 A.D. It was a nearly self-sufficient community, though probably a subsidiary of the larger town at Angel Mounds. (See Evansville Attractions.) No mound was associated with the Southwind site. The excavated site now serves as part of the industrial park for shippers using the Ohio River barge port.

Other prehistoric Indian occupations in the vicinity of Mount Vernon have been discovered in recent years. The Mann Site and the Murphy Archaeological Site are both listed on the National Register of Historic Places. Situated on private property, the sites have been periodically threatened by industrial development in the past.

From Southwind Port Rd., proceed west on IND 62 for *1.2 m.* to Main St. in downtown **MOUNT VERNON** (p. 7,656). In 1798 Andrew McFadden crossed the Ohio River and explored the site that is now the city. He returned with his family and in 1805 erected a log cabin below the present landing on the river. The following year, the McFaddens moved to the bluff at the south end of what is now College Ave. Other settlers soon followed. For about 10 years, the locality was known as McFadden's Bluff. In 1816 John Wagoner platted the west side of Mill Creek, and Aaron Williams laid out the public square and 32 lots. The town grew rapidly after becoming the county seat in 1825, even, for a time, commercially surpassing Evansville. Records are incomplete but indicate that Mount Vernon was incorporated as a town in 1839 and re-incorporated in 1847. Mount Vernon was incorporated as a city in 1865. Today, quiet residential areas with substantial 19th-century homes surrounding a central business district characterize the old river town.

The **Posey County Courthouse** was built in 1876 on a square bounded by Main, Walnut, 4th, and 3rd sts. Architects Vrydale and Clarke designed the three-story brick structure which rises above a Bedford limestone foundation. The handsome dome above a slate roof and the ornamental brackets beneath the eaves are of Italianate style. Rudolph Schwarz, sculptor of the 284-ft.-high Soldiers and Sailors Monument in Indianapolis, designed the Soldiers and Sailors Monument erected on the Mount Vernon courthouse square in 1908.

On the northeast corner of 4th and Main sts., the three-story brick **People's Bank Building** complements the architectural style of the courthouse. The Independent Order of Odd Fellows No. 49 (IOOF) erected the building in 1898, using the third floor for the lodge hall and leasing the first and second floors to various retail stores and offices. The first IOOF lodge in Posey County was organized in 1848. People's Bank has occupied the building since 1908. (*NRHP*)

East of the courthouse, the Masonic Lodge No. 578 occupies the **Hovey house** at 330 Walnut St. Alvin P. Hovey (1821-1891) purchased the two-story brick house of Italianate design in 1871 for his daughter Esther and her husband, G. V. Menzies, a Mount Vernon lawyer and political figure. He later added the front section with a bay area. Hovey began his legal career in Posey County during a dispute over the will of educational reformer William Maclure of New Harmony. A member of the Constitutional Convention of 1850-51, judge of the state Supreme Court, United States district attorney, and Civil War major general, Hovey later served as United States minister to Peru, a congressman, and governor of Indiana from 1889 until his death. In 1921 the Masons bought the house and constructed the back building for use as a lodge.

South of the courthouse, the **Coliseum**, dedicated as a World War I memorial hall in 1926, fronts on 3rd St. The buff-colored brick structure of classical design features Doric order columns, and the interior is of marble with mahogany woodwork. The Coliseum houses the county court, some city offices, and the community auditorium and teen center.

Two blocks south of the courthouse, at the foot of Main St., **Sherburne Park** provides public access to the waterfront on the Ohio River. Jacob Cronbach donated the property for a city park named in memory of his son Sherburne. Just west of the park is the bluff where Mount Vernon's first settler, Andrew McFadden, built his store and second home. A boulder with a bronze plaque at the foot of College Ave. commemorates the site. A nearby roadside marker notes the waterline at 59.2 ft., reached by the Ohio River during the disastrous flood of 1937. Beyond the town's waterworks building, built in 1886, a monument on the riverbank indicates the site of Mount Vernon's first cemetery, used between 1816 and 1973.

From W. Water St., proceed north on College Ave. to 8th St., passing a row of Victorian-era frame houses. Go left one block to Mill St.

then right to 9th St. At 9th and Mill sts. and the Lower New Harmony Rd., a grove surrounds the impressive-looking **Lowrey house**. In 1837 William Lowrey built the three-story brick house with twin chimneys. Called Popcorn Hill and Ferndale by subsequent owners, it provided the setting for a children's mystery novel, *The Treasure of Belden Place*, written by Frances Cavanaugh. Now painted white and trimmed with black shutters, the exterior of the house has changed little, though the interior has been remodeled extensively.

Follow 9th St. east to Main St. and turn right to 6th St. The **City Hall and Police Department** building occupies the southeast corner. The city built the two-story brick building, topped with a cupola, in 1893. On the south half of the city lot stands the old **Carnegie Public Library**, fronted by Doric order columns. Mrs. Matilda Alexander helped organize the Alexandrian Literary Society in 1892, which founded the town's first public library in 1895. A room in the city hall housed the library until 1905. It occupied the building on the east side of Main St. until construction in 1985-86 of a new facility across the street was completed. James Associates of Indianapolis designed the contemporary-style library which features four main sections with numerous skylights, an adult courtyard, and a children's playground area.

A number of well-preserved 19th-century homes and churches still stand along Walnut and Mulberry sts. in the neighborhood west of the old city hall. Two blocks east of Main and 4th sts., on the northwest corner of Mulberry and 4th sts., is the **Sullivan house**, a two-story brick residence of Georgian design. Edward T. Sullivan built this charming house with a front portico between 1847 and 1851 and sold it to John A. Mann in 1855. Robert Keck purchased the house in 1924 and duplicated the original ironwork in 1946 for the long porch on the north side of the house. The Keck-Gonnerman Company, which began as a small foundry in 1873, was Posey County's most important industry at the turn of the century—manufacturing engines, threshers, portable sawmills, and coal mining machinery.

Sullivan also built the **Parke house** at 228 E. 4th St. about 1860. The design of the two-story brick structure topped with a cupola is typical of the architecture popular during the mid-Victorian period. Charles Parke, who married David Dale Owen's daughter Nina, bought

the property and erected a small building in the east yard for use as a private schoolhouse. The main house was later converted into apartments. A real estate company now owns the building.

Return to Main and 4th sts. Continue west for 11 blocks. Turn left on Parke St. and follow IND 69 south for *9 m.*, passing a riverfront industrial complex just outside of Mount Vernon, the village of Hovey, and open farmland.

At the end of IND 69 is the **Hovey Lake State Fish and Wildlife Area** entrance. In 1940 the state and federal governments purchased 885 acres, later increased to 4,298 acres, much of it under water. The preserve is noted for its bald cypress trees, believed to be one of the northernmost stands in the United States. The tall hardwood trees, usually found in the bottomlands of the South, rise from the waters and shoreline of Hovey Lake, giving the appearance of a primeval swamp. Since construction of the Uniontown Locks and Dam began in 1965, the water level of Hovey Lake has risen about 7 ft., and its surface dimensions have increased from 300 to 1,400 acres. Many of the cypress trees have died because their "knees" became submerged year-round in water. Cypress normally grow with their "feet" in water most of the time, yet thrive in drought years when the lakeshore recedes. The Department of Natural Resources has planted hundreds of young cypress trees on higher ground surrounding the lake in an effort to save this natural legacy. Other plant species which have been found in the area include pecan trees, southern red oak, swamp privet, and mistletoe. The lake and wetlands are a stopover for migratory birds and a haven for many kinds of fish and wildlife. The state provides recreational facilities for the public which include campgrounds, picnic areas, boat rentals, and regulated hunting and fishing zones.

At the park exit, turn west and follow the highway south of Hovey Lake for *2.9 m.* to the **Uniontown (Kentucky) Locks and Dam**, located on the Ohio River near former Dam No. 49. The confluence of the Ohio and Wabash rivers, west of the dam, is the lowest point in Indiana. The United States Army Corps of Engineers began construction on the Uniontown locks and dam in 1965. The first boat passed through the locks on December 28, 1970, and the dam began operations on July 9, 1973. About 25 to 30 boats pass through the locks daily, carrying approximately four to five million tons of cargo during a typical month. A series of locks and dams has turned the Ohio River into a string of lakes called navigational pools, which hold back water to maintain a channel for river traffic. The dams are not intended to hold back high water nor to reserve water for dry periods. Recently constructed dams on the Ohio, such as the Uniontown facility, are called "high-lift" dams, because boats passing through the locks are lifted higher than they were at the old dams. A towboat heading upstream through the Uniontown locks is lifted 18 ft. during normal pool conditions.

From the Uniontown Locks and Dam, return to Mount Vernon. At Main and 4th sts. turn left and proceed north *1.9 m.* on IND 69 to the **Bellefontaine Cemetery** situated on the east side of the road. A roadside historical marker notes that Alvin P. Hovey, who died in 1891 while serving as governor, is buried here.

Follow IND 69 north for *9.4 m.* past farms and wooded areas to the turnoff for the **Harmonie State Park**. The park entrance is one mile on the left. Established in 1966, the 3,465-acre park borders the Wabash River about four miles south of New Harmony. The daughters of Elmer E. Elliott, a descendant of Owenite James Elliott, donated the original 700-acre plot for a park, located along a stretch of rapids on the Wabash River. Approximately six miles of hiking trails lead across ravines, wooded areas, grassy plateaus, and country roads. Park facilities include campgrounds, picnic areas, bicycle trails, swimming pool, and playground. The park contains an abundance of whitetail deer, small game, and birds, and a naturalist conducts a variety of activities designed to identify and interpret the natural resources.

Return to IND 69 and continue north for *2.2 m.* to the **Maple Hill Cemetery** on the left, located on the southern edge of New Harmony. A winding road ascends to the summit, overlooking the historic town of **NEW HARMONY** (p. 945), the site of two radical experiments in communal living during the first half of the 19th century.

Only half a dozen settlers lived in the area in 1814 when George Rapp (1757-1847) and his followers came up the Wabash River by flatboat and founded the community of *Harmonie.* In search of religious freedom, the Harmonists, a group of Lutheran dissenters, had left Germany in 1805 and settled in Butler County, Pennsylvania. In 1814 they purchased government land at a location 50 miles south of Vincennes and came to the Indiana Territory. The Harmony Society labored to create a cooperative community bound by the principles of celibacy, obedience to their leader, and Christian communal living. Convinced they were a chosen people, the Harmonists bent thought and practice to preparation for the millennium or Second Coming of Christ which they believed would occur in their lifetimes. Within five years the Harmonists had brought 1,450 acres of land under cultivation and built a community of 180 log and brick buildings, some of which still stand. The almost completely self-sufficient town in the wilderness was a model for planning, order, and cleanliness. Advertised for sale in 1824, the society's total land holdings were about 20,000 acres with an asking price of $150,000. In 1825 Father Rapp sold the settlement with all its improvements to Robert Owen and led his flock back to Pennsylvania. At Economy, the Harmony Society dwindled in numbers as a result of a schism in 1832 and the continued practice of celibacy.

Historic New Harmony, Inc., a nonprofit preservation group managed by the University of Southern Indiana at Evansville, conducts guided walking tours of the community, leaving twice daily (more often during summer months) from the Atheneum at North and Arthur sts. The **visitor center at the Atheneum** also provides maps and tourist information for the New Harmony State Historic Site buildings and the Workingmen's Institute.

From the cemetery, continue north on IND 69 for *.2 m.* to the **Labyrinth**, a re-creation of an elaborate Harmonist garden, on the left side of the road. During the Harmonist period, Frederick Rapp, the adopted son of George Rapp, designed a maze of concentric circles formed with vine-covered fences along paths leading to a small house built of blocks in the center. The winding paths symbolized the Harmonist concept of the devious and difficult approach to a state of true harmony. After 1840 the original labyrinth disappeared from lack of use. A century later, it was reconstructed as a state memorial, adjacent to the original site.

Proceed north on IND 69 (Main St.) for *.5 m.* to the main intersection at Main and Church sts., passing Murphy Park, the former City Hall, and a row of late 19th-century commercial buildings finding new life as shops, stores, and restaurants catering to the tourist trade. New Harmony has been the focus of extensive restoration and revitalization projects made possible through the creation of a state commission and the participation of the Lilly Endowment and local groups dedicated to the preservation of its heritage. Restoration work of the 1970s included the three-story cast iron and pressed-metal facade of the **Owen Block**. Built in 1882 by a grandson of Robert Owen, the Owen Block originally comprised two sections and occupied the southwest corner of Church and Main sts. The connected buildings were used for an agricultural supply business before the end section was torn down to make way for a bank building.

On the east side of Main St. between Church and Granary sts., the Harmonists erected **Dormitory No. Two**, the second of four large dormitories to house their communal society. The three-story structure with dormer windows and gambrel roof was constructed of brick and, typical of Harmonist buildings, insulated with "Dutch biscuits"—3- to 5-ft.-long slats of wood wrapped with straw and mud, inserted between floor joists and wall studs. Completed in 1822, the dormitory accommodated unmarried men. Meals were prepared in the community kitchen bordering Granary St. During the Owenite period these buildings served as a Pestalozzian school and Judge Wattle's Tavern, respectively. An 1821 vertical sundial made of oak boards was removed from Father Rapp's house and now hangs on the south wall of the dormitory. Dormitory No. Two and the kitchen are maintained by the state, fully restored, furnished, and open to the public during the summer months. The building contains educational exhibits representing the Harmonist and Owenite periods. It also houses the printing press of Charles W. Slater, publisher of the *New Harmony Register* which first appeared in 1858.

Hedges and a brick wall almost completely conceal other landmarks remaining from the Harmonist period in the block bounded by Church, Main, West, and Granary sts. Father Rapp erected his brick Georgian residence about 1816 on the northwest corner of Church and Main sts. In the backyard of the former Rapp mansion is a limestone slab of the Paleozoic Age, that George Rapp imported from near St. Louis. The source of human footprints found in the stone has never been determined.

Are they the actual prints of a prehistoric Indian, or an excellent carving, or are they the feet of the Angel Gabriel? A massive stone and brick granary built in 1819, which contained storage vaults for gold and may also have doubled as a fort, still stands in the middle of the block.

New Harmony became the site of Robert Owen's utopian experiment during the two years following the Harmonists' departure. In 1825 Robert Owen, a Welsh industrialist, socialist, and philanthropist, and William Maclure, a Scottish philanthropist, purchased the entire town of Harmonie, which Owen renamed New Harmony, and founded a new social order. They assembled from Europe and the eastern United States a group of renowned teachers and scientists, many of whom arrived from Pittsburgh in January 1826 on the keelboat *Philanthropist*, which docked at the present site of June Barrett Park on the banks of the Wabash River. Among the passengers aboard the celebrated "Boatload of Knowledge" were William Maclure—geologist, educator, philanthropist, and Owen's principal associate and financial partner in the New Harmony adventure; Thomas Say—zoologist, conchologist, entomologist, original member of the Philadelphia Academy of Natural Science, curator of the American Philosophical Society, and professor of natural history at the University of Pennsylvania; and Guillaume Sylvan Casimir Phiquepal d'Arusmont—Pestalozzian teacher known as William S. Phiquepal, who married social reformer Frances Wright.

In 1827 Robert Owen dissolved his community and returned to Scotland. His five children and many participants remained, however, and New Harmony basked in a cultural and scientific afterglow until the 1850s. Drawn to New Harmony were such notable figures of the time as French naturalist Charles Alexandre Lesueur, educator Joseph Neef, inventor and libertarian Josiah Warren, Dutch scientist Gerard Troost, educator Marie Duclos Fretageot, and Swiss artist Karl Bodmer. Believing that education was the key to a new and better way of life, the Owen community made many contributions to society: the first kindergarten in America, the first infant school, the first trade school, the first public school system offering equal education to boys and girls, the first free public library, the first civic dramatic club, and the first headquarters of the United

States Geological Survey. It is also said that the first women's club in America organized with a written constitution and bylaws began in New Harmony.

The children of Robert Owen were destined to take active roles in the field of science and education. Robert Dale Owen, the oldest son, became a philosopher and social reformer, member of the Indiana General Assembly and of Congress, and United States minister to Naples. As a member of Congress, Owen introduced the bill which established the Smithsonian Institution. William Owen was an author, editor of the *New Harmony Gazette*, founder of the New Harmony Thespian Society, and manager of the Owen community during his father's absences. David Dale Owen studied chemistry and geology, earned a medical degree and position of first state geologist in 1837, and directed the United States geological survey in Iowa and Wisconsin in 1847. The youngest son, Richard Owen, became a geologist and doctor. He served as an officer in both the Mexican and Civil wars, was a teacher of geology, chemistry, natural philosophy, and languages, and the first president of Purdue University. Jane Dale Owen married Robert H. Fauntleroy and set up a school for young ladies. Three of the sons—William, David, and Richard—were married in a triple wedding in 1837, and the three couples took their honeymoon trip together.

The **Rapp-Maclure-Owen house** at the northwest corner of Main and Church sts. was built on the foundations of the Rapp mansion, which burned in 1844. Alexander Maclure, the son of New Harmony leader William Maclure, built the present one-story Greek Revival-style residence. From Mexico, Maclure imported the first golden raintrees in New Harmony, which were planted near the gate to the house. Noted for their long sprays of yellow flowers, the golden raintrees blossom in early summer throughout southern Indiana. Ross Lockridge, Jr., borrowed the name for his novel and film *Raintree County*. Behind the house is the tomb of Thomas Say (1787-1834), who brought Osage orange trees to New Harmony. Say devoted his life to the study of natural history. Six volumes of his *American Conchology* were published at New Harmony, 1830-34. Among the subsequent owners of the house was David Dale Owen who lived there 10 years until his death in 1860.

In 1859 David Dale Owen built **Owen Laboratory**, the Gothic Revival-style residence just south of the Harmonist granary between Main and West sts. Architect James Renwick, Jr., who designed Grace Church and St. Patrick's Cathedral in New York, assisted Owen in designing this structure. Owen turned the granary into a museum to house geological specimens. After Owen's death in 1860, the laboratory was converted into a residence, and Owen's immense collection was dispersed among the Smithsonian Institution in Washington, D.C., Indiana University in Bloomington, and the Museum of Natural History in New York City. The house and family papers are now the private property of Owen's descendants. An unusual weathervane, a fish mounted atop a cone-shaped tower on the Owen Laboratory, is visible through the treetops, but the grounds and buildings are not open to the general public.

From Main and Granary sts., proceed north one block. On the northeast corner of Main and North sts. stands the **Barrett Gate House**. About 1815 the Harmonists erected the original log portion of the structure which was moved here from another location. The frame sections were added after the Civil War. It is called the gate house because of its proximity to the gates of the Roofless Church.

The **Roofless Church**, an interdenominational structure of contemporary design, embraces the northwest corner of Main and North sts. Jane Blaffer Owen, a leading figure in the recent development of New Harmony properties, commissioned architect Philip Johnson to design the brick-walled courtyard, completed in 1960, which is open to the sky. Artist Jacques Lipchitz created the striking ceremonial gates and the Madonna sculpture sheltered under a shingled dome in the shape of an open parachute.

Proceed west for one and one-half blocks to North and Arthur sts. Beyond the visitor parking area, the **Atheneum**, an ultramodern structure of gleaming white porcelain squares and shipside railings, rises above the banks of the Wabash. Architect Richard Meier designed the extraordinary building, completed in 1979, to house the New Harmony Visitor Reception Center and conference facilities. In addition, the building contains a museum area, exhibition galleries, a 200-seat auditorium, and multilevel observation terraces.

Owen Laboratory

From the Atheneum, follow the footpath east to the neighboring cluster of historic buildings. Commanding a broad vista, the reconstructed **Macluria house**, also known as the Grayson home, predates the Harmonist settlement. Originally erected about 1775, at a site about half a mile from here, the log dwelling with twin cabins connected by a "dog trot" or breezeway is the oldest structure in New Harmony. It is owned and maintained by Historic New Harmony, Inc., as an orientation center and exhibit area featuring maps and panels about New Harmony land acquisitions.

Just south of the pioneer dwelling is the **David Lenz house** on the northwest corner of North and West sts. Built directly next to the sidewalk with the entrance on the side instead of the front, the frame house is typical of Harmonist construction between 1819 and 1824, following the initial phase of log structures. The Harmonists preferred yellow poplar wood for construction because of its beauty as well as practicality, being naturally resistant to rot. Building techniques such as locking joints in place by inserting square pegs in round holes, called mortise and tenon construction, resulted in sturdy homes which have survived for more than a century. In the 1930s the Colonial Dames of America restored the house and furnished it with Harmonist artifacts.

At the southwest corner of North and West sts. stand a number of reconstructed log structures from the early Harmonist period between 1814 and 1819. Tall fences of stripped saplings surround the single-room dwellings and outbuildings of C. Weber and C. Eigner. The site serves as an exhibition area.

Just west of Granary and West sts. is the **Harmonist Burial Ground**, where more than 200 Rappites were buried in unmarked graves. The Harmonists conducted simple burial services and placed no markers on the graves to emphasize their belief in equality in death as in life. When the 1822 Harmonist church was dismantled in 1874, the bricks were used to erect the 5-ft.-high wall which borders the cemetery. Indians of the Hopewell prehistoric culture used the site for their burial mounds many years before the Harmonists. Charles Alexandre Lesueur, a naturalist of the Owen community, was the first to explore and publish an account of Indian mounds in Indiana.

The **Robert Henry Fauntleroy house**, between the cemetery and West St., stood in the limelight during the Owenite period. The original house, called No. 53, was erected by the Rappites prior to 1823 and occupied by the Pfeil family for 10 years. A succession of owners followed, including Thomas Say, the great zoologist. In 1840 Robert H. Fauntleroy, who married Robert Owen's daughter Jane, purchased the house, which he enlarged and remodeled. In 1859 Constance Owen Fauntleroy, granddaughter of the Owen patriarch, founded the Minerva Society, a women's literary club, in this house. The state of Indiana now maintains the house as a museum containing furniture and memorabilia from the Owenite period.

Proceed south for one block to the New Harmony Public School on the east side of West St. A classic doorway, called the **Door of Promise**, preserved from the Rappite church built in 1822, graces the west wall of the red brick school building, erected in 1915. The Rappite church occupied this site until 1874. Frederick Rapp is believed to have designed and carved the stone pediment. The Golden Rose motif symbolizes the Harmonist anticipation of the millennium foretold in the German Lutheran version of Micah 4:8, which reads, "Unto thee shall come the golden rose, the first dominion."

Continue south for one-half block. On the southeast corner of West and Tavern sts. stands the **Workingmen's Institute, Library, and Museum**, built in 1894. William Maclure founded the institute in 1838 "to bring scientific and all other useful knowledge within the reach of Manual and Mechanical Laborers, without the aid of professional men as teachers" (from Preamble). The members of the New Harmony Workingmen's Institute for Mutual Instruction met four times a month in a wing of the old Rappite school and stocked a reading room with books from London. Maclure died in 1840, leaving a trust which provided funds to begin 144 libraries in Indiana and 16 in Illinois. Dr. Edward Murphy, a successful New Harmony physician, helped the Library Society erect its present building, completed in 1894. George O. Gannser of Chicago designed the brick and limestone Romanesque-style structure which houses a public library, an archive of early New Harmony manuscript collections, and an art gallery and historical museum. It is still owned and operated by the Workingmen's Institute.

Follow Tavern St. east for one block to Main St. The **Lichtenberger Building** occupies the northeast corner. The original building on this site was constructed in 1845, altered in 1870, and remodeled with the addition of the third floor in 1901. The store now houses a lithograph collection of works by Swiss artist Karl Bodmer, who explored the upper Missouri River region in 1832-34. Bodmer and German naturalist Prince Maximilian von Wied-Neuwied conducted the two-year expedition for scientific purposes to record "the primitive character of the natural face of North America." Prince Maximilian filled journals with his observations while Bodmer produced more than 400 watercolors and sketches of people and places. The two explorers spent five months at New Harmony during their trek West.

Behind the Lichtenberger store, on the north side of Tavern St., is the site of David Dale Owen's **Second Geological Laboratory**. In the 1970s archaeologists uncovered the foundations of a Harmonist shoemaker's shop built around 1817, which served in the 1830s as the second of four geological labs by David Dale Owen. A beauty parlor later had been built on the site. It is now an open lot.

On the north side of Tavern St., just east of the laboratory site, is the **George Kepler house**, a Harmonist frame dwelling built about 1822. It houses an extensive geological exhibition from the collection of David Dale Owen, including his geological surveys that were used to open 12 states for settlement and economic development.

The **1830 Owen house**, a two-story brick structure erected by the Vondegrift family, stands at the southwest corner of Tavern and Brewery sts. It is the best surviving example from the Owen period of the brick residential style which was based on English precedents. The house now serves as a museum of decorative arts representing the Owenite period. Sometime before 1840, Jonathan Jaquess built the wing adjoining the west side of the main house. The hall and parlor rooms, restored in the 1970s, feature walls painted with stenciled patterns that were popular at that time.

From Tavern St., proceed north one block to Church St. At the southeast corner, the **John Beal house** is set back from Brewery St. inside a fence. Built in 1829, the house exemplifies building methods used in Tudor England. It has been only partly restored in order to display the early "wattle and daub" wall construction. The Beal house was later occupied by New Harmony's printer and publisher, Charles W. Slater.

Thrall's Opera House and the two buildings at the northeast corner of Brewery and Church sts. comprise New Harmony's present theater complex, maintained by the state of Indiana. The Harmonists built the frame structure on the corner in 1819 as a cooper shop where barrels for packing and shipping were produced. It now serves as an audiovisual showroom and theater museum. The barn behind the cooper shop was built in 1975, using traditional building techniques. It serves as a theater costume and prop shop. Facing Church St., Thrall's Opera House is a two-story brick structure that has been restored to reflect its appearance in 1888 when remodeled by Eugene Thrall. The Harmonists originally erected the building about 1824 as one of four dormitories. Dormitory No. 4 became a ballroom after Owen bought the Harmonist community. It subsequently served as a tenement, school, and grocery and liquor store. The Thespian Society, founded by William Owen in 1827, purchased the building in 1855 and rebuilt it as a theater. In 1914 the stage was removed and the building became a garage. In 1968 the state of Indiana restored the Opera House and revived its stage productions.

From Brewery and Church sts., continue one block to Granary St. On the southeast corner is the **Solomon Wolf house**, a two-story brick structure. Built about 1823 on another location, it was transferred here in 1975. The restored house contains a scale model of 1824 New Harmony with special audiovisual effects. Enter from Brewery St. through the long grape-covered arbor in the backyard.

One block north at the southeast corner of Brewery and North sts. are the remains of a **Harmonist Distillery**—a hop house and shed—used in the 1820s. The Harmonist brewery produced an average of about 500 gallons of beer every other day, and the main distillery, 36 gallons of whiskey daily. A small log still with a pump operated by two dogs treading alternately produced an additional 20 gallons of whiskey per day. Almost all of the whiskey was made for export, some as far south as New Orleans and as far north as Boston. The Harmonists themselves did not consume much liquor, preferring a little homemade wine. The distillery operation is now fenced off and closed to the public.

Diagonally across the street is the Entry House which serves as a meeting room and reception area to the 45-room **New Harmony Inn**, built in 1974. Evans Woollen III of Indianapolis designed the contemporary brick structures to blend with the historic character of the community. All the rooms have yellow poplar floors and simple wood furniture. Some rooms have fireplaces, balconies, or second-story sleeping lofts. None have radios or television sets.

Situated between the New Harmony Inn and Main St., just north of the restaurant complex, is **Tillich Park**. Before his death in 1965, German theologian Paul Johannes Tillich hoped to make New Harmony a center for his teachings in the manner of George Rapp and Robert Owen. A local foundation created the tiny memorial park which contains Tillich's grave and stones engraved with brief selections from his writings.

To leave New Harmony, proceed south on Main St., past Dormitory No. 2. At Church St., go east on IND 66 for *1.6 m.* to IND 68 at the edge of New Harmony. Follow IND 68 for *7.4 m.* northeast to IND 165 at **POSEYVILLE** (p. 1,247). IND 165 bends north-northeast around the Poseyville Cemetery, then becomes Main St., crossing town from west to east. In 1840

Ellison Cale and Talbott Sharp laid out the town, which, like the county, was named for Brig. Gen. Thomas Posey, governor of the Indiana Territory, 1813-16. Until 1852, however, the town was called Palestine. Traditionally, Poseyville has been the shipping center for produce from the outlying agricultural areas. Today the town has little commercial activity besides a pair of antique shops and the single bank. The local Catholic church, St. Francis, erected and partially furnished in 1887 at a cost of $4,100, provides a prominent landmark at the east end of Main St. The organ, purchased in 1907 for more than $1,000, exhibits the craftsmanship of Edmund Giesecke, a prominent German organ builder in Evansville.

From the church, proceed north for *2.2 m.* on IND 165, crossing the I-64 overpass, to the **GIBSON COUNTY** (p. 33,156; 490 sq. m.) line. John Severns, a government surveyor who came from Kentucky to the Northwest Territory about 1789, was the first settler in what is now Gibson County. In 1813, when the southwest corner of the state was organized into counties, Gibson and Warrick were set off from Knox County. The county was named for Brig. Gen. John Gibson, an Indian fighter and secretary of the Indiana Territory, 1800-1816. Though primarily an agricultural area which is noted for its watermelon and cantaloupes, Gibson County has large coal reserves and a booming oil industry. Almost overnight, pump jacks have sprung up like common weeds across the countryside, appearing in backyards, pastures, cornfields, churchyards, and school grounds. Despite the current interest in oil, economic and population growth has remained generally slow but steady. One of the state's larger coal-fired generating plants, capable of producing 155.9 megawatts of electricity, is located in Gibson County, nine miles west of Princeton. A 2,950-acre cooling lake created for the Public Service Indiana facility has been stocked with fish and opened to the public for recreational use.

Continue north on IND 165 for *7 m.* through rolling farmland to Johnson where the highway turns east toward **OWENSVILLE** (p. 1,261). Continue *3 m.* to the Owensville Cemetery on the west edge of town, then *.3 m.* to IND 65. Situated along the old Mount Vernon branch of the Evansville and Terre Haute Railroad (now a part of CSX), Owensville was laid out in 1817 and named after Thomas Owens, a prominent Kentuckian. Although the town has pushed beyond its original boundaries, Owensville retains the atmosphere of a small village characterized by tree-shaded streets, turn-of-the-century architecture, and a centrally located public square.

Follow IND 65 north for *5.9 m.* to IND 64. Turn right and continue east *1.6 m.* to the left turnoff on CR 500W to **LYLES STATION**, an unincorporated area. Located one mile north of IND 64, Lyles Station today is practically deserted. Free Negroes founded the settlement sometime before the Civil War. By the turn of the century, Lyles Station, named in honor of the first settler Joshua Lyles, was a thriving all-black community of about 800 persons with two churches, two general stores, a post office, railroad station, and elementary school. Other than farming, a timber and grain trade was the major commerce of Lyles Station. The devastation accompanying the 1913 flood was the beginning of the end of the community. The termination of railroad passenger service in 1951 sealed its fate. A few farmhouses, a cemetery, and a chapel, said to be the only extant rural African Methodist Episcopal Church in the state, are the last remnants of a once prosperous town.

Continue east on IND 64 for *4.8 m.*, passing the old Louisville and Nashville Railroad depot on the left, to Main St. in **PRINCETON** (p. 8,976). Early Princeton was prominently located at the crossways of a buffalo trace leading westward and the Red Bank Rd. running north and south between Vincennes and Henderson, Kentucky. Broadway (IND 64), running east and west, and Main St. (IND 65), running north and south, now intersect at the center of town. Princeton was chosen the county seat because of its central location. The town was platted in 1814 and named for William Prince, Gibson County's first resident attorney, a legislator, judge, and congressman. Growth in Princeton has not been steady in the past, but it experienced a surge of industrial development in the 1970s which has strengthened the present economy. Hansen Manufacturing Company, Inc., a subsidiary of IMC Magnetics, has been producing timing motors since 1907. Potter and Brumfield, a Division of AMF Inc. and one of Princeton's oldest and largest companies, continues to increase its production of timers, relays, and switching devices. On the east side of town, the Hurst Manufacturing

Corporation produces a variety of electric motors used for banking machines, home computers, robots, Disneyland animated figures, and numerous other purposes.

Judge William Harrington's home served as a courthouse from 1813 to 1815. The first courthouse, constructed of bricks made on the site, was dedicated in 1815. A second courthouse, also of brick, was used from 1843 to 1883. The present **Gibson County Courthouse**, built in 1884, is an impressive brick and limestone structure, with a large central clock tower and smaller decorative towers on each corner. A granite Civil War monument, erected in 1912, stands in the southeast corner of the courthouse square, bounded by Broadway, Main, State, and Hart sts. (*NRHP*) Several commercial buildings surrounding the square have recently been renovated. Though disguised by a modern facade, the Greek Candy Store, founded in 1906, at the corner of Hart and State sts., still contains the original soda fountain and mirrored back bar.

From Broadway and Main sts., return west on IND 64 for *1.8 m.* to the cloverleaf interchange of US 41 and turn north for *3.5 m.* to the turnoff for **PATOKA** (p. 832). Settled by John Severns in 1789 before the organization of the county, Patoka is the county's oldest town. Severns operated a ferry across the Patoka River at a time when a Shawnee Indian tribe led by Chief Old Trackwell occupied the opposite riverbank from Severns's homestead. First called Smithfield, the town became Columbia in 1813 when it was platted. The town shortly thereafter adopted the name of the river. Patoka remains a peaceful little community.

From the Patoka turnoff, continue north on US 41 for *17.7 m.*, crossing the White River bridge at the **KNOX COUNTY** (p. 41,838; 520 sq. m.) line to IND 441 at **VINCENNES** (p. 20,857). Winthrop Sargent, secretary of the Northwest Territory, organized this first Indiana county in 1790 and named it for Maj. Gen. Henry Knox, a Revolutionary War artillery officer and secretary of war, 1785-94. At its inception, Knox County extended to Canada and encompassed all or part of the present states of Indiana, Michigan, Illinois, and Ohio. Many township boundaries and lots were surveyed under the French system of going towards non-cardinal compass points, and Knox is one of only two Indiana counties (the other is

Clark) that was laid out in such a manner. The county is bordered by Sullivan and Greene counties to the north, Daviess to the east, Pike and Gibson to the south, and the Wabash River/State of Illinois to the west. The terrain is basically flat with a good portion of the area consisting of rich bottomland from the valleys of the Wabash and White rivers. Most residents are involved in farming, small manufacturing, or coal mining.

In 1982 Vincennes, the oldest city in Indiana and the capital of the Indiana Territory, celebrated its 250th anniversary. Current documentary evidence indicates that a French fort existed at Vincennes as early as 1732. By that year François-Marie Bissot, the Sieur de Vincennes, a French officer, had arrived there and proceeded to construct an outpost and fur trading center on the banks of the Wabash. The French post later was named in honor of Vincennes, who met his fate at the hands of Chickasaw Indians in 1736 when he was burned at the stake. French traders from Canada settled on the site of Vincennes, and immigrants arrived from Kaskaskia, Detroit, and New Orleans in the 1750s. The Treaty of Paris in 1763 ended the French and Indian Wars, but the British did not actually occupy the post at Vincennes until the late 1770s. Many of the French inhabitants took an oath of allegiance to Great Britain and swore to support the English side of the border disputes which broke out with the frontier settlers. Such was the situation when George Rogers Clark (1752-1818), a young lieutenant colonel from Virginia, appeared on the scene. With the assistance of Father Pierre Gibault, a local priest who persuaded the French inhabitants to switch their allegiance to the Americans, Clark's recruits were able to occupy Fort Sackville, the British name for the fort at Vincennes, on July 14, 1778, without a shot being fired. Col. Henry Hamilton, the British commander at Detroit, retaliated by retaking Fort Sackville on December 17, 1778. When Clark received word that the British had regained control of Vincennes, he plotted his now famous campaign, backed with the financial support of Francis Vigo, to recapture Fort Sackville. After marching from Kaskaskia to Vincennes—a distance of about 180 miles through flooded lowlands—Clark and his band conducted a surprise attack on the fort on February 23, 1779, bringing about a formal surrender two days later. Thus, the capture of Fort Sackville played a decisive part in thwarting British attempts to control the region north of the Ohio and west of the Appalachians.

The **Log Cabin Visitors Center** located on the Vincennes University campus offers tourist information and Trailblazer Train tours of historical attractions in downtown Vincennes situated between the university and the George Rogers Clark Memorial.

From US 41 and IND 441, follow Willow St. west for *2 m.* to the far end of Mount Calvary Cemetery. Turn right on S. 6th St. and go north *.3 m.* to Barnett St. Turn left and proceed west for *.2 m.* to the **George Rogers Clark National Historical Park**. The Visitors Center faces S. 2nd St., and the parking lots can be reached by turning south on 2nd St., then right into the 26-acre park grounds. Construction of the George Rogers Clark Memorial, a part of the national park system, began in 1931. Local laborers built the Classic Greek-style structure designed by F. C. Hirons and F. W. Mellor, a round room encircled by a colonnade of 16 massive Doric columns. The limestone and marble interior features seven large murals painted by Ezra Winter, depicting Clark's western campaign. An 8-ft., 10-in.-tall statue of Clark, sculpted by Hermon A. MacNeil, stands in the center of the rotunda. President Franklin D. Roosevelt dedicated the completed Clark Memorial on June 14, 1936, in a ceremony attended by thousands.

The landscaped grounds surrounding the memorial contain a mall on the site of Fort Sackville overlooking the Wabash River. Near the Clark Memorial is a statue by John Angel of Francis Vigo (1747-1836), a wealthy fur trader who impoverished himself in order to outfit Clark's expedition in 1779. The Visitors Center, dedicated in 1976, offers a 30-minute film about the Battle of Fort Sackville. (*NRHP*)

Adjacent to the park grounds, at the corner of 2nd and Church sts., is the **Old Cathedral**, now the Basilica of St. Francis Xavier. Following the Sieur de Vincennes's tragic death, the next commander of the old fort, from 1736 to 1764, was Louis Groston de Saint-Ange et de Bellerive. In 1749 Saint-Ange de Bellerive, as he was usually known, built a log chapel, named St. Francis Xavier in honor of the 16th-century Basque Jesuit missionary and his namesake, another Jesuit priest, Father Francis Xavier de Guinne, who visited the settlement

from time to time. In 1785 Father Pierre Gibault built the second church on the same site, which also was constructed of logs. He served there as resident pastor until 1789. A statue of Father Gibault executed by Albin Polasek graces the plaza in front of the present cathedral. Begun in 1826 under Bishop Simon William Gabriel Bruté, the cathedral took 14 years to complete. In 1962 the structure of soft red brick topped with a 102-ft.-high frame tower was sandblasted to restore the original finish. Statues of St. Patrick, St. Francis Xavier, and St. Joan of Arc stand in arched niches over the front entrance. Tall pillars of poplar covered with plaster support the interior of the church, and an oil painting of the crucifixion painted by William Lamprecht in 1870 hangs above the main altar. A small bell, brought from France in 1742, still hangs in the belfry, and a crypt beneath the church contains the tombs of four bishops, including that of Bishop Simon Bruté (1779-1839).

Between the cathedral and the parish rectory, the **Old Cathedral Museum Shop** occupies the former St. Francis Xavier Library, built for Bishop de la Hailandière in 1840. Of Classical Revival design, the one-story brick structure features a hipped roof and arched windows with semicircular fanlights. The library now serves as a gift shop.

The **Old French Cemetery** adjoins the cathedral complex to the west. The remains of many pioneer citizens of Vincennes—including priests, parishioners, Indians, soldiers, and slaves—lie in this peaceful spot. The oldest known marker is dated 1800 though the church records note a burial as early as 1750. In the center of the cemetery, a monument honors Father Jean François Rivet (1757-1804), a French missionary commissioned by George Washington to teach language arts and culture to the Indians. Arriving in Vincennes in 1795, Rivet was the first teacher paid with public money in the Northwest Territory.

The new **Old Cathedral Library**, built in 1968, is at the far end of the courtyard behind the cathedral. The library houses more than 11,000 volumes of rare books, some dating from the 15th century, mostly from the collection of Bishop Bruté. The library also displays oil paintings, antique manuscripts, and religious treasures.

St. Rose Chapel, built in 1847, is the only surviving remnant of the first Catholic girls'

George Rogers Clark Memorial, 1934

school in Vincennes. Unused since 1911, the little chapel was completely dismantled and rebuilt on a new foundation just west of the library building in 1982. The Sisters of Charity administered St. Clare's Female Academy, founded in 1823, until 1837, when it was taken over by the Sisters of Providence and renamed St. Rose Academy. Mother Theodore Guerin, founder of the Order of the Sisters of Providence in America, worshiped here. Mother Guerin also began what is now St. Mary-of-the-Woods College in Terre Haute. (*NRHP/HABS*)

From 2nd and Church sts., proceed north to the next intersection, then west on Vigo St. across the **Lincoln Memorial Bridge**. In 1830 Abraham Lincoln and his family crossed the Wabash River by ferry near this location when they moved from Indiana to Illinois. In later years Lincoln returned to Vincennes several times. The Illinois chapter of the Daughters of the American Revolution (DAR) commis-

sioned Nellie V. Walker to sculpt a commemorative monument at the foot of the Lincoln Memorial Bridge on the Illinois side, and it was erected in 1938. A bronze figure of young Abe Lincoln stands before a bas-relief panorama carved in stone illustrating the Lincoln family crossing into Illinois.

From the Indiana side of the Lincoln Memorial Bridge, follow Vigo St. east to 2nd St. and turn left to the 100 block. Two Classic Revival-style buildings designed by John Moore face each other across the street. Built in 1836-38, the **Old State Bank**, 112 N. 2nd St., is believed to be the oldest surviving bank structure in the state. Chartered in 1834, the Vincennes branch of the State Bank of Indiana operated as such until 1858, when it was reorganized as the Vincennes National Bank. It remained in business until 1877. The Francis Vigo Chapter of the DAR purchased the old bank and completed its restoration in 1964. Four 30-ft.-high columns support the front portico, and six fluted columns encircle the inside room beneath a bell dome and cupola. In the early years, trappers and traders exchanged furs for gold in a room adjoining the main banking room. The second floor rooms served as meeting rooms and sleeping quarters for clerks who "lived in" for night security purposes. The old bank vault can still be entered through a massive steel door, imported from France. Today the historic structure is an Indiana Territory State Historic Site owned by the Indiana Department of Natural Resources and houses an art gallery operated by the Northwest Territory Art Guild. (*NRHP/HABS*)

The **Ellis mansion**, a two-story brick structure with a facade of native stone, stands directly across the street from the bank. Judge Abner T. Ellis built the home in 1830, at which time it was considered one of the finest in the state. A Vincennes attorney, Ellis served as a county probate judge and a member of the board of commissioners of Vincennes Academy. He was the first president of the Ohio and Mississippi Railroad, later the Baltimore and Ohio. Abraham Lincoln provided attorney service for Ellis and was a frequent overnight guest in the house. The Pastime Club and the Harmony Society later purchased the building. Since 1938 the interior has been extensively remodeled. (*NRHP*)

From 2nd and Broadway, proceed west one block to 1st St., then north three blocks. On the right side, between Seminary and Hart sts., is the **Old French House** (509 N. 1st St.), a timber structure built between 1786 and 1814. Michel Brouillet, a French-Canadian fur trader, may have erected the one-and-one-half-story house of hand-hewn logs, set upright on a sandstone foundation and daubed with mud. The design of the house—a steeply pitched roof with a single gable and porches adjacent to the front and back doors—is typically French. The interior comprises three rooms, a cellar, and a loft. Following Brouillet's death in 1837, the house was sold. It was still intact in 1853 but modernized in 1899. The original structure was encased in a Victorian cottage when its existence was made known in 1974. The Old Northwest Corporation purchased the house in 1975 and restored it in 1979-80. Visitors can see some of the original plaster made of burned mussel shells, sand, and water in the loft and a section of the posts-on-sill construction where

the plaster has been removed in the front room. The house has been covered with wood siding and furnished with 18th-century period pieces. The **French-Indian Heritage Museum**, behind the Old French House, includes a display of Indian artifacts from prehistoric times to French settlement.

From 1st and Hart sts., proceed east one block, turn left, then continue north on 2nd St. On the right side of 2nd St., between Hart and Shelby sts., stands the **Baty Place**, 617 N. 2nd St., believed to have been the first hospital in Indiana. Samuel Judah, a pioneer lawyer who won a famous land grant case for Vincennes University, built the two-story brick home around 1830. Dr. Jean Isidore Baty, a young French physician, began to practice "medicine, surgery, and dentistry" in Vincennes in 1840 and occupied the Judah house from 1848 to 1865. During that time, Dr. Baty built the three-story addition to serve as a hospital. The older section is in the rear of the building now converted to apartments. The property originally extended to 5th St. and contained an orchard, garden, and vineyard.

Continue north on 2nd St. for two blocks to Harrison St. at the edge of the **Vincennes University** campus. Turn west and proceed one block to the visitor parking area at Harrison and 1st sts. In 1801 Jefferson Academy, the direct forerunner of Vincennes University, was founded. Father Jean François Rivet, a Catholic priest, was the first headmaster of the school. In 1804 Congress approved a land grant for the support of a seminary of learning in Vincennes. In 1806 the First General Assembly of Indiana Territory chartered Vincennes University. The charter provided that Indian students should receive free board, clothes, and education and that provision for the education of women should be made as soon as possible. The university trustees selected a site for the campus, located a few blocks southeast of the present grounds, and completed construction of the first building in 1811. When the first state university was established at Bloomington in 1820, the trustees' hopes for a state-funded institution at Vincennes were dashed. The university faced more hard times in the 1820s, while competing with a rival institution, the short-lived Knox County Seminary. In 1842 the university began a successful legal battle to reclaim the land grant which had gone to Bloomington in the 1820s. In the next 50 years, the university was partially, but never fully, compensated by the state for the federal "land grab." The trustees sold the original campus in 1839 and purchased a parcel of land at the corner of 5th and Busseron sts. This campus served the university until 1953 when it moved to its present site near the Wabash River.

In 1873 the university added courses which provided the equivalent of the first two years of college, though the institution did not identify itself as a "junior college" until 1899. Today, Vincennes University is recognized as the oldest comprehensive junior college in the United States. It offers two-year academic programs in social science, math, science, humanities, and physical education. The occupational division offers more than 50 programs in business education, health occupations, public service, and technology.

In the fall of 1988 a total of 8,285 full-time and part-time students attended Vincennes University and its extensions at Jasper Center, Fort Benjamin Harrison, Grissom Air Force Base, the United States Penitentiary at Terre Haute, and the Crane Naval Weapons Support Center.

The 85-acre campus at Vincennes embraces a mix of old and new buildings. During the 1960s the university experienced a burst of construction which included the **Shircliff Humanities Center** at the northwest corner of Harrison and 2nd sts., completed in 1972. The modern three-story structure houses offices, classrooms, a theater, an art gallery, and several laboratories. Changing art exhibits during the school year are open to the public. Other recent additions to the campus are the public service and social science building, the science center, and the physical education complex with solar panels installed in the roof to conserve energy.

Just north of the humanities building, the university's **Learning Resources Center** faces 1st St. between College and Indianapolis aves. The Curtis G. Shake Library occupies the central building, completed in 1960. The north wing, dedicated in 1967, houses the Byron R. Lewis Library of Historical Collections. It features some 600 volumes from the Vincennes Library Company, organized in 1806 and subscribed to by such prominent early citizens as William Henry Harrison, Francis Vigo, and John Badollet. Another addition, constructed in 1974, houses the Shake Learning Center.

From 2nd St. proceed west on Harrison St. to the second building on the right—the **Maria Creek Church**. Founded in 1809, Maria Creek was the first Baptist church in the area. Early in the 19th century, the church took a strong stance against slavery and allowed blacks to become members. John Morris, a freed slave, was a charter member. In 1963 the university dismantled the old church erected in 1857 and abandoned since 1947. Attempts to rebuild it on the campus failed as the original bricks proved too soft. Therefore, a replica of the first church was built and furnished with the original pulpit and pews. Completed in 1970, the church is now used as an interdenominational chapel.

Directly across the street from the church, a historical park has been set aside from a section of the university campus adjacent to the William Henry Harrison home. The **Log Cabin Visitors Center** at the corner of Harrison and Park sts. provides a gift shop, tourist information, and restroom facilities. Tickets may be purchased here for the Trailblazer Train and for tours of the nearby Indiana Territorial Capitol, Western Sun office, and Maurice Thompson Birthplace.

Just south of the visitors center is the tiny one-room **Thompson house** where James Maurice Thompson was born in 1844. In the 1960s the frame structure was restored and moved from Fairfield, Indiana, to the historical park. Thompson was the author of the historical novel *Alice of Old Vincennes*, published in 1900. The story about the George Rogers Clark expedition was enormously popular at the time. It gave rise to the local supposition that Thompson created the fictionalized character of Alice from the real-life Vincennes resident Mary Shannon Buntin. Thompson also wrote nature sketches, poetry, and with his brother Will, a book on archery which helped popularize it as a sport.

On the east side of Park St. stand two structures from territorial days. Owned by the Indiana Department of Natural Resources, the capitol building and print shop comprise the **Indiana Territory State Historic Site**. When the Indiana Territory was created, Vincennes became the seat of government, and an unpretentious two-story frame building served as the territorial capitol where the General Assembly met between 1800 and 1813. William Henry Harrison was appointed governor by President John Adams and served until 1812. Territorial secretary John Gibson served as acting governor, 1812-13. The capitol originally stood at 217 Main St. The Fortnightly Club of Vincennes restored the historic building and moved it to its present site in 1949. The structure is held together with wooden pegs and contains some of the original furnishings, including a table used by Governor Harrison and the three territorial judges. (*NRHP/HABSI*)

A replica of the Western Sun print shop stands just beyond the old territorial capitol. Elihu Stout began publication of the territory's first newspaper, called the *Indiana Gazette*, in 1804. A fire destroyed the press in 1806, and in the following year the newspaper resumed as the *Western Sun*, a weekly publication. In 1931 it became, through a merger, the *Vincennes Sun-Commercial*. The small frame newspaper office is equipped with a printing press similar to the Adam Ramage hand press which Stout used.

South and west of the historical park, on the northwest corner of Park and Scott sts., is **Grouseland**, the home of William Henry Harrison (1773-1841), 9th president of the United States. Harrison built the Federal-style home between 1802 and 1804 and lived there until 1812. At least 3 of his 10 children were born in this house, including John Scott Harrison, the father of Benjamin Harrison, the 23rd president of the United States. The Harrison family had a long history of political involvement. Born in Virginia, William Henry Harrison was the son of Benjamin Harrison, a governor of Virginia and one of the signers of the Declaration of Independence. As a young man, Harrison served as Anthony Wayne's aide-de-camp in battles against the Miami Indians, was appointed secretary of the Northwest Territory, and elected a territorial delegate to Congress. In 1800, at age 27, he was appointed governor of the Indiana Territory. While governor, Harrison had many dealings with the Indians while trying to acquire Indian land and negotiate peace. Five of the eight treaties he negotiated with the Indians were signed by him at Grouseland. On one occasion Harrison met with Tecumseh and their respective aides on the lawn in front of the mansion. Harrison later defeated the Prophet, Tecumseh's brother and leader of the Indian confederation, at Tippecanoe in 1811. As commander of the Army of the Northwest, Harrison defeated Tecumseh and the British at the Battle of the Thames in 1813. Representing Ohio, Harrison served as a con-

gressman, 1816-19, a state senator, 1819-21, and United States senator, 1825-28. He was also minister to Colombia, 1828-29, and ran for president in 1836. Martin Van Buren defeated him in this race, but four years later Harrison won the presidential election, defeating Van Buren in his bid for reelection. One month after his inauguration, Harrison died on April 4, 1841, having served the shortest term of any American president.

After the Harrison family moved from Vincennes to North Bend, Ohio, in 1812, Grouseland was occupied by Judge Benjamin Parke. Harrison's eldest son, John Cleves Symmes Harrison, and his bride returned to Grouseland in 1819 and lived there for 10 years. After 1852 the house changed hands several times and served as a library, grain storage place, and a hotel before again becoming a private residence. In 1909 the Francis Vigo Chapter of the DAR rallied to save this historic landmark. The house has been restored and furnished with Harrison possessions and period pieces. A portrait of General Harrison painted by John Wesley Jarvis in 1813 hangs in the hallway. Hostesses in period costumes conduct tours of the home. The Harrison mansion is a National Historic Landmark which is owned and administered by the DAR. (*NRHP/HABS*)

Return to Harrison St., turn toward the Wabash River, and follow the road around the edge of the university campus. From Harrison and Chestnut sts., proceed in a northwesterly direction *.4 m.* to Portland Ave. Turn left and continue two blocks to Oliphant Dr. which borders Kimmell Park along the riverfront. Follow Oliphant Dr. north one mile. Cross the CSX Railroad and turn left on Fort Knox Rd. Proceed west for *1.9 m.*, climbing high above the Wabash River valley, to **Ouabache Trails Park**, a 250-acre park operated by the Knox County Parks and Recreation Department. Located in a scenic, wooded area, the park provides picnic and camping facilities, exercise and hiking trails, and an interpretive nature center.

The county park is adjacent to the **Fort Knox II Historic Park**, a public attraction owned by the Indiana Historical Society. The 44-acre historical park is the site of Fort Knox II, one of several outposts built in the Vincennes area. Fort Knox, named after Henry Knox, the first secretary of war, occupied three locations in the Vincennes area. The first fort was built and garrisoned on the northwest edge of the old town between 1787 and 1803. In 1803 Fort Knox II was constructed on this site situated on a hill overlooking the Wabash and operated until 1813. For the first five years, this outpost consisted of little more than a few buildings, but as tensions increased between the American settlers and the Indians the fort was strengthened with a palisade wall and blockhouse. For a short time in 1811 Capt. Zachary Taylor (12th president) commanded the fort. In order to provide more protection for the townspeople, Fort Knox II was dismantled, and the lumber was floated downstream and used for the construction of Fort Knox III, which may have been built on the site of the former Fort Sackville. The property at Fort Knox II subsequently changed hands several times. Public Service Indiana bought the site in 1932 and deeded it to the Indiana Historical Society in 1963. Archaeologists, under the auspices of Glenn A. Black and the Indiana Historical Society, excavated the site, discovering the outline of the fort and a number of artifacts. The Indiana Historical Society has erected a log caretaker's cottage and public restroom facilities, outlined the boundaries of the fort with 3-ft.-high upright logs, and posted signs and descriptive material for self-guided tours of the site. (*NRHP*)

Return approximately *3 m.* to Vincennes via Fort Knox Rd. and Oliphant Dr. At Lyndale Ave., the first street beyond Kimmel Park, turn left and proceed five and one-half blocks to the **Red Skelton Birthplace**, 111 Lyndale Ave. Richard Bernard Skelton (b. 1913) and his widowed mother lived in this modest frame house until he was about 12 years old, when he left Vincennes with a traveling medicine show. The red-haired, cigar-chomping comedian—famous for his portraits of Freddy the Freeloader, Clem Kadiddlehopper, and Dead Eye, among others—later married Georgia Maureen Davis and achieved national recognition as a clown, pantomimist, and TV entertainer.

Continue to N. 2nd St., turn right, and drive south for *.9 m.* to Buntin St. Turn left and proceed east for two blocks to the **Niblack house** at the southwest corner of 4th and Buntin sts. The two-story brick structure with a Colonial-style front porch is now the home of the American Legion, Post No. 73. The old Knox County Courthouse stood on this site from 1813 to 1834 and formed the inner walls

for the Niblack residence, built in 1868. William E. Niblack (1822-1893) represented Knox County in Congress, 1857-60 and 1864-75, and served as state supreme court judge, 1876-89.

Continue on Buntin St. three blocks to 7th St. and turn right. The **Knox County Courthouse** graces the square bounded by 7th, 8th, Busseron, and Broadway. Indianapolis architect Edwin May and his associate Adolf Scherrer designed the limestone courthouse in the central European round-arched mode with Lombard or Tuscan detailing, begun about 1872 and completed in 1876, as a memorial to the soldiers and pioneers of Knox County. Italian sculptor Andrew Barrot carved the figure of George Rogers Clark above a bas-relief memorial to the early settlers. On the opposite side of the building is a 21-ft. marble slab inscribed with names of Civil War soldiers killed in battle beneath the figure of a soldier. The clock in the tower, installed in 1874, has recently been repaired and electrified, retaining the original gear mechanism and faces. On the northeast corner of the square stands a towering Civil War memorial, dedicated in 1914. C. N. Clark of Urbana, Illinois, designed the granite monument topped with a bronze statue of a "color bearer." A mix of private homes and small businesses characterizes the surrounding neighborhood. Thomas S. Emison, a former Vincennes attorney who had offices at 7th and Busseron sts., has been responsible for restoring two historic houses across from the courthouse. About 1847 the Dunn family built the brick house, originally of Federal design, at 815-817 Busseron St. The east addition of the one-story structure dates after the Civil War. At one time the mother of Samuel P. M. Bayard, director of the Evansville and Vincennes Railroad, lived here. Now used as a duplex apartment, the building has always been a two-family residence. In 1876 William B. Robinson, a Vincennes lawyer who served four years as mayor of Vincennes and two terms as the circuit clerk of Knox County, built the two-story Italianate-style house at 825 Busseron St. The house has been converted into apartments.

From 8th and Busseron, go south one block to Main St., then west three blocks to 5th St. At 505 Main St. is the **Bonner-Allen mansion**, now owned by Gardner's Funeral Home. In 1816 Andrew Gardner founded the cabinet and coffin-making shop that today is the oldest continuously operating family business in the state. A sixth-generation Gardner now administers the funeral home. Constructed in 1842, the Gardner residence is a striking two-story Federal-style house. David S. Bonner, a Vincennes cotton mill owner, commissioned the brick house built by Cincinnati contractor Jonathan Spinning. Col. Cyrus M. Allen, Sr., a local lawyer and contractor for the railroad, who was a personal friend of Abraham Lincoln, purchased the house in 1845. A bronze plaque indicates the room in which Lincoln slept while a guest of the Allens. In 1915 the Gardner family bought the mansion which still contains the original 14-in. window sills, front door with large brass locks, hallway wood paneling, and fireplaces. Embossed tin ceilings were installed in 1918. (*NRHP*)

Proceed west one block on Main St., then south one-half block on 4th St. to the **City Hall and Police Department**, a neat two-story brick structure painted green and topped with an eagle-adorned weathervane. The bell from the World War II USS *Vincennes* is mounted in front of the city building. Four naval ships have carried the city's name in the past: the sloop-of-war USS *Vincennes*, a three-masted sailing vessel that circumnavigated the globe in 1829; a heavy cruiser, CA 44, which was lost under Japanese attack in the Pacific during World War II; a light cruiser, CL 64, which successfully served in the Pacific during World War II (it was later scrapped and its bell removed); and an Aegis missile cruiser, commissioned July 6, 1985. This most recent ship to carry the Vincennes name made world headlines when on July 3, 1988, while in the Persian Gulf, and its crew thinking it was under air attack, brought down an Iranian passenger plane, killing all 290 persons aboard.

Return to Main St. and proceed west to the 200 block. The historic **Moore Drug Store**, 221 Main St., with a cast-iron facade and high old-fashioned storefront windows stands on the left. Dr. Reuben G. Moore came to Vincennes in 1866 and established a business in "drugs, paints, toilet articles, etc.," at this location. Next door, the **First National Bank** building, now a restaurant, retains the original four pillars and its name inscribed across the front of the pedimented gable. Dr. John Henry Rabb and J. L. Bayard organized the bank in 1874. Across the street at 200 Main St. is the building formerly occupied by the famous **Gimbel's** department store. Adam Gimbel came to Vin-

cennes in 1842 and founded a mercantile business not far from the ferry landing. His seven sons carried on the trade and later founded the Gimbel Brothers Stores in Milwaukee, Philadelphia, Pittsburgh, and New York. The present building, erected in 1875, was the second Gimbel store on this site.

Continue west on Main St. for one block, then north on 1st St. **St.-Honoré Place**, a tiny shopping mall composed of old buildings with the ambiance of a French quarter, nestles between Main and Busseron. A French restaurant operates across the street, and the Trailblazer Train has a station in front. Much of the early history of Vincennes focuses on this district. Saint-Ange de Bellerive, the French commandant, 1736-64, opened two streets in old Vincennes: one from the front gates of the fort, called Rue de St.-Honoré, and the other which is now Busseron St. Of the former, only the alley between 1st and 2nd sts. entered from Busseron is in use today. Madame Godere, "the Betsy Ross of the Northwest Territory," lived on the corner of 3rd and Church sts. Legend credits her with fashioning a red and green flag to fly over Fort Sackville after it surrendered to George Rogers Clark in 1779.

From 1st and Busseron sts., proceed north one block to Broadway, then east five blocks to 6th St. On the northwest corner of 6th and Broadway stands the **Rabb mansion**, an impressive two-story brick structure, now owned by Goodwin Funeral Home. The original owner, Dr. John Henry Rabb from Rising Sun, Indiana, built the house in 1876. Dr. Rabb helped establish the First National Bank on Main St. in 1874 and served as its first president. The house remained in the Rabb family until 1945, at which time Ross Flummerfelt purchased the property for use as a funeral home. The interior still contains the original fireplace, leaded glass door, decorative plasterwork, and gaslight fixtures.

From Broadway, go north eight blocks on 6th St. to College Ave., east eight blocks to 13th St., and north one block to Wabash Ave. Turn right and follow Wabash Ave. east for .5 m. to the turnoff on the right for the **Sonotabac Prehistoric Indian Mound**. Formerly known as Sugar Loaf, the mound was rechristened Sonotabac in honor of the son of Tabac, the local Piankashaw chief who offered his services to George Rogers Clark at the time of the battle of Vincennes. The 140-ft.-high mound dates back to ca. 300 B.C. when a Hopewell Indian community created it for religious purposes. Adena and Hopewell communities occupied this site until A.D. 2 when a great flood occurred.

From the Indian mound, return to College Ave. and N. 6th St. via the previous route. Proceed north on 6th St. to the cloverleaf interchange at the edge of town. Follow US 50/150 east for *10.5 m.* past Fritchton to **WHEATLAND** (p. 532). In 1806 Richard Steen arrived by wagon from South Carolina and settled in what is now Wheatland. A. Armstrong laid out the town in 1858, and John W. Emison of Bruceville built a mill here in 1865. James D. Williams (1808-1880), politically known as "Blue Jeans" Williams, lived most of his life on a farm near Pond Creek Mills, south of Wheatland. Williams was first elected to the state legislature in 1843. He served many terms in the Indiana legislature in both houses before he was elected to Congress in 1874. Defeating Benjamin Harrison in the contest between "blue jeans" and "blue blood," Williams was elected governor in 1876. He died just before the end of his four-year term and was buried in Walnut Grove Cemetery near the site of his old home. A 30-ft.-high monument was erected in his memory in 1883.

From Wheatland, continue east on US 50/150 for *4.8 m.* to Maysville, crossing an earlier channel of the West Fork of the White River which marks the **DAVIESS COUNTY** (p. 27,836; 432 sq. m.) line. Daviess County is situated at the junction of the east and west forks of the White River. Originally a part of Knox County, Daviess County was formed by the General Assembly in 1816 and named after Capt. Joseph Hamilton Daviess, who was killed leading a charge at the Battle of Tippecanoe. The later formation of Owen, Martin, and Greene counties reduced the dimensions of Daviess County to its present size. The county has plentiful coal reserves and iron ore, sandstone, and limestone deposits in the northern part. The construction of the Ohio and Mississippi Railroad through Daviess County in the 1850s was a major event, because it made the coalfields accessible for exploitation. While in operation, the Wabash and Erie Canal also provided an impetus for development. Now, however, much of Daviess County remains agricultural, and a large Amish settlement farms the area northwest of Loogootee despite encroaching coal mining operations. The horse-drawn buggies of the Amish are a common sight along the rural roads, and many still refuse to hook up electricity or telephone lines to their homes. Some of the more conservative congregations continue to conduct church services in German in their homes instead of church buildings.

At the unincorporated village of **MAYSVILLE**, a state roadside marker for the Vincennes Donation Lands is located along US 50 beside the Maysville United Methodist Church (organized in 1850). In 1788 Congress granted 400 acres of land to heads of French families that had settled in Vincennes. Additional tracts were given to persons for militia service. Most of the donations lie in Knox County, though some are in what is now Daviess County. One of the latter county's earliest settlers, Eli Hawkins, came from South Carolina in 1806 and bought a 400-acre tract near what is now Maysville. John McDonald laid out the town in 1834. Maysville was a thriving Wabash and Erie Canal town for a short time in the 1850s.

Continue east on US 50/150 for *1.2 m.* to **WASHINGTON** (p. 11,325), seat of Daviess County. The town began on the site of Fort Flora, a timber fort erected about 1812 by David Flora at what is now Main and E. 2nd sts. for the protection of a handful of early settlers against the Indians. In 1815 Isaac Galland, George Curtis, and David Flora laid out the town site of Liverpool. In 1817 the county commissioners selected Liverpool, renamed Washington that year, for the county seat. The construction of the Ohio and Mississippi Railroad in 1857 brought a period of rapid growth. Though the line between St. Louis and Cincinnati was completed in 1857 and machine shops were up by 1862, the enlarged shops of the Ohio and Mississippi (later Baltimore and Ohio) Railroad at the west end of Van Trees St. did not open until 1889. (*HAER*) The B and O yards, shops, and division offices once covered more than 100 acres and employed more than 1,000 workers at Washington. In 1965 Evans Railcar Company bought the B and O car repair shops and began production of boxcars. Following a strike in 1980, the operation shut down, and local employment was reduced to a skeleton crew.

One block beyond Meridian St., the dividing line between east and west Washington, is the **Wilson home**, at 103 E. US 50. Architect J. W. Gaddis of Vincennes designed this remarkable Neo-Jacobean-style house for Nelson H. Wilson in 1896. The two-story brick structure features ornate scrollwork at the peak of the gables and elaborate brackets containing whole cartwheels at the lower ends of the roof.

Continue east on US 50 for one block and turn left on 2nd St. Go six blocks to the **Daviess County Courthouse** on the square bounded by 2nd, 3rd, Walnut, and Hefron sts. The first courthouse was a two-story brick structure erected between 1818 and 1824. A log jail containing a debtor's room and a criminal's room was added on the west end of the public square. Construction of a new courthouse began in 1838, was delayed, and finally completed in 1841. Architect George W. Bunting designed the next courthouse, a brick structure finished in 1879. Construction of a jail followed in 1884. The present courthouse, a three-story limestone building, was dedicated in 1927. A monument supporting the figures of three soldiers, dedicated in 1913, stands in front of the courthouse.

From the courthouse, turn left on Hefron St. for one block. On the northwest corner is the **Helphenstine home**, a well-preserved Greek Revival-style residence. William Helphenstine, owner of a pork-packing company, contracted with his brother-in-law Hugh Aikman to build the house in 1847. The exterior has not been altered. The house features a front porch and balcony supported by Doric columns, mortise and tenon construction, and oak/poplar plank floors. The present owner, William Reiners, shows the residence by appointment to persons interested in historic preservation.

Return on Hefron St. to N.W. 1st St., turn left, and continue three blocks to Maple St. The **Robert C. Graham house**, on the southwest corner, is a fine example of the Frank Lloyd Wright "prairie school" of architecture. In 1912 M. D. Kelly commissioned Keith Architects to design the two-story home, featuring overhanging eaves, a tile roof, and wrought-iron grillwork over the windows and front entrance. The Winslow Brothers Company custom designed the side entrance marquee with glass-pane borders. Marshall Field and Company designed the interior, which is highlighted with custom-made cabinets, marble fireplaces, beam ceilings, crystal-glass French windows, mahogany paneling, parquet floors, a skylight in the central hall, and a billiard room and chauffeur's room in the basement. Robert C.

Graham, the Evansville automobile manufacturer (see Evansville essay), later purchased the house. (*NRHP*)

Return south on N.W. 1st St. for five blocks to Van Trees St. Turn east and proceed eight blocks to N.E. 7th St., then south one block to Main St. Turn right. Many lovely old Washington homes line Main St. in this neighborhood. At 608 E. Main St. stands the **Hyatt house**, a two-story brick residence painted a cream color and distinguished by a high French mansard-style roof. Hiram Hyatt, the son of a pioneer family at one time engaged in farming, steamboating, pork packing, timber contracting, and banking, commissioned J. W. Gaddis of Vincennes to design this house in 1880.

Proceed west on Main St. to N.E. 5th St. (IND 57). Turn south and follow IND 57 for *2.1 m.* to Donaldson Rd. Turn left and continue east for *.3 m.* to the two-story red brick schoolhouse on the right with a caboose and a log cabin in the yard. Since 1979 the **Daviess County Historical Society Museum** has occupied the former Jefferson School, built in 1923. The building contains about 15 rooms of exhibits and collections related to Daviess County and Indiana history, including separate rooms for re-creations of a turn-of-the-century schoolroom, a church sanctuary dating back to 1865, a Victorian parlor, a general store, dental and medical equipment, embalming equipment from a local funeral home, fixtures from the Washington National Bank, and an Amish folk exhibit.

Continue about *1.5 m.* to IND 257 and turn right. At approximately *3.5 m.* turn left on CR 500S. Continue *3.6 m.* to CR 600E. Turn right and proceed south for *1.8 m.* to the office and checking station of the **Glendale State Fish and Wildlife Area**. Planning for the 8,021 acres of state-owned land began in the 1950s. Constructed between 1961 and 1965, an earthen dam holds back the water of the 1,400-acre Dogwood Lake. The wildlife area, operated by the Department of Natural Resources, provides regulated hunting for deer, rabbit, quail, squirrel, and waterfowl. Hunting for Canadian geese is forbidden. The dam and a new fish hatchery, which was opened to the public in 1983, can be reached from CR 600S by following CR 500E south for *2 m.* to Hudsonville, then turning left. Revenue from fishing and hunting licenses pays for the operation of the visitor center and outdoor ponds at the East Fork State Fish Hatchery. Dogwood Lake offers good fishing for walleyes, muskies, bluegills, bass, and crappies. Boat launching, camping, and picnicking facilities are available.

Rejoin CR 500E and return north to CR 600S. Follow CR 600S left to IND 257. Go left on IND 257, soon crossing the East Fork of the White River, which marks the northern boundary of **PIKE COUNTY** (p. 13,465; 341 sq. m.). Until 1816 Pike County was a part of Gibson County, and when first organized, included parts of Gibson, Warrick, and Perry counties, and all of Dubois County. The last alteration of Pike County's boundaries was in 1826. The county was named for Brig. Gen. Zebulon Montgomery Pike, discoverer of Pike's Peak in Colorado and a veteran of the War of 1812. The first white settlers in Pike County congregated at White Oak Springs Fort, a small military post along the old Buffalo Trace between Clarksville and Vincennes, which provided the early settlers protection from Indians. About 1815 Hosea Smith laid out a town at White Oak Springs called Alexandria, but refused to donate the land so that it might become the county seat. A modern housing development now occupies the site. The county contains major bituminous coal deposits, and strip mining operations are active. Two modern generating plants—the Hoosier Energy REC, Inc. and Indianapolis Power and Light Company—are located on the White River just north of Petersburg.

Continue south on IND 257 to IND 356 and turn right. This is coal mining country, and approximately *1 m.* west of Algiers pass the huge dragline of the Old Ben Coal Company. Continue to **PETERSBURG** (p. 2,987), the county seat and **home of Gil Hodges**, of baseball fame. Born in Princeton, Hodges (1924-1972) lived in Petersburg as a boy and went on to become a major league baseball player. He signed with the Brooklyn Dodgers in 1943 and went west with the Dodgers to Los Angeles in 1958. He later became manager of the Washington Senators and the New York Mets. The Gil Hodges Bridge across the East Fork of White River is *4 m.* north on IND 57.

The **Pike County Courthouse**, a three-story yellow brick structure, stands in the square bounded by Main, Walnut, 8th, and 9th sts. The first courthouse was constructed of logs in 1818. It was followed by two brick courthouses

erected in 1836 and 1868. Behind the present courthouse, built in 1922, is the old sheriff's office and jail constructed of brick on a limestone foundation and topped with a number of tall chimneys. This building was erected in 1853 and remodeled in 1885.

From Main St., proceed southeast on 8th St. for six blocks to Goodlet St. Between 7th and 8th sts. is the **Morgan-Proffit house**, an old two-story brick structure on a hill. Goodlet Morgan, a merchant and livestock dealer who came to Petersburg in the 1820s, built the house in the mid-19th century. It originally had a tower in the front. George H. Proffit, state legislator, 1831-39, congressman, 1839-43, and minister to Brazil, 1843, later owned the house.

Return to Main and 9th sts. (IND 61 and 57). Turn right and proceed south on IND 61 for *1 m.* Turn left at the road sign for **Pride's Creek Park**. The park entrance is *.5 m.* on the left. Development of this 240-acre recreation area which opened in 1970 was a Green Thumb Project sponsored by the United States Department of Labor. The park and lake have facilities for boating, camping, swimming, and picnicking.

Return to IND 61 and continue south for *2.9 m.* to the **Old Ben Coal Mine No. 2** on the left. The Old Ben and AMAX Coal companies have extensive strip-mining operations in Pike County, employing more than 800 workers and producing some six million tons of coal annually. The local electric plants use much of the coal in generating power; the balance is shipped out. At the Old Ben operation, huge earth movers uncover the coal from two pits. The coal is loaded into a central hopper, then carried by a five-mile-long conveyor belt to the storage site south of Petersburg. Here, in the preparation plant, the coal is separated from rock, washed and crushed, then shipped to order.

Continue south on IND 61 for *4.8 m.* to Center and Main sts. in downtown **WINSLOW** (p. 1,017). In 1837 John Hathaway laid out the town, situated just north of the Patoka River. Development began as a result of its natural location as a shipping and milling center. Flatboats carried local goods downstream until the railroad became the chief means of transportation.

Continue south on IND 61 through Winslow for *2.1 m.* to IND 364. Turn left for *4 m.* through picturesque, hilly, and wooded countryside dotted with rustic-looking homes to the **Pike State Forest**. The Department of Natural

Resources maintains 2,914 acres of wooded land east of Winslow for recreation, timber and wildlife production, and watershed protection. Park facilities include areas for camping, fishing, and picnicking. In addition, the park provides a horsemen's campground and bridle trails through the forest.

Return *3 m.* to CR 300E and turn south for *.9 m.* to the **Patoka State Fish and Wildlife Area**. In 1964 the Indiana Department of Natural Resources initiated a land reclamation program in the coal mining region of southwestern Indiana. The state leased more than 7,400 acres from three major mining companies and assumed responsibility for their development. Old strip mine pits have been stocked with fish and equipped with boat ramps. Leveling and seeding of strip mine spoil banks have encouraged deer and small game to return to the area. Facilities vary at the scattered sites, but hunting and fishing are the major activities offered. The headquarters building provides a 24-hour, self-service information center where maps are available.

Continue south and turn right at IND 64. Proceed west, crossing the county line, to IND 357 in **OAKLAND CITY** (p. 3,301). Turn north on Main St. (IND 357) and proceed *.8 m.* to Washington St. in the center of town. Col. James W. Cockrum and his son-in-law Warrick Hargrove platted the town of Oakland in 1856. When the town was incorporated in 1885, the name changed to Oakland City. From Oakland City came Edd Roush, twice National League batting champion. Roush played for the Cincinnati Reds and New York Giants, 1916-31, and was inducted into the baseball hall of fame in 1962.

From Main St., continue *.4 m.* to **Oakland City College** at the west end of Washington St. The state granted a charter for the college in 1885, and Col. William M. Cockrum donated 10 acres of land for the first building, completed in 1892. The original structure plus an addition erected in 1900 now serve as the administration building. Oakland City College is a private four-year, liberal arts institution affiliated with the General Association of General Baptists. The class of 1922 donated the front gate facing Franklin St. The college chapel, also facing Franklin St., seats 110 persons. It was built in 1968. From Washington and Franklin

sts., go south one block, then west one block on Columbia St. to Lucretia St. The beautiful two-story brick house of colonial design at the northwest corner is the college president's residence. A sign notes that the college is the home of the "Mighty Oaks"—1981 National Little College Athletic Association basketball champions.

From Lucretia and Columbia sts., proceed south one block then west one-half block. **Cockrum Hall**, 627 W. Oak St., now home of the college music department, stands on a hill encircled by oak trees. Col. William M. Cockrum built the two-story brick mansion with a large corner tower in 1876. The house is a copy of an Italian villa. Like his father James W. Cockrum, who settled in Gibson County in 1816 after some time spent running steamboats up and down the Mississippi, William Cockrum was a temperance advocate and abolitionist. In 1907 he published *A Pioneer History of Indiana*. The house has a later addition in the rear and recently underwent restoration.

Return to Washington and Main sts., then go south to IND 357 and IND 64. Proceed west on IND 64 for *1.5 m.* to IND 57. Turn left and proceed south for *7.5 m.* to the village of Buckskin. Turn left on CR 800S, which becomes CR 900S, and go *2.5 m.* east to CR 1050E. Turn left and continue north for *.6 m.* to the parking lot for the **Hemmer Woods Nature Preserve** on the right. The state bought 72 acres of this upland forest in 1974. A nature trail circles through the woods containing large specimens of oak, hickory, maple, elm, mulberry, ash, and sassafras trees, and other smaller growth. Swamp hardwoods grow in the bottomland area below the trail. The forest has been registered as a National Natural Landmark.

Return to IND 57 and continue south for *15.3 m.*, crossing the Warrick, Gibson, and Vanderburgh county lines and passing the unincorporated village of **DAYLIGHT**. The place supposedly acquired its name from a chance remark made by a railroad engineer who said, every evening when he dropped off a construction crew here, "I'll pick you men up at daylight." At the end of IND 57, continue south on US 41 for *4.7 m.* to Walnut St. in Evansville. Turn west and proceed *1.1 m.* to the Civic Center and the end of the tour.

Terre Haute

Terre Haute, French for "high land," is Indiana's ninth largest city (p. 61,125) and the seat of justice of **VIGO COUNTY** (p. 112,385; 405 sq. m.). The city originated in 1816 on a plateau alongside the Wabash River. A prairie, probably created by Indians burning off timber to facilitate hunting, extended east of present 6th St. From about 1720 to 1763 the Terre Haute site lay astride the line dividing the French provinces of Canada and Louisiana. The first indication of permanent white occupation coincided with the construction of Fort Harrison in 1811. A village of Wea (or Ouiatenon) Indians, the future location of Terre Haute, stood a few miles south of the fort. The fort's transient personnel passed the word about the fertility and river proximity of the so-called Harrison Prairie. A few traders and squatters braved the environment of the garrison, but not until 1816 when the doors to settlement officially opened did the marked procession of pioneers begin.

Jackson County's land speculator Joseph Kitchell purchased some 30,000 acres south of Fort Harrison in September 1816. He marketed his holdings to the proprietors of the Terre Haute Land Company: Jonathan Lindley, Abraham Markle, Hyacinth Lasselle, and Cuthbert and Thomas Bullitt. Surveyor William Hoggatt chose the spot for Terre Haute from among the company's properties. Kitchell, an attorney, recorded the plat on October 25, 1816. Despite brisk sales, purchasers often defaulted on loans, and many lots remained unsold. Potential buyers bypassed Terre Haute for the more lived-in look around Fort Harrison.

Terre Haute's survival chances improved when it obtained the county seat in March 1818, two months after the organization of Vigo County, carved from Sullivan County. The proprietors had made provision for a courthouse square, and their foresight, along with a donation of 80 lots and $4,000, won them the county seat. Before long a courthouse and jail materialized, a ferry crisscrossed the Wabash River, and a post office was established.

The county's name honored Col. Francis Vigo (1747-1836). Vigo, born in Sardinia, off Italy, became a prosperous merchant-trader in St. Louis. During the Revolutionary War he supplied George Rogers Clark with information, money, and materials for use in ending British influence in the Northwest Territory. Moving to Vincennes after the war, Vigo, now a naturalized citizen, rendered conspicuous military and civil service. The United States delayed repaying Vigo's crucial wartime loans, and he died practically impoverished. Consequently, Vigo's wish to donate a courthouse bell went unfulfilled until the government compensated his heirs and they subsidized a bell for the 1888 courthouse.

The Terre Haute plat bordered the river for eight blocks and extended five blocks east. The town spread out from its public square at the center of the plat. In 1832 the approximately 1,000 residents voted to incorporate as a town. Officials began making headway in removing trees and underbrush from around the courthouse, grading streets, inspecting packing-houses, and building cisterns and a new jail. By the mid-1840s more than 100 businesses plus churches and schools encircled the public square.

Farming, milling, and especially pork processing constituted the economic backbone of antebellum Terre Haute. A familiar sight was the droves of corn-fattened hogs being coaxed and prodded along city streets toward the numerous slaughterhouses lining the river. The business and industrial expansion of Terre Haute prior to 1860 hinged on the evolution of a transportation system encompassing river, highway, canal, and railroad. The steamboat, *Florence*, docked at Terre Haute about 1823. Soon a stream of packet boats, flatboats, barge fleets, and other rivercraft carried farm produce and passengers southward. The National Rd., the major east-west thoroughfare, reached the city in 1835. The arrival of the Wabash and Erie Canal in 1849 preceded too closely the advent of the more dependable railroad for the waterway to have a significant economic impact. Still, the canal was the principal means of travel to the north for a decade. Even as the canal construction neared Terre Haute, plans went forward to bring rails from Richmond, Indiana, along the course of the National Rd. The Terre Haute and Richmond Railroad, completed in 1852, was the initial line of a rail network that added considerably to the city's reputation as a transportation crossroads. Bridges across the Wabash and its tributaries linked the various transport resources, fostered travel, facilitated business, and extended the city's range of influence.

Terre Haute's economic profile changed after the Civil War. Pork processing declined. The 108,791 hogs processed in 1852 represent the local industry's peak year. The war interrupted pork trade with the South, and with the rise of meat-packing centers in Chicago and Kansas City, Terre Haute's share of the market dwindled. Conversely, railroad needs stimulated the development of nearby iron ore, coal, and oil reserves. The construction and upkeep of railroads required large-scale iron operations fueled by coke. Not until the discovery in 1867 of block coalfields in neighboring Clay County did there exist an easily mined energy supply suitable for iron production. Several iron furnaces started up between 1867 and 1872 in and around Terre Haute, followed by foundries and rolling mills that turned out nails, rails, railroad cars, and bridge iron. By 1870 Vigo County ranked third in the state in coal mining, and fifth in manufacturing.

The city's dream of becoming the Pittsburgh of the West was not realized because of inferior ore and the development of Lake County's steel industry. Over time, the iron furnaces shut down. On the other hand, coal stood second to farm produce as the area's most valuable commodity by 1900. Agriculture predominated, largely due to the role of corn in making alcoholic beverages and food items. The Terre Haute Brewing Company incorporated in 1889, but its roots dated from 1837. Its famed Champagne Velvet beer was registered in 1904. The Hudnut Milling Company, largest of a half dozen local mills, moved from Edin-

burgh, Indiana, to Terre Haute in the early 1860s. It put out hominy grits, corn flour, corn oil, and similar products. By 1880 the city was the nation's fifth most important center for flour and gristmill products, as well as fifth in production of distilled liquor. The oil strikes of the late 1860s and 1889-90 were of little consequence. The anticipation of oil booms aroused the business community, but most wells fizzled. A by-product of oil drilling was unearthing sulfuric waters, sufficiently foul smelling to guarantee their medicinal value and thus profit to owners of bathhouses and sanitariums erected after the discovery of the waters.

The city's burgeoning labor market set in motion a growth in population, which expanded from 4,051 in 1850 to 36,673 by 1900. The mostly native-born residents came primarily from the East, bearing out Horace Greeley's advice to the young to go West, a recommendation Greeley appropriated from a statement of John B. L. Soule in his newspaper, the *Terre Haute Daily Express*, in 1851. An unusual number of persons, however, reverse migrated from Illinois. Terre Haute had the largest percentage of foreign born (11 percent in 1870, for example) in west-central Indiana. Germans slightly outnumbered Irish, who labored on railroads and the canal. The percentage of blacks in the city increased from 2.4 percent to 4 percent between 1860 and 1900.

The proliferation of ironworks, coal mines, brickyards, railroads, breweries, and distilleries afforded abundant opportunities for labor union formation. First came the Typographical Union in 1873. By 1900 unions numbered 27. In 1881 Terre Haute hosted an organizational meeting of Midwest craft unions that led in 1886 to the creation of the American Federation of Labor. Eugene V. Debs, a Terre Haute native who achieved national recognition as a friend of the worker and as the Socialist party's perennial presidential candidate, was influential in several local unions.

In other areas of community life, government officials moved into new offices: City Hall (1874), County Courthouse (1888), and the Federal Building (1887). Fire protection improved with the organization of a fire department, the purchase of steam fire engines, the introduction of the telephone, and the building of an up-to-date waterworks. A city health department and St. Anthony's hospital, both established in 1882, guarded the physical well-being of citizens. St. Anthony's was the city's only hospital until the founding of Union Hospital in 1892. School buildings rose on the average of one every two years. Students wanting advanced business or collegiate education could choose among St. Mary-of-the-Woods (1840), Coates College (1862), the Terre Haute Commerical College (1862), Indiana State Normal School (opened 1870, now Indiana State University), and Rose Polytechnic Institute (1874, now Rose-Hulman Institute of Technology). Churches multiplied more rapidly than schools; for example, 22 churches came into being in the 14 years between 1882 and 1896. To facilitate travel around town the mule-driven streetcars, introduced in 1866, gave way in the 1890s to electric-powered trolleys. The Union and the Big Four railroad depots were erected in the 1890s.

Streetcars and railroads enabled residents to participate in a growing number of amusements: circuses, baseball games, picnics, excursions, vaudeville shows, chautauquas, dramas, and operas. The Naylor Opera House, a massive landmark from 1870 to 1896, sponsored hundreds of operatic and theatrical performances. After the Naylor burned in 1896, the Grand Opera House was built with a seating capacity of 1,500. The famous and odd-shaped Four-Cornered Racetrack, laid out in 1886, drew the finest American trotters and drivers. Its contours, more square than oval, resulted from having to put the required one-mile distance into a limited land area. In 1910 the track was reduced to one-half mile.

Eugene V. Debs was one of a number of persons with Terre Haute connections who carved out eminent careers. Among those were Senator Daniel W. Voorhees, the "Tall Sycamore of the Wabash"; Thomas H. Nelson, minister to Chile and Mexico; John Palmer Usher, interior secretery under President Abraham Lincoln; Richard W. Thompson, dubbed the Ancient Mariner of the Wabash, secretary of the navy under President Rutherford B. Hayes; Edward James Roye, the fifth president of Liberia; Claude Bowers, historian and diplomat; and Congressman Everett Sanders, Calvin Coolidge's secretary. Dr. Lyman Abbott, clergyman, author, and editor of *The Outlook* magazine, held forth at the First Congregational Church from 1860 to 1865.

The city's contributors to the arts include songwriter Paul Dresser, who penned *On the Banks of the Wabash Far Away*, and Theodore Dreiser, Paul's brother, one of this century's most acclaimed novelists. Ida Husted Harper (1851-1931), journalist and biographer of Susan B. Anthony, began her newspaper career in Terre Haute with the *Saturday Evening Mail*. Black author Jane Dabney Shackelford, a Terre Haute teacher, made a major contribution toward informing children of the black heritage when she wrote *The Child's Story of the Negro* (1938). Lawyer-poet Max Ehrmann, whose *A Prayer* and *Desiderata* are still worldwide favorites, was a lifelong resident. Albert Kussner was an internationally known composer, and his sister Amalia achieved fame as a consummate miniaturist. Their parents operated a music store in Terre Haute. Janet Scudder, a sculptor, was most recognized for her bronze fountains and medallions. On stage Marie Roslyn (Rose Fehrenbach) played musical comedy in the world's principal cities. Rose Melville (Rose Smock) toured in stock companies with her sisters until a specially produced play *Sis Hopkins* brought her stardom. Benjamin Sherman (Scatman) Crothers, actor, comedian, and musician, was born in Terre Haute in 1910 and launched his long career in the city's nightclubs. Baseball players Max Carey, Hall of Fame member and record-breaking base stealer, Arthur (Art) Nehf, Vic Aldridge, Paul (Dizzy) Trout, and Tommy John, major-league pitchers, were all Terre Haute natives. Another Hall of Famer, Mordecai "Three Fingers" Brown, while born in Parke County, played for a Terre Haute Three I League team in 1901 and in 1919 and 1920. He lived in the city from 1935 to his death in 1948.

Into the new century Terre Haute's population continued to expand along with its industries and businesses. Reflecting the process of urbanization in the state and the nation, the city's population jumped to 66,083 by 1920. The sprawling metropolis made imperative advances in transportation. The old 1865 wooden covered bridge across the Wabash River was replaced in 1905 with the present-day steel, concrete, and brick span. The new bridge's brick roadway encompassed two sidewalks besides double trolley tracks for use by interurbans, which began local service in 1900.

The burgeoning cities of America required extraordinary vigilance by citizens' groups to counteract vice and political corruption. In the 19th century Terre Haute was reputed to be a "sporting" town, the "Paris of Indiana." The public's indulgence of shady activities changed to anger in the early 1900s. Civic and business organizations joined hands to expose sinister links between crime, special interests, and city hall. At one point the coalition petitioned for state aid and for federal monitoring of elections. Nationwide experiments in city management often granted elected mayors unprecedented appointive powers, therefore inviting misuse of authority. A Terre Haute mayor indebted to a political machine backed by brewery money could make sure his chief of police and his safety board neglected to enforce closing hours of saloons. Fraudulent election practices included repeat voting, stuffed ballot boxes, counterfeit ballots, padded registration lists, bribed election officials and police, extortion, and violence. The tenacity of both the guardians of morality and the beneficiaries of lawbreaking is evident in the replays of official misconduct: Mayor Edwin Bidaman was impeached in 1906; Mayor Louis A. Gerhardt was arraigned for contempt of court in 1911; and Mayor Donn Roberts and 20 others convicted of election fraud in 1915 served time in Leavenworth Penitentiary. Despite these and other court victories, the press stamped Terre Haute as Sin City, thereby fostering an image that has haunted the community.

The exploits of the Johnson brothers were perhaps as interesting to Terre Haute residents as the city hall shenanigans. Harry, Louis, Julius, and Clarence began tinkering with motors in 1903. First they produced inboard boat engines. In 1909 they fashioned and attached an airplane engine to a homemade, single-winged frame. The craft's 30-ft. maiden hop on August 8, 1911, made history as one of America's earliest monoplane flights. The 1913 tornado and flood took 17 lives in Terre Haute and destroyed the Johnsons' boat motor factory. The brothers relocated to South Bend and in 1927 moved to Waukegan, Illinois, where the aviation pioneers began manufacturing the prized Johnson outboard motor. A few years later in 1930 Ellen Church Marshall became the world's first airline stewardess after convincing United Air Lines of the feasibility of using women as hostesses. Between 1952 and 1965 Mrs. Marshall was an administrator at Union Hospital in Terre Haute.

Terre Haute has an interesting connection with the present state of Israel, the seeds of which were planted during World War I. After hostilities had cut off Britain's supply of acetone, an ingredient in explosives, the Russian-born chemist Dr. Chaim Weizmann developed a synthetic product for the British Admiralty. One of the major producers of this synthetic acetone was located in Terre Haute. For Weizmann's war effort the British government issued the Balfour Declaration (1917), a basis for the creation of the modern nation of Israel. The moneys Weizmann received in royalties from the Terre Haute plant, Commercial Solvents Corporation, which held exclusive patent rights, helped Weizmann in 1948 realize his dream of establishing a state of Israel. He became its first president.

Terre Haute's progress could not be sustained after World War I. Liquor prohibition shut down the breweries and distilleries and curtailed bottle making. The departure of the Pennsylvania Railroad's repair shops in 1923 swelled unemployment rolls and impaired small iron and steel firms. The most serious blow stemmed from the decline in coal mining, an outgrowth of mechanized underground digging, the inception of strip mining and its shift to less depleted deposits in far southwest Indiana, coal company consolidations, competition from petroleum, electricity, and cheap coal extracted in nonunion fields in Kentucky and West Virginia. By 1930 some 12,000 fewer men worked the area's coal mines. The Terre Haute Foundation, founded in 1926, snared a few industries, but the city ended the decade with one of Indiana's highest jobless rates and with 3,273 fewer residents than it had in 1920.

Except for severe labor-management problems Terre Haute might have come through the Great Depression relatively unscathed. Belt-tightening had commenced long before the crisis of the early 1930s. Moreover, Terre Haute's light diversified industrial base made it less susceptible to economic downturns than cities dependent on heavy metals and durable goods manufacturing. In addition, with prohibition's repeal in 1933, breweries, distilleries, bottle works, and retail liquor stores reopened, and grain growers prospered.

Since the 1890s industrialists had labeled Terre Haute a bad labor town, one saturated with strong worker organizations. Strikes, lockouts, a conservative Chamber of Commerce, and weak newspapers fostered discord between workers and employers. Pro-labor federal legislation in the 1930s bolstered unionization. Sporadic strikes included three packing plant walkouts that caused livestock markets to close and the city's meat supplies to dwindle. At the Columbian Enameling and Stamping Company plant, management's refusal to arbitrate with the new Federal Labor Union on the matter of a closed shop precipitated a strike on March 23, 1935. After four months of impasse the city's unions announced a "labor holiday" for July 22. The general strike shut down all business except for critical services. Gov. Paul V. McNutt declared martial law and dispatched troops to the city. After two days of some violence and 185 arrests, the strike ended. Martial law, however, remained in effect for six months more. Afterward, the parties regrouped to do battle via the press and the courtroom. The Greater Terre Haute Movement, spearheaded by the newly formed Junior Chamber of Commerce, tried to improve relations by holding informal meetings with all sides represented. Difficulties persisted nonetheless in attracting new industry and in keeping established companies. The city government seemed unable to surmount the economic straits or curb the flourishing vice and gambling.

The Second World War created abnormal economic conditions in many cities, but Terre Haute escaped the problem due to its lack of durable goods manufacturers. Instead, Terre Haute produced peacetime goods, largely food items, and supplied labor to three nearby ordnance plants. The A and P (Great Atlantic and Pacific Tea) Company's Quaker Maid plant was said to have been the world's largest food processing factory under one roof. In one of these plants, the Terre Haute Ordnance Depot, biological agents for antipersonnel bombs would have been produced had the war continued. The city received the nation's 100th United Service Organizations (USO) facility in 1943, and it proudly accepted designation as the country's foremost recruitment center of women serving in the navy (Women Accepted for Volunteer Emergency Service, or Waves). In 1945 when the navy launched the SS *Terre Haute Victory*, a 10,800-ton armed cargo ship, it carried a library and recreational equipment purchased with funds raised in a city campaign.

The rousing activities of the war effort—troop send-offs, victory gardens, bond sales, civil defense drills, parades, and ceremonies—only briefly diverted attention from Terre Haute's almost congenital social and economic plight. In all years but two between 1940 and 1961 the city found itself on some form of federal chronic unemployment list. New factories, such as Pfizer Chemical (1948), Allis-Chalmers (1951), Columbia Records (1954), and Anaconda Aluminum (1959), could absorb only a portion of job seekers from folded businesses. Manufacturing establishments declined from 134 in 1947 to 131 twenty years later. The community lost about 6,000 jobs between 1950 and 1960. The census tally that showed an increase of 9,807 residents in the 1940-60 period masked the loss of workplaces and jobholders. The census figure represented gains through annexations, including the attachment of Harrison Township in 1957, not a net gain of recent arrivals.

National magazines and state newspapers persisted in featuring the iniquities of the city. The image of a debauched community plagued local administrators. Successive mayors tried, more or less, to blot out gambling and prostitution, the volume of which, in any case, had decreased significantly from prewar levels. Isolated incidents, such as the 1957 disclosure that Terre Haute was a base for a large gambling syndicate, stoked the media's fires.

Meanwhile the downtown crumbled financially and physically; the *Saturday Evening Post* depicted it as "shabby" in 1961. Walnut St. was lined with gutted hulks of buildings, the remains of a series of tragic explosions and fires in the early 1960s. Central city residents moved to the suburbs, and merchants relocated into outlying shopping centers. The impact of downtown decay was lessened because of urban renewal in the 1960s and the stepped-up building program at Indiana State University (ISU) in response to a doubling of its student body.

The city's troubles prompted civic groups to organize and to challenge the status quo. The Housewives Effort for Local Progress (HELP), for example, cut through the superficial vice issue and clearly stated what the city lacked: a viable two-party system, municipal leadership, civic planning, community spirit, railroad overpasses, a public auditorium, swimming pools, sewage disposal plant, and pollution control. The development of the Fort Harrison Industrial Park by the Terre Haute Committee for Area Progress (THCAP) paced job growth. In the 1970s, even during the 1973-75 recession, Terre Haute enjoyed one of Indiana's lowest unemployment rates. In 1979 the community was preoccupied with the basketball genius of Larry Bird, College Player of the Year. The French Lick, Indiana, superstar led ISU into the NCAA finals subsequent to signing a pro contract with the Boston Celtics for a wage that made him the highest paid rookie in professional sports history.

The city's apparent healthy glow in the 1970s was misleading. Shocked officials learned that the 1980 census count showed a decade loss of 9,210 persons, a 13.1 percent decline. Not since before the First World War had the population figure stood as low as the 61,125 recorded in 1980. By and large the population reduction stemmed from the exodus of working-age youth, the lack of in-migration to replace the natural attrition within a growing elderly group, an enrollment decrease at ISU, the movement of people and workplaces outside Harrison Township, and cutbacks at Columbia Records, the city's largest employer. The record company finally closed in 1982, eliminating 3,500 jobs. More plant closings, a slumping real estate market, construction curtailments, inflation, and drought reversed the upward trends of the 1970s. By January 1983 unemployment measured 15.5 percent. Manufacturing jobs in the Terre Haute metropolitan area declined by 24.6 percent from 1980 to 1983. The city's population declined by 828 persons between 1980 and 1982. Labor-management disputes involving newspapers, airport, and police aggravated the situation. Crime rates skyrocketed. The demolition of downtown structures proceeded, though one major complex, the Vigo County Annex and Security Center, opened in 1981.

By the mid-1980s considerable headway had been made in Terre Haute to stabilize the economy and enhance community life. In came new stores, factories, and high-tech industrial parks, endeavors urged on by Grow Terre Haute, an organization of city officials and community leaders. Most encouraging was the establishment of the Digital Audio Disc Corporation (DADC), a subsidiary of CBS/Sony, as the first and only American factory designed exclusively to make compact discs and one of only 12 worldwide. Opened in September 1984, the company's first release was Bruce Springsteen's *Born in the U.S.A.* By 1986 employment had tripled, and the factory was producing one million discs per month. Sony's DADC, new construction projects on the campuses of Rose-Hulman and Indiana State, and a major expansion of Bemis Bag and of Ivy Hill Packaging helped to compensate for plant closings including J. I. Case, which phased out its farm and construction equipment production in 1987 with a loss of almost 500 jobs.

In other developments, railroad overpasses eased traffic congestion. A controversial shoot-to-kill police directive reduced incidences of crime in some major categories. Several national and state awards for volunteerism and citizen participation boosted local pride. A multifaceted approach characterized downtown rehabilitation. The construction of a few new office buildings confirmed predictions that the core city would become a professional and business center to complement its governmental, educational, cultural, sports, and entertainment features. Moreover, the architectural commission of Terre Haute Civic Improvement, Inc., outlined goals and performed surveys necessary for a historic preservation district. An inventory of buildings in the central city pinpointed over 125 eligible for inclusion on the National Register of Historic Places. In late 1983 the Register recognized 2 historic districts and 15 individual buildings in the inner city.

Heartened by the turnaround in the national economy and inspired by the demonstrated cooperation of townspeople, business, and government, the residents of Terre Haute, with a new Alliance for Growth and Progress and well-financed Visitor's Bureau, looked forward to the fresh opportunity to develop their town's traditional strengths. Possessing a rich heritage of higher education, agriculture, parks, industry, and cultural institutions, Terre Haute aims at closing out the 20th century on the same progressive note as it began the century.

Terre Haute Attractions

For additional information on Terre Haute's sites and attractions contact the **Terre Haute Convention and Visitors Bureau** in the Honeycreek Square mall, south of downtown, at the junction of I-70 and US 41.

1. The **Vigo County Courthouse**, bounded by 3rd, Ohio, and Cherry sts., is the county's third courthouse and the second on the site. Agitation for a new courthouse began in 1872, but not until 1881 did the public and the county commissioners concur on the need for a larger, costlier, and grander edifice. The Cincinnati firm of Samuel Hannaford and Sons designed the French Neo-Baroque building. The dedication took place June 7, 1888. The imposing limestone structure features a dome 196 ft. above ground level. At one time each of the four projecting columned pavilions had a staircase. Now only the 3rd St. entrance has stairs. (*NRHP*)

On the northeast corner of the courthouse lawn is the county's **Civil War Monument**, erected in 1909-10. Rudolph Schwarz sculpted the five martial figures, including the flag-bearing statue of Indiana's wartime governor Oliver P. Morton, which crowns the memorial. Nearby is the **bust of Richard W. Thompson**, secretary of the navy under President Rutherford B. Hayes. The Thompson sculpture was executed by A. Doyle in 1902 and positioned in 1906.

Just west of the courthouse, near City Hall, is a memorial to Claude L. Herbert, who died after saving several persons in the Havens and Geddes store fire. A bronze statue in honor of his heroic deed was installed at 5th St. and Wabash Ave. Vehicular accidents at this busy corner several times damaged the memorial, which had to be replaced. In 1980 the city moved the fountain to its present location for safekeeping.

2. **Memorial Hall**, 219 Ohio St., is the city's oldest building. It was constructed in 1834-36 as one of the Second State Bank's 13 branches. Edwin J. Peck (1806-1876) supervised the building of the Greek Revival structure with its four tall columns. Peck, whose business ventures included the Indianapolis and Terre Haute Railroad, also oversaw construction of similar styled bank buildings in Madison, Lafayette, and South Bend. The bank was reorganized in the late 1850s, following the termination of its charter, and it continued as a private banking institution until 1867 when new quarters were occupied. After the bank relocated, the building had a succession of uses: residence, music shop, warehouse, and second-hand store. In 1910 it became the headquarters for the local Grand Army of the Republic (GAR). Newly renovated in 1921, it turned into the GAR Memorial Hall, furnished with all kinds of Civil War memorabilia, much of which has vanished over the years. The crowning interior architectural achievement is the art glass dome featuring portraits of 17 prominent Terre Haute bankers and Civil War leaders. (*NRHP*)

3. The **Temple of Labor**, 201 S. 5th St., is the headquarters of the Central Labor Union, set up in 1890, and of a half dozen craft unions. The two-story, red brick Renaissance Revival structure was erected in 1905 as the Phoenix Club, a Jewish men's organization, the initials of which are incorporated in the tile flooring of the front porch. The Terre Haute Labor Temple Association, established in 1912, purchased the Phoenix Club for $36,000 in 1923. Over the years such labor and socialist leaders as Morris Hillquist, Victor Berger, and Norman Thomas have visited the temple. Here, Eugene V. Debs lay in state in 1926. A room in the hall is now named for Debs, and another for Samuel Gompers, a founder of the American Federation of Labor. Both rooms contain memorabilia pertaining to Debs and city unions. (*NRHP*)

Terre Haute Attractions

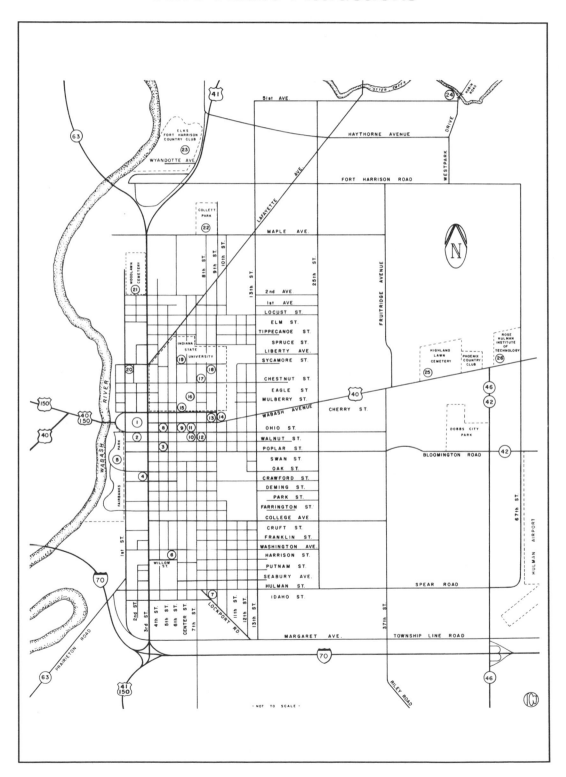

4. **Allen Chapel African Methodist Episcopal Church (AME)**, 3rd and Crawford sts., the city's oldest black religious body, traces its beginnings to 1839 when a group of freedmen established a congregation. The church was named for Richard Allen (1760-1831), the first bishop of the AME denomination, founded in 1816 as America's first major black organization. The Terre Haute worshipers' initial sanctuary went up in the early 1840s on S. 1st St. near Crawford St. The frame building was a stopping place on the "underground railroad," and it housed Terre Haute's first school for blacks. Among the prominent black leaders ministering to the church in this era was Hiram Rhoades Revels (1822-1901), subsequently the first black United States senator, elected by Mississippi voters in 1870. In this same year in Terre Haute the AME church members built an Italianate brick structure on the present site. Severely damaged by fire, an aftereffect of the 1913 tornado, the church had to be almost totally rebuilt. In doing so the church acquired its current Gothic look and Tudor tower. (*NRHP*)

5. **Fairbanks Park**, southwest of the courthouse (enter on Farrington St., off US 41), is the city's only riverside park. In 1916 the Fairbanks brothers, Crawford and Edward, donated riverfront property for the establishment of a park in memory of Henry Fairbanks, their father and a Terre Haute mayor in the late 1870s. Two important historical attractions are situated in the park's 105 acres. The **Chauncey Rose Memorial** incorporates columns and a pediment from the old Federal Building, which stood at N. 7th and Cherry sts. from 1887 to 1933. The wealth and name of Chauncey Rose (1794-1877) has been attached to a number of institutions in Terre Haute: Rose Polytechnic Institute (now Rose-Hulman Institute of Technology), Rose Dispensary, Rose Orphan's Home, Rose Aid Home, and Providence Hospital. He also financially aided Wabash College and charities in Charleston, South Carolina, and New York City. Rose made his fortune as a merchant and promoter of the canal and the railroads. He built the Prairie House, an inn, in 1838, where the Terre Haute House now stands at 7th St. and Wabash Ave., and at one time owned much of what is now downtown Terre Haute. Also in the park is the **Paul Dresser Birthplace**. The famed songwriter and brother of author Theodore Dreiser was born in this two-story brick workingman's home in 1859. The house was opened to the public in 1966, three years after its removal from its original location at 318 S. 2nd St. Its five rooms are furnished with period pieces, but only a glass bowl belonged to the Dreiser family. The home at 1st and Farrington sts. is owned and maintained by the Vigo County Historical Society. (*NRHP*) Besides the historical memorials, Fairbanks Park includes an open-air amphitheater, a 20-station exercise path, boat launching and fishing facilities, and a sunken garden surrounding a new fountain. In the early 1980s city officials spent some $1.5 million on improvements for the park, which is the setting for the annual Banks of the Wabash Festival.

6. The **Historical Museum of the Wabash Valley**, 1411 S. 6th St., occupies the Sage-Robinson-Nagel house. The house represents a building project by three different owners. William H. Sage built the first section in 1868. He sold his home in 1875 to Henry Robinson, who added another part. Clemens W. Nagel bought the house in 1905 and appended the final segment. The Vigo County Historical Society, with funds provided by Anton Hulman, Jr., purchased the structure from Marcella Nagel Lundgren in 1957. The museum officially opened in 1958. Twelve rooms of exhibits on three floors harbor collections of antiques, curiosities, and local memorabilia. Of particular significance to Terre Haute is the Paul Dresser portrait and a piano he played; Francis Vigo's silver pitcher; Chauncey Rose's desk; a display on Max Ehrmann; the Mercury statue from atop the McKeen Bank Building; Punch, a wooden advertising figure from the Biel Cigar Factory; and a painting and a replica of Fort Harrison. The totem pole on the front lawn came in 1963 from the Chapman J. Root estate in nearby Allendale. Called Tootootch, an Indian word for the thunderbird perched on top, the totem was carved in the mid-1930s by Huston Isaacs and Charles Eggleston. They fashioned the object from a 28-ft.-long California pine tree. Chapman Jay Root (1867-1945) headed the Root Glass Company in Terre Haute. From the bottling plant in 1913 came the winning design for the Hobble Skirt, or Mae West, Coca-Cola bottle, which with some modifications remains the standard container. Coca-Cola acquired the bottle's patent in 1937

from Root. The museum displays a copy of the original bottle. (*NRHP*)

7. The **Historical Fire Station No. 9**, 1728 S. 8th St., houses the Fire and Police Museum. Built in 1906, the station acquired in 1910 the state's first motorized fire truck. After June 1980, when it no longer functioned as a firehouse, it was changed into a museum, which opened in June 1981. Retired fire fighter Tom Champion, the curator, led the drive for funds from fellow firemen and the general public to launch the museum. Fire torches, fire hooks, an 1838 rattle alarm, helmets, buckets, uniforms, models of horse-drawn equipment, antique fire trucks, an 1885 police ambulance, and the old blacksmith shop from Fire Station No. 4 are among the items displayed. The original alarm system, still operating, the horse stalls, brass pole, and firemen's quarters remain intact from Station No. 9. Rare movies of fire and police activity in Terre Haute from 1908 to 1910 are available for viewing by groups. At the side of the station is the Memorial Plaza, dedicated in 1982 to the fallen heroes of Vigo County's fire and police departments. The fire bell, from old No. 1 Firehouse built in 1857, is installed on the plaza. (*NRHP*)

8. The **Sycamore Building**, 19-21 S. 6th St., is Terre Haute's tallest structure. The 12-story brick and stone edifice went up in 1921 to house the Citizens Trust Company. At a cost of $318,280, it contained all modern conveniences including high-speed elevators. In 1956, after the bank vacated the building, Emma Herber bought it for $105,000 and leased its office and commercial space. She saw to it that the words Conrad Herber Memorial were engraved on either side of the entrance. Conrad, Emma's husband of 50 years, was a pharmacist, politician, and officer and board member in a variety of businesses and service organizations. He died in the mid-1940s. His wife, it is said, purchased the property in order to memorialize her husband by having his name carved in stone. The building, which underwent a complete exterior restoration in 1982, is presently owned by Sunset Harbor, Inc. (*NRHP*)

Paul Dresser Birthplace, 1968

Indiana Historical Society (Martin Collection 203486)

9. The **Terre Haute First National Bank**, 643-645 Wabash Ave., occupies a building erected in 1904 for the United States Trust Company. Solon Spencer Beman (1853-1914), a Chicago architect, designed the structure. In 1881, ironically, Beman drew up the plans for the company town of Pullman, Illinois, the site in 1894 of the great Pullman Palace Car strike, which propelled the defiant Terre Haute labor leader Eugene V. Debs to national prominence. The First National Bank, so named after a merger in 1960, is the product of some 19 bank combinations and reorganizations stretching back to 1834. In 1927 the building underwent extensive alterations. The local firm of Johnson, Miller, Miller and Yeager devised the present exterior cast-iron and smooth-stone facade with its Neoclassical-style arch. The circular panels on either side of the uppermost part of the arch depict the Indian-head nickel and the Mercury-head dime. Inside the bank around the barrel-vaulted ceiling are eight murals painted in 1927 by Vincent Aderante (1880-1941), an Italian artist principally known for his courthouse murals. The scenes symbolize elements making for economic progress. The airplane, shown in the Modes of Transportation segment, is patterned after Lindbergh's *Spirit of St. Louis*. The use of an airplane in the mural is claimed as a first in the history of this form of artwork. The paintings were refurbished in the mid-1970s.

10. The **Indiana Theatre**, 7th and Ohio sts., represents one of seven grandiose theaters built in the early 1920s in Illinois and Indiana, including the present Indiana Repertory Theatre in Indianapolis. Terre Haute's lavish vaudeville and movie palace formally opened January 9, 1922. Chicago's theater-architect John Eberson designed it, and local businessman T. W. Barhydt supplied the reported $750,000 building expense. The red brick structure, heavily ornamented with terra-cotta trim, particularly festoons and coats of arms, is reminiscent of 17th-century architecture from the Andalusia region of Spain. The Spanish motif continues inside in the ornate ornamentation of the outer lobby rotunda, in the mosaic tile floors, and in the Moorish ceilings. The original Hope-Jones Wurlitzer Organ is at Vincennes University. Still in operation, the theater, currently owned by United Artists Theatre Circuit, seats 1,660 and is claimed to have the state's largest indoor

movie screen. To view the interior is worth the price of a ticket.

11. The **Sheldon Swope Art Gallery**, 25 S. 7th St., opened in 1942 under director John Rogers Cox in the remodeled 40-year-old Swope Block. Sheldon Swope (1843-1929), born in Attica, Indiana, entered the diamond business in Dayton, Ohio, just after the Civil War. Following his arrival in Terre Haute in 1867 Swope launched his jewelry trade, eventually taking Charles T. Nehf as a partner. The three-story Swope Block, one of several downtown structures the jeweler built, adhered to the period's Italian Renaissance spirit in commercial architecture. The brick exterior has a facade of Kentucky's Green River stone. Swope stipulated in his will that a public art gallery be created. Litigations over his sizable fortune obstructed compliance with the bequest, but the accrued interest finally allowed for reworking the Swope Block into an art gallery. The Terre Haute firm of Miller and Yeager designed the gallery and the bronze entry doors, cast by the Ellison Company of Jamestown, New York, in 1941. The museum was incorporated in 1964 and accredited by the American Association of Museums in 1972. Among the local artists represented in the collection is Janet Scudder

Indiana Historical Society (Martin Collection 30290)
Indiana Theatre, 1943

(1873-1940), whose fountain sculpture brought her worldwide recognition. Two of her bronzes are on display. Besides the rotating permanent holdings, primarily American, the gallery schedules special exhibitions. A sales shop and art reference library round out what is one of Indiana's premier museums.

12. The **Scottish Rite Cathedral**, 8th and Ohio sts., was built in 1915-16 as the Hippodrome Theatre. The Chicago-based theater designer John Eberson, along with architect John Reed Fugard, drew up the plans for the vaudeville house, which opened in 1917. Eberson and Fugard employed German-Renaissance architectural features in the three-story structure. Lion heads decorate the shaped gables. The green roof tile, gray-green and light buff terracotta, and gray-brown and red brick present a pleasing exterior color scheme. The 1,000-seat Hippodrome closed in 1929. From 1949 to 1955 it operated as a movie theater, owned by Wabash Theatre Corporation. The Terre Haute Scottish Rite Building Corporation bought the building in 1956 and converted it to a permanent cathedral for the Scottish Rite, Terre Haute Valley. A remodeling removed the marquee and bricked up entrances and show windows. The elaborate ceilings and molding in the lobby and auditorium have remained virtually unchanged. In 1980 Indiana's only Masonic museum and library was established by Earle O. Prater, a prominent local Mason, in the mezzanine hallway off the main lobby. (*NRHP*)

13. The **Terminal Arcade Building**, 820 Wabash Ave., was built in 1911 for the Terre Haute Traction and Light Company. The interurban station housed offices and retail shops on its ground floor and in its basement. Passengers could walk through the central arched passageway to the waiting cars. Most striking is the almost identical front and rear exteriors, which in their large vaulted arches and high relief motifs express that era's enchantment with ancient Roman design. Daniel H. Burnham of Chicago planned the structure, while J. W. Quayle and Fred Edler sculpted the limestone facades. Eventually the arcade's openings were closed and doors installed. Buses replaced the streetcars, and the terminal operated as a bus station from 1949 into the late 1960s. Owned by the Hulman interests the building was vacated in

the early 1970s. Condemned by the city in 1980, the Terminal Arcade has been renovated, and a restaurant, The Terminal, opened in the building in early 1984. (*NRHP*)

14. The **Hulman and Company Building**, 9th St. and Wabash Ave., was built in 1892-93, 43 years after the founding of the wholesale grocery firm by Francis Hulman, a German immigrant, who came to Terre Haute from Cincinnati in 1850. After the death of Francis in 1858, Herman Hulman, Sr., a brother, carried on and expanded the business. He added general merchandise to the grocery line in addition to acquiring the McGregor distillery. In 1892 the senior Hulman sold the liquor concern to his son, Herman Hulman, Jr., and to John E. Beggs. The complex constructed in the early 1890s comprised the main Hulman and Company Building and the Hulman and Beggs Building, 21-25 N. 9th St. Rather than putting up conventional ornate Victorian buildings, Samuel Hannaford, who designed the Vigo County courthouse, elected the more modern and functional Romanesque Revival style. Built of red brick with limestone and granite accents, the structures remain virtually unaltered. When the distillery partnership dissolved in 1898, the Hulman and Beggs establishment served as a warehouse and subsequently as the plant for making Clabber Girl Baking Powder. Clabber Girl became the nation's favored leavening agent in the 1940s following a sales campaign led by Anton "Tony" Hulman, Jr. The city's oldest family business, with its thousands of different products, is presently directed by Mary Fendrich Hulman, widow of Tony Hulman. After 138 years of supplying local and regional merchants and of generous philanthropic activity, not to mention dozens of business ventures, the Hulman name is practically synonymous with Terre Haute.

15. The **Condit house**, Indiana State University's (ISU) oldest structure, stands at the south end of the university's quadrangle, bounded by Chestnut, Cherry, 6th, and 7th sts. The two-story, brick Italianate house with its noteworthy projecting front pavilion was built by Jabez Hedden for Lucian Houriet, a jeweler, in 1860. The Rev. Blackford Condit (1829-1903) purchased the place in 1863. Condit pastored the city's Baldwin Presbyterian Church, 1868-75, and served on the board of trustees of his

alma mater, Wabash College, 1871-96. Besides his Biblical writings, he published the *History of Terre Haute from 1816 to 1840* (1900). Sara Louisa Mills, Condit's wife, was the daughter of Wabash College faculty member Caleb Mills, often mentioned as a founder of the state's common school system. Helen Condit, a daughter, lived in the house until her death in 1961. She bequeathed her home to the university, which first used it for offices. Between 1966 and 1968 it was converted into the president's home. (*NRHP/HABSI*)

16. Charles Fairbanks, local businessman and philanthropist, wished to commemorate his mother by putting up a public bathhouse or a library. Choosing a library, Fairbanks expended $50,000 to have the **Emeline Fairbanks Memorial Library**, 222 N. 7th St., constructed to specifications provided by Terre Haute architects William M. Floyd and Charles E. Scott. The Beaux Arts structure opened August 11, 1906. The library put in practice progressive ideas: patron access to stacks, separate reading and reference rooms, and a distinct children's area. Built of Green River stone from Kentucky quarries, the exterior features a large center portion in the form of a temple pavilion. The chief interior attraction is a stained glass dome, 28 ft. wide, displaying portraits of 15 literary and historical figures, including the Hoosiers Lew Wallace, Daniel W. Voorhees, and James Whitcomb Riley. The library became a part of ISU in 1979 following the opening of a new Vigo County Public Library at 7th and Walnut sts. After a $1.4 million remodeling, Fairbanks Hall, as it is now called, comprises studios, offices, and classrooms for faculty and students of the university's art department.

17. A marker on the northeast corner of 7th and Chestnut sts., in front of Indiana State's University School, indicates **Chauncey Rose's home site**. Rose built his home probably in the 1840s and lived in it until his death in 1877. Miss Susan Hemingway, Rose's niece, held the house until her death in 1909, at which time the property was transferred to Rose Polytechnic school. The house was removed subsequently, and the land became Hemingway Park. The then Indiana State Teachers College purchased the section and constructed its Laboratory School on it. The Lab School (Uni-

versity School) was designed by Miller and Yeager, Terre Haute architects, and it was dedicated in 1937.

18. The **Eugene V. Debs home**, 451 N. 8th St., is a National Historic Landmark and the Eugene V. Debs Foundation headquarters. Union organizer, editor, city clerk, state legislator, and five times the Socialist party candidate for president, Debs (1855-1926) lived in Terre Haute all his life. His parents came from Alsace, France, in 1851 and established a neighborhood grocery. In 1890, five years after Eugene married Katherine Metzel, the couple's mid-Victorian frame dwelling was erected for $4,500. The Debs Foundation purchased the house in 1962, restored its eight rooms and seven fireplaces, and opened the home to the public. A gift of Anton Hulman, Jr., allowed for the attic to be converted to a small auditorium. Joseph Laska, an ISU art professor, painted a chronicle of Debs's life on the slanted attic ceilings. In the Virgil Morris Memorial Garden a back wall exhibits plaques honoring great labor leaders. The Oscar K. Edelman Library is available for serious research on Debs and socialist and labor history. Each year the foundation gives an award to an outstanding leader in labor, public service, or education. (*NRHP*)

19. The **Cordell Room** on the third floor of ISU's **Cunningham Memorial Library**, Center and Sycamore sts., holds the world's largest collection of old and rare dictionaries. Warren N. Cordell, an ISU alumnus and executive with Nielson's TV-rating firm, launched the collection with the presentation of 500 dictionaries to the school in 1970. Since that time the holdings have increased to around 12,000 volumes, the oldest dating back to the 15th century. The interest in dictionaries has led to the establishment of unique courses in lexicography and the formation of the Society for the Study of Dictionaries and Lexicography with headquarters at ISU. The ground breaking for Cunningham Memorial Library took place in 1971. The $6.5 million, five-level structure is named for Arthur Cunningham, who directed the ISU library from 1890 to 1928. The new library opened in 1973 and now has holdings totaling around a million items. Among other important treasures in the Rare Books and Special Collections section, besides the dictionaries, are the papers of Eugene V. Debs and the files

of the Works Progress Administration (WPA) for Indiana.

20. The **Old Indian Orchard Burying Ground** lies on the riverbank next to the Pillsbury Plant at 1 Sycamore St. The common grave site dates from the earliest Indian and white settlement to its abandonment in 1839 with the establishment of Woodlawn Cemetery further north. Three wooden markers at the end of the drive fronting the factory's entrance denote the burial site and three Revolutionary War participants interred there.

21. In the old section of **Woodlawn Cemetery**, at N. 3rd St. between 2nd and 8th aves., repose many of the early citizens of Terre Haute, including the Farringtons, Demings, Condits, and Crufts. Col. (later Brig. Gen.) Charles Cruft organized the 31st Indiana Regiment for Civil War action. Chauncey Rose was buried here in 1877, but his body was reinterred at Highland Lawn Cemetery in 1911. Woodlawn Cemetery was laid out in 1839 on slightly over 12 acres, which cost the taxpayers $620. Two brick guardhouses were built at the entrance. Only one remains. During the Civil War 11 Confederate prisoners died while confined in a makeshift camp in Terre Haute and were buried along the front fence of Woodlawn. Their tragedy was later recognized by the federal government, which erected a 10-ft. stone monument in the cemetery's circle. Amidst the bounty of carved motifs on headstones in Woodlawn are several sculpted urns and female figures, which are purported to be the work of Terre Haute artist Janet Scudder.

22. **Collett Park**, entrance at N. 7th St. and Maple Ave., is the oldest city park, dating from the late 1880s. The 21 acres comprising the grounds were a gift from Josephus Collett (1831-1893), a local entrepreneur, whose business enterprises were spread throughout the nation. In Terre Haute he is particularly remembered for his operation of the Evansville, Terre Haute, and Chicago Railroad, and for his association with Chauncey Rose in the establishment, management, and endowment of Rose Polytechnic Institute. Collett, in addition to the donation of land, made provision for a streetcar line to service the park. Presently, the park's facilities include a playground, tennis courts, softball field, horseshoe and shuffle-board courts, picnic area, and shelters. (*NRHP*) Collett Woods, a six-block residential area that faces Collett Park, has produced a singular number of leaders of American industry and research. Among them are Leroy A. Wilson, president of American Telephone and Telegraph Company; Donald C. Burnham, president of Westinghouse Electric Corporation; Ray R. Eppert, president of the Burroughs Corporation; J. Stanford Smith, vice-president of Sloan-Kettering Institute for Cancer Research; and Maynard S. Wheeler, president of Commercial Solvents Corporation.

23. The **site of Fort Harrison** is in northwestern Terre Haute on the grounds of the Elks Country Club, 3340 N. 4th St. The Benevolent and Protective Order of Elks organized locally in 1892 and purchased in 1937 the 80 acres of what then was the Fort Harrison Country Club. The Elks constructed a new clubhouse on the property in 1970. Several items in and around the Elks facility relate directly to historic Fort Harrison. Apparently some logs from the old fort, which became a boardinghouse after 1822, were carved into canes; however, other pieces were worked into the dividing wall in the lounge of the clubhouse. A small attached plaque tells the story. Nearby, to the southwest, is a bronze marker affixed to a large dome-shaped stone, located at what was the southwest corner of the fort. The Fort Harrison Centennial Association in 1912 erected the plaque to mark the site of the stronghold and to commemorate the 100th anniversary of the garrison's defense in 1812. The depression in the land fronting the marker once cradled the waters of the Wabash and Erie Canal. The slight ridge on the far side of the gully was the towpath. At the south end of the swimming pool is a metal sign indicating the **Burial Ground of Fort Harrison**. Workmen discovered the cemetery while digging a sewer line in 1970. No grave markers are evident, but it is known that Me-chin-quam-e-sha, the Wea mother of Christmas Dagney, a Fort Harrison government interpreter and Indian agent, was buried here in 1822.

24. The **Markle Mill dam and home** can be reached by going north on Lafayette Rd. to the first stoplight after the light at the Otter Creek Junior High School (about 5 miles from the courthouse). Turn east at the light onto 51st

Ave. Continue east 1.2 miles to the millsite on Otter Creek. The address of the Markle house is 4900 Mill Dam Rd. Abraham Markle was one of the five original proprietors of Terre Haute. Markle brought his family to Fort Harrison in 1816, purchased 800 acres around Otter Creek, and built the dam and mill plus a frame home. He combined milling with distilling and general merchandising, and the Otter Creek complex evolved into a major trade center. In 1848 his son, Frederick, put up the present Markle home a short distance behind the original house. The brick Greek Revival residence has 12 rooms, each room with its own fireplace. The home served often as shelter for travelers, including slaves making their way to freedom in Michigan along the Hoosier "underground railroad." The mill changed hands in 1911 and burned in 1938, after which the Hulmans purchased the house and surrounding property. The Hulman family deeded the house to the Vigo County Historical Society in 1977. The costs of upkeep of the old house proved prohibitive, and the society reluctantly sold it in 1983 to private ownership. The dam had deteriorated after the mill fire. In 1983, however, a group of volunteers, lending their professional skills and supported by donations of equipment and supplies, succeeded in largely reworking the stone and concrete dam. A future goal is to rebuild the mill. (*NRHP*)

25. The grave sites of Eugene V. Debs and Max Ehrmann are located in the **Highland Lawn Cemetery**, 4520 Wabash Ave. The cemetery, originally 154 acres, was purchased in 1884 by the city for $15,000 from Ray G. Jenckes, a prominent farmer and miller. The sturdy Debs headstone is located about 200 ft. northwest of the cemetery office, and just behind the Parsons marker, or about 50 ft. directly west of the Elk statue. Max Ehrmann (1872-1945) broke off his long friendship with Debs when Debs began to speak out against American involvement in World War I. Until 1912, Ehrmann, the poet laureate of Terre Haute, combined his writing with lawyering, politicking, or managing the finances of his brother's overall firm, the Ehrmann Manufacturing Company. At age 40 Ehrmann devoted full time to literary production. During his lifetime he published 21 books and pamphlets. His poem "A Prayer" appeared in 1903 and gained fame for its author when the poem was displayed at the 1904 St. Louis World's Fair and when it was published in the *Congressional Record* in 1909. International recognition eluded Ehrmann until long after his death. In 1965 Adlai Stevenson's intended use of Ehrmann's poem *Desiderata* ("Go placidly amid the noise and the haste, . . . ") on a Christmas card directed the nation's attention to the Terre Haute poet. Then, in 1971, a recording of the poem made the Top 10 charts, and it won a Grammy award the following March. *Desiderata*, as a result, became familiar throughout much of the world, as did its author. The bulk of Ehrmann's literary legacy is deposited at his alma mater, DePauw University, in Greencastle, Indiana. To reach the Ehrmann family plot go left at the second drive 200 yds., then 100 ft. to the right. The plot is identifiable by the angel and cross monument next to the large oak tree.

26. The **Rose-Hulman Institute of Technology**, 5500 Wabash Ave., is recognized as one of the premier engineering schools in the world. When founded in 1874 by Chauncey Rose and others it was called the Terre Haute School of Industrial Science. To honor the major benefactor, the school's name changed to Rose Polytechnic Institute in 1875. The school officially opened in 1883. The most recent name change occurred in 1971 after Anton Hulman, Jr., and Mary Fendrich Hulman gave the Hulman Foundation's assets to the school's endowment. The first campus stood on 10 acres at 13th and Locust sts. In 1917 Herman and Anton Hulman donated 123 acres for a new campus about two miles east of Terre Haute. The transfer to the present site took place in 1922. Today, the all-male school stands on 130 acres. Rose-Hulman's abiding interest in the arts is evident in the variety of permanent exhibits on the grounds. In Hadley Hall, the school's administration building located at the end of the entrance driveway, is a fine collection of **Hadley Pottery**. The award-winning utilitarian clayware, mostly white decorated with whimsical designs in sky and earth tones, is the work of Mary Alice Hale Hadley (1911-1965). A Terre Haute native, the artist married George Hadley, a Rose Poly graduate, in 1929, and the couple established the Hadley Pottery in 1940 in Louisville, Kentucky. Hadley Hall, constructed in 1983-84, commemorates the Hadleys' contributions to art and to the school. Also in Hadley Hall is the **Seamon Salon**, dedi-

cated in 1984. Born in Princeton, Indiana, in 1911, D. Omer "Salty" Seamon worked for 23 years as a commercial artist for the Terre Haute firm of Thomson-Symon. In 1954 he began free lance artwork. Like Mary Hadley's pottery, Seamon's watercolors have earned numerous awards and museum status. Another collection of paintings, 115 19th-century **British watercolors**, are displayed in the Chauncey Rose (East) wing of the Hulman Memorial Union. The group was assembled between 1973 and 1975 and acquired through the Logan-Ross-Dougherty Memorial Fund, named for the wives of three Rose-Hulman administrators who initiated the Memorial Art Collection in 1963. The women were killed in an automobile accident in 1966 as the Hulman Union was being completed. Distributed among the paintings are memorabilia associated with Chauncey Rose. Another art exhibit is the **Kappa Kappa Kappa Collection of Hoosier Art** in the John Logan Library. Logan was president of the school between 1962 and 1976, and the library was named for him shortly after his retirement. The library opened in 1974, and the Tri Kappa collection went on display the same year. The collection of the Hoosier art began in 1929. Since that time Tri Kappa has purchased works from professional juried art shows in Indiana. In a glass-walled corner room on the ground floor of the library is an antique drugstore exhibit featuring the furnishings of the old **E. H. Bindley and Company drug firm** begun in Terre Haute in 1864. The company's pharmaceutical paraphernalia came to the college in 1980.

Tour 9

Tour 9 originates at the Vigo County Courthouse in Terre Haute. From the courthouse, travel east on Ohio St./Blvd. *2.9 m.* to Fruitridge Ave., turn right for *.2 m.*, then left onto Poplar St., passing Deming Park and Deming Woods. Proceed *1.4 m.* and turn right onto IND 46.

Continue *5.5 m.* to **RILEY** (p. 269), once an important trade center on the Wabash and Erie Canal. The town was platted by Nathaniel Donham in 1836 as Lockport in reference to the three great canal locks located in the area. When the post office was established four years later, it was discovered that the name duplicated another town in the state; so the name was changed to Riley. It was named for the township in which it is located, a name taken from Riley Township in Butler County, Ohio, earlier home of many settlers. During the canal-building period, the town was nicknamed Battle Row for the numerous fights among Irish immigrant canal workers. Riley was once the site of several flour mills, sawmills, and tanneries. When the railroad succeeded the canal, the town became a grain center and continued as such into the early 20th century. Today Riley is a farming community and a Terre Haute suburb.

Continue east on IND 46 for *3.6 m.* to the **CLAY COUNTY** (p. 24,862; 360 sq. m.) line. The county was organized in 1825 and named for Whig party statesman Henry Clay at the urging of Daniel Harris, Clay County organizer. The county is shaped by 10 right angles and was formed from parts of Vigo, Sullivan, Putnam, and Owen counties. Clay County is 30 miles long and averages 12 miles wide. Topographically, it is located on the elevated lands above the Wabash Valley with a gently rolling terrain and an average elevation of 625 ft. This area was part of what the Indians called the Famous Hunting Ground, which had the reputation of being the best hunting land in the Indiana Territory. The county was part of the land ceded to the United States by the Miami, the Delaware, and the Eel River Indians in 1809 as part of the Treaty of Fort Wayne, also known as the Harrison Purchase.

Coal and clay have been of historical importance to the county's economy. A fine grade of clay, discovered in the 19th century, formed the basis for a number of potteries and brick factories. Coal continues to be mined in Clay County, which in 1986 ranked 12th in coal production of the state's 15 coal-producing counties. Many abandoned strip mines have been transformed into lakes and recreational areas. Agriculture always has been a major source of revenue for Clay County residents. Although no crop is dominant, corn, hay, and soybeans are abundant, while beef cattle, dairy herds, and hogs add to the farm economy. Products manufactured today in the county include truck trailers, electrical cords, door components, and printed business forms.

East of the county line *1.9 m.*, turn right and proceed south *.5 m.* to **CORY**. John S. Donham, Newport Staggs, and Oliver James organized the town in 1872 and named it after Simeon Cory, a Terre Haute pioneer and hardware merchant. Cory was impressed by the gesture of having a town named in his honor and donated enough money for the construction of a town pump and a school. E. A. Doud made Cory famous for its apple orchards. In 1919 he leased a three-acre orchard from Clark Coble and two years later purchased the Coble farm and expanded his operation throughout west central Indiana. By 1942 he owned 280 acres of orchards that yielded 60,000 bushels of 37 varieties of apples. The prosperity Doud brought to Cory continued until his death in 1965. One year later his widow sold the orchards, but the industry died out shortly thereafter. Although there are no longer apple orchards in Cory, the community has held an Apple Festival each fall since 1970.

Return to IND 46 and go east, passing the junction with IND 59 at *5.3 m.* and continuing past several strip mine sites. Prior to World War I most coal was removed by the underground method. By World War II the bulk of Indiana coal came from surface or strip mines, which are generally considered to be more efficient for extracting coal. This process of surface mining involves the removal of the earth covering the coal, termed "overburden," by means of a huge shovel called a "dragline." Once the overburden is removed, the marketable coal is recovered by smaller shovels and hauled away. The excavation is performed in strips that resemble furrows in a plowed field.

Continue east on IND 46 (*5.5 m.* past the junction of IND 46 and IND 59) to **BOWLING GREEN**, the oldest settlement in the county and site of the first county seat. David Thomas, first settler in the area, arrived in 1812 and purchased land on the bluff over the Eel River from the Eel River tribe for two bushels of corn. By 1818 Thomas was conducting a trading post for travelers between Spencer and Terre Haute. The town was founded in 1827 to serve as the newly formed county's center of government. Benjamin Parks, an early inhabitant, named the town after his birthplace of Bowling Green, Virginia. In its early years, Bowling Green was the center of business and civilization in Clay County, but its importance declined when first the National Rd. and later the railroads bypassed it. A petition to remove the county seat to the more prosperous Brazil was successful. To avoid trouble with bitter Bowling Green citizens, a group of men from Brazil crept into the former county seat the night of January 25, 1877, removed the records from the courthouse, and transported them to the newly built courthouse in their town, where they have remained. Today, Bowling Green is primarily a small farming community.

At the west entrance to Bowling Green, on the right, is a historical billboard known as the **Clay County Memorial Tablet**. The 21 x 35-ft. marker was erected from private funds in 1933 and is maintained by the Clay County Memorial Society. It was designed as an open book commemorating the early historical events of Bowling Green. Pictured on the tablet are David Thomas and an Indian chief agreeing to the aforementioned land purchase. Portrait specialist John J. Watts of Brazil painted the figures on the billboard.

Past the memorial billboard *.1 m.* is the **old log cabin** owned by the Bowling Green Historical Society. Constructed in 1836 at Brazil, the cabin was moved to Bowling Green in 1973, when owner Don Bolt donated it to the society. It is now located on the former site of the Farm Bureau Building, which was razed because of fire damage.

In the center of Bowling Green, on the right, is a public park which once served as the **courthouse square**. After the county seat was moved to Brazil, the courthouse building served as a public meeting place until it was destroyed by lightning in 1910. The original steps from this 1853 structure remain on the east side of the square.

Located east of the courthouse square is a brick building that served as the **county jail**. Construction began in 1861; however, its completion was delayed until 1865 because of the Civil War. The structure was built at a cost of $3,750 and served as the jail until 1880. The cells remain intact in the basement.

Return to IND 46, turn left, and proceed *.9 m.* Turn right on a gravel road which cuts through the grade at *.4 m.* of a projected railroad from Blackhawk in Vigo County to Indianapolis. On the right are massive concrete abutments of the railroad's Eel River bridge. The road was projected about 1904 by John R. Walsh, a Chicago banker who developed coal, stone, and mineral spring industries on a grand scale in southern Indiana before his empire collapsed and he was sentenced to prison. The railroad grade crosses many miles of Clay County on a straight line, but no rails were laid.

Return to IND 46, continue west to IND 59, and turn left. Travel *7.1 m.* to **CLAY CITY** (p. 883), an area developed because of its location on the Cincinnati and Terre Haute Railway. Originally the village was referred to as the "Y" for the configuration of tracks on which trains were turned. Barbara Storm, the widow of landowner George Storm, platted the town in 1873. At first, the village was named Markland after a local leader, but it was soon changed to Huntersville, when it was discovered there was already a town in Indiana named Markland. Public dislike for the Huntersville name caused the substitution of Clay City in 1876. The town prospered with the growth of the coal industry, and at one time there were five mines along the Clay City borders.

Tour 9

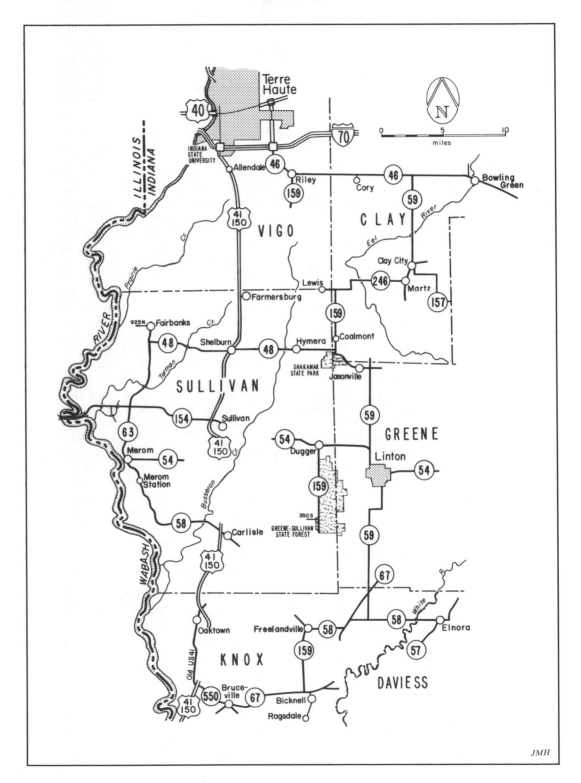

JMH

Continue on IND 59 into Clay City to IND 246 and IND 157. From this junction of three state roads, follow IND 157 (also Fair St. or 9th St.) *.8 m.* south to the **Clay City Pottery Company** on the right side. Beryl Griffith started the operation in 1885, and it may be the oldest continuous business in town. It annually produces 50,000 pieces of pottery.

Return to IND 246, turn south, and travel first through Martz, then straight west for *8.1 m.* to IND 159. Two miles west on IND 246 is **LEWIS**, where a train derailment in 1953 ignited two cars of bulk explosives and one of 105 mm. howitzer ammunition. Damage was heavy, but there was no loss of life and only minor injuries. Return to IND 159, turn right, and proceed south *5.1 m.*, passing through Coalmont, founded in 1900, to IND 48. Turn right *.5 m.* to **SULLIVAN COUNTY** (p. 21,107; 452 sq. m.).

Named for Daniel Sullivan, a Revolutionary War hero who was killed while carrying messages from Vincennes to Louisville, the county was organized in 1816 from a section of Knox County. The original borders included a greater part of the present-day counties of Owen, Clay, and Greene, and all of Vigo. Sullivan County is bordered by Vigo County to the north, Greene and Clay counties to the east, Knox County to the south, and the Wabash River/state of Illinois to the west. The basically flat land is the result of the Illinois Glacier, although the area around the Wabash River is slightly hilly. Oil production, begun in 1906, probably peaked prior to America's entry into World War I. In 1916, 675 Sullivan County wells produced 750,000 barrels of oil. Coal has been mined in the county since around 1816, but coal mining did not assume a dominant economic role until the early 20th century. In 1986, 1.6 million tons of coal were mined in the county. Today, along with agriculture, coal dominates the Sullivan County economy.

West on IND 48 *2.7 m.* is **HYMERA** (p. 1,054). Although there were a number of early settlers and industries in the area, the town was not platted until 1870, when it was named Pittsburg after local landowner William Pitt. The village grew with development of the local coal industry. In 1855 the post office was established as Hymera to avoid confusion with other towns in the state with the same name. In 1890 the town's name officially was changed to correspond with the post office. The origin of the name is not clear. One legend is that John Badders, the first postmaster, named the post office after his unusually tall adopted daughter, Mary, thus High Mary. Another version is that a woman named Mary worked in the post office, and the customers would greet her by saying "Hi, Mary." A third, and more believable, explanation is that it was named after the ancient Sicilian city of Himera. John Mitchell, president of the United Mine Workers of America, stated in 1904 that Hymera was the neatest and most progressive coal-mining town in America.

Continue west on IND 48 about *1 m.* to the **Bethel Cemetery** on the left at the west edge of Hymera. The 10-ft. statue of a Revolutionary War soldier at parade rest atop a 5 ft. inscribed base marks the grave of Nathan Hinkle. Born in 1749, Hinkle enlisted in the Pennsylvania militia in 1776 and served 7 years and 9 months in the militia and Continental Army, participating in the battles of Long Island, Brandywine, and Paoli. The patriot later moved to Sullivan County and died there in 1848 at the age of 99 years and 6 months. The Bedford stone monument was erected in 1904 to correspond with the arrival of United Mine Workers president John Mitchell.

Return east on IND 48 *4.4 m.* On the right is the entrance to **Shakamak State Park**. (Obtain a map at the park gate.) The park was established in 1929 on the former site of strip mines and scrub forests. The area was first named Tri-County Park because its 1,766 acres extend into Sullivan, Clay, and Greene counties, but the name was changed to Shakamak, an Indian word meaning "river of the long fish or eel," when Maumee Collieries donated the land to the state. This peaceful recreation area offers camping, horseback riding, and hiking. An abandoned slope coal mine is visible along Trail No. 2 near the Group Camp. Three manmade lakes provide fishing and swimming, and Shakamak Lake, shaped like the fingers of a hand, once was the site of championship swimming and diving events. Also located on Shakamak Lake are family housekeeping cabins.

The park is an example of the efforts of the state and the coal industry to reclaim stripmined land. Indiana was a pioneer in surface-mine reclamation. Restoration was initiated in 1918 when one Indiana mine operator planted 4,700 fruit trees along the mined area. This was the first recorded instance of surface mining reclamation in the United States. Eight years later, the newly formed Indiana Coal Association voluntarily agreed to a formula for the planting of trees and shrubs on excavated land (a mine owner planted five acres for each shovel or drag line in operation). In the 1941 Surface Mining Act Indiana became the second state in the country to pass coal mine land reclamation legislation. Black locust trees initially were planted to reforest the stripped land, but they proved vulnerable to insects and are now supplemented by black alder, red oak, sycamore, and pine. It takes approximately 40 years to completely reforest a strip-mined area.

East on IND 48 *1.1 m.* from Shakamak State Park is the **GREENE COUNTY** line. Greene County (p. 30,416; 546 sq. m.), the state's fourth largest, was organized in 1821 and named in honor of Nathanael Greene (1742-1786), the Revolutionary War hero. The rectangle-shaped county is roughly divided by the southwesterly course of the White River. East of the river the terrain is fairly rugged, heavily timbered, and veined with limestone. West of the river, the landscape is predominantly rolling farmlands overlying extensive coal deposits. Generally the economy has relied on agricultural, retail, and mining operations. Between 1910 and 1960, the county's population progressively declined by slightly more than 10,000 persons, but this trend has been reversed in recent years.

Travel *.6 m.* southeast of the county line on IND 48 to **JASONVILLE** (p. 2,497), a resort community. The area was settled in the late 1840s by Lewis Rogers, and the village was named in the mid-1850s for his son, Jason, who operated the general store. The name supposedly evolved from a joke: "Uncle Billy" Buckalew dipped a paddle in a bucket of axle grease and wrote Jasonville on the side of Rogers's store. The name stuck. Jasonville was located along the Southern Indiana Railroad but did not progress until the early 20th century with development of the coal industry. The town was devastated by fires in 1914 and 1967.

Continue east *1.5 m.* on IND 48 to IND 59. Turn right, proceed south *6.8 m.* to IND 54, and turn right. West on IND 54 *3.2 m.* is the Sullivan County line, and *.5 m.* farther is the town of **DUGGER** (p. 1,118). Francis M. Dugger and Henry T. Neal laid out the area in 1879 in conjunction with construction of the Dugger Coal Mine, which was located on the east side of town across from the railroad tracks. The

town originally was known as Fairchild after John Fairchild, superintendent of drillers for the Dugger Coal Company, but the name soon was changed to Dugger to correspond with that of the mine operation and its founder. The Dugger economy continues to rely on the local coal industry.

Past the Dugger town limits *.3 m.*, turn left onto 3rd St., travel *.1 m.*, and turn right onto the unmarked main street. The second building on the left is the **Coal Museum**, a former restaurant. Opened in September 1980, the museum traces the history of coal mining in the area with an assortment of items ranging from an old mule harness to a modern-day AMAX (American Metal Climax, Inc.) coal display.

Continue west for *.2 m.* and turn left on IND 159. South *1.5 m.* is the **Greene-Sullivan State Forest** boundary. IND 159 runs through the forest, and there are numerous well-marked turnoffs on the left that lead to various lakes and campgrounds. Like many recreational areas in southwestern Indiana, the state forest is located on the site of abandoned strip mines. The Central Indiana Coal Company started the reforestation process in 1927; in 1936 it donated 3,067 acres to the state. In the late 1930s the Civilian Conservation Corps (CCC) assisted in the tree-planting project, the largest endeavor of its kind in Indiana. Other neighboring abandoned strip mines were donated for forest use by Maumee Collieries, the Sherwood-Templeton Coal Corporation, and the Peabody Coal Company, the latter exchanging land for strip-mining rights on other public lands. The forest presently encompasses 6,764 acres in two counties with more than 100 manmade lakes, many of which are very deep and range in size from 5 to 200 acres. Fishing is permitted in nearly all the lakes, but swimming is prohibited. In addition, there are 5 campgrounds and over 150 primitive campsites located near the lakes. Hunting, picnicking, and horseback riding are allowed in the forest.

Proceed approximately *1 m.*, turn right on CR 350S, and drive *.2 m.* On the left is **Storybook Village**, which originated in the early 1970s when Chester Booker constructed several wooden figures of storybook characters for his grandson Johnny LeDune. The project continued to expand, and in 1976 Booker opened the area to the public as a park. By 1982 Storybook Village had grown to 23 acres that included a small zoo with monkeys, a llama, chickens, peacocks (including the rare white peacock), swans, deer, and goats. Figures of numerous fictional characters are located along a path bordering the nearby woods. A small train is available to transport visitors through the park.

Return north on IND 159 to IND 54 (approximately *3 m.*) and turn left. West *2.2 m.*, on the right, is the road leading *1.2 m.* to the **AMAX Minnehaha Strip Mine**, which opened in the late 1920s as a slope mine but converted to strip mining in 1944. In 1986, 500,000 tons of bituminous coal were extracted from this mine, the smallest of the three AMAX operations. In November 1985 AMAX Coal leased for 20 years 12,000 acres near the mine site to the Department of Natural Resources for a wildlife refuge, named the Minnehaha Fish and Wildlife Area, the state's largest.

Return east to IND 59, turn right, and proceed *1.3 m.* to the city limits of **LINTON** (p. 6,315), the largest community in Greene County. The first settlers arrived in this area around 1816; the settlement originally was known as New Jerusalem. Wickliff Wines, one of the first merchants, is credited with the development of Linton. Laid out in 1850, it was named for William C. Linton, a Terre Haute merchant and politician. The town evolved as a mining center in the 1890s, but its dependency on that industry steadily has dwindled since the 1940s. It now relies on farming, small business, tourism, and manufacturing. Many nearby former strip mines have been converted into parks and lakes. The Linton park system is recognized as one of the best in the state. The community has done an excellent job promoting its attractiveness and has successfully coped with the coal industry decline.

On the right side of IND 59 near the downtown area is a large wrought-iron arch, on top of which is the town's motto, You'll Like Linton. A teenager named Otto F. Harding coined this phrase in 1926 in response to a contest sponsored by the Greater Linton Club, an organization similar to a chamber of commerce. The motto has become a symbol of community pride. Duplicate arches are located along the other main roads leading to Linton.

Continue on IND 59 to IND 54, proceed east one block, and turn right onto 1st St. NE. One block south, at 110 E. Vincennes St., is the **Linton Public Library**. This two-story brick structure, containing elements of Tudor archi-

tectural styling, was built in 1908-9. The land had formerly been the site of the home of Andrew Humphreys, a local businessman, who held various political offices from 1843 to 1904. Funds for the library's construction came from the Carnegie Foundation, although the name Carnegie was not used for fear that the name of an industrialist would discourage the mine laborers and their families from frequenting the facility.

On the second floor of the library is the **Phil Harris/Alice Faye Collection**. Harris, a Linton native, and Alice Faye, his wife, donated many items from their show business careers and private lives for this display. Harris started his career in the late 1920s as a musician and later became nationally known for his music and comedy in radio on the *Jack Benny Show*, 1936-46, and the *Phil Harris/Alice Faye Show*, 1946-54. Children of all ages remember Harris for his voices in Walt Disney animated movies, the most famous of which was Baloo the Bear in the *Jungle Book*. Alice Faye (born Alice Jean Leppert, New York City) gained fame as a singer and movie actress in the 1930s and early 1940s. The Harris/Faye Collection was opened in 1979 and corresponded with the first Phil Harris Scholarship Festival. Since that year, Harris annually returns to Linton the first week in June to participate in the festival. Included are a celebrity golf tournament at the Phil Harris Linton Municipal Golf Course, a celebrity dinner, and a variety show featuring Harris and other famous entertainers.

Return to 1st and A sts. NE and turn east. Approximately *1 m.* on the left is **Linton City Park**. Shelter houses, an Olympic-size swimming pool, tennis courts, and playground equipment are among the present-day features. Just east of the park turn left onto CR 1100 and travel *.7 m.* to the **Conservation Park** entrance on the right. Also named **Lee-Sherrard Park** after two mining officials, it is the largest of Linton's parks with more than 600 acres and 27 man-made lakes. Once the site of a strip mine operated by Maumee Collieries, the land lay dormant from the mine's closing in 1927 until its donation to the Linton Community Conservation Club in 1942, at which time trees were planted and the lakes were stocked with fish. The winding dirt roads were constructed as a joint effort of mine workers and mine bosses during periods of strike negotiations in 1946 and 1947. Conservation Park's terrain and roads are rough, and the area is geared more to the outdoorsman than to the sightseer.

Return to IND 59 and turn left to the Knox County line at *10 m.* (For a description of the county see Tour 8.) Continue south for *2.3 m.* and turn left onto IND 58 and proceed east *3.7 m.* to the White River and the Daviess County border (for a description of the county see Tour 8).

Cross the narrow bridge and proceed *1.8 m.* to IND 57 and **ELNORA** (p. 756). The first settlers arrived in the area around the 1850s and named the region Owl Prairie for the great number and varieties of owls that inhabited the area. The settlers established a few businesses and named the small village Owl Town. The construction of the Evansville and Indianapolis Railroad through the region in 1885 brought an era of progress, and later that year the town was laid out by local merchants William C. Griffith and A. R. Stalcup. When the site was platted, the name was changed to Elnora in honor of Griffith's wife.

Turn left onto IND 57 and travel *.7 m.* to the **Graham Cheese Corporation** on the right. Robert C. Graham, one of three brothers who developed the Graham-Paige automobile and a line of tractors, established the cheese factory in 1928 on his farm, one of the state's largest at the time. This modern operation produces between two and three million pounds of cheese a year, with most of the milk coming from local farmers. Although Graham Farms Cheese is a local operation, the largest portion of the product is sold to a variety of distributors in the Midwest, with the only retail outlet being located at the Elnora plant. The business is presently operated by the third generation of the Graham family. A collection of dairy antiques is on display at the plant's store.

Return to IND 58, head west for *6.5 m.*, and turn left onto IND 67. Travel *1.2 m.*, turn right onto IND 58, and continue *4.5 m.* west to **FREELANDVILLE**. The first settlers in the region were German immigrants who arrived in the 1830s and referred to the hamlet as Bethle-

Indiana Historical Society (Martin Collection 28482)

Coal miners, 1942

hem and Kreuzweg, a German word meaning crossroads. Samuel E. Smith surveyed the land for John Ritterskamp in 1866, and the town was called Freelandsville for local physician Dr. John T. Freeland. The letter "s" later was dropped from the name.

At IND 159 is **Kixmiller's General Store and Red and White Market** on the right. John and Julie Ritterskamp erected the first general store on this site in 1846; it was replaced by the present structure 20 years later. Simon H. Kixmiller, the son-in-law of the Ritterskamps, assumed control of the business in 1890, and he was succeeded in 1943 by William R. Kixmiller, his son. In 1955 the store became affiliated with the Red and White chain. Kixmiller's has always dealt in general merchandise such as groceries, dry goods, shoes, and candy. Much of the store's original decor has been preserved as seen by the rolling wall ladders and the candy counters. (*NRHP*)

Turn left on IND 159 and proceed south for *6.1 m.* to Main St. (IND 159) and IND 67, which marks the limits of **BICKNELL** (p. 4,713). The town was platted by and named for local merchant John Bicknell in 1869. For the first third of the 20th century, the area was one of the largest coal mining centers in the United States. The first mine was sunk near Bicknell in 1873, and by 1926 there were 14 mines nearby. The coal industry declined dramatically after the 1940s, and the town is now a farming and small manufacturing community.

Cross IND 67 and travel south on Main St. for *2.2 m.* through the downtown area and turn right onto an unmarked road, which was known as the old Apraw Rd. Continue *1 m.* on this road and turn left to the village of **RAGS-DALE**. The first settlers arrived from the mountains of western Virginia in the 1830s and named their village Aliceville. However, the community adopted the name Ragsdale when a post office was established in that name in 1917. Ragsdale was named for either a preacher at the local Asbury Chapel United Methodist Church or for the person who owned the land on which the post office was located.

Travel *.2 m.* on this unmarked road past the post office to a stop sign. Straight ahead is a dirt road that leads to the site of the **American No. 1 Mine**. The mine was sunk in 1911, and production began one year later under the ownership of the American Coal Mining Company, later Knox Consolidated Coal. World records

were set for the amount of coal mined in an eight-hour shift in 1917, 1921, and 1924. American No. 1 earned the nickname of the Million Ton Mine when 1,062,000 tons of coal were extracted in 1926. All of these records were set before the age of mechanized mining, when between 800 and 900 men were employed. The coal supply dwindled in the 1940s, and the mine was closed on April 27, 1951. Although the mine site is located on private property, a walk down this dirt road reveals many reminders from the time when this mine was world renowned.

Return to the old Apraw Rd. and turn left. Go *.2 m.* to the **Asbury Chapel United Methodist Church** and adjoining cemetery on the right. Pioneers John and Christiana Horn donated two acres for the church in 1847, and it was named for Mrs. Horn's church near Cedar Springs, Virginia. In 1887 the present brick structure replaced the first log building. A marker commemorates the church's history.

Return to IND 67 in Bicknell, turn left, and pass a coal mine monument on the right. Proceed west *5.8 m.* to **BRUCEVILLE** (p. 646). Maj. William Bruce settled in the area around 1805 and built a small fort on his property six years later for protection from Indian attack. Shortly thereafter, he established a village that was platted as Bruceville in 1829 and flourished as a trading center and way station on the road to Vincennes. The village has not increased in size to any degree since its early days, except for a brief coal boom in the early 20th century, and it remains primarily a farming area.

At IND 550 turn right. Travel *.4 m.* and turn left just past the Christian Church. Continue one block. On the left is a brick marker indicating the **William Bruce homesite**. Bruce constructed a two-story brick structure in 1811, and it served as a tavern and an inn as well as a home for Bruce and his 25 children. In 1844 Abraham Lincoln spent a night in Bruce's house while he was on the campaign trail for Whig presidential candidate Henry Clay. Lincoln spoke that evening at a schoolhouse that was located about one block north on the north side of IND 550. A group of Democrats attempted to disrupt the rally, but a violent confrontation was avoided and Lincoln was able to deliver his speech without disturbance. The house was razed in the 1940s.

Return to IND 550 and turn left. Proceed *2.9 m.* On the left is **Emison's Mill Park**. This seven-acre county park located along the banks of Maria Creek offers picnicking and playground facilities. The park's location was the site of a mill constructed by Thomas Emison around 1808. The mill was among the first in this part of Knox County, and it had the capability to grind corn and wheat. It was operated by water power until 1854, when a steam engine was added. Mill operations ceased around 1891, and the structure was removed a short time later. The land was donated by the Emison family for use as a park, which opened in 1979.

Continue west on IND 550, cross US 41 to the village of Emison, and turn right at the first stop sign onto old US 41. Travel north approximately *5 m.* to **OAKTOWN** (p. 776). In 1867 Samuel E. Smith platted the town for George Bond. Originally named Oak Station, Oaktown, which developed into a shipping center for the local fruit and farming industry, was a stop on the Evansville and Terre Haute Railroad. This area of Knox County is particularly noted for its fruit production, and several large markets remain open to the public along new US 41. Oil and gas wells also were located around Oaktown for the first half of the 20th century.

A Shaker community was once located northwest of Oaktown. The Shakers were a religious sect which began in this area in 1808 and was officially known as the United Society of Believers in Christ's Second Appearing. They were commonly called Shakers for their dance-like movements during their services. Shakers believed in a mother-father God, whose revelations, in order to be fully realized, required the appearance of a male and a female Christ, Jesus and Mother Ann Lee. They practiced celibacy, pacifism, and communal property ownership. Issachar Bates, the father of 11 children before becoming celibate, and other zealots arrived here in 1808. Obtaining 1,300 acres in northern Knox and extreme southern Sullivan counties, they established a society of about two dozen local converts and missionaries. The community was named Busro for Busseron Creek, but it also was referred to as West Union and Shakertown. This area is still known as Shaker Prairie. Busro's population reached about 300 when many faithful from the Eagle Creek Society in Adams County, Ohio, were persuaded to

migrate to the Indiana settlement in 1811. The residents farmed, raised cattle, and operated grist and sawmills as well as a distillery and a hat factory. Indian unrest, linked to the war with England, caused temporary abandonment of the Busro settlement in September 1812. Most of the Believers departed for the larger Shaker settlements in Kentucky and Ohio to avoid the potential problems of Indian raids and the housing of nearby militia. When the Shakers returned to Busro in 1814, they decided to move the settlement closer to Busseron Creek, the site of their mills. Malarial fever, resulting from the community's proximity to swamps, and a general decline in the number of conversions to the Society of Believers led to the abandonment of Shakertown in 1827.

Proceed *.7 m.* on old US 41 to new US 41. Turn left and continue north *1.4 m.* to the Sullivan County line. Proceed *4.7 m.*, turn right on IND 58 (Harrison St.), and enter **CARLISLE** (p. 717), the earliest settlement in Sullivan County. In 1803 James Ledgerwood and his family settled in this area on a large tract granted him by the government for his services during the American Revolution. A short time after his arrival Ledgerwood negotiated a treaty with the local Indian tribes and for his services received an additional 7-sq.-m. site located north of the treaty line bordering his property. Several other families soon joined the Ledgerwoods in the area, and in 1806 French surveyors may have been brought from Vincennes to lay out the future town. Like most of those in Knox County, Carlisle's lots were drawn up on the French system of 45 degree angles paralleling the Wabash. In 1815 the town officially was platted by Samuel Ledgerwood (the son of James), James Sproul, and William McFarland and named either after the town in Pennsylvania from which many of the settlers had come or the Ledgerwood ancestral home in England. Carlisle served as the first county seat from 1817 to 1819, but it then was decided that Merom would be a more advantageous site for the government, probably because of Merom's location on the busy Wabash River. With the advent of the railroad in the mid-1850s, Carlisle developed into a shipping center for local farmers. Coal brought a second boom period to the town in the early 1900s, but with its decline a quarter of a century later, Carlisle settled into a small farming community. John W. Davis, the first congressman from Indiana to become Speaker of the House, 1845-47, lived most of his adult life in Carlisle and is buried in the Carlisle Cemetery north of town.

Continue on Harrison St. for .2 m. to Ledgerwood St. and turn left. Proceed .1 m. On the right, in a building that formerly housed the People's State Bank, is the **Sullivan County Museum**. Opened in 1975, the museum offers both permanent and temporary exhibits relating to the county's history. Featured are displays on housekeeping, farming, and the military. All items were donated by Sullivan County residents or their relatives.

Turn right at the museum onto Eaton St. and proceed one block to Alexander St. On the northwest corner, in an area that originally was laid out as the courthouse square, a rock memorial erected in 1951 commemorates the **Revolutionary War naval skirmish** at a site about eight miles northwest of Carlisle at a double bend in the Wabash River. On February 26, 1779, George Rogers Clark dispatched approximately 50 men under the command of Capt. Leonard Helm up the Wabash in three armed boats to intercept a British flotilla sent from Detroit with men and supplies for the fort. Unaware that Clark's men were in control of the region, the English were surprised at Helm's ambush about March 1 and surrendered without firing a shot. The Americans captured 7 boats, 40 men, and valuable supplies at what is considered the westernmost naval engagement of the American Revolution, and the only one fought in Indiana.

Return to US 41 and proceed northwest on IND 58 (a very crooked road) for *10.9 m.* to the hamlet of **MEROM STATION**. The town sprang up around 1854, when the railroad came through here instead of nearby Merom. Northwest on IND 58 *2.4 m.* is **MEROM** (p. 360). In 1817 the town was laid out on the highest bluff above the Wabash River and named for the high lake along the Jordan River where, in biblical times, Joshua fought a battle against the collected kings. Merom developed into an important trade center along the Wabash and became the county seat in 1819. The town's importance lessened when the county seat moved to Sullivan in 1842, and its commerce further declined when the Evansville and Terre Haute Railroad bypassed it in 1854. Ever since the railroad eliminated the need for

most river transportation, Merom's economy has been based on local agriculture.

Continue on IND 58 *.3 m.* and turn right onto Philip St. Continue *.2 m.* to the south drive to the **old College Hall of Union Christian College**. In 1859 the Rev. E. W. Humphreys opened the college on this site, and Dr. Nicholas Summerbell served as its first president. Affiliated with the New Light Christian Church, this small coeducational, liberal arts institution survived until 1924, when economic woes forced its closing. Twelve years later it reopened as Merom Institute, an ecumenical center supported by 11 Protestant denominations that held seminars, camps, and community activities. In 1977 the Indiana-Kentucky Conference, United Church of Christ, took it over and, in 1984, renamed it Merom Conference Center. The old College Hall, the last remaining building, was constructed in 1859-63. This four-story brick structure with limestone trim combines elements of Romanesque and Gothic architectural styles. The interior is highlighted by a spiral staircase that leads to the observation tower 300 ft. above the river. Francis Costigan, architect of several buildings in Madison (see Madison Attractions), is believed to have designed the staircase. (*NRHP*)

Return to IND 58, turn right, drive about *.3 m.*, and turn left to **Merom Bluff Park**. The wooded area is located on the crown of a 150-ft. bluff above the Wabash that provides a magnificent view of the river and the Illinois countryside. At one time there were steps leading from the park to the foot of the bluff, but most of these have deteriorated or disappeared in the underbrush. When the town of Merom was laid out in 1817, this site was designed as the commons area, and it has always served as a park and meeting place. From 1903 until the 1920s the park also was the scene of one of the largest independently operated chautauquas in the country. Among the featured speakers were William Howard Taft, Eugene V. Debs, Billy Sunday, William Jennings Bryan, Robert M. La Follette, Jeanette Rankin, the first American congresswoman, President Warren G. Harding, and Carrie Nation, the militant prohibitionist. At its height the chautauqua attracted more than 50,000 people over a three-week season. The small cannons at either end of the park were added later to demonstrate the bluff's potential military importance to the control of the river.

North of the foot of the bluff, in an area not easily discerned from the park, is **Paul Lindsey Island**. This 33-acre tract appears to be part of the bank but in reality is separated from the mainland by a channel. The island was named for an outlaw whose gang used the location as a meeting place during and after the Civil War. The area was incorporated into Merom after the war so it could be patrolled by the local law officers, but it was a band of vigilantes that finally raided the island and dispersed the criminals. Lindsey escaped and was never brought to justice.

Return to IND 58 and turn left. Proceed straight at the beginning of IND 63 on the right and continue *.2 m.* to **Merom Cemetery** on the left where several of Maj. Gen. William Henry Harrison's soldiers are buried. Adjoining the cemetery to the north is the site of **Fort Azatlan**. Constructed by the Middle Mississippian culture of mound builders around A.D. 1200, the fort had a circumference of 2,450 ft., was densely populated, and was extremely well protected by natural barriers. The west side bordered a 170-ft. bluff, while deep ravines hindered attack from the east and north. A 30-ft.-thick adobe wall protected the open area to the south, and walls of clay and limestone reinforced various other weak points around the area. Although no trace of these walls remains, there are accounts of sections surviving into the latter part of the 19th century. The interior of the fortification contained the foundations for approximately 45 dwellings, 5 mounds, and 3 water springs. It is not certain how long the fort survived or what became of its inhabitants, but it is believed that both the mound builders and the later American Indian tribes occupied the area for relatively long periods of time. The fortification was named Azatlan by archaeologist Frederick Ward Putnam in 1870 for its resemblance to the earthworks of the Aztecs and the Indian tribes in the southwestern United States. (*NRHP*)

Travel *4.3 m.* north on IND 63 and turn right on IND 154. Proceed east *7.5 m.* to the end of IND 154 at US 41. Cross US 41 and continue *.3 m.* to the **SULLIVAN** (p. 4,774) city limits. The first settlers did not arrive in the area until 1838, and the town was laid out four years later with the specific purpose of serving as the county seat. The site was chosen for its location near the center of the county on the relatively high ground between Buck and Bus-

seron creeks. The town originally was named Benton, but the name soon was changed when it was discovered that there was another Indiana town with that name. William B. Baker suggested the name Sullivan in honor of the county. The railroad went through the town in 1854, but the economy did not expand until the development of the coal industry in the late-19th and early-20th centuries. When Sullivan's last shaft mine was closed in the late 1950s, the town's commerce developed around farming and small industry. Sullivan was the home of movie czar Will H. Hays (1879-1954), chairman of the Republican National Committee, 1918-21; postmaster general under President Warren G. Harding, 1921-22; and head of the Motion Picture Producers and Distributors of America, 1922-45. Theodore Dreiser and Paul Dresser, his brother, spent part of their youth in the town.

Continue on W. Wolfe St. to Section St. and turn right. Drive *.5 m.* and turn left onto Washington St. for one block and turn right onto Court St. On the left is the **Sullivan County Courthouse**, the third courthouse in Sullivan since it became the county seat in 1842. The first log structure was built in 1843, but it was destroyed by fire seven years later. It was replaced by a brick courthouse in 1852, which, in turn, was succeeded by the present Neoclassical Revival-style limestone structure in 1926. In the first-floor rotunda are several plaques and documents highlighting the history of Sullivan County. One plaque was erected in 1937 to honor Sullivan attorney Antoinette Leach, who, in 1893, became the first woman in Indiana to practice law. Much of the exterior beauty around the courthouse square is attributable to a group of Ball State University architecture students, who suggested a more efficient use of parking spaces, traffic islands, and landscaping.

Travel around the courthouse square by way of Court, Jackson, and Main sts. At the northeast corner turn right onto Washington St. Continue *.7 m.* and turn left onto a country road that leads to **Sullivan County Park and Lake**. Opened in May 1969, this recreational site was Indiana's first locally developed multipurpose county park. The $1.7 million cost of constructing the park and lake was obtained from private donations, local taxes, and federal grants. In addition to its role as a fishing, swimming, and boating area, the 461-acre lake serves as a reservoir and conservation area for flood control on Busseron Creek. The 400-acre park includes a 32,000-sq.-ft. beach, boat launching and docking facilities, campsites, and picnic areas. Located to the left of the park entrance, between campsites B and C, is a small coal car and a concrete memorial to those who died in the City, Baker, and Little Betty coal mine disasters near Sullivan. Information on the gas explosions and the names of those who perished are listed on the monument.

On leaving the park turn right onto Leach St. Jog right off Leach and left onto Depot St., then right onto N. Broad St., and after four blocks left onto Wolfe St., which leads back to Section St. (the total distance from the park is approximately *1 m.*). Turn right onto Section St. and travel north *.7 m.* to the American Legion Grounds on the right. On the northeast corner is an open shelter house that served as *Stop 25*, a waiting station on the Terre Haute, Indianapolis and Eastern interurban railroad. A plaque commemorates the line that provided passenger service between Terre Haute and Sullivan for 25 years.

Return to IND 154 and travel west to IND 63 at Graysville. Continue on IND 154 for *1.9 m.* and turn left onto a paved, unmarked country road. Proceed south *.5 m.* to the **Mann-Turman Prairie Cemetery** on the left, where many early graves are located on a large prehistoric Indian mound. The first Caucasians to be buried here were two of William Henry Harrison's soldiers. While Harrison's force was on its way to the Battle of Tippecanoe, they camped near this site on September 28, 1811. Two men from the Kentucky militia continued a family feud and fought to the death. Their graves are unmarked, but apparently they were buried near the mound's summit.

Directly west of the cemetery *.3 m.* is the site of **Fort Turman**, an outpost that served as headquarters for scouts, spies, and mounted rangers during the War of 1812. Pioneer Benjamin Turman farmed the region prior to the outbreak of hostilities, and in 1810 he constructed a blockhouse for protection. Gov. William Henry Harrison acquired Turman's land the following year and ordered the blockhouse expanded into a fortress. During the war with England, Fort Turman was instrumental in maintaining a line of communication between Harrison's army in northern Ohio and Vincennes as well as serving as a base from which

patrols could be dispatched to observe enemy movements as far north as Ontario, Canada. After the fighting the land was sold back to Turman, who later disposed of it to James Mann.

Return to IND 63, turn left, and proceed north *1.5 m.* to the Johnson-Hopewell Cemetery on the left. A roadside historical marker near the **gravesite of Jane Todd Crawford** states that Mrs. Crawford was the first woman to have an ovariectomy. The operation was performed by Dr. Ephraim McDowell at Danville, Kentucky, on December 25, 1809. Mrs. Crawford, who did not receive an anesthetic for the 25-minute operation, later moved to Graysville and spent her remaining years with her son, Thomas, a Presbyterian minister. She died in 1842 at the age of 78.

North *6.3 m.* is the village of **FAIRBANKS**, a farming community founded about 1840 along the old state road between Vincennes and Terre Haute. Benjamin Ernest, James Pogue, and Samuel Myers laid out the town and named it for the township, which, in turn, takes its name from a Lieutenant Fairbanks who commanded a small detachment of troops that were massacred by Indians near here during the War of 1812. The community suffered when it was bypassed by the railroad, a circumstance which partially contributed to its lack of growth. Much of Fairbanks was destroyed by fire in 1913.

Proceed north *.2 m.*, turn left on CR 925N, and go west about *2.5 m.* to the approximate site of the **Fairbanks Massacre**. Lieutenant Fairbanks and nine men were dispatched from Fort Knox with a supply wagon bound for the besieged Fort Harrison. On September 15, 1812, the detachment was ambushed by Indians, and Fairbanks and seven of his men lost their lives. The only survivors were a Frenchman named Purdue, who was able to flee despite being wounded several times, and wagoner John Black, who hid between two logs and slipped away after dark.

Return to IND 48, *1.6 m.* south of Fairbanks, turn left, and go *7 m.* to US 41 at **SHELBURN** (p. 1,259). Paschal Shelburn, a pioneer of the area, platted a portion of his land in 1855 for the town and named it after himself. On May 21, 1949, a tornado caused the deaths of 11 Shelburn residents, injured 83 others, and destroyed or damaged almost half of the town.

Farmersburg, 1948

Take US 41 north out of Shelburn *5 m.* to **FARMERSBURG** (p. 1,240). The settlement evolved in conjunction with the construction of the Evansville and Terre Haute Railroad, and in 1853 it was platted. A major institution in the early town and an important influence on its economy was the Ascension Seminary, established by W. T. Crawford in 1865. The school's significance is reflected in the fact that

the town went by the names Farmersburg and Ascension. The seminary closed at the end of the 1871-72 academic year and moved to Sullivan.

Located near the north edge of Farmersburg on the east side of US 41 is the **Taylor Memorial Prayer Chapel**. This cinder-block structure built in the shape of a cross was erected in 1956 by the Rev. and Mrs. Russell

Taylor as a memorial to the minister's brother and sister, who had been killed in a Texas traffic accident two years earlier. Inside the nondenominational chapel is an altar, a kneeling rail, and pews that can seat up to 18 travelers who wish to stop and pray.

Continue *6.3 m.* on US 41, turn east for approximately *2 m.*, then south *.6 m.* to the entrance to **Fowler Park**, operated by Vigo County. Situated on approximately 230 acres of former strip-mine land, the park was opened in the late 1960s and was named for Capt. Eugene R. Fowler, the first Terre Haute native and the fourth Hoosier to die in the Vietnam War. To the right of the entrance is a restored **Pioneer Village**. The seven log buildings were taken from various locations in Vigo County and reassembled on the site to re-create life in a small Indiana settlement around the 1830s. Since 1972 the village has been the scene of the annual Pioneer Days Festival in the fall. To the south of the Pioneer Village is **Irishman's Covered Bridge**. The 75-ft.-long structure was moved to the park in 1971 from its original location over Honey Creek about three miles west of Riley. Private funds were raised to remove the bridge which had fallen victim to vandalism in its former location. Constructed in 1867, the bridge was designed by C. W. Bishop and named for Adolphus Erisman, one of the owners of land bordering the structure's original location. The name Erisman gradually evolved into Irishman when repeated among the locals. Legend has it that a baby was born on the bridge. Soon after the initial work on the bridge had been completed, a pioneer family was passing through the area on its way west when a storm arose. The travelers sought shelter in the bridge and apparently the birth occurred at this time. Since the sides had not been enclosed yet, the pioneers nailed up pieces of carpeting for protection from the wind and rain.

Extending more than two miles west from US 41 at the Fowler Park Rd. are grounds of the United States Penitentiary. Return to US 41 and continue north *3.1 m.* to the village of Allendale. At the second right past the town limits sign is a road that leads up a hill to the **Carmelite Monastery** on the right. In 1947 Mother Agnes and six sisters from the order of the Carmel of St. Joseph left their Indianapolis convent and established a similar monastery in a converted house outside Terre Haute. An increase in the number of nuns residing in the house resulted in the decision to expand the facility, and Edward D. Pierre of Indianapolis was employed to design the contemporary-style structure in 1958. Based upon the ideas of beauty and practicality, the buff-colored brick building with rose glass inserts serves as the living, working, and dining area for the sisters. The modernistic chapel with the huge gold-plated cross on the facade was a later addition to the complex. With a few exceptions, the nuns are cloistered and vowed to silence.

On the west side of US 41 opposite the monastery is the **Gibault School for Boys**. This educational and residential facility for troubled boys between the ages of 10 and 16 was opened in 1921 and named for Father Pierre Gibault of Vincennes, a pioneer and patriot of the American Revolution. The 100-acre campus is located in a country setting on the former Overbrook estate of Terre Haute distilling executive Fred B. Smith. Part of the land was donated by Smith and part purchased by the Knights of Columbus, a Catholic fraternal organization that continues to provide financial support for its upkeep. The school is operated by the Brothers of the Congregation of the Holy Cross in a family-like atmosphere that combines discipline with kindness.

Located on the grounds of the Gibault School is the **Fred B. Smith house**, now named Columbus Hall. Constructed in 1910-11, the house was designed by Robert C. Spencer, a colleague of Frank Lloyd Wright's in Chicago. It is the only example of the Prairie School of architecture in Vigo County.

Continue north on US 41 for *5.2 m.* to the Vigo County Courthouse.

Tour 10

Begin Tour 10 at the Vigo County Courthouse, located at US 41 (3rd Ave.) and US 40 (Wabash Ave.) in Terre Haute. Proceed east on US 40 for *9.8 m.* to the Clay County line at the junction with IND 340. (For a description of the county see Tour 9.) US 40 rejoins IND 340 at the western edge of Brazil, *4.9 m.* east of the county line. Continue east on US 40 (National Ave.) for *1 m.* to IND 59 (Forest Ave.) in downtown **BRAZIL** (p. 7,852). Brazil has been the county seat since 1877 when the courthouse records were surreptitiously removed from Bowling Green and transported to the newly built courthouse at Brazil. The present **Clay County Courthouse**, a Greek Revival-style structure designed by J. W. Gaddis of Vincennes, was erected two blocks east of Forest Ave. in 1914. It contains a mural with a classical theme and Latin inscription painted by Edgar Allen Payne in 1914. A native of Arkansas, Payne followed the chautauqua circuits, painting advertising posters in the 1900s. Out west his interest turned to painting nature, Indians, and seascapes. The artist died in California in 1947.

When platted in 1844, the town received the name of Brazil from a local citizen who happened to be reading news about Brazil, South America, at the time. The town developed as a coal shipping center in the 1850s, reaching a peak of about 5,000 rail carloads per month in the 1880s. Blast furnaces, utilizing the famous Brazil block coal for smelting iron, flourished in the city. However, imported ore from the mines of the Lake Superior region eventually squeezed native ores out of the market. Among the Brazil coal drillers was John Cleveland Hoffa, whose son, James R., born in the city on February 14, 1913, rose through the union ranks to lead from 1957 to 1971 the International Brotherhood of Teamsters, helping to make it the country's largest union. The Hoffa family lived in Brazil until 1922.

Clay-working plants shared with coal processing the leadership of the local economy. In the early years of the 20th century, for example, nine clay factories produced brick, building block, conduits, tile, crocks and jars, and other useful household containers.

The **Clay County Historical Society Museum**, 100 E. National Ave., occupies the former post office building on the northeast corner of Washington St. and National Ave., one block west of Forest Ave. The museum features many original land grants, Indian relics, and pioneer artifacts from the Clay County area. Memorabilia from Brazil's early interurban electric railway system and samples of clay tiles produced in local plants are also on exhibit. Indiana's first electric interurban line was opened July 16, 1893, and extended from Cottage Hill eastward through Brazil to Harmony, *4.5 m.* Operated by the Brazil Rapid Transit Company, it launched the electric interurban era which revolutionized travel and resulted in a sprawling 1,825-mile network that linked two-thirds of the state's counties and offered short interval service between farm, small town, and city. Except for Ohio, Indiana operated the greatest mileage of traction lines.

From National Ave., proceed south on Forest Ave. (IND 59) for *.6 m.* to Nabuco Dr. at the edge of town. The name honors the Brazilian ambassador to the United States in the mid-1950s. A memorial presented to the town by the country of Brazil as a token of friendship and dedicated May 26, 1956, flanks the entrance to **Forest Park** on the left side of the road. Called the *Chafariz dos Contos*, meaning "fountain of the tales," the granite fountain is a replica of an 18th-century fountain in that South American country. The park also contains two reconstructed 1851 log cabins, a golf course, a swimming pool, tennis courts, a stadium, and a band shell. The property was deeded to the city by the Staubitzer family in 1921. The auditorium was built in 1924 and

Tour 10

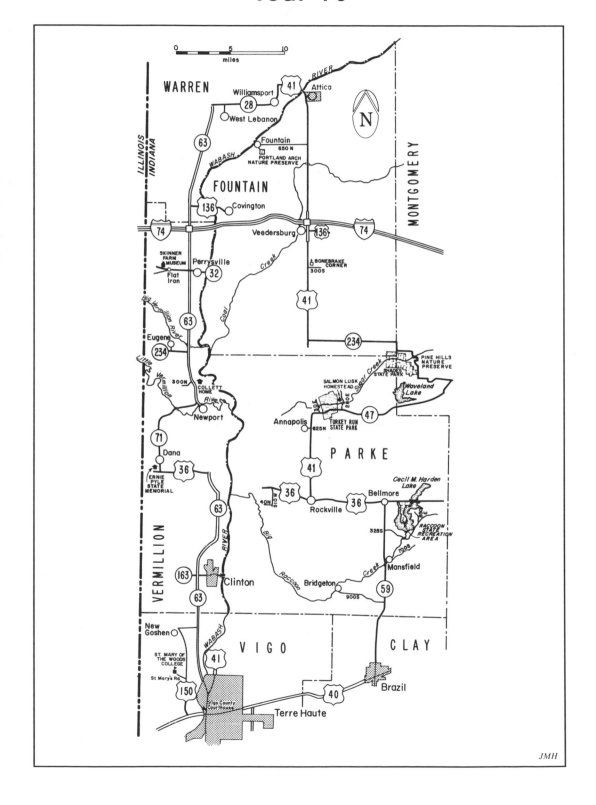

JMH

used for chautauqua productions for several years. The J. Emery Jenkins Nature Trail, which winds through the park, opened in 1982.

Return to US 40 and continue north on IND 59 for *5.6 m.* to the **PARKE COUNTY** (p. 16,372; 444 sq. m.) line. Soon after the Treaty of Fort Wayne in 1809 opened southern portions of the state to settlement, pioneers entered the area via the Wabash River. Parke County was organized in 1821, and the first county elections were held at Richard Henry's house on Henry Prairie. The county was named in honor of Benjamin Parke, a jurist and congressman during Indiana's territorial days and the first president of the Indiana Historical Society. Life in the early communities centered around the mills established along Sugar Creek, Big Raccoon Creek, and their branches. The Wabash and Erie Canal, begun in 1832, reached Lafayette in 1843, Coal Creek in 1847, and Terre Haute in 1849. Montezuma, on the western edge of the county, was once an important canal town, and traces remain of the canal and the basin which was used to store and turn boats. Displacing the waterways as the chief method of commercial transportation, the first railroad entered the county in 1860. Coal-mining operations in Parke County began prior to the Civil War. Although the county still contains coal resources, no coal mines were operating in 1986.

Although the county today supports industry and agriculture, it receives more notice for its turn-of-the-century villages and covered bridges. Thousands of visitors come annually to Parke County for the Maple Syrup Festival in the spring and the Covered Bridge Festival in the fall. Many restaurants, stores, and tourist attractions in the county's small towns are open only during festival time.

Most sugar camps operate in the northern and eastern sections of the county. Buckets and plastic bags hanging from maple trees catch the syrup which men gather in horse-drawn wagons, haul to rustic wooden shacks, and pour into wood-burning vats to boil. More modern operations use a tractor or transport the sap in plastic lines to the evaporating center. It takes about 50 to 60 gallons of sugar water boiled down to produce a single gallon of syrup, hence the retail price of more than $25 per gallon.

Perhaps more so than any other place in the nation, Parke County has preserved its legacy of 19th-century covered bridges. Of the 57 covered bridges built in the county, 34 remain, many of which are still in use. Joseph J. Daniels and J. A. Britton and Sons built the majority. Most bridges took names from families, locations, or creeks. The first known covered bridge in the county was completed in 1854 at Armiesburg. It was washed out in the flood of 1913, but the arches were salvaged for construction of the Cox Ford bridge. Ten bridges have stood more than a century. (*NRHP/ HABS/HAER*)

Continue north on IND 59 for *2.1 m.* to CR 900S. Turn left and follow the signs along county roads for *4.4 m.* to CR 780S and Main St. at **BRIDGETON**. This picturesque little village on the banks of the Big Raccoon retains its turn-of-the-century appearance. Bridgeton has been a mill town since its earliest days. Lockwood and Silliman built a mill that cracked corn about 1823. It later burned and was rebuilt. The second mill also burned and was replaced by the present three-story structure, called **Weise Mill**, in 1869. Buhrstones still grind corn, wheat, rye, and buckwheat into flour during festival days.

Joseph J. Daniels built the **Bridgeton Covered Bridge** adjacent to the mill site in 1868. The two-span bridge is now retired. A roadside park situated just north of the bridge provides a scenic viewpoint for the bridge, mill, and dam. A few feet from the bridge, a historical marker indicates the 1809 treaty boundary, known as the "ten o'clock" line, which ran in a northwest and southeast direction, passing the mouth of Raccoon Creek in Parke County.

Dr. James Crooks settled in Bridgeton in 1856 and treated many cases of "milk sickness" in the town's early days. His office was built in 1875 and the residence added in 1883. The two-story frame house of Italianate design still stands on Main St. just south of the old Masonic lodge built in 1855.

Across the street, the **Bridgeton Country Store**, a red-stained frame structure erected in 1865, continues to sell merchandise over counters dating from the 1890s. Local craftsmen now occupy the **1878 Bridgeton house**, a neat two-story frame building, and cater to the tourist trade.

About *3 m.* southwest of Bridgeton, Raccoon Creek, which occupies an unusually broad and deep valley, reverses its direction to provide one of Indiana's major geological riddles. The stream, which has flowed southwest since its origin, abruptly turns northwest and abandons its valley, laboriously cutting a new valley for nearly 20 miles. Geologists believe that the change was caused by blocking action by the Wisconsin glacier of more than 10,000 years ago.

Return east to IND 59. Turn left and proceed for *2.8 m.* to CR 700S. Turn right and continue *.1 m.* to the village of **MANSFIELD**. Nestled in the hills overlooking the Big Raccoon, Mansfield developed around the early gristmills built in the 1820s. Founded by two Irish immigrants named James Kelsey and Francis Dickson, the settlement was first known as Dickson's Mills. About 1860 the town and mill acquired their present name by the new mill owners from Mansfield, Ohio.

Tex Terry lived in Mansfield during the 1920s before he went to Hollywood and became a cowboy movie star. He later returned to the little town of Coxville in southern Parke County where he operated a tavern during his retirement years. His frequent visits to central Indiana schools were enthusiastically received by students who looked forward to Terry's arrival in a big car decked out with longhorn steer horns, guns, and other Western items.

Just right of the first crossroads in the village, the **Mansfield Covered Bridge** on CR 620S spans the Big Raccoon Creek. Joseph J. Daniels built the 247-ft.-long bridge of burr arch construction in 1867. Side windows provide a picturesque view of the creek and town. The double-span bridge is still in use. (*NRHP*)

G. K. Steele opened a **General Store** at the village crossroads in 1829, which has been in the Kemper family since 1846. Remodeled in 1870, the old general store with a "liar's bench" in the front is still extant.

Upstream from the covered bridge, the **Mansfield Roller Mill**, a three-story yellow poplar board structure, rests on a sandstone shelf. Constructed in 1820 and partially rebuilt in the 1880s following a fire, the mill is still in operating condition. A 15-ft. steel breast waterwheel and two hydraulic turbines provide power for the gears, pulley belts, and machin-

Indiana Historical Society (Covered Bridge Collection)

Mansfield Covered Bridge

ery to grind corn and wheat. Amish carpenters assisted in the recent renovation of the mill.

Return to IND 59. Proceed north for *3.2 m.* to CR 325S. Turn right and continue *1.7 m.* to CR 850E, the road leading to **Cecil M. Harden Lake**. Turn left and go *.3 m.* to reach the hilltop parking area. Formerly known as Mansfield Reservoir and Raccoon Lake, the lake was renamed in 1974 to honor Cecil M. Harden (1894-1984), a five-term congresswoman from this area. In 1960 the United States Army Corps of Engineers completed a 1,840-ft.-long dam across Raccoon Creek, creating the 2,060-acre reservoir. The flood control dam measures 700 ft. across the width of the base and impounds the lake to an elevation of 690 ft. before water goes over the spillway. The road crossing the dam affords a sweeping view of the reservoir to the north and the creek valley to the south. On the far side of the dam is a wooded lookout point dotted with picnic sites.

From the dam at the southern tip of the lake, return to IND 59. Turn right and proceed north for *2.7 m.*, then right on US 36 for *1.6 m.* to the entrance on the right for **Raccoon State Recreation Area** at Hollandsburg. The 4,065-acre recreation area bordering the northwest side of Cecil M. Harden Lake opened in 1961. Noted for its crappie, the lake is also stocked with bass, bluegill, and catfish. Park facilities include a bathing beach, boat ramps, campsites, and picnic areas.

Return west on US 36 through Bellmore and continue an additional *4 m.* Turn right to **NYESVILLE**, *1.5 m.* north. This was the birthplace of Mordecai (Three Fingers) Brown (1876-1948), an all-time professional baseball great and one of the few Hoosiers enshrined in the national Baseball Hall of Fame at Cooperstown, N.Y. In 13 years, 1903-16, mostly with the Chicago Cubs, he compiled a phenomenal pitching record of 239 wins, 129 losses, and an earned run average of 2.06.

Return to US 36, turn right, and drive *1.3 m.* to **Billie Creek Village** on the east side of Rockville. A re-created turn-of-the-century Hoosier village, Billie Creek covers 75 acres and contains reconstructed pioneer buildings moved here from the surrounding area. Village craftsmen demonstrate broom making, blacksmithing, weaving, newspaper printing, and other early trades. Included on the grounds are an operating farmstead, a general store, school-

house, bank, church, doctor's office, newspaper office, covered bridges, and various shops.

Continue west on US 36 for *1 m.* to the **Parke County Tourist Information Center**, housed in a Victorian train station to the south of Ohio St. The restored Vandalia Railroad depot, built in 1886, now houses a gift store and provides visitors with maps and information about the annual county festivals.

Continue west on US 36 for *.2 m.* to the **Parke County Courthouse** between Jefferson and Market sts. at **ROCKVILLE** (p. 2,785). Following the organization of Parke County in 1821, first Rosedale, then Armiesburg, served as temporary county seats before the commissioners selected Rockville in 1824. To seal the act, the commissioners consumed a bottle of whiskey and broke the empty bottle upon a granite rock to christen the town. The first courthouse, a log structure, was completed in 1826. A brick courthouse was built in 1832. Thomas J. Tolan and Son of Fort Wayne designed the present courthouse, a Second Empire-style stone building with a central clock tower, completed in 1882. Boulders at the Ohio St. entrance of the courthouse are reputedly those for which the town received its name.

East of the courthouse, at the northeast corner of High and Jefferson sts., is the **Parke County Jail and Sheriff's Residence**, built in 1879. Courthouse architects Thomas J. Tolan and Son designed the Italianate-style brick building, restored in the 1970s and still in use.

On the southeast corner of Jefferson and Ohio sts., east of the courthouse, is the old **Parke State Bank**, a Victorian-style structure. Organized as the Parke Banking Company, the bank was erected in 1873. A handsome wrought-iron stairway and balcony decorate the north side of the two-story brick bank. The building is now used for law offices.

The **Memorial Presbyterian Church** occupies the northwest corner of Market and High sts., across from the courthouse. The first Presbyterian church at Rockville was built in 1833. The present brick church of Italianate design was erected in 1870, extended in 1893, and restored in 1950. When the Old and New School Presbyterian churches of Rockville united in 1869, the bells from both churches were molded into one. The recast bell now hangs in a tower as a memorial in the yard adjacent to the church.

From the courthouse, proceed west on US 36 for *.2 m.* to the **Parke County Historical Society Museum** on the left side. The museum occupies a brick building erected in 1839 and originally used as a seminary. It subsequently served as an armory during the Civil War, a black elementary school from 1873 to 1924, and a gas station, restaurant, and gift shop before it was purchased by the historical society in 1975. Display cases in two large rooms hold a wide variety of local historical artifacts.

From US 36 and US 41, just west of the museum, continue west on US 36 for *5.5 m.,* then south on 510W *.3 m.* to the **Phillips Covered Bridge** at CR 40N and 510W. Built in 1909 by J. A. Britton, the bridge spanning Big Pond Creek is the state's shortest public covered bridge, measuring only 43 ft. in length. It is still in use.

Return to US 36 and US 41. Turn left on US 41 and proceed north for *6.5 m.* to CR 625N. The boyhood home of Joseph G. "Uncle Joe" Cannon (1836-1926) is situated a mile west of here at Annapolis. Cannon, speaker of the United States House of Representatives from 1903 to 1911, lived in this village between 1840 and 1858. He studied for a law career in Terre Haute and Cincinnati before moving to Illinois and achieving fame in politics. The Cannon House Office Building on Capitol Hill in Washington, D.C., is named for him.

Return to US 41 and proceed north for *1.4 m.* to IND 47. Turn right and continue *.7 m.* to an unmarked, unpaved road which descends north from IND 47 to Sugar Creek, spanned by the **Cox Ford Bridge** at *.6 m.* Built in 1913, the covered bridge on CR 293E is still in service though only a single lane road ascends the creek bank on the far side. J. A. Britton constructed part of this bridge with the arches from a bridge near Armiesburg, built in 1854, that was washed out in the flood of 1913.

Return to IND 47 and proceed east *1 m.* to the entrance for **Turkey Run State Park** on the left. Established in 1916, Turkey Run is the second oldest Indiana state park. The 2,382 acres contain one of the largest stands of virgin timber in the state and public facilities for a number of recreational activities such as tennis, swimming, canoeing, horseback riding, bicycling, and picnicking. The state inn, cabins, and campgrounds provide complete guest accommodations. More than 13 miles of hiking trails traverse the park through wooded ravines, be-

neath sandstone ledges, and past an old quarry and coal mine. A suspension bridge, built in 1917-18, leads across Sugar Creek to the Rocky Hollow-Falls Canyon Nature Preserve, an alluvial forest area highlighted by waterfalls spilling into spectacular gorges where wild turkeys once perched on limestone ledges. Stands of old-growth timber contain fine sycamores, several huge black walnuts, and numerous hickory, hemlock, and evergreen trees.

Near the inn, a monument to Juliet V. Strauss and a memorial to Richard Lieber acknowledge their efforts to preserve this area as a state park for future generations of nature lovers. Known as the "Country Contributor," Strauss wrote a column for the *Rockville Tribune*, published stories in national publications, and compiled a volume titled *Ideals of a Plain Country Woman.* Lieber was the founder and director of the Indiana state park system.

Behind the inn, a log cabin built in 1848 and moved to the park in 1918 now serves as a natural history museum. Nearby Sunset Point provides a bird's-eye view of Sugar Creek beneath steep cliffs. Covered bridges cross the creek at both the western and eastern borders of the park.

From the park entrance proceed east *.8 m.* Turn left on CR 300E and follow the paved road *.7 m.* to the **Narrows Covered Bridge** in a hollow just left of the concrete bridge crossing Sugar Creek. J. A. Britton built the bridge of burr arch construction in 1882. Set against park woods and limestone bluffs, the now retired covered bridge occupies one of the county's most scenic spots.

Located north a short distance in back of the cliffs overlooking Sugar Creek, the **Salmon Lusk Homestead** is reached by crossing the concrete bridge and turning left onto the first side road. A veteran of the War of 1812, Lusk came west from Vermont and settled in Indiana in 1821. He built a gristmill on the banks of Sugar Creek in 1826, which was destroyed by a flood following a quick winter thaw in 1847. A hole for the water-powered wheel shaft is still visible in the rock ledge beneath the concrete bridge on CR 300E. Lusk erected the two-story, Federal-style house of hand-fired brick in 1841, which has been restored and opened to the public as a museum. Salmon's son John occupied the house until 1915. The state acquired it in 1919. (*NRHP*)

Return to IND 47. Turn left and proceed east *5.3 m.* to the Montgomery County line. The Turkey Run Golf Club commands the hillside to the right, and Waveland Lake, formed by a dam erected in 1969, lies to the left.

Created in 1822, **MONTGOMERY COUNTY** (p. 35,501; 505 sq. m.) was located in the western part of the New Purchase. The county was named for Maj. Gen. Richard Montgomery, a Revolutionary hero who died at the siege of Quebec. It is characterized by densely wooded hilly sections to the south and prairie to the north. The northeast section contains lowlands which became fertile farmland when drained. Montgomery County ranks high in the number of hogs sold and in corn produced. It also boasts a major industrial, cultural, and educational center—Crawfordsville.

Continue northeast on IND 47 for *6.6 m.*, past Waveland and Browns Valley, to IND 234. Travel left for *4.8 m.* At the right hand bend in the highway where IND 234 heads north, continue straight ahead for *.7 m.* to the entrance on the right to **Shades State Park**. Established in 1947, the 3,084-acre park is intended primarily for hikers. It features more than eight miles of trails past such romantic sounding places as Shawnee Canyon, Kickapoo Ravine, Lover's Leap, Devil's Punch Bowl, and Maidenhair Falls—much of which cover steep cliffs and rugged terrain. A variety of stories account for how the park acquired its name, but most emphasize the deep shadows of the forests in this area when settlers arrived at this former Piankashaw Indian settlement in the late 1820s. The early name, The Shades of Death, eventually became simply The Shades.

In the 1860s a series of natural springs in a ravine area was developed as a health resort called The Shades. For many years an inn built in 1887 near Devil's Punch Bowl was a landmark in the park. Sugar Creek cuts through the park between high sandstone cliffs creating an outstanding vista from such lookouts as Prospect Point (210 ft. above the creek) and Lover's Leap. For the most part the area has been preserved as a natural park featuring mature forests, deep ravines, and scenic stream beds. Facilities include primitive campsites and the Roscoe Turner Flight Strip, a 120 x 3,000-ft. turf strip for light aircraft use. Also within the park is the Pedestal Rock Nature Preserve.

Return to IND 234 and proceed north for *.8 m.* to the parking lot on the left for the **Pine Hills Nature Preserve**. Craggy hills and deep gorges covered with evergreens and hardwood trees highlight this 470-acre preserve adjacent to Shades State Park. Four narrow ridges called "backbones," remnants from the last glaciers, rise about 75 to 100 ft. above the creek valley floor. Clifty and Indian creeks join at Honeycomb Rock and eventually flow into Sugar Creek. In the 1860s a woolen mill company erected a dam across Clifty Creek and used the impounded water to power a mill. The mill was moved in 1873. The Indiana Department of Natural Resources acquired the Pine Hills tract in 1961.

Continue north on IND 234 for *.6 m.* to the bridge over Sugar Creek. A public canoe launch and parking area are located on the left adjoining the **Deer's Mill Covered Bridge**. Built in 1878 by Joseph J. Daniels, the well-preserved bridge is constructed with two spans of burr arch trusses. It is now retired. (*HAER*)

Continue north and west on IND 234 for *3.3 m.* to the **FOUNTAIN COUNTY** (p. 19,033; 398 sq. m.) line. In 1825 the state legislature approved an act for the formation of Fountain County out of Montgomery and Wabash counties. More than two-thirds of the county's acreage is used for agriculture. The county is named for Maj. James Fountain of Kentucky, who was killed in the Battle of Maumee at Fort Wayne in 1790. The Wabash River forms the entire northern and western boundary of the county. The county seat, Covington, and the county's largest city, Attica, both border the river. Coal Creek and Shawnee Creek are the principal streams. Quantities of coal, sandstone, and limestone are found throughout the county. In the past, water from saline wells was removed and boiled to produce salt for local markets in the lower part of the county. In 1867 Samuel Snoddy built a gristmill on Coal Creek, which still stands on the site of an earlier sawmill dating back to 1828. Snoddy's Mill was a family operation until 1946. It later was leased to the Fountain County Historical Society.

Continue west on IND 234 for *8.1 m.* to US 41 and turn right. In the northeast corner of the first intersection is the Kingman coal mine site, a major strip operation near the northern border of Indiana's coal fields. It produced into the late 1950s. Continue *7 m.* to CR 300S at **Bonebrake Corner Church and Cemetery**. Construction on the building began in 1847. First called "Liberty Chapel," it was a nondenomi-national meetinghouse. Bonebrake was the sur-name of one of the families that held shares in the venture. When still not complete in 1852, the church trustees persuaded the township to finish the building for school purposes with the provision that worship would be allowed. The small rectangular structure became the first brick schoolhouse in Fountain County. Classes were carried on in the church for about 25 years, and services continued until 1901. The Bonebrake Cemetery League, founded in 1932, maintains the cemetery.

Continue north on US 41 for *2 m.* to the north junction of US 136. One mile west lies **VEEDERSBURG** (p. 2,261), the county's sec-ond largest town. Laid out in 1871 by Peter S. Veeder, who with Marshall Nixon opened the town's first warehouse and lumberyard and sold agricultural implements, Veedersburg was an early brick manufacturing center. Locally produced bricks provided the construction ma-terials for many of the town's fine homes and paved streets. Expanding west from the banks of Coal Creek, Veedersburg began as a mill town; its first mill was erected by Oliver Os-burn on Coal Creek in 1829. The town's major industry today is a foundry on the south side which produces gray iron castings.

Along US 41, *1.9 m.* north of US 136, a roadside marker on the right indicates the boy-hood home of Daniel W. Voorhees (1827-1897), one of the state's greatest orators. Born in Butler County, Ohio, Voorhees later prac-ticed law in Covington. He first was elected congressman in 1861, and later as a United States senator he served on the committee that fought for the appropriation of national funds to build the Congressional Library Building in Washington, D.C.

Continue north on US 41 for *5.3 m.* to CR 650N. Turn left and proceed west *4.8 m.* to Portland Arch Rd., going south, in **FOUN-TAIN**. Situated on the Wabash River about seven miles north of Covington, Fountain was laid out as Portland in 1828. It was a trading post town in early days, distributing local goods such as beeswax, tallow, feathers, ginseng, furs, and wild hops for 100 miles up and down the river. Between 1846 and 1875 Fountain partici-pated in trade on the Wabash and Erie Canal along a 376-mile stretch through Indiana from Fort Wayne to Evansville. The towpath still fol-lows the riverbank on the west side of town off Jefferson St.

A sign along CR 650N on the east side of Fountain directs motorists to the parking lot for the **Portland Arch Nature Preserve**, located one-half mile south and east of the village. Bear Creek flows through a deep gorge with sand-stone walls, joins a small tributary stream, and empties into the Wabash River. Near its mouth, Bear Creek has carved an opening through the massive rock formation creating a natural bridge. Situated within the 265-acre na-ture preserve, Portland Arch is a popular attraction. The natural bridge has been desig-nated a National Natural Landmark. Nearby is a landmark known as Tecumseh's Cave. An-other of the natural features within the preserve is the Devil's Tea Table, a rock that looms like a sentry over the surrounding hardwood forest.

From Fountain, return to US 41. Turn left and proceed north on US 41 for *4.8 m.*, passing the Harrison Hills Country Club golf course on the right, to IND 28 in **ATTICA** (p. 3,841). At-tica was laid out in 1825 by George Hollings-worth, who operated a ferry across the Wabash. This ferry and another one established in 1843 were the only means of crossing the river until a covered wagon bridge was erected in 1861. In the early years Attica competed with Coving-ton for trade on the Wabash and Erie Canal, opened to Attica in 1847. The rivalry, however, became moot with the arrival of the Wabash Railroad at Attica and the New Albany and Sa-lem Railroad at Lafayette and the subsequent diversion of commerce. In 1881 the Wabash Railroad opened a branch line from Attica to Covington along the canal's towpath. The lead-ing manufacturer in Attica between 1896 and 1909 was the Sterling Remedy Company, pro-ducer of such medicines as No-To-Bac, Dr. Hobbs Sparagus Kidney Pills, and Gum-to-Bac. No-To-Bac, a 30-day treatment, was guaranteed to cure the tobacco habit or money refunded. Hoosier humorist George Ade wrote advertising copy for the firm at a weekly salary of $12.00 which was later raised to $15.00.

The city's largest employer today is the **Harrison Steel Castings Company**, located off S. Perry St. Established in Converse, Indiana, as the National Car Coupler Company, it moved to Attica in 1906. The firm changed its name in 1927 and gradually diversified its products. Run by the third generation of Harrisons, the company employs 650 persons and plays a major role in the community.

From Council and Jackson sts., proceed east on IND 28 for *.3 m.*, then straight ahead onto Ravine Park Blvd., where IND 28 angles. This leads into **Ravine Park**. The trails of the Kickapoo, Shawnee, Potawatomi, and Ouiatenon Indians once crossed the natural ravines of this 90-acre wooded park. It was a favorite camping ground of the Indians because of its fine springs. The Indians also held their councils in the area. In 1807 Tecumseh and his brother the Prophet represented the Shawnee in a council meeting with the Kickapoo, Potawatomi, Miami, and Winnebago held under a giant oak tree in Attica. Known as the Tecumseh Council Oak, the tree was cut down about 1866. A marker on the south wall of the Attica City Hall at Jackson and McDonald sts., one block west of US 41 and IND 28, identifies the spot.

The first settler in Logan Township, Casey Emmons, built his log cabin in Ravine Park in 1825 and lived there for two years. A tanner by trade, Emmons made clothing and moccasins for the Indians. In the 1830s early settlers ran a distillery on the grounds. Numerous crystal springs provided the town's water supply until the turn of the century. A brick plant operated on the site of what later became a chautauqua pavilion. Discarded bricks formed additional mounds to the already hilly contours of the park. In the 1870s the park was the location of county fairs and horse races. Annual chautauquas were held here in the 20th century.

Return to Council and Jackson sts. Continue west for three blocks. Go south one block to the **Attica Public Library** at Perry and Washington sts. In the front yard is a bronze statue of an American "doughboy" erected in 1927 as a World War I memorial. On the corner of the Carnegie library built in 1904, a plaque honors Attica's illustrious citizen, Dr. John Evans (1814-1897), who came to Fountain County from Ohio in 1839 and practiced medicine here. In 1841 Evans petitioned the state legislature to build a state hospital for the insane. He served as the first superintendent of what is now Central State Hospital at Indianapolis until 1848 when he accepted a teaching post at Rush Medical College in Chicago. He laid out the town of Evanston, Illinois, and there with Orrington Lunt founded Northwestern University. In 1862 President Lincoln appointed Ev-

ans territorial governor of Colorado. He founded a seminary which later became the University of Denver and aided many churches and educational institutions throughout the state.

Many of Attica's finest residences and church buildings line S. Perry St. in the vicinity of the public library and Brady St., one block to the east. Some of the most architecturally important structures are the Greek Revival-style houses surviving from the canal era in the 1850s. The elegant brick Italianate-style mansions reached their height of fashion in the 1870s and 1880s. Both styles reflect the city's earlier era of prosperity and gracious living.

Return to Jackson and Perry sts. in downtown Attica. Follow US 41 west for *.4 m.* to the river bridge leading into Warren County. In 1827 the Indiana General Assembly created **WARREN COUNTY** (p. 8,976; 366 sq. m.). The county was named in honor of Maj. Gen. Joseph Warren, an American Revolutionary War commander who was fatally wounded at Breed's Hill. It is bounded by the state of Illinois to the west, the Wabash River to the south and east, Benton County on the north, and Tippecanoe County on the east. Farmland occupies 89 percent of the total area, with corn and soybeans the principal crops. The county also supports some mining and industry. From the 1890s to the 1940s, a luxurious mineral springs spa called Mudlavia Hotel operated north of Attica, drawing devotees and celebrities from near and far. A stagecoach met the local trains and delivered patrons to the hotel.

Continue west on US 41 for *2.1 m.* then south on IND 28 for *1.4 m.* to Monroe and 2nd sts. in downtown **WILLIAMSPORT** (p. 1,747). Early settlers, mostly from Maryland, Ohio, and Pennsylvania came here by 1827. In 1828 William Harrison, the owner of a tavern and a horse ferry across the Wabash, hired Perrin Kent to lay out the town of William's Port, extending northwest from the river. A year later Isaac Rains laid out the "west addition" on Harrison property donated to the county. This eventually became the local business district. Grain trade and pork packing were important early businesses. A side-cut canal was constructed without permission in 1850-52 so that boats could run to the west side of the river. People called the town the "side-cut city." Williamsport sued to force the canal to pay the cost of the side cut but lost. The Wabash Railroad arrived in 1856, and the new part of town developed north of the tracks whereas the old section fell into decay. William Kent and Elisha Hitchens built a large warehouse near the railroad and stored up to 212,000 bushels of grain per year. In the early 1900s a sandstone quarry operated below the falls just south of the railroad tracks. The stone was used for the construction of many Williamsport homes and businesses.

The original county seat was located at Warrenton, and the first court met at the home of Enoch Farmer in 1828. The following year the county commissioners relocated the seat at Williamsport. William Harrison's log cabin served as the first courthouse. Two courthouses, built in 1834 and 1872, preceded the present **Warren County Courthouse**, erected in 1907, at Monroe and 2nd sts.

From the courthouse, go south one block on Monroe St. and cross the railroad. The **Warren County Historical Society Museum** occupies the corner building in a century-old business block on the left side of the street. Formerly used as a blacksmith shop and later as a machine shop, the old structure has recently undergone restoration. The museum contains several displays depicting the early history of Warren County, and the historical society plans to open a museum dealing with Indiana agriculture in the building next to the Williamsport fire station, also on Monroe St. Volunteers have planted an old-fashioned herb garden behind the museum and built a stairway that leads down to the falls.

Williamsport Falls, the county's most widely known natural landmark, drops a distance of 67 ft. from an overhanging ledge into a rocky ravine. Formed by Fall Branch, the waterfall varies from a mere trickle in the dry summer months to a spectacular torrent during spring thaws. The falls may be reached from the back entrance of the museum or by a narrow driveway around the end of the building.

At the south end of the Monroe St. business block, bear right to cross the Fall St. bridge. Continue south one-half block to the handsome stuccoed-brick **Presbyterian Church** of Gothic design on the left side. The Presbyterians in Williamsport organized in 1850 and built their first church about 1854. They erected the present building with a slate roof and corner steeple in 1890 and used it until 1964. The interior, including the original

oak pews and the outstanding stained-glass windows, has been restored.

Continue south one-half block on Fall St. Turn left on Center St. and proceed two blocks. Turn right. In the middle of the block, at 303 Lincoln St., is the **Tower House Museum**. Elisha Hitchens, a blacksmith and merchant from Chillicothe, Ohio, built this Tuscan-style brick mansion in 1854. The museum takes its name from the tower attached to the 15-room residence. Hitchens came to Williamsport and opened a general store with his son-in-law, William Kent, in 1846. He later engaged in the grain trade and served as the postmaster from 1873 to 1885. The house has been restored and furnished with antiques and collectibles. (*NRHP*) Just east of the Tower House Museum is a house of identical design that was built for Hitchens's daughter and son-in-law. The William Kent house at 500 Main St. was damaged by fire but has undergone restoration.

Go north one and one-half blocks on Lincoln St. to Monroe St. at the Williamsport school. Turn right one and one-half blocks to the **High house** at 404 E. Monroe St. The Ole High Inn now occupies the building. John V. R. High built this sandstone Federal-style building as a tavern in 1853. Fronted by four doors, the stone house is one of the oldest buildings in Williamsport.

Follow Monroe St. northwest across the railroad to 2nd St. at the courthouse. Turn left and proceed west on IND 28 for *5 m.* to IND 263, situated a short distance north of West Lebanon. In 1830 Surveyor Perrin Kent laid out the town of Lebanon, south of what is now **WEST LEBANON** (p. 946). It became the third town in Warren County, preceded by Warrenton and Williamsport, but remained small because of its inland location. When the Wabash Railroad crossed one-half mile north of Lebanon in 1855, new business development moved north, too. The new town was incorporated in 1869.

Continue west for *.9 m.* on IND 28 to IND 63. Proceed south for *10 m.* then east on US 136 for *2.7 m.*, crossing the **David M. Shoup Memorial Bridge** at the county line and turning south on 3rd St., in **COVINGTON** (p. 2,883). The Shoup Memorial Bridge, dedicated November 11, 1983, honors the Battle Ground, Indiana, native, who attended high school in Covington and later commanded the United States Marine Corps. Situated on the Wabash

River, about 15 miles downstream from Attica, Covington is the Fountain County seat. Isaac Coleman laid out the town in 1826. The first **Fountain County Courthouse** was a small frame building built in 1827, followed by a brick building completed in 1833 in the center of the public square. The third courthouse, completed in 1859, was condemned as unsafe in 1933. The present building, designed by architect Louis L. Johnson of Fountain County, was dedicated in 1937.

Artist Eugene Francis Savage, a native of Covington, directed the painting by area artists of the murals which cover the interior walls. Savage personally composed and painted the two canvases on either side of the main entrance. Seven murals and two maps, encompassing more than 2,500 sq. ft., depict the history of Fountain County. Local figures portrayed include Elijah Earl, who invented and manufactured the riding plow and a corn planter; Olive Coffeen, who taught school here for 69 years; and Schuyler LaTourette, a weaver noted for his coverlets. LaTourette's parents came to Fountain County in 1826, carrying the Jarez loom from France. Savage's boldly executed murals at the east entranceway are allegorical representations of social, political, and economic themes. His mother, Ann Savage, was the model for the figure on the north wall representing music. Completed in 1940, the murals were restored in 1983-84.

The courthouse basement contains an exhibit illustrating the history of Fountain County and a bronze bust, cast in 1862, of Maj. Gen. Lew Wallace, by Randolph Rogers. Though born in Brookville, Wallace moved with his family to Covington in 1832 when he was five years old and attended school here. Following service in the Mexican War, Wallace returned to Indiana, passed the bar examination in 1849, and in 1850 opened a law office in Covington, where he practiced for three years. In 1853 Wallace and his wife, with their newborn son, moved to Crawfordsville. (See Tour 13.)

Another important statesman who resided in Fountain County is Edward A. Hannegan (1807-1859). Hannegan settled in Shawnee Township about 1825. He established a law office in Covington in 1831 and became one of the most important criminal lawyers in the state. In the 1840s Hannegan was a participant in the "canal war" over water rights on the Wabash and Erie Canal between Attica and Covington. Believing that the locks at Attica held back the water supply to downstream Covington, a band of irate Covington citizens led by Hannegan marched north and forcibly opened the floodgates. Outnumbered, the Attica men retreated from the locks but retaliated by pitching straw into the canal above the locks, effectively blocking the water's passage. Hannegan served as a congressman, 1833-37, and as a United States senator, 1843-49. President Polk appointed him as minister to Prussia in 1849. During the Polk administration, Hannegan was prominent in the controversy over the Oregon boundary and won fame for his slogan "54-40 or Fight." While a candidate for the presidential nomination in 1852, Hannegan killed his brother-in-law, Capt. John R. Duncan, during a domestic quarrel, which ended his campaign. Hannegan faced a possible manslaughter charge, but the grand jury failed to indict him, and Hannegan was released. He spent the last two years of his life in St. Louis, succumbing to the effects of alcohol and an overdose of morphine.

In the block east of the courthouse is one of the city's oldest houses, the **Hetfield house**, 417 Liberty St. Robert Hetfield built this two-story brick home of Federal design between 1832 and 1837. Hetfield held various state and county offices including that of tax collector, sheriff, county recorder, and Covington councilman. Members of the family owned an interest in the Hetfield flouring mill and the Sugar Grove woolen mills. For a time, the American Legion owned the house. Law offices now occupy the renovated building.

From this house continue on Liberty St., passing a marker near 9th St. designating the grave of Esther Test Wallace, mother of author Lew Wallace, and turn right on 11th St. Follow 11th St. to the I-74 interchange. Go west on I-74 *3.2 m.* to the first exit (Exit 4; IND 63) in **VERMILLION COUNTY** (p. 18,229; 260 sq. m.). Called the "shoe string" county, Vermillion County extends 37 miles north and south between the state of Illinois and the Wabash River. First a part of Vigo County, then Parke County, Vermillion became a separate county in 1824. It averages about seven miles wide. One of the smallest in the state, Vermillion ranks 84th in size of the 92 counties. Nevertheless, it produces nearly twice the corn and soybeans per acre as its neighboring counties, and it has one of the state's largest coal mines, the Universal Mine of the Peabody Coal Company, which produced 2,439,133 tons of coal in 1986. The county is named for the Big Vermillion River which crosses it to join the Wabash River. The greatest density of population is in Clinton near the southern end where Vermillion meets Vigo County, a more industrialized area. Eli Lilly and Company, manufacturer of pharmaceutical and agricultural products, is the county's largest employer, with 900 persons working at its Clinton site.

Turn left and continue south on IND 63 for *4.7 m.*, then right on IND 32 for *3 m.*, passing to the right of the "V" in the road at Flat Iron to the **Skinner Farm Museum** on the north side of the road. Farm owner Norman Skinner has assembled on his property a large collection of Indiana pioneer buildings and early agricultural equipment. Four log cabins, a barn, and a blacksmith shop, all built in the 1820s and 1830s, have been reconstructed and furnished with period pieces. Skinner moved intact the large two-story brick home of his great-great-grandfather David Wittenmyer, a shoemaker and tanner, three miles to his farm. The Skinner family lives in an 1885 frame farmhouse and owns more than 50 different gas tractors and early steam-powered farm machines.

Return to IND 63. Proceed south for *6.5 m.* to the Army Ford Bridge over the Big Vermillion River. A historical marker facing northbound traffic on the highway indicates **Harrison's Crossing**. About 100 yds. from here, Gov. William Henry Harrison led his men across the river on the march preceding the Battle of Tippecanoe in 1811.

Continue south on IND 63 for *.5 m.* to IND 234. Turn right for *1.1 m.* to the Cayuga First Assembly of God at Perry St. in Cayuga (p. 1,258). Turn north and continue *.7 m.* to Eugene. One-half mile north of the unincorporated village is the **Eugene Covered Bridge** built by Joseph J. Daniels of Rockville in 1873. Now retired, the single-span bridge is situated just west of a modern concrete bridge across the Big Vermillion. Stephen S. Collett, who with his brother shipped grain and pork to New Orleans, platted the village in 1827. In the early days a big gristmill operated on the river, and a pork packing plant flourished in the village. Other local industries included a cooper shop, a woolen mill, and a brickyard. The **Alice Craig Fuller house** at the southwest corner of Clay

and Main sts. is the birthplace of the Hoosier author of *Lantern Gleams of Old Eugene* and other poems.

Return to IND 63 and proceed south for *2.1 m.* to the **Collett home** east of the highway near CR 300N. In the 1820s the Collett family acquired extensive property along the Wabash. The grandsons of pioneer John Collett, John and Josephus, planned and endowed the Collett Home for Orphans. The stately two-story Classic Revival-style building, erected in 1901, stands on the old family homestead. The large power plant nearby is Public Service Indiana's Cayuga station, rated at 1,006 megawatts.

Continue south on IND 63 for *3.1 m.* to an unmarked road leading right for *.6 m.* to the **Newport Covered Bridge**. Joseph J. Daniels of Rockville built the bridge in 1885 on the road to Shaw's Mill and Quaker Point.

Return to IND 63 and continue south for *.5 m.* to Market St. at the flashing light. Turn east and proceed *.5 m.* to Market and Main sts. in downtown **NEWPORT** (p. 704). In 1824 the county commissioners selected Newport for the county seat. John Collett laid out the town in 1828 and was important in its early development. He built a hotel at the courthouse square which stood from 1824 to 1957. He also built a dam and gristmill, operated a ferry on the Wabash, and served as the town's second postmaster. Several commercial buildings erected after a fire in 1892 surround the courthouse square. The tavern at the south corner of the block was first used for this purpose in 1870.

The first **Vermillion County Courthouse** was erected in 1824 and replaced in 1831. Architect John F. Bayard of Vincennes designed the present courthouse, which was dedicated in 1925.

One block east of the courthouse at Market and George sts. is the **Vermillion County Jail and Sheriff's Residence**. The first jail was built in 1828 of squared logs. A brick jail replaced it in 1837, followed by a new jail in 1868. The only hanging in Vermillion County took place in the jail yard on April 3, 1879, after a jury convicted 27-year-old Walter Watson for shooting a local storekeeper over a trivial dispute. Architect J. W. Gaddis of Vincennes designed the stone-block jail built in 1895. The old jail was converted into the sheriff's quarters. Both are still in use.

In 1909 Newport was the site of an auto hill climb contest. Participants arrived by train from Evansville, Indianapolis, and Danville, Illinois. The 1,300-ft.-long and 140-ft.-high hill presented a real challenge to the early automobiles, and the event proved popular with the crowds until 1915. In 1963 the hill climb was revived as the Newport Antique Auto Hill Climb. The competition takes place annually on the first weekend in October.

From Newport, return to IND 63. Go north *2 m.* to IND 71. Turn left and follow IND 71 west and south for *9 m.*, passing the World War II Army Ammunitions Plant now operated by Uniroyal Company, to the business district of **DANA** (p. 803). Dana began as a railroad town which sprouted up around the Indianapolis, Decatur and Western Railroad. It was platted in 1875 and named after Charles Dana, a stockholder of the railroad. The town experienced a boom when the government ordnance plant began operations north of here in the 1940s.

Facing the railroad, at Maple St. (IND 71) and Briarwood Ave., is the **Ernie Pyle State Historic Site**. Relocated from its original Helt Township location, the little white frame farmhouse in which the famous World War II correspondent Ernest Taylor Pyle was born on August 3, 1900, now serves as a memorial museum and media center. Pyle lived here for a year and a half, then moved with his family to his grandfather's farm two miles east of IND 71. Pyle attended Indiana University in Bloomington and worked as a reporter for the *La Porte Herald* before going to Washington, D.C., to write for the *Daily News*. His articles written about rural American life at this time were compiled into a book called *Home Country*. Pyle went to England in 1940 and began describing the war. His war assignments took him around the world, and his columns were contained in his books, *Here Is Your War* and *Brave Men*. Pyle wrote about the human side of war. Though a civilian, he received the Purple Heart, the United States Medal of Merit, and the American Legion's Distinguished Service Medal. In 1944 he won the Pulitzer Prize for Correspondence for his coverage of World War II. A movie titled "The Story of G.I. Joe," which premiered in 1945, was drawn from Pyle's writings. Pyle's last assignment was in the Pacific theater where he was killed by a Japanese sniper on the tiny island of Ie Shima near Okinawa in 1945.

Continue south *.5 m.* to US 36. Turn left and proceed east for *2.2 m.* to the **Ernie Pyle Rest Park** on the north side of the road. Shortly after Pyle's death in 1945, soldiers of the 77th Infantry Division erected a monument on the spot where he fell. It was simply engraved "On this spot the 77th lost a buddy." A replica of the monument is in the roadside park. The rest area also contains the Hillsboro Covered Bridge, referred to locally as the Possum Bottom bridge, moved here from Little Raccoon Creek just south of US 36 and original IND 63. The single-span bridge of burr arch construction was built by Joseph J. Daniels in 1876.

Continue east for *2.6 m.* to IND 63, turn right, and continue *4.4 m.* to CR 1050S. On the east side of the highway are the Clinton Laboratories of **Eli Lilly and Company**, the county's largest employer. The plant specializes in producing agricultural products used to prevent poultry disease and to promote better use of feed in beef cattle.

Continue on IND 63 for *5.5 m.* to IND 163 and turn left for *1.7 m.* to 9th St. in **CLINTON** (p. 5,267). Continue on IND 163 to Elm and Main sts. in the business district. Platted in 1829 and named for DeWitt Clinton, governor of New York, Clinton was once a thriving packing center and river port with steamboat lines on the Wabash. By the 1850s the waterfront was almost completely built up with wool and coal yards, grain elevators, mills, warehouses, and pork packing plants.

Between the 1870s and 1920s Clinton drew immigrants of more than 25 nationalities including many Italians who worked in the coal fields. During the height of the coal-mining period, Clinton's population reached about 15,000. Many mine workers were forced to relocate in the 1920s when the mines declined. In the 1940s employment for local workers revived with the opening of the ordnance plant north of the city.

Descendants of Italian immigrants now celebrate their heritage with an annual Little Italy Festival during the Labor Day weekend featuring grape stomps, polka dances, bocci games, ethnic foods, gondola rides on the Wabash, music, and traditional costumes.

One block south of Elm and Main sts., IND 163 turns east and crosses the Wabash River into Parke County. On the west bank, just north of the highway, is a tiny, picturesque park, overlooking the river. The Quattro Stagioni Fontana or **Fountain of the Four Seasons**, erected in 1966, faces the foot of Elm St.

From Elm St., proceed north three blocks on Main St. to the red brick CSX railroad station, which now houses the **Coal Town Museum**. The museum contains historic pictures and mining equipment.

Turn left at the museum onto Vine St., continue west for seven blocks to 9th St., and turn right into Clinton's **Little Italy** section. During the 1920s this neighborhood was a bustling center of Italian-owned shops, restaurants, banks, churches, homes, and theaters. Some of the Old World ambience revives each year during the Little Italy Festival.

At 9th and Clinton sts. is the **Immigranti Piazza**, a tiny park enclosed by a wrought-iron fence with a grapevine design. A mound of black granite in the center of the park supports a statue of a young immigrant carrying a suitcase. The statue and a bull's head drinking fountain were cast in Torino, Italy. The piazza pays tribute to Clinton's early immigrants who came to work in the coal mines.

From Clinton, return to IND 163 and IND 63 and proceed south for *5.6 m.* into Vigo County. Turn right to New Goshen and continue *1.5 m.* to US 150. Turn left and follow US 150 south for *5.6 m.* to St. Mary's Rd. on the right. The entrance onto the main campus of **St. Mary-of-the-Woods College** is *.8 m.* ahead on the right. Mother Theodore Guerin and five Sisters of Providence founded this four-year liberal arts college for women in 1840. It received its charter in 1846. Situated in heavily wooded hills, St. Mary's is the oldest Catholic college for women in the United States. Joseph Thralls deeded the original one-acre tract in the wilderness to Bishop Simon William Gabriel Bruté for $15 to begin a convent and school for the Catholic sisters. At one time the novitiate—living and training quarters for the novices entering the order—housed more than 100 young women each year. Early graduates of St. Mary's taught in nearby Terre Haute schools. The first bachelor of arts degree was conferred in 1899. The school has been a pioneer in developing new career fields for women and now offers more than 20 specialized academic areas. The number of novices has decreased in recent years, but the motherhouse is still home for about 350 sisters.

At the far end of the main boulevard and to the east is the **Church of the Immaculate**

Church of the Immaculate Conception

Indiana Historical Society (Martin Collection)

Conception where the nuns take and renew their vows. Completed in 1886, the chapel is designed in the Baroque Revival style after the motif of La Trinité church in Paris. It features stained-glass windows from the Bavarian Art Institute and religious statuary created by Italian artisan John Rigali. The tomb of Mother Theodore Guerin, who died in 1856, is located beneath the sanctuary.

The **Mother Theodore Guerin Historical Museum** is housed in the Sisters of Providence Motherhouse, adjoining the Church of the Immaculate Conception. The museum provides two display areas for visitors. The Heritage Room contains artifacts related to the history of the community and the state, such as sacred vessels used by early clergy in Indiana. The Diorama Area presents a narrated exhibit of 12 scenes depicting the history of the congregation from 1840 to the turn of the century.

Woodland Inn, the three-story red brick Victorian house in the center of the campus, serves as a home for sisters who are college faculty. Built in 1894, the house was once used as a carriage inn. All of the 11 main buildings were designed by D. A. Bohlen and Son of Indianapolis. Lake and farmland comprise the campus acreage not occupied by the college and motherhouse buildings. In the 1980s St. Mary's received a grant for the renovation and restoration needs of the historic campus.

Return to US 150 and continue south *2.6 m.* to US 40. Follow US 40 east for *1.8 m.*, passing Izaak Walton Lake and crossing the Wabash River bridge to the Vigo County Courthouse in Terre Haute and the end of Tour 10.

Bloomington

Bloomington (p. 52,044) lies approximately 49 miles southwest of Indianapolis. The city, the seat of government for **MONROE COUNTY** (p. 98,785; 385 sq. m.), nestles amidst rolling hills furrowed with stream beds which extend over the northeast boundary of the nation's most productive limestone belt. The lush greenery of the Morgan-Monroe State Forest and the Hoosier National Forest adorn the eastern side of the county. Lake Monroe, southeast of Bloomington, is the state's largest inland body of water and is a favorite recreational spot for many Hoosiers. To the west of the county seat are small farms and pastureland. Indiana University (IU), one of the country's largest state schools, has its main campus here.

The history of Bloomington is virtually synonymous with the history of the university. When the territorial legislature petitioned Congress for statehood in 1815, it asked for a grant of a township of public land, the profits from the sale of which could be used to finance a state university. The Congressional Enabling Act of April 1816, which provided for statehood, heeded the request and vested authority in the new state legislature for the property's disposition. At the Indiana Constitutional Convention meeting at Corydon in June 1816 the delegates accepted the land grant and stipulated that the proceeds from the land sales go only for education. They also prohibited any marketing of the land before 1820. In July 1816 President James Madison designated Perry Township as the "Seminary Township." About this same time settlers began moving onto the future site of Bloomington, just north of Perry Township.

On January 14, 1818, the Indiana General Assembly formed Monroe County, named for President James Monroe, out of Orange County. In April of the same year the county commissioners staked out the county seat which adjoined the seminary township on the north. Bloomington was chosen for the same reasons that were leading other settlers to the site—the elevated terrain appeared secure from floods and healthier than the lowlands. Less rugged than the surrounding landscape, the locale seemed suitable for agriculture. The profusion of wild flowers influenced the naming of the place Bloomington, an appellation a reporter once rhapsodized as "a name sounding in mellow cadences and when once spoken is never forgotten."

In early 1820 the General Assembly provided for the organization of a state seminary at Bloomington. The law named and authorized six trustees to select a location, sell the seminary lands in Perry Township, and construct suitable buildings. The trustees chose to set the school on a promontory about one-quarter mile south of the county seat. At the time Bloomington had a population of around 300 persons. By April 1825, the date of the school's opening, the campus boasted a professor's home and a brick classroom building modeled after Princeton University's Nassau Hall. The first teacher, Philadelphia-born Baynard Rush Hall (1798-1863), supplemented his $250 yearly income as the Greek and Latin instructor by preaching in the Presbyterian Church. The initial student body of 10 young men roomed and boarded in the town. The number of students increased fourfold within two years. Consequently, the legislature rechartered the college as Indiana University. Through the Civil War period funding for the school came from land sales, donations, and student fees. Beginning in 1867 the institution received public support through annual state appropriations. The courageous efforts of a few faculty and friends kept the institution afloat during its first 60 years. Internal factionalism, instigated by student and faculty misconduct and trustee interference, continually threatened to undermine the school. The narrow vision and paternalism of a succession of six "preacher presidents," and the indifference or hostility of the legislature served to perpetuate uncertainties about the nature and function of public education. Periodically the understaffed and underequipped school came close to folding because of attempts to remove it to Indianapolis, or because of meager subsidies, outbreaks of disease, or disastrous fires.

While the university struggled for stability and recognition, Bloomington's residents increasingly realized the physical limitations of their town. The initial prospects for rapid development, predicated on a favorable environment, failed to materialize. At the outset, the town looked as if it would become a transportation center as roads and rails conveyed merchandise and people to and from the county seat. Eventually, however, more and better roads elsewhere dispelled this advantage. Moreover, farming failed to develop to the degree anticipated. It proved a formidable task to retrieve farm space from the densely forested hinterland. The upland earth was seldom put to use because it was often washed away by torrential rains. In addition, the much-touted springs and healthful locale came under attack. Rainwater drained through sinkholes and quickly coursed through the cavernous limestone to the streams. The swift flow of water to the above-ground channels impeded purification processes requiring a prolonged underground stay. The ensuing water pollution contributed to Bloomington having one of Indiana's highest death rates from typhoid. At the same time wells could not get at any quantities of safe water in the pocketed limestone, while below the rock the water happened to be scarce and bitter tasting. A further obstacle to town growth was the delay in establishing a commercial limestone industry. As Bloomington fretted over its deficiencies, the locus of state growth shifted to the central counties and to Indianapolis, thereby putting an end to the town's dream of developing into a regional economic hub.

Symptomatic of the general malaise in the community were the recurrent problems associated with attempts to incorporate. The town voted in 1827 to organize, but it neglected to complete the procedures for incorporation, thus the matter was deferred. By a legislative act of 1845 the town was created again and officers were elected. In 1858, however, townfolk voted to disband the municipal government,

citing excessive costs of maintenance. The following year a state law provided for reincorporation. This time the decision stood. In the mid-1860s the chance to change the town's status to that of a city fizzled due to voter apathy. Another decade passed before city incorporation took place.

In the latter years of the 19th century, both town and gown began to surmount their lackluster past. The occasion for a renewal in the university came after an 1883 fire which destroyed the 10-year-old science building containing David Starr Jordan's valuable scientific collections. The school's trustees seized the moment and decided to rebuild and enlarge the campus on another site. They purchased a 20-acre tract east of Bloomington and erected two main buildings. The new campus and the elevation of Jordan to the presidency in 1884 set in motion a period of administrative reorganization, curriculum expansion, and faculty upgrading. An especially important consequence of these improvements was, at last, public approval for the school. Among Jordan's lasting achievements was his success in impressing on Hoosiers the necessity of a scientific education in a changing society.

The town of Bloomington started to make headway when its most bountiful natural resource, limestone, became an acceptable building material. Among the factors inhibiting development of the limestone industry before 1870 was inadequate transportation, lack of testing, and the competition from lumber and brick interests. Between 1877 and 1896, for a number of reasons sales of limestone increased from 339,000 cubic ft. to nearly 5.5 million. Major urban fires, such as Chicago in 1871 and Boston in 1872, demonstrated the near flameproof quality of the stone. Limestone was an ideal substance with which to build the larger government buildings demanded by an expanding populace. The revival of Gothic or Romanesque architecture prescribed the liberal use of stone. Social fashion influenced the use of limestone in private residences. Improved stonecutting techniques and transport advances eliminated earlier hindrances to efficient marketing.

Prior to 1870 none of the 15 quarries in the limestone belt operated in the Bloomington area. Even in the 1870s carload shipments of limestone originating at Bloomington accounted for only a fraction of the total. In the latter two decades of the century, though, the Bloomington vicinity swarmed with limestone-related activity. By 1909 its quarries employed about 1,400 workers. A local paper reported some 50 quarries, stone mills, and cut-stone plants in the Bloomington neighborhood in 1913. Thereafter, the industry followed a more or less erratic path. It slumped in the years of World War I, rebounded to its all-time peak in the 1920s, de-escalated in the 1930s, recovered slightly after World War II, leveled off between 1955 and 1963, and declined again until now. At present 19 companies employ approximately 900 persons in the Monroe-Lawrence County stone belt.

Fortunately for Bloomington the limestone-quarrying and stonecutting businesses required little water as the city was plagued by water problems throughout its history. The first succession of reservoirs, erected southwest of the city between 1894 and 1915, leaked through their limestone beds. The sagacious university built its own reserve in 1909-11 beyond the reach of the porous limestone. During periodic "water famines," when some people hoarded the precious liquid, the university trucked supplies of water to city residences, but only to those homes boarding students. Consequently, many families quickly overcame a reluctance to house students. Meanwhile, disagreement among civic leaders as to when and where to place the next reservoir delayed progress. The onset of another severe dry season in the early 1920s resolved the matter. The city rushed to build Griffey Creek Reservoir. Griffey, completed in 1924 and expanded in 1940, could not keep pace with the city's growth. Accordingly, in 1953 the construction of Lake Lemon, nine miles northeast, added over six times more water to the city's systems. However, water became scarce again just a few years later. This time the city received promises from the state that it would have first crack at tapping the proposed Monroe Reservoir when finished in 1965. The supplement of more than 10,000 acres of water from Monroe Lake has gone far to reduce anxieties about reoccurrences of water shortages.

Until recently the problem of limited water resources shaped the industrial character of Bloomington. Historically, the major employers, in addition to the limestone industry, have been water-efficient furniture and electronic firms. The Showers Brothers Company, furniture manufacturer, dominated the city's employment picture for much of its 80-year history. In 1940 Showers Brothers sold a portion of its building complex to the Radio Corporation of America (RCA), which planned to build radios. Sarkes Tarzian, the chief engineer of RCA's Bloomington operation, left the company in 1944 to launch his own operation. Sarkes Tarzian, Inc., put on the market an innovative radio system called Hi-Fam, a blend of FM and AM. When this product failed in the marketplace Tarzian turned to the then novel medium of television. His company soon led the nation in the manufacture of television tuners. On Armistice Day, November 11, 1949, the state's second television station, WTTV, a Tarzian enterprise, came into existence in Bloomington. At the time Bloomington was the smallest of 63 cities in the country possessing a TV station. In 1978 Tarzian sold WTTV for $26 million, the largest sum ever to have been paid out for an independent television station.

Across town, William Lowe Bryan, during his 35 years as president of the university, 1902-37, labored to broaden the school's professional base in order to make it more than a teacher training institution. He succeeded to a degree. Indiana University added a graduate school and schools of medicine, dentistry, education, music, and business administration. The changes in the curriculum accompanied expansion of the physical plant. By 1937 the university's campus encompassed about 150 acres and 52 structures. The fivefold increase in buildings during Bryan's tenure came about partially as a result of generous federal grants during the 1930s depression. The faculty count in the same period surged from 65 to 323. Student enrollment rose from 1,334 to 12,557, thereby causing the school to be ranked 13th largest of the nation's 570 colleges and universities. In the meantime the burgeoning institution spread to other parts of the state. Indianapolis, Fort Wayne, and the Calumet area were given university extensions. A university medical center was also placed in the capital city. By 1936 Indiana's roster of extension students was America's third largest.

The pace of campus construction and instructional innovation quickened after World War II. The affable and energetic Herman B Wells, who began his 25-year presidency in 1937, confronted unanticipated educational demands in an increasingly complex and compact world. The postwar influx of veterans over-taxed school facilities. Trailers and army bar-racks encircled the campus as enrollment swelled threefold between 1943 and 1947. A $25 million development program com-menced in 1947.

The challenges of moving the university into a new age of domestic and international relations brought it face to face with the issues of social tolerance and academic freedom. No-where was this most apparent than in the school's concern over the negative reactions to Alfred C. Kinsey's Institute for Sex Research set up just prior to the war. From 1945 into the McCarthy era the university's administration defended Kinsey's published findings on male and female sexuality. Kinsey's champions stressed the scientific and medical benefits of the research, while they endured the barbs of the moralists, gossipers, and, not least, the pop-ularity of Martha Raye's hit record, "Ooh Dr. Kinsey."

In the 1950s, however, most people, no-ticeably students, did not want to grapple with such divisive subjects as personal freedom and public responsibility. Rather, they valued con-formity, security, and comfort. This was not the case in the turbulent 1960s. In the univer-sity the pressures of incessant student unrest over such matters as civil rights, Vietnam, and social mores helped to drive President Elvis J. Stahr from office in 1968 after a six-year term. The campus convulsions did not interrupt uni-versity development. During Stahr's tenure 13 buildings were begun or completed. The worth of the physical plant by 1966 had ballooned to $272 million, nine times the assessment of 1950. The student body increased to about 48,000 on all campuses. The figure jumped an-other 10,000 by 1968.

During the war years Bloomington, unlike most other cities, was not inundated with de-fense contracts. This, and the curtailment of production in many of the local factories, con-tributed to a sluggish economy. Only the thriv-ing RCA plant helped to maintain prewar employment levels. After the war, however, with the matriculation into the university of thousands of ex-GIs, the city's population count jumped 35 percent in the 1940s. By the mid-1950s the press was heralding Blooming-ton as one of the top "boom" towns in the state. In 1959 the National Municipal League selected it as one of 11 "All-American" cities.

Contributing factors in Bloomington's favor included the construction of Lake Lemon, a five-year hiatus in traffic fatalities, and im-provements in the sewer system and in fire pro-tection. While the residents celebrated their All-American tribute, the local courts oblig-ingly postponed investigations into gambling and graft in private clubs.

Bloomington in the 1960s continued to ex-pand and modernize with the construction of 50 retail stores and two shopping centers. Fed-eral urban renewal dollars helped to pay for the leveling of the 80-acre shantytown of Pigeon Hill and its replacement with private and pub-lic housing. A special census in 1966 showed the city with 42,058 residents, more than enough to give it a second-class city status. The magnitude of development in both the univer-sity and the town in a relatively short period of time gave rise to complex problems. A shortage of housing was one such problem. The decision by university officials to let students live in town strained existing facilities but stimulated the housing market. The scramble to build apartments, which one investor called "the best game in town," resulted in 38 apartment build-ings being erected in 1968-69 alone. All this growth stretched the capacities of city utilities. The tide of traffic necessitated constant road maintenance and construction. Water treat-ment and sewer facilities needed enlargement. Other civic improvements discussed included a bus system and downtown beautification. To pay for these the city leaned on land annexa-tions to extend tax responsibilities, and on federal grants and loans, modes of financial recourse guaranteed to heat up election campaigns.

The quickened pace of growth in the 1960s also characterized the 1970s. By 1971 Bloom-ington was reported to be one of the fastest growing cities in the state. The number of res-idents rose to 52,044 by 1980, a 20.3 percent increase. The influx of this many persons caught the city largely unprepared to provide adequate services, make and enforce new zoning laws, and draw up and implement long-term plans. Officials looked for places to ex-pand. The College Mall vicinity on the east side of town was by now a profusion of parking lots, apartments, gas stations, and discount stores. As a consequence, eyes turned westward, and a business and shopping district blossomed in west Bloomington. Later, in the mid-1980s, the so-called "north corridor" would become the center of attention. In 1979, however, the concentration was less on Bloomington's enviable woes associated with too rapid a growth, and more on a movie set. The movie, *Breaking Away*, written by Steve Tesich, an IU alumnus, was for the most part cast and filmed in Bloomington. The film, about the annual Little 500 bike race, was nominated for five academy awards and won the Oscar for best original screenplay.

When the economic recession struck the country in the early 1980s, Bloomington, because of the university's presence, withstood the negative effects of the business inactivity longer than other communities. Even when the layoffs began at the city's two major industries, RCA and General Electric, the expansion of College Mall and the hospital, the arrival of four new plants, the hiring at existing businesses, and construction at IU blunted the blow. Being named in 1982 for a second All-American City award furnished a psychological lift. In any case, double-digit unemployment did not last long. By late 1984 the jobless rate had fallen to 5.6 percent.

By the mid-1980s some of the special matters under consideration by city administrators included revenue seeking, downtown rejuvenation, and public health. A series of planned annexation steps would finally bring several large west-side industries within the tax fold of the city. A number of proposed projects for downtown revitalization were completed, including a restored courthouse, a new Justice Building, parking garages, and renovated buildings around the square. Finally, the polychlorinated byphenyls (PCB) controversy, a live and complex issue since 1975, appeared to be moving toward resolution. Bloomington's Westing-

house plant used PCBs, a suspected carcinogen, in its capacitors. The chemical was discharged into city sewers, eventually flowing into streams and contaminating land. Representatives from all levels of government and from industry have worked for years to agree on a way to clean the sewers and safely dispose of the sludge. Financed by Westinghouse, the cleanup got underway in 1988, but controversy over method lingers.

After 160 years of coexistence, the lines between town and gown have blurred considerably. The university, although the city's major employer, is not on the tax base. Nevertheless, the state-owned school advises and sits on municipal committees, supplies project moneys and space, and supports fire and police protection. A campus of more than 30,000 students and a huge biweekly payroll is of inestimable economic value to the city, even for just nine months of the year. Occasionally town folk not connected with the university express dislike for the cyclical nature of the community's business. Objections are heard, also, about the lack of state aid for the local schools which teach children of non-taxpaying students. Too, the citizens sometimes resent paying for new city projects they feel have been shoved down their throats by a too-progressive university. The disagreeable aspects of the town-gown partnership, however, are more easily digested by the residents because of the enormous economic advantages bestowed by the presence of the university, or when an IU sports team wins a national championship, as the basketball team did in 1987. Certainly of equal worth in cementing harmony between the city and the school is the latter's full schedule of educational, cultural, and sporting activities.

Bloomington Attractions

1. The **Bloomington/Monroe County Convention and Visitors Bureau** at 2855 N. Walnut has available information about the city, county, and university.

2. The sculpture **Red, Blond, Black, Olive** (Four Faces) is located in Miller Showers Park in the 1700 block between College Ave. and Walnut St. The 22-ton limestone sculpture was designed by Jean-Paul Darriau, an IU art professor, and was placed in the park in 1980. The 15-ft.-tall statues depict an African woman facing an Asiatic woman and a Nordic man facing an Indian man.

3. The **Little 500 Stadium/Bill Armstrong Soccer Complex** on the northern edge of campus between Jordan Ave. and Fee Ln. was built in 1981 and replaced the old 10th St. Stadium. Constructed at a cost of $1.7 million, the 20,000-seat stadium is the scene of the "Little 500," the 200-lap (50 miles) bicycle race that inspired the 1980 Academy Award-winning film, *Breaking Away*. Proceeds from this famous annual April event go for scholarships to IU students who are working their way through school. The stadium is also the home of the IU soccer team, a perennial national power. Many experts consider it one of the finest soccer facilities in the nation.

4. The **University Library** is at Jordan and 10th sts. When opened in 1969, the 366,173 sq. ft. of assignable library space made it the largest college library in the country. The exterior of the $15 million structure is a composition of geometrically placed limestone blocks glued to concrete panels. Inside, the walls are glazed and decorated cement blocks that never need painting. The west tower of five stories is devoted to undergraduate reading rooms. Eight of the 12 stories of the east tower contain general stacks. Underlying the towers is a common area which includes the Graduate Library School, a cafeteria and snack bar, and a periodicals room. A building-wide lobby separates the two towers. It features window walls at each end, huge travertine columns, and teak paneling.

5. The **Fine Arts Plaza** comprises buildings committed to culture and the arts. The multipurpose **IU Auditorium**, which cost more than $1 million to erect in 1941, has been the scene of thousands of special lectures, concerts, and theatrical productions. The architectural style of the imposing edifice of Indiana limestone was referred to at the time as a "simple adaptation of collegiate Gothic." Financing stemmed from three sources: a 1938 legislative appropriation, a Public Works Administration grant, and a bond issue. With a spacious three million cubic feet enclosing a 3,788-seat auditorium, the building ably fulfilled the school's need for an adequate assembly hall suitably furnished to attract widely known performers. Prior to the auditorium's appearance, student body activities and cultural functions took place in the Assembly Hall or in the Union's Alumni Hall. Assembly Hall, built in 1898 as a gymnasium and razed in 1939, was the site of the first state high school basketball tournament in 1911. The auditorium opened auspiciously in March 1941. A standing-room-only audience savored the incomparable theatrical duo of Alfred Lunt and Lynn Fontaine acting in Robert Sherwood's "There Shall Be No Night," a drama about the Finnish War.

Within the auditorium are several features worth noting. Visitors enter the building through a stone-walled vestibule into the **Hall of Murals**. The series of large pictures, painted by famed artist Thomas Hart Benton, depicts stages in Indiana's economic and social evolution. The state originally commissioned Benton to paint the tableau for the Indiana exhibit at the Century of Progress International Exhibition held at Chicago in 1933-34. After the exhibition the state stored the paintings at the

Bloomington Attractions

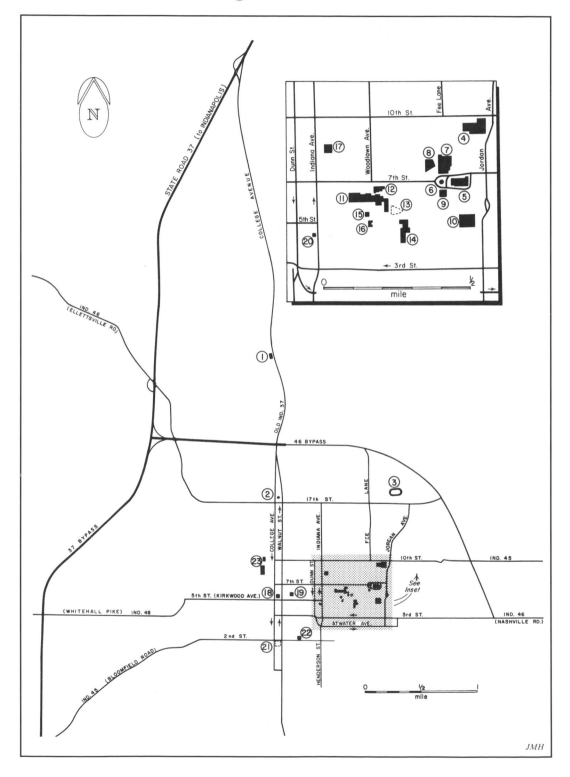

Indianapolis fairgrounds until they were presented to IU in 1940. Benton supervised the installation of the panels. At each end of the Hall of Murals is a marble trimmed grand stairway ascending to the mezzanine and balcony. Enormous golden urns rest on black marble pilasters that extend halfway up the inside wall of each staircase. The placement of these urns, which partially blocked Benton's stairwell murals, infuriated the artist. Calling the Grecian urns "great gilded spittoons," Benton lashed out at architects whom he thought made beautiful structures but then they "dig around in all the junk yards of the past and pick out the most irrelevant decorative accessories they can find and obliterate what they have created."

The auditorium is graced with artwork including statuary by Robert Laurent in the niches of the first floor foyer. Canvases by Indiana artists and others are displayed in the same foyer and in upper floor lounges. Besides magnificent art, the auditorium houses one of the world's greatest organs. H. L. Roosevelt of New York built the instrument in 1889 for the Chicago Auditorium. Dr. William H. Barnes, a Chicago organ architect, bought "The Great Roosevelt Organ" for $1,000 in 1942. He subsequently gave it to the university, which underwrote the cost of rebuilding the teakwood-cased pipe organ by the Aeolian-Skinner Organ Company of Boston. Aeolian-Skinner installed the organ in 1944, and dedication ceremonies took place in 1948. In 1967 the Schantz Organ Company of Orrville, Ohio, redesigned and rebuilt the entire organ. The organ has 88 stops, 76 ranks, and 4,543 pipes.

6. In the center of the plaza is the **Showalter Fountain**. The "Birth of Venus" fountain depicts the goddess of love and beauty and symbolizes the role of the arts in the university's cultural life. The 14-ft., bronze female goddess is shown reclining on a shell encompassed by six water-spouting dolphins. The grey-green patined fish appear to be spiritedly swimming around the muse, heralding her birth. Funding for the sculpture, dedicated in 1961, came from Mrs. Grace M. Showalter in the name of her husband, a retired executive with Eli Lilly and Company. Mrs. Showalter was the first woman on the board of directors of the Indiana University Foundation. The university awarded her an honorary Doctor of Humanities degree in 1967. Robert Laurent (1890-1970), IU pro-

fessor of art from 1942 to 1960, designed and executed the fountain. The French-born Laurent, an internationally recognized stone and bronze sculptor, is best known for the famous "Goose Girl" in New York's Rockefeller Center. A month before he died, Laurent was named to the National Institute of Arts and Letters. His original sketches of the fountain, submitted in 1952, showed a kneeling Venus surrounded by nymphs. A full-size mock-up of this design was deemed too tall, thus Laurent rectified the problem by placing the goddess in a prone position.

7. The **Fine Arts Building** stands on the north side of the plaza. The Fine Arts Department, housed for 20 years in a temporary wooden structure, moved into its new home in 1962. The structure has an interesting facade composed of nine large limestone "screens." Facing south, the building receives an inordinate amount of sunlight. The "screens" effectively diffuse the sun's rays. The main entrance, fronting the plaza, leads directly into the second floor. A rear entrance leads into the first floor, originally set in limestone blasted from the sloping site. The five floors of the building contain galleries, classrooms, storerooms, offices, studios, workshops, and an auditorium. Adjoining the Fine Arts Building to the north is the Radio and Television Building, the communication core of the university.

8. The modernistic **IU Art Museum**, opened in 1983, is the most recent addition to the plaza area. By the middle 1970s the art museum and library had far outgrown their respective spaces in the Fine Arts Building. University trustees approved the construction of a Fine Arts Pavilion to be situated west of the Fine Arts Building. I. M. Pei Associates of New York City, the same firm that designed Columbus's library, was placed in charge of planning the new structure. Pei modeled the structure after the East Wing of the National Gallery in Washington, D.C. The pavilion is in the shape of an isosceles triangle with a connecting right triangle. The three-story building is joined to the Fine Arts Building by a covered gallery on the first floor. In addition to housing the university's over 25,000-piece art collection, the museum also has space for special exhibits, a portion of the art library, and classrooms. The museum is particularly strong in classical Mediterranean

art, Asian art, "primitive" art of Africa, Oceana and America, and 20th-century western European art.

9. The **Lilly Library** is on the plaza's southwest side. In the mid-1950s Josiah Kirby Lilly, Jr., Indianapolis industrialist and philanthropist, agreed to deposit his $5 million private collection of rare books and manuscripts with the university. Lilly made what was considered then the greatest contribution of its kind ever received by an American educational institution, though he did not graduate from IU, nor had he ever visited the campus. The ground breaking for the structure to house the Lilly collection, and others, occurred in March 1958, with its dedication in October 1960. Matching the auditorium in its classical limestone architecture, the richly furnished interior rooms are often designed in keeping with the kind of materials in the rooms. Today, there are nearly 4 million manuscripts, 350,000 printed books, and 100,000 pieces of sheet music in the library. Two of the most cherished items are the Gutenberg and Coverdale bibles. Collections range from Martin Luther's writings to more than 800 British Broadcasting Corporation radio scripts; from material on the Spanish Inquisition to the Starr American Sheet Music Collection. Special events—chamber music concerts, poetry readings, lectures—are scheduled each year in the library.

10. The **Musical Arts Center** south of the plaza houses the music school at IU, the largest, and, by consensus, the finest in the nation. The school, organized in 1921, moved into its own building in 1937 after years of suffering the inadequacies of Mitchell Hall, erected in 1885. Theatrical and operatic performances expanded into the new IU Auditorium after 1941. The postwar student population explosion overran the music building's capacities. Up to five temporary structures were pressed into use. In 1947 a converted warplane hangar from Illinois became East Hall, a 1,000-seat auditorium with 60 practice rooms. A new wing extended from the old Music Building after 1962.

The five-story **Music Annex**, attached by lobbies to the old music building, cost almost $3 million. The circular structure, dubbed the "washer" or "ice box," encloses pie-shaped practice rooms for students and faculty. The shape of the rooms, without windows or parallel walls, is considered ideal for vocal and instrumental rehearsals. Even as construction of the annex neared completion, planning began for a new music facility; planning intensified after East Hall burned in 1968.

After a thorough investigation of theaters and opera houses, including on-site inspection of European opera houses, the university broke ground in 1968 for a new Musical Arts Center. When completed in 1972 the $11 million asymmetrical castle brought IU's music education and enrichment program to its highest level of international recognition. The block and glass building ("itself a performance" noted one observer) is a modern adaptation of antique European fortifications replete with towers and narrow slot windows. The castle motif is meant to evoke a sense of massiveness and the romantic aura of the opera. Evans Woollen III of Indianapolis designed the building. Woollen, who helped plan Clowes Hall in Indianapolis, was the first Hoosier architect to produce an IU building in 30 years. The stark exterior contrasts with the profuse color of the interior. Only Alexander Calder's streetside orange-red abstract sculpture hints at what awaits the visitor or patron. Calder's huge steel work is inexplicably entitled "Peau Rouge Indiana" (Indiana Redskin). Inside, a purple and orange striped carpet accents the glass-enclosed, semicircular lobby. George Ortman's multicolored twin banners hang overhead. The main floor of the oblong bowl-shaped auditorium is framed by three tiers of boxes and balconies and a 90-ft.-wide stage. The auditorium seats 1,500. Its color scheme includes brilliant red sidewalls and a magenta red rear wall. The flowing fronts of the balconies are a white stucco, resembling carpeting. The chandelier is composed of wide golden discs which can be adjusted to enhance the accoustics. Lighting for each performance is controlled by computer. Smaller stages, large and small practice rooms, ballet studios, and workshops take up a majority of the building's remaining space.

11. The **IU Union Building** at 7th and Woodlawn sts., the convenient center of campus life for students, faculty, alumni, and visitors, brings together a variety of accommodations. Included are restaurants, meeting rooms, lounges, a bookstore, barber and beauty shops, bowling lanes, a billiard room, and 200 guest rooms. A terrace overlooks Dunn Meadow and

the Jordan River. Art objects from the union's collection are displayed throughout the building. In 1921 a memorial fund drive began to finance construction of three buildings: a union, a stadium, and a women's dormitory. The latter two opened in 1925. When the union was completed in 1932, the trustees assigned most of the guest rooms for permanent rentals, presumably to faculty bachelors. They also suggested that no tipping be permitted to any employee of the union. Several Civil War veterans were guests of honor at the 1932 dedicatory exercises of the $600,000 memorial to alumni who served in America's wars. In 1959 the union's size tripled with the addition of the Ward G. Biddle Continuation Study Center. Primarily devoted to alumni activities, the center houses the 450-seat Whittenberger Auditorium, guest rooms, and meeting rooms.

12. **Ernie Pyle Hall**, abutting the union at 7th and Woodlawn sts., houses IU's School of Journalism. The building is named for Ernie Pyle, the famed World War II war correspondent of the *Indianapolis Times* and Scripps-Howard newspapers. Before it became journalism's chambers, the structure served as a storage and service building. In 1953-54 the university spent $500,000 renovating the building. Its dedication in 1954 came nine years after Pyle died in the Pacific from a sniper's bullet. In 1976 the limestone edifice underwent a $2.5 million remodeling in response to a burgeoning of journalism majors. Features include a learning laboratory equipped with modern teaching aids, classrooms with television hookups, a photo complex, a library, and an auditorium. The newsroom of the *Indiana Daily Student* is located here. The Ernie Pyle Lounge, on the second floor, contains memorabilia of the journalist.

13. The **Dunn Cemetery**, southwest of the union area, predates the move of the university to its present site. When the university purchased the Dunn's Woods site in 1883 for its new home, the Dunns retained exclusive rights to their 50-year-old family cemetery. To this day, only Dunn family descendants can be interred there. The Dunn ancestors formed the burial ground in the shape of a kite, presumably to augment a latter-day flight heavenward.

Huddled in a corner of the cemetery is **Beck Chapel**. The diminutive Tudor-style inter-denominational chapel, built in 1956, is a monument to the lifetime of service of Dr. and Mrs. Frank O. Beck. Beck, born in Wayne County's Germantown, attended IU in the 1890s where he helped launch Sigma Nu fraternity and generated the drive resulting in the establishment of the yearbook, *Arbutus*. He earned a Ph.D. from Scotland's University of Edinburgh. Returning to Chicago, Beck taught at Northwestern, pastored Chicago-area Methodist churches, and took a lead in the city's welfare programs. He worked with Jane Addams at Hull House and with the derelicts on "Skid Row." His experiences with the city's impoverished were portrayed in his publication *Hobohemia*. He returned to Indiana University in 1934 at the age of 62. Until his death in 1968, at the age of 96, he played a major, if often unofficial, role in the religious activities on the campus.

Plans for the chapel were drawn up in 1941. The next year, at a four-day interfaith conference at Bloomington, religious leaders representing Protestantism, Catholicism, and Judaism planted trees to commemorate their respective faiths and to symbolize an ecumenical desire for a chapel. These trees and explanatory plaques can be seen in the yard beside the chapel. Inside the limestone chapel, light oak pews with a seating capacity of 100 rest on a marble floor. The kneeling bench contains marble pieces from the Sistine Chapel in Rome and St. Paul's Cathedral in London. A circular stained-glass window highlights the altar area. Downstairs are located a small lounge and dressing room. The chapel is primarily used for private devotions and prayers, weddings, baptisms, and memorial services.

14. **Ballantine Hall**, the campus's largest building when completed in 1959, stands west of the music complex. It honors an early faculty member, Elisha Ballantine (1809-1886), professor of Greek, math, and languages from 1854 to 1886. The $9 million, nine-story limestone building provides classroom and office space for the humanities and social sciences. An interesting feature of the giant structure is the geophysical globe on the ground floor. Designed to give a view of the earth from the air in summer, the 6-ft.-diameter globe revolves about 20 times each hour. Another prominent aspect of Ballantine is its first floor walls of marble which came from a 300-year-old French theater. After its

completion Ballantine was designated the emergency statehouse for Indiana in case of a national crisis—a distinction the building no longer holds.

15. and 16. The university's two oldest buildings, **Owen** and **Wylie halls**, were put up when the university moved to its new campus in 1883. Located west of Ballantine Hall, both buildings were designed by George W. Bunting and Son of Indianapolis. The architects erected a number of courthouses and public buildings throughout Indiana and the South. Wylie Hall is named for Andrew Wylie (1789-1851), the university's first president, and for his cousin Professor Theophilus Wylie (1810-1895). Wylie Hall has had a checkered past. Originally it housed the chemistry and physics departments. Almost destroyed by fire in 1900, the rebuilt and expanded hall now functions principally as an office building. Neighboring Owen Hall honors Richard Owen (1810-1890), the son of the reformer Robert Owen and the school's instructor in natural sciences from 1863 to 1879. After being refurbished in 1911, Owen Hall became the medical school until 1937. Today, Owen contains offices, including that of the university chancellor. These buildings are among the nine structures that comprise the Old Crescent Historic District (*NRHP*), a roughly 20-acre, largely wooded tract that was the site of the new 1884 campus. All nine buildings were constructed between 1884 and 1908. Besides Owen and Wylie halls, Old Crescent includes the Old Library (1906-8), the Old Student Building (1905), Maxwell Hall (1890), Kirkwood Hall (1895), Lindley Hall (1903), Rose Well House (1908), and Kirkwood Observatory (1900).

17. The **Glenn A. Black Laboratory of Archaeology**, on the southwest corner of E. 9th and N. Fess sts., was dedicated in 1971 and contains research and lecture facilities and major collections of Indiana artifacts. Glenn A. Black (1900-1964), an Indianapolis native, was a self-educated archaeologist who became the archaeological field director for the Indiana Historical Society and a lecturer at the university. Until 1960 he was the only professional archaeologist in Indiana. He directed much of his labor from 1939 onward to the excavation of the noted Angel Mounds in Vanderburgh County (see Evansville Attractions). The artifacts from Angel

Mounds make up part of the permanent collections of the laboratory, along with the large private collection of materials assembled by Eli Lilly. On the main floor of the two-story, striated limestone building is the museum room, lecture room, a library-seminar room, administration offices, and the Indiana archaeology archives. Changing exhibits are in glass-enclosed cases forming parts of the central corridor's walls. The lower floor is the workshop area for the archaeologists. It includes lab and storage rooms. The **William Hammond Mathers Museum**, adjoining the Glenn Black Lab at 601 E. 8th St., opened in 1983. The museum is really two buildings, a remodeled fraternity house and a modernistic limestone structure constructed by James Associates of Indianapolis. The total cost amounted to $3.3 million. The museum began operation in 1963 as the Indiana University Museum and has been located in a number of buildings before attaining its permanent home. The present name honors one of Frank C. Mathers's sons. Frank Mathers, a former IU chemistry professor, was a major contributor to the museum's building fund. The fraternity house contains the museum offices and the classical archaeology collection. The new wing houses the exhibit hall and the majority of the approximately 120,000-item collection. Among the items are a vintage auto, a log cabin, a 3,500-year-old dugout canoe, and the Robert W. Grafton murals taken from the Hotel Rumely in La Porte. The museum displays both permanent and temporary exhibits.

18. The stately **Monroe County Courthouse**, centered on Bloomington's downtown square, exhibits several uncommon components. Crowning the domed Indiana limestone edifice is a golden fish weathervane. Austin Seward hammered the fish out of sheet copper in 1826, the same year he painted the first permanent courthouse a bright red with white pencilings. Family tradition relates that the fish, over 5 ft. in length, symbolized the reigning Jeffersonian Republican party. In 1908 the fish was reinstalled on the newly constructed present courthouse. The unusual weathervane has become a local landmark and an adopted logo of the city. The courthouse grounds enclose a plethora of monuments. There are several garden variety war memorials. Displayed also is a round stone commemorating Bloomington's designation as the center of population in 1910. There is a

Glenn A. Black Laboratory

drinking fountain appropriately installed by the Women's Christian Temperance Union in 1913 and a Four Freedoms Monument set up in 1952. A most extraordinary sculpture memorializes the eternal quest for peace. The 13-ft.-limestone statue depicts the Mother of Mankind replete with well-chosen peace symbols and inscriptions. Completed in 1979, the work is by the Fort Wayne native, William T. Dahman. Inside the courthouse, years of rearranging have disguised the rotunda that once provided a clear view of the stained glass in the dome. This piece of glass now is the ceiling of a third floor courtroom. A stained-glass window and chandelier can be seen from the marble staircase landing between the second and third floors. (*NRHP*)

19. Barely avoiding destruction in 1977, the old **Carnegie Library** at 202 E. 6th St. is now the **Monroe County Historical Society Museum**. Once again the building is contributing to the city's cultural life as a museum and community center. Andrew Carnegie's gift of $31,000 launched the building's construction in 1918 on the site of the area's first school for blacks. Limestone formed the exterior with roofing of dark red tile, a style *Indianapolis News* colum-

nist Bill Pittman characterized as "early bank vault." The Indianapolis-based architect Wilson B. Parker placed a semicircular fanlight above the main entrance. In so doing, he captured a Carnegie vision of the rising sun symbolizing a doorway to learning. It was Parker's use of the native stone that earned the library a place on the National Register. The all-limestone building represents a benchmark in the growth of the limestone industry. Parker showed it could be used economically for buildings other than ones in large cities or the mansions of the rich. In 1970 a new library, constructed at 303 E. Kirkwood, spelled the eventual demise of the Carnegie library. Three years later the library board sold the building to the Bloomington Redevelopment Department for $125,000. The city developers wanted it removed to make room for a 30-space parking lot. In order to halt demolition plans, an individual donated $50,000 towards the repurchase of the building by a citizens' group. In 1977 The Old Library, Inc., bought the structure. Additional grants helped furnish restoration labor. The museum contains permanent and temporary exhibits dealing with Monroe County history. The old library also houses the Bloomington Area Arts Council. (*NRHP*)

Wylie house, prior to restoration

20. The **Gables**, 114 S. Indiana, is a fast-food establishment that has served as a student meeting point since 1919. Originally called the "Book Nook," the structure has a white-tiled facing topped by three green-trimmed gables. The "Book Nook" was made famous by local songwriter Hoagy Carmichael, for it was here in 1927 that he composed his famous *Stardust*. The restaurant was later renamed the Gables and remained a hamburger/soda establishment until the 1970s when it briefly specialized in Greek cuisine. The Indiana University Foundation purchased the building in 1979, and the foundation, in turn, leased it to a franchise pizza business, perhaps reflecting the changes in the student diet.

21. On the southwest corner of busy 2nd and Walnut sts. is the site of the university's first campus. **Seminary Square**, also the name of a small neighboring shopping center, is now a pleasant little park. Large trees, several picnic tables, and benches grace the old school plot. The university moved from the site in 1883 after fire damaged Science Hall. The one remaining building, dating from 1854-55, was bought by the city in 1897 for $11,500. It became part of the city's educational system until torn down in 1965. The stone columns at the two walkway entrances to the park were contributed by the public school's classes of 1926 and 1950, respectively. (*NRHP*)

22. On the corner of E. 2nd and Lincoln sts. (307 E. 2nd St.) stands the **Wylie house**, the home of the university's first president. Andrew Wylie ordered the construction of the house in 1835. The modified Federal-style brick structure is reminiscent of contemporary dwellings in Wylie's home area of western Pennsylvania. Traditions about the house include its use as a station on the "underground railroad" and its being inhabited with ghosts. The story goes that a workman plastering the new house committed suicide after the death of his wife. Fellow laborers refused to complete his work fearing the deceased would return to haunt them. Later inhabitants of the house did find an unfinished section of plaster leading to an attic. The restoration of the house took

place in 1964-65, a decade after its purchase by the university. Restorers took pains to duplicate materials using lumber from old houses, hand-forging iron work, and hand-tooling replacement shutters. The exterior brick walls were completely re-cemented. Features of the exterior include arched doors and windows. The "captain's walk" on the roof may have benefited the astronomy students or it may have been used to entertain the president's many guests. Inside, the quarter-sawed oak floors and handcarved woodwork frame a galaxy of period furnishings, some belonging to the Wylie family. (*NRHP/HABS*)

23. In west Bloomington around 11th and Morton sts. stands the balance of the old **Showers Brothers Furniture Factory**. Early in the present century the business was considered the world's largest manufacturer of bedroom furniture. The two older Showers brothers, James D. and William N., learned the rudiments of carpentry in their father's coffin shop. In 1869 the siblings bought out their father and began making bedsteads "in the white" (unfinished). The business grew rapidly, and the physical plant expanded only to be reduced to ashes in 1884. Undaunted, the brothers shifted the plant's location to its present site and rebuilt. In 1911 the first brick building with the distinctive "saw tooth" roof was constructed (note the faded S-H-O-W-E-R-S letters across the top of the building). The plant soon comprised a dozen buildings on 70 acres, employed 1,000, and produced a piece of furniture every minute. The locally bought timber forced the brothers to buy so many farms that reportedly William N. Showers at various times owned a fourth of Monroe County. The depression of the 1930s, a depletion of lumber, and competition from southern furniture companies and from RCA for workers undermined Showers by the 1950s. The last of the buildings was sold in 1955 to a maker of juvenile furniture. Later, Indiana University acquired the property for the Indiana University Press and today's storage and service complex.

Tour 11

From the courthouse square in Bloomington, take College Ave. south, bearing left on 2nd St. to Walnut St., and proceed south to IND 37, approximately *6 m*. Turn south onto IND 37. Proceed *6.6 m*. to the **LAWRENCE COUNTY** (p. 42,472; 452 sq. m.) line, observing the picturesque, rolling landscape bordering Lake Monroe.

Many Indiana counties are named for heroes of the War of 1812. Lawrence County, established in 1818, is no exception. In 1813 naval Capt. James Lawrence died on board his ship, the *Chesapeake*, after he sustained wounds in a losing battle with the British frigate *Shannon*. Ordinarily, a wartime defeat and death would not qualify Lawrence for prominence. In this case, however, Lawrence bequeathed to the American navy a deathbed utterance that became a rallying cry in subsequent conflicts: "Don't give up the ship."

Follow IND 37 south *5.9 m*. to IND 54/58. Immediately west is **AVOCA**. A pioneer of Lawrence County and a chief promoter of limestone was the Connecticut-born physician Dr. Winthrop Foote. On the doctor's frequent visits to a spring in the area of future Avoca, he often read to the few inhabitants verses from his favorite poet, the Irish romanticist Thomas Moore. Some of Dr. Foote's favorite lines were, "Sweet Vale of Avoca, how calm could I rest/ In the bosom of thy shade, with the friend I love best." When a small village was platted at the spring in 1819, the founders chose the name Avoca, remembering Dr. Foote's pleasant recitations.

On the south side of the road is the **Avoca State Fish Hatchery**, which produces largemouth bass and bluegills for stocking lakes and streams. It sits on the site of an early gristmill and is fed by a spring which discharges through an enormous underwater cavern. The manager's house dates from about 1823 and is one of the county's oldest structures. The state acquired the property in 1924. Visitors are welcome to view the ponds, enjoy a picnic, or hike a nature trail, but no fishing or swimming is allowed.

Return to IND 37 and proceed south *1 m*. to the next intersection. To the east are the rock-strewn mills of the **Indiana Limestone Company, Inc**. Two limestone eagles guard the entrance. Turn left. Take Main St. into **OOLITIC** (p. 1,495). Oolitic is a geological term meaning eggstone, a reference to the resemblance of the stone's fossils to fish eggs. The Oolitic post office was established in 1892, and the town was platted in 1898. A marker between the Oolitic post office and City Hall commemorates the nearby quarries as "the largest building stone quarries in the world in continual operation since the 1850s." Some years ago one could still hear a native refer to the eastern portion of Oolitic as Spion Kop. For some reason, the residents of what is known as East Oolitic adopted as their neighborhood's designation the name of this famous battle of the Boer War in South Africa in 1900.

On the lawn of the town hall is a 10-ft., 10-ton stone statue of the comics hero, **Joe Palooka, Champion of Democracy**. The Palooka statue symbolizes the American strain of individualism, self-reliance, and direct action. At least these qualities seem to have been behind the creation of the hero by Bedford quarrymen in 1948. Their inspiration came from an incident recorded in the comic strip, in which Humphrey Bennyworth and Virgil Mipply were forced by the government to remove Palooka's image from Mount Rushmore. To redress this blatant misuse of political authority, Bedford stonecutter George W. Hitchcock, Sr., chiseled a likeness of Joe, to remind onlookers of America's hard-won liberties. Hammond E. "Ham" Fisher, the creator of the Palooka character, was on hand to dedicate the statue at Bedford in June 1948 as part of the Indiana limestone industry's centennial celebration. Vandalism of the hero's statue has forced sev-

Indiana Limestone Company, October 1929

eral relocations. It was refurbished and moved to Oolitic in 1984.

A resurgence in the stone industry has pointed up the need for skilled stoneworkers. To this end, the **Indiana Laborers Training Institute** has included classes on stonecutting, carving, and planing. The institute can be reached by taking Main St. back across IND 37 and following the right fork of the road for *1 m.* The students at the institute receive practical training by working on local structures.

Return to IND 37 and head south *3 m.* to the intersection of IND 37 and IND 450. Take IND 450 southwest *9 m.* to the town of **WILLIAMS**, which was platted in 1889, 73 years after the Isaac Williams family arrived in Lawrence County from Tennessee to begin the area's settlement. The town has long been known for Williams Dam, now a state fishing area with facilities for camping and picnicking. To reach the dam, turn left on the first street beyond the Soo Line Railroad crossing and continue to the parking lot. Return to IND 450 and continue beyond the west edge of town. Turn south. Drive through a railroad underpass

and onto the longest covered bridge still in use in the state. Built in 1884 at a cost of $18,700, the bridge stretches for 402 ft., including overhang.

Cross the bridge, ascend the hill, and continue approximately *1.4 m.* to the first road left. Follow this winding blacktop highway generally east, with a south jog at one point, approximately *5.7 m.* to U.S. 50 at Bryantsville. Turn left onto US 50, proceed *3.2 m.*, and turn left on the first county highway (CR 450S at Hartleyville). This leads to **Bluespring Caverns Park**. The cavern is touted as one of the world's 10 largest. The exposure of the cave occurred in the early 1940s when George Colglazier discovered a gaping hole on his farm after a night's heavy rains. Finding the state uninterested in the cave, Colglazier leased the property to Ellis Knoy of Worthington, who developed it as a commercial venture. Opened in 1971, the cave features an hour-long boat ride along the large subterranean river into which flows the more than 21 miles of underground streams. Grounds provide for both trailer and primitive camping.

Tour II

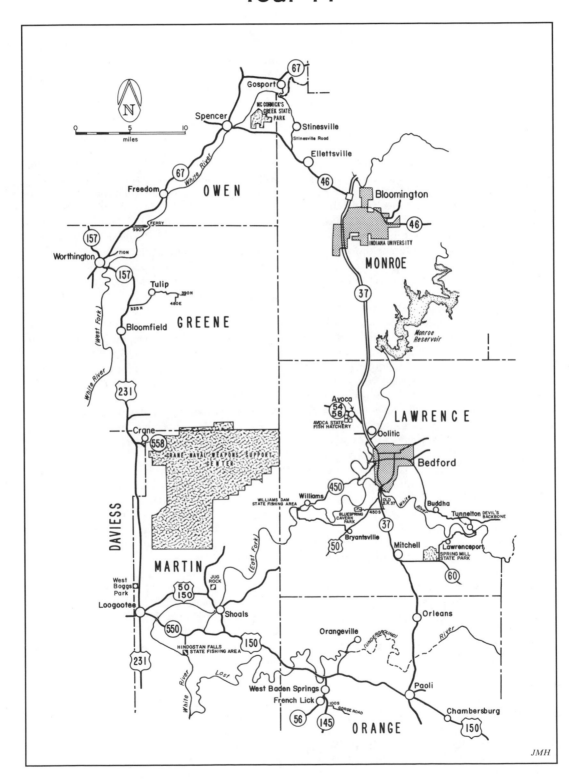

JMH

From the park, return east to US 50. Continue east on the county road *1.3 m.* and cross IND 37. One block east of IND 37 turn left onto Old IND 37 and go *.2 m.* to the **Red Cross Farm**. On the east edge of the road are two crumbling fieldstone columns, flanking a driveway, that once indicated the entrance. A recess in the southernmost post marks the cavity that formerly contained a stone inscribed Red Cross Farm. The stone is now at Spring Mill Park on the third floor museum of the Old Mill. This was once the home of Joseph Gardner, a physician, state legislator, naturalist, astronomer, photographer, inventor, and medical researcher, and his third wife, Enola Lee, an associate of Clara Barton, who founded the American Red Cross in 1881. The newlyweds accompanied Barton on relief expeditions. Gardner's sister married the nephew of Louis Pasteur, renowned French chemist, who discovered the bacterial basis of common diseases. Gardner inherited an 1850s mansion, which he gave to the city and is today the Bedford City Hall at 16th and K sts. Gardner owned 780 acres of prime riverside land near Bedford, which he deeded in 1893 to Barton for her organization's national headquarters. Much of the food and materials needed for worldwide disasters was to be stored there, and some supplies grown. A 44-country Geneva Convention concerning the Red Cross insured the neutrality of the property. Barton noted that "this land . . . will be the one piece of neutral ground in the Western hemisphere. It is a perpetual sanctuary against invading armies, and will be so respected and held sacred by the military powers of the world." The Gardners' large home on the farm became a virtual Red Cross museum. Disillusionment, however, quickly supplanted the auspicious beginnings. A hired overseer mismanaged the farm, and Barton lost interest and allowed tax payments to lapse. In 1904 the Gardners retook possession of the land. The same year Barton resigned from the Red Cross, and the house museum burned to the ground. The cabin the Gardners built for themselves after their house burned is now at Bedford-North Lawrence High School, moved there in 1978 thanks to the efforts of Maxine Hurd, who led the campaign to buy, remove, and renovate the structure, after it was torn down in 1978.

Continue north *1.7 m.* past the farm and bear right onto IND 37. Continue across White River past 16th St. and turn right on 10th St.,

following it about *.5 m.* to the tiny shop of the **Hindostan Whetstone Company** at 2828 Garvey Ln. Though no sign indicates its presence, the company name and its product have an honored place in the state's history, spanning at minimum 160 years and representing one of Indiana's oldest continuing industries. What date whetstones began to be quarried, smoothed, and shaped into "sharpenin' stones" for the world's cutting instruments, remains a mystery. But by the 1820s the hills of northwest Orange County, south of Bedford, bustled with whetstone activity. The thin-bedded sandstone is found in few other places in the world. The little town of Hindostan, once the seat of Martin County, became the hub of the business which centered around the Hindostan Whetstone Company, until the late 1820s when a strange illness made Hindostan a ghost town. In 1859 Louis Chaillaux, a French immigrant, purchased the quarries, and three generations of that family carried on the work. William Ingalls and others bought the whetstone holdings in 1946. Darrell Zink, Ingalls's son-in-law, eventually headed the firm, and he moved the milling end to Bedford in the 1970s. The manufacture of silicon carbide along with advances in synthetic materials reduced the world's demand for natural whetstones. To counter the declining market, Zink developed a small tapered stone for removing fingernail cuticles, and this beauty aid has been the company's mainstay ever since. Zink died in 1982, and Alexander Peacock of Indianapolis acquired the company and launched an aggressive marketing and expansion program for the manicuring products made of "God's concrete." The company continues to make the original whetstone for old customers who prefer the natural sharpener.

Return to IND 37, turn left, and left at 16th St. Proceed into **BEDFORD** (p. 14,410), the county seat, which is Lawrence County's second seat of justice. The first county seat was located on a bluff north of the White River about four miles southwest of present Bedford. The commissioners' choice for the county's capital in 1818 was named Palestine. Nothing remains of the town, but in its initial years it grew rapidly due to its county seat status and perhaps to rumors it might become the next state capital. The building design for the first permanent courthouse called for an octagonal brick structure, but this concept was discarded subsequently in favor of a more traditional, rectangular building. Though blessed by name and hints of future greatness, Palestine turned out to be a malaria-infested death trap. As a result, a new county seat was authorized in 1825. After much rankling over its new location, the county officers chose the Bedford site, at a distance from any waterways. Joseph Rawlins, a prominent pioneer, came up with a name for the new town after visiting Bedford County, Tennessee. Palestine property owners were allowed to transfer their claims to corresponding lots in Bedford, and much bitterness and litigation ensued over the terms of disposal or transfer. Some persons refused to leave Palestine while others decided to migrate elsewhere. Consequently, Bedford developed slowly. Eventually the remnant in Palestine departed, and nature gradually reclaimed the land. The major impetus for Bedford's growth was the maturing of the limestone industry in the late 19th century. Through this period and to World War II Bedford substantiated its reputation as the "Limestone Capital of the World." The postwar decline in the limestone business was offset by incoming light and heavy manufacturing. At present, the largest employer is the Central Foundry of General Motors.

Almost immediately to the right after coming onto 16th St. (IND 450) is the Stone City shopping mall. On the opposite side of 16th St. *.2 m.* is the limestone headquarters of Bedford's **Chamber of Commerce**, a place to pick up literature and ask questions about local sites and attractions.

Continue to M St., turn left for one block, and left again to the **C. S. Norton Mansion** at 1415 15th St. It is locally called the Evans home after the couple who restored it. C. S. Norton was a pioneer limestone operator who organized the C. S. Norton Blue Stone Company in 1888. (*NRHP*)

Head south on O St. to 18th St., then left on 18th St. to L St. and the entrance to the **Green Hill Cemetery**. Indiana is rich in examples of the stone sculptor's craft, and some of the finest specimens of this art are located here. The Stonecutters Monument, a full-sized figure of a craftsman, was sculpted and erected in 1894 by the Journeymen Stonecutters Association of Bedford. It is located in the southeast section. Nearby is the Stone Bench, an exact replica of the worktable of Louis Baker, who

died in 1917. Using a single block of stone, workers in their spare time reproduced his workbench as he left it, including his tools and the unfinished piece Baker was carving at his death. There is a statue of doughboy Michael F. Wallner, with every crease in his uniform preserved. A meticulously carved golf bag complete with clubs stands next to the statue of Tom Bardon. A seven-year-old girl, who died in 1894, rests beneath a tree-shaped monument featuring her high-button shoes and straw hat. Many other testimonies to the stonecarver's delicate skills appear in this remarkable cemetery.

Follow L St. to 16th St. and go east two blocks to the public square and the **Lawrence County Courthouse**. This Neoclassical-style limestone structure, designed by Walter Scholer, is not the large domed and porticoed building we often associate with the county courthouse. It is relatively young, having been erected in 1930. But its style harks back to pre-Civil War days, and it is often characterized as reflecting exceptional restraint and elegance befitting a lesser political unit such as a county. The north wall of the previous limestone courthouse, completed in 1872, is incorporated in this newer model at the request of local stoneworkers who wished to show the durability of limestone. The **Lawrence County Historical Museum** is located in the basement of the courthouse. Now nearly 60 years old, it is one of the state's finest small museums, exhibiting some 5,000 items, mostly from Lawrence County, in its four rooms.

From the courthouse continue east on 16th St. to D St. where a sign on the north side indicates 250 yds. to **Foote's Tomb**. Dr. Winthrop Foote brought into Lawrence County its first stonecutter, a man named Toburn, who, in 1840 cut Foote's burial vault from a large outcrop of stone. The first occupant of the tomb was Winthrop's brother Ziba, a government surveyor, who had drowned in Gibson County in 1806. Winthrop had his brother's body reinterred at Bedford after the completion of the vault. In 1957 the vault was vandalized, and for the first time since Foote's death in 1856 the interior was exposed. Foote had himself buried in a cast-iron casket that appeared "wrapped" to conform to the body in mummy fashion. He took his medical bag with him, and in a stone box at his feet were placed guns and ammunition. His brother Ziba occupied another room of the tomb, and Winthrop's horse was put into a third room. The tomb was resealed and its contents left as they were found.

From Foote's Tomb continue east on 16th St. past Otis Park *1.4 m.* and left at Vocational School Rd. for *.8 m.* to the gatehouse of **Bedford-North Lawrence High School**. Drive straight back from the gatehouse to just beyond the maintenance building where sits a **log cabin that came from the county's Red Cross Farm**. The cabin once was home for Joseph and Enola Lee Gardner.

Return to **Otis Park** at US 50 (16th St.) and the Bedford-Tunnelton Rd. and turn left at the airport sign. At the park's entrance sits the **Civil War-era mansion of William A. Ragsdale**, whose estate at the time covered almost 200 acres. In 1875 the house and grounds were sold to Nathan Hall, who opened the area's first quarry and who is credited with giving Bedford stone a commercial value by shipping it to Chicago by railroad. It is said that Hall's agent in Chicago introduced the building material to members of the building trade by presenting them with paperweights cut from the initial load of stone. Today the house is used as a residence for the park's grounds keeper and for club and civic meetings. In 1935 Fred Otis, publisher of the *Bedford Daily Mail*, purchased the 146-acre site from the Bedford Country Club and donated it to the city for use as a park. The stone bandstand in the park is one of the improvements suggested by Otis at the time. The two-story columned stage was completed in 1938. Stoneworkers, still unemployed in the waning days of the depression, built it. The placement of the six sweeping limestone arches, which form the inner cone of the shell, dumbfounded some construction experts who had not thought stone could be cut and lifted to shape the concavity of the semidome.

South of Otis Park on the Bedford-Tunnelton Rd. *6.6 m.* is **BUDDHA**, a crossroads church and country store hamlet established in 1895 as a post office. It is uncertain how it came to be called Buddha, but accounts of its origin range from the name of a traveling salesman to that of the Hungarian city of Budapest. Apparently, the leader of Buddhism was not considered as a source.

Daniel and Elizabeth Bass lived southwest of Buddha on 175 acres near the southern bank of the White River. To the couple was born, July 21, 1851, a son, Sam Bass, who turned out to be a famous outlaw of the old west. Orphaned during the Civil War, young Bass went to live northeast of Buddha with an uncle. Bass left the area at age 18 and journeyed to St. Louis, Mississippi, and finally to Texas. He launched a violent career of horse stealing and robbing trains, banks, and stagecoaches. He died at age 27 from wounds received in a bank holdup. Years later his sister from Mitchell, Indiana, had erected on her brother's grave in Texas a headstone inscribed "A Brave Man Reposes in Death Here, Why Was He Not True?" Legend has it that Bass buried money in Lawrence County, and many persons have tried unsuccessfully to find it. Sam Bass's mother's maiden name was Sheeks. Her father's log cabin, which Sam probably visited many times, is in Spring Mill Park's Pioneer Village serving as the weaver's quarters.

Continue east on the Bedford-Tunnelton Rd., passing the Tunnelton turnoff at *3.8 m.*, onto the Bedford-Tunnelton route extension, which becomes the **Devil's Backbone Rd.**, a descriptive name intended to indicate the rising precipice the roadway follows. About midway in its four-mile stretch to Fort Ritner, the road hugs the crest of a high ridge. The steep slopes incline to flat farmlands far below. Numerous fatal accidents have occurred on the Devil's spine. In pioneer days a woman and her children were killed when their wagon and team plunged over the side. Years later, reports surfaced of persons continuing to hear the family's screams and the horses' frantic whinnying.

Return to the Tunnelton turnoff and turn left. Isaac Newkirk laid out the town of **TUNNELTON** in 1859, three years after the completion of the Ohio and Mississippi Railroad and its giant tunnel, from which the town derived its name. Through the remainder of the century, the town's development was tied closely to the fortunes of Alfred H. Guthrie (1828-1913), whose stately Italianate brick home stands just north of Tunnelton on the east side of the main access road. Guthrie built a general store in Tunnelton and became the county's largest single landowner, accumulating more than 3,000 acres. He was Tunnelton's first postmaster and served in the state legislature in 1877. He presided over Bedford's Stone City Bank in the early 1900s.

The one-third-mile-long **Big Tunnel** was constructed in 1857. The first train to enter the tunnel stalled partway through, and it had to be pulled out by mules. The rough-cut passage was veneered with brick in 1908 to end the problem of rock falling onto the tracks. The tunnel walls are lined with alcoves, or "manholes," large enough for a person to find refuge from a passing train, and the entrances are decorated with years of graffiti. Young people have always found the trip to and through the tunnel an adventure heightened by such legends as the headless night watchman who stalks the tunnel swinging a lantern at his side. The west entrance to the tunnel is located southeast of Tunnelton. Drive through town on the road that fronts the Guthrie mansion. Proceed under the railroad viaduct and turn east onto the Tunnelton-Fort Ritner road, which skirts the White River to the south and the railroad tracks to the north. East *2.2 m.*, the cut of the CSX (formerly the Baltimore and Ohio) roadbed seems to disappear as the full face of Tunnel Hill becomes visible. The tunnel's entrance is close by, but it takes a hike up a hillside path to see it. Another tunnel was located about *2 m.* west of Tunnelton, but this was daylighted in 1900.

Return to the Tunnelton Rd., turn left, and cross White River and immediately bear right. Follow this scenic road through Lawrenceport, which overlooks White River, angle left about *1 m.* beyond, and right at IND 60 to **Spring Mill State Park**. One of the most popular areas in southern Indiana, the park offers the visitor a variety of historical and scenic vistas to explore. The village of Spring Mill began in 1815 when a Canadian seaman, Samuel Jackson, Jr., built a small mill in the deep valley. Subsequent development by the Bullitts, Montgomerys, and Hamers—each a team of brothers—brought the hamlet to the verge of becoming a permanent Hoosier settlement. The bypassing of Spring Mill by the Ohio and Mississippi Railroad in the 1850s spawned nearby Mitchell but spelled the end of the picturesque little mill town. By the end of the century, Spring Mill was in ruins. When the state launched its park system in 1916, Lawrence countians persuaded the Indiana Department of Conservation to turn the place into a state park. A series of land donations and department director Richard Lieber's vision of a restored village serve as a backdrop to the decades of intelligent reconstruction and preservation evident on the 1,319-acre grounds. Attractions include **Donaldson's Woods Nature Preserve**, an 80-acre virgin stand of predomi-

nantly white oak, beech, and maple. In the park are **Donaldson's Cave** and **Twin Caves**, which offers an underground boat ride. The **Pioneer Village** offers a number of reconstructed log shops and homes and includes the working gristmill of the Bullitt brothers. The **Grissom Memorial**, dedicated in 1971, contains the astronaut Virgil Grissom's space suit, a Gemini III capsule, and a 6-ft.-diameter suspended earth globe. Also available are food and lodging at the Spring Mill Inn, boats, campgrounds, fishing, hiking trails, saddle horses, and an olympic-size swimming pool.

Return to IND 60, turn right, and again at IND 37 and at Main St. to the city of **MITCHELL** (p. 4,641). Mitchell was laid out in 1853 as a direct result of the Ohio and Mississippi Railroad coming through the area. Ormsby McKnight Mitchell, chief engineer and surveyor for the O and M, located the track at the Mitchell site and thereby earned the honor of having the town named for him. Mitchell, a brilliant child, entered West Point at age 15, taught there at age 20, and went on to Cincinnati College as professor of mathematics, philosophy, and astronomy. He acquired major general's rank in the Civil War. Meanwhile, Mitchell incorporated but grew slowly, with industry largely limited to limekilns, which converted limestone to mortar or plaster. In 1902 the Lehigh Portland Cement Company, near Allentown, Pennsylvania, opened the company's first Midwest plants in Mitchell. The demand for the "liquid stone" touched off a decade of boom times for Mitchell. Its population doubled between 1900 and 1910. In 1971 the Mitchell factory shipped its one-millionth barrel of cement. The **Heidelberg Cement Company** of West Germany bought the business in 1979. The plant is at the east end of Main St.

The cement industry fell on hard times during the 1930s, but Mitchell suffered less than anticipated because of an up-and-coming enterprise. Ralph H. Carpenter, a Lawrence County native and blacksmith, came to Mitchell in 1918. He soon was building "hacks" to convey students to the newly consolidated township school. In 1922, with 15 employees, he began manufacturing wood and steel-clad school buses. He introduced the all-steel bus body in 1935. Carpenter had his present factory built in 1938, and two years later he incorporated as the **Carpenter Body Works**. Indiana is a national leader in school bus production, and Mitchell's Carpenter Works ranks among the giants in the field. It is Mitchell's largest employer, and it has continued to flourish during recessions and energy crunches as a result of the vehicle's value as an alternate means of transportation. The sea of buses observable alongside IND 37, between Main St. and IND 60, testifies to the firm's size and importance. The plant is located at 1500 W. Main St., just east of IND 37.

Follow Main St. to 7th and turn left for two blocks to the **Mitchell Opera House**, at the southwest corner of 7th and Brook sts. Built by the county in 1902 as a hall for holding public functions, it became a city possession and was renamed City Hall in 1913. Within three years its general disrepair prompted calls for its demolition. In stepped Menlo Moore. Moore, a seasoned theater impresario and owner, leased and refurbished the building for use as an opera house. From its opening in 1919 to its closing in 1927, the stage reverberated with the sounds of local and imported vaudevillians, chorus lines, thespians, and minstrels. After 1927 the building reverted to a city hall and remained so for most of the passing years until the city offices moved into new quarters in 1979. Local citizens then formed Mitchell Opera House, Inc., which leased the building, financed its renewal, and continues to maintain it. Lennox, Oldham and Matthews Corporation of Indianapolis was in charge of the restoration. The Opera House has reopened for live entertainment. (*NRHP*)

Mitchell boasts a genuine hero in the person of **Virgil I. "Gus" Grissom**, one of the nation's seven original astronauts. Born in Mitchell in 1926, Grissom attended local schools, married a classmate, and joined the Air Force during World War II. After the war he rose to the top echelon of America's test pilots. A pioneer of America's space program, his piloting the Liberty Bell 7 on a 15-minute suborbital flight in 1961 made him the second astronaut to conquer space. In 1965 he commanded the Molly Brown for three earth orbits in the first manned Gemini flight. Grissom was slated to be the first man on the moon before that tragic day, January 27, 1967, when a flash fire aboard the Apollo I test capsule took his life and the lives of two fellow astronauts. Following his death, Indiana constructed at Spring Mill Park a memorial building, dedicated in 1971. Mitchell experienced great diffi-

culties in erecting a monument to its native son. Don Caudill, who grew up with Grissom, spearheaded a movement, beginning in 1967, to put up a replica of the Redstone rocket, which carried aloft his late friend's Mercury Project capsule. The Indiana Limestone Company completed the monument in 1972, but available funds were insufficient for its final placement. The Vietnam War deaths overshadowed Grissom's sacrifice, and, as a result, contributions dried up. Finally, in June 1980 the memorial rocket was positioned. Additional problems, however, plagued the project and delayed the dedication. A crime wave hit Mitchell in late June 1980, and the vandalism included the painting of obscenities on the rocket. This shocking act, plus the cracking and replacement of the capstone, along with time needed for landscaping and for inscribing the stone, postponed the dedication until October 1981. The limestone memorial to Grissom stands 44 ft. high and is 4 ft. in diameter. The details of Grissom's life are recorded on four 10 x 6-ft. wings extending from the base. The monument stands beside the city hall on S. 6th St., four blocks south of Main St. on the right, on the grounds of Grissom's elementary school, which was torn down to make way for the city hall.

Before the elementary school was built, the site was the home of the **Southern Indiana Normal College**. Founded in 1880, the coeducational, nonsectarian school featured innovative curricula, and it mandated no entrance exams or required courses. The school, nicknamed SIN college, usually enrolled more students than Indiana University. In 1900, when the school burned, never to be rebuilt, it had close to 900 students. A marker in front of City Hall on S. 6th St. commemorates the institution.

Continue south on 6th St. to the end, turn right on IND 60, and left on IND 37. Drive *3 m.* and cross into **ORANGE COUNTY** (p. 18,677; 408 sq. m.), organized in 1815, the last of 15 counties established under the territorial government. At the time of its organization the county covered an immense area from south of present-day Morgan County almost to the Ohio River. It comprised parts of five of today's counties. By mid-1818 the county's borders had been reduced to its present 408-sq.-m. shape. The county's topography shades from a classic karst region in the northeast to rugged hill land in the southwest. The land characteristics have discouraged extensive agriculture. The local economy depends chiefly on tourism and small manufacturing. Several years ago it was thought that local tourism might receive a healthy boost when stories circulated that the Disney organization, which operated the famed amusement parks in the Orange counties of California and Florida, was considering a third establishment in Orange County, Indiana. The rumors had no foundation in fact.

Past the county line .7 m. is the **Freeman's Corner historical marker**. The marker calls attention to the corner point of the Vincennes Tract surveyed by Thomas Freeman in 1802-3. Freeman surveyed and established the Indiana land boundaries, which helped property owners secure clear titles to their lands. The actual corner lies 839 ft. north and 48 ft. east of the marker. The Lost River Chapter of the Daughters of the American Revolution (DAR) put up the tablet in 1935. The plaque is affixed to a stone, which faces a small paved semicircular drive beside the water tower on the east shoulder of the highway.

Drive .8 m. past Freeman's Corner, turn east onto Liberty Rd. (by the grain mill), left at the "T," then right, driving 3.5 m. to **Liberty Cemetery** and **Liberty Christian Church**. Ann Todd Tegarden, the aunt of Mary Todd Lincoln, is buried here. Mrs. Tegarden, the wife of Basil Tegarden, died in 1863 at the age of 84.

Pink and white dogwood trees line IND 37 in northern Orange County. The dogwood is the trademark of **ORLEANS** (p. 2,161), 2 m. south of the Freeman's Corner marker. "Operation Dogwood," launched by townspeople in 1966, has succeeded in its goal of having hundreds of the trees planted along roads, in parks, and in yards. The annual Dogwood Festival celebrates Orleans as the "Dogwood Capital of Indiana." Platted in 1815, the town is the oldest in Orange County. Founded two months after Andrew Jackson's victory over the British at New Orleans, the settlers named their town to honor this event. Samuel S. Lewis, one of the founders, became a prominent figure in Texas after he fought for Texas independence from Mexico and served as a senator in the first two congresses of the Republic of Texas under Sam Houston's presidency.

The Orleans town square is called **"Congress Square,"** meaning public place, or it is referred to as "Seminary Square," after the Orleans Academy that stood there from the 1870s to 1963. Whatever it is called, the square has something for everyone: playground equipment, a brick gazebo or bandstand, stone benches, horseshoe courts, and a large sycamore tree. Senator Daniel W. Voorhees, "the tall Sycamore of the Wabash" and a Democratic party leader, spoke in Orleans in the 1880s. His followers planted a tree on the square in tribute.

One of the stories linked with Orleans pertains to the loves of Elizabeth, or Libbie, Shindler. While visiting her uncle in Philadelphia, the young lady from Orleans met the wealthy hat manufacturer and widower John B. Stetson, and they married soon afterwards. Elizabeth became heiress to the Stetson hat fortune after her husband's death in 1906. Elizabeth next married a Portuguese nobleman and lived in a castle near Lisbon. While she was Mrs. Stetson, her husband presented a house to her parents. The house was precut and fabricated in Philadelphia. Imported workers constructed the house in Orleans in 1894. The house is known as the "story book house," or "the house that hats built." The green-shuttered home, which may be one of the first prefabricated structures in the Midwest, is located on Washington St., at the east edge of town just past Stetson St. and opposite the school.

From the north side of the square go west on Jefferson St. four blocks to a cemetery, in which rests a gravestone with this unique inscription: "Charles A. Blalock—America's Greatest Man." Blalock, a railroader, was a companion of the public square group of story swappers. When he died about 1954, his good friend Noble "Zip" Keedy financed the purchase of the headstone and its inscription. Blalock had been all over the country as a railroader, and his buddies kidded him about being America's greatest man. To find the tombstone, go north on 5th St. about 50 ft. The small stone sits in the third row back, west of 5th St. Across the Jefferson St. side of the cemetery is another group of graves, in which lies the body of Edward Jackson, governor of Indiana, 1925-29. Jackson is perhaps best known for his friendship with the Ku Klux Klan and his mid-term trial on bribery charges, for which he was found innocent on a technicality.

Resume the tour south on IND 37. Travel 3.6 m. south of Orleans and cross the dry bed of **Lost River**. The pitted karst or limestone region, comprising over a third of the county, characteristically features subterranean waterways, sinkholes, and caverns. Lost River rises near Smedley's Station in Washington County and courses westward 22 miles above and below ground through Orange County to the East Fork of the White River in neighboring Martin County. The elusive river "sinks" underground southeast of Orleans and courses about eight miles before resurfacing 3/4 mile south of Orangeville. During extreme rains the 22-mile dry channel of the river occasionally has to carry the overflow.

South of the Lost River bridge *2.8 m.* is the county seat, **PAOLI** (p. 3,637), so designated in 1816. The valley town was settled principally by Quakers led by Jonathan Lindley (1756-1828), a wealthy North Carolina businessman. At the age of 55, the former state legislator escorted a large group from Orange County, North Carolina. They settled in the Lick Creek area of present Paoli in 1811. Lindley carved a distinguished place for himself in the state. As a county commissioner and county land agent, he platted Paoli. He held a seat in the first state legislature, helped write the first tax laws, served as a member of the committee to select the site for Indiana University, and served on its first board of trustees. Lindley also was instrumental in the founding of Terre Haute (see Terre Haute essay). Lindley and his friends named Paoli for Pasquale Paoli Ashe, son of North Carolina governor Samuel Ashe. The young Ashe died just prior to the Lindley group's migration from the Tar Heel state.

Descend into Paoli on IND 37. On the city's gently sloping public square rests the much photographed and described **Orange County Courthouse**. The Hoosier author Theodore Dreiser may have thought it "nondescript—a cross between a Greek Temple and a country school," but its preservation as an architectural landmark has been uppermost in the minds of Orange County citizens. The Greek Revival structure was built between 1848 and 1850 for about $14,000. The brick and stone building features a colonnaded entranceway; the six, 4-ft.-thick columns are constructed of concrete-wrapped brick. The unusual outside iron staircases lead from ground level to the portico, and another set of iron stairs rise from the porch to the second floor. (*NRHP*)

A number of memorials on the courthouse lawn enhance the grandeur of the scene. Buhrstones from old country mills are arranged as a monument for Revolutionary War veterans buried in the county. Two cannons guard the courthouse entrance and honor Civil War casualties. A large granite "Gold Star" memorial remembers the "silent ones" of our two world wars. The **Indiana Initial Point Memorial**, dedicated in 1973, calls attention to the point of beginning for all land surveys in Indiana, seven miles south of Paoli off IND 37. The initial point was established by Ebenezer Buckingham, Jr., in 1805. At one time, the area near the initial point bore the tag "Valley of Hog's Defeat," possibly because irate citizens once drove off feeding herds of hogs which threatened to destroy their lands. The memorial, originally dedicated on the spot south of Paoli, was later moved to the courthouse to prevent further vandalism.

The **Orange County Museum of History** is located on the northwest corner of the square in the old Sherrod house, a former academy building and a doctor's office. The museum was established in Paoli in the mid-1980s and is operated by the Orange County Historical Society. In the several rooms of the two-story house the county's history is documented. On display are household items of yesteryear along with Indiana artifacts and agricultural implements. A replica of an old schoolroom is found on the second floor.

Situated on the south side of the Paoli square is the building which used to house the **Landmark Hotel**, formerly the Mineral Springs Hotel. In the late 19th and early 20th centuries, Indiana sprouted with resorts which capitalized on nearby mineral-laden springs to attract the infirm or vacationer. Between 1890 and 1910, dozens of mineral springs resorts existed, the larger portion in southern Indiana. Factors in the health resorts' decline in popularity include false claims made on behalf of the waters, improved health care, purer public water supplies, and expanded transportation choices. In Paoli workers drilled a sulphur well on the south bank of Lick Creek about 400 ft. south of the square in 1895. The three-story brick hotel, completed a year later, offered lodging along with billiards, bowling, and ballrooms. The well water, which state geologist W. S. Blatchley described in 1901 as "quite bitter with the taste of Epsom Salt and hydrogen sulphide," was bottled and sold. The hotel changed hands through the years, experiencing slumps in the 1930s and 1950s.

Immediately south of the courthouse on S. Gospel St. an old single-lane iron bridge with wood flooring spans Lick Creek. Built by the Cleveland (Ohio) Bridge and Iron Company in 1890, it is referred to as the **Gospel St. Bridge**. (*HAER*)

In 1955 Jonathan Lindley's descendants met in Paoli to dedicate headstones to Jonathan and Deborah Lindley. The ceremony took place at the old white frame Lick Creek Friends Meetinghouse, established in 1813. Two former buildings were located 200 yds. east and west respectively of the present church, which dates from 1901. The church and cemetery, along with the **Lindley Memorial**, are located a short distance down a gravel road which leads right from US 150 at *2.4 m.* from the courthouse.

Return to US 150 and turn right for approximately *3 m.* to the hamlet of **CHAMBERSBURG**. Near here, deep in the Hoosier National Forest, a black community thrived in the 19th century. Known as **Little Africa** to whites, but **Lick Creek** to the inhabitants, the community was made up of fugitive slaves in addition to "free" blacks who had migrated about the time the Quakers came from North Carolina. They settled on land deeded to Ishmael Roberts, a black Revolutionary War veteran. Chambersburg established the first school for blacks in Orange County. An old Orange County history states, perhaps mistakenly, that Chambersburg was usually the first stop for escaped slaves after crossing the Ohio River. The question of why the community died out remains unanswered. Sickness, flight, isolation, poverty—any or all could have been responsible. In 1970 Paoli Boy Scouts fixed up the area around the Little Africa cemetery and church site, which is not easily accessible to the public.

Returning to the Paoli courthouse square, drive south on IND 37 *2 m.* to the entrance of the **Pioneer Mothers' Memorial Forest**. The registered natural landmark contains 80 acres of virgin timber unchanged since the days of Indiana's earliest white settlers. More commonly known as Cox Woods, after the pioneer owners Joseph and Mary Lines Cox, the tract of nearly 2,600 trees appeared destined for the lumber mill in 1941 only to be saved by a locally led preservation campaign. The effort, marshaled

by the Meridian Club of Paoli, managed to raise $24,300 in 89 days. The drive met the price and the 90-day deadline set by the accommodating Wood-Mosaic Lumber and Veneer Company of Louisville, the recent purchaser of the Cox estate. The forest's name came from the Pioneer Mothers of Indiana organization who contributed about a fourth of the money to purchase the property. The forest contains a picnic area and trails. Another entrance to the park is *2 m.* southeast on US 150. Vehicles are not permitted, but visitors may park along either highway and walk into the forest. IND 37 overlooks the city of Paoli and affords a spectacular bird's-eye view on the return trip from the forest.

From the Paoli courthouse head west on US 150. To the south, at the west edge of town, *.3 m.* from the square, is the **Marea Radcliffe Rest Park**. The name honors a prominent Paolian who contributed time and money toward the beautification of the city. An old mineral water well, one of the three in Paoli during the prosperous years of the Mineral Springs Hotel, is located in the rest park.

Past the rest park *.6 m.* is the turnoff indicating *1.5 m.* to **Paoli Peaks**, southern Indiana's first snowmaking skiing resort which opened in December 1978.

Just after turning from US 150, the road bends to the right. On the left is the **Lindley home**, a two-story white frame house with green shutters, owned by the Orange County Historical Society. Thomas Lindley, son of Jonathan Lindley, built it in 1869 on a plot of land deeded to his father in 1812. The ground is located almost in the center of the county. Note the first steps on the front and west stoops. They are halves of old buhrstones. (*NRHP*)

Approximately *5 m.* west from the Paoli Peaks turnoff is a north turnoff that skirts the **Ames Chapel United Methodist Church**. The church, established as a union of Nelson Chapel and Smith Chapel, celebrated its centennial in 1979. The original church, built in 1879, burned in 1913. The present sanctuary was dedicated in 1914.

Continue the tour on US 150 west for *3 m.* before bearing left onto IND 56 into the Springs Valley communities of **WEST BADEN SPRINGS** (p. 796) and **FRENCH LICK** (p. 2,265). When approaching West Baden Springs note on the right at treetop level the huge dome of the **West Baden Springs Hotel**. A truly re-

West Baden Springs Hotel

markable architectural achievement, the spa features the world's third largest unsupported dome (the largest are New Orleans's and Houston's sports domes). The structure is often referred to as the "Eighth Wonder of the World." In this century's first three decades, the hotel represented, along with French Lick's famed hostelry, the quintessence of America's adult playgrounds. Its history harks back to 1852 when John Lane constructed his Mile Lick Inn on the West Baden site as a competitor to French Lick's roadhouse. Lane later changed the name of his place to "The West Baden Inn." In 1887 the Monon Railroad built an 18-mile extension to the hotel, portending increased business. A year later, Lee Sinclair, a Salem, Indiana, native, assumed control of the hotel and added an opera house, a casino, and a unique two-deck, covered, one-third-mile oval bicycle and pony track. The electrically lighted baseball diamond in the track's center was spring training headquarters for major league teams. In 1901 the U-shaped, wood frame hotel burned to the ground. With family urging, Sinclair hired a young West Virginia architect, Harrison Albright, to build the world's largest dome. The only architect found who would take the job, Albright completed his task within a year. The rebuilt hotel officially opened in 1903. Guests poured into the hotel to soak in

its mineral waters or drink them bottled as "Sprudel Water." They came to play golf, ride horses or bicycles, attend stage shows, gamble, enjoy the food from the hotel's own farms, dairies, and bakeries, and mingle with the famous and infamous. Paul Dresser composed "On the Banks of the Wabash" here. Al Capone, with his retinue of bodyguards, was a frequent visitor. Prizefighters John L. Sullivan and James J. Corbett trained at West Baden. After Sinclair's death in 1916, his daughter sold the 708-room hotel to Charles Edward Ballard, a local resident, hotel owner, gambler, and an owner of one of the nation's largest circuses, the Hagenbeck-Wallace. During World War I the hotel served as an army hospital. The onset of the depression forced the hotel to close in 1931. Three years later, Ballard gave it to the Jesuits for use as a seminary. The Jesuits dismantled or sold anything that smacked of the hotel's former opulence. Ballard died in 1936 from gunshot wounds administered by a gambling partner. The Jesuits left in 1964. An attempt to reopen the hotel as an opera and art center fizzled. Bought privately at auction in 1966, the building was turned over to Northwood Institute for use as a college. Today, with a little imagination, the tourist can envision the grandeur of the old hotel. The 200-ft.-diameter dome is 130 ft. above a floor composed of about 12 million pieces of tile. Twenty-four steel ribs which support the dome rest on columns 5 ft. thick. Encircling the Pompeian court are six tiers of rooms, some of which open onto balconies overlooking the central hall. A Rookwood tile fireplace adorns one section of the inner wall, while elaborate statues, urns, and plants garnish the mosaic floor. Financial difficulties forced the institute to close its doors after the May 1983 graduation. In the fall of the same year, the institute leased the historic structure to private developer, H. Eugene McDonald, whose renovation of the building to return it to its former resort-hotel status was slated for completion in 1988. (*NRHP/ HAER/HABSI*)

Neighboring West Baden Springs to the south, with a common dividing line, is French Lick. The large, white-columned brick home in the foreground just before the road bears right into French Lick is the old **Ballard home**, built by hotel owner Ed Ballard.

Immediately to the west of the railroad crossing on IND 56 in French Lick is the **Indiana Railway Museum** (IRM), operating out of the former Monon passenger station. The IRM, an organization founded in 1961 to preserve and operate historic railway equipment, was located in Westport, 1962-71, and in Greensburg, 1973-76, before moving to French Lick in 1978. The museum offers rides on its French Lick, West Baden and Southern Railway on weekends to and from Cuzco, nine miles southwest of French Lick. On the trip the old steam-propelled train goes through the state's second longest tunnel, the 2,217-ft. "Barton" or French Lick tunnel, which was built in 1905-6. Laborers bored from both sides of the hill, and tradition says they were only half an inch off center when they met midway.

The IRM also operates an electric trolley that runs between the French Lick Springs Hotel and the former West Baden Springs Hotel. The 1930 trolley, of Portuguese manufacture, reproduces the era between 1903 and 1919 when a similar car made the two-mile round trip. The Springs Valley Electric Railway began operations in 1984.

The Monon station, headquarters of the IRM, has on display a variety of mementos of earlier railway days. The station is also the office of the Springs Valley Area Chamber of Commerce and a tourist information center.

Directly south of the museum are the grounds of the **French Lick Springs Hotel Golf and Tennis Resort** on the right. Long before French Lick acquired its modern repute as an outstanding resort it achieved distinction for the preservative and nutrient qualities of its salt deposits. In 1832 the state sold its saline reserves at French Lick. The salt content of the springs proved inadequate for large-scale salt manufacturing. The principal buyer was a Maryland-born physician and Baptist preacher, William A. Bowles. He built the first French Lick Hotel in 1840—a building later described as "the ugliest and most unsightly building ever constructed in the valley." Despite its unshapeliness, the hotel with its mineral springs brought success to Bowles and the line of lessees who carried on the operation. Bowles is an enigmatic figure. A respected doctor, businessman, and state legislator, he attracted, if not relished, controversy. No stranger to the courtroom, Bowles once sued fellow church members for unpaid medical bills, thereby breaking church law. He faced charges of practicing medicine without a license. He was wrongly accused of cowardice while leading the Second Indiana Regiment in the Mexican War. As an outspoken southern sympathizer and officer in the pro-rebel Knights of the Golden Circle, he narrowly escaped execution through President Andrew Johnson's pardon. He married three times. His sensational second divorce case reached the Indiana Supreme Court. After Bowles's death in 1873 his complex estate required adjudication. The property changed hands several times in the next 25 years. All the while, the old hotel made money, partly because of rail transportation after 1887 and partly because of the increasing popularity of health spas. A disastrous fire in 1897 led to the hotel's purchase in 1901 by a syndicate headed by thrice Indianapolis mayor Thomas Taggart. Taggart rebuilt and expanded the hotel and brought it international fame. As chairman of the Democratic National Committee, briefly an appointed United States senator, and acknowledged political strategist, Taggart drew the political and social elite to his resort. For years, the hotel functioned as the unofficial headquarters of the Democratic party. The resort facilities included a championship golf course, bridle paths, indoor and outdoor swimming pools, and skeet and trap ranges. Only after Taggart's death in 1929 were alcoholic beverages permitted in the hotel. The resort's farm-lands provided exquisite culinary delights. Chief chef Louis Perrin reportedly introduced Americans to tomato juice in 1917. Taggart made "Pluto" water, bubbling from the hotel's primary spring, a household name. The bottled liquid's slogan, "If nature won't, Pluto will," referred to its primary use for "colonic irriga-tion" (laxative). The Pluto operation, situated across from the hotel, became a separate corpo-ration in 1948 and continued bottling the water until the early 1970s. Despite Taggart's refusal to allow gambling on the hotel's grounds, the town of French Lick emerged as America's Monte Carlo. Al Brown's Club, opposite the hotel and now the site of a parking lot, became the most famous of a half dozen or more gam-ing houses—all defying the occasional threats of closure and the raids. The last casino shut down in 1949.

The hotel's erratic economic performance through the depression and World War II led to the transfer of the property in 1946 to a New York hotel group for a reported $4 million. The Sheraton Corporation bought the colossal yel-low brick facility in the mid-1950s, operating it until sold to the Cox Hotel Corporation of New York in 1979. In 1986 the complex was pur-chased by the Kenwood Financial Corporation which launched a multimillion dollar restora-tion of the hotel. Today's attractions on the 2,600-acre resort include 12 indoor tennis courts, two 18-hole golf courses, and a glass-domed all-weather pool. Next to the domed pool is the Pluto water pavilion, the spring still active.

French Lick's national fame as a resort capital has been replaced by its fame as the home of basketball star **Larry Bird**. Nicknamed "the hick from French Lick," Bird starred with the local Springs Valley High School team, led Indiana State University to the NCAA finals in 1979, and is one of the top players in the Na-tional Basketball Association. Bird led the Bos-ton Celtics to the NBA championship in 1984 and 1986 and was three times named the league's most valuable player. The star still res-ides in French Lick in the off season. Note the large basketball-shaped street sign designating Larry Bird Blvd. just east of IND 56 on the north side of the downtown area. In 1979 a portion of Monon St. was renamed Larry Bird Blvd. in honor of the local hero.

Back at the Railway Museum, take Monon St. just north of the station west *2.8 m.* up a steep hill to a gated and fenced roadway which leads to the **Taggart mansion**, completed in 1929 at a cost of around $150,000. The south-ern Colonial-style house replaced the **Mount Aire Tower**, constructed by Taggart in 1917. Hotel guests climbed the tower's seven-story in-ner circular stairway to emerge onto a sheltered and railed deck. Mount Aire, at 909 ft. above sea level and crowned by the 100-ft. tower, af-forded a spectacular view of the surrounding countryside. It was said that through a brass telescope on a clear day, one could see Louis-ville, Kentucky, approximately 60 miles southeast.

The **House of Clocks Museum**, 225 College St. (four blocks southeast of the French Lick Springs Hotel), features nine rooms with over a thousand antique pieces, including a major col-lection of clocks.

Take IND 56 north from the hotel and turn right onto IND 145. At the Kimball Piano Company building go left and follow "Gorge" road, bearing right at times, to the **Sulphur Creek Evangelical and United Brethren Church**, which is *4.2 m.* from IND 56. In the tiny ceme-tery behind the church lie the **Cross Brothers**, Ferdinand and Henry, Hoosier artists. Ferdi-nand (1838-1912) carved stone. Henry (1837-1918) worked with brush and palette. Once on a visit to French Lick, Ferdinand discovered a picturesque ravine replete with cave and over-hanging cliffs. He built a home and studio in the valley. The Cross Mammoth Cave, for-merly a French Lick tourist attraction, is not far from the church on private land. Besides carving tombstones for many of southern Indi-ana's cemeteries, Ferdinand transformed the stone around his home into a menagerie of ani-mals, birds, and reptiles. Only bits and pieces of this remarkable display are extant. He also created a large creature-decorated stone foun-tain which once stood centered under the dome in the West Baden Springs Hotel. Henry, who joined his brother at the cave, excelled in por-traiture. He painted such greats as Lincoln, Grant, Brigham Young, King Edward VIII, Buffalo Bill, Geronimo, and Sitting Bull. A fa-vorite subject was the American bison. Before Henry died in Chicago he requested that his ashes be buried with his brother in the Sulphur Creek burying ground.

Return to IND 56 and proceed through West Baden Springs to US 150 and turn left. Once more, cross Lost River, the water above ground this time. A mile farther is the **MARTIN COUNTY** (p. 11,001; 339 sq. m.) line straddled by an unincorporated spot named Roland. Martin County, formed in 1820 from Dubois and Daviess counties, is noteworthy for its natural splendor. Situated in the Crawford Upland, the most irregular landscape in the state, the county exhibits deep valleys, thick forests, and towering ridges often defined by great lengths of jutting sandstone precipices. A 1964 Indiana University study of the recreational potential of 43 southern Indiana counties noted that Martin County had the location and beauty to become one of the top scenic attractions of the Midwest. Martin is a relatively special Indiana county because no one seems to know how it got its name and because of its transient county seat. In a period of almost 60 years, the seat of justice changed sites nine times as localities repeatedly contended for the prize.

Continue northwest *6.5 m.* from the county line to IND 550 and proceed *5 m.* and turn left *.5 m.* to Hindostan Falls. This is the site of the once prosperous town of **HINDOSTAN**. Settled about 1818 and the first county seat, Hindostan also gave its name to, and served as the processing and shipping point for, the famous Orange County whetstones. In the 1820s a mysterious illness thought to be cholera wiped out the population of the town, never again to be inhabited. Picnic and camping facilities of the **Hindostan State Fish and Wildlife Area** now rest on the site of the once flourishing community. The falls will not be visible if the river is high.

Return to IND 550, turn right, and at *3 m.* turn left to the county seat of **SHOALS** (p. 967), named for its location beside a shallow place in the East Fork of the White River. Shoals received its official name almost 60 years after its settlement in 1815 when the post office changed its name to Shoals in 1868, and the town voted to follow suit four years later. Before 1868 the town was variously known as Dougherty's Shoals, Halbert's Bluff, Memphis, and Shoals Station. The actual courthouse is across the river in what is still referred to as West Shoals, formerly McCormickstown. West Shoals was absorbed into Shoals by annexation in 1902.

In the years between the World Wars, Shoals commanded a large portion of the button production industry. The mother-of-pearl linings from White River mussel shells went into the fasteners. Seven button factories existed in the Shoals area at one time. The better grade of the pearly irridescent substance went abroad for use in handles of knives, guns, and umbrellas. Fabius Gwin (1867-1947), local attorney, industrialist, and five-time state legislator, guided the Shoals button economy and helped establish the Pearl Button Company just prior to World War I. After some peak years in the 1920s and 1930s, the Shoals button industry declined due to the introduction of synthetic button material, elastics, zippers, and the going out of style of wearing long underwear.

Following closely the demise of the button business came the discovery at Shoals of one of the country's richest deposits of gypsum, an ingredient in building materials, particularly dry wall. Two giant companies, **National Gypsum** and **United States Gypsum**, launched rival operations near Shoals in 1955. *Business Week*'s reporting of the Shoals gypsum story in November 1954 helped focus national attention on the "Cinderella town." The potential economic windfall prompted newsman Walter Winchell to hyperbolize that "dwellings will be built solidly from Bedford to Loogootee." Today the Gold Bond Division of National Gypsum and the United States Gypsum plants continue, as they have for more than 30 years, to be major employers in the Shoals neighborhood, averaging about 200 employees each. They are the only two companies presently mining the "white gold" in the state.

National Gypsum's 515-ft. shaft at Shoals is the deepest gypsum mine in the nation. The company is located *2 m.* east of Shoals on US 50. The United States Gypsum Company, of which the Shoals organization is an integral part, dates from 1902 and is the world's largest gypsum producer. Its Shoals plant is *5 m.* east at the end of IND 650, which begins opposite the 6,132-acre Martin County State Forest.

The **Martin County Historical Museum** is located in a Gothic brick residence on the west side of High St. between 5th and 6th sts. Begun in 1966, the museum houses Martin County artifacts.

Directly to the right of the bridge under the sign reading "White River East Fork" is a

cornerstone from Martin County's first span across the river. The names of officials and contractors responsible for the construction in 1880 of the $6,000 bridge are inscribed on the original pier stone. The dedication of the stone took place in 1932 about the time the present bridge was erected.

After crossing the bridge into West Shoals, angle left onto Capitol St., and go four blocks to the **Martin County Courthouse** on the right. The two-story white brick structure dates from 1877. An 1871 courthouse on the same site burned in 1876, some say torched by spiteful residents of communities denied the county seat. Constructed at a cost of around $8,600, the rebuilt courthouse features 18-ft.-high ceilings, an iron-railed balcony off the second floor, and a unique circular stairway. The spiral iron staircase leads from the clerk's office to a courtroom. The jail, next door to the courthouse, was erected in 1878. In 1886 the Archer boys of French Lick were dragged from the jail by an angry mob and lynched from trees standing in front of the courthouse. The Archer brothers had tortured to death a farmer suspected of knowing the whereabouts of someone who had killed an Archer kinsman.

Return on Capitol St. to US 50/150, turn left, and at *.6 m.* pull off right onto a small graveled extension of the road's shoulder. From here the traveler can look down into a forested ravine which harbors the county's most remarkable natural wonder, **Jug Rock**. The almost 60-ft.-high sandstone curiosity appears to balance a huge flat stone on its crown. The name Jug Rock derived from its resemblance to a jug with the capstone representing the stopper. The vertical island of stone, which seems to have sprung upward from the earth, represents the core of an enormous cliff worn down from weathering and decay over thousands of years. In honor of the scenic marvel, sports teams of Shoals schools for years have borne the name the "Jug Rox."

Back on US 50/150, continue west *6.3 m.* to the city of **LOOGOOTEE**, pronounced La-GO-tee (p. 3,100). Thomas N. Gootee homesteaded the site in 1818 and platted the village in 1853. Fifty years later the town received city status, and it remains the only incorporated city in the county. The derivation of the name, Loogootee, remains unsolved. The "gootee" portion is self-explanatory, but the "Loo" has been attributed to Napoleon's Waterloo, to a

Mr. Lowe, a railroad official, to a Mr. DeLoo who surveyed the town tract, and to Lucinda, the wife of Thomas Gootee. The town persistently sought to acquire county seat recognition, and it was granted the distinction briefly in 1867. One of the state's oldest family businesses is still active in the city. The Larkin Brothers Department Store at the public square (actually the public "triangle") celebrated its centennial year in 1982. The large Home Outfitters Store nearby is also a Larkin enterprise, established in 1944. Signs on the outskirts of the relatively small municipality proudly denote that Loogootee had two state high school basketball finalist teams in the 1970s.

North of Loogootee on US 231 is **West Boggs Park**, jointly owned by Martin and Daviess counties. Opened in 1972, the park offers a 622-acre lake, campsites, picnic areas with shelter houses and playgrounds, a nine-hole golf course and a miniature golf course, tennis courts, exercise trail and health center, and a restaurant and snack bar. An old cemetery is located west of the lake.

Proceed *7.6 m.* north on US 231 to the Daviess County line (for a description of the county see Tour 8). Continue *5.6 m.* farther to the IND 558 turnoff on the right indicating *1 m.* to the **Crane Naval Weapons Support Center** and the town of **CRANE** (p. 297) across the county line in Martin County. The huge installation sits on 62,466 acres, a 98-sq.-m. area that takes up nearly the northern third of Martin County and a small section of southern Greene County. The depot for handling, producing, and storing conventional war materials for the Atlantic Fleet was commissioned on December 1, 1941, six days before the attack on Pearl Harbor. The Martin County spot offered isolation and distance from the more vulnerable East Coast. The government already owned more than half of the land, having obtained it as a park and wildlife refuge in the 1930s. The 800-acre man-made Lake Greenwood promised an adequate water supply. The remainder of the land needed was submarginal and could be reasonably purchased, though the government probably did not anticipate some owners' protests over the purchase price. During World War II nearly 10,000 civilian and naval workers supplied the Atlantic Fleet with bombs, rounds of ammunition, flares, and depth charges.

The center supplied the major portion of bombs dropped in Vietnam. In the last 30 years the center has inaugurated a variety of scientific, engineering, and technological programs, including missile research. The center is named for William Montgomery Crane (1784-1846), who was the first chief of the Bureau of Ordnance of the Navy in 1842. Crane committed suicide four years later, presumably despondent over an incident that occurred several years before. In 1844 Crane had refused to attend a test of a new gun, the "Peacemaker," aboard the ship *Princeton* because he was dissatisfied with the weapon. On board, the gun exploded, killing the secretary of state, the secretary of the navy, and several others. Crane held himself somehow responsible for the mishap.

US 231 enters Greene County *.5 m.* farther (for a description of the county see Tour 9). North *8 m.* on US 231 (this road bears to the left *.9 m.* past the county line) is the county seat of **BLOOMFIELD** (p. 2,705), located on a relatively high and well-watered plateau wedged between White River and Richland Creek. Bloomfield's healthy environment prompted county officials in 1824 to transfer their headquarters here from the practically waterless Burlington, the first county seat. Peter Cornelius Van Slyke, Sr., a pioneer of Dutch ancestry and a local distiller, guaranteed the selection of Bloomfield as the new center of county government by donating 62 of his hundreds of acres for its placement. Dr. Hallet B. Dean, a native of Bloomfield, New York, suggested the name for the community. Bloomfield remains a farm trading center with a diversity of small manufacturers, but a large portion of the residents work outside the town in coal fields, at Crane Naval Center, in Bloomington, or in Linton. It is the ninth smallest town in the nation to have a daily newspaper, the *Evening World*. Bloomfield citizens laud their girls' high school basketball team, which finished its 1976 and 1977 schedules among the state's finalists.

The **Greene County Courthouse** on the square cost $60,000 to construct in 1886. George W. Bunting, the architect, belonged to the same family firm that designed Owen and Wylie halls on the Indiana University campus (see Bloomington Attractions). The three-story brick and stone structure underwent extensive interior and clock tower remodeling in 1954-55. When the former courthouse was torn down in 1886, Col. Aden G. Cavins, Civil War veteran and Bloomfield attorney, bought the hex-

agonal cupola for his daughter to use as a playhouse. The slate green-roofed, white tower can be seen in the side yard of Bloomfield's oldest home at 412 S. Seminary St.

Across the street from the Cavins mansion at 340 S. Seminary St. is the former home of Bloomfield's most famous citizen, **Don Herold** (1889-1966). Herold, a celebrated American humorist, published 15 books, including *There Ought to Be a Law* (1926) and *Strange Bedfellows* (1930). A graduate of Indiana University, Herold accepted the presidency of the University's Alumni Association in 1943. He drolly proposed as one of his policy planks the establishment of a Chair of Levity.

Several miles northeast of Bloomfield stands the **Indiana Railroad, formerly Illinois Central Gulf Railroad, trestle**, the state's highest trestle. Constructed in 1905-6 by Italian immigrant labor, the 2,295-ft.-long steel marvel rises at one point 157 ft. above Richland Creek valley. Its 18 spiderweb columns rest on steel reinforced concrete pedestals 8 ft. sq. at the base and 4 ft. sq. at the top. The entire cost was around $1.5 million, including the laying of 167,000 board ft. of pine lumber for a deck. The raising of the bridge created much local excitement as it was rumored that its construction would average one accidental death daily. Fortunately, no fatal accidents occurred during the dangerous project. Despite its size, the bridge is difficult to find without explicit directions. The following course is one of several to the site. Leave Bloomfield on IND 157 north. Go *3.2 m.* to CR 325N and turn right for *1 m.* Drive through a railroad underpass and past the Tulip Church of God on the right. Continue on this country road for another mile and bear right at the sign of the Beechwood Lake Baptist Youth Camp. There is another railroad overpass *.6 m.* farther. On the left within *.5 m.* is a white frame Wesleyan church. One mile from the church turn right onto CR 480E *.5 m.* to the base of the bridge.

Return to IND 157 and proceed north *5.7 m.* to **WORTHINGTON** (p. 1,574), situated west of the Eel and White rivers junction. The proposed linking of the Wabash and Erie Canal with a projected "Central Canal" from Indianapolis accounts largely for the genesis of Worthington. Before the settlement of Worthington, a sizable village lay on the east side of the river intersection. The Allison brothers, J. M. H. and John Fletcher, from Spencer, Indiana, speculated on the intersecting point of the canals and laid out the hamlet of Point Commerce in 1836. The Allisons' merchandise store and produce shipping business stimulated the town's growth. John F. Allison served in the state legislature in the 1840s. After 1849 the extension of the canal on the west side of the river, the prior founding of Worthington, and business misfortunes of the Allisons caused Point Commerce to dwindle and Worthington to develop rapidly. The town was named for a city in Ohio.

Enter Worthington on IND 157 and turn right onto IND 67. Note the old storeside advertisement for the **Why** clothing store on E. Union St. left off IND 67 in Worthington. Early postcards of the town show that it once had two clothing stores named the "Why" and the "When." The origins of the names are obscure, but most likely the appellations were attempts to capitalize on the success of Indianapolis's When store, established in 1875. John Brush, the owner of the capital city store, employed some slick advertising prior to the store's opening to arouse the curiosity of potential customers. He placed in newspapers large black squares containing the word "Where," or "What," or "When," most frequently the last term. After he disclosed the nature of his firm, people refused to call the store anything but "that When Store."

The Worthington area once claimed the nation's largest deciduous tree, **the Big Sycamore**. The sycamore stood 150 ft. high, had a 100-ft. spread, and measured at its base 43 ft., 3 in. in girth. The trunk divided into two sections each around 6 ft. in diameter. The tree became a tourist attraction after its picture was released on postcards after 1911. Eventually, wind and lightning destroyed it. A 20-ft. segment of a branch was saved and installed on a concrete base in Worthington's city park. To get to the park, take Main St. west four blocks and turn right onto Dayton St., which leads to the surviving portion of the tree to the right.

From Worthington, take IND 67 north. After crossing Eel River take the first road right (CR 710N). The road ends abruptly. Turn left and take the next road right to a dead end and go left. The two-story red brick house on the right was built by **J. M. H. Allison**, a founder of Point Commerce.

After rejoining IND 67 proceed north *4 m.* to a right turnoff onto CR 990N. East *2 m.* on

the gravel county road is the unusual sight of a ferryboat. **Farmers Ferry** is county-owned and free to the public but is mostly used to transport farmers and their equipment to and fro across White River. A ferryboat has been operating in these parts since the 1870s. The present ferry negotiates the channel with the aid of a small engine and two guy lines attached by pulleys to an aerial cable which supports and guides the boat. (Operation of the ferry ceased in June 1989.)

The **OWEN COUNTY** (p. 15,841; 386 sq. m.) line on IND 67 is *.1 m.* from the Farmers Ferry turnoff. "Sweet Owen"—so-called by a former congressman elected on the strength of the Owen County vote—typifies many southwestern and south central Indiana counties: it is scenic, forested, sparsely populated, and agricultural. In 1976 roughly 90 percent of the county was about evenly divided between the farm and the timber. Developed land represents only about 1.5 percent. Owen is one of 10 state counties that registers zero percent urban. Its population density per square mile is the eighth lowest of Indiana's 92 counties. The first white settlers in the county arrived in 1816, two years before the county was created from Daviess and Sullivan counties. Its name honors a fallen hero of the 1811 Battle of Tippecanoe, Abraham Owen, a veteran Kentucky militiaman.

Northeast *4 m.* into Owen County, the road goes through the once prosperous hamlet of **FREEDOM**, located on the west bank of the White River. Platted in 1834 and named for its Quaker founder Joseph Freeland, the community languished after the flatboats left the river, the passenger trains no longer stopped, and local trade found better markets elsewhere.

Past Freedom *8.5 m.* is **SPENCER** (p. 2,732), the county seat. The Spencer site was the second choice for the seat of justice. The initial selection of land straddled White River east of Spencer. For some unknown reason the provider of the acreage backed out, and the Board of Commissioners opted for the present location in 1820. Spencer is named for Capt. Spier Spencer who, like his fellow Kentuckian, Major Owen, died in the Tippecanoe battle. Incorporation took place in 1866, and the completion of the Indianapolis and Vincennes Railroad to Spencer two years later accelerated the town's growth.

The present limestone **Owen County Courthouse**, with its green clock-dome, cost $106,000 to construct in 1909-11. Jesse Townsend Johnson, the architect, drew plans for several hundred school, fraternal, and religious buildings in Indiana. After World War I Johnson helped redesign Arlington National Cemetery to include the Tomb of the Unknown Soldier. In 1953 Lieutenant Colonel Johnson received full military honors at his burial in Arlington Cemetery. A jug of whiskey found in the foundation of the old courthouse upon its being razed in 1910, along with a statement of its being deposited there in the 1820s, turned out to be a mischievous act of deception. The whiskey, as correctly reported by the *Saturday Evening Post*, had been sneaked into the courthouse ruins only a few days before its discovery.

On the south side of the courthouse square each Saturday from November into February a large fur bartering market operates as it has done for over a century. From throughout the Midwest, trappers gather to hawk their pelts from truck bed, car top, or trunk.

The famous **Spirit of the American Doughboy** statue, on the courthouse lawn, is the work of Spencer native Ernest Moore "Dick" Viquesney (1876-1946). The son and grandson of expert marble and stonecutters (his grandfather cut some of the intricate detail on the nation's Capitol in the 1840s), Viquesney, a Spanish War veteran, at his death received credit for having designed more war-related statuary than any other American sculptor. One of his best nonwar pieces is Lincoln as a Hoosier Boy. His headstone in Spencer's Riverside Cemetery is a statue he created of his wife titled "**The Unveiling**." To get to the cemetery, go south on Main St. past the public square to Wayne St. Turn right for three blocks to the entrance. The Viquesney grave is toward the rear.

To the right of the Viquesney marker is the large three-tiered flat marble crypt of **Byron Bancroft Johnson** (1865-1931). "Ban" Johnson is remembered as the "father" of baseball's American League. He assumed control of the Western League baseball franchise, a minor league outfit, in 1893, and renamed it the American League in 1900. In 1903 the new league champions played the National League champions in an unofficial "World Series" which was won by the American League. After retiring in 1927, he and his wife purchased a residence in her hometown of Spencer.

Besides Viquesney and Johnson, a number of prominent people have called Spencer their home. Briefly mentioned here, with more to follow, are William Herschell (1873-1939), longtime staff member of the *Indianapolis News* and author of the poem "Ain't God Good to Indiana," among many others; William Vaughn Moody (1869-1910), best known for his play *The Great Divide*; and James H. "Babe" Pierce, a Freedom native and graduate of Spencer High School, who first starred as Tarzan in *Tarzan and the Golden Lion* in 1927, a movie produced by Joseph P. Kennedy, father of the late president. Pierce married Joan Burroughs, daughter of the creator of Tarzan, Edgar Rice Burroughs. Another Spencerite in motion pictures was Fred Burton (1871-1957), who appeared in a number of early films including Douglas Fairbanks's *Ruggles of Red Gap* and *Daddy Long Legs* with Mary Pickford. Hickam Field, Hawaii, prime target of the Japanese attack on Pearl Harbor, honors Lt. Col. Horace M. Hickam, a Spencer native.

Among the several interesting enterprises that located in Spencer, one, the **World Products Company**, became a leader in the carded merchandise field. H. B. Laymon launched his business in 1922 by distributing to roadside stands quantities of aspirin in envelopes or attached to cardboard. Once the largest industry in Spencer, the company later developed carded cosmetics and hundreds of other personal items such as chocolate laxatives, cold tablets, razor blades, and dental cream. Laymon also was a national leader in the production of purebred Berkshire hogs on his thousand plus acres near Spencer and from 1945 through 1948 led the nation in output. He originated the idea of selling livestock by mail and ranked first in the country in this type of merchandising in the 1940s.

Another large employer in this century was the **Spencer Wood Products Company**, which began in 1928 exclusively to manufacture wooden clothespins. The plentiful beech, gum, and sycamore trees in the area supplied the raw material for the millions of clothespins shipped throughout the nation. The Ku Klux Klan bought the factory rejects to clasp handbills, thus facilitating their being thrown on front porches. This technique was later appropriated by politicians and printing firms.

A block west of the courthouse on the southwest corner of the intersection of Franklin and Montgomery sts. stands the historic **John C. Robinson house**, now the home of the Spencer-Owen Civic League. Built before 1850, the two-story frame structure bears a remarkable resemblance to the Lincoln home in Springfield, Illinois, even to its location on an elevated corner lot with stone footings. The Civic League leased the house in 1970 and restored it for use as a community center. The Civic Center provides tourist information and features a county museum, art works for sale, art and craft displays, and meeting rooms.

Across the street from the Robinson house is the Owen County State Bank in which is located the **Owen County Hall of Fame**. The museum contains written and pictorial memorabilia relating to the lives of notable Owen countians.

Just across the tracks, north of the Civic Center, is the **girlhood home of Helen Artie Belles**, mother of the former British Prime Minister Harold Macmillan. Helen, known all her life as Nellie, was born in 1856, the daughter of Spencer physician J. Tarleton Belles. Nellie married first in 1874. After her husband's death six months later she left for Europe to study voice. In London she met Maurice Crawford Macmillan of the publishing firm of Macmillan and Sons. After their marriage they set up housekeeping in London. Harold Macmillan was born in London in 1894. Nellie died in 1937 and is buried beside her husband in Sussex. The prime minister made several nostalgic trips to Spencer in the 1950s and 1960s. He died in 1986.

Continue north on Montgomery St. until it dead-ends at Hillside Ave. Turn left to the 500 block. To the right and directly across from Beem St. is the hilltop **David J. Beem mansion**. Built in 1874, the stately brick home sits on a lofty plateau overlooking the town. Four porches gird the exterior, and high walnut doors open onto rooms with 14-ft.-high ceilings. A Civil War veteran, Captain Beem returned north to build a homestead reminiscent of the southern abodes he so much admired.

Go east on Hillside Ave., cross IND 67, and almost immediately bend left on a gravel road which becomes a driveway leading to the Second Empire-style **Calvin Fletcher estate**. The Fletcher mansion, called Ludlow Hall after the ancestral hometown in Vermont, probably was erected in the 1870s and features a stucco facade hiding thick brick walls. The scrambled interior architecture defies an accurate count of rooms. Published estimates range from 23 to 40. One of 11 children, Calvin Fletcher, Jr. (1826-1903), of Indianapolis, attended Brown University and became immersed in agricultural and horticultural activities. He built turnpikes and was instrumental in completing the Indianapolis and Vincennes Railroad, whereby he became familiar with the Spencer area. He moved from Indianapolis to Spencer in 1869, purchased increasing amounts of land, built his imposing residence, and spearheaded the development of the town. Among his various accomplishments were his tenure as Indiana Fish Commissioner and his dominant part in platting the city of Pasadena, California, which originally was called Indiana Colony. In 1890 Fletcher attempted unsuccessfully to transform his estate into a sanitarium after he discovered mineral water on his property (mineral springs had been actively used in Spencer since the 1870s, and a large sanitarium stood at the north end of Main St.)

In 1900 Fletcher sold his estate to E. Chubb Fuller, publisher since 1881 of the Indianapolis-based farm magazine, the *Agricultural Epitomist*. Fuller turned the house into a publishing plant for his periodical and started an experimental farm on the grounds. After Fuller's death a few years later, the printing operation was moved into Spencer on S. Main St. where the *Epitomist*, later changed to *Farm Life*, continued to be published until 1929. Subsequent journals published in Spencer included the *Breeder's Gazette*, the foremost livestock publication of its day, and various Farm Bureau serials.

Margaret Weymouth Jackson (1895-1974), a Hoosier author, lived in Spencer from age 19 and served as assistant editor of *Farm Life* in 1916 and as women's editor in 1918, her father being the editor. Mrs. Jackson went on to write a half dozen novels, including *Jenny Fowler* (1930) and *First Fiddle* (1932), and to contribute hundreds of feature articles and short stories to practically every popular woman's magazine. She, like so many others in the Spencer area, found employment with the printing firm which once ranked as the largest employer in the county. The Mid-land Press closed its doors in 1973.

In 1915 the Fletcher home and land were purchased by Spencerite Ephraim T. Barnes, the "Dahlia King," an international figure in horticulture whose National Cooperative Show Gardens in Spencer attracted visitors from all over the world. Barnes brought a kaleidoscope of blossoming color to the green terrain, including a multitude of dahlia varieties. Following his death in 1933, the old mansion passed through several hands and functioned for some time as a nursing home. It was sold again in the late 1970s.

Return to the junction of IND 67 and IND 46. Take IND 46 east *1.8 m.* to **McCormick's Creek State Park**. The park is the state's oldest, purchased in the centennial year 1916 for $5,250, a portion of which was contributed by county residents. The rugged woodland, featuring a mile-long, 100-ft.-deep canyon, once offered visitors a sanitarium where the comfortable Canyon Inn now stands, and furnished a view of the quarry from which came the foundation stone for the statehouse in Indianapolis. It is named for the McCormick family who registered the land in 1816. Today, the modernized park provides the usual array of natural attractions and recreational facilities including camp and picnic grounds, family cabins, hiking trails, saddle trails, surrey rides, and a swimming pool. Reasonable food and lodging can be had in Canyon Inn.

Back at IND 67, bear north about *10 m.* to **GOSPORT** (p. 729). Before entering Gosport continue north on IND 67 about *.3 m.* To the left of the highway are two markers. One, a bas-relief limestone slab, depicts the Fort Wayne treaty negotiations of 1809 between William Henry Harrison and Chief Little Turtle. By the treaty's terms, the United States acquired approximately 2,900,000 acres of Indian land at a cost of approximately three cents an acre. A new boundary line, which separated government and Indian properties, runs diagonally from Parke County to Jackson County. It is referred to as the 10 o'clock line because, as legend has it, the line parallels the shadow cast by spears or stakes stuck in the ground at 10:00 A.M. on September 20, 1809. The **10 O'Clock Line Monument**, sculpted by Spencer artist Frederick L. Hollis, was dedicated in 1957. Gosport is the only Indiana town situated directly on the 10 o'clock line. Next to the 10 o'clock monument is a marker indicating the nearby **site of Camp Hughes**, a training camp for the 59th Indiana Volunteer Infantry in 1861-62.

Take 7th St., across from the 10 O'Clock Monument, into downtown Gosport, named for Ephraim and Abner Goss, who laid out the town in 1829. Once a picture of brisk economic life outlined with flatboats, mills, railroads, and livestock, Gosport, like so many small river towns, has dwindled in this century, but its citizens' acute sense of history has not. During its sesquicentennial celebration in 1979, Gosport visitors could take in at least 35 points of interest. Tragically, fires in past years consumed prominent landmarks, including a covered bridge in 1955 and Hezekiah Wampler's imposing Victorian residence in 1968. Also, the Monon passenger and freight station, a rare example of a through-station or "train barn," with tracks passing through the length of the building, was torn down in 1976, despite its *NRHP* status. The destruction of the bridge erased a vital commercial link between Gosport and neighboring Monroe County, and it proved costly to both parties in business closings and population loss. In 1971 an attempt to restore the connection with a secondhand ferryboat proved financially impossible. Owen and Monroe County officials, with urging from citizen groups, began serious discussions in 1977 about a new bridge.

Hezekiah Wampler, wealthy pioneer pork packer, built his massive brick mansion in 1856, convinced it would withstand the fires that had ravaged two previous frame houses. Later used as a funeral home, the 1968 fire so gutted the home it had to be razed.

Historical artifacts of the area are on display in the **Gosport Museum** located in the basement of the Owen County State Bank, at the corner of 4th and Main sts.

An unusual sight is the **Chivalry Trough**, an approximately 8 x 4-ft. concrete receptacle, fed by a spring. As part of the rites of marriage in bygone days, grooms anxiously anticipated a late night dunking in its shivering waters. To see the trough, take Main St. west to 5th St., turn right and go one block to E. North St., turn right again and descend about four blocks until the road fronts on the right the rusted relics of the old Brewer Flour Mill. Next to the road, sometimes hidden by overgrowth, is the trough. About 150 ft. ahead is a railroad viaduct. Beyond the underpass and right are the **sites of the previously mentioned Monon Station and covered bridge**.

On leaving Gosport, take S. 5th St. to its dead end at Goss St., jog right, and enter Monroe County. The road winds along a White River bluff about *4.7 m.* to the town of **STINESVILLE** (p. 227), once a major center of Indiana limestone production. Eusebius Stine laid out the site in 1855. Almost 30 years before (1827), Richard Gilbert opened the first Indiana quarry of record just south of town. The first steam sawing plant in the Indiana stone area was constructed near Stinesville in 1855. Much of the stone used in the Soldiers and Sailors Monument in Indianapolis came from local quarries. The prosperity enjoyed during and after the 1880s began to decline when a 1916 fire destroyed the giant Hoadley stone mill. Soon the demand for limestone faded. The consolidation of the high school into a school at a considerable distance from the town capped its demise.

From Stinesville, take the road crossing the railroad tracks at the south end of town (Stinesville Rd.) *3.4 m.* to IND 46. Go east on IND 46 *2.5 m.* to **ELLETTSVILLE** (p. 3,328). When founded in 1837, the villagers wanted to name it Richland, after the township, but opted to honor local businessman Edward Ellett after being informed that another Indiana post office had preempted the name. Unlike neighboring Stinesville or Gosport, Ellettsville has grown considerably in the last several decades due largely to the expansion of nearby Bloomington, to which most Ellettsville residents commute. Since 1960 the Ellettsville population has nearly tripled. Initially, the community grew slowly until Englishman John Matthews established the first limestone industry in the area in 1862. Matthews, as an apprentice, previously had helped build London's Parliament houses. His wife, a direct descendant of the renowned sailor Sir Francis Drake, reportedly served in the court of Queen Victoria. The

Matthews mansion, dating from about 1870, was the first stone home erected in the county by the Matthews Brothers Stone Company. The two-story, 12-room, French mansard house features the carved faces of four of the Matthews' children above the arched double doored entrance. The house is located north of town. Take Matthews Dr. off IND 46 (Temperance St.) to Mount Tabor and Maple Grove roads and turn right to the first house on the right. The Matthews Brothers Stone Company, situated on Mount Tabor Rd., remained in business more than 125 years until sold in 1979 to the Bybee Stone Company.

Rachel Peden (1901-1975), Hoosier author and columnist, lived northeast of Ellettsville on Maple Grove Rd. Once women's editor for Spencer's *Farm Life* magazine, she later wrote the familiar column "The Hoosier Farm Wife Says" for the *Indianapolis Star*. A spokesperson for the glories of farm living, she penned three books: *Rural Free* (1961), *The Land, The People* (1966), and *Speak to the Earth* (1974).

Leaving Ellettsville east on IND 46, the traveler soon crosses **Jack's Defeat Creek**, so named many years ago, as the stories go, because some horses of a certain Jack Storm became stuck in the creek's mud bottom, because his horses drowned in the swift current, or because a Frenchman, Jacques DeFitt, claimed land in the area.

Continue east on IND 46 to Maple Grove Rd. on the left (*3.2 m.* from the traffic signal on IND 46 at Ellettsville). Take Maple Grove Rd., which immediately curves back west, *.2 m.* to one of the oldest existing houses in the state, the **Daniel Stout house**. Built in 1828, the Federal-style stone house has 22-in. walls. (*NRHP/HABS*)

From the Stout house continue *.7 m.* southeast on IND 46 to the intersection with IND 37 in Bloomington.

Columbus

Columbus (p. 30,614), world renowned as a showcase of contemporary architecture, is the seat of **BARTHOLOMEW COUNTY** (p. 65,088; 409 sq. m.), which was created in 1821 from a section of what had been Delaware County. It was named for Gen. Joseph Bartholomew, one of the county's organizers and a hero at the Battle of Tippecanoe. Its area is rectangular except for a small section removed from the southeastern border with Jennings County. Bartholomew County is bounded by Johnson and Shelby counties to the north, Decatur and Jennings to the east, Jennings and Jackson to the south, and Brown and Jackson to the west. Principal industries are farming and manufacturing. Topographically, the area is basically level with the exception of the hilly west section near the Brown County line and the rolling valleys in the eastern area.

Columbus is situated on rich bottomlands of the East Fork of the White River at the southern tip of the Hawpatch plateau, a flat fertile plain stretching 12 miles northeasterly to Shelby County. Columbus lies approximately 45 miles south of Indianapolis, 80 miles west of Cincinnati, and 70 miles north of Louisville. Positioned within this triangular marketing area, the "Athens of the Prairie" has been the industrial hub of a predominantly agricultural area since the mid-19th century.

John Tipton (1786-1839), a conspicuous figure in the military, economic, and political circles of pioneer Indiana, played a key role in the establishment of Bartholomew County and Columbus. While a state legislator in 1820 and a member of a commission to choose a site for a new state capital, Tipton, with his colleague Senator Joseph Bartholomew, inspected the Hawpatch vicinity. Impressed with what he saw, Tipton purchased several hundred acres. The lawmaker's acquisition came less than two years after the Treaty of St. Marys opened central Indiana to permanent white settlement, and just a year after the arrival of the future county's first settler, Joseph Cox. Tipton was instrumental, as an assemblyman, in determining the boundaries of Bartholomew County. In 1822 Luke Bonesteel and Tipton conveyed 30 acres each to the county in consideration of the selection of their property for the county seat. It has never been determined whether Tipton sold or donated his land. In any case, his political opponents accused him of selfishly engineering the whole affair. Tipton's detractors may have had a hand in having the name of the town changed almost immediately from Tiptona to Columbus. Rebuffed, Tipton left Columbus and his log house on Mount Tipton, the most commanding rise in the local landscape, and rarely visited the town thereafter.

The year 1821 was a banner one for Columbus. It was laid out and given broad streets and alleys. Its 75 x 150-ft. lots sold for between $11 and $211. The public square received a partial clearing, and a two-story log jail went up on the southeast corner. Methodists, Baptists, and Presbyterians organized local congregations. A post office was established. At least three taverns and one general store were in operation. John Lindsey piloted a licensed ferry on Driftwood River. Luke Bonesteel was paid $50 for the use of his log cabin as a temporary county courthouse. The first county-built courthouse was occupied in 1828.

Settlers, mostly from Kentucky, Virginia, and the Carolinas, found a burgeoning little village in the 1820s, but also conditions that made for discouragingly slow growth. The largely swampy and malaria-infested environs invited dreaded frontier diseases. The bottomlands were susceptible to frequent flooding. Periodic financial panics and the general want of stable banking institutions bred uncertainty and errant business transactions. The pioneer family had to overcome these obstacles, plus hack out a homeplace amidst the timber, brush, and briers, and fight off wolves, wild hogs, and grain-devouring squirrels, crows, and pigeons.

For a number of reasons, however, the young settlement not only survived but prospered. The fertile low-lying lands brought forth a bounty of crops. After 1835 a variety of mills went up in the vicinity of present-day Mill Run Park to process the yield. The agricultural surplus contributed to Columbus becoming a regional farm center. In like manner, the demand for the products of a number of nascent domestic industries created considerable traffic in farm and household staples. Flatboatmen found Columbus, conveniently situated on waterways, a source of ready commodities for southern markets. New roads also expedited the delivery of articles. Packhorses gave way to wagons, and teamsters profited. Little wonder that wagon companies resisted the introduction of competitive railroads, yet the latter figured significantly in the community's evolution. The announcement from the state capital in 1836 that a massive internal improvements bill provided funds for a railroad through Columbus excited civic pride and influenced the public to approve in 1837 an ordinance to incorporate the town. Indiana's improvements measure eventually bankrupted the state, but Columbus gained its rail connection. The railway age overtook Columbus one torrid day in July 1844 when a small passenger train from Madison arrived to the cheers of more than 1,000 onlookers.

By virtue of the coming of the railroad, Columbus's prospects brightened considerably. Beginning in 1848 additions were added to the original plat. More railroads followed. The Jeffersonville Railroad reached Columbus in 1852, and the Columbus and Shelby Railroad showed up the next year. The town established a public school system in the 1850s, upgraded its fire-fighting equipment, and witnessed the erection of the area's first steam mill. In 1864 the citizens approved a city charter and elected Smith Jones the first mayor. At the close of the Civil War townspeople could boast of 25 general stores, 17 saloons, 2 breweries, 14 attorneys, 9 physicians, and a 48-acre landscape nursery. The population of the city between 1850 and 1870 more than tripled, from 1,008 to 3,359.

The 1870s began well enough. Gas lights now illuminated the city, a new waterworks promised better fire protection, and a new courthouse was being built. But the city's largest bank, McEwen and Sons, was in serious trouble. It went bankrupt in 1871 and threw the town into near economic collapse. Only a cooperative effort by citizens to prop up their businesses and the establishment of stable financial institutions helped the city withstand the more severe consequences of this bank failure and the subsequent nationwide panic of 1873. In the aftermath, other forms of affliction, such as rate discrimination practiced by the monopolistic Pennsylvania Railroad, confounded recovery efforts.

As in the past, however, talk of a new rail line quickened the local pulse. By the time the Columbus, Hope and Greensburg Railroad, a branch of the Big Four, reached Columbus in 1884 a full-scale boom was under way. A good portion of the doubling of the city's population between 1870 and 1890 can be attributed to the rumors and the materialization of the C, H and G. The rail mania extended to local travel in 1890 with the inception of a mule-pulled streetcar line. Electric cars, 24 ft. long and luxuriously furnished, were placed in operation in 1893. Also partially responsible for the sudden expansion was the development of several industries. Cerealine, Columbus's major contribution to the world's breakfast foods, reached grocery shelves in 1884. In addition, the Reeves family, which had brought its Hoosier Boy Corn Plow company from Knightstown to Columbus in 1875, formed two successful companies in 1888, Reeves and Company and Reeves Pulley Company. M. O. Reeves, a director of the family's businesses, became famous for his inventions. In 1896 he designed an early horseless carriage called the Motocycle, followed the next year by a 19-passenger bus. Built to replace the stage coach in North Dakota, the bus was too wide for the Dakota roads. Reeves also fabricated the six-wheeled Sexto-Auto and the unmarketable eight-wheeled Octoauto. Another industry, the American Starch Works, incorporated in 1880, expanded in 1885, and soon became one of the country's largest processors of cornstarch.

Columbus's thrust of enterprise in the 1880s, undergirded by railroad and factory growth, was relatively short-lived. The national depression in the mid-1890s visited severe unemployment upon Columbus. The city administration began a small public works program but confronted difficulties when the supervisor hired only laborers of his own political persuasion. Another serious blow to the local economy occurred in 1895 with the burning of the Starch Works. The plant was not rebuilt despite pleas from the city fathers.

Columbus advanced at a snail's pace between 1900 and 1920. On the surface the city seemed the embodiment of progress with its diversity of industry, new business blocks, and beautiful residential areas. Its factories produced farm implements, split wood pulleys, dressed leather, tool handles, furniture, work shirts, barrelheads, buggies, canned foods, processed flour, bricks, and lumber. By 1908 interurbans connected Columbus with Indianapolis and Louisville. In fact the first interurban line to enter Indianapolis was owned by Columbus's leading dry goods merchant and banker, Joseph I. Irwin. Establishing a police department in 1910, building in 1917 the state's first county hospital, and motorizing the fire department in 1918 certainly enhanced the community's sense of well-being. For all of these gains Columbus derived little in the way of population growth. In 20 years time the count increased by only 860 persons. Columbus Township grew at a slightly faster pace, an indication of the presence of East Columbus, across Haw Creek. Still the overall growth was negligible due in part to the rush of new manufacturing to Indianapolis and northern Indiana, to a conservative business leadership reluctant to take chances on new technologies or industries, to the failure to keep up, particularly in milling operations, with the modernization of agriculture, and to the lack of ties with automobile makers.

Conditions improved only slightly in the years between the two world wars. The 1920s witnessed the loss of the Lincoln Chair, Orinoco, and Glanton furniture factories, thus ending Columbus's reputation as a center for fine furniture craftsmanship. The decade's business, good or bad, was linked to the frequent changes in the fortunes of farming. Agriculture and a balanced industrial mix served the city well, however, during the depression years of the 1930s. The harsher economic and social realities attending hard times bypassed Columbus. Nevertheless, work projects were needed. By December 1933 at least 500 men in the city and county were employed, reportedly at no federal expense, at such jobs as cleaning and repairing city sewers and streets, constructing a new grandstand at the high school, planting trees in parks, painting public buildings, and fixing up the airport. The programs began phasing out by 1936, and the task of helping the needy largely fell to the newly organized Bartholomew County Welfare Department.

The most encouraging development in the local economy during this 20-year period was the establishment of Cummins Engine Company, Arvin Industries, and Cosco, Inc. The Cummins Engine Company was formed in 1919 by Clessie L. Cummins, a wizard at mechanics and a chauffeur in the Irwin household. With the financial support of William Irwin, Cummins engineered the modern diesel engine and laid the foundation for what would become, and what still is, Columbus's largest employer. Arvin Industries began as a tire pump manufacturer in Indianapolis in 1919. The Indianapolis Air Pump Company began operating in Columbus in 1925. Two years later the firm took the name Noblitt-Sparks Industries, Inc., named for two of the founders, Quintin G. Noblitt and Frank H. Sparks, who went on to become president of Wabash College. In 1931 the company's headquarters moved from Indianapolis to Columbus. In the early days of the business Noblitt and Sparks built a car heater for a Richard Arvin. The heater became popularly known as the Arvin heater, and the Arvin name was applied to a succession of articles. The trade name Arvin Industries, Inc., was formalized in 1950. Over the years the company added to its lines a variety of automotive parts, home entertainment items, and consumer products and expanded its manufacturing facilities to other states and overseas. Presently, Arvin, with Cummins, represents Columbus in the *Fortune* 500. The city's second largest employer, Cosco, Inc., has its roots in the Columbus Specialty Company founded in 1935 by B. F. Hamilton and his three sons, Clarence, Bill, and Earl. The Hamiltons first produced tin matchbox holders, but shifted in the 1940s to making metal juvenile furniture and housewares. The brand name Cosco, a contraction of Columbus Specialty Company, was used after 1941, and in 1946 the company became the Hamilton Manufacturing Corporation. In 1959 the corporate name was changed to Hamilton Cosco, Inc. It became Cosco, Inc., in 1974.

This trio of companies, in due time to be known as the Big Three, would alter the industrial complexion of Columbus, in some ways negatively. The city would not be as industrially diversified as before. The connection of

Arvin and Cummins with car and truck makers tended to make these two giant companies, along with other durable goods manufacturers, especially vulnerable in future recessions. On the other hand, the evolving success of these companies worked upon the entire community, expanding overall employment, fattening payrolls, and stimulating the housing and general retail markets. Furthermore, the ensuing prosperity of the businesses gave them the wherewithal to contribute significantly to the cultural advance of the city.

Despite Columbus's industrial growth of the 1930s, to most observers the county seat remained a provincial village—a convenient rest stop between Indianapolis and Louisville. This perception would change considerably after 1940. The demands of war not only created new plants but forced existing ones to enlarge and expand production. Nearby, the military established Camp Atterbury, a 40,351-acre complex, and Atterbury (Bakalar) Air Base (now Columbus Municipal Airport). From these facilities came thousands of construction workers and members of uprooted farm families to perform duties in the proliferating factories. Meanwhile, personnel from the bases asked for and received from Columbus's retailers and officials more goods and services. The pace of growth scarcely missed a beat with war's end. By 1947, 62 plants were in operation with double the employment rate of 1940. The city's population went up to 18,370 in the 1940s, a jump of 57 percent. More than half of the increase was due to the much-disputed annexation of East Columbus, an inevitable action by Columbus given its growth and the fact that waterways and low marshy land prevented movement in any other direction. To try and bring some order out of this urban sprawl the Columbus Plan Commission was created in 1948 to formulate zoning ordinances and to prepare a comprehensive blueprint for city improvements.

One of the major tasks confronting the Plan Commission and subsequent organizations was the structurally and financially deteriorating downtown. The pressing need for housing, both domestic and business, brought into sharp focus the plight of the city's core. Wedged against the White River, the circumscribed business section, with little growth potential, prompted landlords to lose interest in or vacate their properties, thus accelerating the urban blight. Large shopping centers began being built in 1956 in the northeast suburbs, drawing retail business from the downtown. To combat this, the Columbus Redevelopment Commission was established in 1959 with federal funds. The commission announced plans in 1967 for a $5.5 million renewal project involving one-fourth of central Columbus. Fifty-three acres at the southwest corner of the business district, traditionally called shack town, was acquired and transformed into a park. The project included the relocation of railroad tracks, the making of new streets offering smoother access to the downtown, the restoration of Victorian store fronts, historical buildings, and homes, and the building of a "super block" (the Commons) of shopping and cultural facilities in an enclosed mall, which was completed in 1973.

The construction in 1942 of the First Christian Church, designed by Eliel Saarinen, hinted at another cornerstone of Columbus's soon-to-be renaissance. The Cummins Engine Foundation, through its board chairman J. Irwin Miller, offered to pay architectural fees for much-needed school buildings, providing that distinguished architects be chosen as designers. Beginning in 1957, 11 schools and a number of other buildings have been realized on the basis of this formula. Miller, whom *Time* called "the Medici of the Middle West," and the first layman to head the National Council of Churches, viewed his company's efforts as a way to provide the kind of environment that would attract bright, young, cosmopolitan executives to Cummins. Other companies and civic groups followed Miller's lead so that at present Columbus offers more than 50 examples of outstanding contemporary architecture, an achievement exceeded only in New York City, Los Angeles, and Chicago. For his part in making this happen, Miller was inducted in 1986 into the National Building Museum Hall of Fame in Washington, D.C., as its first living member. Miller joined such notables as Frank Lloyd Wright and Pierre Charles L'Enfant. For three months the museum displayed photographs and 10 architectural models of Columbus's prized structures.

Following the completion of the "super block" in 1973, Columbus, with the rest of the country, was plunged into a recession. Calls went out for new thrusts at economic renewal. The Columbus Economic Development Board was formed in 1974, and within the next eight years 15 companies located in Columbus. More good news about Columbus's performance in the later 1970s surfaced in the early 1980s when a study revealed that during 1979 Bartholomew County had the largest average per person income in the state. In addition, the census figure for 1980 revealed Columbus to have made a substantial gain in population during the 1970s and now exceeded 30,000 residents. The 1980 figure was disappointing only in the sense that Columbus failed to reach the hoped for 35,000 level, which would have made it a second-class city.

In February 1981 Columbus welcomed home Ulric Haynes. Having just resigned his Algerian ambassadorship, Haynes was returning to work at Cummins Engine after assisting in the negotiations for the release of the 52 American hostages in Iran. The only thing that could have detracted from this happy occasion would have been the realization that Columbus was sliding deeper into the nationwide recession. The major companies had begun laying off workers in 1980. As Columbus prepared to welcome Haynes, break ground for an Ivy Tech comprehensive training facility at the airport, begin construction of Cummins world headquarters, and dedicate the new city hall, housing starts dropped to their lowest level in a decade. By April 1982 the county unemployment rate topped 16 percent. Still, through the exertions of the Economic Development Board of the Chamber of Commerce, new industries, several from foreign countries, came to Columbus during the recession years. Also, Indiana University-Purdue University at Indianapolis expanded its Columbus branch. The goal of repopulating the downtown resulted in the conversion to apartments of the second floors of buildings and in efforts to locate parking places for the new tenants.

In March 1983 NBC News began a five-part series on Columbus's recovery from the recession. In the previous month the major industries had begun to recall laid-off employees. By midyear the county registered its second highest level of building activity in its history. On the historic preservation front, the Columbus Historic District, bounded by the Conrail tracks, Chestnut, 3rd, Washington, and Franklin sts., was put on the National Register of Historic Places. Columbus once again turned to making the best of one of its greatest assets, its architecture, and to furthering its already sizable tourist trade. In the late 1980s the completion of St. Peter's Lutheran Church, along with a county jail plus Fire Station No. 5, the renovation of the Sparrell Block Building, the creative adaptation of the old city hall into the Columbus Inn, the planning for additions to Mill Race Park of an earthen amphitheater, expanded water system, and more historic bridges, and the beautifying of corridors into the city testify to Columbus's pledge to enhance its solid reputation in architectural and urban design circles.

With a population that is younger, wealthier, and more educated than that of any other city in the state, the demand is great for continued strides in historic restoration and superior architecture. Not all townspeople, however, have appreciated the new cityscape. Displaced property owners, those with more traditional building tastes, and those who imagine some sort of corporate control of city affairs are among the unconvinced. The detractors have ammunition when they point out the seeming frailty or the unanticipated deterioration of some of the newer buildings. Still, the fact remains that in Indiana, and far beyond, for the size of the town there is nothing quite like Columbus. Approaching almost a half century of engaging the services of major architects, Columbus now has become a significant material document on the trends in 20th-century architectural design.

Columbus Attractions

1. The tour starts at the **Visitors Center (Storey house)** located on the northeast corner of 5th and Franklin sts. The two-story brick, Italianate-style house was designed by James Perkinson of Columbus for local businessman John Vawter Storey around 1864. In 1973 Bruce Adams of Hamden, Connecticut, renovated the building by remodeling the interior to serve as a visitors center and constructing a back addition. The first floor is the home of the Columbus Chamber of Commerce and contains a room for a slide presentation on Columbus architecture, a gift shop, and a general information center. The second floor, called the Second Storey, houses the Columbus extension of the Indianapolis Museum of Art and offers temporary exhibits. The Visitors Center also offers a minibus tour of Columbus for a small charge. The sites described below make up only a portion of the city's architectural attractions.

2. The **Cleo Rogers Memorial Library** (Bartholomew County Public Library) adjoins the Visitors Center at 536 5th St. The building, constructed in 1969, was designed by Ieoh Ming Pei and Partners of New York City, and Kenneth D. B. Carruthers served as architect-in-charge. Named for Cleo Rogers, the head librarian of the old Columbus Public Library from 1936 to 1964, the structure is a brick pavilion with solid east and west walls. Distinguishing features of the library are its off center vestibuled main entrance, its deeply recessed windows, and its rear terrace. The skylight on the second floor allows for an area of trees and foliage and adds to the peacefulness of the interior. Architect I. M. Pei, a native of China who also designed the John F. Kennedy Library Complex in Boston, Massachusetts, implemented the idea of accessibility in a quiet and dignified environment when he chose the location for the building. A $2 million expansion completed in 1987 added an 11,700-sq.-ft. addition. Pei approved the design of James K. Paris of the Architect Group.

3. **Large Arch**, a sculpture by Englishman Henry Moore, stands on the brick and concrete plaza in front of the Cleo Rogers Memorial Library. The arch, a gift of Mr. and Mrs. J. Irwin Miller, was dedicated in 1971 along with the library to mark Columbus's sesquicentennial. I. M. Pei, the library architect, commissioned Moore to do the sculpture. Moore, who was 77 when the work was completed, used the concept of "primitive simplicity" to contrast with the geometrically designed modern library behind it. The arch is 20 ft. tall, 12 ft. wide, and weighs 5 1/2 tons. It was created at Moore's studio in Much Hadham, England, and sandcasted in bronze in 50 sections at the Herman Noack foundry in Hamburg, Germany, where it also was welded together with invisible seams. Moore designed Large Arch to resemble a human torso that could be walked through and around in the style of Stonehenge. The exterior of the arch has a green patina, which gives the bronze a naturally aged look. The library plaza serves as a site for many of the city's concerts and festivals.

4. Next door to the library on the east is the **Irwin home and gardens**. In 1910 Wendell Phillips of Boston, Massachusetts, designed the house for banker and industrialist William G. Irwin. This was the third house built on this site for the Irwin family, the first being constructed in 1864. The present home is covered with tapestry brick, and above each window is a stained-glass transom depicting the gods for the days of the week. The sunken gardens, also designed by Phillips, outshine the house somewhat. Irwin loved flowers and seldom was seen in public without a rose from his garden in his lapel. The garden's motif is Italian, and the garden house was modeled after the Casa degli Innamorati in Pompeii. The four heads carved on

Visitors Center, photographed by Balthazar Korab

the building's columns are the Greek philosophers Plato, Aristotle, Demosthenes, and Diogenes. In the center pool by the garden house is a bronze statue of a boy on a dolphin that was designed in Venice especially for the garden. The upper fountain is modeled after the Vatican Gardens, while the lower level of the garden is taken from a design by Palladio for the Gonzaga of Mantua. The design of the garden's rock wall coping was constructed of stone from the ruins of Pompeii, and the birdbath was cast in Florence by Luigi Romanelli. Only the English sundial and the Japanese large bronze elephant do not fit the garden's Italian design.

5. **Lincoln Elementary School**, built in 1967, is one-half block east of the Irwin home at 750 5th St. Architect Gunnar Birkerts of Birmingham, Michigan, designed the building with the philosophy that a "school is not a building . . . it is an activity . . . it begins at the sidewalk . . . it is an education area . . . designed to stimulate, challenge or arouse curiosity." The school sits on approximately two acres and is

actually two structures. The center is a free-standing multipurpose room constructed of birch walls and laminated wood beams and columns. The exterior building is made of brick and concrete. A 3-ft.-wide skylight joins the roofs of the two structures and allows natural light into the multipurpose room and the corridors separating the two buildings. A play area for the younger pupils lies between the school's exterior walls and the surrounding linden trees. The older children play in an area north of the school which is surrounded by grassy earthworks that separate the playground from the street. A plaque at the school's entrance commemorates a visit by First Lady Mrs. Lyndon B. Johnson on her "Crossroads U.S.A." tour in September 1967.

6. **St. Peter's Lutheran Church**, 719 5th St., is one of Columbus's newest architectural gems, dedicated in 1988. The brick and concrete structure features a conical roof and spire framed in aluminum and clad in copper. A golden sphere supports a golden cross atop the

spire. The sanctuary, lighted by an 18-ft.-diameter chandelier, has the capacity to seat 1,000 persons. The liturgical furniture, pews, and handrails are maple. Gunnar Birkerts was the architect.

7. The **First Christian Church** at 531 5th St. is one and one-quarter blocks west of Lincoln Elementary School and across from the Cleo Rogers Library. Constructed in 1942, it was the first of Columbus's contemporary buildings and one of the first churches in the United States to break with the traditional Gothic and Georgian styles. In 1937 two prominent church members, William G. Irwin and his sister Linnie I. Sweeney, who was also the wife of the pastor, donated the land for the new facility and through the persuasion of their nephew J. Irwin Miller obtained the services of architect Eliel Saarinen. The Finnish-born Saarinen was employed to design a new structure to replace the original Gothic-style First Christian Church built in 1878. Saarinen used limestone and brick in creating this simple, yet dignified, geometrically designed building complex that encompasses almost one block. The main building, which houses the sanctuary, is highlighted by a huge concrete cross above the entrance, which complements another large cross on the south wall of the chancel. The tapestry depicting the Sermon on the Mount, hanging behind the altar, was woven by Saarinen's wife, Loja, and is one of the largest religious tapestries ever made in the United States. A two-story, column-supported "bridge" links the main building with a three-story classroom to the southwest. The church is famous for its 166 ft. (18 story) freestanding bell tower which is a prominent feature in the Columbus skyline.

8. The **Columbus Inn**, 445 5th St., southwest corner of 5th and Franklin sts., is a luxury bed and breakfast hotel in the old City Hall. Charles F. Sparrell designed the brick and limestone neo-Romanesque structure, which opened in 1895. In addition to housing the city government, the building and its auditorium served as a police station, basketball court, ballroom, banquet hall, courtroom, market, and exhibit hall. After the new City Hall opened in May 1981, Cummins Engine Company occupied the old building until the completion of its new headquarters. Cummins then sought a developer to turn the structure into a first-class

inn. In 1985 the Cranston Development Company of Pittsburgh bought the building and put together a team of Pittsburgh firms, including Landmark Design Associates, Architects, to make the conversion. The $1.75 million renovation included total modernization while refurbishing the exterior and preserving the tin ceilings, ornate woodwork, and ornamental tile. The old second-floor auditorium, with its 19-ft.-high ceiling, was divided so that a third floor of guest rooms could be added. The 25,000-ft. facility contains 29 rooms and 5 suites with authentic and reproduction Victorian furnishings. Dining and meeting rooms are on the lower level. Construction was completed in December 1986. In 1988 it was named by *Inn Review* among the 10 best Bed and Breakfast Inns in the country. Also in 1988 it received the "Main Street America Award" for Indiana's best public building restoration. (*NRHP*)

9. A good example of a nicely restored office building is the **Irwin Block** at 422-426 5th St., one-half block west and across 5th St. from the old City Hall. Constructed around 1890 to house the bank offices of William G. Irwin, this Queen Anne-style frame structure is distinguished by its decorative oriels and stained-glass transoms. The building now serves as private offices.

10. The **Irwin Union Bank and Trust Company** can be found by walking one-half block west from the Irwin Block to the northwest corner of 5th and Washington sts. The structure was designed by Eero Saarinen, son of the architect Eliel and a 1930s Yale classmate of J. Irwin Miller, and was completed in 1954. This one-story, flat-roofed building with glass walls was a revolutionary design for a bank building. Traditionally banks were massive stone structures. The new style of bank was intended to present a modern, friendly, and open appearance as exemplified through the limited use of partitions and the elimination of teller cages. The cast-concrete roof of the bank is regularly interspersed with shallow domes which house the interior lights giving variety to the external appearance and to the ceiling height. In 1966 Dan Kiley of Charlotte, Vermont, was employed to complete the landscaping, which is considered part of the architecture. Kiley formed a square around the building through the use of linden

Columbus Attractions

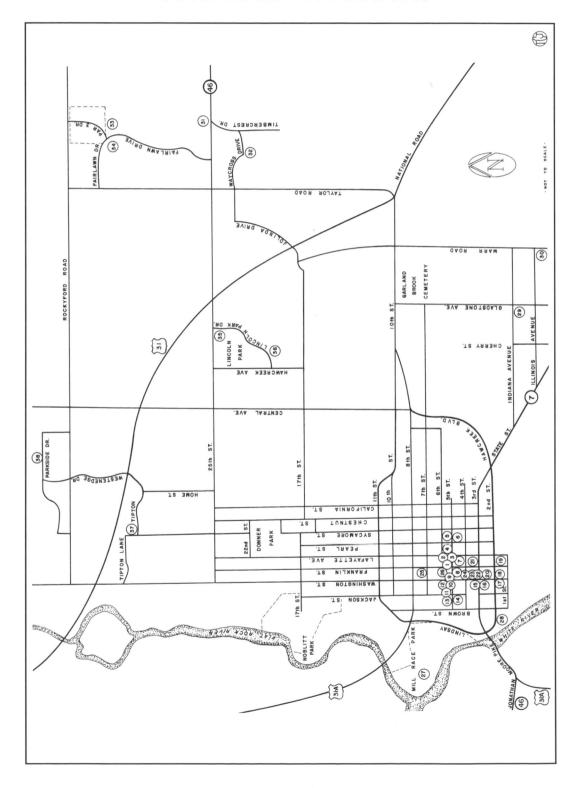

trees and a variety of shrubs and flowers, which help this modern structure to blend in with the surrounding older buildings.

11. Adjoining the Irwin Union Bank and Trust Company on the north and stretching west to Jackson St. is the **Irwin Union Bank and Trust Company Addition**. Designed by the firm of Kevin Roche, John Dinkeloo and Associates of Hamden, Connecticut, in 1973, this three-story building is noted for its "striped" glass. The "striped" effect is created from a special type of laminated glass designed to reduce the amount of heat in the glass corridor absorbed from the sun. Architect Roche was Eero Saarinen's assistant in the construction of the adjacent structure.

12. The **Sparrell Block Building**, 518-524 Washington St., next to the Irwin Union Bank and Trust Company, underwent renovation in 1988. Built in 1885, it is the only commercial structure that Charles F. Sparrell designed among his many creations in Bartholomew County, including the old City Hall, now the Columbus Inn.

13. Continue west one block to the headquarters of **Cummins Engine Company** at the northwest corner of 5th and Jackson sts. This two-block-long modern facility was constructed from 1981 to 1984 at a cost of around $23 million and serves as the world headquarters for the Cummins Engine Company. Located near the center of the massive complex is the former **Cerealine Building** (Mill "A"). Constructed around 1880, the building served as the production facility for Cerealine, the second breakfast cereal in the world produced after rolled oats. This white, flaky corn product was invented (some say by accident) by James Vannoy in the 1870s at the hominy mill owned by T. and J. W. Gaff, Thomas Rush, and Joseph Gent. Cerealine, which was Columbus's first national and international industry, was initially sold for use in food preparation and the making of beer and was not available for sale in groceries under the name Cerealine until 1884. A supposed disagreement with the Pennsylvania Railroad over rate increases probably resulted in the company being moved to Indianapolis in 1892, where it became the American Hominy Company. Clessie L. Cummins and William G. Irwin acquired the struc-

ture in 1919 and used a wing of the building to start the Cummins Engine Company. (This wing of the building has since been demolished.) Cummins has remodeled the historic structure, and it is now used as the company's auditorium. (*HAER*)

14. The **Columbus Post Office** is situated immediately south of Cummins Engine on the southwest corner of 5th and Jackson sts. Kevin Roche, John Dinkeloo and Associates of Hamden, Connecticut, designed this building that was dedicated in July 1970. The Columbus Post Office was the first post office in the United States to be designed by privately funded architects; the Cummins Engine Foundation provided the financial support. This practically maintenance-free structure was constructed of a special salt-glazed tile called Ohio tile that is commonly used in the construction of silos, plus mirrored glass and Cor-ten steel, a special type of steel that rusts to a certain point and then turns reddish-brown, the same color as the tile. The mirrored-glass walls facing Jackson St. present interesting reflections of the surrounding area, and when viewed from the inside, the glass appears transparent. Unlike traditional post offices that are set back from the street on grassy plots, the Columbus Post Office is located close to the street and is highlighted by an arcade supported by huge tile-covered pillars overhanging the sidewalk on Jackson St.

15. The **Commons-Courthouse Center**, a combination civic center and shopping mall completed in 1973, is directly southeast of the Post Office at 302 Washington St. This two-block enclosed area, nicknamed the "super block," is the epitome of the downtown revival project in Columbus. Cesar Pelli, then of Gruen Associates, Inc., Los Angeles, California, designed this structure for the Irwin Management Company. Most of the complex is covered with brown solar glass except for the large area of clear glass on the side of the building facing Washington St. The entrance at 4th and Jackson leads to a shopping area of about 20 retail stores and 1 major department store. A V-shaped skylight in the center corridor highlights the Courthouse Center section of the structure. The Commons or Civic Mall is east of the retail section and was given to the city by Mr. and Mrs. J. Irwin Miller and his sister Mrs. Clem-

entine Tangeman. This civic center consists of an exhibit area, a cushiony astro-turfed "playtank" for children, two movie theaters, a mini-mall of several boutiques, eating areas, meeting areas, a stage, and a general information center. The Commons is also the home of the Driftwood Valley Arts Council, an organization that sponsors many cultural events.

The sculpture **Chaos I** is located in the southeast area of the Commons and is one of the highlights of the building. Architect Cesar Pelli suggested that a major art work be placed in the Commons to serve as a central gathering point for the townspeople. The Millers and Mrs. Tangeman commissioned Jean Tinguely of Zurich, Switzerland, to create the sculpture. Dedicated in 1974, this 30-ft.-high, 7-ton structure, complete with movable parts, was constructed from steel-rimmed wheels, slabs of steel, an old hay conveyor, and other scrap from the Columbus area. Tinguely, known for his humoristic motion works, based **Chaos I** on his philosophy that "Life is movement. Everything transforms itself, everything modifies itself ceaselessly, and to try to stop it . . . seems to me a mockery of the intensity of life."

16. Immediately south of the Commons, on the southwest corner of 3rd and Washington sts., is the fourth **Bartholomew County Courthouse**, built in 1874 at a cost of one-quarter million dollars. Isaac Hodgson, an Irish immigrant who later designed the Marion County Courthouse, created this French Renaissance-style structure that was supposedly the first fireproof building in the state. The courthouse has gone through renovations in 1928, 1953, and 1969, but most of the original decor, such as the spiral staircase and fireplaces, has been preserved. The floors are marble and the terrazzo and the interior trim is wood, plaster, and cast iron. A copper covering replaced the original slate roof in 1954. (*NRHP*)

17. The **Republic** newspaper plant is one block south of the courthouse on the southwest corner of 2nd and Washington sts. Completed in 1971, this glass-walled building was designed by the Chicago-based architecture firm of Skidmore, Owings and Merrill with Myron Goldsmith as design partner. The highly visible interior of the building allows the outsider to view a modern newspaper operation from the advertising and editorial departments at the

west end to the printing press and distribution areas on the east side. The bright yellow offset press also serves as a sort of modern sculpture. The **Republic** plant has two long, high ceilings at the north and south ends with a lower center area of offices and work areas. Modern art highlights several of the white interior walls and partitions in the building.

18. The new **Columbus City Hall** lies directly east of the Republic building on the southeast corner of 2nd and Washington sts. Edward Charles Basset served as the principal architect for the San Francisco office of Skidmore, Owings and Merrill of San Francisco. This new center of city government was dedicated in 1981 and replaced the outdated 1895 structure. The Cummins Engine Foundation paid for the architect's fees while the $5.5 million in construction costs was financed from revenue-sharing funds, city building funds, and the sale of the old City Hall. The building is shaped like a right triangle with the longest side serving as the base. Jutting from the top of this hypotenuse are two 35-ft.-high beams that meet to form an arch over a corridor leading into a semicircular courtyard, of which the glass-walled back leads to the gallery entrance of the building.

Hanging in the City Hall building is an art piece by Robert Indiana of a circle within a square letter. According to Indiana, the painting reflects the architectural highlights of the building: triangular shaped, two suspended building parts that do not meet and glass panels that reflect the sky. The large "C" in the center of the work stands for corn, one of the state's leading commodities.

19. The **Bartholomew County Jail**, bounded by 1st and 2nd sts., Franklin St. and Lafayette Ave., is another recent addition to the modern architectural landscape. The long delayed and controversial project had its ground breaking in March 1988, with its completion expected in 1990. The domed, two-story, 50,000-sq.-ft. jail had a price tag of $7.4 million. Don M. Hisaka of Cambridge, Massachusetts, designed the building and added his name to the lengthening list of major architects contributing to the city's showcase of contemporary building styles.

20. Proceed north two blocks to 3rd St. and turn left. One-half block on the left at 425 3rd

Indiana Historical Society (C4232)
Bartholomew County Courthouse, 1977, photographed by Edward J. Vadas

St. is the **Crump Theater**. Local businessman and farmer John Smith Crump employed Charles F. Sparrell of Columbus to design this structure that opened on October 30, 1889. The building's original facade was highlighted by three arched panels at the top with one word of the theater's name in the center of each panel. The lavish three-storied interior contained a main floor that could seat 400, a balcony, and three levels of side boxes for the city's elite. Much of the theater's charm was lost around 1935 when it was remodeled with a stucco facade in the Art Deco style, but the interior remains a show place.

21. The **Bartholomew County Historical Museum** (McEwen-Samuels, Marr home) is located one-half block east of the Crump Theater on the north side at 524 3rd St. This Italianate-style home was constructed for William McEwen, a prominent Columbus banker, in 1864. Economic hard times forced McEwen to

dispose of the building to David Samuels in 1870. Samuel Samuels, David's son, sold the house to James Marr in 1889 because of financial difficulties. After Marr's death in 1916, there followed a series of owners, and the house fell into a state of decay until it was acquired by the Bartholomew County Historical Society in 1969, restored, and opened as a museum in 1973. The house's parlor has been furnished as a Victorian period entertainment room featuring a working music box and a stereopticon. A bedroom and a nursery also have been furnished, whereas the second story is an exhibit area that includes an 1878 fire engine and an Eastlake clock. (*NRHP*)

22. Return to Washington St. and continue north. **Irwin's Bank**, now the offices of the J. Irwin Miller Management Company, is on the northeast corner of 3rd and Washington sts. The first building was constructed here in 1848, and for many years the site was known as the Old Jones Corner. In 1881 Joseph I. Irwin obtained the building from John V. Storey and remodeled it by adding a cast-iron facade and cornice. Irwin then moved his dry goods store and bank here from 327 Washington St., a location he had occupied since he started his dry goods business in 1850. Irwin's banking business began somewhat by accident when many of his customers asked him to keep their money in the store's safe. In 1871 he incorporated the business as a private bank. By 1907 Irwin had abandoned the dry goods business. He shared the building with Union Starch and Refining Company until 1928 when he sold his interest in the building to the starch company and merged his bank with the Union Trust Company to form the Irwin Union Bank and Trust Company. When Miles Laboratories purchased the starch company in 1966, they sold the building to Irwin Management, who employed Alexander Girard to renovate and redecorate the structure in 1971.

23. **Zaharako's**, a confectionery store, is located about three-quarters of a block farther north on Washington St. A family of Greek immigrants opened the business in 1900, and the second generation of the Zaharako family operates the store. The Neoclassical exterior is overshadowed by an ornate interior that features oak wall panels, glass candy cases, a 50-ft. backbar of solid mahogany supported by Mexican onyx

pillars, and a 40-ft. counter of Mexican and Italian marble divided by a tiffany lamp on an onyx stand. The two Mexican onyx soda fountains were obtained from the 1904 St. Louis Exposition, and the large German pipe organ at the store's rear was acquired in 1908. The Zaharako family still sells its nationally acclaimed candies and ice cream. (*HABS*)

24. Adjoining Zaharako's to the north is the **First National Bank** building at the southeast corner of 4th and Washington sts. Randolph Griffith opened the business in 1865 and moved it to its present location 10 years later. The two-story, limestone structure was completed in 1925 and is an example of the American style of Neoclassical Revival architecture. This architectural design can be seen in the building's four huge columns and plain smooth walls. The closed-in environment of the First National Bank stands in contrast with the spaciousness of the modern Irwin Union Bank and Trust Company one block north.

25. The **Indiana Bell Telephone Company Switching Center** is located three blocks north and one-half block east on the northwest corner of 7th and Franklin sts. The structure was completed in 1978 under the direction of architect Caudill Rowlett Scott of Houston, Texas, with Paul Kennon as design principal, and Jay Bauer as designer. Described as a "non-building" for its all-mirrored glass exterior, the building reflects the residential neighborhood to the north and the business district to the south and, in effect, serves as a transition between the two areas. A two-story trellis containing ivy wisteria and climbing hydrangeas eases the otherwise unbroken line of glass on the south and east sides. Nine huge "organ pipes" of blue, red, orange, and yellow on the west side of the building add color and beauty while cleverly disguising the air conditioning and heating units.

26. The two houses (now offices) known as **Franklin Square** are situated one and one-half blocks south of Indiana Bell on the west side of Franklin St. At 522 Franklin is a Federal-style house built in 1853 for Samuel Harris, a soldier and fine-metal craftsman. The building of Italianate design at 538 Franklin was constructed in 1870 for Dr. William O. Hogue, a physician, pharmacist, and a charter member and director

of the First National Bank of Columbus. In the late 1960s both houses were close to being destroyed when interior decorator David Jones acquired the Hogue house and with support from Mrs. J. Irwin Miller obtained the Harris house and restored both buildings. Many items from other razed structures in the Columbus area were salvaged, such as the stained-glass window from the old Carnegie Library now above the front stairs of the Harris house. Jones was also responsible for the stately garden that separates the two buildings. In the center of the garden is a small wrought-iron, gazebo-like structure that houses a water fountain. The iron fence at the front of the garden originally belonged to an orphans' home in Cincinnati that was built in 1878, and the brick for the back wall came from a local building. The Harris home now houses the American Center for International Leadership (ACIL), founded in 1985 by Sullivan, Indiana, native Stephen Hayes. The center is a privately funded effort to bring together tomorrow's world leaders on American soil and overseas to exchange ideas.

27. **Mill Race Park** at 5th and Lindsay sts., directly west of the Commons-Courthouse Center parking lot, was dedicated on August 21, 1966, as part of the downtown revitalization project. Located along the Flatrock River, the park was once the site of several early mills, but for many years it was an area of poor housing known as Death Valley. This well-maintained city park offers a variety of recreational activities including fishing, picnicking, a playground, and a miniature train ride for children. The park's first covered bridge emplacement, the 1880 Clifty Covered Bridge, was installed in 1966. It burned in 1985 and was replaced the following year by a new bridge, assembled largely of parts from an old Union County span purchased for $1,350 in Indianapolis, where it had been stored since 1974. Architect Alexander Girard of Santa Fe, New Mexico, was responsible for many of the park's improvements during the early 1970s. In the mid-1980s a "People Trails" system of paths for walking, jogging, and biking, with plans for their extension throughout Columbus and vicinity, originated in the park.

28. The former city **Power House** at 148 Lindsay St. was converted by James K. Paris of Columbus, in 1976, to the **Senior Center**, a

building used by senior citizens as a meeting place and recreational facility. The first electric power house was constructed on this site in 1871, but most of the building's current Classical Revival-style features, such as the 17-in.-thick brick walls and the 2-ft.-thick stone slab foundation, were added in 1901. The distinguishing feature of the old power house is its series of arches, including two smaller interior arches that were added during the 1976 renovation to provide easier access between rooms. Located on the East Fork of the White River, the structure served the electrical needs for the city of Columbus until 1952. It later was used as a machine shop where the **Chaos I** sculpture was assembled.

29. **Fire Station No. 3**, 80 S. Gladstone, is a gray concrete block structure, accented with fire-engine-red glazed brick imported from Germany. Designed by the Columbus architect, William E. Burd, of Wood and Burd, the $340,000 station opened in 1983. Unusual features of the building include its brass firepole enclosed in a glass cylinder on the front of the station and its passive solar heating system.

30. The construction of **Columbus East Senior High School** at 230 S. Marr Rd. was based on the concept of individual study with faculty assistance. Mitchell-Giurgola Associates of Philadelphia designed this three-story structure built in 1972 with a 900-seat auditorium at one end and a 4,200-seat gymnasium at the other end. In the center of the building is a two-level gallery that houses a "commons" and a cafeteria which is separated from a terrace by a glass wall. The school also contains a swimming pool, a planetarium, a greenhouse, an animal room for science classes, and a specially equipped industrial arts wing. The school administration provided a program of modular scheduling and team teaching.

31. **Fire Station No. 4**, 4730 25th St. (IND 46 east), was designed by Robert Venturi and John Rauch of Philadelphia, Pennsylvania. Completed in 1967, the trapezoidal-shaped cinder block building has a front facade of red unglazed brick and white glazed brick, with the latter extending up the 36-ft.-high, hose-drying tower, the centerpiece of the project.

32. The **L. Frances Smith Elementary School** is located at 4505 Waycross Dr. Dedicated in 1969 and named for a Columbus elementary education teacher and supervisor, the structure was designed by John M. Johansen of New Canaan, Connecticut. This tri-complex area is constructed of reinforced concrete and Cor-ten steel, a high tin content alloy that builds up a reddish-brown surface rust. Seven brightly colored tunnel-like steel ramps or "tubes" gradually slant upwards and connect the four levels. Each tube's interior is carpeted, which serves to eliminate noise as well as to provide an area for art displays.

33. The **W. D. Richards Elementary School** located at 3311 Fairlawn Dr. is the 1965 creation of Edward Larrabee Barnes of New York City and is noted for its series of radically slanted roofs that adjoin each other and form teeth-like shadows. Four similarly designed 28-ft.-high clerestories above the multipurpose room in the center of the school gives the outline of the structure a spinal appearance. These roofs are sloped so as to provide the maximum amount of natural light through the windows located near the top while allowing for a large amount of classroom wall space. Each of the six grades has its own section of three rooms and an exit leading to a plaza area. Many of the school's facilities are designed with the height of a child in mind. In the main playground behind the building is a 1970 sculpture of 12 miniature horses encircling an ash tree by the Sicilian artist Constantino Nivola; the work was a gift of Mr. and Mrs. J. Irwin Miller. The school was dedicated in 1965 and named for William Dalbert Richards, a Columbus teacher and administrator for 45 years.

34. Situated on a gently sloping knoll at 3300 Fairlawn Dr. is the **First Baptist Church**. Designed by Harry Weese of Chicago and completed in 1965, the church contains elements of the contemporary geometric architectural structure and a traditional religious building. The First Baptist Church is distinguished by its peaked nondimensional bell tower and its steep hand-laid slate-covered roof, which is twice as high as its supporting pink brick walls. An interior wall of pierced brick at the front of the church separates the sanctuary from the choir, organ, and baptistry. All elements in the sanctuary are designed to be off-center except for

the cross which has been described as appearing "to float in midair." Natural lighting for the cross is provided from a row of glass panels in the roof above the chancel. To one side of the main dual leveled, A-frame sanctuary building is a smaller, yet similarly designed, structure that houses the chapel.

35. The **Lincoln Center**, an ice skating rink and recreation center at 2501 25th St., was presented to the city by the Hamilton Foundation in 1958 in the memory of B. F. Hamilton, the founder of Cosco, Inc. Harry Weese of Chicago created this gabled chalet-type structure made from rough-hewn granite, glass, and wood. A circular granite fireplace surrounded by wooden benches and a wood beam ceiling highlight the interior. Weese designed the Lincoln Center as a kind of "Black Forest stage setting" that would combine beauty with practicality.

36. Spanning Haw Creek is the **Quinco Consulting Center** at 2078 Lincoln Park Dr. James Stewart Polshek of New York City designed this facility that handles the problems of mental health patients for a five-county area (hence the name Quinco). This two-story structure was completed in 1972. It is bordered by the Bartholomew County Hospital on one side of Haw Creek and a city park on the other. Built in the shape of two offset rectangles, the center is noted for its angled glass windows which produce a skylight effect on the second floor. The broad middle section contains the main lounge on the first floor and a combination balcony/ bridge on the second floor. The bridge connects the outpatient and office area with that of the inpatient center.

37. The **North Christian Church** on Tipton Ln. and Sycamore St. south of US 31 was the last building designed by Eero Saarinen before his death in 1961. It is one of the most impressive contemporary structures in Columbus. The hexagonal-shaped building is easily distinguished by its 192-ft.-high spire topped by a gold leaf cross. The sloping roof harmonizes with the landscaped mound base and further accentuates the splendor of the spire. The interior is designed "in the round" with the sanctuary in the center and the communion table within it. An opening near the top of the roof and the base of the spire and a space under the edge of the roofline supplies sunlight to the building.

38. **Parkside Elementary School** at 1400 Parkside Dr. was designed by Norman Fletcher of The Architects Collaborative, Inc., of Boston, Massachusetts, and was completed in 1962. The distinguishing feature is the umbrella-like or barrel-vault design of the bus shelter at the front and the central multipurpose section. Fletcher designed the building to respect the individuality of the student as seen by the separation of the lower grades from the upper grades by separate wings. In the courtyard is the sculpture *The Family* by Harris Barron of Brookline Village, Massachusetts. Carved from Chelmsford granite are three angular figures that represent each member of the family.

Tour 12

Tour 12 begins at the East Fork of the White River bridge on IND 46. From downtown Columbus follow 3rd St. to the bridge (sometimes referred to as Tipton Bridge) and take IND 46 west. A *2 m.* stretch of IND 46 was designated the Jonathan Moore Pike in 1976, honoring a Revolutionary War soldier and a member of George Washington's select life guards.

From the bridge travel *1.6 m.* west on IND 46 to I-65. West of the interchange, and across from the West Hill Shopping Center is **Columbus's Tipton Lakes area**. Tipton Lakes, annexed by the city in 1979, is a planned community, the largest in Indiana, encompassing 1,200 acres. In Tipton Lakes is located the ultramodern **Fire Station No. 5** at Goeller Blvd. and Terrace Lake Rd. Susan Torre of New York City was selected to be the principal designer of the firehouse, which opened in the spring of 1987. On the pre-zoned triangular plot, Torre chose to integrate rural motifs—a barn-like roof style and an adjoining "silo" cylinder, which houses a fireman's pole—with the functional requirements of a fire station. Costing over one million dollars, the station will serve the west side of Columbus around the interstate and the vicinity's new housing additions.

Return to the interchange and drive south for *4.6 m.* to the Ogilville-Walesboro exit (IND 58). Drive east *.4 m.* to the **Cummins Engine Company Components Plant** on the right. This 13-acre facility designed by Kevin Roche, John Dinkeloo and Associates of Hamden, Connecticut, maximizes available space by utilizing the roof as the parking lot. The building, completed in 1973, was constructed with the emphasis on a pleasant working environment and the preservation of nature. Each employee has an outside view, and the glass-enclosed landscaped courtyard in the middle of the manufacturing section allows the workers an area in which to relax. Both the office and the manufacturing areas are located on the main level

with the latter being about 3 ft. lower and separated by glass.

Return to IND 46 and proceed west *7 m.* to the Bartholomew-Brown County line. **BROWN COUNTY** (p. 12,377; 312 sq. m.), named for Maj. Gen. Jacob J. Brown, a hero in the War of 1812 and commanding general of the United States Army from 1821 to 1828, was formed from sections of Bartholomew, Monroe, and Jackson counties in 1836. This rectangular-shaped county is bordered by Johnson and Morgan counties to the north, Monroe to the west, Jackson and Monroe to the south, and Bartholomew to the east. Most of the county is hilly, because glaciers stopped at the northern edge of the area and failed to level the hills beyond. Because of the difficult terrain, only about one-third of the land is used for farming. When the residents realized that agriculture would not prosper in the hilly regions, they developed other natural resources, such as timber, salt, and gold. Settlers began the gold-mining industry in 1875 in hopes of discovering large quantities of the precious metal that glaciers deposited in the hills. No major discoveries were ever made, and the industry folded after approximately 50 years. Since the 1930s the Brown County economy has developed a reliance on the tourist trade. It is estimated that each year three to four million visitors converge upon the hills of Brown County to view the breathtaking scenery. Farms and timber still exist in the county, but many residents make their livelihoods on tourism or by commuting to jobs in Bloomington, Columbus, or Indianapolis.

This scenic area at the county line once was known as *Stoney Lonesome*. Until the early 20th century the rough terrain and underbrush made travel through the region treacherous. Compounding the danger were bands of robbers that would hide in the underbrush and ambush settlers or salesmen as they made their way between Columbus and Nashville.

Tour 12

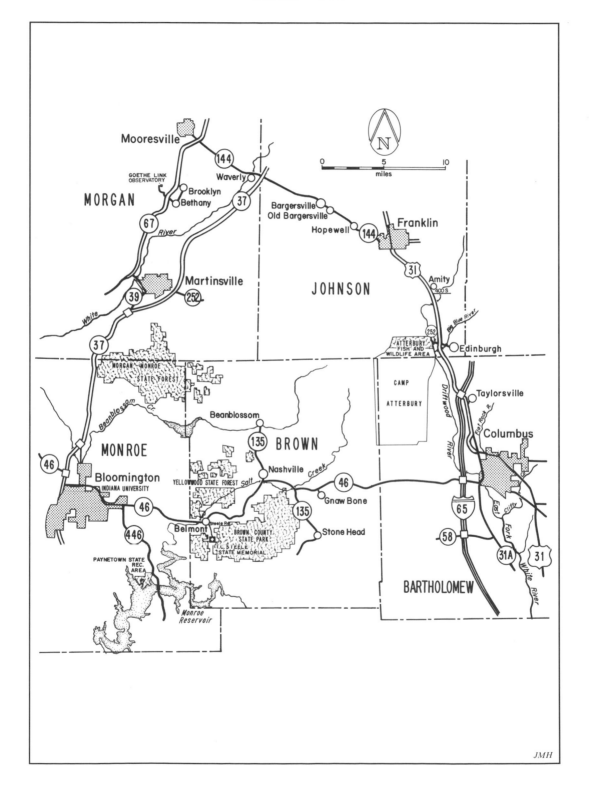

IND 46 has replaced a section of the old road that paralleled a creek bed and the bottom of a valley. The White Caps, a powerful secret organization similar to the Ku Klux Klan, terrorized the area and controlled the local government from the 1880s until 1909.

Continue *4.3 m.* west of the Stoney Lonesome area to the village of **GNAW BONE**. The origin of the town's name is not certain. Several stories involve people or animals "gnawing bones," but the most likely origin is that some of the earlier settlers were French and named the town Narbonne after the city in their homeland, which was later Hoosierized to Gnaw Bone. In later years the village was one of the more depressed areas in the county with numerous wrecked cars dotting the hillside, but more recently it has begun to clean up its surroundings and is now the site of several souvenir stands.

Continue *2 m.* west of Gnaw Bone and turn left onto IND 135. South *5.1 m.* at New Bellsville Pike blacktop is the **Stone Head** road marker in the front yard of a house. The 5-ft.-high work of American folk art is a sandstone carved likeness of a man's head atop a concrete directional marker. Henry Cross, a local farmer and part-time tombstone carver, sculpted the work in 1851 in lieu of his state tax requirement that all males spend six days a year working on public roads or waterways. The likeness atop the marker is supposed to be that of George Summa, the township road supervisor in 1851. Two towns on the road sign—Sparkesferie in Jackson County and Fairfax in Monroe County, now a recreation area on Lake Monroe—no longer exist. Sometime during the 20th century the marker was whitewashed and black enamel paint applied to distinguish the hair and facial features, as well as the directional information at the base of the sculpture. (*NRHP*)

Return to IND 46 and continue west *1.4 m.* to the north entrance of **Brown County State Park**. Immediately outside the park entrance is the **Ramp Creek Covered Bridge**, the only two lane and one of the oldest extant covered bridges in the state. Originally constructed near Fincastle in northwest Putnam County by Henry Wolfe in 1838, the bridge was moved to its present site over the North Fork of Salt Creek in 1932. The structure was remodeled in 1969 and can accommodate cars and light trucks. Brown County State Park opened in 1929 with 1,000 acres and currently is the largest park with 15,547 acres. In the fall of each year the park's 27 miles of paved roads are lined with tourists wishing to view the bright colors associated with the change of seasons. Along the roads are many vistas of the picturesque countryside with its bluish haze that has earned the hills the nickname of the Little Smokies. The area received its appearance as a result of the Illinois Glacier that stopped just north of the present site of Beanblossom. When the glacier melted, the runoff created the beds of Beanblossom Creek and the north and middle forks of Salt Creek and formed a series of ridges in the hills between the two forks that form the bluish haze. The Civilian Conservation Corps (CCC) planted many trees in the park, constructed several structures, and excavated the land for Ogle Lake in the early and mid-1930s. The park includes hiking trails, bridle paths and a horseman's camping area, two man-made fishing lakes, two blockhouses, an olympic-size swimming pool, a nature center, several picnic areas, and campsites. A fire watchtower on **Weed Patch Hill** provides an excellent panorama of the area. A self-guided nature tour is offered at the **Ogle Hollow Nature Preserve**. Maps are available at the start of the trail that describe the various trees and plants visible on the tour. Rare yellowwood trees, found mainly in the south central United States, can be seen along the trail. Brown County State Park is one of the few Indiana locations where these trees are known to exist.

The **Abe Martin Lodge** provides food and shelter for park visitors. Abe Martin was a satirical cartoon character created by Frank McKinney "Kin" Hubbard that first appeared in the *Indianapolis News* on December 17, 1904. The cartoon's setting was placed in Brown County on February 4, 1905, and remained there until Hubbard's death on December 26, 1930. The 23 rental cabins around the lodge are named for characters Hubbard created in the Brown County setting.

Proceed west of the entrance road to Brown County State Park on IND 46 and turn right on IND 135 to **NASHVILLE** (p. 705). The town was founded in 1836 as Jacksonburg in honor of President Andrew Jackson. One year later the name was changed to Nashville after the city in Tennessee that is close to Jackson's home. Over the years economic necessity has induced the townspeople to capitalize on

Indiana Historical Society (C4233)
Stone Head, photographed by the C.R. Childs Company

the natural beauty of the area as a tourist attraction. The lack of manufacturing and the government shelter of thousands of otherwise taxable acres in Brown County State Park have required the emphasis on tourism in order to pay for community services. The town's streets are crowded daily with tourists roaming from shop to shop. A copy of the *Brown County Almanack* which lists all the shops, restaurants, and museums as well as locating them on a map is available at the Nashville Chamber of Commerce on Van Buren St., located on the south side of town, a long two and one-half blocks north of the IND 46 intersection. Nashville's attractions are within easy walking distance of each other, and it is advisable to park near the Chamber of Commerce and proceed on foot.

The **John Dillinger Historical Museum**, located on the southwest corner of Van Buren and Franklin sts., approximately one-half block north of the Chamber of Commerce, opened in 1976 and represents 25 years of collecting and

research by an ex-FBI and Pinkerton agent on one of Indiana's most infamous natives. The museum contains 12 wax figures of criminals and lawmen from the 1920s and 1930s as well as the largest collection of Dillinger memorabilia in the world. Included in the display is the original Dillinger tombstone from Crown Hill Cemetery in Indianapolis.

On the west side of Van Buren St., about one-third block north of Franklin St., is the **Brown County Playhouse**. The original playhouse, located in a combination barn-tent structure, was opened by Indiana University's Summer Theater Department in July 1949. Since that time the university's theater department has offered two summer productions ranging from Broadway plays and musicals to children's classics and original productions. The present Kenneth D. Mock-designed building was opened in July 1977 and features a rustic, village shop-style exterior. Highlighting the playhouse's interior is a thrust stage, which is surrounded by the audience on three sides, and a continental seating design, which features no central aisle.

The atmosphere of an old country store, complete with potbellied stove and cracker barrel, is re-created at the **Nashville House** on the southeast corner of Main and Van Buren sts. Goods available for purchase are arranged in country store fashion. The building also houses a fine restaurant and bakery.

At the southwest corner of Main and Van Buren sts. is the **Hob Nob Corner Restaurant**, formerly the Franklin P. Taggart General Store. Built by Taggart (1838-1907) from 1870 to 1875, the structure with white siding supposedly is the oldest remaining commercial building in Brown County. The two-story general store became a drugstore in 1919, with the second floor being converted to the Red Men's Lodge. Note the 45-starred American Flag wallpaper on the north wall of the first floor interior which dates from around 1900. (*NRHP*)

The **Brown County Courthouse**, built in 1874-75 at a cost of $9,000, is situated on the northeast corner of Main and Van Buren sts. This red brick structure was the third courthouse constructed for the county seat; the first was built in 1837 and the second in 1853. When the second building was destroyed by fire in 1873, the present structure was built on the same foundation with sections of the original walls being retained. On the courthouse

Indiana Historical Society (C4234)

Nashville street, ca. 1930, photographed by the C.R. Childs Company

lawn in front of the building are several highly commercialized Liar's Benches. The original Liar's Bench was immortalized in a 1923 photograph by Frank M. Hohenberger, but it was destroyed as a Halloween prank in 1929. A local merchant obtained the original bench from another businessman in Bartholomew County as a bonus for goods purchased and placed it in front of the courthouse for a place where the men of the town could gather and swap tall tales. Two other benches were taken from an old church and placed on the courthouse lawn to accommodate the increasing number of storytellers. (*NRHP*)

At Gould St. and Old School Way, one block east of Van Buren, is the **Brown County Historical Society Museum Complex**. The complex consists of five buildings, three of which were not built in Nashville. The **Museum** or **Community Building** is a two-story, hand-cut log barn with a drive through in the center. It may have been constructed in the 1840s as a stagecoach station on a section of the old Michigan Rd. The structure was moved to Nashville

in the 1930s by the Works Progress Administration (WPA), and the ownership was transferred to the Brown County Historical Society in the 1960s. The lower room on the east side is used for weaving, and the west side room serves as a gift shop. (*NRHP*) The **Settler's Cabin** was originally constructed by Galen Henry at Spraytown in Jackson County in the 1840s. The cabin was dismantled in 1971 and reconstructed at Nashville without the use of power tools five years later.

Dr. Ralphy's Office represents a typical country doctor's office at the turn of the century. John Eddy constructed the building for Dr. Alfred J. Ralphy at New Bellsville in Brown County in 1898. Ralphy practiced medicine in the New Bellsville area from 1891 until his death in 1928. He was also a taxidermist, naturalist, scientist, and collector of precious stones. The building was moved to the museum complex in 1976 and has been restored and furnished with Ralphy's medical books, instruments, and furniture. The **Old Log Jail** served as the Brown County jail from 1879 to 1919.

Made of hand-cut logs, this 20 x 12-ft., two-story structure replaced the original, smaller 1837 jail. The first floor has two walls of horizontal logs with a wall of vertical logs in the center that made escape nearly impossible. Women were housed in the upper room while men were incarcerated below. (*NRHP*) The small **blacksmith shop** demonstrates the craft as it was practiced in the late 1830s.

Ever since Theodore Clement Steele moved to Brown County in 1907, the area has been a haven for artists wishing to capture the beauty of the local landscape as well as to work in the peaceful, secluded environment of the region. Famous artists such as Steele, Adolph R. Shulz, Glen Cooper Henshaw, Marie Goth, Bill Zimmerman, Jean Vietor, and Dwight Steininger have immortalized the Brown County scenery on canvas. The **Brown County Art Gallery** is located four blocks east of the courthouse on E. Main St. Established in 1926 in a remodeled store building, the gallery allows members of the art colony a place to exhibit their works. A new structure was erected in 1954 on land donated by Adolph Shulz, but it was destroyed by fire in 1966. The present building was constructed on the same site in 1968 and houses both permanent and temporary exhibits. Landscapes, seascapes, portraits, florals, and still life subjects are executed in oils, watercolors, acrylics, pastels, etchings, lithographs, and metal and glass sculptures.

The **Brown County Art Guild** is on the west side of Van Buren St. between Franklin and Main sts., four blocks west and one and two-thirds blocks south of the Art Gallery. Members of the Brown County Art Group, headed by original art colony members Marie Goth and C. Curry Bohm, formed the guild in 1954. Located in the century-old Miner house, which was remodeled in 1976 as a result of the legacy of Ms. Goth, the guild contains a highly selective collection of prominent Brown County artists such as Goth, V. J. Carriani, and Genevieve and Carl Graf. In addition to the gallery and the guild, about 30 local artists open their studios to the public to exhibit and sell their works of art.

One of the legends of Nashville's art world was C. Carey Cloud, a realist painter, who died in 1984 at age 85. A native of Grant County, Indiana, Cloud moved to Nashville in 1948 from Chicago. During his long and productive life, Cloud not only created children's puzzles and pop-up books, but he also designed radio giveaway toys for such programs as Little Orphan Annie and Superman. He is best known, however, as the Cracker Jack artist, who devised many of the playthings found in the containers of caramel popcorn.

North of Nashville *3 m.* on IND 135 on the left side is **Beanblossom Overlook**, a rest park which offers a panoramic view. The stopping point of both the Illinois and Wisconsin glaciers is just to the north. The town of **BEANBLOSSOM** (also spelled Bean Blossom) is about *1.2 m.* north of the rest park and was platted in 1833 as Georgetown after George Grove, the first settler in the area. Around 1913 the village's name was changed to Beanblossom after the nearby creek. The name is either derived from a Miami Indian word meaning "bean" or from a Captain Beanblossom, an officer under William Henry Harrison who drowned in the creek in 1811. The **Beanblossom Covered Bridge**, the only covered bridge built in Brown County, and one of the most photographed and painted bridges in the state, is located on a narrow blacktop road *.5 m.* southwest of the main crossroad in the town. Watch for the sign! Capt. Joseph Balsey built the bridge in 1880 at a cost of $1,200.

Return to the intersection of IND 46 and IND 135 and continue south and west on IND 46. About *1 m.* southwest is the **Little Nashville Opry House**, which features a modern 1,700-seat auditorium that has well-known country music entertainment on weekends. A recent attraction to the Brown County area is skiing. **Ski World** is *3.4 m.* west of the Little Nashville Opry on IND 46. The ski lodge opened in the early 1980s and offers instruction and several slopes with varying degrees of difficulty.

The turnoff for the **Yellowwood State Forest** is *6 m.* west of Nashville on IND 46. Follow the unnamed road north *3 m.* to the entrance to the forest area. This 22,508-acre forest has three lakes, several primitive campsites, rowboat rentals, and numerous trails for hiking and horseback riding. Most of the area was eroded farmland when the federal government purchased it for $9.19 an acre during the depression years of the early 1930s and employed the CCC to reforest it. In 1953 the federal government turned over control of the forest to the state of Indiana, which continues to operate it.

To the south *2.1 m.* past the intersection of IND 46 and the Yellowwood Forest turnoff is

Steele Rd. Follow Steele Rd. *1.5 m.* to the **T. C. Steele State Historic Site** on the right. Situated on 211 acres of picturesque land are the house and studios of Theodore Clement Steele (1847-1926), Indiana's most famous representational artist and one of the founders of the Brown County Art Colony. The Steele residence, called the House of the Singing Winds for the sound made when the wind blows through the trees, was built by Steele soon after his move to Brown County in March 1907. In the furnished 11-room house are many of Steele's paintings and his 900-volume library. There are also two studios which contain additional Steele works. The visitor may walk on several trails that inspired some of Steele's landscape paintings. Also located on the grounds is the **Trailside Museum** (Peter Dewar log cabin). In 1934 Mrs. Selma Steele, T. C. Steele's widow, acquired a two-story, two-room log cabin on land about *5 m.* south of Belmont in a settlement known as the Eel Creek Neighborhood and moved it to her estate. Peter Dewar, a Scottish immigrant, built the cabin around 1871 as a wedding present for his son James. Mrs. Steele gave the 211-acre estate and buildings to the state in 1945. (*NRHP*)

Return to IND 46 and continue west *1.3 m.* to the Monroe County line (for a description of the county see Bloomington essay). Proceed *5.9 m.* and turn south on IND 446 for *6.4 m.* To the right is **Monroe Lake Visitor's Center** and the **Paynetown State Recreation Area**. Located in the Hoosier National Forest Purchase Area is Monroe Lake (Monroe Reservoir), the largest body of water in Indiana with 10,750 acres. This man-made lake was built in 1960-64 as a joint project of the United States Army Corps of Engineers and the Indiana Department of Natural Resources. It was financed primarily by the state. The building of the dam and the reservoir was accompanied by several complications, such as 30 condemnation suits. The Paynetown area includes a beach, boat rentals, campground, concession stand, boat docks, mooring buoys, and a picnic area. Continue south about *1 m.* on IND 446 to the picturesque *.7 m.* causeway that crosses the lake. A stopping point is available south of the causeway on the left. About *3.6 m.* south of the causeway is the **Hardin Ridge Recreation Area** that offers a beach, campground, concession stand, and picnic area.

Return to IND 46 and continue west *5.2 m.* to IND 37. This section of the tour goes through Bloomington (see Bloomington Attractions). Proceed north on IND 37 about *7.1 m.* to **Oliver's Winery** on the right. William W. Oliver, an Indiana University law professor, established the winery in 1972. It is famous for its Camelot Mead, a light, sweet wine made from honey. The other wines produced at Oliver's come from a specially treated strain of French hybrid grapes that give the wines a taste like those bottled in California or Europe rather than most of those produced in the eastern United States. The annual Camelot Wine Festival is held on the winery grounds around the first of June. The festival features demonstrations of medieval combat, period plays, dancing, magicians, mummers, jesters, puppets, and arts and crafts.

Continue north on IND 37 *4.3 m.* and enter **MORGAN COUNTY** (p. 51,999; 409 sq. m.). In 1821 the Indiana legislature created Morgan County from parts of what had been Delaware and Wabash counties. Named for Brig. Gen. Daniel Morgan, a hero of the American Revolution, the county is bounded by Hendricks and Marion counties to the north, Johnson to the east, Monroe and Brown to the south, and Owen and Putnam to the west. Since it is located on both sides of the glacial boundary, the county is a study of geographical contrasts. The agriculturally rich northwest corner is located on what had been a glacial lake, while the southern region is rocky and hilly, marking the glacier's termination. Since most of Morgan County was glacier covered, it is well suited for farming, the county's major business. Corn and apples are among the region's more profitable crops. The greatest number of the Morgan County work force is employed in nearby Indianapolis.

Drive *1 m.* more and turn right at the directional sign indicating the **Morgan-Monroe State Forest**, which is located *3.1 m.* from the turnoff. Straddling the border between Monroe and Morgan counties, the Morgan-Monroe Forest is the second largest forest in the state with 23,463 acres. It has a similar history to that of the Yellowwood Forest in that it was located on depressed farmland purchased by the government for a small price during the depression, was reforested with CCC labor, and later was turned over to the state. The forest contains hiking trails, three small lakes, five shelters, and facilities for camping and picnicking. North of the largest shelter is the 15-acre **Scout Ridge Nature Preserve**, dedicated in 1969, and so named because a Boy Scout can satisfy part of the requirements for a merit badge by walking the three-fourths-mile self-guided tour. In a registration box at the north end of the shelter are brochures with maps that show 27 observation stations along the trail and include information on trees, shrubs, flowers, and life in the forest.

Continue north on IND 37 *4.1 m.* to IND 39 which leads into **MARTINSVILLE** (p. 11,311). Bear right onto IND 39 and follow this road (do not follow IND 39 when it branches off at *1.6 m.*) for *2 m.* until it dead-ends at Main St. Turn left onto S. Main St. and proceed into the downtown area. Established in 1822 and named for one of the founders, John Martin, Martinsville once was known nationally as the Artesian City for its mineral springs and health sanitariums. The mineral springs were discovered when a gas drilling operation owned by Sylvanus Barnard accidently struck artesian water in 1884. According to the legend, the water's potential curing powers were not realized until an old race horse that had been put to pasture in the area drank of the liquid and became revitalized. The sanitarium era peaked during the first years of the 20th century and significantly declined after about 1911. At the height of the craze one could take "the cure" at any of seven facilities. With the decline of the mineral water industry Martinsville reverted to its former reliance on agriculture, but in recent years the area has become the home of many Indianapolis commuters. Former Indiana governors Emmett Branch, 1924-25, and Paul V. McNutt, 1933-37, grew up in Martinsville.

In the heart of the business section is the **Morgan County Courthouse** on the right. Constructed in 1859 at a cost of $32,000, the courthouse is the third building to serve the county. The original 1823 courthouse, a log cabin owned by Jacob Cutler, was replaced by a brick building 11 years later. The current structure is a combination of Victorian and Italianate architecture and is distinguished from other Indiana courthouses by its ornate bell tower. An 1876 fire resulted in the rebuilding of much of the structure, and the annex and bell tower clock are the products of a $1.4 million renovation project in 1977.

Southeast of the courthouse at 539 E. Washington St. is the former **Homelawn Sanitarium**. Homelawn (also called Home Lawn Mineral Springs and Diamondhead) was the most famous of Martinsville's health spas and was the last one to close, in December 1973. The sanitarium was built by Ebenezer Henderson, a Democratic party politician and friend of President Grover Cleveland, in 1889 on four acres of shaded land and could accommodate 200 guests.

From the sanitarium go one block north and head right on Morgan St. *2 m.* to the **Grassyfork Fishery** on the left. Wind through *.5 m.* of woods to reach the ponds. The fishery is considered the world's largest producer of goldfish. It was started by brothers Max and Eugene Shireman in 1899 on farmland inherited from their parents that was unsuited for farming. The business originally had 10 ponds and was launched in response to a soap company's advertising campaign. Today Grassyfork has 400 ponds in four fish farms located within a few miles of each other that produce 25-30 million goldfish a year. At one time the fishery sold both retail and wholesale, but it is now exclusively a wholesaler.

Backtrack on Morgan St. *1 m.* to Hospital Dr. (IND 252). Go southeast *.5 m.* to **Drake's Phonograph Museum**, which is *.1 m.* beyond IND 37. Opened in 1970, the museum claims to be the largest and finest collection of antique phonographs and records in the world. There are more than 600 phonographs and related items in the collection that includes an 1858 phonautograph, an exact copy of an original 1877 Edison phonograph, and an original 1878 phonograph. The collection is owned by E. T. Drake, a retired physician.

Return to Morgan St. and proceed left, through downtown, *1.8 m.* to IND 39. Turn right and drive *.8 m.* to IND 67 and exit right. IND 67 follows the approximate path of the Indian Trace, a trail that ran from Fall Creek near the present-day city of Indianapolis to Vincennes. Continue north on IND 67 for *8.4 m.* and turn right onto Observatory Rd. Proceed *.5 m.* On the right is a narrow road that leads to the biblically-named village of **BETHANY** (p. 127). Watch for the sign as this road is difficult to see. In 1884 members of the Disciples of Christ Church cleared the area, named it Bethany Park, and used it as a camp meeting place. Later, the church members constructed a

2,000-seat tabernacle, a 20-room hotel, and a restaurant on this 40-acre tract of land with an adjoining 8-acre lake. Noted orators such as William Jennings Bryan delivered addresses to huge crowds in the park. When it was not being used for religious or political meetings, Bethany Park served as a weekend resort community for Indianapolis residents. Many attractive log cottages still line the lakefront north of town on Observatory Rd. The hotel and restaurant were destroyed by fire in 1952, and the church soon withdrew its affiliation and dismantled the tabernacle. The mainly self-sufficient, peaceful community became the town of Bethany in 1955.

In the hills west of Bethany is a stream known as **Gold Creek**. The heavy blue clay beds of the creek have been the site of some of the purest gold ever discovered. The first boom came in the period from 1850 until 1855 when three million shares of stock were sold in a company after a few flakes were found in the creek bed. The rush proved to be unsuccessful. The only major discoveries were made in the mid-1870s.

BROOKLYN (p. 889) is located .3 m. north of Bethany on Observatory Rd. The first settler arrived in the area in 1819, and by the 1830s the community was flourishing with several industries along White Lick Creek. The most successful was the distilling industry, which produced brandy and whiskey from pumpkins and potatoes. Frank Landers, one of the leading distillers, platted the town around 1854 and probably named it after the New York City borough. Many of the townspeople opposed the distilleries, and on two occasions they destroyed the local saloon. Because of its local shale deposits, Brooklyn developed a drain-tile factory that survived from 1904 to 1975. The rock is still excavated in the area and transported to nearby tile factories.

Return to IND 67 and travel west on Observatory Rd. for 1.3 m. (the last .6 m. is gravel) and turn right onto a dead-end gravel road. On the right is the **Goethe Link Observatory** of Indiana University's astronomy department. The late Dr. Goethe Link, an Indianapolis physician, started building the observatory for private use in 1937. He donated it and the surrounding 12 acres to the university in 1948. The 36-in. reflector telescope is one of the finest in the country and has contributed to the discovery of two asteroids.

Return to IND 67, continue north 4.6 m., and turn left on Indiana St. (first traffic light) at **MOORESVILLE** (p. 5,349). In 1819 the first settlers arrived in the area, and Samuel Moore, after whom the town is named, settled in 1823, set up a general store, and began acquiring large tracts of land. The following year he laid out the town and attempted to establish a utopian community by giving free lots to those who shared similar educational, religious, and community-spirit sentiments. Primarily a farming community for most of its existence, Mooresville has developed into a commuter suburb of Indianapolis in recent years. Paul Hadley, designer of the Indiana State Flag, was a resident. In 1920 future gangster John Dillinger, then 18, moved with his family from Indianapolis to a farm near Mooresville. Four years later he committed his first crime when he and another man assaulted and attempted to rob grocer B. F. Morgan as he walked by the Assembly of God Church (now Heritage Christian Church) at W. Harrison and S. Jefferson sts. Dillinger soon was apprehended and spent the next nine years in prison.

Drive north on Indiana St. .7 m. and turn left on W. Harrison St. West .2 m. on the left is the Heritage Church site. Continue .2 m. and turn right on Monroe St. One block on the left, at Washington St., is the **White Lick Friends Meetinghouse**. Quakers settled in the Mooresville area as early as 1821 and established the first monthly meeting in 1823. The first meetinghouse, built east of White Lick Creek, was replaced in 1826 with a brick building located on the site of what is now White Lick Cemetery. In 1884 the trustees purchased land on the west edge of Mooresville, and William Macy built the present meetinghouse. In 1903 the building was remodeled—removing the partition that separated men and women and changing the floor plan. The south wing was added in 1954. The Friendship House, a reception room with a large fireplace, was built west of the meetinghouse in 1965. Both buildings stand on attractive wooded grounds.

North one block on the left at 244 N. Monroe is the **Friends Academy**. Built in 1861, it was operated by the Quakers for nine years on a subscription basis though open to anyone who paid the tuition. The Mooresville School Society purchased the building in 1870, which was used by all grades 1-12 until 1908 when the new high school opened. The two-story red brick building now serves as a meeting place for the Morgan County Historical Society. It adjoins the Newby Elementary School and gymnasium built in the 1930s. (*NRHP*)

Return to Monroe and Washington sts. and go left. East on Washington St. two blocks on the left is the **Old Mooresville Cemetery**, which Samuel Moore deeded for a church and cemetery. The first burial was made in 1829. A boulder with a plaque indicates the site of the first Methodist Episcopal church in Mooresville, built in 1839. Moore later helped organize the Old Settlers reunion which has met for a picnic in the old town park on the southeast side of town every August since 1870 except in 1943. When he died in 1889, Samuel Moore was the last person to be interred in the old cemetery.

Continue one block, turn right on Indiana St., and at one block turn left (at traffic signal) onto High St., which is IND 144. Travel east *7.4 m.*, then turn right onto a side road for **WAVERLY**, *1 m.* beyond. The area is noted as the termination point of the Whetzel Trace, a 60-mile path blazed by Jacob Whetzel and his 18-year-old son Cyrus through Delaware Indian country in 1818. The trail started at Laurel in Franklin County. Until 1827 this was the route taken by most settlers who came from the East into central Indiana. The Whetzel family homestead was located on the south edge of town in what is now the Waverly Woods subdivision, which lies straight ahead. The Whetzels are buried in a difficult-to-find cemetery located on top of a small incline on the left about *1.6 m.* from IND 144. The town was established in 1837 when the Central Canal was proposed to extend from central Indiana and Indianapolis to Evansville. The name apparently stemmed from Sir Walter Scott's popular *Waverley* novels. At night, Waverly's saloons served as a popular gathering point for the Irish canal workers. The internal improvement system's collapse forced construction to halt just south of the region the following year.

Return to IND 144, turn right, and enter **JOHNSON COUNTY** (p. 77,240; 321 sq. m.), which was created in 1822 from a section of Delaware County, and was named for John Johnson, a judge of the Indiana Supreme Court. The first settlers found the land covered with forests, undergrowth, and swamps, and a great amount of clearing and draining was required to uncover the county's rich soil. Rectangular in shape, Johnson County is bordered by Marion County to the north, Shelby to the east, Bartholomew and Brown to the south, and Morgan to the west. Most of the county is situated on a broad high ridge that descends southward, with the basic flatness being interrupted only by the bluffs above the White River and the southern hilly region near Brown County. In addition to farming, Johnson County is the home of several small, successful industries. Many county residents live in the fast growing northern area that has become an Indianapolis commuting suburb.

Continue east *.2 m.* to IND 37. The area just north of this site was once the village of **FAR WEST**, also called the Bluffs and Port Royal. Prehistoric Mound Builders once inhabited this region, later occupied by Delaware Indians. French explorers arrived in the late 1700s and established a trading site with the Delaware tribe called Porte Royale. Jesuit missionaries accompanied the French and founded an Indian school that was destroyed in 1791. William H. H. Pinney laid out the town of Far West in 1833; however, it probably was abandoned several years later with the growth of nearby Waverly.

Continue across IND 37 on a county road extension of IND 144 for *5.2 m.* to **BARGERSVILLE** and its neighbor **OLD BARGERSVILLE** (p. 1,647). Bargersville, originally named New Bargersville, developed overnight when the Indianapolis Southern Railroad laid its tracks through the area in 1906. Old Bargersville is southeast of Bargersville at the intersection of IND 135 and IND 144, which resumes. The town was founded in 1850 as Bargersville and was named for a local merchant named either Jefferson Barger or Joshua Bargers.

Continue southeast on IND 144 for *2.6 m.* to **HOPEWELL**, founded in 1876, and proceed east about *2.4 m.* to **FRANKLIN** (p. 11,563), the Johnson County seat and home of Franklin College. Founded in 1823, the town was named for Benjamin Franklin on the suggestion of Samuel Herriott, one of the founders and an admirer of Franklin. George King generally is given credit for the founding, organization, and development of the community, and a marker on W. Jefferson St. at Walnut St. designates the spot where King built his first log cabin in 1823. The town was stagnant until the arrival of the Madison and Indianapolis Railway in 1846, after which time it became a trading and shipping center for nearby farmers. Franklin was featured in a 1940 pictorial essay in *Life* magazine as a typical midwestern town on Saturday night. Governors Paul V. McNutt and Roger D. Branigin were born in Franklin.

About *.3 m.* past the Franklin city limits sign on the left is the 40-acre, beautifully landscaped grounds of the **Methodist Home for the Aged**. Opened in 1957, the facility serves as a nondenominational retirement home for about 245 senior citizens.

Continue east on IND 44, which joins IND 144, through the intersection with US 31, to the center of the city. At W. Jefferson (IND 44) and Court sts. is the **Johnson County Courthouse**. The first county circuit court was held at the house of John Smiley on Sugar Creek (a plaque commemorates the site). The first permanent courthouse was located in a log cabin on the site now occupied by the Artcraft Theatre at 57 N. Main St. The log cabin served as the county seat from 1824 until 1832, when it was replaced by a brick building, which, in turn, burned in 1849. The second brick courthouse also burned in 1874. The present structure was constructed from 1879 to 1882 under the direction of architect George W. Bunting. (*NRHP*) In front of the courthouse facing W. Jefferson St. is the **Vawter Monument**, named for John T. Vawter, a Franklin merchant who paid for the war memorial. Austrian-born Rudolph Schwarz, who designed the Soldiers and Sailors Monument in Indianapolis, also designed the Vawter Monument, dedicated in 1905 to those who fought in America's wars.

From the courthouse go north one block to Madison St. At 150 W. Madison St. is the **Johnson County Historical Museum** and the **Lewis Hendricks Pioneer Log Cabin**. Founded in 1931, the museum was located in the basement of the courthouse until 1961, when Miss Clara Suckow donated her family's house to serve as the permanent museum and the headquarters of the Johnson County Historical Society. More than 8,000 items that date from the 19th century and cover a variety of topics are displayed. Located next to the historical museum is the restored pioneer log cabin. The structure was built by Lewis Hendricks on a nearby farm in 1835 and was moved to its present location in 1974. A former New York Central Railroad right-of-way angles across Franklin near the museum. Earlier the Fairland, Franklin and Martinsville Railroad, it

was completed in 1866 by Maj. Gen. Ambrose E. Burnside of Civil War and side-whiskers fame. In July 1988 the Society purchased the Franklin Masonic Temple, 135 N. Main, and is in the process of moving the museum to this new address.

Return to the courthouse and proceed east to the **Franklin Depot** at 370 E. Jefferson St. The New York Central Railroad constructed the depot in 1906 near Water St., about six blocks from its present site. It was moved and renovated in 1979 and now houses the Franklin Chamber of Commerce, the Johnson County Red Cross, and the United Fund. A railroad museum is located in the depot's lobby and contains several articles of railroad memorabilia including working scales.

Continue east on E. Jefferson St. On the north side *.3 m.* from the Franklin Depot is a marker in front of an apartment house that indicates the former site of the **Dr. Theodore Λ. Pinkney house**. Pinkney, an abolitionist, acquired the house in 1859 and used it as an "underground railroad" station until the first years of the Civil War. He supposedly constructed an underground passage that ran from the house to Hurricane Creek from where the escaping slaves continued their passage north. The building later became the Sigma Alpha Epsilon fraternity house and was destroyed by fire in 1964.

Travel *.1 m.* east from the historical marker, turn right onto Forsyth St., and proceed one block to the east entrance of **Franklin College** on the right (parking is on the left across from campus). This small, church-supported school was chartered in 1834 as the Indiana Baptist Manual Labor Institute. The Rev. Albert F. Tilton and the Rev. A. R. Hinckley opened the school to about 40 students in the winter of 1837-38 on land donated by George King and Harvey McCaslin. In 1841 the institute became the first Indiana college to admit women, and three years later the name was changed to Franklin College in honor of the town. Northern sympathy was high among the students during the Civil War, and the school was forced to close from 1864 to 1869 because of the large number of students who dropped out to enlist. Franklin gained national fame in the 1920s for its basketball team, the "Wonder Five," that compiled a 36-1 record against the nation's best in 1923 and 1924. Among Franklin's distinguished alumni are former Indiana governor Roger D. Branigin, playwright Robert Wise, journalist/author Elmer H. Davis, brain surgeon Dr. Bronson Ray, and sportscaster Joe McConnell. The college is best known for its liberal arts program that includes journalism, theology, and pre-law; however, it also has fine science and business departments.

The eight-acre, tree-adorned campus contains a well-blended mixture of new and old buildings. Among the more recent structures, most of which are located on the east side, are the **Eli Lilly Campus Center** and the adjoining **Spurlock Physical Education Center**. The Lilly Center, a red brick, Georgian-style building, opened in June 1970 and serves as the student union. The similarly designed Spurlock Center was dedicated in April 1975 and houses the gymnasium and athletic department. One of the more impressive modern structures is the **Franklin College Chapel**. Dedicated in October 1976, this multipurpose building was designed by Henry Meier of Indianapolis and was a joint project of the college and the Indiana Baptist Convention. In addition to the 250-seat chapel, the structure is the scene of meetings, dramatic productions, concerts, and films. At the northeast corner of Dame Mall, named for the college's first graduate, John W. Dame, is a bell mounted on a stone. The bell, which formerly had been situated in the Stott Hall bell tower, was removed to its present location in the summer of 1982. It was placed in Stott Hall when either the building was constructed or when it was remodeled in 1903.

The college's older, ivy-covered buildings, including **Old Main** and **Shirk Hall**, are located in the northwest section of campus. Old Main, the administration building, consists of three adjoining buildings constructed at separate times. The three-story north wing, named Chandler Hall for the college's first president, George C. Chandler, was built in 1847 and is the oldest remaining structure on campus. Bailey Hall, the south wing, was constructed in 1859 and named for the second president of the college, the Rev. Silas Bailey. The four-story center building, Stott Hall, was erected in 1887-88 and named for a former college president, William T. Stott. A fire in 1985 seriously damaged the Victorian structure, particularly Stott Hall, but college officials immediately began restoration, which was completed in 1987. Shirk Hall, which honored the Shirk family of Peru, Indiana, was erected in 1903 and served

as the library until 1964, when increasing enrollment resulted in construction of the larger B. F. Hamilton Memorial Library. Symmetrical in shape and Neoclassical in design, Shirk Hall is constructed of brick and limestone. In 1988 the renovated and restored hall became the new home of the college's Pulliam School of Journalism. (*NRHP*)

Additional points of interest on the campus are the **Crawford Wellhouse** and the **Benjamin Franklin Statue**. The brick wellhouse, situated in the middle of campus, was designed by Miss Blanche Crawford and donated by her fellow senior classmates in 1916. Constructed to cover a once active well, it has become a spot for students to meet and lovers to romance. A Franklin College tradition holds that a female student is not considered a coed until she has been kissed inside the wellhouse. The statue of Benjamin Franklin was created in 1930 and was located at the headquarters of the International Typographical Union in Indianapolis. It was given to the college in the summer of 1962 when the union relocated its headquarters to Colorado.

Turn right onto Monroe St. at the edge of campus for *.2 m.*, then left on State St. for another *.2 m.* to the **Indiana Masonic Home** at the intersection of State and South sts. A 360-acre "city within a city," the Indiana Masonic Home was opened on October 28, 1916, to provide food, housing, and clothing for aged and poor Masons, their families, and orphans. In recent years the home has concentrated more on care for the elderly. The complex has its own hospital, powerhouse, public school, dormitories, guest buildings, and a large farm noted for its dairy cattle.

To return to the intersection of US 31 and IND 44 take South St. west to Main St. about *.4 m.*, right on Main St. for *.4 m.* to the courthouse, then left on W. Jefferson St. (IND 44) to US 31.

Proceed south for *4.5 m.* past IND 44 to **AMITY**. Founded in 1855, the village took its name from the French word *amitie* which means "friendship." Amity was a very prosperous trading post until the building of the turnpike in 1860, at which time it ceased to grow. At the south edge of town (*5.6 m.* from IND 44), turn east onto CR 400S (also called Camp Hill Rd.) and drive *1.3 m.* to the grave of a pioneer woman, Nancy Kerlin Barnett, which divides the road. A historical marker commemorates the site. Mrs. Barnett died in 1831, many years before the county road was constructed, and was buried in a grave overlooking Sugar Creek, her favorite view. Later attempts to pave over the grave met with stiff resistance from relatives until legal arrangements assured its protection.

Continue south on US 31 *4.2 m.* from CR 400S and turn right onto Hospital Rd. (also called CR 800S) at the south junction with IND 252. Ahead *1.2 m.* on the right is the beginning of the **Atterbury State Fish and Wildlife Area**, formerly part of Camp Atterbury military base. Camp Atterbury opened in 1942 on 40,351 acres in Johnson, Bartholomew, and Brown counties that had been the site of some of the first homesteads in the area. Named for Brig. Gen. William Wallace Atterbury, an Indiana native who was director general of transportation of the American Expeditionary Forces in France during World War I and served as president of the Pennsylvania Railroad, 1925-35, the base served as the training grounds for 275,000 soldiers during World War II. Among the camp's buildings was the Wakeman Hospital, one of the largest military hospitals in the United States. From the spring of 1943 until 1946, a portion of the base was used to house Italian and later German prisoners of war. Camp Atterbury was deactivated in 1948 but reactivated two years later with the outbreak of the Korean War. The camp again was abandoned in 1954 and remained dormant until 1965 when 1,434 acres were leased to the state as a wildlife area and an additional 1,000 acres were leased for a Job Corps Center on the site of the old hospital center and the adjoining buildings. Four years later the state acquired 5,508 acres north of Hospital Rd. (the entire area except for the Job Corps Center). The land south of the road was taken over by the Indiana National Guard. The Department of Natural Resources razed many old barracks, and the area is now a popular center for sportsmen, picnickers, and hikers. Two large man-made lakes—Pisgah (62 acres) and Stone Arch (25 acres)—provide excellent fishing, and the brush and marsh of the wildlife area conceal an abundance of game. The rock with the inscription Camp Atterbury 1942 on the southeast edge of the area off of Hospital Rd. was carved by Italian prisoners of war.

Continue west on Hospital Rd. to Mauxferry Rd. A major route taken by many early travelers, it was constructed in the early 1820s and ran from Mauckport (formerly Mock's Ferry) in Harrison County to Indianapolis. Proceed west on Hospital Rd. for *2.6 m.* to the gravel Stone Arch Rd. on the right (the stone arch refers to a small bridge supporting the road at its origin). The road is not easily visible! Approximately *1.1 m.* north on Stone Arch Rd. on the right across from Stone Arch Lake is the **Italian Prisoner of War Chapel** (also called the **Chapel in the Meadow**). Built by Italian prisoners in 1943, this 11 x 16-ft. brick and stucco structure is enclosed on three sides, highlighted by religious frescoes painted on the interior walls and ceiling. Because of the wartime paint shortage, the pictures were made from dyes taken from berries, flower petals, and plants, and some of the red supposedly came from the prisoners' blood. Unfortunately, the paintings are fading and cracking almost to the point of being unrecognizable.

Return to the intersection of IND 252 and US 31 and continue east on IND 252 for *.6 m.* to a stop sign. On the right is a marker indicating the site of the Thompson Mill, constructed in 1826 by James Thompson and Isaac Collier on Big Blue River. Continue east on IND 252 to Main St., then right on Main to Main Cross St. in the downtown district of **EDINBURGH** (p. 4,856) (spelled Edinburg from about 1899 until 1977). A plaque in front of the public library at Main and Main Cross sts. notes that Edinburgh, founded in 1822, was the first village in Johnson County. Because of its proximity to Camp Atterbury, the town experienced periods of rapid growth during World War II and the Korean conflict. It was known as Little Chicago during the Second World War because of the escapades of the soldiers from the camp. Today, Edinburgh boasts of being the largest producer of walnut veneer in the United States. The veneer plants are located on the east edge of town. Religion has played a large part in Edinburgh's history. **Holy Trinity Catholic Church**, built in 1883 on a hill about *.1 m.* west of Main and Main Cross sts., is the dominant feature of the town's skyline. One of the early pastors of the First Christian Church, the Rev. Knowles Shaw, composed the religious hymn "Bringing in the Sheaves." There also are several old mansions in town; a particularly interesting one is the former **Thompson house**, 106 N. Pleasant St., built in a Tuscan Villa style in 1867.

Return to US 31, continue south *1 m.*, and enter Bartholomew County (for a description of the county see the Columbus essay). South *3.6 m.* is **TAYLORSVILLE** (p. 1,247). The town originally was called Herod after a local lawyer; however, its negative biblical connotation soon resulted in the name change to honor President Zachary Taylor. At *3.8 m.* south of Taylorsville in the median on US 31 is the **Carter Cemetery**. This fairly modern cemetery was preserved when US 31 went through the area. Continue south on US 31 for *1.4 m.* beyond the cemetery to Washington St. in Columbus, then right *2.1 m.* to the Visitor's Center, one block east on Franklin St. at 5th St.

Indianapolis

Indianapolis, the state capital, is Indiana's largest city. Its 1980 population of 700,807 made it the nation's 13th largest city. Aptly called the Crossroads of America, transportation has been central to the city's development. In the 1830s the Hoosier capital stood at the junction of the National and Michigan rds. Later it became the hub of a railroad network and, briefly, the center of a vast interurban system. The 20th century brought the automobile and the railroad's successful rival, the truck. Today a system of interstate highways extends from Indianapolis in more directions than from any other city in the United States.

The city's location has made it important commercially and industrially. It is not only near the geographic center of the state but also lies within 700 miles of 65 percent of the nation's population. More than 1,400 manufacturing firms are located in the metropolitan area, providing jobs, many transportation related, for over 106,000 (1987) men and women. Another 489,000 jobs are held in the nonmanufacturing sector which, as the nation's economy moves toward service or informational priorities, is expanding faster than manufacturing.

In spite of its size, until a few years ago Indianapolis projected the image of an overgrown town. Located on a plain and possessing wide avenues permitting easy commuting, the city grew outward rather than upward. This small-town atmosphere had both positive and negative connotations. Indianapolis was acclaimed as the comfortable home of the "typical" American and ridiculed as "Indiana-noplace." Regardless of which meaning one placed on it, the accuracy of the then prevailing image changed in the 1980s as city redevelopment, to the tune of several billions of dollars, reshaped it physically.

In 1820 the General Assembly reluctantly recognized that Corydon was an inconvenient location for the state capital. It appointed a commission to find a new site in the unsettled lands to the north. The commissioners agreed on a location at the confluence of the West Fork of the White River and Fall Creek. They thought that this place offered the advantages of a navigable stream, fertile soil, and a central position. The legislature quickly ratified the choice of the site, but argued for several days over a name for the new city. Representative Marston G. Clark earnestly promoted the name Tecumseh, but few found it acceptable. (After all, the great Shawnee war chief had been dead less than 10 years.) Jeremiah Sullivan of Jefferson County finally suggested the name Indianapolis. At first, the legislators greeted the word with derision, but, perhaps worn out from so much talking, eventually adopted it with little dissent.

Alexander Ralston and Elias P. Fordham surveyed the site. Ralston, who had worked with Pierre Charles L'Enfant in laying out Washington, D.C., is probably the man most responsible for the plan of Indianapolis. Some historians claim to see L'Enfant's influence in the wide streets and diagonal avenues of the new state capital. Ralston and Fordham laid out the city on a grid a mile on each side. At its center they placed a circle which was to be the site of the governor's residence. Four diagonal avenues cut inward from each corner of the grid to provide shortcuts to the downtown. Washington St., surveyed 30 ft. wider than the other major streets, was the main thoroughfare of the city. The surveyors reserved space for a courthouse and a statehouse and another tract between Meridian and Pennsylvania sts. for a proposed state university.

The Fall Creek location had limitations as a site for a town. The land was swampy and cut across with ravines filled with stagnant water—excellent breeding grounds for mosquitoes. In the summer of 1821 virtually everyone in the settlement came down with malaria. During that grim summer the settlement lost 25 people, mostly children. The White River proved only marginally navigable. Flatboats and keelboats could make the voyage upriver in the spring, but steamboat travel proved all but impossible. During the 1828-29 season Gov. Noah Noble offered a reward of $200 to the first captain to navigate a steamboat to the capital city, but no one collected. The only steamboat ever to make it all the way to Indianapolis was the *Robert Hanna*, which did so in 1831. The vessel spent six unprofitable weeks on a sandbar on its return voyage, an experience which discouraged later attempts to reach the city.

Samuel Merrill moved the state's properties to Indianapolis in the fall of 1824. It took 10 days for Merrill's wagons to cover the 125 miles from Corydon. By that time the settlement's population had grown to about 100 families. The physical appearance of the town hardly conveyed the image of a state capital. The first view of Indianapolis was disappointing to young Hugh McCulloch, who recalled having seen few towns "so utterly forlorn as Indianapolis appeared to me in the spring of 1833."

A two-story brick courthouse was completed in 1825. It housed not only the county, state, and federal courts, but also served for several years as the statehouse. The first state building was the office and home of the treasurer, located on the corner of what is now Washington St. and Capitol Ave. In 1827 the legislature appropriated funds for a mansion on the Governor's Circle. The building was an impressive two-story structure, but no governor ever lived there, for none wished to reside where his personal life could be so easily scrutinized by the public. The building was used for offices, storage, and in later years, as a hangout for children and derelicts. It was torn down in 1857.

In 1831 the General Assembly authorized the construction of a statehouse. This building was of an unusual style, best described as a Parthenon with a dome. W. R. Holloway, an early historian of the city, disapproved of the Greek style. He regarded it as unsuitable for a flat country and considered the dome an unforgivable error in judgment. A later historian, Jacob P. Dunn, defended the building on the ground that an "American capitol without a dome is inconceivable." Both agreed that the building was constructed of inferior materials, for after a

time it fell into disrepair and presented a shabby appearance.

The completion of the National and Michigan rds. lessened the isolation of the wilderness capital. By the mid-1830s Indianapolis became a major stopping point for traffic moving west on the National Rd. Hopes for the Central Canal which would link the capital to the Wabash and Erie Canal were dashed by the depression of 1837—the only portion of the canal to be finished extended from the village of Broad Ripple to Indianapolis. But railroads succeeded where the canal had failed. The first train, running from Madison to Indianapolis, arrived in 1847. Indianapolis was at last independent of the whims of the weather and unreliable roads. The "long reign of the 'wagoners,' " as Holloway phrased it, was at an end.

The 86-mile line was the first of several to link the city to the outside world. By 1870, 11 railroads led into Indianapolis. At first, each company built its own depot, but this soon proved inconvenient both to the railroads and to the people of the city. In 1850 three of the railroads organized the Union Railway Company, which laid a common track within the city limits and, three years later, built the nation's first union depot. By the end of the 1860s the frame structure, despite enlargements, was no longer adequate for the volume of traffic that it had to handle. In 1888 a massive brick and limestone structure replaced the original depot.

The railroads made Indianapolis an important military assembly center during the Civil War. The old and new fairgrounds became camps Sullivan and Morton. Camp Morton later became a prison for captured Confederate soldiers. Indianapolis's own regiment was the 11th Zouaves, so called because they wore the uniforms and practiced the spirited drill of the French Zouave infantry. Their commander was the flamboyant Col. Lew Wallace. When the ladies of the city presented the regiment with a flag, Wallace, holding the colors aloft, ordered his troops to swear a solemn oath to avenge the humiliation of Buena Vista. (Jefferson Davis, the new president of the Confederacy, had accused an Indiana regiment of cowardice during that Mexican War battle.)

The war acted as a stimulus to the city's growth. Between 1860 and 1870 the city's population grew by 159 percent. In 1865, the first year such statistics were kept, the city issued 1,621 permits for new building construction. The previous year the city had begun its first street railway. In 1873 construction began on a belt line around the city which, linked to a new stockyard, would greatly enhance the city's position as a slaughtering and meat packing center. Construction abruptly stopped after a few months when a severe depression hit the country. It was only through the efforts of Mayor John Caven that the project was finished. Caven persuaded a reluctant city council to pledge the city's credit to the completion of the belt line. The risks of undertaking such a project were great, but in the end proved immensely successful, helping to revive the local economy and providing employment to hundreds of idle workers during the depression.

The depression of the 1870s brought labor unrest and the great railroad strike of 1877. In Indianapolis comparatively little violence accompanied the strike. The 1880s brought recovery from depression, and Indianapolis emerged as an important manufacturing center. Slaughtering and metalworking were the two most important industries. The leading slaughterhouse in the city was Kingan and Company, a firm with plants in several American cities and headquarters in Belfast, Ireland. The Kingan brothers opened their Indianapolis plant in 1862. The company's trademark, a mariner at the wheel of a clipper ship, became a familiar sight to several generations of the city's residents. The pork packing plant remained in the Kingan family until 1952 when it was purchased by the Hygrade Food Products Corporation. Kingan and Company pioneered in the development of a refrigeration system which made it possible to slaughter year-round, instead of only in the winter months. Much of the plant's product was packaged for export to the Liverpool market. Many Irish came to Indianapolis so confident of finding employment at Kingan and Company that they simply addressed their trunks to the plant and showed up for work when they arrived in the city. A lively neighborhood called Irish Hill grew up nearby.

Foundries and machine shops were also an important part of the economy. The Eagle Machine Works began operation the year the Madison and Indianapolis Railroad was completed. The Atlas Engine Works, which in 1880 was the city's largest foundry, specialized in the manufacture of the Corliss steam engine. Other important metalworking industries included the Ewart Manufacturing Company (later Link-Belt); the Nordyke and Marmon works, which made gristmill machinery; and the Indianapolis Malleable Iron Company, founded in 1882. Malleable and Link-Belt were the leading employers of the city's small Eastern European population.

Indianapolis's central location and its excellent rail connections also attracted many other types of businesses. In 1872 Lyman S. Ayres bought out R. N. Smith and Company's Trade Palace and founded the department store chain which has figured prominently in the city's history. Four years later Col. Eli Lilly opened the small laboratory which was to grow into the giant pharmaceutical company. It was natural that the railroads themselves would become important employers. In 1890 railroad car construction and repair shops were the city's fourth largest employer. Probably most important was the Big Four's Beech Grove shops which opened in 1905.

The rise of manufacturing led to a local organized-labor movement. In the 1880s the printers, cigar makers, and iron molders formed the citywide Indianapolis Trades Assembly. By 1892 the Central Labor Union (as the assembly was called after 1883) claimed 83 local affiliates and 11,000 members. Because of the city's central location, several unions chose to locate their international headquarters in Indianapolis, including the influential Carpenters and Joiners Union, the Typographical Union, and the United Mine Workers of America. For a time the headquarters of the infant American Federation of Labor was located in an office building on East Market St. During the first decades of the 20th century Indianapolis's labor movement declined precipitously, partly because of a vigorous open-shop drive launched by the Associated Employers of Indianapolis. This organization claimed credit for the passage of antiboycott and antipicketing ordinances and the defeat of labor candidates in local elections. By 1920 the employers' association claimed that 85 percent of the city's businesses operated as open shops. The local labor movement did not reassert itself until the 1930s.

During the latter part of the 19th century Indianapolis grew into a city of impressive buildings and beautiful homes. A number of imposing buildings were added to the landscape during this period—an ornate three-story county courthouse with a 97-ft.-high clock tower, the elegant English Opera House and Hotel which graced the Circle until 1949, Tomlinson Hall civic auditorium, and a new statehouse completed in 1888 for slightly more than $2 million. In 1902 the city dedicated its new centerpiece, the Soldiers and Sailors Monument. The election of Benjamin Harrison as president of the United States in 1888 seemed a kind of recognition of the rising importance of the young city. In February 1889 a proud Indianapolis sent the new president and his wife off to Washington with a parade that took a full hour to cover the 15 blocks from his home on N. Delaware St. to Union Station.

By 1870 the city had seven streetcar lines operating on 15 miles of track. These mule-powered cars were the main form of public transportation in Indianapolis until 1890 when the first electric cars began operation, an innovation that caused nearly as much excitement as the arrival of the first trains in 1847. The first gas streetlights were installed in the front of the Masonic Lodge in 1851. By 1870 about 40 miles of Indianapolis's streets were illuminated by these lamps. The first electric lights in the city were installed in the old union depot in January 1882. The Indianapolis Brush Electric Light and Power Company, organized by former mayor Caven and others, supplied the power. In 1886 the company constructed five towers topped with arc lamps, which were supposed to illuminate the entire square mile. A private waterworks began operation in 1871, but few customers availed themselves of its services because of the probably accurate belief that its product was unfit to drink. The Indianapolis Water Company was organized in 1881. It sank deep wells and in 1902 built an elaborate sand filtration system which drew water from the old Central Canal. This new system, one of the most modern in the world at the time, provided the city with a reliable source of pure water.

The city was slow in developing good sewer and garbage disposal systems. Perhaps the growing community's greatest problem was the deplorable condition of the streets. Most of the main thoroughfares were paved with cobblestones, a surface which provided a jarring experience for passengers in wheeled vehicles. Less important streets were simply graded and graveled, which meant that in wet weather they were rivers of mud, and in dry weather blanketed with a haze of powdery dust. In 1890 some of the city's leading citizens organized the Commercial Club, with Col. Eli Lilly as its first president, and through the club agitated for a revised charter for the city. The following year the legislature complied, granting a charter that gave more power to the mayor and provided for a Board of Public Works. Under the direction of Mayor Thomas L. Sullivan a major street and sewer improvement program commenced.

Because of the close proximity of the countryside and the rural character of the city itself (during the 1880s cows still wandered free on N. Meridian), the citizenry felt no need for a park system. In 1868 when the heirs of Calvin Fletcher offered Indianapolis 30 acres on the northeast side for development as a park, the offer was turned down. In 1872 the city did acquire land which would become Garfield Park, but the area was not developed until the late 1890s, after a streetcar line was extended to it. Fairview Park, which, beginning in the 1880s was developed by the Street Railway Company into a very successful recreational area, became the campus of Butler University in 1928. In 1897, during the administration of Mayor Thomas Taggart, the city purchased 953 acres of what now comprises Riverside Park and the 82 acres comprising Brookside.

Early in the 20th century Indianapolis became the center of an electric interurban system which covered most of Indiana and extended into neighboring states. The first interurban line to enter Indianapolis was the Indianapolis, Greenwood and Franklin Traction Company, which began operating cars from Greenwood on January 1, 1900. Interurban traffic grew at a dizzying rate. In 1904 over three million passengers entered and left Indianapolis on these electric rail lines. On September 12 of that year the largest interurban station in the world, the Indianapolis Traction Terminal, opened. It included a nine-story office building and train shed sheltering nine tracks. The terminal offered the services of a railroad union station, such as office space for the companies, baggage facilities, ticket counters, and provided passengers with the convenience of a central station in downtown Indianapolis. In 1918, the peak year, 128,145 trains passed through the station and serviced 7,519,634 passengers.

Indianapolis's name also became closely linked with another new form of transportation, the automobile. We may never know the names of all the cars produced in the city, but more than 70 have been identified. Many of the names are now unfamiliar, but others, such as Duesenberg, Stutz, or Marmon, are legendary in automotive circles. The Indianapolis auto industry produced its share of colorful personalities. Most notable was Carl G. Fisher. Born in Greensburg, Fisher quit school at 12 and made his way to Indianapolis where he opened a bicycle shop. Fascinated with speed and the excitement of racing, Fisher became well known as a daredevil cyclist. His interest naturally led him to automobiles, both in selling and racing them. In 1904, in partnership with James A. Allison, he formed the Prest-O-Lite Company which made acetylene head lamps.

Fisher promoted his business interests with spectacular stunts. Once he rode a bicycle across Washington St. on a tightrope. On another occasion he fastened a car to a balloon and soared out across the city. His most grandiose publicity gimmick was his idea of building a racetrack where auto contests would provide advertising for manufacturers as well as serve as a laboratory for testing cars. In 1909 he persuaded James A. Allison and two other partners to join him in purchasing 400 acres of farmland for a track which later became the Indianapolis Motor Speedway.

Allison, Fisher's friend and partner, although a less colorful figure, may have had a more lasting impact on Indianapolis's history. In 1915 Allison opened the Indianapolis Speedway Team Company in a two-story brick building near Prest-O-Lite in Speedway. Initially this plant was little more than Allison's hobby, its main business the repair of race car engines. The company conducted a number of abortive experiments with marine engines (Allison and Fisher avidly raced speedboats) before moving into the field of aircraft motors. In 1929, a year after Allison's death, General Motors purchased the plant, the original structure becoming plant number one of the Allison-GM complex.

Indianapolis earned a reputation as a producer of expensive, luxury automobiles. The Cole, Duesenberg, Stutz, and Marmon were built for the few with the money to enjoy style and high-quality workmanship. Between 1920 and 1935 the Duesenberg plant produced fewer than 1,500 cars. Each was a mechanical and artistic marvel, but the market for such fine-quality transportation was limited and profitability was marginal. Some Indianapolis firms found it hard going even in good times—the Cole Motor Company folded in 1925. The depression of the 1930s proved fatal to the remaining Indianapolis automakers.

The development of the automobile had an enormous impact on the city. Probably most important was the improvement of roads that connected Indianapolis to the rest of the state and beyond. As the popularity of this new form of transportation increased, so, too, did the demand for better roads. Carl Fisher was a leader in the movement for improved highways. He conceived the Dixie Highway, a network of roads which connected the Midwest to Florida. For years this road, which passed through Indianapolis, was known as "Carl Fisher's Highway." In 1925 Congress created a system of United States highways, each marked with its own number, greatly facilitating travel by automobile. Four of these highways passed through the Indiana capital. The automobile had a devastating impact on the fine interurban system that radiated out of the capital. Given a choice, most travelers preferred to go by private automobile, or by the many buses that were more flexible in routing. (In 1925 a 2-mile-long "parade of buses" marked the opening of the city's first bus terminal.) The last interurban service out of Indianapolis, the Indianapolis-Seymour line, discontinued its service in 1941.

The development of the motor truck has probably had as great an impact on the history of the city as the railway. By 1908 a practical heavy-duty truck had been developed and was in use in Indianapolis. In 1914 the stockyards found it necessary to create a division for livestock delivered by truck. Five years later 35 motor express routes operated out of Indianapolis.

During the early decades of the 20th century Indianapolis continued to grow. By 1920 the city's population exceeded 300,000. In that year there were more than 1,000 manufacturing establishments in the city, employing about 50,000 workers. The city's fortunes crashed with those of the rest of the nation in 1929. In October 1933 over 10,000 families were on relief in Marion County. The manufacturing work force sank to about 30,000. The Great

Depression produced in Indianapolis all the signs of distress that could be found in any major city—breadlines, apple vendors, and homeless men sleeping on benches in Union Station. A Hooverville sprang up on the west bank of the White River. A Curtisville (for Vice-President Charles Curtis) developed opposite the Kingan packing plant.

The city responded to the crisis as best it could. Private and public social agencies provided for the emergency needs of victims of the depression. City and county employees contributed 1 percent of their salaries to a municipal soup kitchen which supplied meals twice a day to those in need. The city government and the Chamber of Commerce created an Emergency Work Committee which administered a "make work" program to provide employment to those willing to work. To raise money the committee sponsored a football game between Shortridge and Cathedral high schools on Thanksgiving Day. Despite unusual zero degree weather, the event raised more than $10,000. These funds were put to good use, but were exhausted by January 1931. As the depression deepened in 1932 and 1933 it became obvious that private efforts could not cope with the magnitude of the problem.

The depression brought the federal government into local affairs in a big way. Various New Deal agencies, such as the Federal Emergency Relief Administration, the Public Works Administration (PWA), and the Works Progress Administration (WPA), spent millions in the city through work-relief programs or through grants and loans to the city and county governments. Many of the projects were temporary make-work programs involving such unskilled labor as raking leaves, improving grade crossings, repairing chuckholes, or landscaping parks and hospital grounds. Other projects were monumental public works programs which left a permanent mark on the city's physical landscape. Such projects included the extension of Fall Creek Blvd. east from Keystone Ave., the construction of the State Fairgrounds Coliseum, the completion of the War Memorial Shrine Room, and the building of Lockefield Gardens. Through loans to the Indianapolis Railways, Inc., the PWA enabled the city to rebuild its transit system. Indianapolis pioneered in adopting the trackless trolley and by 1938 had one of the most modern public transportation systems in the country.

The Second World War brought Indianapolis out of the depression. By 1939 the local economy began to improve as the federal government expanded its national defense program. Allison expanded to produce high-speed fighter plane engines, and Curtiss-Wright opened the largest aircraft propeller factory in the United States in the old Marmon auto plant. Bridgeport Brass made artillery, Kingan and Company and Van Camp Packing Company produced army rations, and Eli Lilly made drugs to treat tropical diseases. Labor surplus became labor scarcity. In 1942 the War Manpower Commission declared Indianapolis a "labor shortage area."

The postwar period was one of continued prosperity. Among the new industrial giants to open plants in the city were Western Electric (1950), Chrysler Corporation (1952), and Ford Motor Company (1957). A major change which took place in the city's economy during the 1950s was the decline in the importance of the railroad. During and after the war, the trucking industry began to cut deeply into the railroad freight business. The new federal highway program, begun under President Dwight D. Eisenhower, encouraged this shift. Passenger rail traffic declined even more precipitously than freight service. Union Station, once filled with bustling crowds, by the 1960s stood as an almost unused relic of a bygone era. In 1946, 69 trains left Union Station daily. By 1963 this number had fallen to 18.

During the 1950s Indianapolis became famous as a city that resisted federal intrusion into local affairs. The opposition to federal aid was bipartisan, both Democrats and Republicans shunning federal funding for flood control, urban renewal, and school lunches. The city was able to raise $13 million for hospital construction without seeking federal aid, and the $22 million City-County Building was financed exclusively through local revenue bonds. In 1945 the state legislature created the Indianapolis Redevelopment Commission, which began one of the nation's first slum clearance programs. It was prohibited from accepting federal money to help carry out its work. However, the *Indianapolis Times* noted that while between 1950 and 1959 the city spent nearly $8 million on urban renewal, if it had participated in the federal urban renewal program it could have had an additional $15.5 million. Many felt the city was falling behind in dealing with pressing social problems.

In 1963 Democrat John J. Barton won the mayoral election, running on a platform calling for acceptance of federal aid. The new mayor sought and received federal subsidies for public housing. He also set up the Greater Indianapolis Progress Committee, a blue-ribbon advisory group for planning city development. Under Barton's Republican successors, Richard G. Lugar and William H. Hudnut, Indianapolis has pursued federal aid as aggressively as any city, yet the role of the federal government in local affairs remains limited. Local initiative and local control are still the rule, and federal funds have only supplemented traditional sources of funding—state and local taxes, private investment, and gifts from foundations, most notably Lilly Endowment, Inc.

Under Mayor Lugar the city government underwent a major restructuring. After the 1968 elections the Republicans had the governorship, both houses of the legislature, and the city government. Lugar seized this rare opportunity to push a bill through the legislature creating a consolidated city-county government for Marion County and Indianapolis. Unigov, as it came to be called, eliminated overlapping jurisdictions, created a single countywide legislative body, and strengthened the office of mayor, enabling this official to deal more effectively with metropolitan problems. The reorganization was actually much less than the complete consolidation that its name implied. Legalities and political compromises made it necessary that some governmental units remain unchanged. The city and county continued as separate legal entities, the major county-elected officials remained, the office of township trustee was untouched, and the incorporated cities of Beech Grove, Lawrence, Speedway, and Southport were excluded from the arrangement. Most significantly, the 11 existing Marion County school systems were not disturbed. Unigov was a Republican coup, for it diluted the strong Democratic central city with the votes of the overwhelmingly Republican suburbs. If the Republicans benefited politically, it was also true that Unigov was a characteristically Hoosier reform, forward-looking, but deeply rooted in day-to-day practicalities.

School desegregation became a major issue in Indianapolis in the 1970s. Complaints by blacks of the lack of racial integration in the Indianapolis schools led to a complex court battle which dragged on for years and involved more than two dozen school districts. Judge S. Hugh Dillin of the Federal District Court found the Indianapolis school system guilty of racial discrimination in the assignment of faculty and in the gerrymandering of districts. The faculty integration issue was easily resolved by teacher transfer, but the integration of students proved much more difficult. In Dillin's view, to order the integration of IPS alone would have encouraged a "white flight" which would have eventually resegregated the system. In hopes of preventing this, Dillin ordered one-way busing of black students to virtually every school district within commuting distance of Indianapolis. Court appeals trimmed back Dillin's ruling until his order applied only to IPS and six surrounding Marion County districts. Even in its reduced form, Dillin's order took years to thread its way through an intricate legal maze. It was not until August 1980 that the first busing started within IPS's own boundaries. The following year, with all possible channels of appeal exhausted, the busing of nearly 5,600 black grade school pupils to suburban Marion County school districts began. At the same time, some 17,000 students, both black and white, within the IPS system were reassigned.

On another front, beginning in the 1960s, the city began a dramatic turnaround in its outward appearance. "Indianapolis: A Born-again Hoosier Diamond in the Rust," is the way the *Smithsonian* magazine in 1987 captured the startling transformation of the previous two decades. Leading the attack on "Naptown's" reputation as a drab and declining community was the Greater Indianapolis Progress Committee (GIPC), a citizens' volunteer advisory and research body formed in 1965 through the leadership of banker Frank E. McKinney and then-Mayor John J. Barton. The GIPC, still in existence, was the first of several civic organizations that along with government incentives and the enormous benevolence of Lilly Endowment, spearheaded the city's renaissance, beginning with the establishment on the city's far northwest side of the nearly 5,000-acre Eagle Creek Park and Reservoir, the nation's largest urban park complex.

Large construction projects in the late 1960s and early 1970s included the campus of Indiana University-Purdue University at Indianapolis (IUPUI), the Convention Center, the

Indiana National Bank Tower, the Indianapolis Museum of Art, the Blue Cross-Blue Shield Building, the Hilton Hotel, the Federal Building and a United States Post Office, Market Square Arena, College Park, and Lafayette Square Mall. The city's long-held repute as a leading crossroads for commerce and industry was enhanced at this time by the expansion of Weir Cook Airport and the routing of new interstate highways around and through the city. The city had to wait out the lackluster economy of the mid-1970s into the early 1980s before earnest refashioning of the city could progress. Even in those slack years some prominent improvements took place, such as the bricking of Monument Circle and the construction of Merchants Plaza with its 500-room Hyatt Regency hotel.

Indianapolis had long achieved recognition for its 500 mile race and its hockey and minor league professional baseball teams. The completion of Market Square Arena in 1974 as home of the Indiana Pacers of the National Basketball Association (NBA) followed by four years the movement to Indianapolis of the Amateur Athletic Union headquarters. This blend of amateur and professional athletics struck local leaders in the mid-1970s as the prescription for the city's future. The Hoosier's traditional love of competitive sports in combination with Indianapolis's existing health and recreational facilities seemed tailored to advancing the city to world-class sports status, even becoming the "Amateur Sports Capital of the World." Armed with this vision, the city launched a well-planned campaign to attract sports events and organizations, and provide athletic facilities, jobs that largely fell to the nonprofit Indiana Sports Corporation, founded in 1980.

Within a decade, beginning in 1979, sports fans witnessed the construction of stadiums for tennis, track and field, swimming, professional football, cycling, and of headquarters for sports organizations, at a cost of almost $160 million. Some 20 international, national, and sports-related organizations were based in the city by 1989. The most recent addition is the National Art Museum of Sport which moved in early 1989 to Indianapolis from the University of New Haven in Connecticut. Along with the development and employment of existing facilities, Indianapolis in the 1980s had the capability to host almost any type of athletic activity. Among the events held in Indianapolis in the 1980s were national championships in figure skating, judo and karate, tennis, swimming and diving, rowing, track and field, canoe and kayak, softball, cycling, gymnastics, water polo, flag football, baton twirling, archery, and others. Numbered among the sports spectacles in these years are the National Sports Festival (1982), the NBA All-Star Game (1985), the 1987 10th Pan American Games (the largest sports event in the city's history), and the United States Olympic Diving Trials and the United States Track and Field Trials (1988). The city also is the site in 1991 of the nearly month-long World Gymnastics Championships. Indianapolis, moreover, is home to regularly scheduled sporting events such as the AAU James E. Sullivan Memorial Award Dinner, the GTE/United States Men's Hardcourt Championship, the Indianapolis-Scarborough Peace Games, the United States Nationals Championship Drag Races, the White River Park State Games, and the Larry Bird Pro All-Star Scholarship Classic, not to mention the Indianapolis 500 mile race.

A consensus ranks the acquisition in 1984 of the National Football League's Baltimore Colts and in 1987 of superstar running back Eric Dickerson as perhaps the most breathtaking news stories of the decade. Having a professional football team and a new domed stadium in which to play sent economic ripples throughout the city and state. In 1987-88, the Colts won the Eastern Division of the NFL. Concurrently, the Indianapolis Indians AAA baseball team won the American Association Championship in 1986, 1987, and 1988. In 1988 it went on to win the first "little world series" between the American Association and the International League. Notwithstanding the success of the Indians, the city hopes someday to be the recipient of a major league franchise.

Though sports feats dominated the headlines in the mid-1980s, for some the movement of the Hudson Institute from New York to Indianapolis was equally significant. The world-renowned "think tank," founded in New York in 1961 by Herman Kahn, transferred its headquarters to the IUPUI campus in 1984. Two years later the Institute, which studies public policy issues, moved into the Laurel Hall mansion, 5395 Emerson Way. The 40,000-sq.-ft. house was built in 1911-14 by Stoughton A. Fletcher, Jr. Upon moving, the new base of operations was named the Herman Kahn Center.

With the profusion of athletics in the 1980s came a tidal wave of building that changed the city's skyline. Sports and capital development seemed to nourish one another. Between 1978 and 1988 nearly $2 billion went toward downtown construction or renovation of sports facilities, office buildings, hotels, restaurants, theaters, retail complexes, manufacturing plants, and public space improvements. In this latter category are included such things as the renovated Indiana Roof Ballroom and Union Station, the new Indianapolis Zoo, the development of and around the old canal, the Convention Center plaza, the restoration of the Indiana Soldiers and Sailors Monument, and the construction of White River State Park. The completion of several of these extensive works is projected into the 1990s; they are among the $2 billion worth of additional improvements for the city anticipated after 1988, including the 3 1/2 block, $970 million downtown Circle City Mall, the retail and office construction by Mansur Development Corporation on the Circle and west along Market St., and the 48-story Bank One Center Tower, the state's tallest building. The construction fever in the downtown is matched by that throughout the metropolitan area.

It is generally conceded that as Indianapolis enters the last decade of the century the task will not center on major physical developments. The city has renewed itself. Its image is positive throughout the country. Calling Indianapolis now a "farm with streetlights" has no reference point unless one remembers the not-too-distant past. The National League of Cities ranked it the fifth most successful American city in economic development between 1983 and 1988. From March 1987 to March 1988 it was the nation's 17th fastest growing area for new jobs. Its economy is diversified and is able to withstand, as it did in the early 1980s, any serious national downturn. In the 1990s the city can turn to other matters, such as improving education, revitalizing neighborhoods, housing the homeless, and generally improving the quality of life for all its residents.

Indianapolis Attractions

The **Indianapolis City Center**, located on the ground floor in the Pan American Plaza (the name of the 13-story office building at 201 S. Capitol Ave., its public plaza, and underground parking garage), has available numerous materials pertaining to Indianapolis and surrounding communities. The plaza is located between the Hoosier Dome and Union Station.

1. In 1821 when Alexander Ralston laid out the "mile square" plans for the city of Indianapolis, he placed a circle in the center for the governor's house at the site of what is now the **Indiana Soldiers and Sailors Monument**, Monument Circle. A house was built in 1827, but the governor never occupied it, supposedly because his wife did not want to hang her laundry out for public display. The house was demolished in 1857, and for a time the Circle served as a grazing pasture. Following the Civil War the Grand Army of the Republic began raising money for a monument to commemorate the valor of Indiana's military men. The city held an international competition to produce the design for the Soldiers and Sailors Monument. In 1888 the commission selected the design by Bruno Schmitz of Berlin, Germany. The 284 1/2-ft.-high limestone structure (not counting the 30-ft.-high foundation) required almost $600,000 and 14 years to build. When dedicated in 1902, an estimated 75,000 spectators came for the occasion. Maj. Gen. Lew Wallace emceed the dedication; James Whitcomb Riley read a poem, "The Soldier"; and John Philip Sousa composed a march, "Messiah of the Nations." A 38-ft.-tall, 17-ton bronze statue of **Victory**, though usually called **Miss Indiana**, by George T. Brewster of Cleveland, Ohio, crowns the monument and faces south. The basement contains a museum of Civil War and Spanish-American War memorabilia, including a large collection of battle flags. From the base of the monument an elevator rises up the shaft to a glass-enclosed balcony at the top which affords

a panoramic view of the downtown area. German sculptor Rudolph Schwarz executed the numerous statues clustered about the base of the monument. The two main statuary groups facing east and west represent the themes of War and Peace, respectively. John H. Mahoney of Indianapolis created several bronze statues of famous Hoosiers on the street level. A downtown beautification project completed in 1981 provided the brick streets and sidewalks radiating outward from the Circle. The first phase of a two-phase, $12 million project to restore the Soldiers and Sailors Monument was completed in 1987. At Christmastime the monument is strung with 4,638 lights and touted as the world's largest Christmas tree. (*NRHP/HABS*)

2. Erected in the late 1850s, **Christ Church Cathedral**, on the northeast quadrant of Monument Circle, is the oldest building on the Circle. In 1837 Christ Church, the first Episcopal church in Indianapolis, was organized with the Rev. James B. Britton as its first rector. The original church was a frame structure, dedicated in 1838. In the cornerstone were placed the first silver dimes and half dimes brought into the town. William Tinsley designed the present church, erected on the same site, in an English country Gothic style. Chimes were added in 1861 and the spire in 1869. The recently restored stained-glass windows are in the style of Louis Comfort Tiffany of New York. The congregation repaired the church and dug a basement in the early 1900s. In a niche on the east wall a statue of St. Francis of Assisi with a little bird in his hand honors Albert Splatt, a church groundskeeper. Although the adjoining brick parsonage and the trees are gone, this corner of the Circle looks much the same today as it did during the 19th century. In 1954 Christ Church was named procathedral of the Indianapolis Episcopal diocese. Eli Lilly wrote a history of the church, *The Little Church on the Circle*, published in 1957. The church under-

Indianapolis

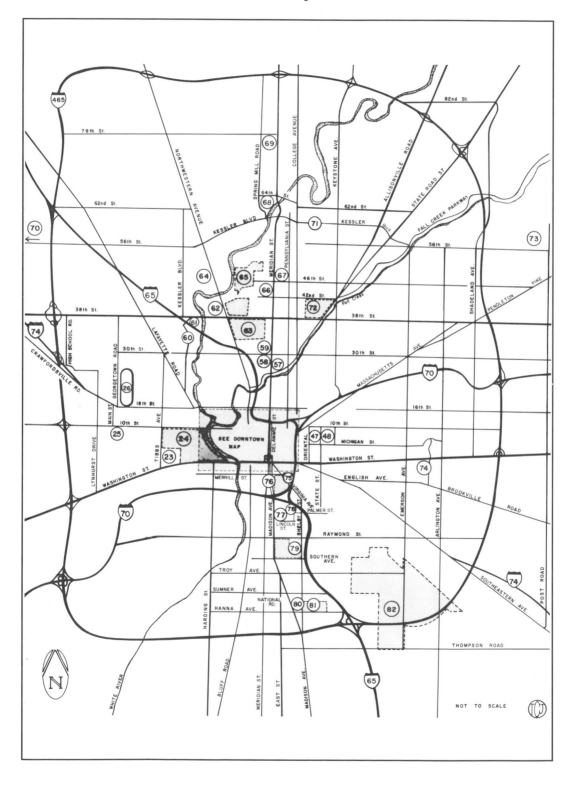

Attractions

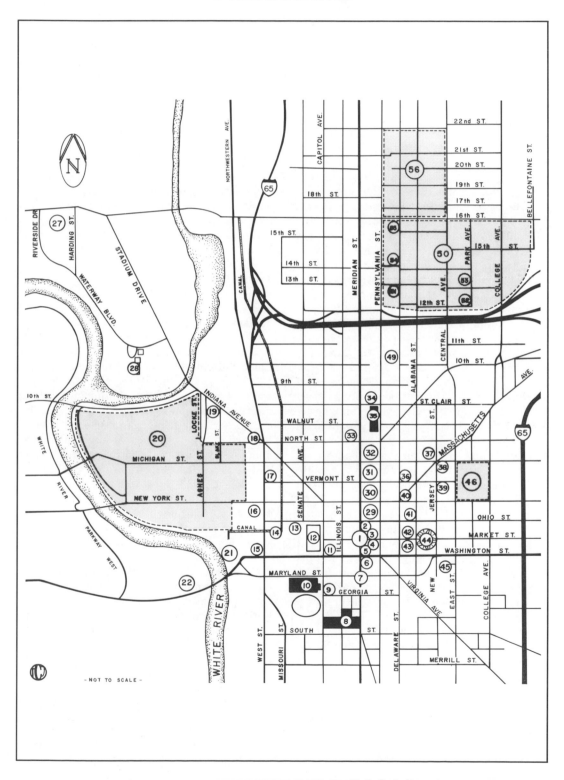

went a $900,000 renovation project in the late 1980s. (*NRHP/HABS*)

3. Founded as a Republican party marching band of 150 men during Benjamin Harrison's presidential campaign in 1888, and incorporated in 1889, the **Columbia Club**, 121 Monument Circle, is the oldest and most widely known private club in Indianapolis. The dedication of the club's second home on the Circle, on New Year's Eve, 1900, was attended by such dignitaries as Benjamin Harrison, James Whitcomb Riley, Charles Warren Fairbanks, Albert J. Beveridge, and several Civil War generals. Rubush and Hunter designed the present 10-story limestone building with leaded-glass windows and a green copper roof. Built for $827,200, it was dedicated in 1925. Alexander Sangernebo carved the English mansard-style stone facade of the building. Club facilities include a walnut-paneled lounge and main lobby with a marble fireplace and staircase on the ground floor, plus meeting rooms, a banquet hall, ballroom, private rooms, and a library on the upper floors. The first woman, Ardath Yates Burkhart, was admitted to the previously all men's club in 1979. In 1985 a five-year project to refurbish the club began, which included restoration of the original Italian floral design hand-stenciled on the ceiling beams and the addition of pressed-glass gaslight fixtures. (*NRHP*)

4. Rubush and Hunter designed the 15-story limestone **Circle Tower Building** on the southeast quadrant of Monument Circle. William Lingenfelter's boardinghouse occupied the site from 1835 to 1873, followed by the 4-story Franklin Insurance Company building. The present structure, completed in 1930, was built in a "wedding cake" design of terraced upper stories to provide an unobstructed view of the monument. It adheres to the height and setback guidelines for buildings on the Circle proposed by city planner George Kessler in 1922. Bronze grillwork in an Egyptian motif glows beneath a sculptured stone archway at the Market St. entrance, and Art Deco panels adorn the upper corners of the exterior facade.

5. Rubush and Hunter designed the **Circle Theatre**, 45 Monument Circle, the first of the city's grand "movie palaces." Built in 1916, the ornate structure with a white terra-cotta facade, classical cornice, and pediments was the scene of elaborate stage productions. It was used for showing movies until 1981. At that time the Indianapolis Power and Light Company purchased the fading movie house. A civic group called Circle Theatre Associates formed to manage its use and conduct a $6.9 million renovation project. Architect Peter van Dijk directed the restoration of the terra-cotta facade and the duplication of the original 1916 marquee. When the interior paint and plaster of 1938 and 1964 renovations were peeled away, the original ceiling was found intact. An example of the Adam style of Neoclassicism, the dusty rose and ivory plasterwork, gilt railings, and Grecian figures have been restored to their original elegance. In 1984 the Circle Theatre reopened as the new home of the Indianapolis Symphony Orchestra under the direction of John Nelson. Raymond Leppard assumed the responsibilities of conductor in the fall of 1987. The ISO, founded in 1930, now houses its administrative offices in a rehabilitated building along Washington St. with direct access to the backstage of the Circle Theatre. (*NRHP*)

6. For half a century the 17-story **Merchants Bank Building**, 11 S. Meridian St., erected 1907-13, was the tallest "skyscraper" in Indianapolis. Architect Daniel H. Burnham based the design of the building on principles of the Chicago School of Architecture. Merchants Bank, founded in 1865, occupies the main floor of the building. The last of the city's grand old bank lobbies is resplendent with bronze and marble. During the 1920s John L. Lewis, president of the United Mine Workers, had his office on the 11th floor. In the late 1940s Indiana's first television broadcast was transmitted over WFBM from a tower on the roof. (*NRHP*)

7. Once the city's **Wholesale District**, the neighborhood bounded by Capitol Ave., Maryland, Delaware, and South sts. contains a large collection of commercial buildings dating from 1863 to 1930. Many of these brick and cast-iron structures are being restored to their Victorian elegance as a result of the district's listing on the National Register of Historic Places, of the urban development associated with the renovated Union Station and the new Hoosier Dome, and of a 1987 preservation plan of the Metropolitan Development Commission and the Indianapolis Historic Preservation Commission.

In 1862 August and Henry Schnull began a wholesale grocery business on S. Meridian St. that eventually expanded the full length of the block. By the turn of the century Indianapolis was home to more than 300 wholesale and jobbing houses in near proximity to the railroad station. As cars and trucks took freight business away from the railroads, wholesale houses moved to the suburbs where parking space was plentiful. With the recent return of commerce to the central city, abandoned stores and warehouses are finding new life as offices, specialty shops, hotels, and restaurants.

Among the 54 historically and architecturally significant buildings in the wholesale district listed on the National Register of Historic Places is the **Hatfield Paint Company Building**, 29 E. Maryland St., erected by Holland and Ostermeyer in 1867 for their wholesale grocery business. Originally part of a block of buildings, the well-preserved structure is the only one remaining. From 1873 to 1876 organic chemists Johnston and Lilly conducted business there. The junior partner, Col. Eli Lilly, left to start his own pharmaceutical company. The Hatfield Paint Company occupied the building during much of the 20th century. Archonics Design/HNTB recently modified the masonry, cast-iron, and timber building for a cable television company.

The greatest number of NRHP buildings in the wholesale district are concentrated within the 100 and 200 blocks of S. Meridian St., known as Meridian Row. **Schnull's Block**, 102-108 S. Meridian St., originally contained four ground-floor storefronts. Bernard Vonnegut designed the building at 110 S. Meridian St. which served as the headquarters for Schnull and Company from 1896 to 1920. Modeled on principles of design of the Chicago School of Architecture, the present building replaced the wholesale grocery store destroyed by fire in 1895.

Volney T. Malott erected the **Brunswick-Balke-Collender Company** building at 118 S. Meridian in 1896-97. The manufacturer of billiard tables and bowling equipment was an early tenant of this Romanesque-style building, which originally was twice its present size. Built in 1866-67 and remodeled in the early 1900s, the Italianate-style commercial building at 124 S. Meridian St. successively housed wholesale stores dealing in hats, boots and shoes, hardware and iron, and groceries. The

House of Crane, a wholesale cigar firm, occupied the building more than 50 years, beginning in 1910.

At 200 S. Meridian St. a fashionable chain restaurant now occupies two commercial buildings erected in the late 1880s. The 1889 **McKee Building** on the corner, designed by architect Robert Platt Daggett and Company, originally housed a wholesale boot and shoe business. A wholesale dry goods firm, D. P. Erwin and Company, owned the L-shaped building next door.

On the southeast corner of Meridian and Georgia sts. the **Byram, Cornelius and Company** building erected in 1871-72 forms part of a restored retail/office complex. The Italian Renaissance-style structure features the oldest remaining cast-iron facade in the city. A candy factory occupied the building after the dry goods firm reorganized as D. P. Erwin and Company and moved across the street in 1890. (*HABS*)

8. The Indianapolis **Union Station**, 39 Jackson Place, is one of the last remaining Victorian train stations in the Midwest. It opened in 1888 on the site of the country's first union station. The first steam train arrived in Indianapolis in 1847, ushering in a new era in transportation. In 1852 construction began on the union station—a simple wooden structure with five tracks inside the passenger sheds and two freight tracks outside. The station served all the city's railroad lines under one roof. In the mid-1880s construction of the present Romanesque-style terminal designed by Thomas Rodd got under way, requiring two years and $500,000 to complete. The imposing three-story brick and limestone building featured a 70-ft.-high barrel-vaulted ceiling in the main concourse with circular rose-colored stained-glass windows at each end. An enormous 175-ft.-tall clock tower crowned the station. The new structure was a showplace with its spacious waiting rooms and modern offices for railroad executives on the upper floors.

After World War II the railroads began their decline as Americans bought cars and built highways. Today Amtrak uses the train shed for service between Indianapolis and Chicago and through Indianapolis connecting Cincinnati, Washington, D.C., and New York. Art Deco-style tile work highlights the concourse, built between 1916 and 1922. In 1983 construction work began on a multimillion dollar project to convert the historic train terminal into a shopping, dining, and hotel complex. Hotel rooms are located on three levels of the train shed and in some restored railroad cars. (*NRHP/HABS*)

9. Architect Diederich A. Bohlen designed **St. John's Catholic Church**, 121 S. Capitol Ave., in a French Gothic style in 1867-71. The rectory around the corner on Georgia St. was erected in 1870. Holy Cross, built in 1840, was the first Catholic church in Indianapolis. The early congregation, composed largely of Irish and German Catholics who worked for the railroad and lived in the neighborhood, erected a church named St. John's in 1850 to replace the overcrowded Holy Cross. The German-speaking members of St. John's eventually wanted a separate church and built St. Mary's Church in 1858; that church later moved to its present location at 317 N. New Jersey St. The Irish members of the congregation erected the present St. John's church. In 1893 the congregation added twin spires above the front towers, imported a marble altar from Italy, and installed a Gothic pulpit, bishop's chair, and choir stalls. Guy Leber painted the angels on the ceiling of the apse. (*NRHP*)

10. The **Indiana Convention-Exposition Center**, 100 S. Capitol Ave., is one of the largest convention headquarters in the nation. The multipurpose facility opened in 1972. Besides a new stadium, the center incorporates 5 exhibit halls, 2 ballrooms, and 55 meeting rooms. The main exhibition hall features movable acoustical walls measuring 300 ft. long by 35 ft. high. The dream of Indiana sports fans came true when the **Hoosier Dome**, an $82 million stadium, opened in May 1984. An adjunct to the Convention Center, the stadium is home to the Indianapolis Colts of the National Football League. It seats 61,000 persons, covers about 8 acres of ground space, and rises to a height of 193 ft. (19 stories). Air pressure from 20 electric fans supports the 514,505-lb. Teflon-coated fabric roof. The billowing white dome creates a bold silhouette on the city's skyline. In addition to football games, the facility schedules a wide variety of activities including rodeos, auto shows, conventions, banquets, trade shows, and baseball and basketball games. The Dome also houses the National Track and Field Hall

of Fame, which was dedicated January 12, 1986. With the 96,000-sq.-ft. floor of the stadium, the Convention Center now has a combined area of nearly 300,000 sq. ft. of available space. Between the Convention Center and the State Capitol is the **Convention Center Plaza**, a block of formal English-style landscaping completed in 1988. The $6 million project, funded by Lilly Endowment, Inc., and designed by Kennedy Brown McQuiston, Inc., of Indianapolis, features fountains, an obelisk, trees, and plants. It rests above a parking garage containing 1,013 spaces. Also completed in 1988 and bordering the plaza on the west is the **Westin Convention Center Hotel**, the city's 26th hotel or motel to open since 1984 and, with 572 rooms, the state's largest.

11. Preston Rubush and Edgar Hunter designed the **Indiana Theatre**, 140 W. Washington St., which was built in 1927 for $1.5 million. Now home for the **Indiana Repertory Theatre**, the former movie palace cost $5.1 million to renovate in 1980. The entertainment center is comprised of a 607-seat main stage theater, a 245-seat upper stage, and a 150-seat cabaret hall. Workers converted the single four-story-high auditorium into space for three theaters by removing the balcony and constructing new floors. Much of the proscenium arch and Arabesque-style interior plaster work has been saved. The lobby's polychrome ceiling, grand staircase, and mural of the Taj Mahal remain the same. Extensive exterior work has restored the gleaming white terra-cotta facade of Spanish-Baroque design, which was sculpted by Alexander Sangernebo. In the 1920s the building contained a billiard room, a basement bowling alley with 16 lanes, and a soda fountain. Also in the theater was a rooftop ballroom known as the **Indiana Roof**. Inspired by the 1926 song "In a Little Spanish Town," architects Rubush and Hunter designed a domed ballroom evoking a Spanish plaza, surrounded by stuccoed house facades, upper story red-tiled roofed open galleries, and ornamental iron railings. Closed in the mid-1970s, the ballroom reopened in 1986 after an extensive renovation by Indianapolis's Melvin Simon and Associates. The ballroom is used for dances and meetings. A hallway connects the Roof with the **Embassy Suites Hotel**, completed in 1985. The 17-story hotel includes the Claypool Shops and three floors of retail shops and restaurants. (*NRHP/HABS*)

12. In 1825 the first state legislature to meet in Indianapolis convened in rented rooms in the Marion County Courthouse, which served as the statehouse for 10 years. From 1835 to 1878 general assemblies met in a Doric-style building with a dome built on the same site as the present capitol. Construction of the existing **Indiana State Capitol**, bounded by Senate and Capitol aves. and Washington and Ohio sts., began in 1878 and was completed in 1888 at a cost of $2,099,794.66 (just over the estimated cost of $2 million). Architect Edwin May of Indianapolis designed the limestone structure in classic Corinthian style. After May's death in 1880 Adolph Scherrer became supervising architect. The building houses the chief offices of the state government and the chambers of the House of Representatives, Senate, Supreme Court, Court of Appeals, and other state agencies. Beneath the 72-ft.-diameter copper dome a blue-hued, stained-glass window imported from Germany illuminates the 234-ft.-high rotunda. Eight Italian Carrara marble statues encircle the third level of the rotunda. Numerous plaques and statues adorn the main floor area. A bronze bust of Col. Richard Owen, commander of Camp Morton during the Civil War, occupies a niche in the rotunda. Former Confederate prisoners commemorated Owen for his courtesy and kindness by commissioning the bust sculpted by Miss Belle Kinney. Portraits of the past governors of Indiana hang in the second-floor hallways. The state stone—an 85-lb. chunk of Bedford limestone mounted on a dolly—occupies a third-floor niche. Original furnishings fill the Supreme Court, and portraits of past justices line the walls. The House chamber, remodeled in 1966, features walnut paneling, a chandelier with 100 lights, and a mural by Eugene Francis Savage entitled the *Spirit of Indiana*. The Senate chamber was remodeled in the 1970s at a cost equal to that of building the entire statehouse in the 19th century. Statues of Thomas A. Hendricks, Oliver P. Morton, George Washington, Christopher Columbus, Abraham Lincoln, and a miner stand on the grounds. The statehouse underwent an $11 million restoration between 1986 and 1988, the work completed in time for the celebration of the building's centennial. The Cooler Group, Inc., of Indianapolis took charge of the restoration. (*NRHP*)

The statehouse anchors a campus of public buildings, mostly just west of the capitol, collectively called the **Indiana Government Center**. The **Indiana Employment Security Division building** is on the northwest corner of Washington St. and Senate Ave. The 3-story, $2.1 million structure went up in 1959-60. Erected about the same time was the adjacent 13-story **State Office Building**. Crews cleared five city blocks and 56 buildings to make way for the $30 million answer to the state's need to centralize its scattered departments. Architects Graham, Anderson, Probst and White of Chicago and Raymond S. Kastendieck and Associates of Gary designed it with some 2,000 windows. A renovation of the building began in 1988. Construction of an $89 million, five-story addition, **State Office Building II**, to the south and west, began in 1988. The newer structure will be two blocks long and will contain 643,000 sq. ft. of space. Plans call for a Market St. extension to begin at the west door of the statehouse and continue 1,000 bricked feet through the "campus" to West St. On the south side of Washington St., between Senate Ave. and West St., is the 3,000-car Government Center parking garage, the largest in the city, completed in 1988.

13. Dedicated in 1934, the **Indiana State Library and Historical Building** at Senate Ave. and Ohio St. is part of the **Indiana Government Center** and represents a monument to Indiana history. Although Classical in style for the most part, the exterior of the building incorporates Art Deco stylized panels sculpted across the upper level. Inside the library the original woodwork, marble, and brass light fixtures have been preserved. The central great hall features a barrel-vaulted ceiling and stained-glass windows. Two murals painted by Scott Williams—*The Winning of the State* and *The Building of the State*—cover the foyer walls. The library specializes in books, federal documents, and early manuscripts dealing with Indiana and Indiana literature, besides housing the state's archives and the **Indiana Historical Bureau**. The west wing of the building, added in 1976, 315 W. Ohio St., houses the Newspaper Division, the Division for the Blind and Physically Handicapped, the Genealogy Division, and the **Indiana Historical Society**. The Society, which celebrates its 160th anniversary in 1990, maintains the William Henry Smith Memorial Library, conducts research, and publishes materials dealing with the state's history.

On the third floor the Smith Library displays a fine copy of Audubon's *Birds of America*, folio edition of 1827-38.

14. The **Central Canal Project** has been one of the more ambitious projects undertaken during the city's 1980s renaissance. For many years there had been talk of creating a new use for the old and idle 1830s canal, that in recent times had turned into a "foul-smelling ditch." A $9 million project was launched in 1984 to rebuild the canal from West St. to 10th St. The object was to stimulate private construction along its banks of condominiums, apartments, shops, hotels, and restaurants. Funding for the canal reconstruction came through grants from the Urban Mass Transit Administration, the Lilly Endowment, Inc., and the Indianapolis Foundation. A two-block portion of the project was dedicated in July 1987. The architectural firm of Browning Day Mullins Dierdorf, Inc., designed a "contemporary Italianate" style for the canal, a Venetian composition, with elements similar to those of the Paseo del Rio (River Walk) in San Antonio, Texas. Most striking at this point of development is the scenic 100-ft.-wide lagoon south of Ohio St., where the canal makes a turn west. The concrete lagoon boasts a 40-ft. geyser, water cascading over a 14-ft.-high wall, a footbridge, walkways, benches, and flower gardens. Here canalboats turn around and are also maintained in the lower portion of the new **Firehouse 13** at the corner of Ohio and West sts. The visitor walks down to the lagoon from the new and more elevated Ohio St. bridge, which like the other new bridges at Michigan and New York sts. is adorned with wrought-iron railings and benches, and new lights. Along a completed two-block stretch, the canal is 4 ft. deep and about 50 ft. wide with sloping sides to allow for extensive landscaping. The channel has been veneered with a black coating to protect its concrete finish, among other reasons. The economic development along the canal has not progressed as rapidly as anticipated, but a 124-apartment complex, Canal Overlook, has been completed at Indiana and Senate, and several more projects are in the works, including Canal Square, a residential and retail complex at West and New York sts. Nearby at Michigan St. and Indiana Ave., will be the **Heritage Preservation Center**, after 1990 the headquarters of the Historic Landmarks Foundation of Indiana, in the historic **Kuhn house**. Built in 1879 by butcher John Charles Kuhn, the Italianate-style house originally stood on the south side of W. Michigan St. on the site of the present American College of Sports Medicine. The onetime funeral parlor and hotel is the only historic building remaining on the canal. A new multistory addition, linked to the old house by a soaring atrium, will include canal-level retail space. Historic Landmarks Foundation of Indiana, incorporated in 1960, was founded by Eli Lilly to aid in the preservation and restoring of sites, buildings, and other structures significant to the historical and cultural development of Indiana.

15. The **Eiteljorg Museum of the American Indian and Western Art**, northwest corner of West and Washington sts., houses one of the nation's outstanding collections of western American and Amerindian art and artifacts. Harrison Eiteljorg, an Indianapolis coal company executive and art patron, began collecting western and Indian art in the 1940s. From 1976 through 1987 a portion of his vast collection was on loan in the Harrison Eiteljorg Gallery of Western Art at the Indianapolis Museum of Art. His desire to assemble in one place all his $40 to $50 million collection led Eiteljorg to establish a downtown museum on ground leased from the White River State Park. Lilly Endowment, Inc., contributed to the project $12.5 million plus funds for museum planning and initial operation. Ground breaking for the $14 million structure took place October 22, 1987. The Indianapolis firm of Browning Day Mullins Dierdorf, Inc., had in mind the mud pueblos of the southwest in designing the exterior. The two-story veined Minnesota dolomite and German sandstone building has a portico supported by trunks of cedar trees imported from British Columbia. Some 23,200 ft. of the 73,000 sq. ft. space is given over to four galleries, three permanent. The collection includes the items from the former Museum of Indian Heritage, which opened in 1967 at Eagle Creek Park. The noted western artist George Carlson sculpted for the new museum's entranceway a 10-ft. Indian with outstretched hands called "The Greeting." The fountain on the grounds, created by California artist Kenneth Bunn, is a model of five deer splashing through the water. The museum opened in the summer of 1989.

16. Bounded by West, Blake, and New York sts. and the canal, **Military Park** has led a varied role in the city's history. In the 1820s the site was used as a militia training field. The annual Fourth of July picnic, a community outing, was held here as early as 1822. The park was the site of the first state fair in 1852, drawing about 30,000 persons over a three-day period. The fair was held here for all except three years until 1860. During the Civil War the grounds were used as a military camp. Many of Indiana's troops bivouacked on the site, renamed Camp Sullivan, including the Zouave Regiment under the command of Col. Lew Wallace. The ground was reduced to its present size in 1868 and became the city's first public park, called Military Park. The property now figures prominently in the plans for the White River State Park. (*NRHP*)

17. **Bethel African Methodist Episcopal Church**, 414 W. Vermont St., is the city's oldest A.M.E. church. The first congregation organized in 1836 and met in the log cabin home of Augustus Turner. In 1841 the congregation built a small frame house on Georgia St. between Senate Ave. and the canal to serve as a place of worship. In 1857 they bought the first Christ Church and moved it from the Circle to Georgia St. The church was destroyed by fire a few years later—possibly at the hands of anti-abolitionists who resented the church members' involvement in the "underground railroad." The present brick building with a gallery and tower was constructed in 1869. Various architectural changes and renovations have been made over the years. A handsome carved pulpit presented by the Rev. Andrew Chambers, an early minister, still remains in the church. The Indianapolis chapter of the National Association for the Advancement of Colored People was organized in this church.

18. The wedge-shaped **Walker Building**, at the triangular corner of Indiana Ave. and West and North sts., is a monument to a famous black businesswoman and a landmark of the once thriving black community of Indiana Ave. Madam C. J. Walker (1867-1919), born in Louisiana as Sarah Breedlove, daughter of ex-slaves, developed a line of cosmetic and hair-care products which she first marketed in Denver, Colorado, with advice and assistance of her husband, C. J. Walker. After their divorce, she brought her business to Indianapolis

and Indiana Ave. where it flourished and made her the nation's first black woman millionaire. After her death, daughter A'Lelia continued the business and had the Walker Building erected in 1927. Designed by Rubush and Hunter, the $1 million, four-story, yellow brick-faced structure, combining African and Egyptian decorations, housed the Walker Company, the Walker Theatre, the Walker College of Beauty Culture, and various shops and offices. Along **Indiana Ave.**, a haven of black culture and commerce, the Walker Theatre along with its Casino stood out as a mecca for top black performers of jazz and the blues, who made their way among dozens of clubs such as Cotton Club, Sunset, Golden West, Paradise, Mitchellynne, and Trianon. On the Avenue, or "Black Broadway," performed such greats as the original Ink Spots, Josephine Baker, Ethel Waters, Cab Calloway, Ella Fitzgerald, Leroy Vinegar, Jimmy Lundsford, Speed Webb, the Hamptons, Frank Clay, Jimmy Coe, the Brown Buddies, J. J. Johnson, Earl Walker, Noble Sissle, Eubie Blake, Freddie Hubbard, Larry Ridley, Jack McDuff, Ben Holiman, and many others. On the "Grand Ol' Street" the "Indy Sound" developed, best exemplified through the guitar of Indianapolis native Wes Montgomery. With the decline of the neighborhood in the middle decades of the century, the Walker Building and Theatre suffered the same fate. The Madam Walker Urban Life Center, Inc., purchased the building in 1979. With the backing of more than $5 million from all levels of government and from Lilly Endowment, Inc., the Center began a three-phase restoration to attract new tenants and provide a catalyst for black culture. Businesses and organizations began leasing space in 1983. The renovated 950-seat theater reopened October 14, 1988, exactly 61 years after it first opened. (*NRHP*)

Across the street from the Walker Building is the new **Center for Nursing Scholarship and International Nursing Library** of Sigma Theta Tau International, a nursing honorary. The Indianapolis firm of Howard Needles Tammen and Bergendoff designed the 37,000-sq.-ft. facility that houses a modern nursing research library. Sigma Theta Tau was founded in 1922 in Indianapolis and currently has about 130,000 members in 264 chapters in the United States, Canada, Korea, and Taiwan.

Future help in reinvigorating the historic avenue also will come with the completion of the 30,000-sq.-ft. **Walker Plaza**, a three-story office building, north of the Walker Building, and the building of a $15 million **headquarters for the Christian Church (Disciples of Christ)** on a triangular site bounded by Indiana and Senate aves. and Michigan St.

19. Another landmark of the Indiana Ave. community is **Lockefield Gardens**, the nation's eighth federal housing project when constructed in 1936 in the 900 block. The original 24 tan-brick buildings, two to four stories in height, contained a total of 748 apartments and covered about four acres out of its 24-acre landscaped site. The buildings were well constructed, airy, and roomy. Their style was adopted from German architectural developments in public housing. The original plans were submitted by Indianapolis architects William Earl Russ and Merritt Harrison to officials in the Public Works Administration (PWA), who modified them. Residents of the $3 million complex took pride in the buildings and grounds, but in the 1950s a less stable population took up housing in the Gardens, which hastened its deterioration. Then, in 1974, Federal Judge S. Hugh Dillin ruled that the Gardens fostered segregation, and he closed them. The idea of some form of renovation paralleled the downtown boom of the 1980s and the need for housing for the Pan American Games. In 1983 the city tore down two-thirds of the buildings to make way for expansion of the campus of Indiana University-Purdue University at Indianapolis. From April 1986 to April 1987 developer Joseph Sexton rehabilitated 199 apartments (*NRHP/HABS*) and built 294 new units. At Walnut St. and Indiana Ave., at the entrance to the Gardens, stands the sculpture "'Jammin' On the Avenue," designed by native Hoosier John Spaulding, newly relocated to Indianapolis from New York City. Dedicated April 24, 1989, the sculpture amasses parts of various kinds of horns around a 13-ft.-high shaft as a reminder of the Avenue's jazz legacy.

20. **Indiana University-Purdue University at Indianapolis** (IUPUI) occupies a 289-acre campus roughly bounded by the White River, 10th, West, and Washington sts. The modern urban commuter campus became an entity in 1969 with the administrative merger of the two universities' Indianapolis facilities. The school serves 24,808 (1988) students and employs 1,300 full-time and 800 part-time faculty, in addition to 5,437 staff. It is one of the five largest employers in Indianapolis. IUPUI offers 165 degree programs in Indiana University's 15 schools in medicine, law, education, business, and the humanities, and Purdue University's 2 schools in science and engineering. Almost half of the student body is in the Purdue programs. Some 1.5 million visitors come to the campus annually for academic or sports events.

Located on the former Fall Creek "bottoms," the IUPUI campus was an Indian hunting ground and Delaware settlement until about 1814. Its location at the confluence of the White River and Fall Creek prompted the commissioners to select this site for the state capital in 1821. An 1821 epidemic was fatal to about one-eighth of the tiny settlement's population who were buried in the "plague cemetery"—now the site of the Medical School Building. The malarial conditions of the "bottoms" persuaded the early settlers to move to higher ground.

Following two smallpox epidemics in 1848 and 1855 Dr. Livingston Dunlap legislated for a hospital that was finally completed in 1859. Built away from the general populace where it "could do no harm," the hospital, called Dunlap's Folly, was considered a "pest house" rather than a place to regain good health. It was used as a house for fallen women and as a military hospital during the Civil War, but for the most part it stood vacant until the city resumed its management in the 1870s. The old buildings were used until the south wing was constructed under the superintendency of William N. Wishard, 1879-87, after whom the hospital was later renamed. **Wishard Hospital** today is a 618-bed public general teaching hospital which houses an outpatient facility, adult burn unit, trauma center, poison center, spinal cord unit, and specialized intensive care units.

In the 1870s the course of Fall Creek was changed so that it went around the campus instead of through it. In 1911 Dr. Robert W. Long donated money for a teaching hospital, which became the first unit of the present **Indiana University (IU) Medical School**. After 1919 the medical school occupied Emerson Hall. The area, however, was not without its problems. A group known as the tribe of Ishmael gave the place a bad reputation. Arriving from Kentucky in 1830, the families intermarried and multiplied, adding assorted tinkers, peddlers, and vagrants to their ranks. The settlement gained notoriety as a haven for gambling, prostitution, and general lawlessness. The residents were forced to move when **Riley Hospital for Children**, still the only one in the state, was built in the 1920s. The School of Dentistry was added in 1925. William H. Coleman Hospital opened as a maternity care facility in 1927—the first intended specifically for obstetrics and gynecology. It closed as a hospital in 1974, and Coleman Hall is now used as the headquarters for the Division of Allied Health Services. The Medical Science Building was constructed in 1958 and expanded in 1980. Regenstrief Health Center, designed for outpatients, was built in 1975. In 1985 the first DNA (deoxyribonucleic acid) bank in the world was established at the IU Medical Center to provide research facilities and services for families with genetic diseases. Today, the IU Medical Center comprises 6 hospitals and 90 clinics, including the IU School of Medicine, the IU School of Dentistry, and the IU School of Nursing. The IU School of Medicine is the nation's second largest in enrollment and campus size. There are about 4.5 miles of tunnels under the medical center, and newer buildings are connected by enclosed walkways. The world's largest **Ronald McDonald House**, 1235 W. Michigan St., houses out-of-town parents of Riley Hospital patients. The IUPUI Medical Research Building and Library, scheduled for completion in 1989, will house on its six levels the School of Medicine Library and research departments for a number of medical specialties.

In addition to the medical buildings, IUPUI has steadily increased its other educational and sports facilities. The Indiana University Indianapolis School of Law, the Purdue School of Engineering and Technology, the University Library, and Cavanaugh Hall were all built in the 1970s. Between the University Library and West Michigan St., east of Cavanaugh Hall, is a large courtyard in which stands three triangular beams of brushed stainless steel, each 55 ft. high with a 45-ft. horizontal bar extending from each base. The $120,000 sculpture was placed on the campus in 1980 and was executed by David Von Schlegell, a Yale University art professor. The "minimalist" (stark or simple) sculpture is made and set

in such a way as to suggest a classic Pythagorean right-angle triangle.

Construction in the 1980s included the School of Education and Social Work and the School of Business and Public/Environmental Affairs. The $26 million Lincoln Hotel was completed at 911 W. North St. in 1987. The 10-story hotel has 278 rooms, restaurants, and a food court. It is attached to the University Conference Center, completed in the same year at a cost of $13 million. The Center provides space for university and corporate meetings and includes a television studio and a 338-seat auditorium. When the corporation that ran the Lincoln Hotel went out of the business in 1988, the complex was renamed the **University Place Conference Center and Hotel**. The second stage of a three-stage Science, Engineering and Technology complex was approved in 1987 for construction. The university community awaits the completion, anticipated in 1991, of a new library. The $32 million structure will have 186,594 sq. ft. on five levels, hold one million volumes, and seat 1,740 persons.

With the construction at 150 Blackford St. of the **Indianapolis Sports Center**, a 13-acre site adjacent to the IUPUI campus, for the 1979 United States Open Clay Court Championships, the campus became the site for other sports facilities. The Sports Center is a $7 million city-owned tennis edifice that features an 8,000-seat stadium court, a 1,500-seat grandstand court, and 23 courts. In preparation for the National Sports Festival in 1982, the **IU Natatorium** went up on W. New York St. The $21.5 million structure houses a 4,700-seat aquatic center with two 50-meter swimming pools, a 1 to 10 meter platform diving pool, and auxiliary gymnasium. Also completed in 1982 was the **IU Track and Field Stadium**, on W. New York St. The $5.9 million, 400-meter rubber track has nine lanes with a seating capacity of 12,111. Included with the above was the laying out of athletic fields on the track's east and west sides. The **National Institute for Fitness and Sport**, built on the east bank of the White River at 901 W. New York St., was completed in 1988. This olympic-class facility houses testing and research labs, a gymnastics center, a track, exercise and conditioning rooms, and meeting rooms. The $12 million building contains 89,000 sq. ft.

21. Plans for the **White River State Park**, a 270-acre urban development project, began in 1977. The 1979 Indiana General Assembly appropriated funds for the initial planning and purchased properties for the downtown site bordering on the White River. Restoration of the historic Indianapolis Water Company Pumping Station built in 1870 at 801 W. Washington St. provided space for the park commission offices and a visitors center while the park is under construction. The brick and slate pump house still contains the old turbine water pumps. Across the street is located a 33-ft.-high stainless steel sculpture, which functions as a sundial, by Rinaldo Paluzzi of Spain. The pumping station is an American Water Landmark. (*NRHP*)

On the east bank of the White River just above the old Washington St. bridge, a 37-ton granite boulder with a bronze historical marker indicates the approximate site of **John McCormick's cabin**. (*NRHP*) Arriving in 1820, the McCormicks were the first pioneers to settle in what is now Indianapolis. When the state commissioners came to this area looking for a future site for the state capital, they boarded at McCormick's home. The documents designating Indianapolis as the state's new capital were signed here on June 7, 1820. The National Rd. laid in 1828 passed near the cabin. Proposals for the completed park include a 30-acre, $95 million family entertainment center on the east bank of the river. The focal point of the center is the old Washington St. bridge, on which plans call for building a glass structure, called the Crystal Bridge, to house a botanical garden and a large public gathering area.

22. The **Indianapolis Zoo** sits on 64 acres west of White River and was the first major construction project in the White River State Park. Ground breaking for the $64 million facility, entirely privately funded, took place on September 8, 1985. The zoo features around 2,000 animals. It opened June 11, 1988, and replaced the city's first zoo that existed from 1964 to 1987 in George Washington Park on the city's east side. At the time of its opening, the zoo's membership of more than 60,000 was the second largest in the country. The zoo's focal point is the marine exhibit, which cost $21 million and includes an aquarium complex and an enclosed Whale and Dolphin Pavilion. The Pavilion includes a lower level glassed gallery for underwater viewing. Another feature is the deserts area, where under a transparent dome the desert environment and animal and reptile inhabitants are put on display. Spearheading the creation of a new zoo was the Indianapolis Zoological Society, founded in 1944.

23. The **Indiana Medical History Museum** is located on the grounds of Central State Hospital at 3000 W. Washington St. Upon entering the east entrance off Warman Ave., ask the gatekeeper for directions to the Indiana Medical History Museum's Old Pathology Building. In 1894 Dr. George Edenharter, superintendent of Central State Hospital (then called the Central Indiana Hospital for the Insane), revealed his plans for a pathology department on the hospital grounds. That department, which opened in 1896, was a 19-room structure containing three state-of-the-art scientific laboratories, a medical photography laboratory, a library, an anatomical museum, and a lecture hall (or amphitheater). At a time when little was known about mental illness, hospital staff used the laboratories to study the causes of mental and nervous disorders. The Medical College of Indiana and the College of Physicians and Surgeons (which merged in 1908 to form IU School of Medicine) used the teaching amphitheater for classes in neurology and psychiatry. IU School of Medicine used the facility for classes until the 1950s; the hospital used the laboratories until the 1960s. Over the years, however, the hospital made few alterations to the building. Thus the laboratories and teaching amphitheater have survived virtually intact since the turn of the century. It is one of the oldest surviving pathology laboratories in the United States. The building is now maintained by the Indiana Medical History Museum, a private, nonprofit organization dedicated to preserving the history of medicine in Indiana. The museum also has a collection of more than 10,000 artifacts which it uses in small exhibits in the museum and traveling exhibits throughout the state. (*NRHP/HABS*)

24. Bounded by 10th St., Washington St., the White River, and Tibbs Ave., **Haughville** became a manufacturing suburb of Indianapolis in 1875 when Benjamin F. Haugh moved his iron-casting factory to the area. Immigrants—primarily from Germany, Poland, Ireland, Great Britain, Slovenia, and Hun-

gary—came to work in the foundries, and the town of Haughville was incorporated in 1883. Many landmarks of the old Haughville ethnic settlements still exist today such as the Slovenian Holy Trinity Roman Catholic Church at St. Clair and Holmes sts., St. Anthony's Catholic Church at Warman Ave. and Vermont St., Firehouse No. 9 at Walnut and Belleview sts., and Christamore House at Tremont and W. Michigan sts. Every September the Grape Arbor Dance is celebrated at the Slovenian National Home at 2717 W. 10th St.

25. The **Allison Divisions of General Motors Corporation** are Indianapolis's top employers in private industry. James A. Allison started the Allison Engine Company in 1915 to fill the need for auto parts in the then-infant automobile industry. The company grew and expanded its line of products from auto parts for early "500" race cars to World War I aircraft engines. In 1929 the company became a division of General Motors. During World War II the Allison Engineering Company produced more than 70,000 aircraft engines. In 1945 it produced America's first gas turbine jet engine, the J-33. Following the war it became the leading manufacturer of power-shift and fully automatic transmissions. The Allison Company merged with Detroit Diesel in 1970. A tour of the Powerama Exhibit includes an extensive, and often technical, display of transmissions, generators, aircraft engines, and mufflers, among other mechanical marvels. In 1983 the aircraft engine operations became a new division named Allison Gas Turbine Division, headquartered at 2001 S. Tibbs Ave., Indianapolis. Groups can contact the Turbine Division offices to schedule a visit to its museum of early piston jet aircraft engines. In early 1988 the transmission operations in Speedway on W. 10th St. became the headquarters of the Allison Transmission Division.

26. Billed as the "greatest spectacle in racing," the 500 mile race at the **Indianapolis Motor Speedway**, 4790 W. 16th St., is traditionally held on the Memorial Day weekend each year. The track opens for practice and official time trials in early May. The Indianapolis Motor Speedway is "unchallenged as the world's oldest continuously operated race course and the site of the largest one-day sports event anywhere."

Cofounders Carl G. Fisher, James A. Allison, Frank H. Wheeler, and Arthur C. Newby pooled $250,000 in capital and filed the articles of incorporation for the Indianapolis Motor Speedway Company in 1909. The 2 1/2-mile racetrack, then situated on 320 acres of land (now 550 acres), was originally intended as a testing and proving ground for the new automobile industry. The first automobile race at the Speedway took place August 19, 1909, on a track paved with oil and crushed stone. By 1910 more than three million 10-lb. bricks covered the track, giving the oval its nickname "The Brickyard." Guardrails went up, and in the 1920s the "railbirds" lounged on their "tin Lizzies" along the main straightaway to watch the "potboilers" roar around the "brickyard." One yard of the original brick pavement remains at the start/finish line although asphalt now covers the rest of the track.

Forty-six cars from around the world entered the first 500 race in 1911, and 40 qualified by reaching 75 miles per hour on the straightaway. Ray Harroun won the first race in an Indianapolis-made Marmon "Wasp" in 6 hours, 42 minutes, at an average speed of 74.59 miles per hour, to share in a total purse of $25,100 in gold. Famed World War I air pilot Eddie Rickenbacker, at age 20, was a relief driver in the first 500. He drove at the Speedway between 1911 and 1916 and owned the racetrack from 1927 to 1945. Today, average speeds reach over 200 miles per hour, and prizes total more than a million dollars. Between 350,000 and 400,000 spectators attend the event. (*NRHP*)

Situated in the Speedway infield, the **Indianapolis Motor Speedway Hall of Fame Museum** occupies a modern white structure fronted by a fountain and a display of checkered flags. Racing, classic, and antique passenger cars including previous 500 winners highlight the spacious showroom. The oldest antique car exhibited is the 1895 Reeves Motocycle, built in Columbus, Indiana. Among the racing cars are three Mercedes—the 1908, 1939, and 1954 Grand Prix winners. A recently installed exhibit pays tribute to Al Holbert and his contributions to racing history. On display are several of Holbert's winning Porsches. Also on exhibit are the four winning cars of racing legend A. J. Foyt and four race cars designed by Harry A. Miller in the 1920s. The Hulman Theatre offers daily showings of a film reviewing the history of the 500 mile race. In 1989 the museum unveiled a permanent exhibit of paintings of the living members of the racing Hall of Fame. There is also an extensive collection of trophies, photos, helmets, goggles, and racing memorabilia of all kinds. The museum conducts a restoration program for donated racing cars. One of the oldest cars that the mechanics have restored is an 1896 Bollée, a French-built vehicle resembling a tricycle. Just west of the museum stands the Louis Chevrolet memorial sculpted by Adolph Wolter, an Indianapolis artist. Bus tours are conducted around the track.

27. The lovely ivy-covered brick walls and the tepee in far center field characterize **Bush Stadium**, 1501 W. 16th St., the home of the Indianapolis Indians, the Triple A farm club of the Montreal Expos. Professional baseball has a long history in the city dating back to 1878. The teams played in a series of ball fields until the present stadium opened September 5, 1931. Norman Perry, a past president of the Indianapolis Power and Light Company, built the $350,000 stadium in memory of his brother James Perry, a former Indians owner, who died in a plane crash in 1929. The Louisville Colonels spoiled the opening day festivities for the 5,942 paid spectators by beating the home club four to three. During World War II the stadium's name was changed to Victory Field. It became Bush Stadium in 1967 in honor of Owen J. Bush, then owner and president of the team. Inside the main gate is the Wall of Fame, a row of larger-than-life paintings of some of the great ballplayers and managers for the Indians. In 1988 the movie *Eight Men Out*, about the infamous Chicago Black Sox scandal in the 1919 World Series, contained scenes shot in Bush Stadium, redecorated for the period film.

28. The **Benjamin Franklin Museum** makes its home in the headquarters of the Curtis Publishing Company at 1100 Waterway Blvd. Founded as the *Pennsylvania Gazette* in 1728 by Benjamin Franklin, the *Saturday Evening Post* suspended publication in 1969. Drs. Cory and Beurt SerVaas bought the *Saturday Evening Post* and its parent publishing firm and moved both from Philadelphia to Indianapolis in 1970. The *Post* underwent a successful revival as a quarterly in 1971, became a bimonthly in 1973, and now publishes nine issues a year. In 1982 the Benjamin Franklin Literary and Medical Society bought the Curtis Publishing Company, leaving the editorial offices at the society's corporate headquarters in Indianapolis. The *Post* magazine is probably best known for its distinctive covers illustrated by Norman Rockwell. The *Post* cover gallery lines the halls of the building. The Franklin Room houses a variety of Benjamin Franklin memorabilia, and the archives contain issues of the *Post* dating back more than a century.

29. Architects John Hall Rankin and Thomas M. Kellogg of Philadelphia designed the **United States Courthouse and Post Office Building**, 46 E. Ohio St. Known as the old Federal Building, the $2 million facility was erected in 1902-5. The north one-third addition was constructed in 1936-38 for just over $1.5 million. Italian Renaissance in style, the four-story limestone courthouse has recessed pediments, a stone balustrade at the top, and Doric columns on all sides. Four statues representing industry, agriculture, literature, and justice by John Massey Rhind flank the front entrances, facing south. The interior features mosaic-tile walls, vaulted ceilings, and a central courtyard. More than 20 different types of marble were used in the original part of the building. Curving marble staircases with self-supporting cantilevered stairs grace the east and west ends of the building. Two paintings by W. B. Van Ingen, *Appeal to Justice* and *Justice and Mercy*, hang in the exquisitely decorated second-floor courtrooms at the southwest and southeast corners of the building. Along the third-floor hallway in the southwest corner of the building are WPA murals painted by Grant Christian in 1936 illustrating *Early and Present Day Indianapolis Life* and *Mail, Transportation and Delivery*. (*NRHP/HABSI*)

30. Bounded by Meridian, New York, Pennsylvania, and Vermont sts., **University Square** was intended originally as the site for a state university. The college never materialized, though a seminary occupied the site from 1834 to 1846. The square was used as a drill ground and assembly point during the Civil War years and was officially laid out as a city park in 1865. Karl Bitter designed the Richard J. Depew Memorial Fountain, sculpted by Alexander Stirling Calder in 1919. The statuary group of dancing children encircling the fountain

forms the center attraction of the park. On either side of the fountain are bronze figures of *Pan* and the nymph *Syrinx*, sculpted by Myra Reynolds Richards of Indianapolis in 1921. Following a series of thefts, the statues were reinstalled with limestone pedestals in 1982.

31. On July 4, 1927, Gen. John J. Pershing laid the cornerstone to the **Indiana World War Memorial** in the square bounded by Meridian, Pennsylvania, Michigan, and Vermont sts. The 210-ft.-high tower of Indiana limestone commemorates the Indiana soldiers killed in World War I. The main entrance is located on the north side, facing Michigan St. Henry Hering's *Pro Patria*, the largest sculptured bronze casting ever made in America, stands over the south steps. A team of Bedford, Indiana, limestone cutters carved the 24 statues standing on the ledges of the memorial's four sides from models made by Henry Hering. The massive war memorial designed by architects Walker and Weeks of Cleveland, Ohio, was patterned after the mausoleum erected ca. 350 B.C. by Queen Artemisia at Halicarnassus, Turkey, for the tomb of King Mausolus. The interior consists of a military museum in the lower concourse, a marble foyer, three small meeting rooms, and an auditorium that seats 450 persons on the main floor. A long set of marble staircases leads upstairs to the Shrine Room, which is surrounded by 35-ft.-tall marble columns, blue stained-glass windows, and a sculptured wall frieze. A 17 x 30-ft. American flag and a star-shaped chandelier hang above the Altar of Consecration, placed on a raised dias in the center of the room. The war memorial plaza covers five city blocks and provides an impressive sight when illuminated at night.

32. Bounded by North, Pennsylvania, Michigan, and Meridian sts., **Obelisk Square**, built in 1923, occupies the area between the Indiana War Memorial to the south and the American Legion Mall to the north. An electric water fountain with two basins of pink Georgia marble plays beneath a 100-ft.-high shaft of Berwick black granite. Henry Hering sculpted the bronzes at the base representing law, science, religion, and education. At the north end of the square, a colorful display of 50 state flags unfurls from electrically controlled poles that operate automatically according to light and temperature conditions.

33. In 1927-29 members of the fraternity of Free and Accepted Masons built the $2.5 million **Scottish Rite Cathedral**, 650 N. Meridian St. George F. Schreiber designed the Tudor Gothic-style structure constructed of Indiana limestone. The downtown landmark is rich in Masonic symbolism. The architect designed the building using a basic measurement of 33 ft. or multiples thereof, symbolizing Christ's time on earth, as well as the 33 Degrees of the Rite. The 212-ft.-high main tower of the cathedral houses a carillon with 54 bells varying in weight from 19 lbs. to 5.6 tons. The total weight of the bells is 56,372 lbs. The interior features an auditorium with White Russian oak woodwork lavishly carved by European craftsmen; a two-story ballroom with a 2,500-lb. crystal chandelier, a mezzanine, and a spring-suspension parquet floor; an entrance hall adorned with Masonic emblems and symbolic figures; a large lounge with eight stained-glass windows; a Jacobean-style library; and a cafeteria and banquet hall in the basement. (*NRHP*)

34. The **Indianapolis Central Library**, 40 E. St. Clair St., was constructed from 1913 to 1916 and is a fine interpretation of Greek Doric architecture. Designed by Paul Philippe Cret of Philadelphia, who won an architectural competition conducted by the Indianapolis School

Indiana Historical Society
Scottish Rite Cathedral, photographed by Mary Ann Ponder

Board, the Bedford limestone library was erected on property partially donated by Hoosier poet James Whitcomb Riley after whom the children's library was named. The present building is the library's fifth home since its founding in 1837. Construction on the five-story annex began in 1975. The restoration of the Main Reading Room and the East and West Reading rooms was completed in December 1985 at a cost of about $1.2 million. A large statuary group created by Richard W. Bock, which adorned the roof of the first public library from 1892 to 1967, has been placed on the west grounds of the current library. (*NRHP*)

35. Indianapolis is home for the **National Headquarters of the American Legion**, 700 N. Pennsylvania St., housed in an imposing four-story limestone building designed by architects Walker and Weeks of Cleveland, Ohio, and erected in the 1950s. Chartered by Congress in 1919, the American Legion now has 2.7 million members in 14,500 posts throughout the world. It is the nation's largest veterans' organization and led the fight for the GI Bill of Rights. The Indiana Auxiliary of the American Legion occupies the former national headquarters building built in 1925 directly across the mall. The first floor of the new headquarters building contains the legion's printing, communications, public relations, and emblem sales facilities. Situated on the fourth floor is the national executive committee room, featuring an original Reni-Mel painting of an American doughboy, autographed by General Pershing and Marshal Ferdinand Foch of France, which was used for the cover page of a 1920s issue of the *American Legion Weekly Magazine*. The Emil A. Blackmore Museum on the fourth floor has exhibits and memorabilia from United States wars in this century. The library, on the same floor, contains extensive material on the legion and on military history. West of the national headquarters, in the **Indiana American Legion building**, 777 N. Meridian St., is the auxiliary's Cavalcade of Memories Museum. Photographs, pamphlets, plaques, and assorted mementos trace the personal histories of women in the organization. Both museums are open to the public. **Cenotaph Square**, in the plaza between the two American Legion buildings, contains a memorial to those who died in World War I. Four columns, each supporting a gold eagle, surround the huge but empty black granite cenotaph.

36. In 1870 the cornerstone was laid for **Roberts Park United Methodist Church** at 401 N. Delaware St. The Methodists of Indianapolis first met in 1825, using the courthouse for their services. In 1845 the congregation dedicated its first church, named Roberts Chapel in honor of Bishop Robert R. Roberts, at Pennsylvania and Market sts. A bell tower and steeple crowned the church, and a special city tax paid for a town clock. Architect Diederich A. Bohlen designed the present Romanesque-style building, which was completed in 1876 and patterned after City Temple in London, England. Renamed Roberts Park, the church houses the bell, made in 1848, from Roberts Chapel. Craftsmen carved the interior woodwork from black walnut trees which grew on the premises. In the 1970s the congregation renovated the church and installed a new organ. (*NRHP*)

37. Built in 1910, the **Murat Shrine Temple**, 502 N. New Jersey St., is one of the largest temples in the world. The temple is the refuge of the Mystic Shrine and home of the Murat Theatre, one of the city's oldest theaters still operating. Oscar D. Bohlen, a descendant of one of the first architects to settle in Indianapolis, designed the temple in a Middle Eastern architectural style featuring yellow and brown brickwork, domes, minarets, parapets, and battlements. A large mosaic-tile mural covers the north side of the building, and the interior carries out the Arabian and Egyptian motifs of the architecture. For the first 20 years at the Murat the Shubert brothers provided top stage productions for Indianapolis audiences. Al Jolson set his box-office record here. Other performers at the Murat included Mary Pickford and Tallulah Bankhead. The annual Shrine Circus has become a tradition here. For more than 30 years the Murat was home to the Indianapolis Symphony Orchestra. In 1975 a $2 million restoration project began at the Murat. The temple's 210 stained-glass windows, one of the largest collections of nonreligious art glass in the state, took Vic Miller and his crew two years to refurbish in the 1980s. The temple is part of the Massachusetts Ave. Commercial District listed on the National Register of Historic Places.

38. Five German immigrants who wished to foster fellowship and German culture in America founded the Turners society in 1851. Originally called *Das Deutsche Haus*, the **Athenaeum Turners**, 401 E. Michigan St., was built between 1893 and 1898. Designed in the south German-Austrian Hapsburg mode, the massive brick building contains a rathskeller with a large fireplace and carved mantel, dining halls, meeting rooms, gymnasium, ballroom, auditorium, biergarten, and a schlossgarten complete with banners and animal heads providing an Old World atmosphere. The Athenaeum's stained-glass windows with nonreligious motifs showing elements of music and recreation—horns, harps, cymbals, bowling pins, and jacks—were imported from Germany. Former home of the Indiana Repertory Theatre, the Athenaeum still contains an antique ticket booth and box office. The club opens to the public every year to celebrate the March Benno Fest, a May winefest, an ox roast in August, a German-American Day in October, and St. Nikolaus Day in early December. The Athenaeum's rathskeller serves lunch daily. It is the city's only remaining 19th-century cultural center still occupying its original building. (*NRHP/HABS*)

39. Architect Hermann Gaul designed **St. Mary's Catholic Church** at 317 N. New Jersey St. in a Gothic-Revival style patterned after the Cologne cathedral in Germany. In 1856 the Rev. Peter Leonard Brandt arrived from Vincennes to organize a congregation among the German Catholics in Indianapolis. Their first church, St. Mary's, was completed in 1858. The parish conducted services in German and maintained Old World traditions. When the neighborhood turned commercial, the congregation bought property at New Jersey and Vermont sts. Under construction from 1910 to 1912, the present church features a facade decorated with gargoyles at the entry portal and towers, a stained-glass window on the north side portraying St. Boniface, the saint who converted the Germans to Christianity, and another window on the south portraying St. Henry, the "church builder." The interior boasts a skylighted apse and is rich in statuary. As the ethnic makeup of the neighborhood changed over the years so did that of the St. Mary's congregation. Masses today are no longer conducted in German, but separate services are held in English and Spanish. (*NRHP*)

40. The **Hammond Block Building**, 301 Massachusetts Ave., exemplifies 19th-century commercial Italianate-style architecture. In 1874 Rezin R. Hammond erected the building, designed in a flatiron shape to fit the triangular corner lot. Over the years it housed a variety of businesses—a doctor's office and residence, a saloon, a laundry, the Central College of Physicians and Surgeons, a liquor store, and, more recently, a sporting goods store. The second and third levels, however, were vacant for 40 years. A law firm now owns the building and occupies the second floor, leasing the first. The architectural firm that directed the restoration of the building occupies the third floor. (*NRHP*)

41. Built in 1909-10, the home of the **Indiana State Museum**, 202 N. Alabama St., served as the City Hall until 1962. Rubush and Hunter designed the massive four-story limestone structure, which is Neoclassical in style. Two eagles flanking the east entrance formerly adorned the interurban traction terminal at W. Market St. Beyond the Doric columns an entry hall features a vaulted, mosaic-tiled ceiling and marble walls and floor. A three-story rotunda with a magnificent oval stained-glass skylight highlights the interior. The Foucault pendulum swings from the ceiling, demonstrating the earth's rotation. Huge metal columns painted to resemble marble support the oval balconies. The museum provides both permanent and changing exhibits that represent the natural and social history of Indiana from prehistoric times to the present. A "birdstone" from the collection of Indian artifacts inspired the design of the museum's logo. In 1982 the museum opened a gallery displaying "ecosystems" from Indiana's past. Its Streets of Indiana gallery exhibits replicas of businesses from the early 1900s to the 1930s era, including Laughner's, Danner's, and a Hook's Drug Store, the latter added in 1988. Also permanently exhibited in the Streets of Indiana is **Freetown Village**, a living history museum of the life and times of Indianapolis's approximately 3,000 blacks in 1870. Created and directed by Ophelia Umar Wellington, the Village began as a pilot exhibit in 1984 before becoming a permanent fixture of the museum. Actors depicting the experi-

ences and culture of the city's blacks perform at selected times daily. Freetown Village also offers tours and puts on dramas, period craft workshops, and special programs, such as the 1870 Wedding and the 1870 Christmas. Freetown Village was the first in the country to portray and teach black history through a living history theatrical group. (*NRHP*)

42. Alexander Ralston planned a site for a **City Market**, 222 E. Market St., in the earliest designs for the capital city. The market at the present site was established in 1832. A new market, designed by Diederich A. Bohlen, was constructed in 1886 next to Tomlinson Hall, built the same year. In the early days both buildings served as a covered market place, and vendors' booths lined the outside sidewalk. The second floor of Tomlinson Hall held about 5,000 seats and was a popular place for sporting events, political rallies, civic meetings, and cultural activities. In 1958 a fire destroyed Tomlinson Hall, leaving only a small section of an archway west of the present market and a brick catacomb beneath the west plaza after the hall was torn down. Renovation of the market was completed in 1977, aided by nearly $4.8 million from Lilly Endowment, Inc. Improvements include two new wings to the east and west of the main structure, miniparks outside, and a mezzanine with space for shops in the old market. The market's original iron columns and roof trusses have been restored. (*NRHP/HABS/HAER*)

43. Built in 1960-62, the 28-story **City-County Building**, 200 E. Washington St., replaced separate facilities for Indianapolis and Marion County government agencies. A new form of government called Unigov made this possible when the city expanded its limits to the Marion County boundaries and merged many city-county services in 1968. Schools, police, and fire departments remained under local jurisdiction. The former City Hall occupied what is now the Indiana State Museum at Alabama and Ohio sts. The old Marion County Courthouse, a Renaissance-style building with a French mansard roof and a 97-ft.-high clock tower, was demolished to make way for the present underground parking garage and pedestrian plaza south of the City-County Building. A tunnel connects the City-County Building with the Marion County Jail. The Indianapolis

Police Department Headquarters is located on the east side of the City-County Building. A public observation deck in the tower provides a panoramic view of the city.

44. Built in 1972-74 as part of a major downtown renewal project, **Market Square Arena**, 330 E. Market St., is a multipurpose stadium capable of seating more than 17,000 persons. One of the nation's largest arenas, it is home for the Indiana Pacers professional basketball team and presents sporting events, concerts, and cultural activities. Elvis Presley gave his last public performance here on June 26, 1977. He died at Graceland, his home in Memphis, Tennessee, on August 16, 1977. The building also provides a restaurant and parking facilities. From a distance, the round-domed building appears to be a gigantic flying saucer hovering over E. Market St.

45. The **Indianapolis Downtown Heliport**, 51 S. New Jersey St., when officially opened May 9, 1985, became the nation's first operational full-service downtown facility, and the prototype of the Federal Aviation Administration (FAA) for planned heliports in other cities. The FAA gave the Indianapolis Airport Authority funds to seek a design for a heliport. James Brown, a former helicopter pilot in Vietnam, submitted the winning design and won the contract to operate a new heliport. Brown is now the president of the Indianapolis Heliport Corporation that leases the building from the Indianapolis Airport Authority. The four-story, $5.8 million structure, situated on a 5.5-acre site, provides a complete array of helicopter services. Its revenue is largely drawn from corporation contracts and repair and maintenance of helicopters. The profitable venture handles about 750 takeoffs and landings monthly. On top of the building is a restaurant bordered by a repair bay and hangars. On weekends a couple can eat in the restaurant and take a ride around Indianapolis in a helicopter for a set fee. In the lobby, the bronze statue of a military pilot is a tribute to those brave men who fought in the Korean and Vietnam wars. It was executed by Brett King, then a student at Herron Art School, assisted by his teacher, Gary Freeman.

46. **Lockerbie Square Historic District** is bounded by College Ave. and Michigan, New York, and East sts. In 1821 Janet and Thomas

City Market, photographed by Mary Ann Ponder

McOuat purchased several "out lots" east of the Mile Square in the western half of the area now known as Lockerbie Square. The McOuats did not settle there until 1830, and Janet's father, a Scottish immigrant named George Murray Lockerbie, joined them a year later. Following the death of her husband, Janet McOuat subdivided her property and named the main street in honor of her father. During the Civil War, people began moving into the neighborhood. George Holler, a plasterer, built the frame cottage at 324 N. Park Ave. in 1863. Johann Ernest Despa, a house painter, erected the Federal-style brick house at 538 Lockerbie St., and the Rev. Thomas Evans, a revivalist and abolitionist, built the frame cottage at 537 Lockerbie St.

Calvin Fletcher, a pioneer lawyer and banker, purchased the eastern half of Lockerbie Square from the state of Indiana in 1835. Timothy Richardson Fletcher bought the property from his uncle in 1841 and began to subdivide it. In 1859 Fletcher sold lots to Joseph W. Staub, a merchant tailor, at 342 N. College Ave., and to Harmon Koch, a boot and shoemaker, at 338-340 N. College Ave. In the 1860s the German residential neighborhood south of Lockerbie Square spread north. About 45 homes were built in McOuat's and Fletcher's subdivisions during that decade alone. The area began to acquire its present appearance with substantial residences interspersed among the smaller cottages. Neighborhood-oriented commercial buildings appeared along College Ave.

The northeast corner of Lockerbie Square was the last section to be developed. In 1869 T. R. Fletcher sold all but three lots of the parcel to the Sisters of Providence as a site for a hospital. In turn they sold the property in 1873 to the Little Sisters of the Poor, an order of nuns dedicated to the care of the old and indigent. A Home for the Aged Poor was completed in 1878. Diederich A. Bohlen designed the three-story brick Gothic-style structure which the Little Sisters of the Poor occupied for more than 93 years. In the same block between Vermont and Michigan sts., the Roman Catholic Diocese of Vincennes purchased land in 1873 to erect St. Joseph's Church. When the German Catholic congregation outgrew its quarters, the Sisters of Charity converted the church into an infirmary for the poor. St. Vincent's Infirmary also outgrew the building and moved in 1889. The Vermont St. buildings stood vacant until 1892 when Bishop Francis S. Chatard razed them and platted a subdivision. Although conceived as a residential area, Chatard's subdivision was sold to the Indianapolis Glove Company for its factory. At the turn of the century Lockerbie Square was a mix of residential, commercial, and light-industrial buildings. During the first half of this century the Indianapolis Glove Company manufactured gloves in the six-story brick building at 430 N. Park Ave. The plant housed corporate offices and served as the company's distribution center until 1982. A $9 million housing project converted the factory into 60 condominiums and erected 54 townhouses on adjacent land in the 1980s.

Lockerbie Square owes much of its preservation to the fact that James Whitcomb Riley's home became a historic landmark. In general the rest of Lockerbie Square experienced a decline following the exodus to the suburbs after World War I. Many of the large houses were converted into apartments with absentee landlords. The frame cottages built in the 1860s decayed rapidly. With the help of the Historic Landmarks Foundation, private residential restoration began in the 1960s. In 1971 state Supreme Court Associate Justice Roger O. DeBruler built a large brick residence at 531 E. Vermont St. and gave impetus to a movement of young professionals and their families into the neighborhood. A cobblestone street, brick sidewalks, and old-fashioned gas lamps were installed along Lockerbie St. The success of the Lockerbie Square renaissance is due to the cooperative efforts of both public agencies and private organizations. Slowly but surely the inner-city neighborhood has made a transformation from a blighted area to a pleasant, viable community. The Indianapolis Regional Office of the Historic Landmarks Foundation of Indiana offers guided tours.

One of the city's oldest houses, located at 544 E. New York St., facing Park Ave., is the **former house of James Brown Ray**, the governor of Indiana, 1825-31. Built in 1835, the two-story frame building originally stood at Pearl and Alabama sts. In 1891 the house was split in two and moved by railroad flatcars to St. Peter St. Fire later destroyed the west wing, and ownership of the main structure changed several times. In 1977 the house was moved to its present site. Completely restored, the house is a fine example of Greek Revival-style architecture.

In 1872 John R. Nickum built the two-story Italianate mansion at 528 Lockerbie St. known as the **James Whitcomb Riley home**. The house remained in the family after Nickum's daughter married Maj. Charles L. Holstein. Hoosier poet James Whitcomb Riley, a close friend of the family, was a paying guest in the Holstein home during the last 20 years of his life. Following his death in 1916, his friends organized the James Whitcomb Riley Memorial Association to purchase the house and preserve it. Miss Katie Kindell, the Holsteins' housekeeper who lived in a cottage across the street, helped to arrange the furnishings as they were when Riley lived there from 1893 to 1916. The house contains many interesting antiques such as a rare 1907 Apollo player piano and a set of unusual silver orange cups on swivel bases. Many of Riley's papers and personal belongings are on display, including a painting of Riley's poodle "Lockerbie" by Wayman Adams. Riley is best known for his poetry depicting familiar Indiana scenes and people. His work had broad appeal, and he gained immense popularity in his time. He wrote "The Old Swimmin' Hole," "An Old Sweetheart of Mine," "Little Orphant Annie," and "The Raggedy Man," among others. Riley's birthday is celebrated every year on October 7. (*NRHP/HABS*)

47. Several historically significant structures were erected as part of a federal arsenal in the years between 1863 and 1893 on what is now the campus of **Arsenal Technical High School**, 1500 E. Michigan St. Six of these remain today—the arsenal building, the guardhouse, the west residence, the barn, the barracks, and the magazine. Four other buildings have been lost to fire and the wrecking ball. The three-story arsenal building of brick and limestone appears on the exterior much the same today as when it was erected in 1865. The archways of the tower

were formerly open so that horse-drawn wagons could pass through and unload. The army used a mechanical hoist to raise and lower supplies in the arsenal. A tower clock with three faces (each 6 ft. in diameter) was installed in 1867. The magazine was built in 1866 with clay bricks made on the premises. It has walls 2 1/2 ft. thick and many chimneys to provide air ventilation for keeping the gunpowder dry. A two-story brick barracks was erected in 1867 to house the soldiers. In 1869 the two-story barn with a grade basement was completed. Officers occupied the three-story brick west residence, built in 1870. A small brick guardhouse, built in 1872, is situated just inside the Michigan St. entrance. Military offenders were once quartered in the basement cells. The army occupied the arsenal until 1903, maintaining a contingent of 50 soldiers and, at one time, storing up to 100,000 rifles.

The facility was auctioned to Winona Agricultural and Technical Institute and converted to a trade school in 1903 (which went bankrupt in 1910). In 1912 Arsenal Technical High School opened its doors. Additional structures have since been built to house classrooms, offices, physical education facilities, and dining/recreation areas. Today the school's administrative offices are housed in the former arsenal. The barn was remodeled for classrooms in 1916, and the guardhouse became a gatehouse. The west residence was converted into a model restaurant as a project of the Career Center. The magazine and barracks are property of the United States government. The former houses Reserve Officers' Training Corps (ROTC) uniforms and equipment; the latter is the headquarters of the school's ROTC unit. (*NRHP/HABS*)

48. On October 2, 1872, James O. Woodruff filed the plat for a 180-lot residential subdivision called **Woodruff Place**, bounded by Arsenal Technical High School and E. 10th, Tecumseh, and E. Michigan sts., which was later incorporated as a town. The original design included three drives with esplanades, fountains, and cast-iron statuary. Woodruff Place experienced a boom in the 1890s when prominent citizens built rambling frame houses along the tree-lined streets with carriage houses and servants' quarters backing the alleys. Among the early residents were Rear Adm. George Brown, a retired naval officer;

Chauncey Butler, the son of educator Ovid Butler; Charles E. Test, president of the National Motor Vehicle Company; and architect Brandt T. Steele, the son of Brown County artist T. C. Steele. Following World War I the neighborhood declined as the owners of large homes moved to the suburbs and the vacated houses were subdivided into apartment units. The process was hastened by the Great Depression and by the housing shortage after World War II.

The turning point in the general decline of this near-eastside neighborhood came in 1952 when residents formed the Woodruff Place Civic League, Inc. The 80-acre community has since shown a steady improvement with the restoration of many vintage houses and public grounds. Woodruff Place is now a showcase of Victorian and Edwardian architecture. One of the oldest structures in Woodruff Place is a Carpenter Gothic-style cottage at 845 Middle Dr., built in 1885. Charles Test built a fine mansion complete with a coach house at 795 Middle Dr. in 1893. Some important pieces of the original statuary dating to the 1870s remain, such as a crouching lion, an urn carved with heads of literary figures, and a vase like a Grecian urn. On the northern edge of Woodruff Place stands the William Prosser house, 1454 E. 10th St. An English decorative plaster worker built the house in the 1880s, applying Classical details to the stucco exterior. (*NRHP/HABS*) The Tudor-style structure at 735 East Dr., built in 1930, was the town hall for 20 years. It was used as a community center after the city of Indianapolis annexed Woodruff Place in 1962. In 1984 it became the home of the Marion County/Indianapolis Historical Society.

49. For many years the **Kemper house**, 1028 N. Delaware St., was known as the "wedding cake" house because of its all-white confectionery appearance and because Charles Clark Pierson, owner of a dental supply company, built the house in 1873 as a wedding gift for his bride. The Piersons lived in the house only one year. John Griffiths, a notable orator and politician, owned the house from 1897 to 1914. After changing ownership many times, the house was purchased in 1962 by Eli Lilly who made possible the expensive restoration and interior redecoration of this fine High Victorian-period house. The house then was presented to the

Episcopal Diocese of Indianapolis and dedicated in memory of the Rt. Rev. Jackson Kemper, Indiana's first Episcopal bishop. The diocese, in turn, gave the Kemper house to the Historic Landmarks Foundation of Indiana in 1977. In 1980 the foundation conducted extensive research to determine the building's original color scheme, then repainted the house with authentic Victorian-period color paints. (*NRHP*)

50. Bounded by I-65 and Pennsylvania, 16th, and Bellefontaine sts., the **Old Northside Historic District** is an inner-city neighborhood that developed in the 1860s as the northern boundary of Indianapolis pushed beyond 10th St. Two distinct neighborhoods grew up within the Old Northside. The first centered around Northwestern Christian University, built in 1855 on land donated by Ovid Butler. A little community developed there that became known as College Corner. The university moved to Irvington in 1875, and although its building was razed in 1904, several early residences remain along the 600 block of E. 13th St. The second neighborhood developed as the city's wealthiest citizens moved northward, seeking larger lots on which to build their mansions. The city's most opulent residences were built along Meridian St., but many were also constructed on Illinois, Pennsylvania, and Delaware sts.

Around the turn of the century a number of wealthy homeowners moved northward to escape the congestion, coal-soot pollution, and encroaching commercialism of the city. The conversion of single-family dwellings to rental units and the changing character of the inner-city neighborhoods are vividly illustrated in Booth Tarkington's novel *The Magnificent Ambersons*. The model for the Ambersons' mansion stood at Delaware and 13th sts., serving first as a single-family residence and then as a clubhouse for the Knights of Columbus. The old house was demolished in 1963. Following World War II the Old Northside decayed rapidly. The downward trend was reversed, however, when restorationists took an interest in the area during the 1970s and began buying homes. Each summer the Old Northside, Inc., a neighborhood organization of property owners and rental residents, sponsors a house tour to display recent restoration and rehabilitation projects. At Christmastime the organization conducts a candlelight tour of neighborhood churches and Victorian mansions. (*NRHP*)

51. The **Benjamin Harrison home**, 1230 N. Delaware St., is both an architecturally and historically important structure. For just over $24,000 Harrison built this Italianate-style home in 1874-75 while he was a practicing attorney in Indianapolis. Born on the farm of his grandfather William Henry Harrison on August 20, 1833, Benjamin received his basic education from a tutor in a log cabin and entered Farmer's College near Cincinnati at the age of 14. He graduated from Miami University in 1852. From 1881 to 1887 he served as a United States senator from Indiana. While campaigning for the presidency in 1888, Harrison sometimes would step out the long parlor window onto a side porch to address political rallies. During the more than 20 years that Harrison lived here, many of his associates moved to the same neighborhood.

Caroline Scott Harrison, his first wife, was a talented artist who designed the china for the Harrison administration. She was the first president-general of the Daughters of the American Revolution (DAR), and her Thursday afternoon teas at home were a popular social event. Following his term as the 23rd president of the United States, Harrison returned to his home on Delaware St. He had lost his wife to tuberculosis and lost his bid for reelection to Democrat Grover Cleveland. He resumed his old law practice and married his late wife's niece, Mary Lord Dimmick. He remained active until 1901, when he contracted pneumonia and died.

From 1937 to 1951 the Jordan Conservatory of Music used the Harrison home as a women's dormitory. The Benjamin Harrison Foundation is responsible for the restoration of the house and its operation as a historic landmark. Many furnishings and artifacts which once belonged to the Harrisons, including some of the White House china designed by Caroline and a rare Moore desk used by President Harrison, have been returned to the house. Docents dressed in period costumes conduct tours through the home. The United States Department of the Interior has designated the home a National Historic Landmark. (*NRHP/HABS*)

52. The **Morris-Butler House Museum**, 1204 N. Park Ave., is a showplace for mid-Victorian decorative arts. In 1864-65 John D. Morris,

who made his fortune selling biscuits to the army during the Civil War, built the prestigious-looking house located in the Old Northside Historic District. Diederich A. Bohlen designed the mansion in the Second Empire architectural style with a central tower, French mansard roof, and Italianate brackets beneath the eaves. A servants' cottage stands in back of the main house. In 1881 Noble Chase Butler, clerk of the United States Supreme Court, purchased the house. It remained in the Butler family until 1958. In 1964 the Historic Landmarks Foundation of Indiana bought the house, restored it, and lavishly furnished it with period pieces. (*NRHP/HABS*)

53. **Ovid Butler**, an Indianapolis attorney best known for his establishment of Northwestern Christian University (now Butler University) in 1850, built his house at 1306 N. Park Ave. in 1848-49 when the area was still covered with forests. The three-story brick mansion incorporates all the major architectural styles of the Victorian period. The west facade features a porte cochere—with two huge griffins—that once was a part of the Bates House hotel. It is reported to be the balcony from which Abraham Lincoln gave a speech in 1861. A carriage house in the rear, now converted to apartments, features carved panels of Queen Anne design on the south gable.

54. In 1890 John W. Schmidt, owner of a brewing company, built the **Propylaeum and Carriage House** at 1410 N. Delaware St., a three-story brick residence with a square tower and porte cochere. The structure combines Romanesque, Neo-Jacobean, and Queen Anne architectural styles. Terra-cotta scrolls adorn the gables and dormer windows. About 1902 Joseph C. Schaf, also a brewer, bought the house. The house became known as the Propylaeum, which means "gateway to culture," when the Indianapolis Woman's Club purchased it in 1923. The house still contains the original servants' quarters and a ballroom on the third floor. Most of the interior, including the original fireplaces, leaded-glass doors, gas lamps, coffered ceilings, and a grand staircase, has been preserved. For many years the converted stable was the teaching studio of artist/sculptor Elmer E. Taflinger. Portrait artist John Robert Dickhaus purchased it in 1981. The adjacent

townhouse was formerly used as an auto garage and the studio of Ruth Pratt Bobbs. (*NRHP*)

55. The **Meredith Nicholson home**, 1500 N. Delaware St., is a fine example of Georgian Revival-style architecture. The famous poet, essayist, and novelist built this handsome house in 1903-4. The house is sometimes called the House of a Thousand Candles from Nicholson's popular novel of the same name, though the house is not the one described in the book. Nevertheless, Mrs. Nicholson began the tradition of placing candles in the windows at Christmas. While the Nicholsons lived there, the house was a favorite meeting place for such literary figures as Booth Tarkington, James Whitcomb Riley, and George Ade. In 1933 Nicholson entered the diplomatic service and left Indianapolis for South America. The house is now the headquarters of the Indiana Humanities Council.

56. Bounded by Central Ave. and Pennsylvania, 16th, and 22nd sts., **Herron-Morton Place Historic District** derives its name from the fact that both Camp Morton and the Herron School of Art were located in this neighborhood. In 1860, 36 acres known as Otis's Grove (bordered by 19th St., Talbot Ave., 22nd St., Central Ave., and fronting Meridian St.) were purchased for the site of the State Fairgrounds. Gov. Oliver Perry Morton designated the fairgrounds for use as a training camp for Union troops in 1861. Within a month 5,000 men were encamped there. A year later Camp Morton was converted into a prisoner-of-war camp, and Col. Richard Owen was appointed commandant. Up to 5,000 Confederates were held in the camp at one time. Between 1862 and 1865 over 1,600 Confederate soldiers died while imprisoned at Camp Morton. After the war the land was reclaimed by the State Board of Agriculture and used as a fairgrounds until 1890. The property later became a prestigious turn-of-the-century suburb called Morton Place. Many prominent citizens lived in this neighborhood, such as Albert J. Beveridge, United States senator, 1899-1911; William H. Block, department store owner; William C. Bobbs, president of Bobbs-Merrill Publishing Company; Willis D. Gatch, inventor of the first mechanical hospital bed; Otto Stark, artist; T. C. Steele, artist; Frank Van Camp, president of Van Camp Packing Company; and William

N. Wishard, superintendent of City Hospital (now Wishard Memorial Hospital).

The **Herron School of Art**, Pennsylvania and 16th sts., got its through a bequest from John Herron in 1895 to the Art Association of Indianapolis, formed in 1883. The bequest provided funds to build an art school and a museum. A Beaux Art/Neoclassical museum, designed by Vonnegut and Bohn, was built in 1905. An art school building was put up in 1907. A new art school facility, designed by Philadelphia architect Paul Philippe Cret, was completed in 1929. The $300,000 Fesler Building, designed by Evans Woollen III, was added in 1962. Now a part of IUPUI, the art school operates a gallery in the old museum building for the exhibition and study of avant-garde art. The Herron Museum of Art moved to its present location on 38th St. as the Indianapolis Museum of Art with the completion of the Krannert Pavilion and Plaza in 1970. (*NRHP*)

57. George Marott, a shoe store owner, built the 11-story **Marott Hotel** at 2625 N. Meridian St. along the banks of Fall Creek in 1926. He lavished the lobby with marble, wood paneling, statuary, and velvet draperies. Visiting celebrities such as Winston Churchill, Bob Hope, Betty Grable, Andre Previn, Marilyn Monroe, Maurice Chevalier, Lauren Bacall, Rose and Ted Kennedy, and several United States presidents stayed at the "grand" hotel. The aging hotel fell on hard times in the 1970s and closed in 1981. Only a shell remained of the building after the furnishings were auctioned off. Following extensive renovations, the landmark hotel reopened in 1984 as a luxury apartment building with fine restaurants. On the exterior, the white terra-cotta tile between the eighth and ninth floors of the twin towers is intact. A lighted marquee and broad foyer doors lead into a spacious lobby complete with a 185-lb. crystal chandelier imported from Italy. A landscaped atrium with arched walkways forms the central dining area. Original marble floors and intricately carved moldings have been restored in the new ballroom. (*NRHP*)

58. Following his term as vice-president of the United States during Theodore Roosevelt's administration, 1905-9, **Charles Warren Fairbanks** returned to Indianapolis and began construction of his home at 30th and Meridian sts. It was completed in 1913. The French Re-

naissance-style mansion originally contained 26 rooms, 8 baths, and 8 fireplaces. During Fairbanks's residency the house was an important political and social center. In the presidential election of 1916 Fairbanks ran against Democrat Thomas R. Marshall of Whitley County for the office of vice-president. His running mate was Charles Evans Hughes. The Hughes-Fairbanks ticket carried the state but lost the national election to Wilson-Marshall. Fairbanks died at his home 19 months later. In 1923 the Indianapolis Life Insurance Company purchased the house. The west wing was added in 1952 and enlarged in 1966. The interior features a 70-ft.-long great hall with vaulted ceilings. Myra Reynolds Richards sculpted the fireplace in Fairbanks's personal library and former drawing room. With the purchase of the Levey mansion the entire block, christened Historic Square, became the property of Indianapolis Life. An $8 million, four-story addition designed by Wright/Porteous and Lowe, Inc., was constructed in 1982.

59. The **Children's Museum of Indianapolis**, 3000 N. Meridian St., which hosts around 1.6 million young and "young-at-heart" annually, is the world's largest children's museum. First housed in 1925 in a rented carriage house behind the Propylaeum at 14th and Delaware sts., the museum moved to larger quarters at Garfield Park's Shelter House the next year. John and Mary Stewart Carey's northside Victorian home contained the museum from 1927 until 1946, when museum officials decided to move to the 35-room St. Clair Parry mansion at 30th and Meridian. Ground breaking for the present museum took place in 1973, and it opened October 2, 1976. The original five-level, $6.8 million building was designed by Wright/Porteous and Lowe, Inc. In the late 1980s, a $14 million expansion began with construction of a new museum entrance and lobby, more exhibition space, classrooms, collection storage area, planetarium, and an innovative gallery for adolescents.

Among the permanent exhibits in nine galleries are the 1868 Reuben Wells steam locomotive, simulated Indiana limestone caverns, international displays, early Indiana housing and occupations, a 15-ft.-long mastodon skeleton found in Hancock County, exhibits of physical science marvels, and many others. The museum's wonderful carousel is a Gustav

Dentzel creation that operated in Broad Ripple Park from 1917 to 1956. The vast toy collection is anchored by the world's largest public display of toy trains and the Caplan Collection of priceless folk art and toys from around the world, donated to the museum by the late Frank Caplan and his wife, Theresa.

During the late 1980s the museum expanded by one-third with the addition of a Welcome Center, a $2 million copper-domed SpaceQuest Planetarium, the Hedback Education Center, a Haunted House, and the museum's largest gallery, the Lilly Center for Exploration. The Welcome Center, a four-story, 55-ft.-tall atrium, opened in 1988. Designed by Evans Woollen III, the museum's entrance is fronted by the brick Edith Whitehill Clowes Plaza, which includes a life-size replica of a Tyrannosaurus Rex, 35 ft. in length, and which borders the Allen Clowes Garden Gallery. In the lobby of the Center is a unique water clock, the world's largest, designed by French physicist and artisan Bernard Gitton. All the conveniences of a major museum—two restaurants, a museum store, rest rooms designed for kids, and handicapped facilities—await the visitor to this cultural and educational landmark of Indiana.

60. **Marian College**, 3200 Cold Spring Rd., was chartered by the state in 1936. It was a merger of two schools operated by the Sisters of the Third Order of St. Francis of Oldenburg, Indiana. Opening in Indianapolis in 1937 as a Catholic college for women, it became, in 1954, the first Catholic coeducational college in Indiana. The campus is composed of estates covering 114 acres that once belonged to three of the four cofounders of the Indianapolis Motor Speedway—James A. Allison, Carl G. Fisher, and Frank H. Wheeler. James A. Allison, then owner of the Allison Engine Company, later a division of General Motors Corporation, hired a team of European craftsmen to build his Lombard-style mansion between 1911 and 1914 at a cost of about $2 million. Called the House of Wonders, the mansion included such innovations as a built-in vacuum cleaner, central steam heat, an indoor heated swimming pool, and stainless-steel kitchen sinks. Allison bought only the finest materials to construct the marble aviary, the oak library with tooled leather paneling, and the music room with two-story-high organ pipes behind handcarved

wood grillwork, the massive fireplaces, the elegant chandeliers, and the fabric-covered walls. The college art department now uses the upstairs. (*NRHP/HABS*) In 1914 Carl G. Fisher, the flamboyant entrepreneur and Speedway promoter, built his home on the property adjoining the Allison mansion. He built a separate house nearby for the mother of his 15-year-old bride. The Park School for Boys converted the main house to classrooms and occupied it from 1924 to 1970. The building now serves as the Student Activities Center. The former estate of Frank H. Wheeler, owner of a carburetor and magneto manufacturing company, is just south of the library. Noted for its extraordinary display of magnolia blossoms each year, the Wheeler property boasts a 324-ft.-long covered colonnade that extends from the house to an outdoor swimming pool. The house exterior is beige brick with a barrel-tile roof. The interior contains an elegant central staircase, a cone-shaped fireplace, and a 16th-century Flemish painting. Following Wheeler's death, the house was owned by Monty Williams, president of the former Marmon Motor Car Company, and by William B. Stokely of Stokely Van Camp, Inc. The Marian College Music department now uses the upstairs bedrooms and servant quarters. The old eight-sided, cork-insulated icehouse on the estate grounds is an interesting relic of the Wheeler estate. The most notable modern building on campus is the Marian College Library, designed by Woollen Associates and built in 1970. A physical education center, designed by Everett I. Brown Company, adjacent to the present gymnasium, was completed in 1983. The coeducational Catholic liberal arts school has over 1,200 students and offers courses in 23 major areas of study.

61. The city-owned **Major Taylor Velodrome**, 3800 Cold Spring Rd., was dedicated July 15, 1982, opening in time to be used in the National Sports Festival. The $2.5 million outdoor bicycle racing facility features a 333.3-meter (almost 1/5 mile) concrete oval with 7 to 28 degrees of banking. The Indianapolis design firm of Howard Needles Tammen and Bergendoff and local contractor Tousley-Bixler built the track into the side of a hill. It is one of a handful of arenas in the country able to host major races. The track is named for Marshall W. (Major) Taylor, a black champion racer born in Indianapolis in 1878. Though learning

the fundamentals while in the city (and acquiring his name "Major" from adolescent trick-riding in military-type garb), he left for more tolerant climes, Massachusetts, at age 17. While confronting and overcoming racism on and off the track, his subsequent racing career took him throughout the nation and to Europe and Australia. Prior to going overseas, he was the American sprint champion in 1899 and 1900, and world titleholder in 1899, only the second black, after boxer George Dixon, to win a world championship. He retired in 1910 and died in 1932. Sydney Taylor Brown, Taylor's daughter, donated a collection of her father's personal memorabilia to the Indiana State Museum in 1988. The Velodrome is administered by the Indianapolis Department of Parks and Recreation.

62. Founded in 1883, the **Indianapolis Museum of Art**, 1200 W. 38th St., occupied the Herron School of Art at 16th and Pennsylvania sts. for many years before moving to its present home in 1970. Richardson-Severns, Scheeler and Associates, and Wright/Porteous and Lowe, Inc., designed the new museum, erected on the 150-acre grounds of the former J. K. Lilly, Jr., estate. The Samuel R. Sutphin fountain (the design of which forms the museum logo) and Robert Indiana's monumental sculpture *LOVE* flank the front of the museum. The building itself contains the Krannert, Clowes, and Showalter pavilions which house the museum's permanent collections. In the back of the museum a concert terrace overlooks the White River. The **Krannert Pavilion**, a massive five-level limestone structure with lofty, spacious rooms, houses the original John Herron library collection, reference library, print study, members' room, major exhibits, rental gallery, and craft shop. Art exhibits range from pre-Columbian to contemporary. The oriental art collection is particularly noteworthy. The museum also owns a permanent collection of paintings by Indiana artists. On the lower level the museum shop offers a wide selection of books, arts and crafts, gifts, and cards. An enclosed breezeway connects the **Clowes Pavilion** to the main building. A courtyard forms the center of the gallery, and paintings by European artists hang along the bordering passages. In a side room a re-creation of the Clowes library contains a collection of paintings by Titian, Rembrandt, and Holbein. An English sitting room with an antique harpsichord houses the Medieval and Renaissance art collection. The J. M. W. Turner Suite, on the second floor, features the largest collection of Turner watercolors outside of Great Britain. On the lower level the **Showalter Pavilion** is the permanent home of the Booth Tarkington Civic Theatre. The Junior Civic Theatre performs children's plays here, and Studio C houses an experimental theater group. Founded in 1914, the Civic Theatre is the oldest continuously operating theater group in the country.

North of the art museum, at the end of an open mall, stands the **Lilly Pavilion of the Decorative Arts**. Hugh McKenna Landon, secretary of the Indianapolis Water Company, was the first owner of the magnificent 22-room mansion, built about 1912 in a French château style featuring a ballroom on the third floor and parquet floors throughout. In 1920 the Olmsted brothers of Brookline, Massachusetts, designed the 54 acres of exquisite landscaping. Frederick Law Olmsted, noted writer and chief architect of Central Park in 1858, originally headed the landscaping firm. Josiah Kirby Lilly, Jr., purchased Oldfields in 1932 to house the family collection of rare books, furniture, and objets d'art. Lilly's children gave Oldfields to the Indianapolis Museum of Art in 1966. The home contains many fine examples of 18th- and 19th-century European and American furnishings. Paintings by the great masters supplement the museum's collection. Adjoining the house are a rose garden, a patio overlooking the White River, winding paths, lawn statues, and a greenhouse—all of which are open to the public.

Located in a wooded setting just east of Oldfields mansion, a restaurant called the Garden on the Green serves luncheons and private receptions. The reduced proportions enhance the charm of this former playhouse and garden retreat, built about 1914. Adjacent to the restaurant is a fountain surrounded by formal gardens and landscaped paths winding through the woods. A variety of bronze sculptures inhabit the grounds. A copy of Bertel Thorvaldsen's *Three Graces* is a part of the original garden statuary included in the Olmsted brothers' landscape plans. South of the restaurant a sculpture field contains such contemporary works as Sasson Soffers's geometric patterns done in dull copper and shiny stainless-steel pipes with open spaces for the viewer to walk through. Additional sculptures can be found behind the Krannert Pavilion. The exhibit space of the museum will increase by some 80 percent in 1990 with the completion of the four-story **Mary Fendrich Hulman Pavilion**. At the same time, both the Clowes and Krannert pavilions will be renovated.

63. **Crown Hill** is the nation's fourth largest cemetery, comprising 555 acres and around 170,000 interments. It is one of the few cemeteries in the nation listed on the National Register of Historic Places (1973). In the midst of the Civil War, it became apparent to civic leaders that the city's burial grounds on the near southwest side, begun in 1821, added to, and collectively called Greenlawn Cemetery, were running out of space, largely due to consignments of war dead. A Crown Hill Association organized in 1863 and purchased a 246-acre tract north of the city that included the farm of Martin Williams. The association added 28 acres in 1864 and dedicated the cemetery June 1, 1864. The following day the first burial took place, that of Mrs. Lucy Ann Seaton, who died of tuberculosis at age 33. The "Crown" of Crown Hill is a 200-ft. elevation, the highest point in the county, which gives a commanding view of the city. Originally called Strawberry Hill because of the strawberry plants adorning its sides, its summit became the resting place of poet James Whitcomb Riley. Near the grave of Oliver Perry Morton, Civil War governor of Indiana, are 700 bodies of Union soldiers transferred from Greenlawn in 1866. The remains of 1,617 Confederate soldiers are buried in a separate section. Among the famous Hoosiers buried at Crown Hill are President Benjamin Harrison, 3 vice-presidents—Thomas A. Hendricks, Charles W. Fairbanks, and Thomas R. Marshall—, 3 vice-presidential nominees, 11 Civil War generals, and several Mexican and Revolutionary War veterans. Among Indianapolis's most prominent citizens buried here are Col. Eli Lilly, Richard Gatling, Alexander Ralston, John H. Holliday, and writers Meredith Nicholson and Newton Booth Tarkington.

Diederich A. Bohlen designed the little **Gothic chapel** built in 1875-77 on a gentle slope in a wooded setting. Adolph Scherrer designed the red brick **Waiting Station** and the stone Gothic-style gateway at the 34th St. entrance of the cemetery, constructed in 1885-86. The funeral procession of Vice-President Hendricks was the first to pass through the gates. In the early years the Waiting Station provided shelter for funeral goers. The carved cherry woodwork of the interior represents a fine example of Victorian craftsmanship. For two decades after 1970, the restored Waiting Station at 3402 Boulevard Pl. served as headquarters for the Historic Landmarks Foundation of Indiana. Among the pieces of art scattered throughout the cemetery, not to mention the astounding variety of monuments, are three statues of Greek goddesses that once stood on the main tower of the old Marion County Courthouse. One of the newest works is the Crown Hill Equatorial Sundial completed on the site in 1987. David L. Rodgers executed the piece, the largest equatorial sundial in Indiana. The nearly three miles of brick and wrought-iron fence surrounding a good portion of the cemetery were completed in the early 1920s. Restoration of the fence began in 1985. (*NRHP/HABS*)

64. The **Toll house** at 4702 N. Michigan Rd. (Northwestern Ave.) is a simple frame structure, built around 1850, that served as a combination post office, country store, toll house, and family dwelling from 1866 to 1892. During this time a toll pole extended across the road, and a small fee was collected by the Augusta Gravel Road Company from persons traveling to and from the Farmers' Market in Indianapolis to pay for the upkeep of the road. No charges were imposed "when families were going to church or to funerals." The second story probably was added to the main building in 1892, followed by a porch on the south side and a rear wing. The store and a porch on the front of the house had to be removed when the highway was widened. Originally unpainted, the house acquired numerous layers of paint over the years. The present multicolor paint scheme conforms to the styles of the Victorian period. (*NRHP*)

65. Founded in 1855 by the Disciples of Christ, **Butler University** at 4600 Sunset Ave. was first named Northwestern Christian University and located at 13th St. and College Ave. on land donated by Ovid Butler. It occupied a Gothic-style building designed by William Tinsley until 1875 when the college moved to Irvington. Ovid Butler was the first president of the board of trustees and the person for whom the university was later renamed. From the beginning the

college admitted both men and women on an equal basis. Students also were allowed to enroll in an elective system rather than in the rigid classical program of study. In 1928 Butler University moved to its present 254-acre site at Fairview Park on the north side of the city. The university offers degrees in more than 80 areas. The first building erected on the new campus was the Arthur Jordan Memorial Hall, built in 1927. The **Hinkle Fieldhouse** opened in 1928 and the Butler Bowl in 1938. The fieldhouse in the past has presented the roller derby, six-day bicycle races, Sonja Henie's Ice Show, Big Bill Tilden's tennis tour, wrestling, golden gloves boxing, and the Shrine Circus, in addition to its famous sporting events. (*NRHP*) At the south end of the stadium is the **Hilton U. Brown Theatre**, a 4,088-seat outdoor facility. The university's radio/television department was established in 1939, and WAJC began daily broadcasting in 1949. In 1951 the **Jordan College of Music** became part of Butler University. Since 1894 the Jordan College of Fine Arts has offered a series of the performing arts. Perhaps the most outstanding example of the university's modern architecture is the **Irwin Library** designed by Minoru Yamasaki and Associates in 1962. A focal point at the north end of the campus, the **J. I. Holcomb Observatory and Planetarium**, was built in 1954. A 24-ft.-diameter aluminum dome replaced the original wooden one in 1984. The observatory offers the public a film and lecture on astronomy and a look through the 38-in. telescope in the tower.

In the wooded area beyond the observatory the **Musetta B. Holcomb Memorial Carillon**, dedicated in 1959, stands above the reflecting pool. Further north in a park-like setting along the Central Canal are located the **J. I. Holcomb Botanical Gardens and Garden House**. Also situated on the Butler campus is the **Clowes Memorial Hall for the Performing Arts**. Since its construction in 1963 the $3.5 million opera house has become a cultural center of the city. For nearly 20 years Clowes Hall was home for the Indianapolis Symphony Orchestra. It now showcases Butler University student productions and various touring companies. Evans Woollen III and John M. Johansen designed the 2,182-seat structure, built in memory of Dr. George Henry Alexander Clowes, research director for Eli Lilly and Company and the first to perfect insulin for production on a mass scale. The splendid architecture and fine acoustics make Clowes Hall an audiovisual delight. In 1958 the College of Religion became a separate institution, **Christian Theological Seminary** (CTS), though still affiliated with the university. Located in modern sandstone buildings along W. 42nd St., CTS holds repertory theater productions in Shelton Auditorium, a wood and plush amphitheater built in 1966.

66. The **Booth Tarkington house**, 4270 N. Meridian St., was built in 1911 by Maria Fletcher Ritsinger Hare, widow of a barrister and an Indianapolis businessman and a relative of Calvin and Stoughton Fletcher. Tarkington purchased the lovely English Tudor-style mansion in 1923. Until that time he had lived in his father's home on Pennsylvania St. and attended Shortridge High School before his family sent him east to Phillips Exeter Academy. Tarkington filled the house with French, Italian, and Spanish antiques from the Renaissance period and converted the third floor into a writing room where he created many of his novels. Two of his books won the Pulitzer Prize for literature—*The Magnificent Ambersons* in 1919 and *Alice Adams* in 1922. Both novels have an Indianapolis setting. Several of his novels were adapted for the stage and screen, and his stories of boyhood in *Seventeen* and *Penrod* remain classics today. Except for summers spent in Kennebunkport, Maine, Tarkington lived in this house until his death in 1946.

67. The rambling brick house on a wooded lot at 4700 N. Meridian St. has served as the **Governor's Residence** since 1970. It has been extensively renovated to make it serviceable for large political and social functions. The heavy oak doors in the covered entranceway came from Central State Hospital. During the Otis R. Bowen administration the Indianapolis Garden Club designed and planted a flower bed to honor Indiana's famous authors. Mrs. Robert Orr, wife of the governor, 1981-89, added the 15-ft.-high wrought-iron gazebo on the south lawn in 1981.

68. In 1916 John H. Holliday, founder of the *Indianapolis News*, donated 80 acres to the city of Indianapolis that is now the site of **Holliday Park** at 6349 Spring Mill Rd. Indianapolis sculptor Elmer E. Taflinger designed the setting

for the *Races of Man* statues by Karl Bitter, which were saved from the old St. Paul Building in New York when it was razed in 1958. The Western Electric Company awarded the statues to the city as a result of Taflinger's sketches. The statues—three figures depicting a black, a Caucasian, and an Oriental at labor—sit on a ledge atop three Doric columns. Behind them is a grotto with a fountain and reflecting pool, dedicated in 1967. Twenty-five Greek columns removed from the former Sisters of the Good Sheperd Convent surround the pool. To the sides are four statues from the top of the old Marion County Courthouse.

The "ruins" were dedicated on the 191st anniversary of the signing of the United States Constitution. The first sentence of the preamble is carved across three large tablets at the east end of the park, representing the history of our country from its beginning as 13 colonies to the present. Three stone seats on a mound in the mall represent the three branches of government. A community center with a meeting room is available for banquets, receptions, and senior citizen activities.

69. Though housed in a relatively new building, the **Second Presbyterian Church** at 7700 N. Meridian St. has played an important part in the city's history. Following a dispute over church doctrine, the Presbyterians divided into two groups in 1838. Henry Ward Beecher came from Lawrenceburg, Indiana, to serve as the first pastor of the Second Presbyterian Church in 1839 and remained until 1847 when he moved to New York. The congregation held its services for a year in the county seminary at University Square, then moved into the lecture room of its new building at the northwest quadrant of Monument Circle, which was completed in 1840. For two decades the first and second Presbyterian churches occupied facilities on the east and west sides of the Circle. The Second Presbyterian congregation constructed a chapel at the northwest corner of Vermont and Pennsylvania sts. in 1867-70, which it occupied until 1959. Architects McGuire, Shook, Compton, Richey and Associates designed the present church as a replica of the 13th-century Sainte-Chapelle of Paris. Adolph Wolter (1903-1980), a German sculptor who came to Indianapolis in the 1930s, executed the two bas-reliefs in the chapel, the angels above the side door, and the figure of a 16th-century reformer at the main door of the magnificent Gothic-style structure. A Tiffany window in the back of the chancel, made in 1902, came from the church on Vermont St. that was demolished to permit completion of the World War Memorial Plaza. In its 150th year in 1988, the church broke ground for a $4.5 million addition designed by Kennedy Brown McQuiston, Inc., of Indianapolis.

70. Located in Pike Township, **Eagle Creek Park and Nature Preserve**, 7840 W. 56th St., contains 3,500 acres of wooded land and a 1,300-acre reservoir. It is the largest city-owned and -operated park and recreation area in the United States. White settlers began to stake claims here after the Land Ordinance of 1785, and David McCurdy built the first gristmill on Eagle Creek. The hilly terrain, however, was not suitable for farming. Near the turn of the century J. K. Lilly, Sr., bought more than 3,500 acres along the creek and maintained it as a nature preserve. In the 1950s the property was donated to Purdue University, which in turn sold it to the Indianapolis Department of Parks and Recreation in 1966. The present **Nature Center** in the northeast section of the park was once Lilly's personal library, and the lodge was his weekend retreat. Just north of the Nature Center stands a beech tree that bears an outline of the territory with an inscription carved by Daniel Boone when he came through Indiana as a United States land surveyor. Within a 38-acre arboretum is a self-guiding nature trail. A renovated horse stable serves as an arts and crafts center during the summer. The park provides complete facilities for boating, fishing, picnicking, and swimming, plus an 18-hole championship golf course.

71. The place now known as **Broad Ripple** developed at first as two separate communities called Broad Ripple and Wellington. The latter gradually lost its identity, and the two became one. In the 1830s a section of the Central Canal was dug through Broad Ripple but was never used commercially. The canal passes through the center of the village, and residents enjoy fishing, biking, and jogging along its banks. Until the 1860s only one road, called the Range Line (now Westfield Blvd.), connected Broad Ripple with downtown Indianapolis. Broad Ripple was incorporated as a town in 1884 and annexed to Indianapolis in 1922. It has, how-

ever, retained its own identity. In the vicinity of N. College and Broad Ripple aves., the village contains an aggregation of boutique shops, art galleries, antique dens, cafés, theaters, flower stands, and craft shops.

From 1886 to 1904 the Dawson family owned the site of what is now Broad Ripple Park. For many years the area bounded by Broad Ripple Ave., Evanston Ave., and 64th South Dr. was a popular picnic spot because of its shaded areas and its proximity to the White River and Central Canal. In 1904 an amusement company built White City Park on the site. The park provided picnic grounds, concessions, rides, and steamboat excursions on the river. Around 1907, Union Traction Company purchased its park. In 1908 a huge swimming pool was built in the park that attracted national attention and drew such celebrities as Olympic swimmer Johnny Weissmuller, know for his Tarzan film roles. In the same year the amusement park, which was mostly built of wood, burned and was subsequently rebuilt by the Traction Company. In 1945 the city of Indianapolis bought 60 acres which became **Broad Ripple Park**. The giant roller coaster and all the old amusement park rides came down. The old swimming pool closed in 1977. A new but smaller pool opened in 1984.

72. The **Indiana State Fair**, E. 38th St. and Fall Creek Pkwy., moved to its current site in 1892. The first statewide agricultural exposition opened in 1852 at what is now Military Park in downtown Indianapolis. During the next several years the fair was held at Madison, Lafayette, New Albany, Fort Wayne, and Terre Haute, as well as Indianapolis. In 1860 the board purchased a 36-acre tract for a new fairground with the main entrance at 19th and Alabama sts. This was the site of Camp Morton during the Civil War years. In 1891 the board bought the 235-acre Voss Farm on the north side of town, opening the fairgrounds the following year. A log cabin stands near the Pioneer Farm Bureau Museum in the same general area where John Johnson homesteaded 80 acres back in 1822.

The fair showcases Indiana's science, art, agriculture, industry, and education. A 10,000-seat coliseum, the present home of the Indianapolis Ice minor-league hockey team, was built in 1939. There are 56 permanent buildings and both 1/2-mile and 1-mile racetracks. The fair-

owned Fox Stake, Horseman's Stake, and Horseman's Futurities are among the oldest continuously run harness races in the nation. The four-and-one-half-acre cattle barn under one roof is reputedly the largest in the world. More than 13,000 farm animals are entered in competition each year. During the winter season harness horses are trained at the fairgrounds, and year-round facilities are available for conventions, trade shows, seminars, sales meetings, and exhibitions.

Located near the 38th St. entrance of the fairgrounds is **Hook's Historical Drugstore and Pharmacy Museum**. The 19th-century drugstore offers a detailed view into America's pharmaceutical heritage. Furnishings from the 1850s include cabinets filled with hand-blown bottles of drugs and patent medicines, glass advertising signs with gold-leaf lettering, a large ceramic container labeled leeches, antique jars, an old-fashioned soda fountain, and a player piano. Visitors may purchase ice cream sodas, old-time novelties, and candies in the drugstore. The historic drugstore and museum opened in 1966 to commemorate the 150th anniversary of the founding of the state of Indiana. In 1900, at age 19, John Hook, son of German immigrants, opened the first Hook's Economy Drug Store in Indianapolis. He began adding new drugstores at an average rate of one per year, and the family business expanded even further under the management of following generations. Hook's claims to be the oldest drug chain in the nation under continuous, successive management. It is the largest drugstore chain in Indiana. Another historical drugstore museum, comprised of furnishings from the first Hook's Drug Store, is on display at the Indiana State Museum.

73. Plans for **Fort Benjamin Harrison**, 56th St. and Post Rd., began in 1903 when the War Department announced that it would purchase 1,833 acres in Lawrence Township to establish an army post. The state militia and the 27th United States Infantry held their training camp at the location in 1904. Since that time the army has annually conducted exercises on the post. It was not until 1906 that Theodore Roosevelt officially named the installation. By 1910 the post covered 2,030 acres and was connected to the city by an electric interurban line. Since then Fort Harrison has served as an infantry post; an officers' training camp during

World War I; an Army Air Corps base; a reception center, general hospital, and prisoner-of-war camp during World War II; and a school center and administration center for the entire United States Army. The fort is self-contained and maintains a small-town appearance. Even the streets change names within its boundaries—Post Rd. becomes Greene Ave., and 56th St. is called Aultman Ave.

There are several buildings of historical significance at the fort. A low brick building that serves as a post office was once an interurban station on the route between Indianapolis and Anderson. The commissary occupies a building that formerly housed mules. In the middle of the post is a cemetery that predates the army post; it is still used occasionally. German and Italian World War II prisoners helped construct the Officers' Club. More recent additions include an area called Camp Glenn with stables, garage rental space, a rod and gun club, and a firing range. Picnic facilities are available at Delaware Lake, New Lake, and Duck Pond. The post has its own newspaper, the *Harrison Post*. An army school is also located on the post. The Defense Information School teaches newspaper, radio, and television communication. The United States Army Soldier Support Center conducts classes in personnel management and administration, finance, comptrolling, and data processing.

The **Maj. Gen. Emmett J. Bean Center**, formerly the United States Army Finance and Accounting Center, stands on Schoen Field—the site of a former air base that opened in 1922—named in honor of army 1st Lt. Karl John Schoen, an Indianapolis aviator killed in action near Verdun, France. Many fliers were trained here during the first and second world wars. The airfield was placed on the inactive list in 1945 and permanently closed in 1950. Ground was broken for the $19 million Finance Center in 1951, and dedication ceremonies were held October 9, 1953. It is the largest single facility (except the Pentagon) that is owned and operated by the United States Army. The center incorporates the equivalent of 14 acres of rooms. It employs civilian and military personnel and publishes its own newspaper called the *Army Dollar*. The Finance Center annually disburses billions of taxpayers' dollars to soldiers on active duty, their dependents, army retirees, the National Guard, and the Army Reserves. The Army Finance Corps

Museum is located off the north lobby of the finance center building. Begun in 1954, the museum houses an extensive collection of military currency and memorabilia dating from the days of the Continental Army to the present. In 1985 the museum was certified by the Office of the Chief of Military History as an official army museum.

74. In 1870 Jacob Julian and Sylvester Johnson of Wayne County created the planned community of **Irvington**, named after American writer Washington Irving, on the far east side of Indianapolis. Julian built his fashionable home in 1871 on the corner of Audubon Rd. and E. Washington St., and Johnson built his house across the street on the west side of Audubon Rd. They modeled the town plan on Glendale, Ohio, a suburb of Cincinnati. In 1987 the whole community with its some 2,000 structures was placed on the National Register of Historic Places. For nearly 20 years, while president of Butler University (formerly Northwestern Christian University), Dr. Allen R. Benton occupied the two-story brick, Second Empire-style house with a French mansard roof at 312 S. Downey Ave. Built in 1873 by Nicholas Ohmer, the house is one of the first five stately homes built in Irvington. The **Irvington Landmarks Foundation** now owns the house and operates it as a museum and meeting place. Volunteers decorate the house at Christmastime with the kind of 19th-century trimmings depicted in Washington Irving's *Sketch Book*. Museum furnishings include 47 chairs with engraved name plates from the Indianapolis Literary Club, bearing names of past members such as Benjamin Harrison, James Whitcomb Riley, Booth Tarkington, and Charles Warren Fairbanks. (*NRHP/HABSI*)

Many notables have made their homes in Irvington, including Hilton U. Brown, publisher of the *Indianapolis News*; David Starr Jordan, biologist and president of Indiana University and Stanford University; George S. Cottman, founder of the *Indiana Magazine of History*; William Forsyth, artist; and Dr. Henry Lee Bruner, zoologist. The English Tudor-style **residences of Frank McKinney "Kin" Hubbard** (creator of the Abe Martin cartoons) and **Helene L. Hibben** (sculptress, dancer, and educator) are located at 5070 and 5237 E. Pleasant Run Pkwy., respectively. Across the street the beautiful **Ellenberger Park** borders the stream.

A wide-spreading 300-year-old burr oak tree on the O. W. Kile property at 5939 Beechwood Ave. is protected by the Irvington Historical Society. There are many fine old houses in Irvington such as the **Eudorus Johnson house** (1876) at 5631 E. University Ave., the **Rev. Robert Blount residence** (1879) at 5470 E. University Ave., and the **Italianate mansion** (1873-76) **of George Julian**, son of the town founder Jacob Julian, at 115 S. Audubon Rd. The Irvington Historical Society sells a walking tour guide of the old section.

Built in 1889, the Greek Revival-style mansion with four towering pillars across the front porch at 5432 E. University Ave. was once the **home of D. C. Stephenson**, former Grand Dragon of the Indiana Ku Klux Klan. In the 1920s Stephenson's organization virtually controlled the state legislature but lost its power when Stephenson was convicted of second-degree murder in the 1925 rape of Madge Oberholtzer, a young Irvington woman who then committed suicide. Subsequent owners of the house reported having heard rumors of secret tunnels and passages from the house but only found a secret room under the driveway that had been filled with concrete. (*NRHP*)

Butler University occupied a 25-acre campus between Butler and Emerson aves. from 1875 to 1928. A commemorative marker is located at the east edge of the former campus, at Butler and University aves. The Disciples of Christ was the first church organization in Irvington in 1875. Built in 1893, the **Downey Ave. Christian Church**, 111 S. Downey Ave., served as the Butler College Chapel for 18 years. The **College of Missions** at 222 S. Downey Ave. opened in 1910 for the graduate training of missionaries. Women of the Christian Church planned, erected, financed, and used the building, though both men and women were students. The modern "building in the round" of the Board of Church Extension of the Disciples of Christ at Downey and Julian aves. was dedicated in 1958. In 1982 a memorial park was dedicated to Hoosier humorist **Frank McKinney "Kin" Hubbard** at New York St. and Emerson Ave. The Irvington History Room in the Hilton U. Brown Library at 5427 E. Washington St. houses a collection of "Abe Martin" books, created by Hubbard.

75. Bounded by I-65, East St., and Lord St., **Fletcher Place Historic District** is an early resi- dential-commercial area on the near south side of the city. Calvin Fletcher, who came to Indianapolis in 1821, bought most of the land in this area. He became the city's first lawyer and served in the state legislature between 1826 and 1833. He helped organize the State Bank and establish the city's health and educational services. Fletcher's Farm, called Wood Lawn, was plotted into individual lots in 1857. Virginia Ave., now the last diagonal street of the original "mile square" plan left intact, linked Fletcher Place with the downtown and Fountain Square to the southeast. Fountain Square was originally called The End because it was at "the end" of the old mule car line. Both large houses and little cottages, representing several architectural styles of the Victorian period, were built in the 1860s. Many of the surviving structures are being restored. (*NRHP*)

Fletcher Place Methodist Church at the intersection of Fletcher and Virginia aves. is the keystone of the historic district. The Fletcher family donated the triangular strip of land that was part of the old family homestead and sugar camp. Dr. Charles Tinsley, the first pastor of the church, directed the construction of the brick Gothic Revival-style edifice between 1872 and 1880. High winds blew down the original church spire, and it was never replaced. Many of the interior features remain intact, such as the fine wooden hammer-beam ceiling work in the sanctuary. In the 1970s local muralist Patrick Flanigan painted a 55-ft.-high rendition of Noah's Ark on the walls.

Neighborhood architectural styles range from simple working-class cottages to elegant two-story residences of Italianate and Queen Anne design. Built in 1863-64, the **Joseph White house** at 441 S. Park Ave. is an outstanding example of Federal-style architecture. In 1982 the Historic Landmarks Foundation of Indiana financed the move of artist **William Forsyth's former home** to 616 Lexington Ave. Built about 1875, the Italianate-style house was altered to its present appearance about 1890. William Forsyth, a member of the Hoosier Group of artists, helped organize several art schools including the Herron School of Art. The Forsyth family owned the house until 1948. Directly across the street is the old **Calvin Fletcher School** at 520 Virginia Ave. The brick building has been altered and expanded since it was originally erected in 1876. The school closed in 1980. It is now renovated and used for office space. In 1984 a neighborhood development group moved the **Caito house** from the expanding Eli Lilly and Company complex to 525 S. College Ave. Sicilian immigrants Philip and Michaelina Caito bought the 1859 brick house in 1900 and used two rooms in the basement to ripen the bananas that they imported and peddled in the city.

Once an extension of Fletcher Place, **Fountain Square Historic District** was cut off by the construction of I-65. An active commercial center since the 1860s, the neighborhood acquired its name from the fountain placed at the intersection of Virginia Ave. and Prospect and Shelby sts. Francis M. Churchman, a partner with Stoughton A. Fletcher in the banking business, erected the fountain as a drinking place for horses in 1890. It was later converted into an ornamental fixture with the sculpture of a maiden. Myra Reynolds Richards executed the present bronze statuary group, depicting a pioneer family, in 1924. Fountain Square was also an entertainment center. With seven theaters, it became the city's first theater district in the 1920s. Still surviving is the former **Fountain Square Theatre** at 1106 Prospect St., designed by Rubush and Hunter. The terra-cotta facade was executed by Alexander Sangernebo.

76. Dedicated in 1969, the **Lilly Center**, 893 S. Delaware St., showcases informative and colorful displays of pharmaceuticals, cosmetics, electronic medical devices, and agricultural products manufactured by Eli Lilly and Company. The Multivision Theatre located on the second floor presents a 10-minute show entitled "The Path We Have Chosen," using 21 projectors and more than 1,200 images shown on a semicircular screen. Two rooms situated on the ground floor commemorate the Lilly Family—the Eli Lilly Room, which contains many personal mementos of the company's founder, and the Lilly Room, which is a partial re-creation of the office of Josiah K. Lilly, Sr., son of the founder.

In 1876 Col. Eli Lilly started his pharmaceutical firm in a small building at 15 W. Pearl St., just west of Meridian St. A family business, Eli Lilly and Company formulated medicines by scientific principles and distributed its products through wholesalers to the medical and pharmacy professions. Following his father's death, J. K. Lilly, Sr., served as president of the company and expanded research to discover

therapeutics for fatal diseases. The Lilly research laboratories developed the first commercial production of insulin from animal pancreases in 1923, and the company also developed a liver extract for the treatment of pernicious anemia.

Eli Lilly and J. K. Lilly, Jr., continued the family tradition of corporate excellence and service to the community. Sound management and marketing practices helped Eli Lilly and Company become a major force in pharmaceuticals in the country in the 1940s. Continued research and development have produced an abundance of products including penicillin, antibiotics, polio vaccine, and medicines for cancer and heart disease. More recently, scientific breakthroughs have been made in the production of biosynthetic human insulin through the use of DNA technology. The company has grown into an international enterprise and has diversified operations to include Elanco agricultural products, IVAC Corporation, Cardiac Pacemakers, Inc., and Physio-Control Corporation medical instruments. In 1985 the company dedicated the **Lilly Corporate Center**, the site of its corporate administration and research facilities. The downtown mall covers a 15-block area and comprises 30 buildings including the Lilly Center and the new $60 million **Biomedical Research Building**. In 1987, Lilly and Company purchased the old Farmers' Market at the southeast corner of South St. and Virginia Ave. The 3.5-acre site, a produce marketplace since the mid-1920s, will be used for expansion of the Lilly complex. The **Lilly Industrial Center** is a complex of production plants strung along Kentucky Avenue and Harding Street on the near southside.

77. Around 1860 Hervey Bates built the first of three sections of the present **Bates-Hendricks house** at 1526 S. New Jersey St. In 1865 Thomas A. Hendricks, a successful trial lawyer and United States senator, bought the house and added the fashionable three-and-a-half story French mansard tower. He also built the north addition featuring a drawing room with floor-to-ceiling windows. No other major structural changes have been made to the 10-room mansion with 6 fireplaces since a service wing was added, ca. 1875. Hendricks sold the house in 1872 upon his election as Indiana's 16th governor. He later became vice-president of the United States under President Grover Cleve-

land but died during his first year in office. (*NRHP/HABS*)

78. The **Sanders-Childers house**, 1020 East Palmer St., opposite Abraham Lincoln School (1901), is Indianapolis's oldest known extant house, built by William Sanders around 1830 on the site of a Delaware Indian sugar camp. Its construction parallels the earliest days of Indianapolis as the state's capital. The two-story brick farmhouse underwent alterations over the years including a major modernization in the early 1920s by Frank R. Childers, Marion County Recorder, 1927-30. He purchased the house in 1914 from James E. Twiname, a contractor and former president of the Indianapolis Builders' Exchange (1891). The house came to the attention of the Historic Landmarks Foundation of Indiana in 1986 when the Childers family offered the property at auction. Historic Landmarks bought the house through its Fund for Landmark Indianapolis Properties (FLIP). It then was sold in 1987 to K. C. Cohen, whose company, RenoTech, performed the restoration. Two housing units have been made from the house and its attached farmhand building. The structure sits askew in relation to Palmer and Barth sts. because no streets had been laid off in this area when the house was built.

79. Founded in 1876, **Garfield Park** at 2400 Shelby St. is the city's oldest park. Originally called Bradley Woods, then Southern Driving Park, it was renamed Garfield Park in memory of President James Garfield following his assassination in 1881. The park was seldom used until after 1895 when it was enlarged to 138 acres and improved by the city during the administration of Mayor Thomas Taggart. Daniel Deupree, a city engineer, planned and designed the stone pagoda with an elaborate wrought-iron trim built in 1903. George Kessler and architects Vonnegut and Bohn executed the formal garden in 1915. A couple of notable monuments have been moved from their original sites to Garfield Park. A statue in tribute to Maj. Gen. Henry W. Lawton of the regular army, who fell in battle in the Philippines in 1899, originally stood in the yard of the old Marion County Courthouse, but it was removed to Garfield Park in 1915. President Theodore Roosevelt attended the unveiling ceremonies in 1907, which followed a reception at

the Meridian St. home of Vice-President Charles Fairbanks, who caused a national scandal by serving liquor to his guests. Another relocated monument is the memorial shaft to the Confederate prisoners who died at Camp Morton. Erected by the War Department in 1912 at Greenlawn Cemetery near the present Diamond Chain Company but moved in 1928 to Garfield Park, the monument lists the names of soldiers now buried at Crown Hill. Adjacent to the park is the **Garfield Conservatory**, built in 1913 and remodeled in 1983. Inside it features a gazebo and a 15-ft.-high waterfall cascading from the roof. On display are more than 500 types of plants from various climates. Garfield Conservatory has held a Chrysanthemum Show every fall for over 50 years.

80. **Alexander M. Hannah** built his two-story Italianate-style house at 3801 Madison Ave. in 1858 with the profits from a trip West in the spring of 1850 during the gold rush. The brick house stood on a 240-acre farm. At that time Madison Ave. was a toll road, and Hannah collected levies. It is said that during the Civil War Hannah used the house as a station on the "underground railroad." (*NRHP*)

81. **University of Indianapolis**, formerly Indiana Central University, 1400 E. Hannah Ave., is a small liberal arts college. In 1902 William L. Elder, a realtor, donated eight acres and a college building to the White River Conference of the Church of the United Brethren in Christ with the stipulation that the church provide buyers for 446 lots in the area of the college, called University Heights. The St. Joseph Conference and the Indiana Conference also cooperated in the arrangement. The first college building, a Classical Revival-style edifice later called Good Hall, was completed and occupied in 1905. The university experienced a period of rapid growth during the 1970s. New facilities added during the decade include a football stadium, a library and audiovisual center, a nursing and behavioral sciences-history unit, a campus park, a carillon, and two dormitories. The **Ruth Lilly Center for Health and Physical Fitness** opened in 1984. The name change occurred in 1987, much to the chagrin of IUPUI supporters who had hoped that the large urban university would become an independent institution and adopt the University of Indianapolis name.

82. Named for the beech trees that once flourished in the area, **Beech Grove** (p. 13,196) sprang up in the middle of former farmland. Much of Beech Grove's growth has been a direct result of railroad construction and repair shops located there. In 1906 when the Cleveland, Cincinnati, Chicago, and St. Louis Railway announced its plans to build "the greatest locomotive hospital in the world" southeast of Indianapolis, the news had an immediate impact on the area. The town of Beech Grove was incorporated the same year, and other businesses such as grain elevators moved to the vicinity. The Big Four Railroad completed its boiler shop in 1908. Most of the other shops were in operation by 1914. The New York Central Railroad acquired the shops in 1922 and expanded the facilities. During World War II the shops employed 5,000 workers. Since then ownership has passed from New York Central to Penn Central and finally, in 1975, to Amtrak. Maintenance services also have been changed from repairing steam locomotives and passenger and freight cars to converting Amtrak's fleet of cars from steam to electric heat and completely refurbishing them. A $29 million modernization program of the major Amtrak repair facility at Beech Grove was completed in the 1980s. Beech Grove has maintained its independent status as a "city within a city." Though geographically located within Marion County, Beech Grove remains governmentally separate from Unigov, which consolidated the city of Indianapolis and Marion County. A historic marker for poetess **Sarah T. Bolton**, author of "Paddle Your Own Canoe" and "Indiana," is located at 107 S. 17th Ave. In 1871 she bought 55 acres in an area called Beech Bank and built a home. In 1930, 32 acres of the old Bolton estate were turned into a public park bearing the Hoosier poetess's name.

Tour 13

Tour 13 begins at the junction of US 421 (Michigan Rd.) and I-465 on the northwest side of Indianapolis. Take US 421 north *1.9 m.* to **BOONE COUNTY** (p. 36,446; 424 sq. m.). Previously part of the New Purchase, Boone County came into being in 1830 as the state's 63rd county. The newly formed county took its name from Col. Daniel Boone, "the pioneer of the west." Jamestown served as the county seat until moved to Lebanon because of the latter's central location. The county has been traditionally agricultural with the leading crops in corn and soybeans. It also ranks high in the sale of hogs and farm machinery. Recent years have seen a growth in light manufacturing, particularly in the Lebanon area.

Continue north on US 421 *.4 m.* and take IND 334 west *.5 m.* to the intersection of E. Sycamore (IND 334) and S. Main sts. in **ZIONSVILLE** (p. 3,948). This picturesque town, situated on the edge of Eagle Creek Valley amidst hills and aged trees, retains its small-town character. In the 1960s the town remodeled the business district to resemble a New England village. Main St., which runs north from IND 334, is paved with brick and decorated with planters and gas lamps. Nineteenth-century homes have been converted into antique shops, restaurants, and boutiques, while newer buildings have been designed to blend with older styles of architecture. The Chamber of Commerce, housed in a tiny cedar shake building at 135 S. Elm St. overlooking the Lions Club Park, publishes a guide to shops and attractions in the village and sponsors an annual tour of private homes in the fall. Horse-drawn carriages provide rides through the downtown area. The homes in the surrounding residential areas feature a variety of 19th-century Victorian architectural styles.

Zionsville was settled about 1830. The town was laid out in 1852 adjacent to the Cincinnati, Indianapolis and Lafayette Railroad and named for its surveyor, William Zion. Just north of the intersection of E. Sycamore St. (IND 334) and Main St., a roadside marker indicates **Historic Block No. 8**—the location of the town's first post office (1853), the first dry goods and grocery stores (1852), and John Miller's home and boardinghouse (1852). The block is now a parking lot with an old frame building once occupied by a lumber company. Additional historical markers along Main St. designate the sites of the town's first livery stable and the first school building.

Five blocks north of IND 334, at the corner of Main and Poplar sts., stands the **First Baptist Church**, which advertises itself as "the old fashioned church preaching the old-fashioned gospel." The Baptists use the former Methodist church, built in 1894. Of Queen Anne-style design, the frame structure features fish-scale shingles, a gabled roof, gingerbread trim, and a bell tower. The Methodists in Eagle Township first met in 1828 and erected a church on the site of the present building in 1854. The Baptists acquired the church in 1962 and conducted restoration work in the 1970s.

One block south of the church, between Main and Elm sts., is the old **Town Hall**, 65 E. Cedar St., a three-story red brick structure erected in 1902. The Knights of Pythias used the second floor for their lodge, and the town hall occupied the lower level. In 1942 the building was converted into a movie theater and later served as a playhouse. In the 1980s the old town hall underwent rehabilitation for commercial use (*NRHP*). The fire station and the waterworks department now occupy quarters in the renovated frame building at the corner of Cedar and Elm sts. The Colonial-style structure features a belfry with a weather vane.

Return to Main St. and continue one block west to **Lincoln Memorial Park** at the southwest corner of Cedar and 1st sts. A railroad station once stood on the site of this tiny park where President-elect Abraham Lincoln stopped en route to Washington. A historical

Tour 13

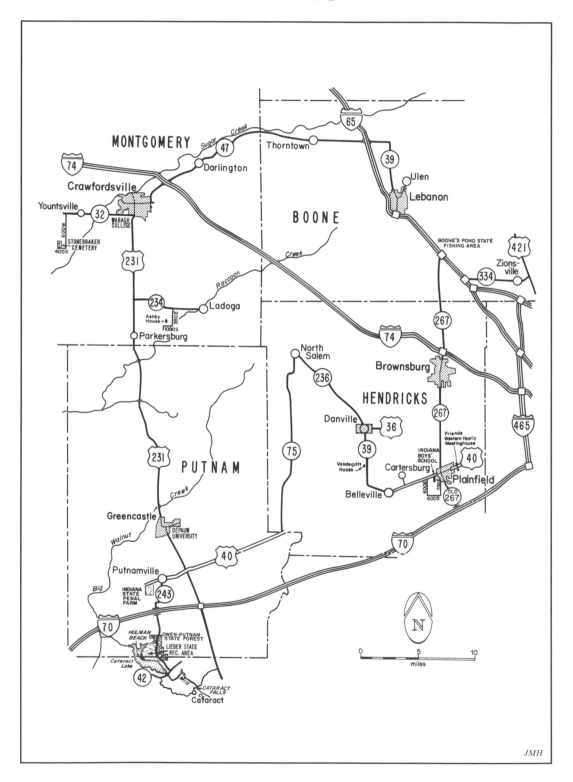

JMH

marker indicates the spot where Lincoln addressed the citizens of Zionsville on February 11, 1861.

From 1st and Oak sts. proceed two blocks south and one block west. In 1957 former schoolteacher Lora Hussey bequeathed to the city the entire 200 block of W. Hawthorne St. except for a house on the west corner. A red brick sidewalk on the south side of this tree-shaded residential street links the art center and the historical museum. In 1974 Mary Elizabeth Hopkins Munce bequeathed the funds to establish the **Munce Art Center**, 205 W. Hawthorne St., in the house built by Lora Hussey's aunts, Laura and Etta Hoffman, in the 1920s. The gallery contains changing exhibits showing arts and crafts produced by Zionsville artists.

The **Patrick Henry Sullivan Foundation Museum**, 225 W. Hawthorne St., was built on the site of the Hussey orchard. Iva Etta Sullivan, teacher and librarian, bequeathed the funds to establish the foundation in memory of her great grandfather, who was the first white settler in Boone County in 1823 and built the first log cabin. Sullivan built a house in 1852 where the library now stands. He died in 1879 and is buried in the Sheets Cemetery on Fords Rd. The handsome brick museum with an arched portico in the front, designed by H. Roll McLaughlin with James Associates of Indianapolis, was erected in 1973. Though used primarily for genealogical research, the facility has a large display area with an extensive collection of local artifacts including some agricultural tools and household furnishings.

Just west of the museum at 255 W. Hawthorne St. is the **Hussey Memorial Library**, established in 1962. The turn-of-the-century frame house of Queen Anne-style design was the home of the Milton and Ella Hoffman Hussey family before becoming a library. The property had been in the family since 1899 when James Hoffman moved to Zionsville and built the residence west of the library.

From 3rd and Hawthorne sts., go north two blocks to Oak St. and turn left. Follow IND 334 west for *4.7 m.* to I-65. Take I-65 north for *8.9 m.* to the second Lebanon exit and turn north on IND 39. Sometime between 1829 and 1831 George L. Kinnard surveyed the Indianapolis and Lafayette Rd., which passed through what is now the city of **LEBANON** (p. 11,456). Kinnard and James P. Drake purchased much of the land adjacent to the road and platted the

town in 1831. They persuaded Abner H. Longley, the town's first permanent settler, to locate there and influenced the county commissioners to select Lebanon as the site for the county seat in 1832 by offering free land for public use. One of the county commissioners, Adam M. French, named the county seat Lebanon, supposedly because it reminded him of the biblical mountain with the famous cedars of Lebanon. Another version of the story says that he named it after his hometown of Lebanon in Ohio.

From I-65 proceed north one mile on IND 39 (Lebanon St.) to the Lebanon courthouse square. Italianate-style commercial buildings and the sandstone and brick county jail, constructed in 1939, face the square. A two-story log structure, erected in 1833, was the first courthouse on the square. A small brick building replaced it in 1840. Indianapolis architect William Tinsley designed an impressive Gothic-style edifice which served as the courthouse from 1856 until 1909. Caldwell and Drake of Columbus constructed the present **Boone County Courthouse**, completed in 1911. The Oolitic limestone building boasts an 84-ft.-high and 52-ft.-wide dome, the second largest in the state. The 35-ft.-tall hand-cut monolithic columns at the north and south entrances are believed to be the largest single-piece pillars in the nation. The structure stands on the Second Principal Meridian Line—a fact noted on a tablet embedded in the center of the rotunda floor. (*NRHP*)

From Main and Lebanon sts. proceed north on IND 39 for seven blocks to Ulen Dr. Turn right and follow the curving road for two blocks to **Memorial Park** on the left. The 40-acre park is the site of the Herr Cabin, built by Nicholas Yount in Perry Township in 1839. It was purchased by Benjamin Herr in 1882 and occupied by the Herr family until 1893. John Herr gave the cabin to the local chapter of the Daughters of the American Revolution (DAR), which in the mid-1930s had it moved to the park and reconstructed by Works Progress Administration (WPA) workmen. Often vandalized, the cabin was presented to the city in 1966 for its protection and preservation.

Adjoining Memorial Park to the northeast is the Ulen Country Club, established in 1924. Turn left on Ulen Blvd., which makes a single loop through the town of **ULEN** (p. 193), incorporated in 1929. Henry C. Ulen designed and built the country club and the surrounding community with all homes within walking distance of the golf course. Ulen built his own house overlooking the ninth hole. Architect Reuben J. Pheiffer designed the stately Mediterranean Revival-style brick house with a barrel-tile roof at 118 Ulen Blvd. A temporary frame shell was erected around the house so that construction work could continue through the winter of 1928-29.

Before his death in 1963 at age 92, Ulen was the corporate director for the Ulen Contracting Company, one of the world's largest international engineering and contracting corporations. In 1929 he relocated the main offices from New York and Paris to Lebanon and built homes alongside the golf course for his staff executives. In the late 1940s Ulen retired from business, and the firm which constructed dams, bridges, railroads, waterworks, and irrigation projects throughout the world later dissolved. The town of Ulen remains, however, one of the most elegant residential areas in the Indianapolis area.

Return to Ulen Dr. and Lebanon St. and proceed north on IND 39 for *4.8 m.* to IND 47. Turn left and continue west *6 m.*, crossing I-65, to a roadside historical marker on the north side of the road. The marker indicates a cemetery which belonged to the Eel River tribe of Miami Indians. Buried here in a square grave are Chief Chapodosia and Chief Dixon, who fought to the death in a conflict among the Indians over the Thorntown treaty. The chieftains were buried in full ceremonial dress and placed in a seated position facing each other. (The burial ground is inaccessible from the road.)

At the junction of Sugar and Prairie creeks, the **THORNTOWN** (p. 1,468) area provided an ideal hunting ground for the Indians. The Miamis named their village Ka-wi-a-ki-un-gi, which means the "place of thorns." The legend which explains the name of Thorntown has several versions. One of the most colorful tells of two young warriors who competed for the hand of a beautiful Indian maiden and killed each other. The heartbroken princess pierced her heart with a thorn from the bushes which grew in the area, and the village thus came to be known as the "place of thorns." In 1818 the federal government granted a 64,000-acre reserve, of which Thorntown was the center, to the Eel River Miamis. The Miami nation ceded

the reserve to the United States in 1828 and left Thorntown the following year. Many of the first white settlers moved into abandoned Indian huts. Few reminders of the Indian heritage remain today.

Continue west on IND 47 for *.8 m.* through the business district to Main and Vine sts. The **Thorntown Heritage Museum**, 124 W. Main St., occupies a one-and-a-half-story Gothic brick house at the northeast corner. The Society for the Preservation of Our Indian Heritage operates a museum in the house which Joseph P. Shipp built for his bride between 1863 and 1867. The house stands on land first deeded to Cornelius Westfall, the town founder. Furnished with antiques, the museum features a display of Indian artifacts found in the Thorntown area.

Among the museum exhibits is the bronze head from a statue which once adorned one of two fountains along Main St. Brig. Gen. Anson Mills financed the town's water and sewage system in 1909 and erected the fountains in honor of his parents. Born in Thorntown in 1834, Mills graduated from West Point, served in the Civil War, and platted the city of El Paso, Texas. He is best known, however, as the inventor of the woven cartridge belt which he designed and manufactured for the army. He died in 1924.

Proceed west on IND 47 for *4.9 m.* to the Montgomery County line (for a description of the county see Tour 10). Continue west on IND 47 for *5 m.* to **DARLINGTON** (p. 811), located on the old Crawfordsville-Thorntown Pike which roughly follows IND 47. Turn right on Madison St. and go *.4 m.* to Main St. Turn right and continue for two blocks to the **Darlington Toll Gate House** just before the Honey Creek bridge. Main St. was formerly a "corduroy" road, and gatekeepers lived in this tiny frame house built in 1880.

Return to Madison St. Proceed straight ahead on Main St. for *1.2 m.* through the business district to CR 600E. Turn left to the **Darlington Covered Bridge** which spans Sugar Creek a short distance downstream from the concrete bridge erected in 1976. The 166-ft.-long covered bridge of Howe-truss design, built in 1867, underwent restoration in the 1970s. The road surface of the bridge paved with wood blocks is still intact though no longer open to traffic. At one time, four mills and factories operated along the banks of Sugar Creek which crosses the northwest corner of the township.

Return on Main St. and turn right on Franklin St. At the next corner stands the National Guard Armory, a fascinating Art Deco building authorized in 1936. Turn left and at one block turn right on Madison St. Proceed to IND 47 and travel west for *7.3 m.* to **CRAWFORDSVILLE** (p. 13,325).

In 1821 William Offield, Montgomery County's first settler, built his cabin near where Offield Creek empties into Sugar Creek about five miles southwest of here. He moved his family West in 1824 as this area became too crowded to suit him. Maj. Ambrose Whitlock of Virginia opened the federal land office and platted Crawfordsville in 1823. He offered every odd-numbered lot to the county, provided that the county seat be located there. He also stipulated that the proceeds from this property be set aside for educational purposes. Whitlock named the town for his friend Col. William H. Crawford, a well-known Indian fighter and Georgia senator who served under Maj. Gen. Anthony Wayne and later with Gov. William Henry Harrison at the latter's conference with Tecumseh at Vincennes in 1811. Crawford was secretary of war, 1815-16, secretary of the treasury, 1816-25, and a candidate for the presidency, 1824, along with Andrew Jackson, Henry Clay, and John Quincy Adams.

Crawfordsville was incorporated as a town in 1834 and as a city in 1865. By 1874 the city had three railroads and a union depot. At the turn of the century, it had a large number of businesses and factories, including a "heading" factory which manufactured barrel heads and staves, coffin factory, wire and nail company, match company, glove factory, creamery, sawmill, body and gear works, foundry, machine shop, brickyard, and many smaller businesses. Midstates Wire, founded in 1900 as the Crawfordsville Wire and Nail Works, is one of the city's largest employers in volume of business and number employed.

Crawfordsville is sometimes called the Athens of Indiana because of its strong cultural interests. It was perhaps the smallest city in the country with a symphony orchestra in the 1930s and has produced many fine artists, writers, educators, and politicians. Local luminaries have included Maj. Gen. Lew Wallace, Henry Smith Lane, Meredith and Kenyon Nicholson, Will and Maurice Thompson, Caroline and Mary Hannah Krout, George Barr McCutcheon, and David C. Gerard. During the nineteenth century E. Wabash Ave. was noted for its elegant homes and prominent citizens.

At IND 32, on the east side of Crawfordsville, continue straight ahead for *.5 m.* to E. Wabash Ave., turn right for *.8 m.*, and left on Mill St. to Milligan Park, which stands on 40 acres of wooded property donated by Henry J. Milligan in memory of his father, Joseph Milligan. The park was dedicated in 1916. The Speed cabin, built in the late 1820s, stands near the Prospect St. entrance. A stone mason from Scotland, John Allen Speed was a fervent abolitionist, said to have been active in the "underground railroad." He served as Crawfordsville's mayor following the Civil War. Originally located at the corner of Grant and North sts., the log cabin was stored in a barn for several years, then reassembled in Milligan Park.

Return to Wabash Ave., turn left, and turn right at Water St. **Lane Place**, 212 S. Water St., between Pike St. and Wabash Ave., is located on spacious grounds once a part of Elston Woods. The grove surrounding the house contains nearly 100 varieties of trees. Henry Smith Lane erected the nine-room Greek Revival-style house from 1836 to 1843, adjoining the two-room cottage built by W. P. Hawkins about 1836. Following a term as congressman, Lane married Joanna Elston, second daughter of pioneer and banker Isaac Compton Elston. He served as chairman of the first National Republican Convention held in Philadelphia in 1856 and was elected governor of Indiana in 1860, but held office for only two days before the state legislature appointed him United States senator in 1861. During the Civil War years Lane lived in Washington and was a friend of President Lincoln. Lane returned to Crawfordsville in 1867 and spent his retirement years at Lane Place. During the 1870s the two porticoes on the north and south sides of the house were added. When Henry Lane died in 1881, the funeral services were held on the west front portico because the house could not accommodate the large number of mourners. Joanna Lane continued to reside at Lane Place until her death in 1913. Helen Smith, Joanna Lane's niece and heir, owned the house until 1931. Since then the Montgomery County Historical Society has operated Lane Place as a museum. Volunteers conduct tours through the house which is furnished with many of the Lanes' possessions. (*NRHP/HABSI*)

Just east and north of Lane Place stands another historic landmark—the **Elston homestead**, 400 E. Pike St. The original owner, Maj. Isaac Compton Elston, a veteran of the War of 1812 and the Black Hawk War, arrived in Crawfordsville in 1823 and began his profitable career as a pioneer merchant, land developer, financier, and banker. When he died in 1867 Major Elston was regarded as one of the wealthiest men in the state. He had been involved in the development of Lafayette and Michigan City, Indiana, and Kankakee, Illinois. In 1850 he formed the Crawfordsville and Wabash Railroad, of which the northern terminus is a town named Elston. In 1853 he opened the Elston Bank, the first and for 10 years the only bank in Montgomery County. E. C. Griffith and Son constructed the limestone Elston Bank building at the southeast corner of Main and Green sts. in 1870. The major's son, Col. Isaac Compton Elston, carried on the family business, renamed Elston and Company, which his sisters Joanna Lane and Susan Wallace joined in 1888.

Major Elston built the stately mansion of Federal design for his growing family of nine children. Though changed by the addition of dormers and wrought-iron porticoes, the two-story house with twin chimneys retains its original classical simplicity and symmetry. The date of construction "1835" is carved in the upper south cornerstone of the west wall. The homestead remained in the Elston family until 1884, then changed hands twice before Major Elston's grandson bought and restored it in 1935. Isaac Compton Elston, Jr., bequeathed the house to Wabash College upon his death in 1964. The house now serves as the residence for Wabash College presidents. (*NRHP*)

Continue one-half block to the east end of Pike St. Surrounded by a brick wall, the **Gen. Lew Wallace Study** and **Ben Hur Museum** stands in the middle of a park. Once part of the Elston estate, the grounds were bequeathed to Wallace's wife, Susan Elston. The entrance with a historical marker at the gate faces Wallace Ave. Maj. Gen. Lew Wallace began building his study in 1896, about 11 years after his return from Turkey, where he served as United States minister, 1881-85. The design of the domed hall and 40-ft.-high tower reflects Wallace's in-

Lane Place

terest in Greek, Roman, and Byzantine archi-tecture. Architect John G. Thurtle designed the library to meet Wallace's specifications. The glazed brick building with a copper roof fea-tures Tiffany stained-glass windows, a tur-quoise skylight, a tower which conceals a huge chimney, and a frieze which depicts the literary characters created by Wallace.

The furnishings of the study include Wal-lace's oil paintings, sketches, Civil War memo-rabilia, gifts from the Sultan of Turkey, and objets d'art which Wallace collected during his world travels. Pictures, books, and other arti-facts trace Wallace's long and varied career as a soldier, author, artist, sportsman, and states-man. Wallace served in the Mexican War, 1846-47, was prosecuting attorney of Indiana's Eighth Circuit 1851-53, organized the Mont-gomery County Guards who adopted the color-ful Zouave uniform in 1856, held a state senate seat, 1857 and 1859, attained the rank of major general during the Civil War, and served as governor to New Mexico Territory, 1878-81.

A bronze statue of Wallace, west of the study, stands on the site of a massive beech tree under which Wallace wrote much of the novel *Ben Hur*, published in 1880. Wallace also wrote *The Fair God* in 1873 and *The Prince of India* in 1893. The bronze is a replica of the original carved from Carrara marble by Andrew O'Connor and erected in the rotunda of the United States Capitol in Washington, D.C. At the southeast corner of the study grounds is the old Wallace stable, built in 1870, a wood frame structure topped with a cupola. A fire in 1964 damaged the "little house," but it has been repaired and now serves as a meeting place. In 1977 the library and grounds were declared a National Historic Landmark. The city owns and operates the study as a historic shrine. (*NRHP*)

From Wallace Ave., proceed west two blocks on Wabash Ave., then north one-half block on Green St. **St. John's Church**, 212 S. Green St., is the first Episcopal church con-structed in Indiana. Bishop Jackson Kemper traveled from Indianapolis to lay the corner-stone on June 7, 1837. Erected on the north-west corner of Water and Market sts., the 30-ft. by 50-ft. frame building was moved with much difficulty to its present location at Green and Pike sts. during the winter of 1872-73. At Water and Pike sts., the rig hauling the church building was mired in the mud from Decem-ber to March. During that time traffic was detoured around the building, and church services were held as usual. In 1873 a Tiffany stained-glass window was installed in the chancel's east wall. Extensive renovations, made in 1917, included exposing the black walnut beams in the sanctuary, excavating the basement, and attaching a three-story tower to the front entrance. In 1961 the congregation removed the tower, added the east annex, and attempted to restore the original Greek Revival architectural design of the "little church." (*NRHP*)

Around the corner to the right is the **Camp-bell-Banta house**, 211 E. Pike St. John P. Campbell, a dry goods merchant, built this two-story red brick residence in 1852. The Greek Revival-style house lies within the Old Town Plat. The original house consisted of only the east wing of the present structure. The Camp-bell family occupied the house until 1883. Sub-sequent owners altered and remodeled it, including the addition of the south wing in 1900. Richard E. Banta, a writer and publisher, bought the house in 1931 and carried out ex-tensive restoration work. The Banta family sold the house in 1971.

Continue north on Green St. for two and one-half blocks to Market St. On the southwest corner stands the recently restored **Otto Schlemmer building**. Dr. Simon Bennage con-structed the two-story brick commercial build-ing in 1854, which Otto Schlemmer renovated and remodeled in 1889. To the Roman arches across the second story, Schlemmer added the stamped metal cornice, frieze work, and central pediment. Between 1854 and the 1880s, a vari-ety of tenants occupied the building including a grocery, a dry goods business, a tobacco empo-rium, a drugstore, and a blacksmith shop. Otto Schlemmer bought the north half of the build-ing in 1882 and the south half in 1885 to use for his wholesale liquor business. The building remained in the Schlemmer family until 1926. A restaurant occupied the building during the late 1920s, but it then became rental property and slipped into neglect and disuse. In 1978 local preservationists saved the historic land-mark, which had already been condemned by the city. The exterior has been meticulously re-stored, and rehabilitation of neighboring build-ings has begun. (*NRHP*)

Circle the block and go west to Main St. The **Montgomery County Courthouse** occupies the northeast corner of Main and Washington sts. The first county courthouse was built of logs in 1823, at a cost of $295. The second courthouse, a two-story brick structure topped with a cupola, stood from 1831 to 1875. When the courthouse was torn down, the bricks were used to build a coffin factory on W. Pike St. and were later reused for the exterior walls of the motel at Pike and Wilhoit sts. Architects Banting and Huebner designed the county's present courthouse, a Neoclassical structure with porticoes on the south and west. The cornerstone at the southwest corner of the Berea sandstone and red brick building was laid on May 6, 1875. The courthouse originally included a 155-ft.-high tower with a four-faced clock and bell which was removed in the 1940s. A monument honoring the war dead was erected in the southwest corner of the yard in 1906.

From Main St., go north two blocks on Washington St. to Spring St. The **Montgomery County Jail and Sheriff's residence**, a handsome Victorian brick and limestone structure, occupies the southwest corner. Erected in 1882, the county's third jail served its purpose until 1973. The first jail, a log cabin constructed in 1823, had two rooms—one for debtors and the other for felons. The second jail, built of brick in the late 1820s, had a cell block in its basement. In the 1882 building the sheriff's family occupied an attractively decorated eight-room apartment in the front section. Doors in the kitchen and dining area led to the jail proper in the rear. W. H. Brown and E. J. Hodgson of Indianapolis designed and patented the unique rotary cell block (one of only seven ever built) that measures about 20 ft. in diameter. A hand-operated crank turns the shaft of the two-story cylindrical cell block which revolves past a single outer opening. Each floor of the cell block is divided into eight wedge-shaped cells. A stationary outer wall of brick and barred windows surrounds the cast-iron cylinder. The design provided maximum security with a minimum of personnel. Though not rotated after 1938, the jail remained in use until 1973. Restored to working condition, it is now owned and operated as a museum by the Montgomery County Cultural Foundation. (*NRHP/HAER*)

Just north of the Old Jail Museum, Washington St. (US 231) crosses Sugar Creek. The city holds an annual canoe race on Sugar Creek in the spring, billed as "the fastest and most scenic in the state." An old Coca-Cola bottling plant, located off Lafayette Ave. on the south bank of Sugar Creek, is used for storage by Clements Canoes, Inc. Between Crawfordsville and Shades State Park, the free-flowing stream runs through areas of rugged terrain and varied vegetation that are most spectacular in May when the redbuds and dogwood are in bloom or in October when the autumn foliage peaks.

Return to Wabash Ave. where some notable structures stand at the intersection. The **Public Library**, on the northeast corner, is a smooth-cut stone building erected in 1902 with Carnegie funds. W. F. Sharpe designed the Classical-style structure featuring gracefully arched windows and Ionic columns at the entrance. The library was remodeled in 1961 and expanded in 1979, when the adjacent Davis building was purchased and remodeled. On the northwest corner stands the **Masonic Temple**. Organized in 1843, the Crawfordsville Masons completed this impressive-looking lodge in 1904. The century-old **Wabash Ave. Presbyterian Church**, on the southwest corner, is a handsome brick edifice of Gothic design with a 100-ft.-high spire. Members of Center Church erected this structure in 1880 when their wooden church built in 1840 became overcrowded. Members of the First Presbyterian Church united with the Center Church congregation in 1921 and changed the church name to Wabash Ave. Presbyterian Church. In 1973 the sanctuary was completely renovated, and the beautiful stained-glass windows were restored.

From Washington St., proceed west on Wabash Ave. for two blocks to **Wabash College**, a four-year private liberal arts college for men. Visitors' parking is available in the lot on the east side of the Admissions Office, 502 W. Wabash Ave. (The main entrance and administrative offices are located off Grant St.) Maps and tour information are available at the Kane house, the red brick house with white columns in front, directly across the street from the admissions office.

Founded in 1832, Wabash College began as the Crawfordsville English and Classical High School located at the corner of Lane Ave. and Blair St. The school became the Wabash Manual Labor College and Teachers' Seminary in 1834. The name was shortened to Wabash College in 1839. The college moved to its present campus following the construction of South Hall in 1838. In the early years, the majority of students at Wabash College prepared for the ministry.

In the northwest corner of the campus, three houses related to the early history of the college have been grouped together. The **Caleb Mills house** was the home of the college's first professor. In 1833 Edmund Hovey wrote to his friend Caleb Mills (1806-1879) in New Hampshire urging him to come teach at the newly organized school in Crawfordsville. The same year Mills conducted the first class at what later became Wabash College. Besides teaching, Mills lobbied for the establishment of a public school system in Indiana. For several years, Mills addressed the Indiana General Assembly at the start of its session to adopt his system. The tracts were published in pamphlet form and distributed throughout the state. A new school system providing a free education for every child in Indiana went into operation in 1852. Mills became the second superintendent of public schools in 1854.

Sarah and Caleb Mills occupied teachers' quarters in Forest Hall until their home was completed in 1838. The Federal-style house reflects their New England heritage. Through the years, many alterations have changed the original floor plan, but Professor Mills's study with an outside door, around the corner of the house from the main entrance, remains the same. Restored and presented to the college in 1926, the two-story white frame house with an adjoining patio and garden recently served as the residence for the Director of Development.

Hovey cottage was the residence of a founder, trustee, and professor at Wabash College. A graduate of Dartmouth and Andover Theological Seminary, Edmund O. Hovey came to Indiana in 1831 as a Presbyterian minister and within a few months organized two churches in Fountain County. Hovey was one of several clergymen who convened in Crawfordsville in 1832 to found a Christian college. Between his duties as an administrator and teacher of chemistry and natural sciences, Hovey traveled East to raise funds for the school and to hire its first president, the Rev. Elihu Baldwin. The Hoveys settled into the little frame house in 1837, which the family occupied until 1897. Restored in 1928, the cottage is now used as office space for the college.

Built in 1833, **Forest Hall** is the oldest structure on the campus. The two-story frame building served as classrooms and living quarters at the school's first campus. About 1850 Forest Hall was relocated and used as a private residence and student dormitory. In 1965 it was moved to its present site and renovated as a headquarters for Wabash alumni.

Despite construction of new facilities such as the student center, library, classrooms, and athletic fields, the campus has maintained its northeastern provincial character. A forest preserve covers the northeast corner of the campus, and nineteenth-century brick buildings surround a landscaped mall, which **Center Hall** dominates. In 1853 Indianapolis architect William Tinsley submitted the plans for Center Hall which were executed in three stages. The center building, completed in 1856, housed "recitation rooms" on the first floor, a science laboratory and lecture rooms on the second, and two rooms for the literary society on the third. The college library and chapel occupied the north wing, completed in 1870, and the south wing, opened in 1871, contained more lecture rooms and laboratories. Today, administrative offices occupy the three-story brick building.

College Chapel at the south end of the campus mall opened in 1929. From 1870 to 1921, the upper hall in the north wing of Center Hall served as the school chapel. Services were conducted in the old exercise room of the gymnasium while the present chapel was under construction. J. F. Larsen of Hanover, New Hampshire, designed the Georgian-style church with a traditional spire. Weekly convocations are held in the chapel, but student attendance at church services is no longer required. Recently renovated, the chapel also serves as a place for concerts, lectures, and weddings.

Across the street from Wabash College stands the **Herron house**, 406 W. Wabash Ave., a brick structure with a wood porch and multicolored gingerbread trim. In 1890 Capt. William Parke Herron built the striking Neo-Jacobean-style house which features a turret, gables, several chimneys, slate shingles, and stained-glass windows. Herron served in the 72nd Indiana Volunteer Infantry during the Civil War and was a friend of Maj. Gen. Lew Wallace, who lived a few blocks east of here. The "gingerbread house" remained in the Herron family until the 1980s.

Continue west on Wabash Ave. and turn left on John Sloan St. to the **R. R. Donnelley and Sons Company**. The company is the nation's largest supplier of commercial printing services such as design, typesetting, color separation and halftone work, plate and cylinder making, presswork, binding, and distribution planning. A limestone sculpture of an Indian head, the company's imprint, fronts the red brick tower looming over the plant. Architects George B. Eich and Elmer J. Fox designed the tower to disguise the water storage tank within. The company has occupied the Sloan St. plant since 1923. In 1941 Crawfordsville officially became Donnelley's book manufacturing center. It is the city's leading industry, employing more than 2,000 workers. The Sloan St. plant specializes in patent (or adhesive) bound books, short-run operations, and sheet-fed press work. The South Plant, located on IND 32, was built in 1964 to accommodate the *World Book Encyclopedia* printing operation. It also produces textbooks and all Smyth-sewn bindings for the company.

Richard Robert Donnelley entered the printing business in 1864. The Great Fire of 1871 burned out his Chicago shop, but he rebuilt by 1873. The company has been printing telephone books since 1886. The Lakeside Press, Donnelley's corporate headquarters in Chicago, prints national magazines such as *Life*, *Time*, and *Fortune*. Since the big book bindery opened at Crawfordsville, it has printed the *Encyclopaedia Britannica*, the *World Book*, the *Holy Bible*, *Reader's Digest Books*, *Time-Life Books*, and other publications. A second Donnelley plant in Warsaw, Indiana, prints catalogs.

From the Donnelley plant turn left, then right at Meadow Ave. Behind a chain link fence is the **Milligan house**, an extraordinary looking residence amidst an industrial setting. Built in 1854, the ornate Gothic Revival-style house is constructed in a T-shape with three gables. Carved wood pendants adorn the peak of the roof and the lower ends of the bargeboards. Joseph Milligan and his family lived here while he was a trustee of Wabash College from 1872 to 1892. R. R. Donnelley and Sons purchased the house to serve as a resident manager's home. It is now used for office space.

Return to Wabash Ave., turn south at Washington St., and west at IND 32 for *3.5 m.* to **Yount's Mill**. A historical marker has been placed on the south side of the road, just west of the bridge over Sugar Creek. The sole remaining building from a once bustling woolen

industry is barely visible between the trees south of the bridge. The bridge also provides a breathtaking view of the creek valley. The present 335-ft.-long concrete structure, erected in 1947, replaces a wooden covered bridge which served the area for 90 years.

In the 1840s Daniel Yount and his brother bought the water rights to a millrace on Sugar Creek and operated a wool carding mill. In 1849 they installed power looms in a new frame structure and began turning out a finished product. Woolen goods were transported by wagon over a gravel road to Crawfordsville where a railroad freight depot opened in 1859. Yount received government contracts for grade A wool used for blankets and uniforms during the Civil War and operated the mill at full capacity. The Yount family also ran a boardinghouse for the factory girls, located above the mill. Erected in 1859, the two-story brick building is now a private residence. In 1864 Yount erected a three-story brick and stone mill with a turbine wheel and added a three-story wing in 1867. The original carding mill became a storage space for wool. At its peak, the mill employed up to 300 workers. When the railroads bypassed Yountsville, the mill suffered from lack of good transportation. Mill operations ceased in 1905. The mill property changed hands several times, and most of the buildings were eventually torn down. The Grimes family restored the old boardinghouse in the 1960s as a residence and saved the 1864 structure of the woolen mill. (*HAER*)

From the bridge over Sugar Creek, continue west on IND 32 for *2.4 m.* through Yountsville to CR 600W. Turn left for *3 m.* to CR 400S and turn right. About *.3 m.* on the right is the **Stonebraker Cemetery**, which contains the grave of George Fruits who died in 1876 at the age of 114 years, 7 months, and 4 days. He is believed to have been the last surviving Revolutionary War veteran in the nation. Fruits married Catherine Stonebraker and settled near here in the 1820s. Another *.3 m.* on the left is the **Stonebraker house**. The two-story brick house with twin chimneys, built in 1827 or 1831, stands on a knoll surrounded by fields and trees. Arriving in the early 1820s, Joseph Stonebraker and Alexander Weir were among the first settlers in the 2-sq.-m.-area of hills and valleys now known as Balhinch. Stonebraker constructed the walls of his house with brick made on the premises, which were laid four deep lengthwise from base to roof. The design of the house is nearly identical to that of Stephen Foster's Kentucky home designed by Thomas Jefferson. The interior features an 8-ft.-wide fireplace in the kitchen, which required a team of horses to haul the back log in place. In 1843 Stonebraker left Montgomery County to prospect for gold in California. He was never heard from again and is believed to have been killed or drowned in the Mississippi River. The house is now owned by Leslie Weir, the great-great-great grandson of the builder.

Descriptions of southwest Montgomery County are a repeated theme in the poetry of James B. Elmore (1857-1942), the Bard of Alamo. The Hoosier farmer-teacher-writer lived and died on a 900-acre farm near Alamo, a rural town of 178 persons. Six volumes of his prose and poetry were published between 1899 and 1907. "The Monon Wreck" was an oft-quoted poem in its time. The actual train crash took place on January 11, 1892. His poems, which ran in the local newspapers, found an appreciative audience as he "fashioned couplets about earthy things such as sassafras and turnip greens and railroad wrecks."

Return to US 231, turn right, and at *7 m.* turn left on IND 234. Proceed east *4 m.* Turn right on CR 350E, continue *1.3 m.*, and turn right on CR 1000S. Set at the far end of a long expanse of grass against a wooded background on the right side of the road is the **Ashby house**, a stately two-story red brick structure. Robert Ashby built the country mansion of Italianate design with a mansard roof and wooden shutters in 1883. The interior features a variety of wood finishes and 11-ft.-high ceilings. In 1902 Ashby moved to Ladoga and operated a grain, lumber, cement, and coal business. The house stood vacant for nearly 20 years before the present owners, Harley Reeder and Olen Gowens, restored it to its former elegance. (*NRHP*)

Return to IND 234 and proceed east for *1.8 m.* to Ladoga. Located in Clark Township, **LADOGA** (p. 1,151) was formerly the site of Shawnee Indian hunting grounds. Lucas Baldwin entered the land which became part of Ladoga in 1826 and built his log cabin where the Nazarene Church now stands. Ladoga came by its unusual name when a group of young people selected it from a geography book which described a lake in Russia called Ladoga. German Baptist Brethren, or "Dunkers" (now Church of the Brethren), from Pennsylvania and Virginia came to this area and held their first meeting in 1832. Ladoga has some fine old houses built with locally-produced bricks. John Myers built the first sawmill in Ladoga on Raccoon Creek in 1832 and later added a four-story flour mill with a double set of French buhrs. Myers platted the town in 1836.

At the northwest corner of Main St. (IND 234) and Harrison St. stands the **old Normal School**, a boarded-up, two-story brick building with a belfry and wood brackets of Italianate design. In 1855 the Baptists established the Ladoga Female Seminary and a nearby boardinghouse which operated for five years. The Central Indiana Normal School and Business Institute conducted classes from 1876 until 1891. It occupied the former seminary until 1878 when the present school building was erected. The school survived the May 10, 1878, removal of practically its entire student body and faculty to Danville (see below, p. 443). The old Normal School served as a public high school, 1897-1971, and as the American Legion Home during the 1970s.

Return west on IND 234 to US 231. Proceed south for *3.5 m.* to **PARKERSBURG**. At the southwest corner of US 231 and CR 1150S is a historical marker commemorating **Chief Cornstalk's Village**. Between 1774 and 1820, the Eel River tribe of Miami Indians lived along Cornstalk Creek about three miles east of here. Chief Peter Cornstalk's village of Snakefish was located near the little Harshbarger family cemetery, and another Indian village known as Dogtown was on Haw Creek. The Indians lived peaceably with the early settlers before moving north to the reservation at Thorntown. In the 1820s Jacob Shuck settled near what became Parkersburg, and a settlement grew up because of the springs in the vicinity. Nathaniel Parker moved to Shucktown and opened a post office in 1835. The town later adopted his name.

Continue south for *2.7 m.* on US 231 to the county line. Situated in an area where the rolling prairies of central Indiana meet the rugged hills of the south, **PUTNAM COUNTY** (p. 29,163; 482 sq. m.) was organized by an act of the General Assembly in 1821 and named for Maj. Gen. Israel Putnam, an officer in the American Revolution. Putnam County is second only to Parke County in the number of its covered bridges, mostly located along Big

Walnut Creek which runs diagonally across the county. It is predominantly agricultural, with corn and hogs its principal products, followed by beef cattle, dairying, and sheep raising. Most of the county's major industries—International Business Machines Corporation, Mallory Capacitor Company, Greencastle Manufacturing Company, and Lone Star Industries, Inc.—center around Greencastle, which is conveniently located midway between Indianapolis and Terre Haute. The southern part of the county bordering Richard Lieber State Recreation Area in the scenic Mill Creek valley is rapidly becoming a resort area. Two of the county's oldest institutions—DePauw University and the Indiana State Penal Farm—provide continuing stability to the economy of Putnam County.

At *15.3 m.* from Parkersburg, just beyond Big Walnut Creek, turn right on a side road. At *.4 m.* turn right onto a winding road *.7 m.* to the **Dunbar Covered Bridge**. Built in 1880, the 174-ft.-long burr arch truss bridge spans Big Walnut Creek. The covered bridge is painted red, in good condition, and open to traffic. In the mid-19th century, grist and sawmills operated along the creek banks. Ice cutting was also a popular business, and wooden storage houses were located along the banks well into the 20th century.

Return to US 231 and turn south to downtown **GREENCASTLE** (p. 8,403). Ephraim Dukes settled here in 1821 and named the area Greencastle after his hometown in Pennsylvania. In 1823 he deeded land in Greencastle for the site of the county seat. The first courthouse was a frame structure built in 1827, replaced by a one-story brick building in 1832 and another with two stories in 1848.

On the square bounded by Indiana, Washington, Franklin, and Jackson sts., the present **Putnam County Courthouse** is a Greek Revival-style building, designed by J. W. Gaddis. Tiles form the date of construction, 1904, at the entrance. A World War I memorial with the figure of a doughboy, dedicated to comrades in arms from Putnam County, stands in one corner of the square and in another corner is a V-1 buzz bomb developed by German scientists during World War II. Mounted on a V-shaped limestone base, the monument was dedicated on Memorial Day, 1947.

At the southwest corner of Washington and Indiana sts., the recently restored **Fleenor**

Building stands on the site of Eli Lilly's first drugstore. In 1835 Capt. William Thornburgh erected the first structure on this site, a brick commercial building used as a dry goods store for more than 20 years. George H. Jordan bought the building in 1857 and leased it to a law firm that, in turn, leased it to Eli Lilly in 1861. The Lilly family moved to Greencastle in 1852, and Eli attended preparatory school at Indiana Asbury College. After working in a Lafayette drugstore for several years, Lilly returned to Greencastle, married Emily Lemon, and opened the drugstore here. Lilly conducted a modest business for a short time before joining the infantry in 1861. In 1862 he was transferred to the artillery, raised a battery, and departed for service in the Civil War. With Eli Lilly as its captain, the 18th Indiana Battery saw action at Hoover's Gap and Chickamauga. Lilly did not reside again in Greencastle. His subsequent career as a pharmaceutical giant in Indianapolis is well known.

Levi Cohn, a French merchant from Cincinnati, bought the 1835 building and replaced it with the present structure in 1865. The building changed owners in the 1870s, becoming a grocery store and then a bank. In 1875 a fire devastated the east and south sides of the square leaving little more than a shell of the bank building. John C. Albin purchased the damaged building and the adjoining sites to the west, later known as the Albin block. He completed reconstruction of the four Italianate-style commercial buildings joined by a single cornice about 1880. The building again changed ownership. It housed a drugstore continuously from 1901 to 1981, including Fleenor's drugstore since 1927. In 1981 the Heritage Preservation Society of Putnam County, 14 S. Indiana St., purchased the building and opened its offices in the rear section. A historical marker on the east side of the building indicates the site of Eli Lilly's first drugstore.

At the west end of the block at 20-24 W. Washington St. is a Victorian Renaissance commercial building built about 1883 as the home for the **Central National Bank**. The front facade contains elements of the Queen Anne style that was popular during the late 19th century. The building, however, gains its notoriety because of the fact that John Dillinger robbed the bank in 1933. The bank building is now used for retail and office space.

From the corner of Washington and Jackson sts., proceed south on Jackson St. for six blocks to Hanna St. Turn left and go three blocks to Locust St., then left into the **DePauw University** campus. Parking lots are located on the east and west ends of the campus if on-street parking space is not available. Founded as Indiana Asbury College by the Methodists in 1837, DePauw University began as both a college preparatory school and a four-year liberal arts college. Women were admitted beginning in 1867. Asbury almost went under financially during the 1880s until Washington Charles De-Pauw, a New Albany business tycoon involved in railroads, banking, grain dealing, gas, and the manufacture of plate glass, rescued the foundering college. In 1884 the school was renamed DePauw University. Today it is considered one of the outstanding small coed colleges in the country.

East College, at the southwest corner of Locust and Simpson sts., is the oldest building on campus and is used for classrooms and administrative offices. Begun in 1869, the four-story Victorian Gothic and Second Empire-style structure, designed by J. A. Vrydaugh of Terre Haute, took nearly 13 years to complete. Following a $2 million restoration project, the magnificent building was rededicated in 1981. Meharry Hall, named for the wife of Jesse Meharry, a school trustee, was the scene of early chapel services, student assemblies, rallies, and lectures. Restoration saved the original oak pews, balconies, and lavish woodwork. The chapel still serves for Friday morning convocations. The building has been updated to provide effective heating and cooling, new wiring and plumbing, elevators, and modern bathrooms and offices. However, an effort was made to retain the original architectural design and decorative details. East College is also the home of two national organizations—Alpha Chi Omega sorority, formed in 1885, and Sigma Delta Chi, the Society of Professional Journalism, formed in 1909. Downey Hall is the new home of the Journalism Hall of Fame. (*NRHP*)

With a few notable exceptions, such as East College, old makes way for the new on the school grounds. The old Bowman Gymnasium has been razed and the site re-landscaped. Three major new buildings—the Performing Arts Center, the Lilly Physical Education and Recreation Center, and the Science Cen-

ter—were completed in the 1980s. The old Carnegie Library, a Neoclassic building at Simpson and College sts., built in 1908, now serves as the **Art Center**. The main floor gallery features ongoing faculty and student displays.

Churches and the Greek houses of numerous fraternal organizations border the campus. Many well-preserved Victorian-style houses built about the turn of the century remain in the neighborhood east of DePauw University along Washington, Walnut, Seminary, Anderson, Hanna, and Bloomington sts.—between Locust and Wood. Several former residences of college presidents and faculty are found in this historic district.

At Simpson and Locust sts., north of East College, stands the **Gobin Memorial United Methodist Church** and **Charter House**, named in honor of Dr. Hillary A. Gobin, a former professor and president of DePauw University. Architect Alfred Grindle designed the late Gothic Revival-style church, built in 1928. The Charter House was added in 1961. On the grounds of Gobin Memorial, **Old Bethel Church** backs against Spring Ave. just south of E. Seminary St. Built in 1807, on Nathan Robertson's farm in Clark's Grant near Charlestown, the single-room cabin is believed to be the oldest Methodist church in Indiana. For several years Robertson's Meetinghouse served as a preaching place for circuit riders, an outpost of Methodism in the Indiana Territory. The little meetinghouse was relocated three times before it was restored and moved to its present site in 1953. It is furnished with reproductions of the original pews and pulpit.

From Spring Ave. and Seminary St., proceed east for three and one-half blocks to Bloomington St. (US 231), turn right, and continue two and one-half blocks to the entrance of **Robe Ann Park** on the east side of the street. John and Anna Robe deeded the land for this 25-acre park to the city in 1928, and the DAR reconstructed the two log cabins here in 1938. The larger cabin belonged to the Vermillion family in southern Putnam County and the smaller one to the Lovetts near Roachdale.

From the park, proceed north six blocks on Bloomington St. to Washington St. Go right one block to Durham, left one block to Franklin St., right three blocks to DePauw Ave., then left one block to the circle intersected by Highridge Ave. Within the circle stands **McKim Observatory**. The white stucco domed building, built in 1884, houses a 9.53-in. clear aperture refracting telescope, equipped with meridian transits. Nearly a mile from the main campus, the observatory was part of a major building project begun by DePauw University in 1884 which also included a law building, a theology building, and two dormitories. Only the observatory, a gift from Robert McKim of Madison, Indiana, remains. Restored in the 1970s, the observatory contains original equipment including a kerosene-lit astral lantern used to teach celestial relationships and a cannon-like brass transit that swivels on its axis to fix star coordinates. (*NRHP*)

Return to Franklin St., then turn east, merging with Indianapolis Rd. (IND 240) at the first intersection. About *.2 m.* up the road, set back on the south side, is a toy shop at 830 Indianapolis Rd., constructed of lumber from the **Halfway House**. The Halfway House was once an inn located on the old National Rd. at Mount Meridian, halfway between Indianapolis and Terre Haute. In 1834 William Heavin erected the original log cabin, which became a regular stagecoach stop. Over the years the wayside inn was enlarged, and a barn was added to accommodate the stagecoaches. The Halfway House continued to operate as a hotel and restaurant long after the stagecoaches and covered wagons disappeared from the National Rd. Eleanore Cammack, a DePauw University archivist, bought the hand-hewn timbers from the Halfway House at an auction in 1946 and used them to build her retirement home. The log house contains six doors and a fireplace mantle from the original building. An addition was made in the 1960s.

Return to US 231 (Bloomington St.) and turn left for about *5 m.* to US 40, then turn right. Located *2.6 m.* west of US 231, **PUTNAMVILLE** was a thriving community in the mid-19th century. The town's importance diminished, however, following a fire in 1878 which destroyed most of the business district. One of the early structures surviving is the Whitehall Inn and Summer Kitchen, located at the northwest corner of Townsend St. and US 40, one block east of IND 243. James Townsend, who laid out the town in 1830, built this two-story brick building of Federal design in 1828. It served as a wayside tavern called the Whitehall Inn for travelers along the National Rd.

On the south side of US 40 at IND 243 (Main Cross St.) stands the **Putnamville Methodist Church**. A Presbyterian congregation, founded by early frontier preacher Isaac Reed, built the Greek Revival-style church with a steeple in 1834. The Methodists bought the building in 1860, which is made of local brick and rests on limestone foundation stones from the quarries west of town. (*NRHP*)

About one mile west of IND 243, the **Indiana State Penal Farm** occupies 3,500 acres of land behind an arched stone entranceway off US 40. Signs posted along the highway warn travelers that "stopping" is prohibited. Stone farm barns within the complex, built about 1880, predate the establishment of the state farm in 1915 (authorized by the state legislature, March 14, 1913). Except for a newly constructed 50-bed maximum security building, most of the prison facilities were built in the 1920s. The state farm once housed about 1,400 inmates though 1,000 is the average figure. Ovens for making bricks are visible from US 40. At one time, prisoners also worked in the shale pit, limestone quarries, furniture factory, and packinghouse. Those products still manufactured in the prison, such as picnic tables, go to state institutions to avoid competition with private industry. The facility continues to keep an orchard and maintain a dairy herd which supplies milk to correctional institutions in the state. Inmate employment is voluntary. In addition, the prison has been a major employer of residents in the Putnamville and surrounding areas since its creation.

Return to Putnamville, turn south, and follow IND 243 for *7.1 m.*, crossing I-70 and passing through a densely wooded section of the Owen-Putnam State Forest to the entrance of **Lieber State Recreation Area**. Established in 1952, the 8,075-acre park was named in honor of Col. Richard Lieber who founded the state park system. The park has become a popular recreation area because of its shaded campsites, lake beach front, woods, and picturesque falls. The state forest consists of scattered holdings, in the developmental stage, used for hunting, fishing, and primitive camping. The road from the park entrance leads to the park office, campgrounds, Hulman Beach, and boat docks on Cataract Lake.

The 1,400-acre lake, also called Cagles Mill Reservoir, was designed primarily for flood control. **Cataract Dam** crosses Mill Creek at the west end of the reservoir and measures 148 ft. high, 950 ft. long, and 630 ft. wide across the base. The overlook at the north end of the dam provides a breathtaking view of the surrounding countryside. The dam can be reached by continuing south on IND 243, past the park entrance, to IND 42 at Cunot. Turn right on IND 42, which roughly follows the contour of the lake and joins with a very rough dirt road leading north to the dam. Proceed with caution.

Also part of the state recreation area, **Cataract Falls** is located at the east end of the lake and reached by following several miles of unmarked country roads. Maps and directions are available at the park entrance on IND 243. The route between the entrance and the falls is picturesque, passing through hilly terrain dotted with small farms and woodlots. One route leads west on IND 42 from IND 243, left on the county road immediately west of the Mill Creek bridge, left at *.8 m.*, left again at *1.8 m.* after crossing the abandoned Louisville and Nashville Railroad right-of-way, then right for *2.1 m.*, recrossing the railroad right-of-way, to the tiny resort of **CATARACT**, located southwest of the falls. Theodore Jennings, the brother of Gov. Jonathan Jennings, arrived here in 1841 while riding horseback from Louisville to Greencastle and bought 1,000 acres, including the falls, the next year. The state purchased the falls in 1967. The United States government had earlier bought part of the lower falls area during formation of the flood control program in the 1950s. The village retains a quality of quaintness with its very old general store, little shops, and summer cottages. At the falls, about *.5 m.* north of the village, are smooth blacktop roads and ample parking and picnic space. Actually a series of drops—the upper falls having a drop of 45 ft. and the lower 30—Cataract Falls creates a spectacular show that changes with each season. At the upper falls, a 140-ft.-long wooden covered bridge, built in 1876, crosses Mill Creek. Still in use, the bridge replaced another which was washed away in 1875.

Cross the covered bridge, take the first right, and at approximately *2.3 m.* turn left on US 231. Turn right at US 40 and proceed *8.5 m.* to IND 75, entering **HENDRICKS COUNTY** (p. 69,804; 409 sq. m.). Of the 30 counties acquired in the New Purchase, Hendricks County was the first to be surveyed because of its location on the meridian. Officially

organized in 1823, Hendricks County was named in honor of William Hendricks, who was then governor of Indiana. Settlers had already come into central Indiana and begun a settlement on White Lick Creek in the spring of 1820. Most of the early population of Hendricks County was concentrated in the southeastern section. The northern and western townships were the last to be settled, mainly because of mosquito-infested swamps. Hendricks County developed as an agricultural center and has remained so. Many "stock stands" opened along the National Rd. (now US 40) to sell corn for the livestock being driven through the county, and farmhouses served as wayside inns to weary travelers. The National Rd. was a heavily traveled thoroughfare for more than 50 years, beginning in the early 1830s, until superseded by the railroads.

Travel north on IND 75 for *18 m.*, passing at *3.8 m.* the town of **COATESVILLE**, which in 1948 was devastated by a tornado which left 20 dead before spending its fury in eastern Indiana. About one mile south of North Salem on the top of a hill stands the **Hadley house**, a beautiful old brick structure. In the 1870s Edmund Hadley led a movement to organize a Grange in Eel River Township. A mystery has surrounded the house since Hadley's death on May 30, 1878, at age 53. Two subsequent owners of the house—Mrs. William Dean and Virgil Osborn—have also died of heart attacks on Memorial Day. The house has been restored by the present owners.

Continue north on IND 75 for *1 m.* to IND 236 in **NORTH SALEM** (p. 581). The town was laid out in 1835 and the post office established in 1839. Stretching west from IND 75 and IND 236, the two-block-long business district includes a general store, the former town hall dated 1891, an Independent Order of Odd Fellows (IOOF) building dated 1882, plus several antique and crafts stores. Many interesting old frame houses remain in the downtown area. In the second block west of IND 75, a wholesale art store on the northwest corner has preserved its old-fashioned cast-iron storefront by George L. Mesker and Company Iron Works of Evansville, Indiana. Next door stands the United Methodist Church, an L-shaped stuccoed Gothic-style structure built in 1923. The first Methodist church at North Salem was one of the earliest churches in Hendricks County.

Cataract Falls

Follow IND 236 southeast for *8 m.*, merging with IND 39 *2 m.* before reaching US 36 in Danville. Turn left on W. Main St. (US 36) and continue east *.4 m.* to the courthouse square. **DANVILLE** (p. 4,220) was laid out in 1824. Judge William Wick, who at that time was holding court, named the county seat Danville in honor of his brother Daniel Wick. The first county circuit court was held in the home of William Ballard, south of Belleville, until the first courthouse in Danville was completed in 1826. A square brick building replaced the log courthouse and jail in 1830. The third courthouse, built between 1859 and 1863, served the county until 1912 when the roof collapsed.

The cornerstone for the present **Hendricks County Courthouse** on Main St. between Jefferson and Washington was laid in 1913. Architect Clarence Martindale designed the Renaissance-style structure of Bedford limestone with a copper roof and art glass skylight in the rotunda.

On the northeast corner of Washington and Main sts., Dinsmore's Basket and Gift Shop occupies a two-story commercial building erected about 1855. The store housed hardware and grocery businesses in the past. Since 1935 Noble Dinsmore has owned and operated the shop as an outlet for handwoven arts and crafts, especially baskets, from around the world. At one time, Dinsmore himself wove many baskets sold in the store. The wood floors, original shelves, and old-fashioned storefront characterize this downtown landmark.

From Washington St. go east one block on Main St. then south one block on Indiana St. to the **Danville Public Library** at Marion St. The Greek Revival-style structure was built with Carnegie funds in 1903. The entire roof was replaced after a tornado damaged it in 1948. A new addition, dedicated in 1980, houses the Indiana Room on the second floor. Established for the preservation and circulation of regional historic material, the Indiana Room features a pair of century-old stained-glass windows removed from the former Methodist Church.

One block west and one block south, on the northwest corner of Washington and Broadway sts., stands the former **Hendricks County Jail and Sheriff's house**. Built in 1867, the stately Victorian brick building housed the sheriff's living quarters and six cells until 1974 when the new jail was constructed. For nearly a century no changes were made to the building, but a juvenile section and small radio room were added in 1966. The Hendricks County Historical Society renovated the building as a museum which opened to the public in 1977. The sheriff's residence is furnished with antiques and historical artifacts gathered from the Danville area. There is a gift store, and tours of the cell blocks are available. (*NRHP*)

Proceed north on Washington St. for three and one-half blocks to the **Hoadley house**, 184 N. Washington St. In 1832 Col. Christian C. Nave built this two-story brick Italianate-style house which stands on a knoll to the left side of the street. Bricks made on the premises were used to construct a two-story apple storage house, sidewalks, three wells, and a cistern, as well as the mansion. Dr. W. J. Hoadley, who served as a county health officer for 19 years, bought the house in 1850. The house was originally a three-story building with 11-ft.-high ceilings, but Mrs. Hoadley had the house remodeled and the top story reduced in 1876. Local lore says that the house was used as an "underground railroad" station in the pre-Civil War days.

Return to Main St. and proceed east for three blocks to the **Danville Junior High School** at the northeast corner of E. Main and Wayne sts. The school and a cemetery in back of the building are situated on a high bluff overlooking the West Fork of White Lick Creek. An old brick building called Hargrave Hall adjoins the junior high school. Built as a science hall in 1915, it is the only building remaining from **Central Normal College**, which, after becoming Canterbury College, closed in 1951. In the 1980s the interior was completely remodeled for use as classroom and storage space.

A county seminary for girls, established in 1829 and believed to be the first private school in Hendricks County, occupied this site until 1856 when the property was awarded to Jesse Matlock in a litigation suit. The seminary built a new school across the street to the south which it operated until 1872. Matlock sold the original seminary building to the Danville Methodist Church in 1858. Danville Academy enrolled 178 students in its first year and built a three-story addition by 1860. The Civil War, however, brought the school financial problems, and the academy was sold at a sheriff's auction in 1864. Danville Academy continued to operate under the auspices of the Methodist Quarterly Conference until declining enrollments forced it to close in 1868. The

Danville Methodist Church used the chapel until its new church was completed in 1878, at which time the school property was transferred to Central Normal College.

Founded as Central Normal College and Commercial Institute at Ladoga, Indiana, in 1876, the early normal school was committed to the educational principles pioneered by Dr. Alfred Holbrook of Lebanon, Ohio. The school practiced an open-door policy which provided an education to students who could not afford one elsewhere. The Ladoga school soon outgrew its single building and moved practically overnight when the facilities of the former Danville Academy became available in 1878. The haste of its departure led to later claims that Danville "stole" or "kidnapped" Ladoga's school. Student enrollment at Central Normal College during its 68 years in Danville varied from a high of 1,308 in the 1921-22 school year to a low of 25 during World War I. The old academy building became Central Normal's Recitation Hall, and a new Administration Building was built in 1903, followed by the Science Hall in 1915 and the Gymnasium in 1924. The Episcopalians became local trustees of the college in 1946. They changed the name of the school to Canterbury College and promoted a liberal arts program to increase enrollment. The attempt failed, and Canterbury College closed its doors in 1951. The buildings became the property of the Danville public school system.

Just east of the junior high school on the north side of E. Main St. is **Ellis Park**. Named in honor of Harvey D. Ellis, who served as park superintendent for 45 years, the 23-acre city park, bordering on White Lick Creek, includes woodlands, sports and picnic areas, a shelter house, and swimming pool.

Continue east on E. Main St. (US 36) to the **Hendricks County Home**—*1 m.* from the courthouse square. Set back north of the road, the old two-story ivy-covered brick building was built in 1868 as a county asylum for the insane. It later evolved into the county home for the indigent. At one time, the orphans' home occupied a frame building on the north side of the highway. The present facility houses an average of 20 residents. The county commissioners manage both the home and an 80-acre farm. In 1981 the state highway department discovered an old pauper cemetery behind the county home when surveying the area for a new highway between Danville and Avon. The contents of the 98 unmarked graves were moved to another cemetery.

Return to the courthouse square and continue west on Main St. for three blocks to Kentucky St. Turn right. Behind the Danville Town Hall, 77 N. Kentucky, the **Danville Standpipe** towers over the surrounding neighborhood. George W. Stuntevauch of Chicago designed the standpipe which measures 100 ft. in height and 12 ft. in diameter and holds 85,000 gallons of water. A foundation of Bedford limestone 8 ft. deep supports the base. Erected in 1892, the standpipe is constructed of heavy steel plates, riveted in place. In 1982 the American Water Works Association selected the Danville Standpipe as an American Water Landmark.

Return to Main St. and continue south on Kentucky St. for three blocks to the **Governor's Mansion**, a large frame house with a concrete block porch next to the northwest corner of Kentucky and Mill sts. Ira J. Chase (1834-1895) lived here while serving as governor of Indiana, 1891-93. He commuted daily to Indianapolis by train. Before becoming governor, Chase fought in the western campaigns during the Civil War, entered the ministry, and served two years as lieutenant governor. Mrs. Chase contracted smallpox while serving as an army nurse, which left her permanently blind. Being blind, she misjudged her son's condition while ill with pneumonia in this house and administered a fatal overdose of morphine. Ira Chase reentered the ministry following his term as governor.

From Mill St. proceed south on Kentucky St. (IND 39) for *3.2 m.* to the **Vandegrift home**, south of Danville. Local residents readily recognize the family name as that of Frances "Fanny" Vandegrift who married the famous author and poet Robert Louis Stevenson. Fanny Vandegrift was born in a house on Indianapolis's Monument Circle in 1840. Her parents purchased the brick house on a hill surrounded by trees within a loop of IND 39 in 1861. Fanny had already married Samuel Osbourne by this time. Apparently the 22-year marriage was a stormy one as Fanny made frequent trips to her parents' home with her three children and finally filed for divorce. In 1875 she traveled to Europe for three years to study art. At that time Fanny met Robert Louis Stevenson, who followed her back to America and married her in California in 1880. For most of

their 14-year marriage Stevenson was plagued by ill health, and they traveled the world seeking healthy climes. He died in Samoa in 1894, and Fanny died 20 years later in California. Her ashes are buried beside Stevenson's grave on a Samoan mountaintop. The former Vandegrift home is now a private residence. Correspondence between the Vandegrifts and the Stevensons is housed in the Plainfield Public Library.

Continue south on IND 39 for *4.9 m.* through Clayton to US 40 in **BELLEVILLE**. In the 1820s Belleville vied with Danville to be chosen county seat but lost. Laid out in 1829, it is the third oldest town in the county. Belleville benefited by its location on the old National Rd. and was once a cultural and educational center. On the west edge of Belleville the new Cascade High School occupies the site of the old Belleville Academy, founded in the 1850s.

Proceed east on US 40 for *2 m.* to Cartersburg Rd. Turn left and continue north for *1.5 m.* to **CARTERSBURG**. John Carter laid out the town of Cartersburg in 1850. The area became a popular resort center in the 1880s and 1890s following the discovery of natural mineral springs on the Dobbins farm north of Cartersburg. A group of businessmen formed the Cartersburg Magnetic Springs Association and bought the farm with the intention of developing it into a multimillion dollar health resort. Despite petty disputes among the board members, the Cartersburg Magnetic Springs prospered for about two decades, drawing wealthy families to the springs for the summer. In September 1906 fire destroyed the hotel and bathhouse, which were never rebuilt. Cartersburg today is a picturesque sleepy village. On the north edge of town a lovely old two-story brick farmhouse stands on a hill to the west of Cartersburg Rd.

Return to Cartersburg Rd. and US 40. Proceed east on US 40 for *2.7 m.* to **PLAINFIELD** (p. 9,191), passing the **Plainfield Elks Club** and the **Edmondson home**, a striking white frame Queen Anne-style house on the north side of the road. In 1820 settlers from Guilford, North Carolina, arrived in what is now Guilford Township and staked their claims along White Lick Creek. Quakers settled a few miles east of the present town of Plainfield. The town was laid out in 1833 and named to reflect the simple values held by the Society of Friends. Plainfield was incorporated in 1839 but soon changed to township rule. The town was incorporated a second time in 1904. The National Rd. initiated rapid growth in the Plainfield area during the 1830s, and it remains the most heavily populated township in the county. Development accelerated even more with the arrival of railroad and interurban lines, placing Plainfield just minutes away from downtown Indianapolis. Today, Plainfield's largest employer is Public Service Indiana, whose headquarters here opened in 1951. Most of the community's work force, however, commutes daily to Indianapolis.

Just before reaching the bridge across White Lick Creek, turn right off US 40 at the entrance to the **Indiana Boys' School**, a longtime institution at Plainfield. Called the House of Refuge for Juvenile Offenders when it was established in 1867, the school changed its name to the Indiana Reform School for Boys in 1883, then the Indiana Boys' School in 1903. By 1913 the school's property included 527 acres of land and 54 buildings. In the 19th century the institution promoted military-like discipline and the manufacture of chairs and shoes. After 1900 an educational program was established, and vocational training was offered. In the 1970s a cottage program with special treatment for emotionally disturbed juveniles and runaways was instituted. Coed activities and volunteer services were also added to the school's program. Full-time counselors and health care specialists followed with the assistance of state and federal grants. Today, the campus consists of 1,038 acres with a physical plant to house about 450 boys.

The administration building, erected in 1893, provides a historic and visual landmark. The stately two-story brick Italianate-style mansion crowns a grassy hill in the center of the campus and serves as the superintendent's residence. The garages south of the house were originally built as a horse barn in 1897. Recent construction includes a maximum security unit, a new diagnostic unit, and several cottages. Two monuments stand on the grounds—a limestone statue of John Greenleaf Whittier's Barefoot Boy sculpted by one of the boys at the school years ago, and a bronze tablet honoring Thomas P. Westendorf, a former school official, better known as the songwriter of "I'll Take You Home Again, Kathleen" in 1875. The road off US 40 crosses through the campus to CR 700E.

At the rear gates of the Indiana Boys' School, turn right on CR 700E and proceed .6 m. to the **Indiana Law Enforcement Academy**. A modern glass and concrete structure stands on a 313-acre tract to the right of the road. Built in the early 1970s, the academy provides specialized training for more than 500 police officers each year. Building and law enforcement training expenses are funded by court costs assessed for law violations. The law violator thus pays for officer training. The academy building contains administrative, instructional, and dormitory space.

Proceed south on CR 700E for .7 m. to CR 600S. Turn right and continue west .1 m. to the **Conservative Friends Meetinghouse** on the north side of CR 600S (Sugar Grove Rd.). Quakers from Virginia and the Carolinas began settling in Hendricks County in the early 1820s, and a Wilburite group established the Sugar Grove Conservative Friends Meetinghouse in 1823. The house next to the present meetinghouse sits on the foundation of the original building. A school operated here until 1928 when it burned. The old cemetery on the hill and the meetinghouse erected in 1870 remain. The meetinghouse was built in the traditional manner with a divided hall for men and women and separate doors so that women could enter on the west side and men on the east. The building has original furnishings and two pot-bellied stoves. It is still used occasionally for meetings, weddings, and special events.

Continue west on CR 600S to CR 600E. Turn right and proceed north to US 40. Follow US 40 east across White Lick Creek to the second intersection in downtown Plainfield. On the southwest corner of Center and Main sts. is the recently renovated building of the **Keeley Institute**. At present the three-story building is used for retail and office space. Stucco was stripped off to expose the original brick, which then was painted beige. Built in 1874 as a hotel called the Hamlet House, the building housed the Keeley Institute for Alcoholism and Drug Addiction from 1891 to 1918. Dr. Leslie E. Keeley began his famous alcohol and drug rehabilitative program at Dwight, Illinois, in 1880. By 1918 he had developed a national chain of "franchised" Keeley Institutes, treating some 400,000 patients. The Keeley "cure" for opium and alcohol addiction partly consisted of a secret compound named Bichloride of Gold. The four to six weeks' treatment also relied on injections to create a repugnance for alcohol or drugs followed by a program of health and appetite building exercises. The institute, run by reputable physicians, claimed that 95 percent of their patients were permanently cured. In 17 years, more than 4,000 persons were treated at the Plainfield facility, many of whom returned for annual reunions of Keeley "graduates."

From Center and Main sts. continue east two blocks to the **Friends' Western Yearly Meetinghouse**, 205 S. East St., set back in a park bordering the south side of Main St. (US 40). The first session of the Western Yearly Meeting at Plainfield was held in 1858 in a one-story 70 x 120-ft. brick building with a wood partition and two doors at each end. Until 1893 separate sessions were conducted for men and women. The present building was erected in 1914 on the foundation of the first meetinghouse, which was destroyed by fire. It serves as a repository for tracts printed by the Friends. In 1881 the Friends' Quarterly Meeting of Plainfield, Fairfield, and White Lick organized Central Academy, holding its first classes in the old town hall. A new school building adjacent to the Western Yearly Meeting grounds opened the fall of 1882 and served the Quaker community until 1919. The Plainfield Public High School subsequently occupied the building. While in operation, Central Academy provided equal educational opportunities to all and quality instruction at a modest cost.

On the grounds of the Friends' Meetinghouse once stood an elm tree, known as the **Van Buren Elm**, which was marked with a tablet as the "tree that spilled a President." In 1842, while making a political swing, ex-President Martin Van Buren arrived in Plainfield via the National Rd. At this site, Van Buren's stagecoach struck the roots of the old elm tree and overturned, spilling the former president indecorously into the mud. Supposedly the accident was rigged because Van Buren had vetoed a bill passed by Congress to improve the highway, and the people of Plainfield wanted to demonstrate the need for repairs. In 1850-51 the National Rd. was converted to planks and by 1923 was paved from Cumberland, Maryland, to Terre Haute.

Return to Main and Center sts. and turn south. Follow old IND 267 for *2.9 m.* to the **Islamic Center of North America**, located in cornfields on the left on 124 acres just north of I-70. The Muslim Students Association was founded in 1963 at the University of Illinois at Urbana and had its headquarters in Gary, Indiana, until 1975. The cornerstone for the national headquarters at Plainfield, serving the United States and Canada, was laid in 1981. The site was chosen for its central location and its receptive environment. A $3.4 million religious and educational center of modern Middle Eastern design officially opened late in 1982. Current membership numbers more than 6,000 and is not restricted to Muslims. Persons wishing to visit the mosque, library, and teaching center may contact the public relations office.

Return to Main St. (US 40) in Plainfield, turn right, and turn left on IND 267 for *11.3 m.* to US 136 in **BROWNSBURG** (p. 6,242). In 1824 James Brown settled in the locale which became Brown Township. The county commissioners later divided the township into two parts, named Brown and Lincoln townships. In 1835 William Harris laid out the town of Brownsburg—first called Harrisburg and later changed to Brownsburg. In 1914 the population was about 900 persons. Because of its near proximity to Indianapolis, Brownsburg has shown a steady population increase in the past few decades. Most of the town's work force commutes to Indianapolis.

The **Hunter building** at the southwest corner of Green (IND 267) and Main (US 136) sts. is one of the oldest commercial structures in Brownsburg. Jesse R. Cope built the L-shaped brick building of Greek Revival design about 1870. It was considered an elegant showplace at the time. Cope and Cyrus Hunt operated a general merchandise store here and added banking facilities between 1873 and 1877—the first bank service in Brownsburg. In 1901 the town's first telephone was installed in the Cope and Hunt store. The next owner, M. T. Hunter, also operated a bank in the building from 1907 to 1932. The large concrete slab which supported the bank vault remains. Subsequent owners changed the facade and constructed an addition at the rear.

From Main St., proceed north *.2 m.* on Green St. On the west side of the street, opposite Franklin St., stands the old **St. Malachy's Church** building—the only Catholic church in Hendricks County until 1914. In 1867 the Catholics erected a small church in Brownsburg, and the first resident priest began services. The church on Green St., a red brick structure of traditional Gothic design, was built in 1903.

From Brownsburg, proceed north on IND 267 for *9.8 m.* to I-65 at Boone's Pond State Fishing Area. Take I-65 south for *3.3 m.* to the exit for IND 334 leading to Zionsville and the tour's end.

Anderson

Anderson (p. 64,695), Indiana's eighth largest city, is the seat of **MADISON COUNTY** (p. 139,336; 453 sq. m.), the state's sixth most populous county. The county lies slightly east of the center of the state. It is generally level with the West Fork of the White River being the principal waterway. Over three-fourths of the land is devoted to agriculture. Soybeans are a major crop. The county ranks high in the state in the production of nursery and greenhouse items. Alexandria, Anderson, and Elwood are the county's three cities. Formation of the county took place January 4, 1823. Its present boundaries were established, after several alterations, by 1838.

Anderson borders White River in a generally level area 37 miles northeast of Indianapolis. The city is situated on the former site of Wapiminskink, translatable as the Chestnut Tree Place, a Delaware Indian village that lay just west of a Moravian mission established in 1801. Kikthawenund, the Delaware chief, was the offspring of a trader named Anderson. Early settlers referred to Kikthawenund as William, or Captain, Anderson, and called his village Andersontown. A prominent Indian leader, Kikthawenund negotiated several major Delaware treaties with the United States. In 1818 he reluctantly signed the St. Marys Treaty, which relinquished Delaware land claims in Indiana. Within the space of three years after the agreement most Delaware had pulled out of Andersontown.

William Conner, a son-in-law of Kikthawenund, sold to John Berry the 320-acre tract that included the abandoned Delaware village of Wapiminskink and its environs. Berry surveyed and platted Andersontown in 1823, the year of the founding of Madison County. The county commissioners initially considered Andersontown for the county seat, but they temporarily held court in nearby Pendleton. Finally, in 1828 the authorities, no doubt influenced by a gift of property from Berry, relocated the county government to the more central Andersontown.

The new Andersontown grew slowly until the canal fever of the mid-1830s generated the first real spurt of population growth and economic prosperity. By 1839 around 350 residents, many in anticipation of the Central Canal coursing through the village, had fashioned rough shelters amid the great hazel thicket which blanketed the vicinity. Nearby, John Renshaw platted Victoria, and J. W. Alley named his creation Rockport, both towns abortive efforts to profit from their neighbor's meteoric rise. The flourishing condition of Andersontown prompted the state legislature in late 1839 to call for its incorporation. Unfortunately, on the heels of this announcement the state ordered a halt to internal improvements, ending work on the Central Canal. This turn of events led to a reversal of the town's fortune. Although a second and larger courthouse went up in 1837-39 and a bridge spanned the river until it washed away in 1847, few new settlers planted roots, and business languished. County officials, tiring of the redundant "town of Andersontown," shortened the name to Anderson in 1848.

Events in the 1850s counteracted Anderson's limited growth of the previous decade. In the 10 years prior to the Civil War, Anderson linked up with its neighbors through a series of transportation and communication improvements. Telegraph lines reached the town early in the decade. In 1852 the Indianapolis and Bellefontaine Railroad extended to Anderson four years after representatives from Madison, Delaware, and Randolph counties met in Muncie to organize the rail company. The arrival of the railroad connected Anderson with the state capital to the southwest and Ohio to the east. On the strength of the line's potential to encourage growth the town incorporated in 1853. A second railroad, from Richmond, Indiana, to Chicago, came through Anderson in 1855.

Road travel in the county was immeasurably improved with the completion of a turnpike from Anderson to Alexandria in the late 1850s. An upswing in population in the 1850s of more than 200 percent paralleled the advancements in shipping facilities and roadways. On the eve of the Civil War 1,196 persons lived in Anderson.

Anderson's development as one of Indiana's leading industrial cities came about during and after the Civil War and went through several phases. First, a covered bridge was built across the White River in 1864. The bridge greatly facilitated the movement of people and goods, which before 1863 had been limited to ferry transportation. Second, a three-ward government was formed based on Anderson's incorporation as a city in 1865. A city designation implied progress and attracted new commerce and consumers. Third, entrepreneurs took advantage of the area's large timber stands to establish a wood products industry, that along with the well-established mills, brought Anderson steps closer to the large-scale market economy already underway on the East Coast. In the 1870s Anderson's wood factories were turning out wagons, carriages, spokes, staves, furniture, porcelain-lined pumps, and related articles. Rapid exhaustion of the raw material, however, soon shut down these firms. Fourth, another natural resource came to Anderson's rescue following the demise of the wood business. The discovery of natural gas in Anderson on March 31, 1887, propelled the city into its next stage of industrial expansion.

Madison County lay at the core of the largest natural gas field in the United States, covering more than 5,000 square miles, or a substantial portion of a block of 17 east central Indiana counties. The extraordinary qualities of this cheap, clean fuel, already demonstrated in Pennsylvania and Ohio, prompted frenzied activity in Hoosierland. The Anderson strike followed the drilling of the county's first gas well near Alexandria in early 1887. In 1930 a former Anderson newspaperman recalled his arrival in the city in 1889: "Flambeaus were burning in every yard and the streets were arched with perforated pipes with thousands of jets all burning freely day and night—a wasteful expenditure of a magic fuel." Throngs of people collected to debate and to dream about a new Anderson. "It was rather a raw congregation of boomers, land agents, factory hands,

and those elements which are drawn to a new community." Another newspaperman remembered a segment of "those elements": "The riff-raff came along with the boom. We were but a farming community. We were not wise enough to cope with a hoodlum element. As a result the rough element was a serious business." Citizens complained, and a former city marshal, Amos Coburn, took the reins of the new police department to allay their fears.

Meanwhile, a hastily formed Board of Trade offered sites and fuel to entice companies to Anderson. New York's Fowler Nut and Bolt firm responded first. By 1890, 22 gas wells and scores of smaller operations and company wells were operating in the city and its vicinity. Thirty-eight new factories had located in Anderson by 1892. The *Anderson Democrat*, which earlier touted the city as the Queen of the Indiana Gas Belt, now claimed for it the title Pittsburgh of White River.

In the score of years between 1880 and 1900 the population increased from 4,126 to 20,178. The enlarged population burdened existing facilities, leading to the establishment of new schools, banks, and churches. The inauguration of a two-car, mule-drawn, street railway in 1888 brought to the city an awe-inspiring but inefficient transport system. Charles L. Henry of Anderson bought the mule line in 1891 and replaced it a year later with one of the state's first electric car lines. In 1897 Henry with Philip Matter of Marion and others formed the Union Traction Company and in December extended the city rails 11 miles to Alexandria. Within a decade the Union Traction Company would operate Indiana's largest intercity railway complex. For his efforts Henry became known as the father of the interurban, the latter term some say he coined.

The proliferation of iron, steel, glass, paper, pottery, tin plate, and nail manufacturers in the 1890s stemmed from Anderson having excellent transportation facilities and a bumper fund of natural gas. Little wonder then that in the first years of the 20th century when the stock of gas rapidly subsided many of these businesses and their suppliers faced bankruptcy as the local economy slid into a recession. The appropriation of alternate power sources, particularly coal and electricity, saved a number of these businesses. But more of a key to Anderson's future was the work of the Remy brothers, Frank and B. P. "Perry," who were providing the infant automobile industry with crudely-made ignition equipment they had developed in a back lot shack in 1896. This new commercial force, the automobile, would shape the character of Anderson in the new century.

Most people cannot recall the names—the Union, the DeTamble, the Lambert, the Rider-Lewis—but they were among at least 14 "magnificent Andersons" rated so highly by the public and by the many other car producers in Indiana. Along with car production went parts manufacturing. Leading the way in parts production was Remy Electric, incorporated in 1901. Remy Electric received national acclaim in 1905 when the new Buick featured a Remy-designed, high-tension magneto. Besides cars and components, including electric headlights, gas engines, and spoke wheels, Anderson's transportation-related industries extended to juvenile vehicles. Hugh Hill, of Anderson, is said to have invented the Irish Mail, a child's wagon propelled by pushing and pulling the handle and steering with the feet. This "triumph of coordination" swept the nation. Viewed as robust and masculine, it seemed the perfect conveyance for young males who thought the tricycle a curiously feminine and sissy contraption. The Irish Mail formed the base of the Hill-Standard Company, founded in 1905, which also made playground equipment and baby carriage wheels. Given Anderson's penchant for fashioning vehicular items, it is not often remembered that at this time two-fifths of the nation's farm silos were assembled in the city.

Anderson's relationship to the fast-growing automotive industry intensified after 1919 when Remy Electric became a subsidiary of General Motors. Earlier, in 1911, the Remy brothers had sold out to Stoughton Fletcher, of Indianapolis, who reorganized Remy Electric and added cranking motors, generators, and ignition distributors to the product line. Remy's main competitor was the Dayton (Ohio) Engineering Laboratory (Delco), which introduced the revolutionary electric self-starter in 1912. In 1916 William C. Durant, the founder of General Motors Company (GM) in 1908, organized the United Motor Corporation in order to bring together several auto parts manufacturers, including Remy and Delco. Two years later the United Motor Corporation, along with Remy and Delco, merged with GM.

Remy's rapid expansion in the 1920s opened up thousands of jobs. By 1923 it was the world's largest producer of electrical equipment for cars. In 1924 Remy began making the famed Klaxon horns, the name derived from a Greek word meaning "to shriek." Remy and Delco consolidated in 1926 under the general management of Charles E. Wilson, subsequently GM chief and President Dwight D. Eisenhower's secretary of defense. Shortly after the formation of Delco Remy, Wilson put on a two-day circus extravaganza in a newly built building to impress GM management with Anderson's industrial development. The event featured the Sells-Floto Circus of Peru, Indiana, and drew thousands of visitors including top brass from Detroit.

GM went into the auto lamp business in 1928 when it bought the Guide Motor Lamp Company of Cleveland, Ohio, the creator of the electric headlamp, and merged it with Delco Remy in Anderson. Guide Lamp (now Fisher Guide) became a separate GM division in 1929. In 1930 all Guide operations were located in Anderson, from where it introduced, over the years, sealed-beam headlights, turn signals, glare reduction rearview mirrors, plastic lenses, two- and four-beam headlights, and an electronic beam selector, among other things.

Under the management of Charles E. Wilson, Delco Remy increased its work force by 5,800 in the 1920s and tripled its payroll. The expansion of GM depended to a large extent on the build-up of adequate living arrangements for present and future employees. To this end both company and private developers invested heavily in land, houses, and apartments. Subdivisions sprang up; GM built new plants; subsidiary and servicing firms came to town; new workers, many educated and professionally trained, moved in—all of which brought economic and cultural benefits to the community. The city's population jumped 33.7 percent in the decade of the 1920s. It could have risen more had not the city, sensing a threat to its municipal light plant and its low taxes, declined to purchase electricity to provide the growing GM complex with an additional source of power. Consequently, in 1928 the Delco Battery Division, originally earmarked for Anderson, went to Muncie instead. Nevertheless, Anderson had earned the right to be called GMsville, Indiana, or the West Point of

General Motors, because it trained so many of the company's executives.

During the 1920s a religious body, the Church of God (Anderson, Indiana), quietly expanded its influence in the community through its educational endeavors. Having already established in Anderson its world headquarters, its publishing house, and the International Camp Meeting, which annually drew thousands of ministers and laity to the city, the church now set about to enlarge and liberalize its infant institution for training clergy and missionaries. The Anderson Bible School opened with 50 students in 1917 as an adjunct of the Gospel Trumpet Company, the publishing arm of the denomination. In 1925 the school separated from Gospel Trumpet and became state-chartered as the Anderson Bible School and Seminary. President John A. Morrison and Dean Russell Olt brought liberal arts courses into the curriculum in 1928, and a year later the name of the school changed to Anderson College and Theological Seminary. In the 1929-30 academic year 232 students attended classes on the campus.

During the early years of the Great Depression, Anderson, like other communities, shouldered the burden of relief for its own and the transient needy. By 1932 the Central Relief Bureau was providing cash, groceries, and coal to 1,000 jobless men who worked one day a week cleaning alleys and streets. The Mellett City Employees Relief Kitchen and the Wayside Cross Mission were among local aid stations which fed, clothed, and sheltered the destitute. A variety of fund raising activities, ranging from charity dances to automatic check deductions of city workers, supported the relief efforts. After 1933 the federal government's distribution of food and jobs eased the strain on local agencies. By 1936 two-thirds of those persons who had lost a job because of depression conditions had been reinstated.

Among events headlining Anderson's history in the 1930s, including winning two state basketball championships and being denied participation in another state basketball tournament because of recruiting violations, was the 1937 sit-down strike at the Guide Lamp plant. Lasting 44 days, the job action threatened the economic recovery of the community. Roughly 4 percent of Anderson's 11,600 auto factory employees had signed up by 1937 with the United Auto Workers of America (UAWA).

The UAWA and the Committee for Industrial Organization (CIO) targeted GM for a nationwide sit-down in an attempt to pressure the giant company into recognizing the UAWA as the exclusive bargaining agent. The strike in Anderson began on December 31, 1936, at Guide Lamp. Delco Remy did not reopen its doors after the three-day New Year's holiday, because, as a result of the national strike of auto workers, its products were not needed by its customers. The sit-down at Guide ceased January 18, with partial plant start-up on February 3, a day following the restart of Delco Remy. Full production at Guide resumed February 15. The strike against GM ended officially on February 11, 1937, with a landmark UAWA victory. In Anderson, however, continued violence led Gov. M. Clifford Townsend to place Madison County under martial law and send in National Guardsmen. On February 23 things began to return to normal, and Townsend pulled his forces out. In spite of the union's success, not until the early 1940s would the majority of workers at Guide or at Delco Remy be union rank and file, a delay that indicates the strength of Anderson's anti-union forces.

During World War II practically all of Anderson's industries converted to war materials production. Madison County ranked eighth among the state's 92 counties in the dollar amount of defense contracts. GM employed around three-fourths of Anderson's wartime workers at its Guide and Delco Remy plants. Both divisions produced airplane parts, and Guide made blackout lamps for motorized war vehicles as well as Browning machine gun barrels, the M-3 submachine gun, and cartridge cases. The inevitable shortages of housing and of skilled workers did not seem to dampen the brisk local commerce, the taxes from which fattened the public coffers and brought forth improved city services. Officials reduced the public debt, raised city workers' pay, put in new streets, improved the water system, and updated police and fire protection.

In the 1950s local sports fans thrilled to the diamond exploits of townsman and Brooklyn Dodger great Carl Erskine, who pitched no hitters in 1952 and 1956 and struck out 14 Yankees in the 1953 World Series, a record that stood for a decade. Erskine is now the president of the First National Bank of Madison County.

A city ordinance passed in 1957 called for annexation of most of Anderson Township to make room for expansion and to create a larger tax base. Not everyone agreed with this solution to the city's problems. Township residents, thinking they were being asked to finance a bankrupt city, dragged the issue through the courts for seven years until the judiciary sanctioned the action in 1963. As a result of the annexation, Anderson's city limits expanded fourfold, and the population jumped 40 percent. By 1970 the city ranked ninth among Indiana's largest urbanized areas.

Civic enhancements, though, waged a losing battle against urban sprawl and downtown deterioration, common maladies in postwar urban America. Urban renewal seemed to be the answer. Time, neglect, and the appeal of shopping centers had rendered the core city fit prey for the wrecking ball. "Anderson," a columnist wrote in 1963, "is not as bad as its downtown looks. It's worse." A million dollar project in 1963 cleared around 50 acres in the central business district and displaced some 50 families. Into the vacuum and spotted throughout the city came new construction, including the Eisenhower Memorial Bridge and government buildings, a city hall in 1969, and a county courthouse in 1973. Whole blocks of houses were rehabilitated. Museums and art centers found lodging in restored homes.

The prearranged face-lift fell short of giving Anderson the needed push to sustain revitalization. It was not unusual in any given year to have one-fifth of the total midtown floor space unutilized. Stores continued to exit the city's core, seeking relief from the high cost and the low returns of doing business there. A series of disasters—fires, collapsed roofs, the new courthouse raining bricks on passersby—inspired the local press to depict the inner city as "a ghost town . . . half of it's burned down, the rest is falling down." To make matters worse, the manufacturing sector in the 1970s experienced fluctuations that added to the instability of the local economy. GM's decision during the recession of 1973-74 to decentralize and relocate some plants to the Sunbelt only indirectly affected Anderson yet created some anxious moments. The years from 1975 through 1979 were generally prosperous ones for Anderson's auto workers. Still, four major nonautomotive companies, including Nicholson File, left the city. High wages at GM and strong unions to guarantee top pay inadvertently forced smaller, uncompetitive firms to vacate. City officials and businessmen, perhaps entranced by GM's success, did not aggressively recruit new industries. On a more progressive note Anderson received an All-American City award in 1977 on the strength of its reorganization of the school system to achieve racial balance; its new senior citizen home, the Isabel Harter House; and its historical restorations, the Gruenewald house and the W. 8th St. Historic District, both listed in 1976 on the National Register of Historic Places. Once again, however, the city's pride was rudely shaken in early 1980 when indictments were handed down naming 23 persons, mostly former city officials, with 100 counts of corruption and fraud. The charges were later dropped due to judicial errors, but the commotion was symptomatic of the troubled community.

Most serious of all Anderson's problems were the deteriorating economic conditions summed up in 1980 headlines which proclaimed Anderson as the nation's leader in unemployment. By mid-1980 Anderson's jobless rate was around 20 percent and rising. Delco Remy had laid off 30 percent of its work force, the Guide, 18 percent. Many blacks and younger workers, those hit hardest by the recession, left town. Thirteen hundred houses sat empty. The adversity rippled throughout the community, necessitating the closing of shops and schools. Drunkenness and domestic squabbles multiplied. Between 1980 and 1983 Madison County lost 5.3 percent of its population, the second largest decrease among all the nation's counties of more than 100,000 inhabitants.

Improved auto production and sales, part of the national business upswing in 1984, brightened the economic picture of Anderson. Delco Remy and Guide began recalling employees. Various civic and commercial development groups launched campaigns to woo prospective manufacturers and thus diversify the city's economic base. The downtown slowly came around. Small retail stores, many started up by laid-off auto workers, occupied long-vacant store fronts. The designation for an Urban Enterprise Zone provided tax and financial incentives to upgrade a 1.8-square-mile tract of the inner city. A new parking garage often filled to capacity as did space in new high-rise buildings. Madison County's new jail opened in May

1988. The recognition by the National Register of Historic Places of the West Central Historic District, roughly bounded by Brown-Delaware, 10th, John, and 13th sts., challenged residents in the near west side neighborhood to preserve and restore their homes.

An event that did much to spark hope was the selection in 1984 of Anderson College's modern athletic facilities for the five-week summer training camp of the Indianapolis Colts of the National Football League. The Colts camp created 130 jobs and brought in thousands of retail dollars from visitors coming to watch the team practice, while the national coverage of the team's training elicited inquiries about convention space. All things considered, the Colts timing could not have been better. Arriving just as the city was passing through another season of adversity, the team's presence contributed enormously to the community's self-esteem. So, too, did the selection of Troy Lewis of Anderson High School to reign as Indiana's co-Mr. Basketball with Michigan City Rogers's Delray Brooks. A basketball powerhouse, the Anderson High School Indians were four times state runners-up in the period 1979-86.

In the later 1980s Anderson experienced a major turnaround in its economy, spearheaded by public and private construction. In March 1985 General Motors announced it would build a $70 million plant on the south side to manufacture the Magnequench, a revolutionary magnet for GM starters with broader applications in the appliance, health care, and computer fields. The Magnequench facility was dedicated in April 1987. The plant's location south of the intersection of IND 9 and I-69 and a $6.5 million drainage project completed in 1987 at this same site spurred a nearby build-ing boom in motels, restaurants, and shopping malls. Between 1984 and 1988, some $78 million of construction flowed into this area. Uptown, the big news focused on developments along Anderson's waterways. A boardwalk system called Indian Trails Riverwalk was completed in 1987 with future plans laid for its linkage with Shadyside Park and Killbuck Creek. Another promising tie with the Riverwalk was the unveiling of ideas by city officials for the River Centre project which ultimately would include a hotel, convention center, and park in the central business district. A new library opened in 1987, and the old Carnegie library was slated for conversion to an exhibition center for artifacts related to Anderson's history and industry. A new campus for Indiana Vocational Technical College, the arrival in 1985 of a branch of Purdue University's School of Technology offering associate degrees in several subjects, and Anderson College's name change to Anderson University in 1987, bode well for the city's educational and cultural environment.

Manufacturing employment in Madison County in the 1980s gradually decreased until it represented only one-third of the work force, down from 60 percent in the mid-1970s. Largely taking up the slack has been the increase in work in nonmanufacturing areas. Though the county continues to lose population, the local economy mirrors a more diverse base, which down the road should stabilize the job picture and halt the outmigration. Meanwhile, the expanding retail sector, the recreational facilities, the opportunities for learning, and the efforts at historical preservation have combined to bring about a fresh confidence in Anderson's tomorrow.

Anderson Attractions

The **Anderson/Madison County Visitors and Convention Bureau**, 6335 Scatterfield Rd. (just south of junction IND 9 and I-69) makes available tour information for the city and the county.

1. The **Delco-Remy Plant One Complex**, 2401 Columbus Ave., dates from 1906 when the first of a number of buildings went up on the site. The five-story office building along Columbus Ave., a south side landmark, was built between July 1928 and February 1929. The 45,000-sq.-ft. headquarters for Delco-Remy was attached to a similar looking five-story building to form a large L-shaped edifice. The first department to move into the new headquarters was the plant's hospital.

2. The **Martin Luther King Memorial Park**, 22nd St., Pendleton and S. Madison aves., was dedicated July 1, 1987. Construction of the small triangular piece of land, preserving the memory of the great civil rights leader, was funded by a Community Development Block Grant of $60,000. More than that was donated for the creation of a statue of King. Ken Ryden of the Anderson University art faculty created an 8-ft., 1,200-lb. bronze statue of King that sits on a 6-ft. granite base. The unveiling of the sculpture took place in October 1988.

3. The **Lambert house**, southwest corner of Hendricks and W. 7th sts., was built in 1899 by John W. Lambert, a pioneer automobile maker. In 1887, while in the family's corn planter business in Ohio, a young John Lambert took out a patent on a gasoline engine, which four years later he attached to a homemade three-wheeled vehicle. Lambert's self-propelled tricycle of 1891 is considered the first gas-powered conveyance built in the United States. Moving his Buckeye Manufacturing Company to Anderson in the mid-1890s, Lambert put up a large factory, still extant, between 19th St. and the rail-road, to make the Lambert cars, beginning in 1905. The largest car ever made in Anderson, the two-cylinder, four or five seat, Lambert was known for its unique friction drive. The inventive Lambert is said to have held 600 patents during his long career. He died in 1952 at age 92.

4. The **Rider-Lewis Motor Car Company**, on the north side of W. 2nd. St. at Sycamore St., was in operation in the period 1908-11. Located in Muncie, the company was persuaded to build a factory in Anderson in 1908. Clifton and Son of Peru, Indiana, constructed the $35,000 building on a site selected by Clermont Rider and bought from W. P. Harter. The company specialized in six-cylinder roadsters and touring cars. The Henry Nyberg Automobile Works took over the factory in 1911 and produced its Nyberg cars there for three years.

5. **Camp Stilwell Marker**, Riverview Dr. N. Shore Blvd., is located at the entrance to the Anderson Country Club, east of the Madison Ave. bridge over the White River. Named for Thomas N. Stilwell, quartermaster of the 34th Regiment, Indiana Infantry Volunteers, this Civil War training camp occupied the present country club site. The 34th Regiment, composed of companies from Madison County and surrounding counties, was organized at Anderson on September 16, 1861. The 34th left Anderson in early October and fought many battles including the Battle of Vicksburg. It fought the war's last battle at Palmetto Ranch, Texas, May 13, 1865, before being mustered out at Brownsville, Texas, February 3, 1866.

6. The **Elmo A. Funk Memorial Park**, on the south side of W. 8th St., just east of Lincoln St., is a tiny pedestrian way station. Its picturesque setting is used for weddings and receptions, or just for resting after exploring historic 8th St. Formally opened in 1973, the park was made

Anderson Attractions

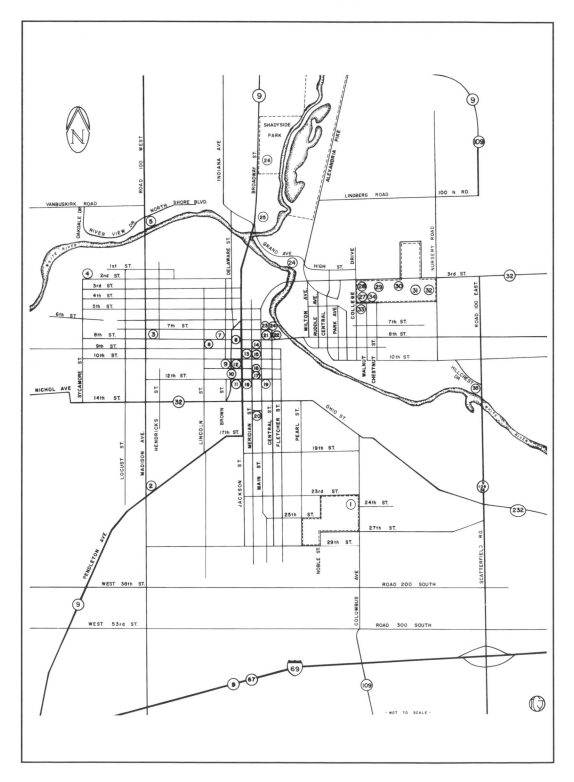

possible through the donation of land by local businessman Thomas C. Funk in memory of his father, Elmo, who at one time lived in the house at 920 W. 8th St. On the park grounds are gas lights, wrought-iron benches and fences, a brick gazebo with a shake-shingle roof, and a brick walkway encircling a fountain.

7. The **Alford house/Anderson Fine Arts Center**, 226 W. 8th St., is a public-oriented facility for the enjoyment and study of the arts. Its calendar of events is packed with art-related activities for all ages: film series, art and theater classes, rehearsals, meetings, lectures, exhibitions, and performances. It also maintains a permanent art collection, a rental gallery, and a gift shop. The center is lodged in the Alford house, so named by Nellie Alford Hill, who donated the house in 1966 in memory of her parents. The two-story brick home was built in 1870 for Neel C. McCullough, founder of Citizens Banking Company in 1855. The Classic Revival-style porch is a 20th-century appendage. The center opened in 1967 with several structural modifications, including transforming the garage into a studio/theater and classroom, and boarding up the large front windows to prevent sun rays from damaging the artwork inside. The monumental steel sculpture on the west lawn is an untitled creation by Phil A. Simpson, a former Anderson resident, and dedicated in 1980.

8. **Historic W. 8th St.** refers to a shaded boulevard lined with stately Victorian homes and more modest cottages of the gas boom era and later. Electrified gas lamps decorate and illuminate the wide, paved street. The Historic W. 8th St. Society oversees the preservation and beautification of the neighborhood. Every year since 1973 the Society has sponsored a Gaslight Festival, a one-day event in mid-June. Historic W. 8th St. is included in the Anderson St. Historical District, which also takes in parts of 7th and 9th sts. W. 8th St. was called Anderson St. in the 19th century. (*NRHP*)

9. The **Miron G. Reynolds house**, 1019 Brown-Delaware St., is an outstanding example of early 20th-century Arts and Crafts style architecture. Miron G. Reynolds, inventor of the gas regulator and manager of the Reynolds Gas Regulator Company, president of the Central Heating Company, and vice-president of the Indiana Silo Company, had the two-and-one-half-story, gabled house built in 1910. Red roman brick faces the first floor exterior with stucco and half timbering above.

10. The **Markt-Jones house**, 129 11th St., southeast corner of 11th and Brown-Delaware sts., was built in 1875. The two-story frame Italianate house, with a wraparound porch, has clapboard siding and a hipped roof. Stephen Markt was an Anderson woodworker, undertaker, and a director of the Peoples State National Bank. Both the Reynolds and the Markt houses are in the **W. Central Historic District**, bounded by Jackson, Brown-Delaware, John, Morton, 9th, 10th, 13th, and 14th sts. The district contains 156 structures in 10 subdivisions on 30 acres platted between 1854 and 1890. The district was officially placed on the National Register of Historic Places on December 6, 1984.

11. The **Stained-Glass Windows of the First United Methodist Church**, 1215 Jackson St., depict the Biblical message from Genesis through Revelations and a critical event in the life of this church. In 1965 fire destroyed the church building, erected in 1900. The congregation's fond memory of the lovely old stained-glass windows led to the emplacement of 14 new windows in the rebuilt church. The inch-thick faceted windows were designed and installed by Henry Lee Willet of Philadelphia. Of special interest is the lower panel in the south chancel (along Jackson St.), which pictures the previous church building engulfed in flames.

12. At the southwest corner of 10th and Jackson sts. once stood the **home of Governor Winfield Taylor Durbin**. Born in 1847 at Lawrenceburg, Durbin moved to Anderson in the early 1870s after a stint in the Civil War and employment in Indianapolis. He married Bertha McCullough, daughter of Anderson banker N. C. McCullough. Durbin helped found the Citizens Bank of Anderson. Active in Republican circles, he was elected the state's 25th governor in 1900. After serving one term, 1901-5, he pursued business ventures in Anderson. He ran again for governor in 1912, but lost. Durbin died in 1928 and is buried in Crown Hill Cemetery in Indianapolis.

13. The **Carnegie Library Building,** on the northeast corner of 10th and Jackson sts., was completed in the spring of 1905. Anderson Mayor M. M. Dunlap had written to Andrew Carnegie in 1901 requesting his aid. Carnegie responded subsequently with an offer of $50,000 provided the city furnish a location and annual support of $5,000. The city purchased the present site for $17,400. The buildings, grounds, and furnishings totaled $72,200. The Carnegie Library was used until the opening of the new library in 1987. It is anticipated that part of the old building will be converted to a local history museum, called the Carnegie Exhibition Center. (*NRHP*)

14. The **Madison County Government Center,** 16 E. 9th St., is the county's fifth courthouse and office building. The previous courthouse, built in 1882, was torn down in 1972. Onlookers of the dignified old courthouse's destruction were given souvenir bricks. The copper vault taken from the five-ton cornerstone revealed that few deposited relics had survived moisture and pests. The edges of the box apparently were not sealed properly. Gerald Ford, then minority leader of the House of Representatives, keynoted the dedication of the new $4 million county building in 1973. A bell tower which displays the bronze bell from the 1882 courthouse crowns the glass-paneled building. A century-old circuit court bench which serves as an information desk graces the foyer.

15. The downtown **Storefront Mural,** on the west side of Main St., between 9th and 10th sts., is a deceptive artwork, painted on the backsides of extant buildings, that depicts a block of realistic shop fronts. Funded by the Anderson Downtown Development Corporation, the project employed 10 artists during the summer of 1983 to design and execute the tricky three-dimensional painting on old pitted bricks and brittle mortar. The real-life quality of the facades has fooled many would-be shoppers. All along the row of shops are little personal touches reflecting the whimsy or humor of the individual artist: the glass front that reflects buildings across Main St., including one previously torn down; a likeness of an artist's daughter in a framed portrait; a spider or bee among the blooms in the flower shop window; and the lone diner at the Nighthawk Cafe, two motifs borrowed by an admiring artist from Ed-

ward Hopper's paintings. The arches and rainbow over the Anderson Trust Company symbolize hope for the city.

16. **WHBU Radio Station,** operating out of the **Union Building,** 11th St. and Meridian Plaza, is Indiana's second oldest commercial station. The station began in 1923 at the corner of 9th and Main sts. In 1927 Citizens Bank, then across the street from the Union Building, purchased the station. The bank constructed a new transmitter and placed the studio in the bank lobby from where, in December 1927, it continued to broadcast. In the early 1930s the bank bought the Union Building and moved the station to its present location. At this time the Union Building became known as the Citizens Bank Building, a name it carried until the early 1980s when the bank relocated to new headquarters at 8th and Main sts. Since then the old Union Building has been called by its original name. The Columbus, Ohio, architectural firm of Richard, McCarthy and Bulford designed the Union Building, constructed in 1902. The six-story structure housed the offices of the Union Traction Company. Gladys and Charles Hollon purchased the Union Building in 1986 and plan a major remodeling of the historically significant building. In 1981 the Indiana Chapter, Society of Professional Journalism, Sigma Delta Chi, designated WHBU an historic site.

17. The **Paramount Theatre,** abutting the Union Building at 1124 Meridian St., is a three-story movie palace constructed in 1929 by George Challace. The Spanish Baroque-style building has lobby floors and walls decorated with eye-catching mosaics. The 1,700-seat theater is outfitted with statuary, twinkling stars, and lush greenery, reminiscent of a Spanish villa. The stage sits over dressing rooms. The colossal Page pipe organ can rise to stage level from its mooring in the orchestra pit. Among the many celebrities who frequented the Paramount stage was Gene Autry. Autry's sidekick in the vaudeville sketches was Max Terhune, an Anderson resident, who played the music halls and appeared in films. Before his career in show business, Terhune worked at Remy Electric. The theater has had a series of owners in recent years and in 1987 was taken over by the county for nonpayment of property taxes. On October 24, 1988, the county accepted an offer

by the Doctors, Lawyers, and Accountant Services, Inc., of $42,000 for the property, which included the theater and the Paramount Building at 1129-1130 Meridian St. The new owners planned to lease the theater to a local arts group and renovate the rest of the building to accommodate restaurants and offices.

South on Meridian below 13th St. is the **State Theatre**, another fine old urban movie house that opened May 30, 1930, to great fanfare. David Graham of Indianapolis designed the showplace, which was part of the Publix Theatres Corporation, to which the Paramount belonged. The 1,580-seat auditorium featured the most up-to-date sound equipment to enhance the new talkies. Its walls were "sound plastered." It carried an air-cooling and -heating system, which gave the moviegoer year-round comfort.

18. The **Remy Historical Marker** on the southwest corner of 12th and Meridian sts. commemorates the site where Frank and B. P. "Perry" Remy founded the Remy Electric Company in 1896. Here in a 280-sq.-ft. building the brothers first developed the magnetos and dynamos for use in automobiles and laid the foundation for Anderson's Delco Remy division of GM.

19. Ground was broken for the new **Anderson Public Library**, 12th and Main sts., on March 3, 1986, and its dedication took place October 25, 1987. The Sears Roebuck Company building and grounds were purchased for $298,000, and the store was totally remodeled and enlarged to give the new library 90,000 sq. ft. of space. The buff brick building has a plaza and fountain at its 12th St. entry, which leads to a lobby below ground level. The book stacks occupy three levels and form the three sides of a reading and study area. Meeting, staff, and special subject rooms make up the rest of the library. The old Sears automobile garage, just southeast of the library at 13th St. and Central Ave., was donated by Melvin Simon and Associates of Indianapolis and converted into an Extension Services building to house the bookmobiles and library services for persons with physical or mental impairments. The entire project, funded primarily through a 13-year bond issue of $5 million, was overseen by Kenneth Montgomery of Montgomery Associates of Anderson. The landscaping was funded through

private donations in a campaign led by local realtors. During the dedication weekend, featured speakers included United States Senator Richard G. Lugar, who gave the dedication address, and novelist Fred Mustard Stewart, an Anderson native, who has written such bestsellers as *The Mephisto Waltz* (1969), *Century* (1981), and *Ellis Island* (1983), the latter made into a television miniseries. Prior to the building of the Sears store in 1947, a series of schools, dating back to 1849, occupied the site, as noted on a marker near the new library's front entrance.

20. The **Big Four Railroad Station**, 29 E. Dillon St. (15th and Main sts.), closed its doors in 1971 after 80 years of service. The building's renovation, begun in 1975, was completed in 1984 after Elsie Perdiue, a Chicago-born Anderson resident, purchased the empty station in 1983 and established the Performing Arts Station for the presentation of dance, drama, music, literature, and the visual arts. Programs in these areas are given in the three studios of the facility, which also includes a dressing room and reception room with kitchen area. In 1984 she remodeled another part of the station and turned it into a railroad museum displaying artifacts and contemporary materials pertaining to railroading.

21. Anderson's **City Building**, bordered by E. 8th, Main, E. 7th sts. and Central Ave., is the center for all municipal departments except fire and police. Standing just south of the Madison County Historic Home, the modern limestone, steel, and tinted glass facility contrasts sharply with the red brick walls and mansard roof of its neighbor. The $2 million building, paid for without increasing local taxes, was completed in late 1969 on the site of the Stilwell mansion that had served the city since 1917. Thomas N. Stilwell, an Ohio native, came to Anderson in 1852 to practice law. He subsequently served in the state and national legislatures, in the Union army during the Civil War, and as President Andrew Johnson's appointee as minister to Venezuela in 1867 and 1868. While president of the First National Bank of Anderson, Stilwell was indicted for embezzlement. Before the trial could begin, Stilwell died as a result of a gun battle with a person he thought to have fingered him for the crime. Inside the City Building, designed by Arthur B. Henning of

Anderson, is a large auditorium used for public events. In the lobby is a plaque indicating the location of Chief Anderson's home.

22. The **Madison County Police and Detention Center**, 720 Central Ave., on the northeast corner of 8th St. and Central Ave., was opened in May of 1984. The $26 million jail can accommodate 145 persons. The demolition of the 1939 jail building next to the new structure began in mid-1984, and in its place rose the police department's administrative headquarters, which was completed in 1985.

23. The **Madison County Historic Home**, also known as the Gruenewald House, 626 Main St., is a marriage of two houses of different styles: an 1860 two-story brick building built by Alfred Makepeace, and a Second Empire town house erected in the early 1870s by Moses Cherry and completed in 1873 by Martin Gruenewald. Gruenewald, a prominent saloon owner, butcher, and real estate investor, lived in the house until his death in 1933 at the age of 94. Following a succession of owners and its near destruction in 1973, the city purchased the property and by means of a matching grant from the Lilly Endowment and a citizens' fund provided for its restoration. The home, restored and furnished with donated 19th-

Indiana Historical Society
Madison County Historic Home (Gruenewald House), 1989, photographed by J. Kent Calder

century furniture, was dedicated in 1976. Besides tours, the home is open for meetings and social events. (*NRHP*)

24. The **Indian Trails Riverwalk** is a one-and-a-half-mile network of paths and boardwalks along the west side of the White River between the Eisenhower and Truman bridges (8th St. to 3rd St.), and along Grand Ave. on the east side of the river between the Truman and Broadway bridges. Dedicated June 20, 1987, the Riverwalk is the anchor in city plans to open a large area of riverfront to recreation and tourism. The White River Development Commission under the chairmanship of James Abraham, established in 1985 as an outgrowth of a White River Task Force, pulled together the resources necessary to complete the $817,221 project, principally a grant from the Department of Natural Resources. Plans call for the extension of the riverwalk and the addition of a hotel and civic center, collectively called the River Centre Project.

25. **Indiana Railroad Headquarters**, east side of Broadway in north Anderson, once housed the main offices of the Indiana Railroad, which came into existence in 1930 and took control of almost all the state's interurban system until the end of the interurban era in 1941. The buildings originally were constructed in 1899-1900 for use as the shops and power plant for the Union Traction Company, incorporated in 1897 and operator of the largest interurban mileage in the state until 1930. The power plant, anticipated to cost $380,000, was touted as the most complete and largest electrical plant west of Niagara Falls. When constructed, the plant not only serviced Union Traction railways but brought electricity into homes and factories in Delaware, Madison, and Grant counties.

26. **Shadyside Park**, north of the Indiana Railroad headquarters on Broadway, is the city's principal playground. The land on which it is situated once belonged to C. L. Henry, Union Traction magnate. The city, influenced by Mayor Blanchard Horne, bought the 32-acre North Anderson tract in 1923 for $18,000 and almost simultaneously annexed North Anderson. The forested and hilly park, lying alongside Killbuck Creek, was dedicated to Madison County veterans of all wars on July 4, 1923.

Indian Trails Riverwalk, 1989, photographed by J. Kent Calder

27. **Anderson University**, roughly bounded by College Dr., 3rd St., Nursery Rd., and 5th St., opened its doors in 1917 as the Anderson Bible School. It became the Anderson Bible School and Seminary in 1925 as it added a higher level of Biblical studies. Four years later the school appended a liberal arts curriculum and changed to Anderson College and Theological Seminary. A Graduate School of Theology came into existence in 1950. In 1964 the name was shortened to Anderson College, and in 1987, 70 years after its organization by the Church of God as a Bible training school, it became Anderson University. The campus covers 95 acres, and its 23 major buildings are largely of recent vintage. Group campus tours can be arranged through the admissions office.

28. The **Charles E. Wilson Library**, 1033 E. 3rd St., dedicated in 1957, houses the papers of Wilson, who led General Motors from 1941 to 1953 and was secretary of defense under President Eisenhower from 1953 to 1957. The $620,000 four-story brick, Georgian Colonial-style library was designed by J. R. Bailey, of Orange, Virginia, and Arthur B. Henning, Anderson architect.

29. The college's **Museum of Bible and Near Eastern Studies** is located in the **School of Theology**, 1123 E. 3rd. St., the next building east of Wilson Library. Established in 1963 by Gustav Jeeninga, a Dutch-born educator, the museum was first housed in Old Main, now gone, then in Wilson Library before its move to the School of Theology in the mid-1970s. Displayed in glass cases in two adjacent rooms is a broad sampling of authentic and replicated artifacts that bring alive the culture of the Biblical world. Around 90 percent of the items are original. The Byrd Memorial Library housed in the School of Theology underwent renovation along with Wilson Library beginning in 1988 with an addition of an underground passageway connecting the two buildings and other amenities which will add 30,000 sq. ft. of space.

30. **Byrum Hall**, 1235 E. 3rd St., is the last of the original major buildings built on the campus. Constructed in 1908, the concrete and stone block building was designed and built by Robert L. Byrum, one of a number of Byrum family members who contributed significantly to the establishment of the Church of God (Anderson, Ind.) and Anderson College. Enoch and Noah Byrum, for example, were respectively

editor and treasurer of *The Gospel Trumpet*, the Church of God's principal publication for many years, and Ruthven Byrum, founder and head of the college's art department from 1936 to 1958, was a well-known landscape artist. A number of his paintings are exhibited in campus buildings. The interior of Byrum Hall, previously used as a tabernacle and gymnasium, underwent complete renovation in 1974. The 500-seat auditorium is used for recitals and other large events.

31. Further east is the sprawling **Krannert Fine Arts Center**, a $4 million complex consisting of five units constructed in 1979. The facility honors Ellnora Decker Krannert (1890-1974). Mrs. Krannert and her husband, Herman C. Krannert (1887-1972), founded the Indianapolis-based Inland Container Corporation in 1925. Their philanthropic work within and outside Indiana was enormous, with major gifts going to medical, educational, cultural, and religious institutions. The Krannert Charitable Trust granted Anderson College $1.25 million to launch fund raising efforts for the center.

The **Bill and Gloria Gaither Music Building**, the northernmost component, is named for the popular writers and singers of gospel music and alumni of the college. Sandi Patti, a 1979 graduate, has dominated this field of music since 1983 when she first was chosen Female Artist of the Year by the Gospel Music Association. Besides her four Gold Albums, the Anderson resident's awards by 1988 included 16 Dove Awards, 4 Grammy Awards, and 5 Artist of the Year Awards. In a ceremony on Indianapolis's Monument Circle, July 2, 1988, Governor Robert Orr presented to the Gaithers and Patti the third Hoosier Pride Award, partially in recognition of the Gaithers writing, and Patti singing, the song "Indianapolis, Indeed."

The **Jessie C. Wilson Art Galleries**, on the second level of the center, is named for the wife of Charles E. Wilson. The Wilson children made possible the art facility. In 1978 a daughter, Rosemary Wilson Austin, gave the college her valuable collection of Boehm porcelain birds, which are permanently displayed in the East Gallery. Also on exhibit is a collection of over 1,500 napkin rings.

32. **Warner Auditorium**, east of Krannert Center, is a Church of God property used primarily for the denomination's annual convention. The

world's first lift-slab dome covers the 268-ft.-diameter building. When constructing the $400,000 structure in 1961, workers poured lightweight concrete over a 40-ft.-high mound of contoured dirt, upon which had been placed slabs of styrofoam and steel reinforcement rods. Next, hydraulic jacks hoisted the three million pounds of concrete and steel some 24 ft. to its resting place upon 36 concrete footings. After leveling the earthen mold, workmen proceeded to build the exterior walls and outfit the interior. The auditorium seats 7,200.

33. The **Robert H. Reardon Auditorium**, College Dr. and 5th St., has brought to the vicinity a much-needed facility for major concerts, theatrical productions, lectures, and conventions. Named for the college's president emeritus, whose presidency extended from 1958 to 1983, the $5.5 million auditorium was dedicated in 1984. The Brooklyn Dodger great and college trustee, Carl Erskine, chaired the fund-raising campaign to which Anderson residents pledged $1.7 million. Gene Autry gave a donation in memory of his old stage associate Max Terhune. The interior color scheme of the 2,200-seat, balconied auditorium emphasizes warm red, beige, and gray tones. The exterior is of red brick. A huge chandelier of 10,000 light bulbs suspends 14 ft. from the downstairs lobby ceiling. The four stained-glass windows in the balcony area were made by local artist John Wiles.

34. Across 5th St. from Reardon Auditorium and just west of Hartung Hall is a life-size cast bronze **statue of Dr. John A. Morrison**, president of the college from 1925 until his retirement in 1958. Ken Ryden of the Anderson University art faculty sculpted the piece which depicts Morrison in academic attire, with Bible in hand. The statue was unveiled June 13, 1988.

35. The **United Auto Workers Local 662 Facility**, 2025 Hillcrest Dr., west of IND 9 and south of 10th St., is the largest local union complex in the nation. The office, recreation, and service areas encompass 20 acres. Local 662 issued from a splintering of old Local 146 following the General Motors strikes of 1937. It received a charter to represent Delco Remy employees in May 1939. It celebrates its 50th year in 1989. In 1979 the then 10,000-member bargaining unit took the occasion to designate its

large park as the Emil Mazey park, after the Detroit-based UAW secretary-treasurer. The Union Hall, dedicated in 1957, includes the Walter Reuther Memorial Auditorium, so named after the UAW president's tragic death in a 1970 plane crash.

Tour 14

The circular tour begins in Anderson at 53rd St. and IND 109 (Columbus Ave.). Drive south on IND 109 *3 m.* to a curious village sign that reads **NEW COLUMBUS** or **OVID**. It recalls a time when New Columbus was the name of the post office in Ovid. In 1837 postal officials instituted the new name, Ovid, to avoid confusion with Columbus in Bartholomew County. The sign acknowledges the persistent use of both names by the state and general public, although the New Columbus post office ceased to exist long ago.

Continue on IND 109 south to US 36 (*1.6 m.*). Follow IND 109 and US 36 east *1 m.* to the hamlet of **EMPORIA**, established in 1891 as a Big Four Railroad station. Follow IND 109 to IND 38 (formerly the Pendleton and New Castle turnpike). Bear east on IND 38 *.6 m.* to **MARKLEVILLE** (p. 427), which John D. Markle laid out in 1852. A mass murder of Indians by whites occurred near Markleville in 1824. To view the massacre's exact location go to the middle of town and turn north on State St. (CR 300E). Proceed *.8 m.* and turn east onto CR 800S. The site of the massacre is located on a farm *.5 m.* on the right. Nine Miami and Seneca trappers, including three women and four children, were killed for no apparent reason by six whites. Either a sense of justice or fear of a Miami reprisal resulted in a strong public outcry for the apprehension of the murderers. The militia was called out, and four of the six criminals were captured. The trial and hanging of three of the whites took place the next year above the falls in Pendleton. The execution of whites for the brutal crime against the Indians is claimed as the nation's first such punishment and forms the basis of Jessamyn West's 1975 best seller *The Massacre at Fall Creek.* Return to the junction of State St. and IND 38. Turn east onto IND 38 and travel *.6 m.* to a marker on the left commemorating the massacre.

IND 38 stretches *13 m.* between Markleville and New Castle and in its entirety crosses Indiana between Lafayette and Richmond. In 1976 the state legislature designated IND 38 the **Bataan Memorial Highway** to honor Hoosier National Guardsmen of the 38th Infantry Division who were instrumental in liberating the Bataan peninsula in 1945. The state has placed a number of memorial highway signs along the route at county lines. One can be seen *1.5 m.* east of the historical marker which stands at the Henry County line.

Named for patriot Patrick Henry, **HENRY COUNTY** (p. 53,336; 395 sq. m.) was organized in 1821, and the early settlers were mostly Quakers. One pioneer Quaker, George Hiatt, defied a Tory command to take up arms in the Revolutionary War. Instead, the pacifist employed the gun as a stick horse and rode about, declaring his innovation to be the best use for the weapon. The building of the Cumberland, or National Rd. (US 40), in the late 1820s accelerated development of the county. Henry County and county seat New Castle took their names from counterparts in Kentucky. The relationship between Henry County and the Raintree County of the famous novel by Ross Lockridge, Jr., is an accepted but unproved tie.

Past the Bataan road sign *4.6 m.* is the tiny town of **CADIZ** (p. 180). Established in 1836, Cadiz took its name from an Ohio town, which, in turn, was named for a city in Spain. Leaving Cadiz, the familiar view of large farms gives way to ranch-style homes dotting the roadside. Continue east approximately *3.4 m.* to the second road right past the IND 234/38 junction. Turn right for approximately *2 m.* on CR 275W to the **Westwood Park Recreational Area**. Under the governance of the Big Blue River Conservancy District, the recreational area includes a 160-acre lake, primitive camping, and picnicking. It opened in 1975.

Return to IND 38 and continue east approximately *2 m.* On either side of the road are

Tour 14

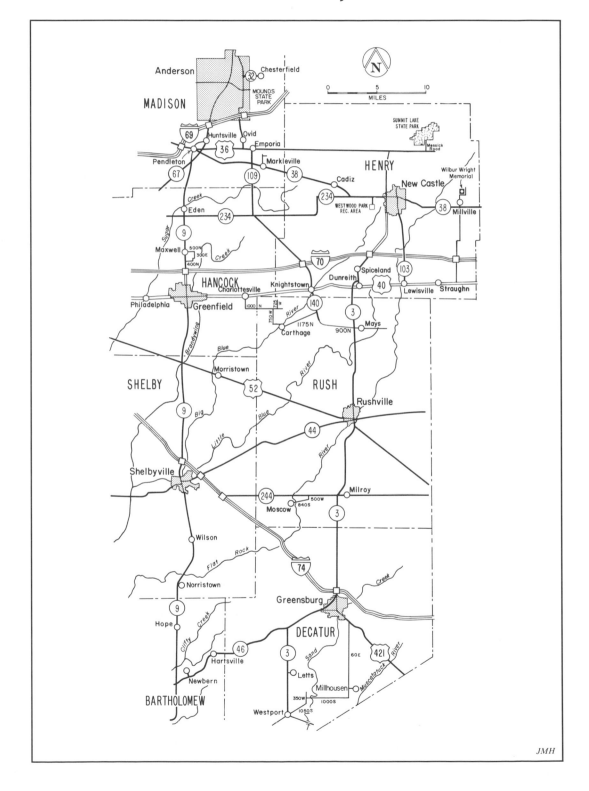

JMH

steel mills. **Ingersoll Steel Division of Avesta** on the right was started as the Indiana Steel Company in the 1910s and has been known by several names. The plant produces stainless steel. At one time Ingersoll was a division of Borg Warner. The **Allegheny Ludlum** plant, producers of cold rolled steel, was opened in 1966 as part of the Ingersoll Steel Division.

The **NEW CASTLE** (p. 20,056) city limits are *.3 m.* farther east on IND 38. The Henry County seat was founded in 1820 and platted in 1836. Named by Ezekiel Leavell, an early settler, for his home in Kentucky, the town grew along agricultural and small business lines. The city became known as the Rose City in this century's early years because it was the major grower and distributor of the American Beauty Rose. The Heller Brothers started the South Park Floral Company in the middle 1890s to produce the rose. The 6- and 12-ft. stemmed roses they exhibited at the 1901 Kansas City International Rose Show created a sensation. At one time more than 50 greenhouses and twice as many florists operated in the city. The general difficulties attending the growing of the species, damage from the 1917 tornado, competition, and export decline with the onset of World War I combined to destroy the city's rose industry. The city's history changed dramatically with the arrival of the auto industry and the establishment of the Hoosier Kitchen Cabinet Company. Starting in 1907 such classic cars as the Maxwell, Lawter, and Universal were produced in New Castle. Chrysler, which purchased the Maxwell plant, continues to be the largest employer. Between 1899 and 1942 the Hoosier Kitchen Cabinet Company was the nation's leading cabinet manufacturer. Today, Hoosier Cabinet is a generic term for all such wooden, self-contained, movable kitchen units. They are eagerly collected and returned to decorative or practical usefulness.

Continue east *.4 m.* to IND 3, turn left, and travel *1 m.* north. On the left is the entrance to **Henry County Memorial Park**, established in the 1920s and later dedicated to those Henry County natives who died in America's 20th-century wars. The almost 300 acres of grounds make it a major non-state park and the largest memorial in Indiana. Along with three artificial lakes providing fishing and boat rental, the park features a number of baseball diamonds, an 18-hole golf course, and buildings for fairs and exhibits. The beauty of the

area is enhanced by the Japanese Garden and the outdoor amphitheater, which is often the scene of weddings. Playground equipment is scattered throughout the park. Six covered shelters are free of charge; small cabins can be rented during the day.

From the park continue north on IND 3 *4.2 m.* to US 36. Turn right and proceed *4 m.* to Messick Rd. Go north on Messick Rd. to the gatehouse of the **Summit Lake State Park**, Indiana's 19th state park, and its newest. The 2,552-acre Summit Lake property, developed with federal and state funds, opened in 1985 as the Summit Lake Recreation Area under the management of the Big Blue River Conservancy District. The state's Department of Natural Resources assumed control on January 9, 1988. The park's facilities include a 500-acre lake for boating, fishing, and swimming. In addition, there are 129 Class-A campsites, picnic areas, and a large shelter.

Return to the IND 3 and 38 intersection, turn left, and proceed *.5 m.* to the **Henry County Courthouse** on the right. Located on the square, the courthouse with its 110-ft. tower dominates the cityscape. This classical Victorian-style structure is the third courthouse on the site, the first having been built in 1824 and the second in 1837. The latter burned in 1864. The present brick and stone courthouse was completed in 1869 at a cost of $120,000. A well-blended addition was finished in 1905. The building bears a close resemblance to the courthouse portrayed by Lockridge in *Raintree County*. (*NRHP/HABSI*)

Continue east and turn south onto 14th St. (IND 103). On the left *.4 m.* is the **Henry County Historical Society Museum**, 614 S. 14th St. The society is one of the oldest in the state, organized November 4, 1887. Benjamin S. Parker (1833-1911), a prominent local bard who penned the poem "The Cabin in the Clearing," chaired the organizing committee. In 1901 the county bought the Grose home for the society's headquarters and museum. Maj. Gen. William Grose (1812-1900) held the highest rank of any county soldier in the Civil War. He built his Italianate-style mansion in 1870. The museum contains a number of authentically furnished rooms and includes a collection of rare Civil War books and extensive genealogy and local history files. (*NRHP*) Located on the museum's grounds are the cornerstone from the high school and the restored interurban waiting station. The high school building, erected in 1895, was later converted into a junior high and was razed in 1973. A private citizen rescued and later donated the stone block to the museum. The interurban waiting station, an open shelter with a pagoda-like roof that originally was located just east of Memorial Park, served commuters between downtown and the park and between New Castle and Muncie until 1941. The deteriorating structure was renovated and removed to the Historical Society Museum. Both items were placed on the museum's grounds in 1979.

Continue south on 14th St. *.6 m.*, turn left onto I Ave., and travel *.2 m.* to the **Chrysler Company's New Castle Plant**. Stretching for more than half a mile, the Chrysler plant encompasses both sides of I Ave. The large red brick building with large glass windows on the south side of the road formerly housed the Maxwell-Briscoe plant. The Maxwell, the classic car immortalized by Jack Benny, had been built at this plant since 1907. In 1925 Walter P. Chrysler acquired the factory and used it in conjunction with his Detroit facilities to form the basis of the Chrysler Corporation. At one time the plant employed over 7,000 workers. The decline of the American auto industry in the late 1970s and early 1980s resulted in mass layoffs at the New Castle plant and a subsequent decline in the town's economy. Despite these cutbacks, Chrysler remains New Castle's largest employer.

Return to 14th St. and continue south *.3 m.* to M Ave. Turn right and proceed *.5 m.* to the **Walter P. Chrysler New Castle High School and Field House**. The new facility was dedicated on November 21, 1959, after using a woefully inadequate gym known as the old Church St. Gym for 35 years. Construction began in December 1957. A portion of the steel framework collapsed in June 1958, halting the work for a brief period. At the dedication ceremonies, Indiana High School Athletic Association commissioner L. V. Phillips declared the structure to be "the largest high school gymnasium in the world." Officially it can seat 9,325, but basketball game crowds often top 10,000. Among the school's star alumni are Kent Benson and Steve Alford. In New Castle, as in almost every Indiana town, high school basketball reigns supreme. Nevertheless, there may have been some concern expressed about the prospects of the game when the first New Cas-

tle team in 1909 lost its opener 59-1 to Lebanon.

Adjacent to the fieldhouse on Trojan Ln. is the **Indiana Basketball Hall of Fame Museum**. The $2.25 million, 14,000-sq.-ft. brick and glass facility opened in 1989 on a five-acre tract. The board of directors of the Hall of Fame, which closed in Indianapolis in 1987 after 25 years existence, chose New Castle as the new site from 13 contesting cities. The split-level gold mine of Hoosier basketball nostalgia is fronted by a huge map of Indiana composed of commemorative bricks purchased by individuals, schools, and businesses. These purchases helped finance the hall's construction.

Return to 14th St. (IND 103) and turn left to Broad St. (IND 38). Drive *6.4 m.* east and turn left onto Wilbur Wright Rd. Travel north *2 m.* passing through the hamlet of Millville. Turn right onto CR 100N and proceed *.5 m.* before turning left onto CR 750E. The **Wilbur Wright Birthplace**, an interpretive reconstruction of the farmhouse where Wright was born in 1867, is *.6 m.* on the left. A fire destroyed the original home in 1884. The state bought the 4.9-acre site in 1929, but it took until 1973 before money was allocated to rebuild the birthplace. Constructed on the original foundation, the two-story mid-Victorian farmstead was pieced together from several old houses. The furnishings were borrowed from state and local museums, and the Wright family contributed one article, a silver pitcher. The smokehouse is original. The memorial opened in April 1974. In 1988 the state, while maintaining ownership of the property, turned the operation of the site over to a local group, the Wilbur Wright Birthplace Preservation Society, Inc.

Return through Millville and continue across IND 38 on Wilbur Wright Rd., jogging west *3 m.* south and again at New Lisbon. At US 40, turn right to **STRAUGHN** (p. 331), approximately *1.5 m.* Platted in 1868 as Straughn's Station after an early settler named Merriman Straughn, the town may have been the model for Waycross, the home of John Wickliff Shawnessy, the hero in the novel *Raintree County*. On the left *.4 m.* east of Straughn is a white Victorian-style house that was the **home of John Wesley Shockley** (grandfather of Ross Lockridge, Jr.) who some believe was the inspiration for the Shawnessy character in the book. The former Shockley home also bears a strong resemblance to the Shawnessy house. John Shockley was a schoolteacher who died before Lockridge was born. The Lockridge children spent several summers in this home visiting their grandmother, and it was here that young Ross developed an interest in his grandfather's letters and writings. The fact that the two possess the same initials seems to be more than coincidental.

Continue west on US 40 *2.9 m.* to **LEWISVILLE** (p. 577). The area was settled because of its location on the National Rd. (US 40), and on Christmas Day, 1829, Lewis C. Freeman recorded the town's plots and named it for himself. Aside from several antique shops, the town's major attraction is the Edwardian-style **Guyer Opera House**, which is located one-third block west of IND 103 on the right. A monument to a local physician, Oscar K. Guyer, the doors first opened in 1902, and everything from stock company productions to rabbit suppers were presented in the following years. No opera productions were ever held at the opera house, but it was called such because the word theater held a negative moral connotation in the early 20th century. After many years as a movie theater the building was closed in 1942 because heating with potbelly stoves violated fire regulations. Under the guidance of the Raintree County Opera House Guild, Inc., organized in 1975, most of the exterior and the first floor have been restored, and it once again functions as a theater and multipurpose building. (*NRHP*)

Travel *4.2 m.* west to **DUNREITH** (p. 184), located at the US 40 and IND 3 junction. Named for the pioneer proprietor, Emery Dunreith Coffin, the original designation, Coffin's Station, was converted to Dunreith in 1865, perhaps for obvious reasons. In January 1968 all residents evacuated the town after damaged tank cars from a Pennsylvania Railroad wreck exploded, destroying a cannery and several houses. Toxic chemicals poisoned a nearby creek, killing fish and livestock. Wreckage blocked busy US 40 for three days.

Continue *.1 m.* and turn north onto IND 3. **SPICELAND** (p. 940), an area settled by North Carolina Quakers in the 1820s, is *2.2 m.* north. In 1828 they petitioned the Duck Creek Monthly Meeting at Greensboro for a local place of worship to be called the Spiceland Meeting, taking the name from the area's spicebushes. Often growing 15 ft. high, the spicebush

once covered central Indiana. Early settlers used the bark and fruit as a substitute for store tea. Folklore dictated that spice tea be consumed only in the spring. If taken in the fall, the blood-thinning brew could lead to chills or worse during the cold months. When the town Spiceland was organized in 1842, it, too, took its name from the local spicebush.

Travel *.3 m.* farther and turn left onto Main St. **Spiceland Friends Church** is *.6 m.* on the left. The present brick structure was erected in 1874, succeeding two earlier meetinghouses. On the southeast side of the church is a marker commemorating the former site of the **Spiceland Academy**. The academy was founded in 1827 by the Friends' Meeting, and by the 1860s it had become one of the leading secondary and college preparatory schools in central Indiana. Over the years several buildings housing the academy had been located on the same site. Dr. Charles A. Beard (1874-1948), an eminent American historian, was a Spiceland native and graduate of the academy. In 1922 the academy was sold to the town and converted into a public high school, continuing to serve until 1973.

Continue west on Main St. *.3 m.* and turn left onto West St. (CR 325). On the right *.3 m.* near the corner of West and Broad sts. is the former **home and observatory of William Dawson**, a pioneer astronomer, weatherman, and occasional lecturer at the academy. At one time the roof contained a tin dome that opened to reveal a telescope for stargazing. Dawson owned the house and observatory during the latter decades of the 19th century, and it was often a favorite spot for the students and faculty of Spiceland Academy to gather and observe the heavens. The roof has since been remodeled, and the building now houses a private residence at 244 W. Broad. Several of Dawson's instruments are housed at the Henry County Historical Society Museum in New Castle.

Return to Dunreith and continue west on US 40 for about *3 m.* On the left is the **Knightstown Spring Rest Park**. The spring has been quenching the thirst of travelers since this portion of the National Rd. was completed in the 1830s. Unfortunately, the water does not pass present regulations of the state board of health, as a sign advises. Next to the warning sign is a marker briefly reviewing the history of the road.

A historical marker *2 m.* farther west on the left commemorates the National Rd. and the early history of **KNIGHTSTOWN** (p. 2,325). (It is *.8 m.* more to the town limits.) Knightstown, second largest population center in Henry County, is situated on the bank of Big Blue River. The town was named after Jonathan Knight, a surveyor and engineer for the National Rd. Hoosier poet William Herschell (1873-1939) picked up the phrase "Ain't God Good to Indiana" to entitle his famous poem about an old-timer fishing in the Blue River east of town. For the nostalgic or the architectural buff, Knightstown is blessed with fine old Italianate and Neo-Jacobean homes, many of which have been restored.

Proceed *.1 m.* and turn right at Washington St. Dividing the thoroughfare is a nicely landscaped **mini-mall** rededicated in 1975-76 to honor the nation's bicentennial. Highlighting the mall is a bandstand, built on the same spot and of the same design as the original structure that had been removed several years earlier and converted into an efficiency apartment.

Proceed north *.3 m.* to Carey St., turn right, and at Adams St. pass the former **Knightstown Academy**, a three-story red brick building constructed in the centennial year of 1876. For many years it served as one of the finest private schools in the state, and it later was purchased by the city for public education. Topping the twin 40-ft. towers of the Second Empire-style structure is a superb model of a telescope and one of a globe, symbolizing education and science. Rising costs of repair and maintenance forced the building's closing in 1981. (*NRHP*) Historic Landmarks Foundation of Indiana purchased the structure in 1989.

Return to Main St., turn right one block, and left onto Washington St. Drive *.3 m.*, turn left onto West Ave. at a Y intersection, and proceed *.2 m.* Situated on a bluff overlooking the Blue River Valley is a Second Empire-style home once known as the **Pesthouse**. The building received its name and notoriety from having lodged victims of a smallpox outbreak. Charles Dayton Morgan, a lawyer, banker, and state representative, had the house constructed in the late 1860s. In 1902 the county bought the building for $2,900 in order to isolate smallpox sufferers. During a six-week span, the pestilence claimed 13 lives and infected 87 others. The house remained vacant for long periods after 1902. Two other families, prior to the present owners, tried to restore the home, but vandals and fire hampered progress. It is now restored and is one of the most impressive homes in town.

Return to Main St. and continue west about *.5 m.* On the left, at 517 W. Main, set off the road and facing a circular drive, is a Federal-style white stucco and brick house with a two-story veranda referred to as the **John Lustig house**. John J. Lehmanowski, a local Lutheran minister, had this home constructed in 1840. No ordinary clergyman, Lehmanowski, a Frenchman of Polish extraction, served as a colonel in Napoleon's Imperial Guard, seeing action in Spain, Russia, and at Waterloo. Escaping a firing squad after the Battle of Waterloo (1815), Count Lehmanowski fled to America, became a Lutheran pastor, and served parishes in Kentucky and southern Indiana before coming to Knightstown. He left Knightstown in 1859 or 1860 and died in Kansas City.

Continue west on Main St. (US 40) approximately *4.5 m.* to Charlottesville, turn left, and cross the abandoned right-of-way of a double-tracked Penn Central main line that once linked St. Louis and New York City but now has been mostly abandoned between Terre Haute and Columbus, Ohio. Enter **RUSH COUNTY** (p. 19,604; 408 sq. m.), which was organized in 1821. It was named for Dr. Benjamin Rush (1745-1813), the renowned physician in the Revolutionary War era. The county's gently rolling and flat landscape, watered by the Flatrock and the Blue rivers and tributaries, has given it, despite its small population, an enviable agricultural history. From its inception, the county has been known for its excellent crops and livestock. Though only 71st in population, the county is among the leaders in the production of corn, soybeans, winter wheat, and hay, and in annual sales of livestock, particularly hogs. About 90 percent of county land is tilled. Furniture making traditionally has been a major force in the county's economy.

Continue south *2 m.*, turn left *1.7 m.* onto CR 1000N, and left at CR 725W. At *.3 m.*, down a long lane to the right, is **Beech church**, which served free blacks who had come into the area by the 1830s with Quakers or friends of Quakers. In 1832 the Beech community residents decided to merge their various religious affiliations and adopt the African Methodist

Episcopal (AME) church as their denomination. A log church was erected in 1838 and replaced by the present white frame building in 1860. The Indiana AME Conference was organized here in 1840. Since 1914 annual homecomings have taken place on the church grounds.

Return to CR 1000N, turn right *.2 m.*, and left on CR 750 for *1 m.* Turn left again and enter **CARTHAGE** (p. 886). Quakers from North Carolina settled Carthage in the early 1830s, and they named their new town for their previous home. Henry Henley, one of the founders, contributed $1,000 to establish a free library. The **Henley Memorial Library**, located on Main St. *.5 m.* west from the town limits on the right and completed in 1902, displays the face of Henry Henley carved in stone high over its front doors. Since 1930 the large Container Corporation of America paper mill has been a fixture at the south edge of town.

Return on Main St. approximately *4 m.* to IND 140, bordering a buildup of modern residences interspersed with excellent restorations and old burial grounds along the rim of the Blue River Valley. Turn right on IND 140 and continue south *.8 m.* to the **Indiana Soldiers' and Sailors' Children's Home** on the left. The state-owned and -operated facility originated in 1866 as a Civil War soldiers' home. In 1867 it admitted veterans and their families. After 1871 it became solely a children's home, veterans being moved to Dayton, Ohio. The population of the home has fluctuated over the years, reaching a high of over 1,000 children during the depression of the 1930s, although usually less than half this number live on the grounds. Interesting historical attractions on the more than 400 acres include the eclectically styled administration building, dating from 1887, and Lincoln Hall, designed by John Hasecoster, dedicated in 1892 as a chapel. Lincoln Hall's two exceptional stained-glass windows, costing $600 each in 1892, feature full-size portraits of a Civil War soldier and sailor, respectively. The windows are visible from the road on the southwest side of the campus.

Continue south on IND 140 past the home (IND 140 ends a short distance past the home and becomes a county road) *2.1 m.* and turn left onto CR 900N. Cross IND 3 at *3.3 m.* and continue *.3 m.* to **MAYS** (town unmarked), founded in 1884 as Mays Station after an early resident. The octagonal **Hall-Crull home** with white siding is on the left *2.2 m.* east on CR 900N. William S. Hall, a school administrator and father of 16, from two marriages, built this structure in 1855 from a design created by Orson Squire Fowler, the famed phrenologist, of New York. Hall, who was an experienced cabinetmaker, employed this rare construction so that the heat could be centrally located. Built from virgin timber cleared from the site, the eight-sided house is distinguished from like structures by its recessed two-story verandas. (*NRHP*)

Return to IND 3, turn left, and proceed south *8.1 m.* to **RUSHVILLE** (p. 6,113). Dr. William B. Laughlin, sometimes referred to as "The Father of Rushville," donated the land for the county seat and requested that it and the county be named for his mentor, Dr. Benjamin Rush. There probably has been no time in Rushville's past when it was without a furniture manufacturer. Former producers and their products include Abe Bowen's "Table Factory," the parlor and library tables of the Park Furniture Company, the bedroom furniture of the Rushville Furniture Company, and the general furnishings of Innis Pearce and Company. The **Schnadig Corporation**, a national leader in upholstered furniture production, came to Rushville in 1935 as the International Furniture Company. Through a series of purchases, the company became the Schnadig Corporation in 1953. It is one of the city's largest employers. The plant occupies two blocks between 11th and 13th sts. on N. George St., located four blocks east of IND 3 (Main St.).

Turn right *.1 m.* past the city limits sign onto Park Blvd. and follow it to the left for *.3 m.* On the right is the **Hackleman log cabin**, located in Rush Memorial Park. The cabin is the birthplace of Brig. Gen. Pleasant Adams Hackleman, the only Indiana general killed during the Civil War. Hackleman died in 1862 from wounds received while commanding a brigade of the Army of the Tennessee in battle at Corinth, Mississippi. Born in neighboring Franklin County in 1814, Hackleman, an aspiring lawyer, moved to Rushville in 1837. A county judge and clerk, the industrious Hackleman also joined with his brother Oliver C. Hackleman in 1840 to start a Whig paper, the forerunner of today's *Rushville Daily Republican*. He served as a state representative but lost two congressional races. Lincoln appointed him to the abortive peace conference that met in Washington, D.C., just prior to the Civil War. The Hackleman cabin was moved to Rushville from Franklin County in 1923 and is maintained by the Daughters of the American Revolution (DAR).

From the Hackleman cabin bear left onto N. Sexton St., drive *.3 m.*, turn left onto 11th St., and right on Harrison to 601, the former **Wendell L. Willkie home**, which served as office and home for Willkie in his 1940 run for the presidency. During the campaign Willkie rented the house and purchased it from his mother-in-law, Mrs. Phil Wilk, in 1942. After her death Willkie continued to maintain the residence, as did his heirs. Willkie, born in Elwood, "adopted" Rushville as his home after marrying a local girl, Edith Wilk, in 1918. While a Republican presidential candidate, Willkie often told audiences that he wanted to give the nation a "Rushville way of living." At the time of his premature death in 1944, he reportedly was the county's largest landowner with five farms, the largest stockholder in the Rushville National Bank, and the owner of four downtown business buildings.

Return to 7th St. and go three blocks east to Perkins St. The **Wolfe house**, on the southwest corner, is restored and available for public meetings and activities. E. H. Wolfe, son of Lt. Col. Joel Wolfe, built the brick Italianate structure in 1869. A single dwelling for numerous families, as the years went by the old house declined, most recently into an apartment house. The Rush County Historical Society purchased the building in 1974. Volunteers and workers under the Comprehensive Employment Training Act (CETA) reversed the deterioration and returned the home to its former usefulness.

Immediately south is the **Rush County Museum** (619 N. Perkins). The museum has delighted residents for over 40 years with its interesting exhibits and is housed in the former residence of the John K. Gowdy family. Gowdy (1843-1918) was a prominent local and state political leader. His successful tenure as chairman of the state Republican Committee in the 1890s brought him to the attention of national party leaders. In 1897 President William McKinley appointed Gowdy consul general to Paris. During his eight and one-half years of service Gowdy received numerous accolades and decorations, including the French Legion of Honor. He was instrumental in having the body of John Paul Jones disinterred and re-

turned to the United States for proper burial at Annapolis. In 1940 Gowdy's Victorian home was deeded to the Rush County Historical Society (organized 1922). The home and carriage house contain an exceptional collection of Indian artifacts and 19th-century memorabilia. Of particular interest is a salesman's sample of a Kennedy covered bridge. For three generations the Rushville-based Kennedy family constructed some of the sturdiest and most picturesque covered bridges in central and southeastern Indiana from 1870 to 1918. The Kennedy salesman would place this model of his company's product between two chairs and stand on it to demonstrate its durability.

Proceed south on Perkins St. to the **Rush County Courthouse** on the right. The present building is the third seat of justice occupying the town square. The Italian Renaissance-style structure cost over a quarter of a million dollars to build in 1896-98. Citizens burdened by the economic depression angrily petitioned against this expenditure, but they failed to sway the county commissioners. A. W. Rush and Son of Grand Rapids, Michigan, designed the building, and P. H. McCormack and Company of Columbus, Indiana, constructed it. The courthouse exterior of buff color Bedford stone rests on a foundation of Niagara limestone. If extended upwards, the outside walls would eventually converge to form a pyramid—a composition intended for strength, elevation, and beauty. The steel-girded interior is faced with marble, quarter-sawed oak, tile, and mosaics. Flanking the entrance to a courtroom on the third floor are two large stained-glass windows. One window depicts the scales of justice, and the other is the largest known rendition of the state seal. On the lawn is a tablet honoring Dr. William B. Laughlin. Note the cornerstone carvings behind the Laughlin marker of a ribbon-tied shock of grain placed between two cornstalks, symbols of Rush County's agricultural preeminence. (*NRHP*)

Return to 3rd St. and turn right to Julian St. On the right is the Knights of Columbus building on the site of the **Rushville Academy**, one of the earliest private girls' schools in the state. Constructed in 1843 as the Rushville Seminary, the building was sold to the city in 1866 for public education.

Just north of the intersection of Julian and 3rd sts. is a long red brick building which once served as a **repair shop and barns** for the Indianapolis and Cincinnati Traction Company interurban cars that ran between Rushville and Indianapolis from 1905 to 1932.

Return to 2nd St. (IND 44) and drive east .6 m. through **Sycamore Row**, so called because of the arch of old Sycamore trees, to **East Hill Cemetery** on the right. Here are buried two famed Rush County residents. The Wendell Willkie plot is in the back center, partially hidden by trees. The grave is marked by a 12-ft.-high North Carolina pink granite cross which sits on a "trinity" base of three steps. Lying open on the ground in front of the cross is a large granite book with quotations carved on the book's pages, chosen by Mrs. Willkie, from Wendell's speeches and from his well-known work *One World*. In *One World* Willkie made a strong plea for postwar cooperation. The visitor can sit on the stone bench near the book and read the citations. Around the east end of the cemetery, near the front, is a huge marble obelisk indicating the grave of Knowles Shaw, a Disciples of Christ evangelist and renowned hymn writer of the last century. Born in 1834, Shaw grew up across from the Big Flat Rock Church near Milroy. In this church he preached his first sermon. His stepfather taught him the fundamentals of music. Shaw published 5 gospel songbooks and over 100 gospel songs. The most popular of his hymns is "Bringing in the Sheaves." He died in an 1878 Texas train wreck.

Return on 2nd St. and drive west to the **Durbin Apartments** on the left. The building marks a succession of inns extending from the 1840s to the late 1970s. Leo and Mary Durbin leased and then in 1926 bought the Lollis Hotel. They developed the Durbin Hotel into a Hoosier landmark, noted for its courtesy, comfort, and cuisine. National recognition came in 1940 when the Willkie national campaign made its headquarters in the Durbin. Four Durbin sons went into the hotel business, prompting a *Newsweek* story to portray the family as a "hotel clan." Hard times came to the hotel in the 1970s. Interstate roads bypassed Rushville, and inflation and the energy crisis cut down on business travelers and vacationers. Under these pressures, the old hotel closed on Christmas Eve, 1979. It was purchased and reopened the next month, but the new owners failed, and its days as a celebrated hotel ended. (*NRHP*) Continue west on US 52 to the **Pioneer Hi-Bred International, Inc.**, on

the right *3.3 m.*, one of the world's largest seed corn production plants.

Return to IND 3 in Rushville and turn right paralleling the New York Central's abandoned Louisville, Kentucky-Elkhart right-of-way *8 m.* through a portion of Rush County's finest farmland to IND 244. Directly east is the town of **MILROY**. The origin of this pleasant rural village's name remains a mystery. Did Roy Miller, a local distiller, permit the town fathers to use a combination of his names? Or, did the men who platted the town in 1830 have knowledge of the exploits of Hoosier pioneer Brig. Gen. Samuel Milroy? The area surrounding Milroy is settled by a number of Amish, and on occasion the traveler will see an Amish horse and buggy.

Go west on IND 244 *3.2 m.* to CR 500W. Strike out on CR 500W south for about *.5 m.* before bearing right onto CR 840S. After *1.2 m.* the roadway makes a sharp bend and disappears into an Emmett Kennedy covered bridge. This 330-ft. structure, built in 1886, is the longest two-span bridge in use in Indiana. Spanning Flatrock River, the bridge is the portal to the languishing but enchanting hamlet of **MOSCOW**, apparently named for the Russian city, but no one knows why. In the Moscow cemetery stands the life-size marble **statue of John Owens**, felled by acute appendicitis in 1896 at age 36. The grief-stricken parents sent to Italy to have the monument carved. The ice and snow of the following winter seemed to Mrs. Owens unmercifully harsh for the bare-headed likeness of her son. The family, therefore, had the Italians sculpt a fedora for the effigy. Unfortunately, through vandalism or normal wear and tear, the head of John Owens is exposed once more to the elements.

Return to IND 3 and resume the tour south *3 m.* to **DECATUR COUNTY** (p. 23,841; 373 sq. m.). Organized in 1821, Decatur County is named for Commodore Stephen Decatur, naval hero of the 1812 conflict with England and the wars with the Mediterranean pirates in 1803 and 1815. An experienced duelist, Decatur died from wounds received in an 1820 pistol confrontation. He is remembered for a patriotic toast delivered in 1816: "Our country! In her intercourse with foreign nations may she always be in the right; but our country, right or wrong." The Eggleston brothers, Edward and George, lived a few years of their youth in Decatur County in the early 1850s. A cloak-and-dagger episode in the Milford area during their residence later formed the basic plot of Edward's famous novel *The Hoosier Schoolmaster* (1871). George's novel *Jack Shelby* (1906) also drew on Decatur County experiences and personages.

The county seat of **GREENSBURG** (p. 9,254) is *7 m.* south of the county line on IND 3. Col. Thomas Hendricks, brother of an Indiana governor and uncle to a United States vice-president, founded the town in 1820. Greensburg incorporated as a town in 1837, and as a city in 1859. Tradition has it that Hendricks's wife suggested the name of Greensburg in honor of her Greensburg, Pennsylvania, hometown, named in honor of Revolutionary War hero Maj. Gen. Nathanael Greene.

Known principally for its live tree protruding from the courthouse tower, Greensburg should also be recognized for the prominent citizens it has shared with the public. For example, Carl G. Fisher (1874-1939), born in Greensburg, left school after the sixth grade, went on to help found the Indianapolis Motor Speedway, to develop Miami Beach, and to spearhead the construction of two great thruways, the Lincoln and the Dixie highways. Another race car enthusiast, Wilbur Shaw (1902-1954), a three-time winner of the Indianapolis 500 and president of the Speedway, spent a portion of his youth in Greensburg. Congressman, state senator, and lieutenant governor Will Cumback (1829-1905) lived 52 years in the city. Hamilton Mercer, editor of the *Greensburg Democrat*, wrote the book *The Reproach of Capital Punishment*, a 1914 polemic against this form of justice. A leading socialist, Julius Augustus Wayland, published his influential paper *Coming Nation* in Greensburg for slightly more than a year, 1893-94. Oscar R. Ewing, one-time federal security administrator, was a native.

Besides its share of interesting personalities, Greensburg also holds a state record—the coldest day. On Groundhog Day, 1951, *3 m.* south of the city, the government thermometer stood at -35 degrees. City fathers, fearing a negative reaction of an "icebox image" by potential employers, moved the weather station to the Municipal Waterworks, hoping for warmer readings. An enduring mystery of the town involves the whereabouts of a 1,500-lb. replica of the city, built in 1949 for display in Belgium. Selected as "The City of Democracy" in 1949

by the United States Junior Chamber of Commerce, Greensburg spent $12,000 to reproduce itself in miniature. In 1951 the display, 44 ft. in circumference, toured the United States as part of a State Department exhibit entitled "America 1950." No one has seen it since.

At IND 46 turn east and continue past the **Delta Faucet Company** on the right. Reportedly the largest factory of its kind in the world, it is Greensburg's principal employer. Continue to the **Decatur County Courthouse** on the left. (Park on Franklin St., just east of the courthouse square.) The building was completed in 1860 at a cost of $120,000 to replace the original 1827 structure. William Jennings Bryan, while on a speaking tour in 1908, reportedly declared the courthouse to be the finest specimen of Gothic architecture he had seen in his travels. Greensburg's most famous landmark is the tree growing from the courthouse tower. A succession of healthy, growing **tower trees** have delighted and puzzled onlookers for more than a century. Theories abound on the reasons for the timber's longevity. Their verification as members of the large-tooth Aspen family led a columnist to jest that the trees' tenacity "was based on their ability to hang on by the skin of their big teeth." The most likely explanation is that rain, seeping through cracks, nourished seeds embedded in a filler of gravel and soil waste transferred to the tower at the time of its construction. When a tower tree becomes so large as to threaten the structure's safety, it is usually trimmed and existing shoots nurtured. (*NRHP/HABSI*)

Walk one block northwest of the courthouse square to 215 N. Broadway, the location of the **Knights of Pythias Building and Theatre**. This storefront-type building was erected in 1899 from St. Louis pressed stone with Bedford stone trimmings. The edifice gained an addition in 1908 with the construction of an opera house, costing around $40,000. The theater's opening night presentation of "The Girl Question" grossed over $7,000 from tickets selling as high as $25 each. Later, the K of P Theatre featured movies, both silent and talkies. It is said that the theater was the first in this part of the state to run sound movies and the first to offer air conditioning for summer comfort. The theater was closed in 1957. However, the building has been remodeled and houses the Decatur County Historical Society Museum, which opened in November 1977. (*NRHP*)

1882 lithograph of Greensburg

Continue north, turn right one block north of Central St., and right on Franklin St. to the former **B. B. Harris home** (the second house on the right north of Central St.). Harris passed through the area while serving as a scout for Morgan's Raiders during the Civil War and returned after the conflict to found the village of Harris City, *5 m.* south of Greensburg. He opened a large limestone quarry there, set up his company town, and delivered stone for use in the Indiana Statehouse, the United States Customhouse in Cincinnati, and other comparable structures. The three-story Greek Revival-style brick home was completed in 1875, shortly after Harris's death. The private residence has been refurbished by the present owners.

Return to Main St. and turn left to **Wilderwood**, a brick and stone house at 446 E. Main St. Brig. Gen. John T. Wilder, who led the unusual fighting force, the "Lightning Brigade," during the Civil War, built this home shortly after his return. Because his brigade often chased Confederate raiders on horseback,

Wilder set his men on mounts, and their swift dispatch earned them their sobriquet. Wilder also armed his band with Spencer repeating rifles. His brigade was the first unit to be so armed in the Civil War. Shortly after the construction of Wilderwood, the general moved to Chattanooga, Tennessee, served once as its mayor, and was buried there in 1917.

Return west on Main St. and left onto Michigan St. (US 421). Proceed *.8 m.*, turn right onto Millhousen Rd. (this road becomes CR 60E), and continue *7.8 m.* to CR 820S. Turn left into the village of **MILLHOUSEN** (p. 214). This remote and picturesque hamlet was founded by German Catholics in the mid-1830s and named for leader Maximilian Schneider's German home. Millhousen quickly became a religious center for southeast Indiana. The first parish in the county was started here in the 1830s, and the first log church was erected in the early 1840s. The majestic **St. Mary's** (also known as Immaculate Conception) **Catholic Church** is *1.5 m.* from CR 60E. This is the third church built on the site, being completed in 1869, and it closely resembles similar Gothic-style structures in Germany. Towering 175 ft. into the air, the 1893-built steeple is visible for miles. In 1899 a Howard tower clock was added to the steeple's facade. Take time to drive around the rolling and winding streets and notice the quantity of locally produced brick used for the buildings.

Return to CR 60E, continue south for about *2 m.*, turn right onto CR 1000S, travel west *5 m.*, and turn right onto CR 350W. On the left *1.2 m.*, in the front yard of a farmhouse, is the marker indicating the **1890 United States Center of Population**. The 9-ft.-tall Bedford stone obelisk was erected in 1891 courtesy of the *Chicago Herald*. More than 10,000 spectators showed up for the marker's dedication. A legend has it that four gold dollars, one at each corner of the 9,500-lb.-marker, were placed on a foundation 5 ft. deep in the ground at the time it was erected. Some believers chipped away at the foundation to find the gold but were unsuccessful.

Reverse direction and proceed south on CR 350W approximately *2 m.* to CR 1050S, and turn right into **WESTPORT** (p. 1,450), a small rural community laid out in 1836 and which grew with the local stone quarry. Turn left onto Main St. and drive *1.7 m.* east. On the left, set off from the main thoroughfare, is the **Westport Covered Bridge**. Built in 1880 by A. M. Kennedy and Sons, the bridge is noted for its ledge stone foundation on the sides that helps to anchor the structure with the bank. This last remaining covered bridge in Decatur County is not passable. (*NRHP*)

Return west on Main St., passing through the downtown area of Westport, and turn right onto IND 3. The hamlet of **LETTS**, an unincorporated town laid out in 1882 and named for Allen Lett, the first postmaster, is *3.6 m.* north. Proceed *5.2 m.* farther and turn left at the intersection with IND 46.

The Bartholomew County line is *6.8 m.* west on IND 46 (for a description of the county see the Columbus essay). The town of **HARTS-VILLE** (p. 370) is *.5 m.* west of the county border. Possibly named for the pioneer Hart family, the town was established in 1832. The Hartsville town square is *.5 m.* farther on the right. Located on the square are several plaques. One inscription denotes the site of **Hartsville College**. The college opened in 1850 as a United Brethren in Christ institution. The

school moved to Huntington, Indiana, in 1897 (Huntington College, see Tour 2) after a schism in the denomination over the admission of members from secret societies. The three-story brick main building, constructed during the Civil War, mysteriously burned six months after its closing. United Brethren Bishop Milton Wright, the father of the Wright Brothers of Kitty Hawk fame, taught in the college from 1868 to 1873. An early professor at the school, Benjamin Markley Nyce, patented the Nyce Fruit Preserving House in 1858—the precursor of the modern refrigerator.

Another historical marker in the square testifies to the good fortune of Pvt. Barton W. Mitchell, whose family moved to Hartsville shortly after he enlisted in Indianapolis for Civil War duty. Mitchell found the famous "Lee's Lost Order" wrapped around a package of cigars in September 1862, while resting from battle at a spot near Frederick, Maryland. Of questionable authenticity is the marker's further statement that the discovery of the order, which detailed Lee's movements, gave the North an opportunity for a victory at Antietam. Private Mitchell is buried in the Baptist cemetery at Hartsville.

NEWBERN, a hamlet established in 1832 and named for New Bern, North Carolina, the hometown of a founder, is *4 m.* west of Hartsville on IND 46 over hills and through woodlands. Drive *1.5 m.* farther. Turn right onto IND 9 and go north *4.7 m.* to the town limits of **HOPE** (p. 2,185). [For an alternate route between Hartsville and Hope, take the road northwest of the square (becomes CR 500N) *4 m.* passing a beautiful lake with a spillway directly facing the road north.] South Carolinian Moravians settled Hope in 1830 as part of the church's mission into frontier areas. Originally designated Goshen (a fertile part of Egypt where the Israelites settled until the Exodus), the Moravians changed the town's name to Hope after discovering another Goshen in Elkhart County.

The **Moravian Church and parsonage** are *.4 m.* past the town limits sign, at the southwest corner of Main (IND 9) and Locust sts. The present church was dedicated in 1875, but the first sanctuary was erected in 1830. Hope's Moravian Church is one of only three left in the state serving this faith. The **Old Iron Gate**, next to the parsonage, commemorates the entrance to the Moravian Seminary for Young Ladies,

1866-81. The plaque adjacent to the gate recognizes several families who reunited annually for over 50 years.

At the end of Locust St., behind the church, is the old **Moravian Cemetery**, established in 1833. In the original section of the cemetery, called God's Acre, row after row of limestone markers are laid flat—flat because Moravians believe everyone is equal in death. Families typically are not buried together. Marital status, age, and sex differentiate the categories of graves (i.e., elderly bachelors, elderly spinsters, single young men, single young women, etc.). Buried in God's Acre is John Henry Kluge, whose gravestone inscription identifies him as the first white child born in Indiana, although historians think only that he was one of the first white children born within the state.

The town square is *.2 m.* north on Main St. On the west side of the town square lawn is the **Indiana Rural Letter Carriers Museum**. This display window type of museum features several items pertaining to early mail delivery, including a mail buggy which was designed by a Hope resident, Albert Hitchcock. The museum is illuminated 24 hours a day. The state's first successful Rural Free Delivery (RFD), and the second in the country, began here in 1896. On the northeast corner of the square is a well-maintained and picturesque bandstand.

Northwest of the square on Jackson St. is the **Yellow Trail Museum**. Located on the south side of the street about one-third block west of Main St., the museum was dedicated in 1975 and contains artifacts of local historical interest. The name was taken from an advertising scheme of a local filling station owner who years ago marked telephone poles with yellow paint, creating a trail which led directly to his place of business.

Continue north on IND 9 for *3.3 m.* to the **SHELBY COUNTY** (p. 39,887; 412 sq. m.) line. Organized in 1821, the state legislature named the new county in honor of the first governor of Kentucky, Isaac Shelby, an appropriate choice because many early county residents migrated from the state to the south of Indiana. Driving north on IND 9, corn and soybean fields issue reminders that no less than 14 international corn king titles have come to Shelby County farmers. **NORRISTOWN** (*1.1 m.* from the county line) is barely more than a crossroads hamlet named for its local physician Dr.

James Norris and platted in 1851. North *2.3 m.* is the turnoff for **GENEVA**. Laid out in 1853 and named for the Swiss city, today's Geneva is safely tucked away along the Flatrock River about *2 m.* east of IND 9. The **Winchester Methodist Episcopal Church and cemetery** are situated *1.7 m.* farther north on the left. The red brick building is dated 1872. Past the church *1 m.* is an unplatted wide place in the road called **WILSON** or **WILSON CORNER**. The small community evolved around a country store operated by the Wilson family.

North on IND 9 *4 m.* is the city of **SHELBYVILLE** (p. 14,989). This county seat is conveniently located *28 m.* southeast of Indianapolis. Over half of the land donated for the establishment of the town in 1822 came from John Hendricks. His son, Thomas A. Hendricks, was the unsuccessful Democratic running mate of Samuel Tilden in 1876 and vice-president under Grover Cleveland in 1885. Hendricks died less than nine months after his inauguration. Besides Hendricks, several other local citizens have received national recognition. Charles Major (1856-1913), a lawyer, is best known for his adventure story, *The Bears of Blue River*, and his 1898 novel *When Knighthood Was in Flower*. The former book is locally set. Seven-ft.-seven-in. Sandy Allen, the world's tallest woman according to the *Guinness Book of Records*, and race car driver Wilbur Shaw (see under Greensburg) are other former Shelbyville residents.

In this century's early decades Shelbyville was primarily a town of a single industry—furniture making. At one point in the 1920s, 19 furniture factories were in operation, making the town deserving of its nickname "Little Grand Rapids." The 1930s depression, along with southern competition and a growing scarcity of white oak and walnut, undermined the furniture business. The Davis-Birely Company, once the world's largest factory exclusively manufacturing tables, folded. A survivor, the Shelbyville Desk Company, closed its doors in 1973 after 88 years of existence. The plant was one of the nation's largest continuous operations among woodworking factories. Fortunately for the town's economic future, the industrial base is far more diversified now, with products ranging from fiberglass insulation to oil gaskets.

Proceed north on IND 9 (Harrison St.). The **Shelby County Courthouse** is *2 m.* on the left. This plain stone building was erected in 1936 on the site of the 1870s courthouse. Unlike most Indiana county seats, Shelbyville's courthouse has not been located on the central square since the 1870s.

Drive *.1 m.* and turn left onto Broadway. Two blocks on the right, between a firehouse and the former Shelbyville High School building, is the **Louis H. and Lena Firn Grover Museum** of the Shelby County Historical Society. The museum opened in 1981 in the former Elks Lodge building (erected in 1950). The museum houses exhibits that relate to specific areas of the life and history of Shelby County.

Reverse direction and proceed east on Broadway. Past the intersection with Harrison St. *.7 m.* is a historical marker on the left indicating the site of **Indiana's first railroad**. Judge William J. Peasley raised the funds for this experimental railroad that officially opened on July 4, 1834. Horse-pulled wooden cars carried passengers over wooden rails for one and one-fourth miles from the east side of Shelbyville to a picnic area on Lewis Creek. The venture was short-lived.

Return to Harrison St. and turn right. The **Public Square** is *.1 m.* north on Harrison. Once a place of beauty, the square had deteriorated over the years to an unattractive and unkempt parking lot. In the late 1970s the area became the first part of a $1.25 million downtown revitalization project, and it was reopened in its present splendor in 1980.

Highlighting the square are two art works. At the south end is the **Joseph Memorial Fountain**. Julius Joseph, a German immigrant and furniture factory operator, donated $5,000 at the time of his death in 1920 to erect a city fountain on the square. George H. Honig (1874-1962), a Rockport, Indiana, native, designed it in 1923. It features a group sculpture of three youths holding various implements of summer fun. Years of neglect resulted in the fountain's removal from the square in 1965, and it was stored in a city garage until the area was refurbished. At the square's north end is an Italian cast **bronze statue depicting Major's *Bears of Blue River* saga**. Designed by Mary Elizabeth Stout in 1929, the sculpture features Balsar Brent, the novel's hero, holding his two pet bear cubs, Tom and Jerry. Stout was living in Paris when she designed the sculpture, and a French boy was employed as the model. Upon its completion, the statue was placed at the en-

trance to the nearby Charles Major Elementary School where it remained until moved to its present location in 1980.

North of the square *.2 m.*, at the southeast corner of Harrison and Mechanic sts., is a historical marker standing in the fenced area of the old Fuller home. It commemorates the site of a **house where Thomas Hendricks resided** before moving to Indianapolis in 1860. Turn right onto Mechanic St., drive *.5 m.* east, and turn left onto Vine St. Proceed *.5 m.* and turn right onto Morris Ave. Straight ahead *.1 m.* is the entrance to the Shelby County Fairgrounds on the right. Located a short distance past the entrance on the left is the **Thomas Hendricks log cabin**. Hendricks was born in Zanesville, Ohio, in 1819, but moved with his family to Shelbyville by way of Madison when he was three. The cabin was reconstructed in 1962 from many of the logs of the first cabin built by his father, John Hendricks, on the east edge of Shelbyville near the point where Michigan Rd. crosses Little Blue River.

The **Cedar Ford Covered Bridge** is situated in the northeast corner of the fairgrounds near the track and grandstand. The 127 ft.-long structure was built by the Kennedy brothers in 1885. It originally spanned the Little Blue River about one and one-half miles northeast of its present location. Vandalism forced its removal to the present location in 1975.

Return to Mechanic St. and IND 9 (Harrison St.), turn right, and proceed north on IND 9. (IND 9 bears right outside of town.) On the right, a short distance beyond Mechanic St., a package liquor store occupies the former one-man factory of the **High-Speed Delivery Fork Company**. In the days before centralized traffic control and radio dispatching, wooden forks with orders tied between the prongs were handed up to crews of nonstop trains. Nearly the entire United States railroad system at one time depended on the forks for delivering train orders. Travel *11.5 m.* north and turn right onto US 52. Proceed east *3.7 m.* to the pleasant town of **MORRISTOWN** (p. 989), which was platted in 1828 and named for one of the founders, Samuel Morrison. The restored **Junction Railroad Depot** that serves as the chamber of commerce is *3 m.* on the right. The building served the Junction Railroad that ran between Shelbyville and Knightstown from 1849 to 1858. In front of the building is a refurbished caboose of a more recent vintage. (*NRHP*)

Continue *.2 m.* farther to the **Kopper Kettle Restaurant**, also on the right. Built as a grain elevator in the late 1840s, it was abandoned when the Junction Railroad was discontinued. The structure was purchased and converted into the Old Davis Tavern and hotel in 1858. The Kopper Kettle has been owned and operated by the same family since 1860. From 1885 to 1923 the restaurant and hotel went by the name of the Valley House. At the latter date, the hotel section was abandoned and the name was changed to the Kopper Kettle. Among the more famous who have dined in the building are James Whitcomb Riley, Henry Ford, Wendell Willkie, Herbert Hoover, and Charles Lindbergh. Although many exterior and interior changes have taken place over the years, the restaurant has maintained its high standards of service and good food in charming surroundings.

Return to IND 9 and turn right to the **HANCOCK COUNTY** (p. 43,939; 307 sq. m.) line, *.4 m.* north. Named for the first signer of the Declaration of Independence, John Hancock, the county was a comparatively late arrival among the central Indiana counties. The settlers, who migrated into the county after 1818, built their rough-hewn dwellings and mills along the banks of Little Swan Creek, Nameless Creek, Little Sugar Creek, and others among 11 quaintly named county waterways. The county was officially organized, effective January 1827. Hancock remains principally an agricultural county ranking high in the state in percentage of land devoted to farming. Bordering on Indianapolis has meant also that many of the county's residents drive west across the line to make a living.

GREENFIELD (p. 11,439), the county seat, is *4.5 m.* north of the county line on IND 9. Practically a suburb of Indianapolis, a substantial portion of the workers commute to the capital. The origins of the name Greenfield are unknown. The name was supplied for the county seat by a legislative committee in 1828, shortly before the town was laid out. On instructions, county commissioners established Greenfield in the center of the county along the National Rd. Tradition says that two founders employed string to measure the east-west dimensions of the county to determine the exact middle. Greenfield's post office was called Hancock until 1833 when Johnson County's Greenfield changed its name to Greenwood. In 1850 Greenfield was incorporated as a town, and as a city in the centennial year of 1876. The gas boom of the 1890s boosted the local economy with an increase of businesses, chiefly glass companies.

Greenfield is synonymous with **James Whitcomb Riley** (1849-1916), and local attractions and events are intimately related to the Hoosier poet's career. Riley's father, Reuben, a lawyer, settled in Greenfield in 1844. He was elected that year as the youngest member of the state legislature at the age of 26. The Rileys named their third child after the governor and senator, James Whitcomb. Young Jim Riley read voraciously but dreaded the boredom of formal schooling. Rather than pursue the scholarly path, Riley turned into a versatile instrumentalist, theatrical performer, and platform entertainer, and he crisscrossed the Indiana countryside painting barns or signs, or selling Bibles. Always playing to an audience, Riley wrote poetry and composed jingles in a down-home dialect that in time brought him riches and fame. Whether, in retrospect, he was the "last sweet sign of the Victorian Age" or a true interpreter of the Hoosier mind and manners, in his day his style of verse accorded him universal recognition. After his death on July 22, 1916, a controversy ensued between Indianapolis and Greenfield over the site of burial. Indianapolis won, and Riley reposes today beneath a stately columned Grecian memorial atop a hill in the northwest section of Crown Hill Cemetery.

Located *1.5 m.* farther north on IND 9 (State St.) is the **Hancock County Courthouse** on the right. Noted for its lofty turreted windows and its bell tower with a Howard clock, this Bedford limestone structure was built by Fort Wayne firms from 1896 to 1898. The fourth seat of justice in Hancock County, the courthouse contains elements of Romanesque and Gothic architectural styles. The cost of the building in 1898 was $242,600.

Situated at the courthouse's north entrance off US 40 (Main St.) is the **Riley statue**. Dedicated in 1918 and cast in bronze by the United Bronze Works in New York, the life-size figure holds a book and is attired in a robe similar to the one worn in 1907 when Indiana University awarded Riley an honorary Doctor of Literature degree. The inscription on the granite pedestal reads "James Whitcomb Riley/Erected by American School Children." Even before his death in 1916, the community's art association had begun collecting funds for a memorial. It deposited into a memorial fund $1 from each order sent by schoolchildren for Riley mementos. The objects included Riley busts, portrait buttons, and reproductions of Andersonian William Bixler's painting *Old Swimmin' Hole*. It was estimated at the time that one million children and 3,400 schools participated. The Indianapolis sculptress, Myra Reynolds Richards (1882-1934), had not completed the statue before Riley's death. She called on famed actor John Drew to model the lower half of the statue. At the unveiling, several old-timers expressed a dislike for the academic garb which they felt misrepresented the Jim they had known.

Turn east onto Main St., travel *.7 m.*, and turn left at Apple St. Immediately on the left is the **James Whitcomb Riley Memorial Park** entrance. The 100-acre city park was dedicated to the poet's memory in 1925. Situated at this end of the park is the Old Log Jail Museum and the nearby Hancock County Historical Society Museum. The **Old Log Jail Museum** is the restored third jail of Hancock County which was used from 1853 to 1874. Operated by the Hancock County Historical Society, the jail is made up of four rooms with 1-ft.-thick walls. An interesting feature is the prisoner room with wood floors heavily laced with old square nails—an imaginative measure to prevent escape by sawing through the logs.

Near the jail is the **Old Chapel**, the former Philadelphia (Indiana) United Methodist Church, a white frame structure topped by a belfry, built around 1865 and abandoned in 1970. The building was acquired by the Hancock County Historical Society, which moved it six miles east to its present location in 1980.

A few yards north of the two museums is a spot on Brandywine Creek designated as **Riley's Old Swimmin' Hole**, located appropriately near the park's modern swimming pool. Brandywine Creek—the creek that inspired Riley's poem "Up and Down Old Brandywine"—threads through the park. The young Riley and his companions swam at various points along this stream. Swimming now is prohibited in Brandywine Creek.

Return west on US 40 *.8 m.* (or one block west of the intersection with IND 9) and turn right onto Pennsylvania St. North one block, on the northeast corner of Pennsylvania and North sts., is the former **Riley Elementary School**. The Neo-Gothic stone structure was erected in 1895 and served as Greenfield High School for many years. Closed as a school in May 1980, the structurally sound building was sold to Historic Landmarks of Greenfield, which converted it into condominiums in late 1982. (*NRHP*)

Go back to Main St., turn right, and travel one block west. The **Riley home**, at 250 W. Main on the right, captures the playful atmosphere of the poet's youth. Reuben Riley built the eight-room house in 1849-50. Reuben's expertise as a carpenter can be seen in the home's semi-spiral walnut stairway. He made use of material from his log home on the same site (the birthplace of James Whitcomb) in the kitchen of the new house. Young Jim grew up under this roof until his mother died in 1870 and financial reverses compelled Reuben to sell the place. Later, in 1893, James purchased the old homestead, renting it until 1912 when his sister-in-law Julia came to live there. The city bought it from Riley heirs in 1936 for $3,500. Remarkably, the Riley Old Home Society refurbished the structure in time for a May 1937 opening. The green shuttered, two-story, white frame home still has that lived-in feeling, and its coziness reflects the warmth of the black walnut woodwork and the charming clutter of a mid-Victorian home. Moreover, the homey touch is a consequence of over 40 years as a restored shrine welcoming thousands of tourists. Among the artifacts in the home is the original plaster cast of the bust of Riley created by Myra Richards. (*NRHP*)

The next door east of the Riley home is the **former home of John F. Mitchell, Jr.** (1883-1972), Riley's close friend. The Mitchell family of Greenfield, beginning with William in the mid-19th century, were pioneers in Indiana journalism. They founded and published the *Hancock Democrat* and later printed works, including Riley's verses, under the label The Old Swimming Hole Press, Inc. John F. Mitchell's mother, Minnie Belle Mitchell, wrote two books about Riley, *Hoosier Boy* and *James Whitcomb Riley as I Knew Him*. The 1893 two-story frame house was bought by the city in 1973. It is now called the **Riley Museum** and is used as an annex to the Riley home and for civic functions.

Among the writings of John F. Mitchell, Jr., is the book *The Rooster: Its Origins as a*

James Whitcomb Riley home

Indiana Historical Society (Peat Collection)

Democratic Emblem (1913). The rooster, the once-popular symbol of the Democratic party, had its genesis in Greenfield during the 1840 presidential campaign. Joseph Chapman, the local Democratic orator and saloon owner, was requested by the state leaders to "crow" (boast) about the party and whip up some votes. The Whigs, learning of the instructions to the silver-tongued speaker, centered their attack on the "crowing" of Chapman. The Democrats turned the phrase "Crow, Chapman, Crow" to their advantage, rallying around it and instituting the rooster as their insignia. A marker on E. Main near the entrance to Riley Park commemorates Greenfield as the birthplace of the Democratic Party Rooster.

Another neighbor of the Rileys was the Vawter family. Will Vawter (1871-1941) was the principal illustrator of Riley's books of verse. Born in Virginia, Will moved to Greenfield with his family at age six. His first illustrations appeared in John Mitchell's *Hancock Democrat*. Riley considered him a "natural" artist. Vawter moved to Brown County in 1908 as a pioneer member of that county's artist colony. He is buried in Greenfield.

Continue west on US 40 *1.3 m.* On the left is the **Eli Lilly and Company Laboratories**, a major factor in the city's economic life since 1913. In that year the Indianapolis-based pharmaceutical firm made its first out-of-city expansion and began construction of a biological division on 150 acres, then *2 m.* west of Greenfield. The Bedford Stone and Construction Company erected three Spanish-style buildings to house the resources used in research and production of antitoxins and vaccines. The design was the idea of then chairman of the board, Josiah K. Lilly, Sr., who first admired the style while visiting California. The middle of the three buildings features a 60-ft.-high tower. The structures functioned partly as barns, lodging a variety of test animals, while the surrounding fields yielded plants for experimentation. The firm led in the production of needed medication and antibiotics during two world wars. In the post-World War II period biological operations gave way to an emphasis on agricultural research. Greenfield annexed a portion of the area in the early 1960s, thereby increasing the city's tax base. The laboratories are housed in 70 buildings located on over 800 acres. It is the largest employer in the Greenfield area. (*NRHP*)

West of the Lilly complex *2 m.* is **PHILADELPHIA**, the former home of Mrs. Mary Alice Gray (1850-1924), the "Little Orphant Annie" of Riley's celebrated poem. Orphaned as an infant, she boarded with the Rileys as a domestic when she was about 10 years old. Although there less than a year, Mary became a cherished playmate of James Whitcomb. Later, Riley undertook a search for his childhood friend—he not knowing she lived nearby, she not knowing he had immortalized her as Annie. At one point, she responded to a newspaper ad placed by Riley, but his illness prevented the long-sought reunion. After his death, Mary, as Annie, thrilled hundreds of children with her school visits. To view the house, continue west *.8 m.* to Spring Lake Rd. at US 40 and CR 250W (just past the flashing yellow lights). Turn south for *.8 m.* The white frame house on the right has undergone remodeling.

Return to US 40 and proceed west *.3 m.* to the entrance of Sugar Creek Park, beside the Philadelphia Cemetery. Here is a marker to the memory of Mary Alice Gray.

Return to US 40 and IND 9 in Greenfield. Turn left, travel north on IND 9 *3.9 m.*, and turn right onto CR 400N. At CR 300E, *1.1 m.* on the left, is the beginning of the **Irving Game Farm**. C. C. Irving of Irving Materials, Inc., a producer of ready-mixed construction materials, developed this 200-acre area of grassy farmland into the home of a surprisingly wide collection of wild animals from throughout the world. Among the animals and birds roaming this scenic, nearly free environment are zebras, camels, llamas, antelopes, ostriches, and deer from China and India. The peaceful, uncaged setting provides a welcome break from the traditionally confined environment of the zoo. Continue *.4 m.* farther east past the intersection of the two county roads. After viewing the preserve's extreme southeastern edge, return to the junction and proceed north on CR 300E through the farm's main area, viewing wild animals on either side of the road.

Drive *1.1 m.* north on CR 300E and turn left at CR 500N. Located *1.2 m.* west is IND 9 at the village of **MAXWELL**. The area was laid out in 1881 as Junction, but it soon became Maxwell after an early railroad builder. Turn right onto IND 9 and drive *2.9 m.* to IND 234. On the northwest corner is the modernly designed **administration building of Irving Materials, Inc.** The company's exterior glass-walled headquarters also functions as a display gallery for Irving's big game trophies. Scores of lifelike examples of taxidermy stand vigilantly posed while animal heads and sprawling pelts line the interior walls.

Immediately north of the intersection is the hamlet of **EDEN**, originally named Lewisburg when platted in 1835. The tour reenters Madison County *3 m.* farther north. (For description of the county see Tour 3.) Continue *2.8 m.* to IND 67 and turn left. On the right *.2 m.* is the tan brick tower and red roof of the **Indiana Reformatory** administration building. Housing several thousand males between the ages of 16 and 30, the reformatory sits on over 2,000 acres, of which 31 are enclosed. A disastrous fire at the original Jeffersonville facility in 1918, and a desire to centralize the institution, led to the selection of this site, officially opened in 1923.

Turn around in front of the reformatory and head northeast on IND 67, turn left at IND 9, and drive north approximately *1 m.* to the **PENDLETON** (p. 2,130) town limits. This "cradle" of Madison County was platted in 1823 by Thomas Pendleton, for whom the town was named. When Pendleton arrived, he found several scores of families who chose to build homes and mills beside the falls of Fall Creek.

Continue north and turn right *.2 m.* beyond State St. into **Pendleton Falls Park**. Long before the city purchased and developed the park in the early 1920s, visitors flocked here to bathe in the pool beneath the picturesque waterfall. The city enlarged the pond area, placing an ornamental lighthouse in the center, and for years children and adults enjoyed swimming in the cool, pure water of the naturally fed pool. Near the falls in 1824, three whites found guilty of killing a group of Indians (see Markleville) were hanged. Here, too, in 1843 former slave and abolitionist leader Frederick Douglass was assaulted for his antislavery views. A large stone marker in the park's front lawn notes these and other occurrences. Bear to the left after entering the park. Located on the right, near the pond, is the park's cannon, Whistling Dick. Set in a stone pedestal, the cannon once was employed as a political as well as a military weapon. Its owner, Stephen "Daddy" Hair, a Civil War artillerist, Republican, and jester,

would shoot the cannon at election time to pro-
voke defeated Democrats. Continue driving on
the road through the park bearing to the left. A
short distance on the left is the **Pendleton Historical Museum, Inc**. Dedicated in 1981, the
two-story remodeled building was formerly the
park's bathhouse. Inside are displays and artifacts of local historical interest.

Continue ahead approximately *.7 m.* to
IND 9 at **HUNTSVILLE**. Enos Adamson and
Eleazer Hunt platted the area in 1830 and
named it for the pioneer Hunt family. Continue
north on IND 9 and 67 which become Business
IND 9 and Pendleton Ave. near Anderson. Proceed *5.7 m.* past Huntsville to the **Fisher Guide**

Plant at 2915 Pendleton Ave. on the outer
fringes of the city. Fisher Guide is the second
largest employer in Anderson (see Anderson essay) and produces a variety of automotive
lighting equipment. The plant celebrated its
50th year as a division of General Motors in
1978. The original building is still in use.

Follow Pendleton Ave. until it becomes
part of 17th St. in Anderson. Proceed *1.5 m.*
northeast from the Guide Plant and turn left
onto Meridian St. Travel north on Meridian approximately *1 m.* and turn right onto 5th St.
Take 5th St. east one block and turn right onto
Main near the Madison County Historic Home
and the end of the tour.

Lafayette-West Lafayette

Lafayette (p. 43,011) is the seat of **TIPPE-CANOE COUNTY** (p. 121,702; 502 sq. m.). Justly famous as the site of the Battle of Tippecanoe in 1811, the county was created in 1826, three years after the first whites settled in the area. The county was named for the Tippecanoe River, which ends its 166-mile journey when it joins the Wabash River above Lafayette. The Wabash River, which drains all the county's streams, enters the northeast corner and flows southwest through the northern half of the county. Small hills bordering the Wabash River and other tributaries provide some relief from the nearly level surface covering the remainder of the county. Highly urbanized with the growth of Lafayette and Purdue University, it is not surprising that educational services, followed by manufacturing and the retail trades, are the leading employers. The university in West Lafayette is the county's largest employer and an important factor in local economic stability. Local industry is diversified, and in addition to many small firms, includes such giants as the Aluminum Company of America (ALCOA), Eli Lilly and Company, Landis and Gyr, Fairfield Manufacturing Company, Caterpillar Tractor Company, and, most recently, the Subaru-Isuzu automobile plant.

The founder of Lafayette was William Digby, a boatman and general ne'er-do-well, whose knowledge of the river gave him the insight to locate a town near the head of navigation on the Wabash. He purchased the land on Christmas Eve, 1824, at the government land office in Crawfordsville. Digby named his town for the Marquis de Lafayette, the French hero of the American Revolution, who at that time was on tour of the United States. Although more of a gambler than a businessman (he sold nearly all of his holdings three days after the town was platted for a mere $240), Digby's choice of a townsite was shrewd. In 1826 the county commissioners chose Lafayette as the seat of newly formed Tippecanoe County. The town's location near the center of the county and its position on a navigable river were obvious advantages, but perhaps a more persuasive consideration was the decision of the town fathers to offer as a gift to the county nearly half of the original town plat.

Lafayette did not inspire much awe in its early years. Crawfordsville residents enjoyed referring to the town as "lay-flat" or "laugh-at." Nevertheless, the town prospered. Lafayette became an important entrepôt for shipping farm produce downstream by flatboat. The steamboat made an early appearance, the first arriving in 1826. Traffic soon increased dramatically. In the spring of 1832, 60 steamboats arrived and departed from the young town.

The construction of the Wabash and Erie Canal further stimulated the growth of the community. The canal, the longest in the United States, eventually ran from Toledo to Evansville by way of Lafayette. The upper section, between Lafayette and Toledo, opened on July 4, 1843. (The lower section was not finished for another 10 years.) Although the canal never made a profit for its investors, the commerce that flowed through it greatly benefited the communities along its course. Lafayette was one of the most heavily used ports along its entire route. Its population increased from 2,600 in 1843 to 6,129 in 1850. As it grew, the community acquired the reputation of a rough and bawdy canal town.

Small settlements sprang up on the west bank of the Wabash soon after Lafayette was founded. In 1847 John Purdue and others financed the construction of a covered bridge at Brown St. which lessened the population's dependence on ferries such as the one operated by William Digby. It was not until 1866 that Chauncey, renamed West Lafayette in 1888, was established.

Although the canal was important in Lafayette's growth, the railroad proved a far more reliable form of transportation. The first line, the Lafayette and Indianapolis, connected the two cities in December 1852. The New Albany and Salem was the second railroad to enter Lafayette. In return for entering the city, this line demanded that it be permitted to run its tracks down any street it chose and, in addition, that the citizens purchase $50,000 of New Albany and Salem stock. Despite some grumbling, the city council agreed, and the railroad built a line down what is now 5th St. Thus began Lafayette's intimate, but not altogether pleasant, relationship with the railroads.

Lafayette prospered as a meat-packing and merchandising center. One of the earliest industries in the town was a slaughterhouse which Henry T. Sample began in 1833. Sample made a fortune slaughtering hogs and shipping them downriver by flatboat and steamboat. In 1870 Leopold Dryfus, a German immigrant, opened a butcher shop, which later grew into the Dryfus Packing and Provision Company. The community's wealthiest men were retailers and wholesalers like Moses Fowler, John Purdue, Adams Earl, Cyrus Ball, and Martin Pierce. Earl, one of the most spectacularly successful, came to Lafayette in 1848 and opened a general store. In partnership with Fowler, he became one of the city's leading merchandisers and one of Indiana's wealthiest men. His interests expanded into banking, railroads, and land speculation. Shadeland Farm, located southwest of Lafayette, became a center for the raising of Hereford cattle, a breed which Earl imported from England in 1880.

An interesting event in Lafayette's history took place on August 17, 1859. This was the launching of America's first official airmail flight. Professor John Wise, a balloonist, theorized that at an altitude of two to three miles the wind always blew to the east. He proposed to carry a bag of mail on his balloon *Jupiter* from Lafayette to New York City. Unfortunately, Wise's balloon floated southwest instead of east, and the professor ended his flight near Crawfordsville. He sent the mail on to New York by train.

Almost as important to Lafayette as the coming of the canal and the railroad was the choice of Chauncey as the site of the state agricultural college. In 1862, under the provisions of the Morrill Act, the federal government granted each state public lands to be used to establish agricultural colleges. Indiana formally accepted the grant in 1865 and immediately be-

came embroiled in a four-year debate over the location of the proposed college. A breakthrough came when John Purdue offered the state $150,000 on condition that the new university be located in Tippecanoe County, that it bear his name, and that he be a member of the board of trustees. Lafayette senator John A. Stein persuasively led the fight for Purdue in the state legislature, which, in special session, acquiesced on May 6, 1869, the date now considered as that of the founding of the university. For the site of the school the trustees discussed several county locations, including Stockwell, Battle Ground, and Shawnee Mound, before choosing a 100-acre plot across the Wabash River and just west of the town of Chauncey.

In the beginning Purdue was a university more in name than in fact. Enrollments were very low, and most students were unqualified for the college course and had to attend preparatory classes. The state proved reluctant to provide adequate appropriations. Despite these problems the university gradually grew. Under James H. Smart, president from 1883 to 1900, student enrollments reached nearly 1,000; academic standards were stiffened; and financial stability was achieved.

By 1870 Lafayette's population exceeded 13,000, but the Panic of 1873 and the ensuing depression put an end to the town's boom era. Industrial production declined during the 1870s and 1880s. Hoping to end this industrial stagnation, business leaders formed the Lafayette Land and Improvement Company to buy up land for a belt railway on the east side of town. Construction of the publicly financed railway began in 1890. The community also persuaded the Monon to locate its shops in Lafayette by pledging public money and gifts of land. By the second decade of the 20th century, Lafayette's industrial economy had revived. Manufacturers such as Duncan Electric, Ross Gear and Tool (now Ross Gear division), Schwab Safe, and Dryfus Packing became an important part of Lafayette's industrial base.

Tragedy interrupted these prosperous years in March 1913 when the Wabash River, swollen by weeks of rain, turned into a raging torrent. A section of the Brown St. bridge collapsed, and the river washed away the Main St. bridge completely. Both Lafayette and West Lafayette were left isolated for several days. The waterworks and gas plant were under water; street lights were out of order; mail service, trains, and streetcars stopped. The floods crested at just under 33 ft. This was the worst flood in the history of Lafayette, and it served to remind the citizenry of the perils of life in a river town.

Lafayette soon recovered from the flood's physical devastation. During the 1920s the city's population grew by more than 16 percent. Purdue University, with an enrollment in 1926 of more than 3,700 students, had established itself as an educational and economic asset to the community. On April 4, 1922, radio station WBAA, authorized to use 200 watts power, went on the air at the university. At the time licensed by the Federal Radio Commission, WBAA is still in operation and is the state's oldest federally licensed radio station. In addition, the local economy with nearly 40 factories was comfortably diversified. On the less positive side, Lafayette had not shaken off its reputation, inherited from the canal days, as a wide-open town. Indeed, during the Prohibition era liquor flowed freely in the city. In 1931 federal agents regarded Lafayette as "one of the wettest cities in Indiana."

Lafayette's diversified economy probably softened the blow of the depression of the 1930s, but the shock was severe nevertheless. By late 1930 signs of economic distress were apparent. In November of that year Mayor John B. Hudson formed a community relief committee to help the needy. The committee raised its funds through private contributions and from the proceeds of high school exhibition games. The Chamber of Commerce organized a 35-acre garden between the Wabash Railroad and Greenbush St. where families could grow vegetables. Employees of the local Sears, Roebuck and Company store contributed one day's pay each month to the relief committee. Faced with massive unemployment in the building industry, the Lafayette Building Trades Council agreed to accept a 10 percent wage reduction. The Lafayette School Board cut teachers' salaries by the same percentage. When Purdue University announced that baseball, track, and other minor sports would be suspended for lack of funds, the Ross-Ade Foundation, established in 1923, came to the rescue by providing the university with financial assistance to continue the sports.

After 1932 Lafayette and West Lafayette were the recipients of aid through such federal work relief programs as the Civil Works Administration (CWA), the Works Progress Administration (WPA), and the Public Works Administration (PWA). These programs, which put thousands to work, included the development of Purdue Airport, the face-lifting of the county fairgrounds, the construction of a swimming pool in Columbian Park, and the building of a fieldhouse at Purdue. A bright spot in an otherwise dismal decade was ALCOA's decision in 1937 to locate a major plant in Lafayette.

World War II brought prosperity back to Lafayette. Even before the United States entered the war, President Roosevelt's rearmament program increased employment at local plants. Perhaps the biggest beneficiary was ALCOA, which produced aluminum for military aircraft. The National Homes Corporation, which began in 1940 as a shoestring operation, grew dramatically in response to the need for wartime housing. Within a decade the company was the nation's largest builder of prefabricated housing. Military training and research programs kept enrollments fluctuating at Purdue. At war's end the campus faced an invasion of veterans who enrolled under the provisions of the GI Bill. Purdue turned down 5,000 applicants in the fall of 1946, and total enrollment that academic year exceeded 14,000. This influx of new students placed an almost intolerable strain on housing in the Lafayette area.

During the 1950s and 1960s Lafayette enjoyed what the *Indianapolis Times* called a "smug" prosperity. Purdue continued as one of the nation's largest and fastest-growing educational institutions. A diversified industrial base kept the community's unemployment rate among the lowest in the state. After a series of scandals in the 1950s, gambling and prostitution no longer flourished openly in the city. Lafayette's problems largely had to do with the state of the downtown—its narrow streets, bad traffic patterns, congestion at railroad crossings, and a depressing slum. The flight of businesses to the suburbs began in 1952, when Mar-Jean Village opened, and accelerated during the 1960s and 1970s. The low point for the city center probably came in 1974 when the J. C. Penney store, located downtown since 1925, closed and moved to Tippecanoe Mall. During the 1960s Lafayette's population growth fell off and in the 1970s actually began to decline. In contrast suburban growth was rapid. Between

1960 and 1980 West Lafayette's population grew by 67 percent.

These developments did not pass unnoticed. In 1966 Lafayette formed a Redevelopment Commission to do something about the decline of the downtown. Early efforts concentrated on the cleaning up of the waterfront with the purchase of a dredge called the *Kleen Mary* and the development of a riverside park complex. Historic preservation also has played an important role in revitalization. Many downtown commercial buildings have been restored and renovated. An example is the former Kresge Building, which has been converted into a retail and restaurant complex called the River City Market. In addition, in the late 1980s, after six decades of attempts to relocate the railroad, rerouting parallel to the Wabash River got under way.

Lafayette has had its share of illustrious residents. Alva Roebuck, co-founder of Sears, Roebuck and Company, was a native. The father of the Mayo Brothers of Mayo Clinic fame practiced medicine here until malaria drove him out of the valley to a better climate. Henry L. Ellsworth lived here. He was later commissioner of patents, and his daughter, Annie, chose the first words to be sent by telegraph, "What hath God wrought." Numerous astronauts have been Purdue graduates, and its Nobel prize winners include Dr. Herbert C. Brown, Edward M. Purcell, Julian C. Schwinger, and Ben Roy Mottelson.

Several important themes emerge in this brief sketch of Lafayette's history. Transportation has always played an important role in the area's prosperity. The railroad and more recently the interstate highway have replaced the river and canal as arteries of commerce, but Lafayette's geographic location and transportation connections ensure its role as an important marketing and distribution center. The diversity of the industrial economy keeps Lafayette's unemployment rate below the state average even during recessionary times. Employment in the high-tech industry and services sector has gained in the 1980s, offsetting losses in manufacturing and construction employment. New industry finds the area attractive. In 1983 the Caterpillar Tractor Company opened a giant diesel engine plant on the east side of town. The Subaru-Isuzu plant under construction in 1987-88 south of town could employ as many as 1,700 persons when completed. Purdue University has 11 major building and beautification projects slated for completion by 1992. The school not only lends prestige to the communities of Lafayette and West Lafayette, but with its 11,000 employees and annual flood of students, it lends economic stability as well.

Lafayette-West Lafayette Attractions

Additional information on Lafayette area sites and attractions can be obtained at the **Greater Lafayette Convention and Visitors Bureau, Inc.**, 3530 IND 26 East. By late 1989 the bureau may be in its new building at 301 Frontage Rd. (I-65 and IND 26).

1. The **Perrin Building**, on the north side of the courthouse square at 330 Main St., is an outstanding example of 19th-century commercial architecture. Built in 1877 by hardware dealers William H. and John O. Perrin, the building at the time of its construction was Lafayette's tallest structure. Italianate in style, as are most of the downtown commercial buildings, it has the only cast-iron facade in the city.

2. The **First Merchants National Bank**, west of the Perrin Building at 316 Main St., is another of the many fine public and business buildings extant in Lafayette. Erected in 1917-18, the Classical Revival-style structure features a limestone and granite shell with a large central arch flanked by Corinthian columns. The elaborately carved stonework is of a Roman motif. The building was later owned by the Purdue National Bank. Both the Perrin and the bank buildings are included in the **Downtown Lafayette Historic District**, one of four Lafayette areas so designated and listed on the National Register of Historic Places.

3. The centerpiece of the Downtown Historic District is the **Tippecanoe County Courthouse**, on the block bounded by 3rd, 4th, Main, and Columbia sts. It is the third courthouse to stand on Lafayette's public square. Completed in 1885, the building was designed by architect James Alexander. The dominant influence is Second Empire, but the building contains elements of Baroque, Gothic, Georgian, Victorian, Beaux Arts, and Neoclassical styles. At the top of the elongated dome, 212 ft. from ground level, is a statue of the Goddess of Liberty who once reputedly held a shield and sword in her hands. (Some local people claim that the statue is actually a depiction of the Goddess of Justice who lost her scales in a windstorm many years ago, but the specifications of the county commissioners refer to the robed lady as the Goddess of Liberty.) Other figures appear on the building in various places. The four female figures standing in niches beneath the clock faces represent the four seasons. Justice appears on the east and west pediments while George Washington, George Rogers Clark, and Tecumseh stand on the north and south pediments. The interior contains a mural illustrating the Battle of Tippecanoe, which was painted by Robert W. Grafton of Michigan City in 1915. The mural occupied the lobby of the Fowler Hotel until 1966. (*NRHP/HABSI*)

The courthouse square was once famous for an artesian well that was drilled in 1857 and located on its northeast corner. Because of its high sulphur content, the water filled the air with the aroma of rotten eggs. Despite this offensive quality, the well was popular because people believed its waters to have curative powers. In 1887 a fountain with a statue of Lafayette, designed by Chicago sculptor Lorado Taft, was erected over the 230-ft.-deep well. The statue was removed in 1936 after it began to lean dangerously. In 1974 it was returned to a place near the original location where it served as the centerpiece for a small rest area. The well itself was capped in 1939 when it no longer produced an adequate flow of water.

4. The **Purdue Block**, 8 N. 2nd St., is the oldest surviving commercial structure in Lafayette. Built by John Purdue in 1845, the block was once part of a row of 12 nearly identical brick buildings along 2nd St. between Main and South sts. Only four remain today. In 1971, while being renovated, the north section of the structure collapsed. Reinforced with steel girders, the exterior of the three-story Federal-style

Lafayette-West Lafayette Attractions

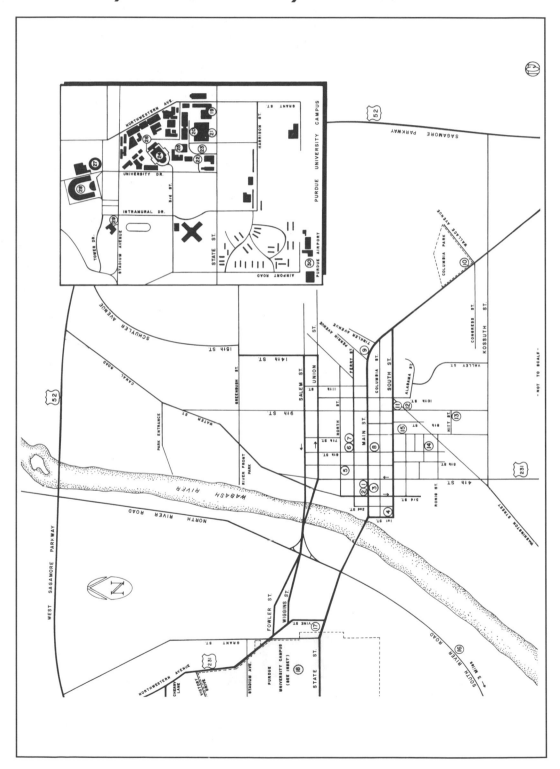

building has been restored to its former appearance. The interior of the restaurant at the south end of the block features exposed brick walls and pressed tin ceilings. Offices and a community center occupy the remainder of the building.

5. The Neoclassical **Monon Station**, 322 N. 5th St., was built in 1901 by the Chicago, Indianapolis, and Louisville Railroad. The structure served as a depot until 1959. It subsequently was used as a Red Shield store by the Salvation Army. The Civic Theatre of Greater Lafayette purchased the building and renovated it into a theater with a thrust stage and flexible seating for 130 to 250 people. Civic Theatre held its first performance in its new quarters on October 9, 1981. The Civic Theatre was founded in 1931 and was originally called the Lafayette Little Theatre. The troupe changed its name in 1965. Since its beginning the group has presented hundreds of plays. In 1959 it produced the world premiere of Sean O'Casey's *The Drums of Father Ned*. An art gallery in the lobby of the theater showcases local talent. The station is in the **Centennial Neighborhood Historic District**, roughly bounded by Union, Ferry, 3rd, 4th, and 9th sts. It takes its name from the Centennial School, built in 1876, which stood on the corner of 6th and Brown sts. until 1950. The area, platted in the 1830s, developed rapidly after the arrival of the Wabash and Erie Canal in 1843 and the railroads in the 1850s. The district contains numerous buildings of historical and architectural significance which range over nearly the entire span of Lafayette history. (*NRHP*)

6. On the south edge of the Centennial District is **St. John's Episcopal Church**, 315 N. 6th St., the oldest church building in Lafayette. The congregation has occupied the same site in different buildings since 1837. George Upfold, the first Episcopal bishop in Indiana, consecrated the structure. The Gothic Revival-style structure was designed by William Tinsley, an Irish-born architect who immigrated to the United States in 1851. Tinsley was well known as an architect of church and college buildings. His work can be seen throughout the Midwest. He designed Christ Church in Indianapolis and the Fountain Square esplanade in Cincinnati. (*NRHP*)

7. The **Samuel Johnson house**, 608 Ferry St., is probably the oldest surviving house in Lafayette. This Federal-style structure was built in 1844 and served as the home of Samuel Johnson, first pastor of St. John's Episcopal Church.

8. The **Long Center for the Performing Arts**, 111 N. 6th St., opened in 1921 as the Mars Theatre. The three-story brick and limestone structure was originally a 1,450-seat vaudeville house. The grand opening featured Ed Wynn in *The Perfect Fool*. As motion pictures became more and more popular, the theater began showing silent films, soon followed by the talkies. In 1929 *The Jazz Singer*, starring Al Jolson, played at the theater. For many years the Mars was a popular motion-picture house, but like many other large downtown theaters it declined during the 1970s. In 1977 Irving Long, its owner, gave the Mars to the city of Lafayette. The theater was renamed the Dennis H. Long Center for the Performing Arts in honor of Irving's father. The Tippecanoe Arts Federation and the city of Lafayette have taken the lead in renovating the theater. In 1983 a 1,280-pipe, three-keyboard organ was installed, and the lobby was reconstructed according to the original theater plans. The facility is the home of the Lafayette Symphony Orchestra and headquarters of the Tippecanoe Arts Federation. (*NRHP*)

9. The **Perrin Historic District** centers on Perrin Ave. between Main and N. 18th sts. In 1873 James J. Perrin, a prominent Lafayette banker, purchased what was then called Stockton's Woods and platted it as Perrin's Addition. Laid out as a residential neighborhood, the streets follow the contours of the hilly terrain, in contrast to the rest of the city's grid pattern. Most of the houses in the district were built between 1875 and 1890 and encompass a variety of architectural styles. Many were the homes of the comfortable 19th-century middle class, but the district also includes examples of the residences of the wealthy and the modest cottages of the working class. (*NRHP*)

10. **Columbian Park**, bounded by Main, Wallace, Park, and Scott sts., was Lafayette's first public park. An entrance is at Park and Wallace sts. The zoo entrance is at Wallace and 24th sts. The park dates from 1876 when the city built a reservoir at the top of Oakland Hill. Originally

called Reservoir Park, the main attraction was boating on the small lakes created in the course of excavating soil to build the reservoir walls. One of these lakes shaped in the form of the letter "G" honored Elias B. Glick, then mayor of Lafayette. In the 1890s the city began developing the park as a recreational area for the residents of housing additions which the Belt Railway Land and Improvement Company had constructed nearby. It was probably in 1892, the 400th anniversary of Columbus's voyage, that the park took its present name. The **Scott St. Pavilion**, near a stop on the Oakland Hill streetcar line, was built in 1899. (*NRHP*) It is the only surviving example of 19th-century recreational architecture in Tippecanoe County. The park's 63 acres include the lagoon, the Tippecanoe County War Memorial Island, outdoor theater, amusement park, stadium, zoo, picnic areas, and playgrounds. The circular swimming pool, built with the assistance of the Works Progress Administration (WPA), opened July 4, 1939.

11. The **Fowler house**, 909 South St., is the home of the Tippecanoe County Historical Association Museum. Moses Fowler built this English Gothic mansion between 1851 and 1852. Fowler, born in Ohio in 1815, came to Lafayette in 1839 at the age of 24 and, with John Purdue, opened a dry goods store. In the mid-1840s, Fowler pursued merchandising on his own and soon became one of the city's leading wholesale and retail grocers. He also was director of the Indiana State Bank and later president of the National State Bank of Lafayette. Fowler speculated in real estate on a grand scale. A land baron by any definition of the term, Fowler owned 25,000 acres of rich prairie soil in Benton and White counties at the time of his death.

Returning to Lafayette after visiting the English Gothic home of a Connecticut business associate, Fowler decided to construct a similar mansion of his own. Working from plans in *The Architecture of Country Homes* by A. J. Downing, Fowler hired a carpenter and, without the assistance of an architect or blueprints, constructed his dream home. The result was this classic Gothic Revival house with ornate carved woodwork both inside and outside. Wilbur Peat in *Indiana Houses of the Nineteenth*

Fowler house

Century called it "probably the finest of the large Gothic residences still standing in Indiana." In 1916 Moses's grandson, Cecil Fowler, remodeled and enlarged the house and transformed the English garden in the rear into a formal Italian garden (since replaced by a parking lot) with a reflecting pool and tea house. (*NRHP/HABSI*)

The Tippecanoe County Historical Association purchased the Fowler house in 1940 from Cecil Fowler and opened it as a historical museum the following year. The house contains Victorian furnishings, portraits of prominent local families, an antique toy collection, and separate galleries to display decorative arts, Indian artifacts, and pioneer wares. The association also operates a gift store and presents an audiovisual tape about the Fowler house. Immediately to the east of the Fowler house is the Wetherill Historical Resource Center. This facility houses the Alameda McCollough Library, which is open to the public for genealogical and historical research.

12. The **Greater Lafayette Museum of Art**, 101 S. 9th St., began in 1909 as the Lafayette Art Association. One of its leading organizers was Laura Ann Fry, a noted ceramicist and sculptor who was professor of Industrial Art at Purdue. The association moved into its present quarters in 1960 and took the name of Lafayette Art Center. Until 1980 when a new wing, the Weil Gallery, opened, most of the museum's permanent collection was scattered in various locations across Lafayette. Many works had never been seen by the public. In 1982 the museum was accredited by the American Association of Museums, and its name was changed to the Greater Lafayette Museum of Art.

In addition to its permanent collections, the museum displays contemporary Indiana and American art as well as traveling exhibits. The museum has a gift shop and a sales and rental gallery offering original works by local and regional artists. A fully equipped photography teaching darkroom facility is also located in the building.

13. The **Cyrus Ball house**, 402 S. 9th St., is an ornate and stately brick building that combines Italianate and Second Empire architectural styles. Judge Cyrus Ball built the mansion around 1869. A successful businessman, Ball came to Lafayette in 1827 where he and his brother opened a general store. Judge Ball served as justice of the peace, associate justice for Tippecanoe County, collector of tolls on the Wabash and Erie Canal, and cashier of the Lafayette branch of the State Bank of Indiana and the Union National Bank. He also was instrumental in the formation of the Lafayette and Indianapolis Railroad. Judge Ball lived in his home until his death in 1893. It is still occupied by members of the Ball family. (*NRHP*)

14. The **Falley home**, 601 New York St., houses the recently formed John Philip Sousa Museum. James B. Falley, a hardware and farm implement company owner, constructed this Italian Villa-style mansion between 1862 and 1864. The garage with a gable roof was added in the 1920s. The main stucco-covered brick structure with a three-story entrance tower and a large carriage house with servants' quarters have been completely renovated. A century-old wrought-iron fence from the grounds of the Lafayette Centennial School surrounds the corner lot. The interior of the house contains period furnishings such as a square piano manufactured in Philadelphia in 1830 and brought to Lafayette via riverboat and a mule-drawn wagon by the second owner of the house, hotel proprietor John Lahr.

The present owner, retired Purdue University band director Al B. Wright, helped establish the John Philip Sousa Foundation, a nonprofit organization which sponsors and administers projects contributing to the excellence of bands and band music throughout the world. The house serves as the foundation's museum and headquarters. Best known as the composer of the *Stars and Stripes Forever*, the March King was leader of the United States Marine Corps Band for 12 years before he formed in 1892 his own group, the Sousa Band, which toured the world until Sousa's death at age 78 in 1932. A large collection of Sousa memorabilia as well as early American band music and scores, phonodiscs, oral history tapes, photos, and special music publications are available for reading, listening, and research. (*NRHP*)

15. **Temple Israel**, 17 S. 7th St., is probably the oldest surviving synagogue building in Indiana. In 1849 the small Lafayette Jewish community formed a burial society called Ahavas Achim, meaning Brotherly Love. The community soon

established a synagogue and school which met in various locations in the city. In 1867 the congregation built this brick and limestone structure as its house of worship. The congregation, which changed its name to Temple Israel in 1919, occupied the building until 1969. The Unitarian Universalist Fellowship restored the structure and rededicated it as a church in 1979. The building still contains the original stained-glass windows. (*NRHP*)

16. **Fort Ouiatenon Historical Park** on South River Rd. is located 3.8 miles southwest of State St. in West Lafayette. In 1717 the governor of New France sent an ensign to establish an outpost among the Wea, a branch of the Miami tribe, near the mouth of Wea Creek on the Wabash River. This was Fort Ouiatenon, the first permanent European settlement in Indiana. The French maintained the fort as a small trading post until 1761 when the British captured it during the French and Indian War. The outpost fell to the Indians in 1763 during Pontiac's Rebellion—a general uprising among the western tribes—and the British never bothered to reclaim it as a garrison. A few French continued to reside at the place until the late 1780s when the Indians began using the old fort as a staging area for raids against settlers in Kentucky. The post may have been burned in 1791 when Brig. Gen. Charles Scott of the Kentucky militia destroyed several villages in the Wabash Valley. Or, more likely, the settlement gradually decayed until its location faded from memory. (*NRHP*)

In 1928, after a careful examination of documents and artifacts discovered in the area, Lafayette physician Richard B. Wetherill concluded that the fort had stood on a small elevation opposite the mouth of Wea Creek. He purchased the land in 1928 and, two years later, constructed a blockhouse for the use of the Tippecanoe County Historical Association. (Wetherill was apparently unaware that the French built their stockades with vertical posts rather than horizontal ones as in his English-style reconstruction.) The property became a county park in 1968. The Tippecanoe County Historical Association operates a gift shop and museum in the blockhouse. Each fall the association sponsors the Feast of the Hunters' Moon on the park grounds. Thousands of participants and spectators gather for this re-creation of an 18th-century trade fair complete with peddlers,

musicians, Indian dancers, military units, craftspeople, and colorful voyageurs.

Not everyone was convinced that Wetherill's site was the true location of Fort Ouiatenon. Over the years, new evidence pointed to another site further downriver. Aerial photographs and an archaeological survey done by Indiana University in 1968-69 show that the French post actually stood about one mile south on the floodplain of the Wabash River. Michigan State University conducted extensive excavations on this location in 1974-79. The true site of the fort is on private property and is not open to the public. There are no markers.

17. **Bank One**, 210 W. State St., is the only building in Indiana designed by the famed Chicago architect Louis Sullivan. Sullivan, whose utilitarian designs followed the dictum: "form follows function," is best known for his pioneering designs of skyscrapers such as the Guaranty Building (1895) in Buffalo, New York, and the Carson, Pirie, Scott and Company Building (1899-1904) in Chicago. The businesslike design of the West Lafayette bank and its rich tapestry brick and polychromed terra-cotta decoration are characteristic of Sullivan's later work. The building, constructed toward the end of Sullivan's career, opened in 1914.

18. **Purdue University**, situated on a 643-acre campus at the junction of US 52/231 and IND 26 in West Lafayette, is one of 68 land-grant colleges founded under the provisions of the Morrill Act of 1862. The university dates its beginning from May 6, 1869, when the legislature voted to locate the institution in Tippecanoe County. Classes began September 16, 1874, with 39 male students enrolled. The Agriculture Experiment Station was established in 1887, followed by the Engineering Experiment Station in 1917. From these modest beginnings Purdue has grown into one of the nation's leading agricultural and engineering schools. The university has regional campuses in Hammond and Westville and offers joint programs with Indiana University in Indianapolis and Fort Wayne. About 10,000 acres of land are under university control for agricultural research. Lafayette campus has an enrollment of more than 33,000 students.

19. The **Purdue Memorial Union** at the northwest corner of State and Grant sts. is the center

FORT OUIATENON, LAFAYETTE, IND.—42

Indiana Historical Society (C4277)

of student social life. It opened in 1924 and was dedicated to the 67 Purdue students who died in World War I (later expanded to include the dead of all 20th-century American wars), commemorated by the Memorial Cross embedded in the floor of the Great Hall. A scale model of the campus is also on display in the Great Hall at the south entrance of the building. The union is entirely self-financed and provides various social services for students, alumni, and faculty. Included are 254 guest rooms, food services, and recreational facilities. Underground walkways decorated with posters connect the Union with Stewart Center, the Krannert buildings, and the parking garages.

20. **Stewart Center**, situated on State St. just west of the Memorial Mall, was opened in 1958 as the Memorial Center but renamed in 1972 in honor of Robert B. and Lillian V. O. Stewart, administrators and benefactors of the university. The building houses facilities for many of the university's cultural and social activities including two theaters, an art gallery, a library, exhibit rooms, lounges, a ballroom, and offices for student organizations. Many outside companies and organizations also use the conference/convention rooms. The huge mural in the west foyer entitled the *Spirit of the Land Grant College 1862-1961* is the work of Eugene Francis Savage. A native Hoosier and artist of inter-

national repute, Savage designed the mural depicting the history of Fountain County in the courthouse at Covington. He also painted the *Spirit of Indiana* on the wall of the House of Representatives in the capitol building at Indianapolis. The Stewart center mural was the gift of Mr. and Mr. Walter Scholer and Mr. and Mrs. Robert B. Stewart.

Among the special collections of the Purdue library located on the second floor of the Stewart Center is a permanent display of some of Amelia Earhart's belongings. In 1929 Earhart founded a women pilots' group, called the 99s, composed of 99 out of the approximately 117 women pilots in the country at that time. The organization, which established the Earhart Collection at Purdue, is now international in scope and numbers about 6,000. The collection of Earhart memorabilia features photographs, maps, medals, scrapbooks, a leather jacket, goggles, scarf, and helmet.

21. Immediately south of Stewart Center is the **Purdue Undergraduate Library**. This unusual structure, two stories in depth, is located almost entirely underground. Designed by Walter Scholer and Associates of Lafayette, the library was placed below ground level so that it would not block the facade of Stewart Center, a campus landmark. The natural insulating properties of the earth make the building energy

efficient and the window wells permit natural light to enter. The facility provides space for more than a million books and seating for 1,300 students. The library opened in June 1982. It houses the independent study center, a 24-hour study lounge, and the journal collection room.

22. Located on Oval Dr. near the center of campus is **University Hall**, Purdue's oldest building and one of seven structures that originally formed the nucleus of the campus. Completed in 1877 and appropriately called the Main Building during its early years, University Hall housed classrooms, administrative offices, and the chapel. Until 1912 the library also was located in the building. James K. Wilson, a Cincinnati architect, designed the building. University Hall was completely remodeled in 1960-61. It is now the home of the departments of history, political science, and philosophy.

23. Immediately in front of University Hall is the **grave of John Purdue**. This Lafayette businessman was the university's first benefactor and the man for whom the university is named. Purdue died on September 12, 1876, the first day of classes in the university's third year. Generations of Purdue students have handed down stories telling how Purdue's body has been disinterred countless times by pranksters and his bones scattered across the state. These stories appear to be little more than campus folklore. There is no evidence that John Purdue has ever been dug up by anybody. As far as anyone knows, his worldly remains still rest peacefully in his grave.

24. Behind the administration building, the **Edward C. Elliott Hall of Music**, east of 3rd and University sts., with a seating capacity of 6,034, is one of the largest performing arts auditoriums in the country. Originally called simply the Purdue Hall of Music, the $1,205,000 building was dedicated in 1940 and renamed for Purdue's president from 1922 to 1945. On the north and south walls of the hall are three figures representing music, drama, and forensics. Above the main stone cornice and below the wall coping are carved panels representing the development of music and opera to radio and cinema. Elliott Hall is the home of the Purdue Music Organizations as well as radio station WBAA, the oldest licensed station in the state.

25. South of the music hall and just east of Stanley Coulter Hall is the **Lion Heads Monument**, a stone obelisk approximately 6 ft. in height that was a gift from the class of 1903. A campus tradition holds that the lion heads mounted on the four sides of the monument will roar when a woman of virtue passes by.

26. **Purdue Mall** fronts on Northwestern Ave. The university's engineering buildings, built in the 1920s for the most part, border the sides of the mall, and the Frederick L. Hovde Hall of Administration, built in 1936, stands at the far end. Hovde Hall was named in honor of the late president of Purdue from 1946 to 1971. Anchoring the mall is a 38-ft.-high water concrete sculpture executed by Robert Youngman, an Anderson resident and professor of art at the University of Illinois. Donations from the Purdue class of 1939 funded the $350,000 project. The fountain, embodying four fin-like forms of varying surface treatments and surrounding a column of water, utilizes a lighting scheme that makes it inviting even in the wintertime when the water is disconnected.

27. Circling the campus in a counterclockwise direction, visitors may see a number of Purdue attractions. Located at the north end on Northwestern Ave. is the **Guy J. Mackey Arena**, dedicated in 1967. Home of Purdue's basketball team, the arena seats 14,123 persons and offers an unobstructed view of the playing floor.

28. Just west of the arena at the junction of N. University and Tower drives is **Ross-Ade Stadium** where the Purdue Boilermakers encounter the Big Ten and other football rivals. Inventor David E. Ross and author George Ade donated $110,000 toward the purchase of land and the building of the $237,500, 13,200-seat stadium in 1924. (Today, the stadium seats 69,000.) Jesse Greene, a Crawfordsville reporter, is credited with first using the term "boilermakers" after a Purdue victory over hapless Wabash College in 1889. Although not meant to be complimentary, the tough Purdue players liked the connotation and adopted it. Two years earlier, before a football game with Butler, a small group of students and faculty

decided the school's colors should be old gold and black.

29. The **Slayter Center of Performing Arts** off Stadium Ave. on the north side of campus was constructed in 1963 and dedicated the following year for donors Games and Marie Slayter, commercial plastic scientists and Purdue alumni. The outdoor concert facility features a side panel design that was modeled after Stonehenge in England. A 220-ton roof suspended from a giant steel tripod shelters the stage. The surrounding grounds provide parking and picnicking space.

30. The **Purdue Airport** is located at the southwest corner of the campus on Airport Rd. A visiting lecturer and counselor for women at Purdue since 1935, Amelia Earhart took off, in March 1937, from this airport in her specially designed Lockheed Electra for Oakland and the start of her fateful around-the-world trip. Funding for the plane's construction came from the Purdue Research Foundation, which received gifts for the project from David E. Ross, J. K. Lilly, airline companies, and public donations. The airport now offers commercial flights to

the Midwest as well as charters and student training planes.

Purdue offers programs in aeronautical engineering and other technical and scientific disciplines required to train personnel for flying and building spacecraft. For its position in the nation's space program, the university has acquired the nickname Mother of Astronauts. The list of Purdue graduates involved with the National Aeronautics and Space Administration (NASA) is long. Several have achieved national prominence for their roles in the space program. Virgil I. "Gus" Grissom was the first person to make two space flights. Roger B. Chaffee, who made his first solo airplane flight at the Purdue University Airport, gave his life with Grissom and astronaut Ed White in a mishap during a ground training session aboard an Apollo space capsule on January 27, 1967. Neil A. Armstrong became the first person to step on the surface of the moon, followed by Eugene A. Cernan, also a graduate of Purdue. In the 1980s Col. Loren J. Shriver and Charles D. Walker were aboard the space shuttle *Discovery*. In 1984 seven Purdue graduates were NASA astronauts.

Tour 15

Tour 15 starts at the northeast intersection of IND 25 and US 52 in Lafayette. Take IND 25 northeast *1.2 m.* and turn right onto CR 200N. Follow this winding road *1.5 m.* to CR 400E and turn right. On the right *.1 m.* is the entrance to the **Jerry E. Clegg Memorial Botanical Gardens** (parking is on the left). Situated on the Clegg estate, the gardens were opened to the public following his death in 1963. The approximately 14-acre wooded area provides a panoramic view of the countryside and contains wild flowers and trees native to Indiana. Rugged nature trails run over glacially formed ravines and hills and along Wildcat Creek. **Lookout Point**, at the top of a climb of 91 railroad tie steps, offers a magnificent view at the park's south edge.

Return to CR 200N and turn right. At *.1 m.* on the left is the **Ely homestead**. Pioneer Henry Ely (1797-1864) came from Ohio in 1825 and constructed this two-story Federal-style brick house in 1847. The homestead, which has been in the Ely family for all but 16 years, received the Tippecanoe County Historical Association Preservation Award in 1973. (*NRHP*)

Return to IND 25 and continue northeast *5.6 m.* IND 25 borders the Wabash River, and the mouth of the Tippecanoe, the largest upper Wabash tributary, can be seen on the opposite side. Continue *5.5 m.* to the **CARROLL COUNTY** (p. 19,722; 372 sq. m.) line. The county was formed in 1828 and named for Declaration of Independence signer Charles Carroll. The land originally was noted for its forests and waterways (the Wabash and Tippecanoe rivers and Wildcat Creek), and until the 1820s a French fur trading post was located just north of the town of Rockfield. The county is primarily agricultural, with about 95 percent of the total acreage being used for farming. Lake Freeman in the county's northwest corner provides a large tourist and recreation area trade (see Tour 16).

At *1.8 m.* turn left on IND 18/39/US 421 at the Delphi city limits, and at *1 m.* pass a marker designating the boundary of the New Purchase, which transferred most of central Indiana from Indian to white ownership.

Cross the Wabash River and immediately turn right into the old canal port of **PITTSBURG**, platted in 1836. A picturesque two-story brick building and other structures on the main street recall the canal days, and a marker explains the town's early significance. Return to Delphi and at the Wabash River look left to the CSX (former Monon) railroad bridge. This replaced an earlier structure in 1949 by a revolutionary engineering method in which the seven spans were launched, one at a time, into the river and dismantled with almost no interruption to rail service as new spans were set into place. The project required about two months and eliminated the need for expensive piling and falsework to support the discarded 93-ton spans.

A short distance beyond the highway bridge, cross the Wabash and Erie Canal bed before entering **DELPHI** (p. 3,042), which was laid out on 100 acres donated by William Wilson in 1828 for the county seat. The town was first called Carrollton, but after nine days the name was changed to Delphi in honor of the ancient Greek city at the suggestion of Samuel Milroy, a leader in the organization of the county. The Wabash and Erie Canal reached the area in 1840, and until the last boat passed through Delphi in the late 1870s, the town was an important port. The railroad replaced the canal as the major means of transport in 1856. Today the community relies on local agriculture, but there are several small industries in the area which produce plumbing fixtures, furniture, truck bodies, containers, and metal fabrications. In 1950 Delphi was chosen as the typical midwestern city by the United States State Department's Voice of America broad-

Tour 15

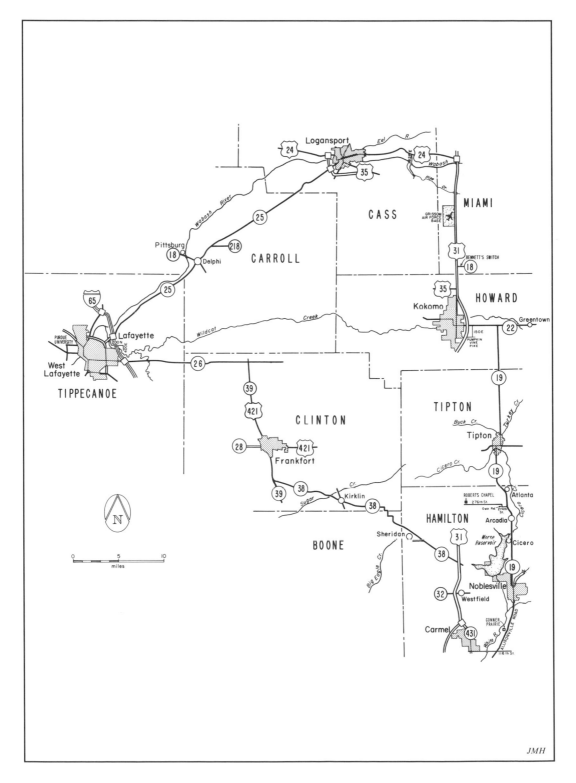

JMH

casts. Actor and television star MacDonald Carey spent some of his childhood in Delphi.

Continue north on IND 25 (Main St.) to the **Carroll County Courthouse** on the left. This three-story, limestone structure was built in 1917 as the third county courthouse. On the main floor is the bell used from about 1841 to 1916 in the former courthouse. It was donated to the museum in 1966. Another highlight is the stained-glass skylight in the rotunda. On the courthouse lawn is a Civil War monument topped with a statue called "The Color Bearer." The memorial was erected in 1888. The **Carroll County Historical Museum**, which contains items of local interest, is located in the courthouse basement.

At the courthouse, turn left on Washington St. and go *.5 m.* to the bridge across the Wabash and Erie Canal bed. This is one of the few easily identified remnants of the canal, which stretched from Toledo, Ohio, to Evansville.

Return to Monroe St., the first street beyond the Norfolk and Western and CSX railroads, and turn left. One block on the left, at the northeast corner of Monroe and Union sts. (203 E. Monroe), is the **Barnett-Seawright-Wilson house**. This Italianate/Greek Revival home was constructed in 1857. Franklin D. Roosevelt once stopped at this house for tea when it was owned by Henry B. Wilson, newspaperman, lumber company owner, prominent state Democrat, and civic booster. (*NRHP*) Delphi has several other attractive 19th-century homes, including an unusual Queen Anne-style home at Union and Franklin sts. and a Gothic Revival-style home at Union and Front sts.

Turn right onto Union St., travel two blocks to Main St., turn right, and proceed one block to Washington St. This area has some interesting examples of 19th-century commercial architecture, including the 1874 Italianate-style **Niewerth Building** at 124 E. Main St. (*NRHP*) Several have unusual window treatments. Southeast *.1 m.* on Washington is the entrance to **Riley Park** on the left. James Whitcomb Riley spent a good deal of time in Delphi, and the city is often referred to as his second home. The picturesque city park borders on Deer Creek, the subject of the Riley poem "On the Banks o' Deer Crick," which depicted the poet's leisurely fishing experiences there.

Return to Main St. and turn right. Continue past the Andersons, a large Ohio-based grain operation near IND 218, *13 m.* on IND 25 to the **CASS COUNTY** (p. 40,936; 414 sq. m.) line. The county was established in 1828 and named for Gov. and Brig. Gen. Lewis Cass of Michigan who negotiated the treaty with the Indians incorporating the area into the United States in 1826. Like most of its neighbors, Cass County relies on local agriculture with about 85 percent of the county's acreage being employed as farmland. Most of the county's varied industrial facilities are located in the county seat of Logansport.

Logansport State Hospital, Indiana's largest mental health facility, is located *5.4 m.* past the county line on the west side of IND 25. The institution was authorized in 1883 and was opened five years later as the Northern Indiana Hospital for the Insane with 300 patients on 281 acres of land. Joseph G. Rogers served as the hospital's first superintendent. The original Administration Building is still standing.

Farther on IND 25 *1 m.* are the city limits of **LOGANSPORT** (p. 17,899). Situated on land acquired from the Potawatomi and Miami tribes, the town was laid out in 1828 and named for James John Logan, a Shawnee chief who was killed fighting for the United States near Fort Wayne during the War of 1812. Supposedly Col. John B. Duret earned the right of naming the new county seat by winning a shooting match. Because of its location at the confluence of the Wabash and Eel rivers, "Logan's Port" rapidly developed as a trade center. Trade and industry blossomed with the construction of the Wabash and Erie Canal in 1838, the year of town incorporation, and continued to progress with the arrival of the railroad in 1855. By 1860 Logansport boasted of being one of the Midwest's largest rail centers. Logansport has been nicknamed the "Bridge City" for its numerous structures over the two rivers. Industry continues to play a prominent role in the Logansport economy, ranging from battery making to meat processing. Other major industries produce wiring, automotive parts, controls, springs, and metal stampings.

Continue northeast on IND 25 to Cicott St., turn left, and cross the Wabash River. Drive *.5 m.* and turn left onto W. Market St. (US 24). Continue *4.6 m.* to the entrance to **France Park** on the left. The 400-acre recreation area features a lake, beach, and waterfalls. Among the activities offered are scuba diving, fishing, swimming, horseback riding, hiking, cross country skiing, snowmobiling, picnicking, water sliding, and camping.

To the immediate left of the park's entrance is a log cabin built by Noah Fouts around 1839 which is now the home of the **Indiana Archery Museum**. The cabin, believed to be the site of the first religious meeting in Deer Creek Township around 1840, was moved from southern Cass County to its present location in 1976.

Return to Logansport and continue east on Market to 3rd St. and turn left. On the right one block, at the northeast corner of 3rd and Broadway, is the **Logan Square** office complex. The Barnes Company constructed this nearly block-long, five-story brick building without the use of wood in 1926. It once housed a 60-room hotel, a theater, and several offices. Cass Investments acquired the structure in 1979 and remodeled it into modern offices.

Turn left, then angle left on Eel River Ave. Along this street, named **Banker's Row**, in what is now designated the Point Historic District, are many Victorian-era homes that once housed Logansport's elite in the late 19th century. Several privately owned mansions have been restored and are open to the public on special occasions.

Turn left on Market St., left on 3rd, and right, after two blocks, on North St., and into the Courthouse Historic District. On the right is the **Cass County Building**, a combination county office, courthouse, and jail. This modern four-story structure was erected in 1978 at a cost of $3.5 million and replaced the 1888 courthouse. Diagonally across the intersection is the architecturally interesting 1896 Romanesque Revival-style Masonic Temple.

Drive one block east (just past the courthouse square) and turn right onto S. 4th St. Three blocks south where 4th St. and Melbourne St. form a "T" is the **Iron Horse Museum**. Housed in the former Vandalia (later Pennsylvania) Railroad depot that dates from 1871, the museum is filled with railroad memorabilia. Included is the original dispatcher's desk, a Pennsylvania Railroad conductor's uniform, a baggage cart, and numerous other railroad items. The depot was scheduled for destruction by Conrail when local railroad enthusiasts obtained it and had it moved from its location north of town to the present site in 1981. The movement and subsequent restoration corresponded with the first Iron Horse

Festival. The festival is held annually in mid-July and attracts thousands of visitors. Highlighting the three days of festivities are crosstown train rides. In 1983 the festival committee obtained the train engine they had been renting, and it is now parked near 6th and Michigan north of town. The engine had been used to haul coal in West Virginia, while the passenger cars had belonged to the Rock Island Line.

Turn left onto Melbourne. Go one block and turn left onto 5th St., which was the Wabash and Erie Canal route, then one more block and right onto Market St., which has several noteworthy houses. The **Pollard-Nelson house**, also known as the **Memorial Home**, a Greek Revival-style structure at 627 E. Market, was constructed by pioneer Philip Pollard in 1844. (*NRHP*) The Gothic-style **Kendrick-Baldwin house**, now called the **Memorial Center**, at the northeast corner of 7th and Market sts. was the Presbyterian Academy site. Built about 1865 and originally named Logansport Female College, the academy was a well-respected educational institution until it closed approximately eight years later. It later was acquired by Daniel P. Baldwin, an attorney, trustee of Wabash College, and former owner of the *Logansport Journal*. (*NRHP*)

Continue east on Market St. approximately three blocks to the **Cass County Historical Society Museum** on the left at 1004 E. Market in the heart of the Riverside Historic District. The 20-room Italianate-style mansion was constructed by local physician George Jerolman in 1853, and it was donated to the historical society by Benjamin Long in 1967. (*NRHP*) The current building is the third structure to hold the historical museum. While the museum contains a wide variety of historical artifacts, it has especially strong Civil War and American Indian collections. On the museum grounds are two log cabins that have been moved from the outlying areas and restored to depict pioneer life in the 1840s.

Continue two blocks east on Market St. and turn left at 12th. One block farther on the southwest corner of Broadway stood the **boyhood home of Sir Henry Thornton**, who was knighted by King George V for his World War I role in administering British railroads. After the war he became the architect and manager of the Canadian National Railways. There are

Indiana Historical Society (Peat Collection)

Cass County Historical Society Museum

numerous examples of early domestic architecture in this area.

Turn left on Broadway, after two blocks turn right on 10th St., and at the end of the street turn right one-half block to **Riverside Park**. The first Logansport city park, Riverside was opened in 1887, but it was little more than swampland before the city started improving the 10-acre area in 1895. Highlighting the park is the **Cass County Carousel**, a merry-go-round that dates from 1892 and features 50 ridable, hand-carved wooden animals. The park also offers picnic areas, shelters, a playground, and other recreational facilities.

Return to Market St., turn left, and continue on US 24 nearly *7 m.* to CR 825E, which is the first right after crossing the Norfolk and Western Railway overpass. Take the next right, cross the Wabash River, and continue south. At the end of the road turn right and continue across Pipe Creek. To the left in the distance can be seen Pipe Creek Falls and the mill which once operated. A dam atop the falls raised the water level, and a foamy cascade can be seen above the dam. Return to US 24, passing on the left a dam at the lower end of the gorge where the water operated two mills. Water attempting to cut through a 325,000,000-year-old

Silurian coral reef is responsible for the falls, which attracted millers as early as the 1850s.

At US 24 turn right and continue *4.9 m.*, crossing the Miami County line, to US 31, and turn south (for a description of the county see Tour 2). On the right *5.7 m.* is **Grissom Air Force Base**. Opened in 1942 as United States Naval Reserve Aviation Base, it served as a training ground for Navy pilots during World War II. The facility was deactivated at the end of the war, and the area reverted to farmland, with most of the buildings being dismantled. The Air Force acquired the base in 1953, constructed new buildings, and reopened it as Bunker Hill Air Force Base the following year. The name Bunker Hill was taken from the nearby town east of the base. From 1953 to 1957 the Air Force used the facility as a tactical base for fighter and bomber units, but in 1957 the base was turned over to the Strategic Air Command. The name was changed to Grissom Air Force Base in 1968 to honor Lt. Col. Virgil I. "Gus" Grissom of Mitchell, Indiana, one of the original seven astronauts (see Tour 11). The 2,868-acre base is the home of the 305th Air Refueling Wing of the Strategic Air Command and two Air Force reserve fighter units. The large, in-air refueling tanker planes, which supply in-flight refueling of Air Force planes throughout the world, easily can be seen from US 31. In 1983 the National Emergency Airborne Command Post was moved to Grissom from Andrews Air Force Base in Maryland. The base now houses a jet the president would use as a flying command post in the event of a nuclear attack.

At *5.7 m.* south of the base, IND 18 leads east *1 m.* to **Bennett's Switch**, ancestral home of stage and screen stars Richard Bennett and his daughters, Constance and Joan. South on US 31 *1.5 m.* is **HOWARD COUNTY** (p. 86,896; 293 sq. m.). Until the county's organization in 1844, the land was part of the southern section of the Miami Indian territory. Originally the county was named Richardville for the Miami chief Jean Baptiste Richardville, the son of a French trader and a Miami princess. Two years after its organization, when the county's future was in doubt concerning name and boundary changes, a compromise was agreed upon. The boundaries remained the same, but the name was changed to Howard in honor of Indiana politician and soldier Tilghman A. Howard. Although Howard County is noted as one of the state's more populous and industrialized regions, it still has a large and profitable agricultural base.

South of the county line *2 m.*, continue straight ahead on Washington St. (Old US 31) to **KOKOMO** (p. 47,808). David Foster, originally from Virginia and the first settler in the county, arrived from Burlington, Indiana, in 1842, obtained land from Chief LaFontaine, and established a trading post on what had been a Miami Indian reservation. Two years later Foster laid out the town and named it for the Miami chief Kokomoko (spelling varies). The settlement was chosen as the county seat for its central location and the fact that Foster donated the land for the courthouse. The town progressed slowly at first because of its location on swampy land, and many early settlers died from disease. The arrival of the Peru and Indianapolis Railroad in 1853 initiated the first era of development, and the city became an industrial leader with the discovery of natural gas in 1886. Kokomo is known as "The City of Firsts" for the number of discoveries and inventions that have taken place within its boundaries. The most famous was the first successful commercially built gasoline-powered automobile in Indiana by Elwood Haynes in

1894. Haynes also discovered stainless steel (1911) and "Stellite" (1906), a high-performance nickel-chromium alloy. Other Kokomo inventions include the pneumatic rubber tire by D. C. Spraker in 1894, the carburetor by George Kingston in 1902, the American howitzer shell and aerial bomb with fins in 1918, and the all-transistor car radio in 1957. In all, 15 major discoveries and inventions have taken place in Kokomo. Since the turn of the century the city's economy has relied on the automobile industry. Today the largest industries are Delco Electronics and the Chrysler Corporation.

Traveling south on Washington St. and before crossing the first railroad note the long brick building on the southwest corner of Washington and Spraker sts. A first section of this building was constructed around 1914 by the Apperson brothers, Elmer and Edgar, as an expansion of their car-manufacturing business. The Appersons established the Riverside Machine Shop on S. Main St. in 1888. From here in 1894 they assembled the first Haynes horseless carriage. On May 15, 1898, the Haynes Apperson Company was incorporated to manufacture "motor carriages." Elmer Apperson withdrew from the company in 1901, and he and his brother formed the Apperson Brothers Automobile Company. The firm remained in business until its dissolution in 1925. Afterwards, a succession of owners used the building until purchased by the Reliance Manufacturing Company. Today it is Delco Electronics Plant 5, acquired in 1951.

Five blocks south of the second railroad, at the northwest corner of Washington and Mulberry sts., was the site of **Elwood Haynes's first home** in Kokomo. Haynes (1857-1925), a Portland, Indiana, native and a graduate of Worcester (Massachusetts) County Free Institute of Industrial Science (later Worcester Polytechnic Institute), came from Greentown to Kokomo in December 1892 to assume the management of the local operations of the Indiana Natural Gas and Oil Company (INGO). While Haynes was living at this site, he built his first successful automobile.

Continue south one block and turn left on Walnut St. On the southeast corner stands the former **City Hall**, a Romanesque Revival building of unusual architecture, now being restored. (*NRHP*) Turn left to the **Howard County Courthouse**. Built in 1936-37, it represented the first time in almost a decade that the citizens of the county had a courthouse. The previous one was judged a fire hazard in 1927, demolished, and its former tenants scattered about the city. With the new $468,000 limestone structure, residents no longer had to suffer the embarrassment of being Indiana's only county without a courthouse. When the cornerstone to the courthouse was being laid in August 1936 observers thought it impervious to harm from natural causes. They had not taken into account manmade forces. On April 14, 1987, a man on trial for drug dealing detonated a briefcase bomb in the courthouse, killing himself and wounding 15 others, and so seriously damaging the courthouse it had to be abandoned for a week before most of the repaired offices could reopen.

Travel west on Sycamore St., which borders the courthouse on the south, five blocks to the **Howard County Museum** at Kingston St. The combination Neo-Jacobean and Romanesque Revival-style home was built around 1890 for Monroe Seiberling, founder of the Diamond Plate Glass Company, forerunner of the Pittsburgh Plate Glass Company. Seiberling paid $50,000 for the construction of this 29-room mansion, which became the home for Indiana University at Kokomo in 1949. The university moved out when a new campus was opened in 1965, and the building was leased to the Howard County Commissioners to house the Howard County Historical Society Museum. Restoration began in 1971, and it was completed three years later. Highlights of the museum are the master bedroom, nursery, military room, and third floor ballroom.

Turn left on Kingston St. (in front of the museum) and left again one block south at Superior St. Continue two blocks beyond Kokomo High School and turn right onto Purdum St. Straight ahead one block is a 10-ft. stone pillar in a fenced area marking a pioneer cemetery and the **grave of Chief Kokomoko**. Several original pioneer tombstones surround the monument. There is some doubt as to the actual location of the Miami chief's grave. The pioneer cemetery was removed to make way for the high school and the neighboring houses.

Return to Washington St. and turn left. Proceed south .6 m. to Markland Ave. Turn left three blocks to Home Ave. and go south on Home Ave. .5 m. to Deffenbaugh St. To the east of this intersection is the **Home Ave. Complex of Delta Electronics**. This complex incorporates the old Haynes Automobile Company build-

ings, in particular its body plant, erected in 1922. By this time the Haynes company was facing serious financial problems from which it never recovered. The company filed for bankruptcy in October 1924, and it was dissolved the following February. In 1935 the Crosley Radio Corporation moved into the Haynes body plant, and the following year the newly formed Delco Radio Division of General Motors purchased the building. In addition to the first transistor car radio, Delco developed the first push-button car radio in 1938 and the first signal-seeking car radio in 1947. Go west on Deffenbaugh St. .8 m. to the entrance to **Highland Park** (originally named City Park). In 1892 the city obtained the park's first 15 acres from George and Mary Gwinn. Over the years the area has been expanded to nearly 100 acres.

In addition to the usual city park attractions, Highland Park also includes several noteworthy historical sites. Near the Deffenbaugh St. entrance on the right is the **Vermont Covered Bridge**. This 117-ft. bridge, including overhangs, was built near the Howard County town of Vermont in 1875 and moved to its present location over Kokomo Creek in 1958. Follow the winding road to the right. On opposite sides are two of the area's more unusual attractions: **Old Ben** and the **Sycamore Stump**. On the right in a shelter with white siding and a picture window stands Old Ben, a large stuffed steer. The crossbred Hereford was born in Miami County in 1902 and raised just north of Kokomo. At age four the steer weighed 4,720 lbs., stood 6 ft., 4 in. tall, was 16 ft., 8 in. in length, and measured 13 ft., 6 in. in girth. Ben was exhibited throughout the country before a broken leg forced him to be destroyed in 1911. On the left in a fenced shelter is a Sycamore stump that once was located on T. A. Harrell's farm near New London, southeast of Kokomo. The 100-ft.-high tree was severely damaged by high winds and flooding in 1915. The stump, which is 51 ft. in circumference and 12 ft. high, was placed in the park in 1916. It was hollowed out and used as a phone booth, and 24 people were able to fit in the stump.

Backtrack on Deffenbaugh four blocks and turn right on Webster St. The **Elwood Haynes Museum** is located six blocks on the right at 1915 S. Webster St. The two-story brick home was built for Haynes in 1915, and it was opened as a museum in 1967. In addition to numerous items relevant to Haynes's life and the rise of the Kokomo auto industry, the museum houses a 1905 Model L Haynes auto. (*NRHP*) The Kokomo Art Association's gallery is in a house next to the museum.

Turn left onto W. Boulevard St. immediately south of the Haynes Museum and continue *1.5 m.* to US 31, crossing Washington St. one block north of the Indiana University at Kokomo campus. Just south of the intersection of US 31 and E. Boulevard St. are Kokomo's major auto plants: the **Chrysler Corporation** on the west side of US 31 and the **Delco Electronics division of General Motors** on the east. Chrysler Corporation came to Kokomo in 1937, taking over and remodeling what was called the Davis Building unit of the Haynes Automobile Company. The plant produced over five million standard transmissions for Chrysler until 1955 when it was converted to a die-casting facility and the present transmission plant constructed. Delco, meanwhile, continued to expand its Home Ave. complex until in 1964-65 it constructed its Bypass plant.

On Boulevard St., at the southeast corner of the intersection, a marker relates the story of Haynes's first horseless carriage run. Continue east on Boulevard St. (Pumpkinvine Pike) *.4 m.* On the northeast corner at CR 150E (Goyer Rd.) at the base of a flag pole in front of the Foursquare Gospel Church is a marker commemorating the site of **Elwood Haynes's first test drive** on July 4, 1894. A horse-driven carriage towed the car from the Appersons' machine shop on Washington St. to this location three miles outside of the city because local officials feared the auto would either explode or the noise would frighten the horses. The clutch-driven, gasoline-powered vehicle with an electronic ignition traveled about six miles, achieving a speed of six or seven miles an hour. Haynes's most consistent work was in metallurgy. He experimented for many years with nickel, chromium, and cobalt steel alloys, which led to the discovery of Stellite, a high-strength metal. He also was an early developer of stainless steel and has a valid claim to its discovery.

Turn left onto CR 150E, travel north *1 m.*, and turn right on IND 22/US 35. East on this road *6.5 m.* is **GREENTOWN** (p. 2,265). The town was laid out in 1848 and incorporated in 1873. Accounts of the origin of the community's name vary. The settlement was named for either a patch of green meadow in the wilderness or for the Miami Indian town located on the site and called Green's Village for a Miami chief. The town grew with the gas boom but reverted to a farming community when the natural gas supply was exhausted.

Proceed *.5 m.* and turn left onto Meridian St. One-half block on the right, in the old city hall building, is the **Greentown Glass Museum**. With the discovery of natural gas in the area came the construction of the Indiana Tumbler and Goblet Company in 1894 under the direction of D. C. Jenkins, Jr. The town donated land near the railroad to entice the business. This small, independently owned glass company manufactured tumblers, goblets, tableware, and souvenir glassware. Colored glass production was started in 1897, and two years later the company merged with 19 companies to form the National Glass Company. Glass chemist Jacob Rosenthal came to the Greentown plant in 1900, and it was his unusual color creations for which Greentown Glass received its national reputation. Rosenthal's best-known creations were chocolate brown and golden agate (holly amber) colored glassware. The plant was destroyed by fire in 1903 and was never rebuilt. The museum was opened in 1970 to correspond with the first annual Greentown Glass Festival. Almost 1,000 pieces of Greentown Glass are displayed in the museum. The Glass Festival, which is held in early June, attracts thousands of visitors and provides revenue for the museum.

Return to Main St. and turn left. One block east at the southeast corner of Howard St. is the restored **Hy-Red gasoline station**, now occupied by Brad Howell Ford, which includes such early devices as hand-operated, gravity flow gasoline pumps. (*NRHP*)

Continue two blocks east, turn left on Mill St., and right at the end on Uncle Tom St. (which was named for a relative of the Jenkins family) to the **Indiana Tumbler and Goblet Company** factory site, where a marker on the left relates the factory's history.

Return to Main St. and go west on IND 22/US 35 *3.7 m.* to IND 19 and turn left. South *5 m.* on this road is the **TIPTON COUNTY** (p. 16,819; 261 sq. m.) line. Prior to its organization in 1844, the northern half of the county was part of the Miami Indian reservation, and the southern half belonged to Hamilton County. The county was named for military hero and United States Senator John Tipton.

Most acreage originally was covered by swamps, but once the settlers drained the land, it became one of the state's leading agricultural counties with Pioneer Hi-Bred Corn Company the leading industry. Auto parts also are produced.

Continue south on IND 19 *7 m.* and turn right onto Division Rd. On the right *.4 m.* is the **Sisters of St. Joseph Motherhouse**. The first sisters arrived in Tipton from New York in 1888 and established a girls' school, St. Joseph's Academy, and the convent just outside Tipton on Mill St. The academy, which served grades 1-12, was dedicated in 1891, and the first class graduated the following year. In 1904 the school and convent were moved to the present location on the former grounds of St. Anthony's Farm, named for Father Anthony Kroeger, the school's first spiritual director. The academy building dates from the year of the move, and the convent building was constructed in 1910. The most recent structure, the Motherhouse Building or administration center, was erected in 1957. Declining enrollments forced the school to close in 1972, but the facility continues to serve as the motherhouse for the order in Indiana. The Sisters of St. Joseph operate hospitals and train teaching sisters for schools.

Continue west *.1 m.* and turn left on Main St. *.5 m.* to the county seat of **TIPTON** (p. 5,004). The settlement was founded by Samuel King in 1839 and named Kingston. When Tipton became a separate county in 1844, the site was chosen as the seat of justice, and the name was changed to Canton for pioneer John D. Smith's former home in Ohio. Because of a duplication it was renamed Tipton after the county. It has remained small throughout its history, and although there are several industries in the area, it basically serves the need of the local agricultural community. At one time it was a state leader in tomato production and supported numerous canning factories.

Continue to the **Tipton County Courthouse** at the southeast corner of Main and Jefferson sts. The Romanesque-style building was constructed in 1893-94 as the third county courthouse. Adolph Scherrer of Indianapolis was the architect, and Pierce and Morgan of Indianapolis were the contractors. Scherrer also supervised the construction of such Indianapolis landmarks as the State Capitol, the Blind Institute, and the Central State Hospital. The sand-

stone structure is 66 ft. high to the cornice and 206 ft. to the top of the flagstaff on the bell tower. Although no longer used, the 3,000-lb., specially made bell is still housed in the tower. (*NRHP*)

Located on the courthouse's ground floor is the **Tipton County Historical Society Museum**. Exhibited along the hallways are display cases containing items of local historical interest with a concentration on Indian artifacts. The museum was opened in the courthouse in 1951. A tablet mounted on a boulder in the north courthouse yard shows the intersection at Tipton of Indian trails connecting the Wabash and White rivers. Continue south on Main St. (IND 19) and pass the City Park on the right. It contains picnic areas, a swimming pool, tennis courts, and a golf course.

Drive south on Main St. (IND 19) *4.2 m.* to **HAMILTON COUNTY** (p. 82,027; 398 sq. m.). The region was organized in 1823 and named for patriot and statesman Alexander Hamilton. Much of the county has developed into a residential suburb of Indianapolis in recent years with a dramatic rise in population. The 1980 population is more than three times that of 50 years ago, and by the year 2000, the population is projected to double that of 1980. Although Hamilton County has experienced a population boom, over 75 percent of the area's land is used for farming, and many communities have retained a rural atmosphere.

Turn left on the county line road to **ATLANTA** (p. 657) and at *.4 m.* turn right on Walnut St. and left on Main St. The scene of a recent fascinating economic experiment, Atlanta was founded as Buena Vista in 1854, although a post office named Shielville had been established there in 1845. It was renamed Atlanta in 1886. The town was dying slowly until Mr. and Mrs. Robert Layton of Noblesville purchased nearly all of the two-block-long downtown between 1972 and 1976, restored it, and converted it into a tourist mecca of boutiques, unusual shops, and restaurants. Despite the attraction of an annual festival, two devastating fires have reduced the community's vitality.

Return to IND 19 and proceed south *2.4 m.* and turn right on 274th St. Travel west *1.1 m.*, then right on Gwin Rd. Proceed *.2 m.* and turn left on 276th St. On the right *3.8 m.* is the **Roberts Chapel and Cemetery**, remains of the **Roberts Settlement**. Hansel Roberts established the community comprised of people who were an unusual mixture of white, black, and Cherokee Indian blood in 1838. He was descended from a black valet who came to America with an Englishman named Roberts who had set up a plantation in North Carolina. When he died without heirs the valet assumed his name. The valet and his descendants remained in the area until local pressure forced the families to move north in the 1820s. Roberts Chapel dates from approximately 1860, and Hansel Roberts is buried in the cemetery. During the last decade of the 19th century, the Roberts settlers concluded that their land had become overcrowded and would no longer support them adequately. Consequently many moved to eastern or midwestern cities where they carved distinguished careers in medicine, education, law, and the ministry. These included a president of the National Medical Association, a college president, the first black elected to the Illinois senate, and the pastors of some of the nation's largest African Methodist Episcopal churches.

Return to IND 19 and continue south *.8 m.* to Main St. in **ARCADIA** (p. 1,801). John Shafer and Daniel Waltz laid out the village in 1849. The name was probably taken from a region of ancient Greece. Arcadia primarily has been a farming community throughout most of its history, except in the 1890s and early 1900s when it was a gas boom town. The fuel attracted a glass factory which was well known and respected, and Arcadia glass items are sought by collectors.

Turn right on Main St. for *.4 m.*, then left on Washington St. for one block, and right on South St. On the left is the **Heritage Center**, a restored railroad depot that dates from 1869. The Peru and Indianapolis Railroad came through Arcadia in 1852, and the depot was constructed under its ownership. In 1887 the railroad was acquired by the Lake Erie and Western, and it in turn became the Nickel Plate, then the Norfolk and Western. The last passenger purchased a ticket at the depot in 1932. The facility was restored in the late 1970s and is used as a library, museum, and meeting center.

Go back to IND 19 and turn right. On the left *1.9 m.* is the **Indiana Academy**, a coeducational boarding school operated by the Indiana Conference of Seventh-day Adventists serving grades 9-12. The denominational school, which has an average enrollment of 150 students from

throughout the United States, was opened in 1919 on 100 acres of woods and farmland.

The extreme northeast tip of **Morse Reservoir** is located *.2 m.* past the Indiana Academy on the west side of IND 19. This man-made lake was created by the Indianapolis Water Company in 1956. Seven billion gallons of water fill the 1,463-acre reservoir. Recreational activities on the lake include fishing, boating, and sailing. Most of the shore area is lined with private homes. For a panoramic view of the reservoir, continue *.7 m.* to the flashing light at Jackson St., turn right, and continue *.3 m.* A causeway crosses the water. Return to IND 19 and turn right.

South on IND 19 *4.8 m.* is the city of **NOBLESVILLE** (p. 12,056). William Conner and Josiah F. Polk surveyed and platted the area in 1823 as the Hamilton County seat. Legend has it that Polk named the settlement for his fiancé, Lavinia Noble, but it may have been called Noblesville to honor United States senator James Noble. The town was a farming community prior to the arrival of Firestone Industrial Products in 1936.

Continue on IND 19 for *.3 m.* and turn right into **Forest Park**. The 180-acre park was constructed by the Works Progress Administration (WPA) during the depression. Offered in the complex are cabins, camping facilities, picnic area, hiking trails, and a swimming pool. Located *.6 m.* past the park's entrance on the left is the **Indiana Transportation Museum**. The museum was organized in 1960 and was moved to its 10-acre Forest Park site five years later. Though small, the museum has an excellent collection of railroad equipment, vintage autos and trucks, buggies, and wagons. Among the rail collection are operating electric interurban railway cars, locomotives, a dining car, and a railroad president's private car. Other items include a mule-drawn streetcar, a 1921 Stutz hook and ladder fire truck, and a 1926 Model TT Ford one ton truck. The museum operates former Chicago-area interurban cars over nearly a mile of track and uses for an office the former Nickel Plate Railroad station at Hobbs (Tipton County).

Travel south on IND 19 for *.7 m.* and turn left on Logan St. to the **Hamilton County Courthouse** at the southeast corner of 8th St. The French Renaissance-style structure was built in 1878, but the current tower dates from 1968. In 1925 the courthouse and Noblesville gained national attention as the site of the D. C. Stephenson trial. The Grand Dragon of Indiana's Ku Klux Klan was convicted of second degree murder in the death of Madge Oberholtzer, a statehouse secretary, and given a life sentence. (*NRHP*)

The former **Hamilton County Jail** is situated on the southwest corner of the courthouse square. The two-story brick and stone structure was erected in 1876 and housed local criminals until 1977. D. C. Stephenson was imprisoned in the building during his trial. The sheriff's residence side of the jail is now a historical museum operated by the Hamilton County Historical Society.

Travel east on Logan St. two blocks and turn left on 10th St. North *2 m.* on the left is **Potter's Covered Bridge**. The 259-ft. bridge spans the West Fork of the White River and was constructed by Josiah Durfee and Company in 1871. It was rebuilt in 1937 but has since been closed to traffic.

Return south on 10th St. (Allisonville Rd.) *6.5 m.* to the **Conner Prairie Pioneer Settlement** on the right. This 55-acre open-air museum is situated on the former William Conner homestead in an area known as Horseshoe Prairie.

Conner (1777-1855) acquired the land from the Delaware tribe in 1802 and constructed a log cabin and fur trading post. He later married Mekinges, the daughter of the Delaware Chief Anderson, but in 1820 the Indian princess went west with the rest of her tribe. A few months earlier in 1820, the commissioners selected to choose a site for a new state capital met in Conner's cabin and agreed on that of the present-day city of Indianapolis. Conner married Elizabeth Chapman in 1820 and constructed the area's first brick home for her in place of the log cabin. Among those who visited the Conners in their new home were Washington Irving, James Fenimore Cooper, and John Jacob Astor. In 1824 the house and farm served as Henry Clay's western campaign headquarters. Conner served as a state representative, 1829-32 and 1836-37. At the later date he sold his farm and moved into Noblesville. Eli Lilly, the pharmaceutical manufacturer, obtained the decaying farm for use as a hog breeding project in 1934, and he soon restored the brick home and added several other structures. In 1964 Lilly donated the farm to Earlham College, which continued the restoration process and opened it to the public as an outdoor museum.

Indiana Historical Society (Peat Collection)

William Conner house

In 1973 Conner Prairie took on a new flavor when the guides assumed settlers' roles. The settlement depicts everyday life from the year 1836, with each guide contributing a distinct character and profession. Many of the village's thirty-nine buildings were moved to Conner Prairie from other parts of the state and were painstakingly restored to period authenticity. The blacksmith's house comes from Lewisville (Henry County), the doctor's house from 86th St. and Allisonville Rd. (Marion County), the Doan house from Westfield, and the Cedar Creek covered bridge from south of Auburn (De Kalb County). The Golden Eagle Inn, a tavern and boardinghouse moved from Westfield in 1975, has been restored to resemble a Pennsylvania German inn. In 1988 Conner Prairie unveiled its **Museum Center**, a 65,000-sq.-ft., nearly $8 million facility. Besides a permanent gallery, the museum, designed by the Everett I. Brown Company of Indianapolis, contains a revolving exhibits gallery, meeting rooms, library, restaurant, gift shop, theater, storage, and administrative offices. Protected by a copper roof, the ultramodern building of rubble stone and glass contrasts sharply with the historical setting around it. The copper fountain in the foyer was crafted by Hoosier artist Donald Robertson. A two-story airy atrium is the main reception area. Also of new construction are the crafts and maintenance buildings north of the museum.

Proceed *2 m.* south on Allisonville Rd. and turn right on 116th St. The city limits of **CARMEL** (p. 18,272) are *2.1 m.* west on 116th St. The village was established in 1837 as Bethlehem, but when the post office was started nine years later, it was discovered that another Indiana community had the same name. The post office then was named Carmel after the biblical site, and the town followed suit in 1874. The area once was noted for its feed, grain, and livestock, as well as for its manufacturing, with such industries as ready-mix concrete, lighting accessories, machine products, pet accessories, and metal stampings, but from the late 1960s into the 1980s, it has developed into one of Indianapolis's more affluent suburbs. Carmel's population growth from 1960 to 1980 has been phenomenal with an increase of nearly 17,000 residents.

On the right *.2 m.* past the city limits sign is the **Flowing Well**. Joe Carey discovered the artesian spring by accident while drilling for natural gas in 1902. This popular attraction is usually crowded with enthusiasts wishing to obtain the mineral water from the free-flowing fountain. The well area was beautified, and an enclosure with blue siding was added in 1983.

Continue west *2.2 m.* and turn right on Range Line Rd. Proceed north *1.6 m.* to Main St. This intersection was the site of one of the country's **first electric traffic signals**. Leslie Haines, a Carmel native who learned electrical engineering while in the Navy, designed the signal in 1923. The light was disconnected in 1933 and removed from its cone-shaped base the following year. In 1975 the signal was given to the Carmel-Clay Historical Society.

Turn right on E. Main St. and proceed *.9 m.* to the **John Kinzer house and cabin** on the left, in one of Carmel's more elite areas. Kinzer, an Ohio native, settled in the region in 1828 and constructed the log cabin two years later. The Federal-style wooden house with white siding dates from about 1835. There is an unsubstantiated story of buried treasure on the property. The Delaware tribe received a large sum of gold from the United States government for the land cession in the Treaty of St. Marys (1818). Before the Indians left the region, they supposedly buried the gold on the land later acquired by Kinzer. Despite efforts by Kinzer and others, no gold was ever unearthed. (*NRHP*)

Return *.2 m.* and turn right on IND 431 (N. Keystone Ave.). Travel north *4 m.*, merging with US 31, and turn right on 169th St. at **WESTFIELD** (p. 2,783). This Quaker settlement was laid out in 1834 and probably named for another community. Westfield was a major stopping point on the "underground railroad," and several older homes concealed runaway slaves making their way to Canada. Today the region is noted for its livestock and feed grain.

Drive east *.3 m.* and turn left on Westfield Blvd. (Union St.). The **Union Bible Seminary** is located *.3 m.* on the right. The two-story, red brick building was constructed in 1861 as the Friends Academy (later Union High School). At its peak in the 1870s, this Quaker-maintained school had an enrollment of several hundred students and was recognized as one of the premier secondary schools in the state. The school later became public-supported and was closed in the 1890s. It was reopened in 1911 as the Union Bible Seminary, an institution concerned with Bible study and related topics for male and female missionaries. The seminary was reorganized and expanded in 1924, and it has developed a national reputation for the training of fundamentalist students of elementary and high school age interested in becoming missionaries. Additional buildings have been constructed recently.

Continue north .3 m., turn left on Main St. to US 31, and turn right. At 3.6 m. turn left on IND 38 (Bataan Memorial Highway). Travel northwest (a very crooked road in several places) through **SHERIDAN** (p. 2,200) and briefly cross the extreme northeast corner of Boone County (for a description of the county see Tour 13) to the **CLINTON COUNTY** (p. 31,545; 405 sq. m.) line (11.5 m. from US 31). Clinton County was organized in 1830 and named for DeWitt Clinton, the canal-supporting governor of New York. The largest portion of the county's rolling land is used for agriculture, but the region's overall economy is diversified with several major manufacturers, particularly in and around the Frankfort area.

Proceed northwest 18.9 m. on IND 38, passing through **KIRKLIN** (p. 662), to IND 39. Turn right and travel north 2.7 m. to **FRANKFORT** (p. 15,168). The town was laid out in 1830 for the specific purpose of becoming the county seat on land donated by John Pence and his brothers. The community was named either for the Pences' ancestral home of Frankfurt am Main in Germany or for Kentucky's state capital. The town grew slowly until arrival of the Terre Haute and Logansport Railroad in 1870, when it blossomed into one of the region's leading manufacturing centers. One of these industries, the Kemp Brothers Packing Company (later Del Monte), claims to have marketed the country's first commercially canned tomato juice in 1928. Other major industries in Frankfort include Frito-Lay snack foods, Indiana Brass, and National Cigar. Agricultural processing is also a major industry. Most larger manufacturers are located about 2 m. west of town on IND 28.

Travel 1 m. past the city limits sign on S. Jackson St. (IND 39 & 38) to the **Clinton County Courthouse** on the left. The cornerstone of this third county courthouse was laid in 1882, and the building was completed in 1886 at a cost of $200,000. The classically styled structure is made of Indiana Oolitic limestone. George W. Bunting of Indianapolis was the architect, and Farman and Pearce were the build-

ers. The three-story building is distinguished by its tower and clock, reaching a height of 165 ft. Parts of the courthouse were remodeled in 1975-76. (*NRHP*)

Turn right on Clinton St. immediately south of the courthouse and proceed one block to **"Old Stoney"** on the right. This former high and junior high school building was opened in 1892 and represents a rare combination of several architectural styles projecting a castle-like appearance. The structure receives its nickname from its sandstone exterior. Among those who attended high school in the building was the late Hollywood actor Will Geer, a Frankfort native. In 1974 the junior high moved to a new building and "Old Stoney" became vacant for two years until renovation was initiated to convert the historic structure into a home for the Clinton County Historical Society Museum and several offices and businesses. In 1980 the building was reopened with the Historical Society and Museum occupying an area on the second floor. (*NRHP*)

Continue east on Clinton St. .2 m. to the **Kelly Home and Antique Museum** on the left at 804 E. Clinton. This home was constructed in 1899 and is noted for its wood carvings and woodwork. This private residence contains numerous antiques.

Return west to Main St. (on the west side of the courthouse) and turn left. One block on the right, at the southwest corner of Walnut St., is the **Goodwin Funeral Home**. Located in a former garage at the building's rear and scattered throughout the house is director William Goodwin's outstanding and unusual antique collection. Goodwin started the hobby in 1956 when he acquired a horse-drawn antique hearse to celebrate the 100th anniversary of the funeral home's founding by his grandfather, George William Goodwin. The largest part of Goodwin's varied antique collection consists of autos, bicycles, and Lincoln memorabilia. Among the more unusual items are Gen. Omar Bradley's Cadillac limousine and a motorized wheelchair once owned by President Franklin Delano Roosevelt.

Travel .2 m. north on Main St. to Morrison St. Located in a brick building at the northeast corner is the **National Cigar Corporation**, the nation's largest producer of dark Connecticut broad leaf cigars. The operation was started in its present location by Noah "N. N." Smith in 1919. Smith later sold out to the John Burger and Son Company, and in 1977 the name was changed to the National Cigar Corporation. At its inception, the cigars were hand-rolled, but automation has since replaced the older method, although the company claims not to engage in the mass-production techniques of the larger firms.

Continue north on Main St. *.4 m.* to Kyger St. and turn left on US 421/IND 39. Continue to IND 26 at Rossville (p. 1,148) and turn left. Continue *9 m.* and reenter Tippecanoe County, then travel *8.6 m.* farther to the intersection with US 52, the tour's termination point.

Tour 16

Tour 16 begins at IND 26 (State St.) and IND 43 (River Rd.) in West Lafayette. Located on IND 43, *3.7 m.* north of State St. in West Lafayette, is the **Indiana State Soldiers' Home Historic District**. In 1886 the Grand Army of the Republic, an organization of Civil War veterans, began lobbying for a state home for destitute or disabled veterans and their widows. These efforts bore fruit in 1895 when the legislature established the Indiana State Soldiers' Home and designated the present location of the Indiana Veterans' Home as its site. The historic district included three buildings: the Commandant's Residence, the Lawrie Library, and the Administration Building. The Commandant's Residence, with its impressive white pillars, is the focal point of the district. No longer the residence of the administrator of the home, the two-story Greek Revival-style house has been renovated and is available as a meeting place for community groups. Although the building has been painted white for many years, the original colors were probably red with white trim. The Administration Building, which flanks the Commandant's Residence on the left, is currently used for state offices. The Lawrie Library is empty.

In the early 1970s these buildings were threatened with demolition or extensive remodeling. (The State Board of Health wanted to cover the Commandant's Residence with aluminum siding and remove the massive pillars.) Through the efforts of preservation groups such as the Wabash Valley Trust for His-

Indiana State Soldiers' Home, Commandant's Residence, 1937

Tour 16

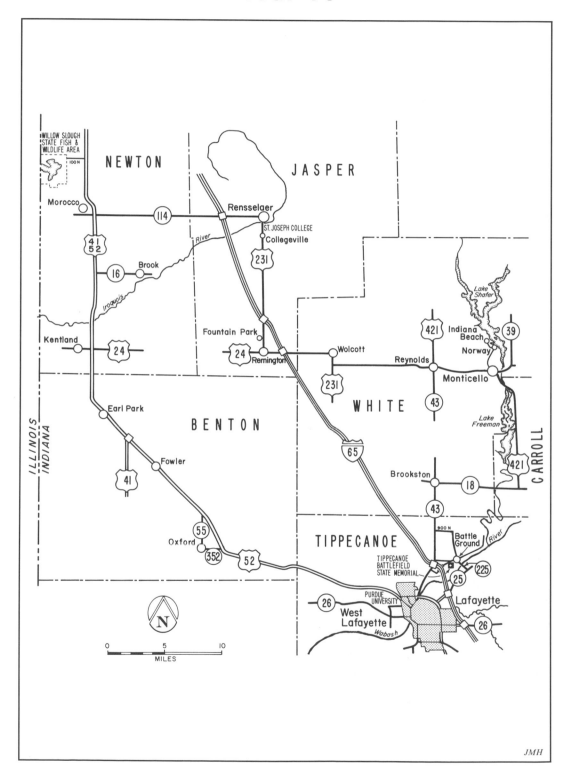

JMH

toric Preservation the buildings were saved and placed on the National Register of Historic Places in 1974. The properties, no longer part of the Indiana Veterans' Home, are administered by the Department of Natural Resources as a state memorial. Proceed northeast on IND 43 *1.6 m.*, make a sharp right turn onto Burnette Rd., and left at *.4 m.* to 9th St. (Railroad St.). Drive *1.6 m.* to the **Tippecanoe Battlefield** entrance on the left. In the early morning of November 7, 1811, a force of between 600 and 700 Indians made up of a confederation of the Potawatomi, Shawnee, Kickapoo, Delaware, Winnebago, Wea, and Wyandotte tribes under the direction of Tenskwatawa, the Shawnee Prophet, attacked an encampment of more than 900 United States regulars, militia, and volunteers under the command of territorial governor William Henry Harrison. Although 95 percent of the United States troops had no combat experience, they repelled the surprise attack in several hours. While generally regarded as a less than decisive military victory, Tippecanoe resulted in the loss of the Prophet's power within the Indian confederacy. The battle also represented the first major conflict between Indians and whites in the Old Northwest since the Battle of Fallen Timbers in 1794. According to the monument, United States casualties at Tippecanoe, dead and wounded, numbered 188. At least 35 Indians lost their lives during the fighting, but probably the number was much higher.

Much of the historical significance surrounding the Battle of Tippecanoe evolved after the actual fighting. Ten Indiana counties bear the names of men who fought at Tippecanoe. The battlefield was the site of a Great Whig Rally on May 29, 1840, when presidential candidate William Henry Harrison launched his successful campaign in front of some 30,000 supporters. The battle became immortalized by the Harrison campaign slogan of "Tippecanoe and Tyler Too."

In 1829 John Tipton, a veteran of Tippecanoe, acquired the battleground for the purpose of making it a memorial. He transferred the tract to the state in 1836, which enclosed it with a wooden fence in 1851. An iron fence replaced the wooden structure 22 years later. The 92-ft. granite obelisk with a life-size statue of Harrison at the north end was erected in 1908. The Buffalo, New York, based firm of McDonnell and Sons constructed the memorial

at a cost of $24,500. Smaller markers also were erected at various locations on the field to indicate the approximate sites where officers were killed. The park, which is a National Historic Landmark as well as a state memorial, has been expanded over the years so that now it encompasses about 100 acres. Among the features are hiking trails and a retreat center for overnight groups. A museum, the most recent addition, contains exhibits and a slide presentation on the battle and the Harrison campaign of 1840. (*NRHP*)

Turn left onto Railroad St. upon exiting the battlefield. Drive *.1 m.* to Prophet St. and turn left. Ahead on the right *.7 m.* is a stone marker pointing out the trail to **Prophet's Rock**. Atop this ledge on the bluffs of Burnett's Creek, the Prophet is said to have given the command for his forces to attack Harrison's troops. Tenskwatawa did not take an active part in the fighting. During the battle he remained in relative safety at this site chanting to the Master of Life for the safety and success of his warriors. When the Prophet saw his braves retreating, he also fled to Prophetstown. Trails may be walked from the battlefield to this area.

Return to the intersection of Prophet and Railroad sts. and turn left. Drive *.2 m.* to the main intersection in **BATTLE GROUND** (p. 812) and make a sharp right turn onto IND 225. Proceed *1.1 m.* southeast to a historical marker on the right indicating the former site of **Prophetstown**. In the spring of 1808 the Shawnee half brothers Tecumseh and Tenskwatawa moved from their Ohio lands to establish this town just below the mouth of the Tippecanoe on the north bank of the Wabash. The settlement was laid out along regular street lines and contained two public buildings as well as a guest lodge. While not a tribal center, Prophetstown served as the capital of the Indian confederacy and was the training ground for more than 1,000 warriors. The threat that this Indian stronghold posed to white expansion, together with Tecumseh's absence at the time recruiting tribes in what is now Arkansas, induced Harrison to march from Vincennes to Prophetstown. The village was abandoned immediately after the defeat at Tippecanoe, and it was burned at Harrison's orders the day after the battle. The Indians blamed their defeat on the false promises of the Prophet, who narrowly escaped from his former followers with his life. An attempt was made to rebuild Prophetstown in the spring of 1812, but it was destroyed in November of the same year by another United States expedition under the command of Maj. Gen. Samuel Hopkins.

Return to the intersection in Battle Ground and turn right onto Main St. Drive northeast (the name changes to Pretty Prairie Rd. outside of town) *2.6 m.* to the junction with Tyler Rd. This region once was the site of **Keth-tip-pe-can-nunk**, a settlement built by French and Indian traders from Ouiatenon around 1780. At one time it was the most powerful Indian town on the Wabash containing around 70 buildings. In 1791 President George Washington ordered Brig. Gen. Charles Scott and a force of about 750 into this area in an effort to break down Indian resistance to white expansion. A part of this detachment under the command of Col. James Wilkinson destroyed Keth-tip-pe-can-nunk on June 3 of the same year.

Head back to Battle Ground, turn right onto Jefferson St. (*2.5 m.* from Pretty Prairie and Tyler rds.), and drive *1.6 m.* to the entrance to **Wolf Park** on the right (Jefferson St. becomes Harrison Rd. *.2 m.* from the Main St. turnoff). Dr. Erich Klinghammer of Purdue University developed the park to allow scientists and students to observe and record the habits of wolves.

Continue northwest on Harrison Rd. *1 m.* and turn left onto CR 900N at Ash Grove. Proceed *1.1 m.* and turn right onto IND 43. Drive *.9 m.* and enter **WHITE COUNTY** (p. 23,867; 506 sq. m.). The county was formed in 1834 and named for Col. Isaac White, who was killed at the Battle of Tippecanoe. Rich soil that yields large crops of corn, oats, wheat, and soybeans covers most of the county. While farming is the primary occupation, food products, furniture, tools, and plastic products also are manufactured in White County.

Proceed *2.7 m.* and turn right at IND 18 in **BROOKSTON** (p. 1,701). The distinguished journalist Horace Greeley arrived here on a freight and livestock train in 1853 after missing his passenger train in Lafayette. The 14-mile trip required three hours, but the worst was yet to come. The engine broke down, and Greeley, in a desperate attempt to keep a speaking date in La Porte, commandeered a handcar and rode at night across the eerie Kankakee swamp. He reported the experience to his *New York Tribune* in vitriolic rage and began a lifelong dis-

dain for Hoosiers. He described Brookston as a village of three houses. Drive east on IND 18 *5.1 m.* and cross the Tippecanoe River to enter Carroll County (for a description of the county see Tour 15). Go *2.1 m.* and turn north onto US 421/IND 39. Off this road to the left is **Lake Freeman**. This man-made body of water was created in 1925 when the Insull Company (the forerunner of Northern Indiana Public Service) along with the Army Corps of Engineers constructed the Oakdale Dam on the Tippecanoe River to provide hydroelectric power. Named for Roger M. Freeman, chief engineer of the Oakdale Dam at the south end of the lake, Lake Freeman shares its 50 miles of shore with White and Carroll counties. Principal activities on the 1,547-acre lake are boating and fishing. Since this resort lake is private, a good portion of the lakefront property is owned by individuals who have constructed summer or weekend homes.

North *9.6 m.* on US 421/IND 39 from IND 18 the tour reenters White County at **MONTICELLO** (p. 5,162). The county seat was laid out on the bluffs overlooking the Tippecanoe River in 1834 and named for Thomas Jefferson's home in Virginia. The city has been hit by numerous tornadoes including one in 1974 that devastated the area causing an estimated $100 million in damage and taking several lives.

On the left at Broadway and N. Main sts. *1.5 m.* farther is **White County Building** (county courthouse). This is the fourth or fifth building to house the county government, with the first log structure being completed in 1837. The previous 1895-constructed courthouse was destroyed in the 1974 tornado. Two years later the present modern, three-story brick and concrete building was completed at a cost of $2.5 million. Robert Longardner of Longardner and Associates, Inc., of Indianapolis was the architect.

The **James Culbertson Reynolds house** is located *.3 m.* north on the right at 417 N. Main St. The Italianate-style home was constructed in 1872 by the G. P. Randall Company of Chicago for James Culbertson Reynolds (1816-1877), a farmer, church elder, merchant, and politician who settled in the area from his native Ohio in 1843. (*NRHP*)

Turn left onto Pierce St. just north of the Reynolds house, drive west one block, turn left onto N. Illinois St., and continue *.3 m.* to Broadway (US 24) and turn right. Proceed west *.6 m.* and turn right onto 6th St., which leads to the west bank of **Lake Shafer**. Other than being created two years before Lake Freeman, Lake Shafer and Lake Freeman have almost identical histories. Lake Shafer, named for Indianapolis engineer John A. Shafer, was formed when the Insull Company constructed the Norway Dam on the Tippecanoe River north of Monticello to provide electricity. The 1,291-acre lake has about 50 miles of shoreline and is four miles in length with an average depth of 15 ft. Shafer is probably better known for its fishing and boating than Freeman and is more geared to the tourist trade, although there are numerous private residences along the lake.

North *3.3 m.* from Broadway is the turnoff on the right for **Indiana Beach**, the state's largest privately owned summer resort, which is somewhat glamorously referred to as "The Hoosier Riviera." E. W. Spackman started the operation in 1926 with a bathhouse and a small beach where he rented fishing boats. Originally called Ideal Beach, the area has grown to a 156-acre vacationland that contributes heavily to the area's tourist economy. Spackman built a ballroom in 1930 that once featured big bands such as Glenn Miller, Benny Goodman, and Tommy and Jimmy Dorsey. The ballroom (now called the Roof Garden) is still used for contemporary musical groups. The hotel was constructed in 1933, and the rides along the beach were added in 1946. The one-half-mile-long boardwalk with its rides, games, and restaurants is the beach's featured attraction along with the paddlewheel boat, the *Shafer Queen*, that offers rides. Ski shows are performed during the summer at the Aqua Theater. In addition to the hotel, there are 43 family cottages and a 1,000-site campground.

Return to Broadway (US 24), turn right, and drive *13.8 m.* to **WOLCOTT** (p. 923). The town was platted by and named for Anson Wolcott in 1861. Wolcott (1819-1907), a New York native and nephew of Declaration of Independence signer Oliver Wolcott, sold most of his holdings in 1858 and purchased as much as 10,000 acres of farmland in north central Indiana. In the 1850s many eastern land speculators acquired large land tracts from the federal government in this rich farm area. Most of these "land barons" remained east and either leased the land to tenant farmers or sold it to the railroads. Wolcott was an exception in that he moved west to live on his property. In addition to his landholdings, Wolcott was a prominent lawyer and politician. He served as Gov. Oliver P. Morton's representative in Washington during the Civil War and was the Greenback party candidate for governor in 1876.

Bear right on US 24/231 *.5 m.* past the town limits sign and proceed *.7 m.* to the **Anson Wolcott home** on the left. The two-story Italianate house with an observatory was constructed by T. Tilly of Chicago for Wolcott in 1860, but probably not completed until 1864. Certain aspects of the house reflect a Southern mansion influence since Wolcott spent part of his youth in Louisiana. It is said that the men, lumber, and materials for the home were imported from Chicago. Wolcott's descendants gave the house to the township in 1956, and it was restored two years later as a community center. (*NRHP*)

Continue west *3 m.* and enter **JASPER COUNTY** (p. 26,138; 561 sq. m.). This agriculturally reliant county was formed by statute in 1835, organized in 1838, and named for American Revolutionary War hero Sgt. William Jasper of South Carolina. About 84 percent of the county's basically flat terrain is used for farmland. Most of central and northern Jasper County was water-logged, much of it in the famous Kankakee swamp, and awaiting speculators who would drain and develop it. Chief among these was Benjamin J. Gifford of Rantoul, Illinois, who amassed approximately 35,000 acres for as little as $4.50 an acre, ditched it, and produced prodigious quantities of corn and oats and such muck crops as onions and potatoes. Gifford operated on such a grand scale that he built his own 32-mile railroad, the Chicago and Wabash Valley, which was known popularly as the "Onion Belt," to haul produce and livestock. Additional wealth lay just beneath the surface, and a turn-of-the-century oil boom generated approximately 100 active wells by 1900. They tapped a field at the incredibly shallow depth of approximately 100 ft. A town, appropriately called Asphaltum, was founded, and a refinery and oil well equipment manufacturers located there. The boom and the industries died quickly, but 50 years later farmers continued to grease machinery with the heavy petroleum that still oozed from abandoned wells.

Near the Jasper County line, the Atchison, Topeka and Santa Fe Railroad intermodal facility stands on the left, convenient to trucks operating on nearby I-65. The railroad built the terminal after its subsidiary, Toledo, Peoria and Western, had bought a castoff Pennsylvania Railroad line and then found its Logansport connection eliminated by Conrail abandonments. Continue *2.9 m.* and turn right on US 231 in **REMINGTON** (p. 1,268). Drive *1 m.* north and turn left onto CR 1600S. On the left *.4 m.* is the entrance to **Fountain Park**, one of the few remaining chautauquas in the country. The first chautauqua was held in New York in 1874 to train Sunday school teachers. At the height of the movement around the turn of the century, there were hundreds of local assemblies each attracting thousands of participants. A special feature of the chautauquas were addresses by some of the best-known political and religious orators of the day. Since 1895 people have been meeting at Fountain Park for several weeks each summer for spiritual, social, and educational sharing. The village is located on 17 acres and includes a 35-room hotel that dates from 1898, a 600-seat, open-air tabernacle built in 1959, and an art colony. Surrounding the village are 65 private cottages dating from around 1900 and a 35-site campground.

Continue north on US 231 *9.8 m.* to **St. Joseph's College** at **COLLEGEVILLE** (p. 1,059). This Catholic Church-supported school was incorporated in 1889 under the direction of the Society of the Precious Blood. The first students (54) enrolled in the fall of 1891, and the first graduation took place in 1896. Father Augustine Seifert served as the school's first president. In its early years St. Joseph's was on two educational levels: a high school and a junior college. Young men were trained for professional schools and the religious life as well as for teaching and business careers. From 1925 to 1931 St. Joseph's was used as a minor religious seminary only, before returning to its previous status, and it was not until 1936 that the institution became the four-year liberal arts college that it is today. With a few exceptions, St. Joseph's remained all male until the fall of 1968. The campus served as the preseason training camp for the Chicago Bears of the National Football League from 1944 to 1974. The team's former practice field can still be seen on the southwest edge of campus. One of the school's dormitories, Hallas Hall, was named for the former owner and coach of the Bears,

George S. Hallas, a major contributor to the college.

Highlighting the 130-acre campus with 30 buildings is the Romanesque-style brick and stone **Chapel** which is near the entrance. Completed in 1910, the chapel with its twin bell towers is symbolic of St. Joseph's. Enhancing the beauty of the chapel is the bordering reflecting pond and fountain, which date from the college's early days.

Near the rear of the campus is the **Halleck Student Center**, the union building. The cornerstone of this $1.5 million building was laid by former President Dwight D. Eisenhower in 1962. Named for former congressman and St. Joseph's trustee Charles A. Halleck, the structure houses the student dining room, lounges, meeting rooms, and administrative offices.

The **Lourdes Grotto** at the southwest corner of the campus was started by a student, Faustin Bernard Ersing, in 1898. It was enlarged in 1931 with the construction of the interior shrine containing the Carrara marble statue of Christ in Gethsemane.

Set off the road on the east side of US 231 is **Drexel Hall**. This three-story brick structure once served as the main building for St. Joseph's Indian Normal School. It was erected and the school was started in 1888 by the Bureau of Catholic Indian Missions under the direction of Msgr. Joseph A. Stephan. Philadelphia, Pennsylvania, heiress Katharine Drexel donated $50,000 for its construction. She later became Mother Katharine, the founder of the Sisters of the Blessed Sacrament. The school was located on 420 acres of farmland and was designed to provide young Indian men with training in industry (farming, tailoring, and carpentry), practical hygiene, religion, and patriotism. From the beginning, the school's location presented a problem. Since there were no longer Indian tribes in Indiana, students had to be transported from Michigan, Wisconsin, Minnesota, and the Dakotas. Distance, legal problems, and family breakups discouraged many potential pupils. Homesickness resulted in a high number of runaways among those who did come, and the school averaged a 50 percent turnover rate. Only 6 out of the first class of 50 completed the designed five-year program. The highest enrollment at the Indian School was 74 in 1892. The government cutoff of funds to sectarian Indian missions forced St. Joseph's to close in 1896. The building and the grounds were acquired by St. Joseph's College. Over the years the old main building was used for a variety of purposes until it was remodeled into a residence hall housing about 100 in 1937 and was named for Mother Katharine Drexel. In 1971 the building was dedicated as an Indiana historic site. The only exterior changes have been the removal of the bell tower and the dormers. Economic reasons forced the school to close the hall in 1978. (*NRHP*)

Proceed north on US 231 *.3 m.* to **RENS-SELAER** (p. 4,944), the county seat and largest city in the area. The first settlers to the region, the Joseph D. Yeoman family, arrived in 1836. In 1838 James Van Rensselaer, a merchant from Utica, New York, obtained part of Yeoman's land and constructed a gristmill. Van Rensselaer laid out the town as Newton in 1839, but its name soon was changed to honor its founder. Throughout its history Rensselaer has been an agricultural center with a few small industries, whose principal products are electrical equipment, mattress innersprings, and cabinets. James F. Hanley (1892-1942), the composer of "Indiana" (better known as "Back Home Again In Indiana," with lyrics by Ballard MacDonald), was born in Rensselaer, and his 1917 hit song apparently was inspired by his home as a youth. Hanley also was the composer of such hits as "Zing Went the Strings of My Heart" and "Second Hand Rose."

Continue north on US 231 (Washington St.) and bear right *.5 m.* ahead to stay on Washington St. On the left is a small area known as **Milroy Park**, named in honor of Maj. Gen. Robert H. Milroy (1816-1890), a military hero and member of the 1850-51 Indiana Constitutional Convention. Milroy, who was serving as the circuit court judge in Rensselaer when the Civil War began, organized a company of local volunteers. Milroy and his troops are best known for their stand at Winchester, Virginia, which retarded Lee's invasion into Pennsylvania. His appearance and heroics earned him the nickname "Gray Eagle." After the war Milroy became a trustee of the Wabash and Erie Canal and later the Indian agent to the state of Washington. The park is located on the Milroy homestead site. The large bronze statue of the general was erected in 1910. Miss Mary Washburn, a Rensselaer native, was the sculptress.

The **Jasper County Courthouse** is located *.2 m.* farther on the right at Van Rensselaer St. This Romanesque/Late Gothic-style building was constructed by Alfred Grindle and Charles R. Weatherhogg of Fort Wayne from 1896 to 1898. The four-story stone structure is highlighted by a 140-ft.-high central tower with a four-faced clock. (*NRHP*)

Turn left onto N. Cullen St. (IND 114) just north of the courthouse, drive *.3 m.* northwest, and bear left when IND 114 follows W. Clark St. Ahead *1.6 m.* on the left is the Jasper County Fairgrounds, location of the **Historical Log Cabin Museum**, which dates from 1872 and is furnished with period pieces.

Proceed west to the **NEWTON COUNTY** (p. 14,844; 401 sq. m.) line (*4.8 m.* from the fairgrounds). The state legislature created the county in 1835, but it soon became part of Jasper County and remained so until 1859, making Newton the last county organized in Indiana. It is named for Sgt. John Newton, a Revolutionary War hero who served with Francis Marion in the Carolinas. Ninety percent of the county's basically flat land is farmed, with grain and cattle production leading the way. Many farms are large operations, and Newton leads the state in average size per farm. At one time it contained two farms of 17,000 acres each. Stone is quarried in the Kentland area.

Drive west *8.3 m.* and turn right onto US 41. Proceed north *5.3 m.* and turn left onto CR 100N, opposite the end of IND 14. On the left *1 m.* is an entrance to **Willow Slough State Fish and Wildlife Area**. (A second entrance is located on CR 275S just north and west of the IND 114/US 41 intersection.) This 9,670-acre area was opened in 1953 for public fishing and hunting. The high sand ridges and underbrush provide an abundance of fur-bearing game, while the watery lowlands and marshes are a haven for waterfowl. The 1,500-acre man-made J. C. Murphy Lake is stocked with fish. (Fishing is not allowed during the fall waterfowl season.) Camping and picnicking are available at the south end of the lake. Willow Slough is a restored remnant of Beaver Lake, a vast shallow outpost of the Kankakee swamp, which covered much of northwestern Newton County. Before it was drained in 1853, it covered 36,000 acres to a depth of 3.5 ft.

Return to US 41 and travel south to **MO-ROCCO** (p. 1,348) on the right at *5 m.* John Murphy laid out the town in 1851. This was the home of Edgar (Sam) Rice, a 20-year American League outfielder who was one of the few Hoosiers elected to the national Baseball Hall of Fame. Rice, who played from 1915 to 1934, had a .322 lifetime batting average and set defensive records.

From Morocco continue *5.5 m.* to IND 16 and turn left. Drive east *5.9 m.* through **BROOK** (p. 926) to the George Ade home, **Hazelden**, on the right. A Kentland native, Ade (1866-1944) is best known as a playwright, humorist, author, and newspaper columnist. In the early 1900s he became the first author to have three plays simultaneously run on Broadway, a feat only Neil Simon has since matched. Ade's best known literary work was *Fables in Slang* (1900). Hazelden, named for Ade's grandparents, was constructed in 1904 at a cost of $25,000 and quickly became a nationally known social and political mecca. William Howard Taft opened his successful bid for the presidency here in 1908 before 25,000 partisans, and a party for 800 members of the Indiana Society of Chicago became a legend because of the vast amounts of food consumed. Among those who visited Ade at Hazelden were Will Rogers and President Theodore Roo-

Indiana State Library

George Ade, 1923

sevelt. Restoration on this English Manor/Tudor-style house began in the mid-1960s at a cost of $100,000. Some of the rooms have been restored to their original condition, complete with memorabilia from Ade's life. (*NRHP*) A marker in Brook designates the first courthouse site, *2.3 m.* south. Brook was also the home of Hess Witch Hazel Cream, a popular skin lotion of the 1920s and 1930s, created by local druggist Elmer (Mack) Hess.

Return to US 41 and continue south *6.1 m.* to **KENTLAND** (p. 1,936). The Newton County seat was platted as Kent by town founder and major landowner Alexander J. Kent in 1860. The name later was changed to Kentland when it was discovered that it duplicated another Indiana town. The town has always relied on agriculture for its prosperity, although local industry produces aluminum and food products. In addition to being the birthplace of George Ade, Kentland also was the home of Warren T. McCray (1865-1938), Indiana governor, 1921-24.

One of Kentland's major industries is the **Edward J. Funk and Sons** hybrid seed corn company. The operation began in 1938, and it annually produces over 600,000 bags of seed corn, taken from 10,000 acres of farmland in a 70-mile area around Kentland. The company's modern corporate headquarters building is located on the west side of US 41 near the north edge of town. This contemporary earth-colored structure was designed by Leroy Troyer and Associates of Mishawaka, Indiana, in 1978. The one-story, 14,000-sq.-ft. building received special recognition from the Indiana Society of Architects. After passing at *.6 m.* on the right a section of the Alexander Kent mansion, which is now part of the **Nu-Joy Restaurant**, continue to the Funk production plant at the southwest corner of US 41/52 and US 24 (E. Seymour St.), *.8 m.* south of the corporate building. Stop at the reception desk to obtain a map for a self-guided plant tour. There are five stations where recorded messages explain the various production steps.

Travel west on Seymour St. (US 24) *.4 m.* and turn right on 3d St. North one block on the right is the **Newton County Courthouse**. This Neoclassical-style buff brick and limestone structure was constructed in 1905-6 at a cost of $30,525. Joseph T. Hutton of Hammond, Indiana, was the architect, and Eric Lund was the contractor. This building replaced the first county courthouse constructed in 1861.

Return to Seymour St. (US 24) and US 41/52 and continue east *2.6 m.* to the **Newton County Stone Company** on the right. A section of this excavation revealed a geological phenomenon. Studies revealed that a tremendous amount of force had uplifted a square mile of solid rock nearly 1,500 ft. closer to the surface than it should have been, earning it the name "The Kentland Crater." As early as 1883, the first owners of the stone company noticed that the rock strata extended vertically rather than in the normal horizontal pattern. Theories on the cause have varied from a meteor to a volcano or an earthquake.

Return to US 41/52 and turn left. South *2.2 m.* the tour enters **BENTON COUNTY** (p. 10,218; 407 sq. m.). Organized in 1840, the county was named for Missouri politician Thomas Hart Benton. As is the case with most of its neighbors, the county's economy is almost entirely reliant on agriculture. Corn, cattle, and hogs are the main products in this county where almost 100 percent of the land is farmed. On the average, Benton County farms are the richest in the state. It has one of the lowest population densities in Indiana.

An early land speculator in Benton and adjoining counties was Henry L. Ellsworth, a New Englander who became commissioner of patents and whose daughter selected the first words to be sent over the telegraph. Ellsworth believed so strongly in the potential riches of the unbroken prairie soil that he purchased nearly 90,000 acres in Benton County and additional thousands in other prairie counties during the 1830s. On the strength of his optimism, many other New Englanders, including Noah and Daniel Webster and members of the Boston Cabot family, also bought land. They were referred to in Benton County as the "Yale Crowd." Many years after most New Englanders had become disillusioned and sold out, and Ellsworth had bequeathed much of his land to Yale, the university owned nearly 10 square miles of Benton County, in addition to nearly 5,000 acres in other Indiana counties, mostly on the Grand Prairie of northwestern Indiana. As the "Yale Crowd" and their contemporaries disappeared, the cattle barons moved in. These men operated vast farms, following the pattern set by Ellsworth and his friends, and relied on tenants, meanwhile living

on a scale that exceeded the southern planter aristocracy. Moses Fowler fattened as many as 2,000 cattle at a time on his 20,000-acre Benton County farm, and his brother-in-law, Adams Earl, established America's foundation herd of purebred Herefords. The cattle barons left their names on the land in such Benton County towns and villages as Fowler, Earl Park, Raub, Atkinson, Boswell, Chase, and Templeton.

South *3.4 m.* is **EARL PARK** (p. 469). The main section is located about *.5 m.* west of US 41/52. This agricultural area is known for its towering old maple trees. Chief Parish (Pierrish) of the Kickapoo tribe fell to his death from one of these trees, and the area in the southwest corner of town is named Parish Grove in his memory. Parish Grove Township is on the county's west side, but Earl Park is not in it. Earl Park was named for Lafayette landowner Adams Earl who helped found the town in 1872. Its main claim to fame was its involvement in a historic 1922 court case concerning the legality of Indiana's "blue law," forbidding the showing of movies on Sunday. From 1919 to 1922 the Earl Park theater defied the state law by showing moving pictures on Sunday night. The court ruled in favor of the theater, but the judgment proved to be the establishment's undoing. Since Earl Park was no longer the only place to see Sunday night movies, the theater's crowds dwindled, and it was forced to close one year later because of the competition from movie houses in the more populated areas. East of Earl Park *7.5 m.,* the tiny settlement of Wadena produced a record number of professional baseball players in the first third of this century. Fred (Cy) Williams twice led the National League in home runs, Otis (Doc) Crandall had a .623 lifetime pitching average in the National and Federal leagues, and his two brothers played in the American Association and International leagues.

Proceed south on US 41/52 *2.7 m.* and follow US 52 to the right for approximately *4 m.* to **FOWLER** (p. 2,319), the county seat. Lafayette businessman Moses Fowler laid out the town in 1872 in hopes of attracting a railroad. Two years later the county seat was moved from Oxford to Fowler. The change came about partially because of Fowler's more central geographic position and its location on a high spot on the Grand Prairie and partially because of

Moses Fowler's contributions of the land and $40,000 for construction of the courthouse.

Turn left onto 5th St. (IND 55) *.4 m.* past the town limits sign. On the right *.4 m.* is the red brick and limestone **Benton County Courthouse**, constructed in 1874-75. Unlike most county courthouses which are centrally located, this Second Empire-style building is situated on the east edge of town, the result of a miscalculation by Fowler, who believed that the railroad would locate further east than it did. When the railroad came, the town developed around the station area instead of the courthouse.

Turn right on S. Lincoln Ave. just west of the courthouse, drive south one block, and turn right on E. 6th St. The **Ella Grant Lawson Home/Benton County Historical Society** is located on the left at 404 E. 6th. George A. Matthews (1859-1953) constructed this Neo-Jacobean-style house with white siding in the 1890s. Matthews was a local building contractor, merchant, and farmer. After two ownership changes, Ella Grant Lawson acquired the house in 1922. Lawson, a local socialite and philanthropist, bequeathed the house to the Woman's Club of Fowler upon her death in 1957. In 1971 the Woman's Club leased the house to the Benton County Historical Society. Although the building's exterior has undergone several style alterations, the historical society restored much of the interior to its original elegance. The house is mainly used for meetings.

Return to US 52, turn left, drive *5.6 m.*, and turn right onto IND 55 (CR 400E) *2.2 m.* to **OXFORD** (p. 1,327). The first settler, Judge David J. McConnell, arrived in 1834, but the town was not platted until 1843 when it was chosen to be the county seat. Within one year the town had undergone three name changes. It was first called Milroy after one of the founders, then Hartford after the Connecticut city, and finally Oxford at Judge McConnell's suggestion when it was discovered that the first two names already were being used by other Indiana communities. The derivation of the name Oxford is not clear. It was probably named for the English city and university, although local legend attributes it to oxen-driven wagons that forded nearby Pine Creek. For

many years Oxford was the only settlement in the county, but in 1873 the county courthouse was condemned, and the seat of justice was moved to Fowler. The town square is the only reminder of the building's former location.

Oxford's most famous son, or horse, was the trotter **Dan Patch** (1896-1916). Out of Zelica by Joe Patchen, the famed horse was born at Kelly's livery stable on IND 352, immediately south of IND 55. This white barn, on the left, is easily distinguished by the words "Dan Patch 1:55" spelled out in the green shingled roof. The horse's first owner was local merchant Dan Messner, and the trainer was another local, John Wattles. From the time the trotter started racing in 1900 until he stopped racing against competition in 1909, Dan Patch did not lose a race and finished second in only two heats. Because of a lack of competition, the horse often raced in exhibitions against the clock, and in 1905 he set the world's record for the mile of 1:55 1/4 at Lexington, Kentucky, a record that stood for 33 years. The time of 1:55 was an unofficial record set at the 1906 Minnesota State Fair. From 1909 to 1916 Dan Patch raced only in exhibitions at such places as fairs and special events. Despite his numerous racing accomplishments, the stallion was best known for his sometimes humanlike character. Although not a classic racing horse in terms of beauty and grace, the trotter was gentle, easy to handle, and often played the showman to the crowd. Dan Patch earned over $2 million for his owners, Messner, 1896-1901, M. E. Sturgis of New York, 1901-2, and M. W. Savage of Minneapolis, Minnesota, 1902-16. When the horse died in 1916, he was found to have an enlarged heart resulting from his years of racing. It weighed nine pounds, two ounces, while an average horse heart was five pounds. Dan Patch preceded owner Savage in death by one day.

Continue on IND 352 (Benton St.), turn left just past the Dan Patch birthplace, and proceed east *1.7 m.* to US 52 east. Turn right and drive *6.7 m.* to the Tippecanoe County line. Tour 16 ends *9.5 m.* farther where US 52 separates from US 231/IND 43A north of West Lafayette.

South Bend-Mishawaka

ST. JOSEPH COUNTY (p. 241,617; 459 sq. m.) lies at the heart of what is informally known as Michiana—that part of southern Michigan and northern Indiana that makes up a distinct social and economic unit. The state legislature created the county in 1830, giving it administrative jurisdiction to the state's western boundary, a large territory with but 287 residents. Not until 1850, and after five alterations, did the county assume its present shape and size, and there would be another act in 1931 to redefine the border between La Porte and St. Joseph counties. The county took its name from the St. Joseph River which crosses the northeast quarter of the county. This stream flows in a southwesterly direction out of Michigan and then loops abruptly north to recross the state line and empty into Lake Michigan. The county's topography is generally level except for moderate sloping in the southern part. Drained marshlands in the Kankakee River Valley provide rich farmland, where fruit and grain are the principal crops.

The county's industry is concentrated in the adjoining communities of South Bend (p. 109,727) and Mishawaka (p. 40,201), the county's two incorporated cities. South Bend, the seat of St. Joseph County, takes its name from its location on the southernmost bend of the St. Joseph River. Mishawaka also takes its name from its geographic location, but the precise meaning of the word is unclear. Of Potawatomi origin, the word may mean "thick woods rapids" or "country of dead trees." South Bend-Mishawaka began as a few scattered and isolated outposts, but blessed with abundant water power and imaginative leaders, the area soon grew into an important industrial center. Studebaker, Oliver Plow, Bendix, Singer, Uniroyal, and Reliance Electric are only a few of the important names in manufacturing that have been associated with the two communities.

In 1679 René-Robert Cavelier, Sieur de La Salle, and a small party of explorers paddled their canoes up the St. Joseph River and crossed the Kankakee-St. Joseph portage to continue down the Kankakee to the Illinois country. Although trappers, missionaries, soldiers, and explorers frequently used the portage throughout the 18th century, Europeans did not settle permanently in the area until the early 1800s. The earliest to come were fur traders. In 1820 Pierre Navarre, an agent of John Jacob Astor's American Fur Company, established a trading post on the east side of the river. Navarre moved west in 1840, but returned afterwards. Alexis Coquillard, who built a trading post called Big St. Joseph Station in 1823 near the bend of the river, is commonly considered the founder of South Bend. Another trader, Lathrop M. Taylor, opened a post in 1827. The little settlement that grew up in the vicinity of these two posts received a boost in 1828 when the route of the Michigan Rd., the state's first north-south highway, was surveyed through the area. In June 1829 Taylor became postmaster of Southold, a name changed a year later to South Bend.

Coquillard and Taylor bought most of the land in the vicinity of their posts and in 1831 platted a town. When the legislature designated St. Joseph, an infant community two miles downstream, as St. Joseph County's seat of government, the two traders, with generous offers of land for county buildings and a gift of $3,000, persuaded the county commissioners to move the county government to South Bend. Shortly thereafter, the rival town of St. Joseph withered and died. Other towns challenged South Bend's pretensions as the dominant community along the St. Joseph River. In 1834 Judge Elisha Egbert platted Portage near the St. Joseph-Kankakee crossing. He established a ferry and planned to build a college, but his dreams died in the depression following the Panic of 1837. Upstream, near the head of the

Mishawaka rapids, Alanson Hurd platted the town of St. Joseph Iron Works in 1833. The community took its name from the company which Hurd and others organized to manufacture iron from the bog ore found in nearby swamps. In 1835 William Barbee platted another town, called Mishawaka, immediately to the east. The next year Fowler's Addition and Indiana City were laid out on the opposite side of the river. In 1838 the legislature consolidated these four communities into one town and named it Mishawaka.

The economic life of the young towns of South Bend and Mishawaka depended on the river. By 1833 at least 10 keelboats regularly made the trip up and down the St. Joseph between Three Rivers, Michigan, and the lake. The keelboat era proved short-lived, for in 1833 the first steamboats reached South Bend. Soon a small fleet of such vessels was navigating the St. Joseph as far north as Three Rivers. The first major industry located along the river was the St. Joseph Iron Works. Its blast furnace was completed in 1834, and the company produced iron until the supply of bog ore was exhausted in 1856. The owners of the iron works built a dam at the head of the Mishawaka rapids (the first across the St. Joseph), which supplied water power to other industries. In South Bend Coquillard sold the rights to dig a millrace to a group of New York investors who also obtained a charter from the legislature to build a dam across the St. Joseph. These projects failed in the Panic of 1837, and a few years later the South Bend Manufacturing Company completed the dam and built races on both sides of the river.

Technological and political changes accelerated industrial growth in South Bend-Mishawaka at mid-century. The coming of the railroad released the two communities from the uncertainties of river and road transportation. In 1851 the Michigan Southern and Northern Indiana Railway Company built a line from Toledo to Chicago by way of South Bend and Mishawaka. On October 4 of that year, to the cheers of an enthusiastic crowd, the first train, pulled by the diminutive locomotive *John Stryker*, passed through the two communities. The Civil War accelerated South Bend and Mishawaka's economic development. Wagon manufacturers such as the Milburn Wagon Company of Mishawaka, which had received military contracts even before the war, were the

special beneficiaries. In 1857 George Milburn, unable to handle an army order, subcontracted 100 wagons to Henry and Clement Studebaker, who had opened a small horseshoeing and wagon repair shop in 1852. In 1862, after the outbreak of the war, the brothers signed their first contract directly with the government. At war's end the Milburn and Studebaker works were the largest in South Bend-Mishawaka.

Industrial growth in South Bend soon outpaced that in Mishawaka, which suffered a devastating fire in 1872 and lost its major manufacturer, the Milburn works, in 1874. By the mid-1870s the Studebaker wagon works, the Oliver Chilled Plow Works, and the Singer Sewing Machine Company dominated South Bend's economy. Studebaker, claiming to be the largest wagon works in the world, made over 11,000 wagons per year. The success of Oliver Plow, which turned out 300 plows a day, rested on James Oliver's patented process for "chilling" the iron as it was poured to form the moldboards of plows. The Singer factory, which manufactured wooden cabinets for sewing machines, moved to South Bend in 1868 because of the abundance of walnut and oak in the area. Together the three plants employed about 2,000 workers, about 15 percent of the population of the entire city.

The growing industries of the area were a magnet for European immigrants who came in search of work, most taking unskilled jobs in large plants such as Oliver's or Studebaker's. Most important in terms of numbers were the Poles and Hungarians. Ethnic neighborhoods appeared in both South Bend and Mishawaka. "Polonia" was located on South Bend's west side. Chapin St. became known as "Little Budapest." In Mishawaka a "Belgian Town" of neat homes grew up on the south side. By 1910 South Bend's population was nearly 25 percent foreign born while Mishawaka's was 15 percent.

During the winter of 1884–85, South Bend had its first taste of labor conflict. When James Oliver reduced his labor force and cut wages, the largely Polish workers responded by forming a labor union (the Polish Labor League) and attempted to block the plant gates. In January a riot left a dozen people injured and considerable damage to the Oliver plant. This disturbance, as unsettling as it was to South Bend residents, was an exception to the community's normally quiet labor relations.

Throughout the 19th century, South Bend-Mishawaka's small organized labor movement remained weak and conciliatory in its attitude toward management.

The substantial buildings constructed in South Bend and Mishawaka during the late 19th century symbolized the respectable prosperity that the two communities had achieved. In 1874 the Studebaker brothers built an imposing brick building to house their carriage works and offices. In 1884 James Oliver began work on the Oliver Opera House, a combination office building and theater with seats for 1,253 people. Oliver also had constructed the elegant Oliver Hotel, which the *South Bend Tribune* described when it opened in 1898 as the "best in any city of 40,000 inhabitants in the world!" The mansions of the area's successful capitalists were testimony to the wealth created by local industry. Most impressive were Clement Studebaker's Tippecanoe Place, built in 1886, and Copshaholm, the residence of Joseph D. Oliver, completed in 1895.

The new century brought rapid growth to Michiana. The population of South Bend nearly doubled between 1900 and 1920, while Mishawaka's almost tripled. The area's leading industries adapted and profited from changing circumstances. In 1901 Studebaker employed well over 2,000 workers. The market for wagons remained strong, but the younger generation at Studebaker saw the horseless carriage as the way of the future. In 1908 Studebaker began marketing cars produced by the Everitt-Metzger-Flander Company of Detroit. The success of the car prompted Studebaker to buy all the E-M-F stock and go into auto manufacturing in a big way. In 1916 the company began constructing a modern automobile plant in South Bend that would be capable of producing 700 cars a day. The switch to the internal combustion engine also had a tremendous impact on the manufacture of agricultural implements. By 1915 Oliver Plow began perfecting a new line of plows to be used with the Fordson, a low-cost tractor built by the Ford Motor Company.

World War I acted as a stimulus for industrial growth. Studebaker manufactured military wagons, harnesses, artillery saddles, drinking water carts, artillery wheels, ambulances, and tracks to be used for tanks. Although domestic auto production was cut in half, Studebaker president Albert Russell Erskine put his engineers to work developing a new line of cars for the postwar market. The wartime demands for foodstuffs, the scarcity of farm labor, and the military use of horses accelerated the transition from the horse-drawn plow to the tractor. This in turn created a tremendous demand for tractor plows, which by the end of 1917 Oliver supplied at the rate of 200 per day. Between 1917 and 1920 the Oliver plant underwent the largest physical expansion in its history.

At least one event in the early 1920s harbingered a genial future. Radio station WGAZ (now WSBT) signed on July 2, 1922. Now, WSBT is Indiana's oldest commercial station, and its debut in 1922, with a classical music program, is considered the first commercially sponsored radio broadcast in the United States (an achievement recognized in March 1989 with a Golden Mike Award from the Broadcast Pioneers Foundation). The local economy, however, was not as upbeat as expected after the booming prosperity of the previous two decades. The sluggish performance of the area's two industrial giants, Studebaker and Oliver Plow, was a premonition of the 1930s. After a peak year in 1923 Studebaker sales began to fall. Erskine began to dip into the company's operating capital and reserves to maintain dividend payments. Oliver Plow also faced financial difficulties. A severe agricultural depression hit the nation in 1921, reducing the demand for farm equipment. It was not until the mid-1920s that the plow works began to show a modest profit again. In 1928 the company received another blow when Ford discontinued production of the Fordson tractor, depriving Oliver of a lucrative market. Faced with stiffening competition, in 1929 Oliver merged with two other agricultural implement manufacturers to form the Oliver Farm Equipment Company. Although the firm remained an important South Bend employer, the merger signaled the end of family control of the business.

While South Bend companies struggled with their problems, Vincent Bendix brought a new industry to the community. Bendix was an inventor and entrepreneur who had developed a device—the Bendix Drive—which made electric self-starters feasible in automobiles. He later purchased the patents for a four-wheel braking system devised by the French engineer Henri Perrot. It was these brakes, which became standard equipment on all automobiles, that the new South Bend plant manufactured. The growth of the company was dramatic. In 1926 Bendix changed the name of his corporation to the Bendix Aviation Corporation and began moving into the manufacture of aircraft components.

The depression of the 1930s hit South Bend-Mishawaka with sledgehammer blows. During the winter of 1930–31 perhaps as many as half of those employed in 1929 were out of work, and many of those who did have jobs worked less than a full week. In South Bend and Mishawaka, the depression abruptly halted the population growth that had long characterized the two communities. Loss of sales during the depression forced the already weakened Studebaker Corporation into receivership. It was something of a miracle that the company survived at all. Under court supervision production continued on a month-to-month basis until 1935 when the courts declared the company solvent. The depression was a rough period even for the diversified Bendix Corporation. The company's stock, which sold for $104.37 a share in 1929, fell to $4.37 in 1933.

The 1930s saw the unionization of many of the area's workers. The decade was a period of industrial unrest with often bitter strikes breaking out in the major plants. Only Studebaker, where labor-management relations were unusually good, weathered the tumultuous 1930s without a major strike. South Bend workers played an important role in national labor history during this period. On November 17, 1936, about 1,000 workers at the Bendix plant sat down by their machines and refused to leave the plant when ordered to do so. This was the first sit-down strike in the history of the American automotive industry. The strike, which ended peacefully and with important concessions from Bendix management, provided the United Auto Workers (UAW) with valuable lessons which it put to good use in the Flint sit-down strike of the following year. Both the Bendix and Studebaker locals, formed in July 1933, were leaders in the movement for an independent auto workers union. The UAW became an international union at a convention held in South Bend on April 27, 1936. Two months later the new organization abandoned the American Federation of Labor to affiliate with the newly formed Congress of Industrial Organizations.

World War II put an end to the depressed local economy. Of all Indiana cities only Indianapolis received more military contracts than South Bend. Bendix Aviation, where the work force expanded from 3,800 to 14,000 during the war, produced automobile brakes, universal joints, aircraft carburetors, as well as gun turrets for B-25 and B-17 bombers. Studebaker manufactured a heavy-duty truck for the army as well as an amphibious vehicle called the Weasel. In a new facility especially constructed for that purpose, the company also manufactured the Wright Cyclone engine used on B-17 bombers. United States Rubber in Mishawaka made raincoats, fuel cells, footwear, fire-fighting suits, and other rubber products for military use.

During these wartime years of labor scarcity, South Bend began to attract large numbers of blacks. In 1930 only about 3 percent of the city's population was black. Thirty years later this figure had increased to 10 percent. (Mishawaka's black population remained very small.) Like the Poles, Hungarians, Italians, and other European immigrants that came before them, blacks filled unskilled jobs in the large plants in the area. At the time of its closing approximately 20 percent of Studebaker's work force was black. South Bend's blacks settled in distinct neighborhoods.

Reconversion to peacetime production was a traumatic experience. Studebaker began laying off employees one day after the Japanese surrender. Before the end of August 1945, approximately 15,000 workers in the South Bend-Mishawaka area were out of work, but this painful adjustment period was only temporary. By January Studebaker had resumed domestic production with the introduction of the sleek 1946 Champion. Most other local industries made a successful transition to peacetime work.

Despite the company's recovery immediately after the war, trouble lay ahead for the Studebaker Corporation. Sales lagged in 1954, and the company found it increasingly difficult to compete with the Big Three automakers in Detroit. In the first six months of that year, the company laid off 15,000 workers. A merger with the Packard Motor Car Company and a wage cut kept the company from going out of business, but many residents worried that South Bend might never recover from the closing of the auto plant. In response to these fears, local business and civic leaders formed the "Committee of 100" which was charged with the responsibility of bringing new industries into the area to help diversify the economy. In the process the committee discovered not only that other businesses found South Bend an attractive location but also that the community's dependence on Studebaker had been exaggerated. By the mid-1950s Bendix, which opened an aerospace systems division in Mishawaka in 1951, was the largest employer. Studebaker, the committee discovered, accounted for less than 25 percent of the employment in the area.

When Studebaker finally closed, South Bend's residents were prepared psychologically for the blow. The announcement came on December 9, 1963. About 8,000 workers were affected, 9 percent of the total employment in the St. Joseph County area. The federal, state, and local governments as well as private business groups provided relief as well as retraining and new jobs for the former Studebaker employees. The general prosperity of the times assisted these community efforts. By early 1966 eight companies employing some 2,500 workers operated out of the old Studebaker plant buildings. Other industries such as Bendix or Uniroyal and plants in nearby communities absorbed many of the laid-off workers. The closing may have crippled South Bend temporarily, but it hardly proved fatal. By the beginning of 1966 unemployment in the community stood at less than 3 percent.

South Bend-Mishawaka's passage through the 1960s and 1970s was rocky. After two decades of growth South Bend experienced a population decline. Between 1960 and 1980 the number of the city's residents fell by about 18 percent. While Mishawaka did not lose population, the city's growth was considerably slower than it had been in the 1950s. Flight to the suburbs accounts for much of this loss. In the inner city a number of problems began to fester. Urban blight began to spread through some of South Bend's neighborhoods. During the summer of 1967 the city had its own version of the race riots that swept through America's major cities. The issue of school desegregation hung over the community from the mid-1960s until 1980.

In 1968 Mayor Lloyd M. Allen unveiled a sweeping urban renewal plan to put an end to the deterioration of the downtown. Problems and delays plagued the ambitious program from the beginning. For many years, "the hole"— a vacant space where the redevelopment commission had demolished an entire city block—symbolized the city's stalled program. Although far behind schedule, the plan did move forward, but its progress was not always in accordance with Mayor Allen's original scheme. The impressive multifunctional First Source Bank Center, which includes the Marriott Hotel, now fills the infamous "hole." The Bank Center opened in 1982. Other centerpieces of downtown revitalization include the formidable convention complex, Century Center, completed in 1977, the One Michiana Square office building, constructed in 1985–86, and the East Race Waterway of the St. Joseph River, part of a 52-acre redevelopment project that encompasses several creative adaptations of older buildings. Some $80 million has gone into new downtown projects in the 1980s, transforming what was primarily a shopping zone into a governmental, cultural, and office district.

Manufacturing remained an important source of employment in South Bend-Mishawaka during the 1960s and 1970s. However, in the recession of the early 1980s a number of industrial operations moved out or closed down, including large durable goods manufacturers. The local economy might have been more severely affected had it not been for its diversity, which helped soften the problems that usually arise from an excessive dependence on the automotive industry. A sluggish manufacturing sector continued to plague the communities during the late 1980s, relieved occasionally by the announcement of a new company moving to town or the awarding of a new defense contract. For example, in 1985 the Mishawaka plant of LTV Missiles and Electronic Group (AM General Corporation) received a $1.2 billion army contract for 57,000 "Hummers," a four-wheel drive troop- and cargo-carrying vehicle.

By early 1987 less than one-fourth of South Bend's jobs were in manufacturing. The rest were in services, reflecting a trend experienced by many midwestern cities, where the once-dominant industrial base was being replaced by retail, wholesale, and professional activities. The generally rosy nationwide economy during the middle and late 1980s not only supported the establishment of a viable services sector but also initiated a major upswing in housing and real estate sales. Add to these favorable signs of community progress the continued impact of a variety of post-secondary educational institutions with a total student enrollment of around 20,000, and it appears that South Bend-Mishawaka can look forward to enhancing its traditional role as the retail and commercial center for the Michiana area.

South Bend-Mishawaka Attractions

1. **Century Center**, 120 S. St. Joseph St., is located on the banks of the St. Joseph River in downtown South Bend. The New York architectural firm of Philip Johnson/John Burgee designed this convention and cultural center, which opened to the public on November 1, 1977. The most striking feature is the immense (17,200 sq. ft.) Great Hall, whose east window wall offers a magnificent view of the whitewater rapids on the old west race. In addition to the convention facilities, the center is home of Discovery Hall Museum, which is devoted to exhibits relating to the industrial past of South Bend-Mishawaka. The museum features life-size photomurals, audiovisual programs, and buggies, wagons, and automobiles from the Studebaker Historic Vehicle Collection. The center also contains a performing arts center with the 718-seat Bendix Theatre, rehearsal halls, dressing rooms, and an electric music lab. Art Center, Inc., occupies three floors with 11 classrooms for teaching arts and crafts and two galleries, which feature rotating exhibits. Exit the building from the rear of the Great Hall and cross the footbridge to Island Park. To the right, mounted on a platform on the spillway of the dam, is Mark di Suvero's *Keepers of the Fire*, erected in October 1980. The modernistic orange-colored sculpture, made from steel I-beams and stainless-steel plate, towers 32 ft. over its pedestal. Di Suvero, who lives in California, is an internationally known creator of abstract sculpture.

2. The **East Race Whitewater Rapids** follow the course of the old east race, running parallel with the St. Joseph River between Madison St. and Jefferson Blvd. The original race was completed in 1844 to provide water power to the factories crowded along its banks. When manufacturers switched to other sources of power or moved elsewhere, the race was abandoned and eventually filled in. The city spent $4.5 million to rehabilitate the old race as a recreational waterway featuring artificial rapids. Formally opened on June 30, 1984, the whitewater rapids drop 13 ft. along the concrete-lined race, providing a world-class competition course for canoeing and kayaking.

3. The **Morris Civic Auditorium**, 211 N. Michigan St., is of Spanish Renaissance design. The building opened on November 2, 1922, as the Palace Theatre. Seating 2,486 in its auditorium, the building was originally a vaudeville and stage theater, but soon became a motion picture house. The Palace—along with three other South Bend theaters—hosted the 1940 premiere of "Knute Rockne—All American," which starred Ronald Reagan as the Gipper. The theater fell on hard times during the 1950s and narrowly escaped demolition when Ella Morris, South Bend civic leader and philanthropist, purchased the property and gave it to the city in 1959. Today the building is the home of the South Bend Symphony Orchestra. The Broadway Theatre League brings several Broadway shows to the facility each year. (*NRHP*) Mounted on a fountain across the street is the sculpture *Violin Woman*. Created by Harold Langland of Indiana University at South Bend, the sculpture was erected in 1982 to mark the 50th anniversary of the South Bend Symphony Orchestra.

4. The **Northern Indiana Historical Society Museum**, 112 S. Lafayette Blvd., is housed in the building which served as St. Joseph County's second courthouse from 1855 to 1896. This Greek Revival structure of a distinctive cream-

South Bend-Mishawaka Attractions

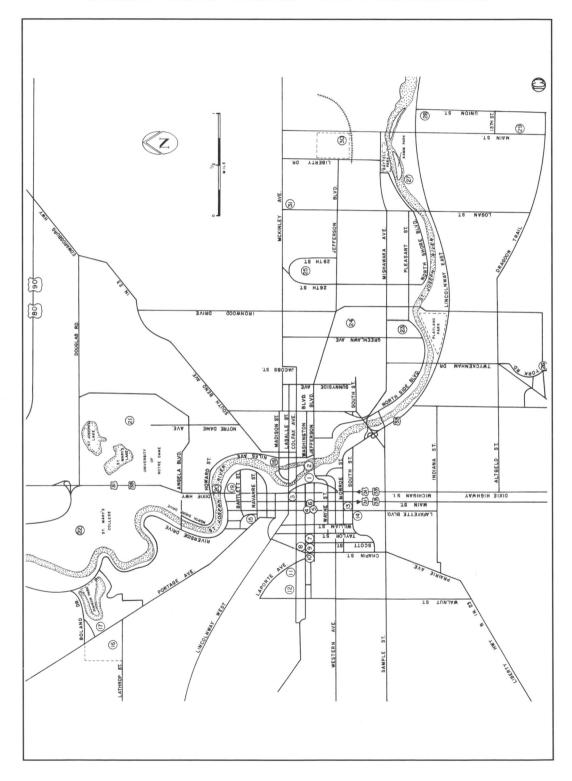

colored Lemont limestone was designed by John Van Osdel, Chicago's leading architect at the time. Many of Van Osdel's buildings were destroyed during the Chicago fire of 1871, and the old courthouse is one of the few surviving examples of his work. In 1896, to make way for construction of the new courthouse, the building was moved with horses from its original site facing Main St. to its present location. The Northern Indiana Historical Society has occupied the building since 1907. Exhibits tell the story of Indian tribes, pioneer days, and local trades, crafts, agriculture, and transportation. A segment of a blazed tree from the 1679 La Salle landing, excavated in 1897, is also displayed. Personal articles—letters, pictures, a cane, a gown worn by his wife to the 1869 inaugural ball—belonging to United States vice-president and South Bend resident Schuyler Colfax occupy an entire room. In addition to a museum, the society maintains a small research library. (See No. 10 below.) (*NRHP/HABS*)

5. South of the museum, on the northeast corner of S. Lafayette and Jefferson blvds. (227 W. Jefferson Blvd.) stands the **County-City Building**. In use since December 1, 1969, the $8 million, 14-story, steel, glass, and brick structure was designed by the South Bend firm of Ogden, Maurer, Van Ryn and Natali.

6. The present **St. Joseph County Courthouse**, 101 S. Main St., is a Beaux-Arts Classicism-style structure of Bedford limestone and granite, designed by Chicago architect Charles A. Coolidge and completed in 1898. In the second-floor rotunda are two murals done at the New York studio of H. F. Huber Company by Arthur Thomas, a noted painter of historical subjects. The murals depict La Salle on his first crossing of the St. Joseph-Kankakee portage in 1679 and on the occasion of the Miami treaty in 1681. The courthouse plaza is part of the **West Washington Historic District**, placed on the National Register of Historic Places in 1975. The district runs west about 10 blocks along Washington Blvd. and includes about 2 blocks to the north and south of the avenue. Once one of South Bend's most elegant neighborhoods, W. Washington Blvd. had by the 1960s fallen into an advanced state of decay. In 1974 a private group formed the Southold Heritage Foundation (since renamed the South Bend Heritage Foundation), which has focused specifically on the rehabilitation and preservation of buildings in the W. Washington Historic District.

7. **Tippecanoe Place**, 620 W. Washington Blvd., was built by Clement Studebaker, one of the five founding brothers of South Bend's most famous industry. Completed in 1889, the mansion is in the Richardson Romanesque (Romanesque Revival) style and made of Indiana fieldstone. Henry Ives Cobb, an architect who planned the Newberry Library as well as several buildings on the University of Chicago campus, designed the mansion. The building has 40 rooms and 20 fireplaces—each of a different design. The source of the name Tippecanoe Place probably derives from Studebaker's friendship with Benjamin Harrison, 23rd president of the United States and grandson of William Henry Harrison, victor of the Battle of Tippecanoe. The Studebakers occupied the building until 1933 when George Studebaker, Clement's son, moved out after declaring personal bankruptcy. During World War II the mansion served as the headquarters of the Red Cross. Afterwards it housed the E. M. Morris School for Crippled Children. In 1975 the Morris family gave the building to Southold Restorations, which maintained it until 1980 and then sold it to Continental Restaurant Systems of San Diego, California. The firm renovated the interior of the building and transformed it into an elegant restaurant. (*NRHP*)

8. The **DeRhodes home**, 715 W. Washington Blvd., was built in 1906. Frank Lloyd Wright designed the house for a prominent local businessman, Kersey DeRhodes, and his wife, Laura. The building—with its horizontal lines, wide roof overhangs, and bands of windows—is a good example of Wright's early Prairie-style homes. In 1954 the Avalon Grotto, a fraternal order, purchased the building and used it as a lodge for many years. In the late 1970s the lodge sold the house, and it became a residence again.

9. The **Bartlett house**, 720 W. Washington Blvd., is the oldest building in the W. Washington Historic District. John Bartlett, a grandson of Josiah Bartlett (a signer of the Declaration of Independence), a staunch antislavery man, and the city's first baker, moved to South Bend from New Hampshire in 1837. Constructed in

1850 by Bartlett's brother-in-law Jonathan Webb, the house is in the Federal style and embellished with Greek Revival window and door pediments. The building features unusual cast-iron lintels and pediments. The walk to the house is paved with bricks from the oven in Bartlett's bakery. Set into this walk is a marble stone bearing the inscription "J. G. Bartlett," which once was over the door of his bakery.

10. **Copshaholm**, 808 W. Washington Blvd., was the home of Joseph D. Oliver, son of James Oliver, founder of the Oliver Chilled Plow Works. The building is named for the Scottish village where James Oliver was born. The 38-room, three-story, fieldstone mansion, which combines Romanesque and Queen Anne styles, was completed in 1896. The architect was Charles Alonzo Rich, who designed the homes of many prominent easterners, including Sagamore Hill, Theodore Roosevelt's mansion at Oyster Bay, Long Island. The last of the family to occupy the house, Joseph D. Oliver, Jr., passed away in 1972 at the age of 80. Caretakers resided in the home surrounded by a stone wall and maintained it in pristine condition until 1988 when the heirs donated the house and contents to the Northern Indiana Historical Society. The society is planning to move the museum from the old courthouse to a new building to be constructed next to the Oliver home. (*NRHP*)

11. **St. Paul's Memorial United Methodist Church**, 933 W. Colfax, is a Gothic Revival structure, designed by the Cleveland church architect S. R. Badgley. It was built with funds contributed by Clement Studebaker in memory of his father-in-law, George Milburn. Studebaker, who passed away in 1901, did not live to see the church—dedicated on March 15, 1903—completed. The outstanding feature of the building is a 30 x 18-ft. stained-glass window, created by the art glass works of Mayer and Company of Munich, Germany, which depicts St. Paul preaching on Mars' Hill in Athens. In the window, standing on the balcony behind the governor of Athens, are the likenesses of Clement Studebaker and his valet "Old Tom." Another art treasure in the church is a Byzantine-style baptismal font dating from A.D. 821, which was once used by St. Cecilia's Church in Rome. The font was a gift of John Mohler Studebaker in memory of his brother.

12. The entrance to **City Cemetery**, South Bend's oldest burial ground, is on Elm St. off Colfax Ave. The wrought iron gate at the entrance dates to 1899. The fence that encloses the cemetery was erected in 1905. The land for the cemetery was a gift of Alexis Coquillard and Lathrop Taylor, the founders of South Bend. To the left, immediately past the entrance, is the grave of Schuyler Colfax (1823–1885), the city's most famous native son. Colfax was editor of the Whig paper, the *St. Joseph Valley Register*, speaker of the United States House of Representatives from 1863 to 1869, and vice-president of the United States under Ulysses S. Grant. Also buried in the cemetery are James and Mary McKinley, grandparents of President William McKinley. Turn left at the third road past the entrance. This road crosses a small stone bridge. In 1835 Coquillard began constructing a canal that was to connect the St. Joseph and Kankakee rivers, thus providing an unlimited source of water power. The project proved impractical and was abandoned. The line of this canal passed through the cemetery. The stone bridge is all that remains of "Coquillard's Folly."

13. The beginnings of the **Studebaker National Museum**, 515 S. Main St., took place on June 22, 1966, when the Studebaker Corporation gave more than 50 historical vehicles, as well as the company's archives, to the city of South Bend. The company stipulated that the collection remain permanently in South Bend and that the vehicles remain on continuous display. It was 20 years, however, before the vehicles found a permanent home. In 1982 Mayor Roger O. Parent appointed a commission which selected the present location for the museum. The Freeman-Spicer Building has historic ties to the Studebaker Corporation. Studebaker constructed the building in 1919 and used it for offices and a company-operated dealership. In 1931 the Scherman, Schaus, Freeman Company purchased the building and sold Studebakers there until the corporation stopped making automobiles. The museum opened in 1983. In addition to the Studebaker wagons and automobiles, the collection includes some non-Studebaker items such as the carriage in which Lincoln reputedly rode on the night of his assassination and the one that the Marquis de Lafayette used on his visit

Studebaker residence

Indiana Historical Society (C545)

to the United States on the 50th anniversary of the American Revolution.

14. To the southwest of the museum at 635 S. Lafayette Blvd. can be seen the massive six-story building of the former **Enclosed Body Plant of the Studebaker Corporation**, designed by Albert Kahn and completed in 1923. Just to the north of the Studebaker plant is the **New York Central Union Station**, 326 South St. The New York firm of Fellheimer and Wagner designed the $1 million barrel-vaulted, Art Deco terminal, which was dedicated May 27, 1929.

15. The **Chapin house**, 601 Park Ave., was built in 1857 by Horatio Chapin, an early South Bend merchant and banker. This Gothic Revival building, which originally stood a few hundred feet to the northwest, was moved to its present location in 1891. The wrought-iron fence in front of the house, installed in 1968, once stood at St. Stanislaus Church. (*NRHP*) The Chapin home is the oldest house in the Chapin Park Historic District. Placed on the

National Register of Historic Places in 1982, Chapin Park, centering on winding Park Ave., was once an exclusive neighborhood of South Bend's leading citizens. In the 1940s the neighborhood began to decline, and many of the large homes were subdivided into apartments. The Park Ave. Association took the lead in revitalizing the area.

16. Highland Cemetery, 2257 Portage Ave., is the location of the **Council Oak**. It was under this tree, according to local tradition, that the French explorer La Salle met with the Miami and Illinois Indians in 1681 and persuaded them to enter into an alliance with the French against the Iroquois. Take the middle fork of the road into the cemetery and follow it to the tree. A tablet placed at the spot by the Northern Indiana Historical Society marks the tree.

17. At the northern outer edge of Riverview Cemetery, at about 2800 N. Portage Ave., is a granite tablet marking the location of the **portage** where La Salle crossed from the St. Joseph

River to the Kankakee River in December 1679. La Salle's journey across the northwestern corner of the state was the first recorded visit of a European to the area that later became the state of Indiana. La Salle was on his way to the Illinois country where he hoped to explore the upper Mississippi Valley and find new sources of furs.

18. The **Madison Center**, 403 E. Madison, occupies the first building constructed for the Singer Manufacturing Company complex. Built in 1868, the year the Singer Cabinet Works came to South Bend, the three-story brick structure was used by the sewing machine firm until 1901. The H. D. Lee Company, which made overalls, resided there from 1917 to 1964. The Hickey Construction Company purchased the building in 1964, restored it (including sandblasting some 50 coats of paint off of the brick walls), and renamed it Riverview Building. In 1977 the Mental Health Center of St. Joseph County, a private firm, moved to the building. The official name of the Mental Health Center was changed to Madison Center in May 1981.

19. **Leeper Park**, US 33 North at Riverside Dr., was named for David R. Leeper, mayor of South Bend, 1892–93, who died in 1900. In 1895 the city of South Bend purchased the site as a location for a pumping station and improved the surrounding grounds. Pierre Navarre, a fur trader and South Bend's first white settler, built the tiny one-room log cabin, located in the part of the park east of Michigan St., in 1820. The cabin originally stood on the north bank of the St. Joseph River near the Michigan St. bridge but was moved to its present location in 1904. Navarre moved west with his Potawatomi wife in 1840 but returned many years later to spend his last days in South Bend. On the grounds of Leeper Park is the North Pumping Station, built in 1912. In 1980 the city council declared the Beaux Arts Classicism-style structure a historic landmark.

20. Continuing north from Leeper Park on US 33 North the St. Joseph River is crossed by way of the **Leeper Bridge**. South Bend and Mishawaka have many fine bridges, and the Leeper Bridge is one of the most photographed and artistically portrayed of the pre-1930 concrete spans. Its three spans measure a total of 276 ft.

21. The **University of Notre Dame**, Angela Blvd. at Notre Dame Ave., was founded by Father Edward F. Sorin, a French priest, and a handful of brothers of the Congregation of the Holy Cross in 1842. The intrepid band had accepted a tract of land on the shores of St. Mary's Lake from Célestine de la Hailandière, the bishop of Vincennes, on condition that they establish a college in two years. St. Joseph County was still a rugged frontier area and an unlikely site for a new college, but Sorin was a determined leader, and the group triumphed over innumerable obstacles. The first students enrolled in the fall of 1844, and the following January the legislature granted the college, called Notre Dame du Lac, a charter.

The university grew slowly, surviving a constant lack of funds and a fire in 1879 that destroyed the main campus building. By the beginning of the 20th century the university had acquired a national reputation. Under the leadership of Knute Rockne, who became coach in 1918, Notre Dame emerged as a well-known football power. The university's 1924 team with its backfield of Harry Stuhldreher, "Sleepy Jim" Crowley, Don Miller, and Elmer Layden—the legendary Four Horsemen—was undefeated. Notre Dame ended that season with its only Rose Bowl appearance and defeated Stanford, 27 to 10.

Coaches such as Frank Leahy, 1940–43 and 1946–53, and Ara Parseghian, 1964–74, have kept football at the center of campus life, but Notre Dame also has acquired a distinguished academic reputation. In 1952 the Rev. Theodore Hesburgh became president and set about transforming it into an outstanding academic institution. In 1960 Notre Dame was one of six American colleges (and the only Catholic one) to receive a $6 million challenge grant from the Ford Foundation to implement the school's proposed development program. In 1967 the Congregation of the Holy Cross relinquished direct control of university governance to a lay board of trustees. Five years later, after a merger with St. Mary's College failed to materialize, Notre Dame accepted its first undergraduate women students. Hesburgh's service on such bodies as the United States Commission on Civil Rights, the International Atomic Energy Commission, and the Carnegie Commission of the Future of Higher Education has greatly enhanced the university's image. In addition to some 30 courses of study leading to the master's degree and more than 20 leading to the doctorate, Notre Dame has a Graduate School of Business and a Law School.

The University of Notre Dame is a pedestrian campus. Visitor parking is available near the main gate at the north end of Notre Dame Ave. A good place to begin is at the **Administration Building** located at the north end of the main quadrangle. (Both the main and south quadrangles of the campus were placed on the National Register of Historic Places in 1978.) The building is easily recognized by a dazzling gold leaf dome. The statue at the top is *Our Lady of Notre Dame*, a gift of St. Mary's College. It is a replica of a statue erected by Pope Pius IX in the Piazza di Spagna in Rome. The building houses the university's principal offices, including that of the president. Constructed in 1879 after the college's first main building was destroyed by fire, the structure once housed virtually the entire university. On the second floor walls are a series of 12 murals depicting the life of Christopher Columbus. The painter, Luigi Gregori, was a Vatican artist who came to Notre Dame in 1874 to paint the Stations of the Cross for the Sacred Heart Church and remained until 1891 as artist-in-residence. Gregori customarily used Notre Dame faculty as models for the figures in his paintings. In 11 of the murals Father Thomas Walsh, president of the university from 1881 to 1893, served as the model for Columbus. In the 12th mural, depicting Columbus on his death bed, Father Sorin served as the model for the Italian mariner.

To the west of the Administration Building is **Sacred Heart Church**. Construction of this Gothic-style building began in 1870, replacing the wooden church that stood on the same site. The interior was renovated in 1967 in keeping with the liturgical reforms of the Second Vatican Council. The 42 stained-glass windows were created and donated to Notre Dame by the Carmelite sisters at Le Mans, France. Several Gregori frescoes decorate the walls. One of them, *The Presentation of the Blessed Virgin in the Temple*, includes likenesses of the artist and his family. The church is also the location of Ivan Mestrovic's group sculpture, *The Descent from the Cross*. The Croatian-born Mestrovic, a renowned sculptor of religious art, came to Notre Dame as a professor of fine arts in 1955 and remained until his death in 1962. Mestrovic sketched the plans for this work of art on butcher paper while a prisoner of the Nazis in Zagreb during World War II. Notre Dame has the largest collection of Mestrovic's works outside of Yugoslavia. In the chapel behind the main sanctuary is the so-called Bernini altar. This baroque altar is not the work of the master himself but was probably designed by Bernini's students several years after his death. Orestes Brownson, a 19th-century writer and convert to Catholicism, is interred in the Sacred Heart crypt. A small museum displaying artifacts from the history of the Congregation of the Holy Cross and of Notre Dame is located in the sacristy.

Continue west along the walkway in front of Sacred Heart Church to a road that runs alongside St. Mary's Lake. Walk southwest until you reach the **Old College**. This is the oldest building on the Notre Dame campus. Notice the historic marker on the southwest wall. In the spring of 1843 Father Sorin had this building erected to house a dormitory, classrooms, a dining room, and a kitchen. Originally consisting of two stories, it was later expanded to four. The brick building was intended only as an interim structure until a larger main campus building was completed. It has been in continuous use since its construction.

Immediately to the southwest of the Old College is the **Log Chapel**. When Father Sorin arrived at the shores of St. Mary's Lake during the winter of 1842, the only buildings on the grounds of what would become the University of Notre Dame were a log chapel built by Father Vincent Badin, a missionary priest, in 1831, and a clapboard house occupied by an Indian interpreter. The log chapel that stands today is a reconstruction built in 1906 of Badin's 1831 structure. Sorin and the brothers that accompanied him used the attic as a chapel and the ground floor as living quarters.

Walk east along the road bordering St. Mary's Lake to the **Grotto of Our Lady of Lourdes** on the right. Contructed in 1896, the grotto is a reproduction, on one-seventh scale, of the famous shrine in Lourdes, France, where in 1858 a peasant girl named Bernadette Soubirous claimed to have seen the Virgin Mary.

Exit the grotto at the rear and walk east across the campus to reach the **Notre Dame Memorial Library**. This 14-story building, constructed in 1963, symbolizes the academic excellence achieved by the university since

Indiana Historical Society (C4276)
Sacred Heart Church

Theodore Hesburgh became president in 1952. On the south wall is the mural *The Word of Life* by the artist Millard Sheets. This giant work of art, 134 ft. high and 68 ft. wide, contains 143 natural shades of granite. Sheets gathered the 6,700 pieces of granite that make up the mural from 16 different countries. The mural is a depiction of Christ the teacher surrounded by a procession of figures representing the history of the Catholic Church. A plaque at the south end of the reflecting pool describes the figures in the mural.

From the library, follow the walk south to **Notre Dame Stadium**. This 59,074-seat stadium was built in 1930. Sod from Cartier Field, the previous stadium where Notre Dame did not lose a home game in 23 years, was used in the new facility.

East of the stadium is the twin-domed **Athletic and Convocation Center** dedicated on December 8, 1968. Designed by Ellerbe Architects of St. Paul, Minnesota, the huge structure covers more than 10 1/2 acres under one roof. The building is used both for athletic and a variety of cultural and entertainment events. The center has a 12,500-seat basketball stadium, ice rink, baseball diamond, tennis courts, an Olympic-size swimming pool, a track, and facilities for intramural sports. Display cases of Notre Dame sports memorabilia including numerous trophies and photographs are housed on the second floor.

Northwest of the stadium is the **Snite Museum of Art** which opened on November 9, 1980. The new facility is an extension of O'Shaughnessy Hall, which once served as the university's museum. The old quarters are now used for temporary and rotating exhibits. The former studio of Ivan Mestrovic is also part of the museum and has been renovated to display the artist's drawings and sculptures. The museum's collections include 14,000 pieces worth approximately $30 million.

22. **St. Mary's College**, a 275-acre campus on the west side of US 33, is the second-oldest Catholic women's college in the United States. St. Mary-of-the-Woods near Terre Haute is the oldest. In 1843 four Sisters of the Holy Cross arrived in Notre Dame. The sisters lived in the loft above the chapel and attended to the college's domestic work. Sorin planned to establish an academy for the education of young women, but Bishop de la Hailandière vetoed this idea because the Sisters of Providence had already established one in his diocese. The undaunted Sorin, with the permission of the bishop of Detroit, established St. Mary's Academy in 1844 just across the state line in Bertrand, Michigan. By 1850 the academy had an enrollment of 50 girls. The arrangement was not an ideal one for the sisters, who continued to do the domestic chores at Notre Dame. Bishop de la Hailandière's successor did not oppose the existence of a second girls' academy in his diocese, and in 1855 St. Mary's Academy moved to its present location on the banks of the St. Joseph River near the University of Notre Dame. Points of interest on the campus include Moreau Hall, which houses classrooms and studios for art, music, and theater, as well as the 1,300-seat O'Laughlin Auditorium. The first performance in the auditorium was the world premiere of the NBC Opera Company held on October 11, 1956. At the entrance of the auditorium are 14 frescoes by the French-born muralist Jean Charlot. Also on the campus is the Cushwa-Leighton Library dedicated

on September 3, 1982. The library's Rare Book Room is famous for its outstanding Dante collection.

23. **Indiana University at South Bend**, 1700 Mishawaka Ave., began as an extension of Indiana University in 1933. It became a regional campus in 1966. IU at South Bend began granting Baccalaureate degrees in 1967.

24. On the grounds of **Potawatomi Park** are the **Ella Morris Conservatory** and the **Muessel-Ellison Tropical Garden**, 2105 Mishawaka Ave. The conservatory was dedicated in 1964 and houses a wide variety of tropical plants. The Muessel-Ellison Tropical Garden was built in 1973 to provide a home for a valuable cacti and succulent plant collection which the Rev. Joseph S. McGrath, C.S.C., a Notre Dame chemistry professor, gave to the park department. A breezeway connects the conservatory and tropical garden. The facilities include meeting rooms, office space, and exhibit areas for flower shows. Also located in Potawatomi Park is **Potawatomi Zoo**, 500 S. Greenlawn. The entrance to the zoo is on the east side of the park at Wall St. The zoo has a learning center and features animals from five continents.

25. **Walnut Grove**, between McKinley Ave. and Jefferson Blvd. east of 26th St., is one of three wartime housing projects built in South Bend to provide shelter for war workers' families. Completed in March of 1942, the project of the Federal Works Agency was placed, over protests of affluent Jefferson Blvd. homeowners, on some 80 acres of the Birdsell estate, purchased for a reported $32,000. Unlike the barracks type of housing at the other sites, the Walnut Grove settlement contained one-family units: 250 families housed in 157 buildings including 93 one- , two- , and three-bedroom doubles, and 64 two-bedroom single family dwellings. Roy A. Worden and Karl R. Swartz, local architects, designed the flat-roofed, split-level houses and placed them on cul-de-sacs at angles best suited for weather conditions. Henke Construction Company of Chicago landed the $910,903 building contract. Extensive landscaping gave a park atmosphere to the development.

26. The **Herman T. Mossberg house**, 1404 Ridgedale Rd., is on the corner of Ridgedale

and York rds. Designed by Frank Lloyd Wright, the brick and cypress Mossberg home, in contrast to his early Prairie-style DeRhodes home, is an example of his later work. Built in 1949, the home is in Wright's Usonian style, which differed from the Prairie style in the greater use of glass, open patios, flat roofs, and one-floor design. Wright built his first Usonian home in 1937. At the time critics considered the design a radical break with architectural practice. Herman Mossberg owned a local printing firm.

27. The **100 Center**, 700 block of Lincolnway East, Mishawaka, is the site of the old Kamm and Schellinger Brewery. John Wagner built the first brewery on the location around 1853. In 1870 Adolph Kamm and Clemens Dick, both German immigrants, bought the business. Ten years later Kamm's brother-in-law, Nicholas Schellinger, acquired Dick's interest. The Kamm and Schellinger Brewery produced a popular beer (except for the Prohibition years when it switched to soft drinks) until 1951 when competition from larger companies forced it to close its doors. In 1968 a group of local investors purchased the old buildings and converted them into a restaurant and shopping complex. (*NRHP*)

28. The **Beiger mansion**, 317 Lincolnway East, Mishawaka, is a fine example of post-Victorian architecture. Martin V. Beiger, founder of the Mishawaka Woolen Manufacturing Company, which later became Uniroyal, contracted to have the 22-room Neoclassical mansion constructed. Beiger died in 1903 and never lived in his dream home, which was not completed until 1909. His widow, Susie Higgins Beiger, stipulated in her will that the building be used as a home for "deserving elderly women." It served this purpose from 1930 to 1967. In 1973 the Beiger Heritage Corporation purchased the building and saved it from demolition. In 1975 a tragic fire extensively damaged the structure and destroyed many valuable antiques that had been part of the building's original furnishings. Although many thought the building damaged beyond repair, the Beiger Heritage Corporation has restored the structure. The mansion now is used as a cultural and community center. Craft shops are also located in the building. (*NRHP*)

29. The **Hannah Lindahl Children's Museum**, 1402 S. Main St., began in 1946 with a single

room in Mishawaka's Mary Phillip's School. By 1955 the collections were moved to the former John B. Niles home at 410 Lincolnway East. The museum remained there until 1983 when it moved into its present facilities located in the south end of the Emmons Elementary School building. Operated under the auspices of the city school system, the children's school museum reopened in 1985. Exhibits include a re-creation of a 19th-century village with a schoolroom, general store, clothing store, family dwelling, and natural history gallery. To honor Mishawaka's sister city of Shirogiri in Japan, a Japanese house and garden with life-size models in traditional costumes have been constructed. The museum also provides a unique program called "Survive Alive," designed to teach children how to escape from a burning house. On-duty firemen conduct a simulated fire with strobe lights, heat, and chemical smoke as part of the fire drill.

30. Mishawaka **City Cemetery**, located in the 1300 block of N. Main St., contains some of the city's oldest graves. In 1836 when Joseph Battell and the brothers Grove and James Lawrence laid out the town of Indiana City, they donated a tract of land to the community as a burial place. The cemetery is the resting place of Willard Aldrich, a gambler and horse trader who died on September 7, 1882. Before he passed away, Aldrich stipulated that he be buried in a seated position with a deck of cards, bottle of whiskey, pipe, tobacco, matches, his favorite boots, and a shotgun. The vault containing Aldrich's remains is covered by huge stone slabs hoisted in place by a derrick. After entering the park from Main St., drive to an island in the road where a flagpole stands. Aldrich's grave is on the right.

31. **Bethel College**, 1001 W. McKinley Ave., Mishawaka, is a small liberal arts college that is affiliated with the Missionary Church. The college opened in 1947. The Otis R. and Elizabeth A. Bowen Library, completed in 1984, houses the papers of the former governor.

Tour 17

Linked by I-80/90, US 20, and US 33, Elkhart County's largest city, also named **ELKHART** (p. 41,305), is located 15 miles east of South Bend. The early settlement spread out from around what is now called Island Park, situated at the confluence of the Elkhart and St. Joseph rivers. To the Indians, the shape of the island resembled an elk's heart and inspired the original name for the river, which was later translated to French, then English. Potawatomi Indian Chief Pierre Moran selected the site of what is now the city of Elkhart for a reservation in accordance with terms of the Chicago Treaty of 1821, and his tribe occupied this land for the following 10 years.

ELKHART COUNTY (p. 137,330; 466 sq. m.) was officially created in 1830. Most early settlers entered the county via the road from Fort Wayne and by river routes from Michigan. The county commissioners selected Elkhart as the first county seat in 1830, but Goshen soon became a rival for the position, eventually winning out because of its central location.

In 1831 Dr. Havilah Beardsley acquired a land grant to property along the St. Joseph River. He built a gristmill on the north bank and in 1832 platted the village of Elkhart on the south side. Elkhart was incorporated as a town in 1858 and as a city in 1875. Until the railroad arrived in 1851, Elkhart was an active river port that shipped flour, pork, and other produce down the St. Joseph to Lake Michigan. About 1870 Elkhart became a railroad division terminal, and the Lake Shore and Michigan Southern Railroad erected roundhouses and repair shops. Some 50 tracks now owned by Conrail enter the freight classification yard on the west side of town. A majority of Elkhart's work force is employed in manufacturing, and the county's unemployment rate is one of the lowest in the state.

Known as the "band instrument capital of the world," Elkhart is a center for musical instruments manufacture. Following a lip injury,

C. G. Conn produced a rubber mouthpiece for his cornet and in 1873 began selling them. A flamboyant promoter who brought to Elkhart well-known musicians such as John Philip Sousa, Conn made and lost a fortune. Nearly all of the subsequent band instrument factories in Elkhart have been offshoots of the Conn empire. Major concerns still operating include United Musical Instruments, E. K. Blessing Company, Emerson Instrument Company, J. J. Babbitt Company, Inc., Gemeinhardt Company, Larilee Woodwind Company, Selmer Company, and Walter Piano Company.

Elkhart is also called the "recreational vehicle capital of the world." More than 200 firms in Elkhart manufacture mobile homes, campers, or other recreational vehicle-related products. Founded in 1964, Coachmen Industries, Inc., is one of the county's largest RV manufacturers. It seems fitting that Elkhart should have earned such a standing with its recreational vehicles because in earlier days it commanded respect as an auto manufacturing center. More makes (at least 27) were produced here than in any Hoosier city except Indianapolis. These included the Elcar, Crow, Royal, Sterling, and Komet. Production began with the Elkhart Electric in 1906 and continued until 1932, when the last Elcar was produced. Two of the plants still stand: the Elcar plant at Michigan St. and Beardsley Ave., now occupied by Excel Industries, and the Crow plant at Main and Simonton sts., now the home of several small industries.

Miles Laboratories, Inc., heads the city's pharmaceutical industry. Dr. Franklin Miles began to market his home remedy, a sedative called Dr. Miles Restorative Nervine, in 1884. About 1900 Dr. Miles moved his dispensary into the Bucklen Opera House at Main and Harrison sts. and worked there for a few years before leaving the active management of the company to the Miles, Beardsley, and Compton families and establishing a plantation in

Tour 17

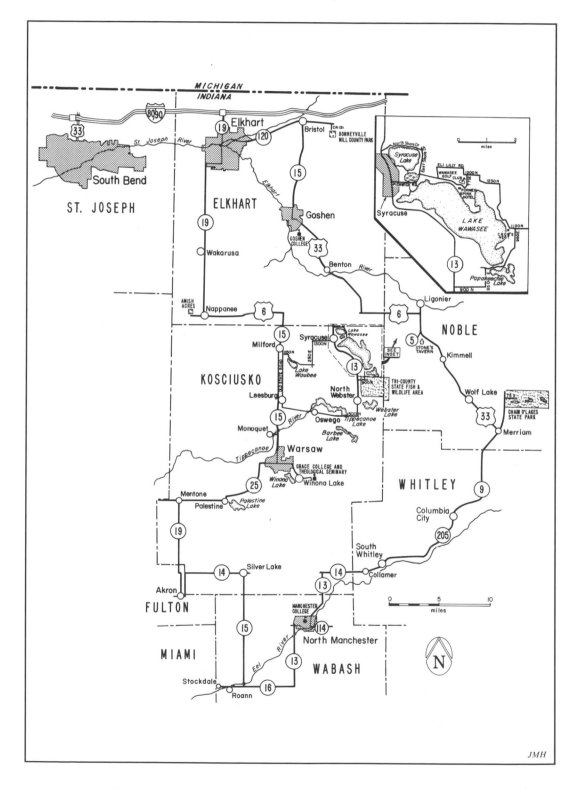

JMH

Florida. Between 1900 and 1940 the company published almanacs, calendars, health guides, and booklets. In the 1930s the company achieved fame as the producer of Alka-Seltzer. In the 1960s Miles Laboratories opened a research center and added One-A-Day vitamins and S.O.S. steel wool pads to its products. In 1978 Bayer AG of West Germany, which developed the popular Bayer aspirin, acquired the company. Miles Laboratories today is a billion-dollar high-tech firm that employs more than 2,500 persons at its headquarters in Elkhart. Its archives center in the Centennial Building, 701 Randolph St., features a film about the company's history and an exhibit of its current products.

In contrast to Elkhart's image as a modern industrial and commercial center, Amish farms in the surrounding countryside reflect 19th-century life-styles. The Amish and the Mennonites first migrated to northern Indiana from Pennsylvania and Ohio in the 1840s. There are large concentrations of Old Order Amish, the most conservative sect, east and southwest of Goshen. These groups are bound by strong religious and family ties and practice a New Testament Christianity which emphasizes brotherly love, nonviolence, and a plain, simple life. Many use no church buildings but worship in barns during the summer and homes in the winter. Most continue to use horses rather than tractors to operate their farms, and their plain black horse-drawn carriages are a common sight on Elkhart County roads.

The Amish wear simple unadorned clothes, not unlike those of their ancestors, with white caps and long solid-color dresses required for the women and broad-brimmed hats and coats with hooks and eyes instead of buttons for the men. The women use no cosmetics, and the men grow beards after marrying. The Amish maintain an agrarian way of living and speak Pennsylvania German in the home.

Many prominent early Elkhart citizens built their homes in the area north of the St. Joseph River. In 1848 Dr. Havilah Beardsley (1795–1856), the town founder, erected Elkhart's first brick residence, a two-story Italianate-style house that has been well preserved, at the northwest corner of Beardsley Ave. (IND 19) and Main St. Beardsley established the first sawmill in the area in 1831, followed by a flour mill in 1832, a carding mill in 1835, a second flour mill in 1845, and a paper mill in 1847.

Because of his many business and real estate interests, Beardsley did not practice medicine in the community very long. In a triangle one block west of Main St. at Riverside Dr. and W. Beardsley Ave. stands a bronze and marble statue of Dr. Beardsley, erected by Albert R. Beardsley in 1913.

From Main St., proceed east for two blocks to **Ruthmere** on the northeast corner of Beardsley Ave. and Grove St. Albert R. Beardsley (1847–1924), a nephew of Elkhart's founder and a director of Dr. Miles Medical Company, commissioned the construction of this elegant mansion, built between 1908 and 1910. Architect E. Hill Turnock, a student of Frank Lloyd Wright, designed the three-story yellow brick and stone structure combining elements of the Beaux Arts and Midwestern Prairie schools of architecture and using American building materials as much as possible. Albert and Elizabeth Beardsley named their home Ruthmere in memory of their only child, Ruth, who died in infancy. The Beardsley family occupied the house until 1944. The Andrew Hubble Beardsley Foundation purchased it in 1969.

In the 1970s O'Hara Decorating Service of Chicago restored the interior which features elaborate hand-painted ceilings, ornate frieze designs, native wood floors and paneling, brocade wall coverings, velvet wall murals, gilded moldings, and stained-glass windows. Original patterns and color schemes have been preserved. Furnishings include a Choralcelo organ in the music room, silk and satin draperies, and Tiffany lamps. A 1916 Milburn Light Electric car is parked in the garage. Ruthmere opened as a 1910-period house museum in 1973. (*NRHP*)

Return to Beardsley Ave. and Main St. From the St. Joseph River bridge proceed south one and one-half blocks. At the southeast corner of Main and Sycamore sts., a historical marker indicates the island to the east which the Indians thought resembled an elk's heart and describes early river navigation. A footbridge at the end of Sycamore St. leads to **Island Park**, a tranquil wooded site featuring a giant old sycamore tree at the entrance. James Rufus Beardsley donated the land to the city for this lovely little park in 1887. The Miles Centennial Footbridge, a 270-ft. span constructed in 1984, connects Island Park with Pulaski Park, situated on a bluff overlooking the St. Joseph River. The park is the site of the early village of Pulaski established along the old Fort Wayne Rd. a few years before Elkhart was laid out.

Return to Main St. and proceed south. The **Midwest Museum of American Art**, a nonprofit organization established in 1978, occupies the former St. Joseph Valley Bank building at 429 S. Main St. The first home of the bank was a château-style stone structure at 214 S. Main St., built in 1885. The Hoggson Brothers designed and erected the limestone museum building in 1922, which architects Wiley and Miller remodeled in 1960. The 1960 bank vault has been incorporated as a part of the museum. Two large rooms on the first floor serve as a display area for the permanent collection of 19th- and 20th-century American art. In 1984 the second floor was converted into additional gallery space, financed by gifts in memory of Barbara McClelland Kirk, a former docent of the museum.

Continue south on Main St. through the business district to the railroad. East of Main St., in the 2000 block of Middlebury St., is the **SRM Vintage Cars Museum**, housed in a separate building east of the plant on the 50-acre grounds of the Atlas Die Company. S. Ray Miller, Jr., owner and president of the company, began his vintage car collection in the 1970s and now owns more than 40 restored cars, including a 1928 Elcar rumble seat roadster manufactured by the Elkhart Motor Company, which produced cars from 1915 to 1931. The museum also contains a rare Model J Duesenberg with a custom body and a 1920 Kissel Kar with a single door and an impact-absorbing bumper. Miller's 1985 addition to this private collection is a 1909 Sterling with all-brass trim which also was produced in Elkhart. Displays include automotive memorabilia, old advertising signs, license plates, and a gas pump.

Return west on Middlebury St. to Prairie St. Turn south and proceed *1 m.* to the traffic light at W. Lusher Ave. Turn right and continue *2 m.*, then follow S. Nappanee St. (IND 19) south *9.1 m.* Turn west on CR 40 (E. Waterford St.) and go *1 m.* to CR 3 (Elkhart Ave.) in the center of **WAKARUSA** (p. 1,281). Platted in 1852, Wakarusa was named after a stream in Kansas. Wakarusa is an Indian word meaning "knee deep in mud," which the townspeople thought best described the nature of the boggy soil in that area. The village was incorporated in 1897. Most industry is related to rec-

reational vehicles and furniture products manufacturing, though the surrounding area remains primarily agricultural.

From Waterford St., proceed south on Elkhart Ave. for two blocks through Wakarusa's historic area of 19th-century commercial buildings featuring fine examples of pressed-tin facades. Turn left on Wabash St. and continue southeast for three blocks to Railroad St. The **Wakarusa Historical Society Museum** is located on the southwest corner. The historical society maintains the old Wakarusa depot, a board and batten frame structure built in 1892, as a museum for railroad memorabilia. Also on the site are a Pullman car which has been converted into a movie theater and a 1917 wooden caboose. A tiny frame building which served as the medical office of Dr. S. C. Wagner from 1910 to 1919 and the veterinary office of Dr. C. C. Clay from 1919 to 1942 has been moved next to the depot and now houses an exhibit of local historical artifacts.

Continue south *.5 m.* and turn left. At IND 19, the first crossroad, turn right and continue south *5.5 m.* to US 6 (Market St.) in the business district of **NAPPANEE** (p. 4,694). The town's name is an Indian word of uncertain origin but may have been brought by an early settler from Napanee, Ontario, spelled with a single letter "p." Unlike Elkhart to the north, which was a thriving river port in its early days, Nappanee grew along the Baltimore and Ohio Railroad. Nappanee rivaled nearby Locke Town for location on the B and O, but after the railroad bypassed Locke Town, it declined rapidly in business and population, though for a time it operated a train station at the railroad's nearest access point two miles away. When platted in 1874, Nappanee almost surrounded Locke Station, which was soon closed, and Nappanee's future development as a transportation center was assured.

Nappanee's first industry was a sawmill, erected in 1873, which the three Coppes brothers purchased in 1876. By 1885 the Coppes mill was sawing lumber at the rate of 75,000 ft. per week. Though the mills disappeared in the 1920s, at least four companies in Nappanee today are major producers of custom-built wood kitchen cabinets. Tourism and the manufacture of recreational vehicles and related products, wiring harnesses, and boats also support the economy.

Located *.9 m.* west of IND 19 on US 6, **Amish Acres** is an 80-acre farm which Christian and Moses Stahly bought in 1874. It is now a popular tourist attraction. The main buildings include the original farmhouse, the Gross Dawdy house (the grandparents' home), and the great Schwietzer barn. Several historic buildings which actually were used by the Amish years ago have been moved to the grounds to create the appearance of an Amish community. Additional buildings have been constructed to provide accommodations for visitors such as the barn restaurant, gift store, soda and candy shop, cider mill, and cheese and meat shop. The farm is a living museum in which the architecture, farming, husbandry, and household methods of the Old Order Amish are depicted. Women carry out everyday domestic tasks such as quilting, candle dipping, and baking in the outdoor oven. The farm still produces maple syrup, apple cider, sorghum, and dried foods.

Return to Nappanee and continue east on US 6 for *8.2 m.* to IND 15. Turn right and proceed south *1 m.* to the **KOSCIUSKO COUNTY** (p. 59,555; 540 sq. m.) line. Kosciusko was part of Elkhart County and was called Turkey Creek Township until 1833 when the Indians ceded this territory to the United States. The county boundaries were established in 1835, and the county was organized officially in 1836. Stands of walnut, hickory, maple, and oak trees once covered most of the southern part of the county, whereas the northern sections were mostly prairie. Ditching and draining created rich farmland from the lowlands. The county contains some 90 lakes, varying in depth from 10 to 123 ft., including Indiana's largest natural lake—Wawasee.

Agriculture is big business in Kosciusko County. Two major businesses in the county are agriculture-related, the Maple Leaf Duck Farms near Milford and the Creighton Brothers hatchery west of Warsaw. The Creighton Brothers firm has more than 1.3 million laying hens and markets about 3.2 million dozen eggs per year. At the Crystal Lake Products plant, specialized machinery separates the egg yolks from the whites. The facility distributes shell and processed eggs to restaurants, institutions, and grocery stores. The Warsaw and Mentone area is called the Egg Basket of the Middle West.

The county is named in honor of Thaddeus Kosciusko, a Polish general who fought in the American Revolution, and the county seat after Warsaw, the capital of Poland. A contest for permanent location of the county seat took place at various times among Oswego, Leesburg, and Warsaw, but Warsaw was selected in 1843.

From the county line, continue south on IND 15 for *1.9 m.* to Emeline St. (at the stoplight) in **MILFORD** (p. 1,153). The first permanent white settlers in the county chose the fertile level prairie land around Milford, Leesburg, and Clunette. In 1836 Judge Aaron M. Perine platted Milford and opened a hotel. The town came of age with the arrival of the Cincinnati, Wabash and Michigan Railroad (now Conrail) in 1870, crossed by the Baltimore and Ohio in 1874. At the railroad junction, just north of town, a community emerged, named Shakespeare, but later changed to Milford Junction. The town of Milford was incorporated in 1880.

Turn left and follow Emeline St. east to Old State Rd. (Main St.). Proceed south *.6 m.* to CR 1150N, turn east for *.5 m.* to Camp Mack Rd., then go south for *.2 m.* to **Lake Waubee**. Miami Indian chiefs Wawasee and Papakeechie and their followers made their homes along the shores of Lake Waubee (meaning Half Moon) before moving to the larger Lake Wawasee. The spring-fed lake has a surface area of 117 acres and a depth of 51 ft. mainly due to dredging by a cement company for the lake's marl deposit. Situated to the right of Camp Mack Rd. is Waubee Park, which is equipped with a public boat ramp and picnic and playground areas.

Continue around the lake for *.7 m.* to the wooded grounds of **Camp Alexander Mack**. Owned and operated by the Church of the Brethren, it is a lakefront summer camp and winter retreat. The camp, named in honor of Alexander Mack who founded the Church of the Brethren in Germany in 1708, is used for church assemblies and large group meetings, serving many nonprofit organizations for religious and educational purposes. Development of the 212-acre site began in 1925 with the construction of Deeter cabin, the original administration building. During the depression volunteer workers erected Becker Lodge and most of the cabins at the camp. Shultz Chapel, constructed of fieldstones in 1948, stands on a bluff overlooking the lake. Stained-glass windows form the east chapel wall, and the west end is open to the lake. Quinter-Miller Auditorium is a large wood and stone structure with dirt floors and simple wooden benches, erected between 1933 and 1940.

The auditorium houses a remarkable mural measuring 180 x 5 1/2 ft., divided into two 90-ft. sections containing six panels each. The Rev. Medford D. Neher, who studied art at Manchester College and theology at Bethany Bible Seminary, painted the mural over a five-year period. Completed in 1949, it traces the history of the Church of the Brethren from its founding through the various stages of its development in the United States, to its place in the atomic age.

Return to the camp entrance, turn right, and at *1.3 m.* turn left on CR 250E. Continue *2 m.*, then turn right on CR 1300N for *2.6 m.* to IND 13 at **SYRACUSE** (p. 2,579) and turn left onto Huntington St. Located on Syracuse Lake, a 564-acre bay at the northwestern end of Lake Wawasee, Syracuse was settled in the early 1830s. The town was platted in 1837, and a hotel called the Rough and Ready House opened in 1848. Other early businesses included two distilleries, a cowbell factory, a tin shop, and a barrel-making factory. The town was incorporated in 1876. Though the town retains permanent residents, year-round business, and boat manufacturing industries, the area is considered primarily a summer playground. Every summer the population swells as tourists rush to the lakeshore seeking water-related activities. The town of Syracuse has four parks—all near the water. The business district caters to the tourist trade.

Take Huntington St. (IND 13) to Washington St. Follow Washington St. to the right and turn right on North Shore Dr. and continue along Syracuse Lake to the end of the road. Turn right onto East Shore Dr. and proceed *.7 m.*, cross the CSX (former Baltimore and Ohio) Railroad, turn left and continue *.6 m.*, and turn right. **Lake Wawasee** is on the right. Covering a surface area of 2,618 acres, Lake Wawasee is the largest natural lake in Indiana. Called Turkey Lake in the early days, it was named for the Miami Indian chief Wau-wa-aus-see. More than 10,000 years ago receding glaciers formed the hilly moraines and kettle holes of the lake region of which Lake Wawasee is a part. Several hundred years ago, Lake Wawasee was 7 or 8 ft. deeper, and much of the present marshland was then lake bottom. A dam built at Syr-

acuse in 1834 raised the water to its present level. Surrounded by hotels, camps, cottages, boat liveries, riding stables, golf courses, and a repertory theater—the lake has become a vacationer's paradise. The growing popularity of winter sports has helped even more to expand the region's recreational opportunities.

Continue *.4 m.* after passing the marker on the right which notes that you now are at the boundary of Chief Papakeechie's reservation, which once extended into Noble County. Nearby is the three-story, 350-ft.-long **Spink Hotel** and gambling casino, which rose on the waterfront site in 1925. The George Spink family of Indianapolis owned the 130-room luxurious hotel, a rambling pink stucco building. A religious order, the Crosier Fathers of Fort Wayne, operated a seminary and preparatory school there from 1948 until the 1970s. For several years the Lake Wawasee landmark stood vacant before it was turned into condominium apartments in 1984–85.

Turn left on CR 775E. Lying primarily to the left is the **Wawasee Golf Club**, founded by Col. Eli Lilly in 1891. In his book *Early Wawasee Days*, the colonel's grandson, Eli Lilly, describes life at Lake Wawasee around the turn of the century—train rides from Indianapolis, summer days spent swimming, fishing, and yachting, and evenings dancing at the Wawasee Yacht Club. J. K. Lilly, son of the colonel, built the residence, called Anchors Aweigh, across the road from the club. Constructed in 1936, the gracious two-story brick home is sequestered by an iron picket fence and brick gateway. The original cottage which Colonel Lilly built in 1886 is out of sight from the road at the south end of the property. It was one of the first summer homes built on the lake. Just west of Anchors Aweigh is the former home of Indianapolis Speedway founder James A. Allison—a Greek Revival-style frame house. A. H. Nordyke, manufacturer of the early Marmon Wasp, and later John Noll, of cough syrup fame, owned the lakeside property adjoining Lilly's cottage.

At *.4 m.* turn right onto CR 1300N and continue for *1.4 m.* before turning right on CR 900E or Papakeechie Rd., which leads past the east shore of the lake. Continue south *1.7 m.*, passing the turnoff to the Enchanted Hills Playhouse housed in an old barn. At *1.1 m.* beyond is the **Crow's Nest Yacht Club**, a picturesque old house with fieldstone porches, built by Na-

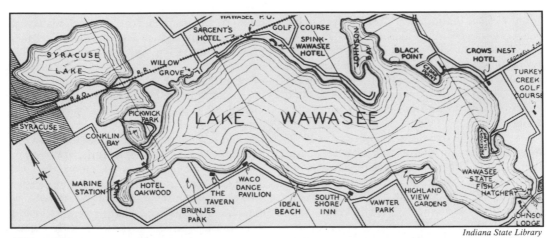

1938 map

thaniel Crow. The house became one of seven hotels on Lake Wawasee operating in the 1930s. It later served as a nursing home, health spa, swim and cabana club, and now a clubhouse for the yacht club. A number of short-lived yacht clubs have flourished at Lake Wawasee since the 1890s. The Wawasee Yacht Club, formed in 1935 and still in operation, has existed the longest. Since 1949 club members have competed in a regatta each year for the *Cynthia's Cup.*

At *.4 m.* beyond, turn right on CR 950E and continue past the site of a fish hatchery, which the state operated between 1914 and 1950 on land between Lakes Wawasee and Papakeechie. Before the construction of an earthen dam in 1910, **Papakeechie Lake** was six small lakes surrounded by marshland. It is now a 300-acre, privately owned lake. Papakeechie, whose name translates "flat belly," was a Miami Indian chief and the brother of Wau-wa-aus-see. It is said that Papakeechie customarily wore a small fish bone inserted through the cartilage of his nose, replaced by a silver ring for important occasions.

Continue a short distance to CR 850E and turn left. Proceed *1.2 m.* to the **Tri-County State Fish and Wildlife Area**. This 3,486-acre game preserve encircles 39 natural and man-made lakes and ponds. Used primarily as a public hunting and fishing area, the property also offers trapping, hiking, and mushroom hunting. Located within the wildlife area is a 10-acre woodlot formerly owned by Jethro Grider. It was also part of Chief Papakeechie's reserva-tion between 1828 and 1834. Now a nature preserve, Grider's Woods contains a self-guiding nature trail.

Return to IND 13 by way of CR 900N and turn left. At *.4 m.* a marker on the left designates the Continental Divide between the Mississippi valley and Great Lakes watersheds. Continue south for *2.3 m.* to Washington and Main sts. in **NORTH WEBSTER** (p. 709). Thomas Boydston came here from Ohio in 1842 and operated a sawmill and gristmill until 1850 when he joined the California gold rush. He returned in 1853. The mill, rebuilt in 1856, was a family operation until the 1920s. North Webster, incorporated as a town in 1937, and Webster Lake were known earlier as Boydston's Mill and Boydston's Pond, respectively. The mill burned in 1949 and was not rebuilt. In 1907 the Ruth chain-drive automobile was manufactured in North Webster. Mack Mock, Charlie Daniels, and Henry Outcelt, each of whom had a daughter named Ruth, were the principal operators of the short-lived enterprise.

Located just east of the town, **Webster Lake** covers 585 acres and reaches depths of 45 ft. Weimer Park was a very popular camp meeting site on Webster Lake around 1915. The *Dixie*, a diesel-powered, double-deck stern-wheeler, has plied the lake waters since 1929. A trip around the lake takes about one hour. Reached by Epworth Forest Rd. off IND 13, the grounds of the Indiana Conference of the Methodist Church, organized in 1924, are located at Epworth Forest Park on the lake's north shore. The park was named to honor

John Wesley, the founder of Methodism, who was born in Epworth, England, in 1703.

With a few exceptions such as the White Front Grocery, a traditional white frame building of Greek Revival design on the northwest corner of Washington and Main sts., the storefronts in downtown North Webster have assumed the concrete and plastic appearance of "Camelot." The transformation began in 1973 when the **Counting House Bank** (now Trustcorp Bank) and the **International Palace of Sports** replaced the old Farmers State Bank, chartered in 1925. O. J. Simpson, Johnny Weismuller, Jesse Owens, Pancho Gonzales, Dick Weber, and about 40,000 sports fans were on hand for the dedication in 1974. At Camelot Square, the southeast corner of Main and Washington sts., a 20th-century Arthurian castle complete with battlements and turrets houses the bank, fountain of fame, and wax museum. The museum contains life-size wax figures of internationally famous sports figures such as Mark Spitz, Bruce Jenner, and O. J. Simpson. Each year a King of Sports is selected, and a wax replica of the chosen person is dedicated. Donations to the organization provide scholarships for disadvantaged young people.

Continue on IND 13 for *.6 m.* beyond the south edge of North Webster and turn right onto CR 500N, which becomes Armstrong Rd., for approximately *5.7 m.* to **OSWEGO**, passing between the Barbee Lakes chain on the left and Tippecanoe Lake. Laid out in 1837 by Willard Barbee and Ezekiel French, the village, at the west end of Tippecanoe Lake, is on the site of a former Indian reservation occupied by Chief Musquabuck and his people. By 1843 the village contained a tannery, gristmill, blacksmith shop, and John Pound's store and post office. Fed by the Tippecanoe River, the lake stretches six miles east from Oswego and has a surface area of 707 acres. It is the state's deepest natural lake. Camps and parks border the northern shore.

Located at Armstrong Rd. and 2nd St., the two-story white frame structure known as **Pound's Store** is the oldest business establishment in Kosciusko County. French and Barbee built the store in 1838, but for many years John Pound used the building as a general store and post office. Now maintained by the Kosciusko County Historical Society, Pound's store contains many original furnishings and fixtures used until 1943. The Society operates a museum in the store, featuring local historical items such as Indian artifacts, early ledgers from the store, Civil War memorabilia, and pioneer farm implements.

Continue west *3.1 m.* on Armstrong Rd. to its end and turn right to **LEESBURG** (p. 629). The oldest town in Kosciusko County, Leesburg also served as the first county seat. Levi Lee laid out 48 lots in the wilderness between Big Turkey Creek and Little Turkey prairies in 1835. The first county court session took place in the Lee home in 1836, but the following year the county business moved to Warsaw. Leesburg was an early commercial center. David Roudabush erected the township's first flour mill at Leesburg in 1857. In 1871 the Cincinnati, Wabash and Michigan Railroad, a predecessor of the Big Four (now Conrail), was completed through Kosciusko County. The mills at the east end of Van Buren St., opposite the depot, were built in 1899. The frame depot in Leesburg still stands at Old State Rd. and Van Buren St.

Turn left and cross the railroad. Follow Van Buren St., a tree-shaded street paved with bricks, west *.5 m.* through the town's single-block-long business district to IND 15 (Main St.). Turn south and proceed *4.8 m.* to the **WARSAW** city limits (p. 10,647), which Christopher Lightfoot and W. H. Knott surveyed and platted in 1836. It has served as the county seat since 1837. After competing with Leesburg and later with Oswego, Warsaw eventually won out, due in part to its central location. In 1854 Warsaw was organized as a town and about 1875 as a city. Theodore Dreiser, author of *An American Tragedy*, once lived with his family in Warsaw and attended high school here. He later described Warsaw and other towns where he lived in *A Hoosier Holiday*, published in 1916.

Much of the city's economic stability is a result of its diversified industrial base. The city's largest employer is the book printing and distributing plant of R. R. Donnelley and Sons, which opened in 1959. Also seven manufacturers and many suppliers and subcontractors contribute to the orthopedic industry which began when DePuy Manufacturing Company was founded in 1895. An employee of DePuy, J. O. Zimmer, formed his own company in 1927, which is now perhaps the world's largest producer of appliances used for the treatment of bone fractures. Warsaw's industrial community also includes manufacturers of iron castings, plastics, containers, movie-projection screens, X-ray equipment, and glass and auto parts. The United Telephone Company of Indiana has made Warsaw its headquarters since 1931.

Continue south on IND 15 for *2.1 m.*, passing Center Lake on the right and Pike Lake on the left, covering 120 and 203 acres, respectively. The city maintains a public beach and park at each location. Swimming, boating, and fishing facilities are available. The city pavilion at Center Lake Park is a restored building from the 1930s.

At IND 15 (Detroit St.) and Main St., turn right and go west two blocks to Indiana St. On the southwest corner the old county jail, a Gothic castle-like structure of limestone block, now houses the **Warsaw Museum and Genealogical Library** of the Kosciusko County Historical Society. Architect George O. Garnsey designed the jailhouse erected in 1870. The north wing, of a similar style, was added in 1937. Eight rooms at the front of the building, adjoining the prison, originally served as the sheriff's residence. One small room now features a Civil War-era display. (*NRHP*)

Proceed one block west to the **Kosciusko County Courthouse** on the square bounded by Main, Center, Lake, and Buffalo sts. Jacob Losure's log cabin, built in 1836, served for a time as the first courthouse as well as a hotel and town hall. A two-story courthouse was erected in 1837 and was replaced in 1848. The present limestone structure was begun in 1881 and completed in 1884. Architects T. J. Tolan and Son designed the handsome French Second Empire-style edifice which was restored following a fire in 1980. The third-floor courtroom retains its original fireplaces, and the decor has been re-created. A tunnel connects the old courthouse to the new county justice building at the southwest corner of Lake and Main sts. The new facility, dedicated in 1982, features a large stained-glass window designed by Joan Hector in the second-floor foyer. The Kosciusko County Courthouse drew nationwide attention in 1921 during the six-day trial of the Culver Bank bandits. Clarence Darrow of Chicago defended the four men who received sentences of life imprisonment for the robbery of the bank and the murder of a police officer.

Across the courthouse square, at the northeast corner of Buffalo and Center sts., the **Saemann Building** is a fine example of urban restoration. The century-old brick commercial building is of Italianate design. Stained-glass transoms and cherry and walnut woodwork enhance the first floor. The old-fashioned storefront windows have been retained. The Masonic Lodge originally occupied the third floor, and the Fraternal Order of Eagles met on the second floor of the building next door to the east on Center St. The Saemann project has stimulated interest in downtown renovation and the preservation of other historic buildings. In 1982 the two-block area which includes the courthouse, the old county jail, and the Saemann building was officially designated a historic district. (*NRHP/HABSI*)

One block east at the northeast corner of Center and Indiana sts. is a tiny urban park situated on the **site of the first Kosciusko County Courthouse**, 1837–48. Proceed two blocks east on Center St. to Detroit St. Turn right and continue south for four blocks to Pope St. One of the city's oldest businesses, the **Warsaw Cut Glass Company** has occupied the two-story brick factory building on the southeast corner since 1911. The building is constructed of street paving bricks from the Brazil Brick Works. The second floor still houses the original grinding wheels used to produce the company's famous etched glass, and the first floor is used for a showroom and antique glass exhibit which is open to the public.

Between 1911 and the 1930s, at the height of production, the company employed up to 65 workers—40 of whom worked as glass cutters in the upstairs room. The company produced a heavy deep-cut crystal which was sold to major department stores and hotels, but today owner Randy Kirkendall and his assistant use a lightweight glass, due to inability to obtain heavyweight glass. They employ shallow cuts to create the company's traditional glassware patterns. The handcrafted crystal is sold on a retail or made-to-order basis. (*NRHP*)

From Pope St. return one block and turn right. Proceed east for *1.6 m.* on Winona Ave. to Argonne Rd. and Park Ave. at **WINONA LAKE** (p. 2,827). Known as the "western Chautauqua," Winona Lake in the early years of the 20th century was the popular meeting place for a number of Christian religious groups. The Pittsburgh, Fort Wayne and Chicago Railroad served the lakeside town, bringing thousands from New York and Chicago. The Winona Interurban Railway provided easy access to Warsaw. During the summer months visitors flocked to the lakeshore for swimming, boating, fishing, picnicking, golf, and chautauqua entertainments. The Winona Lake Christian Assembly was in session during the summer, and the Bible Conference lasted 10 days, featuring lectures, music, and readings at the Winona Auditorium. The famous baseball player and evangelist, Billy Sunday, drew crowds to the lake to hear his "fire and brimstone" sermons, filling to capacity the large auditorium named after him. His influence was felt throughout the community, and Christian sanctions against smoking, drinking, or creating a disturbance were strictly enforced.

Continue to the right on Park Ave., following the shoreline of **Winona Lake**. First known as Eagle Lake because its shape was roughly that of an eagle with outspread wings, Winona Lake covers 478 acres and attains a depth of 80 ft. The Winona Lake Christian Assembly operates the old Winona Hotel on the left overlooking the lake. It is the only building on Chestnut St. west of 4th St. to survive a devastating fire in 1914.

Founded by the Presbyterians in 1894, the Winona Assembly and Summer School Association developed the mile-long strip of lakefront property between Winona Ave. and 12th St. The Winona Lake Christian Assembly, Inc., became interdenominational in 1938 and now shares its facilities with other religious groups. Situated on Christian Assembly property along Park Ave. are motel and apartment facilities, a wooded park, an administration building, the white frame Billy Sunday Tabernacle, and the brick-and-glass Homer Rodeheaver Auditorium. Between 1906 and 1938 a biological station of Indiana University was maintained on the grounds. The final chautauqua program was held in 1943.

At 12th St., turn left and drive up the hill to Sunday Ln. Turn left into a narrow residential street which leads to the rear of the **Billy Sunday home**, 1111 Sunday Ln., a modest frame bungalow facing the waterfront. William Ashley Sunday was born near Ames, Iowa, in 1862. He played National League baseball eight years for the Chicago, Pittsburgh, and Philadelphia teams before deciding in 1896 to make evangelism his lifework. He became a Presbyterian minister, preaching in the days before radio and television. His dynamic sermons captivated and converted thousands. Tempo-

rary wooden buildings with sawdust floors such as the Billy Sunday Tabernacle were built with volunteer labor to accommodate his huge audiences. When converts came to the altar, they were said to be "hitting the sawdust trail." Choirs of 1,000 to 4,000 members accompanied his performances. Billy Sunday and his wife came to Winona Lake in 1910 to make their home between campaigns, and he often preached at the nearby tabernacle until his death in 1935. His home, now a museum, and the tabernacle still draw visitors.

Continue north on Sunday Ln. to 9th St. Turn right and proceed one block past the Free Methodist Church on the right and the International Friendship House on the left to the yellow brick **Free Methodist Church World Headquarters** facing College Ave. The Free Methodists founded their international headquarters at Winona Lake in 1935 and purchased the Mount Memorial Building of the defunct Winona College, 1908–18, and the Winona Lake School of Theology, 1920-35, for use as a publishing house, called the Light and Life Press. The Free Methodist press continues to operate, publishing mostly Bible School curriculum materials and church newsletters.

From 9th St., turn right and proceed south on College Ave. for two blocks to Publishers Dr. On the northeast corner is the distribution center for **The Word, Inc.**, the music publishing company founded by Homer Rodeheaver in 1910. A singer and musician, Rodeheaver sang baritone and played the trombone at Billy Sunday's revival meetings. He was Sunday's choir director for 22 years. He also composed religious songs and helped popularize "The Old Rugged Cross." His company became the nation's largest publisher of gospel songs and still operates with royalties from Rodeheaver's copyrighted songs. It is now owned by the American Broadcasting Company. Corporate offices are located at Waco, Texas.

Proceed east one block to Kings Highway and turn left. The 150-acre campus of **Grace College** and **Grace Theological Seminary** extends to the east between Publishers Dr. and Wooster Rd. (7th St.) Located in Akron, Ohio, for two years, the seminary was founded in 1937 and moved to Winona Lake in 1939, where it established Grace College in 1948. The college is a liberal arts school with majors in Christian ministries, business, teaching, and nursing. The seminary offers master degrees in divinity and theology and a doctorate in theology. Both schools are affiliated with the Fellowship of Grace Brethren Churches. A recent expansion includes a fine arts complex with a 2,500-seat auditorium.

Follow Kings Highway north and west to Argonne Rd. where it becomes Winona Ave. Continue west until Winona Ave. becomes IND 25 in Warsaw. Proceed west and south on IND 25 for *7.5 m.* to **PALESTINE**, an unincorporated village of about 150 persons in a scenic lakeside setting. A turnoff road to the left leads to a public access site on **Palestine Lake**, a 232-acre shallow lake with a gravel bottom. The lush vegetation surrounding the lake provides ideal conditions for breeding fish, and fishermen find an ample supply of bluegills, largemouth bass, perch, and crappies. A water-powered gristmill, advertised as the home of "Straight Goods" flour, stood on the bank of Trimball Creek in the middle of the village from 1838 until 1983 when it was razed. For a time Palestine was a thriving mill town but failed to prosper after the Pittsburgh, Fort Wayne and Chicago Railroad (now Conrail) bypassed it to the north.

From Palestine, continue west on IND 25 for *4.7 m.* to downtown **MENTONE** (p. 973). A 3,000-lb., egg-shaped concrete monument built in 1946, on the southeast corner of IND 25 (E. Main St.) and Morgan St., announces that you are in the Egg Basket of the Midwest. Mentone is also the birthplace of aviation pioneer Lawrence D. Bell (1894–1956), founder and owner of the Bell Aircraft Corporation of Buffalo, New York. Founded in 1935, the company recorded many "firsts" in the field of aviation such as production of the nation's first jet propelled airplane, the world's first commercial helicopter, the world's fastest and highest flying airplane, the first aircraft to shatter the sound barrier, and the first jet vertical takeoff and landing airplane. Bell devoted 44 years to the aircraft industry and won numerous awards for his contributions, but he never forgot his home town. Bell bequeathed the funds to build a memorial for his parents, the **Bell Memorial Public Library**, 306 N. Broadway, dedicated in 1959.

The **Lawrence D. Bell Aircraft Museum**, completed in 1979, is located on Oak St. two blocks west and two blocks south of IND 25 and IND 19. In the 1970s the townspeople raised the money to erect a museum specifi-

cally to house Bell's personal collection of aviation memorabilia, papers, aircraft models, and other artifacts. The display reflects the development of aviation from the early years of barnstorming to the dawn of the space age.

From Mentone, proceed south on IND 19 for *9.8 m.* to IND 14 in downtown Akron in **FULTON COUNTY** (p. 19,335; 369 sq. m.). The county was formed in 1835, organized in 1836, and named in honor of Robert Fulton, inventor of the steamboat. The county commissioners selected Rochester, centrally situated one-half mile northwest of Lake Manitou and two miles south of the Tippecanoe River, as the county seat. In a series of treaties with the federal government, Chief Aubbeenaubbee of the Potawatomies had relinquished the rights of his tribe to property in the northwest corner of the county, and by 1839 nearly all Indians had been removed. The principal towns of Akron and Kewanna were laid out and platted in 1838 and 1845, respectively.

AKRON (p. 1,045) is the second largest town in Fulton County. Dr. Joseph Sippy came here in 1835 and returned the following year with a party of 47 from Ohio. When the group arrived at the crossing of the trails (now IND 14 and 19) they stopped to give thanks to God. Their leader said, "This is the New Ark, consummating the covenant seeking homes in a new land." In 1838 Dr. Sippy and Hiram L. Welton platted the town of Newark. Because of a post office in southern Indiana with the name Newark, the name of the town was later changed to Akron.

At Mishawaka and Walnut sts., one block north of the main intersection, stands the **United Methodist Church**. Architect A. D. Monler of Huntington designed the Gothic-style edifice with a bell tower, dedicated in 1904. The cornerstone weighs 1,400 lbs. and contains a tin box filled with historic memorabilia. The church, the third building on the site, has been restored. Next door the former **Hotel Akron** was erected in 1905 by John H. Grindle, the same man who built the church.

Continue south to the northwest corner of Rochester and Mishawaka sts., where a plaque mounted on the former state bank building marks **the Indian trails crossing** at the site of the original white settlement in 1836. The 19th-century brick building now serves as the Akron post office.

Akron's first industry was a shovel factory, later the American Fork and Hoe Company, begun in 1923. It is now the site of Sonoco Products Company just east of IND 19 at the south edge of town. The paper converting plant produces spirally wound paper tubes and cores for industrial use.

Akron is also the headquarters for Pike Lumber Company, founded by a Quaker, Jonathan Pike, who logged with oxen in Wabash, Indiana. Incorporated in 1904, it is the largest of the company's three Midwest mills. The company ships Indiana hardwood lumber both domestically and internationally.

Take IND 14 east for *9.4 m.* to **SILVER LAKE** (p. 576) in the center of dairy country. Turn south on IND 15 and go *11.1 m.* to IND 16, entering Wabash County (for a description of the county see Tour 2). Turn west and go *1.8 m.* to Chippewa Rd. in **ROANN** (p. 548), situated on the Eel River about 15 miles downstream from North Manchester. Joseph Beckner from Virginia settled here in 1836 and operated a tavern on Chippewa Rd. Beckner employed Elijah Hackleman to survey the original plat in 1853 and created the name for the new town, Roann, after his hired cook, Ann Roe, and his daughter, also named Ann. The Detroit, Eel River and Illinois Railroad arrived in 1871, spurring the economy. In 1881 Roann was incorporated as a town.

Ross Franklin Lockridge, author of numerous books on Indiana history and for a time supervisor of the Work Projects Administration (WPA) project which compiled the 1941 edition of *Indiana: A Guide to the Hoosier State*, was born in Miami County three miles southwest of Roann in 1877. His son, Ross, Jr., wrote the best-selling novel *Raintree County*.

Just north of IND 16, on Chippewa Rd. (CR 770W), is the **Roann Covered Bridge**, one of two left in Wabash County. The Smith Bridge Company of Toledo, Ohio, constructed the Roann bridge in 1872 with two spans of oak trusses in the design patented by William Howe in 1840. Three previous bridges across the Eel River at Roann, built in 1841, 1845, and 1856 or 1858, were washed away. Through traffic has been diverted to a new concrete-and-steel structure 500 ft. upriver. (*NRHP*)

Proceed west one mile on IND 16 to **STOCKDALE**, near the Wabash-Miami county line, where parking is available at a public access site on the south bank of the Eel River.

Once a Potawatomi Indian village called Squirrel's Village, Stockdale was platted by Thomas Goudy in 1839, the same year he built the first gristmill, which was washed away by high waters in 1856. Baker and Ranck erected the present water-powered flour mill at Stockdale in 1858, but rollers replaced the original buhrstones in 1881. The Deck family operated the mill until 1964; the machinery is still intact. Constructed with 60-ft.-long beams, hand-hewn by broadax and fitted together by notches, the large weatherboard building stands unused and fenced off on private property along the north bank of the Eel River. The prosperous village of Stockdale began to dwindle when the railroad bypassed it in 1871. By 1920 only the roller mills and a cement products factory were still in business.

Return east on IND 16 *7.9 m.* to IND 13 and turn north for *6 m.* to IND 114. Turn east and proceed *1.4 m.* to downtown **NORTH MANCHESTER** (p. 5,998). Situated on the great bend of the Eel River, North Manchester is an attractive town of wide tree-lined streets and well-tended homes. Peter Ogan laid out the original plat bounded by Elm, 4th, and Wayne sts. and the Eel River, recorded in 1837. Early industry focused on the riverfront. Sawmills and a brickyard south of town provided the materials for North Manchester's stately mansions.

The Detroit, Eel River and Illinois Railroad arrived in 1871, followed by the Big Four line. A planing and band sawmill operated adjacent to the railroad on the west side of town. For a short time in 1908–9, V. L. DeWitt manufactured automobiles at a factory which was later destroyed by fire. The DeWitt auto featured 40-in.-diameter spoke wheels made of hickory with solid rubber tires. The North Manchester Historical Society possesses a replica of the DeWitt auto, produced by a local company owned by Russell Egolf.

North Manchester's largest employer is Eaton Controls. Other manufacturers are United Technologies, which produces wiring harnesses, and the Heckman Bindery. The Heckman family has been binding books and magazines since 1931 and is a major producer of library bindings.

Several century-old buildings with distinctive architectural styles stand along W. Main St. Built in 1882, the **Zion Evangelical Lutheran Church** in the 100 block is the second home of the North Manchester congregation, organized in 1846. The brick Gothic-style church features a 100-ft.-high bell tower. Art glass windows were installed in 1900. The parsonage adjacent to the church was added in 1950. Renovations of the church were completed in 1966. Dr. Lloyd C. Douglas, author of *Magnificent Obsession* and *The Robe*, preached here from 1903 to 1905 while writing his first book, *More Than a Prophet*.

Continue east on Main St. for two blocks through the center of North Manchester's early business district. Turn right and follow Mill St. south and east for two and one-half blocks to the North Manchester **Covered Bridge**, spanning the Eel River. The Smith Bridge Company of Toledo, Ohio, built the plank floor and oak beam structure about 1872. The single-lane bridge with a walkway was renovated in 1966 and is now closed to traffic. The Potawatomi Indians called this river the Kenapocomoco, which means "snake fish." Chief Pierrish (Parish) and his tribe had a village near the river on the north side of North Manchester. (*NRHP*)

Return to Main St. Go west one block to Walnut St. Turn north and proceed past the 100 block, a row of recently renovated turn-of-the-century commercial buildings housing a colorful variety of boutiques and offices. At the northwest corner of Walnut and 2nd sts. stands the historic **Hotel Sheller**. (*NRHP*) Henry Lantz built this landmark as a stagecoach inn and saloon in 1847. Rufus Grimes purchased the hotel in 1881. He moved the original building to the west and erected a new two-story structure on the site, joining the two sections as one large hotel. The exterior is of Franco-American design with a French mansard roof and Italianate-style cornices and brackets. The interior contains many original Victorian furnishings. H. B. Sheller bought the hotel in 1892. He erected a new wing on the north side and converted the attic into a third floor of rooms. Sheller's daughter-in-law continues to operate the 20-room hotel. The hotel guest register boasts an assortment of well-known names, including William Jennings Bryan, Jesse James's brother Frank, Lillian Russell, Lloyd Douglas, and Vice-President Thomas R. Marshall.

Continue north on Walnut St. Turn left at 7th St. and continue .5 *m.* to the **Peabody Retirement Community**, which is approached through a beautiful arch of trees. Established in 1930, it is one of Indiana's early retirement homes. Return to Walnut St. and turn north. The squat frame cottage, now encased with shingles, at 902 N. Walnut St., was the **birthplace of Thomas Riley Marshall** (1854–1925), the man who became governor of Indiana, 1909–13, and vice-president of the United States, 1913–21, during the Woodrow Wilson administration. Built in 1848, the house originally stood at 126 E. Main St. and was moved several times before reaching its present site in 1898. In 1925 Marshall returned to his hometown to give the commencement address at Manchester College. He died 10 days later on the first of June.

From 9th and Walnut sts., proceed north two blocks to College Ave. and turn right. **Manchester College**, an independent, coeducational college, began as Roanoke Classical Seminary, founded by the United Brethren Church in 1860. The seminary became Manchester College in 1889 when it moved to North Manchester. The Church of the Brethren purchased it in 1895. It gradually evolved into a college of liberal arts, and the academy division, established in 1907, was discontinued in 1923. Mount Morris College in Illinois, founded as a Methodist Seminary in 1839, merged with Manchester College in 1932. Students of all faiths now attend the college. The four-year curriculum offers a variety of professional and pre-professional areas of study and a graduate study program leading to the Master of Arts degree in Education. Paul Flory, a Manchester College graduate, was the 1974 Nobel laureate in chemistry.

The Administration Building stands in the middle of the original campus, a 10-acre wooded plot fronting College Ave. between Wayne and East sts. Built in 1889, the east end of the Administration Building, known as College Hall, housed the entire school operation. The Bible School Building, erected in the 1890s, is now the west end of the Administration Building. The present campus covers more than 100 acres and offers a number of modern facilities, including a new gymnasium. The school quadrangle is flanked by the 1,300-seat Cordier Auditorium, built in 1978, on the north and the cruciform-shape Petersime Chapel, built in 1962, on the south. Guest parking is available on the south side of College Ave. opposite the Administration Building.

From Manchester College, turn left and follow East St. north for *.5 m.* to IND 13. Turn right and continue northeast for *4.3 m.* to IND 14, crossing the Kosciusko County line at *2.3 m.* Turn right for *3 m.* to the **WHITLEY COUNTY** (p. 26,215; 336 sq. m.) line. Following the Indian treaties of 1826 and 1828 at Wabash, the county's first land sales began in 1833 and lasted until 1848. Though both the Miami and the Potawatomi Indians claimed property in the territory, they actually had established only one settlement, Seek's Village, the last section to be placed on the market. Little Turtle (ca. 1752–1812), the great Miami warrior and chieftain, was born in what is now Union Township, about five miles east of Columbia City.

Carved from Allen and Huntington counties, Whitley County was formed in 1835, organized in 1838, and named for pioneer and Indian fighter Col. William Whitley of Kentucky, who was killed at the Battle of the Thames, Canada, in 1813. The Wabash and Erie Canal, which opened from Fort Wayne to Huntington in 1835, helped develop the southeastern corner of the county. Once the land was cleared of forests, agriculture became the county's major occupation. From 1900 through the 1920s Whitley County competed with Noble County in growing onions, and Collins, northeast of Columbia City, claimed to be the onion capital of the nation. The northern part of the county is noted for its picturesque lakes. Seven miles north of Columbia City, a 100-acre state nature preserve is maintained on the east side of Crooked Lake. In the tri-lakes region—around Cedar, Round, and Shriner lakes—resorts flourished during the 1920s. Once almost "fished out," the lakes have been replenished thanks to the Department of Natural Resources. In the northeast corner, **CHURUBUSCO** (p. 1,638) is the second largest town in Whitley County. Originally the twin towns of Union and Franklin, Churubusco united as a single town in order to gain a post office and took its name from the 1847 Battle of Churubusco, a decisive American victory during the Mexican War. In the 20th century the county has witnessed extensive industrial development. Products manufactured include tools, dies, molds, electrical and auto parts, rubber and plastic products, grey iron castings, fertilizers, boats, sails, kitchen cabinets, musi-

cal instruments, nuts and bolts, and industrial soap.

From the county line, proceed east on IND 14 for *3.2 m.*, passing through Collamer, to IND 5 in **SOUTH WHITLEY** (p. 1,575). Laid out in 1837, South Whitley was first called Springfield, but the name was changed to Whitley in 1839 because of a name duplication. Whitley then became South Whitley in 1842 to distinguish it from the Whitley courthouse in Columbia City. In recent years South Whitley has acquired the designation of "bed race capital of the world" because of its annual festival in September. Competing teams of five persons, four pushing and one riding, race beds mounted on casters through the downtown area. South Whitley is the hometown of the award-winning country recording artist, Janie Fricke.

The nation's largest producer of high-quality bassoons is **Fox Products Corporation**. Hugo E. Fox, first bassoonist in the Chicago Symphony from 1922 to 1949, founded the company in 1949 in a converted barn and chicken house on the Fox farm. Today the family-run operation, which exports musical instruments around the world, occupies a modern plant *.8 m.* south of IND 14 off IND 5 on the southern edge of town and employs three dozen craftsmen and professional tuners.

One of South Whitley's most important businesses is situated at the corner of State (IND 5) and Broad sts., *.3 m.* north of the Eel River. The Grip Nut Company, now called **Gripco Fastener**, moved here from Chicago in 1905. For many years the makers of fasteners and lock weld and clinch nuts occupied the former Springfield Academy building at Broad and Maple sts. which served as a school between 1867 and 1869.

Proceed north *.3 m.* on IND 5 to IND 205. Turn right and travel *9.3 m.* to **COLUMBIA CITY** (p. 5,091). IND 205 merges with IND 9 which becomes Main St., running roughly north-south through the city. Continue north on IND 9 for *.7 m.* to Van Buren St. In 1839, county officials selected land owned by Elihu Chauncey for the county seat, and they appointed Richard Collins to lay off the new town, called Columbia. The name of the town was not officially changed to Columbia City until 1854. Most of the city's industrial development is on the south side near the Conrail Railroad. Products manufactured include screw machine, auto, and molded plastic parts, wiring, and pontoon boats. Ralph F. Gates (1893-1978) was born in Columbia City and practiced law here both before and after serving as governor of Indiana, 1945–49. Gates spent his retirement at his home on Crooked Lake, where the Ralph Gates Nature Preserve was dedicated in 1978.

The first **Whitley County Courthouse** erected on the square bounded by Main, Chauncey, Market, and Van Buren sts. was a two-story frame building on the west side of Chauncey St. It was built in 1841 and used until a brick courthouse was erected on the square in 1848–50. The present courthouse, designed by architect Brentwood S. Tolan of Fort Wayne, was built between 1888 and 1890 for a little under $150,000. The Renaissance-style sandstone structure has unusual cylindrical projections at the corners and intricate detail work on the clock tower. Between 1979 and 1981 the county spent more than $450,000 to sandblast the exterior, repair the copper dome, and extensively refurbish the interior. (*NRHP*)

On the west side of the courthouse square, the **Clugston Building**, erected by merchant David B. Clugston in 1889, occupies the southwest corner of Chauncey and Van Buren sts. From 1889 to 1908 the second floor of the dry goods store housed Thomas R. Marshall's law firm. The legal partnership dissolved when Marshall went to Indianapolis to take office as governor in 1909.

Continue north two blocks on Chauncey St. At the turn of the century, this residential section was known as **Silk Stocking Row** because the city's early merchants and professional people erected their fashionable homes here. The Clugston family, local bank and department store owners, built three of the most elegant mansions. The white frame house of Dutch Provincial design at 317 N. Chauncey St. was originally the home of Philemon H. Clugston, the oldest son of David B. Clugston, a partner in the law firm of Marshall, McNagny and Clugston, and the mayor of Columbia City, 1889–93. His fiancée, Emma Thatcher, gave the house to him as a wedding present in 1898. David B. Clugston, Jr., who operated the Clugston dry goods business at Larwill, built the Queen Anne-style house at 319 N. Chauncey St. in 1890. The white frame house, featuring a large veranda, now serves as the First Presbyterian Church manse. The regal Greek Revival-style house at 323 N. Chauncey St. was the home of David B. Clugston, the family patriarch. Built in 1915, the white frame structure boasts a front portico with massive two-story-high pillars.

From Chauncey and Jefferson sts., proceed east one-half block to the **Whitley County Historical Society Museum** at 108 W. Jefferson St. Located one-half block west of N. Main St., the two-story white frame house was the home of Thomas Riley Marshall from 1877 to 1909. Born in North Manchester, Marshall lived in Pierceton from the age of six until he entered Wabash College. Marshall studied for the bar under Walter Olds and began practicing law in Columbia City in 1875. Two years later he formed a law partnership with William F. McNagny, later joined by Philemon H. Clugston, which lasted until Marshall was inaugurated governor in 1909. Meanwhile, Marshall had married Lois Kimsey in 1895 and brought his bride to the house on Jefferson St. Marshall ran a dry campaign on the Democratic ticket for governor and, while in office, pushed for a child labor law and voters' registration. He also led a fight against capital punishment and convinced many industries to buy Indiana coal. His attempts to have the state adopt a new constitution failed. Marshall served as the United States vice-president during the Woodrow Wil-

Indiana Historical Society (Bass Photo Collection)
Thomas Riley Marshall

son administration. At Washington, he became known for his dry sense of humor and is often remembered for his remark, delivered as an aside during a Senate debate on the country's needs, "What this country needs is a really good five-cent cigar." Examples of Marshall's wry wit abound in his autobiography, *Recollections: A Hoosier Salad*, published in 1925. Marshall was reelected vice-president and often acted as ceremonial head of the nation during Wilson's absences and illnesses. After he left the vice-presidency, Marshall joined the law firm of Walker and Hollett and settled in Indianapolis.

Today the Whitley County Historical Society operates the Marshall home as a museum. The house contains some Marshall furniture, numerous mementos, and a collection of pioneer relics from the area. Restoration work in the 1980s followed the 1896 blueprints which Marshall used in remodeling the home. Old-fashioned street lamps surround the house, and the yard contains a millstone from the Liggett Mills, which operated between 1878 and 1917, and a highway marker with a copper medallion of Abraham Lincoln. (*NRHP*)

From Jefferson and Main sts., proceed north four blocks to North St. At the northwest corner is a historical marker indicating the **birthplace of Lloyd C. Douglas** (1877–1951). Douglas's father was the pastor of Grace Lutheran Church. At the age of 5 he moved with his parents to Kentucky and returned at age 16. He later attended Wittenberg College and Hamma Divinity School in Ohio and became a Lutheran minister. While serving as the pastor of Zion Lutheran Church at North Manchester, Douglas married Besse Io Porch of Columbia City. His publications were primarily of a religious nature. He gained much success on the lecture circuit and held several posts outside Indiana. His novel, *Magnificent Obsession*, was published in 1929 and achieved immediate recognition. Several later novels were produced as movies, most notably *The Robe*, published in 1942. Douglas died in Hollywood, California, at age 73.

Continue north on Main St. and follow IND 9 *9.7 m.*, crossing the Noble County line (for a description of the county see Tour 1), to US 33 at **MERRIAM**, an unincorporated village of about 75 persons. Continue northeast on IND 9 for *4 m.*, then turn right on CR 75S. Proceed one mile to the **Chain O'Lakes State Park**, a 2,678-acre park established in 1960. The park encompasses a chain of lakes called "kettle lakes," which were formed by glaciers approximately 10,000 years ago. Melting ice from receding glaciers created the streams which connect most of the lakes in the park. The park offers many water-related activities (boating, fishing, canoeing, swimming), and rustic cabins provide family accommodations. Camping is available and a nature interpretive center is housed in a one-room schoolhouse, built in 1915. Rolling hills and open fields offer ideal cross-country skiing terrain during the winter.

Return to US 33 at Merriam and turn right for *4.3 m.* to **WOLF LAKE**. Patrick C. Miller and Andrew Stewart platted the town in 1836, about the same time that Noble County was organized. As early as 1833, Stewart operated a hotel of sorts in the area. It is possible that Wolf Lake was previously laid out in 1832 while still a part of Lagrange County. During the early 20th century, the mucklands around Wolf Lake became the center for onion growing in Noble County. Today, the lake area provides a quiet summer vacation spot.

In a cemetery *1.1 m.* west of IND 109 and US 33, then a short distance north, is the **grave of Marvin Kuhns** (1867–1907), Noble County's infamous outlaw. During his criminal career, Kuhns three times broke out of the Noble County Jail, twice deserted the United States Army, once fled the Ohio State Penitentiary, and several times fought gun battles with law officers. When not serving time behind bars, Kuhns chalked up a record in Indiana and Ohio for drinking, carousing, playing pranks, robbing stores, stealing horses, and, in one instance, for murder. Alerted on the party line telephone, farmers converged on Kuhns, after he stole a horse and buggy, and gunned him down in Van Wert County, Ohio. Since his death, Kuhns's exploits have gained widespread notoriety.

From Wolf Lake, follow US 33 north for *8.4 m.* to IND 5. Nestled in a grove of trees to the left, **Stone's Tavern**, a museum operated by the Stone's Trace Historical Society, is a relic from pioneer days. Richard Stone built a double log cabin for his family in 1831 and lodged travelers who passed along the old Goshen-Fort Wayne Trail, a former Indian trace, now US 33. Another early trail known as the White Pigeon Rd. is today's IND 5. In 1839 Stone erected the present two-story frame structure which was used as a stagecoach inn until 1862. In the 1840s it served as a courthouse, post office, jail, and schoolhouse. Stone sold the tavern in 1860, and it changed hands several times before the Stone's Trace Historical Society acquired it in 1964. The tavern underwent extensive restoration before opening as a museum. The parlor contains original wood plank flooring, salvaged from the ground-floor rooms, and a reconstructed fieldstone fireplace. Period furnishings help to re-create the atmosphere of the 19th-century tavern with its taproom and upstairs bedrooms. (*NRHP*)

From Stone's Tavern, follow IND 5/US 33 north for *2.3 m.*, crossing US 6, to the Lincolnway triangle at Union St. in **LIGONIER** (p. 3,134). In 1835 Isaac Cavin, a native of Ligonier, Pennsylvania, laid out the village. It was incorporated as a town in 1864 and as a city in 1892. The Michigan Southern and Northern Indiana Railroad arrived in 1858, giving impetus to Ligonier's growth as a grain market. Ligonier's leading industry today is Monsanto Company, which manufactures plastics.

Following the lead of Prussian immigrants Solomon Mier and Frederick Straus, who arrived in Ligonier in 1854, a Jewish community began to form which had a profound influence on the business and financial development. By 1880 the Jewish population had grown to more than 200, making Ligonier one of the largest Jewish settlements in Indiana. The number of Jews in Ligonier slowly dwindled in the 20th century until 1981 when the town's last Jewish resident, Durbin Mier, died. Ligonier has had three Jewish heads of government.

IND 5 (Lincolnway South) merges with Cavin St. at the triangle. Continue north for one block, then west on 6th St. for one block to Main St. and turn right. A tree-lined residential street featuring many of the city's finest homes, Main St. did not become a business street as intended because the bridge crossing the Elkhart River and providing through traffic was located on Cavin St.

At 503 S. Main St. stands the **Ahavath Shalom Reform Temple**. Organized in 1867, the congregation met in the Hostetter Building until a small synagogue was erected in the same year. In 1888 the congregation built a new temple and moved the old building to the rear of the new structure. For a time, the small building served several Protestant churches, but as

of 1989 it is the property of the Ligonier Public Library, which transferred its collection of material on Ligonier Jews, along with other local artifacts, to the temple for exhibition. The **Ligonier Jewish Cemetery** is located in the south side of the city across from the Ligonier Monument Company, 1274 Lincolnway South. There are 180 Jews buried in the cemetery. (*NRHP*)

At 210 S. Main St. is the **Jacob Straus house**, a stately Greek Revival-style mansion with front and side porches supported by pillars and with an oversized carriage house in back. Straus came from Germany in 1854 and settled in Ligonier, entering the mercantile business. In 1868 he founded the Citizens Bank. He also prospered in real estate and owned a carriage factory. His elegant home was one of many fashionable houses erected along Main St. by successful merchants and bankers in the community. (*NRHP*)

Return to Cavin St. and Lincolnway South (IND 5) and proceed south for *.9 m.* to US 6/33. Proceed west for *5.8 m.*, crossing the Elkhart/Noble county line, and turn north on US 33 for *5.7 m.* to **BENTON**, one of the county's first settlements. Matthew Boyd located here in 1828 and operated a ferry across the Elkhart River when the water was high. Nearly all early settlers crossed the ford at Benton. Boyd also opened an inn in 1830 which he ran more than 40 years. In 1832 Capt. Henry Beane platted Benton, which was named for Senator Thomas Hart Benton of Missouri. Though settled early, Benton failed to develop into a major city because the first railroads bypassed it for Goshen to the north, and the business establishments followed.

Continue north for *4.8 m.* to College Ave. in **GOSHEN** (p. 19,665). Platted in 1831 and incorporated in 1854, Goshen is the second largest community in the county. Oliver Crane named it for his hometown of Goshen, New York. Goshen is a Biblical term for "the land of plenty." Many early settlers in the Goshen area were Mennonites from Ohio and Pennsylvania. Goshen has traditionally been an agricultural trade center, known for its dairy, poultry, and mint products. It is also a large gladiolus-producing area. Goshen industry is varied and composed of mostly small companies. Woodworking plants followed by rubber factories lead the industrial sector. Items produced include boats, kitchen cabinets, automatic controls, ladders, rubber and plastic parts, mobile homes, and recreational vehicles.

At College Ave., turn west and proceed *1.3 m.* to **Goshen College** between 9th and Main sts. In 1894 the Mennonite Church founded the Elkhart Institute of Science, Industry and the Arts, a private preparatory school. The institute moved to the 135-acre campus at Goshen in 1903, becoming Goshen College. Now a fully accredited four-year liberal arts institution, Goshen College has expanded to 17 buildings, including the recently constructed John S. Umble Center for the Performing Arts and the 900-acre Merry Lea Environmental Learning Center located about 30 miles southeast. Situated on the northwest corner of the quadrangle, the administration building and the visual arts building, erected in 1903, are the oldest structures on campus. The Mennonite Historical Library, which has an extensive collection of books dealing with this denomination, is now housed in the new Harold and Wilma Good Library. The Mennonite Chapel is also a modern building featuring a round sanctuary. Approximately 70 percent of the students are Mennonite, and the college is still owned by the Mennonite Church. Since 1968 the college has required all students to enroll in an international education program which provides firsthand experience in another culture by living 14 weeks in a developing nation. In 1980-81 Goshen College became the first American undergraduate school to negotiate an educational exchange with a college in the People's Republic of China.

From College Ave. proceed south four blocks to Westwood Rd. and turn right. At *.3 m.* the drive ends at the Elkhart River dam and millpond. **Shoup-Parsons Woods**, across the river, is a rich natural area used extensively by Goshen College biologists and known for its record number of bird species.

Return to College Ave. and continue north *.9 m.* on Main St. (IND 15) to Purl St. Turn right and continue *.3 m.* to the **Goshen Sash and Door Company**, situated just east of the Conrail Railroad. Founded by Reuben Whitmer in 1869, the original factory producing wood windows, sashes, doors, and blinds was located on the then-newly constructed hydraulic canal. The firm operated on the millrace for 24 years before moving to its present location in 1893 and is one of the few surviving industries from that era. The first factory at this loca-

tion, a two-story brick building, is still in use. A second building, similar to the first, was erected in 1903, and a third in 1941. The company offices and showroom are housed in the east building.

Return to Main St. and continue north for *.4 m.* to the **Elkhart County Courthouse**. A bronze Neptune statue and fountain donated by J. Polezoes in 1912 grace the front of the well-preserved courthouse on the square bounded by Lincoln Ave. and Main, 3rd, and Clinton sts. Architects J. H. Barrows and George O. Garnsey designed the Greek Revival-style structure with an Italianate-style center dome. Built in 1870, the present brick and limestone courthouse replaced the courthouse erected in 1833. (*NRHP*) A new jail has been constructed recently on 3rd St. across from the courthouse, and a county office building has been added a block west on 2nd St. Goshen has numerous examples of outstanding 19th-century domestic architecture, including the Rowell-Champion house, a Greek Revival-style structure, next to the jail.

In front of the courthouse, an **octagonal limestone booth** occupies the northwest corner of Main St. and Lincoln Ave. The WPA erected the booth across the street from the bank following Dillinger's widely publicized robberies in neighboring cities. City police manned the bullet-proof enclosure from 1939 to 1969. It is now used as an information center by local realtors.

Proceed north on IND 15 for *9.7 m.* to IND 120 at **BRISTOL** (p. 1,203). Located on the St. Joseph River, Bristol was settled by Yankee farmers from New York State and New England. Samuel P. Judson, Lewis Alverson, and Hiram Doolittle platted the town in 1835, and it developed as a river port until the railroad arrived in the 1850s.

Most of Bristol's industry is now located on the south edge of town. Several recreational vehicle-related industries opened in the 1970s and 1980s. The town's largest employer, however, is E.S.I. Meats, Inc. Formerly located in Goshen, the large southside meat processing plant supplies the Ponderosa restaurant chain.

The backside of a Greek Revival-style frame building known simply as the "old store" at 110 E. Vistula St. can be seen from the Division St. bridge, just north of Vistula St. (IND 120). In 1849 Aaron Kline, a grain merchant, built the facility for use as a warehouse and wharf. It is now occupied by Reproduction Technologies, Inc. Return to Vistula St. and go two blocks east to Apollo St. and turn left to a public access site on the river.

A collection of structures dating from the town's early days can be found in Bristol. Two blocks south of Vistula St. at the northwest corner of Charles and St. Joseph sts. stands the **Thomas Wheeler house**. Built in 1834, the compact frame house of Greek Revival design originally stood on a site nearer to the river. Wheeler and his partners operated a flour mill and sawmill during the 1840s when Bristol was an active wheat-shipping river port.

Return to Vistula St. and turn east. Restored in the 1960s, the **Bristol Opera House** at 212 E. Vistula St. first opened in 1897. The frame building trimmed with Italianate brackets once contained a post office at the west end. In past years the opera house was a stop for traveling theatrical troupes and medicine shows and recently has revived its stage productions on weekends.

Continue east on Vistula St., which follows part of the road (now IND 120) constructed in the 1830s between South Bend and Vistula (now Toledo), Ohio. Just east of Chaptoula St., at 601 E. Vistula St., is **St. John of the Cross Episcopal Church**, a white frame Gothic-style chapel. Constructed of ash wood and assembled with wooden pegs, it was completed in 1851. Built about the same time is the parish hall across the street, a former Presbyterian church. Both buildings are still in use. (*NRHP*)

From the church, proceed east on IND 120 for *2.5 m.* to CR 131 on the right, leading to the **Bonneyville Mill County Park**. Within this 155-acre park is the state's oldest gristmill in continuous operation. In 1832 Edward Bonney constructed a dam on the narrow Little Elkhart River and erected the water-powered mill to grind the grain of local farmers. The mill had a vertical shaft with a turbine-type wheel lying flat against the water flow instead of the usual overshot waterwheel. (*NRHP*) Bonney led a checkered career following his early years as a miller. In 1842 he was arrested for counterfeiting. He escaped from prison and turned up with his family near the Mormon community of Nauvoo, Illinois, in 1844. According to a published autobiographical account of his experiences, which Bonney titled *The Banditti of the Prairies or the Murderer's Doom!!—A Tale of the Mississippi Valley*, Bonney worked for the newly organized Allan Pinkerton Detective Agency and led a 13-month chase after nine thieves and murderers across a four-state area. Bonney served in the 127th Illinois Infantry during the Civil War. At age 59, he died in 1863, and his body was returned for burial near the mill. Restored in the 1960s, the mill is still grinding buckwheat flour, which is sold to visitors. The park also offers facilities for picnicking, fishing, hiking, sledding, and cross-country skiing.

Return to Bristol and continue west to the 300 block of W. Vistula St. (IND 120). On the right, the old Washington Township High School, which opened in 1904 and closed in 1966, houses the **Rush Memorial Center**. Howard Rush donated the 10-room school building to the county parks department. The Elkhart County Historical Society offers a museum featuring displays of early Bristol—a typical pioneer kitchen, elementary school room, blacksmith shop, dentist's office, general store, and other exhibits. Complete Tour 17 by returning *5.4 m* west to IND 19 (Main St.) in Elkhart via IND 120.

Tour 18

From Michigan St. and IND 2 (Western Ave.), at the south edge of South Bend's downtown business district, follow IND 2 west for *13.1 m.* to Timothy Rd. Turn south and continue *.4 m.* to the entrance of the **Bendix Woods County Park**.

The 195-acre park situated at the eastern edge of the Valparaiso Moraine opened in 1966 on the site of the former Studebaker Corporation Proving Grounds. Studebaker acquired the property in 1926 and constructed specially designed roads for testing cars under all possible driving conditions. It also reforested much land which had been cleared for agriculture in the 1860s and planted 8,200 pine trees over an area 250 ft. wide and a half-mile long to form the name Studebaker, a sight which can be appreciated only from the air. When the Studebaker Corporation went out of business in 1963, the Bendix Corporation bought the proving grounds and donated a portion for a county park. The company still maintains an office building east of the park.

Adjacent to the proving grounds, the park operates a **nature center** and book shop in a two-story brick structure erected in 1926 as an exclusive clubhouse for the drivers and engineers of Studebaker cars. Following World War II, the house was remodeled to provide working space for 25 to 30 engineers and draftsmen. In the 1960s Studebaker president Sherwood Egbert lived with his family on the second floor and drove his custom-built Avanti on the company proving grounds. The exterior is basically unchanged. Once an executive lounge and library, the east wing now accommodates exhibits of stuffed birds and area nature objects.

In the southern portion of the park, a 30-acre nature preserve has been set aside to protect an impressive old stand of American beech and maple trees. Numerous native tree species grow in Bendix Woods, and specimen plantings have been labeled for identification near the nature center. Park facilities also include a visi-tors center, nature trails, picnic shelters, ski slopes, and winter sports activities.

Return to IND 2 and proceed east *8.5 m.* to the US 31 South Bend By-pass. Turn south and continue approximately *11.9 m.* to IND 4 at **LAKEVILLE** (p. 629). Turn right and proceed west *4.7 m.* to the entrance on the right for the **Potato Creek State Park**. Potato Creek, which rises just south of the park, is part of the Kankakee drainage system. Potawatomi Indians once lived along the creek, and wild potato plants grew on the banks. During pioneer days, at least six mills lined Potato Creek, two of which were located inside what is now state property.

In the 1970s the state erected a dam to form **Worster Lake**. The 327-acre lake is named for Darcey Worster, a naturalist who promoted the idea of the lake as a recreation facility. Dedicated in 1977, the 3,840-acre recreation area provides bicycle, hiking, and horse trails, cross-country skiing and ice skating areas, cabins, campgrounds, boat rentals, and picnic areas. The state has set aside Swamp Rose Nature Preserve, a 100-acre area of swampland and round-topped glacial mounds in the northeast corner of the park.

From the park exit, continue west on IND 4 for *3.4 m.* to IND 23 (State St.) in **NORTH LIBERTY** (p. 1,211), laid out by Daniel and James P. Antrim in 1837 and incorporated as a town in 1894. Follow IND 23 south for *4 m.* On the left is a covered bridge on a private road leading to the Lightning Dude Ranch. Continue *1.1 m.* to Tyler Rd. East of the highway *1.5 m.* on the Stuntz-Hostetler Pines property is the **Stuntz Museum**. The author of four books about Indiana's Indians, Ervin Stuntz built the museum on his Christmas tree farm to house the Indian artifacts which he has collected for many years. The exhibit includes numerous arrowheads and an ivory knife, reputed to be over 2,000 years old, that was discovered when a pond here was excavated.

Tour 18

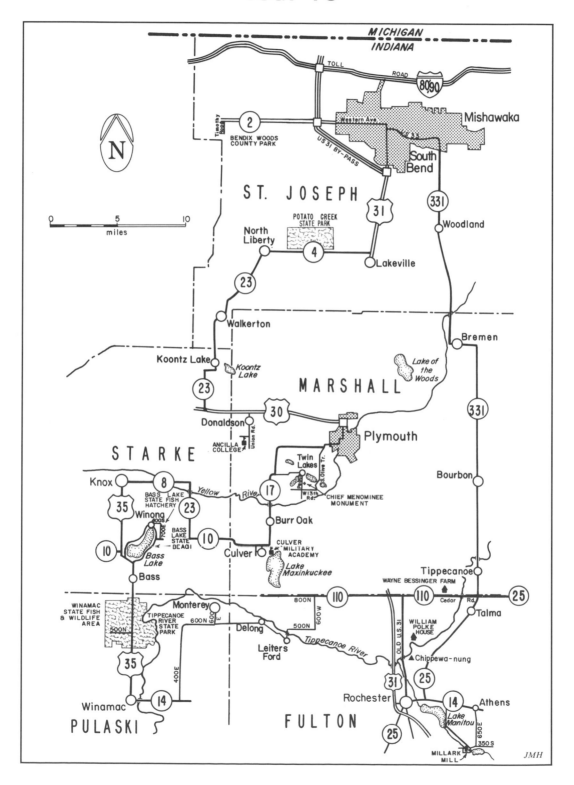

JMH

Return to IND 23 and continue south for *2 m.* to US 6 in **WALKERTON** (p. 2,051). In 1856 railroad surveyors platted the first lot in Walkerton, named for railroad promoter John Walker, who contracted the construction of the Cincinnati, Peru and Chicago Railroad. Born in Walkerton, Dr. Harold Clayton Urey won the Nobel Prize for Chemistry in 1934 for his discovery of a heavier isotope of hydrogen. A marker dedicated to Urey has been placed in the tiny park located along Roosevelt Rd. in the center of town, one block east of the US 6 junction.

Continue south through Walkerton on IND 23 for *2.7 m.* to the **STARKE COUNTY** (p. 21,997; 309 sq. m.) line. Formed by statute in 1835 and organized by a legislative act in 1850, the county was named for John Stark, a Revolutionary War hero whose action led to the defeat of Maj. Gen. John Burgoyne at Saratoga. The county seat was located at Knox. The Yellow River flows through the center of the county and empties into the Kankakee River which forms the northwestern border. Before drainage systems were developed in the 1890s, water covered much of Starke County. The southwest corner of the county is now noted for its fertile farmland, producing lucrative crops of mint which are converted into oils that flavor chewing gum, confections, and toothpaste.

Continue south on IND 23 for *1 m.* to **Koontz Lake**, located *.4 m.* east of IND 23 via Cherokee Rd., where a landing provides public access to the lake. Private cottages surround its wooded shoreline. Return to IND 23 and proceed south for *4.2 m.* to US 30. Turn left and continue *2.2 m.* to the **MARSHALL COUNTY** (p. 39,155; 444 sq. m.) line. Formed in 1835 and organized in 1836, Marshall County was named for United States Supreme Court Chief Justice John Marshall who died in 1835. Marshall County was originally a part of the territory belonging to the Menominee tribe of Potawatomi Indians, included in the government purchase under the 1832 treaty of Tippecanoe River. The most interesting geological features of the county are its lakes; several of the most attractive ones are Lake of the Woods, Twin Lakes, and Lake Maxinkuckee. The Yellow River flows in a southwesterly direction through the middle of the county, and the Tippecanoe River crosses the southeast corner. The county ranks high agriculturally. Onions,

mint, corn, oats, potatoes, and hay grow in the muck created by draining the marshlands. Orchards dot the highlands at Culver, Pretty Lake, and Twin Lakes.

Continue east on US 30 for *1.1 m.* to Union Rd. Turn right and continue south for *1.8 m.* through Donaldson to the front gates of **Ancilla Domini Junior College** on the right. A central drive lined with sycamore trees leads to the cloistered convent-villa-college campus located on Lake Galbreath. The administration offices are housed in a beautiful Gothic-style structure, surmounted with a 140-ft.-high tower sheathed in copper. Founded in 1937, the two-year coed commuter college of about 300 students offers associate degree programs in accounting, business administration, liberal arts and sciences, and nursing and pre-medicine. The Ancilla Domini Sisters, an order of the Poor Handmaidens of Christ founded in 1851, established the Ancilla complex. The 160-acre campus occupies the site of a resort, active in 1916, which featured the 42-room Lake Galbreath Hotel. A small museum contains native wildlife specimens, Indian artifacts, a geological display, and an exhibit of items collected by Catholic missionaries from various cultures around the world.

Return to US 30, passing the Sports Complex, housed in a former Catholic institution, turn right, and continue east for *7 m.* to the **PLYMOUTH** (p. 7,693) exit. When platted by James Blair, John Sering, and William Polke in 1834, Plymouth had only two streets—the Michigan Rd. and the Yellow River Rd. It was established as the county seat in 1836, incorporated as a town in 1851, and reached city status in 1873. Early industries in Plymouth included sawmills, a plow company, a grain elevator, novelty works, a tannery, and a sash, door, and blind factory. The city's major employers today are McCord Heat Transfer Corporation (auto radiators), United Technologies (automotive wires), Aker Plastics (bathroom fixtures), and Hehr International (recreational vehicle parts). Principal agricultural products of the area are livestock, tomatoes, pickles, and grain. Sand, gravel, and clay are the principal mineral resources.

From US 30, proceed south on IND 17 (Michigan St.) for *1.1 m.* Turn left on Jackson St. and continue east one block to **Magnetic Park**, at the end of the street. Situated along the Yellow River, the 16-acre wooded park provides picnic facilities. In 1936–37 the Works Progress Administration (WPA) erected the stone archway along Water St., the stone lodge, and the shelter for the water well. The park takes its name from the magnetic qualities found in the water of the flowing well.

Return to Michigan St. Proceed south three blocks then west one block on Jefferson St. (Old US 30). The **Marshall County Courthouse** occupies the square bounded by Madison, Jefferson, Walnut, and Center sts. Unlike most courthouses, the one in Plymouth is surrounded by residences rather than businesses. The new jail stands across the street north of the courthouse and the new county office building to the east. A one-story structure built in 1840 at the corner of Adams and Michigan sts. served as the first courthouse. The cornerstone for the present courthouse was laid in 1870. Architect Gordon P. Randall of Chicago designed the brick and stone building of Georgian Revival design with a central clock tower, completed in 1872 and remodeled in 1914. (*NRHP*)

At the northwest corner of Madison and Walnut sts. stands the **Simons house**, a handsome brick residence now owned by the Van Gilder Funeral Home. A state legislator in 1895–96, Millard W. Simons, who had inherited a fortune from his brother, a Fort Wayne capitalist, erected the home and adjacent carriage house in 1896. Shortly thereafter, Simons suffered financial reverses and was forced into litigation. In 1906 he died, penniless, in a mental hospital at Denver, Colorado. The property was tied up in the courts for years and owned by the Holzbauer family for several years before the Van Gilders purchased it about 1945.

North and west of the Simons residence, the former carriage house now serves as the **Marshall County Historical Museum**, 317 W. Monroe St. The front yard contains 19th-century gristmill wheels, farm implements, and a bell and cornerstone from the old Linkville School. Museum exhibits include a parlor setting and child's bedroom from about 1885, cooper tools, and Potawatomi Indian artifacts. The museum is also noted for its local history and genealogy research facilities.

Return to Jefferson and Center sts., along the east side of the courthouse square, then proceed south two blocks to Washington St. **Plymouth Fire Engine House** on the southeast corner was erected in 1875. The red brick fire station surmounted with a watchtower cur-

rently houses the city's emergency service organization. The town's first fire alarm bell, dated 1879, is mounted in front of the station. The building originally served as both the city hall and the engine house. (*NRHP*)

Continue south two blocks to La Porte St., turn left, and go east one block to Michigan St. On the northwest corner, a wall plaque notes the **site of the first house in Plymouth**, built by Grove Pomeroy in 1835. The first county board of commissioners met here in 1836. Later called the Plymouth Hotel, the house served as a station on the stage line between Logansport and Niles, Michigan.

Continue east on La Porte St. for three blocks to a cantilevered footbridge which spans the Yellow River. The **Iron Footbridge**, or "footpath of iron" as it was called, and an iron vehicle bridge on Garro St., one block north, built to replace the old wooden one, were erected by W. B. Bassett of the Rochester Bridge Company, in 1898, for a total of $2,950. The footbridge measures approximately 100 ft. long, 6 ft. wide, and 20 ft. high. Before construction of the bridges, the area on the east side of Michigan St. was largely undeveloped. Following completion of the bridges, however, it grew into a commercial center. The vehicle bridge was replaced in the 1920s, but the pedestrian bridge is still in use. (*NRHP*)

Return to Michigan and La Porte sts. and proceed west on IND 17 for *1.7 m.* to S. Olive Trail. Go south *3.1 m.* to W. 13th Rd., turn right, proceed *1.2 m.* to S. Peach Rd., and turn right to the **Chief Menominee Monument**, *.4 m.* north on the right. In 1909 a life-size granite statue was erected in memory of Chief Menominee and his tribe of 859 Potawatomi Indians who were marched from here to a western reservation. Menominee unsuccessfully attempted to defy Gov. David Wallace's order for their removal from the Twin Lakes region. In the summer of 1838 a company of soldiers under the command of Maj. Gen. John Tipton led the Indian men, women, and children on a 900-mile trek to Kansas, the infamous Trail of Death. More than 150 Indian lives were lost along the way to disease, fatigue, and the effects of winter. Stricken with typhoid, Chief Menominee was among the dead. Following their removal, the Indians' land was opened to white settlement.

Continue on S. Peach *.8 m.* past the lakefront to W. 12th Rd. Turn left and proceed west for *2.7 m.* to IND 17. Continue west and follow IND 17 for *5.7 m.* across the Yellow River and through the village of Burr Oak to IND 10 at **CULVER** (p. 1,601). Bayless L. Dickson, an early settler whose farm bordered on Lake Maxinkuckee, laid out Union Town in 1844, but a new survey was made in 1851, and it was renamed Marmont in honor of Auguste-Frédéric-Louis Viesse de Marmont, one of Napoleon's marshals. In 1895 the town commissioners changed the name to Culver to honor Henry Culver, a prominent citizen. Culver today is a thriving resort area. The town embraces **Lake Maxinkuckee**, the second largest natural lake in Indiana, which is noted for its beauty and for its chief landmark—the Culver Military Academy.

From IND 10, the town of Culver lies straight ahead via Lake Shore Dr. Proceed south *.2 m.* to Academy Rd. Turn left and follow the road which bends around the western edge of the **Culver Military Academy**, passing many classroom buildings. Henry Harrison Culver, a businessman from Missouri, came to Lake Maxinkuckee in 1894 and on its shores established what has become one of the country's leading prep schools. Culver Military Academy and the Culver Girls Academy now occupy 1,500 acres along the lakefront. The Culver Girls Academy was established in 1971. Today all classes and campus facilities are coeducational. Among the alumni are playwright/director Joshua Logan, United States Senator Lowell P. Weicker, astronaut John Finley, and ex-Cincinnati Reds owner Louis Nippert.

The Eugene C. Eppley Foundation donated the funds for the three classroom buildings which comprise Gignilliat Memorial Quadrangle. Eppley Auditorium, built in 1959, seats 1,500 persons. Culver Legion Memorial Library was constructed in 1924 and dedicated to the memory of Culver graduates who gave their lives in the First World War. The Culver Memorial Chapel, constructed in the 1950s, is a magnificent Tudor-Gothic-style structure with a 156-ft.-high spire. Vaulted ceilings and stained-glass windows crafted in England grace the interior. On the waterfront, the Culver Inn occupies the former Palmer House built in the 1890s. Formal dining facilities are available for students and their guests.

Public appearances of the school's famous Black Horse Troop began in 1898, and it participated at President Woodrow Wilson's inaugu-

rations of 1913 and 1917. More recently, the troop led President Ronald Reagan's inaugural parades in Washington in 1981 and 1985. The cavalry unit has more than 130 horses. On most Sunday nights during June and July, the Black Horse Troop conducts parades for the public on the campus. The academy also has a complete student flight-training program with a fleet of planes and a private airport just east of the campus.

Each year, the Culver Summer Camps offer more than 1,400 girls and boys ages 9-17 a program in sailing, riding, aquatics, soccer, scuba, rifle, hockey, tennis, golf, wrestling, reading skills, volleyball, basketball, aviation, and gymnastics. A separate facility in a wooded setting just east of the main campus includes cabins, a dining hall, library, observatory, and museum. The woodcraft camp was inspired by a suggestion from Lord Baden-Powell, founder of the Boy Scouts of England, to Brig. Gen. Leigh R. Gignilliat, third director of the academy. The summer program began in 1912. Daniel Carter Beard, the head of the Boy Scouts of America, worked there from 1912 to 1915. The summer facilities became coed in the 1960s. The Culver Woodcraft Camp Indian Lore and Nature Museum located off IND 10 just east of IND 17 features an extensive display of Indian artifacts. The camp presents authentic Indian dances for the public on Saturday evenings from late June through July.

Return to IND 17 and IND 10, turn left, and proceed west on IND 10 *5.9 m.* to IND 23, crossing the Starke-Marshall county line. Follow IND 23 north for *4 m.* to IND 8 then west for *5.1 m.* to US 35 in **KNOX** (p. 3,674). Named for Maj. Gen. Henry Knox, a Revolutionary War officer and secretary of war under George Washington, the town of Knox became the county seat in 1850. During the same year, Carter D. Hathaway laid out the town. Knox was incorporated in 1871. Its principal industries produce trophies, lumber products, gloves, and molds.

Proceed north on US 35 (Heaton St.) for *.7 m.* to Washington St. Turn left and continue one block to the **Starke County Courthouse**, situated on the square bounded by Main, Pearl, Washington, and Mound sts. The first courthouse was a small frame building used until 1863, when the next courthouse was completed. The second courthouse was moved away in 1896. Architects Wing and Mahurin of

Y.M.C.A. Building, Culver Military Academy, Culver, Ind. 1 C.L.

Indiana Historical Society (C4283)

Fort Wayne designed the present courthouse, a Richardsonian-style limestone structure with Gothic detailing, completed in 1898. (*NRHP*)

From the courthouse, proceed south beyond the business district to the **Starke County Historical Society Museum**, 401 S. Main St. The museum, which opened in 1977, occupies the former home of Henry F. Schricker, publisher of the *Starke County Democrat*, 1908–19, and two-term governor of Indiana, 1940–44 and 1948–52. The museum features official Schricker papers, plaques, clothing, and pictures.

Continue south on Main St. for *.4 m.* to W. Culver Rd. (IND 8). Turn left for two blocks then right on US 35. Proceed south *5.1 m.* to IND 10 at **Bass Lake**, Indiana's third largest natural lake. Indians called it Winchetonqua, meaning "beautiful waters," and surveyors named it Cedar Lake. To avoid duplication, it was renamed Bass Lake for the abundance of black bass. Most of the 1,345-acre lake is only about 7 ft. deep. It is unique among Indiana lakes. It is an elevated lake, occupying the top of a ridge, and is fed by underwater springs and flowing wells. Its miniscule drainage area cov-

ers 937 acres. A circular drive follows the shoreline. At the turn of the century, the lake was a popular fishing resort with a steamboat operating daily among the hotels along the shore. Sculptor Charles J. Mulligan lived near Gull Point for a time, drawing celebrities from the arts and humanities to the area. In the 1920s Chicago politicians owned cottages and entertained lavishly. Numerous summer cottages still surround the lake. Follow IND 10 east for *1.9 m.* to the **Bass Lake State Beach**. Established in 1931, the 21-acre state facility provides swimming, picnicking, and camping opportunities.

Continue on IND 10 *2 m.* and turn left on CR 700E for *.7 m.* to the **Archbishop Andrew Sheptytsky Museum** located on the grounds of the St. Andrew Missionary Apostolate. Msgr. Jaroslav Swyschuk organized the museum, which opened in 1979, to honor the Ukrainian archbishop who promoted church unity among the Roman Catholic, Eastern Orthodox, and Protestant churches. Before his death in 1944, Sheptytsky helped thousands of Jews escape the Nazis occupying the Ukraine during World War II. Stone busts of popes and important

Catholic figures line the front of the museum. The building contains an extensive collection of Russian, Greek, and Ukrainian icons from the 16th and 17th centuries. It also features items from India and the Holy Land, wood carvings from Africa, and a sculpture of Pope Pius XII by Ivan Mestrovic, a professor at the University of Notre Dame.

Continue *.3 m.* and turn left. At *.6 m.* is **WINONA**, laid out by Abner Hay and John Shoup in 1891. **Bass Lake Fish Hatchery** is located here. Established in 1912, the state-operated hatchery occupies 14 acres and has 12 ponds for hatching and raising fish. Situated on the site of the Shoup Farm, it is the oldest hatchery in the state and represents one of the first serious moves by the government to restock lakes and streams that almost had been fished out. The basic design of the ponds remains much like the original. The hatchery produces primarily smallmouth and rock bass.

Turn right and continue west and south around the lake to US 35. Turn right and proceed *2.1 m.* to the **PULASKI COUNTY** (p. 13,258; 435 sq. m.) line. Created from portions of territory belonging to Cass and White counties by an act of the legislature in 1835, Pulaski County was officially organized in 1839. The county was named for Casimir Pulaski, a soldier from Poland, who served heroically during the Revolutionary War. The farming of soybeans, corn, and mint is the main source of income.

Continue south on US 35 for *3 m.* to CR 500N. Turn right and proceed *1.5 m.* to the **Winamac State Fish and Wildlife Area**. In 1959 the Indiana Department of Natural Resources acquired 3,710 acres of federal land to create a fish and game area. Characterized by sand ridges and oak forests, the property was not suitable for farming but provided a prime habitat for quail, deer, and other upland game species. The wildlife area covers 4,592 acres, including three small marshes totaling about 90 acres. Regulated hunting is available to the public. Facilities also include three rifle ranges, a skeet range, and an archery range.

Return to US 35 and continue south for *.7 m.* to the **Tippecanoe River State Park** on the left. The WPA of the 1930s developed more than 6,500 acres of recreational and wildlife property covering both sides of US 35 and bordering on the Tippecanoe River. At one point an estimated 300 men worked on the project and received 40 cents per hour in wages. Of the land, 2,761 acres became the Tippecanoe River State Park, established in 1943. A new visitors center and park office opened in 1979. Trails lead through oak forests, sand dunes, and open fields. Camping, canoeing, bicycling, fishing, and picnicking facilities are available. At the north edge of the park is the Sandhill Nature Preserve, a 60-acre area of sand hills formed during the Wisconsin glacial period.

From the state park, proceed south on US 35 for *4.3 m.* to IND 14 (11th St.) in **WINAMAC** (p. 2,370), which was named in honor of the Miami Indian chief whose tribe lived in this area before the first settlers arrived in the 1830s. William Polke, John Pearson, Jesse Jackson, John Brown, and John B. Niles laid out the original town in 1839. In the past, Winamac's economy depended primarily on agriculturally related services and businesses. Today, the city's labor force is almost equally divided between manufacturing and nonmanufacturing positions. Winamac's major employers are Eaton Controls Corporation of America (automotive switches and controls), Winamac Division of N I Industries (agricultural equipment), Galbreath, Inc. (waste disposal equipment), Plymouth Tube Company (tubing), and Braun Corporation (specialized equipment for the handicapped).

Continue south on Monticello St. (US 35) for four blocks to the **Pulaski County Courthouse** on the square bounded by Monticello, Main, Market, and Jefferson sts. The county commissioners selected Winamac as the county seat and met for the first time in 1839 at the log house of John Pearson. A frame courthouse building was erected on the public square during the 1840s. This was replaced with a brick building, completed in 1862. Architects A. W. Rush and Son designed the present Romanesque-style courthouse built in 1894. Constructed of Bedford limestone with a slate roof, the building features a central clock tower. In 1980 the Pulaski County Circuit Court drew national attention during the Pinto trials. The Ford Motor Company was accused of causing death by manufacturing a defective product—the fuel tank system of a 1973 Pinto which exploded upon impact, killing three teenagers. Although the verdict found Ford not guilty of reckless homicide, the 10-week historic legal battle was significant in showing that a corporation could be held criminally liable for faulty products.

At the northeast corner of Market and Main sts., an elegant three-story Victorian brick commercial building faces the courthouse square. Built in 1882, the **Vurpillat Building** originally contained retail stores on the first floor, offices on the second, and an opera house on the third. A bank later occupied the building, which now houses a drugstore.

From Main St., proceed south one block on Market St. and turn left on Jefferson St. to Riverside Dr. Opposite the intersection is the **Pulaski County Historical Museum**, which occupies a four-room annex in the back of the modern public library and county office building. The museum, which opened in 1985, features a variety of historical items collected by local citizens such as a wooden immigrant's chest dated 1846 and numerous 19th-century tools and artifacts donated by Verlin R. "Itch" Meyer, the town cobbler.

Northeast of the museum is the **Memorial Bridge**, a 4-ft.-wide, 200-ft.-long pedestrian bridge spanning the Tippecanoe River. In 1923 Russell E. Nutt constructed the steel cable suspension bridge as a memorial to Pulaski County war veterans. The "swinging bridge" leads to the 43-acre city park on the east river bank. On the west bank is an artesian well discovered when crews drilled for gas in the 1880s. The well is still in use.

Follow Riverside Dr. north *.5 m.* then proceed east on IND 14 (13th St.) for *4.1 m.* Turn north on CR 400E and continue *6 m.* At CR 600N, turn right and proceed east for *2 m.* to CR 600E. Turn left and go north for *1 m.* to CR 700N (Main St.) in **MONTEREY** (p. 236). In 1849 Eli and Peter W. Demoss laid out the town of Buena Vista, renamed Monterey. Both names derived from Mexican War battle sites. Once a thriving village, Monterey was the location of a limburger cheese factory in the 1870s. It is now the terminus of the Tippecanoe Railroad, a 16-mile independent remnant of the 998-mile Erie-Lackawanna line, which extends to North Judson. Just west of town, a 1980 archaeological dig uncovered the 10,000-year-old skeleton of a mastodon once weighing 2 1/2 tons and measuring 19 ft. long. The remains are now exhibited at the Indiana State Museum in Indianapolis.

Return on CR 600E to CR 600N and travel east *5.1 m.* reentering Fulton County (for a description of the county see Tour 17), going under IND 17 and angling southeast, passing through the village of Delong before reaching **LEITERS FORD** on Olson Rd. Gilbert Bozarth, John Mahler, and Jesse Bailey were the first settlers in the area in 1836-37. William Hunter arrived in 1840 and settled beside the Tippecanoe River. In 1845 John Leiter, who had a family of 21 children, purchased Hunter's property and founded the town of Leiters Ford.

At the flashing light in the center of town turn right and go south about two blocks. The **Leiters Ford Depot Museum**, a compact frame structure with a railroad signal in front, sits back from the road about one-half block to the right, just west of its original site along the Erie-Lackawanna Railroad. At the turn of the century, a creamery, a pickle factory, and a livestock yard operated along the railroad. The present depot, built in 1880, has never had running water. Woodie and Wilma McGlothlin deeded the property to the Fulton County Historical Society in 1977. It contains an extensive collection of railroad equipment and memorabilia. The former freight room serves as the township history room and features a statue of Chief Aubbeenaubbee.

Return to the flasher and continue on CR 750W about three blocks to the Tippecanoe River bridge. A plaque on a boulder on the right just south of the bridge notes that William Hunter built his log cabin near this site, which was used as a ford in the 1840s. The first bridge at Leiters Ford was built in 1885. The present iron-truss bridge, erected in 1941, provides a scenic view of the river. The 166-mile-long Tippecanoe River, the clearest stream in the state, derives its name from the Potawatomi word Ki-tap-i-kon-nong or "place of the buffalo fish."

Cross the river, turn right at the "T," continue *1.4 m.* to the end of the road, and turn left. At *3 m.* turn right on CR 800N (IND 110). Proceed *6.7 m.*, crossing US 31, to Old US 31. Turn right *1.2 m.* to the **Larry Paxton Round Barn** on the right. Built in 1924 by the Kindig Builders, the barn measures 60 ft. in diameter and was the last round barn erected in Fulton County. The popularity of round barns reached its height around the turn of the century, when their construction was promoted by agricultural experts and farm publications. Contractors claimed that the round barns could be constructed more cheaply per square foot of enclosed space and used more efficiently than the conventional rectangular barns. The unusual design also appealed to many farmers, and the round barns became almost a fad in some areas. Kindig Builders was in business for 62 years beginning in 1900 and erected 11 of the 15 round barns in Fulton County. The county boasts one of the highest concentrations of round barns in the country. Nine working barns are shown annually during the Round Barn Festival in July.

Continue south for *2.8 m.* to the **William Polke house** on the left, where a historical marker provides a description of the county's oldest house. The first white settler in Fulton County, William Polke (1775–1843) came in 1832 to superintend the surveying of the Michigan Rd. On the south bank of the Tippecanoe River Polke built a log cabin and trading post which housed the county's first post office. About 1833 he built a frame house on the north bank which also served as a stagecoach inn. Governor Wallace appointed Polke to conduct the last band of Potawatomi Indians from the

Indiana state line to Kansas in 1838 when they were removed from the state. In 1841 Polke moved to Fort Wayne to manage the federal land office there. Ownership of the property remained in the Polke family for 113 years.

Continue south *.7 m.* to the two roadside markers on the left situated on the south bank of the Tippecanoe River. A bronze plaque on a boulder indicates the site of the Potawatomi Indian village of **Chippewa-nung** where treaties were signed selling Indian land to the United States government. Soldiers and Indians camped here before moving on to Twin Lakes during the removal of the last Potawatomis. In the summer and fall of 1838 the Indians were marched over 900 miles in 61 days from northern Indiana to Kansas. So many died along the way that it is called the Trail of Death. Every year the Fulton County Historical Society sponsors a commemorative program in recognition of the Indians' ordeal. The Trail of Courage Rendezvous Site is situated on 35 acres along the north bank of the Tippecanoe River just west of US 31. On the north end of this property, at the corner of the first county road

Indiana Historical Society (C4281)

north of the Tippecanoe River, is located the **Fulton County Museum**. Besides an extensive display of historical domestic and agricultural items, the museum features items related to the culture and history of the Potawatomi Indians and a large collection of genealogical materials on Fulton County.

A second historical marker notes that the **Michigan Rd.**, Old US 31, extending from the Ohio River at Madison north to Michigan City, was constructed with funds received from the sale of former Indian land. Begun in 1832, the road helped open the northern part of the state to settlers.

Follow Old US 31 south for *2.3 m.* to the railroad at **ROCHESTER** (p. 5,050), where it becomes Main St. and continues south for *.5 m.* to the center of town at IND 14/25. Founded in 1835, Rochester served as a trading center for Indians from among the villages in the surrounding areas. These were the tribes removed to Kansas in 1838. Rochester was incorporated as a town in 1853. A gristmill, sawmill, and ironworks were the first industries. Those factories closely related with agriculture have been the most successful over long periods of time. Other industries have come and gone, such as the Rochester Shoe Factory which occupied the site later used by the Rochester Bridge Company and the Cole Brothers Circus. Today the McMahan-O'Connor Construction Company, a major road building firm, has its offices on the site. The Cole Brothers Circus had its winter headquarters in Rochester between 1935 and 1940. Some performers, such as high-wire artist Willie Lamberti, continued to live here after the disastrous fire which closed down the circus. Other famous performers included lion trainer Clyde Beatty, clown Emmett Kelly, and cowboy star Ken Maynard. Local stories still abound, 50 years later, about elephants running down Main St. and a cowboy riding his horse into a small café. In 1915 Armours opened a butter factory in Rochester and established a duck farm along Mill Creek. The Armour and Company processed cheese factory, sold in 1959, was one of the largest in the world. Rochester's major employers are Hartmarx, formerly Hart Schaffner and Marx (clothing), and Rochester Metal Products (castings).

The **Fulton County Courthouse** stands on the square bounded by 8th, 9th, Main, and Madison sts. Architects A. W. Rush and Son of Grand Rapids designed the Richardsonian Romanesque-style building erected in 1895–96. The two-and-a-half story structure of quarry-faced stone features a hipped roof with gables and a central clock tower. Ten stone lions surround the courthouse. Renovated in 1975, the building is the county's third courthouse.

A historical marker in memory of **Rochester College** is mounted above a limestone cornerstone dated 1895 at the southwest corner of the courthouse square. Dr. Winfield S. Shafer and Professors George Suman and W. H. Banta founded the Rochester Normal University in 1893 and dedicated the school building in 1895. Because of financial problems, the college closed in 1912, and the structure was razed in 1923.

From the courthouse square proceed east for *.7 m.* on IND 14 to **Lakeview Park**. In the 1920s the site was called Millrace Park and used as a tourist camp. WPA workers erected the stone bridge and gates at the entrance, left of the highway, during the 1930s. What now appears to be a dried-up lake basin was a fish hatchery operated by the United States government between 1933 and 1965. The hatchery was abandoned because the low ground was too porous and the ponds leaked. The site became city property, and a golf course and swimming pool were installed.

The Fulton County Historical Society provides two museums, located at the west end of Lakeview Park. The **Rochester Depot Museum** occupies a frame building erected by the Chicago, Cincinnati and Louisville Railroad Company (now the Norfolk and Western) in the 1870s. The depot was repaired and opened as a museum in 1972. It contains a century-old loom, a handmade model train, stuffed birds, arrowheads, Rochester College and Cole Brothers Circus memorabilia, and other local artifacts.

The **Pioneer Woman's Log Cabin Museum** was constructed in 1975, using logs from two cabins built in the 1860s which belonged to Samuel Collins and George Washington Alspaugh of Fulton County. The cabin is furnished with century-old furniture, including a rope bed, and kitchen utensils to demonstrate how pioneer women kept house.

One block west of Lakeview Park, at 8th and Race sts., a plaque mounted on a boulder indicates the location of the **Millrace**. Dug about 1840, it originally extended from Lake

Manitou to the north end of Rochester and flowed into Mill Creek after providing water power to local factories before the use of electricity began in the 1890s. The county's first railroad passed nearby. Icehouses used to cool the refrigerator cars stood at IND 25 and the millrace until 1925. Early industries along the race included an ironworks, flouring mills, sawmills, woolen mills, a planing mill, and a steam elevator. All but about a half mile of the millrace which passes in front of Lakeview Park was gradually filled beginning in 1912.

Return to IND 14/25 in front of Lakeview Park and proceed east for *.1 m.*, angle right, and continue *.3 m.* to the lakefront. A historical marker in the roadside park designates the mill and dam site at **Lake Manitou** and the first white settlement in the county, **TIPTON-VILLE**, named for Indian agent John Tipton. In 1826 the Treaty of Paradise Springs was signed at Wabash, and the federal government agreed to build a gristmill on the Tippecanoe River and support a miller for benefit of the Potawatomi Indians. A blacksmith shop also was to be erected and manned by the government near the mill. The mill, however, was built on a tributary of the Tippecanoe, and the dam enlarged several small lakes into the present 713-acre Lake Manitou. The Algonquian word *manitou* means spirit or supernatural force. According to Indian legend, the lake was the home of Meshekenabek, a serpent-like water creature which wreaked havoc on the nearby Indians. The Indian brave Messou, seeking vengeance for the death of his cousin, killed the monster and bound his companions to the caverns at the bottom of the lake.

After white settlers arrived at Tiptonville during the 1830s, sightings of some sort of monster or fish in the lake were reported in the Logansport newspapers. An editorial battle between the *Telegraph* and the *Herald* ensued over the credibility of the stories. Following a 10-year silence about the monster issue, the *Logansport Journal* reported in 1849 that a 7-ft.-long fish weighing several hundred pounds, believed to have been the basis for the legend, was captured when it ran aground in shallow water.

In the 1920s Lake Manitou was a popular summer resort with more than 200 cottages, 4 summer hotels, and a large amusement park called White City. Double-decker excursion boats operated on the lake, and big name bands played at the open-air dance pavilions. The resort business, however, declined after the 1920s. Today, summer cottages surround the lake, and residents support an active yacht club. The Department of Natural Resources protects more than 100 acres of wetlands at the south end of the lake. The Manitou Islands Nature Preserve is accessible by boat only.

Return to IND 14/25 and go east on IND 14 for *4 m.* to CR 650E in Athens. Turn right and proceed south *3.5 m.* to CR 350S. Turn right and continue *.2 m.* around the north end of the pond to **Millark Mill**. Henry Hoover settled here in 1836 and established a gristmill, sawmill, and lumberyard in the 1840s. A fire destroyed the mills in 1859, but Hoover's sons rebuilt them the following year. An undershot waterwheel powered the mill until the owner installed an electric motor in 1942. The gristmill remained in operation under a number of owners until 1967. In the 19th century a thriving community which included a small tool factory, blacksmith shop, icehouse, and whiskey business surrounded the millpond. Little remains of the early settlement of Millark other than the mill. In 1976 Skidmore, Coplen, and Fansler bought the old mill and renovated it with cedar siding.

Return to IND 14 and CR 650E at Athens. Turn left and return to IND 25 on the east side of Rochester. Turn right and go north *4.4 m.* to the roadside marker for **Cincinnatus Hiner Miller** (ca. 1839–1913) on the left. Celebrated as the "poet of the Sierras," Miller spent his boyhood in Indiana before trekking west with his family to Oregon and California where he gained his reputation as a poet and an author. Miller recalled his life in Fulton County in several poems he wrote later. He took the pen name Joaquin after the Mexican bandit and revolutionary Joaquin Murietta. He is best known for the poem "Columbus."

Continue north on IND 25 for *3.4 m.* to **TALMA**. A marker on the right notes that this is the "only town in the U.S. named Talma." Originally called Bloomingsburgh, the village officially became Talma in 1896. William Roundtree Kubley petitioned the government to replace the name of the post office with a shorter one and selected the word Talma from a word puzzle in a farm magazine.

Continue north on IND 25 for *1.4 m.*, then turn left on IND 110, the boundary between Fulton and Marshall counties, and proceed *1.3 m.* to the **Wayne Bessinger Farm**, 10622 Cedar Rd. A wildlife conservationist, Bessinger has developed a 40-acre wildlife area, including a 15-acre marsh, on his 600-acre farm. He also has implemented a forest management plan and planted more than 10,000 trees and shrubs as cover and food for wildlife. Bessinger conducts tours of his farm to promote wildlife habitat programs with other landowners. His home is a spacious log cabin perched on a knoll, overlooking duck ponds and farmland.

Return to IND 25, continue east, and at *.3 m.* turn north on IND 331, entering Marshall County. At *4 m.* on the right, after passing through Tippecanoe and Old Tip Town, is the Lions and Kiwanis Wildlife Park. Proceed *4.5 m.* to downtown **BOURBON** (p. 1,522). In 1836 James Parks and his family came here from Bourbon County, Kentucky, and named their new home Bourbon. The Parks residence, located along the mail delivery route between Fort Wayne and Chicago, served as a post office beginning in 1843. Samuel Thomas and J. S. Neidig laid out the town in 1853. Three years later, the Pittsburgh, Fort Wayne and Chicago Railroad arrived, stimulating growth of the community. Twenty-five lumber mills opened here and shipped their timber by rail. After the Civil War, timber-related industries such as the furniture, butter tub, and boat oar manufacturers began operating in the Bourbon area. Although the county remains primarily agricultural, many Bourbon residents find employment in industry. The major employer is Biomed, Inc., which produces artificial joints and fracture treatment devices.

At Center and Main sts. (Old US 30 and IND 331), the **Old Town Pump** and stone water trough stand in a park on the northwest corner. The present pump was dedicated in 1929 in remembrance of the town's original landmark at this location.

Proceed *11.9 m.* north to IND 331 (Plymouth St.) and Center St. in downtown **BREMEN** (p. 3,565). About 1836 Germans settled in the area situated along the Yellow River and named the town New Bremen after the seaport in Germany. In a short time the word New was dropped from the name. George Beiler laid out the town in 1851. By the mid-1850s the community supported two mills, a tannery, several trade shops, a tavern, and a general store. The town was incorporated in 1871. Three years later the Baltimore and Ohio Railroad leading to Chicago was laid through Bremen. It was used primarily for shipping grain, livestock, and lumber from the surrounding areas. M. Brown and Sons Company, established in 1908, and Wm. Leman, Inc., established in 1911, producers of peppermint and spearmint oils, are longtime businesses in Bremen. The leading manufacturers here are the auto industry suppliers and recreational vehicle components producers.

The **Dietrich-Bowen house**, 304 N. Center St., is located three blocks north of Plymouth St. (turn right at the first stoplight). The prosperous Dietrich family, department store owners, built the elegant Queen Anne-style home in the early 1900s. In 1946 Dr. Otis R. Bowen established his medical practice in Bremen and in 1953 purchased the house, which he used as a medical office until he entered state politics. Bowen served as the state representative from Marshall County, 1957, 1961, 1963, 1965, 1967, 1971–72, governor of Indiana, 1973–81, and secretary of health and human services in President Ronald Reagan's cabinet, 1985–89. (*NRHP*)

Continue north on Center St. for two blocks to **Shadyside Park** on the right. Situated in a wooded area along the Yellow River, the city park contains the largest black walnut tree in Indiana, according to the Department of Natural Resources in 1976. It measures over 75 ft. tall with a limb spread of over 66 ft. and a trunk circumference of 20 ft. Park facilities include a shelter house, picnic area, and playground.

Return to Plymouth St. Go west one block then south on Jackson St. for one-half block to the **Bremen Water Standpipe** on the west side. Contractor James Madden erected the elevated water storage tank encased with bricks in 1892. It served to maintain the town's water pressure at the proper level until 1955. The American Water Works Association recognized the standpipe as an official American Water Landmark in 1975.

Return to Plymouth St. Go west *.4 m.* then north at Bowen Ave., which is IND 331. Continue north for *2.2 m.* to St. Joseph County (for a description of the county see South Bend essay).

From the county line, proceed north on IND 331 for *6 m.* to New Rd. at **WOODLAND**. This area was settled late, about 1840, because of marshlands and dense forests. German immigrants cleared the lands and sold the lumber. Once drained, the property became productive farmland. A rural community, Woodland was never laid out as a town although it functioned as one. By 1880 it contained a grocery store, post office, wagon shop, blacksmith shop, doctor's office, a school, and two churches, but in the 1890s began to lose commerce and population to Wyatt, a town located on the Wabash Railroad two miles south.

Continue north on IND 331 for *6.8 m.* to US 33. Turn west and follow US 33 for *4.2 m.* to the center of South Bend and the end of Tour 18.

Calumet Region

The Calumet Region is that part of northwestern Indiana and northeastern Illinois drained by the Grand Calumet and Little Calumet rivers. In Indiana, the Region is usually identified with the northern portions of Lake and Porter counties lying along the southern tip of Lake Michigan. Broader definitions include all of Lake County, most of Porter County, and the cities of La Porte and Michigan City in La Porte County to the east. The narrower definition, however, is the one most commonly accepted. In this area there are more than 500,000 people and 19 incorporated places of more than 2,500 residents. The largest cities are Gary (p. 151,953) and Hammond (p. 93,714). Traditionally, these two cities, along with Whiting and East Chicago, constituted the heart of Indiana's Calumet Region. In the last two decades, though, attention has begun to shift southward to the east-west corridor along US 30, which is emerging as the Region's "Main Street." (Interestingly enough, this route was one of the major trails through the Region in the earliest days of settlement.) Commercial development of the land straddling the highway, commencing at the intersection of US 30 and I-65, has attracted residents from the lake cities and has spawned dramatic growth of communities.

Gov. Thomas R. Marshall once said that he would be relieved to learn that, during some night, the city of Gary had slipped off into Lake Michigan. Though impolitic, this remark expressed sentiments held by many Hoosiers that the Calumet Region was not really "Indiana." Indeed, the belief that the Calumet is different is probably held most firmly by the inhabitants of the Region itself. This sense of being at odds with the rest of the state has sometimes taken extreme forms such as that when, in 1935, Lake County solons introduced a bill in the state legislature to establish the county as the 49th state. The bill made it to the second reading! The residents of the Region have regarded themselves as more truly a part of the greater Chicago metropolitan area than of Indiana, and, in fact, much of the life of the Calumet Region revolves around that great city. Even the streets of Hammond, Whiting, and East Chicago follow Chicago's numbering system.

The dissimilarity between the Calumet Region and the rest of Indiana is not of recent origin, but has its roots in geography itself. The Grand Calumet and Little Calumet rivers, two sluggish and reed-choked streams, flow east and west rather than north and south, offering no access to the interior of the state. To the south, the great Kankakee marsh, a forbidding and impassable swampland until the late 19th century, made direct contact with the Calumet virtually impossible from that direction. Because of this obstacle, the Michigan Rd., Indiana's first north-south highway, completely bypassed the Region to connect with the lake at Michigan City. The land itself was not inviting, consisting of ancient dunes and sloughs covered over with a thick undergrowth of vegetation. John Tipton, surveying the area in 1821, doubted that it would ever "be of much service to our state."

On the other hand, geography has conferred on the Calumet some of its greatest assets. Historically, its location at the tip of Lake Michigan made the Region the shortest land route between points east and west of the lake. The difficult terrain limited travel across the Region to a few important routes. The most famous was the Sauk (or Sac) trail, which cut across La Porte, Porter, and Lake counties into Illinois. This is the route that US 30 (the Lincoln Highway) and CR 330 (old Lincoln Highway) follows today. Other trails farther north followed the Calumet and Tolleston beaches, sandy ridge lines laid down when Lake Michigan was a much larger body of water. Another trail followed the lakeshore itself where the compacted sand, especially in winter months when it was frozen, made travel relatively easy.

It is this same geographical placement that to-day provides visitors to the Region an enormous variety of natural attractions, from the lakeshore to inland protected prairies, nature preserves, numerous parks, and rare wildlife. The Calumet Region is much more than its industry.

Settlers began to move into the southern reaches of the Region in the 1830s, but few ventured into the inhospitable lands further north. In 1850 less than 100 people lived north of the Little Calumet River. Beginning in the 1850s, the railroads, cutting across the area to the growing city of Chicago, slowly began to erode its isolation. The railroad companies built stations at various points where locomotives could take on fuel and water and passengers could stretch their legs. Tiny settlements grew up at these locations whose residents made their livings supplying wood to the railroads, working on the tracks, or providing refreshments to passengers. Dyer, Miller, Whiting's Crossing, West Point (later Gibson Station), and Tolleston began in this fashion.

The Region did have some natural resources, and the railroad made it possible to exploit them. Sand, white pine and cedar, huckleberries and cranberries, fish, ducks, the pelts of mink and muskrats, and ice cut from the Region's many streams and lakes found ready markets in Chicago. The unspoiled character of the Calumet wilderness and its proximity to Chicago made the area popular among wealthy sportsmen. In 1873 Chicagoans incorporated the Tolleston Club and bought and leased 5,000 acres along the Little Calumet River. The club built a retreat, located at what is now 25th Ave. and Clark Rd. in Gary, and fenced off its property as a private hunting preserve. In 1885 another group of sportsmen built the Calumet Gun Club on the present site of the United States (US) Steel works. The club buildings survived to provide comfortable lodgings for the engineers who laid out the mill.

As cheap land grew increasingly rare in Chicago, the Calumet became an attractive location for industry. This was especially so for so-called nuisance industries, which were either too offensive to the senses or too dangerous to be located near populated areas. The first major factory established in the Calumet Region was George H. Hammond's State Line Slaughter House built in 1869. Hammond, a pioneer in the shipping of refrigerated beef, constructed

his packinghouse on the Michigan Central Railroad near the Grand Calumet River.

State Line was not a pleasant place. Huge piles of animal carcasses surrounded the slaughterhouse, and an unsavory stench always hung in the air. Hammond, who lived in Detroit, cared little about conditions at the slaughterhouse, but Marcus M. Towle, Hammond's partner, saw the potential benefits of developing a town. In 1875 he purchased several acres near the slaughterhouse, platted a town, and sold 50-ft. lots to his employees. He loaned the purchasers lumber to build homes and sold the structures to them on time at $10 a month. Towle renamed his little community in honor of the man who had opposed its birth. In 1884 he became its first mayor. Because of the large number of German butchers who worked in the slaughterhouse, Hammond had a distinctively Teutonic character.

Unlike cities that later grew up in the Calumet, Hammond did not remain a one-industry town. The W. B. Conkey Printing and Bookbinding Company came to Hammond in 1898 through the influence of George H. Hammond's brother, Thomas "Honest Tom" Hammond. In 1906 the Standard Steel Car Company, manufacturers of railroad cars, began to construct a plant. The factory soon employed more than 3,500 workers and for many years remained the city's leading employer.

Towle did not restrict his interests to Hammond. In 1887 he and several other investors formed the Standard Steel and Iron Company, which, despite its name, did nothing but sell real estate. Purchasing 637 acres, the company cleared and leveled 110 acres between what is now 151st St. and Chicago Ave. in the southwest part of East Chicago and began promoting the land as an industrial site. These efforts were rewarded when the William Graver Tank Works purchased land for a plant to manufacture oil storage tanks in 1888. By 1889 the locality had attracted enough residents to incorporate as the town of East Chicago. Other factories soon came. These included the C. A. Treat Car Wheel Works, the National Forge and Iron Company, and the Chicago Horseshoe Factory. By 1910 East Chicago's industries (not including those in the Indiana Harbor area) employed more than 3,600 workers.

The same year that East Chicago became a town, Standard Oil began secretly purchasing land for a refinery a few miles away near the hamlet of Whiting's Crossing. The new facility was to process oil piped from the fields centering on Lima, Ohio. Standard Oil might have built the refinery in South Chicago had Lima crude, known as "skunk oil," not been so offensive to the sense of smell. In May 1889 an army of laborers arrived at Whiting to begin the arduous task of clearing the land and constructing the refinery. The work, considering its difficulty, was completed with remarkable speed. On Thanksgiving Day, 1890, the first tank cars loaded with kerosene rolled off to market. Whiting, once a cluster of cabins surrounding a general store, suddenly became a boom town. Construction workers crowded into bunk houses built by the company or rented space in houses owned by enterprising residents. A business district sprouted up along the trail that became 119th St. Once the refinery became operational, Standard Oil laid out a small town complete with wooden sidewalks and running water (but no saloons) for its supervisory personnel.

In 1901 Inland Steel began construction of a large mill in that part of East Chicago bordering Lake Michigan. This was the largest steel mill yet built in the Calumet Region. By 1904 it employed 1,200 men. In 1901 a group of wealthy Chicagoans organized the East Chicago Company and launched an ambitious plan to develop this area as an industrial site. The company laid out a business and residential area and began construction of port facilities. They also began work on the Indiana Harbor Ship Canal that would provide easy access to the lake for industry. Isolated from the rest of East Chicago by the canal and railroad switchyards and possessing its own commercial district, Indiana Harbor soon took on its own identity. Although municipally part of East Chicago, in almost every other respect it was an independent municipality. By 1910 Indiana Harbor had 19 industries employing 2,919. Inland Steel was by far the largest, with a work force of over half the total.

In 1905 the US Steel Corporation decided that if it were to maintain its position as the nation's leading manufacturer of steel, it would have to build a new plant in the Midwest. For a time, corporate officials considered locating the plant in Waukegan, Illinois, but because of cheaper real estate prices and superior transportation connections, settled on an empty tract of land east of Hammond and East Chicago. The undertaking was on a gigantic scale. The corporation bought up more than 9,000 acres, an expanse of land measuring some seven miles along the shore of Lake Michigan. The mill would be the largest in not only the US Steel empire but also the entire world. Plans called for not only the mill but also a city. One enthusiast described the project as "the largest enterprise of the human race in all history."

The company constructed the mill on the lake and the town further south. The Grand Calumet River served as a moat between factory and city. In effect, the mill was an impregnable fortress, secure against its own employees during strikes. The plant site was leveled and raised some 15 ft. by sucking sand from the bottom of Lake Michigan and spreading it over the uneven terrain. Three railroads were relocated and provided with elevated crossings. A huge switching yard and a harbor were built. The Grand Calumet River was moved more than 1,000 ft. south and confined to a narrower and straighter channel. The formal opening of the Gary Works took place July 23, 1908, with the arrival of the first ore boat.

The town also was laid out on an impressive scale, but corporate officials candidly admitted that it was of secondary importance. The corporation installed a network of sewers, water lines, gas mains, and a waterworks designed to accommodate a city of 200,000. The company obtained water by digging a 6-ft. tunnel 8,000 ft. into the lake. Explaining that it was not in the resort business, the corporation provided for only two small parks (one the site of the pumping station and water tower). It refused to reserve any part of the shoreline for recreational purposes. By the end of 1910, the steel corporation had spent about $70 million for the construction of both mill and town.

The town was named after Elbert H. Gary, chairman of the board of US Steel. The company's relationship to the town was to be one of "limited involvement." The planners recognized that workers had to be provided with a place to live, but wanted to avoid the costly and unpopular paternalism of the type, such as at Pullman, Illinois, where the company owned stores, libraries, and homes. Through its subsidiary, the Gary Land Company, US Steel sold lots to employees and others who built their homes according to strict standards. To set an example, and to encourage sales, the corporation built 500 homes for company officials and skilled workers. For lower-paid employees, the company built 50 smaller homes in the northeast corner of the townsite. These homes attracted mostly single, male immigrant workers who shared lodgings and neglected the property. Eventually, the land company evicted these renters and restricted the homes to American-born workers with families. Thereafter, the corporation made no effort to provide housing for its unskilled, immigrant workers.

The high price of the company's homes and lots forced unskilled workers to seek lodgings outside of US Steel's holdings, thus creating a lucrative market for local developers. South of the Wabash Railroad, the southern limits of US Steel's property, a section known as the Patch grew up. Here, unrestrained by even the most elementary housing codes and sanitation regulations, speculators constructed a jungle of cheap housing. In this area there was no city water, sewers, and few paved streets. Saloons went unregulated, and prostitution flourished. The Patch, in short, was a notorious and bustling slum. Thus, from the very beginning, there were two Garys, the company-owned section of substantial homes of skilled workers and corporate officials and the section south of the tracks, made up of flimsy boardinghouses and tar-paper shacks inhabited by the unskilled, poor, and mostly immigrant workers.

Despite its flaws and imperfections, Gary was rightly considered the wonder of the era. Incorporated as a town on July 14, 1906, in a wilderness of dunes and scrub oak, by 1909 it had become a full-blown fifth-class city of 12,000 residents, who enjoyed paved streets, cement sidewalks, a modern sewer, water, a gas system, and electric lighting. Gary had banks, hotels, churches, three daily newspapers, a complete business district, and its complement of lawyers, doctors, and other professionals. It was an instant city, compressing into a short space of three years decades of growth. Thomas E. Knotts, president of Gary's first town board in 1906, became the city's first mayor in 1909.

Other than the modern steel mills themselves, Gary was probably best known for its innovative school system. The new town's educational program was largely the work of William A. Wirt, who served as superintendent of schools, 1907-38. Wirt, a disciple of John Dewey, established a work-study-play system

in the Gary schools. Under this system one half of the student body of a school studied traditional subjects in classrooms during part of the day while the other half participated in special activities such as athletics, shop, music, industrial arts, and so on. The groups then reversed. This arrangement made it possible not only to diversify and enrich the curriculum but also to maximize use of school facilities. Under the platoon system, the capacity of the average building was increased about 40 percent.

In Gary there were no separate schools for elementary and secondary grades. All included students from kindergarten through high school. Wirt considered these "complete" schools a much more economical unit. The superintendent also considered it uneconomical to provide each student with his or her own desk. Instead, students moved from classroom to classroom, using lockers in the hallways to store their books and personal possessions. The Gary schools attracted international attention. A constant stream of educators visited Gary to view the system in operation. Numerous school systems adapted parts of the Gary model to suit their needs. The New York City system was one of the earliest to do so. A 1929 survey showed that 1,068 schools across the nation had adopted some form of Wirt's plan.

The heavy industry of the Calumet depended in large part on unskilled foreign labor. In 1910 East Chicago's population was about 53 percent foreign born, Gary's 49 percent, Whiting's 43 percent, and Hammond's 26 percent. This was in sharp contrast to the state as a whole, where the foreign-born population averaged less than 6 percent. Few cities in the state, even industrial ones, had foreign-born populations comparable in size to the cities of the Calumet. In 1910 South Bend's foreign-born population was 25 percent and Michigan City's 24 percent, but Indianapolis had only 8 percent, Fort Wayne 11 percent, Terre Haute 7 percent, and Evansville 6 percent. Many immigrants came from Eastern and Southern Europe. East Chicago, Hammond, Gary, and Whiting became the homes of thousands of Poles, Czechs, Slovaks, Hungarians, Serbs, Croatians, Slovenes, Romanians, Greeks, Russians, and Italians.

Many immigrants who came to America fully intended to return home and use their earnings to buy land, pay debts, get married, or to establish themselves in some way in their native lands. Some did exactly this. Others crossed and recrossed the Atlantic several times, while still others never returned home. Because they did not intend to remain in America, the early immigrant population was overwhelmingly male. These workers tolerated inferior and overcrowded living conditions because they hoped to save as much as possible. Immigrants held the hardest, dirtiest, most dangerous, and lowest paying jobs in the plants.

Organized labor failed to gain a foothold among these immigrant workers. The leading industries that came to the area, such as Standard Oil and US Steel, were defiantly anti-union. Many Chicago companies, seeking escape from that strong union city, found northwest Indiana particularly attractive. The Conkey Printing Company built its plant in Hammond, where it could hire nonunion labor, but kept its business office in Chicago.

World War I changed the labor picture. At the same time that orders began to pour in from Europe, the hostilities cut off the flow of immigrant workers, and unskilled labor suddenly became a rare commodity. Fearful that labor conflict might imperil war production, the federal government took unprecedented steps to protect the interests of labor, recognizing the right of workers to organize and providing administrative machinery to mediate labor disputes. After the armistice, labor and management prepared for a major confrontation. Unfortunately for the workers, their germane bread-and-butter issues took a back seat to the largely hollow issue of Red radicals instigating labor unrest. In 1919 a great wave of strikes swept over the nation, several taking place in the Calumet Region. Particularly bitter and violent was the Standard Steel Car strike in Hammond. Of greater national significance was the steel strike which the American Federation of Labor (AFL) began in September to organize the industry. At the US Steel works in Gary, about 85 percent of the force of 18,000 joined the strike. There were also walkouts at Inland Steel and the Mark Manufacturing Company in East Chicago. On October 4 violence broke out in both Gary and East Chicago. The following day, a detachment of state militia arrived to restore order. The intervention of the troops put an end to the strike in East Chicago, but only seemed to intensify the situation in Gary. In defiance of Mayor William F. Hodge's anti-

parade order, approximately 2,000 strikers, some of them in uniform, staged a peaceful march through the city.

This "outlaw parade" was the occasion for the intervention of some 1,500 federal troops sent by Maj. Gen. Leonard Wood, commander of the Central Military District at Fort Sheridan, near Chicago, and placed under the command of Col. William S. Mapes. The troops moved in with fixed bayonets, machine guns, and field artillery. General Wood promulgated rules against public gatherings that were so rigid that picketing became almost impossible. The military occupation of the city ended the strike in Gary. Faced with similar failures in other districts, the AFL organizing committee formally ended the walkout on January 8, 1920. The campaign for unionization of the steel industry was a failure.

The 1920s was a period of growth for the Region. The population of the four Calumet cities increased from 137,494 in 1920 to 230,650 in 1930. The bustling new city of Gary soon eclipsed its sister cities. In 1920, with a population of 55,378, it took Hammond's place as the largest city of the Region. Everything in Gary (at least outside of the slums) seemed to reflect growth and promise. Its mills, the most modern in the world, appeared to guarantee its prosperity. The decade of the 1920s was the city's golden age of construction. Besides countless apartments and private dwellings, construction included three 10-story buildings, the Hotel Gary (1927), the Gary State Bank building (1929), and the imposing Knights of Columbus building (1929), plus the massive City Methodist Church (1926). New public structures also graced the landscape, most notably a civic auditorium seating 5,000 persons and the Gary Gateway complex at 4th and Broadway which included the Gary City Hall, the Gary office of the Lake County Courthouse, and a 10-acre esplanade. The city also built two parks, one along the lakeshore in Miller, called Marquette Park, and the other, Gleason Park, along the Little Calumet River. The newness of the city, its 1,800 hotel rooms, and its sources of entertainment (licit and illicit) made Gary an important convention center.

Two important ethnic groups began to arrive in the Region during World War I and the 1920s. When the war interrupted European immigration, the steel mills began actively recruiting Southern blacks as an alternative labor source. In 1919 the companies brought many blacks north as strikebreakers. After Congress ended European immigration with the passage of the National Origins Act of 1924, blacks continued to arrive in the Region in increasing numbers. Blacks filled the lowest positions in the mills and were offered virtually no chance of advancement into skilled or supervisory work. Despite the large number of blacks who came to the Region to find work, the mills apparently established hiring quotas. From 1920 to 1934, US Steel's black work force rarely exceeded 15 percent of the total.

Black life in the Region followed rigidly structured patterns of segregation. In 1920 more than 77 percent of the Region's black population lived in Gary, making up 9.6 percent of the city's population. In fact, Gary's percentage increase of blacks in the two decades between 1910 and 1930 was more than any American city, and its 17.8 percent black population in 1930 ranked it higher than any northern industrial city. In Gary, blacks moved into the Patch. The Wabash tracks to the north and the Little Calumet River to the south were the limits of black settlement.

Most of the Region's public accommodations were segregated. Gleason Park in Gary was divided into white and black sections. Marquette Park, Gary's only lakeside park, was closed to blacks. Gary's vaunted public school system, except for Froebel School, where blacks attended separate classes, was segregated. In 1927 about half of the 2,800 white students at Emerson School successfully struck to exclude 18 blacks who had been transferred from an overcrowded facility. In Indiana Harbor, the school administration refused to segregate the schools. The issue never arose in East Chicago proper, where no blacks lived.

Mexicans began to arrive in the Calumet at about the same time as blacks. Beginning in 1916, some of the railroads in the Region hired Mexican laborers for their track crews. By 1923, more than half of the Indiana Harbor Belt Line crews were Mexicans. During the 1919 strike, the steel mills began sending agents to the southwest to recruit Mexican workers as strikebreakers. Although several companies, including the various plants of US Steel and Youngstown Sheet and Tube, hired Mexicans, Inland Steel became the leading employer. In 1925 almost 25 percent of Inland's work force

was Mexican, making the company the largest employer of Mexicans in the United States.

The Indiana Harbor section of East Chicago became the center of the Region's Mexican population. In 1930 more than 5,000 Mexicans resided in East Chicago and more than 3,000 in Gary. In Gary, Mexicans, like blacks, were confined to the Patch. In Indiana Harbor, a *colonia* formed along Block and Pennsylvania avenues and immediately outside the gate of Inland Steel on Michigan Ave. and Watling St. By the late 1920s, the Mexican community had become a permanent part of the Region. As workers brought their spouses north, families developed and the Mexican neighborhood stabilized. A small middle class formed as Mexicans established businesses to cater to the tastes and needs of their countrymen. In the pattern of immigrants before them, Mexicans formed mutual aid and protective societies and, as soon as the size of the population justified it, their own churches. Our Lady of Guadalupe Church in East Chicago dates from 1927.

The depression dealt the Calumet Region a devastating blow. In 1929 the Gary works of US Steel operated at near 100 percent capacity. By the end of 1932, no steel mill in the Region ran at more than 15 percent of capacity. Between 1930 and 1932, 33 Lake County banks closed. The entire city of Hammond had no banks at all during 1932. In Gary, only the Gary State Bank stayed open. With their assets frozen in failed banks and with tax revenues declining, municipalities resorted to issuing tax anticipation warrants—"shin plasters"—to pay their creditors. The number of people needing relief overtaxed the resources of the township trustees. At the end of 1930, North Township of Lake County (Whiting, Hammond, East Chicago) led the state's 1,016 townships in the amount of money spent for poor relief. Calumet Township (Gary) ranked third. By December 1932 approximately half of East Chicago's population received aid in some form.

The depression caused a realignment in the area's politics. Until the 1930s, the Calumet had been consistently Republican, both on the county and municipal levels. Republicans, who had taken credit for prosperity during the 1920s, found themselves shouldering the blame for the lack of it during the 1930s. In the 1930 Lake County elections, every Democratic candidate was elected. After 1932, Democrats found that their best campaign strategy was simply to proclaim their loyalty to Franklin D. Roosevelt's New Deal. As the *Gary Post-Tribune* ruefully commented following the 1934 municipal election, " 'Me and Roosevelt' was the campaign cry of every Democratic candidate."

The depression also brought the unionization of the Region's industries. Steelworkers took the lead in this movement. Between 1935 and 1937, the industry had begun to make a dramatic recovery from the depression. Encouraged by these improved conditions and by the favorable attitude of federal, state, and local governments, workers began to press for higher wages. The steel companies, hoping to neutralize this rising militancy, organized company unions which they expected to control. US Steel, which never before had countenanced even company unionism, was the first to establish an employee representation plan.

The time seemed ideal for another attempt to organize the steel industry. In June 1936 the Congress of Industrial Organizations (CIO) formed the Steelworkers Organizing Committee (SWOC) to orchestrate this campaign. Because of its size and importance, US Steel, as it had been in 1919, was the target. SWOC adopted the unusual strategy of working through the company unions hoping to encourage them to become more independent and eventually to come over to SWOC. Lake County was particularly fertile ground for this effort, for the employee associations in the Region had refused to remain docile puppets of management and had demonstrated an unseemly independence.

US Steel surprised the nation on March 2, 1937, when it announced that it would recognize SWOC as the bargaining agent for the workers in its plants. Clearly, the corporation hoped to avoid a costly strike at a time when the industry was recovering from the worst depression in history. It also demonstrated a realistic conviction that unionization would come eventually and that resistance would be costly and in the long run pointless. The decision of the steel corporation converted SWOC overnight into one of the nation's largest and most powerful labor unions.

Most of the nation's steel industry followed US Steel in signing agreements with SWOC, but one important group of companies did not do so. Known collectively as Little Steel, these manufacturers included Bethlehem, Republic, Youngstown Sheet and Tube, Inland, National, and American Rolling Mill. Little Steel, led by Tom Girdler of Republic, was determined to resist unionization. The young union was very strong in the Inland and Youngstown plants in Indiana Harbor. When SWOC called a strike in May 1937, 20,000 workers walked off the job, and the two mills shut down completely. The strike was much less effective outside of Indiana, and even there the strike ended in defeat for the workers. It was not until 1941, after rulings by the National Labor Relations Board, that the Little Steel companies recognized SWOC as the bargaining agent for their employees.

The organization of the steel mills laid the groundwork for a massive redistribution of wealth in the Calumet Region. Between 1935 and 1939, the wages of steelworkers, nationally, rose some 27 percent. In 1939 Lake County ranked 11th among all counties in the nation in the amount of wages paid by industry. The prosperous war years brought even more advances for steelworkers in the areas of union security, working conditions, and fringe benefits such as paid vacations and sickness and accident insurance. The growth of the CIO in the Calumet Region is testimony to the success of the union drive. In 1943 the industrial unions claimed to have a membership of over 30,000 in Lake County. Thirty percent were in locals of the steelworkers' union. The AFL also grew. In 1939 there were 90 craft unions affiliated with the labor federation in the Region.

During the postwar era, manufacturing continued to be the leading economic activity of the Calumet Region, but important changes began taking place within the context of the industrial economy. Following a national trend, the percentage of the Calumet's work force engaged in manufacturing declined. Several important plants closed, including Pullman Standard, Gary Bridge Company, Cities Service Petroleum, Universal Atlas Cement, and Graver Tank. By the mid-1980s nonmanufacturing was clearly sharing the burden of upholding the Region's economy. Between 1979 and 1986, northwest Indiana experienced a 42.5 percent loss in manufacturing employment. This fall in the industrial work force has come mostly at the expense of oil and steel. Steel, the traditional backbone of the Region's prosperity, or lack thereof, faced a serious crisis by the end of the 1970s brought on by declining automobile sales, high wage scales, work stoppages, and competition from overseas and from mini-mills. By mid-1987 some 50,000 steel jobs had been lost in the Region. However, changes in the international money market in the late 1980s made American steel economical, and all the area's plants showed profits. By mid-1988 the Region's steel production amounted to almost one-third of all steel produced in this country, and the local unemployment rate dropped to its lowest in almost nine years.

Though steel has rebounded somewhat, the economic strength of the Region has diversified with medium-sized and small firms, a plethora of retail establishments, and services. Much of the business and residential growth has been the result of a general movement to the suburbs. This settlement away from the big lakeside cities began in the postwar period as good economic times and widespread car ownership enabled workers to live away from the grimy, smoky neighborhoods near the mills. Communities which were little more than villages at the end of the war blossomed into substantial residential areas. Munster, for example, grew from 4,753 in 1950 to 20,671 in 1980. With the construction of several industries around the new Burns International Harbor, built in the late 1960s, the suburban area expanded into Porter County. The town of Portage, unincorporated in 1950, grew to 27,409 over the next 30 years. The most dramatic example is that of Merrillville. Not even incorporated until the end of 1971, the town had a population of 27,677 in 1980. Schererville went from 3,663 residents in 1970 to 13,209 in 1980, a 261 percent increase. By 1987, almost all of the commercial building in Lake County had taken place in south Lake County, and almost half of the county's population resided outside of its three major urban centers, which have had to grapple with urban decay, declining tax revenues, and escalating crime rates. Gary has suffered more than most cities. Between 1963 and 1975, one quarter of the city's retail stores closed, many of them moving to the new Merrillville shopping complex. The city's last major department store, Goldblatt's, shut down in 1981.

The suburban movement deepened divisions in a region that has always been characterized by a lack of harmony. Those who left

the cities were almost all white. No suburban community included more than a handful of blacks. Merrillville, typical of the others, had only 36 blacks in 1980. The community's Hispanic population, although substantially larger, still represented less than 5 percent of the whole. As the whites fled, the percentage of Gary's population that was black increased markedly. In 1950 Gary was less than 30 percent black, but by 1970 this figure had grown to 53 percent and in 1980 to 70 percent.

The new black majority in Gary created the possibility that blacks would some day win control of the city government. Since the end of World War II, Gary had been ruled by a Democratic machine dominated by eastern and southern European ethnic groups. By the early 1960s, the power of the machine had begun to wane, a victim of not only demographic changes but also the exposure of widespread corruption within its ranks. The civil rights revolution of the 1960s produced a new generation of blacks eager to win political power. A young attorney and city councilman, Richard G. Hatcher, emerged as the champion of Gary's black population.

Hatcher declared his candidacy for the Democratic mayoral nomination in 1967. In a difficult primary campaign, with an organization much smaller than his opponent's, Hatcher won a plurality of the vote. Normally, the capture of the Democratic nomination was the equivalent to victory in the fall general election. In 1967, however, the Democratic machine repudiated its own party candidate and joined the Republicans in branding Hatcher as an extremist and an agent of the Kremlin and Fidel Castro. Although failing to win the support of the local Democratic party, Hatcher did attract the backing of major national party figures such as Vice-President Hubert Humphrey and Senators Robert Kennedy and Birch Bayh. Several black celebrities such as Harry Belafonte, Sammy Davis, Jr., Bill Cosby, and Dick Gregory helped raise funds for the challenger. In an election in which the Justice Department intervened in order to ensure an honest outcome, Hatcher won by 2,000 votes. He gained the support of 96 percent of the black voters.

Elected on the same day, Richard Hatcher and Carl Stokes of Cleveland were the first black mayors of major northern cities. Hatcher proved to be a remarkably durable political leader, serving as the city's mayor for 20 years before his primary defeat in 1987 to Thomas V. Barnes, the Calumet Township Assessor, who went on to become Gary's second black mayor. As one of the first black mayors, Hatcher acquired a national stature far beyond that normally accorded the chief executive of a medium-sized city. This enabled him to speak out on issues important to urban blacks and also enhanced his ability to attract millions of federal dollars to his beleaguered city.

To help with the revitalization of Gary's hard-hit business district the Hatcher administration launched a construction program, the focus of which was the building of the Genesis Convention Center, a multi-event facility in the heart of Gary's downtown. The center's important link with the Sheraton Hotel, which in 1979 moved into the building vacated by the Holiday Inn, was severed when the Sheraton closed in May 1988. Plans also called for a National Civil Rights Museum and Hall of Fame, which did not see the light during Hatcher's tenure but remains a goal. The downtown was made more accessible by the construction of an Indiana Toll Road interchange at Broadway and a new South Shore Commuter depot. On a regional basis promising news has come from a variety of sources. The proposed conversion of the Hatcher Gary Regional Airport into the third major airport in the greater Chicago area was a prime topic of conversation in the late 1980s. The House of Representatives approved in 1988 $3 million for further improvements of Indiana Dunes National Lakeshore. Consideration is also being given to converting some 250 miles of abandoned railroad rights-of-way in Lake, Porter, and La Porte counties to networks of trails for bikers, hikers, walkers, motorcyclists, and cross-country skiers. In 1985 the Indiana General Assembly created the Lake Michigan Marina Development Commission, a major step for aiding local communities. The commission's master plan for marina development along with a subsequent state appropriation has led to the construction and expansion of marinas in Hammond, East Chicago, Gary, Portage, and Michigan City. Meanwhile the building of shopping centers, plazas, and strip malls along the US 30 growth area continues unabated, with some one million feet of new stores constructed in 1988 alone. Over a century has elapsed since the Calumet Region began the transition from wilderness to steel

mills. Along the way a number of talents, at one time or another, have called the Region home: actors William Marshall and Karl Malden; athletes-turned-actors Alex Karras and Fred Williamson; football's Tom Harmon and Hank Stram; baseball's Charles O. Finley and Ron Kittle; boxing great Tony Zale; sports announcer Bill Fleming; gymnast Dianne Durham; astronaut Frank Borman; Noble Prize winner Paul A. Samuelson; treasure hunter Mel Fisher; and screenplay writer Steve Tesich. Some would say that the Region's chief gift to the world has been Gary's musicians, from the peerless gospel groups working out of the Gary Local Quartet Union, to Vivian Carter, founder of the Vee Jay record label in Gary that gave the Dells, Spaniels, Staple Singers, and Jerry Butler, their starts, to Deniece Williams, the Jackson Five, and these siblings' world-famous brother, Michael Jackson.

Though steel production revived in the late 1980s, it would no longer dominate the Region's economy. The diversity of the Region can now be fully and truthfully advertised. It is not just an area of steel mills, but one of lakefronts, rivers, farms, small towns and large cities, parks, natural and historical sites. This ethnic-rich district—crisscrossed with superhighways and small country lanes—has so much heterogeneity that it makes the much-vaunted southern Indiana appear one-dimensional. Its very multiformity can produce seemingly contrasting national media images as when, in the summer of 1988, *Money* magazine listed the Hammond-Gary area as the 41st best place to live among 300 American cities, and the best in Indiana, while *U.S. News and World Report* ranked Gary-Hammond as the most segregated of the nation's 60 metropolitan areas. When weighing the import of the Region's diversity and historical development, it seems doubtful that Lake County's three northern townships could ever merge into one governmental unit creating one huge city, the state's second largest, as recommended in 1986 by the Center for Government Services at Indiana State University. Its location does, however, bring a semblance of unity to the area. In the minds of most Hoosiers, the Calumet will continue to be set apart from the rest of Indiana by its location, its steel mills, and its history. The residents of the Region will continue to view themselves as Indiana's stepchildren, and

Hoosiers to the south will continue to regard that strange land with awe and suspicion.

Calumet Region Attractions

The Calumet area is rich in industrial, ethnic, natural, and historical sites and attractions. The selections below, while significant, are but a few of the many interesting places in the Region. For additional tourist information see No. 32 below.

1. The **State Boundary Marker** is located in the uppermost western corner of the state where Indiana meets Illinois. In 1821 John Tipton, a commissioner appointed to determine the state line, placed a stone marker by the shore of Lake Michigan. The 15 1/2-ft. boundary stone, restored and rededicated in 1988, now stands across the Elgin, Joliet and Eastern Railroad from the entrance to the Commonwealth Edison Company of Indiana power plant at Hammond. It stands in a small park named for the late Allen J. Benson, a Commonwealth Edison executive who led his company's involvement in the restoration efforts. To reach it by car you must enter Illinois. Drive into Chicago on Indianapolis Blvd. (US 12, 20, and 41) to Ewing Ave. Turn right, go under I-94 and Conrail and CSX railroads, and turn right at 100th St. Cross the Elgin, Joliet and Eastern Railroad, turn right, and continue one-half mile to the plant entrance.

2. The **State Line Generating Unit No. 1**, housed in the Commonwealth Edison State Line Power Station in Hammond, is the only Historic Mechanical Engineering Landmark in Indiana. For 25 years the 208,000-kilowatt turbine-generator, built in 1929, was the largest electrical production unit operating in the world. The American Society of Mechanical Engineers designated it a landmark in 1977.

3. The **Whiting Community Memorial House**, or the Whiting Community Center, as it is locally known, at 1938 Clark St., is a monument to Standard Oil Company employees who died in World War I. In 1923 the company constructed the brick Italianate Villa-style building with its marble and limestone exterior details of Romanesque design. Owned by the city since 1973, the building contains meeting rooms for local organizations, gymnastic facilities, 12 bowling lanes, a crafts room, club rooms, and a senior citizens' room. Of particular interest is a meeting room which is richly paneled with wood from the Black Forest of Germany. The auditorium, which seats 750 persons, is attractively decorated with elaborate cast-plaster moldings. (*NRHP*)

4. The **Whiting Public Library**, 1735 Oliver Ave., was built in 1905 through funds from Andrew Carnegie and the donation of the site by the Standard Oil Company. The two-story brick facility is of Romanesque design with an octagonal tower. In the 1980s the structure underwent renovations which included the creation of a rotunda in the main chamber and a new wing carefully designed to match the old section architecturally.

5. **Calumet College of St. Joseph**, 2400 New York Ave., began in 1951 as a two-year "Calumet Center" branch of St. Joseph's College at Rensselaer. It became a four-year degree-granting institution in 1960. After a lengthy tenure in commercial buildings of East Chicago the Catholic liberal arts college run by the Precious Blood Fathers officially separated from St. Joseph's in 1973 and in 1976 moved to its present campus on land and in facilities once occupied by the Amoco Oil Company. The buildings were renovated and equipped to serve the commuter student body. The main academic building houses a chapel, art gallery, library, and bookstore on the first floor which are open to visitors. The college has satellite campuses in Merrillville, Portage, and Hammond.

Calumet Region Attractions

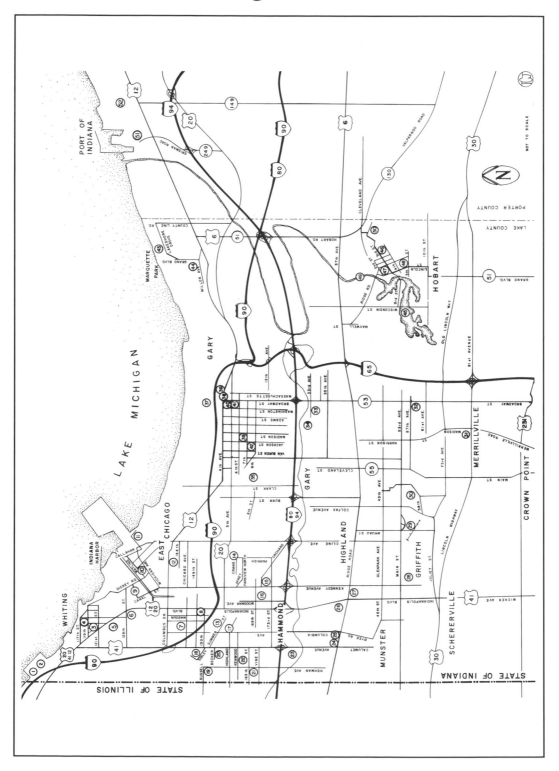

6. The administrative offices of **Amoco Oil Company**, 2815 Indianapolis Blvd., oversees the operations of the nation's sixth largest refinery, which sits on approximately 1,700 acres of land. In 1889 the Standard Oil Company started a refinery at 129th St. and Indianapolis Blvd. to process crude oil piped in from Lima, Ohio. The refinery was located on 235 acres of dunes and marshland near a railroad crossing at Whiting. The foul-smelling crude had a high sulfur content which Standard extracted by means of a copper-oxide process developed in 1887 by Herman Frasch, a German-born chemist. Subsequently known as the American Oil Company and, finally, the Amoco Oil Company, it became the Midwest's largest refiner following development of the Burton-Humphreys Thermal Cracking Process in 1912. Dr. Robert E. Humphreys, its chief chemist at Whiting, managed to quintuple the gas yield by successfully experimenting, at bodily risk, with refining oil at previously untried levels of heat and pressure. His achievement, a landmark in the annals of modern invention, assured an adequate gasoline supply, thus opening the door to America's automotive age. In 1982 Amoco completed construction of a $55 million hydrotreater that improved the company's ability to process crude oil products and reduce environmental pollution.

7. The **Robert A. Pastrick Branch of the East Chicago Public Library**, two blocks west of Indianapolis Blvd. at Baring and Chicago Aves., is a Carnegie library built in 1912 and recently given the name of the city's longtime mayor (1972-present). It houses a mural painted in the 1930s under the sponsorship of the Works Progress Administration (WPA). Ernest Kasas, a radio announcer in Gary, painted *The Gift of Culture* and *The Gift of the Book to Mankind*, two 34 x 64-in. panels, mounted above the library reference room.

8. **St. Stanislaus Catholic Church**, 4935 Magoun Ave., one block west of Indianapolis Blvd. near 150th St., is East Chicago's first Polish church. It was founded in 1896. Originally called St. Michael's, the church, built in 1900, was moved a block east to its present location. At that time, the name of the parish was changed to St. Stanislaus. A small parish school, a rectory, and a convent were built on the new site. During the 1920s all of the parish

facilities were replaced with new buildings. A fire destroyed the school in 1958, but a new school and hall opened in 1961.

9. **Marktown**, bounded by Pine St., Dickey and Riley rds., and 129th St. in East Chicago, is an example of a planned worker community. Two-story, stucco, pastel-colored homes press closely on narrow streets, which serve as walkways for the residents who park their cars on the sidewalks, a unique characteristic of the town noted in Robert Ripley's *Believe It Or Not* years ago. Clayton Mark, founder of the Mark Manufacturing Company, constructed the 190-acre town in 1917 to provide company housing. The self-contained community of about 16 square blocks, shut off from other communities by the mill, was designed by Chicago architect Howard Van Doren Shaw and built on former marshland. The original plan included Tudor Revival-style single-family houses, duplexes, and four-unit row houses for workers and their families and two boardinghouses for single men employees. Though intended to accommodate 8,000 persons, the town never reached completion. Ninety-four buildings were constructed, however, all of which remain standing. The steel plant and Marktown were absorbed by the American Sheet and Tube Company in 1920, which in turn was bought out by Youngstown Sheet and Tube Company of Ohio, now LTV Steel, in 1923. The similarly styled homes have been privately owned since 1942, and the working-class neighborhood of about 650 residents is designated a historic district. (*NRHP*)

10. The Indiana Harbor Works of **Inland Steel Company**, 3210 Watling St., began in 1893 as a small plant in Chicago Heights, Illinois, using secondhand machinery from a defunct steel mill. After a shaky start, Inland's sales increased as the demand grew for steel plows and side rails for metal beds. In 1897 Inland Steel bought the East Chicago Iron and Steel Company. Then, in 1901, when the Lake Michigan Land Company offered 50 acres to induce a steel company to build an open-hearth plant in East Chicago, Inland Steel accepted the offer. It sold the steel company to Republic Steel, and in 1902 the first steel ingots produced in open-hearth furnaces in Lake County were poured. A month later the blooming mills started operations, and the sheet and bar mills followed. In 1907 Inland Steel constructed the first blast

furnace in the Calumet Region. Today, it is East Chicago's largest employer. The Indiana Harbor Works produces sheet and strip, bars, plates, and structural steel products used primarily for the automotive and appliance industries. The company's No. 7 Blast Furnace, dedicated in 1980, is one of the largest and most highly computerized blast furnaces in the country, producing up to 10,000 net tons of molten iron per day. The plant, built on 1,900 acres of landfill jutting two miles out into Lake Michigan, includes iron ore docks, blast furnaces, and coke ovens.

11. **Indiana Harbor**, situated near the lake and between Michigan and Cline aves., is a settlement of workers' residences built when Inland Steel began construction of its Indiana Harbor Works in 1901. An earlier settlement of a few Germans, destroyed by fire in 1871, was never rebuilt. In the early 20th century, houses, restaurants, saloons, hotels, and small businesses sprang up almost overnight. Although a part of East Chicago, Indiana Harbor retained its own identity. In 1920 the Indiana Homes Company, a subsidiary of Inland Steel, began to develop low-cost rental housing in a section called the Sunnyside addition of Indiana Harbor to accommodate the increasing number of workers at the steel mill. Today, Indiana Harbor is a predominantly Hispanic neighborhood. The churches of the community remain as a record of the ethnic groups that have settled here. St. Patrick's Catholic Church, founded in 1902, was the first parish in Indiana Harbor. The first black church was St. Mark A.M.E. Zion Church (now the Second Baptist Church) built in 1917. More recently established was the Midwest's first Mexican church named Our Lady of Guadalupe, completed in 1927, and rebuilt at another location in 1940 after a disastrous fire. Needing more room, a new church arose nearby at 3510 Deodar St. in 1976.

12. **Washington Park**, bounded by 142nd St., Grand Ave., 144th St., and Parrish Ave., contains the nursery for the entire East Chicago park system. On the 17-acre grounds are a greenhouse, conservatory, and a garden with flowers and herbs labeled for the blind. Flower shows are held annually in the spring and fall. Across the street is the E. J. Block Stadium—a facility for soccer, softball, baseball, and football—and a swimming pool.

13. The **Gibson Rail Yards** at Hammond, which included a large roundhouse and machine shops, began operations in 1906. The rail yards reached from Columbia Ave. east almost to Kennedy Ave. The Indiana Harbor Belt Line, which started in 1901, still uses the roundhouse for its diesels though the coal chute stands idle. In 1923 four employees of Indiana Harbor Belt, George Hannauer, E. M. Wilcox, Garner Grills, and John Marsh, developed a mechanical car retarder to slow the speed of freight cars as they rolled into individual classification tracks, thus eliminating the necessity of brakemen riding cars and manually controlling their speed. First used in the Gibson Rail Yards, the invention was adopted nationwide. The original installation is now in the Smithsonian Institution in Washington, D.C. The yard's Administrative Offices, housed in a four-story brick building, remain just off Kennedy Ave. to the west.

"West Point," or "Gibson," a railhead/ stagecoach station, was the western terminal of the Michigan Central Railroad which came through the Calumet Region and reached Chicago by 1852. Joseph Hess, an Alsatian baker, opened a restaurant at Gibson station in 1851. He soon moved south one mile and assembled a general store, post office (1857), cattle business, and log school, thus planting the seed for the village of Hessville.

George H. Hammond, along with Marcus M. Towle, Caleb Ives, and George W. Plummer, owned and operated a slaughterhouse adjacent to the Michigan Central Railroad between 1869 and 1901. Known as the State Line Slaughter House, the meat packing plant occupied a 42-acre site between the Illinois-Indiana border and Hohman Ave. Hammond and Towle pioneered in the use of transporting finished beef by rail in refrigerated cars newly developed by the Davis brothers of Detroit. A post office established near the slaughterhouse in 1873 took the Hammond family name. In 1875 Marcus Towle bought property near the plant and platted "Hohman," a town for the workers. Additional subdivisions led in 1883 to the incorporation of the town of Hammond, and its reorganization as a city in April 1884. The city acquired its present boundaries with the formal annexation, in 1923, of Hessville and the southern parts of Hammond to the Little Calumet River.

14. The **Gibson Woods Nature Preserve**, situated east of Kennedy Ave. in the Hessville section of Hammond at 6201 Parrish Ave., is a 120-acre tract of wildlife and rare plants and features hiking trails and a nature center. It contains the longest undissected dune ridge in Indiana, outside of the National Lakeshore. Dedicated in 1981, the site is the county's first nature preserve.

15. The **Little Red Schoolhouse**, 7205 Kennedy Ave. in Hammond, was built in 1869 in Hessville to replace the log school. Half of the building was constructed with limestone, but it was completed with clay bricks which were less expensive to transport to the site. The school was used until 1896, after which it became a private dwelling. A local group purchased the building in the early 1970s, refurbished it, and moved it onto a new foundation in **Hessville Park**. It is now operated as a living museum by the Hessville Historical Society. Here are the original tower bell, desks, and other period furnishings. Schoolchildren are invited to attend classes conducted in a 19th-century manner. The basement provides a community meeting room. A monument of two tree trunks representing Joseph and Elizabeth Hess stands in the family burial plot at the old **Hessville Cemetery**, 169th St. and Arizona Ave.

16. The **Purdue University Calumet Campus**, situated on the east side of Indianapolis Blvd. at 2233 171st St. in Hammond, is a modern and expanding regional institution. In 1943 Purdue University established a series of technological programs in the Calumet Region to meet the increased demand for skilled craftsmen and technicians during World War II. In 1946 the university appointed a resident faculty and offered regular undergraduate courses. Two years later Purdue purchased 167 acres on which to build a permanent campus. The first building was occupied in 1951. The Industrial Research Institute building was completed in 1954. A special attraction, on permanent loan from the city of Hammond, adorns the south entrance wall of the Student-Faculty Library Center—the majestic Art Deco-style bronze doors which fronted the Hammond City Hall from 1935 to 1976. Alfonso Iannelli sculpted the doors to "represent the industrial worker laboring to fulfill his physical needs tending machinery and his spiritual needs in tolling the church bell."

17. The **Standard Steel Car Company's housing for workers** comprises a neighborhood, now a historic district, east of Columbia Ave. at Highland St. Homes were put up shortly after the Pennsylvania-based company built its large Hammond plant in 1906. Exterior features of the duplex and single-family dwellings, constructed along curved streets, include facades of stone, brick, stucco, and shingles; return-style roofs; and arched entryways. Tenement housing for men erected along Columbia Ave. was removed in 1939 as part of the city's low-cost housing program. Most of the homes remaining were built in 1917 when the company offered housing facilities as an inducement to recruit management during World War I. The Pullman Company purchased Standard Steel in 1930, creating Pullman-Standard of Hammond. Pullman, Inc., discontinued production of passenger cars and closed its plants in Hammond and South Chicago in 1981.

18. The **Hammond Public Library**, located between Sohl and Hohman at 564 State St., is a modern limestone structure featuring spacious rooms and galleries along the upper terrace. Organized in 1902, the library was housed first in the Bloomhoff Millinery Store and then the Chicago Telephone Company on Ribach Ave. A Carnegie library building in Central Park was occupied between 1905 and 1965. Architects Besozzi, Carpenter, and Ignelzi designed the present library building which opened in 1966. The Calumet Room, dedicated to Lafayette School principal Renal Ames, contains a noteworthy collection of papers, pictures, and artifacts related to the history of the Calumet Region.

19. **St. Joseph's Catholic Church**, 5304 Hohman Ave., was built in 1912. The original parish, composed primarily of German-speaking Catholics, was formally established in 1879. Caroline Hohman, the wife of Hammond's first settler, donated the land on which the first church was erected. The first parish school opened in 1885. A three-story rectory, built in 1904, is still in use. The present church is a striking Romanesque-style brick building with twin towers and a large circular stained-glass window. The church interior features a high al-

tar made of Carrara marble from Pietrasanta, Italy. A huge mural painted by John A. Mallin of Chicago treats an interesting combination of religious and contemporary themes, including a scene of steelworkers from the Calumet Region.

20. The Hammond **Civic Center**, 5828 Sohl Ave. between Becker and Eaton sts., was erected by the WPA in 1937 for $400,000. Originally planned as a community center for basketball and other sports, the semiclassical-style brick and stone building designed by L. Cosby Bernard, Sr., has an auditorium which seats approximately 5,700. From October to May, it is used for sporting events, concerts, circuses, revivals, and music shows. During the summer, the facility is used for such activities as a boxing program and dog training classes. Across the street is an outdoor exhibit of Nickel Plate Railroad equipment. The "Old 624" steam locomotive and coal car, a refrigerator car, caboose, and a watchman's tower are on display.

21. **"Church Row,"** between 165th and 173rd sts., is an impressive display of Hammond's newest and finest churches, built literally in a row along the east side of Hohman Ave. Located here are the First Presbyterian Church, the First United Methodist Church, the First United Lutheran Church, Temple Beth-El, St. Demetrios Greek Orthodox Church, Congregation Beth Israel, the First Church of Christ Scientist, and the Trinity Evangelical Lutheran Church. One church, not present here but deserving of mention, is the huge **First Baptist Church** at 523 Sibley St., in downtown Hammond on the northeast corner of Sibley St. and Oakley Ave. The third church building on the site since 1888, the year after the church was organized, its auditorium seats 6,400 worshipers. First Baptist has grown to become one of the largest churches in the nation. By the early 1980s it claimed a membership of 60,000 and an average of 26,000 in its Sunday School. In October 1973, *Christian Life Magazine* named First Baptist as having the "World's Largest Sunday School." Among its formidable network of other ministries is the Hyles-Anderson College established in 1972 and moved to its present campus in 1974 at 8400 Burr St., south of US 30 about one-half mile in Crown Point.

22. **Oak Hill Cemetery**, 227 Kenwood St., is a 21-acre wooded site bordering Hohman Ave. between 165th and Kenwood sts. It is the oldest cemetery in Hammond, formally established in 1885. Most of the city's founding fathers are buried here, including Thomas Hammond, Marcus M. Towle, the first mayor and postmaster, and Ernst and Caroline Hohman, Hammond's first settlers, who moved from Chicago in fear of cholera and in 1851 built a log cabin on the north bank of the Grand Calumet River.

23. The **Indiana Botanic Gardens**, at 626 177th St. (near I-94 and Calumet Ave.), houses a processing plant, a mail-order facility, and a small retail store. In 1910 Joseph E. Meyer established a herbal plant operating from a one-room, mail-order office. He was a printer by trade but wanted to operate his own business so he collected herbs, dried and packaged them, and sold them through mail-order ads. He printed trade books and pamphlets such as *The Old Herbal Doctor* and *Nature's Remedies*. He also printed a 130-page exposé of gambling practices. Meyer built the present Tudor-style building of brick, stucco, and stone on E. River Rd., designed by John Broughton, in 1924. The garden along the Little Calumet River once produced the herbs processed by the company. Today the garden serves as a bird sanctuary and wildlife refuge, and the company imports most of its herbs. The company packages about 1,500 different herbal products and publishes its own sales catalogs and *The Herbalist Almanac*, established in 1925.

24. The **Munster Town Hall**, 1005 Ridge Rd., is composed of three colonial-style buildings connected by breezeways, which serve as the administration building, police, and fire departments. This Lake County community was founded by Dutch farmers. Dingernon Jabaay was the first settler in the area to arrive from the Netherlands. In 1855 other members of his family joined him, along with the Munster family. By 1860, 55 persons of Dutch extraction, most of whom were farmers, lived in Munster. In the 1870s Dutch-owned truck farms began producing crops of cabbage, sweet corn, tomatoes, cauliflower, potatoes, parsnips, and melons for the Chicago markets. Onions became a major product of the Region. The town received its name from Jacob Munster who ran

the post office in his general store on Ridge Rd. beginning in 1892. The "town on the ridge" was incorporated in 1907, and Cornelius P. Schoon, a leading onion farmer, was elected town clerk. During the depression years the local food processing plants closed, and truck farming diminished. Munster gradually evolved as a suburban town, and new residential sections prospered after 1935. The present municipal center was completed in 1982.

25. **Rotary Park**, at the northwest corner of Ridge Rd. and Columbia Ave. in Munster, features a metal sculpture garden titled "Yesterday and Today for Tomorrow" created by Holly Ores. Dedicated in 1976 during the bicentennial celebrations, the sculpture arrangement is composed of three 15-ft.-high figures depicting a steelworker, a farmer, and an Indian. At the southeast corner of the intersection, a historical marker notes the site of the **Brass Tavern**. David Gibson built and operated an inn along the "old highway," now Columbia Ave., between 1837 and 1845. Allen Brass used the timbers from the old inn to construct a tavern which served travelers going between Fort Dearborn and Fort Wayne. Johann Stallbohm purchased the property in the 1860s and maintained the inn until the turn of the century. The Region's first telegraph office was housed in the tavern, and the news of President Abraham Lincoln's assassination first reached Lake County here. The tavern was destroyed by fire in 1909. A private residence now occupies the site.

26. **Wicker Park**, located at US 6 and US 41 in Highland, just south of Hammond, covers 240 acres along the Little Calumet River. In 1927 President Calvin Coolidge dedicated the park as a memorial to Lake County's deceased World War I soldiers and sailors. Situated in a wooded setting, the park facilities include a clubhouse and pavilion, an 18-hole golf course, a swimming pool, picnic grounds, and recreation areas.

27. The **Highway of Flags Memorial**, at the southeast corner of US 41 and Ridge Rd. in Highland, was dedicated in 1975 as a national shrine to honor the American flag and all servicemen and women of all wars and conflicts. In 1971 the National Council for the Encouragement of Patriotism received proclamations from the governors of eight states designating the entire length of US 41, from Michigan to Florida, the Highway of Flags. The monument, a concrete semicircle, bears the flags and insignias of the eight states.

28. **Hoosier Prairie** lies east of Kennedy Ave. north and south of Main St. (which divides Highland and Schererville), and about 2 1/2 miles south of Ridge Rd. The prairie is a 335-acre tract of virgin land. In 1977 the bit of land was declared a state nature preserve and a national natural landmark. Hoosier Prairie represents the ecology of the area as it was before civilization encroached upon the land. The preserve is mostly prairie and wetlands with an abundant mixture of typical prairie wild flowers and grasses, but also some oak woods and savannahs. It is an excellent window onto the native habitats of birds and animals, many rare in Indiana.

29. The **Grand Trunk Depot Museum**, just north of the tracks at 201 S. Broad St. in Griffith, has many ties to the early history of the community. Griffith developed after the Michigan Central Railroad reached the area in 1854. German railroad workers settled in the vicinity of the tracks. The town takes its name from a railroad surveyor, Benjamin Griffith, who prepared maps of the region. Peter Govert, a railroad agent, built the white frame house, one of the earliest in town, at 338 S. Broad St. in the 1870s. At one time five lines converged at Griffith—the reason for it being known as "the town that came to the tracks."

30. The **Oak Ridge Prairie County Park**, 301 S. Colfax St. in Griffith, is Lake County's newest park. The attractive 592-acre man-made facility opened in 1984. It provides a nature preserve with a two-mile channel surrounded by marshland and special areas designed for picnicking, hiking, fishing, canoeing, sledding, and cross-country skiing. The parking lot is located .4 mile south of 53rd Ave. on Fairbanks St.

31. More than 1,300 Greek-American families from the Calumet Region worship in the **Greek Orthodox Cathedral of SS. Constantine and Helena** and the **Hellenic Cultural Center**, 8000 Madison St., north of US 30 in Merrillville. In 1912, 10 families of Greek immigrants organized Lake County's first Greek Orthodox

Church and used the Byzantine-style church at 13th Ave. and Jackson St. in Gary until the present church complex in Merrillville was completed. Construction of the Hellenic Cultural Center began in 1971. The cathedral, built between 1974 and 1976, features a 56-ft.-high x 100-ft.-diameter rotunda and has a seating capacity of 1,063. The interior offers a rich display of mosaic murals, icons, and stained-glass windows depicting the fathers, martyrs, and patron saints of the cathedral—Constantine the Great and his mother, Empress Helena.

32. The **Lake County Convention and Visitors Bureau**, located north of I-65 and 61st Ave. at 5800 Broadway, Suite N, in Merrillville, is the county's newest tourist information center. It offers free brochures, calendars of events, and information about the Region.

33. **Indiana University Northwest**, at 3400 Broadway, is conveniently located south of I-80/90 in the city of Gary. The Gary Extension Division of Indiana University offered the first college-level courses in Lake County at Jefferson High School in 1920. Five years later the extension center moved its offices to the Memorial Auditorium in Gary. Gary College, founded by Superintendent of Schools William A. Wirt in 1932, became a part of the extension division in 1948. Quarters were occupied at Gary's City Methodist Church until 1959 when Indiana University Northwest moved to its present site. The $9 million Library-Conference Center, a repository for the Calumet Regional Archives, was dedicated in 1980. Today the college has more than 4,500 students and offers more than 150 degree programs including a master's degree in Public and Environmental Affairs.

34. **Gleason Park**, west of Broadway on 30th and 33rd aves., covers about 600 acres of former marshland, extending to Grant St. along the Little Calumet River. Originally called Riverside Park, it was renamed Gleason to honor William P. Gleason, the first superintendent of the United States (US) Steel Corporation's Gary Works and longtime park board president. At 30th Ave. between Broadway and Harrison is a marshland preserve which is the habitat for many birds, including one of the few nesting places in the state for the yellow-headed blackbird. On the surrounding floodplain are

ball fields, playgrounds, and a nine-hole golf course reputed to be the first such facility for blacks in the country. In the next decade, Gleason Park is to be incorporated into a major regional greenway park of around 3,500 acres being developed from the Illinois state line to Burns Waterway in Porter County.

35. **Brunswick Park Savanna**, 765 Clark Rd., is a 49-acre park on the west side of Gary. It is listed on the Indiana Natural Area Registry and protected in its natural state. Rare plants that have been safeguarded in the preserve include black oak, zaric uplands savanna and bluejoint grass, prairie cordgrass, and prairie sunflowers. In 1976 the city built on the grounds a multipurpose community center with a gymnasium, day care center, classrooms, and office space. Outdoor facilities include tennis courts, baseball diamonds, and picnic areas.

36. The **Gary Land Company** was established in 1906 by the US Steel Corporation (now USX) to lay out and build a "company town." The original land office, the oldest building in Gary, now stands at 216 E. 4th Ave. in Gateway Park between Massachusetts and Pennsylvania sts. At its first site near 3rd and Broadway, the Gary Land Company shared the two-story frame structure with the town hall. The building also housed the city's first post office. Following World War I the building was sold to a private buyer who moved it to 6th and Jefferson and used it as a boardinghouse. In 1955 the Gary Historical Society purchased the building and moved it to Gateway Park. A fire in 1979 caused heavy damage, but the land office has been repaired and reopened as offices for the Gary Historical and Cultural Society. (*NRHP/HABS*)

37. The **Gary Works of the US Steel Corporation (USX)**, 1 N. Broadway, and the city of Gary were founded and developed simultaneously. US Steel bought 9,000 acres along the southern shore of Lake Michigan because of its proximity to Chicago railroads and its potential as a harbor. After the immense project of building a steel mill in the middle of a wasteland began in 1906, the company found it necessary to provide homes for the workers. The Gary Land Company (see above) was established and constructed houses between 1909 and 1919. The first steel was poured at the

Gary Works in 1909. At that time the US Steel plant became the largest and most modern steelmaking facility in the world, and Gary was called "the steel city." The city's economy has fluctuated with the rise and fall of steel production. In the past two decades, US Steel has invested heavily in modernization and renovation projects and in pollution control equipment. The company, with 7,700 employees, is the largest employer in Gary. In 1984 the Gary Works poured its 350 millionth ton of steel, the most produced by any steel plant in the world, according to US Steel officials.

38. **Gary City Hall**, 401 Broadway, is a four-story limestone structure built in 1927. Gary's first "city hall" shared a frame house with the Gary Land Company near 3rd Ave. and Broadway. In 1909 a brick building was erected at 7th Ave. and Massachusetts to house the city hall as well as the police and fire departments. The present building is part of a complex which encompasses the three-story limestone courthouse across the street and the city park to the north. In front of the city hall is a statue of Elbert H. Gary (1846-1927), chairman of the board of US Steel and for whom the city was named, at his insistence.

39. The **Gary-Hobart Water Tower**, in Borman Square, 650 Madison St., is one of Gary's oldest landmarks. The imposing 40-ft.-high concrete and stone block octagonal tower contains a 30-ft.-diameter steel tank which holds 290,000 gallons of water. In 1906 a vast waterworks system was begun to serve the needs of both the city and the steel mill. A 6-ft.-diameter intake tunnel, three miles long and 38 ft. below water level, was dug into Lake Michigan. A pumping station then moved the water to the storage tower at 7th and Madison sts. The Gary Heat, Light, and Water Company completed in 1910 the network of shafts and tunnels designed by the Chicago engineering firm of Alvord and Burdick. In 1970 the tower was designated an American Water Landmark by the American Water Works Association.

40. Gary's **Genesis Convention Center** in the 400 block of Broadway—a $13.4 million facility built with Federal moneys—opened in December 1981. Designed by Wendell Campbell and Associates, Inc., of Chicago, the convention center contains 142,000 sq. ft. of exhibit space and meeting rooms on two levels. The auditorium seats 7,500 spectators with additional seating available within the arena.

41. **City Methodist Church**, a massive limestone structure of Gothic design at 575 Washington St., was completed in 1926. A Methodist class first met in Gary in 1906, holding its service at Binzenhof Hall. The Rev. William Grant Seaman became pastor in 1916 and was instrumental in the construction of the present church—the "downtown cathedral" of Gary. The church complex, which covers a city block, originally comprised three sections: the church, a four-story educational building with administrative offices and recreational facilities, and a three-story commercial unit. The Gary Extension Division of Indiana University held classes here from 1948 to 1959 when the college moved to its present site. Church membership peaked at 3,000 during the 1950s. Following a decline in membership, the church closed in 1975.

42. Now **a historic district**, the old **westside neighborhood** near downtown Gary along 6th, 7th, and 8th aves., between Jackson and Van Buren sts., was part of the "company town" built by US Steel Corporation beginning in 1906, intended for the use of company officials and supervisors. Although a planned community, the neighborhood reflects a variety of architectural styles. Best known is the white stucco house with green trim at 669 Van Buren designed in the Prairie School style of architecture made popular by Frank Lloyd Wright.

43. **Marquette Park**, on the lakefront at Grand Blvd. and Forest Ave. in Miller, was a gift to the city of Gary in 1919 from US Steel. The 120-acre park was named for Père Jacques Marquette. While traveling through the Great Lakes region as a missionary in 1675, Marquette is believed to have camped at the mouth of the Grand Calumet River in the area of the present park. A bronze statue of Marquette designed by Henry Hering of New York stands near the entrance. Before becoming a city park, the wild-looking sand dunes had been the location for the making of silent films such as *The Conquest of Mexico* and *Lost in the Desert*. During the 1920s the city developed the beach front and built a pavilion and bathhouse. Chicago architect Jens Jensen landscaped the

Indiana State Library
Boulder with plaque in Marquette Park commemorating Octave Chanute

dunes surrounding the lagoon area. The city also created picnic facilities, bridle paths, hiking trails, and a gun club. In 1981 the city renovated the pavilion—a brick structure with twin towers and a grand entrance flanked by columns—at a cost of $670,000. Just south of the pavilion, next to the parking lot, a boulder with a bronze plaque commemorates **Octave Chanute's glider experiments**. A retired railroad civil engineer from New York, Chanute (1832-1910) moved to Chicago in 1889 and conducted some of his early glider flights from isolated sand dunes near here in 1896. He developed the world's first reasonably stable glider. His experiments preceded those of the Wright brothers, and his design for the biplane glider became the model upon which the first successful powered airplanes were built.

44. **Miller Town Hall**, 6306 Miller Ave. at Grand Blvd. and Old Hobart Rd., is a local historic landmark. An early sand dune settlement and a former fishing and ice-harvesting center, Miller was incorporated as a town in 1907. The modest two-story brick town hall was constructed in 1910 as an electric lighting substation for the community. The first floor housed the station's equipment, and the second floor served as the town meeting hall. After Miller was annexed to Gary in 1918, the building served as a fire station. Renovation work begun

in 1976 has returned the structure to its original character. (*NRHP*)

45. **Lake George**, Hobart, was formed in 1846 when George Earle built a dam across the Deep River for his three-story wooden gristmill and sawmill. In 1849 Earle platted the town of Hobart and named it for his brother Frederick Hobart Earle. The town now surrounds the 270-acre lake, and attractive park areas border the north and south shores.

46. The **Hobart Historical Society Museum**, 706 E. 4th St., occupies a charming Carnegie Library building constructed in 1914-15. The Hobart Women's Reading Club was instrumental in getting the project under way, and Ingwald Moe, a Gary contractor and builder, erected it. The two-story, Tudor-style structure exhibits nine colors of brick along with a slate roof and leaded windows. The building served as a library until 1968. The museum offers displays depicting life in the Hobart area, an art gallery featuring three paintings (ca. 1867) by town founder George Earle, and a research library containing an extensive collection of local newspapers. The downstairs display includes the printing press used to put out the *Gazette* in 1889, a replica of a blacksmith shop, and numerous farm implements. Upstairs are a variety of Indian artifacts and early settler household items. (*NRHP*)

47. The **Hobart Post Office** is located at 221 Main St. George Earle established Hobart's first post office in his gristmill at Front and Main sts. in 1847. In 1861 post office operations moved to Joseph Black's trading post. The present post office, built in 1936, stands on the site of the trading post. In 1938 William Dolwick of Cleveland, Ohio, painted a WPA-sponsored mural in the post office lobby. Titled *Early Hobart*, it represents the town as it might have appeared in 1870.

48. The **First Unitarian Church**, 497 Main St., was the first church erected on town property when dedicated in January 1876. Hobart's Unitarians officially organized in 1874, meeting in a schoolhouse. The congregation leased a hall until the present church was completed. A. D. Pollard and Company constructed the ivy-covered brick building of traditional Gothic design. A parish hall in the back was added in

1956. The church cupola contains a very old bell cast in England and presented to the Hobart church by United States Senator George F. Hoar of Massachusetts from the sister Unitarian church at Concord.

49. The **Pennsylvania Railroad Bridge** was built over the Deep River in Hobart in 1854. The unusual stone arch span can be seen in the distance by looking east from the bridge north of the Hobart Wastewater Lift Station on Old Ridge Rd., which becomes Center St. in Hobart. (*HAER*)

50. The **Pennsylvania Railroad Station**, located in Pennsy Park on Lillian St. in northeast Hobart, was built in 1911 and opened in January 1912. Price and McLanahan of Philadelphia were the architects of the $25,000 terminal, the third depot erected on the site. The single-story building constructed of pressed brick with ceramic tile inserts (prior stations were frame) housed the passenger waiting room and freight office. In 1983 the Save Our Station Committee purchased it from Conrail on behalf of the Hobart Historical Society for its use as a rental property and for its post-renovation dedica-

tion, which occurred in March 1987. Although the station is occupied by a retail firm, Amtrack picks up its passengers here for its daily commuter service to Chicago. (*NRHP*)

51. **Burns Waterway**, a drainage channel completed in 1926, made possible the development of some 20,000 acres where a large industrial harbor at IND 249 and US 12 called **Burns International Harbor**—the **Port of Indiana**—was built between 1965 and 1969. Burns International Harbor is a man-made, deepwater port, built specifically to handle St. Lawrence Seaway ocean-going traffic. A 4,600-ft.-long breakwater shelters the open-water approach and provides direct access to the Great Lakes. Within the harbor, a 28-ft.-deep turning basin allows large freighters to turn about without the assistance of tugboats. Nearby railroad lines and interstate highways provide rapid transportation of goods to and from the ships. Burns International Harbor is flanked by **Bethlehem Steel** on the east and **Midwest Steel** on the west. The $21.5 million grain elevator constructed by **Cargill, Inc.**, is capable of handling more than 40 million bushels of grain per year and has a 3.4 million-bushel storage capacity.

Northern Indiana Public Service Company, 1962

Indiana State Library

The **Paul Dee Company**, at Burns International Harbor, imports oyster shells by barge from the Gulf of Mexico and processes them for use as a calcium supplement to chicken feed. Just east of Bethlehem Steel, the **Northern Indiana Public Service Company (NIPSCO)** began constructing in 1970 a nuclear electric generating station, the ill-fated Bailly Plant. Located adjacent to the Indiana Dunes National Lakeshore Park, it succumbed to public protest, rising costs, and stringent building codes; the project was abandoned in 1981. South of the port, near the intersection of IND 149 and I-94, **Union Carbide** operates an oxygen plant. The plant's twin towers are the largest air-separation columns in the world, capable of producing more than two million cubic feet of liquid nitrogen and argon daily.

52. **Bethlehem Steel Corporation's** Burns Harbor Plant is located east of IND 249 between Lake Michigan and I-94. Part of the steelworks is visible from US 12. Built in 1965 on 3,300 acres, the Burns Harbor plant is one of the newest and most technologically advanced steel mills in the country. An automatic conveyor system moves ore, limestone, and coke from the waterfront directly to two blast furnaces (each 25 stories high), where the ore is reduced to molten iron. After the iron is refined further, it is poured into a "continuous castor" which converts the molten steel to a solid slab, eliminating the traditional procedure of forming slabs with ingot molds. More than five million tons of steel are produced each year. The Burns Harbor Works employs more than 6,000 workers.

From the entrance to Bethlehem Steel, return west on IND 12, *11.1 m.*, to I-65. Proceed south about *15 m.* to the US 231 exit, south of Merrillville. Go northwest on US 231 *3 m.* to the center of Crown Point where the narrative for the large circular tour around the Calumet Region begins.

Tour 19

LAKE COUNTY (p. 522,965; 501 sq. m.) is a land of contrasts. Its terrain varies from shoreline sand dunes in the north to farmland, lakes, and rolling prairie in the central section to densely vegetated lowlands in the south. The northern part of the county is mostly urban and industrial, crisscrossed with a maze of highways, railroads, and high-tension cables. (See Calumet Region Attractions.) Fast-growing suburban towns inch southward along US 41 and I-65, edging away from congested cities. In the southwest corner of the county, the Indiana Department of Natural Resources has preserved a stretch of virtually untamed marshland along the Kankakee River as a natural fish and wildlife habitat.

Father Jacques Marquette, the French explorer-Jesuit priest, is believed to have been the first white man to set foot on what is now Lake County when he camped on the shore of Lake Michigan around 1675. Four years later René-Robert Cavelier, sieur de La Salle, explored the southern boundary as he led an official expedition down the Kankakee River. An ancient Indian route, called the Great Sauk Trail, that passed through the central portion of the county, also provided a means of access for early white settlers of the region.

When Indiana was organized as a state in 1816, Congress extended the new state's northern boundary by 10 miles above the "old Indian boundary line," creating frontage on Lake Michigan. The government purchased the 10-mile strip from the Potawatomi Indians by a treaty signed in 1826. The remainder which makes up Lake and Porter counties was purchased in 1832, and settlers began arriving shortly after. In 1835 Porter County was formed by statute and the following year was organized by a legislative act. Lake County was formed in 1836 from the western portion of Porter County and was organized in 1837. The county's first election was held in 1837, and Liverpool, a settlement founded by George Earle, was established as the first county seat in 1839. A year later this honor was transferred to Crown Point. Industrial development of the north did not begin until the late 19th century, and the central and southern portions of the county have remained primarily agricultural to the present.

Centrally located in Lake County about 15 miles south of Lake Michigan, CROWN POINT (p. 16,455) spreads out from the junction of IND 55 with US 231 and IND 8. The area was known as Robinson's Prairie until 1840 when it became the county seat, and a committee, including Solon Robinson, renamed it Crown Point.

The **Old Lake County Courthouse** at Main and Joliet sts., a brick structure with a clock tower and smaller domes, dominates the center of the business district. Designed by John C. Cochrane of Illinois, the courthouse was built in 1878-79. The north and south wings were added in 1907-8. After the county government agencies moved to new facilities in the 1970s, the Lake County Courthouse Foundation, a nonprofit organization, began restoring the Georgian and Romanesque-style building. The foundation electrified the clocks, renovated the basement for commercial use, and converted the first floor to five rooms of museum space for the Lake County Historical Society. The historical museum features the antique radio collection of H. W. Cauley, which includes early radios, tubes, amplifying horns, telegraph equipment, and other components. It also contains a variety of local artifacts including a feed mill grinder made by the Letz Manufacturing Company. Restaurants and boutiques occupy the basement. The silent film star Rudolph Valentino got his marriage license at this courthouse in 1923. Thousands of instant civil weddings were performed in the years following World War I when waiting-period restrictions were relaxed and "marrying justices"

Tour 19

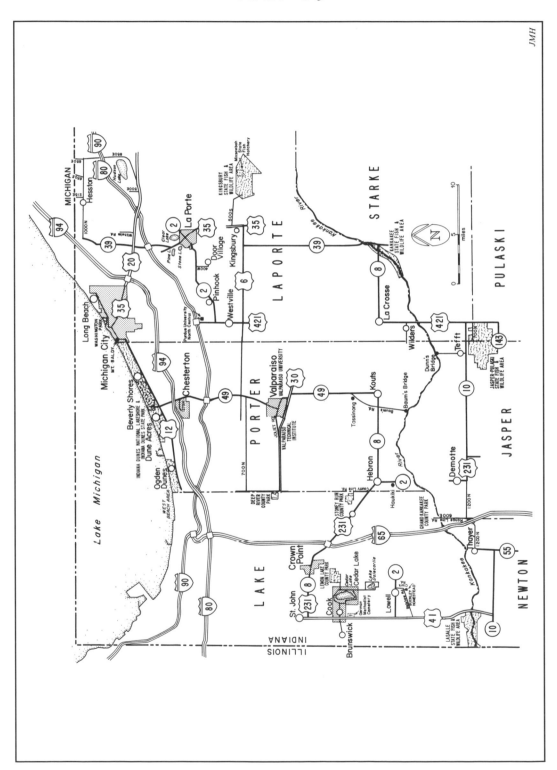

were readily available. Crown Point was known as the "marriage mill" of the Midwest. Local justices of the peace married such celebrities as Colleen Moore, Red Grange, Tom Mix, Ronald Reagan, and Joe DiMaggio to their respective spouses. (*NRHP/HABSI*)

In 1971 the county built the new **Lake County Government Complex** on a 70-acre tract at 93rd Ave. and Main St. on the far north end of town. A modern three-building complex of steel and glass houses the jail, courts, and administrative offices. An additional two rooms provide a display of model trains collected by the Hoosier Line Model Railroad Company.

Near the northwest corner of the downtown courthouse square, in front of the old Crown Point Board of Education Building, 105 N. Court St., a historical marker indicates the **site of the Solon Robinson homestead** where the "squatter king" of Lake County erected his log cabin in 1834. Robinson acquired his nickname after 1836 when a group of early settlers met in his home to form the Squatters Union to protect their property from future land speculators, once land sales began. One of the county's first settlers, Robinson served as the first justice of the peace and later became the agricultural editor of the *New York Tribune*.

A block south of the courthouse square, at 227 S. Court St., is **Ye Old Homestead**—Crown Point's first clapboard house. Wellington A. Clark, a native of New York, built the six-room cottage in 1847. Clark also owned a dairy farm and cheese factory north of town. The Greek Revival-style house is one of the oldest remaining unremodeled homes in the county. The Clarks' granddaughter, Claribel Clark Beven, deeded the property to the city to become a historic residence for the public to visit. Most of the furnishings belonged to the Clark family and other early settlers of Crown Point. It opened as a museum in 1966.

Several blocks south of Ye Old Homestead, on S. Court St. between Greenwood and 121st Aves., the **Lake County Fairgrounds** cover land near the crest of the Valparaiso Moraine, a 10,000-year-old glacial formation extending from southwestern Michigan to northeastern Illinois. This glacial deposit or drift has the highest elevation in Lake and Porter counties and is the natural divide between the Great Lakes and the Mississippi River drainage system. The 120-acre park surrounding Fancher Lake is open year-round for recreational activi-

ties. In 1933 the State Highway Commission moved a covered bridge built by A. M. Kennedy and Sons in 1878 from Rush County to its present site on the fairgrounds.

At the southern end of the county fairgrounds, where S. Court St. intersects with 121st Ave. and Franciscan Rd., the first **St. Anthony Home** stands on the southeast corner. Indian trails once crossed the property, and early pioneer roadways probably formed the five-point intersection. In 1912 Johanna and Michael Williams built the three-story building, designed by Joseph McCarthy, which originally served as a private residence on a 40-acre farm. In 1939 stucco was applied over the original clapboard exterior, and the Williams farm subsequently was used as a home for the aged, 1939-66, a clinic for children, 1974-79, and a child care center, since 1981. The recently renovated building now houses the Holy Family Child Center.

Return to the downtown area by way of Court St. One block east of the courthouse square at East and Joliet sts. is the **Crown Point Post Office**, erected in 1935. It features a Works Progress Administration (WPA)-sponsored mural painted by George Mellville Smith in 1938, which illustrates the Solon Robinson family greeting newcomers to Crown Point in the 1830s.

Just off the courthouse square to the south, the old **Carnegie Library, Criminal Courts Building, Sheriff's House**, and **County Jail** line S. Main St. The library building is now Carnegie Center, 223 S. Main St., and serves as public meeting rooms run by the public library. The Criminal Courts Building was built in 1926. A small park with a gazebo beautifies the rear of the building. At 228 S. Main St. is the sheriff's house, built in 1882, and attached county jail in the rear. Now boarded up, the jail once confined the infamous John Dillinger. On March 2, 1934, after one month's imprisonment in the Lake County jail, Dillinger escaped, armed with a handcrafted fake revolver. Dillinger made his getaway in the car of Lake County sheriff Lillian Holley, taking a jail garage mechanic and a deputy sheriff as hostages. On July 22, 1934, FBI agents gunned him down outside the Biograph Theatre in Chicago.

South of the sheriff's house is the **Fifield Mansion**, 302 S. Main St., built in 1897. For many years, the well-preserved Queen Anne-style house served as a funeral home. In the

1970s it was converted to a restaurant. The house retains many of the original features: 10-ft.-high ceilings, fireplaces, wainscot moldings, and stained-glass windows.

From the Lake County Courthouse, proceed west on US 231/IND 8 for *5.5 m.* to US 41. Turn right and proceed north *2 m.* to 93rd Ave. in **ST. JOHN** (p. 3,974). In 1846 residents of the settlement, known as Prairie West, petitioned for a post office to be named St. John in honor of John Hack, a devout Catholic. By the 1840s St. John had the largest German Catholic population in Lake County. The congregation of **St. John the Evangelist Church** erected a brick church in 1855. The present church, which stands on the southwest corner of 93rd Ave. and US 41, was built in 1923. The school and parish hall were added later. The **oldest Catholic church building in Lake County** occupies a site adjoining a cemetery at the south end of the St. John's church parking lot. Pioneer John Hack built the log cabin church in 1839 on his homestead east of here. Craftsmen from the Capuchin Seminary of St. Mary, located five miles northeast of St. John, restored the old church and moved it to its present site. Old pews and an altar provide the only furnishings for this historic church. The cabin is still used occasionally for special services.

From US 41 and 93rd Ave., go south one block then east on Joliet St. for *.5 m.* Just before the second set of railroad tracks, set back on the south, is the **John Hack Cemetery**. Hack and his family settled here in 1837, five years after the land was purchased from the Indians. He built a log church and deeded the property to the bishop of Vincennes. A stone archway and a monument with a cross, adjoining the cemetery, designate the original site of the church.

From St. John, take US 41 south for *4.8 m.* to 133rd Ave., turn right, and drive *2 m.* to **BRUNSWICK**. Established about 1858, the village was named for the state and city in Germany. On the right, the **Perfection Musical String Company** occupies a two-story white frame house. The century-old building originally served as a schoolhouse. In operation since 1910, the little factory has achieved international recognition for the quality of its violin, viola, cello, and bass viol strings. Local women spin silver or aluminum casings around beef or sheep gut cores with winding machines designed and built on the premises. At the in-tersection west of the string factory, turn south on Calumet Ave. and continue *.3 m.* On the left stand two **round barns** built in 1909 and a well-preserved farmhouse that is also built in the unusual round shape.

Return to US 41 and proceed east on 133rd Ave. for about one block to **Holy Name Catholic Church**, located in the unincorporated village of **COOK**. The attractive Romanesque-style church with a tower and large circular stained-glass window was built in 1932. The church grounds contain a school, a rectory, and an early German cemetery in the rear. On the west end of the church property, a historical marker designates the site of Hanover Center, the name given by German immigrants who settled here around 1855. When the New York Central Railroad arrived in 1906, D. A. Cook, a water service man working out of Gibson Yards in Hammond, lent his name to the depot and by 1920, the name Cook had replaced Hanover Center.

Continue east on 133rd Ave. for *.8 m.* to Parrish Ave. Turn north on Parrish Ave. and drive *.4 m.* to the **Franciscan (Polish) Monastery** on the right. Flanked by grottoes on the east and west sides, a two-story structure topped with a cupola houses the Stella Maris retreat. Dedicated in 1938, the monastery occupies the former George Einsele Hotel, a brick building with screened-in porches and a Colonial-style portico, situated on a crest overlooking a lake. Religious statuary graces the center of the lake, and the stations of the cross adorn the shoreline.

Return to 133rd Ave. and proceed east for *.2 m.* to the triangle on the right just before the Monon Railroad underpass. A centennial marker on a boulder designates the site of **ARMOUR TOWN**, founded in 1870. Now a residential area, Armour Town was a thriving community between 1880 and 1920 with at least 18 private homes, several businesses, 4 hotels, 4 icehouses, and an ax handle factory. Peter Scholl, grandfather of the famous Dr. William Scholl of foot comfort fame, operated a shoemaker shop in Armour Town where his grandson apprenticed when he was 17. Ice barns built along the lakeshore in the 1880s were the major industry, and the Armour brothers cut ice from the lake and hauled it by train to Chicago to supply their meat packing company. As many as 150 workers came from the city and surrounding area each winter to cut and haul blocks of ice. Industry abandoned Armour Town after World War I.

From the Armour Town marker, follow W. Lake Shore Dr. for *.5 m.* to the north end of **CEDAR LAKE** (p. 8,754). The 281-acre lake was formerly called the Lake of the Red Cedars for the trees which covered its shores. Continue east *.5 m.*, turn north on Cline St., and proceed *.3 m.* to the 77-acre campus of the former **Salesian Prep School**, operated by the Society of St. Francis de Sales, which was founded by St. John Bosco. The once beautifully landscaped grounds with two ponds contain an old chapel, gymnasium, and wooden dormitories. The school closed in 1979. Good Shepherd Home, Inc., a nursing home, now occupies the site. The statues have been removed, and a modern administration building has been erected.

Return to W. Lake Shore Dr. and follow the road east *.8 m.* to W. 133rd Ave. on the east side of the lake. Turn left and continue *.7 m.* to the entrance to the 296-acre **Lemon Lake County Park**, which spreads across a bluff east of Cedar Lake. In the 1870s a community of immigrants from Bohemia settled in this area, then heavily wooded with indigenous red cedars, and farmed the land. Until the 1930s Lemon Lake, a natural sinkhole, was part of a marsh. Today, much of that farmland has been subdivided except for the open land and the enlarged lake within the county park. Park facilities include picnic areas, nature trails, a physical fitness trail, a Braille trail for the blind, baseball diamonds, tennis and basketball courts, and fishing on the lake.

Return to W. Lake Shore Dr. which merges with Morse St. and go south for *.7 m.* to the **Cedar Lake Town Park** on the right at Constitution Ave. The Cedar Lake Town Hall occupies the former site of the Lake Christian Assembly Place, a 20-acre lakeside religious campground from 1940 to 1975. Cedar Lake residents established a post office as early as 1839, but they did not resolve problems of incorporating the town until 1967. Built in the 1970s, the town hall houses the police department, clerk's office, and a meeting room. The Cedar Lake Historical Association also occupies office space in the town hall and maintains the historic hotel next door.

The 65-room **Lassen Hotel**, on the Town Complex Grounds, is the lone survivor of Cedar Lake's "hotel era" which began in the 1890s and ended with the 1929 depression.

During the 1920s Chicago gangsters, tourists, and prominent persons flocked to the resort town by train for swimming, fishing, boating, and dancing at the pavilion on the lake behind the hotel. The hotel was one of 42 clustered around the lake. The east section, built in 1890, originally was owned by the Armour brothers and used to house hoboes and laborers who cut ice on the lake for the Chicago meat-packers. In 1920 that section was moved across the frozen lake from the west side, and a new front was added. Later, this was remodeled and extended again. Chris Lassen operated the building as a summer resort hotel until World War II when the Lake Region Christian Assembly purchased it for a summer camp hotel. The Cedar Lake Historical Association now leases the old hotel from the town. A historical museum in the hotel contains displays related to the town's ice industry and summer resort days. It also has equipment used by Dr. William Scholl. (*NRHP*)

Return to Morse St. and turn right. For a short side trip to scenic **Lake Dalecarlia**, take Morse St. south for *1.9 m.*, then turn left on 153rd Ave. for *.8 m.*, crossing the northern end of the lake. Pleasant residential areas with wooded lots and winding roads border the lake, which is noted for its absence of commercial and tourist facilities. The southeast side of the lake was first settled in 1833 by Peter Surprise, who lived there until his death in 1903 at the age of 109 years, 6 months, and 3 days. The early settlement was known as Pleasant Grove and later as Wonder Lake. Swedish stockholders in a land development company renamed the lake after one in their native land during the late 1920s. An artificial lake, Lake Dalecarlia was created from the Carsten and Foley millponds. A dam controls the overflow from Cedar Lake, and spill waters drain into a little tributary of Cedar Creek. Springs provide a supply of fresh water to the lake. The private lakeside community remains unincorporated.

Return to Cedar Lake and turn left on 145th Ave., following the road *2 m.* around the south end of the lake. At 139th Ave., on the west side of the lake, is the entrance to the **Cedar Lake Bible Conference Center**. Cottages elbow for space on this 20-acre tract that the Chicago, Indianapolis and Louisville Railway Company (later the Monon Railroad Company, now CSX) developed as a lakeside park and picnic grounds beginning in 1882. The railroad from Chicago to Cedar Lake brought hordes of summer vacationers directly to a platform in front of the park. In 1907 the Marshall Field employees' picnic alone drew 7,000 persons to Monon Park—by then well established with concessions along a midway, four large hotels, a lakefront pier, numerous cabins, and game areas. In 1914 the railroad gave the park to Paul Rader, representing the Moody Bible Institute of Chicago. Within a few years, the character of the grounds changed from an amusement park to a Bible study camp dotted with big chautauqua tents. In 1919 carpenters cut the Glendenning Hotel into two sections and moved it onto park property. Other permanent buildings, named after church members, such as Wooley Hall and Torey Hall, were added. Road signs indicate those areas on private property.

Follow 139th Ave. west for .5 m. to Parrish Ave. Turn right and continue .4 m. to the **Jane Ball Memorial**. At the north end of the Jane Ball Elementary School, a marker on a boulder commemorates the first schoolteacher in Lake County and designates the location as the site of the old Ball log school built in 1838 (torn down in 1904). Jane Ball and Judge Hervey Ball homesteaded on the shore of Cedar Lake in the 1830s. Their son, the Rev. Timothy Ball, became the renowned historian of Lake County.

Turn left and go west 1 m. to US 41. Turn left and proceed south for 2 m. to the **German Methodist Cemetery Prairie Nature Preserve** on the left side of the highway. A German Methodist church built in the 1850s occupied part of the two-acre plot. The rest of the property was set aside as a cemetery, but only half of it was ever used. The Nature Conservancy has fenced off the acre of black soil virgin prairie for its protection. Visitors may drive through the cemetery to the edge of the prairie.

Continue south on US 41 for 1 m. to 157th Ave. Turn left and proceed .1 m. to the first farm on the right. A turn-of-the-century **iron windmill** mounted atop a weatherboard structure stands over a 30-ft.-deep well. The building contains a water storage tank and two wood shops which are powered by the shaft of the windmill. Steel windmills became popular, especially on the prairies, around 1880, by which time cast-iron pump manufacturers were well established. Windmills hitched to water pumps were a common sight until they were sup-

planted by rural electrical service in the 1930s and 1940s. A few farmers kept windmill pumps much later as standby or auxiliary water suppliers.

Return to US 41 and proceed south for 3 m. to IND 2. Turn left and proceed 2.6 m. to **LOWELL** (p. 5,827). First settled by Samuel Halstead in 1835, the town was laid out in 1853 and named for Lowell, Massachusetts. A mill town in the early days, Lowell now serves as a mecca for antique hunters. Many 19th-century houses have been converted to commercial enterprises. Turn left on approaching the CSX Railroad and turn right after one block at Washington St., which angles. This is the "old downtown" section of Lowell. View the storefronts on the north side of the 100 block.

Continue onto Commercial Ave. and turn left on Mill St. After two blocks, turn left on Main St. to the **Melvin A. Halsted house**, 201 E. Main St. Melvin Halsted (no relation to Samuel Halstead), a native of New York state, came to Lowell in 1848 and operated a sawmill on Cedar Creek west of the house. The family lived in a cabin while Halsted made the bricks for a two-story house, built in 1849. It is believed to be the oldest brick house in Lake County. The Three Creeks Historical Association now owns the house. (*NRHP*)

In 1852 following a trip to California in search of gold, Halsted built a flour mill. He was influential in the construction of a school in 1852 and laid out the town in 1853, giving his workers property to promote settlement. With bricks made at the pit and kilns located north of W. Main St. and just west of Cedar Creek, Halsted built a large three-story building to be used as a woolen mill. The venture failed, however, because of the rise in the cost of wool and the decline in sales of the finished product. By 1865 Halsted owned three mills and controlled the dam-trapped waters coming downstream from Cedar Lake. About the turn of the century, the mills became obsolete, and the chain of lakes between Cedar Lake and Lowell was allowed to drain.

Reverse direction and continue three blocks to the old **Lowell Grade School**, 525 E. Main St. The four-room brick schoolhouse, built in 1896 and later enlarged, served the community until 1975. It now houses a variety of gift and antique shops. The interior features exposed wood beams and original floors.

Return one block to Fremont St. and turn left for two blocks to Commercial Ave. opposite the police station, which occupies the old town hall, erected in 1933.

Across the street, a wrought-iron picket fence encloses a white frame house, known as the **Grandfather's house**, 427 E. Commercial Ave. A Dr. Bacon built this charming house with arched windows, shutters, and a widow's walk in 1861 and made his home and conducted his medical practice here. Three generations of the Bacon family occupied the house before Robert Hein, a public accountant, bought and renovated it for business purposes. The fireplaces were removed and the central staircase turned around.

Adjoining the town hall, Senior Citizens Park contains the **Three Creeks Monument**, a 25-ft.-high granite shaft crowned with a statue of a Union soldier, dedicated in 1905 in honor of all soldiers who fought in the wars of the 1800s. Just beyond, the **Town Hall**, 512 E. Commercial Ave., occupies the former Carnegie Library built in 1920 and renovated in 1971. In 1909 Chicago promoters attempted to create a Western Vanderbilt road race on a 23.6-mile course between Lowell and Crown Point. A crowd of 200,000 was anticipated, and though the actual number fell far below that figure the area was inadequately equipped to deal with the crowds and confusion generated by the two-day racing event. Louis Chevrolet won the race, driving 402 miles in a Buick at an average speed of 49.26 m.p.h. For many years Murrell Belanger operated a farm implement store on Mill St. in Lowell and built race cars on the second floor between 1945 and 1966. Belanger's famous No. 99 won the Indianapolis 500 race in 1951 at an average speed of 126.244 m.p.h. The building later housed a drugstore which was destroyed by fire in 1976.

Continue east approximately *1 m.* to Clarke Rd. which runs along the east edge of a shopping center. Turn south and continue *.9 m.* to Belshaw Rd., then turn left. Open fields afford an unobstructed view of the Kankakee River Valley. One of the finest marshland hunting areas in the world during the 1880s, the valley is now a rich agricultural area. Continue for *.7 m.* to 3606 Belshaw Rd., where the 160-acre **Buckley Homestead**, settled by Catherine and Dennis Buckley in 1849, has been adapted for use as a living history farm by the Lake County parks and recreation department. The struc-

tures depict three periods of early Lake County history and include a six-bedroom clapboard house, a large barn, a log house, several smaller buildings including a hog barn, tool shed, carriage house, milk house, granary, hired-hand quarters, and a turn-of-the-century schoolhouse. Interpreters wear period costumes. (*NRHP*)

Return west on Belshaw Rd. *4.3 m.* to US 41 and turn left. Continue *5.7 m.* to the east entrance of the **La Salle State Fish and Wildlife Area**—a 3,640-acre state-owned site along the Kankakee River, named after the French explorer La Salle who canoed down the river with his men in 1679. Remnants of the Grand Kankakee Marsh that once stretched along the river from South Bend, Indiana, to Momence, Illinois, remain in this protected area. Following the construction of drainage ditches, beginning in 1858, most of the swampland was converted to agricultural purposes. Through careful management by the Division of Fish and Wildlife, some of the timbered area along the river, the bayous, and the wildlife population have been saved. Hunting, trapping, fishing, and bird-watching are the main attractions. A 600-acre marsh provides excellent waterfowl habitat along the river. The entrance leading to the headquarters and check-in station is located in Newton County *1.6 m.* south of the US 41 entrance and *1.5 m.* west on IND 10.

From US 41 and IND 10, proceed east for *6.2 m.* to IND 55. Turn north and drive *2 m.* to CR 1200N in **THAYER**. Established in 1882, Thayer was a resort noted in the early days for fishing on the Kankakee River and hunting on Beaver Lake. Turn east and continue *6.1 m.* northeast, then north, as CR 1200N becomes Range Line Rd. and turns into a gravel surface. A bridge built in 1927 and jointly owned by Jasper, Lake, and Newton counties leads to the visitors center at the **Grand Kankakee Marsh County Park**. Dedicated in 1979, the 930-acre park bordering six miles of the Kankakee River contains a wildlife refuge, campgrounds, canoe livery, and waterfowl hunting area. Once a sportsmen's paradise on an international scale, drawing such Indiana notables as Benjamin Harrison, Lew Wallace, and Oliver P. Morton, the river and bayous still support one of the nation's prime habitats for fish and game within the state and county preserves. The maze of waterways also provides ideal conditions for canoeing and studying wetland ecology systems.

Retrace Range Line Rd. for *2.3 m.* to CR 1200N, crossing the Conrail Railroad. Turn left and proceed east *4.1 m.* to US 231, passing **DEMOTTE** (p. 2,559). Descendants of Dutch settlers still farm the land surrounding Demotte, which is noted for its asparagus production. Continue east on US 231 *2.3 m.*, then east on IND 10 for *9.5 m.* to 400E (Tefft Rd.), passing IND 49. Go north *2.3 m.*, passing through the village of Tefft, to **Dunn's Bridge.** The old bridge, situated to the left of, and parallel with, the Tefft Rd. Bridge, is closed to pedestrian and auto traffic. In 1884 Nancy and Isaac Dunn laid out the town of Dunnville. Because the name of the town was confused with Danville, it was renamed for Mr. Dunn's brother-in-law, Dr. Tefft. Several years later Dunn built a bridge across the Kankakee River.

Return to IND 10. Turn left and proceed east *4 m.* to US 421. Turn right and continue south *2 m.* to CR 700N and the entrance to the tree nursery of the **Jasper-Pulaski State Fish and Wildlife Area** on the right. The state Division of Fish and Wildlife began the nursery in the 1930s. The main entrance to the camping and picnic areas, park headquarters, shelters, and parking lots is located *1.5 m.* south of the nursery road on US 421 and west on IND 143. The 7,995-acre area includes a large wetland area as a haven for birds, such as the rare sandhill cranes which stop here while migrating to and from Florida. There are two observation towers for bird-watching in the field. At the game farm, display pens contain white-tailed deer, elk, bison, and several varieties of game birds. The farm hatches 20,000 ring-necked pheasants each year. Although state-controlled hunting and fishing are available, absolutely no hunting is permitted in the waterfowl nesting area of this preserve of wetland and upland forest in Jasper, Starke, and Pulaski counties.

Return to US 421 and proceed north *8.3 m.* to the Kankakee River, the **LA PORTE COUNTY** (p. 108,632; 600 sq. m.) line, passing the junction with IND 10 and the town of San Pierre. In 1830 the state designated all of northwestern Indiana from near the present Elkhart County to the state line as St. Joseph County. Five districts were formed; the center one, Descheim, later became part of what is now La Porte County. La Porte became a separate county in 1832. The southwestern corner of the county, when first organized, belonged to Starke County, but the people in that area had difficulty crossing the Kankakee River to pay their taxes in Knox, so in 1842 it was annexed to La Porte County. The present boundaries of the county were formed in 1850 when 20 sections of land were removed from St. Joseph County on the east and added to La Porte County.

Continue north on US 421 for *4.1 m.* to **LA CROSSE** (p. 713). The town began at the crossing of the Cincinnati, Louisville and Chicago and the Louisville, New Albany and Chicago railroads. Many early buildings were erected on the railroad rights-of-way or on stilts because of constant flooding. The region, however, became fertile farmland following drainage of the marshlands. The grain elevators at the former railroad crossing have been the main business of La Crosse since the turn of the century.

Turn east on IND 8 and proceed *7.6 m.* to the **Kankakee State Fish and Wildlife Area.** A hunting and fishing area with picnic and restroom facilities is situated on the north side of the road just west of IND 39. In 1928 the Department of Conservation established the wildlife area in Starke and La Porte counties and employed transient laborers to develop the site. The floodplain in the Kankakee and Yellow River Valley is noted for quality duck hunting. Each fall, more than 1,500 acres are flooded for the waterfowl migration. Fishing, deer hunting, camping, and canoeing are other popular activities. The park headquarters is located two miles south of IND 8 and IND 39 on Jordan Ditch Rd. In 1983 the Department of Natural Resources purchased a 1,100-acre estate adjacent to the state wildlife area, increasing the park's total acreage to more than 3,400. Once an international sportsmen's mecca and home of the Art Gumz Duck Club, this property, once part of English Lake, provides some of the best duck hunting ground in the state.

Turn north and proceed *14 m.* on IND 39 to US 6. Turn right and proceed east *2.2 m.* to **KINGSBURY** (p. 329). In the late 1830s pioneers from Kingsbury, New York, settled here, building a gristmill at Mill Pond and operating a fulling mill to process wool. With the advent of the railroad, Kingsbury became a shipping point for grain from the surrounding farms.

From US 6, go north one block on US 35 and turn right on Hupp Rd. at the large sign for the **Kingsbury Industrial Park**. In 1941 the United States government constructed the Kingsbury Ordnance Plant here on 13,454 acres of farmland. It was one of 73 ordnance plants in the country operating during World War II. The government provided housing for workers at nearby Kingsford Heights. At peak production, the KOP employed over 20,000 workers (nearly half of them women) to assemble point-detonating fuses, load high-explosive shells, and pack ammunition. Testing sites, barracks, bunkers, and dormitories blanketed the countryside, crisscrossed with railroad tracks and highways. At the war's end, the KOP shut down, to reopen briefly during the Korean War. Parts of the complex today are used as an industrial park. The United States Army Reserve Center occupies a building near the park entrance, and reminders of the old ordnance plant can be seen from Hupp Rd.—deserted army buildings, fields of grass-covered bunkers, vacant ammunition plants, rail supply lines, and off-limit signs for contaminated test sites behind barbed-wire fences.

Return to US 35 and proceed north for *1 m.* to CR 500S. A sign on the right indicates the **Kingsbury State Fish and Wildlife Area**. Continue east *4.5 m.* to the park entrance, then *.2 m.* south on Hupp Rd. The 6,060-acre wildlife area provides bow and arrow deer hunting, game hunting, camping, hiking, fishing, and wetland trapping. Blinds are available for waterfowl hunting. The Department of Natural Resources acquired the property from the ordnance plant when it closed. Located within the Kingsbury Fish and Wildlife Area, the **Mixsawbah State Fish Hatchery** produces salmon and trout for Trail Creek and the Little Calumet River. Visitors may see the fish in outdoor tanks. To visit the hatchery, proceed *1.8 m.* northeast on Hupp Rd. from the park entrance and continue despite turns and jogs to IND 104, passing CR 500S and crossing the Norfolk and Western Railroad in Stillwell. Turn south on IND 104 and continue *2.1 m.* to CR 675E and a sign for the hatchery. Turn right and follow the road *1.1 m.* to the visitor parking area.

Return to US 6 and US 35 in Kingsbury. Proceed west on US 6 for *10.1 m.*, crossing IND 39 and passing the towns of Wellsboro and Union Mills, to US 421. The **Beatty Memorial Work Release Center** stands in the distance on the west. The medium-security state prison farm, the area's largest employer, occu-

pies the former state mental hospital built in 1951. Take US 421 north for *1.5 m.* to Main St. in downtown **WESTVILLE** (p. 2,887). Settled in 1836, the town was not platted until 1851. Westville was a thriving community noted for its fine school system in the 19th century. Today, Westville is a commuter town, centrally located between La Porte, Valparaiso, and Michigan City. The public library and some century-old buildings—notably, the Odd Fellows Lodge and the United Methodist Church, erected in 1868—line the tree-shaded street.

Proceed north on US 421 for *2.9 m.* to the 264-acre campus of **Purdue University North Central**, located north of IND 2 and just south of the I-90/80 interchange. Following World War II, Purdue University offered classes in borrowed facilities at Michigan City and La Porte. Increased enrollment and educational demands contributed to the need for a regional campus. The Education Building of this modern complex opened its doors in 1967, followed by an addition in 1968 and the Library-Student-Faculty Building in 1975. Enrolling nearly 3,000 students, the university provides educational opportunities related to the nature of the surrounding community and the industrial development of the area. The school promotes an "open admission" policy and offers associate degree programs in nursing, general business, and various fields of technology; a bachelor's degree curriculum in supervision and liberal studies; and a limited selection of graduate-level courses. Students generally complete their first two years at the North Central Campus, then transfer to a larger university to meet requirements for the bachelor's degree.

Return to IND 2, turn left, and proceed *2.1 m.* to the **Pinhook Community Church** and adjoining cemetery on the left. The Methodists built the frame building in 1847. It is the oldest standing church in La Porte County. For many years the Pinhook church shared a minister with Door Village. The church celebrated its centennial in 1946, but shortly after that it closed and has not reopened.

Established in 1837, **PINHOOK** was originally known as New Durham, but supposedly as a result of a feud with the neighboring village of Flood's Grove, two miles south, the name became Pinhook. In the heat of an argument, residents of New Durham called Flood's Grove "Squat Ham." In response, the latter community called New Durham "Pinhook," and the name stuck. Flood's Grove has since disappeared. Although Pinhook survives, the final business of a once thriving community, a grocery store, recently closed.

Pinhook today is probably best known for its bog, which is a Registered Natural National Landmark and a part of the Indiana Dunes National Lakeshore. Take Wozniak Rd. approximately *3.7 m.* north of IND 2 to the site on the right. **Pinhook Bog** is a bowl-shaped depression, thought to be a glacial kettle, surrounded by wooded hills. A thick mat of vegetation covers 400 acres of trapped water left by retreating glaciers centuries ago. Some portions of the quaking bog can support a person's weight but others cannot. A boardwalk has been constructed to span the bog. Wozniak Rd. was originally built as the Southern Plank Road from Michigan City to the Kankakee River.

From the Pinhook Community Church, follow IND 2 east for *4.7 m.* to CR 400W. Turn right and proceed south *1.3 m.* to Joliet Rd. in **DOOR VILLAGE**. When French explorers and fur traders arrived here, a natural opening through the forest served as a gateway to the prairies beyond. They called this opening La Porte, meaning "the door," from which the county received its name. Turn east and follow Joliet Rd. for *.5 m.* to the **Door Village Methodist Church**. The original church, erected in the early 1830s, was one of the first Protestant chapels north of the Wabash River. The present church, built in 1965, adjoins the old cemetery which has a number of white bronze markers.

Continue east on Joliet Rd. for *.5 m.* to the **historical marker** mounted on a boulder on the left. The marker designates the site of a stockade which pioneers erected in 1832 as a defense against a possible attack by Black Hawk and his Sac warriors. The Indian "invasion" never materialized. Once a segment of the **Great Sauk Trail**, Joliet Rd. witnessed the traffic of many Indians and pioneer wagons in the early days. In La Porte County the Sauk Trail passed just south of Hudson Lake and then through the present-day towns of La Porte, Door Village, and Westville. In the 1830s the trail from Detroit to Westville was upgraded into the famous Chicago Rd.

Return to IND 2 and proceed east for *2.3 m.* to the Northern Indiana Public Service Company (NIPSCO) building on the left at **LA PORTE** (p. 21,796). During the Civil War, **Camp Colfax**, a drilling camp for new recruits,

occupied this site. The 9th Indiana Regiment was quartered here. Known as the Bloody 9th, the regiment suffered heavy losses while serving under the command of Gen. Ulysses S. Grant in the Battle of Shiloh, Tennessee, in 1862. The 9th and 29th regiments from La Porte were destined to fight the bloody battles from Shiloh all the way to the final conflict at Appomattox Courthouse.

Follow IND 2 east (which becomes Lincoln Way) for *1.3 m.* to the **La Porte County Courthouse** at US 35 (Indiana Ave.). When La Porte County was organized in 1832, the town of La Porte was chosen as the county seat because of its location on the east-west Sauk Trail. The present courthouse, built in 1892, is the third courthouse to stand on this site since 1835. Brentwood S. Tolan of Fort Wayne designed the Richardsonian Romanesque-style building constructed of red sandstone blocks from Lake Superior. The grand old building surmounted with gables and a large clock tower forms a visual as well as historic landmark in downtown La Porte. Well-preserved Victorian storefronts facing the courthouse enhance the square. The downtown area roughly bounded by State, Jackson, Maple, and Chicago sts. has been designated a historic district. (*NRHP*)

Dedicated in 1978, **Independence Plaza** provides an urban park area between the courthouse and the new La Porte County Annex and Security Center to the north. At the west end of the brick plaza, an 18-ft.-high copper figure of a Potawatomi Indian holds aloft a broken spear which symbolizes the peaceful coexistence between the Indians and the early settlers of La Porte. The statue, sculpted by Howard A. DeMyer, a native of La Porte, towers over a reflecting pool and fountain at its base. At a lower level of the plaza is the bell which hung in the second county courthouse, 1848-90, the city hall, 1890-1907, and the firehouse, 1907-70.

The **La Porte County Historical Society Museum** occupies the annex on the north side of the plaza. Two floors of modern and spacious facilities house a wide variety of displays. The W. A. Jones antique gun collection, probably the best-known acquisition, came from a Chicago industrialist and world traveler who spent most of his life collecting and cataloging rare and unusual firearms. He bequeathed to the city over 850 pieces, believed to be one of the finest weapon collections in the world.

Other highlights include authentic furnishings of a pioneer log cabin, a Victorian parlor, a turn-of-the-century doctor's office, a carpenter's shop, and a 1920s model kitchen. Numerous display cases hold coins, combs, china, musical instruments, battle relics, dolls, papers, photos, and documents. There is an interesting photo exhibit of the infamous Belle Gunness who supposedly murdered at least a dozen men and buried their dismembered bodies in the yard of her La Porte farm, just north of the city, before 1908.

The museum also contains documents relative to the Chicago-New York Electric Air Line Railroad, which served La Porte from 1907 to 1917 with conventional electric interurbans. Promoters planned to link Chicago and New York by a virtually flat railroad with no rail grade crossings or curves negotiable at less than 90 miles per hour. The road would offer a 10-hour service on a route 150 miles shorter than any in existence. The line, through feeders, eventually connected La Porte and Hammond, but went out of existence in 1917 with the reorganization of the electric railroads in northwest Indiana. La Porte also received the world's first commercial dial telephone system, installed in 1892, and the museum displays the first of the 52 Strowger automatic phones put in place that year. The system was improved and enlarged, but reconversion to manually operated phones occurred in the early 1900s.

Within walking distance of the courthouse are several historically important landmarks. At the foot of Michigan Ave., which borders the east side of the courthouse, the **New York Central passenger depot**, built in 1909, faces the railroad. The Michigan Southern and Northern Indiana Railroad reached La Porte in 1852, and its machine shops, north of the tracks, were the city's major industry until 1870 when the shops moved.

Near the corner of Michigan Ave. and Washington St., a **historical marker** indicates the site of the first homestead within the present city limits. The Girl Scouts' 1932 centennial cabin is a near replica of the log cabin that George Thomas erected in 1832 on the shore of Clear Lake, which at that time extended south of its present boundaries. Before La Porte was laid out, three villages called Laketon, Hail Columbia, and Independence stood near the downtown area.

Maple Ave., three blocks south of the courthouse, represented the southern boundary of La Porte when it was laid out in 1833. Many of the city's finest homes and churches line Michigan and Indiana aves. south of here. In the 1850s Sebastian Lay planted the maple trees in this area which led to the city's nickname, the Maple City. The city paid Lay 50 cents for each of the 2,400 trees he planted on Michigan and Indiana aves.; State, Harrison, and Washington sts.; Maple Ave.; and Noble St., which included a "mall" of trees down the center.

At 1118 Michigan Ave., **Dr. William Hailmann**, a native of Switzerland, built a Queen Anne-style house with the pitched roof typical of his homeland. While superintendent of local schools in the 1880s, Hailmann established the free kindergarten system. The building behind the house (now used as a garage) served as a kindergarten, believed to be the second west of the Alleghenies.

According to local legend, the **Pulaski King house**, 1200 Michigan Ave., was used as an "underground railroad" stop before the Civil War. A tunnel connected the main house to one of seven workers' cottages on Indiana Ave. Built between 1852 and 1859, the brick house originally had a single-story veranda across the front. When remodeled in 1903, the house acquired its present 18-ft.-high fluted columns and southern plantation appearance. An insurance company now occupies the house.

Continue south to the **Ruth C. Sabin home**, 1603 Michigan Ave., a two-story brick building set back from the road on the southeast corner of Michigan and South aves. In 1889 Mrs. Sabin, a Quaker widow, opened this 35-room home where elderly women could spend their last years comfortably. At age 88, she was the first occupant. The house originally had only fireplace heat and a minimum of furnishings, but it has been modernized over the years. A sun porch and three upstairs rooms were added in 1924. Wrought-iron porches and a porte cochere replaced the original veranda in 1959. Today the house is furnished with antiques and still is used as a home for older women.

From Michigan and South aves., go west one block then south on US 35 (Indiana Ave.) to an interesting **octagonal barn** on the left, *1.8 m.* from the La Porte County Courthouse. The historic red barn stands on private property. Marion Ridgeway built the much-photographed Door Prairie barn around 1876. Each of the eight horse stalls had its own outside entrance, and hay was dumped from the loft into a central area. Ridgeway raised Percheron and Clydesdale horses imported from Scotland.

Return to downtown La Porte via US 35 (Indiana Ave.) which passes many old mansions, such as the **Ingersoll house**, 1202 Indiana Ave. Rear Admiral Royal R. Ingersoll built this magnificent home in 1908. Architect George Allen designed the front to resemble the captain's bridge of a ship. The window in the back is from the designs of Andrea Palladio, the 16th-century Italian architect whose work inspired Thomas Jefferson's plans for Monticello. The interior design is of the Georgian Colonial period, featuring beautiful enameled woodwork. The admiral's son, Royal Eason Ingersoll, served as commander of the United States Atlantic fleet, 1942-44.

Continue north to the **Cutler Funeral Home**, 1104 Indiana Ave. George Allen also designed this house, built for La Porte businessman Seth Eason in 1898. The two-story brick house with a garland design wood trim features onyx-tiled fireplaces, French plate-glass windows beveled and set in copper, crystal chandeliers, and cherry woodwork. The Cutler family began its funeral business in 1896 and has used the Eason house since 1936. The frame house next door, 1108 Indiana Ave., belonged to John Alstyne Secor while he was chief engineer for the Advance-Rumely Company.

On the northwest corner of Indiana and Maple aves., the **Swedenborgian Church**, also called the La Porte New Church, opened its doors in 1859. The legendary Johnny Appleseed supposedly spread the doctrine of Emanuel Swedenborg among the early settlers of western Ohio and Indiana while traveling by horseback from cabin to cabin through the wilderness between 1838 and 1845. Carrying apple seeds from Pennsylvania cider presses in leather bags, he set out on a self-imposed mission to plant apple orchards on the farthest reaches of white settlements and to bring the "news right fresh from heaven." The La Porte Swedenborgians held their first meeting in 1851. The original 1859 wood frame structure has been changed by the installation of stained-glass windows, addition of the entry at the front, and application of stucco on the exterior since the turn of the century.

From Indiana Ave. (US 35) and Lincoln Way (IND 2), go west one-half block. George Allen designed the **People's Savings and Trust Bank**, 912 Lincoln Way. Built in 1912, the building features a striking facade with fluted columns, stone entablature, and a recessed arch. In 1926 four men, reportedly Charley Fitzgerald's gang, robbed the bank of $30,000 cash and $60,000 bonds. Before the bank could recover its losses, the depression struck, forcing it to close in 1930. The bank building was subsequently occupied by a series of retail stores and is now a tavern.

Set back from the north side of Lincoln Way, between Chicago and Madison sts., **La Porte Hospital** sprawls across a two-block area. In 1966 Holy Family and Fairview hospitals joined to form La Porte Hospital, Inc. The new hospital opened in 1972. The main thresher plant of the **Rumely Company** once occupied this site, and Clear Lake covered the tract now occupied by **Allis-Chalmers Corporation** on Pine Lake Ave., just north of the hospital. A plaque at the base of the hospital flagpole marks the site of Meinrad Rumely's blacksmith shop.

Meinrad and John Rumely began a small foundry in 1853 to manufacture corn shellers, horse-powered machines, and iron castings for the railroad shops. Their first threshing machine, built in 1857, was powered by horses driven in a circle around a drum which operated the machinery. It was the predecessor of the famous Advance-Rumely Ideal Separator of later years.

Many immigrants, especially from Germany, worked in the Rumely shops. The Rumelys developed a portable steam engine in the 1870s capable of running a thresher. In the 1880s Meinrad bought out his brother's interest and incorporated under the name M. Rumely Company. After Meinrad's death in 1904, the well-established company carried on, later under the name Advance-Rumely Company with plants in La Porte, Battle Creek, Michigan, and Toronto, Canada.

It took John Alstyne Secor 15 years to develop for the M. Rumely Company the economical kerosene-burning engine which powered the Rumely Oil-Pull. Marketed in 1909, the Oil-Pull was the first piece of kerosene-powered farm equipment to revolutionize agriculture on a worldwide scale. In the next 25 years, Rumely manufactured more than 56,000

Oil-Pulls in 16 different models, ranging in weight from 3 to 14 tons. In 1931 Allis-Chalmers Corporation bought out the Advance-Rumely Company and eventually discontinued the manufacture of the famous Oil-Pull tractors as smaller, more versatile equipment took over the market. The Allis-Chalmers farm equipment plant, where 1,000 people once worked, closed in 1983.

La Porte has a diversified industrial base and stable economy and is the location for more than 70 industrial concerns. Two recent additions to the city's manufacturing family are Hedwin Corporation, producers of thermoplastic industrial containers, and Howmet Turbine Components Corporation, which makes precision investment castings for gas turbine engines. Principal manufactured products are castings, rubber and plastic products, food equipment, and heaters and blowers.

From Lincoln Way, follow Madison St. south for four blocks to 1st St., which crosses diagonally. A number of historic sites are located in this near-southwest-side neighborhood. The streets are marked numerically running east-west and alphabetically north-south. Turn right on 1st St. and proceed one block. The two-story red frame building on the southwest corner of 1st and C sts. once served as a **Civil War hospital**. Built in 1861, the hospital treated wounded soldiers returning from the battlefields and recruits from Camp Colfax and Camp Jackson. After the war La Porte had no hospital until 1900 when the Holy Family Hospital was built at the corner of E and 2nd sts. The hospital was razed in 1981.

Go south one block, then east one-half block on 2nd St. The **Sage Ice Cream Company**, 204 2nd St., has been making and selling ice cream in La Porte for more than 80 years. The original factory was next door in a three-story building. The family business moved to its present location in 1922, and much of the original ice cream parlor equipment, such as the soda fountain, wooden back bar and mirror, depression-era glasses, and light fixtures, is still used. The owner claims, "Only the price has changed with time."

Return to Indiana Ave., then north to the county courthouse, and continue *.6 m.* north on Indiana Ave. (US 35) across the Conrail overpass. At the first traffic signal, turn right on Truesdell Ave., which borders the north shore of Clear Lake. La Porte is sometimes called the City of Lakes because of the numerous lakes within its boundaries. Two of the city's finest parks have lakeside locations. WPA funds and workers accomplished much of the city's park and lakeside construction. **Fox Memorial Park** nestles in a wooded area along the north shore of Clear Lake. In the 1880s "Doctor" Samuel B. Collins of opium cure fame ran a private club here where members could drive their carriages along the lakeshore. Collins also built a private residence and sanitarium on Pine Lake Ave. He advertised a "painless" cure for opium addiction and attributed his healing abilities to clairvoyance and psychic powers. Hundreds of patients came to La Porte to avail themselves of Collins's secret formula. The Fox family purchased the property and donated it to the city in 1912. In 1864 Samuel Fox cofounded the La Porte Woolen Mills, which became one of the country's largest producers of woolen goods. The business remained in the family until the 1930s. Besides a waterfront location, the park features baseball fields, picnic facilities, and a band shell.

Return to Pine Lake Ave. (US 35). Just west of here, a residential area called **Weller's Grove** developed along the east shore of Stone Lake. In 1855 the Rev. Henry Weller, first minister of the La Porte Swedenborgian Church, built a home in a grove of trees near the lake. The area became a popular campsite for church members.

Proceed north on Pine Lake Ave. (US 35). Waverly Rd., to the left, leads to the **Soldiers Memorial Park**, situated on a high ridge between the south end of Pine Lake and the northern tip of Stone Lake. The city-owned park consists of 356 acres, part of which once belonged to an ice company. The John Hilt Ice Company operated on Pine Lake from 1883 to 1932, harvesting up to 100,000 tons of ice each winter. Workers equipped with saws and pike poles cut the ice which was stored in a huge icehouse, then shipped to the stockyards in Chicago and Kingan and Company pork packing plant in Indianapolis. The land became a park in 1938. Facilities include a swimming beach, boat launch, and picnic grounds.

During the 1880s and 1890s resort hotels and cottages sprang up around the lakes, and Capt. T. J. Harding operated two steamboats on Pine and Stone lakes. On the northern bluffs of Pine Lake, the Baptists held assemblies every summer. Before the water level of the lakes fell in the early 1900s, vacationers could sail from Clear Lake to North Pine Lake via connecting channels.

Return to Pine Lake Ave. (US 35) and proceed north to Severs Rd. (to the east) and Johnson Rd. (to the west), *2.5 m.* from the La Porte County Courthouse. The entrance to the **Pine Lake Cemetery**, which opened in 1856 when the original La Porte graveyard became too small for the growing city's needs, is on the right. A mass grave in the southwestern section contains many unidentified bodies transported from the old cemetery. In 1916 the family of Seth Eason commissioned architect George Allen to design the lovely stone Gothic-style memorial chapel near the main entrance.

From the cemetery, proceed north on US 35 *.7 m.* to the estate on the right of **Charles O. Finley**, former owner of the American League baseball team, the Oakland Athletics. On the left at *.8 m.* stands Pinehurst Hall, home of **Pine Lake Grange No. 1044**, 3042 N. US 35, the oldest remaining Grange (of the National Grange of the Patrons of Husbandry) in La Porte County. The two-story white frame meeting hall was built in 1914. The Pine Lake Grange, founded in 1876, previously met in a schoolhouse on the same site. Within two years after the formation of the first Grange in Indiana in 1872, about 3,000 locals with 60,000 members were organized throughout the state. (*NRHP*)

Return to Pine Lake Cemetery and take Severs Rd. east, bordering the cemetery, to IND 39. Turn north for *3 m.* On the left, just before US 20, stands the **Springville Free Methodist Church**. Built in 1891, the frame church adjoins a pioneer cemetery. German immigrants settled this area in the early 1830s. After the Michigan Southern and Northern Indiana Railroad laid its tracks to La Porte in 1852, bypassing Springville, the town ceased to grow.

Continue north on IND 39 for *4.9 m.* Turn right at CR 1000N and proceed east for *2.3 m.* to the **La Porte County Historical Steam Society**, on the left, at Hesston. The steam society offers an outdoor exhibit of a wide variety of steam-powered machines. In its collection is a square cylinder steam engine and winch, recovered from the deck of the *J.D. Marshall*, a ship which sank in Lake Michigan in 1911. Another eye-catcher is a restored steam locomotive built in Scotland in 1889, rebuilt in 1908 for service in India, and later shipped to the United States

for retirement. A train powered by a steam locomotive on a two-mile-long track runs through 155 acres of fields and forests. East of the steam train museum *.1 m.* on CR 1000N stands the **old schoolhouse** of Galena District No. 2, now owned by the Steam Society. The small brick school was built in 1892.

This part of La Porte County is noted for its fruit orchards. Road stands along CR 1000N sell apples, peaches, blueberries, apricots, raspberries, blackberries, grapes, cherries, plums, strawberries, nectarines, and pears—in season—plus cider and honey. Many of the fruit growers have "pick-your-own" arrangements for the public.

Continue east for *1 m.*, passing the Galena Baptist Church and the Heckman Memorial Cemetery on the right. Turn left on CR 215E and drive north *.2 m.* to the driveway for **Hesston Gardens and St. Paul's Monastery**, in a lovely wooded setting. The gardens, planted and cared for by the Rev. Joseph G. Sokolowski, display a profusion of flowering plants, shrubs, and trees from spring to fall. Religious statuary adorns the forest floor, and a winding path leads to a rustic little chapel in the pine woods. Another chapel in the house features a rare collection of religious paintings, Russian icons, missals, relics, jeweled chalices, and closets full of ornate chasubles.

Return to CR 1000N and continue east for *1.5 m.* On a knoll overlooking the valley, Posey Chapel stood from 1855 until 1972 when vandals destroyed it. The Rev. Wade Posey was the first minister of a log cabin church erected on the same site in 1841. Only the pioneer cemetery shaded by pines and white beech trees remains on **Posey Chapel Hill**. The cemetery offers a fine panoramic view of the surrounding countryside.

Continue east on CR 1000N for *2.8 m.* to CR 650E. On the southwest corner stands a one-room schoolhouse built in 1890, now used as the parsonage for the **Maple Grove United Methodist Church**. Just east of CR 650E, the 1867 church and cemetery are situated on a hill to the north. One of the oldest churches in La Porte County, it is furnished with the same pews, altar chairs, and lectern used in 1867.

Continue east on CR 1000N for *1.9 m.* to CR 850E (Hudson Lake Rd.). Turn right for *2.8 m.* past the east side of the lake to Chicago Rd. Joseph Bay and Joseph W. Lykins were early settlers in the **Hudson Lake** area, then called Lac du Chemin. Several Mormon families lived on the northwest bank before moving on to Illinois and Utah. A Baptist mission, operating on the east side of the lake in the late 1820s, tried to christianize the Potawatomi Indians still inhabiting northwest Indiana.

In the early days the Chicago Rd. was an important route that ran from Detroit to Chicago, roughly following the Great Sauk Trail. Stagecoaches and freight wagons passed through Hudson Lake, and many people stayed because of the rich soil and timber. The railroad arrived in the 1850s but established a station in New Carlisle instead of Hudson Lake, thus thwarting its development. Hudson Lake experienced a revival in the 1890s when the summer resort business prospered. The South Shore Railroad brought vacationers from Chicago to the hotels and a casino on the lake. The resort trade declined during the depression.

Turn right and follow Chicago Rd. south for *2.2 m.* to a fork in the road. Bear left for *.1 m.* to US 20, turn west toward Michigan City, and continue *2.2 m.* **ROLLING PRAIRIE**, to the north, was settled in 1831. Known first as Nauvoo, the town was platted under the name of Portland in 1853, then changed to Rolling Prairie with the arrival of the post office in 1857.

Turn right and follow the sign for *1.7 m.* to the **Le Mans Academy**, 5901 N. CR 500E, a residence and day school for boys, grades 5-9. Run by the Brothers of the Holy Cross, the Catholic school offers a Christian environment, small classes, and supervised study. It was established in 1956.

In 1907 Dr. Edward Rumely organized the Interlaken preparatory school for boys in La Porte. In 1911 the school moved to the 700-acre estate on the shores of Silver Lake north of Rolling Prairie. The setting lent itself to Rumely's idea of combining the boys' physical and academic activities with the freedom of country life, and the curriculum emphasized experience drawn from the practical world. The boys lived in tents while they constructed their own school buildings. They made frequent field trips to factories and businesses in the surrounding communities and attended cultural events in Chicago. John A. Secor, an inventor, spent a year at Interlaken developing his internal combustion engine. Students saw its first successful test and watched its progress.

After Rumely's school closed, the federal government used the grounds for an army training camp during World War I. The school buildings subsequently were used for a summer camp for children from Chicago, then were moved or dismantled. In 1922-23 the Brothers of the Holy Cross built St. Joseph's Novitiate, which has housed the Le Mans Academy since 1968.

Return to US 20 and continue west for *6.2 m.* to Wilhelm Rd. Turn right and proceed north *1.4 m.* to the **La Lumiere School**, 6801 N. Wilhelm Rd. The entrance to the offices and residence halls is located just east of Wilhelm Rd. off CR 650N. The athletic complex is north another *.4 m.* on Wilhelm Rd. Established in 1963 by a group of Midwest Catholic laymen, La Lumiere is a college preparatory boarding and day school for boys and girls, grades 9-12. A huge physical education building, classrooms, and five dormitories occupy 150 acres of the original 487-acre former estate of Chicago executive Edward La Lumiere. The campus features woodlands, landscaped grounds, and a lake. The school offers a liberal arts curriculum, and average enrollment is around 100 students.

Return to US 20 and proceed west for *5.1 m.* to I-94, crossing IND 39 and merging with US 35. Just west of I-94 is the **La Porte County Convention and Visitors Bureau**, 1503 S. Meer Rd. Brochures and tourist information are available at the Visitors Center.

Proceed west on US 35 *2.9 m.*, then north *.3 m.* on Carroll Ave. to the Chicago, South Shore and South Bend Railroad crossing. The **Carroll Ave. Repair Shops and Station** at Michigan City have served the South Shore Line since the early 1900s. Located on the site are the South Shore's corporate and freight operating offices, maintenance shops, and yard facilities. Constructed in 1908, the electric railway connects South Bend and Chicago by way of Michigan City, Gary, East Chicago, and Hammond. It is the country's last interurban still in operation—the only survivor of a once vast electric railway system.

In 1925 public utilities tycoon Samuel Insull purchased the line and rehabilitated it. Big orange steel coaches built by Pullman Car and Manufacturing Company replaced the old wooden railway cars. The new equipment, repaired and remodeled at the Michigan City shops, ran on the northwest Indiana corridor

more than 50 years. In 1949 three 273-ton locomotives were added to the rolling stock.
Among the largest electric engines ever built,
the "Little Joes" originally were intended for
Russia. In the 1980s a new fleet of stainless
steel cars was purchased. Built in Japan and
assembled by General Electric, the 85-ft.-long
cars seat 93 passengers each. In addition to passenger cars, the line carries heavy unit trains of
coal to the power-generating plants and steel
mills along its route.

Federal, state, and local funds helped to revitalize the line, owned by the Chicago, South
Shore and South Bend Railroad since 1925.
The original main shop building at Carroll Ave.
was superseded as a maintenance and overhaul
facility by the construction of a new shop in
1930-31. A new automatic car washer
recently opened.

Continue north *.2 m.* on Carroll Ave. Take
Springland Ave. west *.1 m.* to Liberty Trail on
the right, which leads into the **Krueger Memorial Park**. Named for Martin T. Krueger, six
times mayor of Michigan City, the park is the
site of several historically significant events. In
1675 the French Jesuit missionary Father Marquette came here to visit the Potawatomi Indian council ground and took shelter by the
spring below the bluff, now known as Marquette Spring, upon his return from Chicago to
St. Ignace in upper Michigan, just before
his death.

A historical marker in the park indicates
that near here the Battle of Trail Creek took
place on December 5, 1780. While returning to
Illinois from a raid on Fort St. Joseph at Niles,
Michigan, a party of about 16 Frenchmen and
Americans led by Capt. Jean Baptiste Hamelin
were overtaken and badly defeated by British
soldiers and Potawatomi Indians led by Eti-
enne Champion. It was the only skirmish of the
American Revolution to occur in northwestern
Indiana. Today the Krueger Memorial Park
contains a forest preserve dedicated to the
memory of the Michigan City men who died in
World War I. There are also a timber lodge and
picnic facilities available for the public.

Down in the valley just south of the park
off Liberty Trail is a botanical park which
opened in 1938. Clarence Stauffer created the
International Friendship Gardens as a way to
bring nations together through plants and flowers. At its peak, the garden featured 130 acres
of plant displays representing 65 countries, including replica gardens of England's Royal
Garden with formal sculptured hedges, the Persian Rose Garden, Holland's tulip fields, and a
Roman Garden with classic marble columns.
Though less elaborate than originally, the gardens remain a popular spot for summer weddings and continue to draw flower lovers from
everywhere.

Return to Springland Ave., proceed west
.5 m. to 8th St., and continue west *.5 m.* on
8th St. to US 35. Follow US 35 (Michigan
Blvd.) north *.6 m.* to downtown **MICHIGAN
CITY** (p. 36,850). The first settler on the site of
Michigan City was Samuel Miller, who came
from Chicago and settled by the first bend of
the creek. In 1831 Maj. Isaac C. Elston, a businessman from Crawfordsville, bought land near
the mouth of Trail Creek and in 1832 platted a
town, which he named Michigan City. The
town was the terminus of the Michigan Rd.,
which opened for travel in 1832, and Elston
hoped it would become the county seat. The
early business district developed along Front
St., and the town limits reached only to 9th St.

The harbor at the mouth of Trail Creek developed gradually between 1836 and 1875. On
the west bank at the present NIPSCO generating plant location stood a nearly 200-ft.-high
sand dune called **Hoosier Slide**. Once visible
from Chicago, the mountain of sand was leveled between 1890 and 1920 for use in glassmaking by the Ball Brothers of Muncie and
Pittsburgh Plate Glass of Kokomo and as landfill for the Illinois Central Railroad right-of-
way in Chicago. An estimated 13.5 million tons
of sand were shipped off.

The land on the east bank of the harbor
supported huge stacks of lumber for the bustling lumber port and rail center. Both freight
and excursion steamers used the harbor until
the 1920s. The lake port experienced an industrial slump after the Michigan Central Railroad
repair shops moved to Niles, Michigan, in
1917, but the economy recovered partly as a
result of the Chamber of Commerce promoting
the tourist and convention trade. Commercial
activity virtually ceased in the harbor following
the depression. In the 1960s Indiana joined
Michigan and Wisconsin in rehabilitating Lake
Michigan by stocking it with trout and salmon
imported from Washington and Oregon. The
project was a tremendous success. Charter
boats began taking tourists sport fishing on
Lake Michigan for coho and chinook salmon

and trout. Today Michigan City calls itself the Coho Capital of the Midwest. New growth in condominiums promises to bring a revival of lakefront development.

In the 1840s and 1850s Lodner D. Phillips developed and launched the first submarine on the Great Lakes at the Michigan City harbor. Phillips eventually produced a 40-ft.-long craft with a 4-ft.-diameter, capable of reaching depths of 100 ft., which he used to take his family on a three-mile underwater cruise of Lake Michigan. He also developed a torpedo-launching submarine and another for salvage work. Phillips attempted to interest the United States Navy in his inventions and unsuccessfully petitioned for construction of a navy shipyard at Michigan City. He received patents for more than 40 inventions including a mobile diving suit and diving bell. The Old Lighthouse Museum displays some scale models of Phillips's submarines and other naval artifacts.

At the foot of E. Michigan Blvd. (US 35), bear north toward the lake, negotiating a semicircle around the Michigan City Police Department, and cross the bridge over Trail Creek to Lake Shore Dr. at **Washington Park**. At the park entrance stands the Civil War Memorial, a vertical stone shaft erected by Indiana state senator John Humphrey Winterbotham in 1893 and dedicated to the city. From 1919 until 1945, the Smith Brothers operated their cough drop company near the entrance to Washington Park. It was one of two plants in the country, the other being at Poughkeepsie, New York. The factory was torn down in 1966. In the early days, Michigan City attracted many manufacturers because of cheap labor available from the nearby Indiana State Prison. Manufacturers of shoes, cigars, bicycles, and overalls had contracts with the prison until a law passed in 1904 forbade the practice. Today Michigan City has more than 90 manufacturing plants including Anderson Company (windshield wipers), Sullair Corporation (air compressors), Weil-McLain (castings and heating equipment), Dwyer (gauges and switches), and Jaymar-Ruby, Inc. (men's dress slacks, clothing, and sportswear).

Washington Park covers 90 acres of lakefront property. Public facilities include a fishing pier, picnic areas, a swimming beach on the famous "singing sands" of Lake Michigan, and a zoo. The old municipal bandstand, dedicated in 1911, has been restored recently. Area res-

idents began the zoo in 1928. Most construction was funded by the WPA during the depression. The zoo is noted for its Bengal tigers. On top of a sand dune at the end of a long trail, WPA workers erected a 75-ft.-high limestone observation tower, restored in 1980, which offers a panoramic view of the city and the waterfront.

Just west of the bridge, the **old lighthouse** still stands at the harbor on Trail Creek. In 1858 the federal government constructed the stone and brick lighthouse, equipped with a sperm-oil lantern visible for 15 miles, to replace a tower built in 1837. It is Indiana's only lighthouse with a keeper's dwelling. In 1861 Miss Harriet Colfax became the lightkeeper, a political appointment, through the influence of her cousin Schuyler Colfax, vice-president under Ulysses S. Grant. She held the post for 43 years. Beacon lights were later installed on the east and west piers built in 1904. The Michigan City east pier, headlight tower, and elevated walk have been placed on the Indiana State Register of Historic Sites and Structures. A major addition to the north side of the lighthouse was made in 1904. In 1971 the Michigan City Historical Society restored the lighthouse, placing a replica of the original lantern tower on the roof. The museum contains 19th-century furnishings, shipbuilding tools, ship models, shipwreck relics, and other memorabilia. The antique Fresnel lens that served as a beacon at the Michigan City harbor for 82 years now resides in the museum. (*NRHP/HABS*)

For an optional seven-mile trip through lakefront residential and resort areas, continue east of the zoo along Lake Shore Dr. and enter **LONG BEACH** (p. 2,262). Here John Lloyd Wright (1892-1972), the second son of architect Frank Lloyd Wright, designed several homes and public buildings between 1923 and 1946. He earlier achieved success as the creator of the popular "Lincoln Logs" wooden construction toy for children. The Long Beach homes illustrate Frank Lloyd Wright's philosophy of organic architecture which emphasizes the natural landscape, indigenous materials, and functional structure. The John Lloyd Wright homes reflect the beauty of the dunes by utilizing natural-colored stucco, stained-wood shingles, and multifloor levels to conform to the hilly terrain. Some of Wright's experiments in design include the all-tile inte-

1858 Lighthouse

rior of the house at 2935 Ridge Rd. (reached from the 2900 block of Lake Shore Dr.), the seven floor levels of "Shangri-La" at 2920 Ridge Rd., and the dramatic beach view from "The Pagoda" at 2602 Lake Shore Dr. Wright also designed the Long Beach Elementary School and the Long Beach Town Center on Oriole Trail. In 1946 Wright and his third wife moved to California.

Return on Lake Shore Dr. to Washington Park. Recross the Trail Creek bridge and proceed to the railroad station to the west at 100 Washington St., which is housed in the **old Michigan Central Railroad Depot**. The renovated depot, built around 1910, offers a sweeping vista of boats coming and going on Trail Creek. On May 1, 1865, at N. Franklin St., the funeral train bearing Abraham Lincoln's body from Washington, D.C., to Springfield, Illinois, stopped in Michigan City. The train arrived at the original Michigan Central depot, built in the 1850s, opposite the present station.

Proceed south toward the business district, bearing right around the complex of municipal buildings. At the southeast corner of Washington St. and Michigan Blvd., a historical marker mounted on a boulder commemorates the com-

pletion of the Michigan Rd. in the 1830s. The old courthouse building, now adapted for commercial use, stands on the north end of the original town square.

Continue south one block then east one-half block on 4th St. to the **Michigan City Public Library**. C. F. Murphy Associates designed the ultramodern steel and fiberglass structure completed in 1977. Bright-colored exposed pipes and a sawtooth-shaped roof suggest the appearance of an industrial plant.

Return to Washington St. and proceed south for three blocks to the **Barker Mansion and Civic Center**, 631 Washington St. Industrialist John H. Barker, Jr., built the 38-room Jacobean-style mansion, copied after an English manor house, in 1905 and furnished it luxuriously with imported art objects. His daughter, Catherine Barker Hickox, donated the mansion to the city for cultural purposes in 1968. It now serves as a meeting place and historical museum. (*NRHP*)

The Barker home was built within walking distance of the "car shops" which occupied a 100-acre site between 4th and 8th sts. off Wabash St., one block west of Washington St. In 1855 John H. Barker, Sr., entered the railroad car manufacturing firm of Sherman, Haskell and Company, incorporated in 1852. Within a few years, the name became the **Haskell-Barker Car Company**. Between 1852 and 1970 the factory was the city's largest employer. John H. Barker, Jr., became general manager of the company in 1869 and president in 1883. With shrewd business management and imported labor, Haskell-Barker was producing more than 1,000 freight cars per year by 1879. The rate of production increased to 15,000 cars per year in 1908. The company merged with the Pullman Company in 1922 and manufactured sleeping cars for the Allied troops during World War II. Pullman-Standard closed the Michigan City plant in 1970, and a fire destroyed most of the facilities in 1973. Today only one Pullman-Standard building still remains at 8th and Wabash sts.

South of the Pullman-Standard plant at the southwest corner of 10th and Buffalo (parallel to Washington, two blocks to the west) is one of the oldest churches in continuous use in Michigan City. In 1867 the Irish Catholics of St. Ambrose's Church and the German Catholics from St. Mary's united to form **St. Mary's of the Immaculate Conception Parish**. German architect John Renkawitz designed the brick Gothic-style church, erected in 1869. In 1954 the church exterior was faced with permastone, and a mural painting by Murillo was placed over the main altar. Marquette Hall was built in 1955.

From 10th and Buffalo sts., proceed west for five blocks to Chicago Rd., then southwest on Chicago Rd. to the **Indiana State Prison**. The fortress-like stone walls of the prison can be viewed from the outside by following the perimeter roads around the site. Construction of the Indiana State Prison began on a 100-acre site in 1860-61, using convict labor. Until the early 1900s local businessmen contracted inmates for inexpensive labor, especially in wood-related trades such as barrel, wagon, and chair making. In 1930 prisoners began making license plates, a function they performed for more than 50 years. John Dillinger served time here from July 1929 to May 1933, when he received parole. Today prisoners produce such products as clothing and maintenance supplies toward the support of the institution.

From the state prison, return to Chicago and 10th sts. Continue east on 10th St. to Franklin St. (US 421), then north one block to 9th St. The churches at 9th and Franklin sts. form a historic and visual focal point at the south end of the **Franklin Square Mall** which extends from 9th to 5th sts. Franklin Square, dedicated in 1969, began as a measure to halt the departure of retail businesses from the downtown area to the suburban shopping malls along US 421 on the south side of town. It has been moderately successful as a service and financial center intermixed with assorted specialty shops.

In 1867 the German-Americans built Sankt Johannes Evangelischer Lutheranischer Kirche at the southwest corner of 9th and Franklin sts. In 1875 a schism took place within the congregation, resulting in the construction, in the following year, of a separate church named **St. Paul's Lutheran Church** at the northeast corner of 9th and Franklin sts. The St. Paul's congregation still worships in this church, now one of the oldest churches in the city in continuous use. In 1882 the St. John's congregation built a school and parsonage adjoining their church. They conducted classes and services in German until 1919. In 1925 it officially became Saint John's Evangelical Church, and in 1957, after several denominational mergers, it became Saint John's United Church of Christ. The congregation moved to new facilities on the south side of town in 1968. Since 1969 St. John's church and parsonage have served as a summer theater, and the school has been converted into a German-style restaurant.

From 9th and Franklin sts., proceed east on 9th St. for five blocks to York St. Philip Zorn, a German immigrant, established a brewery in the brick buildings between 8th and 9th sts., which produced up to 15,000 barrels of beer per year. **Zorn Brewery** operated from 1871 to 1934. The 19th-century buildings have been renovated imaginatively for office space by Ken Fryar Associates. One new occupant is the Dunes Art Foundation, the oldest and largest cultural organization in Michigan City. The foundation owns 33 acres in Michiana Shores with a summer theater, a pavilion for classes and fairs, and a large pottery kiln. The old brewery houses its workshop for winter programs, classes, and experimental theater.

From the brewery, go west on 8th St. for two blocks to the **John G. Blank Community Center for the Arts**, 312 E. 8th St., between Spring and Cedar sts. Erected in 1897, the Indiana limestone edifice with a marble interior served as the public library until the 1970s. The center offers visual and dimensional art exhibits.

From the art center, proceed south on Spring St. for four blocks to Detroit St. Installed in the north entrance foyer of **Elston High School**, 317 Detroit St., is a mural painted by Robert Grafton in 1925, restored in 1984. The mural, composed of two 4 x 10-ft. side panels and a 32 x 10-ft. center section, depicts the harbor at the mouth of Trail Creek in the late 19th century.

A portrait of Maj. Isaac C. Elston painted by Gen. Lew Wallace in 1865 hangs in the second floor hall just outside the administrative office. In 1831 Major Elston purchased the land on which Michigan City was built at a cost of $1.25 per acre. Wallace was married to Elston's daughter Susan. Other historically significant books and paintings are housed in the high school's Learning Center.

From the high school, go west one block. Take Pine St. north nine blocks to Michigan St. Turn west and follow US 12 to the eastern end of the Indiana Dunes National Lakeshore, *1.7 m.* from Michigan City. **Mount Baldy** rises 135 ft. above the lake on the north side of US

12. Sand dunes, which were mined away in the 1920s, once covered the lakefront between the park and the harbor on Trail Creek.

Pushed by wind and wave action, Mount Baldy is an active sand dune, moving southward at a rate of about 4 ft. per year and burying an oak woodland in its path. When wind conditions are right, the moving sand makes a low, humming sound, like the drawing of a bow over the strings of a bass viol—the area's famous "singing sands." A trail ascends the wooded ridges to the west side of the dune, allowing access to the beach. From the summit, Mount Baldy provides a good view of Michigan City and the lakeshore.

Continue west on US 12 for *.4 m.* to the **PORTER COUNTY** (p. 119,816; 419 sq. m.) line. Established in 1835, the borders of Porter County reach from Lake Michigan in the north to the Kankakee River in the south. The county takes its name from Commodore David Porter, a naval commander in the War of 1812. Valparaiso is the county seat. In the past, the main source of income for the county has come from agriculture. At a time when La Porte and Lake counties to the east and west of Porter County show loss or little growth in population, Porter has experienced a 37.5 percent increase be-

Indiana State Library (Hohenberger Collection). Reprinted with permission of Indiana University Foundation

Indiana Dunes

tween 1970 and 1980. Most of this can be attributed to the industrial expansion associated with the development of the Midwest, the Bethlehem steel mills, and Burns International Harbor. Increasing numbers of tourists visiting the Indiana Dunes and city dwellers moving to the suburbs also account for the county's population and income growth, particularly in the northern half of the county.

Proceed *5.5 m.* west on US 12 to the **Visitors Center of the Indiana Dunes National Lakeshore**, located on the southwest corner of US 12 and Kemil Rd. The visitors center conducts a variety of free programs for the public, including ecology lectures, hikes, exhibits, interpretive activities, and a slide show about the park.

The **Ly-co-ki-we Trail**, a 3.5-mile loop for hiking, cross-country skiing, and horseback riding, begins and ends a mile south of the visitors center at the parking lot just east of Kemil Rd. on US 20. The trail wanders through lowlands, which were once the bottom of a glacial lake, and sand dunes, which were formed about 14,000 years ago. Vegetation now covers these dunes, providing shelter for birds and other wildlife. Camping is not allowed in the national park, but accommodations are available in nearby communities and the state park. Future development plans include the construction of an environmental center, east and west transit centers, and a campground. The Paul H. Douglas Center for Environmental Education was dedicated in September 1986 and serves schoolchildren of Indiana, Illinois, and Michigan.

In 1916 the National Dunes Park Association organized to raise funds for purchasing land to be turned over to the federal government as a national park. Operating as a national park since 1972, the Indiana Dunes contain 14,000 acres of sand dunes, bog, and wooded areas along the shoreline from eastern Lake County to northwestern La Porte County. To date, only the West Beach has been fully developed for public usage although beach sites with limited parking are located at Kemil Rd., Beverly Shores, and Mount Baldy. The park is dedicated to preserving the ecology of the sand dunes, which represent 15,000 years of botanical and geological history. Strange landscape features and rare combinations of plants exist here as a result of glacial movements—advancing, retreating, and depositing their

remnants. This collision of climatic zones and environments has produced a wide variety of plant life that differs from dune ridge to dune ridge. The dunes are also a haven for birds and animals. Great blue heron find shelter in a 368-acre rookery near the headwaters of the Little Calumet River.

Return to US 12 and Kemil Rd. Proceed north on State Park Rd. (Kemil Rd.) for *1.3 m.* to Lake Front Dr. in **BEVERLY SHORES** (p. 864). Until 1927 only one person lived within this six-mile stretch of land along Lake Michigan. The area was previously used for farming cranberries and blueberries. In the 1920s a Chicago realtor promoted land speculation, but the depression slowed actual development. In 1934 a Michigan City land developer bought several buildings from the 1933 Chicago World's Fairgrounds and transported them by barge across the lake to Beverly Shores. Twelve replicas of historic structures from the Colonial Village exhibit were placed in town. Only two remain: the Old North Church on W. Beverly Dr. and the Wayside Inn on Jameson Ave. off Broadway.

Five modern houses from the Home and Industrial Arts exhibit were hoisted ashore and reassembled along Lake Front Dr. Between E. State Park Rd. and Broadway, the **House of Tomorrow** clings to the hillside above the road. The black, geometrically shaped, multilevel structure with a central steel frame and floor-to-ceiling glass windows designed by George Fred Keck still appears modern in concept though now half a century old. Just west, the **Armco Ferro house** is made of prefabricated steel and was designed by Robert Smith, Jr. Robert Law Weed designed the flamingo pink stucco home, called the **Florida Tropical house**, on the lake side of the road. An overhanging balcony facing the lake provides an impressive view for the occupants. To the west sits the **Rostone house** made of a synthetic cast stone. East of the House of Tomorrow, the rooftop of the **Cypress house** with a birdhouse at the peak emerges between evergreen trees. The Southern Cypress Manufacturers built the rustic-looking cabin to demonstrate various finishes and construction styles which could be applied to their natural product. The five houses were placed on the *NRHP* in 1986.

At Lake Front Dr. and Broadway, turn right and drive *.1 m.* to Beverly Dr. Beverly Shores was incorporated as a town in 1947.

Lithuanian families own many homes and support cultural activities. Today the town is like an island, with parkland on three sides and Lake Michigan on the other. Sentiments of the townspeople are split between the desire for preservation of the dunes and for industrial development of the area.

Return to US 12 and Kemil Rd. Proceed west for *3.2 m.* to IND 49, passing the old resort town of Tremont. Turn south and follow the road signs for *.7 m.* to the **Indiana Dunes State Park** entrance. Beyond the gate at the right side of the entrance to the main parking lot, a historical marker indicates the approximate site of Le Petit Fort, built at the mouth of Fort Creek in 1750. Near this point, a minor battle of the American Revolution was fought in 1780. The 2,182-acre park contains three miles of sandy beach and a 1,530-acre nature preserve. Facilities include a bathhouse and pavilion, observation tower, picnic shelters, campsites, and hiking and cross-country skiing trails. The Calumet Trail, a nine-mile-long bicycle path between Dune Acres and Mount Baldy, passes through the state park.

The state park features many natural wonders accessible only by foot trails. **Mount Tom**, the tallest point of land along Indiana's shore, rises 192 ft. above the beach. Nearby **Mount Holden** and **Mount Jackson** measure 184 ft. and 178 ft., respectively. In contrast, the surrounding lowlands contain dunal prairies and primeval swamps. Each supports habitats for plants and wildlife characteristic of its terrain and climatic conditions, yet all coexist within a short distance. **The Pinery**, in the eastern section of the park, contains the last virgin pine trees left in the area. Woodland covered much of the swamps between the Dunes and the Detroit-Chicago road before the timber boom that began in the 1850s. Lansing and Gilbert Morgan, Edwin Furness, and other early settlers operated sawmills along the lakeshore and shipped the timber to Chicago.

Within the nature preserve are three major saucer-like depressions called "blowouts," eroded by wind currents from the lake and devoid of vegetation. **Big Blowout** is the largest and best-known. In the **Tree Graveyard**, wind action has uncovered the remains of a pine tree forest which grew there hundreds of years ago before the advance of the dunes. **Furnessville Blowout** has a long, narrow shape rather than a circular one. **Beach House Blowout** is located east of Mount Tom where the Prairie Club of Chicago leased a large tract of land and built a clubhouse in 1913. When Mount Tom was threatened with extinction by industrial interests, a "save the dunes" movement began in 1916. In 1923 a bill passed to purchase lakefront property for a state park, established by 1925. The Indiana Natural Resources Commission approved the creation of the Dunes Nature Preserve within the state park in 1971.

Return to US 12 and proceed west for *1.3 m.* to Mineral Springs Rd. **Cowles Bog**, a registered natural landmark, is just north of US 12 on the left side of the road. At the turn of the century, Henry Chandler Cowles, a botanist at the University of Chicago, made an intensive study of plant life in the tamarack swamp which now bears his name. The Save the Dunes Council owns and protects Cowles Bog.

In 1923 a group of Gary businessmen leased 582 acres just north of Cowles Bog and laid out a town called **DUNE ACRES** (p. 291) in a tract containing some of the highest dunes along the Indiana shore. A guard keeps uninvited visitors out of this exclusive residential area where commercial establishments are prohibited.

Return to US 12 and proceed south on Mineral Springs Rd. for *.6 m.*, past the park headquarters, to the parking area on the right for the **Bailly Homestead**, **Bailly Cemetery**, and **Chellberg Farm**. A two-mile-long trail that begins and ends at the parking lot links these historic landmarks within the National Lakeshore. Joseph Bailly, a French-Canadian fur trader who had passed through here as early as 1794, was the first white man to settle in northwest Indiana. He arrived in 1822 and built a trading post near the Little Calumet River where the North Sauk and Potawatomi trails converged. For 10 years it was one of only two posts between Fort Dearborn (at the present site of Chicago) and Detroit. Bailly's first wife was the daughter of an Indian chief, and his second wife, Marie Le Fevre, was the daughter of a French merchant and an Ottawa Indian. He took considerable interest in christianizing the Indians and even translated the New Testament into the Potawatomi language. Though living in a wilderness, Bailly sent his four daughters to Detroit and Fort Wayne to receive formal educations. He began construction of the main house a few months before his death in 1835. His granddaughter Frances Howe later erected the family vault at the cemetery and assembled some of the old log buildings belonging to Bailly Post, which included the one-and-one-half-story house, the chapel, and a fur storehouse. She also ordered the construction of the two-and-one-half-story frame house, the coachman's house, and the brick dwelling. The former has been restored to appear as it did in 1917. Bailly family descendants occupied the 42-acre homestead until 1918, after which time it served as a Catholic retreat, then passed through private hands before it became a part of the national park in 1971. Joseph Bailly and his family are buried in the old cemetery at Oak Hill, situated at the northernmost end of the trail. (*NRHP/HABS*)

Adjacent to the Bailly Homestead is the **Chellberg Farm**, a turn-of-the-century restoration. Swedish immigrants had already settled in this area when Anders Chellberg arrived in 1863. Chellberg was a farmer, tailor, and deacon of the local Swedish church. He built the present farmhouse in 1885 to replace an earlier building destroyed by fire. He also erected the granary and the peg-and-beam frame barn, designed in a Swedish architectural style. Outbuildings such as the chicken house, corncrib, and sugarhouse were constructed later. Chellberg died in 1893, and his descendants operated the farm until 1972 when it became part of the national park. The farm is the site of an annual maple sugar festival, and the sugar shack where syrup was processed during the 1930s still houses much of the original equipment.

Return a short distance to the first crossroad, Oak Hill Rd., and turn left. At *.7 m.*, on the right, is the tiny **Augsburg Swensk Skola**, a white frame building also known as Burstrom Chapel. Measuring but 14 1/2 x 20 1/2 ft., the structure was built as a tool shed but donated to the Augsburg Swedish Lutheran congregation in 1880 by Frederick Burstrom and moved to its present location for use as a school. In 1930 it was rededicated as a church and was renovated in 1970. It has been called Indiana's smallest church. (*HABS*) Continue on Oak Hill Rd., turn left on US 12, and proceed approximately *4 m.* to Ogden Dunes on the right, passing Bethlehem Steel Company, the Port of Indiana, and National Steel Company. Promoted simultaneously with Dune Acres, **OGDEN DUNES** (p. 1,489), just west of the present Port of Indiana, was developed when a

Gary syndicate purchased 513 acres of the Francis A. Ogden estate and laid out the town in 1925. A 240-ft.-high ski slide was erected here in 1927, which was used for annual competition until 1932. The lakeside community has gained attention because of the legends surrounding Diana of the Dunes, a recluse who lived several years in primitive simplicity among the dunes. The object of curiosity was actually Alice Mabel Gray, daughter of a Chicago physician, graduate of the University of Chicago, and wife of a beachcomber. She lived alone in a driftwood shack for about four years before she married Paul Wilson in 1920 and moved to a shack which they called Wren's Nest in the western part of Ogden Dunes. Diana died in 1925, and her husband left the dunes shortly thereafter. Access to the town is limited.

Continue on US 12 approximately *1.5 m.* to County Line Rd. and turn right to the **West Beach Area** of the Indiana Dunes National Lakeshore, where a three-and-one-half-mile-long stretch of sandy beach has been developed for public usage. Facilities include a bathhouse, concessions, picnic areas, and a hiking trail. The West Beach Area contains the largest of the interdunal ponds, Long Lake, reached by a trail from the parking lot. The area is a natural habitat for an abundance of wildlife, and the wetlands attract many birds.

Return east on US 12, which follows the **Calumet Beach Trail**, once a major Indian route between the Great Lakes and the Mississippi River. In 1831 a military route was established between Chicago and Detroit along the former Indian trails. Messrs. Converse and Reeves operated a stage line along this route, beginning in 1833. The settlement of Porter County followed. The Dunes Highway opened in 1923, providing "the shortest route from the Atlantic to the Pacific." In the triangle at the intersection of US 12 and IND 49, a historical marker commemorates the highway's opening.

Proceed south on IND 49 for *2.2 m.* to Indian Boundary Line Rd. (CR 1275N), past the I-94 overpass. Turn west for *.4 m.* to Calumet Rd., then south *.4 m.* to the central business district of **CHESTERTON** (p. 8,531). The Chesterton area was first called Coffee Creek after the post office and nearby stream of that name. Arriving in 1833, James Morgan was the first settler and postmaster. Mau-me-nass, a Potawatomi squaw, possessed many of the original land deeds. An early settler, William Thomas, ran a store at the corner of Calumet Rd. and Broadway and in 1852 platted the village which he named Calumet. In 1869 the town was incorporated as Chesterton, supposedly because the name Calumet was associated with two rivers and the region as a whole. Chesterton abandoned incorporation in 1878 because taxes proved insufficient to support a town government. It reincorporated in 1899 on the strength of population and industrial growth.

The economy of the early community centered around the Lake Shore and Michigan Southern Railroad, which shipped grain from surrounding farmlands. Irish railroad workers built St. Patrick's Church on the north side of Chesterton in 1857. **Thomas Centennial Park** and the town band shell at the corner of Calumet Rd. and Broadway occupy the site of the Lake Shore and Michigan Southern Railroad's former woodyard where farmers stacked cords of wood to fuel the wood-burning locomotives. A number of old railroad buildings along Broadway between 3rd and 4th sts., including the old depot and freight station, have been converted to shops and commercial offices. In recent decades Chesterton has become a popular community for artists and craftsmen whose shops lend color to the business district.

At the northwest corner of Broadway and 4th St., the Chesterton Post Office stands on the site of the **Hillstrom Organ Company** which moved here from Chicago in 1880. The company produced about 40,000 organs, distributed worldwide, and employed as many as 125 workers. After the turn of the century, the popularity of reed organs diminished as pianos became fashionable. Production at the Hillstrom plant declined, then stopped completely after 1920. A cereal company occupied one of the buildings for a short time. During World War I the Gary Chemical Company produced explosives here for the government, but the company converted to dye making after the war. In 1923 fire destroyed the old Hillstrom factory.

From Broadway, follow Calumet Rd. south four blocks to Porter Ave. Proceed west to the **George Brown house** at 700 Porter Ave. A native of England, Brown migrated to Indiana in the 1850s and took up farming in Porter County. He also operated a grain and livestock business and supplied most of the cordwood used in the kilns of the brickyards in Porter. In 1885 Brown built this Queen Anne-style mansion of local brick. Elaborate gingerbread-trimmed porches and balconies originally surrounded the two-and-one-half-story gabled structure designed by Chicago architect Cicero Hine. Italianate-style brackets along the roof line and an ornate etched-glass door panel suggest the ornamental type of architecture popular before the turn of the century. The small portico in the front is a later addition. The Browns died in the 1890s, and the house eventually became the home of Dr. Gerald Gustafson. The Duneland School Corporation purchased the house in 1963 and converted it into administrative offices.

Part of the original Brown property is now the site of Chesterton Park. For many years the park was the home of the **Chesterton Turtle Derby** founded in 1939 by the Chesterton Lions Club. A 50-ft.-course was laid out in concentric rings, and the event was sometimes covered by Chicago radio stations and newspapers. Any size turtle was eligible to enter the race provided that its owner was under 17 years old. In 1948 the race moved to Chesterton Park and drew more than 300 entries the first year. Though smaller in scope, the race has been held in Hawthorne Park in the town of Porter since the 1970s.

Return east on Porter Ave. to Calumet Rd. In the 1850s Calumet Rd. was a plank or corduroy road connecting Chesterton with Valparaiso to the south and City West, once a thriving village and stagecoach stop on the Detroit-Chicago road, to the north. Continue east on Porter Ave. for *.5 m.* to IND 49 and proceed south for *3.8 m.* to US 6. A side trip east of here provides a scenic view of a particularly picturesque farming valley. Take US 6 east for *2.6 m.* to CR 400E, then turn south on Old Suman Rd. which overlooks the valley.

Return to US 6, drive west to old IND 49, then south *1 m.* Turn right on CR 700N and continue *5.1 m.* to Juniper Rd., where the **Seven Dolors Shrine** is situated on 160 acres of landscaped grounds maintained by Franciscan friars who established a monastery here in 1929 and gradually cleared the land. The settlement encompasses the main grotto dedicated in 1931, the friary built in 1935 and expanded in 1953, the modified Gothic-style chapel dedicated in 1959, the parish house erected in 1967, the altar of St. Francis of Assisi, the 14 stations of the cross, and religious statuary throughout.

Picnic facilities and a gift shop are located on the grounds.

Continue west *1 m.* to CR 450W. In 1875 **Josephus Wolf**, the son of early settler Jacob Wolf, built the stately Italianate-style house, crowned with a cupola, which stands on the northwest corner of the intersection. The main part of the house contained family rooms and a farm office. The rear ell comprised a carriage house and workmen's quarters. The house was restored in 1970. (*HABS*)

Continue west *3.5 m.* to the Lake County line (County Line Rd.), turn left, and proceed *3.8 m.* to **Deep River County Park**, which covers 900 acres of wooded land at the site of an Indian mound and early pioneer settlement. The park offers a wide range of outdoor activities including hiking, canoeing, horseback riding, and picnicking. The old Christian Church, built in 1900, houses the park's interpretive nature center. Among its displays are the 8,000-year-old bones of a mastodon found near Leroy, Indiana.

John Wood (1800-1883) came to this area in 1835 and erected a log cabin along the Deep River. Woodvale Cemetery, established in 1836, is near the cabin site. Wood built a sawmill in 1837 and the first gristmill in Lake County in 1838. The village of Deep River, named for the nearby stream, sprang up in the vicinity. The gristmill's first source of power was a water turbine, but it later was powered by steam and finally by electricity. The three-story red brick mill closed in the 1920s and stood unoccupied until 1975 when it was restored as a bicentennial project. John Wood's Old Mill now serves as a museum and country store, where the public may purchase stone-ground cornmeal. Numerous gift display cases, arrangements of early American furniture and farm implements, and craft exhibits fill the interior. The Ross Township Historical Society has provided the museum with a collection of historical artifacts from the area. (*NRHP*)

From the park, continue *.7 m.* southeast to US 30, turn left, and continue *3.4 m.* to CR 330 (Joliet Rd.), which leaves US 30 on the left and roughly parallels it. At approximately *3.7 m.*, immediately after crossing the Conrail Railroad, enter **VALPARAISO** (p. 22,247), the seat of Porter County. Residents call their city Valpo. The county seat began as Portersville, named after the county and platted in 1836. The following year a party of visiting sailors

from the South Pacific renamed the city after the port of Valparaiso, Chile, near where Commodore David Porter fought the British. The Spanish name means Vale of Paradise.

Near the city entrance, at Lincoln Way and Chicago and Center sts., is the campus of **Valparaiso Technical Institute**, founded in 1874 as the Dodge Institute of Telegraphy. It is the oldest technical institute teaching electronics in the country. The institute offers basic and advanced electronics programs and an associate degree in engineering electronics. The **Wilbur H. Cummings Museum of Electronics**, named after the first president of VTI's Alumni Association and curator of the museum, is located on campus in the WNWI-1080 (AM Radio) Station building. The museum features exhibits of electrical and electronic artifacts that range from the telephones and radios of the 1920s to the sophisticated equipment of today, including an early "portable" radio made in 1924, the first version of a clock-radio console, a 1938 Seeberg jukebox, a 4-ft.-tall calculator built in the 1940s, and some early television studio cameras and videotape equipment.

Valparaiso maintains a diversified industrial base. I G Technologies began producing magnets in 1910 and is one of the world's largest suppliers. Urschel Laboratories began making canning machinery in 1910. James H. McGill started the McGill Manufacturing Company in 1905. McGill's bearings and electrical specialties factory is the city's largest employer. Clyde McMillen, a Hoosier inventor, developed an improved nozzle for firefighting and moved his firm to Valparaiso in 1976. Most of the city's industries are located on the outskirts, whereas central Valparaiso retains an old college town atmosphere with tree-shaded streets and well-preserved 19th-century homes.

Continue east on Lincoln Way to Campbell St. in the west part of the city, turn left, and left again at Harrison Blvd. to Ogden Gardens and Forest Park. The park provides an overview of the crest of the **Valparaiso moraine**—a great mass of glacial drift composed of sand, boulders, and clay—now mostly overgrown with trees and vegetation. The ridge forms the watershed between the Great Lakes and the Mississippi River drainage system. From its highest elevation of about 885 ft. above sea level in La Porte County, the main crest extends west to Crown Point in Lake County.

Return on Harrison Blvd., crossing Campbell St., to Washington St. At 308 N. Washington St. stands the old Immanuel Lutheran Church, built in 1891. Following a fire in 1975, the brick Gothic-style church was restored to its original appearance and renamed **Heritage Lutheran Church**. (*NRHP*) The parish hall, built in 1930, faces Institute St.

Turn right on Washington St. Go one block and turn left on Erie St. for two blocks. At 208 N. Michigan Ave., at the corner with Erie St., stands the former **home of Edgar Crumpacker**, Valparaiso's first congressman. A La Porte County native, Crumpacker served as prosecuting attorney, 1884-88, Indiana appellate judge, 1891-93, and congressman, 1897-1913, then resumed the practice of law in Valparaiso until his death in 1920. Built about 1890, the large brick house has been well preserved by its present owners.

Turn right on Michigan St., continue three blocks to Lincoln Way, and turn right. One block west, between Franklin Ave. and Washington St., stands the **Porter County Courthouse**, a handsome Indiana limestone structure. Built in 1882-83, the courthouse was remodeled following a fire in 1934 which left only the outer walls. Builders added a fourth floor and lowered the main entrance to the ground level. Fred Frey created the welded sculpture *Caritas* on the courthouse lawn. The contemporary design of the sculpture, dedicated in 1978, initially stirred discontent in the community but has now earned general acceptance.

At the southeast corner of Franklin and Indiana aves., on the south side of the courthouse, a distinctive brick and stone building houses the **Old Jail Museum**. Built in two parts in 1871, the brick front portion served as the sheriff's quarters, and the Joliet stone rear portion was the jail. The massive stone walls and towers of the jailhouse create an imposing appearance in contrast to the Italianate-style design of the front residence. The Historical Society of Porter County operates the museum. The restored jailhouse and sheriff's residence contain period furniture and exhibits of historical papers, documents, and photographs. (*NRHP*)

Next door to the Old Jail Museum stands an equally impressive structure—the **Memorial Opera House**, 122 E. Indiana Ave. Erected in 1893 as a Civil War memorial, the opera house attracted many well-known performers in the early years. The brick and limestone building with a grand arched front entrance is one of 74 buildings designed by local architect Charles F. Lembke, a pioneer in fireproof construction. The Community Theatre Guild currently contracts with the county to maintain and occupy the opera house.

Proceed east on Indiana St. two blocks to Morgan Blvd. Go north two blocks to Jefferson St. The **Henry Baker Brown house** stands on a hill at 303 E. Jefferson St. In 1873 Mr. Brown opened the Northern Indiana Normal School and Business Institute, which became Valparaiso University. He served as its president for 44 years. The Browns built this 22-room white frame house in 1880 and entertained here many famous people including William Jennings Bryan. Brown's son remodeled the house extensively in the 1920s and converted it to three apartments in the 1930s. The original property was much larger, and terraces extended to the corner of Morgan and Jefferson sts. The house later became a single-family residence again. It now serves as the White House Restaurant.

Turn right on Jefferson St. and continue five blocks to Garfield Ave. and turn right. At 156 S. Garfield, on the right in the second block, is the **Octagon house**, one of only six remaining octagonal houses in the state. In 1860 businessman David Garland Rose commissioned the construction of the octagon house based on the designs of Orson Squire Fowler in his book *A Home for All*, first published in 1849. Most of the octagonal houses in the Midwest were built during a Victorian building fad which lasted only about one decade, 1850-60. Fowler, an amateur architect and New York phrenologist, was a colorful figure. Besides his progressive ideas for home building, he took to the lecture circuit to spread his views advocating dress reform, vegetarianism, and abstinence from alcohol. He also published a number of health and sex manuals. His own octagonal house with its three stories and glass-domed cupola, built in 1853, amazed his Hudson River Valley neighbors. Valparaiso's Octagon house incorporates Gothic Revival elements in its steeply pitched roof and ornamental bargeboard. A pendant motif adorns the gables. The unusual eight-sided house was renovated and converted into a duplex in 1983-84. (*NRHP*)

Continue south to Union St., turn right, and go about four blocks to the city cemetery. Here, near the west edge, is the remarkable **tombstone of William G. Talcott**, which displays a lengthy epitaph done in a phonetic spelling system which Talcott invented. A Universalist minister, founder of a commune near South Bend, and a newspaper publisher, he also was a judge and an early advocate of women's rights.

Return on Union St. to College and turn right. Directly ahead is the entrance to the **Heritage Park Campus** of **Valparaiso University**. Founded in 1859 as a Methodist college, the Valparaiso Male and Female College operated on a very modest scale until 1871, then closed. In 1873 Henry Baker Brown opened the Northern Indiana Normal School and Business Institute. In 1900 the school was rechartered under the name Valparaiso College, and in 1907 it became Valparaiso University. During Brown's 44-year administration, Valparaiso University became known as the "poor man's Harvard." In 1914-15, student enrollment peaked at 6,000, second in size only to Harvard itself. The college experienced financial difficulties following World War I and Brown's death in 1917. Brown's son, Henry Kinsey Brown, managed the college briefly. A public announcement was made that the faltering university had been sold to the Ku Klux Klan, but the purchase was not consummated, and in 1925 the Lutheran University Association acquired the facilities.

The west campus contains several turn-of-the-century buildings in a park-like setting. **Heritage Hall** is the oldest building on the university campus. Built as a boarding dormitory in 1875, the brick structure had three floors before a fire destroyed the top story. The rear wings were added in 1918 and 1946. Originally known as Flint Hall, the building was renamed after Richard A. Heritage, professor of music, 1878-94, and served as the college library, 1925-59, then as classrooms and offices. The flattop building with arched windows and a paneled double-door entrance beneath a fanlight was remodeled in the 1980s to house law school student services, publications, and organizations. (*NRHP*)

From the campus return to Union St. and turn right to the **East Campus**. Construction began in 1956. The School of Law building, the science center, and a number of residence halls were dedicated in the 1960s. Ground breaking for the new Athletics-Recreation Center and for the Academic Computer-Communications Center took place in 1984. Known for its fine law school, Valparaiso University offers more than 70 different fields of study leading to undergraduate and graduate degrees. It is the nation's largest Lutheran university. The school has produced a long list of distinguished alumni of which radio commentator Lowell Thomas is one.

Dedicated in 1959, the **Chapel of the Resurrection**, designed by Charles Edward Stade and Associates of Park Ridge, Illinois, towers over the 310-acre campus. The chapel, which seats more than 3,000 persons, features modern lines in stone and wood, mosaic murals, and magnificent stained-glass windows designed by Peter Dohmen Studios of St. Paul, Minnesota. A roof shaped like a nine-pointed star tops the glass-enclosed chancel. Nearby, a 143-ft.-high freestanding campanile sounds out the class hours and calls to worship with an electronic carillon. Scheduled musical events are provided on the chapel's Reddel Organ.

Across the street, the **Henry F. Moellering Memorial Library**, dedicated in 1959, houses the university's outstanding Sloan collection of more than 250 American paintings. Percy Sloan, son of Junius R. Sloan, endowed to the university a wide-ranging selection of his father's paintings produced in the Hudson River Valley and Illinois by the 19th-century portrait and landscape artist. The art collection will move to the university's new Performing Arts/ Museum Center when construction is completed in the 1990s.

From the east gate of the university campus, proceed south on East Dr. to US 30. Take US 30 east to IND 49 and turn right. About *1 m.* south is the **Porter County Exposition Center**, a 23,000-sq.-ft. building which contains 104 trade show booths. It is part of the new fairgrounds complex which succeeded about 1985 the in-town location which had been occupied since 1872.

Since 1979 Valparaiso has drawn huge crowds for its annual popcorn festival. Orville Redenbacher, the bespectacled native of Brazil, Indiana, and Purdue University graduate whose gourmet popcorn TV commercials helped make Valparaiso the popcorn capital of the world, presides over the opening parade. The Orville Redenbacher popcorn factory, a subsidiary of Beatrice/Hunt-Wesson, Inc., had its beginnings here in 1952 when Redenbacher bought the George F. Chester and Son seed corn company.

Follow IND 49 south for *5.5 m.*, then angle right on Baum's Rd. and continue another *.1 m.* to the historical marker on the right. This area is the site of a Potawatomi Indian village called **Tassinong** when the first white explorers arrived in 1673. Jesuit missionaries camped near here while canoeing up the Kankakee River. The French used the site for a mission and trading post which was burned and captured by the British before becoming American territory. Settlers arrived about 1833 and established the first post office in 1838. The village included two stores, an inn, a church, and two blacksmith shops which were abandoned when the railroad bypassed them for another village. Infrared photography of the settlement shows the outline of building foundations. Archaeologists also have found evidence of two Indian wars, perhaps boundary disputes, about 1491 and 1776. All that remains today to indicate this historic site is the roadside marker.

Return to IND 49 and continue south *2 m.* to **KOUTS** (p. 1,619). About 1865 Bernard Kouts laid out the town at the crossing of the Erie and Pennsylvania railroads. Railroad workers who boarded at Kouts's home named the place Kouts Station. The name was changed to Kouts in 1890. The town became a shipping center for lumber, livestock, and grain. The Heinold feed and fertilizer elevators, now owned by Cargill, have been landmarks along the now-abandoned Pennsylvania Railroad for many years. The Heinold Hog Market, just south and east of the former railroad, has operated at the end of Mentor St. since 1948. Continue west on IND 8 for *1.5 m.* and turn left on Baum's Rd. to Baum's Bridge, which crosses the Kankakee River at *3.3 m.*

Return to IND 8 and proceed west for *7.2 m.* to **HEBRON** (p. 2,696). Hebron began as a road crossing called the Corners. In 1844 John Alyea laid out the town, and it was named for the biblical city of Hebron. James McCune built the **Stagecoach Inn** in 1849 on one of three one-acre lots owned by early settler John Alyea, located on Main St. (IND 2), one-half block north of Sigler St. (IND 8). The lumber for the saltbox-style building was hauled by wagon from Michigan City. It was the first frame house in the community and served as a stagecoach inn on the Detroit to St. Louis route until the railroad arrived in 1857. Passengers traveling on the old Pennsylvania Railroad from Chicago to Logansport used it as a hotel until 1870. It then became a private residence. Louis Alyea purchased the Stagecoach Inn and remodeled it as a museum and community meeting place, dedicated in 1970 as a memorial to his son Donald Alyea, who gave his life in World War II.

The **Hebron Public Library**, located on the northwest corner of Washington and Sigler sts., one block west of IND 8 and IND 2, was dedicated in 1922. It may have been the last of 149 Indiana libraries built with the help of the Carnegie Foundation. A historical marker is posted in front of the two-story yellow brick structure of Tudor Revival design.

From IND 8 and IND 2/US 231, go south for *1.6 m.* to the historical marker on the right indicating the site of **Haukiki**. This is believed to be the location of the oldest and largest Potawatomi Indian village along the Kankakee River. It served as the tribe's winter home until 1838. Old Indian Town was a popular fur and game center at the turn of the century when sportsmen flocked to the Kankakee Valley for hunting and trapping.

Return on US 231 for *4.9 m.* Turn right (due north), going *.4 m.* to the end of the road. Turn right and continue *1.6 m.* to the entrance of **Stoney Run County Park**. Dedicated in 1973, the 271-acre park at 142nd Ave. and Union St. has picnic shelters, wooded areas, and a physical fitness trail. A Vietnam veterans monument in the park, started by the family of a war victim, was dedicated in 1984. From the park, return to US 231 and continue northwest for *7 m.*, passing Leroy and the I-65 overpass, to Crown Point. The tour ends at the courthouse square in Crown Point.

Index

This index includes topical main entries on the following subjects: Automobiles, Banks, Bridges, Canals, Cemeteries, Churches and Temples, Circuses, Creeks, Dams, Educational Institutions, Forts, Hospitals, Hotels, Indians, Interurbans, Lakes, Libraries, Mills, Museums, Parks, Railroads, Religious Orders, Reservoirs, Riverboats, Rivers, Ships, Sports, Theaters, and Treaties.

A. Booth Tarkington
B. Ernie Pyle
C. Wendell Willkie
D. Madam C. J. Walker
E. James Whitcomb Riley

F. Benjamin Harrison
G. Abraham Lincoln
H. Gene Stratton-Porter
I. Col. Eli Lilly
J. Lew Wallace

Cover by Garry Nichols